Pope John Paul II greets a crowd on his visit to San Juan de los Lagos, Jalisco, Mexico in May of 1990.
(© Sergio Dorantes/CORBIS. Reproduced by permission.)

NEW
CATHOLIC
ENCYCLOPEDIA

NEW CATHOLIC ENCYCLOPEDIA

JUBILEE VOLUME
The Wojtyła Years

GALE GROUP

Detroit
New York
San Francisco
London
Boston
Woodbridge, CT

in association with
THE CATHOLIC UNIVERSITY OF AMERICA • WASHINGTON, D.C.

THE NEW CATHOLIC ENCYCLOPEDIA: JUBILEE VOLUME, THE WOJTYŁA YEARS

Gale Group Staff

Peter M. Gareffa, *Managing Editor*
Laura Standley Berger, Joann Cerrito, *Senior Editors*
Thomas Carson, William Harmer, *Editors*
Stephen Cusack, *Associate Editor*
Erin Bealmear, Jason Everett, Laura S. Kryhoski, Margaret Mazurkiewicz, Christine Tomassini, *Contributing Editors*
Ryan McNeill, Shannon Ringvelski, *Editorial Assistants*

Mary Beth Trimper, *Manager, Composition and Electronic Prepress*
Dorothy Maki, *Manufacturing Manager*
Evi Seoud, *Assistant Manager, Composition Purchasing and Electronic Prepress*
Rhonda Williams, *Buyer*

Kenn Zorn, *Design Manager*
Michelle DiMercurio, *Art Director*
Michael Logusz, *Graphic Artist*
Randy Bassett, *Image Database Supervisor*
Robert Duncan, *Imaging Specialist*
Pamela A. Reed, *Imaging Coordinator*
Dean Dauphinais, *Senior Image Editor*
Leitha Etheridge-Sims, Mary Grimes, *Image Catalogers*

Maria L. Franklin, *Permissions Manager*
Edna Hedblad, *Permissions Specialist*

Library of Congress Cataloging-in-Publication Data
New Catholic encyclopedia: jubilee volume / [by the Catholic University of America].
    p. cm.
  Includes bibliographical references and index.
  ISBN 0-7876-4787-x (hardcover)
  1. Catholic Church—Encyclopedias. I. Catholic University of America.

BX841 .N44 2001
282'.03—dc21   00-060991

Frontispiece photograph © Sergio Dorantes/CORBIS. Reproduced by permission.

Printed in the United States of America
10 9 8 7 6 5 4 3 2

Table of Contents

Editorial Advisory Board

Mary Collins, OSB, Ph.D.
Prioress, Mount St. Scholastica
Atchison, Kansas

Rev. Raymond F. Collins, S.T.D.
Professor of New Testament
The Catholic University of America

John J. Convey, Ph.D.
Provost and Professor of Education
The Catholic University of Amcrica

Antoine Garibaldi, Ph.D.
Provost and Chief Academic Officer
Howard University

John F. Haught, Ph.D.
Professor of Theology
Georgetown University

Monika K. Hellwig, Ph.D.
Executive Director
Assoc. of Catholic Colleges and Universities

Rev. Joseph Komonchak, S.T.L., Ph.D.
The John C. and Gertrude P. Hubbard Professor of
  Religious Studies
The Catholic University of America

Rev. James H. Provost, J.C.D.
The O'Brien-O'Connor Professor of Canon Law
The Catholic University of America

Lourdes Sheehan, RSM, Ed.D.
Secretary for Education
United States Catholic Conference

Rev. Msgr. Robert Trisco, Hist. Eccl. D.
Professor *Emeritus* of Church History and
Editor, *The Catholic Historical Review*
The Catholic University of America

Rev. Msgr. John F. Wippel, Ph.D.
Professor of Philosophy
The Catholic University of America

Editorial Staff

Executive Editor
Berard L. Marthaler, O.F.M.Conv.

Assistant Editors
Richard E. McCarron
Gregory F. LaNave

Contributing Editors
Katherine I. Rabenstein
Salvador Miranda

Director of The Catholic University of America Press
David J. McGonagle

Foreword

History therefore becomes the arena where we see what God does for humanity. God comes to us in the things we know best and can verify most easily, the things of our everyday life, apart from which we cannot understand ourselves (Pope John Paul II, *Fides et ratio*, 12).

We who lived in the twentieth century, now past, witnessed a remarkable period of history. We have, indeed, seen something wonderful that God has done for humanity in the person and pontificate of Pope John Paul II. Without exaggeration, this man of God has dominated the world stage since assuming the papacy in 1979 in many areas of endeavor. Seen and heard by more people than any other human being in the history of the world, he has become, truly, part of our everyday life and has helped us understand ourselves in God, in Christ, and in his revelation "offered to every man and woman who would welcome it as the word which is the absolutely valid source of meaning for human life" (*FR* 12).

It is with great pride and profound appreciation for the contributions of our Holy Father to the Church and the world that The Catholic University of America Press in collaboration with Gale Group dedicates this Jubilee Volume of the *New Catholic Encyclopedia* to His Holiness, Pope John Paul II. As the authors represented herein suggest, history will judge his pontificate to be the critical time when the noblest hopes and ambitions of humankind found a voice, a heart, and a soul to express them as we cross the threshold into a new millennium.

Very Reverend David M. O'Connell, C.M., J.C.D.
President
The Catholic University of America

Preface

In two important ways this volume initiates a new stage in the development of the *New Catholic Encyclopedia*. The original 15-volume edition was published in 1967 and after more than three decades continues to be a standard reference guide for the general public, especially readers who have a special interest in Roman Catholic history, teachings, and practice. Subsequently in 1972, 1978, 1988, and 1995 the editors prepared supplements aimed at keeping the encyclopedia current. This Jubilee Volume, however, is designed not so much as a supplement to the original edition as a *propaedia*, a preamble, to the revised edition of the *NCE* that will follow in due course.

It is called the Jubilee Volume because its publication date coincides with the beginning of a new century and new millennium. Pope John Paul II designated the year 2000 as a "Jubilee Year" in the spirit of the jubilee years of ancient Israel that were seen as a time for taking stock, redressing old grievances, and beginning anew. In focusing on the pontificate of John Paul and events in the last decades of the twentieth century, this Jubilee Volume is a registry of people and issues that shaped the Church in the period after the Second Vatican Council. Their importance lies in the influence they have had on the future of the Church as it crosses the threshold (a favorite metaphor of John Paul) from one millennium to the next.

The Jubilee Volume has two distinctive parts. The first is a series of interpretative essays that survey developments and analyze the principles that have determined church policy in the years of Pope John Paul's pontificate. They trace political and cultural influences that fashioned the outlook and formed the values which Karol Wojtyła brought with him from Poland to Rome and to the world. Each of the authors fastens on a particular aspect: his personalist philosophy, approach to theology, social thought, implementation of Vatican II, and ecumenical concerns. The essays show that Pope John Paul II's sphere of vision and influence transcends theological issues and extends well beyond the institutional Church to basic human rights and family values, to the arts and sciences, to economics and geopolitics.

Part two of the Jubilee Volume reports the hard data that one expects to find in a reference work: dates, place names, information about people, institutions, and events. A major section of this second part presents thumbnail sketches of hundreds of the saints and *beati* declared by Pope John Paul II. These brief accounts provide information that is not readily available in most hagiographies, and, taken together, they illustrate how the Jubilee Volume continues in the best tradition of encyclopedias. It presents a "circle of learning" with one article and entry referencing and enhancing another. The hagiographies, though brief, include men and women from every continent. They include married and single, old and young, academics and illiterate. They are from every walk of life from prelates to bankers, social workers to journalists. John Paul II has used the process of canonization and beatification to highlight the catholicity of the church and give new meaning to the universal call to holiness. For him the saints and *beati* underscore the virtues and values that he advocates for society as a whole.

There is a second important way that this Jubilee Volume marks the beginning of a new chapter in the history of the *New Catholic Encyclopedia*. In addition to serving as a preamble to a revised edition of the *NCE,* it introduces a new publisher. The Gale Group, based in Farmington Hills, Michigan, and the Catholic University of America Press have entered into a working relationship designed to insure the existence and enhance the quality of the encyclopedia for years to come. As publisher the Gale Group, whose name is well known in academic circles and by librarians, will oversee the production and marketing of the *New Catholic Encyclopedia,* and the Catholic University of America Press will continue to be responsible for the editorial content.

BERARD L. MARTHALER, O.F.M.CONV.

Part I: From the Poland of Karol Wojtyła to the World of John Paul II—Thematic Essays

Introduction

The twelve essays that follow explain the principles and policies that define Karol Wojtyła, the man and his vision. Although the authors, outstanding scholars, most with international reputations, worked independently, their essays reinforce one another. They agree that a remarkable consistency of thought has colored the papacy of John Paul II. It is characterized by a coherent philosophy of the human person and comprehensive view of world affairs that was observable in Wojtyła's formative years. He moved to Rome but he never left the Poland of his youth—its deep piety and devotion to Mary, the Jewish companions of early years, interest in theater and the arts, his ties to the academic world of Lublin. The Solidarity movement that frustrated the communist regime has become, in the writings of the Polish pope, a principle in theology and public policy. The way that the brother saints Cyril and Methodius incarnated Christianity in Slavic culture is the model for John Paul's "new evangelization." In light of Pope Wojtyła's elaborate plans to cross the threshold into the third millennium, preparations for the millennial celebration of Polish Christianity in 1966 now appear as a dress rehearsal. The thematic essays, each in its own way, paint a portrait of a man whose spiritual and intellectual life, whose sensitivity to cultural and political forces, prepared him well for the role of universal pastor.

George Weigel begins these essays by displaying the Poland in which Karol Wojtyła grew up and became cardinal archbishop of Kraków. The "unique history" of Poland under communist rule made it a centerpiece of Pope John Paul's vision of the transformation of society.

Karol Wojtyła was a poet and dramatist before he became a philosopher and remained an artist even after he received his training in philosophy. **Bolesław Taborski** examines Wojtyła's literary works, from his biblical and historical poems to his last play, *Radiation of Fatherhood.* **Kenneth Schmitz** looks at young Fr. Wojtyła's dissertation in philosophy, and explains how the union of metaphysics and phenomenology can be used to understand the ethical action of the person.

Karol Wojtyła was more a philosopher than a theologian, but it would be more precise to say that his work shows throughout a concern with the truth of man, revealed in Jesus Christ. **Peter Phan** discusses the new pope's Trinitarian triptych of encyclicals (*Redemptor hominis, Dives in misericordia,* and *Dominum et vivificantem*) as testimony to this pastoral outlook.

Like his predecessors, Pope John Paul has found occasion to assert his influence in the public-policy debates of society, both in his writings and in the direct involvement of the Holy See in world organizations. The constant theme in such interventions is the good of the person. **Gregory Baum** examines the pope's social encyclicals (*Laborem exercens, Sollicitudo rei socialis,* and *Centesimus annus*) and concludes that his economic teaching calls for a free-market society regulated by the demands of the common good and transformed by a culture of solidarity. **Helen Alvaré** sees that Pope John Paul's writings on the family and the Holy See's decisive engagement in the international conferences at Cairo and Beijing "have substantially clarified the stakes for the family in the twenty-first century."

First as auxiliary and then as archbishop of Kraków, Bishop Wojtyła took part in every session of the Second Vatican Council and made well-known contributions to the documents *Gaudium et spes* and *Dignitatis humanae.* **Paul McPartlan** argues that the future pope saw the council as "removing the distinction between doctrine and practice," revealing the truth of the faith in action. McPartlan shows how the substance of the council has come to fruition in Pope John Paul's pontificate.

Vatican II confirmed the Church in its pursuit of ecumenical and interreligious dialogue. **John Radano, John Borelli,** and **Eugene Fisher** show how this process has been carried out vigorously in Pope John Paul's pontificate, from the opening of the Orthodox-Catholic dialogue (1980) to the World Day of Prayer for Peace in Assisi (1986) and the pope's visit to the Holy Land during the Great Jubilee Year 2000. Fisher speaks of the pope's lifelong concern for the Jewish people, culminating in his dramatic visit to and prayer at the Western Wall in Jerusalem. ''Jewish-Christian relations will never be the same.''

Pope John Paul's openness to the world has included a keen interest in culture, manifest in the work of philosophers, artists, and scientists. **George Coyne** speaks of the ''new view'' from Rome with respect to the sciences. Though this has received most attention through the reexamination of the Galileo case, its real fruits lie in an ongoing discussion between the Church and science on questions of ultimate meaning.

Lawrence Cunningham brings this set of essays to a close with reflections on the pope's tremendous dedication to the universal witness to the truth of the gospel in the blood of the martyrs. Pope John Paul has beatified and canonized more people than any other pope in history,

thus emphasizing the universality of the call to holiness. He has also expanded the notion of martyrdom to include not only those who are killed precisely on account of their faith, but also those unjustly put to death, whose lives ''stood in direct and dramatic counterpoint to forces of evil and untruth.''

In subtle and not-so-subtle ways, the foregoing essays make it clear that, however much history has shaped this pope, he has left his own stamp on history and the papacy. The program of his pontificate has not been to change substantially the Church's institution, teaching, and practice—yet in a sense everything has changed. He has given a new model of the office of the pope; he has exemplified a new engagement with culture; he has renewed the Church's commitment to its universal mission. In sum, he has given a new articulation of what it means to be a Christian in the modern world.

[EDITORS]

The Church, the Collapse of Communism, and the Challenge of New Democracies

George Weigel, Senior Fellow Ethics and Public Policy Center, Washington, D.C., is the author of Witness to Hope: The Biography of Pope John Paul II *(New York 1999).*

During the three decades following the Second Vatican Council, the Catholic Church in Poland lived a unique history that had important effects on the Church's life throughout the world, especially in central and eastern Europe.

Poland ignited the Revolution of 1989, the nonviolent upheaval that marked the terminal crisis of European communism and ended both Stalin's external empire and, eventually, the Soviet Union. And it would be impossible to imagine the Revolution of 1989 happening when it did, and how it did, without the leadership of the Polish Church throughout the communist period (1945–89). For during the years when a foreign-dominated communist party usurped the politics of the Polish state, the Polish nation found its principal institutional defender and its resonant public voice in the Catholic Church. That same Polish Church also gave world Catholicism its first non-Italian pope in 455 years when, on 16 October 1978, the archbishop of Kraków, Karol Józef Wojtyła, was elected bishop of Rome. And in the years after communism's demise, the Church in Poland tested the answer to an historic question: whether a democratic polity and a free-market economy could be built, simultaneously, on the foundations of a largely intact Catholic culture.

The Polish experience of Catholicism in the second half of twentieth-century history thus brought into sharp relief many of the great questions that confronted the Church at the opening of the third Christian millennium: Catholic identity; the relationship between traditional piety and modern life; Christian mission amidst rapid secularization; and the defense of human rights and religious freedom against political tyranny and false humanisms.

A Most Catholic Nation. When the Great Powers, meeting at the Crimean resort town of Yalta in January 1945, moved post-war Poland some one hundred fifty miles west on the map of central Europe, they simultaneously created the most "Polish" Poland that had ever existed. Although the identification of Catholicism with Polish nationhood dated back to the baptism of the Piast prince, Mieszko I, in 966, ethnic Poles composed only 65% of inter-war Poland (which was born in 1918 and crushed by the combined forces of Hitler and Stalin in 1939); significant minorities of Jews (15%), Ukrainians (9%), Byelorussians (5%), and Germans (2%) shared the Second Polish Republic with its Polish majority, often uneasily. Polish Jewry was destroyed during the Holocaust; the Ukrainian areas of inter-war Poland (seized by Stalin in 1939) were remanded to the "Ukrainian Soviet Socialist Republic" (and thus to the Soviet Union) by the Yalta accords; and the German population in the new western Polish lands was expelled to Germany. Thus postwar Poland was almost entirely Polish and Catholic, a demographic fact that made Poland the most indigestible of the Soviet satellite states. (Stalin once remarked that introducing communism to Poland was like "fitting a cow with a saddle.") A generation after the communist take-over, the regime's failure to alter the historic character of the Polish nation was aptly demonstrated by the fact that Poland was arguably the most intensely Catholic country in the world: some 95% of the population had been baptized, vocations to the priesthood and religious life were multiplying, and both parish churches and national pilgrimage sites were filled to overflowing on Sundays and feast days. This demographic reality set the stage for the high drama to follow.

The "Great Novena" and Vatican II. Cardinal Stefan Wyszyński, who was named Primate by Pope Pius XII in 1948 and is remembered throughout Poland as the "primate of the millennium," was the dominant figure in the Polish Church in the years immediately preceding and following the Second Vatican Council. According to Polish tradition, the primate served as the *interrex,* or acting head of state, between the death of a Polish king and the election of a new monarch by the nobility. Cardinal

Pope John Paul II waves to a crowd of Solidarity proponents. (Reuters/Luciano Mellace/Archive Photos. Reproduced by Permission.)

Wyszyński revived this ancient role during the communist period, and served, in effect, as *interrex* of Poland for over thirty years.

Vatican II occurred while Poland was completing the "Great Novena," nine years of catechetical and spiritual preparation for the millennium of Polish Christianity in 1966. Planned by Wyszyński during his three years of imprisonment and house arrest in 1953–56, the Great Novena was designed to culminate in a national act of consecration by which the people of Poland would dedicate their country to Mary, Queen of Poland: an act of dedication that Wyszyński hoped would be received in person by Pope Paul VI. As it happened, the communist regime refused the pope a visa; at the millennium liturgy at the Jasna Góra monastery on 26 August 1966, the pope's portrait, wreathed in red and white roses, sat on an empty chair next to the altar.

Concerned about the brutal effects of the Nazi occupation and the communist attempt to redefine Polish his-

tory and culture, Wyszyński conceived the Great Novena as a nine-year-long period of national spiritual revitalization, involving the systematic re-catechesis of the entire country according to a special theme chosen for each of the nine years (faith, the Ten Commandments, the family, the moral life, social justice, and so forth). Pilgrimages to Poland's major shrines and other traditional pious practices were also encouraged; but perhaps the greatest pilgrimage of the Great Novena was the pilgrimage of the Black Madonna throughout the country. This, in fact, was the symbolic heart of Wyszyński's pastoral plan of spiritual renewal—for nine years, a special copy of Poland's most famous icon (blessed by Pius XII) would travel throughout Poland, diocese by diocese and church by church, and at each parish a special day- or night-long vigil of prayer and reconsecration would be held during the hours while the Madonna was in residence. After some years of this, the Polish authorities "arrested Mary," as one Polish priest later described it, took the icon back to Częstochowa, put a guard on it, and told the Church that the icon could not leave the Jasna Góra monastery. Cardinal Wyszyński responded by sending the icon's empty frame from parish to parish, where it was met with the same fervor as the icon itself.

The Great Novena was an exercise in national religious restoration that had great public (and, ultimately, political) consequences. It revived the nation's spirits in the midst of fifty years of totalitarian occupation, and gave the hard-pressed Polish people an experience of their country's traditional role as the *antemurale Christianitatis,* the "rampart of Christendom." It deepened popular memory of the true history of the Polish nation and its culture during a period when the communist regime was systematically rewriting (and falsifying) that history for purposes of ideological indoctrination and political control. And it educated a generation of young people in the basics of Catholic faith and Catholic morality: an act of spiritual and cultural formation that would have an historic political impact in 1980, when the youngsters who had learned their catechism and the truth about their Polish heritage in unheated church buildings during the Great Novena were striking against the regime at the Lenin Shipyard in Gdańsk and elsewhere.

The Polish reception of the Second Vatican Council was complex, as might have been expected given the Polish Church's distinctive circumstances. Cardinal Wyszyński was concerned that some of the council's structural reforms might be manipulated by the regime in order to disrupt the Church's unity, which he had labored hard to preserve and which he regarded as the most effective line of defense against communism. Thus while the Polish Church might be strengthened by the introduction of the Polish language to its liturgy, the episcopate declined to institute, during the communist period, conciliar-approved practices like the permanent diaconate and parish councils, precisely in order to avoid the danger of the Church's being penetrated by the secret police.

On the other hand, according to Polish church leaders, several council documents were crucial in supporting the Church's struggle to maintain both its independence and the cultural integrity of the Polish nation under communism. The two most frequently cited documents in this regard are *Dignitatis humanae* (the Declaration on Religious Freedom) and *Gaudium et spes* (the Pastoral Constitution on the Church in the Modern World). The council's affirmation of the fundamental right of religious freedom in *Dignitatis humanae* was of obvious importance to a persecuted Church; the declaration's stress on the Church's respect for the dynamics of human freedom also created circumstances in which the Church could open a dialogue with all who were concerned with the

moral truth about the human person, whether they were believers or not. Thanks in part to *Dignitatis humanae,* the Church in Poland became the defender of the basic human rights of all Poles, not only the religious freedom of Polish Catholics. *Gaudium et spes,* in a complementary fashion, provided the Polish Church with the outline of a true Christian humanism (in the fields of culture, family life, and the economy) with which to challenge the false humanism of Marxism-Leninism. The young archbishop of Kraków, Karol Wojtyła, played a significant role in the preparation of both *Gaudium et spes* and *Dignitatis humanae* at the council. Later, as cardinal-archbishop, Wojtyła convened the archdiocesan Synod of Kraków to implement the council's dual program of *ressourcement* and *aggiornamento.* The preparation for the synod involved a systematic reading of the Council's documents throughout the archdiocese; Cardinal Wojtyła also wrote a personal commentary on the conciliar constitutions, decrees, and declarations (later published in book form in English as *Sources of Renewal: The Implementation of Vatican II*).

Lay-oriented renewal movements flourished in Poland in the years after the council. One of the most influential was the Light-and-Life (*Światło i Życie*) movement; its charismatic leader, Father Franciszek Blachnicki, articulated a distinctive Polish liberation theology that was focused, during the communist period, on the development of what Blachnicki described as a "diaconate of liberty through truth." Light-and-Life work included "Oasis" summer camps for young people and families, during which religious instruction, liturgy, and common prayer were combined with recreation; the movement also conducted a ministry to the physically handicapped. From the mid-1970s through the late 1980s, some 300,000 Polish youngsters received a Light-and-Life spiritual formation, which stressed the *light* of God's Word as the key to the renewal of the *life* of God's people; and by the end of the 1980s some 40% of the Church's religious vocations were coming out of the movement. The Institute of the Immaculate Mother of the Church, a secular institute for women whose name combined traditional Polish piety with the Mariology of Vatican II, was closely affiliated with Light-and-Life and its various works.

Duszpasterstwo Akademickie ("Academic Pastoral Care"), a chaplaincy to Catholic university students, played an important role in the formation of a Catholic intelligentsia in Poland during the communist period (like the "Oasis" summer camps, it was regularly badgered by the secret police). The *Klub Inteligencji Katolickiej* ("Club of the Catholic Intelligentsia," or *KIK*), formally recognized by the communist regime in 1956, was instrumental in healing the breach between the Church and anti-clerical Polish intellectuals; *KIK*'s monthly journal, *Więź* (''Link''), was edited for many years by Tadeusz Mazowiecki (who in 1989 became Poland's first non-communist prime minister since World War II). Traditional patterns of Polish devotional life, including massive pilgrimages to the Jasna Góra monastery in Częstochowa, home of the icon of the ''Black Madonna,'' also continued in the years after the council. The foundations were being laid, in and through the Church, for an unprecedented coalition of workers and intellectuals in opposition to communism.

Prelude to Revolution. Archbishop Karol Wojtyła was created cardinal by Paul VI at the consistory of 1967, after which the communist regime intensified its efforts to drive a wedge between the more traditional style of Cardinal Wyszyński and the reforming tendencies of the archbishop of Kraków. Such efforts were singularly unsuccessful. For, even as Cardinal Wojtyła was becoming a major figure in international Catholic life (through his work at the Synod of Bishops' general meetings in 1969, 1971, 1974, and 1977, by his participation in the 1976 Eucharistic Congress in Philadelphia, and by a series of philosophical lectures at major universities throughout the world), he was also conducting a vigorous public ministry in Kraków that complemented, in more contemporary forms, the leadership of Cardinal Wyszyński. Perhaps the symbolic centerpiece of that ministry was the epic struggle, successfully conducted over twenty years, to build a church in Nowa Huta, the steelmilling suburb of Kraków constructed by the communists as a ''model workers' town''—which meant, of course, without a church. The strikingly modern ''Church of the Ark of Our Lady, Queen of Poland,'' which was consecrated by Wojtyła in 1977 after ten years of voluntary labor, and another Nowa Huta parish, the Church of St. Maximilian Kolbe, dedicated in 1983, would become centers of anticommunist resistance during the years leading up to the Revolution of 1989.

Through his writings in the Kraków-based newspaper *Tygodnik Powszechny* (''Universal Weekly''), his philosophical studies and publications, his teaching at the Catholic University of Lublin, and his work with the Kraków *KIK* group, Wojtyła also helped broaden and deepen the post-conciliar conversation between the Polish Church and Polish intellectuals (who, since the eighteenth century, had nurtured a proud tradition of anticlericalism). That rapprochement reached a crucial point of public visibility when, in 1977, the historian Adam Michnik, a secular activist of Jewish background, published *Kościół, Lewica, Dialog* (''The Church, the Left, and Dialogue''), which claimed that the situation had changed dramatically: ''For many years now, the Catholic Church in Poland has not been on the side of the powers-that-be, but has stood out in defense of the oppressed. The authentic enemy of the left is not the Church, but totalitarian power, and in this battle the Church plays a role which it is impossible to overestimate.'' Michnik's argument was seconded by the distinguished philosopher Leszek Kołakowski (another nonbeliever) who, from exile, wrote in 1979 that the ''most powerful source of moral authority'' in Poland, and thus the most powerful source of opposition to communism, was the Catholic Church.

Cardinal Wojtyła's election as pope on 16 October 1978 sent profound shock waves throughout every level of Polish society, and decisively broke the pattern of ''humiliation'' that British historian Norman Davies once described as ''the essence of Poland's modern experience.'' But it was Wojtyła's return to his Polish homeland as Pope John Paul II in June 1979 that began the decisive phase of the Polish Church's struggle with communism.

Wojtyła had designed the Synod of Kraków so that it would conclude in 1979 with a celebration of the 900th anniversary of the martyrdom of St. Stanisław, the first bishop of Poland's ancient capital. The communist authorities balked at that celebration being the occasion for John Paul II's return to Poland (Stanisław had died because of his resistance to the civil power of his day, and the parallels were undoubtedly uncomfortable for politicians already unsure of their grip on power); and so it was decided that John Paul, rather than coming to Poland for two days in May, would come for nine days in June, and would visit six cities rather than just Kraków and Warsaw.

It was during that pilgrimage, 2–10 June 1979, that Poland turned irreversibly toward a non-communist future, in a pivot whose effects would ultimately be felt throughout central and eastern Europe. In speaking to almost one-third of the Polish nation (some thirteen million people) in person, John Paul created what political scientist Bogdan Szajkowski would later call a ''psychological earthquake, an opportunity for mass political catharsis.'' But it was a distinctive kind of political upheaval, in that the pope's sermons, addresses, and spontaneous remarks during the pilgrimage were determinedly Christocentric in content, challenging the people of Poland to live ''in the truth'' about the God-given dignity of the human person, a truth that had been definitively revealed in the life, death, and resurrection of Jesus Christ. In Warsaw, Gniezno, Częstochowa, Opole, Mogila, and Kraków, John Paul preached what Adam Michnik would remember as a ''great lesson in dignity,'' precisely by being a Christian evangelist.

The Solidarity Revolution. The enormous public impact of the pope's pilgrimage became clear the following year. In early August 1980, workers at the Lenin Shipyard in Gdańsk, led by the charismatic electrician Lech Wałęsa, struck in protest against the dismissal of Anna Walentynowicz, a veteran independent labor activist. Aided by advisers like *Więź* editor and *KIK* activist Tadeusz Mazowiecki, the workers' strike committee demanded, and eventually won, the right to form the independent, self-governing trade union "Solidarity" (which, by mid-1981, had over ten million members throughout Poland).

The very name, "Solidarity," was deliberately chosen to reflect the catechesis of John Paul II. Moreover, the union's struggle to be born was supported by the Church at several key points of confrontation with the regime. In the last week of August 1980, with the specter of Soviet intervention hanging over the negotiations in Gdańsk, the Polish bishops' conference issued a communiqué citing *Gaudium et spes* (n. 68) on the "fundamental right" of individuals to "form themselves into associations which truly represent them and are able to cooperate in organizing economic life properly." Two months later, when another crisis broke out over the legal registration of Solidarity, Cardinal Wyszyński assured Warsaw Solidarity chief Zbigniew Bujak, "I am with you." Perhaps most dramatically, on 16 December 1980, John Paul II wrote a private letter to Soviet leader Leonid Brezhnev, after receiving American intelligence information indicating that a Soviet-led Warsaw Pact invasion of Poland, aimed at crushing the nascent Solidarity movement, might be imminent. In the letter, the pope, reminding the Soviet leader that Poland's independence had been guaranteed by the 1975 Helsinki Final Act, suggested that he was prepared to denounce any Warsaw Pact invasion by moral analogy to the Nazi invasion of September 1939.

The year 1981 was one of great difficulty for the Polish Church. On 13 May 1981 John Paul II was seriously wounded in an assassination attempt that was widely assumed, although never conclusively proven, to be linked to events in Poland and the threat those events posed in Moscow. Two weeks later, on 28 May, Cardinal Wyszyński died of cancer; he was succeeded as primate by his former secretary, Józef Glemp, then bishop of Warmia, who was named archbishop of Gniezno and Warsaw on 7 July. On 5 September Primate Glemp was principal concelebrant at the Mass that opened Solidarity's first national congress (during which a recuperating John Paul II issued the social encyclical *Laborem exercens*). In October, General Wojciech Jaruzelski, who was already Poland's prime minister and minister of defense, became first secretary of the communist party as well, thus drawing all the levers of power into his hands. A few weeks later, John Paul II met in Rome with a delegation of Polish intellectuals who were supporting Solidarity.

Amidst the general apprehension that something ominous was at hand, the pope assured the group that, in his judgment, the movement toward freedom in Poland could not be reversed. Men and women who had regained a sense of their dignity would not continue to acquiesce in their enforced absence from public life. Communism, the pope suggested, was dying, no matter how long it took for the end-game to be played out.

After months of rising tensions between the trade union that was really a political opposition, and a regime being hard pressed by its Soviet "ally," General Jaruzelski imposed martial law in Poland on the night of 12–13 December, with virtually all of the Solidarity leadership being placed under arrest.

In retrospect, it seems that this crude attempt to return Poland to the status quo ante-1979 was doomed to failure from the outset. But another eight long years had to pass before the Solidarity revolution was completed in 1989. Those eight years of struggle were punctuated by two more papal pilgrimages, as John Paul returned to Poland in June 1983 and June 1987. The 1983 pilgrimage took place when the pall of martial law still lay heavily over the Polish nation. In a private conversation with General Jaruzelski, the pope argued that re-opening a dialogue on the agreements that had been reached during the Solidarity revolution was the only path to genuine social renewal in Poland. The pope also rebuffed the government's tacit offer to have the Church, in effect, replace Solidarity as the expression of the Polish people's political aspirations. Publicly, John Paul preached the virtue of hope to a people depressed by the deteriorating economic and political situations. He also gave the Poles two new icons of resistance, beatifying the Carmelite Rafał Kalinowski and "Brother Albert" Chmielowski, both of whom had been involved in a nineteenth-century anti-czarist revolt before embracing religious life. By the time of the 1987 papal pilgrimage, it was clear that communism in Poland was just about finished, and John Paul spent a week laying the philosophical and theological foundations for the revival of Solidarity. The energy for national renewal, he suggested, would be generated by a re-emerging Polish nation freeing itself "from the inheritance of hatred and egoism" and the contemporary "disease of superficiality"; the crumbling facade of the Polish communist state was largely ignored as the pope drove home the theme of social solidarity in a series of addresses along the Baltic Coast, the first home of Solidarity.

During the years between the imposition of martial law and the Revolution of 1989, the Church developed a multifaceted resistance ministry, aimed at sustaining the independent life of Polish culture during a time when the Polish nation was denied any political expression of its aspirations to independence.

One key locale for that ministry of non-violent resistance was the Church of St. Stanisław Kostka in the Żoliborz section of Warsaw, where a dynamic young curate, Father Jerzy Popiełuszko, inaugurated a monthly ''Mass for the Fatherland'' in January 1982, shortly after the imposition of martial law. Popiełuszko's services were attended by as many as fifteen thousand Poles from all over the country; the priest posed such a threat to the regime that he was murdered by the secret police on the night of 19 October 1984. Father Popiełuszko was buried in the churchyard at St. Stanisław Kostka, which immediately became a Solidarity sanctuary, or what one activist would later call ''a piece of free Poland.''

Lech Wałęsa's church in Gdańsk, St. Bridget's, was another center of Solidarity's underground life, as was the Kolbe Church in Nowa Huta, which sponsored debates, ''evenings of independent Polish culture'' (including classical and jazz concerts, art exhibitions, and theater), an unofficial Christian university, and, toward the end of the 1980s, an independent television station (operated by people who had been fired at the state-run network). These sites embodied a distinctive feature of the Polish Church's life during the mid-1980s: just as embassies enjoy ''extraterritorial'' legal status in the host country, resistance churches in Poland enjoyed a kind of ''moral extraterritoriality'' in which they became virtual embassies from Polish society to itself.

The Church's resistance to a communist regime that was slowly collapsing throughout the 1980s was not without cost; in 1988 and early 1989, for example, five priests died violently under suspicious circumstances. But by then it seemed certain that the regime's days were indeed numbered. In April and May 1988, workers in Nowa Huta and Gdańsk struck, and their demands included the legal restoration of Solidarity. Demonstrations followed in Warsaw, Kraków, Łódź, and Lublin, with young students and workers chanting, ''There's no freedom without Solidarity.'' In desperation, the regime tried to engage the Church as its primary interlocutor, bypassing the Solidarity activists. The Church leadership refused to interpose itself, and thus helped force the government to resume a dialogue with the trade union/political opposition it had banned in 1981. Round Table negotiations began on 6 February 1989, and as a result of those negotiations, partially free elections were held on 4 June 1989 (certain seats in the Sejm, the lower house of the parliament, were reserved for communist party members). Solidarity candidates won all 161 freely-contested elections for the Sejm, and took 99 out of 100 seats in the newly-created Polish Senate. After months of further maneuvering, Tadeusz Mazowiecki was sworn in as prime minister of Poland on 24 August 1989.

The Resistance Church Elsewhere. John Paul's influence on the collapse of European communism was not limited to his role in Poland. Indeed, the pope's impact could be felt throughout both the external and internal Soviet empires, in the years before their collapse.

From the beginning of his pontificate, the Polish pope urged the Czechoslovak Church to take a more assertive position in the face of one of east central Europe's most repressive communist regimes. The Czech primate, Cardinal František Tomášek, had been rather timid in his relations with the government prior to October 1978; sensing the personal support of the pope, the octogenarian cardinal became one of Czechoslovak communism's most determined and feared opponents during the 1980s, growing older and tougher at the same time. The government refused a visa that would have permitted John Paul to participate in the celebrations of the 1,100th anniversary of the death of St. Methodius, which were held in Velehrad in July 1985; but the pope made his presence felt anyway by sending a letter to all Czech and Slovak priests, who in turn made the Methodius anniversary the largest demonstration of Catholicism's public presence in Czechoslovakia in four decades. John Paul also used his disciplinary authority to good advantage in the struggle against communism in Czechoslovakia: a 1982 instruction from the Congregation for the Doctrine of the Faith forbidding priests from participating in partisan politics was crucial in destroying the influence of ''Pacem in Terris,'' the regime-friendly organization of Czechoslovak clergy. By 1987, the Church in Bohemia, Moravia, and Slovakia had been reborn in resistance, to the point where a Moravian farmer, Augustin Navrátil, could organize three nationwide petitions for religious freedom. In the ''Velvet Revolution'' of November-December 1989, Catholic lay and clerical leaders were in the front ranks of the democratic resistance, and the election of President Václav Havel, the dissident playwright who had been jailed earlier in the year, was marked by a national ''Te Deum'' in Prague's St. Vitus Cathedral.

The more alert Soviet leaders quickly perceived that Pope John Paul II would pose a grave threat to the internal Soviet empire as well as to the Soviet position in the Warsaw Pact. Lithuania, the key to the Soviet position on the Baltic, and Ukraine, without which the Soviet Union would cease to be a great power, were the two cases in point within the USSR. And in both instances, John Paul's influence, however indirect, helped support a reinvigorated resistance Church that eventually made its contribution to the recovery of national independence.

A group of activist Lithuanian clergy, religious, and laity (many of whom had previously been involved in publishing the underground *Chronicle of the Catholic Church in Lithuania,* one of contemporary Catholicism's most remarkable martyrologies) launched a Catholic

Committee for the Defense of Believers' Rights within months of John Paul II's election. Many of these activists were later sent (or returned) to Gulag labor camps, and another dissident priest was murdered in a 1986 "road accident." But John Paul's personal support for the Church in Lithuania (to whose principal Marian shrine, Ostrabrama, he had clandestinely sent his red cardinal's zuchetto after his election as pope) inspired other clergy and laity to take up the cause of Lithuanian religious freedom, which was also rekindled in the Lithuanian diaspora in North America. By the time Lithuania declared its independence from the Soviet Union in 1990, few observers, including those in the Kremlin, doubted that the Catholic Church had helped keep the Lithuanian nation alive during fifty years of an intense Soviet effort to destroy Lithuanian national consciousness.

Ukraine was the linchpin of the internal Soviet empire that Lenin and Stalin had consolidated on its original czarist foundation. The guardian of Ukrainian national identity, especially in western Ukraine (Galicia), was the Greek Catholic Church, which had been bitterly persecuted since Stalin's day. Unlike some other Polish clergy, Karol Wojtyła had shown himself sympathetic to the Greek Catholic cause, and as pope, he quickly signaled his support for a hard-pressed local Church by meeting with the exiled Ukrainian cardinal, Josyf Slipyi, in November 1978, a month after his election. The full complexities of the situation, which involved ecumenical as well as political issues, were revealed the following year, when both the Russian Orthodox patriarchate of Moscow and the Kremlin reacted negatively to the pope's March 1979 letter to Cardinal Slipyi, in which John Paul cited the Universal Declaration of Human Rights in support of religious freedom for all in Sovict Ukraine. In March 1980, a synod of all of Greek Catholic bishops from the Ukrainian diaspora throughout the world met in Rome (the bishops from the underground Church in Ukraine could not, of course, participate). The synod made provision for the succession to the aging Cardinal Slipyi, electing Archbishop Myroslav Lubachivsky of Philadelphia as Slipyi's coadjutor. But the ecumenical situation remained unresolved, in part because, under Soviet law, the Greek Catholic Church in Ukraine did not exist, legally. That fact, coupled with historic animosities of a particular ferocity, made any serious ecumenical engagement between the Greek Catholics of Ukraine and their Orthodox brethren very unlikely. John Paul tried to turn the 1988 millennium of the baptism of Rus', which both Greek Catholics in Ukraine and Russian Orthodox claimed as their particular anniversary, into a moment of ecumenical rapprochement; he was, in the main, rebuffed. After an independent Ukraine had secured its independence in the aftermath of the 1991 Soviet crack-up, Cardinal Lu-

bachivsky (who had succeeded Cardinal Slipyi in 1984) and other Greek Catholic leaders in Ukraine tied to follow the pope's ecumenical lead, but their efforts were made even more difficult by the fact that, in post-Soviet Ukraine, the Orthodox Church itself splintered into three competing factions. In a 1995 apostolic letter marking the fourth centenary of the Union of Brest, by which the Greek Catholic Church in Ukraine had been reunited to Rome while retaining its Byzantine liturgy, John Paul proposed that the fidelity that had once caused the Ukrainians to bind themselves to Rome now "commits [the Greek Catholic Church] to fostering the unity of all the Churches." The martyrdoms and persecutions of the past, he wrote, should be a "sacrifice offered to God in order to implore the hoped-for union" of Catholicism and Orthodoxy at the end of the second millennium. It was a hope easier to enunciate than to realize. The pope had kept faith with a persecuted eastern-rite Church, but in doing so, he had immensely complicated the ecumenism to which he was just as firmly committed. Here was a sad truth of history that even so forceful an advocate as John Paul II could not overcome.

John Paul II and Russia. Karol Wojtyła was singularly free of the mutual antipathies that have marked (and scarred) Polish-Russian relations for centuries. As pope, John Paul read extensively in modern Russian philosophy and theology, including the works Vladimir Soloviev, a late-nineteenth-century prophet of East-West reconciliation, and the writings of former Marxists (like Nicolai Berdyaev, Sergei Bulgakov, and Simon Frank) who had embraced Orthodoxy prior to the Bolshevik Revolution. These authors, and an ongoing series of private conversations with Russian intellectuals, convinced the pope that there was a religious core to Russian culture from which the whole world could benefit. John Paul's initiatives towards Russia and Russians, however, were frequently more successful with political than with religious leaders.

No dialogue with the Soviet leadership was possible until the generation formed in the Stalin era—Leonid Brezhnev, Yuri Andropov, Konstantin Chernenko—had passed from the scene. The ascension of Mikhail Gorbachev in 1985 opened up the possibility of a Holy See/Kremlin dialogue, an opportunity the pope was eager to seize. In June 1988, a Vatican delegation led by Cardinal Agostino Casaroli came to Moscow for the public celebrations of the millennium of Christianity in Rus'. (The patriarchate of Moscow had made it clear that the pope himself would not be welcome.) Casaroli and his delegation were received in the Kremlin by Gorbachev, to whom they presented a long letter from John Paul II in which the pope expressed his desire for a more forthright and normal relationship between the Soviet state and the Holy See. Gorbachev replied positively, and came to the

Vatican for a historic meeting with the pope on 1 December 1989. Earlier that year, John Paul had encouraged the Soviet Nobel laureate, Andrei Sakharov, in his work as a democratic reformer in the new Soviet parliament. The new Soviet law on religious freedom of October 1990 was, in some part, a fruit of the pope's efforts. The collapse of the Soviet Union in 1991 ended the dialogue with Soviet political leaders, but Russian president Boris Yeltsin met with the pope twice during his years in power.

The frustration of his ecumenical initiatives with Russian Orthodoxy must rank as among the great disappointments of John Paul's pontificate. The brusque, even hostile, reactions to the pope's efforts by the Moscow patriarchate were perhaps understandable during the Soviet period, when the patriarchate was closely controlled by the Soviet government. But the difficulties did not end with the collapse of the Soviet Union. The resurgent Greek Catholic Church in Ukraine was regarded by Russian Orthodox leaders as both a western political salient and a Roman ecclesiastical invasion in historic Russian and Orthodox lands, as was the establishment in April 1991 of four apostolic administrations for the pastoral care of Catholics in Russia. Attempts to resolve the ecumenical crisis at a meeting in Balamand, Lebanon, in 1993 created a framework for future discussion between Rome and Orthodoxy, but did little to ease the situation on the ground in Ukraine and elsewhere. A hoped-for meeting between the pope and Patriarch Alexei II of Moscow in Vienna in June 1997 was canceled because of intra-Orthodox tensions, and Alexei made clear in the two years following that he did not look favorably on the possibility of a papal pilgrimage to Russia. Moreover, the rigidity of the leadership of Russian Orthodoxy, world Orthodoxy's largest Church, made matters more difficult for the somewhat more ecumenically minded Ecumenical Patriarch of Constantinople, Bartholomew I, while reinforcing the anxieties and nervousness of other Orthodox Churches about the Roman ecumenical embrace. Yet it was precisely during this period of ecumenical tension that John Paul, determined to pursue his vision of a Church once again breathing with both its lungs, built the "Redemptoris Mater" Chapel in the Vatican, the first to be decorated in the Byzantine iconographic style. The chapel was both the pope's monument to the Great Jubilee of 2000 within the Apostolic Palace and an enduring memorial to his great millennial hope.

The Post-Communist Period. Like virtually every other institution in the post-communist societies of central and eastern Europe, the Catholic Church struggled to define its role in the democratic circumstances of the 1990s. After decades of oppression in which it had sometimes held a monopoly on institutional virtue, in Poland and elsewhere, the Church found itself compelled, by the logic of its own social doctrine, to work for the day when that monopoly was broken. For were free societies to be built in central an eastern Europe according to the model defined by John Paul II in the 1991 encyclical *Centesimus annus,* there would necessarily exist many virtuous public institutions.

Although the Catholic Church in central and eastern Europe had come through the stirring events of 1989–91 with its public reputation at perhaps a historic peak, there was still a massive work of reconstruction to do in the years after the communist crack-up. Diocesan structures and the organization of episcopal conferences required considerable attention, as did the legal relationship between the Church and the new democracies. In Poland, for example, a new concordat between the Holy See and the government of the Republic of Poland was signed on 28 July 1993, but intense debate continued over the legal definition of Church-state relations in a new Polish Constitution. The Church's educational ministry required renovation at all levels; work was underway throughout the 1990s to develop new catechetical materials and practices and to review the curricula of central and eastern Europe's seminaries and houses of religious formation (many of which, of course, had to be rebuilt from scratch). Religious publishing, long conducted underground or in highly constrained circumstances, now enjoyed unprecedented access to the public, but had to make its way in a free economy. The Church's ministry of charity and social service experienced new demands as the new democracies made the transition from communist welfare statism to democratic capitalism, at a time when financial pressures on the Church were great. Consideration also had to be given to those structural reforms of Vatican II (such as the permanent diaconate and lay consultative bodies) whose implementation had necessarily been delayed during the communist period.

Public controversy over the Church's role in the new democracies centered in the 1990s on abortion law, religious education in public schools, the content of programming in the media, and the role of the clergy in partisan politics. The Polish situation was, once again, a microcosm of the entire region. In 1956, the Gomułka regime had enacted a highly permissive abortion law, in a deliberate assault on the moral authority of the Church; given that history and the Church's consistent teaching on the subject, it should have come as no surprise that, after the communist collapse, the Church leadership wished to see that law replaced by a statute protective of unborn life. The controversy that ensued was shaped not only by the substantive issue, but also (and perhaps even primarily) by concerns that certain Church leaders had not fully internalized a commitment to democratic persuasion in public life. Similar concerns about the style of the hierarchy's intervention in legislative debate effected the argument over voluntary religious education in public schools and the role of "Christian values" in the media, especially television.

In his address to the Polish bishops during their *ad limina* visits to Rome in January 1993, John Paul II stressed that the Polish Church, while being fully engaged in public life as a moral mentor, must also be a non-partisan Church in the new Polish democracy. "The Church is not a political party," John Paul insisted, "nor is she identified with any political party; she is above them, open to all people of good will, and no political party can claim the right to represent her." On 27 June 1993, a letter from the Polish bishops was read in all parishes at Sunday Mass, three months prior to national elections; following the pope's lead, the letter insisted that the Church could not be identified with any party, coalition of parties, or candidate, and emphasized the role of the laity in carrying the social teaching of the Church into political life.

Despite these difficulties and controversies, the Church in central and eastern Europe crossed the threshold of the third Christian millennium in a distinctive position to test the capacity of Catholic social doctrine to inform and shape national processes of democratic and market transition. Skeptics, in the region and elsewhere, argued that Polish, Czech, Slovak, Lithuanian, and Ukrainian Catholics would be no more immune to the tides of secularization than their Spanish, Portuguese, and Irish brethren had been in their post-authoritarian periods of democratic and capitalist consolidation. But those inclined to look at these matters more hopefully could point several countervailing facts. In Poland, religious practice, and recruitment to seminaries and religious communities remained exceptionally high in the decade after the communist collapse. In western Ukraine, a vital Greek Catholic Church had not only emerged from under the rubble of more than five decades of underground life and intense persecution, but was growing. The Church in Bohemia, in the aftermath of the Velvet Revolution, was in its strongest public position in centuries. Moreover, with *Centesimus annus* John Paul II had positioned the teaching authority of the Church ahead of the curve of debate in post-communist societies, and the Church throughout central and eastern Europe was thus positioned to act as a magnet toward responsible reform.

See Also: AD LIMINA VISIT, AGOSTINO CASAROLI, CENTESIMUS ANNUS, ALBERT CHMIELOWSKI, MYROSLAV LUBACHIVSKY, RAFAEL KALINOWSKI, JERZY POPIEŁUSZKO, JOSYF SLIPYJ, STEFAN WYSZYŃSKI

Bibliography: J. KUBIK, *The Power of Symbols Against the Symbols of Power: The Rise of Solidarity and the Fall of State Socialism in Poland* (University Park, Pennsylvania 1994) A. MICEWSKI, *Cardinal Wyszyński: A Biography* (San Diego 1984). B. SZAJKOWSKI, *Next to God . . . Poland. Politics and Religion in Contemporary Poland* (New York, 1983). G. WEIGEL, *The Final Revolution: The Resistance Church and the Collapse of Communism* (New York 1992); *Witness to Hope: The Biography of Pope John Paul II* (New York 1999).

[GEORGE WEIGEL]

Karol Wojtyła: Poet, Playwright, Philosopher, and Patriot

Bolesław Taborski, M.A. (Bristol), is a poet, writer, and theater critic. He is the author of Karola Wojtyły dramaturgia wnętrza (The Inner Theatre of Karol Wojtyła) *(Lublin 1989) and editor of* The Collected Plays and Writings on Theater of Karol Wojtyła *(Berkeley 1987).*

The unique imprint of John Paul II's pontificate is largely due to his personality, his way of thinking and seeing things. This in turn stems not only from his native roots, but from his upbringing and seminary education in a country with a specific brand of religious tradition. Just as important is his artistic creativity and his skill as a writer, which he was developing from his early youth. His love of literature and theater, based on the best achievements of Polish culture, had a liberating influence on young Wojtyła, who soon transcended the need for self-expression. His poetry developed with the man, as it were: from somewhat conventional beginnings he came to achieve the stature of a major religious poet for our time through the crystallization of his own deep spirituality. Similarly, his plays gradually led to a concept of "inner theater" which, though never explicitly defined, replaced external action with his protagonists' tormented search for spiritual values.

In his plays and in his long philosophical, contemplative poems he strives to reach under the surface of events and to look for links between them in God's, albeit flawed, world. It is worth noting that Wojtyła continued writing plays until 1964 (when he was an archbishop), and poetry until the time of his election to papacy. It can be argued that even now his literary works are helpful in gaining a better comprehension of their author's philosophy, views, and actions.

The Poet

One may call Wojtyła's poetry religious in its deepest, innermost sense. But the phraseology and imagery is by no means devotional or superficially "religious." It should be remembered that his poetry spans four decades.

As time went by it reflected more and more his main task of a concerned and committed pastor. His poetry has always been one of ideas rather than images, notwithstanding its striking and beautiful imagery. It could be said that with the passage of time he transcended poetry, as it were, in the sense that while formal aspects, like rhythm or line pattern, remained, to some extent the poems were simply philosophical and religious reflections. But this would not be altogether true.

The future direction of his poetry can already be seen in his *juvenilia,* written in his late teens, for the main part unpublished: an early collection of ballads, and another called *Renaissance Psalter*, both written in 1938–1939, from which seventeen sonnets were published only in 1955. The young poet looks back to the "golden period"'of Polish literature in the sixteenth century, and his style is indebted to the early twentieth-century Young Poland movement. But his thoughts are already maturing in a remarkable way, and are rooted firmly in Christian tradition. Even the form shows strong signs of originality, particularly in the longer poems: *Word-Logos,* the second version of *Mousike*, and *Magnificat* (this last was one of only a couple included in his works published after 1978).

Still unpublished remain the long poems written during the Second World War. *The Harpist* is religious in character; its subject is the biblical King David. *The Avengers* is connected with the patriotic strain in his writing, and *Proletariat* with his social awareness. *The Breakthrough* seems to reflect the impending change in his life. The war-time poems form a transition to his mature poetry, which emerged in 1944 at the time that he embarked on the road to priesthood. Poetry, one has the feeling, was to him something very intimate. He never brought it to the open, published infrequently and with reluctance in periodicals, and never under his own name.

The fourteen great poetic structures that followed are written mainly in free, blank verse, with a changeable, often long line, which sometimes in later poems passed into poetic prose. As a rule they are long poems, divided into parts and sections. They form elements of a complex, multi-layered construct and only the whole poem has the full intended impact. Complex also is the way in which the author uses his material. The subject described is seen directly, and at the same time becomes the centerpiece of a grand metaphor spreading through the entire fabric of the work; the detailed images at the same time form part of a large canvas.

Wojtyła's poetry is directed to universal values. Unlike most poetry written today it is not self-centered, or even in a wider sense anthropocentric, but theocentric, God-orientated (though the actual word God is not often mentioned; the poet is very sparing in employing religious terms). This theocentricity does not mean that his poetry neglects man. On the contrary, it is hard to find poetry more caring for man. But man is considered here not just in relation to his earthly matters, or to history, but also to his ultimate destiny which, as far as this poet is concerned, lies in God. It is also an intensely personal poetry in that it expresses his deeply felt emotions and thoughts about his and other people's place in the world. On becoming a priest, Wojtyła continued writing poetry because it still seemed a natural means of expression for an important aspect of his personality; for the poet who was still in him. But naturally it had to be connected with his religious vocation and pastoral work. For such a totally committed person, it would be strange if it were not so.

On the other hand, Wojtyła's poems never become just philosophical or theological dissertations, clothed in the form of poetry. On the contrary, although some early poems are complex, resounding with echoes of his reading of mystics and theologians, later poems contain striking images, lyrical passages of great beauty, and direct, simple statements. This is poetry written truly of the inner necessity of both mind and heart. It also provides proof, if one were needed, that Wojtyła himself was one of those writers whom he had in mind when on his first pilgrimage to Poland as Pope John Paul II, in 1979, he said: "Christian inspiration continues to be the main creative source of Polish artists. Polish culture still flows with a broad stream of inspiration that has its source in the Gospel."

In very broad outline the poems encompass three major themes: religious, biblical and those dealing with aspects of Polish history, in particular with development of Christianity in Poland. These groups are, of course, closely related. I will, albeit briefly, consider them in this thematic, rather than strictly chronological order.

Religious Themes

EUCHARIST

Song of the Hidden God (1944), Wojtyła's longest poem, is divided into two distinct parts. The first, "Shores of Silence," is in the nature of religious reflection; the second, "Song of the Inexhaustible Sun," has the form of a prayer in that it is addressed to God. It is a deeply contemplative poem, closely connected with the author's desire to enter the Carmelite novitiate. There are echoes of his readings of Spanish mystics, particularly of St. John of the Cross, who a year later became the subject of his dissertation at the university seminar of dogmatic theology. In the poem, however, the author contemplates God on the basis not only of faith, but above all—love. Love, personified in God, is the dominant theme, leading to adoration of God in his own greatness and in the mystery of the Eucharist, as well as in the beauty of Nature. In its deepest essence, as the very title suggests, it is a poem about Eucharist. As always with this poet, external landscapes are closely bound with the landscape of the inner soul and one passes into the other. We have the impression throughout that the young poet simply communicates with God (even though with his usual reticence he does not mention the word). As in the well-known medieval legend an acrobat prayed to Our Lady with his dancing, here the poet adores God with his poetry. The poem has a simplicity of form almost unparalleled in Wojtyła's work. A musical phrase dominates; the poem is, indeed, a song: a song of the soul.

CONFIRMATION

If at the core of *Song of the Hidden God* is the Eucharist, as approached by the pious young seminarist, some sixteen years later another sacrament, that of Confirmation, is made the subject of a poem written by a bishop. *Birth of the Confessors* (1961) is closely connected with its author's mission and is, as it were, a spiritual account of one of his pastoral journeys in the diocese.

The poem consists of two symmetrical parts, based on a simple, yet original idea: the sacrament of Confirmation is successively reflected upon by the bishop who administers it in a mountain village (part 1) and by a man who receives it (part 2). The bishop thinks about the hidden sources of energy with which the world is charged, from the mountain stream to the stream of thought, and he realizes that he himself is the giver, who touches forces in man which ought to rise; the electricity which is a fact in nature but also a symbol. In part 2 of the poem the man who is being confirmed wonders how he is to be born anew, since he is like a wanderer walking along the mountain stream, with all the hazards of that journey. He realizes that man must preserve truth with his life, that the sacrament of confirmation establishes harmony between God, nature, and man.

Birth of the Confessors is not limited to narrow "theological" deliberations, but is wonderfully open to man and the world, subtly directing the reader's attention to problems of faith. A remarkable achievement is also the author's use of two lyrical subjects.

DEATH AND NEW LIFE

The theme of *Meditation on Death* (1975), Cardinal Wojtyła's last published poem before his election to the papacy, is the Christian attitude to death. The eschatological reflections here are those of a poet, thinker, and pastor, conscious of his responsibility for human souls, but there is no trace of moralizing or "pontificating." The poem is in fact a very personal statement on the drama of human existence. To overcome the fear of death is possible, but not at all easy: it requires an effort, a conscious act, and cooperation with the mystery of grace.

The author considers first the dilemma facing man: exactly at a point when he reaches full maturity based on life's experience, he nears death. But though maturity means fear, fear of death, it also means love. Though the passing of life on earth cannot be halted, the way out of the dilemma can be seen in the view of life as the mystery of passing from death to a new life. The poet also considers the drama of passing, witnessed every day in the history of our planet, and insists that God alone can retrieve our bodies from earth. In conclusion the poet again reiterates that though "death is an experience of the end and has something of annihilation in it," the struggle can be won, for hope placed in HIM (God) will lead to resurrection.

Meditation on Death abounds in striking juxtapositions and reveals contradictions because man's striving and achievements (cosmic rockets are mentioned) do not allow him to surpass his limitations, unless he does it on a non-material level.

THE PASTOR: POETIC HARVEST OF THE SECOND VATICAN COUNCIL

The most significant and seminal event in the life of the Catholic Church in the twentieth century was the Second Vatican Council. The newly elected capitular vicar of the metropolitan see of Kraków, Bishop Karol Wojtyła, took a very active part in the first session of the council (11 Oct.–8 Dec. 1962). It was not only the pastor, however, who went to the council but also the poet. Less than a year later the Kraków Catholic monthly *Znak* published a poem signed with the cryptonym A.J., entitled *The Church—Pastors and Sources.* The subtitle defined the place and time when it was written: "St. Peter's Basilica, autumn 1962." Perhaps more than Wojtyła's other works, *The Church* could be regarded as a cycle of poems rather than one long poem, but for its unifying theme of the church, understood in a dual sense: material, as a place of worship, in this instance the principal church of Christianity, whose various parts the poem evokes; and spiritual, as the congregation of the faithful constituting the mystic body of Christ.

The poem consists of nine short parts, or poems, of six to twelve lines each. The subtitle calls it "fragments." We may assume that duties of a father of the council, more absorbing and responsible as it progressed, made the poet give way to the bishop. Still, what we have remains a significant poetic evocation and record of his council experiences. His impressions of the architectural splendour of the basilica are closely intertwined with reflections on its meaning for man and his destiny; observations on his fellow members of the council, like the African bishop to whom he addresses one of the poems; or the eternal message of the gospel which they are all trying to serve by the grave of St. Peter. Written in verses of simple beauty it is the most remarkable poetic account of the council, an event that was an important lasting experience for him, as well as a spiritual journey to the sources of the Church he served and would go on serving.

Biblical Themes

The most prolific and consistent thread in Wojtyła's poetry has been connected with the Bible: half a dozen of his poems are concerned with events or persons described in the Old Testament or the Gospels (in one case early Christian tradition). But as biblical echoes and quotes abound in virtually all his other poems, the Bible can be called a springboard for his ideas and reflections on important aspects of Christian life and doctrine, though employed more imaginatively than would be done by a priest in a sermon. For the most part, though, these Bible-inspired poems are spiritual treatises imbued with lyrical substance.

JACOB FIGHTS THE ANGEL

One such poem is *Thought is a Strange Space* (1952). "Jacob's fight with the Angel" becomes here the springboard for its wholly modern application. The word *space* in the title—a common image in Wojtyła's poems and plays means the inner space in the mind and soul of man rather than external physical space. The human space in the poem ostensibly applies to Jacob; but in fact the poem's protagonist is modern man who has inherited Jacob's problem and carries it in himself.

The poet begins with a statement that sometimes "we confront truths for which we lack words, we lack gestures and signs." And so we must fight like Jacob. It may well be—the poet continues—that man suffers so that fundamental changes may be brought about. But he

inspired a great poem, so his experience in the Holy Land found artistic expression in a work that was equally profound. The poem *Journey to the Holy Places* (1965), similar in its form to *The Church,* is by no means a geographic or illustrative description of external observation but a journey to the interior of the human soul. In confrontation with the places visited, the dominating factor is reflection on their meaning for Christians. The places themselves, though existing in reality, are also signs of events that created our faith, and symbols which are to strengthen it in us today.

Thus looking at the Mount of Olives, the poet addresses Christ and recalls "a fragment of earth still seen by you," while in the desert of Judea he contemplates the land, which in itself is not beautiful, but it was here that "He who Is became Father to us." In the longest central part, called "Identities," the author analyzes the identity of the places of two thousand years ago, places at the root of our faith—our own "pilgrimage to identity". He then traces the rise of religion from the biblical wanderings of Abraham to the rise of Christianity, the development of man through the tree of the Cross, and defines the place of man: "My place is in You. Your place is in me." The external places where God used to walk on earth, where he died but where he also established the sacrament of the Eucharist, lead us to understand and define the inner place "where You give yourself and accept me." It is highly significant that the concluding part of the poem is also a prayer.

Themes from Polish History

Karol Wojtyła's deep attachment to his native Poland is well known. It has always been based on the equally profound conviction that the country's development is intrinsically connected with its Christian roots and spirit. Adherence to it made the country great; departure caused decay and eventual downfall. This thought underlies his four poems on Polish themes.

A WORKER'S PRAISE OF LABOR

The Quarry (1956) was published in *Znak* in June 1957. A year before workers in the city of Poznań demonstrated in the streets, demanding their basic rights and improvement in working conditions. Tanks were brought out by the communist authorities, and over fifty people lost their lives. The Poznań events could well have contributed to the poem having been written at that time, yet it is not a political work. Let us recall the title: *The Quarry.* For five years during the German occupation of Poland in World War II, young Karol Wojtyła was employed as a manual laborer in the Solvay chemical works near Kraków, first as an assistant in blasting rocks. A dozen or so years later he recalled those experiences

in order to express his innermost feelings with regard to physical work and the men engaged in it. In spite of lapse of time, his memory of those days produced vivid images and emotional commitment of great intensity. As in many of his poems the subject described is both seen directly and made the focus of a grand metaphor. To the Stalinist axiom that the present generation of workers should sacrifice everything for the good of future generations, the author opposes the Christian view that every man is a unique *person* and must not be exploited in this way.

After all, however, *The Quarry* is a hymn in praise of human labor, its value and meaning. In part 1, "The Material," the poet defines the nature of work in a quarry, showing how human energy cuts and shapes the stone for the use of man. But he adds that "the whole greatness of this work is within man." There are images of striking beauty—for example, "hands are the landscape of the heart." This particular image is then connected with the main theme, that of manual labor. Part 2, "Inspiration," analyzes the motivation behind human toil. Love which should be at the basis of work finds its supplementation in anger, he adds, possibly in a veiled reference to the recent events in Poznań. Part 3, "Participation," a beautiful sequence of eight quatrains, while continuing reflections on the essence of labor, expresses also the poet's enduring solidarity with his fellow-workers, subtly pointing to the different tasks allotted to different people:

> I know you, magnificent people, people without
> manners or pretence. . . . Some hands are for toil,
> some belong to the cross.

And he makes a virtually prophetic statement:

> The young search for the road. The roads of them
> all strike straight at my heart.

The final part of the poem, dedicated "To the memory of a fellow-worker" brings a vivid description of a worker's death ("the stone crushed his brow and cut the ventricles of his heart"), his being carried away by fellow-workers, the coming of the bereaved family, and his conclusions:

> Is his anger only to spill over to others? Had it not
> grown in himself with his own love and truth? Is
> he to be used only as raw material for other gener-
> ations, deprived of his most profound substance,
> uniquely his own?

But it should be remembered, the poet adds, that in the "world's inner structure" he has taken with him, "love will explode the higher, the greater the anger that permeates it."

An actual event remembered from the time when he himself worked in a quarry may have inspired a dirge for the killed workers of Poznań. But, like the rest of the poem, it is universal in its appeal. Both in its intellectual substance and on artistic level, *The Quarry* is outstanding in the body of poetry devoted to human labor. It is also a proof of how fruitful and meaningful for its author was the heavy physical work that he had of dire necessity to perform during the war. He had the strength, the will, and the capacity for full commitment to it, like to so many other tasks he has undertaken during his life. At a time when he wrote the poem as a young priest it was a personal and fully credible statement, and a comment on the abuse of the enforced Marxist approach to labor in his country. Today, his voice sounds just as genuine when he talks about problems of human labor and social justice at the Vatican and in course of his travels to so many countries.

CHRIST'S RESURRECTION GIVES MEANING TO HISTORY

In the April 1966 issue of *Znak,* the then metropolitan of Kraków, Karol Wojtyła, published, under the cryptonym A.J. a long poem entitled *Easter Vigil 1966.* The date in the title was highly significant. It was the millenary year, celebrated in Poland with solemnity but, unfortunately, with a duality characteristic for a communist-ruled Christian country. The authorities celebrated the thousandth anniversary of the Polish state; the Church reminded with its celebrations that this was also the millennium of Christianity in Poland and that the country's history, even though its present rulers would rather forget this, was from its beginnings bound with the history of the Church. The poem was Wojtyła's offering for the millennium and will remain as one of the most impressive literary monuments of that occasion.

In a striking manner *Easter Vigil 1966* combined meditation on the mystery of Christ's Resurrection with the view of Poland's history from the perspective of the millennium. Associations of this kind have a long tradition in Polish literature. Notably in romantic poetry Poland, the Christ of nations, buried by her enemies, was to rise from the grave like the Savior. It would be wrong, though, to suppose that in his poem Wojtyła follows a traditional romantic "messianism." His is rather a philosophy-of-history kind of poem, in which the poet, tracing the course of human history, particularly that of his country, aims at discovering the deeper sense of man beyond history: man in God.

In the first part, "Invocation," the poet defines his attitude, as that of a modern man, to the visions of old chroniclers and historians. He then analyzes the transience of man on earth against the background of history written by God and asserts that though human body in history dies, more often and earlier than the tree, man endures beyond the threshold of death, endures in God. In the second part, "The Tale of the Wounded Tree," the poet goes back to the beginnings of the Polish state and evokes a striking vision of its first ruler, Mieszko, who introduced Christianity to Poland, planting his orchard for future generations. The poet uses this image as a metaphor for the development of Christianity, tracing the wounded tree's beginnings from the tree of the Holy Cross. He then sketches the spiritual development of the nation which gave the world Copernicus, who altered our vision of the world. In subsequent parts he considers in an illuminating way the problem of freedom, so well known to his countrymen. He points out to the abuses of freedom which after a thousand years resulted in "riches of defeats." In the name of freedom violent and wrong deeds were also committed, until in the end freedom "remained a great vacuum to be filled." The part entitled "Ritual" is a great hymn in praise of our earth which for the poet "has become a ritual," all-embracing, life-giving and leading man, through his seeming transience, to eternal Wisdom.

The short final part is entitled, like the whole poem, "Easter Vigil 1966." The tangled history of man, considered in the poem, finds its resolution on Easter night:

> keeping watch by Your grave we are the Church more than ever—it is the night of struggle between despair and hope within us; a struggle imposed on all struggles of history.

Everything now falls into place because:

> On that Night the earth's ritual reaches its beginning. A thousand years is like one Night: the Night of keeping watch by your grave.

In this prayer-like conclusion the poet gives us to understand that it is in the mystery of Christ's death and resurrection that the meaning of a millennium of history is made clear. His view of history, so concerned with the lot of man, is theocentric.

HIS BELOVED COUNTRY

Two further poems, which remained unpublished till after Cardinal Wojtyła's election to the papacy, continued the thoughts of *Easter Vigil.* In *Thinking My Country* (1974) the author expresses through poetic images his feelings and thoughts relating to the country where he was born and his great concern for its proper development. The six parts are in turn very short lyrical poems and longer reflections with a historiosophic slant. He analyzes the significance of his country's tongue, which identifies and distinguishes its people among the nations on earth. Though the language limits them in human space, "embraced every day by the beauty of our language we do not feel bitter that on the world markets our thought is not bought because of the high price of words.

. . . A people living in the heart of its own speech remains for generations a mystery of the thought unfathomed to the end.'' (Thus writes the unparalleled linguist among popes, we may add). The poet then evokes lyrically the landscape and life of his native countryside and amplifies his earlier thoughts on the history of his country where the abuse of liberty led to captivity and to the struggle for true freedom. Good and bad grew in the country's history, but history ''cannot flow against the current of conscience.''

The author then goes on to significant observations, whose validity has been tested over and over again, before and since: ''We must not consent to weakness. . . . Weak is the people that accepts its defeat, if it forgets that it has been sent to watch until its hour comes. The hours keep returning on the great clock face of history.'' He ends his poem with an apostrophe to earth and concludes that throughout history we learn new hope and, on the way to the new earth, we raise the old earth, ''as fruit of the love of generations that outgrew hate.'' It can easily be discerned that *Thinking My Country,* far from being limited to one people's problems, opens up to all humanity, and its direct message is pertinent to any people, any country, though particularly to those that have had more than their share of suffering.

STANISŁAW AND BOLESŁAW OR CHURCH AND STATE CONFLICT RESOLVED

It is fitting that the last published (1979), perhaps also the last written, poem by Cardinal Wojtyła concerns St. Stanisław, bishop of Kraków. The author was his successor at that bishopric. The poem is only one of the many statements defining his attitude toward Bishop Stanisław Szczepanowski, and his view of a close connection between the drama that took place nine hundred years earlier and the history of the nation as well as the Church in Poland. This struggle between king and bishop has long been the subject of debate. On the one hand, some historians argue that the bishop plotted with the king's enemies and was justly tried and executed. Others maintain that the king killed St. Stanisław because he was enraged by admonitions regarding his immoral behavior. This medieval conflict between lay and ecclesiastical powers fueled those ideologists who stressed the irreconcilable antinomy between Church and State. The ''manipulators'' intended to divide the people, but the result was the opposite: a spiritual unity of the people around the anniversary celebrations.

Wojtyła sees clearly the ever-valid model of St. Stanisław as someone loyal both to his country and to the Church. But he sees also the strange interrelation of the two protagonists: Stanisław and Bolesław. The mission and martyrdom of one, the crime and penitence of the other, have both influenced the history of the Polish people and can be somehow considered positively. This is the view adopted in the poem. The author describes the very moment of martyrdom, the blow that struck when—as tradition has it—St. Stanisław was saying Mass. The poet speculates on the king's thoughts which, strangely enough, may have been that ''the Church . . . will be born of the spilled blood.'' Stanisław, in his last moments, may have thought that if ''the word did not convert, the blood will.''

The second part begins with a lyrical invocation of the Polish land, and its contemplation prompts the poet to ponder on ''the land of hard unity. The land of people seeking their own roads''; the land where freedom was first abused, then lost, land torn from the maps but ''the land through its having been torn apart united in the hearts of the Poles like no other.'' The poem concludes with words on the enduring validity of the name given to Stanisław, ''for him, for the bishops' see in Cracow, for King Bolesław, for the twentieth century.''

Thus, with nine hundred years of history bridged in a flash, ends *Stanisław* and, possibly, the poetry of Karol Wojtyła, before a new phase opened in his life. From then on there seems to be room for only one of the threads which has always been present in his poetry: the poetic prayer.

The Theater

Karol Wojtyła's plays were closely connected with his poetry. They were, for the most part, poetic dramas. One could claim also that his poetry crossed the boundary of drama in that it was charged with dramatic tension, was constructed almost in the manner of plays, while the text took very often the form of dialogue or monologue, dramatic in character. Before commenting on the plays, it is necessary to mention, albeit briefly, Wojtyła's connections with the theater. This was not just a ''passing phase'' with superficial connotations. Through his manifold participation as dramatist, theoretician, and sometime performer, he contributed to the development of a specific kind of theater, to which some of his plays also bear witness.

Young Karol engaged very actively in school theater in his native Wadowice: he invariably performed leading parts in, and co-directed some of, a dozen plays, mainly Polish romantic and neo-romantic classics. He continued this activity as a student at Kraków University in the year 1938–39. The most important of his theater contacts was his association with Dr. Mieczysław Kotlarczyk, who had been a teacher and theater pioneer in Wadowice before World War II, and at the beginning of the war moved to Kraków. Together they co-founded the Rhapsodic Theater, whose first performance took place in August 1941. The group consisted of three women and two men. During the war years they put on seven productions of dramas and poems—again taken from the romantic and neo-romantic repertory. Because performances took place clandestinely in private houses, the visual aspects had to be reduced to the minimum, and the arrangement of the limited space counted a great deal.

The Rhapsodists created a theater of imagination. The chosen works were carefully arranged into scenarios, by extracting passages most significant and relevant to the audience and performers alike. Thus a kind of 'synthesis' of a literary work was presented. Actors suggested rather than "performed" their parts. There emerged a kind of ritualized theater, where spectators and performers united in a common ritual, through the thoughts and words of the great masters, spoken in defiance of the grim war-time reality. Kotlarczyk and Wojtyła agreed that they had to "revolutionize the theater through the word," by which they meant that in the era of total debasement of words (need one mention Hitler's speeches, for instance?) one had to revalue the word, give it back its meaning. After all, the Greek word *logos* meant both "word" and "thought." Kotlarczyk had even earlier been opposed to spectacle in theater. The war-time limitations transformed necessity into virtue, and the only thing that counted for the Rhapsodists was to transmit, with the minimum of movement and decor, the meaningful thoughts of great writers through the spoken word.

Towards the end of the war Wojtyła switched from philological to theological studies but his interest in theater continued. Once, as a student priest in Rome, he gave a one-man performance. Later when he became for a while an assistant priest in a country parish, he immediately founded a parish theater group, directing and acting in a religious play. Above all he maintained close links with the Rhapsodic Theater. In 1950 he consecrated the ground of their future premises. But the Rhapsodic Theater was suppressed in 1953, because its patriotic and religious aims were frowned upon by the communist authorities. It was reopened in 1956 with the political "thaw." Wojtyła attended and reviewed its performances. When the Rhapsodic Theater was forcibly closed again in 1967, Cardinal Wojtyła protested strongly, to no avail. He wrote a preface to Kotlarczyk's book *The Art of the Living Word,* published in Rome in 1975. Three years later, in a strongly worded speech at Kotlarczyk's funeral, he again took the authorities to task for that unjust action.

The reviews and other essays by Father, Bishop and Archbishop Wojtyła from 1952 to 1964 (mostly published under a *nom-de-plume* in the Catholic *Tygodnik*

Powszechny) were few in number. Nonetheless they expounded the idea of a theater based on the word, appropriately used, with a minimum of decor, props, or action, in order to stimulate thought; the actor was to carry problems rather than "act." This did not mean that movement was to be neglected. The word, if it is to live, cannot be conceived without movement—not a nervous, chaotic movement, but a sparing simple gesture which acquires its rhythmic pattern from the rhythm of the words, helping to bring out the inner tension of the thoughts expressed. It is a non-naturalist movement, akin to dance, which complements the speech. This approach prevents actors from imposing themselves on the text in a destructive manner. It gives them an inner discipline, so that they are a group of people, free yet unanimous in their service of the great poetic words and the noble ideas behind them.

Analyzing the Rhapsodists' practice in this way, their one-time colleague and all-time friend formulated the theoretical base of a particular kind of theater, very much needed in a country, whose rulers were imposing their lie on an unwilling people. After the enforced suppression of their theater the Rhapsodists dispersed, but their style and achievements passed into the mainstream of theater in Poland that is still to be seen today. The plays of Karol Wojtyła reflect a similar approach.

THE TEENAGE PLAYWRIGHT: PROPHETS

David: **The Lost Play.** The first three plays were written in a fairly quick succession by the nineteen-year-old Wojtyła between late fall 1939 and early summer 1940. They were all poetic dramas on biblical subjects and were a result of his extensive reading of the Old Testament in the first year of the war: *David, Job,* and *Jeremiah.* The text of the first of these has not been found but we know of it from the author's description in a letter written 29 December to Kotlarczyk (who at that time still lived in Wadowice): "I have written a drama, or more precisely, a dramatic poem. It is called *David.* Many things dormant in my soul have been revealed in it. I wonder what you would think of it. *David* is written in prose, in blank verse, in rhymed verse—it touches the heart." This is as much as we know of it, from the author himself.

Job: **A Play on Suffering.** *Job* is written entirely in verse, partly blank verse, part rhymed. The line is short, eight to nine syllables, a versification popular with poets and poetic dramatists of the Young Poland movement, under whose influence Wojtyła the poet then was. The language is also indebted to the Young Poland style, but moderately so. Considering that apart from a couple of cycles of early poems it is the earliest literary text of

Wojtyła's that we have, it is an amazingly mature work, particularly in its structure and in the substance of its thought. Its simplicity, seriousness, unpretentious sincerity and a singular dramatic force in the character of Job has much to commend it. There are ten characters and a chorus (first of Job's guests then mourners). The plot follows fairly closely the biblical story of Job, who lost his family and all his possessions and endured great suffering, but to whom, in the end, God restored everything.

It is not, however a straightforward dramatization of the Book of Job. In a letter to Kotlarczyk he calls his play "Greek in form, Christian in spirit, eternal in its substance, like *Everyman.* A drama about suffering." In a short semi-poetic introduction, the author declared that the action took place "before the coming of Christ, but it also happens today, at Job's time for Poland and the World, the time of expectation, imploration for judgement, longing for Christ's testament, time of Poland's and the World's suffering." We find veiled references to the war then raging (like "camps") in the Prologue and Epilogue. Still, the play aims at more universal, Christian significance. The author introduces a young prophet Elihu, who in the presence of Job has a prophetic vision: he sees Christ's Passion, Garden of Olives, Mount Calvary, and the Cross. Only Job shares in his vision, thus learning the positive value of suffering.

There was nothing strange about a young Polish poet writing a play about Job at a time when the country had been stricken by a bloody war and ruthless occupation—like Job, deprived of everything. This was in keeping with the long Messianic tradition of Polish literature. To the Romantic poets of the nineteenth century the dismembered Poland after the partitions had been the incarnation of the suffering Christ. History now repeated itself. And Job, after all, was the Old Testament pre-figuration of Christ. To Wojtyła, who had lost his mother and only brother as a child, the suffering of the country combined with personal suffering was something close and intimate, something he had to resolve for himself.

***Jeremiah*: Prophecies for Israel and Poland.** Unlike Job, *Jeremiah* is not an entirely biblical play. The action takes place in seventeenth-century Poland, a crucial period in the country's history. External wars and internal anarchy reduced one of the greatest powers on the continent of Europe to a powerless wreck. It is in this period that historians see the causes of Poland's subsequent fall and disappearance from the map of Europe in the next century. That was exactly the reason why young Karol set his drama in the early years of the period, but the action projects the future decline, through prophecies and warnings. It is not strictly a historical play, as it does not present external events, though it alludes to them, but rather ideas and attitudes, a vision of Polish history.

The protagonist is the Jesuit priest Piotr Skarga (1536–1612), a fervent preacher and writer who uttered many shattering warnings that Poland would fall if her house was not put in order. The other two main characters are Hetman (commander-in-chief of the crown forces) Stanisław Żółkiewski (1547–1620), great general and patriot, who after many victories was killed in an unequal battle with the Turks at Cecora, and Brother Andrzej (Andrew) Bobola (ca. 1591–1657), Jesuit and martyr, declared a saint in 1939. But there are also a number of biblical characters, the principal of whom is the prophet Jeremiah. The story of his opposition to the elders of Israel and his prophecies of Jerusalem's fall is shown in the visions of Father Piotr and develops alongside the main action as an analogy to the Polish situation. The play is set in the cathedral during services of the Holy Week. Palms are distributed on Passion Sunday. Father Piotr preaches an impassioned sermon to the King and nobles, referring to Jeremiah's prophecies from his visions. The monks chant Jeremiah's laments while Easter Tenebrae are being celebrated. News is brought of the defeat and death of Hetman Żółkiewski. But as Easter approaches the Hetman appears after death. He and Piotr speak of the Covenant, concluded earlier for the protection of Jerusalem from destruction. The Hetman assures Piotr that an avenger will come, and departs to God's judgement.

Just as Blake saw a new Jerusalem in England, the idealistic strand in Polish thinking attributed this role to Poland: the Polish-Lithuanian *respublica* saw herself in her golden age as the defender of Christianity against the heathen Turks and Tartars. The biblical analogies to Jeremiah did not seem far-fetched. On a more immediate level, the Avenger was to be Hetman Żółkiewski's descendant King Jan Sobieski, who in 1683 (sixty-three years after the battle of Cecora) decisively defeated the Turks, raising their siege of Vienna and stopping their advance into western Europe.

The play, as written by the twenty-year-old Wojtyła, is a tour-de-force. It is diversified stylistically in the highest degree. He uses all possible kinds of verse (rhymed, blank, long and short lines, varying the accents, number of syllables, etc.) suiting them to the scene and speaking characters. There is also a somewhat heightened prose, and extensive stage directions are employed to suggest some visual scenes performed as tableaux (e.g., the royal court and the nobles are so arranged). Jeremiah's laments are spoken in turn—sometimes together by the monks, who are given Hebrew names for the occasion. But Jeremiah and the elders of Israel are shown as themselves in dramatic exchanges after two sculpted angels on the cathedral altar have come to life and pulled back the curtains.

Jeremiah is a work dominated not so much by action as by spatially composed images. Within those images the characters express—in a poetic, somewhat flowery language—their forebodings and visions. Such a structure already forecasts Wojtyła's later plays. If the literary allusions, liturgical and historical references, not to mention an over-idealistic view of history, may limit its appeal, there is another side to it. The play could be taken as a general metaphor of forces of good winning over those of evil in politics; and the analogy to ancient Israel could have a more universal application than just the particular Polish situation.

OUR GOD'S BROTHER: CHARITY VERSUS REVOLUTION

Father Wojtyła completed the play *Our God's Brother* from earlier drafts in 1949, when he was at his first posting in a country parish. The subject of the play was a very remarkable man, Adam Chmielowski (1845–1916) who as a youth took part in the anti-Russian Rising of 1863, was wounded, and had part of a leg amputated while in captivity. Having evaded exile to Siberia, he studied in Paris and Munich, opened his studio in Kraków and became a well known painter. But in time he became more and more dissatisfied with art and—as he thought—its social uselessness. This prompted him to help the poor and to embark on religious life. He founded a congregation known as the Albertine brethren, and was since known as Brother Albert. He gave up fashionable society and spent the rest of his life in poverty with his fellow-brethren and the poor they cared for.

The play, written in a somewhat heightened prose, is not meant to be a biographical account of Albert's life. The author's aim was to give an insight into the inner history of Adam Chmielowski's spiritual struggles and his progress to sanctity. The main problem for Adam was to "overcome the artist in himself"; in his wish to sacrifice his life for the poor he had to consider the struggle for social justice, even revolution. Though Adam chooses the way of Christian charity for himself, the author closes the play with a significant conclusion: that there is no contradiction between the great just anger "which will endure" and the choice of "a greater freedom" by Brother Albert. It is a positive synthesis at the end of the struggles within the hero of this drama.

Such "inner approach" to his hero by the author had in its turn important consequences for the style of the work. He rejected flat realism and straight chronology. As in *Jeremiah,* he introduced here the relativity of time, which makes it possible for characters and events from the past and future to appear on stage in the present. Although the characters are authentic, external events have been condensed, transposed in time, and many have been left out. What we see on stage is the projection of Adam's states of mind, memories, besetting doubts.

In fact Wojtyła adopted a convention derived from the Christian mystery theater, where human life—both external, and that which develops in a man's soul—is seen from the vantage point of Providence, as totality, not as a succession of moments in time. This is most clearly marked in the longest middle act called "In the Vaults of Anger," where even the semblance of realism has been abandoned. Some of the scenes seem to take place in concrete venues: in the poor-house where Adam is first rejected, then grudgingly accepted by the crowd of the homeless; in the street, where he talks to his *alter ego,* who tries to deflect him from his growing resolve; in the confessional, or in his studio, where he considers his doubts further. But in reality, these scenes happen "everywhere and nowhere"—in Adam's inner space.

As we have already noted, *space* is a word often used in Wojtyła's poems and plays. Out of that space people emerge, in it they surround the hero—sometimes menacingly—and into it they depart. It is more psychical and spiritual than physical: it is the space of the inner life. Mysteries have no limitations imposed by narrowly conceived realism. They take place within the spacious limits of the Christian cosmos, as well as within the human soul; they take place in the past as well as in the future, focused into one point of stage present. Such a perspective exists already in *Our God's Brother*—a play whose "epilogue," uniquely in the history of world drama, was added forty years later, when its author, now Pope John Paul II, proclaimed his protagonist a saint of the Catholic Church (12 Nov. 1989). But at the time it was written, this play marked a clear beginning of a new phase of Wojtyła's "Inner Theater."

THE JEWELER'S SHOP: LOVE AND MARRIAGE

In his last two plays Wojtyła moved even closer to the mystery formula, and also to the Rhapsodic Theater as his model. In 1960 he wrote to Kotlarczyk: "I must send you the fruit of my current literary activities. For some time now I have essayed in the 'Rhapsodic' style which seems to me to serve meditation rather than drama." The play was *The Jeweler's Shop,* soon to be published in *Znak* under his *nom-de-plume.* Subtitled "A Meditation on the Sacrament of Matrimony, Passing on Occasion into a Drama," it is quite clear that this meditation on one of the most dramatic aspects of human existence, expressed in love and marriage, contains more drama than the modest subtitle admits. In 1960 even the play's dramatic form was innovative. Apart from a couple of very short scenes, the play is composed of monologues spoken by people seemingly together but not talking directly to each other, though the monologues connect, refer to one another, and impel the action, such as it is. This is a drama not of external action but of moral attitudes, chances taken or missed.

The Jeweler's Shop is a poetic drama, though there are also passages of prose and excerpts from letters. Somewhat heightened, this prose is in keeping with the mood and reflective character of the play. In addition to definable characters, a Chorus appears twice. Its lines are short, poetic imagery more direct; certain phrases are repeated like refrains in a song. For the most part, though, the play consists of long lines of free-flowing blank verse with changing rhythms and uneven numbers of syllables. Apart from the style of versification, the author achieves his purpose with an unusual dramatic structure, developed through interrelated monologues.

Free from obvious stage conventions, the play's structure is nonetheless carefully worked out and lucid. No direct sequence of scenes develops in concrete time and space, not at least in linear terms. Voices emerge from nowhere and disappear into a void, after uttering a remark which usually echoes a character's thoughts. Snippets of dialogue recount recollections in the minds of the main characters. The inner development in *The Jeweler's Shop* is dramatized in both past and present, as if to reflect a metaphysical perspective. Even more than *Our God's Brother* this play suggests that God sees the entirety of human life at once, not just the moment in which a person finds himself or herself at any given time. But the drama of *The Jeweler's Shop* is also presented from a metaphysically human viewpoint: the Jeweler and his shop are there or not there, depending on our need or willingness to perceive them.

The timeless, nonlinear structure of *The Jeweler's Shop,* with its unique imagery and oblique reasoning, makes for complexity. But on another level the play is simple enough. In its three parts the stories of three couples are intertwined, not so much in time, and only rarely in space, as in theme. In Act I Teresa and Andrew become betrothed and marry. Act II reveals Stefan and Anna's marriage in an advanced stage of breakdown. Deeply hurt by Stefan's indifference Anna attempts to make contact with other men and tries to sell her wedding ring which the Jeweler rejects: "This ring does not weigh anything . . . only both together will register" on his scales. In Act III the children of the two marriages are in love and marry, but theirs is no easy match. Monica, the daughter of Anna and Stefan, is highly strung and difficult; Christopher, the son of Teresa and Andrew, born after his father's death in the war, was brought up (at least in the spiritual sense) by Adam, his father's friend. Adam happens to be also the mysterious stranger who restrains Anna from an adventure with a man. Adam, too, toward the close of the play, addresses all the other characters (including Andrew, who, in the timeless, metaphysical perspective is present as if physically alive). He tries to make the other characters see the essence of their lives

and relationships. He performs the role of a spiritual guide and confessor and has something of the author in him. Father Wojtyła had been a confessor and adviser to many young people who accompanied him on vacation trips to lakes and mountains, trips whose echoes we find in the play.

If Adam can be called the confessor, another character, even more enigmatic, is present in the play without actually appearing in the flesh. His actions are described, his words quoted, by other characters: the Jeweler. He seems to stand for Divine Providence, for the power of moral judgement. The wedding rings, which he does not so much sell as dispense and refuses to buy back, symbolize the obligations of marriage. His presence is felt but not imposed. But another interpretation is also possible. If Adam can be called a confessor, the Jeweler can be called the voice of conscience. A conscience is both innately human and God-given. The characters act always in the sight of God. The Jeweler sees our thoughts and actions through his shop window, which is also the window of our conscience. Surely, what God knows our consciences ought to know.

Although the author sets out his views and principles, the play is not *piece a these*; it does not impose any theological solutions. The author treats his characters and their problems with warmth, understanding and delicacy. He writes with insight, at times with great power, about human love. The play concludes with no easy solution, no conventional happy ending, but with encouragement. As one of the young newly-weds says:

> Love is a constant challenge, thrown to us by God,
> thrown, I think, so that we should challenge fate.

There is hope, if only we can reach out, see the true face of the other person, and hear the signals of a Love that transcends us. God does not force us into this state of mind and heart, but invites us.

RADIATION OF FATHERHOOD: CHILDHOOD AND PARENTHOOD

In *Radiation of Fatherhood* (1964), Wojtyła's inner theater came to full fruition. It is openly subtitled "a mystery" and continues some of the themes of *The Jeweler's Shop,* broadly in similar style, with free blank verse based on long lines. But there are also differences. Parts 1 and 3 are written entirely in heightened prose, reflective, philosophical in character. Part 2, written in verse, in addition to monologues contains dialogue, absent in the former play. The plot is almost non-existent, characters enigmatic; there is something of archetypes about them. But this work is much more than a treatise. The drama of human existence and relations is for the author not only a subject of discourse, but also images.

In part 1, entitled "Adam" (symbolizing all men), the author analyzes the metamorphoses of "ego," loneliness, and the substance of fatherhood. Mother, symbolic of the mother of all men, comes to console him. During their monologues, according to stage directions, "Adam's space suddenly fills with people." Some mimed scenes are played out. Static monologue spoken by one actor is thus joined to the movement of a mime group, creating theater possibilities. Movement complements the word, and is subordinated to the thought. This concept is repeated in part 3, "Mother." Again groups of people appear and perform mimed scenes to supplement the monologue of Mother. She concludes that bodily parenthood and spiritual parenthood become one. "In me will survive the heritage of all men implanted in the Bridegroom's death." The Bridegroom, of course, is Christ the Redeemer.

In the amazing part 2, "The Experience of a Child," mime images have been replaced by poetic images. This middle part of the drama (considerably longer than the other two together) abounds in lyric quality and is written in verse. In a series of images, as if based on a family album, we witness a moving evocation of childhood memories and family life, spoken by Monica, the Child. The opening scene "in the room" almost imperceptibly changes into her excursion with Adam through the forest, which at the same time is a trip to man's inner soul. (The room and the transition of the scene to the forest are described in the author's long stage direction in concrete theatrical terms.) Two kinds of images, metaphors, descriptions—relating to the external world of nature, and to the strivings within the human being—constantly interchange, and one leads to the other. The cool forest stream in which Monica and Adam are wading turns into the SOURCE, from which everything takes its beginning; which embraces and takes them to a new birth through baptism. It is one of many extended metaphors that at the same time carry the philosophical load of the work in a natural way.

Radiation of Fatherhood is equally the work of a philosopher/theologian and an artist. It is a treatise, but also a modern mystery play, a profound reflection on the drama of human existence through poetry and unusual theater means. Adam expresses the dilemma of today's man in the first sentence of this play: "For so many years now I have lived as a man exiled from my deeper personality, and yet condemned to probe it."

It is significant that the plays of Karol Wojtyła, written over a quarter of a century, for all their stylistic differences, are in some respects monolithic, particularly in their themes and moral import. They are coherent in what I would call their inner form. Even though some of the early plays are externally stylized, from the very beginning Wojtyła the playwright was no one's debtor, but consistently constructed his own vision of the drama of human existence: man's place on earth and in the divine plan of creation. In his plays he referred to the highest values of our culture and, at the same time, in the days when word and language were totally degraded and devalued by ideologies that demanded subservience to shallow, often inhuman purposes, he aimed at the revaluation of words, and meanings behind them. With a remarkable consistency he developed also a modern form of theater that is religious without being devotional. They are a gift whose acceptance ambitious theaters might seriously consider.

Bibliography: Works by KAROL WOJTYŁA: *Collected Poems,* translated with an introductory essay and notes by JERZY PETERKIEWICZ (New York: Random House, 1982); *The Jeweler's Shop,* translated by BOLESŁAW TABORSKI (New York: Random House, 1980); *The Collected Plays and Writings on Theater,* translated with introductions by BOLESŁAW TABORSKI (Berkeley and Los Angeles: University of California Press, 1987); *Opere Letterarie—Poesie e Drammi,* introductions and notes by BOLESŁAW TABORSKI (Vatican City: Libreria Editrice Vaticana, 1993). Works about KAROL WOJTYŁA: BOLESŁAW TABORSKI, *Karola Wojtyły dramaturgia wnętrza* [The inner theater of Karol Wojtyła] (Lublin: Catholic University of Lublin, 1989). JERZY PETERKIEWICZ, trans. *The Place Within: The Poetry of Pope John Paul II* (London: Hutchinson, 1995).

[BOLESŁAW TABORSKI]

The Personalist Philosophy of Karol Wojtyła

Kenneth L. Schmitz, Ph.D., professor Emeritus of Philosophy and Fellow of Trinity College, University of Toronto, is the author of At the Center of the Human Drama: The Philosophical Anthropology of Karol Wojtyła/Pope John Paul II (Washington, D.C., 1993).

The seminarian Karol Wojtyła was introduced to philosophy by way of a scholastic manual in metaphysics. In its dry pages he discovered a new world of thought, distinct from his interests in philology and literature. In his dramas (associated with what came to be known as the "theater of the living word"), he had already addressed issues of philosophical relevance, such as the nature of truth and love, and the relation between time and eternity. These dramatic intuitions were to receive methodic expression in and through his philosophical studies. Because of the unsettled circumstances of his education, however, he never took a classroom course in philosophy. Despite that, after his ordination and the completion of a theological dissertation on the notion of faith in St. John of the Cross, he was assigned the task of a second doctoral work, so that he might fill the position of professor of ethics at the newly reorganized Catholic University of Lublin. He taught there from 1954 to 1957 and continued to hold the chair in ethics until his elevation to the papacy.

Background: Kant and Scheler

The topic suggested for his doctoral work was the possibility of founding a Christian ethics based upon the philosophy of Max Scheler, the early-twentieth-century phenomenologist. Wojtyła was drawn into a comparison of Scheler's theory of value with the ethical thought of Immanuel Kant. In contrasting the two thinkers, he found much that contributed to his own thought, but he also found an offsetting defect. In approaching the issue of moral action, Wojtyła agreed with Scheler's criticism of Kant's exclusion of the emotions and passions from the consideration of ethical action. Kant's restriction of ethical value to purely rational duty, performed out of respect for the moral law, left aside the full experience of moral action, in which the emotions played an important role. More seriously still, Kant had introduced a division within the human person that did not reflect the actual experience of ethical action. This dualism had been brought about in Kant's thought by his prior rejection of metaphysics as the science of our knowledge of things as they really are. At the same time, despite Kant's restriction of cognition to phenomena, Wojtyła saw in Kant's thought a respect for the person, who must never be treated as a mere means but always as an end.

Turning to Scheler, Wojtyła appreciated the phenomenologist's rejection of Kant's extreme rational formalism. Instead, Scheler recovered the fuller and richer experience of values in what he referred to as a "material" ethics, that is, a descriptive understanding of the experience of value that gave full play to the emotions and the objective content of various values. Scheler further described a hierarchy of values, ranging from the lower values of pleasure to the highest values of the experience of the sacred. According to Wojtyła, however, what was underplayed in Scheler's material ethics was the factor of action and the decisive role of the will. Scheler rejected the view that a person could elect ethical values directly, and argued that they emerged in experience as an accompaniment to other experienced values.

For Wojtyła, on the other hand, the decisiveness of will and the exercise of freedom issuing in action were the very heart and soul of ethical life. In summing up his comparison of the two philosophers, Wojtyła located their opposing differences in a defective relation to actual ethical experience. This defect was brought about, he argued, by a prior "methodological reservation" which blinded both philosophers to the full disclosure of ethical experience. Both ignored constitutive factors in experience: Kant excluded the role of the passions, and Scheler all but ignored the role of willed decision. The effect of both philosophers was a reduction of the full ethical experience of the person.

Foundations: Metaphysics and Phenomenology

It is not, Wojtyła argued, reason alone nor experience but the whole person who deliberates, selects, decides, and performs a moral action. It is with the integrity of the whole person in mind, therefore, that in his *Lublin Lectures* the young professor undertook a tour through the history of philosophy, gathering up the factors that enter into the constitution of the person who acts. He gathered these metaphysical factors first from Plato, who highlighted the Good as the supreme value in which the person is called to participate. While Aristotle retained the finality of the good, he also inscribed it in the rational nature of the individual. Moreover, Aristotle provided an account of how one becomes good, moving from the potentiality to the good to its actualization through action. Augustine drew upon Plato, but recognized the highest good as personal, so that Platonic participation is transformed into Augustinian love. The significance of Thomas Aquinas for Wojtyła is that he rooted the foregoing dynamic structure in the deepest source of actuality: in existential act (*esse*), so that what is good and true is so by virtue of its actual existence. Wojtyła continued his tour, spending considerable time in a critical study of Hume and Bentham; but the positive elements of his analysis are drawn from the metaphysical philosophers already mentioned. In sum, it is not the will or the consciousness, but the person, constituted in the unity of his being, who is the *suppositum,* the concrete, existing agent of moral action.

Having assembled his metaphysics of the person as the underlying foundation of ethical action, Wojtyła turned to phenomenology in order to analyze the action from within the agent. Because the horizon of understanding in metaphysics, and consequently its vocabulary, is comprehensive, embracing everything insofar as each is a member of the community of being, the intimate and interior experience of action itself does not fall within the principal concern of metaphysics. Phenomenology, on the other hand, in its adaptation to the experience of values by Scheler, provides a method by which reflection can articulate ethical action precisely as experienced from within the action itself. Wojtyła employed the method in his work *Love and Responsibility* (1959), which yielded a frank and realistic discussion of sexual love. It is in his major philosophical work, *Osoba i czyn* (1969; translated into English as *The Acting Person*; it is now in its third Polish edition), however, that one finds his methodical consideration of ethical action.

Wojtyła's Solution: Ethical Action and the Person

In *Osoba i czyn* Wojtyła alerts his readers that he is not writing an ethics, which would set forth the norms of conduct for a moral life. Instead, he is setting forth the philosophical basis of such a life. This fundament is the human person as the concrete subject (*suppositum*) of human action, so that *Osoba i czyn* is a work in philosophical anthropology. In considering the whole scope and fundamental character of human ethical action, the philosopher Karol Wojtyła anticipated the encyclical of Pope John Paul II on *The Splendor of Truth* (*Veritatis splendor*), which is unprecedented in papal writings in that it considers, not this or that specific moral issue, but the entire span of ethical life.

Drawing upon ordinary ethical experience, Wojtyła in *Osoba i czyn* sets out to describe the precise character of ethical action. Such action differs from other activity in that it redounds upon the person, transforming him or her for better or for worse. Ethical values, then, differ from other values. I may have a fine technical skill, be a first-rate engineer or musician, and yet be a bad person; or conversely, I may be a poor piano-player and yet a good person. Only ethical values determine the worth of the person as a whole and precisely as a person.

In setting forth the elements of his method, Wojtyła begins with the phenomenological device of *bracketing*. He places consciousness "before the brackets" and the various elements of the composite human person within the brackets: these include his or her physiological processes, feelings, drives, the subconscious tendencies, the cognitive processes—all fall within the brackets. In this way, Wojtyła avoids excluding these factors in the way Kant had done. It is, after all, the whole person who is engaged in a fully ethical and human action. The purpose of the bracketing is twofold: it permits us to interpret the elements within the brackets from the point of view of lived consciousness; at the same time, it relativizes consciousness in that it considers consciousness as an aspect from which to view the other components of the human person. This relativization is crucial to Wojtyła, since his criticism of modern thought, especially in its idealistic versions, is that it has absolutized consciousness. The fault, here, is that it thinks of consciousness as the agent. But in truth, consciousness does nothing; it is the person who acts by way of consciousness. To refuse to relativize consciousness commits us to idealism, or at best to objectivism (as in the case of Scheler).

The focus of Wojtyła's reflection is not just any and every action, nor all aspects of action, but precisely that quality in the action that in the metaphysical tradition is called *actus humanus* (*czyn*). What distinguishes such acts from other operations and processes in the human person is that such action arises from our freedom. It is action that comprises deliberation, selection, decision, and performance. The human person is a composite of other dynamisms, which Wojtyła terms "activations" or "happenings." They are not the result of our free will. They include the physiological processes of the body (somato-vegetative dynamisms), and the feelings, drives, and emotions (psycho-emotive dynamisms). In addition, he recognizes the subconscious, and while he accepts the repressive role assigned to it by Freud, he sees a more positive role for it. Indeed, he encourages artists and educators to find a rich deposit in the subconscious, to be teased out into explicit form. And he marvels at the way in which such images strive to come into the light of fully human expression.

In the *actus humanus,* to be sure, cognition plays a significant role. Unlike many phenomenologists, however, he refuses to identify consciousness with the intentional relation to objects, but he does recognize the role of intentionality in determining the presence of objects "in the field of consciousness." This is the avenue to the truth, to which conscience in ethical action testifies, for only in and through cognition, is the action able to be in harmony with the structure of reality and its genuine goods. In human action, however, the truth is apprehended precisely under the aspect of the good; or more precisely, as value, that is, the good insofar as it offers itself to the agent as the objective norm of the action.

Wojtyła asks further: What is the character of consciousness *as such* in the domain of action? He describes two non-temporal phases. There is first what he terms "reflecting" consciousness. This is the mode in which consciousness accepts the objects presented to it in the field of consciousness by means of the intentional processes of cognition. But reflecting consciousness "mirrors" the objects, thus translating them into its own immanent, conscious mode of being. At the same time, it cooperates with the cognitional objects to fashion a self-image of the person in relation to the world in which it dwells. This self-image accompanies the person's action and provides a quasi-objective polarity in the action.

It is, however, in the second phase, in "reflexive" consciousness, that the core (*eidos*) of consciousness discloses itself. It is that in and through which each person experiences himself or herself as the originator of new being, that is, as a free agent, endowed with self-determination, self-governance, and self-possession. This freedom is not, however, without an inbuilt directive, for it is in and through the conscience that truth manifests itself to the person, calling for a free surrender to the truth as normative for the action. And it is this practical truth that presents itself to the person as both a true good in itself and as perfective of the acting person. It is this perfective power that is efficacious in bringing the person to an inner threshold beyond which he or she becomes more fully a person in truth.

Since it is not only consciousness as such that is the source of such freedom but the person as such, and since the whole person is a composite of many dynamisms—for example, the somato-vegetative, the psycho-emotive, the subconscious, each possessing its own dynamic pattern and immediate objective—each acting person is faced with the task of integrating the many dynamisms within any particular action. It is here that the normative character of the truth is especially important, since the truth that presents itself as normative for the action includes the truth of the person himself or herself. In answering to that truth in the freedom of its own originating causality, the person transcends his or her present condition. In carrying out the task of integration in and through the action the person experiences a transformation that is a crossing of the threshold to a new state of being. Efficacious action, through self-determination, self-governance, and self-possession results in self-transcendence of and within the person.

From the foregoing analysis we can recognize that human action is a dramatic affair in which the fulfillment or non-fulfillment of the human person is at stake. For in presenting the action as a positive fulfillment of the person, the analysis implies the possibility that we may fail in the task of integration and transcendence with the consequent diminution of our personhood.

Fortunately, we are not called upon to act in isolation. As persons we are open to intersubjective, interpersonal relations. What is more, our very fulfillment as persons is to be realized in "acting together with others," who are not simply members of this or that organization, but whose well-being is inscribed in our motivation (solidarity). Each is our neighbor, and in acting together with others, we realize our own personhood as participants in the community of persons. In sum, the interplay of metaphysics and phenomenology in his thought has resulted in grounding the person objectively in the community of beings, while at the same time permitting him to enter into the lived experience of the person as an existential subjectivity.

Papal Writings

The ideas expressed philosophically have received continued expression and development in John Paul II's theological and doctrinal works. In his first encyclical, *Redemptor hominis,* which is the emblem of his pontificate, the person of Jesus is central within the Trinity of persons. The radical worth of the person is also reflected in his encyclical on life (*Evangelium vitae*), his exhortation on the family (*Familiaris consortio*), and his letter on the dignity and vocation of women (*Mulieris dignitatem*). His emphasis on interiority is especially evident in his encyclical on work (*Laborem exercens*), in which he speaks of work, not so much in terms of productivity and products, (themes he addresses in *Centesimus annus* and *Sollicitudo rei socialis*) as in terms of the inherent dignity of the worker and the work itself. The breadth of his sense of participation and community is expressed in his ecumenical teaching (*Ut unum sint, Slavorum apostoli, Orientale lumen*), and in the outreach to the whole of humanity as his neighbor (*Tertio millennio adveniente*). Philosophically, what is especially determinant of his thought is the profound relation he sees between freedom and truth (Veritatis splendor), and between faith and philosophical reason (Fides et ratio). It is in living in the truth disclosed to reason and revealed fully in faith that the person finds the perfection of his or her freedom and person.

Bibliography: Works by John Paul II: K. WOJTYŁA, *Lubliner Vorlesungen* (Lublin Lectures); *Love and Responsibility* translated by H. T. WILLETTS (San Francisco: Ignatius Press, 1993); *The Acting Person,* translated by ANDRZEJ POTOCKI (Dordrecht and Boston: D. Reidel, 1979); recommended translations of the *The Acting Person*: *Persona e Atto* (Italian), *Person und Tat* (German); various essays in *Analecta Husserliana* (during the 1970s); *Person and Community: Selected Essays,* translated by THERESA SANDOK (New York: Peter Lang, 1993). Studies of Pope John Paul II: R. BUTTIGLIONE, *Karol Wojtyła: The Thought of the Man Who Became Pope John Paul II,* translated by PAOLO GUIETTI and FRANCESCA MURPHY (Grand Rapids, Mich.: Eerdmans, 1997).K. L. SCHMITZ, *At the Center of the Human Drama, The Philosophical Anthropology of Karol Wojtyła/Pope John Paul II* (Washington, D.C.: The Catholic University of America Press, 1993). A. WOZNICKI, *A Christian Humanism: Karol Wojtyla's Existential Personalism* (New Britain, Conn.: Mariel Publications, 1980). G. WILLIAMS, *The Mind of John Paul II: Origins of His Thought and Action* (New York: Seabury, 1981). G. WEIGEL, *Witness to Hope: The Biography of Pope John Paul II* (New York: HarperCollins, 1999). W. GRAMATOWSKI and Z. WILIŃSKA, *Karol Wojtyła negli scritti: Bibliografia* (bibliography of pre-papal writings in Latin and Polish).

[KENNETH L. SCHMITZ]

God in the World: A Trinitarian Triptych

Peter C. Phan, S.T.D., Ph.D., D.D., is the Warren-Blanding Professor of Religion and Culture in the School of Religious Studies at the Catholic University of America, Washington, D.C.

It is indicative of the centrality of the doctrine of the Trinity in John Paul II's thought that his first encyclical, which outlines the program of his papacy, is part of a trilogy on the Trinity. *Redemptor hominis* on God the Son (4 March 1979) was followed by *Dives in misericordia* on God the Father (13 Nov. 1980) and *Dominum et vivificantem* on God the Holy Spirit (18 May 1986). That the doctrine of Jesus as the Redeemer and together with it Trinitarian theology lie at the center of John Paul II's mind and heart was candidly acknowledged by the pope himself. Some fifteen years later, he explained how the encyclical was written so soon after his election to the papacy: "You will remember that my first encyclical on the Redeemer of man (*Redemptor hominis*) appeared a few months after my election on 16 October 1978. This means that I was actually carrying its contents *within me*. I had only to 'copy' from memory and experience what I had already been living on the threshold of the papacy" (John Paul II 1994, 48).

The centrality of the Trinity in John Paul II's theology is also revealed in his call for the celebration of the jubilee of the year 2000. As he himself has said explicitly, "Preparing for the Year 2000 has become as it were a hermeneutical key of my Pontificate" (*Tertio millennio adveniente* 23). However, this hermeneutical key, which is eschatology, is deeply shaped by the Trinitarian mystery. In organizing the three-year preparatory activities, from 1997 to 1999, the pope said that "the thematic structure of this three-year period, *centered on Christ,* the Son of God made man, must necessarily be theological, and therefore *Trinitarian*"(TMA 39). Indeed, John Paul II assigned each divine person as the theme for theological reflections for each year of the triennium: Jesus Christ in 1997, the Holy Spirit in 1998, and God the Father in 1999.

In this essay I will examine John Paul II's understanding of the Trinity, following the order he adopted in his apostolic letter *Tertio millennio adveniente* (1994), that is, "from Christ and through Christ, in the Holy Spirit, to the Father" (TMA 55). It differs in approach but not in content from the order of his Trinitarian encyclicals which begin with Christ the Redeemer as the way to the Father, who is rich in mercy, and ends with the Holy Spirit, the Lord and giver of life. My treatment will focus on his Trinitarian trilogy and will explore how this Trinitarian theology shapes his vision of the world, especially his anthropology. I will conclude with reflections on how the pope's Trinitarian vision enriches and can be enriched by contemporary Trinitarian theologies.

In Christ and through Christ, the Redeemer of Humanity

TWO FUNDAMENTAL PRINCIPLES OF TRINITARIAN THEOLOGY

Like many contemporary Catholic theologians, John Paul II begins his reflections on the Trinity, not from the inner and eternal relations among the three divine persons (the "immanent [or better, transcendent] Trinity"), but from the Christian experiences of each divine Person's presence and activities in the history of salvation (the "economic Trinity"). Accordingly, the pope's Trinitarian trilogy deals first with Christ as the *Redeemer of humanity*. As a result, his Trinitarian theology is profoundly soteriological and more precisely, anthropocentric in character.

Furthermore, in implicit agreement with the majority of contemporary Catholic theologians, John Paul II emphasizes the identity between God who acted in history (the economic Trinity) and God "in himself" (the immanent Trinity). Already in his commentary on Vatican II, the archbishop of Kraków highlights this identity and maintains the necessity of reflecting on both dimensions of Trinitarian theology:

> The mystery of the Godhead, the most holy Trinity, lies open to the consciousness of the Church

The Trinity with Christ Crucified located in the National Gallery, London (©National Gallery Collection; By kind permission of the Trustees of the National Gallery, London/ CORBIS)

not only as the supreme and complete truth concerning God "in himself" as it is professed by the Church, but also as the truth concerning salvation, to which man is called and invited by God. It is likewise the truth concerning the Father who from eternity begets the Son who is the Word, and who with the Son is the eternal source of the Spirit who is Love. Again, it is the truth concerning the Father who works in human history through the visible incarnation of the Son and the descent of the Holy Spirit, to whom the Council refers as an "effusion" because he exists in a continuous and invisible manner. (Wojtyła 1980, 58–9)

This statement of Wojtyła is not only an accurate summary of the teaching of Vatican II as well as of Christian Tradition on the Trinity but also a succinct synthesis of the Trinitarian vision which the future John Paul II would develop at length in his numerous papal pronouncements.

These two principles—methodological and theological—must be constantly kept in mind as we proceed to examine John Paul II's Trinitarian thought. The first principle—that Trinitarian theology must be rooted in the Christian experience of salvation—will explain why the pope's treatment of the Trinity differs markedly from that of Neoscholastic manuals on the Trinity, with which he is very familiar, not only in matters of theological language and categories, but, more importantly, in the profoundly soteriological orientation of his Trinitarian

theology. The second principle—that the "economic Trinity" is identical with the "immanent Trinity"—leads John Paul II to correlate his Trinitarian theology with a host of other theological themes that at first blush seem to be totally unrelated to it. The pope's incorporation of these themes into his theology of the Trinity have provoked puzzlement in some professional theologians who are accustomed to maintaining clear-cut academic specialization and disciplinary boundaries, and it has caused them to criticize what they perceive as meandering diffuseness in the pope's approach.

JESUS AS THE FULL REVELATION OF THE TRINITY

John Paul II's decision to begin his Trinitarian reflections with Jesus Christ flows from his deep conviction that in Jesus of Nazareth the mystery of the Trinity is fully revealed. In an eloquent paragraph replete with biblical citations, the pope describes Jesus' function in the revelation of the Trinity: "We must constantly aim at him 'who is the head,' 'through whom are all things and through whom we exist,' who is both 'the way and the truth' and 'the resurrection and the life,' seeing whom, we see the Father, and who had to go away from us—that is, by his death on the Cross and then by his Ascension into heaven—in order that the Counselor should come to us and should keep coming to us as the Spirit of truth" (RH 7).

In spite of its explicit concentration on Jesus, *Redemptor hominis* is not and should not be read as a conventional treatise on Christology. There is in it no detailed treatment of staple themes of Christology such as Jesus' life, ministry, parables, miracles, death, and resurrection. Nor is there a systematic discussion of the eternal origination of the Word from the Father and of his relation to the Holy Spirit within the immanent Trinity, in the manner of Augustine and Thomas Aquinas. Rather these Christological doctrines are presupposed as part of the Christian faith and are dealt with in the pope's later encyclicals. In *Redemptor hominis,* however, the pope casts these traditional doctrines in a new light by placing them in relation to the life of Christians and even non-Christians:

The Church does not cease to listen to his words. She rereads them continually. With the greatest devotion she reconstructs every detail of his life. These words are listened to also by non-Christians. The life of Christ speaks, also, to many who are not capable of repeating with Peter: "You are the Christ, the Son of the living God." He, the Son of the living God, speaks to people also as Man: it is his life that speaks, his humanity, his fidelity to the truth, his all-embracing love. Furthermore, his death on the Cross speaks—that is to say it expresses the inscrutable depth of his suffering and abandonment. The Church never ceases to relive his death on the Cross and his Resurrection. (RH 7)

Clearly, then, John Paul II's theology of the Second Person of the Trinity is deliberately and almost exclusively soteriological, and more radically, as will be shown shortly, anthropocentric. The pope's stated purpose in writing his Christological encyclical is to provide an answer to the question he sets for himself: "What should we do, in order that this new Advent of the Church connected with the approaching end of the second millennium may bring us closer to him whom the Sacred Scripture calls 'Everlasting Father,' *Pater futuri saeculi*?" (RH 7). It is in the light of this soteriological question that John Paul II develops his Christology. His favorite name for Jesus is *Redemptor,* as the titles of two of his later encyclicals, on Mary (*Redemptoris Mater*) and on the Church's mission (*Redemptoris missio*), indicate.

THE DIVINE AND HUMAN DIMENSIONS OF REDEMPTION

In explicating the import of Jesus' redemption, John Paul II highlights its two dimensions. On the divine dimension, Jesus' redemptive work reconciled humanity to God: "He it was, and he alone, who satisfied the Father's eternal love, that fatherhood that from the beginning found expression in creating the world. . . . He and he alone also satisfied that fatherhood of God and that love which man in a way rejected by breaking the first Covenant and the later covenants" (RH 9). Jesus' uniqueness and universality as Redeemer and Savior, so strongly affirmed here, was emphasized again in *Redemptoris missio*: "Christ is the one mediator between God and humankind. . . . No one, therefore, can enter into communion with God except through Christ, by the working of the Holy Spirit. Christ's one, universal mediation, far from being an obstacle on the journey toward God, is the way established by God himself, a fact of which Christ is fully aware. Although participated forms of mediation of different kinds and degrees are not excluded, they acquire meaning and value *only* from Christ's own mediation, and they cannot be understood as parallel or complementary to his" (RM 5).

In this context, John Paul II explains the meaning of Jesus' death on the Cross. It was, he says, "a fresh manifestation of the eternal fatherhood of God" (RH 9), a revelation that "love is greater than sin, than weakness, than the 'futility of creation'; it is stronger than death; it is a love always ready to raise up and forgive" (RH 9). Anticipating the central theme of his next encyclical, *Dives in misericordia,* the pope adds that Jesus' death on the Cross

manifested God's love as *mercy*: "in man's history this revelation of love and mercy has taken a form and a name: that of Jesus Christ" (RH 9).

On the human dimension, Christ's redemption created humanity anew and revealed to humans their true nature: "In this dimension man finds again the greatness, dignity and value that belong to his humanity. In the mystery of Redemption man becomes newly 'expressed' and, in a way, is newly created" (RH 10). This recovery of human dignity through Christ's redemption is another central theme of *Dives in misericordia,* to which we will return in our discussion of the pope's teaching on God the Father.

ANTHROPOCENTRIC ORIENTATION

What is most distinctive of John Paul II's Christology, however, is its pronounced anthropocentric orientation. For him, Jesus Christ is "the chief way for the Church" (RH 13). The Church, he emphatically and repeatedly insists, must travel with humanity: "Man in the full truth of his existence, of his personal being and also in his community and social being—in the sphere of his own family, in the sphere of society and very diverse contexts, in the sphere of his own nation or people (perhaps still only that of his clan or tribe), and in the sphere of the whole of mankind—this man is the primary route that the Church must travel in fulfilling her mission: *he is the primary and fundamental way for the Church,* the way traced out by Christ himself, the way that leads invariably through the mystery of the Incarnation and the Redemption" (RH 14).

The fundamental reason for this anthropocentric character of John Paul II's Christology is his profound conviction, derived from the Second Vatican Council, that through his Incarnation and Redemption Christ has united himself personally with every human being, whether he or she is aware of it or not: "This man is the way for the Church—a way that, in a sense, is the basis of all other ways that the Church must walk—because man—every man without any exception whatever—has been redeemed by Christ, and because with man—with each man without any exception whatever—Christ is in a way united, even when man is unaware of it" (RH 14).

It is this anthropocentric character of his Christology, in addition to his acceptance of the identity between the "Economic Trinity" and the "Immanent Trinity," that allows John Paul to broach a variety of themes that might seem out of place in a treatise on the Trinity. One of these themes is anthropology, which constitutes, as is well known, the central focus of the pope's philosophy. In his view, "the man of today seems ever to be under threat from what he produces, that is to say from the result of the work of his hands and, even more so, of the work of his intellect and the tendencies of his will'' (RH 15). Among these threats the pope singles out nuclear extinction, the uncontrolled development of technology with disastrous consequences for the ecology, the growing gap between the rich and the poor, and the abuse of human rights. Contemporary humanity is characterized by a pronounced distancing ''from the objective demands of the moral order, from the exigencies of justice, and still more social love'' (RH 16).

The remedy John Paul II proposes against these threats is ''an honest relationship with regard to truth as a condition for authentic freedom'' (RH 12), that is, a correct understanding of human freedom, which sees it as dependent on truth, and which the pope elaborates at great length in his encyclical *Veritatis splendor* (1993). In this conception of freedom, humans must realize that their dominion over the visible world consists ''in the priority of ethics over technology, in the primacy of the person over things, and in the superiority of spirit over matter'' (RH 16). The Church, which is ''the social subject of responsibility for divine truth'' (RH 19), is called to satisfy humanity's ''creative restlessness . . . the search for truth, the insatiable need for the good, hunger for freedom, nostalgia for the beautiful, and the voice of conscience'' (RH 18).

In the Holy Spirit, the Lord and Giver of Life

John Paul II's encyclical on the Holy Spirit—the last of his Trinitarian trilogy—was a response to Vatican II's call for a new study on the Holy Spirit and a commemoration of the sixteenth centenary of the First Council of Constantinople. Disclaiming an exhaustive treatment of pneumatology and any preference for a particular solution of outstanding controversies in this area of systematic theology (e.g., the *Filioque*), the pope intends, by using the resources of Vatican II and the theological tradition of the Oriental Churches, ''to develop in the Church the awareness that 'she is compelled by the Holy Spirit to do her part towards the full realization of the will of God, who has established Christ as the source of salvation for the whole world''' (DV 2). Just as *Redemptor hominis* is not a complete Christology, so *Dominum et vivificantem* is not a complete pneumatology. Rather, the pope highlights aspects of pneumatology that in his judgment would be most helpful for the Church's preparation for the celebration of the Jubilee Year 2000, which, as the pope has said, is the hermeneutical key to his pontificate. Hence, the orientation of *Dominum et vivificantem* is primarily spiritual and pastoral.

THE UNITY OF THE MISSIONS OF THE SON AND THE SPIRIT

Following a theological tradition that dates back to St. Irenaeus in the second century, John Paul II forcefully emphasizes the unity of the mission of the Son and that of the Holy Spirit:

> There is established a close link between *the sending of the Son* and *the sending of the Holy Spirit.* There is no sending of the Holy Spirit (after original sin) without the Cross and the Resurrection: ''If I do not go away, the *Counselor* will not come to you.'' There is also established a close link *between the mission of the Holy Spirit and that of the Son* in the Redemption. The mission of the Son, in a certain sense, finds its ''fulfillment'' in the Redemption. The mission of the Holy Spirit ''draws from'' the Redemption: ''He will take what is mine and declare it to you.'' The *Redemption* is totally *carried out* by the Son as the Anointed One, who came and acted in the power of the Holy Spirit, offering himself finally in sacrifice on the wood of the Cross. And this Redemption is, at the same time, *constantly carried out* in human hearts and minds in the history of the world—by the Holy Spirit, who is the ''other *Counselor.''* (DV 24)

John Paul II explicates this unity between Jesus and the Holy Spirit by appealing primarily to Jesus' discourse during the Last Supper as related by the Fourth Gospel. He highlights the role of the Holy Spirit as ''another Counselor,'' as teaching the Christians ''all things'' and reminding them of what Jesus has said, as bearing witness to Jesus, as guiding the faithful into all the truth, and as taking what is of Jesus and declaring it to the believers. For the pope, ''in the farewell discourse at the Last Supper, we can say that *the highest point of the revelation of the Trinity* is reached'' (DV 9).

The intimate link between Jesus and the Holy Spirit is further illustrated by five additional factors. First, John Paul II points out that the Redemption accomplished by Jesus is transmitted by the Holy Spirit, in such a way that Christ's ''departure'' is an indispensable condition for the sending and the coming of the Holy Spirit. As the pope puts it pointedly, ''the Holy Spirit comes *at the price of* Christ's 'departure''' (DV 14). Second, Jesus is the Messiah, anointed with the Holy Spirit. Invoking Isaiah 11:1–3 and 61:1 the pope suggests that the prophet was presenting Jesus as ''the one who *comes in the Holy Spirit*, the one who possesses *the fullness of this Spirit in himself* and at the same time *for others*, for Israel, for all the nations, for all humanity'' (DV 16). Third, not only was Jesus anointed by the Spirit but he was ''exalted'' in the Spirit as well, particularly at his baptism in the Jordan by John, when the Spirit descended upon him in bodily form. John Paul calls this moment "a *Trinitarian theophany*" (DV 19). Fourth, quoting Luke, the pope points out that during his ministry Jesus was "full of the Holy Spirit" and "led by the Spirit." With a special reference to Luke 10:21, John Paul II says: "It is another revelation of the Father and the Son, united in the Holy Spirit. Jesus speaks only of the fatherhood of God and of his own sonship—he does not speak directly of the Spirit, who is Love and thereby the union of the Father and the Son. Nonetheless *what he says of the Father and of himself—the Son—flows* from that *fullness of the Spirit* which is in him, which fills his heart, pervades his own 'I,' inspires and enlivens his actions from the depths" (DV 21). Finally, the Risen Christ, who is himself the gift of the Father, gave the gift of the Spirit: "Already the 'giving' of the Son, *the gift of the Son,* expresses the most profound essence of God who, as Love, is the inexhaustible source of the giving of gifts. The gift *made by the Son* completes the revelation and giving of the eternal love: *the Holy Spirit,* who in the inscrutable depths of the divinity is a Person-Gift, through the Son, that is to say by means of the Paschal Mystery, is given to the Apostles and to the Church in a new way, and through them is given to humanity and the whole world" (DV 23).

THE SPIRIT WHO CONVINCES THE WORLD CONCERNING SIN

As in his Christology John Paul II emphasizes the anthropological dimension of Redemption, so in his pneumatology he highlights the special function of the Holy Spirit in the human person's self-consciousness and self-understanding. On the basis of John 16:8–11, the pope argues that the Holy Spirit's special role vis-à-vis humans is to convince them of sin: "And when he [the Counselor] comes, he will convince the world concerning sin and righteousness and judgment: concerning sin, because they do not believe in me; concerning righteousness, because I go to the Father, and you will see me no more; concerning judgment, because the ruler of this world is judged."

To understand John Paul's thought here, it is necessary to take the three aspects—sin, righteousness, and judgment—together. The pope believes that the reality that the Scripture calls "hardness of heart" today takes the form of the "loss of the sense of sin" (DV 47; see also his apostolic exhortation *Reconciliatio et paenitentia*). This loss of the sense of sin the pope regards as the equivalent of the "sin against the Holy Spirit," which is "the refusal to accept the salvation which God offers to man through the Holy Spirit, working through the power of the Cross" (DV 46). In preparation for the Jubilee, the pope wishes to reawaken this sense of sin and argues that no one can bring this about except the Holy Spirit. The

reason for this, he points out, is that in order to arrive at a genuine sense of sin, one must acknowledge the evil that brought about the Cross, and given the intimate connection between the mission of Jesus and that of the Holy Spirit, as shown above, only the Holy Spirit can convince the world of sin: "The Holy Spirit also convinces of every sin, committed in any place and at any moment in human history: *for he demonstrates its relationship with the Cross of Christ.* The 'convincing' is the demonstration of the evil of sin, of every sin, in relation to the Cross of Christ. Sin, shown in this relationship, *is recognized in the entire dimension of evil* proper to it, through the *'mysterium iniquitatis,'* which is hidden within it" (DV 32). In this connection, John Paul II draws attention to the fact that only the Holy Spirit "can fully 'convince concerning the sin' that happened at the beginning, that sin which is the root of all other sins and the source of man's sinfulness on earth, a source that never ceases to be active" (DV 35).

The Spirit's conviction of sin, however, is not for its own sake. Its ultimate purpose is to lead to righteousness, which is the second task of the Holy Spirit: "This convincing is *in permanent reference to 'righteousness'*: that is to say to definitive salvation in God, to the fulfillment of the economy that has as its center the crucified and glorified Christ" (DV 28). Finally, thanks to this salvation, there came about the judgment of the prince of this world, the third element of the mission of the Holy Spirit.

John Paul II goes on to explain the two ways in which the Holy Spirit moves from convincing the world concerning sin to achieving righteousness for the sinner and judgment of the prince of this world. First, the Holy Spirit reveals the suffering of God caused by sin. While pointing out that God as the most perfect being cannot feel pain "deriving from deficiencies or wounds," the pope notes that the Bible speaks of God, in the face of human rejection, as "a Father who feels compassion for man, as though sharing his pain. In a word, this inscrutable *fatherly 'pain'* will bring about above all the wonderful economy of redemptive love in Jesus Christ, so that through the *mysterium pietatis* love can reveal itself in the history of man as stronger than sin" (DV 39). The pope suggests that the Holy Spirit, directing the sacrifice of the Son to the Father, introduces pain into the "divine reality of the Trinitarian communion" but at the same time, being the love between the Father and the Son, the Holy Spirit is able to draw from this divine suffering "a new measure of the gift made to man and to creation from the beginning" (DV 41). This new measure consists precisely in the coming of the Holy Spirit as Love and Gift upon Jesus' sacrifice upon the Cross and consuming "this sacrifice with the fire of love, which unites the Son with the Father in the Trinitarian communion" (DV 41). In this way, the Holy Spirit is revealed as the Love animating the Paschal Mystery, as the source of the salvific power of the Cross of Christ, and as the gift of new and eternal life.

Second, the Holy Spirit, made present in the Paschal Mystery "in all his divine subjectivity" is able to bring about the conversion of the human heart by penetrating into the conscience of the human person and producing the remorse for the sin he or she has committed. John Paul II sees this remorse as "an echo of that 'reprobation' which is interiorized into the 'heart' of the Trinity and by virtue of the eternal love is translated into the suffering of the Cross, into Christ's obedience unto death" (DV 45). He goes on to say: "When the Spirit of truth permits the human conscience *to share in that suffering,* the suffering of the conscience becomes particularly profound, but also particularly salvific. Then, by means of an act of perfect contrition, the authentic conversion of the heart is accomplished" (DV 45).

THE HOLY SPIRIT, GIVER OF LIFE

Christian Tradition has always associated the Holy Spirit with sanctifying grace. Following the pneumatology of the Oriental Churches and the consensus of contemporary Roman Catholic theology, John Paul II privileges the ontological priority of the Holy Spirit as "uncreated Love-Gift" (DV 10) over created, sanctifying grace: "As such he is given to man. And in the *superabundance of the uncreated gift there begins* in the heart of all human beings that particular *created gift* whereby they 'become partakers of the divine nature' . . . . Thus there is a close relationship *between the Spirit* who gives life and *sanctifying grace* and the manifold *supernatural vitality* which derives from it in man: between the uncreated Spirit and the created human spirit" (DV 52).

According to John Paul II, by dwelling in the human person, within and "outside the visible body of the Church" (DV 53), the Holy Spirit first of all confronts the tensions in the human heart between "spirit" and "flesh." This resistance of the "flesh" against the "spirit" does not remain within the interior and subjective dimension of the human person, but also manifests itself in the external dimension, especially in the philosophical ideology of materialism. There is also a conflict between "life" and "death," the latter taking the contemporary forms of, for example, nuclear self-destruction, poverty and famine, abortion, war, and terrorism.

These spiritual conflicts and symptoms of death may lead to despair. However, John Paul II is deeply convinced that the dark shades of our materialistic civilization, and especially the contemporary signs of death, are a more or less conscious plea to the life-giving Spirit and

that with the Holy Spirit as Gift and Love the human world will be transformed: "The Triune God," who 'exists' in himself as a transcendent reality of interpersonal gift, *giving himself in the Holy Spirit as gift to man, transforms the human world from within,* from inside hearts and minds. . . . Gift and love: this is the eternal power of the opening of the Triune God to man and the world, in the Holy Spirit" (DV 59).

THE HOLY SPIRIT, THE PRINCIPAL AGENT OF MISSION

Pentecost, with the coming of the Holy Spirit, initiates the era of the Church. Following Vatican II, John Paul II describes the Church as the sacrament or sign and instrument of humanity's union with God and of the unity of the whole human race. While not denying that the Church is the sacrament of Christ, making him continuously present in the world, especially through the celebration of the sacraments, the pope expands this definition of the Church in the context of his pneumatology by calling the Church the sacrament of the Holy Spirit. Insisting on the intimate unity between Christ and the Spirit, the pope affirms that "the Church is the sign and instrument of the presence and action of the life-giving Spirit" (DV 64). Furthermore, the Church is the sacrament of the Holy Spirit, not only in bringing about humanity's union with God, but also in realizing the unity of all humans among themselves: "In the same universal dimension of Redemption *the Holy Spirit is acting,* by virtue of the 'departure of Christ.' Therefore the Church, rooted through her own mystery in the Trinitarian plan of salvation, with good reason regards herself as the 'sacrament of unity of the whole human race.' She knows that she is such through the power of the Holy Spirit, of which power she is a sign and instrument in the fulfillment of God's salvific plan" (DV 64).

In his encyclical on mission, John Paul II expands further his notion that in and through the Church, "the Holy Spirit remains the transcendent and principal agent for the accomplishment of this [salvific] work in the human spirit and in the history of the world" (DV 42). Referring to the mission *ad gentes* specifically, the pope states that the Holy Spirit is "the principal agent of the whole mission of the Church" (RM 21). The reason for this is that when Jesus entrusted the apostles with the "missionary mandate," he sent them forth in the power of the Spirit, so that "under the impulse of the Spirit, the Christian faith is decisively opened to the 'nations' . . . . It is the Spirit who is the source of the drive to press on, not only geographically but also beyond the frontiers of race and religion, for a truly universal mission" (RM 24).

The Church's mission is truly universal because, John Paul II points out, the Holy Spirit is already present and active not only in all human beings but also in society and history, in cultures and religions. This universal presence of the Holy Spirit must not be separated from, much less opposed to, his particular activity in the Church, since "it is always the Spirit who is at work, both when he gives life to the Church and impels her to proclaim Christ, and when he implants and develops his gifts in all individuals and peoples, guiding the Church to discover these gifts, to foster them and to receive them through dialogue" (RM 29).

To God the Father, Who Is Rich in Mercy

"To the Father, through Christ, in the Holy Spirit": God the Father is the destination of humanity's pilgrimage. John Paul II begins his encyclical *Dives in misericordia* by reaffirming his trademark principle that every human being is the way for the Church. However, the pope points out, "in Jesus Christ, every path to man, as it has been assigned once and for all to the Church in the changing context of the times, is simultaneously an approach to the Father and his love" (DM 1). Accordingly, the pope rejects any opposition between "theocentrism" and "anthropocentrism"; in addition, he believes that it is the Church's mission to link them together in a deep and organic way.

GOD THE FATHER, "WHO IS RICH IN MERCY"

Of all the attributes of God John Paul II singles out mercy and makes it the focus of the last panel of his Trinitarian triptych, because in his judgment God's mercy is what "humanity and the modern world need so much. And they need mercy even though they often do not realize it" (DM 2). The reason for contemporary humanity's urgent need of divine mercy is rooted in its ironic situation. On the one hand, thanks to the spectacular progress in science and technology, humans have been able to produce new material goods. On the other hand, as John Paul II had already pointed out in his earlier encyclicals, the contemporary world is threatened by various evils: the danger of mass destruction by nuclear arms, totalitarianism, the loss of interior freedom, world-wide hunger, and the growing gap between the rich and the poor. In the face of these injustices, there have recently been calls for restoring justice. But the pope notes that very often programs inspired by the idea of justice end up in spite, hatred, and even cruelty: *summum ius, summa iniuria.* Hence, the necessity of mercy: "The experience of the past and of our own time demonstrates that justice alone is not enough, that it can even lead to the negation and destruction of itself, if *that deeper power, which is love,* is not allowed to shape human life in its various dimensions" (DM 12). The key issue is to understand how justice, love, and mercy, though distinct from each other, must go hand in hand in our contemporary world.

THE REVELATION OF GOD'S MERCY

As has been said above, John Paul II's Trinitarian theology is deeply soteriological and anthropocentric. In light of humanity's sinfulness and divine Redemption, it is natural for the pope to emphasize that God's love and justice have been revealed as mercy and mercifulness, or as "the mystery of God the 'Father of mercies'" (DM 2). This revelation of God's mercy already took place in the Old Testament, among the Jews, who had "a special experience of the mercy of God" (DM 4). Out of this experience came a host of terms to describe God's mercy. In a display of linguistic sophistication, the pope explains in an unusually lengthy footnote the various Hebrew terms for mercy: *hesed, rahamim, hamal, hus,* and *'emet.* In sum, for John Paul II, mercy as *hesed* highlights God's "masculine" fidelity to self and "responsibility for one's own love," whereas, as *rahamim,* mercy highlights God's "feminine" gratuitous love characterized by goodness and tenderness, patience and understanding, and readiness to forgive.

Furthermore, the pope acknowledges that in the Old Testament God's mercy is in a certain sense contrasted with God's justice. But he hastens to point out that "mercy differs from justice, but is not in opposition to it" (DM 4). The difference exits because mercy is rooted in love, which is "greater" than justice: "Love, so to speak, conditions justice and, in the final analysis, justice serves love. The primacy and superiority of love vis-à-vis justice—and this is a mark of the whole of revelation— are *revealed precisely through mercy*" (DM 4). Hence, mercy is more powerful and more profound than justice.

The revelation of God's mercy was brought to its fullness by Jesus: "Not only does he. speak of it and explain it by the use of comparisons and parables, but above all he *himself makes it incarnate* and personifies it. *He himself, in a certain sense, is mercy.* To the person who sees it in him—and finds it in him—God becomes 'visible' in a particular way as the Father 'who is rich in mercy'" (DM 2).

DIVINE MERCY AND HUMAN DIGNITY: JUSTICE, LOVE AND MERCY

One of the parables that John Paul II uses to illustrate God's mercy at length is that of the prodigal son. The pope acknowledges that the terms "justice" and "mercy" are not used in the parable, but he contends that *"the relationship between justice and love, that is manifested as mercy,* is inscribed with great exactness in the content of the Gospel parable" (DM 5). The pope is aware that contemporary men and women have two objections against mercy. First, confusing mercy with pity, they think that mercy implies a relationship of inequality between the one offering mercy and the one receiving it.

To be an object of someone's pity is to be stripped of one's dignity. Second, they think that mercy is a round-about way of dispensing with the demands of justice, and prefer to build social relationships on justice rather than gratuitous mercy.

John Paul II believes that the parable of the prodigal son answers these two objections against God's mercy fully. First, with regard to human dignity, the merciful father in the parable, the pope notes, remains faithful to his paternal responsibility, and because of this faithfulness, he continues to treat his prodigal son as his son, and in this way preserves and restores his filial dignity. Similarly, God's merciful love towards sinners preserves and restores their dignity as children of God which they have lost by sinning: "Mercy—as Christ has presented it in the parable of the prodigal son—has *the interior form of the love* that in the New Testament is called *agape*. This love is able to reach down to every prodigal son, to every human misery, and above all to every form of moral misery, to sin. When this happens, the person who is the object of mercy does not feel humiliated, but rather found again and 'restored to value'" (DM 6).

Furthermore, John Paul II observes that in the practice of mercy, there is an interpersonal encounter—an *admirable commercium*—between the one showing mercy and the one receiving it: "In reciprocal relationships between persons merciful love is never a unilateral act or process. Even in the cases in which everything would seem to indicate that only one party is giving and offering, and the other only receiving and taking . . . in reality the one who gives is always also a beneficiary" (DM 14). This mutuality in mercy, the pope suggests, is also at work between God and sinners: "In a special way, God also reveals his mercy when he *invites man to have 'mercy' on his only Son, the Crucified One*" (DM 8). Even Christ himself, the pope says, is "the one who stands at the door and knocks at the heart of every man," asking for solidarity with and mercy for himself (DM 8).

With regard to justice, merciful forgiveness "does not cancel out the objective *requirement of justice*. Properly understood, justice constitutes, so to speak, the goal of forgiveness. In no passage of the Gospel does forgiveness, or mercy as its source, mean indulgence toward evil, toward scandals, toward injury or insult. In any case, reparation for evil and scandal, compensation for injury, and satisfaction for insult are conditions for forgiveness" (DM 14). John Paul II sees this demand for justice fulfilled in the death of Jesus on the Cross: "In the Passion and death of Christ—in the fact that the Father did not spare his own Son, but 'for our sake made him sin'— absolute justice is expressed, for Christ undergoes the Passion and Cross because of the sins of humanity" (DM

7). However, because this justice "springs completely from love, from the love of the Father and of the Son" (DM 7), and because "the Cross upon which Christ conducts his final dialogue with the Father, *emerges from the very heart of the love* that man, created in the image and likeness of God, has been given as a gift" (DM 7), it brings about the redemption of sinful humanity. In this way, mercy, "love's second name" (DM 7), reveals that love is more powerful than death and more powerful than sin.

From these reflections on God the Father as rich in mercy John Paul II concludes that the essential mission of the Church is to profess and proclaim the mercy of God and seek to put mercy in practice: "The Church lives an authentic life when she *professes and proclaims mercy*—the most stupendous attribute of the Creator and of the Redeemer—and when she brings people close to the sources of the Savior's mercy, of which she is the trustee and dispenser" (DM 13). Of course, the task of the Church is to promote justice, but the pope points out that it is mercy that creates "the most perfect incarnation of 'equality' between people, and therefore also the most perfect incarnation of justice as well" (DM 14). The reason for this is that whereas the equality brought about by justice is restricted to extrinsic goods, the equality that love and mercy produce regards the basic dignity of the human person. In this sense, in every interpersonal relation, "justice must, *so to speak, be 'corrected' to a considerable extent* by . . . *merciful love*" (DM 14).

The Drama of Trinitarian Love

As has been mentioned above, John Paul II's trilogy does not intend to offer a comprehensive theology of the Trinity. His primary concern is pastoral. The preparations for the celebration of the Jubilee Year 2000 focus on the missions of the divine Persons in the world. An eschatological outlook dictates the pope's choice of aspects of the Trinitarian doctrine to be treated in his three encyclicals. This does not mean that his Trinitarian theology is idiosyncratic or utilitarian. On the contrary, he develops his reflections on the Trinity mainly on the basis of Scripture and Vatican II. Indeed, in his basic methodological and theological principles, John Paul II stays very much within the compass of contemporary Catholic theology, his rooting of Trinitarian theology in the Christian experience of salvation and with his emphasis on the identity between the "economic Trinity" and the "immanent Trinity."

Nevertheless, thanks to his soteriological and anthropocentric orientation, John Paul II is able to introduce into his Trinitarian theology fresh accents and novel themes which usually are not found in a traditional treatise on the Trinity. Mention has been made of his original way of linking Trinitarian theology with anthropology, in particular human freedom; of uniting the mission of Jesus with that of the Holy Spirit; of relating the task of recovering the sense of sin ("convincing the world concerning sin") and the theology of original sin to the Holy Spirit; of considering the Holy Spirit as Giver of life in relation to the tensions between "spirit" and "flesh" and "life" and "death" in the human heart; of presenting the Holy Spirit as the principal agent of the Church's mission *ad gentes*; of highlighting the mercy of God the Father in relation to God's love and justice and to human dignity; and of relating the Trinity to the concrete life of Christians and the Church in general. All these themes and others will enrich contemporary theology of the Trinity which still tends to be abstract and removed from the daily life of Christians.

On the other hand, to formulate a comprehensive theology of the Trinity, John Paul II's reflections must be expanded to include valid insights of various contemporary theological movements such as liberation, feminist, and ecological theologies. Not that these insights are absent from John Paul II's trilogy: the pope does speak of the "suffering" and "pain" of God, hint at the "feminine" dimension of God (God's *rahamim*), and affirm the intrinsic relationship between faith in the Triune God and the work for justice and liberation. Nevertheless, these still are fleeting insights, and it is incumbent upon theologians to integrate them into John Paul's overall Trinitarian theology.

Because of the priority he has chosen to give to the economic Trinity, one aspect of Trinitarian theology that John Paul (and he is much aware of it) has not developed is the immanent Trinity or the operations *ad intra*. Only once in the three encyclicals does he offer reflections on the inner life of God, when he distinguishes between "essential love" in God and "personal love" which is the Holy Spirit:

> In his intimate life, God "is love," the essential love shared by the three divine Persons: personal love is the Holy Spirit as the Spirit of the Father and the Son. . . . It can be said that in the Holy Spirit the intimate life of the Triune God becomes totally gift, an exchange of mutual love between the divine Persons, and that through the Holy Spirit God exists in the mode of gift. It is the Holy Spirit who is *the personal expression* of this self-giving, of this being-love. He is Person-Love. He is Person-Gift. . . . At the same time, the Holy Spirit, being consubstantial with the Father and the Son in divinity, is love and uncreated gift from which derives as from its source (*fons vivus*) *all giving of gifts* vis-à-vis creatures (created gift): the gift of existence to all things through creation; the

gift of grace to human beings through the whole economy of salvation. (DV 10)

And yet, John Paul II's philosophical and dramatic writings offer a rich source for developing a theology of the immanent Trinity. Space does not permit an elaboration of this theme here, but there is no doubt that if John Paul's notion of "person" as developed in his plays and his philosophical *magnum opus, The Acting Person,* is pressed into service, a dynamic and "dramatic" theology of the Trinity will result and will make an original and substantive contribution to Trinitarian theology.

In *The Jeweller's Shop,* a three-act play that Karol Wojtyła published in 1960 under the pseudonym Andrzej Jawień, the author offers his reflections on love and marriage through the stories of two couples and their children. The first couple, Andrew and Teresa have a short but happy marriage; the second couple, Stefan and Anna, have a long marriage broken by anger and rancor. Christopher, the son of the first couple, is planning to marry Monica, the daughter of the second couple. The play centers on three marriages, the first loving but short, the second long but failed, and the third about to happen in fear and hope.

In and through these protagonists and especially the Christ figure of the Bridegroom and the Everyman figure of Adam, Wojtyła explores the nature of human love, especially conjugal love. Rocco Buttiglione summarizes succinctly the theme of *The Jeweller's Shop*: "This is the lesson of *The Jeweller's Shop*: to love truly, to generate and to be generated as a person, it is necessary to incorporate one's own human love into the infinite love of God, transcending the sphere of emotions and sensibility and turning toward the core of the person, where one's relationship with God makes him what he is. This calls for an encounter with the Incarnation. But it also allows one to enter into the Trinitarian reality, into the eternal process within which the Father generates the Son out of himself and all of the Persons subsist fully in the other, without residue" (Buttiglione 1997, 265).

As always, for Wojtyła, the fundamental issue is the human person. In his view, it is impossible to understand the human person without reference to God, and more precisely, the God who is Father, "rich in mercy," who sent his Son as "Redeemer of humanity" fulfilling his redemptive mission by the power of the Holy Spirit, "Lord and Giver of life." In a later drama entitled *Radiation of Fatherhood: A Mystery,* Wojtyła turns to the theme of fatherhood in the figure of Adam with his daughter Monica. Adam, the Everyman, suffers from loneliness. But he is called to leave his loneliness by becoming a father, a call he resists because he wants to be independent of everything. Having to choose between self-subsistence and relatedness, he opts for self-sufficiency and autonomy. Still, Adam struggles with the challenge of becoming a father, and when the Woman-Eve comes to him and conceives a child by him, he begins, by himself becoming a father, to understand the radiation of the fatherly love of God who also from all eternity gives birth to his Son. Furthermore, Adam also realizes that he can accept the radiation of Love from the Father only in and through the Son, and therewith by becoming himself a son of God. For Wojtyła, the trinity of father, son, and love in the human person reflects the Trinity in God: Father, Son, and Love.

Wojtyła's philosophy of the person came to fruition in his *The Acting Person.* In this work, widely recognized as extremely difficult, the author attempts to combine the phenomenological method and the Neoscholastic analysis of the human act in order to arrive at a satisfactory anthropology. Wojtyła argues that what is distinctive about the human person is not that he is a *suppositum entis* but that he is an "acting subject." First, through an analysis of human consciousness, Wojtyła shows that human persons are aware that they are the cause of their actions, that is, that they are the subject of action. Second, in their action human beings transcend themselves, that is, in completing an action, the person simultaneously realizes himself or herself. In action human persons reveal themselves to be subjects though their capacity for self-government and self-possession, which in turn imply freedom and responsibility for their action. Third, in their action, human persons integrate their bodies and their psyches, since action belongs neither to the body alone nor to the psyche alone but to the personal unity which integrates all these aspects. Fourth, in action humans become intersubjective and social beings through participation. The person becomes what he or she is only on relationship with an other. Against individualism and totalism, Wojtyła maintains that individual and community mutually imply each other. What binds individuals and community of acting individuals together is the common good, which is the realization of the persons through their actions.

It is not difficult to see that the figure of Jesus Christ is present on every page of *The Acting Person.* As has been said above, for John Paul II, Jesus reveals the true identity of the human person. Indeed, the ideal person as described by Wojtyła is fully embodied in Jesus whose death on the Cross is the one act deliberately integrating all his dimensions in obedience to and love for his Father and in solidarity with us. Nor is it difficult to make use of Wojtyła's conception of the person as an acting subject to explicate the eternal relations among the divine Persons in the immanent Trinity (of course, without the third element, which presupposes bodiliness). The divine Persons are constituted by their actions ("processions," to use a Scholastic term) which in turn produce mutual relationships characterized by the Source of action (the Father), the Truth of the action (the Son), and the Love and Freedom of action (the Holy Spirit).

The emphasis on acting and action in Wojtyła's conception of the person, when applied to the immanent Trinity, has the advantage of presenting the Trinity as an eternal drama which unfolds in the history of salvation as a "theodrama" in which humans are invited to play a role. The "economic Trinity" then is nothing other than the revelation-in-beauty of the "immanent Trinity" manifesting itself as Being, Truth, and Goodness.

See Also: DIVES IN MISERICORDIA, DOMINUM ET VIVIFICANTEM, RECONCILATIO ET PAENITENTIA, REDEMPTOR HOMINIS, REDEMPTORIS MATER, REDEMPTORIS MISSIO, VERITATIS SPLENDOR

Bibliography: GIACOMO BIFFI, "The Action of the Holy Spirit in the Church and the World," in *John Paul II: A Panorama of His Teachings* (New York: New York City Press, 1989). ROCCO BUTTIGLIONE, *Karol Wojtyła: The Thought of the Man Who Became Pope John Paul II,* translated by PAOLO GUIETTI and FRANCESCA MURPHY (Grand Rapids, Mich.: William B. Eerdmans, 1997). PINCHAS LAPIDE, "*Dives in Misericordia*: An Encyclical for Christians and Jews," *Journal of Ecumenical Studies* 18 (1981): 140–42. JOHN M. MCDERMOTT, ed., *The Thought of Pope John Paul II: A Collection of Essays and Studies* (Rome: Editrice Pontificia Università Gregoriana, 1993). ANTOINE E. NACHEF, *The Mystery of the Trinity in the Theological Thought of Pope John Paul II* (New York: Peter Lang, 1999). PAUL L. PEETERS, "*Dominum et Vivificantem*: The Conscience and the Heart," *Communio* 15 (1988): 148–155. JOHN SAWARD, *Christ is the Answer: The Christ-Centered Teaching of Pope John II* (Edinburgh: T & T Clark, 1995). KENNETH L. SCHMITZ, *At the Center of the Human Drama: The Philosophical Anthropology of Karol Wojtyła/Pope John Paul II* (Washington, DC: The Catholic University of America Press, 1993). ANGELO SCOLA, "'Claim' of Christ, 'Claim' of the World: On the Trinitarian Encyclicals of John Paul II," *Communio* 18 (1991): 331–332. GEORGE HUNSTON WILLIAMS, *The Mind of John Paul II: Origins of His Thought and Action.* (New York: Seabury, 1981). KAROL WOJTYŁA, *Sources of Renewal* (London: Collins, 1980).

[PETER C. PHAN]

John Paul II's Economic Teaching: A Call for Spiritual, Moral, and Structural Conversion

Gregory G. Baum, D. Th., is professor emeritus at the Faculty of Religious Studies, McGill University, Montreal, Canada.

"The needs of the poor must take priority over the desires of the rich, the rights of workers over the maximization of profits, the preservation of the environment over uncontrolled industrial expansion, and production to meet social needs over production for military purposes." (John Paul II, on his visit to Canada, 1984)

Pope John Paul II's social teaching is theologically grounded. He has developed his ideas in continuity with antecedent papal teaching and in critical dialogue with secular thought, but the basis of his teaching is the gospel. This differs from papal teachings in the past which were based on natural law reasoning and bracketed reference to divine revelation. Previous popes did this in the hope of finding a common ground with non-Christians. Pope John XXIII was the first pope to mention the gospel in his social teaching. It was John Paul's II "cosmic Christology," the idea that through Incarnation and Redemption Christ is related in some way to every human being, that accounts for the theological orientation of his social teaching. He proposed this Christology in his first encyclical, *Redemptor hominis* (1979), expanding upon ideas set forth by the Second Vatican Council, and often referred to it at subsequent occasions. We have here the retrieval of a theological current of the ancient Christian authors, especially in the East, according to which through Incarnation and Christ's death and resurrection the whole of humanity, or even the entire cosmos, has been elevated and assigned a supernatural destiny. On the basis of this theology, Pope John Paul speaks confidently of Christian principles, trusting that if they are expressed in simple language, people outside of the Church will understand them.

A practical consequence of this theological approach is that the Christian's commitment to social justice receives a new location in the life of faith. When the Church's social teaching was based on natural law theory, social justice belonged to the order of the natural virtues and did not involve the order of faith, hope, and love. Spirituality and the intimate life of faith did not include commitment to justice and the transformation of society. The spiritual books in use in seminaries and religious communities testify to this: they did not trouble their readers with the problems of their society. With John Paul's social teaching, universal solidarity and commitment to social justice have been lifted into the life of faith, hope, and love and thus become a part of Catholic spirituality. There is a mystical dimension in the sorrow over the suffering of others and the public engagement to reconstruct the social order. The pope's teaching, one might add, reflects the religious experience of vast numbers of Christians committed to social justice in various parts of the world.

Since Pope John Paul II has produced an extensive literature developing his social teaching, a single article cannot cover the full range of his thought, but will have to focus on a particular topic. I wish to concentrate on a theme in his teaching, often overlooked in the North America, that made him a critic of Eastern communism and Western capitalism. I wish to call this "the double orientation" of his teaching. During the Cold War, John Paul II adopted a position, rarely defended in North America, that called for the spiritual, moral, and structural conversion of communism and capitalism. While he opposed the totalitarian regimes in the Soviet bloc countries, denounced their militant atheism, and criticized the imperialist outreach of the Soviet Union, he did not envision the collapse of these systems, but advocated their reform. Nor did he think that the world was threatened by Soviet imperialism alone. In *Redemptor hominis* he denounced the involvement of the two superpowers in Third World countries, accusing them of exploiting the local populations, fomenting conflicts between them, supplying them with weapons to wage war, and exercising neocolonialism of one kind or another. Then he added that this criticism is likely "to offer both 'sides' an occasion for mutual accusation, each overlooking its own faults" (16).

Since John Paul II's social teaching is so bold and so rarely heard, I offer many quotations from his speeches and encyclicals, to reassure the reader that these radical ideas are indeed found in his writings and are not drawn from other sources. First, I deal with the pope's encyclical *Laborem exercens* (1981) in support of the Polish labor movement, *Solidarnosc,* which called for reforms in the existing communist and capitalist societies. Second, I offer a brief account of Rome's relation to Latin American liberation theology. Third, I shall describe the encyclical *Sollicitudo rei socialis* (1987), which offers a critical analysis of the two superpowers and, far from anticipating the collapse of communism, urges the reform of the two existing economic systems. Finally, I examine the pope's teaching after the collapse of Eastern European communism in 1989 both in his encyclical *Centesimus annus* (1991) and his speeches delivered in Poland and other countries formerly members of the Soviet bloc.

Laborem exercens

I begin with a brief account of the political philosophy of the Polish Solidarity movement supported by both secular and Catholic workers. In her detailed study, *The Polish Solidarity Movement,* Arista Maria Cirtautas has examined Solidarity's affirmation of social rights and its relation to capitalism. She offers a careful analysis of the debate among workers and intellectuals over the basis for their opposition to Poland's communist government and then shows that they eventually agreed on a value-rational position that she designates as "a fusion of communist and Catholic humanism" (Cirtautas 1997, 166). She confirms this conclusion in her study of the writings of Adam Michnik, the influential secular socialist, and of Jozef Tischner, the Catholic social thinker. These intellectuals articulated humanistic positions that, though distinct, were close enough to lay the foundation for solidarity in a joint struggle for communist reform. In *Laborem exercens*, John Paul II, conscious of this secular-Catholic cooperation, expressed his thought in a Catholic discourse that addressed at the same time the secular workers. The pope's message was fully heard as support for the joint struggle. Responding to the encyclical in the name of his colleagues, Michnik wrote that the pope did not confront them with a choice between faith and atheism; instead he proposed a set of common values with which they readily identified.

What was the aim of the Polish labor movement? It was certainly not to introduce Western-style capitalism in Poland. *Solidarnosc* fought for independent labor unions, a more participatory society with freedom of speech, a more open space for economic initiatives and the creation of free markets; at the same time, it supported a strong central government to regulate the economy and assume the redistribution of wealth. Thinking that communism was reformable, the movement struggled for a socialism with a human face.

In *Laborem exercens* John Paul II defines human beings as workers: "Work is one of the characteristics that distinguishes humans from the rest of creatures, whose activities for sustaining their lives cannot be called work. Only humans are capable of work, and only human work, and in doing so occupy their existence on earth" (intro.). "Human life is built up every day from work, from work it derives its specific dignity, yet at the same time work contains the unceasing measure of human toil and suffering and also of the harm and injustice which penetrate deeply into social life within the individual nations and on the international level" (1). John Paul writes his encyclical "to highlight—perhaps more than has been done before—that human work is a key, probably the essential key, to the entire social question" (3). This is in fact a new discourse in papal social teaching.

The encyclical introduces the important distinction between the *objective* and the *subjective* poles of labor. The objective pole refers to the product of work, which in one way or another transforms the earth, while the subjective dimension refers to the self-realization of the workers through their work. It is to the latter that the pope attributes priority. "Human beings work as persons, performing various actions belonging to the work process. Independently of their objective content, these actions must all serve to realize the humanity of the workers, to fulfill the calling to be persons that is theirs by reason of their very humanity" (6). Humans are divinely destined to realize and constitute themselves through their work. What follows from this is that workers are *subjects* and not *objects* of their work. "The sources of human dignity of work are to be sought primarily in the subjective dimension, not in the objective one" (ibid.).

This understanding of human work respects what the pope refers to as "the primacy of the spiritual." This primacy, we note, is not an otherworldy principle; it refers rather to the preeminence of the spiritual dimension in the constitution of human beings and their societies.

Continuing his argument, John Paul II writes, "At the beginning of the industrial age, work was understood and treated as a sort of 'merchandise' that the industrial worker sells to the employer, who is the possessor of the capital, i.e. of all the working tools and means that make production possible" (7). When workers are not respected as subjects, their work is deeply alienating—that is, their work prevents them from fulfilling their human vocation. The encyclical argues that workers' movements and social reforms were able to transform the original situation at the beginning of the industrial age and produce various forms of capitalism and socialism. Still, "the danger of treating work as a special kind of 'merchandise' or as an impersonal 'work force' needed for production always exists, especially when the whole way of looking at the question of economics is marked by the premises of materialistic economism" (ibid.).

Is the pope here speaking of the communist East or the capitalist West? Here is what he says: "When the human is treated as an instrument of production . . . whatever the program or name under which this occurs, should rightly be called 'capitalism'" (ibid.). By implication, the pope here accuses the existing communist society of being a form of state capitalism. "The error of early capitalism can be repeated wherever workers are treated on the same level as the whole complex of the material means of production" (ibid.). John Paul II here formulates an ethical principle that is applicable to all industrial systems, namely "the priority of labor over capital" (12).

At the industrial revolution, "a break occurred" through which "labor was separated from capital and set in opposition to it, and capital was set in opposition to labor, as if they were two impersonal forces" (13). "Considering human labor solely according to its economic purpose, was a fundamental error that can be called . . . economism" (ibid.). "It was this practical error that struck a blow first and foremost against human labor, against the working man, and caused an ethically just social reaction" (ibid.), "an impetuous emergence of a great burst of solidarity between workers, first and foremost industrial workers" (8). This outburst of solidarity, as we shall see further on, produced reform movements within capitalism and generated socialism in various forms, most of them affected by the same economistic error. This error is corrected by the application of "the priority of labor over capital."

Almost the entire social teaching of John Paul II in the period of Cold War was formulated in such a manner that it offered a theologically grounded, ethical critique of the existing communist and capitalist societies. This does not mean, of course, that he put the two competing superpowers and their allies on the same level. The totalitarian regimes of the Soviet bloc countries and their militant atheism created oppressive conditions over against which the Western democracies appeared as realms of freedom, despite their own oppressive practices. Yet, as we shall see, the pope did not overlook the imperialism exercised by the superpower of the West.

To illustrate the pope's brilliant double-oriented economic and political ethics in this encyclical, I give two examples, (1) the ongoing need for a labor movement supported by all who love justice and (2) the conditional character of the ownership of the means of production.

First, since in all industrial societies the subjectivity of labor and the living conditions of workers continue to be threatened, labor movements, including the unionization of labor, are indispensable elements of society, gifted with a historical vocation. "In order to achieve social justice in the various parts of the world . . . there is need for ever new movements of solidarity of the workers and with the workers. This solidarity must be present whenever it is called for by the social degrading of the subject of work, by exploitation of the workers and by growing areas of poverty and even hunger. The Church is firmly committed to this cause, for its considers it to be its mission, its service, a proof of its fidelity to Christ" (8). That this struggle differs from the Marxist idea of class war is clear: first, this social struggle does not aim at the conquest of the owning classes but at conditions of greater justice, and second, this struggle calls for the solidarity of workers and the solidarity with workers of all citizens who love justice and hence transcends its location in the working class.

The second example is the pope's bold interpretation of ownership that radicalizes what was taught on the subject by previous popes. Applying the principle of "the priority of labor," the encyclical argues that unless the ownership of the means of production, whether it be personal or collective, intends to serve labor, or more widely the laboring society, the ownership loses its legitimate title. This is a subversive principle questioning both capitalist and communist societies. "Isolating the means of production as a separate property in order to set it up in the form of 'capital' in opposition to 'labor'—and even to practice exploitation of labor—is contrary to the very nature of these means and their possession. They cannot be possessed against labor, they cannot even be possessed for possession's sake, because the only legitimate title to their possession—whether in the form of private ownership or in the form of public or collective ownership—is that it should serve labor" (14). Implicit in this understanding of ownership is the realization of the ancient Christian teaching usually formulated as "the universal destination of good and the right of common use of them" (ibid.).

Laborem exercens had a strong influence on the social teaching of the Canadian bishops, especially on their *Ethical Reflections on the Economic Crisis* (1983). When the pope visited of Canada in 1984, he supported the radical critique of the existing economic order by a number of strong statements—for example, "Poor people and poor nations—poor in different ways, not only lacking food, but also deprived of freedom and other human rights—will sit in judgement on those people who take these goods away from them, amassing to themselves the imperialistic monopoly of economic and political supremacy at the expense of others.'' The pope calls for the conversion of heart and mind of the powerful élites. His radical call for the reconstruction of the global society recognizes the primacy of the spiritual.

Liberation Theology

The evaluation of Latin American liberation theology by Pope John Paul and the Congregation for the Doctrine of Faith is a complex one, not free of contradictions. On the one hand, Latin American liberation theology has been able to shift the focus of ecclesiastical teaching—at the Latin American Bishops' Conference at Medellin (1968), at the second general assembly of the Synod of Bishops (1971) and in Paul VI's *Octogesima adveniens* (1971). Pope John Paul II himself has repeatedly endorsed ''the preferential option for the poor,'' a concept taken from Latin American liberation theology. Sometimes the pope prefers to speak of ''the preferential love of the poor,'' which is an option within the order of charity, demanding that in its pastoral and charitable service the Church assign priority to the poor. ''The preferential option for the poor'' belongs to a different order. It is implies a double-commitment: (1) to read historical events and the texts associated with them from the perspective of the poor and (2) to give public witness to their struggle for greater justice. This is what the pope has done on many occasions. On his visits to Third World countries, he has sided with the poor, the great majority, and told them that, in their name, he denounces the unjust structures that oppress them.

A famous example is his speech at Cuilapan, Mexico (1979), addressing several hundred thousand Native peoples from Oaxaca and Chiapas. Here the pope promised that he would be their voice, the voice of those who cannot speak or who are silenced, expressing their prolonged suffering and their disappointed hopes and accusing the men in power responsible for the oppressive conditions that cause hunger and misery among the poor and rob them of their dignity as God's children. The pope read Mexican society from the perspective of the poor and gave public support for their struggle for justice. He proclaimed the Christian gospel as God's merciful act of love rescuing the people from the enemies of their lives.

The pope used a different emphasis in his opening statement at the Latin American Bishops' Conference at Puebla (1979). He insisted that the starting point of Christian reflection must be the doctrines of the faith; the second step is the turn to the misery of the poor inflicted by unjust conditions. He criticized liberation theology and even a trend among the bishops to regard solidarity with the poor as the first step, taken in the name of Jesus, and then only to explore the meaning of Christian doctrine from the perspective of these oppressed people. After his criticism followed two declarations of the Congregation for the Doctrine of the Faith (1984, 1986); the first was highly critical of liberation theology, suggesting that it made ''an insufficiently critical use of Marxism,'' while the second adopted a more positive approach, even while warning against the adoption of Marxist principles. It is not clear to what extent these critical observations apply to the different types of liberation theologies produced in Latin America. In a letter to the Brazilian bishops (13 March 1986) who were puzzled by the Roman position, John Paul II seemed to clarify his own attitude: ''The theology of liberation can and must exist . . . we must proceed with this reflection, update it and deepen it more and more.'' Liberation theology is acceptable, he continued, as long as it respects the primacy of the spiritual, recognizes the struggle of the poor for social justice as grounded in Christian values, and remains faithful to the Church's social teaching. The pope's concern here is the same as in *Laborem exercens*: the struggle against injustice and oppression must preserve the primary of the spiritual and understand itself as an ethically grounded movement sustained by the gospel, and not as the necessary product of the class conflict built into the material dynamics of history as Marxists have interpreted it.

Rome's position vis-à-vis liberation theology deserves a major study, taking into account both the various ecclesiastical texts and the differences among liberation theologians. The topic is even more complicated since Rome also seems to have criticized Latin American bishops for their own social teachings, even though these were more moderate than the social messages of liberation theology. New bishops appointed by Rome were often conservative churchmen who did not share the spirit of Medellin and did not follow the option for the poor as expressed at Puebla. Some students of this period, puzzled by the shift in Roman policy, have attributed it to the opposition of the U.S. government.

Solicitudo rei socialis

The encyclical *Solicitudo rei socialis* was published in December 1987, commemorating Paul VI's *Populorum progressio* written twenty years earlier. In 1987, it was already clear that a shift had taken place in the orientation of the Western economy. Under the impact of the policies adopted by Margaret Thatcher, prime minister of the United Kingdom, and Ronald Reagan, president of the United States, the national economies in the countries of the West had abandoned the Keynesian policies favoring regulated capitalism and the welfare state and instead introduced monetarist policies that called for the deregulation of capital, the privatization of public goods, and the globalization of the free market. The encyclical concludes that since 1967 the conditions of the poor countries have deteriorated.

What is also remarkable is that the encyclical in no way anticipates the collapse of Eastern European communism that was to take place less than two years later in 1989 (see *Centesimus annus* 22). In 1987 John Paul II still believed, as he did in *Laborem exercens,* that the two opposing economic systems and their respective societies could be reformed, made more just and more human, and then live peacefully side by side. In 1987 the pope was still preoccupied with the impact of the Cold War, especially on the countries of the Third World. "If their situation is examined in the light of the division of the world into ideological blocs . . . and in the light of the subsequent economic and political repercussions and dependencies, the danger is seen to be much greater" (10).

John Paul II's social teaching in *Sollicitudo reo socialis* is bold and original. The encyclical begins with a survey of the contemporary conditions focusing especially on the Third World (11 19). Using several statistical criteria, such as the production and distribution of foodstuffs, hygiene, health, housing, availability of drinking water, working conditions (especially for women), life expectancy, indebtedness, and other social and economic indicators, the pope concludes that the gap between rich and poor is increasing and that the majority of humanity is now worse off that in 1967 when Paul VI published *Populorum progressio.*

Among the oppressive features of contemporary society, John Paul II mentions the spread of unemployment in capitalist countries and the suppression of people's right to economic initiative in communist countries. In this context the pope expands the concept of "subjectivity," already applied to workers in *Laborem exercens,* to all citizens and, more generally, to members of any organization. No institution has the right to suppress the spirit of initiative, reliance on personal creativity, and the sense of co-responsibility, for these belong to a person's "subjectivity." The immediate reference is here to the command economy in communist countries that stifles people's economic initiative and fails to recognize the indispensable role of markets. The pope adds an interesting sentence on bureaucratic domination that has universal relevance. "In the place of creative initiative there appears passivity, dependence and submission to the bureaucratic apparatus which, as the only 'ordering' and 'decision-making' body—if not also the owner—of the entire totality of goods and the means of production, puts everyone in a position of almost absolute dependence, which is similar to the traditional dependence of the worker-proletarian in capitalism" (15).

According to the encyclical, the situation of Third World peoples is strongly affected by the tension between the two superpowers:

> the existence of two opposing blocs, commonly known as the East and the West. The reason for this description is not purely political but is also, as the expression goes, geopolitical. Each of the two blocs tends to assimilate or gather around it other countries or groups of countries, to different degrees of adherence or participation. The opposition is first of all political, inasmuch as each bloc identifies itself with a system of organizing society and exercising power which presents itself as an alternative to the other. The political opposition, in turn, takes its origin from a deeper opposition which is ideological in nature. In the West there exists a system which is historically inspired by the principles of liberal capitalism which developed with industrialization during the last century. In the East there exists a system inspired by Marxist collectivism which sprang from an interpretation of the condition of the proletarian classes made in the light of a particular reading of history. Each of the two ideologies, on the basis of two very different visions of man, and of his freedom and social role, has proposed and still promotes, on the economic level, antithetical forms of the organization of labor and of the structures of ownership, especially in regard to the so-called means of production. It was inevitable that by developing antagonistic systems and centers of power, each with its own form of propaganda and indoctrination, the ideological opposition should evolve into a growing military opposition and give rise to two blocs of armed forces, each suspicious and fearful of the other's domination. International relations, in turn, could not fail to feel the effects of this "logic of blocs" and of the respective "spheres of influence." . . . Sometimes this tension has taken the form of "cold war," sometimes of "wars by proxy," through the manipulation of local conflicts and sometimes it has kept people's minds in suspense and anguish by the threat of an open and total war. (20)

John Paul II has further developed the analysis expressed in the above paragraphs at other occasions. He argues that because industrial capitalism produced both wealth and freedom for the middle classes, they were tempted to turn private property and the free market into a principle of universal validity, an ideology, that accounted for the evolution of history and defined its orientation toward the future. Ideologies are deadly—the pope refers to them sometimes as "idols"—because they are taken as infallible guides for policies and actions without attention to their destructive empirical consequences. John Paul II is fully aware that thanks to the labor movement and reform-minded political parties capitalism has assumed new forms, sometimes allowing workers substantial degrees of participation.

Conversely, the pope argues that the ethically justified struggle of workers to achieve more just conditions and the respect of their rights has tempted Marxists to turn the working-class struggle into a principle of universal validity, an ideology, that accounts for the evolution of history and defines its orientation toward the future. Again, this ideology has become deadly because it guides policies and actions without attention to the devastation they produce. The struggle of workers for greater justice, the pope holds, is an ethical undertaking, an outburst of solidarity, that deserves the support of all classes and the Church itself. In line with the Polish Solidarity movement, the pope believes that an ethical, non-ideological form of socialism is a political possibility. The rigidity of communist governments has prevented this from happening.

The opposition between the two superpowers, John Paul II argues, has been transferred to the developing countries, creating hostilities between them and prompting them to arm themselves, prepare for war, and spend their limited resources on the expansion of their military. "This is one of the reasons why the Church's social doctrine adopts a critical attitude towards both liberal capitalism and Marxist collectivism" (21).

While the East-West tension seems to be presently declining, the pope believes that a new development has begun to threaten the well-being of the developing countries, namely the global interdependence between rich and poor countries or the globalization of the free-market system, unrestricted by any ethical principles. "The results are disastrous consequences for the weakest. Indeed, as a result of a sort of internal dynamic and under the impulse of mechanisms that can only be called perverse, this interdependence triggers negative effects even in the rich countries" (17). "*Populorum progressio* already foresaw the possibility that under such a system the wealth of the rich would increase and the poverty of the poor would remain" (16).

John Paul II is not opposed to the process of globalization brought about by the development of technology and universal exchange. On the contrary, he praises globalization as long as it is regulated by social justice, respect for the culture of others and a universal commitment to solidarity.

In *Sollicitudo rei socialis,* John Paul II touches upon many issues of great importance such as the international debt, the arms trade, refugees, unemployment, the culture of consumerism, population policy, abortion, and threats to the natural environment. He is encouraged by some positive developments (26): the attention to human rights fostered by the United Nations and other international organizations, the growing awareness of the limits of nature and the need for environmental protection, and the growing realization that the entire globe is vulnerable to the same threats, that humanity shares a common destiny and that universal solidarity is indispensable.

The pope also offers a theologically grounded theory of human development that takes the economic dimension with utmost seriousness and at the same time emphasizes the primacy of the spiritual. The spread of global interdependence must be guided by the spirit of solidarity. There are no solutions of the world's problems and no remedy for the human suffering caused by these problems, apart from a commitment to universal solidarity. What is required is a conversion of the heart and mind.

Sollicitudo rei socialis places considerable emphasis on "evil mechanisms" and "structural sins" that create and perpetuate injustices and damage the lives of human beings. Thus we read in reference to the international debt that changes made in the international financial markets "have turned into counter-productive mechanisms" (19). "The mechanisms intended for the development of peoples has turned into a brake upon development instead, and in some cases has aggravated underdevelopment" (ibid.). Or we read that "a world divided into blocs, sustained by rigid ideologies, in which instead of interdependence and solidarity different forms of imperialism hold sway, can only be a world subject to structures of sin" (36). What we must wrestle against demands therefore collective action and public engagement to reconstruct institutions that do grave harm to people. The primacy of the spiritual may not be interpreted as if the divine summons to social justice simply means that each person should become more holy in his or her private life. What is needed are social movements grounded in preferential solidarity with the victims and oriented towards the renewal of human society as a whole.

Centesimus annus

Centesimus annus (1991) is the first of Pope John Paul's encyclicals written after the "unexpected" collapse of Eastern European communism in 1989. It is not surprising that the demise of the Soviet bloc gave him great joy. The totalitarian regimes with their official atheism were overcome, and the doors opened for the public celebration of the Christian faith and new social and economic developments in the liberated countries. What I wish to show in the following is the continuity of the pope's social teaching, that is, the continued relevance of *Laboren exercens* and *Sollicitudo rei socialis* after collapse of the Soviet bloc.

We read in *Centesimus annus* that in the world of 1991, Pope John Paul sees three distinct sociopolitical projects that people or their governments attempt to translate into reality (19). One of these projects the pope dismisses very quickly. There are governments, he writes, that oppose Marxism for ideological reasons and set up "systems of national security aimed at controlling the whole of society in a systematic way in order to make Marxist infiltration impossible" (ibid.). These societies sin, the pope argues, as did the Marxist system by robbing the citizens of their freedom.

A second societal project is "the affluent or consumer society that seeks to defeat Marxism on the level of pure materialism by showing how a free market society can achieve greater satisfaction of material human needs than communism, while equally excluding spiritual values" (ibid.). Although it is true that the existing socialist societies were economically inefficient, the ideological defense of capitalism "reduces man to the sphere of economics and the satisfaction of material needs" (ibid.). It is based on an economistic misunderstanding of the human being. "There is a risk that a radical capitalist ideology could spread which refuses to consider that vast multitudes are still living . . . in great material and moral poverty, in an *a priori* belief that . . . blindly entrusts the solution of these problems to the free development of market forces" (42). Or again, "it is unacceptable to say that the defeat of 'real socialism' leaves capitalism as the only model of economic organization. It is necessary to break down the barriers and monopolies which leave so many countries on the margins of development" (35).

The pope is preoccupied with two issues related to this second societal project: the market as possible "idol" and the culture of consumerism. While markets are absolutely necessary in a free and economically efficient society, they have their limits. "There are collective and qualitative needs which cannot be satisfied by market mechanisms. There are important human needs that escape its logic. There are goods that by their very nature cannot and must not be bought and sold. Certainly the mechanisms of the market offer secure advantages . . . yet they carry the risk of 'idolatry' . . . ignoring the existence of goods . . . which cannot be mere commodities" (40). The encyclical offers high praise for the free market. "On the level of individual nations and of international relations, the free market is the most efficient instrument for utilizing resources and effectively responding to needs" (34). This positive evaluation is immediately followed by a paragraph emphasizing the limits of the market. First, the free market is acceptable only for things that are by nature "marketable"; second, the free market is a useful instrument for the distribution of goods only among people who have money to pay the price. For the

distribution of basic needs to the poor, one must find institutions other than markets. "It is a strict duty of justice and truth not to allow fundamental human needs to remain unsatisfied and to allow those burdened by such needs to perish" (ibid.).

In what the pope calls liberal, rigid, or ideological capitalism, the logic of the market invades every sphere of human life and creates a culture where "having" has priority over "being." Consumerism occurs "when people are ensnared in a web of false and superficial gratifications rather than being helped to experience their personhood in an authentic way" (41). The culture of consumerism is promoted with the help of mass media by industrial and commercial institutions intent upon extending the market and increasing their profit. "Alienation is also found in work, when it is organized so as to ensure maximum returns and profits with no concern whether the worker, through his own labor, grows or diminishes as a person, either through increased sharing in a supportive community, or through increased isolation in a maze of relationships marked by destructive competitiveness, in which he is considered only a means and not an end" (ibid.).

This second societal project described in the encyclical—which I shall call Model A—appears to refer to the neo-liberal globalization of the free market which, as I indicated above, was already being promoted in 1991. Model A is brought about by the deregulation of capital, the privatization of publicly own goods, the unlimited rights of private property, the unrestricted global mobility of capital and goods, and the reliance on market forces to regulate education, public health, and cultural development and to solve the problems created by ecological damage, social inequality, and the exclusion of the poor.

The pope describes the third societal project as "democratic societies inspired by social justice" (19). Such societal projects, he writes, try to preserve the free-market mechanisms, the harmony of social relations, and the citizens' economic initiative to build a better future for themselves and their families. At the same time, these societal projects "avoid making the market mechanisms the only point of reference for social life; they also tend to subject these mechanisms to public control which upholds the principle of the common destination of material goods" (ibid.). These societies recognize the role of labor unions, provide welfare for the needy, and encourage political participation. These societies enhance "the subjectivity" of their members. This third societal project, which I shall call Model B, is characterized by what the pope calls "a modern business economy" (32). Freedom is exercised in the economic field as it is in other fields; at the same time, economic activity is only one sector in a great variety of human activities. The market is surrounded by other social forces, and competition is restrained by a culture of cooperation and solidarity. Moreover, "it is the task of the state to provide for the defense and preservation such as the natural and human environment, which cannot be safeguarded simply by market forces" (34).

At one point in *Centesimus annus* John Paul II asks whether, after the failure of communism, capitalism is now the one victorious social system that should be the goal of countries that presently wish to rebuild their economy (42). His answer is very clear. If capitalism is understood as referring to Model A—with its rigid capitalist ideology, its unregulated free market system, and its economistic concept of the human being—then the answer is negative. But if capitalism is understood as referring to Model B—with its free market economy regulated by government and contained by labor organizations and a culture of solidarity—then the answer is positive.

Since Model A remains predominant—or, in the pope's words, "since marginalization and exploitation remain in the world, especially the Third World, and alienation continues to be real in the more advanced countries" (ibid.)—the struggle for greater justice must continue, "to which the Church lends her voice" (ibid.). That is why the labor movement continues to play an essential role in society: it must wrestle against Model A capitalism. "It is right to speak of a struggle against an economic system, if the latter is understood as a method of upholding the absolute predominance of capital, the possession of the means of production and of the land, in contrast to the free and personal nature of work" (35) The pope here refers back to *Laborem exercens*. To struggle against such a system, he writes, is not an attempt to reconstruct the old socialism, which in fact was state capitalism, but to create a society of free work, enterprise, and participation. "Such a society [i.e., Model B] is not directed against the market, but demands that the market be appropriately controlled by forces of society and by the state, so as to guarantee that the basic needs of the entire society are satisfied" (ibid.).

According to John Paul II, the experience of the Polish labor movement offers an important lesson for contemporary social movements that struggle against the unjust structures of society (24). First, such movements must engage in their struggle with non-violent means; second, they must understand their struggle as not simply aimed at greater economic benefits, but also and above all as oriented towards a more dignified and responsible human existence; and third, such movements must set a limit to their demands allowing them to opt for negotiations at the right time.

With *Laborem exercens* and *Sollicitudo rei socialis, Centesimus annus* calls for a commitment to solidarity with the excluded and unjustly treated at home and abroad.

Speeches in Formerly Communist Countries

In the speeches of John Paul II given in countries formerly integrated into the Soviet bloc, we find repeated warnings—in line with his encyclicals—against Model A capitalism with its consumerist culture. This capitalism is promoted by forces in the West and has begun to appeal to great numbers in the East. Against this trend, the Pope calls for a political commitment to a socioeconomic project in keeping with Model B.

In a speech given in Poland on 8 June 1991, John Paul II cites with approval a paragraph written by an Italian political thinker, Rocco Buttiglione, whom he greatly esteems. "The Polish people could either enter the [European] consumer society and occupy there the lowest place before this society closes its doors to new arrivals . . . or they could contribute to the discovery of the great, profound and authentic tradition of Europe by opting simultaneously for the free market and for solidarity." Speaking to the bishops of Poland in 1991, the pope said, "In the past, Poles found in the Church the defense of their human rights; now Poles find in the Church a defense against themselves, against a bad use of their freedom, against wasting a great historical moment." In a sermon delivered in Poland in 1997, the pope said, "Political leaders and men of the economy have the grave responsibility for a just distribution of the goods on the national and international level . . . . Solidarity must conquer the unbridled desire for profit and the application of the laws of the market that do not take people's human rights into account."

Addressing the an audience at the University of Riga, Latvia, in 1993, John Paul II made the following observations. "While the Church has vigorously condemned 'socialism,' it has also, from Leo XIII's *Rerum novarum* [2] on, distanced itself again and again from the capitalist ideology, holding it responsible for grave social injustices. In his *Quadragesimo anno* [109] Pius XI employed clear and strong language to denounce the international imperialism of money. This line of thinking has been confirmed by the most recent magisterium, and after the historical collapse of Marxism, I have not hesitated myself to raise serious doubts regarding the validity of capitalism, if one understands by this not the simple 'market economy,' but a system where the freedom in the economic sphere is not circumscribed by a juridical framework capable of making the economy serve integral human freedom."

In the same speech the pope spoke about Marxism. ''The problems from which Marxism historically arose were very grave indeed. The exploitation which an inhuman capitalism had inflicted on the proletariat from the beginning of the industrial age represented a social evil that was openly condemned by the Church itself. This protest is the grain of truth in Marxism, thanks to which it could present itself as a solution attractive even in the countries of the West. But this solution proved a total failure.'' According to John Paul II, wrestling for justice in solidarity with the exploited and marginalized remains an abiding task.

In 1997, the pope called upon the Polish people to examine their conscience. He warned them that ''the decadent forms of the concept of the human person and of the values of human life have become more subtle and, for this reason, more dangerous. What is needed today is great vigilance.''

Despite the pope's warnings, Poland and other countries formerly of the Soviet bloc have opened themselves to Western-style capitalism with the inevitable result of unemployment and a growing gap between rich and poor. In his book on John Paul II published in 1994, Alain Vircondelet wrote, ''Seduced by the European economy, Poland no longer listens to warnings of the Pope against the capitalist system which is today the source of major evils in the world, the damage of which has affected Africa as well as America itself'' (Vircondelet 1994, 530).

What follows from the above sections is that the critique of Western capitalism in *Laborem exercens* and *Sollicitudo rei socialis* is taken up and extended by John Paul II in *Centesimus annus*. What he recommends for the present is above all a conversion of the heart, a commitment to social solidarity. What we should struggle for, following his teaching, is a free-market society in keeping with Model B, where the market forces are regulated by government so that they serve the common good and where the logic of capital is contained by the labor movement and a culture of solidarity. There are only hints in these encyclicals recommending greater citizens' involvement, the strengthening of civil society, the importance of solidarity movements at the base, and the promotion of community economic development, topics discussed in today's critical literature that have already received the attention of some bishops' conferences. With the globalization of the free-market system the world has become a new and dangerous ball game, the consequences of which reach into every area of human life. The world is deeply troubled by many as yet unanswered questions. The brilliant social teaching of John Paul II supports social movements that reach out for the globalization of solidarity from below and aim at the reconstruction of society in greater conformity with God's will.

See Also: CENTESIMUS ANNUS, LABOREM EXERCENS, PUEBLA, SOLIDARITY, SOLLICITUDO REI SOCIALIS, JOZEF TISCHNER

Bibliography: GREGORY BAUM, *The Priority of Labor: A Commentary on ''Laborem exercens''* (New York: Paulist Press, 1982). GREGORY BAUM and ROBERT ELLSBERG, eds., *The Logic of Solidarity: Commentaries on Pope John Paul II's Encyclical ''On Social Concern''* (Maryknoll, N.Y.: Orbis Books, 1989). GERARD BEIGEL, *Faith and Social Justice in the Teaching of Pope John Paul II* (New York: Peter Land, 1997). CARL BERNSTEIN and MARCO POLITI, *His Holiness: John Paul II and the History of His Time* (New York: Penguin Books, 1996). ARISTA MARIA CIRTAUTAS, *The Polish Solidarity Movement* (London: Routledge, 1997). CONSTANCE COLONNA-CESARI, *Urbi et Orbi: Enquête sur la géopolitique vaticane* (Paris: La Découverte, 1992). CHARLES CURRAN and RICHARD MCCORMICK, S.J., eds., *John Paul II and Moral Theology* (New York: Paulist Press, 1998). KEVIN DORAN, *Solidarity: A Synthesis of Personalism and Communitarianism in the Thought of Karol Wojtyła/John Paul II* (New York: Peter Lang, 1996). DONAL DORR, *Option for the Poor: A Hundred Years of Vatican Social Teaching* (Maryknoll, N.Y.: Orbis Books, 1992). JUDITH A. DWYER, ed., *The New Dictionary of Catholic Social Thought* (Collegeville, Minn.: The Liturgical Press, 1994). JONATHAN KWITNY, *Man of the Century: The Life and Times of Pope John Paul II* (New York: Henry Holt, 1997). MARVIN L. K. MICH, *Catholic Social Teaching and Movements* (Mystic, Conn.: Twenty-Third Publications, 1998). KENNETH MYERS, ed., *Aspiring to Freedom: Commentaries on John Paul II's Encyclical ''The Social Concern of the Church''* (Grand Rapids, Mich.: Eerdmans, 1988). UGO COLOMBO SACCO, *John Paul II and World Politics* (Belgium: Peeters, 1999). TAD SZULC, *Pope John Paul II* (New York: Scribner, 1995). ALAIN TOURAINE, *Solidarity: The Analysis of a Social Movement: Poland 1980-1981* (New York: Cambridge University Press, 1983). ALAIN VIRCONDELET, *Jean Paul II* (Paris: Julliard, 1994). MICHAEL WALSH, *John Paul II* (London: HarperCollins, 1994). GEORGE WEIGEL, *Witness to Hope: The Biography of Pope John Paul II* (New York: HarperCollins, 1999).

[GREGORY BAUM]

From Rome to Cairo and Beijing: John Paul II on Family and Human Rights

Helen M. Alvaré, Esq., *professor of Law in the Columbia School of Law, Catholic University of America, Washington, D.C., is former director of Planning and Information for the National Conference of Catholic Bishops' Secretariat for Pro-Life Activities.*

Although family life has figured prominently in Catholic social teaching over the past century, it is Pope John Paul II's distinctive contribution to have linked family issues and human rights in an unprecedented way. His writings and pronouncements focus the attention of Catholics on the family as a foundational unit in society, and many others—Christians and non-Christians alike—see him as a champion of traditional family values and relationships. He constantly reminds all who will hear that population growth and family planning are not merely or even chiefly economic concerns.

The pope's words echo in international meetings dealing with human rights and the role of women in society. He makes the Church's presence felt in policy decisions taken by the United Nations, most notably at the Cairo Conference on Population (1994) and the Beijing Conference on the Status of Women (1995). The Vatican's delegation at the United Nations, in alliance with Arab countries and many developing nations, has consistently promoted strengthening the stability of families and promoting policies that strengthen family stability as a cohesive force in society.

John Paul II has had profound, widespread, and very practical influence upon family life during the course of his papacy. This influence is likely to continue well into the future for three reasons. First, his letters, encyclicals, and talks on the subject of family constitute a significant portion of his writings during his papacy. Taken together, they articulate an entire framework for thinking about the family—including the family as a unit, as individuals with mutual responsibilities to one another—and the family in the life of society. Second, the Holy See's participation in two United Nations' conferences concerning family garnered massive media attention and brought the Church's teachings about family life as expounded by John Paul II to a worldwide audience. Third, families have taken John Paul II's words "to heart," taken them personally in the way they order family life.

There is a sense in which families feel that the Holy Father knows their situation and accurately grasps the challenges families face in the modern world. His encyclicals and letters often speak with the voice of a close friend or family member who takes their spiritual welfare quite seriously. They also contain personal reflections about his own upbringing in a family. Families sense that he has a deep love for family life. That he knows and champions the importance of individual members to each other and of family units to their communities and even their nations. Because of his teachings, families are more aware of their important and irreplaceable roles, how they ought to aspire to act, and the shape of the threats they face. Families feel both challenged to live up to his ideas and strengthened for the task. All this is evident in the number of family organizations, not only in the Catholic community, but in other faith communities and in the secular culture as well, which welcome and even celebrate the Holy Father's teachings on family.

Of course, family life has figured in Catholic social teaching documents written by earlier popes. For example, in *Rerum novarum, Quadrigesimo anno, Centesimus annus,* and *Laborem exercens* the Church spoke about the relationship between work and family life. *Humanae vitae* spoke about marriage and parenting in the context of reaffirming the Church's teachings on responsible family planning. The career of John Paul II has demonstrated a length, breadth, and depth of involvement with family themes that merit special consideration.

Marriage and Trinitarian Love

As recounted in the papal biography, *Witness to Hope* (Weigel 1999), even as a priest and then a bishop in his native Poland, Father Karol Wojtyła was noted for his many personal friendships with married couples and

John Paul II stands before the United States Capitol building, 1979. (Corbis-Bettmann. Reproduced by permission.)

families, taking the time frequently to marry them and to baptize their children. In his 1960 play *The Jeweler's Shop,* he took up the subject of married love, in particular, the necessity in marriage of the daily work of self-giving. He portrayed married love in uplifted terms and first expressed in writing his lifelong teaching that married love provides an introduction to understanding the communion of love that is the Holy Trinity.

Father Wojtyła's concern for marriage and family life resulted also in the publication in 1960 of *Love and Responsibility.* In it, he wrote about the positive context in which the Church's teachings on sexual morality should be viewed: the obligation to love (the fundamental Christian imperative) and to love the other "responsibly," i.e., with the spouse always as an "end" in themselves, never as a means or a thing. He redefined chastity as a goal far richer than abstinence: Chastity prevails when one person loves another in accordance with the truth about the meaning of love, the truth that reveals the nuptial meaning of the human body and the necessity of complete and mutual self-donation in loving.

Women and Family

John Paul II is the first pope to consider at length some of the new questions confronting women in the

modern world. He treats this topic quite regularly in the context of reflections about family life. In 1981, he wrote in the apostolic exhortation *Familiaris consortio* about women's "lofty dignity" and their rights and roles in the public square and in the family. In the 1988 apostolic letter *Mulieris dignitatem,* he offered a lengthy scriptural reflection on the equal dignity of women and their different and complementary roles with respect to men. He condemned unjust discrimination against women as evidence of original sin and called on women to adopt "justice and charity" to overcome discrimination, not domination. He also identified marriage as the "indispensable" place for the transmission of new life and celebrated women's role as mothers: "God entrusts the human being to women in a special way. . . ."

During the pontificate of John Paul II, the Holy See has also been visibly and influentially involved in international gatherings devoted to the subject of the status of women, including the United Nations' 1994 International Conference on Population and Development (Cairo) and the United Nations' 1995 Fourth International Conference on Women (Beijing). These will be treated at length below.

Papal Writings on the Family

During his papacy, the Holy Father has devoted portions of many different teaching documents to the subject of family and an entire apostolic exhortation *Familiaris consortio* (1981) to the subject. This exhortation was drafted after the 1980 Synod of Bishops on the "Role of the Christian Family in the Modern World." It is a lengthy response by John Paul II to modern forces tending to "destroy" and "deform" families—couples living together, civil marriages, separation, and divorce—while reviewing Catholic teaching about family life from Scripture and Tradition. The exhortation exposed those forces masquerading as "freedom" and offered a model of family life that can achieve real freedom and happiness for all family members. *Familiaris consortio* first emphasized families' tremendous importance in God's eyes; families are "willed by God in the very act of creation." The pope called on society and government to recognize women's right of equal access to all "public functions" but stressed that the greatest social advancement would be policies recognizing women's irreplaceable function in the home. He denounced government interference in couples' decisions about the number and spacing of their children, including where international aid programs are made conditional upon acceptance of some forms of family planning. Government interference in matters of practicing and teaching the faith is strongly denounced. He recognizes families as children's primary educators generally, a role not to be usurped by the state. The pope recommended the principle of subsidiarity to governments that leaves to the family all functions they can perform on their own.

The theme of the family is taken up in the context of other papal teaching. *Laborem exercens* (1981) asserted that families are the important reality around which work life ought to be fashioned and proposes greater recognition for the work women often perform in their homes and with their children. In his 1985 apostolic letter to the youth of the world, John Paul II exhorted young people to form marriages and families according to the Christian model, rejecting a modern paradigm dominated by materialism and consumerism, in which love is reduced to mere pleasure and children to annoyances. *Sollicitudo rei socialis* (1987) condemned international programs of development that disrespect families. It judged that some of these programs are carried out with animus against the poor and against families of certain races. The encyclical labeled as "contemptible means of development" those programs acting against families' cultural and religious identities or families' freedom to decide the number and spacing of their children in accordance with natural means.

The apostolic exhortation *Christifideles laici* was issued in 1988 following the 1987 Synod on the Laity. Amid ample treatment of various forms of lay ministry, family life was called the "first form of communion between persons" and the place where persons' duty to society "primarily begins." John Paul II called for the defense of marriage and family as a lay vocation, primarily "in those times when human egoism, the anti-birth campaign, totalitarian politics, situations of poverty, material, cultural and moral misery" threaten the very foundations of family life.

In *Centesimus annus* (1991), John Paul II called the family the "fundamental structure for proper human ecology," the environment in which human beings are most ideally nurtured. In 1994, John Paul II wrote his "Letter to Families for the International Year of the Family." This is a "lengthy meditation" on family, considering the breadth of scriptural teachings about family and holding up the family as essential to individual salvation, as well as to the well-being of communities and nations. "The history of mankind, the history of salvation, passes by way of the family. . . . [T]he family is placed at the center of the great struggle between good and evil, between life and death, between love and all that is opposed to love. To the family is entrusted the task of striving, first and foremost, to unleash the forces of good, the source of which is found in Christ, the redeemer of man."

In 1995, *Evangelium vitae* considered the threats to human life itself within families—particularly abortion, euthanasia, and assisted suicide—and urged Catholics and others to build up a new culture respectful of human life, particularly the life of the most defenseless. In 1995, John Paul II also published a letter to women, delivered in advance of the United Nations' Fourth World Conference on Women to be held in Beijing in that year. Here, the pope addressed women in all walks of life, opined that the process of women's liberation had been "substantially a positive one," though not without mistakes, and affirmed the importance of mothers' work as well as women's work in the public square. This latter contribution, said the pope, makes public institutions "ever more worthy of humanity."

The Pontifical Council for the Family, relying heavily upon the writings of John Paul II, issued *The Family and Human Rights* in 1999. This document celebrates the 50th anniversary of the Universal Declaration of Human Rights issued by the United Nations in 1948. It called to the world's attention the fundamental and irreplaceable role assigned to the family in the UN declaration. The letter called on those who work for human rights on both national and international levels to remember that protection of the rights of families is an indispensable part of protecting human rights.

The Cairo and Beijing Conferences: An Introduction

Although the above body of writing about the family would, by itself, make John Paul II a noteworthy contributor on the subject, perhaps his most widely received contribution came about as a result of the Holy See's participation in two United Nations' Conferences, the first on population and development (Cairo, 1994) and the second on the status of women (Beijing, 1995). The Holy See, in its status as Permanent Observer at the United Nations (UN), was present and very active at both of these conferences. In the course of both, delegations from certain nations and influential non-governmental organizations (NGOs) sought to undermine the importance of family life and to champion in opposition to the family, individual rights, and flawed notions of women's rights, particularly rights related to sexual expression. The Holy See and its allies resisted.

At Cairo, it became apparent that the United States' delegation was the leading voice for those who wished to overturn traditionally accepted notions about family life. In turn, the Holy See became the leading voice opposing U.S. views. It found allies among many Latin American and Islamic countries. The Holy See became a public target not only for those delegations and some NGOs supporting legal abortion, population control, and homosexual rights, but for the media as well. During a public session of the Cairo conference, the Holy See was openly booed by delegates opposed to its views. Holy See delegation members were also taunted privately, highly unusual behavior in the diplomatic setting of the UN. Media regularly reported the conference as if the dynamic were obvious: The Holy See was opposing progress generally, and women's rights and sexual freedom in particular.

In the struggles that ensued right to the last moments of both the Cairo and the Beijing conferences, the teachings of the Church about family life were regularly exposed in the media, if not always accurately. Media tended to dwell on those topics related to sex and to ignore the important contributions made by the Holy See in other areas related to family, women, population, and development. Still the teachings of the Holy See received worldwide exposure over the course of both the Cairo and the Beijing conferences.

In the years since these conferences and influenced largely by the witness of the Holy See at these, many NGOs have taken up the Church's teachings with a new urgency and sought to influence subsequent actions of the UN on family life, as well as domestic policies about the same. In a very practical way, the Church, particularly since Cairo and Beijing, has become a guiding force in the arena of family, shaping the issues, not only within the Church, but also in secular arenas and on an international basis.

Foundations for Cairo and Beijing: Catholic Teaching on the Family

Before considering the specific positions on family publicly articulated by the Holy See at these international fora, two preliminary topics will be addressed: first, the basic elements of the Church's theology about marriage and family out of which the specific teachings of the pope emerged and second the context in which the United Nations' Cairo and Beijing conferences occurred, i.e., a brief history of the UN's involvement with family policy in the twentieth century.

The fundamental principles of the Catholic teaching on marriage and family are outlined in the *Catechism of the Catholic Church* (nos. 2201–2231), the document that is perhaps the most enduring legacy of John Paul II's pontificate. According to the Catechism, marriage between a man and a woman is a fundamental human institution, created by God simultaneously with the creation of the very first man and woman, according to the Genesis accounts. "Family" is constituted by a man and a woman united in marriage, together with their children. This institution is prior to public authority, which has an

"obligation to recognize it." Larger communities such as the state should not usurp family prerogatives or interfere with their life.

The married couple is intended to reflect God as Trinity, in communion and in complementarity. From the New Testament, one learns that husbands and wives are also to love each other and their children in a way that gives witness to the love between God and the People of God: "Husbands, love your wives, as Christ loved the Church" (Eph 5:25). They are to serve one another in mutual self-giving.

The first premise of Christian teaching about children is that one cannot understand fully the relationship of husband and wife without understanding their relationship with children at the same time. Children are the natural fruit of conjugal love, something springing from "the very heart of that mutual giving." The central metaphor for children in the Christian tradition is "gift." They are the "supreme gift of marriage" and a "sign of God's blessing."

Parents are children's first and most important educators. They have a right to form their children in the Christian faith. Children have their own intrinsic dignity. They are first and foremost "children of God" who must be "respected as human persons"; they are not extensions of their parents. Families should maintain a generous openness to children, as integral parts of marriage and family life.

The United Nations and the Family

Recent UN conferences concerning family life can best be understood against a backdrop of the UN's involvement in the subject in twentieth century. In 1948, the UN declared the family the basic social unit. It stated that the family in general and motherhood and childhood in particular are entitled to the special protection of society and the state. The Declaration affirmed that every person has the right to marry and establish a family and that workers are entitled to a standard of living suitable for themselves and their families. It affirmed also spousal equality and a prior right of parents to choose the education of children. Individual persons were viewed in this document as persons situated within families.

According to Archbishop Renato Martino, head of the Holy See's Permanent Observer mission to the United Nations in 2000, it was not until 1992 at a UN conference in Brazil that a "radical feminist" perspective appeared at the UN, urging dramatic changes in the UN statements about families (Martino 1998). By 1994, proponents of a certain strand of feminism had become deeply entrenched in UN bureaucracies and into influential lobbying organizations that had become close to the UN. These proponents posited family and motherhood as primarily oppressive institutions for women and even for children, and they would address this "oppression" in the first instance with unlimited recourse to birth control and abortion.

In 1994, following two decades of "doomsday predictions" (Martino 1998) about world overpopulation, the UN Fund for Population Activities (UNFPA) spotlighted the topic of "women's reproductive health" at the Cairo Conference on Population and Development. The chair of the conference, Dr. Fred Sai was the former director of the International Planned Parenthood Federation, the world's foremost provider and promoter of birth control and abortion. In the view of many observers, the UNFPA's focus, which included abortion on demand, widespread distribution of contraception in developing countries, and homosexual rights, eclipsed the attention given to the fundamental issues of the economic development necessary for human dignity and demographic stability. These "sex issues" at the Cairo eventually received vast international publicity and brought media attention to this conference larger than any that had attended prior UN conferences. But media were also attracted to the controversy because the chief opponents appeared to be the United States and Holy See delegations, and because large numbers of NGOs attending the Cairo conference that were strongly supportive of U.S. and UNFPA perspectives had many public relations resources at their command.

In the end, however, despite intense pressure from the United States and other more developed countries to achieve consensus for a vision of family life deeply at odds with the Christian tradition, the views of the Holy See had significant impact. A substantial number of the amendments supported by the Holy See and its allies were incorporated into the document. The Holy See was able to join in a "partial consensus" on the final "Program of Action" while expressing enough reservations about the final Platform for Action to reduce substantially its weight on the world stage.

In 1995, the UN Committee on the Status of Women issued its draft of the Platform of Action for that year's Fourth World Conference on Women, to take place in Beijing. The sponsor of this conference was the UN's Committee on the Status of Women, a group that strongly favored a model of family life and sexual freedom starkly opposed to traditional models and to Christian teachings. In this draft platform, marriage, motherhood, and family life were rarely mentioned. When they were mentioned, it was often in a negative light.

Information coming out of the preparatory meetings for this conference indicated that Beijing would have the same potential for controversy over the same topics as the Cairo conference. Representatives of the Clinton White House took steps in advance of the conference to appear ready to work with the Holy See because the U.S. delegation had not received entirely positive coverage of its tactics in Cairo. John Paul II issued his Letter to Women several months in advance of the conference, which was supportive of efforts to end discrimination and secure equal rights for women. The Holy See appointed as leader of its delegation an influential and internationally recognized scholar in the area of family law, Mary Ann Glendon, the Learned Hand professor of Constitutional Law at Harvard University.

At the Beijing conference, a group led by the European Union (EU) attempted to secure in the Beijing document the abortion and other "sexual rights" that they could not achieve in the Cairo document. The Holy See argued that this agenda, which included broadening the meaning of "family" and stripping families, especially mothers and children, of any special consideration by the state, was inimical to the Universal Declaration of Human Rights. Finally, the Holy See delegation broadcast a press release to the major European papers pointing out the differences between EU delegates' positions and the positions taken in their own nations' laws and constitutions. The EU delegation relented. In the end, the Holy See was able to support many parts of the final Program of Action treating poverty, literacy, education, and women's equal access to capital. It denounced, however, those parts of the document that treated family life as inimical or irrelevant to women and distorted and disproportionately elevated the significance of sexual and reproductive issues in women's lives.

John Paul II, Cairo, and Beijing

The Holy See was a lightning rod for controversy at the Beijing and Cairo conferences. Only forty years ago the positions advocated by Holy See delegates at these conferences would have easily achieved consensus in the international community and among families across religious faiths. But by 1994, the ideas proposed by the most economically developed nations on the subject of family had changed. Thus the Holy See found itself the preeminent defender and promoter of longstanding Western traditions on these matters. Since 1994 much of the discussion about family, women and development that has taken place nationally and internationally has proceeded according to the categories the Holy See helped create at those two conferences.

Papal contributions to the conferences are presented here according to a series of themes: "family" *versus* "families" or "individuals"; family as positive reality;

daily necessities of family; human sexuality; population; and family planning. In the context of each theme the section will refer to events at international conferences to elucidate what the Holy See was seeking to accomplish and what it was working to defeat.

"Family" v. "Families" or "Individuals"

At the Cairo and Beijing conferences, delegations from some of the developed nations, such as the United States and the EU undertook strong efforts to remove the traditional family from the central place it had held in the scheme of international human rights. First, it was proposed that *individuals,* and not *families,* should be at the center of human rights protections. Second, instead of recognizing one form of family as natural and advantageous for couples and children, many possible "forms" of family would be recognized as acceptable. In the draft document proposed to international delegations at Beijing, for example, nearly every mention of "family" had appended to it the phrase "in all its forms."

As against this, the Holy See proposed that the family structure is "founded upon the very nature of the human person. It is the "proper setting for the conception, birth and upbringing of children." At Cairo, the Holy See urged that the Conference document ensure that the family receives from society and the state "the protection to which the Universal Declaration on Human Rights says it is entitled." It proposed, in fact, that social policies should have the well-being of families as a principal object. The pope himself took the occasion of his exhortation following the Synod for Africa to recall that importance of the family that the Cairo document sought to undermine. Recalling that the UN conference was held on African soil, he echoed the urgent appeal of bishops of Africa to all the world's heads of state: "Do not allow the African family to be ridiculed on its own soil! Do not allow the International Year of the Family to become the year of the destruction of the family!" (*Ecclesia in Africa,* no. 84).

Family, Negative or Positive Reality?

The draft conference documents presented to the delegates at both the Cairo and Beijing conferences downplayed the role of women in the family or by the family in women's lives. It even derogated the family, stressing the possibility for sexual abuse and other violence by a spouse, without a context of positive references to marriage. During the Beijing conference, delegates from the EU fought virtually all positive references to family and parental authority.

The Holy See responded by agreeing to those propositions condemning sexual violence and other violence

and mutilations directed against women. But it also succeeded in getting some positive references to family included in the final Beijing document so that such condemnations could be made, without appearing to mar all of marriage and family life.

The Holy See also proposed language praising the work of mothers and urging social support—including economic recompense—for their critical work in society and through the family. Regarding children, the Holy See proposed that family life be seen as positive, and indeed indispensable for children, since the family is the place most conducive to children's well-being. The Holy See also tried to achieve consensus on the issue that children are a positive reality for families; they are a family's true riches and the promise of the future. This affirmation of children contradicted the suggestion that children are primarily "another mouth to feed," whose numbers ought to be reduced, and the proposal that they be viewed as independent from their families, particularly where questions about sex and "reproductive rights" were involved.

Narrow Agendas versus Daily Necessities

Enormous attention during both the Cairo and Beijing conferences was paid to the narrow agendas of powerful delegations on the controversial subjects of birth control, abortion, and "sexual rights," including the rights of homosexuals. Issues essential to the conferences' promised agendas were neglected. Thus, it often fell to the Holy See to speak more forcefully about women and families' most basic and daily needs. In its preparatory documents for the Beijing conference on women, for example, the United States spoke first of the necessity of obtaining for women worldwide access to birth control and abortion. Only second did the United States speak of improving the rights and status of women. Regularly the Holy See delegates raised subjects such as discrimination against women, poverty, freedom of religion, access to basic health care including pre-and postnatal care, clean water, and access to education and financial credit for females.

Family Life and Human Sexuality

The Cairo and Beijing conferences showcased the current thought of the most developed nations about human sexuality. These views of sex had little or nothing to do with marriage and children, and they treated sex through the lens of public health alone. They had no opinion regarding a proper context for sexual relations (i.e., marriage), save that sexual intercourse should always be voluntary. In its preparatory documents for Cairo, the United States, for example, proposed universal access to family planning and "safe, legal, and voluntary abortion as a 'fundamental right' of all women.'' The United States proposed that these services be available to adolescents as well as adults in order to reduce unintended pregnancies and sexually transmitted diseases. Parents were not to be informed of their minor children's use of these services in case it might make minors reluctant to use them.

The Holy See responded to such proposals clearly and directly. It chided the conference for paying disproportionate attention to ''reproductive health'' and almost no attention to major health problems suffered by millions of people in less developed countries, especially mothers and mothers-to-be. It noted that the vast majority of paragraphs in the conference document treating maternal health concerned preventing reproduction, not safeguarding it for women and children. It suggested that such impulses reflected more an animus against the poor than a desire to promote their authentic development. Particularly lacking was any attention to maternal health and safety.

The Holy See objected strongly to the inclusion of very young women in such a ''reproductive health'' agenda. And doing so without parental involvement and authority. In early versions of the Beijing document, parental involvement was even called ''interference.'' The Holy See endorsed the idea of some form of sex education for adolescents so long as it was respectful of parents' authority, age appropriate, maturity enhancing, and sensitive to cultural, religious, and moral values.

Regarding abortion, the Holy See objected strongly to any language making abortion a human right or suggesting that any country ought to legalize it. The Holy See eventually secured language in the final Program of Action at Cairo placing abortion in a negative light, affirming that it should in no way be used as a form of birth control. This was preserved against tremendous odds in the Beijing document as well.

Family Planning

The Beijing and Cairo conferences were dominated by rhetoric about ''overpopulation.'' In both cases, the draft conference documents were prepared by UN committees wed to the notion that massive birth control programs were a necessary first response to this crisis.

The Holy See did not attempt to achieve language at either Beijing or Cairo that would legally ban artificial birth control. Yet it did object strongly to the emphasis placed on implementing and funding birth control programs and the pressure placed on families in certain countries to strictly limit the number of their children. The Holy See proposed instead that families be safe-

guarded in their ''liberty to decide responsibly, free from all social or legal coercion, the number of children they will have and the spacing of their births.'' The Holy See did not deny that governments could ''create the social conditions which will enable [families] to make appropriate decisions in the light of their responsibilities to God, to themselves, to the society of which they are a part and to the objective moral order.'' It proposed, in other words, a model of responsible parenthood that is ''not a question of unlimited procreation or lack of awareness of what is involved in rearing children, but rather the empowerment of couples to use their inviolable liberty wisely and responsibly, taking into account social and demographic realities as well as their moral criteria.''

While the conference document called for billions of international dollars to be spent for reproductive health and family planning, a specific dollar amount of seventeen million was proposed. As to the rest of the program for bringing about ''development'' in the poorest nations, the document only ''vaguely conceded'' that '''additional funds' would be needed for development'' (Martino 1998).

Population

Under John Paul II, the Holy See has put forward a nuanced view on ''the population question.'' It acknowledges that there are areas of the world where suffering is related to population difficulties, some because of a low birth rate and some because of a high birth rate. It does not see the answer in vast programs of birth control distribution. This resistance is not simply because of moral opposition to artificial birth control. Rather, the Holy See recognizes as more credible economic analysis that concludes that development does not arise out of population control. Population problems stabilize in the presence of real economic, social and political progress, such as better access to education, better health care, stable governments, and equality for women. When, in the Cairo document, the word ''population'' was used in isolation, the Holy See tried to add the words ''and development.'' It wanted to keep before the governments of the world the primacy of development versus bare control over numbers of people.

After Cairo and Beijing

In the judgment of the Holy See's Permanent Observer Mission to the UN, the Cairo and Beijing conferences were catalysts for real progress in women's ''political, economic and social rights.'' On other hand, since these conferences there has been an increase in a certain type of sex education in the school systems of developing countries, education not at all in conformity with the Christian vision of human sexuality. Contraception use has increased around the world, and population control programs have been instituted in 70 percent of the UN's member states. There has also been some, but not great, increase in the passage of more permissive abortion laws. Since 1996, the UN campaign to decrease pregnancy and delivery-related deaths may have involved itself in providing abortions, and deaths from pregnancy and delivered related causes actually rose from 1990 to 1998.

The UN's developmental work since Cairo and Beijing has been strongly influenced by those conferences. The UN's Commission on Status of Women and its Committee on the Elimination of Discrimination against Women have tried to press the more radical aspects of their agendas. Even the United Nations International Children's Fund, long known for its care for the most vulnerable children around the world, after 1996 began to involve itself in delivering contraceptives and Western-style sex education to children. Since Cairo and Beijing, the UN's High Commissioner for Refugees has begun to provide "emergency reproductive health services" including post-coital contraception and assistance with "incomplete abortions" (understood practically to include all abortions) in refugee camps. The new field manual for this group supports sex education for adolescents with no provision for involving parents or religion.

At a 1999 diplomatic conference sponsored by the UN to establish an International Criminal Court for those committing war crimes and crimes against humanity, a handful of developed nations attempted to include "forced pregnancy" among the list of crimes against humanity, referring it also to abortion's unavailability or illegality. After intense negotiations involving the Holy See, this concept was defined so as to include the phrase: "This definition shall not in any way be interpreted as affecting national laws relating to pregnancy."

Defender of the Dignity of the Family

During a crucial time in history when family life has been denigrated, ignored, and experimented with, John Paul II has been a brilliant defender and promoter of the family. His ideas are consistent with the ways families have traditionally understood themselves for generations and around the world. At the same time, the pope has offered up a vision of family life that transcends traditional teachings. John Paul II celebrates marriage as the sacrament coincident with the creation of the human person. He teaches that marital and family communion offers insight into the communion of love, which is the Holy Trinity. He offers fathers, mothers, and children dignified visions of their individual vocations as members of a family and their mutual vocation as a family unit. He

urges governments to enact laws recognizing, promoting and even compensating motherhood. He has almost single-handedly called attention to the increasing power international bodies are attempting to wield over the family. Consequently, he has inspired thousands of people to become active on behalf of the family at the international level.

Since the Cairo conference, many groups not previously interested in UN activities acquired official NGO status at the UN. They now participate in the international conferences and in the more mundane working meetings at the UN. At the Beijing conference, about 200 of the 4,000 NGOs present were prolife. Many were formed in the wake of the Holy See's witness at the Cairo Conference. Also after Cairo, a group formed at the United Nations called the Catholic Family and Human Rights Institute. It observes closely the activities of the UN relevant to the family and human rights and mobilizes Catholics and others to act when necessary. When a public relations effort was launched in 2000 by a large proabortion group to strip the Holy See of its permanent observer status at the UN, hundreds of groups, mobilized by the Catholic Family and Human Rights Institute, came together on a petition in support of the Holy See. Many of the groups were Protestant or nondenominational in origin.

The most vocal opposition to the thought of John Paul II on family life seems to arise in large part out of a certain strand of feminism that grew up in the United States and Europe beginning in the1970s. It views women's progress as an individual proposition. Thus it casts the family and domestic life as largely harmful to women. Children, in this perspective, are a threat to women's progress and are rejected by means of birth control and/or abortion. Birth control and abortion, in fact, often become the very centerpieces of this view, and many issues of fundamental importance to women are simply neglected.

Over the last three decades of the twentieth century, many groups struggled against this view of family and sought to restore a more balanced view inclusive of egalitarian ideas about women's roles in the family and in society. There is no question that the writings of John Paul II, as well as the Holy See's participation in the Cairo and Beijing conferences, have substantially clarified the stakes for the family in the twenty-first century and presented a vision of family life worth struggling for. In the words of John Paul II, "The history of mankind, the history of salvation, passes by way of the family."

See Also: CATECHISM OF THE CATHOLIC CHURCH; CENTESIMUS ANNUS; CHRISTIFIDELES LAICI; ECCLESIA IN AFRICA; EVANGELIUM VITAE;

FAMILIARIS CONSORTIO; MULIERIS DIGNITATEM; SYNOD OF BISHOPS (FIFTH AND SEVENTH GENERAL ASSEMBLIES)

Bibliography: *Catechism of the Catholic Church,* (Washington, D.C.: United States Catholic Conference, 1994). MARY ANN GLENDON, ''Family and Society: International Organizations and the Defense of the Family'' *Origins* 27 (30 October 1997): 343–48. RENATO MARTINO, ''The Rio, Cairo and Beijing Conferences and Current Developments,'' *Familia et Vita* 3, no. 3, 1998 (Vatican City: Pontificium Consilium Pro Familia): 88–98. G. WEIGEL, *Witness to Hope* (New York: Cliff Street Books 1999).

[HELEN ALVARÉ]

The Legacy of Vatican II in the Pontificate of John Paul II

Paul McPartlan, S.T.L., D.Phil., is lecturer in systematic theology at Heythrop College, University of London.

Pope John Paul II participated in the Second Vatican Council from start to finish. As its texts matured, so, by his own testimony, did his participation mature (Pope John Paul II 1994, 158). In 1962, he was a young auxiliary bishop; by 1965, he was archbishop of Kraków and a major figure. To read the book *Sources of Renewal: Study on the Implementation of the Second Vatican Council,* which he wrote in 1972 to mark the tenth anniversary of the start of the council and to guide his own newly launched archdiocesan synod, is to appreciate the understanding that he had, first, of the council's teaching as a highly integrated whole; second, of its purpose as being to enhance *faith*; and third, of his responsibility as a bishop "to elicit that response of faith which should be the fruit of the Council and the basis of its implementation" (Wojtyła 1980, 11). If such was his task as a bishop, we can safely assume that the same writ large was how he understood his new role as pope in 1978.

The first conciliar passage quoted in Sources of Renewal is from the Constitution on Divine Revelation, *Dei verbum*: "as the centuries go by, the Church is always advancing towards the plenitude of divine truth" (DV 8). Wojtyła comments: "The enrichment of faith is nothing else than increasingly full participation in divine truth. This is the fundamental viewpoint from which we must judge the reality of Vatican II and seek ways of putting it into practice" (Wojtyła 1980, 15). He quickly makes it plain that, for him, the reality of Vatican II is what we might call doctrine in practice, or *lived* doctrine. So it is that when the bishops perform the "essential task" of teaching about "faith and morals," these are not really two separate areas but one: "on the one hand doctrinal acts of the magisterium have a pastoral sense, while on the other pastoral acts have a doctrinal significance, deeply rooted as they are in faith and morals." "These pastoral acts contain the doctrine that the Church proclaims; they often make it clearer and more precise, striving in-

cessantly to achieve the fulness of the divine truth (cf Jn 16:13)" (ibid., 17).

It is in this deep sense of (almost) removing the distinction between doctrine and practice that Cardinal Wojtyła understood Vatican II to have been "pre-eminently a pastoral Council," as Pope John XXIII many times emphasized that it should be (ibid., 16). As such, the council resonated with his own philosophical convictions. In his book *The Acting Person* (1969) he set himself firmly against the cognitive approach of Descartes by asking: "does man reveal himself in *thinking* or, rather, in the actual *enacting* of his existence?" It is not by "speculating" or "reasoning" that man reveals himself, but "in the confrontation itself when he has to take an active stand upon issues requiring vital decisions and having vital consequences and repercussions" (Wojtyła 1979, vii viii). We might summarize that in human life it is not simply true that *by their deeds shall you know them;* rather we should say of human beings, *by their acts shall they know themselves.* Our very identity is at stake in our every action; much of John Paul's pontificate is foreshadowed in the words just quoted, not least the unshakable stand that he personally has taken on doctrinal and moral issues.

There is a significant hint of his own weighty philosophical background in Cardinal Wojtyła's indication of the specific character of Vatican II. "A 'purely' doctrinal Council would have concentrated on defining the precise meaning of the truths of faith," he says, "whereas a pastoral Council proclaims, recalls or clarifies truths for the primary purpose of giving Christians a life-style, a way of thinking and *acting*." His purpose as a bishop was expressly to foster the "attitudes" that Christians "should acquire." "These attitudes, springing from a well-formed Christian conscience, can in a sense be regarded as true proof of the realization of the Council" (Wojtyła 1980, 18, emphasis added), and the fundamental attitude, to which we shall return below, is one of "self-abandonment to God" (ibid., 20).

The mold-breaking document that most epitomizes Vatican II as a pastoral council, in the radical Wojtyła sense, is, of course, *Gaudium et spes.* It is no coincidence that this was the document upon which the future pope worked most. It is with this document that we must start.

Gaudium et spes

The key to the pontificate of John Paul II lies in *Gaudium et spes,* the council's final document, which he himself wanted to be styled the *Pastoral Constitution* on the Church in the Modern World. In late November 1965, a quarter of the assembled bishops still wanted this most unusual text, being hastily completed, to be called simply a "Declaration" or a "Letter," but Archbishop Wojtyła, who had worked intensely on the draft since 1964 and was now a key member of the mixed commission finalizing it, spoke up in favor of the title that emphasized both the high status and the great newness of the document. "The document is really a 'Constitution' but one that is 'pastoral.' This latter term should be carefully explained. It is much more concerned with life than with doctrine" (Rynne 1999, 550).

Speaking of the document at the end of the international symposium on the implementation of Vatican II, held in Rome, 25–27 February 2000, Pope John Paul said: "The Pastoral Constitution *Gaudium et spes* which posed the fundamental questions to which each person is called to respond repeats to us still today words which have lost nothing of their relevance." The words he had in mind are the opening words of no. 22: "it is only in the mystery of the Word made flesh that the mystery of man truly becomes clear" (Flannery 1981, 922). Highlighting their programmatic importance for him personally, Pope John Paul commented: "These are words as dear to me as ever, that I have wanted to set forth repeatedly at fundamental points in my magisterium. Here is found the true synthesis to which the Church must always look when in dialogue with the people of this or of any other age: she is aware of possessing a message which is the vital synthesis of the expectation of every human being and the response that God addresses to each one" (*L'Osservatore Romano,* English edition, 28–29 Feb. 2000, p. 1)

A more recent translation of the key passage goes as follows: "it is only in the mystery of the Word incarnate that light is shed on the mystery of humankind" (Tanner 1990, 1081; unless otherwise indicated, quotations of Vatican II documents are taken from this translation). The translation of the Latin word *homo* by "humankind" loses something of the stark solitude conveyed by the singular "man," or "woman," a solitude which is itself an essential part of the human predicament that *Gaudium et spes* analyzes. "Quid est homo?" it asks repeatedly (GS 10, 12), what is this solitary creature, man or woman?

Each is a "mystery" (GS 10) and a riddle: "each individual remains to himself or herself an unsolved question . . . dimly perceived" (GS 21), "divided interiorly" (GS 13), "weak and sinful" (GS 10) yet "thirsting for a life which is full and free and worthy of human beings" (GS 9). The answer must fundamentally be an answer to solitude, because God made us not as solitaries but as social beings (GS 12). However, the council insists on the need for a true answer and its words seem even more apt in this Internet age: "people's relationships are multiplying continually, and at the same time *socialization* is introducing new relationships without necessarily promoting *personalization,* or a maturing of the person and genuinely personal relations" (GS 6; cf 23).

The true answer lies in *communion,* and the Christian revelation has much to contribute to promoting what is truly a life of communion between persons (GS 23). "The outstanding feature of human dignity is that human beings have been called to communion with God" (GS 19, cf. 21), called, indeed, into "the everlasting communion of . . . incorruptible divine life" (GS 18); the all-important no. 22 specifies that "it is in Christ that the truths stated here find their source and reach their fulfilment." Christ himself has ended our individual isolation: "by his incarnation the Son of God united himself in some sense with every human being," and this communion of each now with Christ is doubly revelatory. In a sentence made tighter by the repetition of words, the text goes on to say, "Christ, the last Adam, in the very revelation of the mystery of the Father and his love, fully reveals man to man himself and brings to light his most high calling" (my translation). After quoting the second of these two extracts from *Gaudium et spes* 22 in *Sources of Renewal,* Cardinal Wojtyła says, "We seem here to have reached a key point in the Council's thought" (Wojtyła 1980, 75). Italicizing them both for emphasis in his first encyclical, *Redemptor hominis,* Pope John Paul refers to the section of *Gaudium et spes* 22 in which they occur as "this stupendous text from the Council's teaching" (RH 8 9). Echoes of the text abound in his later letters (e.g., *Redemptoris missio* 2; *Tertio millennio adveniente* 4).

Gaudium et spes quotes *Lumen gentium*'s celebrated chapter on "The People of God" to reinforce its message: it "pleased God . . . not to sanctify and save [human beings] individually, without mutual relationships, but to make them into a people which would recognise God in truth and serve God in holiness" (GS 32; cf LG 9). This purpose is achieved in Christ: "As the firstborn of many brothers and sisters, by giving his Spirit after his death and resurrection he set up amongst those who accept him in faith and love a new communion of kinship, his body, which is the church, in which all as members of each other would serve each other in accordance with the various gifts imparted to them'' (GS 32). It is notable that Bishop Wojtyła's one intervention at the second session of the council was in favor of the decisive change to the draft of *Lumen gentium* that put the chapter on the people of God *before* the chapter on the hierarchy. His speech suggested that ''people are what the Church, in the end, is all about'' (Szulc 1995, 230).

Recalling the final stages of work, in 1965, on the draft of *Gaudium et spes,* Pope John Paul says that, among all the bishops and theologians with whom he had the ''good fortune'' to work, he is ''particularly indebted to Father Yves Congar and to Father Henri de Lubac,'' both of whom, we may note, he subsequently nominated as cardinals (in 1994 and 1983, respectively). He specially singles out de Lubac: ''I still remember today the words with which the latter [de Lubac] encouraged me to persevere in the line of thought that I had taken up in the discussion. . . . From that moment on I enjoyed a special friendship with Father de Lubac'' (Pope John Paul II 1994, 159). De Lubac's own recollection of their meeting during the drafting of ''Schema 13,'' which became *Gaudium et spes,* is enlightening: ''We worked side by side. . . . It did not take long observation to discover in him a person of the very highest qualities. He knew my works, and we were soon on good terms'' (De Lubac 1993, 171).

In the early 1950s, Father Wojtyła had been on leave for two years in order to prepare for the examinations to qualify for university teaching, which he passed with a thesis on Max Scheler, the founder of modern personalism. He spent some of that formative study period in Paris and probably became familiar with de Lubac's writings at that time. The newly ordained Father Wojtyła may well have heard of de Lubac already from the director of the doctoral dissertation that he wrote on ''The Problems of Faith in the Works of St John of the Cross'' at the Angelicum University in Rome (1948). His director was Fr. Reginald Garrigou-Lagrange, a Dominican whose influence in Rome was already then stoking up suspicion of de Lubac, as a leader of what he termed the ''*nouvelle théologie*'' (ibid., 60).

De Lubac's controversial book *Surnaturel* (1946), had just appeared, in which he had used the term ''*nouvelle théologie*'' in criticism of the theory of ''pure nature,'' expounded by Neoscholastics such as Garrigou-Lagrange, that eradicated the intrinsic bond between the supernatural and human nature and, thereby, kept the Church hermetically sealed off from the world at large. De Lubac showed that the theory, presented as the teaching of Aquinas, was in fact a catastrophic distortion of his authentic doctrine of the natural desire in every human

being for the supernatural vision of God, which perfectly aligned with the famous words of Augustine at the start of his *Confessions,* ''You have made us, Lord, for yourself, and our hearts are restless until they rest in you'' (see McPartlan 1993, chap.2; McPartlan 1995, chap.4).

Tad Szulc says that Fr. Wojtyła was ''disturbed . . . that Garrigou-Lagrange, his mentor, had turned on the New Theology . . . with uncontained rage,'' and that he himself visited France in the summer of 1947, became aware of the alarm felt there at the gap between the Church and the world, and had great regard for the worker priests who tried to bridge the gap (Szulc 1995, 146–148). *Gaudium et spes* was a most authoritative denial of any grounds for such a gap, and a reassertion, from its opening sentence, of solidarity between the Church and the world. As the primary cause of the alienation which had arisen was the theory of ''pure nature'' (see Komonchak 1990, 580), so *Gaudium et spes* enshrined in no. 22 a vindication of de Lubac's unyielding opposition to it, showing thereby that it was Garrigou-Lagrange's *théologie* that was *nouvelle.* After quoting the above words of Augustine in no. 21, the council fathers simply and clearly stated in no. 22 that ''in truth there is one ultimate calling, which is divine, for all people'' (my translation).

Already in his first book, *Catholicisme* (1938), de Lubac gave voice to the traditional understanding that unites Augustine and Aquinas when he said, ''the vision of God is a free gift, and yet the desire for it is at the root of every soul'' (de Lubac 1988, 327). In his own powerful words which directly and strikingly foreshadow those used in *Gaudium et spes,* he then stressed, however, that it is Christ who lays bare this desire:

> By revealing the Father and by being revealed by him, Christ completes the revelation of man to himself. By taking possession of man, by seizing hold of him and by penetrating to the very depths of his being Christ makes man go deep down within himself, there to discover in a flash regions hitherto unsuspected. It is through Christ that the person reaches maturity, that man emerges definitively from the universe, and becomes conscious of his own being. Henceforth, even before that triumphant exclamation: *Agnosce, O Christiane, dignitatem tuam* [Recognize, O Christian, your dignity], it will be possible to praise the dignity of man: *dignitatem conditionis humanae* [the dignity of the human condition]. (Ibid., 339–340)

Here are seeds, nurtured at Vatican II in *Gaudium et spes* and in the Declaration on Religious Freedom, *Dignitatis humanae,* and richly harvested in the pontificate of John Paul II. In a sense, the whole program of his pontificate could be said to derive from de Lubac's foundational work on nature and grace. Because all human beings are graced with a call to a single destiny, which is divine, the Church has a mission to all and must defend the dignity of people everywhere, including their right to religious freedom, not just as one right among others, but as the right that underpins all others (see Boeglin 2000, 53–58). At Vatican II, Archbishop Wojtyła was a persuasive advocate of clear teaching on the controversial subject of religious freedom, not only in *Gaudium et spes* (Vorgrimler 1969, 38, 50) but also in a specific Declaration, on the grounds of its importance for the Church behind the Iron Curtain. If the Church wanted to claim religious freedom for itself when in conflict with hostile regimes, then it must be prepared to espouse it generally (Rynne 1999, 463). As pope, he greeted with "deep love and respect" the many representatives of Christian traditions and world religions who responded to his invitation to a World Day of Prayer for Peace held in Assisi on 27 October 1986 (*L'Osservatore Romano,* English edition, 3 Nov. 1986, p. 3).

In his letter on preparation for the Jubilee year 2000, *Tertio millennio adveniente* (1994), Pope John Paul II urged "the son and daughters of the Church" to repent of "the acquiescence given, especially in certain centuries, to intolerance and even the use of violence in the service of truth." "From these painful moments of the past a lesson can be drawn for the future, leading all Christians to adhere fully to the sublime principle stated by the Council: 'The truth cannot impose itself except by virtue of its own truth, as it wins over the mind with both gentleness and power' (*Dignitatis humanae* 1)" (TMA 35). The Day of Pardon celebrated by the pope on 12 March 2000, the first Sunday of Lent, duly made sorrowful mention of the Crusades and the Inquisition.

The Day of Pardon also addressed "sins regarding relations with the people of the first Covenant, Israel: contempt, hostility, failure to speak out . . .," words which were read not just publicly by a curial cardinal that day in St Peter's, but also in the intense privacy of prayer at the Western Wall in Jerusalem by Pope John Paul himself on 26 March 2000, at the end of what many saw as the most deeply significant of the nearly one hundred pilgrim journeys he has made worldwide. Following custom at the Wall, he placed the paper containing these words and signed by him into the Wall itself, from where it was subsequently taken to the Yad Vashem Holocaust memorial.

Following Pope John XXIII's removal of reference to the "perfidious Jews" from the Good Friday Liturgy, the council's Declaration on the Relation of the Church to Non-Christian Religions, *Nostra aetate,* specifically stated that, "Although the Jewish authorities with their followers pressed for the death of Christ, still those things which were perpetrated during his passion cannot be ascribed indiscriminately to all the Jews living at the time nor to the Jews of today" (NA 4). Having had close contact and friendly relations with Jews since his childhood in Wadowice, where his parish priest already preached that "anti-Semitism is anti-Christian" (Szulc 1995, 68 69), and coming from a country where the Jewish population of three million was almost wiped out by the Holocaust, Pope John Paul was remarkably qualified to understand and address the pain of the Jewish people, particularly the pain caused by the Church. In 1986, he visited the Rome synagogue and particularly singled out the following words from the Declaration as "a decisive turning point in relations between the Catholic Church and Judaism": "[the Church] deplores the hatred, persecutions, and displays of anti-Semitism directed against the Jews at any time and by anyone" (NA 4). When he then said, "I repeat: 'by anyone,'" he was interpreted by some as turning the spotlight onto the papacy itself (*Accatoli* 1998, 116–117).

"Unlike his twentieth-century predecessors," John Paul II is "a foreign policy activist and the chief guide of Vatican diplomacy"; he has been credited for beginning, in 1991, the process that led to Holy See's diplomatic recognition of the state of Israel (Szulc 1995, 449–453). An initial agreement establishing diplomatic relations was signed in Jerusalem in December 1993 and full relations were established the following June. On 7 April 1994, the fiftieth anniversary of the Warsaw Ghetto uprising, Pope John Paul invited around a hundred concentration-camp survivors to the Vatican and spoke to them individually, before a concert commemorating the Holocaust and attended by the Chief Rabbi of Rome. He likewise mingled with survivors at the Holocaust memorial on 23 March 2000, when he finally fulfilled his dream of visiting Jerusalem and paid homage to the millions of Jews murdered in the Holocaust.

Lumen gentium

Just as human beings are revealed and known by their acts, so too is the Church. Thus, although Pope John Paul refers to *Gaudium et spes,* on the Church in the modern world, as complementing and completing *Lumen gentium,* on the Church in itself (Wojtyła 1980, 35, 69), he specifies that it does so "because it reveals what the Church essentially is." "The redemptive work of Jesus Christ which determines the inmost nature of the Church is in fact the work of the redemption of the world." In short, the Church is essentially outward-looking, and *Lumen gentium* simply describes the inner reality of such a Church.

The concept of the Church as *sacrament* illustrates the link between the two documents. This concept, repeatedly set forth by *Lumen gentium* (1, 9, 48), is identified by *Gaudium et spes* as the key to understanding the purpose of the Church in the world. "Every benefit the people of God can confer on the human family during its earthly pilgrimage derives from the church's being 'the universal sacrament of salvation'" (GS 45, my translation). John Paul II's papal teaching on mission reflects the same priority of action. *"The Church is missionary by her very nature"* (*Redemptoris missio* 62), he says with emphasis, and this mission derives "from the profound demands of God's life within us" (RM 11).

The council emphasized that God's life is a Trinitarian life of communion, and taught that the Church is first and foremost a mystery (cf. the title of chapter 1 of *Lumen gentium*) because it is "a people made one by the unity of the Father and the Son and the Holy Spirit," as Cyprian said (LG 4). What is then distinctive of this *people* (cf. chapter 2 of *Lumen gentium,* "The People of God") is that it is "a communion of life, love and truth" (LG 9). Cardinal Wojtyła wrote at length on the Church as the People of God in *Sources of Renewal* (Wojtyła 1980, 1127–200), but emphasized that "the link uniting the Church as People of God" is *communio* (ibid., 133 146). It is true, as the second extraordinary assembly of the Synod of Bishops (1985), called to assess the impact of the council twenty years after its close, acknowledged, that use of the term "People of God" for the Church has waned. But what has dislodged it is what Cardinal Wojtyła regarded as the essential idea behind the term, namely, the idea of the Church as *communion*. To the people of Kraków he said that, "both *ad intra* and *ad extra*," the Church must "seek ways of realizing 'communion' among human beings" (ibid., 146). The synod itself reflected the same understanding when it said in summary: "The Church as communion is a sacrament for the salvation of the world" ("Final *Relatio,*" II.D.1, in *L'Osservatore Romano*, English edition, 16 Dec. 1985, p. 9). Service of this communion is in fact the measure of ecclesial action: "in the society of the Church itself all must measure their behavior according to the principle of communion, whose theological meaning and importance have been re-emphasized by Vatican II" (Wojtyła 1980, 146).

Reflecting on the thirtieth anniversary of the beginning of the council, Pope John Paul said that Vatican II would "go down in history *primarily as an ecclesiological Council*" and that, since it understood the Church as being rooted in the mystery of the Trinity, the council itself was also *"profoundly Trinitarian."* He particularly highlighted the "exchange of gifts" that ought to characterize a Trinitarian Church set in a universe itself filled *"with the mystery of divine communion."* Ad extra, missionary activity is the "privileged place" in which the

exchange of gifts between the Church and the world takes place "with an ever greater richness"; and *ad intra*, "under the inspiration of that divine communion," "the mystical Body of Christ is one in the multiplicity of Churches spread over the face of the whole earth" ("Christmas Address to the College of Cardinals," in *L'Osservatore Romano,* English edition 6 Jan. 1993, pp. 6–7).

By its highlighting of the Trinitarian mystery of the Church, not only in *Lumen gentium* 4, but also in *Gaudium et spes* 24 and the Decree on Ecumenism, *Unitatis redintegratio,* 2, Vatican II played a significant part in the renewed appreciation of the Trinity that was a striking feature of many Christian traditions in the twentieth century (see Wainwright 1998). Pope John Paul clearly wants to carry forward this conciliar theme, and his comments above enable us to identify two outstanding "Trinitarian" characteristics of his pontificate *ad intra:* the Trinitarian framework of his encyclical letters and of the years of preparation for the millennium, and the multiplicity of meetings of the Synod of Bishops not just those continuing the already established program of general (i.e., worldwide) assemblies, but his own program of regional assemblies of bishops from the local churches in different continents, all of which enable an exchange of gifts among the churches.

In 1986, Pope John Paul recalled the Trinitarian greeting taken from the letters of St. Paul and used in the celebration of the Eucharist: "The grace of our Lord Jesus Christ and the love of God and the fellowship of the Holy Spirit be with you all" (2 Cor 13:13), and said that he was now completing, with his encyclical on the Holy Spirit, *Dominum et vivificantem* (cf. 2), the Trinitarian program inspired by it and already begun with the encyclicals *Redemptor hominis* (1979) and *Dives in misericordia* (1980). In 1994, he directed that the three years of immediate preparation for the Great Jubilee should be devoted to reflection on Jesus Christ (1997), the Holy Spirit (1998), and God the Father (1999), respectively (TMA 30 54). He also announced that, following upon the special assemblies of the Synod of Bishops already held for Europe (1991) and Africa (1994), there would be further continental synods, for the Americas (1997), Asia (1998), and Oceania (1998). Meanwhile, the regular program of general assemblies of the Synod has been pursued, with synods on the Christian Family (1980), Penance and Reconciliation (1983), the Vocation and Mission of the Lay Faithful (1987), the Formation of Priests (1990), and the Consecrated Life (1994).

The Synod of Bishops was established by Pope Paul VI, implementing the decision made in favor of such a body by Vatican II in its Decree on the Pastoral Office of Bishops in the Church, *Christus Dominus* (5). It is, of course, an exercise of episcopal collegiality, but a restricted one. Defining collegiality, after stressing that the pope has "full, supreme and universal power over the whole Church," Vatican II said that "the order of bishops, which succeeds the college of the apostles in teaching authority and pastoral government, and indeed in which the apostolic body continues to exist without interruption, is also the subject of supreme and full power over the universal Church," but it specified that this was so only "provided it remains united with its head, the Roman pontiff, and never without its head": "this power can be exercised only with the consent of the Roman pontiff" (LG 22).

In 1983, Pope John Paul promulgated the new *Code of Canon Law,* to which, together with the subsequent *Code of Canons for the Eastern Churches* (1990), he has referred as being, "in a certain sense . . . the last documents of Vatican II." He added that "something similar could be said (and perhaps even more rightly so) of the *Catechism of the Catholic Church*" (see "Christmas Address," above), which arose from the extraordinary assembly of the Synod in 1985 and was published in 1992. The codes are indeed intimately related to the council. When he announced the forthcoming council in 1959, Pope John XXIII also announced a complete revision of the Church's canonical discipline. The existing code for the West dated from 1917 and some provisions for the Eastern Churches had been promulgated in 1948, but there was no complete code for the Eastern Churches. The new codes are therefore not only landmarks in the overall life of the Church, but more specifically achievements of major importance for the implementation of Vatican II, by giving a legal framework for the life of the post-conciliar Church. We should associate with them also the apostolic constitution *Pastor bonus,* of 1988, which restructured the Roman Curia, building upon the initial reform undertaken by Pope Paul VI at the behest of the council (cf CD 9 10).

Writing of the Synod of Bishops with reference to the new code, Cardinal Joseph Ratzinger clarified its exact status and specified that it "advises the pope; it is not a small-scale Council, and is not a collegial organ of leadership for the universal Church" (Ratzinger 1988, 46). Such an organ might perhaps be envisaged in the ongoing implementation of Vatican II, to exercise the authority over the universal Church that the college of bishops together with the pope has, as *Lumen gentium* taught, but the Synod is certainly not it. Synods are undoubtedly a most significant new feature of the post-conciliar Church, greatly fostered by Pope John Paul II, to the benefit of a real collegial spirit among the bishops, but their limited status must be recognized. Synods, even

the regional assemblies, are held in Rome and their deliberations are finally submitted to the pope who in due course personally issues a post-synodal apostolic exhortation.

In spite of its reform in 1988, the curia is still criticized for impeding the exercise of collegiality. In 1996, Archbishop John Quinn (former archbishop of San Francisco) pointed to the danger that "in place of the dogmatic structure comprised of the pope and the rest of the episcopate, there emerges a new and threefold structure: the pope, the curia and the episcopate." The curia, he said, can see itself "as exercising oversight and authority over the College of Bishops', instead of being at the service of the pope and the college. To the extent that this is so, he warned, "it obscures and diminishes both the doctrine and the reality of episcopal collegiality" (Quinn 1998, 12–13).

The distant origins of the curia lie in the twelfth century, when it was formed to manage the papal territories at a time when the Church was becoming increasingly centralized under a much more directive papacy. The Gregorian Reform, initiated by Pope Gregory VII (1073 1085), culminated in the pontificate of Pope Innocent III (1198 1216), the first to style himself the "Vicar of Christ." The Dominican scholar Yves Congar has shown how the rise of the new mendicant orders at that time, with their immensely influential theologians, the great Scholastics (e.g., St. Thomas Aquinas, St. Bonaventure), contributed to a decisive shift away from a communional ecclesiology of local churches towards a universal ecclesiology. As mendicants, the members of the new orders did not fit into the stable structure of local churches and were much criticized. "Clearly, they needed to justify themselves and they did so by invoking a canonical mission received from the bishops . . . or better, received from the pope. This entailed their developing the theology of a power of the pope amounting to a properly episcopal authority over all the faithful, whatever diocese they belonged to." "All of the mendicant theologians developed these ideas," Congar says, "which, it must be admitted, became those of the Catholic Church." The Church is one people, with one head, not just invisibly in heaven, but visibly on earth. As each local church has a bishop at its head, so also the Church as a whole has a bishop at its head. "Such an ecclesiology immediately entails an affirmation of the pope's universal jurisdiction" (Congar 1964, 244–245).

The Orthodox Churches have continued resolutely to resist such ideas, which they believe still to be operative in the Catholic Church. Pope John Paul's own practice of sending a letter to all the priests of the world on Holy Thursday each year leans in that direction. To all priests, in his first such letter in 1979, he said (adapting the words of St Augustine): "For you I am a bishop, with you I am a priest" (*Novo incipiente nostro* 1). Vatican I, indeed, declared that the pope has ordinary and immediate episcopal jurisdiction over all the shepherds and faithful of the Church (DS 3060), but left unresolved the difficulty of explaining how this power does not impede but rather confirms the ordinary and immediate episcopal jurisdiction that each bishop has in his own diocese (DS 3061). Vatican II greatly improved on this drily juridical account by emphasizing once more the Church's Eucharistic life. The bishops are high priests, presiding at the Eucharist of their local churches (Constitution on the Sacred Liturgy, *Sacrosanctum concilium,* 41; also, LG 21, 26), and they are all "vicars of Christ" (LG 27). Their collegiality (LG 22) fits with this renewed patristic understanding and is rooted in the Eucharistic communion of their churches. The fundamental Eucharistic ministry in the Church is that of the bishops, whom priests, normally called "presbyters" by Vatican II, represent (SC 42; also, Decree on the Ministry and Life of Priests, *Presbyterorum ordinis,* 5). It could perhaps be said that a thoroughgoing application of this idea would mean that a bishop would say to his presbyters not so much that he was a priest with them but that they were priests with him.

Although Vatican II wanted to show the Catholic Church's integration of Eucharistic and universal ecclesiology, in order to refute Orthodox claims that these two models were incompatible (McPartlan 1986, 327), the two were left rather juxtaposed in its documents (Kasper 1986, 111), particularly with regard to the papacy. The pontificate of John Paul II has seen remarkable efforts to integrate the papacy itself into a Eucharistic understanding of the Church, as a service rendered amid the local churches to the overall harmony of their Eucharistic witness. The 1992 Vatican text *Communionis notio* says that "the existence of the Petrine ministry . . . bears a profound correspondence to the Eucharistic character of the Church" (11) and the *Catechism of the Catholic Church* makes a similar connection (CCC 1369).

Cardinal Ratzinger regretfully notes that the "most crucial development" that occurred in the Latin West as it entered the Middle Ages was "the increasing distinction between sacrament and jurisdiction, between liturgy and administration as such" (Ratzinger 1987, 254). Most of the major divisions that still mark the Church, beginning with that between Catholics and Orthodox, have occurred since that time and been related to this development. We can therefore see the prime ecumenical importance of removing that distinction, not only, as Vatican II did, with regard to bishops, by restoring a Eucharistic understanding of their ministry, but also with regard to the pope.

Against the background of the historical developments described by Congar and Ratzinger, two rather contrasting features of the pontificate of John Paul II particularly stand out. First, he has given encouragement to the many new "movements" that have sprung up in recent decades. Their rise at the end of the second millennium invites comparison with the rise of the mendicant orders at its beginning, for they too have a strongly universal focus in their ecclesiology and often rather weak or strained relations with local bishops. Pope John Paul addressed a huge gathering of members of over fifty movements and communities, both great, like the Neo-Catechumenate and Comunione e Liberazione, and small, on Pentecost eve, 1998, in Rome. Second, however, in a quite unprecedented way he has placed his own ministry into discussion and, in his encyclical letter on ecumenism, *Ut unum sint* (1995), invited leaders and theologians of other Christian traditions to engage in "a patient and fraternal dialogue" with him about it, in order to help him exercise it in a way that will be recognized by all as "a service of love" (UUS 95 96). The encyclical has already prompted many constructive responses (see, e.g., Puglisi 1999).

Two further points must be made in connection with this encyclical. First, it testifies to the sustained, total commitment to ecumenism that is one of the principal ways by which Pope John Paul has implemented the Second Vatican Council, at which "the Catholic Church committed herself irrevocably to following the path of the ecumenical venture" (UUS 3). Looking at the period since the council, he himself says: "it can be said that the whole activity of the local Churches and of the Apostolic See has taken on an ecumenical dimension in recent years" (TMA 34). This is, in no small measure, thanks to his own leadership. Ecumenical meetings have been an integral part of his many international visits, and *Ut unum sint* itself catalogues the progress and accords achieved across the wide spectrum of Christian relations, not least with the Oriental Orthodox Churches, from whom there has been the most long-standing separation, dating back to the Council of Chalcedon in 451.

Sadly, largely for the reasons indicated above, the pope's greatest ecumenical desire, namely the restoration of full communion between the Catholic and (Eastern) Orthodox Churches, has not been realized. Only a year after his election, he visited the Ecumenical Patriarchate in Constantinople and expressed his hope for full communion between Catholics and Orthodox by the dawn of the third millennium. Nevertheless, there has been great progress in theological dialogue between the two Churches and also many blessed moments, such as the visits of Ecumenical Patriarchs Dimitrios and Bartholomew to Rome in 1987 and 1995, respectively, on both of which occasions the Creed was recited by pope and patriarch together in St Peter's without the controversial *filioque.*

Second, in *Ut unum sint,* Pope John Paul asks forgiveness for the pain caused by the papacy to other Christians, and associates himself with Pope Paul VI in doing so (UUS 88). In fact, this willingness to recognize faults and ask forgiveness, that has been such a feature of the pontificate of John Paul II (see *Accatoli* 1998) and has been promoted by him throughout the whole Church, particularly in preparation for the Great Jubilee of the year 2000, can be traced back to Pope John XXIII in his very calling of the council, and indicates the profound moral continuity between these recent popes. Pope John made it clear that he wanted the council to advance the cause of Christian unity and, only days after calling it, specified: "We do not intend to set up a tribunal to judge the past. We do not want to prove who was right and who was wrong. Responsibility was divided. All we want to say is: 'Let us come together. Let us make an end of our divisions'" (Leeming 1966, 19).

Self-Abandonment to God

The past deeds of the Church for which Pope John Paul has consistently wanted to ask forgiveness, culminating on the Day of Pardon itself, are essentially deeds that have "sullied her face, preventing her from fully mirroring the image of her crucified Lord, the supreme witness of patient love and humble meekness" (cf. TMA 35). Asking forgiveness is essentially a process of purification, so as to reflect the image of Christ more faithfully in the world. It deeply accords with the opening of *Lumen gentium,* which specifies that Christ is the light of the world, and that the Church's desire is to let that light shine through it for all. Asking forgiveness is an intrinsic part of the self-abandonment to God that, as we saw above, Pope John Paul regards as the fundamental Christian attitude, an attitude that he is charged to promote.

"In the lives of those who, while sharing our humanity, are nevertheless more perfectly transformed into the image of Christ (cf. 2 Cor 3:18), God makes vividly manifest to humanity his presence and his face." From these words of *Lumen gentium* 50 we can readily understand the crucial importance of the saints to Pope John Paul, as examples of the very self-abandonment that he is called to foster in all. He clearly believes that a prime way of fostering it is to furnish the faithful with fresh examples of it. A striking feature of his pontificate is the vast array of three hundred new saints and a thousand new *beati* that he has given to the faithful around the world as patterns of self-abandonment. His own self-abandonment is amply reflected in his motto, *Totus tuus.*

Perhaps especially to young people has he wanted to teach the message of Vatican II that, made as we are in the image of God, each human being can fully discover himself or herself "only in sincere self-giving" (GS 24). Millions have gathered with him in different countries for World Youth Days, and been challenged to find fulfilment in this way, with Christ as guide (cf. RH 13). It is a challenge communicated not just by Pope John Paul's words, but, in accordance with the core principle of his own philosophy, by the outstanding witness of his own life.

See Also: YVES CONGAR, NEOCATECHUMENAL WAY, HENRI DE LUBAC, PASTOR BONUS, JOSEPH RATZINGER, REDEMPTOR HOMINIS, REDEMPTORIS MISSIO, SYNOD OF BISHOPS (VARIOUS ESSAYS), TERTIO MILLENNIO ADVENIENTE, UT UNUM SINT

Bibliography: LUIGI ACCATOLI, *When a Pope Asks Forgiveness,* translated by JORDAN AUMANN. (New York: Alba House, 1998). JEAN-GEORGES BOEGLIN, *Les droits de l'homme chez Jean-Paul II* (Paris: Salvator, 2000). YVES CONGAR, "De la communion des églises à une ecclésiologie de l'église universelle," in *L'Episcopat et l'Eglise universelle,* eds., Y.CONGAR & B.D.DUPUY (Paris: Cerf, 1964). AUSTIN FLANNERY, ed., *Vatican Council II. The Conciliar and Post Conciliar Documents* (Dublin: Dominican Publications, 1981). POPE JOHN PAUL II *Crossing the Threshold of Hope* (London: Jonathan Cape, 1994). WALTER KASPER, "Church as *Communio,*" *Communio* 13 (1986): 100–117. JOSEPH A. KOMONCHAK, "Theology and Culture at Mid-Century: The Example of Henri de Lubac." *Theological Studies* 51 (1990): 579–602. BERNARD LEEMING, *The Vatican Council and Christian Unity* (New York: Harper & Row, 1966). HENRI DE LUBAC, *Catholicism,* (San Francisco: Ignatius Press, 1988); *At the Service of the Church* (San Francisco: Ignatius Press, 1993). PAUL MCPARTLAN, "Eucharistic Ecclesiology." *One in Christ* 22 (1986): 314–31; *The Eucharist Makes the Church: Henri de Lubac and John Zizioulas in Dialogue* (Edinburgh: T & T Clark, 1993); *Sacrament of Salvation: An Introduction to Eucharistic Ecclesiology* (Edinburgh: T & T Clark, 1995). JAMES F. PUGLISI, ed., *Petrine Ministry and the Unity of the Church* (Collegeville, Minn.: The Liturgical Press, 1999). JOHN R. QUINN, "The Exercise of the Primacy and the Costly Call to Unity" in *The Exercise of the Primacy,* eds., PHYLLIS ZAGANO and TERENCE W. TILLEY (New York: Crossroad, 1998). JOSEPH RATZINGER, *Principles of Catholic Theology,* translated by SISTER MARY FRANCES MCCARTHY SND (San Francisco: Ignatius Press, 1987); *Church, Ecumenism and Politics,* translated by ROBERT NOWELL (Slough: St Paul Publications, 1988). XAVIER RYNNE *Vatican Council I.* (New York: Orbis, 1999). TAD SZULC, *Pope John Paul II: The Biography* (New York: Scribner, 1995). NORMAN P. TANNER, ed., *Decrees of the Ecumenical Councils* vol. 2 (London: Sheed & Ward; Georgetown: Georgetown University Press, 1990). HERBERT VORGRIMLER, ed., *Commentary on the Documents of Vatican II,* vol. 5 (London: Burns & Oates; New York: Herder & Herder, 1969). GEOFFREY WAINWRIGHT, "The Ecumenical Rediscovery of the Trinity." *One in Christ* 34 (1998): 95, 124. KAROL WOJTYŁA, *The Acting Person,* definitive text established in collaboration with the author by ANNA-TERESA TYMIENIECKA and translated by ANDRZEJ POTOCKI (Dordrecht, Boston & London: D. Reidel, 1979); *Sources of Renewal* (London: Collins, 1980).

[PAUL MCPARTLAN]

Ut Unum Sint: John Paul II's Ecumenical Commitment

John A. Radano, S.T.B., M.A., Ph.D., is the head of the Western Section, Pontifical Council for Promoting Christian Unity, Vatican City.

Pope John Paul II reiterated the Catholic Church's ecumenical commitment, as well as his own, on his inauguration day, assuring Orthodox, Anglican, Protestant, Old Catholic, and World Council of Churches (WCC) representatives of his "firm resolution to go forward along the way to unity," and "not stop before arriving at the goal, . . . this unity which Christ wishes for the Church." "The commitment of the Catholic Church to the ecumenical movement . . . solemnly expressed in the Second Vatican Council, is irreversible" (Pontifical Council for Promoting Christian Unity, *Information Service (IS)* 38 [1978]: 56). In 1999 he could say to the Holy Synod of the Romanian Orthodox Church, "I have sought unity with all my strength and I will continue to do all I can until the end to make it one of the priority concerns of the Churches and of those who govern them in the apostolic ministry" (*IS* 102 [1999]: 224).

According to John Paul, ecumenism is at the heart of the Church: it is a pastoral priority which the church "cannot and will not abandon" (IS 102 [1999]: 198). In *Ut unum sint* (1995), the first papal encyclical ever on ecumenism, he emphasized that it is "not just some sort of appendix . . . added to the Church's traditional activity. Rather . . .[it is] an organic part of her life and work (which) must pervade all that she is and does" (*Ut unum sint* 20). Because "it corresponds to the will of God and the prayer of Christ," and because "the value of prayer and the need for conversion and purification have been repeatedly emphasized and must always be so, the challenge of ecumenism is a call to holiness" (*Insegnamenti di Giovanni Paolo II,* VII, 2 [1984]: 1045). Thus, restoration of unity "must be above all a restoration of the inner dimension of the Christian life—a wholehearted personal commitment to Jesus Christ which makes intolerable any separation among those who share that commitment" (*Insegnamenti,* VIII, 2 [1985]: 1421).

Ecumenism is integrated into John Paul's daily ministry. He mentions it in statements during Wednesday general audiences, Sunday Angelus, and *ad limina* visits of bishops, as well as to ecumenical guests at private audiences and on receiving credentials from ambassadors to the Holy See. Early on, he indicated the critical relationship, for advancing toward unity, between ecumenical renewal within the Church and the reception of the results of dialogues undertaken with other churches. Commending the Secretariat for Promoting Christian Unity (SPCU; renamed a Pontifical Council [PCPCU] in the 1988 reform of the curia) in 1978, for promoting over thirteen years a "mind and spirit loyally at one with the wishes of the Council," he said that without this "the positive results achieved in the various dialogues could not be received by the faithful" (IS 39 [1979]: 2).

"My fondest hope," he prayed in a homily in Romania in 1999, "is that Jesus' prayer . . .: 'Father, that they may all be one' (cf Jn 17:21) will always be on your lips and, never cease to beat in your hearts" (*IS*102 [1999]: 228).

Fostering Bonds of Communion with Other Christians

ACKNOWLEDGING A SHARED CHRISTIAN HERITAGE

The pope has emphasized that what Christians share in common is far more important than what divides them. Visiting the WCC in 1984, he stated that the Catholic Church and WCC member churches have "never ceased to have in common many of the elements and endowments which together build up and give life to the Church"—our common baptism, the Word of God, etc. He also mentioned differences, on ethical questions for example. "But what unites us already allows us to hope that a day will come when we shall arrive at a convergence on this fundamental ground" (*IS* 55 [1984]: 39 41). More broadly, Christians share the faith confessed in the Nicene Constantinople Creed (381). "The teaching of the first Council of Constantinople is still the expression of the one common faith of the whole of Christianity" (*Insegnamenti,* VII, 2 [1984]: 715).

Pope John Paul II together with Archbishop of Canterbury George Carey (to his right) and Metropolitan Athanasius of the Ecumenical Patriarchate, kneeling before the Holy Door at the Roman Basilica. (L'Osservatore Romano Photo Service.)

Sharing in Redemption. Christians share in, and witness to, Redemption in Christ. John Paul has particularly highlighted the great gift of Redemption, and the person of the Redeemer, drawing out ecumenical implications. His first encyclical, *Redemptor hominis* (1979), called Christian unity "the will of Jesus Christ himself" (6). The encyclicals *Redemptoris Mater* (1987; see nos. 30, 31) and *Redemptoris missio* (1990; see no. 50) each had important ecumenical aspects. The pope designated 1983–84 as the special Holy Year of the Redemption, marking the 1950th anniversary of the redemptive act of Christ's death and resurrection, and initiated in 1994 a program of preparation, with significant ecumenical aspects, for the Jubilee 2000, intended as thanksgiving "for the gift of the Incarnation of the Son of God and of the Redemption which he accomplished" (*Tertio millennio adveniente* [1994] 32). "Celebrating the Redemption" he said of its ecumenical implications on the eve of the Holy Year 1983, "we go beyond historical misunderstanding and contingent controversies, in order to meet each other on the common ground of our being Christian, that is, redeemed. The Redemption unites all of us in the one love to Christ, crucified and risen. This is above all the most valid [ecumenical] meaning" (*IS* 50 [1982]: 119; cf. *IS* 54 [1984]: 13).

Ecumenism of Saints and Martyrs. "The finest expression of the gift of the Redemption, which ransoms man from sin and gives him the possibility of new life in Christ" is the wealth of holiness in the history of the Church (*L'Osservatore Romano,* English weekly edition, 6 October 1999). Saintly witness is a shared Christian heritage binding separated Christians together. "Perhaps the most convincing form of ecumenism, is the ecumenism of the saints and of the martyrs. The *communio sanctorum* speaks louder than the things which divide us" (TMA, 37). *Ut unum sint* takes shared heritage in sanctity further. The incomplete communion among Christians "is truly and solidly grounded in the full communion of the Saints—those who at the end of a life faithful to grace are in communion with Christ in glory. These Saints come from all the Churches and Ecclesial Communities which gave them entrance into the communion of salvation"(84).

Renewed relations after the Second Vatican Council between the Ecumenical Patriarchate and the Church of Rome have benefited by recalling their shared apostolic heritage, represented by their patronal saints, the apostles and brothers Peter (with Paul), for Rome, and Andrew, for Constantinople. Of particular significance was John Paul's 1980 proclamation of Sts. Cyril and Methodius, apostles of the Slavs, as co-patrons of Europe, along with St. Benedict (*Egregiae virtutis* [1980]). They carried out their missionary service in the ninth century, before the

John Paul II prays during a Mass for the Saints Peter and Paul festivities at the Vatican, 29 June 1999. (Reuters/Vincenzo Pinto/Archive Photos.)

division between the East and West, "in union both with the Church of Constantinople, by which they had been sent, and with Peter's Roman See, by which they were confirmed" (ibid., 1). One motivation for the pope's recognition of them was precisely ecumenical. After centuries of division, the Catholic and Orthodox Churches entered, also in 1980, "the stage of a decisive dialogue." The pope's act was "intended to make this date memorable"(ibid., 3). He also wanted to stress the common heritage of Eastern and Western Christianity. "As in Saint Benedict, so in Saints Cyril and Methodius, Europe can rediscover its spiritual roots. Now . . . they must be venerated together as the patrons of our past and as the Saints to whom the Churches and nations of Europe entrust their future" (UUS 54).

In Anglican-Catholic relations, John Paul's contacts with archbishops of Canterbury have been occasions for recalling "the common heritage," as he and Archbishop George Carey said in 1996, "of Anglicans and Catholics rooted in the mission to the English people which Pope Gregory the Great entrusted to Saint Augustine of Canterbury" (*IS* 94 [1997]: 21). Renewed relations between Rome and Nordic Lutherans have been aided by mutual acknowledgment of Nordic saints: for example, Sts. Olav of Norway (cf. *IS* 60 [1986]: 2), Henry of Finland (*Insegnamenti,* VIII, 1 [1985]: 32), and Bridget of Sweden. The pope has presided twice at ecumenical services in St. Peter's Basilica with the Lutheran archbishops of Uppsala and Turku, commemorating St. Bridget: in 1991, on the 600th anniversary of her canonization; in 1999, when she was named one of three co-patronesses of Europe.

Orthodox and Catholics. John Paul's statements, or joint statements with Orthodox leaders, have reiterated a common shared heritage of the same sacraments, "above all, by apostolic succession, the priesthood and the episcopal ministry." During Ecumenical Patriarch Dimitrios I's 1987 visit to Rome, the two stated together that, "each of our churches has received and celebrates the same sacraments" (*IS* 66 [1988]: 29).On Dimitrios's arrival for that visit, the pope said that "we are brothers by the grace of baptism and of the priesthood" (*IS* 66 [1988]: 10). John Paul addressed the bishops of the Holy Synod of the Romanian Orthodox Church as "Brothers in the Episcopate" (*IS* 102 [1999]: 223), and said to the Ethiopian Orthodox Patriarch that (cf. UR 15) "our Churches remain very closely linked, above all in virtue of apostolic succession, the priesthood and the Eucharist" (*Insegnamenti,* IV, 2 [1981]: 446). He described the dialogue between Catholics and Orthodox to Dimitrios I as "based on a common sacramental conception of the Church" (*IS* 59 [1985]: 27) and said to Polish Orthodox leaders that to speak of one another as "'Sister Churches' is not just a polite phrase but rather a fundamental ecumenical category of ecclesiology" (*IS*77 [1991]: 39).

AN ECUMENISM OF PERSONAL ENGAGEMENT

Pope John Paul II has also fostered bonds of communion through personal contacts. He has visited or has been visited by international leaders of other churches and communions, and, since each of his pastoral journeys to the Catholic Church across the world ordinarily includes an ecumenical meeting, he has had many personal contacts, too, with regional, national, and local leaders and faithful.

Pope John Paul continued relations well established by Paul VI with the Ecumenical Patriarchate, and, like Paul VI, he met with a Greek Orthodox patriarch of Jerusalem. But his were the first personal papal contacts with the patriarchs of Alexandria and All Africa, Antioch and All the East, the Romanian Orthodox Church, and the Orthodox Church of Georgia, and with metropolitan archbishops of the Czechoslovakian Orthodox Church and the Orthodox Church of Albania. Despite the difficulty in arranging personal meetings between the pope and the patriarchs of Moscow, Serbia, Bulgaria, or the archbishops of the Autocephalous Churches of Greece and Cyprus, there have been many high-level contacts and/or significant correspondence with them. Such visits and contacts comprise a "dialogue of love," helping to overcome centuries-long hostility toward one another, and to support the Orthodox-Catholic international theological dialogue which began in 1980. Common declarations with some patriarchs—Constantinople, Romania, and Georgia—represent initial efforts of common witness. No less important have been the personal relationships. There were a variety of significant events during meetings with Dimitrios I. Ecumenical Patriarch Barthololomew I wrote meditations (1994) for the "Way of the Cross" the pope leads on Good Friday at the Roman Colosseum, the first from another Church to do so (cf. UUS 1). Parthenios III, Greek Orthodox patriarch of Alexandria and Africa, was the first patriarch to participate in an assembly of the Synod of Bishops in Rome, as a fraternal delegate (special assembly for Africa [1994]). And when John Paul invited Christian and other religious leaders to a World Day of Prayer for Peace in Assisi (1986), representatives of many Orthodox Churches participated.

Concerning Oriental Orthodox Churches, John Paul II, like Paul VI, had personal contacts with patriarchs of the Coptic, Syrian, and Armenian Churches. John Paul made the first papal contacts with Ethiopian Orthodox patriarchs, with a catholicos of the Malankara Syrian Orthodox Church, and with a patriarch of the Assyrian Church of the East. Common declarations made with the Syrian, Armenian, and Assyrian patriarchs were decisive in resolving Christological problems. Armenian patriarch-catholicos of Etchmiadzin Karekin I wrote meditations for the papal "Way of the Cross" for Good Friday 1997. Mar Dinkha IV, Assyrian Church of the East, participated personally at the Assisi Day of Prayer for Peace.

Pope John Paul, like Paul VI, met two archbishops of Canterbury, and presidents of the Lutheran World Federation (LWF). He was the first pope to receive, on a visit to Rome, a President of the World Methodist Council (WMC), a President of the Baptist World Alliance, and the General Minister of the Christian Church (Disciples of Christ) (CC [DC]). Further ecumenical steps include: common declarations issued with two archbishops of Canterbury; the scope of contacts with Archbishop Runcie; and the participation of the archbishop of Canterbury (George Carey), the President of the Union of Utrecht of Old Catholic Churches (Archbishop Antonius Glazemaker), the presidents of the LWF (Bishop Christian Krause) and the WMC (Dr. Frances Alguire), and the General Minister of CC (DC) (Dr Richard Hamm), in the special ecumenical service for the opening of the Holy Door of the Roman Basilica of St. Paul Outside the Walls (18 Jan. 2000).

Perhaps John Paul II's longest, most constant ecumenical contacts were with Ecumenical Patriarch

Dimitrios I (from 1978 until his death in 1991) and with Archbishop Robert Runcie (during his tenure, 1980 1991). The pope "considered it one of the first duties of my pontificate to renew personal contact" with Dimitrios I (UUS 52). At their first meeting (Istanbul 1979), they announced the beginning of the international Orthodox/ Catholic theological dialogue. Annually, for thirteen years, they exchanged substantial messages, each sending a delegation to celebrate the patronal feast of the other (Sts. Peter and Paul [29 June], and St. Andrew [30 Nov.]), and for ecumenical discussion. Pope John Paul wrote to Dimitrios on particular occasions, such as the sixteenth centenary of the First Council of Constantinople (1981), underlining the Nicean-Constantinopolitan Creed's importance and asking for dialogue on historical controversies regarding the doctrine of the Holy Spirit, particularly the eternal relationship of Son and Spirit (*IS* 46 [1981]: 56-57). During Dimitrios's visit to Rome (1987), at Mass on 6 December, pope and patriarch proclaimed together the Nicean-Constantinopolitan creed in the original Greek without the *filioque* (as did John Paul II and Bartholomew I in 1995). During that same visit the pope first made the significant proposal that pastors and theologians of both sides study together the forms in which the ministry of unity of the bishop of Rome might accomplish a service for all. And each underlined again the common Marian heritage shared by Orthodox and Catholic Churches, as Dimitrios said, "like a common bond and common tradition" in a "common dogmatic and theological heritage" even though for "certain unilateral actions of a dogmatic nature" dialogue is necessary (*IS*66 [1988]: 20–21).

Pope John Paul and Archbishop Runcie on two occasions met while each was on a pastoral visit: in Accra, Ghana (1980), publishing a joint statement (*IS* 44 [1980]: 90); and in Bombay, India (1986). In *Ut unum sint* (24), the pope recalled "with profound emotion . . . praying together, with the Primate of the Anglican Communion at Canterbury Cathedral (May 29, 1982)." In a common declaration they initiated a second Anglican Roman Catholic International Commission to examine "outstanding doctrinal differences which still separate us with a view toward . . . restoration of full communion" (*Insegnamenti* V, 2 [1982]: 1944). During 1984–85, they exchanged cordial but frank correspondence concerning difficulties arising because of ordination of women by Anglicans (*IS* 61 [1986]: 106–07). In 1986 Archbishop Runcie personally accepted Pope John Paul's invitation to the Assisi World Day of Prayer for Peace. For the "Christian Prayer" at the third part of the day, the pope, Archbishop Runcie, and representatives of the Ecumenical Patriarchate and the LWF presented together the Christian prayer (*IS* 62 [1986]: 173–74). In his 1988 address at Lambeth Conference, Runcie, on the basis of the Assisi experience, proposed that all Christians reconsider the primacy of the bishop of Rome. In a fraternal spirit he sent the pope an account of issues discussed at Lambeth Conference (*IS* 70 [1989]: 59). Runcie visited Rome in 1989. The two highlighted, as in 1982, the Catholic and Anglican common heritage of the sixth-century evangelization of England entrusted by Pope Gregory to St. Augustine, Runcie repeated his proposal concerning the papal primacy (*IS* 71 [1989]: 117, 118).

Towards Healing Bitter Memories. Healing bitter memories is also indispensable for building bonds of communion, requiring personal and communal metanoia. John Paul has addressed this often, saying to French Protestants in Paris (1980), "our personal and community memory must be purified of the memory of all the conflicts, injustice and hatred of the past. This purification is carried out through mutual forgiveness, from the depths of our hearts" (*IS* 44 [1980]: 84). He made similar statements to Swiss Protestants (1984); to Reformed Christians in Hungary (1991); to Orthodox Christians in Poland (1991); to both Reformed and Catholics in the Czech Republic (1995), asking them to extend mutual pardon for violence inflicted during the seventeenth-century European religious wars; and within the Catholic Church, especially in the preparations for the Jubilee 2000 (cf. TMA, 33, 34, 35).

Since healing of memory requires purification by recognition of the truth, John Paul II called for the common historical study of Reformers and the Reformation. In 1983, he asked for accurate historical work concerning Luther, "to arrive at a true image of the reformer, of the whole period of the Reformation, and of the persons involved in it" (*IS* 52 [1983]: 83). Concerning Zwingli and Calvin, the pope expressed the hope in Switzerland in 1984 that Swiss Catholics and Protestants would "write the history of that troubled and complex period together" with objectivity rooted in charity (*IS* 55 [1984]: 47). In Czechoslovakia in 1990, he challenged experts, "to define more precisely the place which John Hus occupies among the reformers of the Church" (*IS* 75 [1990]: 139). Addressing participants in a 1999 international symposium on Hus, in Rome, he expressed gratitude for progress made in that historical study thus far, and "deep regret" for the death inflicted on Hus and the resulting wound of conflict and division imposed on the minds of the Bohemian people (*L'Osservatore Romano*, English weekly edition, 22 December 1999).

Dialogue and Reception: Taking Steps toward Unity

John Paul II's pontificate coincides with a time of transition in the ecumenical movement. While dialogue continues, the reception of dialogue results has increased (cf. UUS 80). More ecumenical cooperation has been undertaken. Some important steps toward unity have been made, to which the pope has contributed.

Theological Dialogue. Seeing ecumenical dialogue as "an outright necessity, one of the Church's priorities" (UUS 31), the pope supported international bilateral dialogues already in place in 1978 between Catholics and Lutherans, Anglicans, Methodists, Reformed, Disciples of Christ, Pentecostals, Coptic Orthodox, Evangelicals, and the multilateral dialogue of Faith and Order (WCC). New international dialogues began after 1978, also touching further geographical areas, between Catholics and Orthodox, with Baptists, with the Malankara Syrian Orthodox and also the Malankara Orthodox Syrian Churches in India, with the Assyrian Church of the East, with Mennonites, and also consultations with the World Evangelical Fellowship.

Ut unum sint also offers a theological interpretation of dialogue which, like ecumenism itself, must be influenced by the quest for sanctity. Dialogue must be a "dialogue of consciences" because dialogue is marked by a "common quest for truth." Since truth forms consciences, truth demands that Christians divided from one another "be inspired by and submissive to Christ's prayer for unity" (33). Ecumenical dialogue must also be a "dialogue of conversion." "Dialogue cannot take place merely on a horizontal level" of meetings, but has also "a primarily vertical thrust, directed towards the Redeemer, who "is himself our Reconciliation." This vertical aspect "lies in our acknowledgment, jointly and to each other, that we . . . have sinned," creates in separated Christians "that interior space where Christ, the source of the Church's unity, can effectively act, with all the power of his Spirit" (35), enabling conversion to take place.

Reception of Dialogue Results. John Paul II has fostered favorable conditions for reception of dialogue results and taken a personal role in it. He discusses reception in *Ut unum sint,* indicating that it serves to transform dialogue results into "a common heritage" and to strengthen "the bonds of communion" between divided Christians (80). Dialogue reports need to be studied within the sponsoring churches, so that the faithful can see how new light is shed on long-standing theological conflicts. Decisive is the Church's formal authoritative response to a dialogue report, involving a precise evaluation process which usually includes widespread consultation within the Church, the contribution of theologians, collaboration between appropriate offices of the Holy See, particularly the Pontifical Council for Promoting Christian Unity and the Congregation for the Doctrine of Faith, leading to an authoritative decision on the matter, with the resulting response approved by the pope.

During the pontificate of John Paul II the Catholic Church formally responded to several important dialogue reports. The WCC Faith and Order text *Baptism, Eucharist and Ministry* (*BEM*)(1982), resulting from 55 years of dialogue between Orthodox, Catholic, Anglican, and Protestant theologians, showed significant convergences, though not full agreement, on issues long disputed by divided Christians. The 1987 Catholic response pointed to areas needing continuing study, but generally assessed *BEM* as an ecumenical step forward; John Paul II made positive comments about *BEM,* and publically supported the formal response process. Also, after the Anglican Roman Catholic International Commission completed its "Final Report" on Eucharist, ministry and ordination, and authority in 1981, John Paul called for its evaluation, approved both the formal response (1991), and additional "Clarifications" (1994) to points raised in the response. While acknowledging that further work was needed on the question of authority, he recognized affirmatively the convergences and agreements reached between Anglicans and Catholics on the meaning of the issues of Eucharist and ministry. The pope has also contributed to significant steps taken recently, aided by dialogue, toward resolving conflicts stemming from the fifth, eleventh, and sixteenth centuries.

TOWARDS HEALING DIVISION BETWEEN EAST AND WEST

In John Paul's view, reconciliation of Christian East and West would uniquely benefit the whole ecumenical movement, as reflected in his oft-cited expression that the Church must breath again with "both lungs," Eastern and Western. "I am convinced" he said to the SPCU in 1980 "that a rearticulation of the ancient Eastern and Western traditions and the balancing exchange that will result when full communion is found again, may be of great importance to heal the divisions that came about in the West in the 16th century" (*IS* 43 [1980]: 67).

The international Orthodox-Catholic dialogue fosters the growing renewed recognition of each other, by Orthodox and Catholics, after centuries of isolation, as "Sister Churches." This designation, based on a common understanding of the sacramental structure of the Church (cf UR 14–18) was mutually used at the time of Vatican II by Pope Paul VI and Ecumenical Patriarch Athenagoras who also took other steps towards the healing of memory in regard to the sad events in 1054 (cf. UUS 52–7). In efforts to reestablish full communion between Catholics and Orthodox, states John Paul, "the traditional designation of 'Sister Churches' should ever accompany us along this path" (UUS 56).

Dialogue reports published in 1982, 1987, and 1988 underlined common views on ecclesiology and sacramentality. *Ut unum sint* expresses the pope's approval of certain results: for example, the dialogue's conclusion "that the Catholic Church and the Orthodox Church can already profess together that common faith in the mystery of the Church and the bond between faith and sacraments" (59), and the commission's acknowledgment (1988) that "in our Churches apostolic succession is fundamental for the sanctification and the unity of the people of God" (ibid.). These affirmations "are important points of reference for the continuation of the dialogue" and they "represent the basis for Catholics and Orthodox to be able from now on to bear a faithful and united common witness in our time, that the name of the Lord may be proclaimed and glorified" (ibid.).

When changes in Eastern Europe in 1989 enabled Eastern Catholic Churches, suppressed under communism after the Second World War, once again to practice their faith openly, priority in Orthodox/Catholic relations was given to solving concrete questions. The Orthodox insisted that the theological dialogue, which had before it a discussion of primacy and synodality, address the question of "Uniatism," and over the next decade published only one statement: "Uniatism, Method of Union of the Past and the present search for full communion" (1993). Reacting to the tensions, John Paul II wrote a "Letter to the (Catholic) Bishops of Europe on the Relations between Catholics and Orthodox in the New Situation of Central and Eastern Europe" (31 May 1991), explaining the steps taken to normalize situations of both Latin and Byzantine Catholic Churches, describing tensions, especially the disposition of places of worship formerly belonging to Byzantine Catholics, and urging dialogue to settle these issues. Based on *Unitatis redintegratio* 15, relations with the Orthodox Churches, he said, "are to be fostered as between Sister Churches." This means recognizing the leaders of those Churches as pastors of that part of the body of Christ confided to them, rejecting all undue forms of proselytism, and promoting coexistence with mutual respect.

These ideas found an echo in the 1993 dialogue statement "Uniatism," which, without mentioning it by name, *Ut unum sint* describes as "a significant step forward with regard to the very sensitive question of the method to be followed in re-establishing full communion between the Catholic Church and the Orthodox Church," laying "doctrinal foundations for a positive solution to this problem on the basis of the doctrine of Sister Churches." The method to be followed is the dialogue of truth supported by the dialogue of love. Also, recognition of the Eastern Catholic churches' right to have organizational structures, to carry out their apostolate, and their actual involvement in the dialogue "will promote fraternal esteem between Orthodox and Catholics and foster their commitment to work for unity" (UUS 60).

HEALING FIFTH-CENTURY CHRISTOLOGICAL DISPUTES

John Paul has been deeply involved in restored relations, which began after Vatican II, "with Ancient Churches of the East which rejected the dogmatic formulations of the Council of Ephesus [431] and Chalcedon [451]." "Precisely in relation to Christology, we have been able to join the Patriarchs of some of these Churches in declaring our common faith in Jesus Christ, true God and true man" (UUS 62). Theological clarifications in the 1960s and early 1970s regarding Christological controversies led to the signing of Christological agreements, in 1971 by Pope Paul VI with Syrian Orthodox patriarch of Antioch Jacob III, and in 1973 by with Coptic Orthodox pope Shenouda III. John Paul confirmed and drew on the first "for the development of dialogue with Pope Shenouda" (ibid.). In 1988 both Churches developed a "Brief Formula" giving the 1973 agreement, as John Paul wrote to Shenouda, "a simpler and more popular form in order to make it accessible to all the faithful in Egypt" (*IS* 76 [1991]: 12). In a 1984 Christological declaration John Paul II and Syrian Orthodox patriarch Mar Ignatius Zakka I built on their predecessors by adding provisions for pastoral collaboration in particular situations—for example, members of one Church without access to a priest could request sacraments of Penance, Eucharist and Anointing of the sick from a priest of the other. The declaration made clear that this particular pastoral step was possible, even though complete identity in faith does not exist yet, because the two churches hold these sacraments together "in one and the same succession of Apostolic ministry" (*Insegnamenti* VII, 1 [1984]: 1902–1906).

During John Paul's pontificate, four other Oriental Orthodox Churches became involved in this reconciliation process. Dialogue with the Malankara Syrian Orthodox Church (autonomous Church under the authority of the Syrian Orthodox patriarch of Antioch) produced a 1993 mixed-marriage agreement. Approved by the authorities of both Churches, it builds on the 1984 common Christological declaration and pastoral arrangement. Another dialogue, with the Malankara Orthodox Syrian Church, produced a 1989 joint statement authoritatively approved by both Churches, affirming their common faith in Jesus Christ. Although no common Christological declaration was signed with the Ethiopian Orthodox Church, John Paul II witnesses that during the 1993 visit of Patriarch Abuna Paulos, "together we emphasized the deep communion existing between our two Churches." Addressing the patriarch, he said "today, moreover, we can affirm that we have the one faith in Christ, even though for a long time this was a source of division between us" (UUS 62). The 1996 common declaration of

John Paul II and Armenian patriarch-catholicos Karekin I of Etchmiadzin confirmed "fundamental common faith in God and in Jesus Christ" such that "the unhappy divisions" which had followed divergent expressions, "should not continue to influence the life and witness of the Church today" (*Insegnamenti* XIX, 2 [1996]: 1021); this was reaffirmed in a common declaration between the pope and Armenian Catholicos Aram I of Cilicia in 1997.

Finally, concerning the division after the Council of Ephesus (431) the pope and Patriarch Mar Dinkha IV, Assyrian Church of the East, signed a common Christological declaration in 1994: "taking into account the different theological formulations, we were able to profess together the true faith in Christ" (UUS 62).

Together, according to Cardinal Edward Idris Cassidy, President of the PCPCU, these declarations "illustrate the virtual resolution of the Christological controversies, as far as the Catholic Church and the Oriental Orthodox Churches are concerned, resulting from reactions to the Councils of Ephesus and Chalcedon in the fifth century" (*IS* 101 [1999]: 158).

JOINT DECLARATION ON THE DOCTRINE OF JUSTIFICATION

Since the doctrine of justification was at the heart of Martin Luther's conflict with Church authorities in the sixteenth century, one of the most dramatic ecumenical events of the 1990s was the development and official acceptance by the Lutheran World Federation and the Catholic Church of the *Joint Declaration on the Doctrine of Justification (JD),* cosigned at Augsburg, Germany, on 31 October 1999. The level of consensus achieved on this doctrine, said Cardinal Cassidy, making public the official Catholic response in 1998, "virtually resolves a long disputed question at the close of the twentieth century" (*IS* 98 [1998]: 97). JD itself (43) points to other matters still to be clarified between Lutherans and Catholics as the two continue to move toward unity.

The pope's numerous contacts with leaders of the LWF and of Lutheran churches in Germany, USA, and Nordic countries (cf. UUS 25, 72) encouraged Lutheran-Catholic dialogue. His constructive comments about Luther (*IS* 52 [1983]: 83), appreciation expressed for the Lutheran Augsburg Confession (AC) which carries a concise definition of justification (4), helped create a good atmosphere as well. In 1980, the 450th anniversary of AC, he mentioned it on numerous occasions, saying for example to the Council of the German Evangelical Church in Germany that reflecting on AC helps us realize that we profess together biblical truths about Salvation in Jesus Christ (*IS* 45 [1981] :6). John Paul II also pressed for official evaluation of Lutheran Catholic dialogue results "to see how far . . . dialogues have taken us towards unity in faith" (*Insegnamenti* XII, 1 [1989]: 1512).

This challenge was taken up in regard to justification. Presenting, concisely, the results of over thirty years of dialogue, JD states that "a consensus in basic truths of the doctrine of justification exists between Lutherans and Catholics" (40) and that "the teaching of the Lutheran churches presented in this Declaration does not fall under the condemnations from the Council of Trent. The condemnations in the Lutheran Confessions do not apply to the teaching of the Roman Catholic Church presented in this Declaration" (41). The pope repeatedly voiced his support of the JD as it was being developed. When it was made public, the pope stated that "we can now rejoice at an important ecumenical achievement." On 31 October 1999, almost simultaneously with the formal signing of JD, the pope publically expressed gratitude. "In Augsburg, Germany," he said "a very important event is taking place at this moment," calling the signing of JD "a milestone" on the difficult path to re-establish full unity among Christians," "a sound basis . . . for addressing the remaining problems with a better founded hope of resolving them in the future," and "a valuable contribution to the purification of historical memory and to our common witness" (*L'Osservatore Romano,* English weekly edition, 3 Nov. 1999).

The Petrine Ministry: From "Gravest Obstacle" to Ecumenical Challenge?

"The Pope, as we well know" said Paul VI in 1967, "is undoubtedly the gravest obstacle in the path of ecumenism" (*IS* 2 [1967] :4). John Paul tried in three ways to raise the question of the papacy to the level of serious ecumenical dialogue and challenge.

First, in initiating dialogue he explained the evangelical purpose of papal primacy as a service to the unity of the Church for the sake of the gospel. Thus he described to Lutherans in Finland (1989) his personal spiritual journey: in baptism united with Christ; "without any merit" on his part "called to the priesthood, then ordained a bishop in pastoral care of God's people;" in God's design becoming "Bishop of Rome, the successor of Peter in whom, according to Catholic teaching the Lord instituted a permanent . . . visible source and foundation of unity of faith and fellowship." He preaches "no other message but the Gospel. I proclaim the name of Jesus Christ . . . and bear witness to the cross" (*Insegnamenti* XII, 1, [1989]: 1510–11). At greater length, *Ut unum sint* (4, 88 97) summarizes salient aspects of Catholic teaching on this ministry, a "servus servorum Dei" (esp. 94, 97), and outlines its biblical basis in the ministry of Peter. Like Peter, the pope needs Christ's mercy and personal conversion before being able to strengthen his brethren; his authority is completely at the service of God's merciful plan, totally dependent on the Lord's grace. This ministry is entrusted to him within the college of Bishops. As Peter spoke in the name of the apostolic group, serving the unity of the community, this function of Peter must continue in the Church, so that under her sole Head, Christ, she may be visibly present in the world as the communion of all his disciples.

Second, John Paul II made an effort to exercise this office precisely as "a primacy in action and initiative in favour of that unity for which Christ so earnestly prayed" (*Insegnamenti* XII, 2 [1989] :713) in several ways: (1) in common witness *mutually initiated* with other Christian leaders, as in signing common declarations; (2) through invitations *initiated by the pope* to other leaders to join him in common witness (e.g., the Assisi World Day of Prayer for Peace). Notable in this regard was the reaction of Archbishop Runcie, based on his Assisi experience: "In Assisi" he said "we saw that the Bishop of Rome could gather the Christian Churches together. We could pray together, speak together and act together for the peace and wellbeing of humankind, and the stewardship of our precious earth." Thus Runcie proposed: "Could not all Christians come to reconsider the kind of primacy the bishop of Rome exercised within the Early Church, 'a presiding in love' for the sake of the unity of the Churches in the diversity of their mission?" (*IS* 71 [1989]: 118). This service also includes (3) *responding to initiatives from other leaders* (e.g., incorporating into Roman Catholic Jubilee 2000 calendar Patriarch Bartholomew's suggestion that Christians around the world offer prayer services at the vigil of the Transfiguration of Christ [6 August 2000]).

Third, John Paul invited other Christians to dialogue with him on the ministry of the bishop of Rome. He expressed hope for such dialogue in 1984 at the WCC (*IS* 55 [1984]: 39). In 1987 in the presence of Ecumenical Patriarch Dimitrios I he first made the specific invitation, repeated in *Ut unum sint* 95, that we "seek—together of course—the forms in which this ministry may accomplish a service of love recognized by all concerned." This invitation in general has been mostly well received. In a limited way dialogue has begun, since some churches, communities, and ecumenical bodies have now formulated written responses.

The Jubilee Year and the Future Agenda

The goal of ecumenism remains the unity which Christ has bestowed on his Church and which "stands at the very heart of Christ's mission" (UUS 9). The full communion to which Christians are called involves, in the Catholic view, a "unity constituted by the bonds of the profession of faith, the sacraments and hierarchical communion" (ibid.).

As John Paul promoted ecumenism in many ways, so too some Jubilee 2000 celebrations reflected an ecumenical agenda. On 18 January 2000, leaders or representatives of Orthodox, Oriental Orthodox, Anglican, Old Catholic, and Protestant churches and the WCC accepted the pope's invitation to the Roman Basilica of St. Paul Outside the Walls for an ecumenical ceremony featuring the opening of the Basilica's Holy Door, the first time this jubilee event took place in an ecumenical service. Pope John Paul, Metropolitan Athanasius of the Ecumenical Patriarchate, and Archbishop George Carey of Canterbury together pushed open the Holy Door. All representatives, with the Pope, walked through it. As a new century began, all witnessed together to the words of the Redeemer. "I am the gate. Whoever enters by me will be saved" (Jn 10:9).

Pope John Paul's words and actions set an agenda and establish priorities for the twenty-first century. Ecumenical achievements illustrate that Christians are much closer to overcoming divisions, and therefore more able to witness together to the gospel than previously. *Christians are called to increase the opportunities for common witness, to the extent that they can now, for praising the Redeemer together before the world.*

Theological dialogue must continue in order that Christians together can be loyal to the "faith that was once for all entrusted to the saints" (Jude 1:3). Contemporary dialogues are focusing on various issues, some related to ecclesiology (e.g., ministry, authority in the Church, sacraments, primacy and synodality). Ethical questions are presenting new challenges for the churches. In the twenty-first century these and others are "in need of fuller study before a true consensus of faith can be achieved" (cf. UUS 79).

Besides ongoing theological dialogue, the healing of memories, too, has continuing priority for the twenty-first century, requiring a deep spirituality. Christians "cannot underestimate the burden of *long-standing misgivings* inherited from the past, and . . . are called to re-examine together their painful past and the hurt which . . . continues to provoke even today" (UUS 2). A second Jubilee event, the "Day of Pardon" (12 March 2000), highlighted a "Universal Prayer" concerning "Confession of Sins and Asking for Forgiveness," celebrated by the pope within the Eucharistic liturgy for the First Sunday of Lent. In this unique service, John Paul II led the Church in a public confession and prayer before the world, addressing seven categories of sins committed during the history of the Church, especially during the second millennium, one category being "Confession of Sins Which Have Harmed the Unity of the Body of Christ" (cf. TMA 34; UUS 34, 82). It set a tone and spirit for supporting a healing of memories and ecumenical relations in the future, reflected in the prayer of confession, which expressed deep regret before God and one another for the sin of division:

> Merciful Father, . . . believers have opposed one another, becoming divided, and have mutually condemned one another and fought against one another. We urgently implore your forgiveness and we beseech the gift of a repentant heart, so that all Christians reconciled with you and one another will be able, in one body in one spirit, to experience anew the joy of full communion.

A third Jubilee event was the "Ecumenical Commemoration of Witnesses to the Faith in the Twentieth Century" (7 May 2000) at the Roman Colosseum. The pope presided and representatives from Orthodox, Oriental Orthodox, Anglican, and Protestant churches, and the WCC, participated. "The witness to Christ borne even to the shedding of blood has become a common inheritance of Catholics, Orthodox, Anglicans and Protestants" (TMA 37). Separated Christians redeemed by Christ are also linked to one another in their witness to faith in the Redeemer, and to the Cross. In the pope's view, "the greatest homage which all the churches can give to Christ on the threshold of the third millennium will be to manifest the Redeemer's all powerful presence through the fruits of faith, hope and charity present in men and women of many different tongues and races who have followed Christ" (TMA 37). This commemoration was a reminder that the search for Christian unity in all its aspects is deeply interrelated with the search for sanctity; which should be the first priority for all Christians, in the twenty-first century, and from age to age.

See Also: ASSISI; EDWARD IDRIS CASSIDY; JOHN PAUL AND INTERRELIGIOUS DIALOGUE; A PILGRIMAGE OF RECONCILIATION; REDEMPTOR HOMINIS, REDEMPTORIS MATER; REDEMPTORIS MISSIO; SLAVORUM APOSTOLI; TERTIO MILLENNIO ADVENIENTE; UT UNUM SINT

Bibliography: EDWARD IDRIS CASSIDY, "*Ut Unum Sint*: Three Years Later" in *Oriental Lumen II Conference 1998 Proceedings* (Fairfax: Eastern Christian Publications, 1998). EDWARD IDRIS CASSIDY and PIERRE DUPREY, "Ecumenical Advances 1960–1999: Towards The New Millennium." The Pontifical Council For Promoting Christian Unity, Vatican City *Information Service,* no.101 (1999):155–65. COLIN DAVEY, "*Ut unum sint*: Responses within Britain and Ireland to Pope John Paul II's Encyclical Letter on Commitment to Unity" *One in Christ* 4 (1999): 339 382. PIERRE DUPREY, "Les Gestes Oecuméniques de Paul VI." *Proche Orient Chrétien* 48, fasc. 1–2 (1998):145–67. ELEUTERIO F. FORTINO, "Comments on the Encyclical Letter *Ut unum sint*," Pontifical Council For Promoting Christian Unity, Vatican City, *Information Service* 89 (1995): 85–7. *Insegnamenti di Giovanni Paolo II* (Vatican City: Libreria Editrice Vaticano, 1978). WALTER KASPER, "Das Petrusamt in Okumenischer Perspektive," in *Papstamt,* LOTHAR LIES and SILVIA HELL, eds. (Innsbruck: Tyrolian Press). JAMES F. PUGLISI, ed., *Petrine Ministry and the Unity of the Church: "Toward a Patient and Fraternal Dialogue"* (Collegeville, Minn.: The Liturgical Press, 1999). E. J. STORMON, ed., *Towards the Healing of Schism: The Sees of Rome and Constantinople. Public Statements and Correspondence Between the Holy See and the Ecumenical Patriarchate 1958–1984,* Ecumenical Documents 3 (New York and Mahwah: Paulist Press,1987). THOMAS F. STRANSKY and JOHN B. SHEERIN, *Doing the Truth in Charity: Statements of Pope Paul VI, Popes John Paul I, John Paul II, and the Secretariat for Promoting Christian Unity 1964–1980,* Ecumenical Documents 1 (New York and Ramsey: Paulist Press, 1982). Pontifical Council for Promoting Christian Unity, *Information Service* 38 (Vatican City 1978)ff. JOHN A. RADANO, "The Catholic Church and BEM, 1980–89." *Mid-Stream* 30, no.2 (April 1991): 139–56.

[JOHN A. RADANO]

John Paul II and Interreligious Dialogue

John Borelli, Ph.D., is associate director of Secretariat for Ecumenical and Interreligious Affairs, National Conference of Catholic Bishops, Washington, D.C.

According to Pope John Paul II's grand design, laid out in *Tertio millennio adveniente*, dialogue and relations with followers of other religions were essential activities for Christians preparing for and celebrating the Jubilee Year 2000. Leading a church into a new millennium, renewed and redirected by the Second Vatican Council (1962–65) which spoke clearly about dialogue with other religions, John Paul II called for interreligious activity in every phase of preparation for the Jubilee. He identified its appropriateness as one of the contexts for the preliminary examination of conscience by the church (TMA 35–6) and underscored its importance as a theme of the continental synods of bishops of Africa, Asia, and elsewhere he was convening in conjunction with preparations for the third millennium of Christianity (TMA 38). He singled out "the increased interest in dialogue with other religions" in the program for 1998, the year of the Holy Spirit (TMA 46), and, for 1999, the year of God the Father, he prayed that "God grant that as a confirmation of these intentions it may be possible to hold joint meetings in places of significance for the great monotheistic religions" (TMA 53). He concluded his letter with a vision, drawn from the council's constitution on the church and enhanced by Pope Paul VI's encyclical on the church (*Ecclesiam Suam*), of all peoples called to the Catholic unity of the new people, already belonging to it or related to it in various ways, and through it participating in the means of salvation (TMA 56).

For John Paul II, the Second Vatican Council "gave a fundamental impulse to forming the church's self-awareness by so adequately and competently presenting to us a view of the terrestrial globe as a map of various religions" (*Redemptor hominis* 11). The positive and inventive approach to other religions is intimately connected with other new directions and initiatives resulting from the council, especially the renewed understanding of the church as a communion of persons called by God into a dialogue of salvation, a fresh approach to Christian unity, an innovative emphasis on religious liberty, a reinvigorated social and public involvement of the church in the world especially for the causes of justice and peace, and a redirection of missionary activity as a service to all humanity. To comprehend Pope John Paul's leadership in the sphere of interreligious relations, one must combine his understanding of all these achievements of the Second Vatican Council with three hallmarks of his papacy: the preeminent leadership of the papacy under him, his emphasis on the fundamental role of the Holy Spirit, and his formulation of the essential link between interreligious dialogue and the evangelizing mission of the church.

World Leader

For John Paul II the Second Vatican Council was "a providential event whereby the church began the more immediate preparation for the jubilee," "a council similar to earlier ones, yet very different," "a council focused on the mystery of Christ and his church, and at the same time open to the world," "the beginning of a new era in the life of the church," and "a profound renewal" (TMA 18). On innumerable occasions he has firmly reiterated that "no council had ever spoken so clearly about Christian unity, about dialogue with non-Christian religions, about the specific meaning of the old covenant and of Israel, about the dignity of each person's conscience, about the principle of religious liberty, about the different cultural traditions within which the church carried out her missionary mandate and about the means of social communication" (TMA 19). He saw that "the council's enormously rich body of teaching and striking new tone in the way it presented this content constitute as it were a proclamation of new times" (TMA 20).

Unquestionably, the reconsideration of relations of the Catholic Church with other Christians, with peoples of all faiths, and veritably with all humanity led to momentous steps, reflected especially in the conciliar documents on the church, ecumenism, interreligious relations,

John Paul II with Britain's Archbishop of Canterbury, Robert Runcie, during their 1989 meeting. (AP/Wide World Photos.)

and religious liberty. Karol Wojtyła participated in the Second Vatican Council, first as auxiliary bishop, then as archbishop of Kraków, and devoted particular attention to the schemas that became the documents on the church (*Lumen gentium*) and the church in the modern world (*Gaudium et spes*) and to the two sections of the draft on ecumenism, eventually partitioned into distinct texts on relations with other religions (*Nostra aetate*) and religious liberty (*Dignitatis humanae*). The channel of his interest in interreligious relations might well have been his deep-rooted concern, arising from his life in Poland, for how Christians should improve their understanding of their relationship with Jews. His own deeply personal stake in the promotion of religious freedom, as a pastor during the Cold War, focused his interest on how the church identifies and develops principles for engaging the public and social realities of contemporary life, including the increasing experience of religious and cultural diversity.

Including "all men and women of good will" in the salutation of his first encyclical (*Redemptor hominis*) was a sign of new times. The document was issued less than five months after his election following the thirty-three-day papacy of John Paul I. After noting his predecessor's unprecedented choice of a double name, he explained that he too was signaling the same new starting point "to continue, in a certain sense together with John Paul I, into the future, letting myself be guided by unlimited trust in and obedience to the Spirit that Christ promised and sent to his church" (2). He harnessed the new directions of the council with the prevailing guidance of the popes from Pius XII to himself, "The rich inheritance of the recent pontificates struck deep roots in the awareness of the church in an utterly new way, quite unknown previously, thanks to the Second Vatican Council" (3). Referring to Pope Paul VI's foundational encyclical *Ecclesiam Suam*, issued at a pivotal point during the council, because it illustrated how the church as the communion of persons can engage in the dialogue of salvation through the image of a series of concentric circles increasingly encompassing the whole of humanity, John Paul II reasserted the necessity of dialogue with all Christians, with peoples of all faiths, and with all humanity. The conspicuous citation of Paul VI's initial encyclical in his own first encyclical and observation that ''Paul VI gave us his personal example'' (6) signaled John Paul II's intention to lead by example along the same paths.

The personal example of Paul VI, especially his disarming candor and spontaneity on occasions of historical importance, was already legendary. In 1963, at the opening of the second session of the council, Paul VI asked God's pardon and that of the separated Christians of the East who were offended in the past by the Catholic Church. In 1964, he embraced Ecumenical Patriarch Athenagoras on the Mount of Olives. In 1966, he removed the episcopal ring from his finger and handed it to the archbishop of Canterbury. In 1975, he kissed the feet of the bishop envoy bearing news of Orthodox agreement to proceed with a formal theological dialogue. On Pentecost Sunday 1964, he expressly welcomed to Rome from that day forward every pilgrim from other religions through the establishment of a Secretariat for Non-Christians (now Pontifical Council for Interreligious Dialogue). Later that year in India he prayed the ancient words of a Hindu sacred text while speaking to religious leaders. In 1978, at what was to be his last public meeting with representatives of other religions, he was moved to conclude a greeting to the visitors from Japan with these words, ''We thank you again for your visit and pray to the Lord that we may always be worthy to love you and to serve you.''

Pope John Paul II's acts of leadership in the promotion of Christian unity are on the same scale: he was the first pope to visit the Lutheran church in Rome and to preach from a Protestant pulpit, to renew baptismal vows in Canterbury Cathedral with the archbishop, to share the pulpit with the Ecumenical Patriarch (Dimitrios) at a papal mass, to visit a monument to twenty-four Protestant martyrs of the Reformation in Slovakia (this after noting their example of conscience at the canonization of three Catholic martyrs of the Thirty-Years War), and to write an encyclical on ecumenism. Extraordinary as these acts are, his leadership in interreligious relations is nothing but phenomenal. He is the first pope to visit Oświęcim (Auschwitz). He visited the Catholic community in Ankara, Turkey, and urged now ''when Christians and Muslims have entered a new period of history, to recognize and develop the spiritual bonds that unite us.'' In Casablanca, in 1985, he addressed a stadium filled with young Muslims and explicitly reaffirmed, ''We believe in the same God, the one and only God, the living God, the God

John Paul II and Jordanian King Abdullah II, right, upon the pontiff's arrival in Amman on 20 March 2000. (AP/Wide World Photos. Photograph by Arturo Mari.)

who creates worlds and brings creatures to their perfection.'' Twice he traveled to India and twice he went to Raj Ghat, the spot where Mahatma Gandhi's remains were cremated. John Paul II began his first pilgrimage to India there in 1986, paying homage to the Hindu leader as a ''hero of humanity,'' a devotee of God, and a revealer of the human heart who urged all to cling to the truth with respect for the unique dignity of every human being.

In 1986, John Paul II was the first pope to go inside the synagogue of Rome. As the guest of the chief rabbi and the Jewish community of Rome, he observed that ''this gathering . . . brings to a close . . . a long period which we must not tire of reflecting upon in order to draw appropriate lessons from it.'' He also observed on that occasion that ''the general acceptance of a legitimate plurality on the social, civil and religious levels has been arrived at with great difficulty.'' These and other such initiatives can also be seen as expressions of good will in preparation for the much exalted interreligious event of 27 October 1986: the World Day of Prayer for Peace which he hosted in Assisi.

The pope announced his intention to hold the day of prayer at the conclusion of the annual week of prayer for Christian unity—25 January 1986, the twenty-seventh anniversary of John XXIII's announcement of his intention to call the Second Vatican Council, and at the same place, St. Paul's Basilica. He spoke at length about the ecumenical movement and its goal of restoration of Christian unity, and then announced that he was "initiating opportune consultations with the leaders, not only of the various Christian churches and communions, but also of the other religions . . . to organize with them a special meeting of prayer for peace" and predicted that it would be one of the "most significant and important moments" in spiritual ecumenism.

If the Second Vatican Council was the epochal step for Catholics into interreligious relations, the World Day of Prayer for Peace was its boldest implementation. The generous response of Christian, Jewish, Islamic, Hindu, Buddhist, and other religious leaders to join Pope John Paul II to fast, to walk, and to pray for peace made it an event of singular importance in the history interreligious relations. Over sixty leaders, most of whom were not Christians, spent the day with him in Assisi, praying together in their respective religious families and coming together to pray in the presence of one another.

The day of prayer in Assisi has been commemorated since that day, in some form or another, each year at the end of October (on or near the anniversary of the passage and promulgation of *Nostra aetate* [28 October]). At the concluding service of an interreligious assembly on 28 October 1999, the Assisi scene was re-enacted. The members of the assembly (over 200) spent three days in discussions at the synod hall with a break for a trip to Assisi. They came together for a final service at the center landing on the steps of St. Peter's Basilica with the representatives of various religious groups arranged semicircularly to the pope's sides and behind him; the candlelit ceremony included testimonies, hymns, prayers, and the reading of a message prepared by the assembly. Religious leaders gathered around a pope will long be remembered as a picture of the papacy of John Paul II.

His personal example extends beyond his role as a host of interreligious dialogues and as a pilgrim to the shrines of holy places of religious communities. On his visit to the synagogue of Rome he restated the words of *Nostra aetate* that the church "deplores the hatred, persecutions, and displays of anti-Semitism directed against the Jews at anytime and by anyone," and then added emphatically the last two words, "I repeat: 'by anyone.'" On 23 March 2000, at Jerusalem's Yad Vashem Holocaust memorial, he stated, "I assure the Jewish people that the Catholic Church, motivated by the Gospel of truth and love and by no political considerations, is deeply saddened by the hatred, acts of persecution and displays of anti-Semitism directed against the Jews by

Christians at any time and in any place." Three days later, he left at the Western Wall a written request for God's forgiveness for the centuries of mistreatment of the Jewish people by Christians.

Pope John Paul has made admissions and offered statements of remorse to other cultural and religious groups as well. In 1984, he admitted to native peoples of Canada that their encounter with the gospel had not always enriched them and acknowledged that there had been difficulties and blunders. In 1987, he observed to Catholic Native Americans in Phoenix that not all the members of the church lived up to their Christian responsibilities and called on all to learn from the mistakes of the past for reconciliation and healing. In 1992, in Santo Domingo for the 500th anniversary of Columbus' first voyage, he declared to the indigenous people, "In all truth, there must be a recognition of the abuses committed due to a lack of love on the part of some individuals who did not see their indigenous brothers and sisters as children of God, their Father." In 1993, while in Izamal, Mexico, in a message for all indigenous peoples from Alaska to Tierra del Fuego, he was even more explicit about how the richness of their cultures has not always been respected and how the shadow of sin was cast over America too in the destruction of many artistic and cultural creations and violence against native peoples.

Buddhists have been received with respect and honor at the Holy See, and the Dalai Lama was given a place of prominence next to the pope during the day of prayer in Assisi. The pope's book of personal reflections *Crossing the Threshold of Hope* (1994), included some negative interpretations to Buddhist doctrines, which provoked some reactions in the Buddhist world. In January 1995, the pope said in Sri Lanka, "I come *as a pilgrim of goodwill,* with nothing but peace in my heart." He then expressed his highest regard for Buddhists and referred to certain teachings, in particular compassion, equanimity, loving kindness, and empathetic joy. He concluded with a quotation from a Buddhist text, *Dhammapada*: "Better than a thousand useless words, is one single word that gives peace." The strain in Buddhist-Catholic, caused by the passages in *Crossing the Threshold of Hope* and events surrounding the papal trip to Sri Lanka, including the statements of some Buddhist leaders that they refused to attend certain interreligious events, led to the establishment of an consultation between the Holy See and Buddhist teachers and scholars. It met in July 1995 and again in July 1998.

To the young Muslims in Morocco, John Paul II acknowledged the lessons of history: "in general we have badly understood each other, and sometimes, in the past, we have opposed and even exhausted each other in polemics and in wars.'' It has become customary for the president of the Pontifical Council for Interreligious Dialogue to send greetings to all Muslims at the end of the month of Ramadan; in 1991, the pope chose to send the greetings himself. In the aftermath of the Gulf War, against which he had spoken firmly, he wanted to express to those who had lost loved ones his sympathy and solidarity, and to all Muslims the readiness of the Catholic Church to aid the victims and to build structures of lasting peace. In a highly symbolic gesture, he quoted a message of Pope Gregory VII, written eighteen years before the first crusade was preached, to the Muslim ruler of present-day Algeria, emphasizing that Christians and Muslims agree that God wishes all to be saved and that after loving God we should love one another, not doing unto others what we do not wish done to ourselves. In 1995, referring to mentality behind the crusades, he said, ''Today we ought to be grateful to the Spirit of God, who has enabled us to understand even more clearly that the appropriate way to deal with problems that can arise between peoples, religions and cultures, one which is also in harmony with the gospel, is that of patient, firm and respectful dialogue.''

After the Gulf War, Dr. M. Hamid Algabid, Secretary-General of the Organization of the Islamic Conference, wrote to the pope praising his efforts for peace and acknowledging that ''the Muslim world has been aware of Your Holiness' repeated appeals for peace in the Gulf region, for a peace founded on rights, justice and fairness . . . and following with great respect your continuous valuable endeavors to encourage the Christian church to make a concrete contribution toward establishing peace in the Middle East and consolidating an Islamic-Christian dialogue.'' Three years later, at the opening session of the sixth assembly of the World Conference on Religion and Peace in November 1994, in Rome, Dr. Ahmed Muhammad Ali, Secretary-General of the Muslim World League, publicly thanked the pope for his leadership during the preparatory phase of the United Nations Conference on Population and Development convened the previous September in Cairo. Such public recognitions by the chief staff officers of pan-national and political Islamic organizations were unprecedented. Formal dialogues with religious leaders on papal trips had not happened so prominently before John Paul II's pontificate. Also during his papacy, the first mosque in Rome was completed and inaugurated in 1995, and interreligious dialogues between the Holy See and various Islamic organizations and agencies have prospered.

When Pope John Paul arrived in Egypt on 24 February 2000, he was greeted by Grand Sheik Mohammed Sayyid Tantawi of al-Azhar University, whose presence in the welcoming party with Coptic Orthodox bishops

and the Catholic Coptic Patriarch was reported to be not part of the original program and a special sign of respect for John Paul II. Sheikh Tantawi, one of the most highly regarded authorities in Islam, later that day hosted the pope at al-Azhar university and announced that he would make an unprecedented visit to the Vatican the following fall. Pope John Paul began his address on his arrival at the airport with the familiar Arabic greeting used by Muslims worldwide, ''As Salaam Alaikum'' (Peace be with you). He explained that he wanted his pilgrimage to Egypt and especially to Mount Sinai, where Moses received the Ten Commandments, to be ''a moment of intense prayer for peace and for interreligious harmony.''

Of particular interest to many Muslims was the pope's visit to the Senegalese island of Goree in February 1991, where millions of Africans had been sold into slavery for transportation to America, an enterprise he described as ''a shameful commerce, involving the participation of baptized people who did not live according to their faith.'' He said, ''this human sin against human beings, this human sin against God, should be confessed in all truth and humility.'' His apostolic letter on the approach of the third millennium developed more extensively the need for Christians to begin preparing for this opportunity for renewal by confessing the sins of Christians and recalling with sorrow ''all those times in history when they departed from the spirit of Christ and his Gospel and, instead of offering to the world the witness of a life inspired by the values of faith, indulged in ways of thinking and acting which were truly forms of counterwitness and scandal'' (TMA 33). He noted especially ''acquiescence given, especially in certain centuries, to intolerance and even the use of violence in the service of truth'' (TMA 35). On the first Sunday of Lent in the Jubilee Year 2000, he led a service requesting God's pardon for ''the infidelities to the Gospel . . . for violence some have used in the service of the truth and for the distrustful and hostile attitudes sometimes taken toward the followers of other religions.'' The service specifically mentioned ''the words and attitudes caused by pride, by hatred, by the desire to dominate others, by enmity toward members of other religions . . . .''

His expressions of sorrow and acts of affection have created a positive environment for interreligious relations. Religious leaders who spent the day of prayer with him in Assisi spoke of the informal moments together when he would linger with several of them, listening attentively to what they had to say. At the end of his encyclical on mission, John Paul II added a personal observation: ''My contact with representatives of the non-Christian spiritual traditions, particularly those in Asia, has confirmed me in the view that the future of mission depends to a great extent on contemplation'' (*Re-*

demptoris missio 91). His affection for spending time with religious leaders was illustrated again in the assembly of the World Conference on Religion and Peace in 1994. This occurred just after the close the special assembly of the Synod of Bishops on consecrated religious life. He arrived at the synod hall, entered up the stairs, looked out over the audience of various representatives in their diverse ceremonial attire, and observed how this was like another synod of Rome. After his address, he sat with other religious leaders at the front desk listening to the speeches, praying his rosary as a Buddhist sat next to him fingering his beads, and a Muslim on the panel was praying with his. Finally, after much urging from Vatican officials, he got up to make his next appointment for which he was already late. The participants also rose and pressed towards the main desk. After shaking a few hands, he expressed his regret that he could not greet everyone personally but exclaimed, ''Come back, Rome is always open.'' Over two hundred guests returned to Rome five years later on the eve of the Jubilee Year 2000 for an interreligious assembly. At the concluding ceremony on 28 October, 1999, Usha Mehta, an elderly Hindu woman had been one of Gandhi's disciples, apologized to the pope and to all Christians for any abuse committed against Christians in India and joined her wishes with those of other Indians in welcoming John Paul II to India in the next few days. On that November 1999 pilgrimage to India, his second, he came as a silent, elderly pilgrim to Raj Ghat, bent over with age and barefooted, pausing for a prayer.

The Spirit and the Religions

In *Redemptor hominis,* Pope John Paul indicated a particular theme he would emphasize for interreligious relations: discernment of the Spirit working among peoples of other religions. First, he listed the various activities by which Christians may come closer to representatives of non-Christian religions—''through dialogue, contacts, prayers in common, investigation of the treasures of human spirituality, in which, as we know well, the members of these religions also are not lacking''—and then he reiterated this conciliar teaching: ''the firm belief of the followers of the non-Christian religions . . . is also an effect of the Spirit of truth operating outside the visible confines of the Mystical Body'' (6). Drawing from the Gospel of John (3:8), he urged respect for everything that has been brought to humanity by the Spirit that ''blows where it wills,'' and pointed out how this teaching was succinctly stated in the conciliar text on the church in the modern world (*Gaudium et spes* 22). His message to the peoples of Asia, delivered from Manilla in 1981, refers to ''praiseworthy elements of spiritual growth'' and ''the potential for spiritual living

which so deeply marks the traditions and cultures of whole societies.'' In that text, he delved into the theological implications of the universal importance of the need for prayer: ''wherever the human spirit opens itself in prayer to this Unknown God, an echo will be heard of the same Spirit, who, knowing the limits and weakness of the human person, himself prays in us and on our behalf.'' In 1986 the encyclical *Dominum et vivificantem* (1986), issued several months before the day of prayer in Assisi, he returned to both the gospel and conciliar texts in a passage on the action of the Holy Spirit ''in every place and at every time, indeed in every individual'' (53).

The pope devoted his 1986 annual December message to the Roman Curia entirely to the world day of prayer for peace in Assisi, calling it ''the religious event that attracted the greatest attention in the world in this year'' and marveled at how ''at Assisi, in an extraordinary way, there was the discovery of the unique value that prayer has for peace. . . . the prayer of all, each one in his own identity and in search of the truth.'' The event graphically illustrated the emphasis he had been placing on the role of the Holy Spirit: ''We can indeed maintain that every authentic prayer is called forth by the Holy Spirit, who is mysteriously present in the heart of every person.'' In *Redemptoris missio* he reiterated these observations, cited his observations on Assisi, and drew attention to the mysterious work of the Holy Spirit that touches every individual. He commended other religious traditions for providing their followers with an experience of the Spirit that ''enlightens them in a way which is accommodated to their spiritual and material situation'' (*Redemptoris missio* 10). In the section on interreligious dialogue, Pope John Paul clarified that work of the Spirit is not simply an action on all individuals apart from the collective value of their religious traditions for God ''does not fail to make himself present in many ways, not only to individuals but also to entire peoples through their spiritual riches, of which their religions are the main and essential expression'' (*Redemptoris missio* 55). This is, perhaps, the most explicitly commendatory statement in papal teaching about the value of other religions and suggests that the religions themselves may participate in the mediation of salvation. The pope alluded to this possibility earlier in the encyclical: ''Although participated forms of mediation of different kinds and degrees are not excluded, they acquire meaning and value only from Christ's own mediation, and they cannot be understood as parallel or complementary to this'' (*Redemptoris missio* 5).

Evangelization and Dialogue

The encyclical on mission marked the twenty-fifth anniversary of the conciliar text on mission (*De gentes*) and the fifteenth anniversary of Paul VI's apostolic exhortation on evangelization (*Evangelii nuntiandi*). Paul VI had reminded Catholics that "neither our respect for these religions nor the high esteem in which we hold them nor the complexity of the question involved should deter the Church from proclaiming the message of Jesus Christ to these non-Christians" (53). John Paul II's words in *Redemptoris missio* are more direct: "Interreligious dialogue is part of the Church's evangelizing mission," "the Church sees no conflict between proclaiming Christ and engaging in interreligious dialogue," and "dialogue should be conducted and implemented with the conviction that the church is the ordinary means of salvation and that she alone possesses the fullness of the means of salvation" (55).

The link between a genuine desire for interreligious dialogue and the firm responsibility to proclaim the gospel as two distinct though interconnected aspects of evangelization has been another resounding message of John Paul II. In his first address to the Secretariat for Non-Christians he noted how "the Secretariat is a symbol and expression of the Church's will to enter into communication with every person" and commented how "a Christian finds it of the highest interest to observe truly religious people, to read and listen to the testimonies of their wisdom, and to have direct proof of their faith" like Jesus commending the centurion's faith in the gospel (Mt 8:10). He recalled the testimony of the apostles on Pentecost and the "tremendous responsibility and the immense joy" of recalling the mighty works of God for the salvation of all, especially in Jesus Christ.

John Paul II has often undertaken journeys for the stated dual purposes of evangelization and dialogue. From the start of his first pilgrimage to Africa, he greeted all the inhabitants of Africa, first all Catholics and other Christians and then all "inspired by religious sentiments, intent upon submitting their lives to God or seeking his presence" ("submitting to God" is a translation of word "Islam"). He said he was coming to Africa as a spiritual leader and servant of Jesus Christ on a mission of evangelization to strengthen the members of the church in the true faith and as a man of religion with esteem for "the religious sense so deeply rooted in the African soul." Three days later he spoke with Muslim leaders in Kenya and combined the themes of witness and dialogue: "As the Catholic Church makes every effort to sustain religious dialogue with Islam on the basis of existing bonds, which she endeavors every more to reflect on, she likewise extends the invitation that her own heritage be fully known, especially to those who are spiritually attached to Abraham, and who profess monotheism."

The pope was giving theological importance to a simple fact of interreligious dialogue, namely, that it is a sustained and intentional encounter between persons of different religious convictions and traditions. Its goals are mutual understanding and respect, cooperation in the service of humanity, a common search for the truth, and the mutual enrichment resulting from the exploration of one another's spiritual paths. Thus persons of conviction dialogue while witnessing to one another their beliefs. In *Redemptoris missio* he cautioned that "these two elements must maintain both their intimate connection and their distinctiveness; therefore they should not be confused, manipulated or regarded as identical, as though they were interchangeable" (55). He continued for two more paragraphs on the nature of dialogue, which he says "does not originate from tactical concerns or self-interest." The pope calls other religions "a positive challenge for the church" for they challenge Christians to acknowledge what is true and good within others and to examine themselves more deeply about how well they bear witness to what is true and good. Thus, he says, "those engaged in this dialogue must be consistent with their own religious traditions and convictions, and be open to understanding those of the other party without pretense or closed-mindedness, but with truth, humility and frankness, knowing that dialogue can enrich each side." Returning to his other theme of the discernment of the action of the Holy Spirit in the lives and traditions of others, he concludes these reflections with the observation that "dialogue leads to inner purification and conversion, which, if pursued with docility to the Holy Spirit, will be spiritually fruitful" (56).

The pope expressed his strong support for interreligious dialogue, offered his positive evaluation of the religious and cultural traditions of all peoples, and explained very carefully the principles for dialogue in his encyclical on mission for several reasons. Not only are missionaries often engaged in interreligious dialogue, but so too are many Christians today, whether in lands where their numbers are proportionately small or in societies that are religiously diverse, are daily in contact with peoples of other faiths. Also, very often many Christians today have internalized interreligious dialogue, for Christians in Asia, Africa, Oceania, and among indigenous peoples live as Christians and as persons of their cultures. Therefore in their formation and education they already are learning the interaction between their faith as Christians and their lives as peoples of their cultures. Those who enter their environment as missionaries should receive correct and edifying information on the religious and cultural traditions.

Church teaching on inculturation, the mutual interaction and enrichment between the gospel and the people of a particular culture, arises out of the documents of the Second Vatican Council on interreligious dialogue, missionary activity, and the church in the modern world. John Paul II's discussion of inculturation in *Redemptoris missio* comes immediately before his discussion of dialogue with peoples of other religions. Perhaps his fullest treatment of inculturation appears in the apostolic exhortation *Ecclesia in Asia* (1999), based on the work of the special assembly for Asia of the Synod of Bishops. In several places in *Ecclesia in Asia* he reports how the Asian bishops who attended the synod drew attention to the positive values of the religions and cultures of Asia because the Holy Spirit "continually sows the seeds of truth among all peoples, their religions, cultures and philosophies" and thus these "are capable of helping people, individually and collectively, to work against evil and to serve life and everything that is good" (15). The pope cites the difficulties the bishops listed during the synod in the proclamation of Christ and the inculturation of the gospel for daily life on Asian soil. Inculturation, he notes, allows Christians to transmit the truth and values of their faith, aids the renewal of cultures from within, and enriches the whole life and development of the church. (21) On the same trip to India, he spoke to religious leaders and reaffirmed the nature of genuine dialogue: "This means that when wee hold firmly to what we believe, we listen respectfully to others, seeking to discern all that is good and holy, all that favors peace and cooperation."

In June 1991, six months after *Redemptoris missio,* the Pontifical Council for Interreligious Dialogue and the Congregation for the Evangelization of Peoples issued as a joint document, *Dialogue and Proclamation,* as a sign that the pope's sentiments about evangelization and its two interrelated yet distinct aspects of dialogue and witness would become further institutionalized in the structure of the church. With the publication of the *Catechism of the Catholic Church* (1992), the theological principles for interreligious relations and dialogue were further incorporated into the life of the church (27–8, 39, 839, 84–43, 846–48, 856, 1149, 2104, and 2569).

The momentous steps taken by Pope John Paul II in promoting interreligious dialogue, especially incorporating interreligious relations as a defining characteristic of his leadership of the Catholic Church in the third millennium of Christianity, may insure that this direction taken by the Second Vatican Council will occupy a significant place in the mission of the church and in the hearts of the peoples of faith whom he has touched for decades to come. Referring to the interreligious assembly hosted in Rome in November 1999 as "another step on that journey," he concluded his address with a prayer of hope: "In all the many languages of prayer, let us ask the Spirit of God to enlighten us, guide us and give us strength so that, as men and women who take their inspiration from their religious beliefs, we may work together to build the future of humanity in harmony, justice, peace and love."

See Also: ASSISI; DOMINUM ET VIVIFICANTEM; ECCLESIA IN ASIA; A PILGRIMAGE OF RECONCILIATION; REDEMPTOR HOMINIS; REDEMPTORIS MISSIO; TERTIO MILLENNIO ADVENIENTE; UT UNUM SINT; UT UNUM SINT: JOHN PAUL II'S ECUMENICAL COMMITMENT

Bibliography: Pontifical Council for Interreligious Dialogue, *Interreligious Dialogue. The Official Teaching of the Catholic Church (1963–1995),* edited by Francesco Gioia (Boston: Pauline Books and Media, 1992). Contains excerpts and entire texts of papal addresses and all documents of the Second Vatican Council and the Roman Curia on interreligious relations up to 1995. Subsequent documentation and pertinent articles and other materials can be found in other sources, *Pro Dialogo, Origins, CNS Documentary Service,* and *Catholic International.Pro Dialogo.* A bulletin issued approximately three times a year by the Pontifical Council for Interreligious Dialogue. Current issue: No. 103, 2000/1. Nos. 1–69 (1966–88) appeared as Bulletin, issued by the Secretariat for Non Christians. Nos. 70–84 (1989–93) appeared as *Bulletin,* issued by the Pontifical Council for Interreligious Dialogue.POPE JOHN PAUL II, *Spiritual Pilgrimage. Texts on Jews and Judaism* 1979–95, ed. by EUGENE J. FISHER and LEON KLENICKI (New York: Crossroad, 1995). LUIGI ACCATTOLI, *When a Pope Asks Forgiveness. The Mea Culpa's of John Paul II,* translated by JORDAN AUMANN, O.P., (Boston: Pauline Books and Media, 1998). JOHN BORELLI, "Catholics and Interreligious Relations," *MID Bulletin* (Monastic Interreligious Dialogue), no.64 (May 2000), special edition: "Christ of the 21st Century" Papers: 6–13. JOHN BORELLI, "The Catholic Church and Interreligious Dialogue," in *Vatican II. The Continuing Agenda,* edited by ANTHONY J. CERNERA (Fairfield, Conn.: Sacred Heart University Press, 1997), 89–111. WILLIAM R. BURROWS, *Redemption and Dialogue, Reading Redemptoris Missio and Dialogue and Proclamation*(Maryknoll, NY: Orbis Books, 1993). JACQUES DUPUIS, S.J., *Toward a Christian Theology of Religious Pluralism* (Maryknoll, NY: Orbis Books, 1997). DONALD W. MITCHELL, "The Making of a Joint Buddhist-Catholic Statement," *Buddhist-Christian Studies* no. 16 (1996): 203–8. "Special Feature Interreligious Dialogue," *The Living Light* 32, no. 2 (Winter 1995): 4–72. Quarterly Review published by the Department of Education, United States Catholic Conference. FRANCIS A. SULLIVAN, S.J., *Salvation Outside the Church? Tracing the History of the Catholic Response* (New York: Paulist Press, 1992).

[JOHN BORELLI]

A Pilgrimage of Reconciliation: From Wadowice to the Wailing Wall

Eugene J. Fisher, Ph.D., is associate director of Secretariat for Ecumenical and Interreligious Affairs, National Conference of Catholic Bishops, Washington, D.C.

In the Jubilee Year 2000, Pope John Paul II fulfilled a dream that he had spoken of since early in his pontificate, to visit the Holy Land, the sacred geography where Jesus, the Jew of Nazareth, was born, preached his saving truths, and died at the hands of the Roman Empire. In so doing, he fulfilled another dream as well, quite consciously and purposefully, a dream also of the Jewish people, and at the same time a dream of the Fathers of the Church gathered for the Second Vatican Council thirty-five years earlier: the dream of reconciliation between the Catholic Church and the Jewish people. Few pilgrimages in the two millennia of Christian history have had such pregnant hopes and such significant results.

John Paul II's pontificate has seen more progress in Catholic-Jewish relations, and certainly more dramatic gestures toward the Jewish people by the bishop of Rome than occurred during the reigns of all of his predecessors combined. This remarkably open Pope has worn his heart on his sleeve, telegraphing his hopes for all to see, yet moving with magisterial prudence, step by step, toward goals that appeared impossibly distant on the horizon when he assumed his office in 1978.

The pope has spoken on Judaism on numerous occasions and in a remarkably wide range of locations throughout the world. Virtually wherever he has traveled, there exists a Jewish community, whether large, as in the United States, or tragically small, as in the tiny remnant of the once-flourishing Jewish community of Poland; and wherever he goes he seeks out those communities to reach out to them in reconciliation and affirmation of the infinite worth of Judaism's continuing proclamation of the name of the One God in the world.

The papal talks and gestures discussed here provide a record of a profound spiritual pilgrimage for the pope and the Church, almost two millennia after the Church's birth as a Jewish movement in the land and among the people of Israel. One finds in them a growth and development in the pope's understanding of and appreciation for how "the Jews define themselves in the light of their own religious experience" (Commission for Religious Relations with the Jews, *Guidelines and Suggestions for Implementing the Conciliar Declaration "Nostra Aetate," No. 4* [1974], prologue, cited by the pope in his first address to representatives of Jewish organizations, 12 March 1979 [Fisher and Klenicki 1995, 5]). This development teaches the Church how it too must reinterpret its relationship to the Jewish people as "people of God."

Motivation

The pope has spoken of the Jewish friends of his youth on many occasions, including in his personal reflection, *Crossing the Threshold of Hope,* and in meeting with some of the few survivors among them during his prayerful visit to Israel's memorial to the victims of the Holocaust (Shoah), Yad VaShem, on his Jubilee pilgrimage there in 2000.

The pope grew up in Wadowice in the 1930s, one of many Polish towns which, like much of Poland, has endured shifting sovereignties over the centuries. Had he been born thirty years earlier, Karol Wojtyła would have been considered an Austrian citizen, though indubitably a Pole at heart. Jews made up a substantial minority of Wadowice's citizens in Wojtyła's youth, as they had for centuries. Poland, indeed, at that time enjoyed the distinction of having the world's largest Jewish population and the greatest concentration of Jewish centers of learning in Jewish history. Jews had been welcomed into Poland throughout the late Middle Ages when they were exiled from most of the countries of Western Europe. By the time of Wojtyła's youth they had been an integral part of Polish society and history for nearly a thousand years, enriching it culturally, intellectually, and (though not all Poles would acknowledge this) spiritually as well. There were antisemitic Catholics in Wadowice, of course, but according to Jerzy Kluger, one of the pope's childhood

The destruction of the Warsaw Ghetto in the spring of 1943. (AP/Wide World Photos. Reproduced by permission.)

friends, these were relatively few and normally contained by other Polish Catholic youth.

When Nazi Germany invaded Poland, a centuries-long and mutually beneficial co-existence of Polish Jews and Polish Catholics was forever destroyed. In an astonishingly brief period of time the ancient Polish-Jewish community, and many close friends of Wojtyła's youth, were systematically hunted down by the Germans, "concentrated" first in newly erected ghettos and then into "labor" camps, and finally, just as systematically murdered. Poles who know their history say that this loss of the significant Jewish segment of "Polonia" represents one of the greatest tragedies of Polish history.

This great loss happened on Polish soil to its Polish citizens of Jewish descent. For Wojtyła, the loss was both national and personal. And it was unhealable. Poland would never, could never, be the same again. John Paul II remains to this day quite attached to the friends of his youth, having organized and continued regular class reunions of his high school classmates—those who survived the war—not only as archbishop and cardinal, but even as pope. When he speaks of feeling still the presence of the Jewish victims of Nazi genocide, as he did for example at the 1994 Vatican concert memorializing them on Yom HaShoah that year, he is to be believed. The Holocaust, for this pope, was a personal event. It happened not to "them," but to him, to his friends and to his friends' parents, relatives, families. It is no wonder, then, that no one, Jewish, Christian, or secular-academic, has done more to defeat so-called "Holocaust denial" than John Paul II.

He evoked this sense of personal loss and remembrance poignantly during the Yom HaShoah Concert at the Vatican (1994), commemorating the Holocaust:

> Among those who are with us this evening are some who physically underwent a horrendous experience, crossing a dark wilderness where the

John Paul II celebrates mass at the traditional site of the Last Supper on Mount Zion, 23 March 2000. (AP/Wide World Photos. Photograph by Arturo Mari.)

very source of love seemed dried up. Many wept at that time, and we still hear echoes of their lament. We hear it here too; their plea did not die with them but rises powerful, agonizing, heart-rending, saying, "Do not forget us!" It is addressed to one and all. Thus we are gathered this evening to commemorate the Holocaust of millions of Jews. The candles lit by some of the survivors are intended to show symbolically that this hall does not have narrow limits. It contains all the victims: fathers, mothers, sons, daughters, brothers, sisters, and friends. In our memory they are all present, they are with you, they are with us (Fisher and Klenicki 1995, 188–89).

Rabbi James Rubin, one of the organizers, was standing quite close to the pope when John Paul spoke these words. The pope, Rabbi Rudin reports, could see real faces of real people in his mind as he spoke. He spoke the words to them, the murdered friends of his youth.

The pope's personal "stake" in what happened to the Jews of Europe, the families and the friends of his youth, explains much about the concentration on Catholic-Jewish relations that has so marked his pontificate.

His personal caring also launched him on a journey of theological discovery, of careful reconsideration of the essential nature of the Church's understanding of its relationship with the people of Jesus and Mary, the Jews, and of the faith they have held dear through centuries of discrimination and persecution.

Building a Theological Bridge of Hope and Reconciliation

The ongoing papal reconsideration over the years and gradual, step-by-cautious-step redefinition of ancient theological categories represent the fruits of a painstaking effort, supported by the efforts of Catholics and Jews in dialogue throughout the world, as the pope has acknowledged ("Historic Visit to the Synagogue of Rome" [1986], no. 4; Fisher and Klenicki 1995, 60 73), to articulate anew the mystery of the Church in the light of a positive articulation of the abiding mystery of Israel. The results are as breathtaking as they have been painstaking.

Progress since the Second Vatican Council has been measured in small steps: a word uttered here to clarify an awkward phrase there; a slightly less ambiguous wording to replace a more ambiguous, potentially misleading theological formula; and so forth. But the direction is clear and the basic message starkly unambiguous: The Church is not alone in the world as "People of God." The Church is joined by the Jewish people in its proclamation of the oneness of God and the true nature of human history, which Jews and Christians alike pray daily, and through their prayers, proclaim universally (cf. Commission for Religious Relations with the Jews, *Notes on the Correct Presentation of the Jews and Judaism in Catholic Preaching and Teaching* [1985] II, 9 11). The following thematic categories serve to organize some of these small steps and interventions by which the pope has sought to frame and to move forward the Church's side of historic dialogue between Catholics and Jews.

The Spiritual Bond between the Church and the Jewish People. The notion of a "spiritual bond" linking the Church and the Jewish people ("Abraham's stock") was central to the Second Vatican Council's Declaration on the Relationship of the Church to Non-Christian Religions, *Nostra aetate.* It has become a major theme of John Paul II's own reflections on the subject over the years, one that he has constantly tried to probe and refine. In his first address to Jewish representatives, for example, he interpreted the conciliar phrase as meaning "that our two religious communities are connected and closely related at the very level of their respective identities" (Fisher and Klenicki 1995, 4), and he spoke of "fraternal dialogue" between the two.

Using terms such as *fraternal* and addressing one another as *brothers* and *sisters* reflect ancient usage within the Christian community. They imply an acknowledgment of a commonality of faith, with liturgical implications. It was an ecumenical breakthrough, for example, when the Second Vatican Council and Pope Paul VI began the practice of addressing Orthodox and Protestant Christians in such terms. John Paul II's extension of this terminology to Jews is by no means accidental. The relationship reaches to the very essence of the nature of Christian faith itself, so that to deny it is to deny something essential to the teaching of the Church (cf. *Notes,* I, 2). The spiritual bond with Jews, for the pope, is properly understood as a "'sacred' one, stemming as it does from the mysterious will of God" (Fisher and Klenicki 1995, 56).

In bringing this lesson home, the pope has used startling and powerful language. In his important allocution to the Jewish community of Mainz, West Germany (1980), for example, he likened the relationship to that between "the first and second part" of the Christian Bible. The dialogue between Catholics and Jews is not a dialogue between past (Judaism) and present (Christianity) realities, as if the former had been "superseded"

or "replaced" by the latter, as certain Christian polemicists would have it. "On the contrary," the pope made clear in Mainz, "it is a question rather of reciprocal enlightenment and explanation, just as is the relationship between the Scriptures themselves" (cf. *Dei Verbum,* 11; Fisher and Klenicki 1995, 15).

In this vein, the pope has also moved Catholics to formulate more sensitive biblical terminology. The pope cautions against interpreting the "old" in "Old Testament" to mean that it has been abrogated in favor of the "new;" he suggests using the term "the Hebrew Scriptures" ("Address to the Jewish Community in Australia" [1986]; Fisher and Klenicki 1995, 83).

In the pope's view, so close is the spiritual bond between the two peoples of God that the dialogue is properly considered—unlike any other relationship between the Church and a world religion—to be "a dialogue within our Church" (Mainz, 1980; Fisher and Klenicki 1995, 15). Interpreting *Nostra aetate* during his visit to the Rome Synagogue, the pope brought these themes to a dramatic culmination:

> The Church of Christ discovers her "bond" with Judaism by "searching into her own mystery" (*Nostra Aetate,* 4). The Jewish religion is not "extrinsic" to us, but in a certain way is "intrinsic" to our own religion. With Judaism, therefore, we have a relationship which we do not have with any other religion. You are dearly beloved brothers and, in a certain way, it could be said that you are our elder brothers (Rome, 1986; Fisher and Klenicki 1995, 63).

A Living Heritage. The phrase, "elder brothers," used here with caution, raises the question of how the pope has dealt with the sometimes awkward (for Christians) question of the Church's spiritual debt to Judaism. This debt has been acknowledged, traditionally—as in medieval canon law's exception allowing Jews freedom of worship (within certain limitations), a right granted to no other religious group outside Christianity.

Yet the acknowledgment often came negatively. For many Christians over the ages, for example, the application of the term *elder brother* to the Jews would have conjured images of apologetic interpretations of the younger/elder brother stories of Genesis in which the younger brother takes over the heritage or patrimony of the elder (e.g., Esau and Jacob). The powerful imagery of the Gothic cathedrals of Europe is another example of this. Juxtaposed on either side of the portals of many medieval cathedrals is a statue of the Synagogue (portrayed in the physical form of a woman), her head bowed, holding a broken staff of the Law, with the tablets of the Ten Commandments slipping from her fingers, and a statue of the Church, resplendently erect and triumphant. The pairings symbolized for the medieval artists the passage of the covenant from Judaism to Christianity.

The pope has sought to reinterpret ancient apologetics and to replace negative images with positive affirmations. In his address to the Jewish community in Mainz, he cited a passage from a declaration of the bishops of the Federal Republic of Germany, issued earlier that year, calling attention to "the spiritual heritage of Israel for the Church." He added to the citation, however, a single word that removed any possible ambiguity and opened up a new area of theological reflection, calling it "a *living* heritage, which must be understood and preserved in its depths and richness by us Catholic Christians" (Mainz, 1980; Fisher and Klenicki 1995, 14).

In March 1982, speaking to delegates from episcopal conferences gathered in Rome from around the world to discuss ways to foster improved Catholic-Jewish relations, the pope confirmed and advanced this direction in his thought:

> Christians have taken the right path, that of justice and brotherhood, in seeking to come together with their Semitic brethren, respectfully and perseveringly, in the common heritage, a heritage that all value so highly. . . . To assess it carefully in itself and with due awareness of the faith and religious life of the Jewish people *as they are professed and practiced still today,* can greatly help us to understand better certain aspects of the life of the Church (Fisher and Klenicki 1995, 18–19; italics added).

The "common spiritual patrimony" of Jews and Christians, then, is not something of the past but of the present. Just as the Church, through the writings of its doctors and saints and the statements of its councils, has developed a rich tradition interpreting and clarifying its spiritual heritage, so has Judaism developed, through rabbinic literature and the Talmud, through Jewish philosophers and mystics, what was given to it in its founding by God (see *Notes,* VI). The pope calls us to understand the "common spiritual patrimony" not only positively but assertively as a joint witness of God's truth to the world: "Jews and Christians are the trustees and witnesses of an ethic marked by the Ten Commandments in the observance of which man finds his truth and freedom" (Rome, 1986; Fisher and Klenicki 1995, 65).

Permanent Validity of God's Covenant with the Jewish People. Underlying the previous considerations is a central message, implicit in the teaching of the Second Vatican Council, that John Paul II has made explicit. Not only *Nostra aetate* but also the Dogmatic Constitution on the Church, *Lumen gentium,* drew upon the strong

affirmation of St. Paul in Rom. 11:28–29 when seeking to define the role of the Jewish people in God's plan of salvation, even after the time of Christ: "On account of their fathers, this people [the Jews] remains most dear to God, for God does not repent of the gifts He makes nor of the calls He issues" (*Lumen gentium* 16).

Logically, the conciliar affirmation means that Jews remain God's chosen people in the fullest sense ("most dear"). This affirmation, the pope teaches, is unequivocal and in no way diminishes the Church's own affirmation of its own standing as "people of God." In Mainz, the pope addressed the Jewish community with full respect as "the people of God of the Old Covenant, which has never been revoked by God," and emphasized the "permanent value" of both the Hebrew Scriptures and the Jewish community that witnesses to those Scriptures as sacred texts (Mainz, 1980; Fisher and Klenicki 1995, 15).

In meeting with representatives of episcopal conferences, the pope stressed the present tense of Rom. 9:4–5 concerning the Jewish people, "who have the adoption as sons, and the glory and the covenants and the legislation and the worship and the promises" (Rome, 1982; Fisher and Klenicki 1995, 18), while also affirming "the universal salvific significance of the death and resurrection of Jesus of Nazareth" (ibid.). The pope does not seek a superficial reconciling of these two great truths but affirms them both together, commenting: "This means that the links between the Church and the Jewish people are founded on the design of the God of the Covenant" (ibid.).

The pope's remarkable formulation in Australia distills years of theological development: "The Catholic faith is rooted in the eternal truths of the Hebrew Scriptures and in the irrevocable covenant made with Abraham. We, too, gratefully hold these same truths of our Jewish heritage and look upon you as our brothers and sisters in the Lord" (Australia, 1986; Fisher and Klenicki 1995, 83).

Catechetics and Liturgy. The pope insists that this renewed vision of the relationship between Judaism and Christianity must permeate every area of church life. In his address to representatives of episcopal conferences, for example, the pope stressed the need for Catholics to know the Jewish roots of their liturgy, and for catechesis to involve a full appreciation of the Jewish heritage (Rome, 1982; Fisher and Klenicki 1995, 19). In his response to the International Conference of Christians and Jews, the pope noted that the "great common spiritual patrimony" shared by Jews and Christians rests on a "solid" foundation of "faith in a God . . . as a loving father . . . in a common basic liturgical pattern, and in a common commitment, grounded in faith, to all men and women in need, who are our 'neighbors' (cf. Lev. 19:18, Mark 12:32, and parallels)'' (Rome, 1984; Fisher and Klenicki 1995, 42). Catechesis and the liturgy itself have as a primary goal making clear the ''spiritual bond'' that links the Church to the people Israel (cf. *Notes,* II, VI). Also needing to be made clear to Catholic youth is the often tragic history of Christian-Jewish relations over the centuries (Rome, 1984; Fisher and Klenicki 1995, 42).

At the time of his visit to the Rome Synagogue, the pope reminded ''my brothers and sisters of the Catholic Church'' of the 1974 *Guidelines* and the 1985 *Notes* issued by the Holy See's Commission for Religious Relations with the Jews. The pope concluded that ''it is only a question of studying them carefully, of immersing oneself in their teachings, and of putting them into practice'' (Rome, 1986; Fisher and Klenicki 1995, 64).

The *Catechism of the Catholic Church* duly reflects these papal concerns flowing out of the Second Vatican Council. In the section on the Creed, ''Jesus Christ Suffered under Pontius Pilate, was Crucified, Died and Was Buried'' (571–98), the Catechism devotes considerable attention to a nuanced discussion of Jesus' relationship to his people, Israel; to God's Law, the Torah; to the Jerusalem Temple; and to ''Israel's Faith in the One God and Savior.'' Rather than pillorying ''the Jews'' as earlier catechisms might have done, it stresses the ''ignorance'' of ''the Sanhedrin's tragic misunderstanding'' (591). It is noteworthy that the Catechism speaks specifically of certain ''religious authorities of Jerusalem,'' as did *Nostra aetate,* rather than collectively of the Jews as a people. The Catechism reminds the reader of the depth of the mystery of salvation in Christ, and, indeed, of the ''act of faith'' itself. It stresses the ''divisions among Jewish authorities concerning Jesus' death,'' so that readers will not stereotype the religious leadership of the Jews of Jesus' time, much less the people as a whole. The Catechism devotes two very strong paragraphs to debunking any remaining temptation that Christians might have to blaming the Jews as a people, then or now, for Jesus' death: ''Jews are not collectively responsible for Jesus' death'' (597) and ''all sinners were the authors of Christ's passion (598).

Paragraphs 839 and 840 similarly summarize both papal themes and those of statements of the Holy See's Commission for Religious Relations with the Jews, especially the 1985 Notes. The Jewish People are called (following the wording of the revised Good Friday Prayer for the Jews of the Roman Missal) ''the first to hear the Word of God.'' ''The Jewish Faith,'' the Catechism states, ''unlike other non-Christian religions, is already a response to God's Revelation in the Old Testament.'' Jews and Christians, the section concludes are similarly posed in the perspective of the history of salvation: ''When one considers the future,'' Jews and Christians ''tend toward similar goals: expectation of the coming (or the return) of the Messiah.'' The Catechism represents the official teaching of the magisterium and as such provides a solid doctrinal basis for theological dialogue between the Church and the Jewish People leading toward joint witness to sacred truths we share in common, as well as joint action for the betterment of humanity.

Condemnations of Anti-Semitism and Remembrances of the Shoah

In his first audience with Jewish representatives, the pope reaffirmed the Second Vatican Council's repudiation of anti-Semitism ''as opposed to the very spirit of Christianity,'' and ''which in any case the dignity of the human person alone would suffice to condemn'' (Rome, 1979; Fisher and Klenicki 1995, 5). The pope has repeated this message in country after country throughout the world, calling on Catholics, especially in Europe, to remember, ''in particular, the memory of the people whose sons and daughters were intended for total extermination'' (''Homily at Auschwitz'' [1979]; Fisher and Klenicki 1995, 7). From the intensity of his own experience, the pope is able both to articulate the *uniqueness* of the Jewish experience of the *Shoah* and to revere the memory of all of Nazism's millions of non-Jewish victims. (The pope would, it may be appropriate to say, agree unreservedly with the formulation of Elie Wiesel: ''Not every victim of the Holocaust was a Jew, but every Jew was a victim.'')

In his 1987 address to the Jews of Warsaw, the pope acknowledged the priority as well as uniqueness of Jewish suffering in the *Shoah*: ''It was you who suffered this terrible sacrifice of extermination: one might say that you suffered it also on behalf of those who were likewise to be exterminated'' (Warsaw, 1987; Fisher and Klenicki 1995, 99). From this, he derives the very significant theological insight that the Jewish witness to the *Shoah* is for the Church as well as for all of humanity, a ''saving warning,'' indeed a continuation ''in the contemporary world'' of the prophetic mission itself. The Church, in turn, is called to listen to this uniquely Jewish proclamation and to unite its voice to that of the Jewish people in their continuing ''particular vocation,'' one may say, to be a light to the nations.

The order of the pope's theological reflection on the *Shoah* is important. As he stated in a letter to Archbishop John L. May (1987), an ''authentic'' approach first grapples with the ''specific,'' and therefore specifically Jewish reality of the event. Only then, and with this continually in mind, can one begin to seek out its more ''universal meaning'' (Fisher and Klenicki 1995, 100–101).

In Miami, the pope spoke of the "mystery of the suffering of Israel's children," and he calls on Christians to learn from the "acute insights" of "Jewish thinkers" on the human condition and to develop in dialogue with Jews "common educational programs which . . . will teach future generations about the Holocaust so that never again will such a horror be possible. Never again!" (Miami, 1987; Fisher and Klenicki 1995, 108). From "the suffering and martyrdom of the Jewish people," understood within the context of their "constant progression in faith and obedience to the loving call of God" over the centuries, then, our remembrance of the *Shoah* may lead to "a much deeper hope . . . a saving cry of warning for the whole human race" (Vienna, 1988; Fisher and Klenicki 1995, 121), a prophetic "prick of conscience" that may tell us "what message our century [can] convey to the next" (Mauthausen, 1988; Fisher and Klenicki 1995, 118).

Over the years, Pope John Paul has issued strong statements of condemnation of acts of terrorism against synagogues and Jewish communities, sending messages of sympathy for their victims. He has also seldom missed a chance to remind Europeans of the *Shoah*. He has frequently cited the statement of the Thirteenth International Catholic-Jewish Liaison Committee meeting held in Prague with its call for Christian "*teshuvah* (repentance)" for anti-Semitism over the centuries and its statement that anti-Semitism is "a sin against God and humanity" (cited in Pontifical Council on Christian Unity, *Information Service*, no. 75, 4:172–78), in order to place that joint statement firmly within Catholic teaching. On 26 September 1990, in his annual Jasna Góra meditation celebrating the feast of Our Lady of Częstochowa, the pope spoke as a Pole to his fellow Poles, reminding them:

> There is yet another nation, a particular people, the people of the Patriarchs, of Moses and the Prophets, the heirs of the faith of Abraham. . . . This people lived arm and arm with us for generations on that same land which became a kind of new homeland during the Diaspora. This people was afflicted by the terrible deaths of millions of its sons and daughters. First they were marked with special signs, then they were shoved into ghettos, isolated quarters. Then they were carried off to the gas chambers, put to death simply because they were the sons and daughters of this people. The assassins did all this in our land, perhaps to cloak it in infamy. However, one cannot cloak a land in infamy by the death of innocent victims. By such deaths the land becomes a sacred relic. The people who lived with us for many generations has remained with us after the terrible death of millions of its sons and daughters. Together we await the Day of Judgment and Resurrection" ibid., 4:172).

In September 1997, John Paul II convened in Rome a symposium of theologians and historians to analyze the relationship between Christian anti-Judaism and modern, racial antisemitism. He saw the former as at least a contributing cause leading to the development of the latter, though by no means the only (or even the main) cause. He spoke of how centuries of Christian anti-Judaic teachings based upon serious "misunderstandings" of the New Testament itself, had by the twentieth century so "lulled the consciences" of many Christians in Europe that when the test came with the rise of Hitler and his ideology of antisemitic hatred, they "failed to act as the world had a right to expect."

Similarly, the 1998 Vatican document *We Remember: A Reflection on the Shoah* noted the distinction between Nazism's racist ideology and traditional Christian theological polemics against Judaism and the "blindness" of the Jews themselves, on the hand, and by implication the historic fact that the latter paved the way for the former by its constant, centuries-old attribution of negative stereotypes to Jews and Judaism, lulling the conscience, as it were, of a continent.

The document concluded with this call to repentance:

> At the end of this millennium the Catholic Church desires to express her deep sorrow for the failures of her sons and daughters (toward the Jews) in every age. This is an act of repentance (*teshuvah*), since as members of the Church we are linked to the sins as well as the merits of all her children. . . . It is not a matter of mere words, but indeed of binding commitment. . . . We pray that our sorrow for the tragedy which the Jewish people has suffered in our century will lead to a new relationship with the Jewish people. We wish to turn awareness of past sins into a firm resolve to build a new future in which there will be no more anti-Judaism among Christians or anti-Christian sentiment among Jews, but rather a shared mutual respect as befits those who adore the one Creator and Lord and have a common father in faith, Abraham." (*Catholics Remember the Holocaust*, Washington, DC: U.S. Catholic Conference, 1998).

In the week prior to his Jubilee Year pilgrimage to Israel, on the first Sunday of Lent, 2000, during the Mass at St. Peter's, the pope modified the penitential rite into a prayer for forgiveness for the sins of Catholics throughout the past millennium. The prayer is remarkable in many ways. It divides the sinfulness of the repentant Church into seven categories, one of which is the centuries of sins against the Jews. A few days before the pope's liturgical prayer, the International Theological Commission, chaired by Cardinal Joseph Ratzinger, issued a lengthy document that defines with greater specificity what the calls for God's forgiveness meant in each case. Section 5.4 of the document, referring to *We Remember,* quite specifically raises the question of the Church's ancient teaching of anti-Judaism and the Holocaust: "it may be asked whether the Nazi persecution of the Jews was not made easier by the anti-Jewish prejudices imbedded in some Christian minds and hearts."

Finally, at Yad VaShem, Israel's memorial to the victims of the Holocaust during his historic pilgrimage to the Holy Land, the pope observed a moment of prayerful silence and then intoned:

> In this place of memories, the mind and heart and soul feel an extreme need for silence. Silence in which to remember. Silence in which to try to make some sense of the memories which come flooding back. Silence because there are no words strong enough to deplore the terrible tragedy of the Shoah. My own personal memories are of all that happened when the Nazis occupied Poland during the war. I remember my Jewish friends and neighbors, some of whom perished while others survived. . . . We wish to remember. But we wish to remember for a purpose, namely to ensure that never again will evil prevail as it did for millions of innocent victims of Nazism. . . . As Bishop of Rome and successor of the Apostle Peter, I assure the Jewish people that the Catholic Church, motivated by the gospel law of truth and love and by no other consideration, is deeply saddened by the hatred, acts of persecution and displays of antisemitism directed against Jews by Christians at any time and in any place. In this place of solemn remembrance, I fervently pray that our sorrow for the tragedy which the Jewish people suffered in the twentieth century will lead to a new relationship between Jews and Christians. Let us build a new future in which there will be no more anti-Jewish feeling among Christians or anti-Christian feeling among Jews, but rather the mutual respect required of those who adore the one Creator and Lord, and look to Abraham as our common father in faith. (Jerusalem, 23 March 2000)

Many Israelis in attendance, survivors and politicians, religious leaders and security officers, cried. Prime Minister Ehud Barak, himself a former general not given to sentimentality, spoke equally from his heart:

> When my grandparents, Elka and Shmuel Godin, mounted the death trains at Umschlagplatz near their home in Warsaw, headed toward their fate in Treblinka—the fate of three million Jews from your homeland—you were there, and you remembered. You have done more than than anyone else to bring about the historic change in the attitude of the church toward the Jewish people, initiated

by the good Pope John XXIII, and to dress the gaping wounds that festered over many bitter centuries.

Land and State of Israel

On 30 December 1993, representatives of the Holy See and the State of Israel signed in Jerusalem the *Fundamental Agreement* that would lead the way to full diplomatic "normalization of relations" between the two. On 16 August 1994, the apostolic pro-nuncio, Archbishop Montezemolo, presented his credentials to President Chaim Weizman of the State of Israel as the first ambassador of the Holy See to the Jewish State. As the *Fundamental Agreement* acknowledged, this was not just a moment of international diplomacy between two tiny Mediterranean states. It was a theologically significant moment in the nearly two-millennia-long history of the relationship between the Jewish people and the Catholic Church.

The pope's references to Israel over the years have been positive ones, as they have been positive as well toward the Palestinians as a people. This essentially supportive attitude was expressed as early as his apostolic letter *Redemptionis Anno* (1984), and was cited by him many times after that.

The implications for Catholic religious education preaching of this papal affirmation of the right of the Jewish State to existence and security were drawn out in theological terms in the 1985 *Notes,* which distinguished between land, people, and State of Israel, affirming each appropriately. In the process, the Vatican document gave a positive theological interpretation of the Diaspora as Israel's universal and "often heroic" witness to the world. Christians are invited to understand this religious attachment of Jews to the land of their forefathers, which finds its roots in biblical tradition, without, however, making their own any particular religious interpretation of this relationship. The existence of the State of Israel and its political options should be envisaged not in a perspective which is in itself religious but in their reference to the common principles of international law.

Over the years the pope has increasingly expressed his deep concerns over and profound hopes for the Holy City: "Jerusalem, called to be a crossroads of peace, cannot continue to be the cause of discord and dispute. I fervently hope that some day circumstances will allow me to go as a pilgrim to that city which is unique in all the world, in order to issue again from there, together with Jewish, Christian and Muslim believers, [the] message of peace" (Rome, 1991; Fisher and Klenicki 1995, 144). "What a blessing it would be if this Holy Land, where God spoke and Jesus walked, could become a special place of encounter and prayer for peoples, if the Holy City of Jerusalem could be a sign and instrument of peace and reconciliation'' (Rome, 1992; Fisher and Klenicki 1995, 162).

This is, again, language redolent with theological nuance in Catholic terms. ''A sign and instrument of peace and reconciliation'' is specifically *sacramental* language. To use it of an earthly city, albeit one with a ''heavenly'' analogue according to both Jewish and Christian traditions, is breathtakingly daring from one point of view. Catholic reverence for the Holy City of Jerusalem is not political but born of the sacredness of the city expressed in the psalms that the Church prays daily.

In March 2000, the Holy Father made a historic and, for him, long-awaited trip to the Holy Land, stopping en route at Mt. Sinai in Egypt (where God revealed the Ten Commandments to the Jewish people). He prayed at the ancient monastery there with the Greek Orthodox monks who keep penitential vigil at the foot of the mountain.

The papal pilgrimage took John Paul first to Bethlehem and Jericho in the Palestinian Authority. Then he came as a pilgrim to Nazareth and Jerusalem, sites pregnant with sacred memories for Jews and Christians alike. As a pilgrim he prayed, not only at Christian sites but at Jewish ones: the Western Wall (the ''Kotel''), the only remnant of the Temple of Jerusalem at which Jesus prayed and which he sought to cleanse, and Yad VaShem, Israel's profoundly moving memorial to the six million lives so brutally ended by Nazism. Despite the hoopla of the media and the various ongoing differences in viewpoint between Catholics and Jews, the pope's prayers were healing ones, offering reconciliation to both ancient communities.

While the visit to Yad VaShem understandably and rightly garnered the central attention during the pope's trip, it may well be that in the long run it was his simple prayer at the Western Wall that will have the longest and most profound impact. For this gesture marked the definitive end of the ancient polemical stance of the Catholic Church toward Judaism: the aptly named ''teaching of contempt.'' According to this teaching, the Jews were not only ignorant of the true fulfillment of ''their'' (yet also ''our'' Christian) Scriptures in the New Testament, they were willfully so.

For nearly two millennia, Jews have prayed at the Western Wall, all that was left of the Jerusalem Temple compound after the Romans destroyed the city following the second Jewish revolt. Now came the bishop of Rome, the successor of St. Peter, to pray at the Kotel, as a humble pilgrim who acknowledges the full validity of Jewish prayer at the site on its own terms over the centuries. The Western Wall is for Jews the central physical remnant of biblical Israel, that is, the central symbolic referent for Jews as a people and for Judaism as a four-to-five-thousand-year-old faith tradition. There is no hesitation in the pope's religious affirmation of Judaism, no political, theological, or social caveat. Once the pope prayed at the Wall, Jewish-Christian relations would never be the same.

In Jerusalem as well, the pope met with the two chief rabbis of Israel. It was a meeting of dialogue not diatribe, a meeting of reconciliation after centuries of alienation. It was a meeting neither the pope's nor the chief rabbis parents' could have dreamed to be possible in their wildest imaginations. The pope seized the opportunity not just of a lifetime but of the millennium.

Controversies and Dialogue

While the pontificate of John Paul II is marked by the most solid and extensive advances in Catholic-Jewish relations, it has also seen some vocal controversies. These revolve, not surprisingly, around the two key events of Jewish history in this century: the Holocaust and the State of Israel. The substantive position of the pope on both of these issues has been stated already. A series of incidents with regard to the *Shoah* greatly increased awareness of the fragility of the contemporary dialogue between the two communities.

In 1982 the pope met with Yasir Arafat, the leader of the Palestinian Authority who at the time was seen by many—and all Jews—as nothing more than a terrorist. In 1987 the pope met with Kurt Waldheim, the newly elected President of Austria whose hidden Nazi past was then being revealed. The 1987 meeting with Waldheim precipitated a crisis for Catholic-Jewish relations in the United States because it came just weeks before the pope's visit, which was scheduled to open in Miami with a meeting with several hundred Jewish leaders from around the country.

Also controversial was the beatification in 1987 and canonization in 1998 of Edith Stein, Sr. Benedicta of the Cross, a Jewish convert whose canonization raised questions in Jewish minds about the Church's intentions with regard to proselytism as well as its memory of the Holocaust. Was the Church about to launch a missionary effort targetted at the Jews? Was the Church trying to ''appropriate'' the *Shoah* to its own lexicon of suffering, thus whitewashing Christianity's role in paving the way for the death camps? (Papal statements on Edith Stein, along with Catholic and Jewish commentaries can be found in John Sullivan, OCD, ed., *Holiness Befits Your House: Documentation on the Canonization of Edith Stein* [Washington, DC: ICS Publications, 2000]).

Although the Holy Father had nothing to do with the problem but only with its resolution, the Auschwitz convent controversy of the late 1980s absorbed a huge amount of energy and painful reflection, especially among the European Catholic hierarchy. In 1984, Carmelite nuns in Poland established a small, cloistered convent in an abandoned building adjacent to the Auschwitz-Birkenau death camp complex. A well meaning priest in Belgium, without the knowledge of the nuns, decided to raise money for it. The flyer he sent around to do this contained language speaking of the convent as representing "the triumph of the Cross over Auschwitz." Auschwitz is the world's largest Jewish cemetery and, for Jews, symbolic of the *Shoah.* Again, Jews feared that the Church was trying to "take over" the Holocaust for its own purposes, blurring the Jewish specificity of the *Shoah.*

Controversies arose over the causes of canonization of two popes, Pius IX and Pius XII. Pius IX may have been put forward by the Congregation for the Causes of Saints of the Holy See for the understandable reason of reminding Catholics of the importance of continuity in Catholic Tradition, since he was the pope who called the First Vatican Council. The memory of Pius IX is quite negative in the Italian Jewish community. At the beginning of his pontificate, Pius IX freed Jews from the ghetto of Rome, but later reinstated it. To make matters worse, there was also the case of Edgardo Mortara, a young Jewish boy whose Catholic nanny swore she had secretly baptized when he was an infant. Because of this alleged baptism, Pius IX ordered the papal police to take the boy from his parents. He was raised in the Vatican, despite a world-wide outcry, became a priest, and died in 1942 in Belgium shortly before the Nazi invasion of the Lowland countries. The Mortara family was and is a very prominent one in the Italian Jewish community. The memory of their bitter loss of their child is still very fresh to them. The criticism of Pius XII was that he failed to speak out with sufficient explicitness on the fate of the Jews and that the Holy See did not do enough to prevent or oppose the Holocaust. Father Pierre Blet, one of the editors of Vatican archival material documenting Pius's policies concerning the deportation of Jews strongly repudiates the charge, and some Jewish scholars are persuaded by the evidence.

Each of these controversies has its specifics and, especially on the symbolic level for the Jewish perspective, commonalities with the others. Indeed, some Jewish commentators have perceived a rather ominous sort of pattern in these incidents: an attempt not so much to deny as to appropriate the Holocaust for the Church.

It must be said, first, that in each of these events there has been, if one takes the time to look, a papal response.

The Holy See's responses tend to address the substance of Jewish concerns, and do not always have an eye to "media relations." In the meeting with Arafat, for example, the Vatican Secretariat of State on the day of the meeting issued a tersely worded statement defining the meeting as not intending to give any credence whatsoever to PLO claims, and that the pope was meeting with Arafat to express humanitarian concerns for the Palestinian people and to exhort him to eschew violence against Jews. The Catholic press picked this up, but neither the Jewish nor the secular media did much with it. The result was that, to this day, many Jews will speak of the pope "embracing" Arafat. He did not; the photo shows only a rather distant handshake, nothing like an "embrace" at all. Catholics, on the other hand, were rather satisfied that the pope, while meeting with Arafat, took the occasion to lambast him about PLO terrorism.

Likewise, a careful reading of the text of the pope's homily in beatifying Edith Stein reveals that, far from seeking to foster conversionism, as some have charged, the pope took the occasion to acknowledge the uniqueness of the *Shoah* for the Jews and to urge Catholics to greater sensitivity to the trauma suffered by the Jewish people. Again, the Catholic press tended to emphasize these healing elements of the pope's talks while the Jewish press expressed concern over what they saw as the possibility of a new wave of proselytism.

So, too, with the pope's visit to Austria in 1988. What the pope actually did and said during his meeting with the Jewish representatives in Vienna and later that same day in Mauthausen was reported very differently by and for the two communities. Understood on their own, which is to say Catholic, terms, the pope's actions in these very authentically sensitive areas for Jews do not carry the symbolic weight or intent that the Jewish community appears to derive from them. For Catholics, the pope's meetings with Arafat and Waldheim did not in any way give credence to either figure as such; in the course of his pastoral work, the pope, like any priest, meets all sorts of unsavory characters, one may say, and like any head of state has meetings with numerous people of whom he may or may not personally approve.

But it must also be said that this is exactly the problem. Catholics do not understand sufficiently the suffering and trauma that lie behind these largely symbolic (for Jews more so than for Catholics) actions on the part of the pope. The symbolism is very different on both sides. And while John Paul II, perhaps more than any other pope, is sensitive and open to Jews and Judaism, he acts, as in a very real sense he must act, as a Catholic. We need, then, both understanding of each other's symbolic referents and a very real measure of mercy on and with each other's words and gestures.

A Vision for the Future: The Call to Joint Witness and Action in History

Central to Pope John Paul's vision of the Christian-Jewish relationship is the hope that it offers for joint social action and witness to the One God and the reality of the Kingdom of God as the defining point of human history. In his address in Mainz, the pope calls this "third dimension" of the dialogue a "sacred duty": "Jews and Christians, as children of Abraham, are called to be a blessing for the world [d. Gen. 12:2ff] by committing themselves to work together for peace and justice among all peoples" (Mainz, 1980; Fisher and Klenicki 1995, 16).

Such joint action, for John Paul, is far more than simple "good neighborliness." It is a fulfillment of what is essential to the mission of both Judaism and Christianity, for, "certainly, the great task of promoting justice and peace [cf. Ps. 85:4], the sign of the messianic age in both the Jewish and Christian tradition, is grounded in its turn in the great prophetic heritage" (Rome, 1984; Fisher and Klenicki 1995, 32). The possibility of a joint proclamation by word and deed in the world, which yet avoids "any syncretism and any ambiguous appropriation" (Rome, 1986; Fisher and Klenicki 1995, 64), is seen by the pope as no less than a divine call: "The existence and providence of the Lord, our Creator and Saviour, are thus made present in the witness of our daily conduct and belief. This is one of the responses that those who believe in God and are prepared to 'sanctify his name' [*Kiddush ha-Shem*] [cf. Matt. 6:9] can and should give to the secularistic climate of the present day" (Rome, 1985; Fisher and Klenicki 1995, 54).

This way of collaboration "in service of humanity" as a means of preparing for God's Kingdom unites Jews and Christians on a level that, in a sense, can be said to be deeper than the doctrinal distinctions that divide us historically. "Through different but finally convergent ways we will be able to reach, with the help of the Lord, who has never ceased to love his people (Rom. 11:1), true brotherhood in reconciliation and respect and to contribute to a full implementation of God's plan in history" (Rome, 1982; Fisher and Klenicki 1995, 20). That "full implementation" the pope defines in religious terms. It is a "society . . . where justice reigns and where . . . throughout the world it is peace that rules, the *shalom* hoped for by the lawmakers, Prophets, and wise men of Israel" (Rome 1986; Fisher and Klenicki 1995, 65). To use the words of the 1985 *Notes* to summarize Pope John Paul II's thoughts on Christian-Jewish relations, one can say that it is his vision that through dialogue:

> We shall reach a greater awareness that the people of God of the Ancient [Hebrew] Scriptures and the New Testament are tending toward a like end in the future: the coming or return of the Messiah—even if they start from two different points of view. Attentive to the same God who has spoken, hanging on the same word, we have to witness to one same memory and one common hope in Him who is the master of history. We must also accept our responsibility to prepare the world for the coming of the Messiah by working together for social justice, respect for the rights of persons and nations, and for social and international reconciliation. To this we are driven, Jews and Christians, by the command to love our neighbor, by a common hope for the Kingdom of God, and by the great heritage of the Prophets.

The note that Pope John Paul placed in the Temple Wall in Jerusalem in 2000 was, by prior arrangement, immediately taken to Yad VaShem to be preserved and displayed there for future generations of Jews and Christians.

> God of our fathers, you chose Abraham and his descendants to bring your Name to the Nations. We are deeply saddened by the behavior of those who in the course of history have caused these children of yours to suffer, and asking your forgiveness, we wish to commit ourselves to genuine brotherhood with the people of the Covenant. (26 March 2000)

The note distills in simple language much of what the pope had come to Israel to say to the Jewish People as the head of the Catholic Church and, in this instance, undoubtedly for all of Christianity. Jewish-Christian relations will never be the same.

See Also: CATECHISM OF THE CATHOLIC CHURCH; JOHN PAUL II AND INTERRELIGIOUS DIALOGUE; JOSEPH RATZINGER, EDITH STEIN, PIUS IX, UT UNUM SINT; UT UNUM SINT: JOHN PAUL II'S ECUMENICAL COMMITMENT

Bibliography: EUGENE J. FISHER and LEON KLENICKI, eds., *Spiritual Pilgrimage: John Paul II on Jew and Judaism* (New York: Crossroad, 1995).

[EUGENE J. FISHER]

The Church in Dialogue with Science: The Wojtyła Years

George V. Coyne, S.J., Ph.L, S.T.L., Ph.D., is the Director of the Vatican Observatory (Specola Vaticana).

Historical Background

From the very beginning of his papacy, Pope John Paul II has advocated a view of the relationship of science and faith that has differed in important respects from that which he inherited. In order to see what is new and in what the newness consists, it will be helpful to summarize three periods which together set the background: (1) the rise of modern atheism in the seventeenth and eighteenth centuries, (2) anticlericalism in Europe in the nineteenth century, (3) the awakening within the Church to modern science in the twentieth century.

It was paradoxically precisely the attempt in the seventeenth and eighteenth centuries to establish a rational basis for religious belief through arguments derived from the natural sciences that led to the corruption of religious belief (Buckley 1987). All of the great figures at the birth of modern science, including Galileo, Kepler, Brahe, Leibniz, Descartes, and Newton, were religious believers and they were inclined to think that the existence of God must be so well established from scientific arguments that evidence derived from religious experience itself became secondary or even forgotten. In the seventeenth century, with Galileo as a principle protagonist, the experimental method was perfected, and the application of mathematics to scientific research was begun. With Isaac Newton we come to the real beginning of modern science. Although the Galileo case, as it is called, provides the classical example of confrontation between science and faith, it is really in the misappropriation of modern science by such as Isaac Newton to try mistakenly to establish the foundations for religious belief that we find the roots of a much more deep-seated confrontation. From these roots, in fact, sprang the divorce between science and faith in the form of modern atheism.

An example of the influence of nineteenth-century anticlericalism on the development of the relationship between science and faith is seen in the founding of the Vatican Observatory in 1891 by Pope Leo XIII. His words show very clearly the prevailing mistrust of many scientists for the Church: "So that they might display their disdain and hatred for the mystical Spouse of Christ, who is the true light, those borne of darkness are accustomed to calumniate her to unlearned people and they call her the friend of obscurantism, one who nurtures ignorance, an enemy of science and progress" (Leo XIII 1891, 207). He terminates this *motu proprio* in which he established the Observatory by stating a very strong, one might say even triumphalistic, view of what the Church does:

> in taking up this work we have become involved not only in helping to promote a very noble science, which more than any other human discipline, raises the spirit of mortals to the contemplation of heavenly events, but we have in the first place put before ourselves the plan . . . that everyone might see that the Church and its Pastors are not opposed to true and solid science, whether human or divine, but that they embrace it, encourage it, and promote it with the fullest possible dedication. (Leo XIII 1891, 210)

The awakening of the Church to modern science during the twentieth century is best seen in Pope Pius XII. He was a man of rich culture and even in his youth he had become acquainted with astronomy through his association with Fr. Giuseppe Lais, Oratorian, who was an astronomer at the Vatican Observatory from 1890 to 1921. Pius XII had an excellent gentleman's knowledge of astronomy, and as pope, he frequently discussed astronomical research with the staff of the observatory. Yet, he was not immune from a rationalist tendency, and his understanding of the then most recent scientific discussions concerning the origins of the universe led him to a somewhat concordant approach, seeing in these scientific results a rational support for the scriptural (and by derivation doctrinal) interpretation of creation. This tendency was first revealed in the address "Un'Ora," delivered to the Pontifical Academy of Sciences on 22 November 1951 (Pius XII 1951, 73 84) in which he attempted to examine the scientific results from which arguments for the existence of God the Creator might proceed. Even at that time the papal discourse created a great deal of negative comment.

The specific problem arose from the tendency of the pope to identify the beginning state of the Big Bang cosmologies, a state of very high density, pressure and temperature, which was at that time thought to have occurred about one to ten billion years ago, with God's act of creation. He had stated, for instance, that:

> contemporary science with one sweep back across the centuries has succeeded in bearing witness to the august instant of the primordial *Fiat Lux,* when along with matter there burst forth from nothing a sea of light and radiation. . . . Thus, with that concreteness which is characteristic of physical proofs, modern science has confirmed the contingency of the Universe and also the well-founded deduction to the epoch when the world came forth from the hands of the Creator. (Pius XII 1952, 41, 42)

Georges Lemaître, a respected cosmologist, President of the Pontifical Academy of Sciences and a Catholic priest, had considerable difficulty with this view. Solid scientific evidence for Lemaître's theory of the Primeval Atom, which foreshadowed Big Bang cosmologies, was lacking at that time, and the accusation was made that his theory was born of a spirit of concordism with the religious concept of creation. In fact, it was only with the discovery in 1965 of the cosmic background radiation that persuasive scientific evidence for the Big Bang became available (Dicke et al 1965; Penzias and Wilson 1965). Lemaître insisted that the Primeval Atom and Big Bang hypotheses should be judged solely as physical theories and that theological considerations should be kept completely separate (Lemaître 1958).

From what has been said of these three historical periods we can conclude the following. First, as an inheritance from the origins of modern atheism in the seventeenth and eighteenth centuries, there has been within the Church a tendency to associate scientific research with atheism. Second, a type of "siege" or triumphalist mentality characterized the thinking of the Church at the time of the foundation of the Vatican Observatory. Third, when enlightened about the magnificent progress in scientific research in the twentieth century, the Church wished too hastily to appropriate the results of science to its own ends. In the papacy of John Paul II we see a view of the science-faith relationship that contrasts in a significant way with these antecedent views.

The New View from Rome

THE ABANDONMENT OF TRIUMPHALISM: THE GALILEO CASE

The views of John Paul II on the relationship of science and faith can be essentially derived from five of his messages: (1) the discourse given to the Pontifical Academy of Sciences on 10 November 1979 to commemorate the centenary of the birth of Albert Einstein (John Paul II 1986, 151), (2) the discourse given on 28 October 1986 on the occasion of the fiftieth anniversary of the Pontifical Academy of Sciences (John Paul II 1986, 193), (3) the message written on the occasion of the tricentennial of Newton's *Principia Mathematica* and published as in introduction to the proceedings of the meeting sponsored by the Vatican Observatory to commemorate that same tricentennial (Russell, Stoeger, and Coyne 1995), (4) his message on evolution to the Plenary Session of the Pontifical Academy of Sciences on 22 October 1996 (John Paul II 1996), and (5) the encyclical *Fides et ratio* (John Paul II 1998).

The public view of the first two discourses has emphasized the statements made by the pope concerning the Copernican-Ptolemaic controversy of the seventeenth century and especially the role of Galileo in those controversies. These statements have certainly set the stage for a new openness of the Church to the world of science. In his statements concerning Galileo the pope essentially does two things. He admits that there was wrong on the part of churchmen and apologizes for it, and he calls for a serene, studious, new investigation of the history of that time. In fact, he requests that specific tasks be undertaken:

> I hope that theologians, scholars, and historians, animated by a spirit of sincere collaboration, will study the Galileo case more deeply and, in loyal recognition of wrongs from whatever side they come, will dispel the mistrust that still opposes, in many minds, the fruitful concord between science and faith, between the Church and the world. I give my support to this task which will be able to honor the truth of faith and of science and open the door to future collaboration. (John Paul II 1986, 153)

A pontifical commission on Galileo was set up in 1981 to carry out the pope's wishes. In a discourse on 31 October 1992 (John Paul II 1992) the pope accepted the closure of the commission's work. On several previous occasions, notably in his discourse of 10 November 1979, John Paul II referred to the Galileo controversy as a "myth." He did so again in 1992:

> From the beginning of the Age of Enlightenment down to our own day, the Galileo case has been

a sort of myth, in which the image fabricated out of the events was quite far removed from reality. In this perspective, the Galileo case was the symbol of the Church's supposed rejection of scientific progress, or of dogmatic obscurantism opposed to the free search for truth. This myth has played a considerable cultural role. It has helped to anchor a number of scientists of good faith in the idea that there was an incompatibility between the spirit of science and its rules of research on one hand and the Christian faith on the other. A *tragic mutual incomprehension* has been interpreted as the reflection of a fundamental opposition between science and faith. The clarifications furnished by recent historical studies enable us to state that this sad misunderstanding now belongs to the past. From the Galileo affair we can learn a lesson that remains valid in relation to similar situations which occur today, and that may occur in the future. (John Paul II 1992, no. 10; emphasis added)

In the pope's discourse, and in that of Cardinal Poupard, who presented the commission's conclusions, the "tragic mutual incomprehension" is specified by what may be identified as the four principal conclusions of the discourses: (1) Galileo did not understand that, at that time, Copernicanism was only "hypothetical" and that he did not have scientific proofs for it; (2) "theologians" were not able, at that time, to correctly understand Scripture; (3) Robert Bellarmine understood what was "really at stake;" and (4) when scientific proofs for Copernicanism became known, the Church hastened to accept Copernicanism and to implicitly admit it erred in condemning it. It would be useful to discuss each of these four conclusions in turn.

In the papal discourse we read:

> like most of his adversaries, Galileo made no distinction between the scientific approach to natural phenomena and a reflection on nature, of the philosophical order, which that approach generally calls for. That is why he rejected the suggestion made to him to present the Copernican system as an hypothesis, inasmuch as it had not been confirmed by irrefutable proof. Such, therefore, was an exigency of the experimental method of which he was the inspired founder.(John Paul II 1992, no. 5, para. 1).

There is an ambiguity involved in this characterization of the scientific method and Galileo's use of it. The word "hypothesis" has two distinctly different meanings: a mathematical expedient to predict celestial events or an attempt to understand the true nature of the heavens. There is no doubt that Galileo understood his own investigations to be an attempt to understand the true nature of things. It is well known that he preferred to be known

as a philosopher of nature rather than as a mathematician. It can be debated as to whether Galileo himself was ever convinced that he had irrefutable proofs for Copernicanism (involved in that debate would be the very meaning of proof for him and, indeed, for us), but it cannot be denied that he sought evidence to show that Copernicanism was really true and not just a mathematical expedient. Galileo rejected that Copernicanism was a hypothesis in the former sense. He sought to find experimental verification of it in the latter sense. He can certainly not be accused of betraying the very method "of which he was the inspired founder."

As to the incomprehension on the part of the Church, fault is placed by the pope, echoing the conclusion of Cardinal Poupard, exclusively on theologians. There is no mention of the Roman Inquisition or of the Congregation of the Index, nor of an injunction given to Galileo in 1616 nor of the abjuration required of him in 1633 by official organs of the Church. Nor is mention made of Paul V or Urban VIII, the ones ultimately responsible for the activities of those official institutions.

In contrast to these theologians, Bellarmine is said by the pope, again echoing Cardinal Poupard, to have been the one

> who had seen what was truly at stake in the debate [since he] personally felt that, in the face of possible scientific proofs that the earth orbited around the sun, one should "interpret with great circumspection" every biblical passage which seems to affirm that the earth is immobile and "say that we do not understand rather than affirm that what has been demonstrated is false." (John Paul 1992, no. 9, para. 2)

This interpretation of Bellarmine's position is based on only a partial and selective reading of the *Letter to Foscarini*. In the passage immediately preceding the one cited by the pope, Bellarmine had taken a very restrictive position by stating that

> Nor can one answer that this [geocentrism] is not a matter of faith, since if it is not a matter of faith "as regards the topic," it is a matter of faith "as regards the speaker;" and so it would be heretical to say that Abraham did not have two children and Jacob twelve, as well as to say that Christ was not born of a virgin, because both are said by the Holy Spirit through the mouth of the prophets and the apostles. (Fantoli 1996, 183)

Clearly if geocentrism is a matter of faith "as regards the speaker" then openness to scientific results and circumspection in interpreting Scripture are simply ploys. They lead nowhere. Furthermore, at the end of the *Letter to Foscarini* Bellarmine appears to exclude any possibility of a proof of Copernicanism by stating that our senses clearly show us that the sun moves and that the earth stands still, just as one on a ship senses that it is the ship that is moving and not the shoreline. A further indication of this conviction of Bellarmine is had in the fact that he supported the decree of the index which was aimed at excluding any reconciliation of Copernicanism with Scripture. If Bellarmine truly believed that there might be a demonstration of Copernicanism why did he not recommend waiting and not taking a stand, a position embraced, it appears, by Cardinals Barberini and Caetani?

John Paul II accepts the judgment, given by Cardinal Poupard in his discourse, that "the sentence of 1633 was not irreformable" and both seek to establish that a reformation actually started as soon as the scientific evidence for Copernicanism began to appear. As a matter of fact, the works of Copernicus and Galileo remained on the index until 1835, more than a century after the discovery of the aberration of starlight by James Bradley in 1728, which may be considered a proof of the Earth's motion.

The record on the Galileo case is therefore mixed. It is clear that the pope envisaged a just resolution of the controversy. Unfortunately, the picture given in the discourses of 31 October 1992 does not stand up to historical scrutiny and, consequently, the commission did not fulfill the pope's desire that "a frank recognition of wrongs from whatever side they come, [might] dispel the mistrust that still opposes, in many minds, a fruitful concord between science and faith" (John Paul II 1986).

A NEW DIALOGUE: THE COMMON QUEST OF SCIENCE AND FAITH

The message of John Paul II to the Pontifical Academy of Sciences on evolution is characteristic of his openness to dialogue with the sciences. While Pius XII's encyclical *Humani generis* (1950) considered the doctrine of evolution a serious hypothesis, worthy of investigation and in-depth study equal to that of the opposing hypothesis, John Paul II states in his message: "Today almost half a century after the publication of the encyclical [*Humani generis*], new knowledge has led to the recognition that the theory of evolution is no longer a mere hypothesis" (John Paul II 1996, no. 4, para. 2; the English translation of this sentence in *Origins* is incorrect).

The sentences that follow this statement indicate that the "new knowledge" to which the pope refers is for the most part scientific knowledge. He had, in fact, just stated that "the exegete and the theologian must keep informed about the results achieved by the natural sciences." The context in which the message occurs strongly supports this. As the specific theme for its plenary session the Pontifical Academy of Sciences had chosen *The Origin and Evolution of Life,* and it had assembled some of the most

active researchers in the life sciences to discuss topics ranging from detailed molecular chemistry to sweeping analyses of life in the context of the evolving universe. Only months before the plenary session of the academy the renowned journal *Science* published a research paper announcing the discovery that there may once have existed primitive life forms on the planet Mars. Furthermore, within the previous two years a number of publications had appeared announcing the discovery of extra-solar planets. This ferment in scientific research not only made the plenary session theme very timely, but it also set the concrete scene for the papal message. Most of the scientific results cited were (not surprisingly) very tentative and very much disputed, but they were very exciting and provocative. The pope wished to recognize the great strides being made in the scientific knowledge of life and the implications that may result for a religious view of the human person; but at the same time he had to struggle with the tentative nature of those results and their consequences, especially with respect to revealed, religious truths.

The pope's argument progresses in the following way: The Church holds certain revealed truths concerning the human person (e.g., created in the image and likeness of God, fully revealed in Christ). Science has discovered certain facts about the origins of the human person. Any theory based upon those facts that contradicts revealed truths cannot be correct: "the theories of evolution which, because of the philosophies which inspire them, regard the spirit either as emerging from the forces of living matter, or as a simple epiphenomenon of that matter, are incompatible with the truth about man" (ibid., no. 5, para. 2). Revealed truths are given an antecedent and primary role in this dialogue, yet they are not wholly determinative; the pope wishes to remain open to a correct theory based upon the scientific facts. The dialogue proceeds, in anguish as it were, between these two poles.

If we consider the revealed, religious truth about the human being, then we have an "ontological leap," an "ontological discontinuity" in the evolutionary chain at the emergence of the human being. Is this not irreconcilable, wonders the pope, with the continuity in the evolutionary chain seen by science? An attempt to resolve this critical issue is given by stating that "the moment of transition to the spiritual cannot be the object of this kind of [scientific] observation, which nevertheless can discover at the experimental level a series of very valuable signs indicating what is specific to the human being" (ibid., no. 6, para. 2). The suggestion is being made, it appears, that the "ontological discontinuity" may be explained by an epistemological discontinuity. Is this adequate or must the dialogue continue? Is a creationist, interventionist theory required to explain the origins of the spiritual dimension of the human being? Are we forced by revealed, religious truth to accept a dualistic view of the origins of the human person, evolutionist with respect to the material dimension, creationist and interventionist with respect to the spiritual dimension? The pope's message gives strong indications in its last paragraphs, on the God of life, that the dialogue is still open with respect to these questions.

The principal thrust of John Paul II's encyclical *Fides et ratio,* which in the twilight of his papacy summarizes his thinking on the relationship of faith and reason, is a plea that we not lose the search for ultimate truth. He writes, for instance: "She [the Church] sees in philosophy the way to come to know fundamental truths about human life. . . . I wish to reflect upon this special activity of human reason. I judge it necessary to do so because at the present time in particular the search for ultimate truth seems often to be neglected" (FR 5).

In this search there are various ways of knowing and among them he contrasts philosophy with the natural sciences:

> It may help, then, to turn briefly to the different modes of truth. Most of them depend upon immediate evidence or are confirmed by experimentation. This is the mode of truth proper to everyday life and to scientific research. At another level we find philosophical truth, attained by means of the speculative powers of the human intellect. (FR 30)

It is clear that philosophy and the natural sciences must each have their autonomy:

> St. Albert the Great and St. Thomas were the first to recognize the autonomy which philosophy and the sciences needed if they were to perform well in their respective fields of research. (FR 45)

Later on the pope laments the "lack of interest in the study of philosophy" and "the misunderstanding that has arisen especially with regard to the human sciences" and he says:

> On a number of occasions the Second Vatican Council stressed the positive value of scientific research for a deeper knowledge of the mystery of the human being. But the invitation addressed to theologians to engage the human sciences and apply them properly in their inquiries should not be interpreted as an authorization to marginalize philosophy or to put something else in its place in pastoral formation. (FR 61)

A further contrast between science and philosophy is given when he writes:

> Reference to the sciences is often helpful, allowing as it does a more thorough knowledge of the

subject under study; but it should not mean the rejection of a typical philosophical and critical thinking which is concerned with the universal. (FR 69)

The pope expresses a rather critical view of science:

> Science would thus be poised to dominate all aspects of human life through technological progress. The undeniable triumphs of scientific research and contemporary technology have helped to propagate a scientistic outlook which now seems boundless, given its inroads into different cultures and the radical changes it has brought. (FR 88)

While the encyclical's principal focus is not upon the natural sciences, it does make a serious attempt to lay the foundations for dialogue. The view presented of the natural sciences is somewhat limited. Scientific research, especially in our day, cannot be excluded from the search for ultimate meaning. Today scientists, within their own well-determined methodology, are asking such questions as: why is there anything rather than nothing? is the universe finite or infinite in time and in space? is the universe fine-tuned to the existence of intelligent life? did humans come to be through necessary processes, chance processes, or some combination of the two in a universe fecund enough to allow both processes together to fructify?

Mathematical physics has played, and continues to play, a key role in addressing these questions of ultimate meaning. From Plato to Newton the contest as to what part mathematics has had in coming to a scientific understanding of the universe took place in a religious framework. After a period of what might be called "atheistic rationalism" we again hear the refrain of discovering "the mind of God" coming from scientists (Davies 1992). Among scholars there has been a serious attempt to evaluate that long previous history and to make sense of its echo in our times. It is no longer sufficient to dismiss any possible meeting between science and faith as only apparent, with the excuse that their distinct methods do not allow for dialogue. It is clear that the methodology of modern science is evolving into what might be called a new physics (Heller 1996). I would suggest that the dialogue envisioned by the pope requires that the methodology of theology must also be in flux. As an effort at coming to a rational understanding of revealed truth, theology is subject to all of the vagaries of human thought. And revealed truth, granted that it first occurred at a privileged time and to chosen persons, is incarnate and must be continuously rethought and reacquired. What is revealed is deeply imbedded in the way we think and the understanding of it is, therefore, evolving. Furthermore, all rational knowledge of God is analogous, and it would, therefore, be appropriate that concepts from the new physics be taken as analogies in the search to understand God. The methods of theology have always been very determined by prevailing philosophies; since the Middle Ages, Christian theology has been very much attached to the Aristotelian-Thomistic tradition, and especially to the concept of final cause. Thus such notions as purpose and design have dominated the Christian view of the world. Might philosophers and theologians not apply themselves to an attempt to understand God, the creator of a universe where purpose and design are not the only, nor even the dominant, factors but where spontaneity, indeterminacy (even at a macroscopic level), and unpredictability have contributed significantly to the evolution of a universe in which life has come to be?

Philosophers and theologians should critically evaluate and embrace, according to that evaluation, the nonteleological approaches of the new physics. They would reflect upon the evolving universe, and in particular upon the evolution of life in that universe, as we know it from the new physics. In so doing theologians must beware of a serious temptation. Within the culture of the new physics God is essentially, if not exclusively, seen as an explanation and not as a person. God is the ideal mathematical structure, the theory of everything. God is Mind. It must remain a firm tenet of the reflecting theologian that God is more than intelligence and that God's revelation of himself in time is more than a communication of information. God is love. Even if we discover ''the mind of God'' we will not have necessarily found God. The very nature of our emergence in an evolving universe and our inability to comprehend this even with the new physics may be an indication that in the universe God may be communicating much more than information to us. We might come to see the universe of the new physics as a unique revelation of God. There will, of course, always be a tension between science and theology because of the transcendental (i.e., beyond reason) character of the latter, but considering the somewhat Platonic quest in the new physics for the ''mind of God,'' for ultimate meaning, that very tension could be the source of a creative dialogue. It need not be excluded that such dialogue could take place even on the level of ultimate meaning.

Summary

John Paul II has taken a position on the relationship between science and religion that is compellingly different from the one he had inherited. In his message on the occasion of the tricentennial of Newton's *Principia Mathematica* he clearly states that science cannot be used in a simplistic way as a rational basis for religious belief, nor can it be judged to be by its nature atheistic, opposed to belief in God

> Christianity possesses the source of its justification within itself and does not expect science to

constitute its primary apologetic. Science must bear witness to its own worth. While each can and should support the other as distinct dimensions of a common human culture, neither ought to assume that it forms a necessary premise for the other. The unprecedented opportunity we have today is for a common interactive relationship in which each discipline retains its integrity and yet is radically open to the discoveries and insights of the other. (Russell, Stoeger, and Coyne 1995, M9)

The pope furthermore states:

> science develops best when its concepts and conclusions are integrated into the broader human culture and its concerns for ultimate meaning and value. . . . [Scientists] can come to appreciate for themselves that these discoveries cannot be a substitute for knowledge of the truly ultimate. Science can purify religion from error and superstition; religion can purify science from idolatry and false absolutes. Each can draw one another into a wider world, a world in which each can flourish. (Russell, Stoeger and Coyne 1995, M13)

Nothing could be further from the antagonism of Leo XIII, born of the anticlericalism of the seventeenth and eighteenth centuries, than the following words of John Paul II:

> By encouraging openness between the Church and the scientific communities, we are not envisioning a disciplinary unity between theology and science like that which exists within a given scientific field or within theology proper. As dialogue and common searching continue, there will be growth towards mutual understanding and gradual uncovering of common concerns which will provide the basis for further research and discussion. (Russell, Stoeger, and Coyne 1995, M7)

The newest element in the new view from Rome is the expressed uncertainty as to where the dialogue between science and faith will lead. Whereas the awakening of the Church to modern science during the papacy of Pius XII resulted in a too facile appropriation of scientific results to bolster religious beliefs, Pope John II expresses the extreme caution of the Church in defining its partnership in the dialogue: ''Exactly what form that (the dialogue) will take must be left to the future'' (Russell, Stoeger, and Coyne 1995, M7). This is clearly the newest and most important posture that the modern Church has taken in its approach to science. It is diametrically opposed to accusations of atheism, to a posture of antagonism; it is awakened but expectant.

In his message on the occasion of the tercentenary of Newton's *Principia* the pope raises the question: ''Can science also benefit from this interchange?'' (Russell, Stoeger, and Coyne 1995, M7). The answer is not clear.

In fact, it is very difficult to see what the benefits to science as such, that is as a specific way of knowing, might be. In the papal message it is intimated that the dialogue will help scientists to appreciate that scientific discoveries cannot be a substitute for knowledge of the truly ultimate. In what way, however, do scientific discoveries participate, together with philosophy and theology, in the quest for that ultimate? This is a serious and open question. The new view from Rome is not a claim to have all the answers, but an invitation to a common quest.

See Also: FIDES ET RATIO, PAUL POUPARD

Bibliography: M. J. BUCKLEY, *At the Origins of Modern Atheism* (New Haven: Yale University Press, 1987). P. DAVIES, *The Mind of God* (London: Simon and Schuster, 1992). R. H. DICKE, "Cosmic Black Body Radiation," *Astrophysical Journal* 142 (1965): 414. A. FANTOLI, *Galileo for Copernicanism and for the Church,* translated by G. V. COYNE, 2d ed., (Vatican City: Vatican Observatory Publications, 1996). M. HELLER, *The New Physics and a New Theology* (Vatican City: Vatican Observatory Publications, 1996). JOHN PAUL II, *Discourses of the Popes from Pius XI to John Paul II to the Pontifical Academy of Sciences* (Vatican City State: Pontificia Accademia Scientiarum, 1986. Scripta Varia 66). JOHN PAUL II, "Discourse on the Occasion of the Plenary Session of the Pontifical Academy of Sciences and the Conclusion of the Work of the Study Commission on the Ptolemaic-Copernican Controversy," in *Discorsi dei Papi alla Pontificia Accademia delle Scienze* (Vatican City State: Pontificia Accademia Scientiarum, 1992). JOHN PAUL II, "Message to Pontifical Academy of Sciences on Evolution," *Origins* 26, no. 22 (14 Nov. 1996): 349–52. G. LEMAÎTRE, "The Primeval Atom Hypothesis and the Problem of Clusters of Galaxies," in *La structure et l'evolution de l'universe* Bruussels: XI Conseil de Physique Solay, 1958). LEO XIII, "Ut Mysticam" (1891), in SABINO MAFFEO, *In the Service of Nine Popes, One Hundred Years of the Vatican Observatory,* translated by G. V. COYNE (Vatican City State: Vatican Observatory Publications, 1991). A. A. PENZIAS and R. W. WILSON, "A Measurement of Excess Antenna Temperature at 4080 Mc/s.," *Astrophysical Journal* 142 (1965): 419. PIUS XII, "Un'Ora" (1951), in *Discourses of the Popes from Pius XI to John Paul II to the Pontifical Academy of Sciences* (Vatican City State: Pontificia Accademia Scientiarum, 1986, Scripta Varia 66). PIUS XII, "Le prove della esistenza di Dio alla luce della scienza naturale," *Acta Aposto;icae Sedis* 44 (1952): 31–43. R. J. RUSSELL, W. R. STOEGER, and G. V. COYNE, *Physics, Philosophy and Theology, A Common Quest for Understanding,* 2d rev. ed. (Vatican City State: Vatican Observatory Publications, 1995).

[GEORGE V. COYNE]

The Universal Call to Holiness: Martyrs of Charity and Witnesses to Truth

Lawrence S. Cunningham, Ph.D., is Professor of Theology, Department of Theology, University of Notre Dame, Notre Dame, Indiana.

Chapter five of the Vatican II's Constitution on the Church, *Lumen gentium,* underscores insistently that the call to holiness is, in fact, a universal one. Christ preached holiness of life to each of the disciples regardless of their situation (no. 40); everyone is justified by faith, is forgiven, is called as God's chosen ones (ibid.); in all the various types and duties of life one and the same holiness is cultivated by "all who are moved by the Spirit of God" (no. 41) whether they be bishops, clergy, religious, married persons, the widowed or single, laborers or those who live in privation (ibid.). Decades after the close of Vatican II, Pope John Paul II would describe this universal call to holiness as a call to universal love stipulating that this "vocation to universal love is not restricted to small groups of individuals" (*Veritatis splendor,* no. 18). In fact, the pope, in his 1994 letter on the coming millenium *(Tertio millennio adveniente)* takes explicit pains to remark on the wide range of witnesses to holiness in the Church; beyond the martyrs there are "teachers of the faith, missionaries, confessors, bishops, priests, virgins, married couples, widows, and children" (no. 37).

The orientation of *Lumen gentium* with its emphasis on universal holiness created the subsequent obligation for finding ways in which people in the Church, beyond the primary resources of the ascetical, spiritual, sacramental, and liturgical life, could find paths of spirituality proper to the real situations in which they found themselves. The council itself, in its decree on the laity *(Apostolicam actuositatem)* already recognized the necessity of diverse forms of Christian formation since lay formation "takes its special flavor from the distinctively secular quality of the lay state and from its own form of spirituality" (no. 29). This recognition of the need for diverse forms of spirituality is at least as old as the opening pages of *An Introduction to the Devout Life* (written between 1602 and 1608) where Saint Francis de Sales insists on an appropriate form of Christian living adapted to the state and capabilities of the individual.

The fundamental model for all paths of spiritual formation is the supreme model who is Jesus, but as Vatican II points out in *Lumen gentium,* there is a whole tradition of witnesses from every era and every social situation—the saints—who attest to the fact of holiness in the Church (no. 40). In the Constitution on the Sacred Liturgy *(Sacrosanctum concilium)* the Fathers at Vatican II conceive of the saints not just as characters whose lives and deeds are an historical memory but as part of the living Church; by their veneration in the liturgy we "hope for some part and fellowship with them" (no. 8). The witness of the saints is one way in which the eschatological nature of the Church is made manifest. That same witness, as the saints are invoked, reminds us that the Church is not simply an institutional reality but a *communio* that is meta-historical.

In its reflections on the universal call to holiness, *Lumen gentium* pays particular attention to the concrete evidence of holy people who show forth, almost sacramentally, the holiness of the Church. The holiness of the Church "is expressed in multiple ways by those individuals who, in their walk of life, strive for the perfection of charity and thereby help others to grow" (no. 39). That witness further shows that everyone of "whatever rank and status are called to the Christian life . . ." (no. 40), and finally, despite the "various types and duties," it is "one and same holiness [that] is cultivated by all who are moved by the Spirit of God and who obey the voice of the Father, worshiping God the Father in spirit and in truth" (no. 41).

In the midst of this discussion of the universal call to holiness and the exemplarity of Christ, the council then singles out one particular paradigm of holiness to which few are called: martyrdom. The council sees martyrdom in the light of love, even the love shown to persecutors after the model of the forgiving Christ. The council further links the gift of the martyr with the sacrificial gift of Christ on the cross. The Church thus considers martyrdom as an exceptional gift *(donum eximium)* and the highest proof of love *(suprema probatio caritatis)* (no.

John Paul II blesses the faithful gathered at the Piazza del Campo in Siena, 30 March 1996. (Reuters/Luciano Mellace/ Archive Photos, Inc. Reproduced by permission.)

42). A passing observation in the Pastoral Constitution of the Church in the Modern World *(Gaudium et Spes)* will amplify the martyr's gift of life as love by hewing more closely to the fundamental sense of the martyr as witness by seeing the martyr as one who testifies to the truth of the faith (no. 21). Such witnesses exhibit in their witness the greatest of the *charismatic* gifts in the sense that their sacrifice is not only for their salvation but as a grace given for the strengthening of the whole Church.

The fact that the council speaks of the luminous witness of faith given by the martyr both in the past tense and in the present (i.e., they continue to give witness) is a passing but almost parenthetical observation about the persecuted Church of the times. Indeed, one could argue that the declaration on religious freedom *(Dignitatis humanae)* was a plea for the kind of human freedom that would render otiose the need for martyrs, but given the realities of a sinful world, that desire will find its fulfillment only in the *eschaton.*

Pope John Paul II has dispelled the unfortunate tendency on the part of many people to think of martyrs as persons who lived only in the distant past. Those distant lives have been enshrined in hagiographical legends patinated by a sea of pious iconography: compliant virgins standing before roaring lions in a Roman arena or kneeling quietly under the sword of the pagan executioner. The fact is that our century has been unparalleled for the sheer number of violent deaths in a range of large-scale and small wars, vendettas, civil disturbances, and man-made atrocities of various kinds. The litany of those modern atrocities is a lugubrious one: acts of genocide that range from Armenia to Western Europe; civil wars from Nigeria to the Sudan to Eastern Europe; engineered famines in the Ukraine and Russia; the terrible tolls of world-wide and regional wars; the direct attempts to exterminate whole peoples during the Nazi and Stalinist periods.

One of the sad novelties of martyrdom in this century, as the liberation theologians in Central and Latin America like to point out, is that martyrs are also found in societies that claim to be Catholic, and further the perpetrators of this violence against believers claim that they are acting in the announced hope of saving "Christian" civilization from "godless" communism. Many of those death-dealing events had within them impulses derived from hatred for religious faith—impulses that created situations in which people of faith had to give their lives in the name of Christ. To put the matter starkly: The iconography of martyrdom today would have to depict electric cattle prods, gas chambers, the hangman's noose, the bullet behind the ear, the rape of women, the murder of children, and judicial "disappearances" as a contemporary counterpart to Catherine's wheel or Laurence's gridiron. How many died in this fashion as witnesses to Christ is almost impossible to calculate but we do know that masses of Christians died of whose names we only number the more famous.

It should not come as a surprise that Pope John Paul II has a special interest in modern martyrs who stand as part of that "cloud of witnesses" (the *nephos marturōn* of Heb 12:1) who are so conspicuous in contemporary Christianity. His interest derives from a kind of triangulation of three intersecting events in his own life. First, he came to maturity when the Nazis had control of his native Poland with the attendant elimination of the Polish intelligentsia (including, conspicuously, priests and religious; estimates are that twenty percent of the Polish clergy were killed during the Nazi occupation of Poland), the genocide waged against the Jews in his native Poland and Poland as the final repository for millions of other European Jews, and the mass conscription of ordinary Poles into slave labor battalions. Second, his life as a priest in postwar Poland and his rise to the rank of the episcopacy occurred in tandem with the most repressive years of a Stalinist regime in Poland that actively and openly persecuted the Church. Finally, on assuming the papacy he was in a position to understand not only the continuing persecution of the Church in the Eastern bloc but had access to reliable sources about the situation of Christians in China, in parts of Africa, in countries under authoritarian regimes in Central and South America, and in those areas of the world, preeminently Eastern Europe, where Christians were a persecuted minority or, in the case of his native land, a persecuted majority.

As a person from Eastern Europe, shaped by close contact with two of the most demonic socio-political cultures of the modern era, the pope was disinclined to view the history of this century through the sunny lens of the Enlightenment prism of progress and scientific optimism. Conspicuously in his 1995 encyclical letter *Evangelium vitae* (The Gospel of Life), he even began to speak more generally of our modern condition as deeply infected with a "culture of death." Indeed, in his 1994 apostolic letter *Tertio millennio adveniente* detailing his hopes for the preparations for the coming millennium celebrations, the pope sees an explicit parallel between the first period of persecution and martyrdom that ended only in the fourth century and the modern era: "In our own century the martyrs have returned, many of them nameless, 'unknown soldiers,' as it were in God's great cause." (no. 37). The pope goes on to say that the memory of those martyrs must not be permitted to disappear. He puts on the local churches the duty of recording as much as possible the memory of those who died for the faith in this century. The pope reiterated that same theme in his 1999 apostolic exhortation *Ecclesia in America,* where he says that the example of the martyrs "must not only be saved from oblivion, but must become better and more widely known among the faithful of the continent (no. 15). The strategies suggested by the pope for keeping their memory alive, apart from local efforts, is a topic to which we will return.

Suffice it to say that this was hardly the first time the pope singled out the martyrs as being a significant *topos* in his thinking. When one looks back over the years of Pope John Paul's Petrine ministry, there is a persistent theme concerning the martyrs, especially modern martyrs. To look back on this theme is to see that the pope approaches the subject of martyrdom from a diversity of angles that raise issues about the papal understanding of martyrdom, the paradigmatic role martyrs play in evangelization, and the symbolic role that martyrs play in the papal understanding of culture. Each of these topics deserve some detailed investigation.

Canonization and Martyrdom

In 1983 John Paul II issued his apostolic constitution *Divinus perfectionis magister* that revised and simplified the procedures and norms to be used for the canonization of saints. This was the first major revision of these proce-

dures that hitherto reflected (in the old Code of Canon Law) processes derived from the work of Prosper Lambertini (later Benedict XIV) in the eighteenth century. John Paul's reform of procedures follows on the 1969 reorganization of the curia by Pope Paul VI who created a separate congregation for the causes of the saints that had hitherto been under the aegis of the Congregation of Rites. Essentially, the new apostolic constitution substituted the old adversarial system that utilized the *Promotor Fidei* (the so-called "Devil's Advocate"), who argued against the case for canonization proposed by his opposite by establishing a procedure in which the postulator(s) for the person's cause would write a detailed narrative for the heroic virtue of the life of that person. This narrative *(relatio)* would base itself on the all of the preliminary investigation done at both the local and Roman level. The completed *relatio,* in essence, would be the document in which the case for canonization would be set out before the Congregation for the Cause of Saints and for the pope for his final decision. The *relatio,* of course, was presented in tandem with evidence of miracles performed through the intercession of the person nominated.

Martyrs for the faith were generally considered the "easy" cases for canonization since they demonstrated with their very lives, fidelity to the Gospel, heroic virtue, self-giving, and so on. In the case of martyrs considered for beatification and canonization the necessity of intercessory miracles was waived. The issue of what constitutes a martyr, however, is not always so easy to determine. The rule of thumb for the martyr had been stipulated centuries ago by Saint Augustine: martyrdom derives, not from the punishment inflicted, but the reasons for the punishment *(non poena sed causa).* Although such a rule seems straightforward, it is not always so in actual practice. Saint Thomas Aquinas, for example, points out that John the Baptist was a martyr because he denounced adultery; hence he was a martyr for the sake of the "truth of faith" *(Summa Theologiae,* IIa IIae, q.124 art. 5).

The complexity attached to the term *martyr* is easily illustrated in two canonizations celebrated during John Paul's papacy. John Paul II canonized Father Maximilian Kolbe, a Franciscan friar, in 1982, just a scant year before the new norms for canonization were published. Kolbe (1894–1941) had volunteered to take the place of a married man in Auschwitz in a punishment bunker; after two weeks in starvation conditions Kolbe was still alive; he was given a lethal injection of phenol that killed him. The issue is this: Was he killed for the sake of his faith or was he simply killed as part of the routine sadism of his Nazi captors? His punishment seems to have been as an exemplary act to maintain discipline in the camp by inflicting ruthless punishment on randomly chosen prisoners. The answer seems to have been supplied by Pope Paul VI at Kolbe's beatification in 1971, when the pope hailed him as a "martyr of charity," further stipulating that he would henceforth be venerated also as a martyr. Pope John Paul II ratified that decision at the canonization 1982. The rubric "martyr of charity" then was a new way of understanding how one is to conceive of the word martyr in its etymological sense of witness; Kolbe witnessed in the ultimate gesture of love or charity. In that sense, he died for the "defense of the faith" as Aquinas described it.

The far more contentious case was the canonization of Edith Stein (Sister Benedicta of the Holy Cross), a Carmelite contemplative who had been sent to the same Nazi death camp in a roundup of converted Jews in Holland, where she lived in the Dutch Carmel of Echt after leaving her Carmel in Cologne under the pressure of Nazi anti-Semitism. Pope John Paul II beatified Edith Stein (1891–1942) in Cologne, Germany on 1 May 1987, after her cause had been presented to him as a woman of heroic virtue, a confessor, and as a martyr. When the pope canonized her (16 October 1998), he wore the red vestment used for liturgies venerating martyrs and, in fact, declared her to be one. He took up explicitly her Jewish background arguing in his homily that she died both as a daughter of Israel and as a person of Christian faith. That act brought forth a cry of consternation from Jews who argued that Edith Stein was killed for the simple reason that in the eyes of the Nazis she was a Jew; her death (and that of her sister Rosa) had nothing to do with her Christian faith.

Yet, as many commentators have noted, Edith Stein was deported to Auschwitz as part of a program of retaliation against the Dutch Church whose hierarchy had spoken out against Nazi atrocities; in that sense, the Nazis attacked the Church through its members as part of their explicit desire to demonstrate their *odium fidei*. It is also worthwhile noting that Edith Stein did not convert from Judaism to Christianity; even though she was Jewish, she had been a convinced atheist from the age of fourteen. In Edith Stein (whom the pope would name a patroness of Europe along with Saints Catherine of Siena and Brigid of Sweden in 1999) John Paul saw someone who was, in his words, a "synthesis of history"—a Jew by birth, a Christian by conviction; an intellectual who converted from atheistic humanism; an intellectual who was a contemplative.

In addition to the cases of Maximilian Kolbe and Edith Stein mention might also be made of the issue raised by the determination of the pope to canonize the seventeenth-century Czech martyr Jan Sarkander

(1576–1620), which he did while on a visit to the Czech Republic in May of 1995. Sarkander was tortured and died from those tortures during the religious wars of the early seventeenth century. Czech Protestants vigorously protested Sarkander's canonization alleging that he was party to those who forced conversion to Catholicism during his missionary work in Moldavia. In other words, Sarkander may well have been the victim of torture (partially inflicted to obtain confessional secrets), but he was hardly a model of Christian understanding or tolerance. The pope was only able to defuse the tension built up over this canonization by using Sarkander's canonization to plead for mutual forgiveness; Catholics forgiving Protestants for horrors done during the religious wars of the past and asking Protestants to do the same for injuries inflicted on Catholics. The pope used the occasion both to testify to the fidelity of Sarkander and as an opportunity to use the example of a martyr to advance ecumenical understanding and forgiveness. Such sentiments helped defuse an ecumenical impasse in 1987 when the pope beatified eighty-five martyrs of England and Wales. The Anglican primate Robert Runcie noted that such an event would have caused controversy and pain at an earlier time but "today we can celebrate their heroic Christian witness and together deplore the intolerance of the age which flawed Christian convictions."

It is further clear, in both the case of Maximilian Kolbe and Edith Stein, that the pope had a more nuanced view of martyrdom than that which is usually proposed. He understood martyrdom to be more in the way of a public witness even unto the death for the truth of the Gospel, even when the explicit reason for the martyr's death is not a refusal to apostasize by denying the faith. It is not to be wondered that in his encyclical letter *Veritatis splendor* (1993), which emphasizes norms of moral behavior that have no exceptions, the pope will call upon the witness of the martyrs who underscore the solidity of Christian truth even at the cost of their own earthly lives. The martyr, the pontiff writes, is one whose "fidelity to God's holy law, witnessed to by death, is a solemn proclamation and missionary commitment *usque ad sanguinem*" Neither the sacrifice of a life for the sake of another (Kolbe) nor the death of one out of racial hatred (Stein) is what makes them martyrs. The reason(s) why the pope sees them as martyrs is that their lives stood in direct and dramatic counterpoint to forces of evil and untruth. In their particular cases, it was, as it were, that they became public anti-signs to the evil that confronted them. In a broad sense, one could say that the pope sees in the martyrs a manifestation of the sacramental: they are signs that give grace.

One could argue that sections 91–94 of the encyclical *Veritatis splendor* constitutes the fullest "theology" of martyrdom to be found in the papal corpus of writing. The pope sees the martyr as the one who rejects any compromise with evil (no. 91); he cites examples of those who will never fail when tempted to commit one mortal sin (no. 91). He sees their witness as twofold: for God's law and for human dignity and, as such, as giving the lie to those who think that there are exceptions to divine law (no. 92; a conviction that he repeats in *Donum vitae,* no. 60). Finally, he links the sacrifice of the martyr to the theme of the holiness of the Church (no. 93).

The canonizations of Father Kolbe and Edith Stein are among the more famous of the hundreds of canonizations and beatifications proclaimed during John Paul's papacy. In that huge list of canonized saints and beatified servants of God (more than all the canonizations and beatifications done in the last two centuries) there are any number of martyrs. In a 1996 visit to Germany he beatified two anti-Nazi martyrs, the priests Bernhard Lichtenberg and Karl Leisner, while recalling Protestant martyrs of the same era like Count Helmut Moltke and Dietrich Bonhoeffer. He beatified twenty-six Spanish religious in 1989 (in 1999 he canonized ten of these martyrs in Rome) who were martyred in Spain's civil war, while a year earlier he did the same for Miguel Pro, SJ, who was shot by the violently anti-clerical Mexican authorities in 1927 (providing the only photograph of an actual martyrdom we possess as Father Pro stood before a firing squad). In 1981 he beatified Lorenzo Ruiz a missionary martyred in Japan. Three years later, in 1984, the pope canonized the 103 Martyrs of Korea.

In 1985 on his second trip to Zaire Pope John Paul beatified the religious sister Anuarite Nengapeta who had been murdered in 1964 by the *Simbas* in what was then the Congo. The slaughter of religious in that period was part of a long simmering native hatred for the Belgians in general and the religious orders that represented the West in particular. At the beatification ceremonies, the pope singled out four reasons why he considered Sister Anaurite a martyr: her commitment to her religious community (the Sisters of the Holy Family); her fidelity to her vows; her life of intense prayer; and the mutual support between her and her fellow sisters and superiors. It was, in short, fidelity *usque ad mortem* that caught the attention of the pontiff.

Holiness of the Church throughout the World

The sheer geographical spread of the canonizations and beatifications mentioned above (they are only representative examples) provides a partial reply to the question about why the pope is so lavish in his celebrations of the saints in general and the martyrs in particular. The short answer to that question is to recall the central notion

of the universal holiness of the Church that is a centerpiece of John Paul's thinking as he received it from his own experiences at the Second Vatican Council. In essence, canonizations and beatifications are empirical evidence of the holiness of the Church.

When one looks at the list of those beatified and canonized since John Paul first began such processes in 1979, it is evident that he is quite cognizant of the geographical diversity of those who have suffered martyrdom. He also follows the criterion of naming the martyrs by the country where they suffered rather than by reason of their nationality. Thus, to cite one conspicuous example, when the pope canonized the 117 martyrs of Vietnam in 1988, their group included persons who were native Vietnamese, Spanish, and French spanning a period from 1745 to 1862. Other group beatifications include eighty-five martyrs who suffered in England, Scotland, and Wales in the late sixteenth and early seventeenth centuries (1987); missionary martyrs in Ethiopia (1988); groups of religious who died in various parts of Spain were beatified in 1989, 1990, 1992, 1993, 1995, 1997, 1998, and 1999. In that same period the pope beatified martyrs who suffered during the French Revolution (1984) and another group from the same country in 1995 as well as martyrs who died in Thailand (1989); Ireland (1992); Mexico (1992); and Poland (1999). On 6 March 2000, during the Jubilee year, the pope beatified forty-four martyrs in Rome ranging from seventeenth-century martyrs in Brazil, the Philippines, and Vietnam to ten Polish nuns who gave their lives in exchange for other hostages and were shot by the Nazis on the border of Belarus in 1943.

The pope also has a partiality for celebrating beatifications and canonizations *in situ*—that is, he likes to make such proclamations in the countries where the person(s) lived and died. In that way he is able to give concrete expression not only to the universal call to holiness but to demonstrate that such holiness is characteristic of each local church and an impetus to fidelity and growth. Toward the finish of his apostolic exhortation *Ecclesia in Asia* (6 November 1999) the pope said:

> May they [i.e., the ancient and modern martyrs] stand as indomitable witnesses to the truth that Christians are always and everywhere to proclaim nothing other than the power of the Lord's cross. And may the blood of Asia's martyrs be now as always the seed of new life for the church in every corner of the continent.

Sentiments such as those uttered in Asia are part and parcel of the papal message. When the pope visited Lithuania in September of 1993, he reminded the audiences there that in the period after the war as many as four bishops, 185 priests and as many as a quarter million of lay people were deported to Siberia or put in prison camps. Their very existential state as exiles or prisoners was a form of witness and a stark sign of those godless forces against which the Gospel struggles.

Martyrdom and Theological Reflection

Lumen gentium (no. 42) places martyrdom within the context of the Church where the council sees this charism as having its deepest meaning. It is the Church, after all, that perceives martyrdom to be an "exceptional gift" and the "highest expression of love." One expression of this ecclesial sense of martyrdom is the roll call of martyrs who are named in the Roman canon of the liturgy who stand conspicuously as part of the witness of the Church that celebrates the Eucharist proclaiming the "Lord's death until he comes" (1 Cor 11:26).

When the Church reflects upon the person of the martyr, it not only recalls what has happened in the past as an historical event but seeks further understanding about the significance of the martyr's gesture. Again, *Lumen gentium* (no. 42) gives us the appropriate clue: "By martyrdom, a disciple is transformed into an image of His master, who freely accepted death on behalf of the world's salvation, he [i.e. the martyr] perfects that image even to the shedding of blood." To put it boldly, the martyr acts in imitation of Christ who gave himself even unto death. The paschal mystery of Christ is the complete template for the Christian. In that sense we can link the theme of the imitation of Christ to the rich Pauline insight that the very being of a person "in Christ" is a recapitulation of the Christ story; the martyr actualizes Paul's insight that "if we have died with Christ we believe that we shall also live with him" (Rom 6:8). That insight is surely background for the ancient custom of remembering the day of the martyr's death as a birth day *(dies natalis)* and surrounding the deeds of the martyr with the iconography of the palm of victory, the crown, and the language of overcoming.

Some contemporary theologians have seen the martyr in terms of "expressive" and "performative" language. The martyr's gesture is expressive in the sense that martyrs provide by their actions a language that utters a clear message. It is that expressive nature of the martyr's message that seems to have captured the imagination of John Paul II. The martyr's expressiveness contains both a prophetic "No!" to those who stand for the anti-human, the repressive, the demonic, and resistance to the Gospel, just as it utters a prophetic "Yes!" as an alternative to those negative forces. That dialectic of "yes and no" stands behind the pope's insistent calling to mind those who suffered from antireligious regimes as well as his insistence in places like *Veritatis splendor* that martyrdom can sometimes be demanded of those who remain steadfast in affirming the irreducible truths of faith.

If martyrdom is expressive language, it is also a form of performative language. The rubric of "performative" language comes to us via the philosophy of language where it has long been recognized that certain forms of speech (think of oaths in a courtroom or wedding vows) actually change a situation by their very utterance. Theologians have taken over that insight to note, quite rightly, that the sacred scriptures is not simply a book to be read but a text to be performed. After all, everything from acts of Christian charity to the sacramental and liturgical life of the Church can be understood as a performance of what is contained in the word of God. In that way we can say that the performance of the Word of God is a species of biblical exegesis in the sense that the very acting out of the Word of God is an attempt to uncover the deepest meaning of the text by actualizing it in life.

The martyrs perform the Word of God at a number of different levels. There is, of course, the fundamental template of the passion of Christ who is the martyr par excellence. That *imitatio Christi* has run as a leitmotif in the accounts of martyrs from the second-century *Martyrdom of Polycarp* down to accounts of our own day. Adopting that understanding allows us to see that the passion of Christ becomes recapitulated not only in the liturgy but also in the witness of those who live (and die) in the imitation of Christ. All performance of the Word of God is, in a very real sense, an exegesis of the scriptures, an "uncovering" and "unveiling" of the hidden meaning of the Word of God.

If we think of the performative character of the Christian life as a species of scriptural unveiling we begin to see the aptness of Daniel Boyarin's recent observation that martyrdom can be thought of as a discourse that is a "practice of dying for God and of talking about it, a discourse that changes and develops over time . . ." (Boyarin 1999, 94). The point Boyarin makes is that when the martyr gives his or her life "for God" that act enters into the tradition as another example of how the first template (Jesus Christ) becomes remembered and honored in the tradition. We tell the martyr's story either in the liturgy or in hagiography or in commemorative acts precisely because they contribute to the unfolding of the Paschal Mystery in time. It is for that reason, to reiterate a point, why John Paul II in *Tertio millenio adveniente* (no. 37) insists that "this witness should not be lost to the Church." He then concludes in that same section of his letter that

> the greatest homage which all the churches can give to Christ on the threshold of the third millennium will be to manifest the Redeemer's all-powerful presence through the fruits of faith, hope and charity present in men and women of many different tongues and races who have followed Christ in the various forms of the Christian vocation.

The theme of the ecumenical spread of martyrs in our century, touched on in *Tertio millennio adveniente,* gets a fuller treatment in the encyclical on ecumenism *Ut unum sint.* In fact, the pope opens that ground-breaking encyclical by noting that the long list of Christian martyrs in the twentieth century gives new impetus to those who seek Christian unity. The pope notes, in a strong rhetorical passage, that believers in Christ following in the footsteps of the martyrs of our day can hardly remain divided among themselves (no. 1). Later in the same encyclical the pope calls the witness of the martyrs as opening up a "vast new field" for ecumenism (no. 48).

Martyrdom and the Great Jubilee

The committee appointed by John Paul II for the celebration of the Great Jubilee in Rome published two small booklets for pilgrims coming to the Holy City during the celebrations after the opening of the Holy Door in Saint Peter's Basilica on Christmas Eve 1999. One booklet *Pellegrini a Roma* ("Pilgrims in Rome") is an artistic-spiritual guide to the holy places in Rome; the other, *Pellegrini in preghiera* ("Pilgrims at Prayer"), is a manual of prayers and devotional exercises for those who make the Holy Year pilgrimage. The former volume provides, among other things, a guide to the major catacombs, traditionally venerated as the burial place of many martyrs, while the latter has a beautiful section on prayers in honor of the martyrs.

Pellegrini provides a meditation on the martyrs of Rome in its reflection prefacing a discussion of the catacombs. The author cites two observations that span Christian history. Saint Athanasius, the fourth-century bishop of Alexandria, once wrote that the witness offered by the blood of the martyrs speaks louder than any sermon. Sixteen centuries later the radical Florentine priest, Primo Mazzolari, observed with his customary sharpness that the head of Saint John the Baptist spoke more loudly on a platter than it ever did when it was attached to his neck! In keeping with the wide sweep that characterizes John Paul's understanding of martyrdom, the same reflection looks not only to those martyrs in Rome whose names are invoked with such honor in first Eucharistic Prayer, but to those of our own day like Maximilian Kolbe, Edith Stein, Titus Brandsma, Oscar Romero, and the martyred Trappist monks of Algeria, and also those other Christians like Dietrich Bonhoeffer or non-Christians like Mohandas Gandhi.

In the Jubilee Year 2000 Pope John Paul presided over a liturgy in the ancient ruins of the Roman Colosseum honoring by broad category those Christians who died for their faith in the modern period. On 8 May a procession went to the Colosseum for a prayer service that included Orthodox, Protestant, Lutheran, Methodist, Anglican, and Evangelicals. Without naming specific persons they honored and prayed for persons who died for the faith in eight regions of the world: victims of the Soviet Union and its satellites, those who suffered under Nazism and Fascism, martyrs in Oceania and Asia, Spanish and Mexican witnesses to the faith, martyrs in the Americas, witnesses in Africa, and those who suffered in other parts of the world. The pope ended the service by asking the world to keep the memory of those martyrs alive. The definitive list submitted by local churches will be published in due time.

That ceremony gave flesh to the desire for the pope to keep alive the memory of those who witnessed even unto death the truth of the Gospel. The ceremony stands as a counter sign to the liturgical ceremony in Saint Peter's basilica on the first Sunday of Lent, when the pope affirmed the repentance of believers for the manifold failings of Christians in ages past who acted, through the Inquisition, through forced conversions, for acts of crusading war, through bigotry towards the Jews and others, in a manner incommensurate with the imperatives of Christian discipleship. The lifting up of the martyrs is a public gesture to illustrate that the cultivated field of this world will contain both weeds and wheat until the eschatological harvest.

The Colosseum ceremony, further, gave flesh to the ancient custom of memorializing the martyrs in a public fashion both by liturgical celebration (by their commemoration in the Mass and in the *Opus Dei*) and by the living tradition of hagiography that keeps close to the heart of the Church the martyrologies compiled over the past two millennia. Hence, it is not mere rhetoric for Saint Augustine to write that "the Church everywhere flourishes through the glorious deeds of the martyrs. . . ." (*Sermo* 329).

Pope John Paul's attention to the tradition of the martyrs fulfills the task of the good householder of the scriptures who brings forth things both old and new. We have celebrated the martyrs from the time when Saint Stephen was honored as the protomartyr in the Church to the present day, when martyrs most likely live hidden (but not forgotten) in the basement of jails, in exile, and in the Gulags of our unhappy times. Their blood, as Tertullian wrote millennia ago, is the seed of the Church.

See Also: TITUS BRANDSMA, DIVINUS PERFECTIONIS MAGISTER, ECCLESIA IN AMERICA, ECCLESIA IN AMERICA, EVANGELIUM VITAE, MAXIMILIAN KOLBE, OSCAR ROMERO, JAN SARKANDER, EDITH STEIN, TERTIO MILLENNIO ADVENIENTE, UT UNUM SINT, VERITATIS SPLENDOR, VIETNAM (MARTYRS OF). THIS VOLUME CONTAINS A SECTION THAT CONTAINS

SAINTS AND BLESSED CANONIZED AND BEATIFIED BY POPE JOHN PAUL II.

Bibliography: L. ACCATTOLI, *Man of the Millennium,* trans. J. AUMANN (Boston: Daughters of St. Paul, 2000). SUSAN BERGMAN, ed., *Martyrs* (San Francisco: HarperSanFrancisco, 1996). DANIEL BOYARIN, *Dying for God: Martyrdom and the Making Christianity and Judaism* (Stanford: Stanford University Press, 1999). LAWRENCE S. CUNNINGHAM, "Saints and Martyrs: Some Contemporary Considerations," *Theological Studies* 1999, 60: 529–537. R. FISCHELLA and R. LATOURELLE, ed., *Dictionary of Fundamental Theology* (New York: Paulist Press, 1995, s.v. "Martyrdom." N. LASH, "What Might Martyrdom Mean?" in *Suffering and Martyrdom in the New Testament,* ed., W. HORBURY and B. MCNEIL. (Cambridge: Cambridge University Press, 1981). ROBERT ROYAL, *The Catholic Martyrs of the Twentieth Century* (New York: Crossroad, 2000). GEORGE WEIGEL, *Witness to Hope: The Biography of Pope John Paul II* (New York: Cliff Street Books, 1999). KENNETH WOODWARD, *Making Saints* (New York; Crossroad, 1990).

[LAWRENCE S. CUNNINGHAM]

Part II: John Paul II and His Pontificate

The Life of John Paul II: A Chronicle

INTRODUCTION

Pope John Paul II is a biographer's dream. Journalists have a way of turning his childhood and early life into a melodrama set against the background of totalitarianism and foreign domination. Writers with a hagiographical bent, understandably moved by his traditional piety and moral rectitude, would beatify him in his lifetime. Pundits and editorial writers track his political activity and impact on international affairs. Historians of all stripes are challenged by the way religious, economic, cultural, and personal factors converge to define his papacy. Church historians note his every innovation in ritual and deviation from custom. Protestants welcome his ecumenical drive. Non-Christians resonate with his spiritual outlook that embraces everyone as a child of God. Secular writers struggle to explain the attraction and influence of this eminently religious man to a world that does not share his beliefs. Photo journalists and the electronic media have captured his life on film and tape, picturing the dramatic meetings and moments of this most public papacy. There is a biography of Pope John Paul II for people of all interests and tastes.

The pages that follow provide the raw data and dates from which biography is made, but it is not a biography. They begin with a brief sketch of his early years up to his election as pope. The account that follows is in the form of a chronicle, a detailed year-by-year report of significant events of the pontificate. The first two parts of the chronicle are taken from earlier volumes of the *New Catholic Encyclopedia,* one written in 1988, the other in 1995. In the first, Professor George H. Williams, himself an early biographer of Karol Wojtyła, recounts the extraordinary pilgrimage activity undertaken by Pope John Paul from the beginning of his papacy, as well as his prolific output of magisterial teaching. In the second, the foreign editor of the Catholic News Service William Pritchard continues the year-by-year account of the pope on the world's center stage, tracking his global travels, reporting the many contacts he made with other religious leaders, and recording his admonitions to both East and West about the moral responsibility of society after the fall of the Berlin Wall. Finally, CNS international editor Barb Fraze reports in detail the years leading up to the Great Jubilee Year 2000, including the regional assemblies of the Synod of Bishops called for by *Tertio millennio adveniente,* the pope's self-reflection on the twentieth anniversary of his ascendancy to the papacy, and his unprecedented visit to Cuba. The chronicle ends with the opening of the Holy Door and an account of the great events of the Jubilee Year itself.

The chronicle presented here does not replace the several very fine existing biographies of Pope John Paul, which in varying degrees probe his spiritual and intellectual development and evaluate his achievements. The thematic essays in part 1 of this volume interpret the pope's vision and actions. The following section is intended as a reference tool, designed to present a detailed timeline that relates the pope's travels, pronouncements, and other activities to each other and to contemporary world events.

[EDS.]

KAROL WOJTYŁA: EARLY YEARS

Born 18 May 1920, in Wadowice, an industrial town in the Archdiocese of Kraków, Poland. He was the third child of Karol Wojtyła and Emilia Kaczorowska. His elder brother, Edmund, died in 1932 at the age of 26. An older sister died in infancy. The elder Karol Wojtyła, an officer in the Polish army, retiring as a captain in 1927, was regarded by friends and superiors alike as a just and religious man of great integrity. Both his piety and his love of Polish literature had great influence on young Karol.

As a high-school student in Wadowice, Wojtyła planned a career as an actor under the tutelage of a local teacher, Mieczysław Kotlarczyk. Kotlarczyk's vision of a "theater of the inner word," in which power of drama

Karol Wojtyła, seated on ground, with his father and friends in 1930. (Roger Viollet/Liaison Agency.)

was centered in the word of the actor, presenting a universal, transformative truth to the audience, rather than in plots, sets, and gestures, shaped much of Wojtyła's later literary work and nourished his philosophical and theological insights. In 1938 he moved with his father to Kraków (his mother had died nine years earlier) and entered the Jagiellonian University, concentrating on poetry and drama, though he also began to study philosophy. During the Nazi occupation he worked in a quarry, then in a chemical plant, where he became a spokesman for better working conditions. Despite the relentless attacks of the Nazis on the Church and Polish culture, young Wojtyła's religious and artistic life flourished. In 1940 he met Jan Tyranowski, a lay mystic, who had begun the "Living Rosary" organization—a lay effort (most of the local priests had been arrested) to minister to the spiritual needs of other young men. Tyranowski also introduced him to the spirituality of St. John of the Cross. From 1939 on he helped to create an underground theater—a movement that reached a definitive shape in 1941 when Kotlarczyk moved to Kraków and established the Rhapsodic Theater, with Wojtyła as one of its first actors. In February 1941 his father died. Over the course of the next year and a half, he decided that his vocation was to the priesthood.

The Nazis had closed the Kraków seminary, forcing Wojtyła and the other candidates for the priesthood to study theology secretly, under the direction of the archbishop, Adam Stefan Sapieha. After the war he completed his studies in the seminary, was ordained 1 November 1946, and was immediately sent to Rome, where he spent the next two years earning a doctorate at the Angelicum under the direction of R. Garrigou-Lagrange. His thesis was entitled "Quaestio fidei apud S. Joannem a Cruce." Though he successfully defended the thesis, he was not granted the degree because he could not afford to have the thesis published. When he returned to Kraków, he was assigned to pastoral work in parishes and with university students. (He also submitted his thesis at the Jagiellonian University, which granted him a doctorate in theology.) The next few years saw the beginning of a number of pastoral initiatives by Fr. Wojtyła that would become lasting themes of his ministry. In 1950 he initiated the first-ever marriage preparation program in the Archdiocese of Kraków; in retreats and conferences with young couples he began to articulate his understanding of love as the gift of oneself to another, a theme that he would develop philosophically in *Love and Responsibility* (1960), and that would be fundamental to his papal catechesis on *The Original Unity of Man and Woman*. In his work as university chaplain he attracted a circle of intellectuals that marked the beginning of a dialogue with modern culture that has continued throughout his career.

EARLY YEARS–TIMELINE

1920	18 May Karol Józef Wojtyła born in Wadowice, Poland
1938	August Enters Jagiellonian University in Kraków
1942	October Begins seminary studies for archdiocese of Kraków
1946	November Ordained a priest; begins graduate studies in Rome
1953	October Begins lecturing at Jagiellonian University
1954	12 October Joins the philosophy department of the Catholic University of Lublin
1956	December Appointed to chair of ethics at the Catholic University of Lublin
1958	4 July Consecrated auxiliary bishop for Kraków
1960	January First edition of *Love and Responsibility* published
1963	5-15 December Pilgrimage to the Holy Land 30 December Named archbishop of Kraków
1962-65	Attends sessions of the Second Vatican Council
1966	Celebration of the millennium of the baptism of Poland
1967	28 June Created a cardinal by Pope Paul VI
1969	December *Person and Act* published
1972	Establishes archdiocesan synod of Kraków for implementation of Vatican II and publishes *Sources of Renewal: Implementing the Second Vatican Council*
1978	16 October Elected pope; takes the name John Paul II

In 1953 he began an annual custom of a two-week-long kayaking trip with young families, making it a pastoral opportunity to minister to a community by active engagement in its life and thought. His literary work (plays, poems, and essays) from 1946 to 1960 reflect a similar concern for following Christ in transforming culture from within.

In 1951 Fr. Wojtyła began to study for a doctorate in philosophy, writing a habilitation thesis for Jagiellonian University (which would allow him to teach at the university level). His thesis, *An Evaluation of the Possibility of Constructing a Christian Ethics on the Basis of the*

System of Max Scheler, involves a serious confrontation with phenomenology, which appeared to him to offer great hope of an evangelical ethical understanding—one that could issue a convincing appeal to modern man—provided that it be coupled with a truly metaphysical appreciation of the objectivity of truth. Shortly after he earned his degree, in 1954, the communist government suppressed the faculty of theology at Jagiellonian; thus he became a lecturer in ethics and moral theology at the Catholic University of Lublin, the only Catholic university behind the iron curtain. Father Wojtyła became recognized in the academic world through the more than 300 articles he published in scholarly journals, especially in the area of Christian ethics. In the progress of his own thought he integrated the methods and insights of phenomenology with his strong grounding in the thought of St. Thomas Aquinas.

In 1958 Pius XII consecrated Fr. Wojtyła titular bishop of Ombi (ancient Egypt) and auxiliary to Archbishop Eugeniusz Baziak, apostolic administrator of Kraków. (The see had been vacant from 1951 because of obstruction by the communist regime.) When Archbishop Baziak died, in 1962, the regime continued to exercise its veto right over proposed successors to the see; the first nominee found to be acceptable was Bishop Wojtyła. On 13 January 1964 Pope Paul VI named him archbishop of Kraków and on 26 June 1967 created him cardinal.

Bishop Wojtyła took an active part in the Second Vatican Council. His most prominent interventions concerned the documents later promulgated as *Dignitatis humanae* and *Gaudium et spes.* He expressed the fundamental motivation of the Church's mission to man in this contemporary world: "Every pastoral initiative, every apostolate, of priests and laity alike, has as its purpose that the human person in every relationship—with self, with others, with the world—should perceive and actually express the truth of the human being's integral vocation" (*Acta* v. 4, pt. 2, 660). The personalism so characteristic of his thought he perceived as the gospel understanding of the worth and dignity of man and that was the basis on which he wished the conciliar affirmation of religious freedom to be expressed (ibid., 11–13). He also gave clear enunciation to the total range of the Church's mission on behalf of human dignity. "The way in which God, through the Cross, has made the work of creation become part of the work of Redemption has settled forever how the Church accepts the meaning of the term "world; the Church's service brings to the world truth and morality, but always in accord with the transcendence that Redemption means" (ibid., 661).

After the Council he dedicated himself completely to its implementation. In 1972 he published a book on the foundations of Vatican II renewal and convened an archdiocesan pastoral synod. This synod included the laity and religious as well as the clergy of the archdiocese; their task was, simply, to renew the life of the Church in the archdiocese by a communal effort to implement the teaching of the Council. The synod lasted seven years; Wojtyła, as Pope John Paul II, presided over its solemn closing in 1979, during the course of his first papal visit to Poland.

On the national level, Cardinal Wojtyła quickly became a prominent figure. He was vice-president of the Polish episcopal conference, president of its committees on ecclesiastical studies and on the laity; in March 1978 he issued the report of the doctrinal committee critical of the communist regime's imposition of materialism and secularism, in violation of the cultural and religious heritage of the Polish people. With Cardinal Stefan Wyszyński, the Polish primate, Cardinal Wojtyła became a leading figure in the Polish Church's stand for its own rights. The stage had been set for a renewal of Catholic life throughout Poland some years earlier. In 1957 Cardinal Wyszyński had proclaimed a nine-year "Great Novena" to prepare for the celebration of the millennium of the Church in Poland—an evangelical enterprise that undoubtedly influenced Pope John Paul's vision of the whole Church renewing itself, particularly through the Council, on the eve of the third millennium.

Internationally, Cardinal Wojtyła was well known to his peers. He participated in all assemblies of the synod of bishops (except for the first, in 1967, when he refused to attend out of respect for Cardinal Wyszyński, who had been denied permission to attend by the Polish government) and was elected one of the three members for Europe on the synodal *Consilium.* In the 1974 synod, he was appointed *relator.* His published monographs and his leadership as archbishop were matters of record; he was known in the United States from several visits, particularly to the Philadelphia Eucharistic Congress in 1976. In August of 1978 he participated in the conclave that elected Cardinal Albino Luciani as Pope John Paul I. After the Pope died, a month later, he again participated in the conclave. He was elected on the fourth ballot: 16 October 1978. He took the name John Paul II, and was inaugurated six days later.

[T. C. O'BRIEN/EDS.]

PAPACY: 1978-1988

By his choice of name, John Paul II honored his immediate predecessor of thirty-three days and, like him, pointed to the two popes of Vatican II, John XXIII and

Paul VI. The choice was a clear signal that he intended to continue the implementation of the council's work, as he stated in his first major address of 17 October 1978. In that and other addresses and gestures following his election, John Paul II signaled the style and substance that would become characteristic of the first decade of his pontificate. He identified episcopal collegiality as "the special cohesion" that unites the bishops of the world with the Bishop of Rome in the magisterium. In speaking to the diplomatic corps accredited to the Holy See, he called for freedom of religion for all. In an address to journalists he called for proportionate coverage of "the spiritual aspects of the Church." He signaled his emphasis on Marian devotion in the design of his papal coat-of-arms that features a large M under the cross. In the formal enthronement on 22 October 1978, he eschewed the tiara. In its absence, in his inaugural homily he meditated on its three crowns as plausibly reflective of the threefold office of Christ as prophet, priest, and king, a motif he related to the Vatican II references to the People of God as "a kingdom of priests."

From the outset John Paul II abandoned the sovereign "We," intending thereby to affirm the continuity of John Paul, the pope, with Karol Wojtyła, the bishop, priest, artist, and scholar. In testimony of this, he authorized the publication of the bilingual, analytical *Karol Wojtyła negli scritti* (1980). The collection arranged his 1,490 titles in seven languages under the headings "poet, philosopher, theologian, pastor." Verbal and conceptual currents from these writings, though uncited, remained detectible in his papal pronouncements for several years. On 12 November he took liturgical possession of St. John Lateran, his cathedral see as Bishop of Rome, completing thereby the inaugural formalities of his pontificate, and beginning what would turn out to be the intensive and extensive discharge of his primatial duties in Italy by many visitations in Rome and throughout the Republic (70).

Early in his pontificate, John Paul II made two appointments that signaled the direction of his policy and thinking in political and doctrinal matters. He appointed Agostino Casaroli to succeed the deceased Secretary of State, Cardinal Jean Villot. Named a cardinal in June 1979, Casaroli had previously distinguished himself as chief negotiator of the Vatican in Eastern Central Europe. The other figure who was to have high visibility in the first decade of John Paul's papacy was Cardinal Joseph Ratzinger, formerly archbishop of Munich, appointed Prefect of the Sacred Congregation for the Doctrine of the Faith in 1981. Ratzinger, a *peritus* at Vatican II and an established theologian in his own right, gave the Congregation new energy in its efforts to safeguard the integrity of Church teaching. This zealous concern for orthodoxy, already evident under his predecessor Cardinal Franjo

John Paul II (Catholic News Service.)

Seper, was manifest in the disciplinary action that the Congregation initiated against such prominent theologians as Jacques Pohier, Hans Küng, Edward Schillebeeckx, and Charles Curran. The first apostolic constitution issued by John Paul, *Sapientia christiana* (May 1979), regulates the appointment of faculty in pontifical universities; actually a dozen years in formulation, it unmistakably bears his stamp.

John Paul on Pilgrimage. In the first decade of his pontificate, John Paul II undertook 37 trips to about 50 countries, to several more than once. In the course of these travels, the pope has developed a certain ritual—a pattern of visitation. Upon arriving in a country for his first visit, he kisses the ground (usually the airport tarmac). He is received at some point as a temporal sovereign by the head of state; he addresses the diplomatic corps, the bishops, the priests, the religious, and besides the lay faithful in and outside cathedrals, the general population in stadiums and other places of assembly. He singles out special groupings: youth, farmers, urban workers, the poor, the sick, the handicapped. He visits at least one Marian shrine, meets at least once with the local Polish community, and seeks out minority groups, often speaking in their language when different from that of the majority (indigenous peoples, the ethnically marginalized, undocumented workers, refugees). He makes an effort to have at least one intra-Christian and one interfaith ecumenical conference and among the faithful, he solemnizes at a beatification of local servants of the Church or announces forthcoming canonizations in Rome.

On every major pilgrimage it has come about, following the model that emerged on his first (to Mexico to address the Latin American Episcopal Conference), that the local itinerary and some of the themes are worked out with the regional or national episcopal conferences. John Paul at junctures along the route responds to a series of position papers submitted in advance and studied by him in Rome well before his arrival. His own prepared responses and major addresses, seldom modified in actual delivery, take on the aura of encyclical letters in that he later cites himself from this growing body of globally delivered instruction, counsel, and exhortation. The pilgrimages gain him direct access to the attention of the media, and this further extends his audience to Catholics and non-Catholics alike, and allows him to admonish, persuade, and engage readers, listeners, and viewers to hear his message.

In the course of these papal visitation there are typically three eminences (in whatever pragmatic sequence): the Bishop of Rome listens to, confers with, and instructs the assembled bishops of the land; the Sovereign of Vatican City meets with the head of state or his deputy to discuss issues that sometimes touch on relations of Church and State, but more often on broad humanitarian and social questions; and the Supreme Pontiff and *pastor omnium* celebrates the liturgy with the people and commits the country visited to the protection of the Virgin Mary.

Mexico, Poland, the U.N. and the U.S. In his first "pilgrimage of faith" beyond Italy (25–31 January 1979) he kissed the tarmac in Santo Domingo on the island of Hispaniola, where Mass was first celebrated by Spaniards in the New World, and then flew on to Mexico to give the keynote address in Puebla at the Third General Assembly of Latin American Bishops (CELAM). The pope deplored in liberation theology the interpretation of Jesus as solely a prophet in the OT sense of social critic. Warning against any construing of political, economic, and social liberation as coinciding with salvation in Jesus Christ, he defended the sole magisterium of bishops and their truth that brings with it an authentic liberation, and warned against "parallel magisteriums" in misguided seeking to implement the preferential love of the poor by an over-socialized and politicized gospel.

The messages he delivered in Mexico related thematically to his impending inaugural encyclical, *Redemptor hominis* (March 1979). He reminded priests that they "are not social directors, political leaders, or officials of a temporal power." He clarified the triple mission and office (*triplex munus*) of the Redeemer in the Church and the world amid a rich tapestry of themes, then dealt scripturally with Christian anthropology and promoted the ongoing dialogue of salvation within and beyond the Church.

John Paul returned to Poland (2–10 June 1979) on the occasion of the ninth centenary in Kraków of the slaying of Bishop Stansislas (d. 1079). Notable was the more than a minute of utter silence of over a million in the meadows of Kraków meditating on the presence of their former archbishop and Pope among them. He reiterated the theme of his first encyclical that humanity cannot be understood fully without Christ at the center of history. Within European history he stressed the spiritual unity of Old Christendom, Catholic and Orthodox, and (at Gniezno) on his own providential role as the first Slavic Pope with responsibility under the direction of the Holy Spirit "at this precise moment" to lead Europeans back to their Christian sources. Although John Paul made no direct allusion to the communist system, he was so devotedly, attentively, and peaceably received by such masses of his fellow Poles that his first visit to Poland is widely credited retrospectively with having energized and channeled the national labor movement Solidarity in achieving by peaceful means an extraordinary (if temporary) reordering of Polish society, its industry and agriculture.

It was in response to the invitation of Kurt Waldheim, the Secretary General of the United Nations, that John Paul conceived of his third journey abroad, which lasted from 29 September to 7 October 1979. En route he stopped for two days in Ireland where he and the Cardinal Primate agreed he would deal straightaway with the stubborn and urgent Irish problem. At Drogheda on the River Boyne, close to the Republic's border with Northern Ireland, he solemnly and firmly called for an end of terror and pointedly insisted that violence on either or any side should never mask itself as Christian, being instead ongoing fratricide.

He gave six addresses to the United Nations community in New York, including an address to the XXXIV General Assembly. He expressed the wish that the U.N. never cease to be the forum for the global discussion of problems, called for the primacy of spiritual values in the behavior of individuals, among professionals of all kinds, and in societies at large, appealed to the Universal Declaration of Human Rights as both an inspiration for, and a test of, appropriate international and domestic behavior. He also called for "the just settlement of the Palestine question" and renewed the call of his predecessor for a special statute under international guarantee for Jerusalem, sacred to three religions. He expressed growing concern for Lebanon, encouraged the reduction of arms, and dealt systematically with the current and long-range threats to human rights and peace, including neocolonialism and societal and other "structures" that condemn persons adhering to spiritual or transnational values to the status of second or even third-class citizenship in a materialistic society.

In the United States, familiar to him from two earlier visits as cardinal, his instructions, exhortations, and admonitions dealt with political-constitutional issues (freedom of conscience and of religion), on life-family issues, and on socio-economic issues ("consumerism," migrants, the unemployed). The themes were not new, for he was drawing on papal precedent, Vatican II, and on his own pre-papal teachings; but he was explicating them for the first time on a large and challenging scale in a religiously, ethnically, and constitutionally pluralistic society, conveying his views as engagingly and winsomely as possible in the idiom of citizens of a superpower.

In his address in Yankee Stadium, New York, he appealed to Americans to take from their substance and "not just from their abundance" for the poor in their own country and in the Third World. In Philadelphia before the representatives of diocesan priests, he held up the eternal vocation of the priest, who as a "man for others" leads the congregation *in persona Christi* in eucharistic worship. In the cathedral of the Immaculate Conception in the presence of the archbishop of the Ukrainians, Myroslav Ivan Lubachivsky, he placed the vocation of the various Catholic rites and jurisdictions in a larger setting, reminding all Byzantine-rite Catholics that in their traditions they "are called to adhere with love and respect to certain particular forms of discipline," alluding here to the imposition of clerical celibacy in the diaspora and other accommodations in an adapted canon law, which he and his predecessors, he said, "have judged necessary for the well-being of the whole body of Christ."

In Des Moines he addressed the world of the farm belt. In Chicago, among others, he addressed the assembled bishops of the U.S., recalling his own gratification in working through a national episcopal conference, stressed the collegiality formulated by Vatican II as the completion of Vatican I, and then emphasized points already made by the bishops in their pastoral letter of 1975: on civil rights regardless of race or ethnicity, on five life-family issues (faithful monogamy, divorce, contraception, homosexual activity, abortion, euthanasia; to which would later be added a seventh magisterial instruction on genetic and embryological technology). He underscored the decisive and indisputable roles of each bishop as authoritative teacher with respect to both priests and non-episcopal theologians (the magisterial issue), recalling the fourth bishop of Philadelphia, St. John Neumann, as an ideal; and he called upon each as the liturgical president to see to it that any development in the parish services should remain "theocentric," that intercommunion not be resorted to as a means of achieving ecclesial unity (one of the several ecumenical issues), and that the priests under them adhere to the proper limits of general absolution and concertedly foster the Sacrament of Reconcilia-

tion. Welcomed in Washington as a head of state, he was received by the President and Mrs. Carter in the White House. He addressed diplomats, journalists, and the Catholic University community of the U.S. on the campus of The Catholic University of America in Washington.

Second Pontifical Year. On the first anniversary of his pontificate, John Paul issued the apostolic exhortation *Catechesi tradendae* in response to the request of the 1977 Synod of Bishops (in which he had participated as cardinal). It highlighted the need for systematic catechesis, adapted to the needs of the modern world. At the end of November 1979, John Paul was in Turkey, visiting Ankara, Istanbul and Meryam Ana (the Marian shrine near the site of ancient Ephesus). He was received as a head of state by the government, and he reminded the small Catholic community of moral values held in common with Muslims. The climax in Istanbul of the intra-Christian fellowship took place in the cathedral of St. George in the Phanar, when in the course of the liturgy, presided over by the Ecumenical Patriarch Demetrios I, the Pope called for a new dialogue of charity, looking forward to full intercommunion, and co-announcing the establishment of two theological commissions to help to this end.

Early in 1980 John Paul convoked two extraordinary national synods in Rome. In the unprecedented particular synod of the Dutch bishops (14–31 January) he was instrumental in the formulation of a document that pulled back the Dutch church from a number of positions advanced by some leaders. In the synod of Ukrainian Catholics (24–27 March), their archbishop in Philadelphia was made coadjutor to Major Archbishop Cardinal Joseph Slipyi, but the erection of a patriarchate (controversially presumed by the Cardinal) was synodally rejected for, among other reasons, it would exacerbate the condition of the underground Uniates in the Soviet Union. In May 1980 the Pope told the Italian bishops' conference that they were "in charge of the Church of Italy."

For his part, he had already begun the process, foreseen by his predecessors in the revision of the concordat with the Republic of Italy, of distancing official Catholicism from the Christian Democratic Party. In May John Paul entered upon his first pilgrimage to black, primarily equatorial, Africa. At the outset in Kinshasa (Zaire) he declared that "Christ, in the members of His Body, is Himself African," a phrasing he would come to adopt for many non-European peoples. A distinctive theme, in addition to extensive treatment of life-family issues, as he moved across Zaire (during the centennial of its church), the Congo Republic (Brazzaville), Kenya, Ghana (during the centennial of its church), Burkina Faso (Upper Volta), and the Ivory Coast, was inculturation, specifically the appropriate Africanization of the gospel. He warned against its vagaries, particularly being reserved about some excesses in liturgical accommodation. He took cognizance of polygamy, observing that monogamy was not a European but rather originally a "Semitic" ideal of conjugal love and partnership. In addressing heads of state and diplomatic corps he underscored the independence and universality of the Church and the propriety of plenary freedom in the exercise of religion as consonant with all legitimate national and decolonializing aspirations.

The first visit to France was occasioned by the invitation of the director general of UNESCO. In a major address to UNESCO's executive council in Paris (2 June 1980) he summoned the leaders of science, technology, and government to promote the highest of cultural values and notably the dignity of every person in whatever the form of society. He warned against the misuse of wealth and technology, and the disfigurement of global life by inappropriate concentration of wealth and power.

From 30 June to 12 July he was in Brazil. In thirteen cities and sites in the most populous Catholic country in the world, he participated in the tenth National Eucharistic Congress (Fortaleza), in the silver jubilee of CELAM (Rio de Janeiro), and in the concentration of the new basilica of the principal Brazilian Marian sanctuary (Aparaceda). Among his emphases distinctive to the Brazilian scene, he noted the harmonious melding of different indigenous, imported, and immigrant ethnic groups and cultures in a pluralism that could be dangerous, however, if all norms and standards were dissolved in relative and mutual selfishness. Going beyond his positions at Puebla, he provided unambiguous support for the progressive sociopolitical orientation of the Brazilian bishops, endorsed labor unions working not exclusively through a single party (Sao Paulo), acknowledged the ecclesial character of the base communities, and defended the much reduced indigenous population in their traditions and in their jungle habitats (Manaus).

In his apostolic letter, *Sanctorum altrix* (11 July 1980) on the fifteenth centenary of the birth of St. Benedict, John Paul reminded the people of the continent of Europe of its saintly patronage and deplored the new paganism in the very lands where pioneering monks had held aloft the dignity and discipline of work, prayer, and stability.

Third Pontifical Year. John Paul convened the sixth general assembly of the Synod of Bishops (26 September–25 October 1980) on the theme of the family. He embodied the important points of its deliberation, close to his mind and heart from prepapal days, in the apostolic exhortation *Familiaris consortio* 22 (November 1981), and endorsed them in another form, The Charter of Family Rights (late 1983).

Momentous was the Pope's seventh pilgrimage abroad, to the Federal Republic of Germany (15–19 November). He observed that the scheduling of his pastoral visit was occasioned by the seventh centenary of the death of Albert the Great, and he took notice of the fact that his visit coincided with the 450th anniversary of the imperial diet that received the Augsburg Confession. He said that, as Martin Luther had once been a pilgrim to Rome, so he came as a pilgrim to Germany, "to set with his pilgrimage a sign of union in the central mystery of faith." To Catholic theologians assembled in the Marian shrine of Altötting he observed that Vatican II's Decree on Ecumenism, in recognizing "a hierarchy of truth," did not intend thereby to be reductionist, and thus he upheld as wholesome the ongoing disputation, fraternal dialogue, and openness among theologians, so long as they understood theology as derived from revealed Scripture, as transmitted and understood in the tradition, and so long as they acknowledged that "the magisterium and theology have two different tasks to perform." He articulated most emphatically the recurrent "magisterial issue," namely the unique teaching of bishops in collegiality with the Bishop of Rome. The Pope was notably warm in his expression of universal gratitude to the German "genius" in the history of culture and scholarship, and currently in the generous aid to the Third World.

His second encyclical, *Dives in misericordia* (30 November–2 December 1980) continued a theme of his inaugural encyclical. He concentrated on the role of the Church in reflecting the divine mercy and on the necessity of mutual human acts of forgiveness, "especially in this modern age," based on the recognition of God as "our model of mercy," alike in Judaism, Christianity and Islam.

John Paul spent February 16 to 27, 1981, in Asia. In Karachi, Pakistan, he alluded to the Five Pillars of Islam when he emphasized three of them as common to Catholic Christianity, and tactfully clarified what was both similar and different on the remaining points. John Paul spent six days in the Philippines, where he addressed himself thematically to "the reckless exploitation of nature." In Manila he beatified sixteen martyrs, among them a Filipino, the first time a Pope officiated at a beatification outside Rome (or Avignon). He forcefully addressed the disparities of wealth and poverty and impediments to human rights (President Ferdinand Marcos present), while counseling nonviolent socioeconomic change, addressed the Muslim leadership (Davao) in hope of mutual mercy between Muslim and Christian, and in an address to Chinese Catholics (in Manila) from various lands he signaled his hope that Catholics in mainland China could be regarded as both patriotic and loyal to Rome. In the space of four days in Japan, he met with the Emperor, met with Buddhist and Shinto leaders together, had a notable exchange with young adults in Keruan Stadium partly in Japanese (as he had previously said Mass for three months in transliterated Japanese) and on all stops (Tokyo, Hiroshima, Nagasaki) he stressed the theme of peace and nonviolence and the proper office of science and technology. He returned to Rome via Guam and Anchorage (greeted there by a delegation of Catholic prelates and President Ronald Reagan).

After a general audience on 13 May 1981, while he was riding slowly through St. Peter's Square, an attempt was made on the Pope's life by Mehemet Alí Agça, the Turkish rightist and convicted killer of a Turkish editor. The stricken Pope was rushed to Gemelli Polyclinic Hospital in peril of life from abdominal wounds. He was kept there until 23 May and was obliged to return for viral infection and foreseen restorative surgery (3 June–14 August). He recuperated with reduced duties at Castel Gondolfo. He would never again be able to be so accessible to crowds, a heavily guarded "popemobile" henceforth impairing the icon of the Universal Pastor among his flocks.

At an emotion-drenched trial, Agça, an escaped accomplice in the Piazza, and several other suspects (some in absentia) were accused, among other charges, of a conspiracy allegedly masterminded by the Bulgarian secret police. Agça was given a life sentence by the Italian court. In a dramatic act of personal reconciliation, the Pope visited Alí Agça in his cell in Rebibbia Prison (27 December 1983). The published photograph of the confidential exchange between the Christian victim-priest and the repentant Muslim assassin-by-intent served globally among Catholics and others as a powerful icon of penance in the confessional and absolution and in this case of extraordinary, exemplary mutual reconciliation. At another level of reconciliation, having addressed to Jan Cardinal Willebrands a letter on the occasion of the fifth centenary of the birth of Martin Luther, calling for a joint Catholic-Lutheran effort to study afresh the schism, John Paul visited the Lutheran church in Rome (11 December), to pray with its minister and congregation, an act unique in papal history.

In the midst of his convalescence there took place two major conciliar anniversaries: the 16th centenary of the Council of Constantinople (381) and the 1550th anniversary of the Council of Ephesus (431). During these observances (6–7 June 1981) concurrent in Rome and Istanbul, John Paul was able to appear for a five-minute message, in which he repeated a portion of the Nicene Creed as it had always been for the Greeks: without the Western addendum of *filioque*. In this, possibly the theologically most significant intra-Christian ecumenical event of his pontificate to date, there were representatives of five non-Catholic communions besides the Orthodox and a staff-member of the World Council of Churches (WCC).

The main achievement of the closing months of the third year of his pontifical was his third encyclical *Laborem exercens*, originally conceived as celebrative of the ninetieth anniversary of *Rerum novarum* (Leo XIII's great social encyclical). He theologically reconceived toil by the sweat of the brow not so much as punishment for the Fall but as a way to earthly perfection and mutual care and affirmed the workbench as the nexus of human life and a source of human dignity in the earthly calling of labor and service.

Fourth Pontifical Year. John Paul undertook seven trips abroad in 1982, undaunted by the attempt on his life. His tenth pilgrimage as Pope was his second to equatorial Africa (12–19 February), where he dealt afresh with inculturation, lauding the vitality and enthusiasm of the African soul, but insisting on monogamy along with his other life-family themes, while he upheld the universal character of the Catholic Church, whose authority should not be diminished under the pretext of safeguarding African values from foreign tutelage.

His pilgrimage to Portugal (12–15 May) had a poignant personal intention, for he wished to appear before the Virgin of Fatima on the anniversary (13 May 1982) of the attempt on his life. On the eve preceding, after the Rosary, a maddened priest of the Latin-rite Fraternity of Archbishop Marcel Lefèbvre at Econe, Switzerland, wielded a knife as the Pope approached, shouting, "Down with the Pope and Vatican II." At the Mass the next day commemorating the 65th anniversary of the appearance of the Virgin to the shepherd trio (the one survivor, the Carmelite Sister Lucia being present), the Pope, recalling the motherly severity of the original messages of 1917, reconsecrated the whole world to the Virgin and asked that she intercede for its deliverance from hunger, sins against life, injustices and from the incalculable destruction of nuclear war.

His pilgrimage to Great Britain (28 May–2 June 1982) was an act of apostolic valor, for it was during the war of Britain with Catholic Argentina over the Falkland Islands (Malvinas). From Westminster, to Edinburgh, to Cardiff, John Paul made the celebration of all seven sacraments (from Baptism through First Communion and Ordination) thematic in his pastoral visitation of his English, Scottish, and Welsh flocks. His ecumenical celebration with Archbishop Robert Runcie in Canterbury cathedral was notable in the festive renewal together of common baptismal vows and an exchange of tokens against the background of the recent acceptance (the month before) of the final report of the Anglican-Catholic International Commission (ARCIC). Notable too, was the ecumenical coordination of services in the two nearly facing cathedrals in Liverpool.

Within scarcely more than a week John Paul was in Argentina on a mission of peace (11–12 June), deploring the war, as he had in Britain, urging a more rational and constructive patriotism, and conferring earnestly with the ruling junta in the presidential palace. Within days (15 June) he was in Geneva, where he addressed the sixty-eighth annual conference of the International Labor Organization, lifting up themes of his encyclical on work and proposing solidarity among government, workers, and employees, yet upholding the right of independent unions. His sixth trip of the year was to autonomous San Marino.

The Pope's seventh trip of the year was his twice-postponed visitation of Spain, 31 October to 9 November. Near Basque country, he was firm in his appeal to eschew violence however noble the cause, speaking with the voice of "one who has suffered personally from violence." He successively venerated the sites of SS. Teresa and John of the Cross. In the cathedral of Santiago de Compostella, in the presence of the King and especially invited representatives of the Common Market, he set forth his vision of a culturally united Europe, based upon shared Christian values, and he exhorted Europe, as one of the seven continents, to redeem the war torn past and to resume collectively its role as "the guiding light of civilization."

Fifth Pontifical Year. With the apostolic constitution, *Sacrae disciplinae legis* of 25 January 1983, John Paul promulgated the *Codex Iuris Canonici*, revised as mandated by Vatican II.

Between 2 March and 10 March, John Paul visited all seven countries of Central America and Haiti. His overriding concern in Nicaragua was the emergence of a divided Church, nearly schismatic, "charismatic," "a people's church," thereby imperiling the role of the universal Church. In Managua he publicly reprimanded one of the five priests in the government. Taunted by an intemperate throng with the shout: "We want peace," the Pope thundered back "The Church is the first to ask for peace." In the seven Central American societies, many of which were in progressive disintegration, in widespread fear, repression, hunger, violence, urban congestion, and despair, and where fundamentalist and stridently anti-Catholic missions overtly supported sever-al oppressive regimes and where many bishops and priests were defending the much abused rights of Indians and of the impoverished and the threatened generally, John Paul specifically chided the arrogantly born-again proselytizing sectaries. He did not, however, choose to draw attention to the differences between "a people's church" (self-distancing itself from the magisterium and oversight of a bishop and therefore more prone to governmental pressure) and the congeries of base communities (which, extending from Brazil, represent a communal Catholic modality of accommodation to the needs of deracinated, fearful, or marginalized populations, yet independent of state control and accessible to priestly ministry). His visit to Haiti coincided with a national eucharistic congress.

He visited Poland again (16–23 June), comforting a people loyal to their bishops and primate, but despondent at the closing down by martial law of Solidarity, which had sprung up in hope after his first visit. In Częstochowa, "where we have always been free" (an allusion to historic or imminent invasion from East or West), he presented to the Virgin as sovereign of Poland his sash torn by a bullet in the attempt on his life. Rural folk around Poznan were encouraged in defense of private farms. In two meetings with Wojciech Jaruzelski, neither side gave in the fundamental issues. But the Pope was permitted to meet privately for several hours with Nobel Laureate Lech Walesa and his family.

For the vigil and feast of the Assumption, John Paul was at Lourdes. He was in Austria (10–13 September), an interval coinciding with the closing year's program there of Christian renewal. He observed the third centenary of the lifting of the Turkish siege of Vienna through the heroism of Polish king John Sobieski, but he took the occasion of the Christian victory to deplore "the equal shame" for atrocities committed on both sides (with evident contemporary allusion). On other occasions, too, he emphasized the special vocation of Austria between Eastern and Western Europe.

The sixth general assembly of the Synod of Bishops (29 September–29 October) attended to the theme of penance and reconciliation. A year later, in his own apostolic exhortation, *Reconciliatio et paenitentia,* John Paul distinguished three valid meanings for social sin, but eschewed the concept of systemic or institutional sin, and rejected any reduction of mortal sin to an act of "fundamental option" or contempt of God or neighbor and urged that general absolution be kept to limited times and occasions.

Sixth Pontifical Year. In January 1984 the establishment of full diplomatic relations between the Holy See and the United States was announced, while in February the Vatican-Italian agreement on the revision of the Lateran Accords was signed, bringing Italy into roughly the same relation to the Holy See as other traditionally Catholic states. Later (June) John Paul paid his first visit as sovereign of Vatican City to the presidential palace, the Quirinale.

On Good Friday in April, John Paul dated his apostolic letter on the status of Jerusalem, a decade after Paul VI's visit there, as he noted, observing that it represented geographically the confluence of three continents and religiously the sacred city of three world religions but still without peace. He called again with urgency for resolution of the seemingly "insoluble" antagonism between Israelis and Palestinians. He reiterated the papal position on an internationally guaranteed "special status" for the City of Peace. While reflecting on communal suffering and peace, John Paul wrote two apostolic letters: *Salvifici doloris* (February) on the redemptive role of suffering and *Redemptionis donum* (March) on the three evangelical counsels of male and female religious in the contemplative orders.

The principal goal of the pope on his twenty-first journey abroad (2–12 May) was to celebrate in Korea the bicentennial of the arrival of Catholicism there. In Seoul, he canonized Korea's 103 martyrs, and met with a dozen Buddhist and Confucian leaders. His official meeting with Protestants was limited to a specialized group of scholars engaged with Catholics in a common Korean version of the Bible, he himself having exerted himself to use Korean at his masses. He renewed his support for the reunification of Korea and deplored the failure of the North Korean government to permit him contact with any Catholics there. He flew on to Papua, saying Mass in English and in Pidgin in the capital and in the highlands, addressed the joint bishops' conference of Papua and of the Solomon Islands on common socioeconomic and bureaucratic problems of the two recently decolonized states, and went on to the capital of the second state, Honiari on Guadalcanal (a week earlier it had voted to establish diplomatic relations with the Holy See). In Thailand, he paid tribute in Bangkok to the king and to the high priest of Thai Buddhism for the patrimony of tolerance. He commended Buddhists for the renunciation of violence, while reminding them that the Church rejects nothing that is true and holy in any non-Christian tradition. He invited Thai Catholics to consider their native land especially fertile terrain for the word proclaimed uniquely by Christ to take root. At a camp he counseled Indochinese refugees in transit to host countries to retain the old language and culture but, while waiting, to acquire a new one.

Within a month of his second Asian visitation, John Paul was in Switzerland for the second time (2–12 June) but now on a "necessary ecumenical" trip, implicitly mandated by Vatican II. A sidelight that made it notable was that the Pope was greeted and throughout protected by his own uniformed Swiss guards.

At the headquarters of the World Council of Churches in Geneva, he acknowledged the ecumenical movement as "irreversible." He urgently raised the ecclesiological issue of the papal ministry, his understanding of the Church as itself a mediator between God and humanity, his opposition to sharing the Eucharist prior to the achievement of visible unity, his sense of the utter difference between Catholic and particularly Reformed spirituality (Zwingli, Calvin), his opposition to any change in the Catholic canons concerning the priesthood, and his anxieties over the modalities of social change fostered by the WCC. At the end of the day the Pope visited the Orthodox center at Chambesy and there expressed the hope that "soon" they and Catholics would be in intercommunion.

At the Catholic University of Fribourg John Paul lauded the theologians "in the great act of tradition" and urged them to accept the fact that from their level they cannot solve all the problems presented, just as pastors, he said in another meeting, cannot always find satisfactory resolutions to life's problems. Picking up problems distinctive of Switzerland as a whole, the Pope called for the "powerful world of money" and of arms exports to be subject to the consciences of all in their democratic society, and in every town and field greater concern for guest workers among them.

His twenty-third trip abroad was to Canada, 9–20 September, 1984 (he had paid a visit in 1969). John Paul spent his first three days in Quebec Province, then went on to the Maritimes. In Toronto he made a major ecumenical effort, lauding and encouraging all sides. Besides his life-family themes and spirituality he gave, especially in the western provinces, ringing denunciations of the arms race and the economic disparity between the hemispheres. On several occasions he emphasized the rights of native Canadians, twice acknowledging the earlier mistakes of missionaries among the Indians, exculpating the gospel itself. As in the first visit to the United States, he reserved to the end his appearance at the capital, exhorting Canada's bishops assembled in Ottawa to uphold the life, family, and social teachings of the Church, the full sacramental ministry (Penance and Eucharist), and to overcome the "conspiracy of silence" about the abuse of religious freedom in many lands.

As John Paul made plans for another flight to Hispanic America, the Congregation of the Doctrine of the Faith published the apostolic instruction *On Certain Aspects of the Theology of Liberation* (3 September), an uncommonly spirited argumentation, clarification, and rejection of any "Catholicized" Marxism. This document cited John Paul's addresses with phrasings also reminiscent of his pre-papal writings in its disentanglement of Catholic truth from the new Marxicising context of a praxis with a motivating principle in class struggle. On the first leg of the visit to Latin America, (10–13 October), in Spain John Paul made reference to the fifth centennial of the opening of the New World to Catholicism when Columbus landed in Hispaniola in 1492. Upon leaving the basilica of Our Lady of Pilar in Saragossa whence, he said, came "the light of faith" to the New World, he flew to Santo Domingo and set forth in the presence of a hundred representatives of the Latin American Bishops' Council his broad vision of working for a civilization of love in the avoidance of the idols of power, violence, wealth, and hedonism.

Seventh Pontifical Year. John Paul undertook his fifth trip to Latin America, 26 January to 6 February 1985, visiting Venezuela, Ecuador, and Peru, and where he clarified "the Church's preferential but not exclusive option for the poor." He upheld the rights of the Incans and other Indians, and in Peru appealed to the Maoist Sendero Luminoso guerrillas to reject "the pitiless logic of violence." In many gatherings from among the industrialized and more prosperous segments of the various populations he warned against consumerism, dehumanizing technologies, and a sensate culture. After a visit to an Ecuadoran shantytown, in Guayaquil, he undertook the beatification of Mother Mercedes de Jesus, the foundress of Ecuador's first religious institute, the Sisters of Mariana of Jesus. The nuns serve as missionaries and educators, especially among orphaned and abandoned children. "In her," he said, "the true preferential option for the poor clearly shines."

In many of his pilgrimages and audiences John Paul singled out the young for special attention and instruction. In conjunction with the U.N.-sponsored Youth Year, he issued an apostolic letter *To the Youth of the World,* making the Ten Commandments central; and he addressed young people assembled in St. Peter's Square, 31 March, urging them to shout to all humanity that Christ is indispensable to the world.

After having earlier met with American Jewish leaders and earlier received the prime minister of Israel (February), John Paul, accepting the invitation of the chief rabbi of Rome, joined him in the synagogue in a service of song and prayer, a first in papal history (13 April 1986). He there reflected in the presence of the Holy One of Israel on the momentous significance of his visit, a solemnly joyful betokening of the general acceptance of "a legitimate plurality [of faith communities] on the social, civil, and religious levels." He connected his visit with an earlier gesture of John XXIII, evoking *Nostra aetate* of Vatican II as the decisive grounding of the new relation between Catholics and Jews, and recalling his own words of universal anguish when he visited Auschwitz in 1979. He looked for perennial respect of "the identity of each divergent Biblical tradition and sustaining community," beyond any syncretism and any ambiguous appropriation. He referred Catholics to the guidelines of 1974 and 1985 on the presentation of Jews and Judaism in Catholic preaching and catechesis, which theologically presupposes that the relationship between the Church and the Jewish people is "founded on the design of the God of the Covenant" and that instruction on Judaism is not marginal but essential to Catholic instruction and with that it affirms "the existence of the State of Israel" on the basis of "the common principles of international law." This political aspect of papal instruction was not alluded to in the synagogue by the Pope, who stressed rather the religious and moral bonds and also the benignly but firmly held differences in scriptural interpretation.

The twenty-sixth papal pilgrimage, to the Benelux nations, 11–21 May, proved difficult. In all three countries he faced articulate disagreement with the papal magisterium ranging in expression from bishops deploring the pain of those who conscientiously found it hard to stay in the Church, all the way to boycott and even violent hostility from youth in street demonstrations (Utrecht). He held up Christ as "the tutor of adult conscience" in faith and morals against the claims of the autonomous conscience. Going first to the Netherlands, then Luxembourg, and finally to Belgium, he had to be tactful also on the linguistic front, Dutch-Flemish, German, and French. Of all his intra-Christian ecumenical encounters, the one that took place in The Hague was the most critical. The spokesman of the Dutch Reformed Synod charged that his policy was slowing down the ecumenical movement. Elsewhere urging mutual forbearance within the Church of diversity, when it meant complementarity, John Paul admonished Dutch theologians against creating a spurious "parallel magisterium" to that of bishops and enjoined them in turn not to isolate themselves from the universal collegial unity. Before the World Court John Paul called for measures to strengthen the rule of law among nations and took the occasion that he had not yet been afforded by a trip to Southern Africa to condemn apartheid. In all three countries he warned against local xenophobia and urged an embracing sense of economic fair play on the part of the nations of the Northern hemisphere for those of the Southern.

Participation in the forty-third International Eucharistic Congress in Nairobi was the special motive of his third trip to Africa (11–21 May), to seven countries, two for the second time, and Kenya for the third. Nairobi had taken as its theme the Eucharist and the Christian Family. John Paul closed the Congress at a Mass on 18 August, in English and Swahili, declaring that "the power of Christ's gospel has been revealed in Africa." He took the occasion of the place and the Congress to press very hard and specifically against the policy of the Kenyan government on reducing population growth. In several of the countries he had ecumenical meetings with other Christians and with Muslims, sometimes together, and for the first time he prayed with a group of animists (in Togo). Notable was the royal invitation extended to him to visit Morocco, and for the first time and at the explicit request of Hassan II, to address a stadium full of young Muslims, a dramatic implementation of the principle of dialogue with non-Christians, he said, endorsed by Vatican II.

In June John Paul turned to the Slavic east of Europe with his fourth encyclical *Slavorum apostoli*, on the eleventh centenary of the death of St. Methodius. He had already declared SS Cyril and Methodius "pioneers in inculturation" and co-patrons of Europe with St. Benedict, observing that the cultural, political, and religious mission (Cyrillic alphabet, Bible, and liturgy) of these two Greeks had been under the joint auspices of Constantinople and Rome while still in full communion.

The second extraordinary assembly of the Synod of Bishops was convened by the Pope 24 November to 8 December, to commemorate the twentieth anniversary of the close of Vatican II, to assess it, and, in John Paul's concluding words, "to avoid divergent interpretations." Later in this year he appointed a commission, recommended by the Synod to prepare a compendium of Catholic teaching or universal catechism to embody "the teachings of Vatican II considered in their continuity and complementarity with all the preceding magisterium of the Church."

Eighth Pontifical Year. Invited to India by its president and its episcopal conference, and encouraged by the Catholic spouse of the prime minister, John Paul in the first ten days of February visited 14 cities of a vast state, less than two percent of which is Catholic. He said that his visit was a pilgrimage of good will and peace in the fulfillment of a desire to experience personally the "soul" of India and its "various spiritual quests for the Absolute." He was there also to address social and moral issues common alike to Christians and non-Christians, to preside over and exhort various Catholic flocks, celebrating Mass in more than one rite (the Syro-Malabar, for instance, going back to the tradition of Thomas the Apostle). He began his pilgrimage at Raj Ghat, dedicated, he observed, "to the Father of the Nation and the apostle of non-violence. I have come here to pay homage to Ma-

hatma Gandhi, hero of humanity." In retrospect he declared: "I have evangelized the Indian people through the words of Mahatma Gandhi." In the Indira Gandhi Stadium in New Delhi he addressed by name Hindus, Muslims, Sikhs, Buddhists, Jains, Parsees, and fellow Christians, asserting his conviction that "India's great contribution to the world can be in offering it a spiritual vision of man." He celebrated Mass among 150,000 tribal hill peoples in Assam, many of them sill animists, observing that Christianity can transform without doing violence to indigenous culture. He solemnized the beatification at Kottayam of two Indians of the Syro-Malabar rite, a Carmelite father of the 19th century and a sister of the Immaculate Conception (Lithuanian, d. 1946). In Bombay toward the close of his pilgrimage he entrusted the people of India to the intercession of Mary.

In *Dominum et vivificantem*, his sixth encyclical (30 May 1986), John Paul carried further his teaching on the Holy Spirit as the Second Counselor and he meditated on how the Spirit is sent by the Father and by the Son in comforting and also convalidating the teaching of Christ. Observing that Vatican II was an "ecclesiological and hence also a pneumatical council," he unfolded in the encyclical the gifts of the Spirit from creation through regeneration. He especially reflected on the development of the role of the Spirit through the apostles and the episcopal magisterium to priests and to the faithful. The Spirit, he pronounced, upholds the original divine truth in shaping and constraining conscience in such a way that human beings are, for the most part, held back from passing beyond the limits of licit behavior into the presumption of becoming through class, nation, race, or ideology "an independent and exclusive source for deciding about good and evil. . . . When God is forgotten the creature itself grows unintelligible."

On the eve of his thirtieth pilgrimage, his sixth to Latin America, the Vatican released three related letters by John Paul, Archbishop Runcie of Canterbury and Cardinal Willebrands, in effect slowing down Catholic-Anglican rapprochement. Willebrands firmly articulated the Catholic position regarding the ordination of women in some provinces of the Anglican Communion as an increasingly serious obstacle to intercommunion: "The [male] priest represents Christ in his saving relationship with his body . . . not primarily . . . the priesthood [male-female] of the whole people of God."

The visit to Colombia (1–7 July) emphasized the healing of a nation rent by civil war, overwhelmed by the drug traffic, and grieving from a succession of spectacular natural disasters. The descendants of African slaves who constitute the major strand in the population inland from Colombia's Pacific coast heard John Paul honor St.

Peter Claver, SJ, who before his death (1654) had cared for and converted 300,000 black slaves as "a sign of the authentic theology of liberation." He also honored Luis Bertand, O.P. (d. 1581), missionary to Africans and Indians, patron saint of Colombia. The Pope returned to Rome after a stop at the island nation of Santa Lucia.

For the sixteenth centenary of the conversion of St. Augustine, John Paul wrote an apostolic letter (August), reflecting on the affirmation of the Carthaginian doctor of the Church: "I should not believe the Gospel unless I were moved to do so by the authority of the Catholic Church."

The third pilgrimage to France, 4–7 October, was occasioned by the bicentennial of the birth of St. John Vianney, the Curé of Ars, patron of parish priests. At Ars (near Lyons) he delivered a series of three meditations during a day of recollection for 5,800 priests, deacons, and seminarians, drawing upon the saint as model. He celebrated Mass at the basilica of Paray-le-Monial of the Visitation Nuns, recalled the visions of St. Margaret Mary Alacoque (1673–75), which shaped the devotion to the Sacred Heart of Jesus, and afterwards handed a letter to the superior general of the Jesuits, urging his order to promote devotion to the Sacred Heart. In Annecy he praised the cofounders of the Visitation Nuns (1610), SS. Francis de Sales and Jane de Chantal. He met with forty-five Protestant Brothers of Taizé. In Lyons, in the ancient amphitheater site of the martyrdoms of A.D. 117, he addressed a gathering of Armenians, Orthodox, and Protestants, urging "boldness" in implementing the gains of the ecumenical movement on the parish level. There he unexpectedly appealed for truces everywhere in the world during the forthcoming world day of prayer for peace.

This day was observed at Assisi under the patronage of St. Francis whom John Paul had already denominated patron of ecology (1979). At the invitation of John Paul 150 representatives of a dozen world religions (including animist, Hindu, Buddhist, Parsee, Jewish, and Muslim) joined him and many leaders of diverse Christian tradition, including the metropolitan of Kiev, in a world day of prayer for peace on 26 October (with some actual cessation of hostilities out of respect and longing), the most significant interfaith ecumenical event of the nine years of his pontificate.

Near the beginning of summer in the Southern hemisphere, John Paul undertook a pastoral trip into Oceana, 18 November to 1 December. Although he made stops in the capital of Muslim Bangladesh, in Singapore, at Suva, capital of Fiji and seat of the Francophone Pacific Conference of Bishops, and at the capital of Seychelles, the principal mission of the Pope was to New Zealand and Australia. More pointedly than elsewhere he appealed for the return of wayward Catholics (Sydney). At the capital (Canberra) of the country whose physicians pioneered *in vitro* fertilization (also in Brisbane and Melbourne), he carried much further than on any other pilgrimage his warning against all kinds of genetic and embryological experimentations and euthanasian practices, anticipatory of the Apostolic Instruction on Respect for Human Life (issued by the Congregation of the Doctrine of the Faith in the ensuing March).

Ninth Pontifical Year. His fifth encyclical, *Redemptoris Mater*, dated on the feast of the Annunciation (25 March), was a comprehensive scriptural, conciliar, and theological meditation on the Mother of God, directed to all Christians. The encyclical explained her subordinate mediatorial role, her role as model of mother and obedient expectant follower of the divine will. It cited the Marian piety as a common tradition binding Catholics and the Orthodox together. John Paul II used the encyclical to announce a Marian Year that would extend until the solemnity of the Assumption in August 1988.

From 31 March to 12 April the Pope was off on his seventh trip to Latin America. In cathedral in Montevideo, Uruguay, he went further than ever before in defining the preferential option for the poor to mean primarily the spiritually impoverished who are suffering because of sin and being cut off from the divine. In the course of his stay in Chile he met thrice with General Augusto Pinochet, its autocratic president. His clearest public stricture was at the welcoming in Santiago, when in response to the president's account of his own achievement in defense "of the Christian West" against Marxism and his hope for a transition to democracy, the Pope said: "I am not an evangelizer of democracy . . . [but] if democracy means human rights, it also belongs to the message of the Church." When he heard one archbishop speak openly about a "culture of death" in the country, he voiced his outrage at such victimizations. In answer to a youthful deplorer of the state of his nation, the Pope referred to it as Lazarus, trusting that he would be understood to mean that he was hoping for a resurrection of the nation. In reiterating his rejection of violence and hatred, he condemned any sympathy with "programmed class struggle" as the dialectic solution to social injustice, whether of the urban poor or the Indians. In Argentina he defended the same indigenous groupings, asked workers not to confuse labor union and political action. On his arrival he commended socialist President Raul Alfonsin for "full re-establishment of democratic institutions," and took other occasions to rejoice that the preceding period (1976–83) of the miliary culture of death, terror, and "the youthful disappeared" had come to an end. In farewell to Argentina, he entrusted the whole nation to its patroness, the Virgin of Lujan.

On the Thursday after Easter he was on his second visit to West Germany, 30 April to 4 May. A sustained theme was the role of Catholics under Hitler. Occasionally implying that more corporate and individual opposition might have only exacerbated conditions under "the treacherous tyranny of National Socialism," he emphasized three figures from the horrendous period, beatifying (in Cologne) the Carmelite Edith Stein as "a daughter of Israel" (d. Auschwitz, 1942). He prayed at the tomb (in Münster) of Clemens August Cardinal Count von Galen as a prelate who had been a swift and outspoken opponent of the policy of euthanasia for the insane and imbecile. He came close to saying that abortion and euthanasia for the terminally comatose today are but subtle manifestations of the more dramatic threat to human dignity and basic rights under the Nazis. While admonishing on some points, he expressed again high regard for German society in extricating itself from the tragic past and winning new respect among the nations. In the cathedral in Augsburg, which gives its name to the principal Lutheran confession (1530), he went further than on his first visit and acknowledged that the Reformation, despite many dire consequences for Christendom, had the effect of renewing the Church and intensifying the papal ministry. He reiterated before the bishops his call for the re-evangelization of Europe and within Europe in particular the world of workers.

John Paul's third pilgrimage to Poland, 8–14 June, fitted into the national Eucharistic Congress and climaxed in a closing procession of one million people on the Sunday before the feast of Corpus Christi in Warsaw. John Paul beatified two Poles, a peasant girl, killed while resisting rape by a Russian soldier (d. 1884), and a bishop who was injected with poison in Dachau (d. 1943). He was able to visit several cities not hitherto accessible to him, notably his own Catholic University in Lublin, where he addressed world scientists assembled by the invitation of his own former rector, ordained 46 priests, and visited the vast suburban concentration camp of Majdanek. He prayed at the tombs of Primate Wyszynski and the priestly martyr of Solidarity, Jerzy Popieluszko. He met with Jews, with the ecumenical council, with Lech Walesa, and twice with General Jaruzelski amid expressions of cool correctness on either side. Yet the ground was prepared for the resumption of the social dialogue between the government and the hierarchy (with legalization and a concordat at issue).

In Kraków John Paul had prayed before the relics of Queen Jadwiga and at the tomb of her Lithuanian spouse (King Jagilas), who on acceptance of Christian Baptism promised the conversion of his nobles and peoples (1387). In Rome, during the celebration of the sixth centenary of the Christianization of the Lithuanians (19 June), for which he had issued his apostolic letter *Christianitas*, he beatified the scholarly priest of conjoined Polish and Lithuanian heritage, George Matulaitis, the "splendid model" bishop of Vilnius (1918–25).

In the same month the Pope received the president of Austria, Kurt Waldheim, who had invited the Pope to the U.N. (1979). Waldheim's visit called forth protests particularly from American Jews because of persistent allegations of his involvement in Nazi crimes. John Paul, of whom the Jewish community had within the preceding season expressed the highest praise for progress in interfaith relations, sensed the urgent need of a substantial assuagement of their fears. He arranged meetings with Jewish representatives, 31 August and 1 September, in the Vatican and in Castel Gondolfo lest misunderstanding blemish an important interfaith encounter with Jewish leaders (Miami), foreseen for near the outset of his second pastoral and ecumenical visitation to the United States.

On his itinerary from Miami, to Columbia, New Orleans, San Antonio, Phoenix, Los Angeles, Monterey, and San Francisco to Detroit (10–19 September), John Paul gave special attention to the ethnic pluralism of the country and of the Church. He more than once used Creole, French, and Spanish; he spoke to Hispanics, Haitians, Indians, and Eskimos (to the indigenous peoples, both in Phoenix and Fort Simpson in the Northwest Territories, fulfilling there a plan foiled by bad weather on his first trip to Canada), and perhaps most notably (in New Orleans) an assembly of black bishops and 1,800 priests. His interfaith and intra-Christian ecumenical encounters were substantial. His meeting (in Columbia, S.C.) with heads of more than a score of denominations and communions ranging from the Armenian Apostolic to Southern Baptist was something new in his pilgrimages, in that he responded to a nationally prepared, representative interdenominational paper on the state of society in the perspective of Christian responsibilities among citizens of a world power. He had chosen Columbia to witness to common scriptural bonds and even solidarity between Catholics and Evangelical Protestants and the Orthodox. After addressing by name the twenty-four denominations engaged in worship in the university stadium of 60,000, and preaching from the Bible-centered podium, interpreting the interrelated texts on the family and civic life, he declared: "You cannot insist on the right to choose without also insisting on the duty to choose well, the duty to choose in the truth." From the outset of his second visit, John Paul made it clear in several addresses, climaxing in his response to four presentations before the United States bishops (Los Angeles), that appropriate or licit inculturation (formerly "Americanization") would have to eschew any "merely sociological view" of the relationship of the local churches to each other and to their center in Rome, to refrain from any selective adhering to the magisterium in moral theology and praxis, and instead to yield to tradition and canon law on the role women hold in the Church, and to resist pessimism about the shortage of priests and vocations to the life of religious and the entertainment of uncanonical strategies to cope with a passing phase.

Many of the concerns of the laity and bishops presented with poignancy during his second American visit recirculated in the deliberations of the seventh general assembly of the Synod of Bishops, 1–30 October, conceived as a review of the impact of Vatican II on the vocation and mission of the laity in the Church and the world.

Determined to commemorate the twentieth anniversary of *Progressio populorum*, John Paul, surely moved by the cumulative impact of his thirty-seven pilgrimages, issued his seventh encyclical, *Sollicitudo rei socialis* (30 December 1987). He reviewed the advances and setbacks in economic, social and moral development in the twenty-year interval. The Pope deplored the division of the Northern hemisphere between the geopolitical blocs of East and West, of Marxist collectivism and liberal capitalism, and the intrusion of the largely extraneous conflicts into the Southern hemisphere and the Third World. He identified as the Fourth World the bands of poverty, homelessness, and joblessness created by the perverted mechanisms of the systems, cropping out even in sectors of the First World itself. He identified the encyclical as a theological and moral reflection on the human condition and not as some third way between the two principal economical-philosophical systems. He insisted that the proper distribution of superabundance of the individual and the society belongs to the less well off not out of charity but in fair distributive justice. He placed his vision in the global perspective of the four ''worlds'' in interdependent development moving toward mutual respect, solidarity, and collaboration. For the first time a papal encyclical was formulated in direct address to, besides the Catholic faithful, all Christians in their churches and ecclesial communities and eleemosynary organizations, to the Jews, and to the Muslims as all heirs of Abraham, and to the devotees of all the world religions.

Overall Achievements. By the time John Paul II entered the tenth year of his pontificate in October 1987, he had significantly turned the papal ministry into a global mission beyond anything envisaged in the era of Vatican II. He had expanded the international representation in the College of Cardinals and the Roman Curia. In three consisteries (1979, 1983, 1985), John Paul named cardinals from every continent, including a half-dozen or more

from North America: Archbishops Gerald Emmett Carter of Toronto, Joseph Bernardin of Chicago, Bernard Law of Boston, John J. O'Connor of New York, James A. Hickey of Washington, Edmund C. Szoka of Detroit, Paul Gregoire of Montreal, Louis Albert Vachon of Quebec, and Metropolitan Myroslav Ivan Lubachivsky of the Ukrainian Rite. The College of Cardinals has worked with the Pope in finding a solution to the depressed finances of the Vatican, faced with increased overhead and declining revenues. John Paul's pontificate has been plagued with fiscal problems inherited from his predecessors that are said to have resulted from unwise investments and alleged banking irregularities. He took the occasion of the consistory in 1988 to issue the apostolic constitution *Pastor Bonus* which reorganized the Roman Curia.

By a phenomenal output of official teaching, with a detectible personal input and distinctive emphasis, and by having exerted himself in endless travel, celebrating all the Sacraments with flocks great and small around the world, John Paul II has gone far toward transforming the perception of the papal ministry from seeming to be distant and magisterial and diplomatic into an immediate sacerdotal ministry of pastoral caring and social concern. Moreover, by his regular general audiences on sustained themes addressed in several world languages, by his receptions in audience of heads of state and government at the Vatican, by his regular addresses on pilgrimage to the international diplomatic corps accredited to the given capital, and to the U.N. and its related institutions (UNESCO, the World Court, Labor) and perhaps especially by exchanges, often without the intermediation of his nuncios, with the heads of government in their own capitals, the Polish Pope has enormously enhanced the world impact of papal diplomacy. Indeed he has come to exercise direct spiritual sovereignty amongst the heads of government or their envoys by his sacral presence and power, by his moral authority, and by his enhanced vision for having visited and talked with so many parts of the world. With the Holy See a signatory of several international accords, notably that of Helsinki and of nuclear nonproliferation, by a Vatican presence at state funerals (e.g. at the Kremlin for general secretaries), by international mediation (the Beagle Channel Accord between Chile and Argentina), by frequent global and regional appeals, exhortations, and intrafaith and interfaith prayer convocations, by his *Urbi et Orbi* and New Year's messages, John Paul II has made of the Apostolic See a major force in East-West relations in the North Atlantic and between the Northern developed and the underdeveloped Southern hemisphere.

[G. H. WILLIAMS]

PAPACY: 1988-1994

Tenth Pontifical Year. Pope John Paul made four trips outside Italy in 1988. From 7–18 May he visited four countries in South America: Uruguay, Bolivia, Peru and Paraguay. He spoke frequently on themes of social justice, human rights, solidarity, and the common good. In Bolivia he lamented the temptation toward violence as a means of redressing structures that are considered unjust, and he urged action to stop drug-trafficking that "leads to the most terrible forms of servitude." The government of Paraguay where President Alfredo Stroessner has been in power for thirty-four years attempted to cancel a scheduled speech to civic leaders in Asunción for fear that it turn into an anti-government demonstration. When the Vatican protested, the government relented. John Paul took the occasion to stress the importance of democracy and citizen participation in decision-making. While in that country Pope John Paul canonized the first Paraguayan saints, the native-born priests Roque Gonzalez and Alfonso Rodriguez, and Spanish-born John del Castillo. All three were Jesuit missionaries who were martyred because of their ministry among the indigenous people. Gonzalez and the others organized a network of Christian communities, "reductions," that brought them into conflict with both the Indians and the Spanish colonists who saw them in terms of economic competition. During the canonization ceremonies the pope defended the work of the early missionaries in the region. During a trip to Austria, 23–27 June, John Paul visited the site of the former concentration camp at Mauthausen and later met with leaders in the Austrian Jewish community. The pope spent 10–19 September in Africa, making stops in Zimbabwe, Botswana, Lesotho, Swaziland, and Mozambique with an unplanned detour through South Africa. He ended a three day visit to France 8–11 October with a speech to the European Parliament in Strasbourg in which he recalled Europe's "underlying religious and Christian fabric."

Earlier, in January 1988 Pope John Paul II published an apostolic letter, *Euntes in mundum universum,* commemorating the millennium of the baptism of Vladimir the Great in 988 and the conversion to Christianity of the people of Kievan Rus. The pope took the occasion to make another plea for unity of the Churches of East and West as a means of breaking down the walls that divide people and hinder world peace. On the feast of Sts. Cyril and Methodius, 14 February, John Paul issued *Magnum baptismi donum,* a special message to the Ukrainian Church, suppressed by the Soviet authorities. He pointed to the millennial observances as an ecumenical moment for dialogue between Catholics and Orthodox Christians. He emphasized that Eastern Rite Catholic Churches are not "an obstacle to full communion with our Orthodox

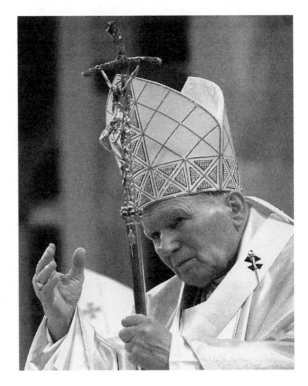

John Paul II (Catholic News Service.)

brethren." The pope sent a high-level delegation headed by Agostino Cardinal Casaroli, Vatican secretary of state, to the millennial observances celebrated by the Russian Orthodox in Moscow. The importance of the event, said Casaroli in a brief address in the Bolshoi Theater, has "not escaped the attention of public opinion" and expressed hope that "a new breath of wind will animate the entire relationship of the Soviet state with religion as a whole." Casaroli was warmly received in the Kremlin when he delivered a six-page letter from Pope John Paul to Mikhail Gorbachev.

On 8 April Pope John Paul addressed a letter to Cardinal Ratzinger, prefect of the Congregation for the Doctrine of the Faith, in which he expressed a desire for a continuation of efforts to heal the division brought about by Archbishop Marcel Lefebvre and the Priestly Fraternity of St. Pius X. Pope Paul VI had suspended Lefebvre from priestly duties in 1976 because the archbishop rejected certain positions and reforms directed by Vatican II. In 1988 Lefebvre was threatening to ordain other bishops who would carry on his movement. Most of the pope's letter to Cardinal Ratzinger is devoted to a discussion of conservative and progressive tendencies in the post-conciliar Church. On 5 May Cardinal Ratzinger and Archbishop Lefebvre signed a protocol that was to be the basis of a reconciliation, but when Archbishop Lefebvre proceeded, in defiance of a formal canonical warning, John Paul excommunicated him. In the apostolic letter, *Ecclesia Dei,* of 2 July the pope described the unauthorized ordination as an act of disobedience, and a "schismatic act" that implied a rejection of the Roman primacy.

On the feast of the Assumption the pope brought to a close the Marian Year that had begun fourteen months earlier. It was the occasion of the apostolic letter on the dignity of and vocation of women, *Mulieris dignitatem.* He cast it in "the style and character of a meditation," reflecting on the exploitation of women, marriage, motherhood, the value of religious consecration, virginity, the suffering of women, female gifts, and the ordination of women.

Pope John Paul named twenty-five new cardinals from seventeen countries. In the group who received the red hat on 28 June were American archbishops James A. Hickey of Washington and Edmund C. Szoka of Detroit. Father Hans Urs von Balthasar of Switzerland died 26 June, before the installation ceremonies.

Eleventh Pontifical Year. John Paul began his second decade as pope on 28 October 1988. In the eleventh year of his pontificate he was to return to Africa 28 April–6 May 1989 with stopovers in Madagascar, the French possession Reunion, Zambia, and Malawi. From 1–10 June he visited Scandinavia (Norway, Iceland, Finland, Denmark, and Sweden). John Paul spent 19–21 August in Spain, and 6-16 October in the Far East, visiting Korea, Indonesia, East Timor, and Maurilius. In Seoul, South Korea, he attended the closing ceremonies of the Forty-fourth International Eucharistic Congress.

At the end of January 1990 the Vatican released Pope John Paul's *Christifideles laici,* his apostolic exhortation based on the 1987 Synod of Bishops that had as its theme "Vocation and Ministry of the Laity in the Church and the World 20 Years after the Second Vatican Council." The pope rehearsed the synod's discussion and noted, among other points, "the ministries and church services entrusted at present and in the future to the lay faithful, the growth and spread of new movements' alongside other group forms of lay involvement, and the place and role of women both in the church and society."

Women's issues were a theme that ran through many of the pope's discourses and speeches both in Rome and as he traveled around the world. The discussion took a new twist and complicated Anglican-Roman Catholic efforts at unity at the Lambeth Conference in July–August 1988. On 5 July 1988 the Church of England synod had voted to propose ordaining women as priests. The conference urged the various members of the churches of the Anglican communion to respect one another's decisions to ordain women as bishops. It occasioned an exchange of letters from His Grace, Robert Runcie, archbishop of Canterbury, and Pope John Paul. In a letter dated 8 December 1988, the pope wrote that the ordination of women to the priesthood and "the right of individual provinces to proceed with the ordination of women to the episcopacy, appears to . . . effectively block the path to mutual recognition of ministries." Later in the year when Runcie paid a visit to the Vatican 29 September–2 October, the archbishop and the pope issued a common declaration in which they reaffirmed their commitment to "the urgent quest for Christian unity," acknowledging that the ordination of women to the ministerial priesthood "prevents reconciliation between us even where there is otherwise progress toward agreement."

At the end of August, John Paul recalled the fiftieth anniversary of the outbreak of World War II that began with the Nazi invasion of Poland, 1 September 1939. He issued an apostolic letter that criticized Nazi paganism, Marxist dogma, and, in reference to hostility against Judaism, "every form of racism." The letter echoed the message John Paul sent the day before, 26 August, to the Polish bishops. His reference to the massive extermination of the Jews, gas chambers, and racial hatred came at a time that the Polish Church was embroiled in a dispute over the continued existence of a Carmelite convent on the site of the former concentration camp at Auschwitz. The sisters had agreed to move in 1987, but as of 1989 they were still in place.

Twelfth Pontifical Year. John Paul made his sixth and seventh trips visits to Africa in 1990, bringing to ninety-seven the number of countries he visited to this point in his pontificate. He spent 25 January–1 February in Cape Verde, Guinea-Bissau, Mali, and Burkina Faso; 1–10 September in Tanzania, Rwanda, Burundi and the Ivory Coast. In between he travelled to Czechoslovakia, 21–22 April; Mexico and Curaçao, 6–13 May; and Malta, 25–27 May.

John Paul's carefully orchestrated *Ostpolitik* gradually won concessions on freedom to practice religion in communist bloc countries. The pope found an ally in Mihail Gorbachev who visited the pope on 1 December 1989. As a result of the meeting, diplomatic ties were established between the Holy See and Moscow, and the Roman Catholic Church was permitted to function openly and establish hierarchies in various states of the Soviet Union.

From the beginning of his pontificate Pope John Paul took an interest in the identity and mission of Catholic universities. In 1985 the Congregation for Catholic Education initiated a series of consultations that, after several drafts, resulted in *Ex corde ecclesiae,* the apostolic constitution published by Pope John Paul at the end of September 1990. The constitution discusses among other issues, the mission of Catholic universities, their relationship to the magisterium and the local bishop. After several drafts and consultations, the constitution set down norms that became effective with the 1991 academic year. Earlier in the year, 26 June, the Congregation for the Doctrine of the Faith with the approval of the pope issued the "Instruction on the Ecclesial Vocation of the Theologian."

Thirteenth Pontifical Year. In 1991 John Paul traveled to Portugal, to Poland twice, to Hungary, and to Brazil. The visit to Poland 1–9 June provided the pope an opportunity to meet with many bishops from Ukraine, Byelorussia, Lithuania, Moscow, and Kazakhstan as well as other European countries. It also had an ecumenical dimension that afforded the pope an opportunity for common prayer with Orthodox and with Lutherans. He also met with representatives of the Jewish community in Poland. His second trip to Poland in August was occasioned by the celebration of World Youth Day in Częstochowa. On his return he stopped over in Hungary. John Paul's visit to Brazil 12–20 October was the fifty-third foreign trip of his pontificate.

John Paul's intervention in international affairs moved on several fronts. Threats of war had caused him to make more than fifty appeals to government leaders to find a peaceful solution to the crisis in the Persian Gulf. In August 1990 he had condemned Iraq for invading Kuwait, and in January 1991 he criticized the UN for invading Iraq. From 4–6 March, less than a week after the cease-fire, John Paul arranged a summit meeting of Vatican officials and church leaders from countries most directly involved in the Persian Gulf War, seven Middle East patriarchs and eight heads of bishops' conferences. Later the pope communicated the concerns for the region expressed by the participants to the UN secretary general. John Paul stressed the summit's hope that interreligious dialogue between Muslims and Christians and Christians and Jews would contribute to the cause of peace.

With the disintegration of the Soviet empire, the pope envisioned new hopes for a Europe that could "rediscover its soul" and reunite around "human and Christian values." Old antagonisms, however, cast a shadow over the special assembly of the Synod of Bishops for Europe held to examine the role of the Church in a changing Europe. Catholic bishops from Eastern and Western Europe gathered in Rome for this purpose 28 November–14 December 1991, and though they had been invited, the Orthodox Churches boycotted the meeting. The Orthodox in places such as Russia itself, Ukraine, Romania, and Bulgaria felt threatened by evangelizing efforts and opposed returning church property confiscated under communist regimes to the Catholics.

John Paul issued his eighth and ninth encyclicals. *Redemptoris missio,* released 22 January 1991, carries the subtitle, "On the Permanent Validity of the Church's Missionary Activity." Stressing the urgency of evangelization *ad gentes,* the encyclical also explores new frontiers for missionary activity in modern society and in traditional Christian areas that need to be re-evangelized. *Centesimus annus,* as the title suggests, was issued to mark the hundredth anniversary of Pope Leo XIII's ground-breaking social encyclical *Rerum novarum.* Like Leo's classic work, *Centesimus annus* addresses "new things": new forms of ownership, new technology, the collapse of communism in Eastern Europe, that are influencing today's social order.

The pope inducted twenty-two new members into the College of Cardinals 28 June. They included the archbishops of Los Angeles and Philadelphia, Roger M. Mahony and Anthony J. Bevilacqua.

Fourteenth Pontifical Year. Despite surgery in July 1992 for a precancerous tumor and removal of his gall bladder, John Paul continued his travels. He spent 19–26 February in West Africa visiting Senegal, Gambia, and Guinea, and in June he returned for a week touring Angola, São Tome, and Principe. In October he made stopovers in Mexico and Belize en route to Santo Domingo in the Dominican Republic for a meeting of the Latin American Bishops' Conference (CELAM) in conjunction with the five hundredth anniversary of the arrival of Christianity on the island of Hispaniola.

Fifteenth Pontifical Year. Pope John Paul made his tenth trip to Africa, visiting Benin, Uganda, and Sudan during the week of 19–26 February. On 25 April he flew to Albania for a thirteen-hour visit, and attended the concluding ceremonies of the International Eucharistic Congress in Seville 13 June and stayed on in Spain until 17 June. While in Madrid he canonized a Spanish priest, Enrique de Osso y Cervello (1840–1896), known for his zeal in catechetical work. In August en route to the World Youth Day in Denver, the pontiff stopped in Jamaica and Mexico. In Mexico he was greeted by President Carlos Salinas de Gortari and in Denver by President William Clinton. He spent the week of 4–10 September in the Baltic countries, Lithuania, Latvia, and Estonia. Less publicized were Pope John Paul's travels within Italy. His one-hundred-ninth pastoral visit to locales outside Rome took him to Sicily 8–10 May. He took the occasion of his third visit there to denounce the Mafia.

One of the most ambitious projects of Pope John Paul's pontificate has been the publication of the *Cate-*

chism of the Catholic Church. The French text was released 7 December 1992, was soon translated into Italian and Spanish, and almost immediately became a worldwide best-seller. The idea for a new catechism had been proposed by the special assembly of the Synod of Bishops that met in 1985 to mark the twentieth anniversary of Vatican II. The pope introduced the catechism, traced its history, and outlined its purpose in the apostolic constitution *Fidei depositum* that serves as a preface to the text that runs almost 600 pages in the American edition.

In his tenth encyclical, *Veritatis splendor* ("The Splendor of Truth"), John Paul reaffirms "the universality and immutability of the moral commandments, particularly those which prohibit always without exception intrinsically evil acts." The foundations of moral theology, separated from faith, are, he says, "being undermined by certain present-day tendencies" that set freedom in opposition to truth.

Sixteenth Pontifical Year. In April 1994, John Paul underwent a hip replacement after a fall in his bath. Despite his physical pain, in September the pope flew to Zagreb, Croatia. He had planned also to visit Sarajevo, Bosnia, and pray for peace with Catholics, Moslems, and the Serb Orthodox, but a fresh outbreak of hosilities forced him to cancel it at the last moment.

John Paul continued to promote better Christian-Jewish relations. On 30 December 1993 Israel and the Holy See signed an agreement establishing full diplomatic relations. On 7 April 1994 the pope presided over a ceremony in the Vatican commemorating the those who had died in the Warsaw Ghetto uprising fifty years before.

Despite his failing health, the pope presided over two assemblies of the Synod of Bishops. The first, a Special Assembly of the Synod of Bishops for Africa, came about largely because of John Paul II's direct intervention. It met in Rome 10 April–8 May 1994 and had as a general theme, "The Church in Africa and its Evangelizing Mission toward the Year 2000: *You shall be my witnesses* (Acts 1:8)." The second, a scheduled assembly of the synod now set for every three years, met 22-29 October. It had as its theme "The Consecrated Life and Its Role in the Church and in the World."

In May Pope John Paul released an apostolic letter addressed to bishops, *De sacerdotali ordinatione viris tantum reservanda* ("On Reserving Priestly Ordination to Men Alone"). Although it was not presented as infallible teaching, the pope made it clear that according to "the constant and universal tradition of the Church and firmly taught by the magisterium in its more recent documents," women cannot be ordained priests. Furthermore, the matter is no longer open to debate.

Seventeenth Pontifical Year. John Paul began the seventeenth year of his pontificate 28 October 1994 in frail health, but it did not deter him from travelling to Asia 12–21 January to celebrate World Youth Day in Manila. En route he stopped in Australia, Papua New Guinea, and Sri Lanka. On 20 May he flew to Prague in the Czech Republic and made still another pilgrimage to Poland. In Olomouc, a town in the Czech Republic near the Polish border, John Paul presided a liturgy at which he canonized Jan Sarkander, a Catholic priest tortured to death by the Protestants in 1620. His sixty-fifth trip outside Italy took him to Belgium for an overnight trip. At a mass in the Koekelberg neighborhood of Brussels on 4 June he beatified Damien (Joseph) de Veuster, known as the "apostle of the lepers."

Even as John Paul II showed increasing physical frailty, he continued to capture world headlines. *Crossing the Threshold of Hope,* a collection of essays that he wrote in response to questions posed by the Italian publisher Vittorio Messori, became an international best-seller late in 1994. He sharpened his critique of abortion, euthanasia, and other anti-family policies that he saw as symptomatic of a "culture of death." His strong moral voice and high visibility around the world made John Paul *Time* magazine's choice for "Man of the Year" in 1994.

A warning against the "culture of death" was a principal theme of John Paul's eleventh encyclical, *Evangelium vitae* ("The Gospel of Life"). The encyclical reaffirms the value and inviolability of human life "in the light of present circumstances and attacks threatening it today." The pope contrasts the "culture of death," with the "culture of life," implicit in the gospel message. Within months of *Evangelium vitae,* the pope published another encyclical, *Ut unum sint* ("That All May Be One"), that sought to re-energize efforts toward Christian unity. It identified five areas that need further study before a true consensus of faith can be reached: the relationship of Scripture and Tradition, the Eucharist, priestly ordination, the Church's teaching authority, and the role of the Virgin Mary. In a bold stroke, John Paul II, acknowledging that the papal authority itself is an obstacle to unity, suggests that the Churches engage in open and fraternal dialogue on how that authority might be exercised in today's world.

At the sixth consistory of the College of Cardinals held on 24 November 1994 Pope John Paul added thirty new members to the group. It was the largest single increment ever, and shifted the balance so that for the first time there were fewer cardinals from Europe than from the rest of the world. Among the countries represented by the new members were Albania, Belarus, and Bosnia. The list included four from North America: Archbishop Adam J. Maida of Detroit, Archbishop William H. Keeler of Baltimore, Archbishop Jean-Claude Turcotte of Montreal, and Archbishop Juan Sandoval Iñiguez of Guadalajara. Two priest-scholars, both over eighty, Yves Congar, OP, and Alois Grillmeier, SJ, were also named to the college.

Towards the Third Millennium. In the course of his long pontificate John Paul has gradually changed the composition of the Catholic hierarchy. All but a few of the cardinals of voting age, that is, younger than eighty years, have been named by him, and he has appointed most of the active bishops, including well over half the bishops in the United States. In the first fifteen years of his pontificate, he beatified 596 individuals and canonized 267 saints. Pope John Paul asserts that the Second Vatican Council has set the direction for his papacy. Vatican II inspired the interfaith meetings he has had with the world's religious leaders, and the council plus his own war time experience in Poland is evidenced in the special warmth he has shown Jews. His public pronouncements and private correspondence give evidence that he envisions dramatic meetings with Orthodox and Protestant leaders and the healing of divisions within the Church. The pope from Eastern Europe gave priority in the first years of his pontificate to the struggle for human rights and religious freedom in Communist bloc countries. With the collapse of the Soviet Empire, in which he had a hand, John Paul has turned his attention more to the relativism, permissiveness, and consumerism of Western democracies. His frequent visits to Africa and his regular attendance at World Youth Days indicate where he sees the future of the Church. For all his warnings about the culture of death, John Paul always holds out hope. The pope celebrated his seventy-fifth birthday 18 May 1995. It is the age at which bishops are required to offer their resignations, but this pope sees it as his mission to lead, or if not lead, prepare the Church for the third millennium.

[W. PRITCHARD]

PAPACY: 1995-2000

Eighteenth Pontifical Year. In the eighteenth year of John Paul's pontificate, beginning 28 October 1995, he presided over a special assembly of the Synod of Bishops for Lebanon and continued to be an active international traveler. Despite several bouts of fever and an increasingly noticeable hand tremor, in 1996 John Paul visited Guatemala, Nicaragua, El Salvador and Venezuela 5–11 February, Tunisia 14 April, Slovenia 17 May, Germany 21–23 June, Hungary 6–7 September, and France 19–22 September. He preached a message of reconciliation in Latin America. In Tunisia, he appealed for tolerance across Muslim North Africa. In Slovenia and

John Paul II addresses a crowd in Denver in 1993. (AP/Wide World Photos. Reproduced by permission.)

Hungary, he spoke of the new emptiness settling over post-communist Europe and urged patience when dealing with the current difficulties. To Germans, he encouraged a spiritual renewal to parallel the economic and political renewal of the reunited country. In France, he marked milestones of the country's evangelization. At the special assembly for Lebanon in November-December 1995, convened after seventeen years of Lebanon's civil conflict, the pontiff told citizens to forgive and forget the wounds of war. Much of the synod's focus was on relations with other churches, and for the first time Muslims were among a synod assembly's fraternal delegates.

John Paul continued to speak out on world issues. When addressing Vatican diplomats in January 1996, he urged a total ban on nuclear testing, and when the test-ban treaty was approved in September, the Vatican was among the first to sign it. In April, before an international conference on updating a conventional weapons convention, John Paul called for a global ban on anti-personnel land mines. In June, just before an international housing conference, he criticized the economic inequities that lead to the rapid growth of urban slums and said the "right to a house and the right to honest work are part of a plan of social harmony that should provide a dignified life for everyone, without discrimination."

In February, John Paul issued a sixty-five-page apostolic constitution, *Universi dominici gregis,* updating the rules for a conclave electing a new pope. Among changes, the document allows the cardinals, after thirty-three ballots, to drop the two-thirds majority needed to elect a pope and opt for a fifty percent majority plus one.

On 8 October 1996, doctors removed John Paul's appendix, confirming that the inflammation had produced recurring symptoms of fever and nausea. Doctors ruled out the presence of other pathogens and said that within three days of the surgery, the seventy-six-year-old pontiff was eating solids, walking, and meeting with aides. Within three weeks of the surgery, John Paul sent a message to the Pontifical Academy of Sciences, giving the church's blessing to the theory of evolution, and saying it must be recognized as "more than a hypothesis."

Nineteenth Pontifical Year. On 3 December 1996, marking the fiftieth anniversary of the formal establishment of the Chinese Catholic hierarchy, John Paul sent a message to Chinese Catholics via a Vatican Radio broadcast. He urged restoration of "visible unity among all" Chinese Catholics and full communion with Rome. Although he did not mention the government-approved Chinese Catholic Patriotic Association, which spurns Vatican ties, he said bishops must lead their faithful "in full freedom and with independence from any local authority."

The same month, he met at the Vatican with His Grace George R. Carey, archbishop of Canterbury, spiritual head of the worldwide Anglican Communion. Although the two pledged to continue to support Catholic-Anglican dialogue, they wrote in a joint declaration of "the obstacle to reconciliation caused by the ordination of women as priests and bishops in some provinces of the Anglican communion" and said "it may be opportune at this stage in our journey to consult further about how the relationship between the Anglican Communion and the Catholic Church is to progress." In June 1997, John Paul sought a first-ever meeting with Russian Orthodox Patriarch Alexei II of Moscow, but Ecumenical Patriarch Bartholomew of Constantinople reacted by boycotting the European Ecumenical Assembly that was to follow, and Alexei canceled the meeting with the pope. Bartholomew later broke a twenty-year tradition by announcing that he would not send a delegation to the Vatican for the papal Mass marking the feasts of Sts. Peter and Paul.

In a visit to war-shattered Sarajevo, Bosnia-Herzegovina, 12–13 April, John Paul appealed to the majority Muslims and minority Croats and Serbs to find forgiveness in their hearts and heal the wounds left by interethnic fighting. "Never again war! Never again hatred and intolerance!" was his cry upon his arrival and departure from the city. Shortly before his arrival, police discovered and deactivated twenty-three mines and a radio-controlled detonator under a bridge along the papal motorcade route, prompting increased security. The pope took a similar message of reconciliation to Lebanon 10–11 May and presented his apostolic exhortation *Une esperance nouvelle pour le Liban,* formally closing the special assembly of the Synod of Bishops for Lebanon.

In visits to the Czech Republic 25–27 April and to Poland 31 May–10 June, John Paul cited St. Adalbert as a model for faith, church-state cooperation, and Christian unity throughout Central Europe. He mentioned the saint in a meeting in Poland with the presidents of Germany and six formerly communist Central European states, a meeting that included discussion of including former Warsaw Pact members in the international community. John Paul traveled to France 21–24 August for World Youth Day and the beatification of Frederic Ozanam, founder of the St. Vincent de Paul Society. In Brazil 2–5 October, John Paul promoted social justice, highlighting the imbalances between the country's rich and poor, and rallied Catholics to defend and strengthen family bonds.

Twentieth Pontifical Year. John Paul celebrated the twentieth anniversary of his election as pope with an emotional Mass of thanksgiving in which he asked whether he had done all he could to lead the church well. He spoke to 70,000 people gathered in St. Peter's Square 18 October 1998: "After twenty years of service on Peter's chair, I cannot help but ask myself some questions today. . . . Have you been a diligent and vigilant teacher of the faith in the church? Have you tried to bring the great work of the Second Vatican Council closer to the people of today? Have you tried to satisfy the expectations of the church's faithful, and also the hunger for truth that is felt in the world outside the church?" The Mass capped a week of celebration that included best wishes from international leaders and ordinary Catholics, special concerts, media specials, and a series of books on the papacy. It also capped a year that saw the pope continue his international travels, name new cardinals, write an encyclical and two apostolic letters and preside over two synods of bishops despite an advancing neurological disorder that affected his posture, speech and movements.

On 15 October, the pope released his encyclical *Fides et ratio,* in which he warned that a growing separation between modern thought and the "ultimate truths" of religion was leading people to despair and to ethical confusion. The document called for a renewed harmony between theology and philosophy: John Paul asked the church's theologians to recover the "metaphysical dimension of truth" in their work and to help return the truths of the faith to Catholics' moral lives. He asked intellectuals to rise above the current vision of life and allow transcendent truths to guide them. The previous summer, the pope issued two apostolic letters: *Apostolos suos,* on the authority of bishops' conferences, and *Dies Domini,* on the religious observance of Sunday.

The special assemblies of the Synod of Bishops for America, 16 November–12 December 1997, and for Asia, 19 April–14 May 1998, were part of a series of regional synods John Paul convened in Rome to revitalize Catholic identity worldwide and to prepare for the new millennium. He presided over the general meetings of the assemblies. In the end he told delegates from the Americas that the synod was "a new point of departure" for evangelization of their continents. Opening the Asian synod, John Paul announced that he had invited two Chinese bishops to attend; the Chinese government did not permit the bishops to travel to Rome, and John Paul expressed his disappointment at the end of the synod.

Visiting four cities in Cuba 21–25 January 1998, John Paul defended the church's right to take the gospel to all areas of social life and said spiritual renewal was the answer to Cuba's problems. He appealed for the release of political prisoners, consoled the sick, and urged young people not to leave the island. Many church and international leaders hoped the papal visit would open opportunities for the island-nation's Catholics, and as rain began to fall on the last day of his visit, John Paul remarked that perhaps it signaled a new beginning for Cuba. John Paul also visited Nigeria 21–23 March, Austria 19–21 June, and Croatia 2–4 October.

In January 1998, John Paul named twenty-two new cardinals, including two *in pectore* (i.e., he did not reveal their names). He waived the limit on the number of cardinals under age eighty and for a brief time allowed more than 120 cardinal-electors eligible to vote. Among North Americans named were Archbishops Francis E. George of Chicago, Aloysius M. Ambrozic of Toronto, Norberto Rivera Carrera of Mexico City and J. Francis Stafford, the president of the Pontifical Council for the Laity.

Twenty-First Pontifical Year. John Paul focused on the approaching millennium, beginning 29 November 1998, when he formally proclaimed 2000 a holy year in a papal bull, *Incarnationis mysterium*. In the document, he introduced the ideas of global solidarity and church-wide soul-searching, focusing on repentance and forgiveness, in addition to maintaining the spiritual aspects of holy years, such as indulgences. The bull was accompanied by an appendix explaining how the faithful could obtain indulgences during the holy year, which was to run from 24 December 1999 to 6 January 2001. From encouraging Roman officials to complete their 2000-related construction projects to urging Lenten penitence and conversion to prepare for the jubilee as well as Easter, the pope kept the focus on the holy year.

He presided over the last two special assemblies of the Synod of Bishops before the holy year—for Oceania in December 1998 and Europe in October 1999—and officially closed the 1997 Synod of Bishops for America by issuing his apostolic exhortation *Ecclesia in America* in Mexico City during a 22–26 January visit. To spread Christ's message, John Paul said in the exhortation, individuals must be awakened to conversion and societies must be led to justice. He appealed for protection of human life in all its forms and for defense against modern evils such as abortion and the death penalty. In a 27 January stop in St. Louis, John Paul met with the governor of Missouri and obtained clemency for a convicted murderer scheduled to be executed that day.

Other papal travels highlighted various aspects of his pontificate. After twenty years of promoting Christian unity, John Paul made his first visit to a predominantly Orthodox nation, Romania, 7–9 May. Romanian Orthodox patriarch Teoctist, who invited the pope, attended Catholic Masses, and John Paul attended Orthodox liturgies, but neither received Communion from the other. One Vatican official said the level of Teoctist's and John Paul's joint activity was unprecedented. John Paul said at one Mass, "I am here among you pushed only by the desire for authentic unity." He also acknowledged how much minority Catholics had suffered for their religious beliefs, especially under communism, but added that their well-tested faith in Christ must give them the strength to overcome their differences with the Orthodox and work with them to spread the faith.

From 5–17 June John Paul made his longest visit to his homeland, touching twenty-one cities in sixteen dioceses. It was a visit of memories, including a stop in his hometown of Wadowice, where he spoke of childhood friends and the cream-filled pastries he used to eat. But in mid-visit, John Paul fell and cut his head, needing three stitches, and days later a fever and bout of the flu forced him to cancel appearances at a Mass attended by more than a million people in his former archdiocese of Kraków and at a nearby prayer service. It was the first time in more than twenty years of papal travel that he had canceled a full day's activities because of illness. The pope also canceled a short trip to Armenia to visit Catholicos Karekin, head of the Armenian Apostolic Church, who died of cancer a few days later.

On a one-day visit to Slovenia in September, John Paul urged ethnic groups of the former Yugoslavia to replace nationalism with love of country and culture that does not rely on hatred of others. Slovenia was John Paul's eighty-eighth trip outside the Vatican since the beginning of his pontificate.

Twenty-Second Pontifical Year. In the twenty-second year of John Paul's pontificate, he ushered the church into the new millennium, an event for which he had felt destined since his election as pope. He opened the Great Jubilee of the Year 2000 Christmas Eve 1999, when, walking unsteadily and wavering, he pushed open the holy door at St. Peter's Basilica. After it opened, he knelt in prayer. Among the first to follow him in were lay people from various continents, a symbol of the church's global nature.

The 24 December ceremony was the beginning of a sometimes continuous stream of activity for John Paul. He opened the holy doors at Rome's other three major basilicas, and, opening the door to the Basilica of St. Paul Outside the Walls at the beginning of the Week of Prayer for Christian Unity, he was helped by George Carey, archbishop of Canterbury, England, and Orthodox metropolitan Athanasios of Helioupolis and Theira, a representative of the Ecumenical Orthodox Patriarchate.

In a Jubilee Lenten Mass, the pope sought forgiveness for the past and present sins of Christians, including sins against Christian unity and against society's weakest members, the use of violence in serving the truth, hostility toward Jews and members of other religions, and the marginalization of women in the church. Weeks later, at Jerusalem's Western Wall, John Paul placed in a crack a signed piece of paper with a reading from his repentance liturgy, asking God to forgive the actions of all those who have "caused these children of yours to suffer."

The Holy Land visit was a dream come true for the pope, who for years had expressed his desire to visit the sites of major biblical events during the Jubilee year. When Iraqi authorities said security concerns and a continuing Western embargo made it impossible for the pope to visit the country, John Paul remained at the Vatican and took a spiritual pilgrimage of prayer to the ruins of Ur, birthplace of the patriarch Abraham. The following day he left for a 24–26 February trip to Egypt, where he prayed at the foot of Mount Sinai, where Moses received the Ten Commandments. The visit to the Western Wall in Jerusalem, the most sacred place in Judaism, came in late March, during a trip to Jordan, Israel, and the Palestinian territories. John Paul visited holy sites of the Old and New Testaments, walking in the footsteps of John the Baptist in Jordan and on the shores of the Sea of Galilee in Israel, traveling to Jerusalem's Church of the Holy Sepulcher to Manger Square in Bethlehem, where the Muslim call to prayer briefly interrupted the end of a papal Mass.

At each stage of the pilgrimage, John Paul reached out to other religious leaders. In Egypt he visited Pope Shenouda III, the patriarch of Egypt's Coptic Orthodox Christians. The pope said it was only right that the successor of St. Peter should visit the successor of St. Mark the Evangelist, who is held by tradition to have evangelized Egypt before being killed for the faith there. Grand Sheik Mohammed Sayyid Tantawi greeted John Paul at the Cairo airport and later announced he planned to visit the Vatican the following fall to participate in Catholic-Muslim dialogue sessions. In Jerusalem, a city sacred to Muslims, Christians, and Jews alike, John Paul called Christian disputes over the holy sites "scandalous" and urged a new spirit of harmony among Christian leaders. The same day that the pope visited the chief rabbinate and Yad Vashem Holocaust memorial and met with the Israeli president, John Paul also met with members of the Christian, Muslim, Jewish, Druze, and Bahai faiths.

Throughout the holy year, John Paul presided over many smaller Jubilee celebrations dedicated to different members of the church. In May, he combined his eightieth birthday celebration with the Jubilee for Priests, concelebrating a Mass with some 8,000 priests in St. Peter's Square. On the Jubilee for Workers, he called for a resolution to labor inequality and injustice throughout the world. He met with artists and journalists, police and children, deacons, scientists, and the sick. Closing the Forty-Seventh International Eucharistic Congress at the Vatican, he linked the Eucharistic and the worldwide mission of proclaiming the gospel.

In May, he traveled to Fatima, Portugal, to beatify two of the shepherd children to whom Mary appeared in 1917. On the nineteenth anniversary of his assassination attempt, he had the Vatican secretary of State, Cardinal Angelo Sodano, announce that he believed the so-called Third Secret of Fatima referred to the attempt on his life and the twentieth-century struggles against communism. The Vatican later published the secret.

As numbers of cardinals dwindled, Vatican officials looked for John Paul to name new members of the college. And in a year that saw trips to India, Georgia, and the Holy Land, John Paul was making plans for a visit in 2001 to Oceania, to officially close its special assembly. At eighty, an age when most Vatican officials are forced to retire, John Paul continued a hectic schedule. Slowed by age and a neurological disorder, he sometimes appeared more frail than ever, but many in Rome were impressed by his resilient spirit and steadfast manner.

[BARB FRAZE]

The Synod of Bishops

INTRODUCTION

The Synod of Bishops is a permanent institution, established by Pope Paul VI with the *motu proprio* entitled *Apostolica sollicitudo,* 15 September 1965, in response to the desire of the Fathers of the Second Vatican Council to keep alive the positive spirit engendered by the conciliar experience. The Second Vatican Council affirmed Paul VI 's initiative and made explicit reference to *Apostolica sollicitudo* in *Christus Dominus,* the Decree on Bishops (no. 5).

Literally speaking, the word "synod," derived from two Greek words *syn* meaning "together" and *hodos,* meaning "road" or "way," signifies a "walking together." The synod, generally speaking, represents the Catholic episcopate—pope and bishops—which is convoked by the pope to seek counsel in the governance of the universal Church. In this way, it is a particularly fruitful expression and instrument of the collegiality of bishops.

The "synodal principle" can be traced to the early days of the Church when Roman synods were called to examine serious problems. In the first millennium similar manifestations of the communion and collegiality of the episcopal college can be found in apostolic visits, pastoral letters and synods of various types (metropolitan, regional and patriarchal). The Code of Canon Law adopts language from Paul VI's *motu proprio* in describing the administrative structure, membership, procedures, and authority of the Synod of Bishops, but changes some provisions found in *Apostolica sollicitudo* (cc. 342–348).

The purpose of the Synod is "to foster a closer unity between the Roman Pontiff and the bishops, to assist the Roman Pontiff with their counsel in safeguarding and increasing faith and morals and in preserving and strengthening ecclesiastical discipline, and to consider questions concerning the Church's activity in the world" (c. 342). The Synod of Bishops, a standing ("permanent") institution, meets in general assembly when convoked by the pope. Its membership consists of bishops elected to represent their episcopal conferences as determined by the special law of the synod (*ex electione*), other bishops designated by this law itself (*ex officio*) and bishops (*ex nominatione pontificia*) according to the norms of the special law. To this membership are added some priests—religious elected in accord with the norms of the same special law (c. 346). As an institution, the synod has a permanent general secretariat presided over by a general secretary appointed by the Roman Pontiff, who is assisted by a council made up of bishops, some of whom are elected in accord with the norm of its special law by previous general assembly of the Synod of Bishops and some of whom are appointed by the pope. The responsibilities of all members cease at the beginning of a new general session (c. 348). The synod is directly under the authority of the pope who calls the synod into session, ratifies the election of its members, determines the topics for discussion and the agenda, and presides over the proceedings either in person or through delegates. He alone has the power to conclude, transfer, suspend, or dissolve the synod (c. 344).

Similarly, the Code of Canons of the Oriental Churches states that the Roman Pontiff is assisted in exercising his office by the bishops who aid him in various ways, among these is the synod of bishops. Regarding membership, the participation in the Synod of Bishops of patriarchs and other hierarchs who preside over Churches *sui iuris* is regulated by special norms established by the Roman Pontiff (c. 46, § 2).

Canon law envisages three types of synods: in addition to general assemblies which meet in either ordinary or extraordinary sessions, there are "special" sessions (c. 345). As a general rule, the ordinary general assemblies since 1971 have met every three years. They address particular topics affecting the good of the Church worldwide, selected by the pope who through the general secretariat elicits input from individual episcopal conferences and bishops. A synod of bishops gathered in extraordinary general session deals with matters "requiring a speedy solution." Special sessions convoke bishops to deal with regional issues; most bishops attending a special assembly are from that particular region (c. 346).

John Paul II opens the 1999 Synod of Bishops for Europe. (© Livio Anticoli/Liaison Agency.)

Once the pope settles on the theme of a synod, the general secretariat with the assistance of the council members prepares the *lineamenta,* a broad "outline" of the topic, presented in such a way as to generate suggestions and observations on the local level. To provide guidance and a structure for formulating responses, a series of questions appears at the conclusion of the document. On the basis of the responses to the *lineamenta,* the general secretariat, assisted by this same council drafts the *instrumentum laboris* or "working paper" for submission to the Holy Father for his approval. This document becomes the point of reference for discussions in the synodal assembly. In the case of special assemblies, the Holy Father appoints a Pre-Synodal Council which collaborates with the general secretariat in preparing the above documentation as well as formulating a criteria for participation, for ultimate approval by the Holy Father, according to the foreseen categories, i.e., members *ex officio, ex electione, ex nominatione pontificia,* fraternal delegates, experts and observers.

The *Indictio,* that is, the Holy Father's official act of convocation, establishing the dates of the assembly, is communicated by the Secretary of State to the General Secretary, who in turn sees to contacting those concerned as well as rendering the information public. Technically speaking, the Holy Father is president of the general secretariat as well as president of each synodal assembly. Though present at plenary sessions of the synod, he customarily appoints presidents-delegate to oversee the proceedings in his name. He also appoints, the general *relator,* one or more special secretaries and other officials responsible for the day-to-day working of the synodal assembly, as well as specialists (*periti*) in various church and academic disciplines to assist the general relator and special secretaries, not to mention non-voting observers (*auditores*). Customarily, representatives from churches, church and ecclesial communities and other religions—depending on the character of each synodal assembly—have been invited to participate as fraternal delegates.

The working sessions of the synod consist of general congregations (*congregatio*) at which the synod fathers give their presentations (*interventiones*) and listen to those of others on some aspect of the synod topic as found in the *instrumentum laboris.* In this period, the fraternal delegates are also invited to speak. To further assist the synod fathers in their discussion, similar sessions (*auditiones*), depending on time, are also provided for the observers. The discussion period is followed by small groups (*circuli minores*) that focus attention on particular points raised in the general congregations. Subsequently, the small groups make a report to the plenary session and then reconvene to formulate recommendations (*propositiones*) which, after an initial presentation in plenary ses-

SYNOD OF BISHOPS-TIMELINE

29 September-29 October 1967; First General Assembly

11-28 October 1969; First Extraordinary Assembly

30 September-6 November 1971; Second General Assembly

27 Sept.-26 October 1974; Third General Assembly

30 September-29 October 1977; Fourth General Assembly

26 September-25 October 1980; Fifth General Assembly

14-31 January 1980; Particular Assembly of Dutch Bishops

24-27 March 1980; Particular Assembly of Ukrainian Bishops

29 September-29 October 1983; Sixth General Assembly

24 November-8 December 1985; Second Extraordinary Assembly

1-30 October 1987; Seventh General Assembly

30 September-28 October 1990; Eighth General Assembly

28 November-14 December 1991; First Special Assembly for Europe

10 April-8 May 1994; Special Assembly for Africa

2-29 October 1994; Ninth General Assembly

26 November-14 December 1995; Special Assembly for Lebanon

16 November-12 December 1997; Special Assembly for America

19 April-14 May 1998; Special Assembly for Asia.

22 November-12 December 1998; Special Assembly for Oceania

1-23 October 1999; Second Special Assembly for Europe

sion, are returned to the small groups for possible amendments. A final list of recommendations, compiled by the general relator and special secretary in collaboration with the relators of the small groups and experts, are then submitted to the vote of the synod fathers before they are finally submitted, with the results going to the Holy Father as the primary work of the synodal assembly. Popes Paul VI and John Paul II have used these recommendations, along with the entire synodal documentation, in drafting a post-synodal apostolic exhortation (*exhortatio apostolica post-synodalis*), which has become the customary concluding document to a given synodal assembly. It has also become common practice for a synodal assembly, before adjourning, to issue a "Message to the People of God" (*nuntius*), as the first "collegial'' fruit coming from the assembly, to offer encouragement to the Church on points related to the synod topic. Though the responsibilities of a synod assembly ceases at its conclusion, during each synod assembly the elected bishop-members usually form a council, which is composed of bishops chosen by the synod and those appointed by the Holy Father. This council, through the general secretariat, provides assistance to the Holy Father in analyzing the recommendations and drafting the text to the concluding document, as well as evaluating the follow-up of the synod assembly and attending to related matters.

The First Ordinary General Assembly of the Synod of Bishops (1967) considered a number of timely questions: the preservation and strengthening of the faith, the revision of the Code of Canon Law, and pastoral questions, including seminaries, mixed marriages and the liturgy. Pope Paul VI convoked three more ordinary sessions to deal with the ministerial priesthood and justice in the world (1971), evangelization (1974) and catechesis (1977). Paul VI called the First Extraordinary General Assembly (1969) to examine issues of episcopal collegiality vis-à-vis papal primacy.

Bibliography: For the Latin text of *motu proprio* by POPE PAUL VI that is entitled *Apostolica sollicitudo,* see: *Acta Apostolicae Sedis* 57 (1965): 775–780. *Ordo Synodi Episcoporum celebrandae recognitus et auctus* (Vatican City: Typis Polyglottis Vaticanus, 1971). J. A. CORIDEN, T. J. GREEN, and D. E. HEINTSCHEL, *The Code of Canon Law: A Text and Commentary* (New York/Mahwah: Paulist Press, 1985). JAN P. SCHOTTE, *With the Church Towards the Third Millennium: The Second Vatican Council and the Synod of Bishops, Bishops' Conference of Malaysia and Singapore* (1986); "The Synod of Bishops: A Permanent Yet Adaptable Church Institution," *Studia Canonica,* 26 (1992): 289–306; "The Synod of Bishops: History, Work and Recent Experiences," in *The Bishop and His Ministry* (Vatican City: Urbaniana University Press, 1998), 375–390.

[JOHN A. ABRUZZESE]

EXTRAORDINARY ASSEMBLY

SYNOD OF BISHOPS (SECOND EXTRAORDINARY, 1985)

The Second Extraordinary Assembly of the Synod of Bishops (24 November to 8 December 1985) was called by Pope John Paul II to commemorate the 20th anniversary of the Second Vatican Council. The Pope expressed the hope that the synod would revive the conciliar experience of episcopal collegiality, provide an occasion for an exchange of information on the effects of the Council, and promote its further study and implementation.

Preliminary Discussions. The months between the pope's announcement on 25 January 1985 and the opening of the synod saw a rather passionate debate, not so much on the council itself but on its impact within the Church. Much of this debate was focused by the apparently unconnected publication of an interview given by Joseph Cardinal Ratzinger, Prefect of the Congregation for the Doctrine of the Faith, in which he proposed a decidedly negative evaluation of postconciliar developments. This debate was to echo within the synod itself.

The preparations for the synod began with a letter sent out in March to all the episcopal conferences asking them to report on the steps taken to make the council known and implemented, on problems and difficulties encountered in the meantime, and on what might be done to remedy evils and to promote the council even further. The bishops were asked to concentrate on the council's four constitutions: on the Liturgy; on the Church; on Divine Revelation; and on the Church in the modern world.

By the time the synod opened, ninety-six responses had been received from around the world, of which only about twenty were made public. These provided valuable surveys of the council's impact on the local and particular churches. The assessments were generally favorable, with many respondents speaking of the council as a great gift of God to the Church, showing its fruits in the liturgical life of the Church and in a growing awareness of the Church as a communion of believers. The reports also mentioned problems in the postconciliar Church, cautioning, however, against blaming them on the council itself and indicating that the solutions must lie in a greater effort to make the council's teachings better known and more fully implemented. Among frequently mentioned difficulties were an over-accommodation to modern cultural norms and political ideologies and a failure to implement the council's call for greater autonomy for the local Churches.

As at the First Extraordinary Assembly of the Synod in 1969, the episcopal conferences were represented only by their presidents and not by elected delegates. Bishop James Malone of Youngstown represented the U.S. conference of bishops, Bishop Hubert of St.-Jean-Longueuil, Quebec, the Canadian conference. Cardinal John Krol of Philadelphia was one of the three co-presidents of the synod appointed by Pope John Paul II.

The synod proper opened with the initial report of Cardinal Godfrey Danneels of Brussels, the synod's *relator,* summarizing the reports received from the churches. The first week was devoted to oral and written interventions by the members of the synod. Most of these simply repeated in summary form the written reports of the churches the members represented. At the end of the first week, Cardinal Danneels provided a synopsis of the proceedings to that point, and proposed a set of subjects for

Pope John Paul II (C), flanked by cardinals and bishops, in St. Peter's Square on their way to St. Peter's Basilica at the 1985 Synod. (© Reuters/CORBIS)

the second week's discussions in the small language-groups.

Since the topics suggested for discussion concerned mainly problem areas, it is not surprising that the reports of the language-groups tended to be less optimistic and confident than the first week's interventions. The final report, which, along with a brief "Message to the People of God," was the only official document issued by the synod, reflects more the tone and emphases of the second week's discussions than that of the first.

The Final Report. The synod bishops structured their final report around a programmatic statement already anticipated in Danneels' initial report: "The Church, under the Word of God, Celebrating the Mystery of Christ for the World's Salvation." The emphasis, thus, was ecclesiological. The report began with a brief celebration and reaffirmation of the council as "a grace of God and a gift of the Holy Spirit" and with a commitment to continue to foster it. It then passed to a discussion of the "deficiencies and difficulties in the acceptance of the council," among which it gave special prominence to the sense of alienation from the Church common in developed nations. Among the causes of this it listed a technological ideology, materialism, and superficial interpretations of the council, particularly one-sided readings of its ecclesiology.

As a remedy for these defects, the final report called for a deeper reception of the council, which would require greater knowledge, an interior assimilation, and fuller implementation of its teachings. Norms for the interpretation of the council insisted on retaining its integral teaching, the central role of the four constitutions, attention to its pastoral character, a refusal to separate its "spirit" from its "letter," and the need to read it in the light of the earlier tradition.

The final report then turned to particular themes of the council. It began with a great stress on the Mystery of the Church, which it proposed not only as central to the council's vision but also as especially appropriate in contemporary conditions where a new thirst for the sacred is discerned. Linked with this emphasis on mystery is a call for a greater awareness of the council's teaching on the universal call to holiness.

The sources of the Church's life were then briefly considered, first, in a recall of the teaching of *dei verbum* on the relationship between scripture, tradition and magisterium, and then in a stress on the primary tasks of evangelization. A very brief section followed on the Liturgy, with emphasis especially on its interior and spiritual dimensions.

The next section introduced the synod's other primary ecclesiological emphasis: the Church as communion.

(The most remarkable weakness of the final report is the very little attention given to the central conciliar theme of the Church as the people of God.) The report recalls the Trinitarian and sacramental bases of communion and then passes to consider its implication for the questions of uniformity and pluriformity, the Eastern rite Churches, collegiality and episcopal conferences, participation, coresponsibility, and ecumenism.

The last section concerned the Church's mission in the world. While stressing the importance of *gaudium et spes*, the final report argues that the signs of the times have changed for the worse since the council, which requires a renewed emphasis on the theology of the cross. This is the context for brief paragraphs on *aggiornamento*, inculturation, dialogue with non-Christian religions and non-believers, the preferential option for the poor, and human development.

Throughout the final report, several suggestions are made for further promotion of the council. Among the more specific of these are calls for a universal catechism or compendium of Catholic doctrine, for textbooks to be used in the teaching of theology, for a speedy promulgation of a code of canon law for the Eastern Churches, and for study of the theological status of episcopal conferences and the applicability of the principle of subsidiarity in the Church. After the synod, Pope John Paul II appointed commissions to carry out the suggestions with regard to the catechism, episcopal conferences and subsidiarity.

In the end, the synod proved to be much less dramatic than many had anticipated. It provided an opportunity for a needed assessment of the council's impact on the Church, and this assessment, at least gathered from all the reports and interventions and not just from the final report, was as balanced and as full as could be expected in two short weeks. Taken as a whole, the synod in many ways illustrated the epochal significance of the Second Vatican Council.

See Also: GODFRIED DANNEELS, JOHN KROL, JOSEPH CARDINAL RATZINGER

Bibliography: G. CAPRILE, *Il Sinodo dei vescovi: Seconda assemblea generale straordinaria 24 novembre–8 dicembre 1985* (Rome 1986). G. ALBERIGO and J. PROVOST, eds.,*Synod 1985—An Evaluation* (Edinburgh 1986). A. DULLES, *Vatican II and the Extraordinary Synod: An Overview* (Collegeville, Minn. 1986). P. HEBBLETHWAITE, *Synod Extraordinary: The Inside Story of the Rome Synod, November–December 1985* (Garden City 1986). X. RYNNE, *John Paul's Extraordinary Synod: A Collegial Achievement* (Wilmington 1986). *Synode Extraordinaire: Celebration de Vatican II* (Paris 1986). J. RATZINGER with V. MESSORI, *The Ratzinger Report: An Exclusive Interview on the State of the Church* (San Francisco 1985). Texts relating to the Second Extraordinary Synod published in *Origins* include various interventions, *Origins*

15, no. 26 (12 Dec 1985); the final message, *Origins* 15, no. 27 (19 Dec 1985): 441–44; and the report to the pope, *Origins* 15, no. 27 (19 Dec 1985): 444–50.

[J. KOMONCHAK]

ORDINARY ASSEMBLIES

SYNOD OF BISHOPS (FOURTH GENERAL ASSEMBLY, 1977)

The Fourth General Assembly of the Synod of Bishops met in Rome, Italy 29 September–28 October, 1977, the meeting occurring on the tenth anniversary of the first synod, 1967. As in the case of all the synods to date, the members were those cardinals and bishops selected by episcopal conferences throughout the world, representatives of the Eastern Churches, those appointed by the pope, the heads of the major offices of the Roman Curia, and representatives of various religious orders of men. The American members of this synod included four selected by the National Conference of Catholic Bishops (Cardinal John J. Carberry, Archbishops Joseph J. Bernardin and John F. Whealon and Bishop Raymond A. Lucker), two Metropolitans of the Eastern Rites (Archbishop Stephen Kocisko and Bishop Joseph Shmondiuk), Cardinal Timothy Manning (appointed by the pope), Abbot (now Archbishop) Rembert Weakland, Primate of the Benedictines, and Cardinal John J. Wright, Prefect of the Congregation for the Clergy, the Vatican office responsible for, among other things, worldwide catechetics.

Theme: Catechesis

The 1977 synod had as its theme Catechetics. Catechesis comes from the Greek word "to make resound" or "to echo." It is a precise word for what the Church has been doing since the days of the apostles. It refers to the witnessing, proclaiming, preaching, or teaching of Christ's message, the "good news," in such a way as to produce an "echo" of Christ in those who hear it. Catechetics is the art or discipline concerned with the what and the how of catechesis. Catechesis implies more than religious education, which has come to refer to the academic discipline of religion. In this sense religious education can mean the intellectual appreciation of a subject much like one would learn mathematics or biology. The synod spoke of catechesis rather than religious education. As urged by the Synod, the term refers to every activity intended to help people grow and mature in the faith.

Another way of defining catechesis is to call it the active witnessing of Christ by word and deed. When catechesis is described as witness it is easy to see that it is not limited to bishops and priests. It is true, as the synod documents point out, that all individual testimony to the truth revealed in Jesus Christ must find its touchstone of authenticity in terms of the teaching of the Church through her official witness. But it is also correct to say that the obligation to bear testimony concerning all that Jesus did and said falls to every believer. Hence all the faithful are called to be catechists (*Message to the People of God*, Synod 1977, n. 12; hereafter Message).

Deliberations. When the bishops faced the issue in the synod aula, they seemed intent on moving beyond immediate controversies regarding methods of teaching the faith to confront underlying issues and point to the solutions. The synod began its deliberations with a study of the working paper that grew out of earlier episcopal consultations. The Synod Office prepared a draft document and sent it to all the episcopal conferences. Reactions and suggestions to this paper were followed by the second paper, that was sent to the synodal members in time for them to study it before they met in Rome to open the discussions.

Catechizing. In particular, the bishops examined catechetics with a special reference to the teaching of the faith to children and young people. As the meeting's original working draft (*instrumentum laboris*) pointed out, "it is precisely children that can often be one of the most powerful reminders to the whole Christian community and individual members of the faithful to be attentive to their own vocation and their own educational responsibilities" (*instrumentum laboris* 7). The synod here spoke of the essential teaching mission which reaches out to all, both young and old. "In our time, even more than ever, there is needed a catechetics that accompanies Christians throughout their lives with due regard to their concrete situation of faith" (ibid. 6). In turn, catechetics is seen as one aspect of the great evangelical mission of the Church; the bringing of Christ to all men and women. For this reason, there is a strong relationship between the work of the 1974 synod on evangelization and the 1977 synod on catechetics. The synod's final public document, *Message to the People of God*, states that "it is the Church's task to proclaim and accomplish Christ's salvation in the whole world. This is the work of evangelization of which catechetics is an aspect. It is centered in the mystery of Christ. Christ, true God and true Man, and His saving work carried out in His incarnation, life and death and resurrection, is the center of the message" (Message 7).

By the time the 1977 synod met, there was a waning of the polarization and polemics that had marked the field of catechetics after Vatican Council II. The division in theory and approach that plagued much of the work in teaching the faith, particularly to the young in many of the European nations and North America, was not so much in evidence in the discussions of this synod.

Synod Message to the People of God. The general assumption that seemed to support nearly all of the speeches made from the floor—and certainly reflected in the final public text—was that catechetics as instruction of others in faith is essentially the transmission of a message. Thus, the document, issued in the name of the bishops of the synod, tends to stress primarily the idea of content. But it must be remembered that content includes the understanding that living out the faith is also a part of the Church's teaching. Method, techniques, and pedagogical devices are only tools in the much more important task of telling others of the teaching of Christ (Message 7 and 8). The synod insists that this teaching is to be in its fullness, for otherwise the learner, the instructed, would be left with an incomplete faith. "Fidelity in handing on the integral gospel message and the authenticity of the catechetical mode of communication through which faith is transmitted are both to be discerned through the reverent attentiveness to the magisterial and pastoral ministry of the Church" (Message 8). The synod's public document considers catechesis as the manifestation of the salvation of Christ. The center of catechetics is the mystery of Christ: "The Church insists that it is the bearer of the message of salvation destined for all mankind . . . [that] Jesus Christ is the focal point and foundation of our faith and source of our life" (Message 7). According to the synod, catechetics has as its primary function the proclamation of the faith; the mystery of Christ. The communication of faith in and knowledge of Christ, the central reality of the Church's proclamation, can be seen, according to the synod's text, under three headings; word, memory, and witness.

Catechesis as Word. As word, catechetics is concerned with the message received from Christ. "The integral, vital substance handed down through the creed provides the fundamental nucleus of the mystery of the one and triune God as it is revealed to us through the mystery of God's Son, the Incarnate Savior living always in His Church" (Message 8). The model of catechesis as word is found in the preparation for adult baptism. The liturgical exemplar of this manner of teaching the faith is found in the special formation which prepares an adult convert for the profession of faith during the Paschal Vigil. During this preparation the catachumen receives the Word of God in the form of the gospels and its ecclesial expression, the creeds.

Catechesis as Memory. As memory, catechesis is concerned with the action by which the church recalls in each age the "good news" about Christ. For this reason the synod insists that certain elements of the Church's belief and heritage can be committed to memory and that religious education contain this element. The synod notes that "normally, things should be memorized as part of the formation; such as biblical texts, especially from the New Testament, certain liturgical formulae which are the privileged expressions of these texts, and other prayers. Believers should also make their own expressions of faith—the living fruit of the reflections of Christians over the centuries—that have been gathered in the creeds and principal documents of the Church" (Message 9).

The aspect of catechesis shows its connection with the whole life of the believing community. For it is precisely as in living, effective memory of Christ that the Church celebrates the Eucharist. The value of words and actions today or at any time within the Christian family have effect and lasting meaning only inasmuch as they show forth the Lord Jesus and unite men and women with him. Thus, in doing so within the collective and individual memory of him, catechesis is connected with the entire sacramental and liturgical life of Christ's Church.

Catechesis as Witness. As witness, catechesis translates the word "which is rooted in living tradition" into the "living word for our times" (Message 10). At this point the synod indicated that the faith cannot remain without fruit. By the believer—by the one who bears the Word of God—there must be not only a faith-acceptance of it but a translation of that faith into action. Thus, there is required a serious commitment. The believer must follow the law of Christ in terms of moral action. Because this is so the synod text continues: "We must affirm without ambiguity that there are laws and moral principles which catechesis must teach. In addition, we must affirm that the moral doctrine of the gospel has a specific nature which goes far beyond the demands of mere natural ethics" (Message 10).

The three realities, faith, witness, and the Church are inseparable. None can function in a vacuum. Witness must be a constant declaration of the faith and this implies a communion with all those who hold the same faith. That community is the Church. Witness is always founded upon what it receives within the Church and falls back on that same Church for the authentication of the content of all to which it testifies. As the one principal witness, the Church has the obligation to testify to the faith and see that it is spread over the face of the earth. In the Church's unique position as the extension of Christ, all believers are called to participate. Some share this ministry as official spokesmen for the Church, local or universal, others as believers whose personal witness is united to the Church. The communion and unity of their witness rests on the one Spirit who gives life and truth to his one Church (Message 10).

The Synod Propositions

In addition to its public document, *Message to the People of God*, the 1977 synod offered to the Holy Father a series of thirty-four considerations or propositions (Prop.) related to catechetics. This material was forwarded to the pope in the hope that he would use it in the preparation of his own public statement, an apolistic exhortation or encyclical (Prop. 1). Although they are not presented as a complete text, they do offer a good summary of what had preoccupied the bishops during the month-long meeting.

In the propositions the bishops note the existence of new catechetical methods and the reasons for or scope of catechetics (Prop. 2–3). According to the propositions, the faith must be understood as living in Christ. For this reason, commitment to the faith is most important in those who are to teach others the way of the Lord (Prop. 4–6). Authentic catechesis requires, however, more than just commitment. It must be founded on a clear and complete knowledge and presentation of the faith—which in turn is centered on the person of Christ (Prop. 7–8). Proper catechesis implies the presentation of the full and entire faith content and its implications for Christian living. It must also inspire one to want to live the Christian way of life in all its ramifications (Prop. 10–13). Teaching the faith takes into consideration the situation of the listener and attempts to use available methods that will help reach him or her (Prop. 14–20). Every believer is by nature a catechist—a teacher of the faith—but parents have a special role to play as they are the first teacher of the faith in the life of a child. Those who prepare the young in the grasp of the faith also have a place in the mission of the Church (Prop. 21–25). The Christian community of believers is the home of the faith; it is, therefore, within the community that the believer learns the faith. The next section of proposition speaks of the role of the larger Christian community, the Church itself, in teaching the faith, and then of the place of smaller cells of community life. It notes that the family, the parish, the schools, and still other smaller communities are natural places for learning the faith (Prop. 26–29). There are various problems that arise in teaching within a given diocese, and all should remember that the ultimate responsibility for the proper catechesis of the local Church rests with the bishop, who is the principal teacher of the faith in that Church. Those who undertake this task do so in collaboration with him (Prop. 30–34).

Particular Issues. In *Message to the People of God*, the synod stressed the need for catechesis to help families face the contemporary cultural breakdown. It speaks of the need to catechize couples before and after marriage concerning their responsibilities to each other and for special programs to assist parents in giving catechesis to their children.

Another major theme was the importance of small communities of faith as settings for catechesis. The hope expressed is to form small groups of Christians who support and encourage one another to live out their faith more fully.

In his final address, Pope Paul emphasized that he looked to the synodal Fathers to be a leaven inspiring their fellow bishops to action. He also referred to the General Catechetical Directory, issued in 1971 by the Congregation for the Clergy and sent to all episcopal conferences with the hope that it would be made the basis for catechetical texts and teaching. He also called upon the faithful to take up the task of catechetics—the mission of passing on the faith.

Assessment

Of particular value in this synod was the frank appreciation of the problems that had divided catechists in the years following the council. The synod noted the two areas of focus, content and emphasis, and opted for a statement that insisted on content-conscious catechetics while also urging the adoption of relevant techniques in teaching the faith. The synod's balance is seen in its call for content—the knowledge of the faith—as well as an understanding of the need for methods of teaching that reach men and women, young and old, where they are today. The theme of catechetics as word, memory, and witness adopted by the synod offers a brief summary of the way the synod approached its subject and is a tool for understanding the nature of catechetics as it is lived within today's Church.

See Also: CATECHESI TRADENDAE

Bibliography: G. CAPRILE, *Il Sinodo dei vescovi: Quarta assemblea generale* (Rome 1978). For the Latin text of *Catechesi tradendae,* see: *Acta Apostolicae Sedis* 71 (1979): 1277–1340. Texts relating to the 1977 Synod published in *Origins* include the *instrumentum laboris* 5, no. 47 (13 May 1976) 741–751; and various interventions in *Origins* 7, nos. 17–21 (13 Oct–10 Nov 1977). *The Living Light* 15 (1978) 1–127, contains a summary of the *Instrumentum laboris,* as well as the text of "Message to the People of God" and the thirty-four propositions of the Synod.

[DONALD W. WUERL]

SYNOD OF BISHOPS (FIFTH GENERAL ASSEMBLY, 1980)

The Fifth General Assembly of the Synod of Bishops, held in Rome from 26 September to 25 October 1980, had for its principal theme "The Roles of the Christian Family in the Modern World." There were 148 elected representatives of episcopal conferences. The

Pope John Paul II seated at the presidency table in the Synod Hall during session works of the Fifth World Synod of Bishops. (© Bettmann/CORBIS)

bishops from the developing countries of Africa, Asia and Latin America held a clear majority with 94 attendees. Among the appointed participants, there were 13 representatives from the Eastern Churches, 24 papal appointees, 20 delegates from the curia, 10 superiors of religious orders and 43 official auditors.

In addition, ten ''special auditors'' or *periti* were appointed to be of service to the special secretary of the synod, Bishop Lozano Barragán (Mexico City). Cardinal Joseph Ratzinger (Munich) was appointed *relator* for the synod and Cardinals Primatesta (Cordoba), Picachy (Calcutta) and Gantin (president of the Pontifical Commission for Justice and Peace) were named alternating presidents. Members selected from the National Conference of Catholic Bishops of the United States (NCCB) included: Archbishops John R. Quinn (San Francisco, President of the NCCB), Joseph Bernardin (Cincinnati) and Robert Sanchez (Santa Fe), and Auxiliary Bishop J. Francis Stafford (Chairman of the U.S. Bishop's Family Life Commission). Other Americans were the *ex officio* major metropolitan of the Byzantine rite, Archbishop Stephen Kocisko (Pittsburgh), two superiors of religious communities, Rev. Paul Boyle (Passionist) and Rev. Stephen

Tutas (Society of Mary), and a papal appointment, Cardinal Terence Cook (New York).

Theme of the Synod. In May 1978, the advisory council of the secretariat for the synod, a group of fifteen bishops (twelve elected at the end of the previous synod in 1977 and three appointed by the pope) met for the first time, chaired by Cardinal Karol Wojtyła (Kraków). The advisory council suggested to Pope Paul VI that ''The Family in the Modern World'' be the topic taken up in the Fifth General Assembly. After Paul VI died, his successor, Pope John Paul II (Cardinal Wojtyła) determined that the topic would be ''The Roles of the Christian Family in the Modern World.''

The subtle shift in this designation implied a change of emphasis. Following the crisis occasioned by *Humanae vitae* in 1968, there had been a desire on the part of many to investigate further the theology of marriage of the family, in order to ground the teaching of the magisterium in a ''fuller, more organic and more synthetic explanation'' (speech of Paul VI, 31 July 1968). While this appears to have been the intention of Paul VI, John Paul II preferred to emphasize the ''roles'' of the family in the mission of the Church. The preparatory documents reflected this emphasis and suggested that the source of the family's unique role was to be found in God's Divine Plan.

In May 1979 the secretary general of the synod, Bishop Władyslaw Rubin (Gniezo, Poland), sent the *lineamenta* (outline), to the leaders of the hierarchy of the Church. The ensuing dialogue resulted in a significant number of suggestions to the secretariat. A new secretary general, Joseph Tomko, integrated these suggestions into the document that served as a working paper (*instumentum laboris*) for the synod. This working paper, which closely resembled the *lineamenta*, was sent to the individual members of the synod in June 1980.

Methods and Events. After the formal opening of the synod, which included a homily by Pope John Paul II, Bishop Tomko delivered a report on the activities of the general secretary since the previous assembly. One of the points brought up by Bishop Tomko was that there were still a number of questions concerning the function and the status of the Synod of Bishops itself. The first *relatio* by Cardinal Ratzinger summarized the pre- synodal documents. The assembly then heard 162 spoken and received 51 written interventions about various aspects of family life. So far-ranging were these interventions that Cardinal Ratzinger's *relatio altera*, delivered 6 October, reflected a significant change in the concerns of the bishops. The participants then divided into eleven smaller groups (*circuli minores*) and met for discussion from the 6–10 of October. Each group delivered its report to the general assembly at the beginning of the third week. The synod then attempted to draw up its final documents.

After some delay, the *circuli minores* were again called together to present suggestions for a list of propositions. These suggestions were delivered 17 October by the *relators* of the eleven groups, and in conjunction with Cardinal Ratzinger they drew up the final version of the text. It was presented to the assembly 20 October. The final week of the synod was devoted to rewriting the "Message to Christian Families" (going through three drafts), originally composed by five of the bishops, and making further amendments to the *propositiones* (recommendations). The *propositiones* received between 750 and 800 suggestions (*modi*), approximately 150 of which were incorporated into the final version.

During the synod there were also two "academic sessions" on 10th and 22nd of October, held outside of the official meetings, and one "World Day of the Family" celebrated on 12 October.

Text and Results. The "Message to Christian Families," drawn up by a small, ad hoc committee of bishops and published at the close of the synod, did not reflect the full range of discussion of the four week meeting. The message first described the "Situation of Families" (par. II), then invoked "God's Plan for Marriage and the Family" (par. III) as normative, and finally implied that even the most pressing pastoral problems could be worked out through the "Family's Response to God's Plan" (par. IV) or the meditation of "The Church and the Family" (par. V). More representative of the bishop's work were the forty-three *propositiones* submitted to John Paul II for his consideration. These recommendations were published unofficially in various translations and revealed the deep concern of the synod bishops for the many dimensions of marriage and family life. Issues calling for more investigation and pastoral solicitude ranged from personal questions of marriage preparation, divorce, and the regulation of fertility, to the global concerns of social justice, sexual roles, threats and support systems for the family, the diversity of customs, and human rights. Perhaps the most significant ideas discussed were specifically theological: marriage and sacramentality, the role of faith, the domestic church, mixed marriages and the question of inculturation. The discussions did not lead to many concrete conclusions, but numerous suggestions were made for continued research and dialogue.

Pope John Paul II addressed four of these issues in his closing homily: divorce and remarriage, contraception and "gradualism," inculturation, and the role of women. The homily foreshadowed the apolistic exhortation *Familiaris consortio*, published 15 December 1981. A document of more than 30,000 words, it reflected the emphasis of John Paul II on the centrality of "God's Plan for the Family," and on the role of that plan in the Church's mission of evangelization and catechesis. At least one-half of the original recommendations appeared in *Familiaris consortio*, and most of the issues suggested by the bishops were given consideration. In the final analysis, however, the papal assessment of these issues remained normative. Few controversial questions were left open for further inquiry. As a whole *Familiaris consortio* forms a compendium of traditional doctrine with respect to marriage and the family.

Two other events related to the 1980 synod were the establishment of the Pontifical Council for the Family, and the publication of the "Charter of the Rights of the Family." Pope John Paul II established the pontifical council in a *motu proprio* on 9 May 1981. The council supercedes the former committee on the Family set up by Pope Paul VI on 11 January 1973. The first president named for the new council was Cardinal John Knox, an Australian prelate who was the prefect of the Sacred Congregation for Sacraments and Divine Worship.

See Also: FAMILIARIS CONSORTIO, BERNARDIN GANTIN, JOSEPH RATZINGER

The inauguration of the 1983 synod at St Peter's Basilica in the Vatican City. (© Vittoriano Rastelli/CORBIS)

Bibliography: G. CAPRILE, *Il Sinodo dei vescovi: Quinta assemblea generale* (Rome 1981). For a Latin text of *Familiaris consortio*, see: *Acta Apostolicae Sedis* 74 (1982): 81–191. USCC, *Charter of the Rights of the Family* (Washington, D.C. 1983). J. GROOTAERS and J. SELLING, *The 1980 Synod of Bishops "On the Role of the Family"* (Louvain 1983). Texts relating to the 1980 Synod published in *Origins* include the *Lineamenta* 9, no. 8 (19 July 1979): 113–128; the *Instrumentum laboris* 10, no. 15 (25 Sept 1980): 225–233. Various interventions can be found in *Origins* 10, nos. 17–21 (16 Oct–6 Nov 1980), and the final "Message" in *Origins* 10, no. 21 (6 Nov 1980): 321–325.

[J. A. SELLING]

SYNOD OF BISHOPS (SIXTH GENERAL ASSEMBLY, 1983)

The Sixth General Assembly of the Synod of Bishops was called by John Paul II to discuss and offer advice on the theme "Reconciliation and Penance in the Mission of the Church" from 29 September to 29 October, 1983. Participants included: 13 from the Oriental Churches; 149 representing the 100 episcopal conferences throughout the world; 10 superiors general of religious communities of men; 20 heads of dicasteries in the Roman Curia; the General Secretary (Archbishop Joseph Tomko); and 23 papal appointees.

Organization. The episcopal conference of the United States was represented by four elected delegates: Archbishop John R. Roach of St. Paul-Minneapolis (NCCB President); Cardinal Joseph Bernardin of Chicago; Archbishop Patrick F. Flores of San Antonio; and Auxiliary Bishop Austin B. Vaughan of New York. Other U.S. citizens eligible to vote were Cardinal William Baum, Prefect of the Congregation for Catholic Education; Metropolitan Stephen Sulyk of the Ukrainian Archeparchy of Philadelphia; Archbishop Stephen Kocisko of the Archdiocese of Pittsburgh (Byzantine Rite); as well as two papal appointees: Cardinal Timothy Manning and Archbishop Edmund C. Szoka of Detroit. Nine invited auditors included Sr. Catherine Magdeleine, Superior General of the Dominican Sisters of Brittany; Sr. Agnes Walsh, Superior General of the Institute of the Blessed Virgin Mary, English-Irish Branch; and Mr. Gerald P. Hughes of the Cursillo Movement (U.S.).

Although 221 bishops were eligible to vote, not all could attend. Illness explained the absence of Cardinal Joseph Parecattil. Four others, however, had been denied their government's permission to travel to Rome: the representatives from the episcopal conferences of Latvia, Lithuania, and Laos, and the papal appointee from

Czechoslovakia. In accordance with Synod procedures, the Pope named three Cardinals to preside in turn over plenary sessions (congregations): Joseph Cordeiro of Karachi; Timothy Manning of Los Angeles; and Joseph Ratzinger, Prefect of the Congregation for the Doctrine of the Faith. The *relator* was Cardinal Carlo Martini of Milan.

Synodal Themes. The Synod conducted its business in three stages, the first a general discussion of the themes of reconciliation and penance. In all 173 spoke—each having eight minutes to address the assembly. Pope John Paul II attended all but one of the morning and evening sessions, and although he led the opening and closing prayers, he otherwise limited his participation to paying careful attention to what each speaker had to say. At times he availed himself of copies of the prepared texts that all were required to submit prior to speaking—for the sake of facilitating simultaneous translation and press releases. His presence was not intimidating with regard to the free exchange of views. This was clear from the discussion of general sacramental absolution.

The pope's strong, repeated assertion of the need for individual confession was well known at the time. Some speakers urged a strict construction of the Church's teaching and law regarding general absolution, including Cardinal Ratzinger, who made the matter the subject of his report from the Congregation for the Doctrine of the Faith. Nevertheless, others who made interventions expressed a contrary view—convinced that through a wider authorization of general absolution the Sacrament could be adapted to meet more pastoral needs without violating the *jure-divino* requirements with regard to the confession of sin.

For their part the four elected delegates of the United States episcopal conference gave individual addresses to the assembly on various subjects. Jointly they submitted a written text, in which attention was drawn to the fact that Christians need: 1) to be healed of spiritual maladies; 2) to grow in their individual and personal lives; 3) to receive counsel and guidance with regard to the promotion of that justice which is required by the social nature of sin and forgiveness; 4) to hear the promise of forgiveness from the divine family (the Church) and God; and 5) to submit themselves to the judgment of God's people through its ordained ministers, who are charged with determining the authenticity of one's turning from sin and ascertaining whether divine compassion is better expressed by conferring or delaying absolution.

These five needs, the delegates said, provide the grounds for the Church's requirement of individual, integral confession of mortal sins. The U.S. delegates asked—without presupposing the answers—that the Synod discuss the following questions regarding general absolution: 1) How long is the *diu* (long time) required by Church law for licit recourse to general absolution? 2) Has the Church already given a taxative list of the circumstances in which it wishes to give or may give authorization to confer general absolution? 3) Are there grounds for thinking there is indiscriminate use of general absolution? 4) Could fear of abuses be keeping ministers from imparting general absolution even when the Church's teaching office would (or at least might) consider this legitimate and conducive to the good of the faithful? 5) How can it be made plain that when the Church urges the obligatory character of a subsequent confession of mortal sins forgiven through general absolution, it is concerned with human needs and rights as well as with the saving structure of the Sacrament? [*Origins* 13 (1983) 328–330]

Other areas cited as in need of reconciliation and penance included: the arms race and the toll it takes on all peoples; justice and rights for those oppressed on the basis of race, creed, and sex; ecology and the need to respect the integrity of nature; exploitation of poor nations by richer ones; loss of a sense of divine transcendence and of sin; the need for compassion with regard to priests who have left the active ministry and Catholics involved in canonically invalid marriages. Christian unity figured in the discussion as well, very notably as the theme of the intervention of Archbishop John Roach. The need to improve Catholic-Jewish relations was singled out by Cardinal Etchegaray. Nor were Islam and other world religions forgotten.

Group Discussions and Final Message. In the second phase of the Synod the participants divided up into small discussion groups: three groups for each of the following languages: English, French, and Spanish-Portuguese with one each for German, Italian, and Latin. Each group elected its own chairman and secretary. The goal was the same for all: to engage in the discussion of mutual concerns and to agree on a set of propositions to set before the whole assembly on the theme of reconciliation and penance in the mission of the Church. Twelve sets of propositions resulted from these discussion groups.

Those propositions that were approved by the assembly formed the advice the Synod offered the pope, though they were not made public. The Synod did however approve and make public a *nuntius* or message drawn up by members charged with the task of formulating a document in which it might speak to the world. For his part, John Paul II received the bishops' advice and on 2 December 1984, issued an apostolic exhortation *Reconciliatio et paenitentia.*

For some of the Synod's participants, emphasis on social or structural sin seemed called for; failure to attend to this matter, they felt, would lead to even greater evils, including the resistance of individuals to their own reconciliation and repentance. Others stressed the alienation of individuals and groups from the practice of Christianity—an alienation that keeps those so affected from being agents of imperative social change. Both groups shared a conviction about the power of the gospel of Jesus Christ to change hearts and structures. How best to nuance that conviction was the source of debate and found no ready or simple answer.

See Also: JOSEPH BERNARDIN, WILLIAM BAUM, ROGER ETCHEGARAY, CARLO MARTINI, JOSEPH RATZINGER, RECONCILIATIO ET PAENITENTIA, EDMUND SZOKA, JOZEF TOMKO

Bibliography: G. CAPRILE, *Il Sinodo dei vescovi: Sesta assemblea generale* (Rome 1985). For the text of *Reconciliatio et paenitentia,* see: *Acta Apostolicae Sedis* 77 (1985): 187–275 (Latin); *Origins* 14 (1984): 432–458 (English). C. J. PETER, "The Synod of Bishops in 1983: Some Facts, Opinions, and Hopes," *Theological Dimensions in the Human Religious Quest,* vol 1, ed., J. ARMENTI, (Ann Arbor, Mich.): 246–55. Texts relating to the 1983 Synod published in *Origins* include the "Lineamenta," *Origins* 11, no. 36 (18 Feb 1982): 565–580; various interventions, *Origins* 13, nos. 18–22 (13 Oc–10 Nov. 1983); the final "Message," *Origins* 13, no. 22 (10 Nov 1983): 369–371; and the report on the 63 propositions given to the Pope, *Origins* 13, no. 22 (10 Nov 1983): 371–373.

[C. J. PETER]

SYNOD OF BISHOPS (SEVENTH GENERAL ASSEMBLY, 1987)

The Seventh General Assembly of the Synod of Bishops, originally scheduled to meet in 1986, was delayed a year in order to accommodate the Extraordinary Assembly that commemorated the twentieth anniversary of the closing of the Second Vatican Council. The Seventh Assembly had as its assigned topic, "the vocation and mission of the laity in the Church and world twenty years after the Second Vatican Council." The discussions continued many of the themes of the Extraordinary Assembly, especially the theme of communion ecclesiology.

Over two hundred Synod Fathers and sixty lay observers were on hand to hear the greetings of Pope John Paul II at the first general congregation on October 1. When the Seventh Assembly of the Synod adjourned on 30 October, there had been in all twenty-nine general congregations with the pope present at most of them. Participants in the general assembly included bishops select-

ed by episcopal conferences throughout the world, representatives of the Eastern Churches in communion with Rome, papal appointees, the heads of the major offices of the Roman Curia, and representatives of religious orders of men. The prominence of the lay observers was one of the distinctive features of the Seventh General Assembly of the Synod. The archbishop of Dakar (Senegal), Cardinal Hyacinthe Thiandoum, was the special secretary or principal *relator.*

Among the U.S. prelates in attendance were the four elected delegates representing the National Conference of Catholic Bishops: Archbishop John May of St. Louis, Cardinal Joseph Bernardin of Chicago, Archbishop Rembert Weakland of Milwaukee, and the chairman of the NCCB Laity Committee, Bishop Stanley Ott of Baton Rouge. Among the other Americans were two papal nominees, Archbishop Roger Mahony of Los Angeles and Bishop Anthony Bevilacqua of Pittsburgh; Archbishop John P. Foley, President of the Pontifical Commission for Social Communications; Cardinal William Baum, Prefect of the Congregation for Catholic Education; Ukrainian Metropolitans Stephen Sulyk of Philadelphia and Cardinal Lubachivsky; and Archbishop Stephen Kocisko of the Byzantine Rite. Religious orders of men were represented by three American generals: Paul Boyle of the Passionists, Thomas Forrest of the Redemptorists and John Vaughn of the Franciscans. Among the lay auditors were Virgil Dechant, Supreme Knight of the Knights of Columbus, and his wife Ann, and Mrs. Albina Aspell, president of the Catholic Press Association. Another American, Mr. Walter Sweeney, was the only permanent deacon in the Synod Assembly. Of the twenty theologians appointed by the Holy See three were from the United States: Dr. William May, Joseph D. Fessio, SJ, and Mary Milligan, RSHM.

The 1987 Synod followed the format and procedures that governed previous General Assemblies. The first two weeks were given chiefly to hearing reports and eight-minute interventions by most of the participants. During the third week, the Synod carried on its discussions in small language groups—the *circuli minores*—which provided the basis for a statement by the bishops—their "Message to the People of God"—and the fifty-four propositions that summarized the main points and, in some cases, called for action. At the end of the four weeks, the Assembly turned over to the Holy Father all the documentation collected in the course of their work, and requested that he prepare "at an appropriate time a document on the vocation and mission of the laity in the church and in the world."

THE ISSUES

In the opening congregation Archbishop Jan Schotte, the Secretary General of the Synod of Bishops, summa-

Cardinals Paul Poupard (left) of France and Rosalio Jose Castillo Lara of Venezuela converse at a session of the 1987 Synod of Bishops. (AP/Wide World Photos.)

rized events leading up to the Seventh Assembly. He reported that in the spring of 1984 the Secretariat Council of the Synod recommended and Pope John Paul II approved that the next general assembly focus on the role of the laity in the Church and the world. In February 1985, the Secretariat prepared and circulated outlines—the *lineamenta*—of the issues to be covered, asking the episcopal conferences and Oriental Synods for their input. Originally the deadline for their replies was September 1985, but that date was pushed back when it was decided to postpone the Seventh General Assembly to the following year 1987. On the basis of the replies and suggestions, the Secretariat prepared the working paper—*instrumentum laboris*—that was to be the basis for the discussions. It was published in the *L'Osservatore Romano* on 28 April 1987.

Schotte's report highlighted the participation of the laity in the synodal process. Although laity had been present at previous assemblies of the Synod, their prominence in sessions that would deal specifically with their vocation and mission had particular significance. Schotte stressed the fact that laity had collaborated in the preparation of the Seventh Assembly through various channels, including diocesan and group meetings, and reports submitted to their episcopal conferences. The sixty lay observers—*auditores* and *auditrices*—invited to be present at the General Assembly itself represented a cross-section of men and women from every walk of life. On three different occasions—in the fourth, tenth and seventeenth general congregations—lay representatives were able to make twenty-minute interventions, the so-called hearing of the laity (*auditio laicorum*), and they participated in the discussions of the small groups (*circuli minores*) that took place in the third week.

At the third general congregation Cardinal Thiandoum gave an initial report based on the replies sent in by the episcopal conferences. It consisted of two parts: the first outlined basic theological principles and focused on the fundamental issues that would run through the discussions. The basic premise on which there was general agreement was that all Christians share a common vocation and mission by reason of their Baptism. There remained, however, broad issues that the Synod needed to address: granted that all the baptized partake in the mystery of Christ's redemption and share in his prophetic, priestly and kingly office, what is the proper sphere of activity of the laity in the exercise of these offices? The mission of the Church is not the exclusive preserve of the laity or the hierarchy alone, said Cardinal Thiandoum, but the question is how to define each one's personal vocation so that it is in keeping with the Church's global mission.

In the second part of his report Cardinal Thiandoum cited the *instrumentum laboris* as evidence that the teaching of Vatican II needed revision on some points regarding the role of the laity. He singled out four specific problems that the Synod needed to address: the secular nature of the vocation and mission of the laity; lay associations and their relationship with pastors; ministries that can be properly exercised by the laity; the vocation and mission of lay women in the church and the world.

Vocation and Mission of the Laity. Vatican II defined the lay vocation primarily in terms "of bringing the gospel and holiness to men, and . . . penetrating and perfecting the temporal sphere of things through the spirit of the gospel" (*Apostolicam actuositatem*, 2). The apostolic exhortation *Evangelii nuntiandi* issued by Pope Paul VI after the 1974 Synod took the position that pastors have the primary responsibility for ecclesial structures, and the laity for bringing the gospel into the marketplace of politics, economics, science and the arts, mass media and professional life. Although many bishops reiterated this position at the 1987 Synod, others argued that it is improper to define the vocation of the laity by focusing on what they must do in the world. There is a common Christian vocation and it is a false dichotomy to divide it into two opposing blocs so that the clergy are charged with responsibility for the things of heaven and the laity with the things of earth. It is proper that lay Christians take an active part in the interior life of the ecclesial community, and the vocation of some may well be a call to ministry. On the other hand, bishops and clergy do not usurp the role of the laity in the secular sphere by taking a stand on social and political issues.

The propositions drawn up by the bishops at the end of their deliberations reflect the tension, but they offer little in the way of a clear solution. Propositions 3 and 4 speak of the secular character of the lay vocation, and the latter says that this character "is not to be defined only in a sociological sense, but most especially in a theological sense." Part II (propositions 10 through 19) addresses the role of lay Christians within the Church and in relation to ministry. Part III deals with their mission in the world and society.

Lay Associations. The tension between the local church and a number of new lay movements like Opus Dei and Communion and Liberation was mostly a concern of Spanish and Italian hierarchies, but the other issues implicit in the controversy were of broader interest. Opus Dei was represented at the Synod by its Prelate su-

perior, Msgr. Alvaro del Portillo, and Communion and Liberation by its founder, Msgr. Luigi Giussani. Their defenders referred to them as "movements of the Spirit," and attributed the tension to the efforts that these movements were making to renew the Church, to put new wine into old wine skins. Their critics saw them as undermining the authority of bishops and the integrity of the local church and creating an elite in the Church.

The broader issues were the viability of the traditional parish and the autonomy of the local church. Many bishops, including Archbishop May, speaking for the NCCB, saw the parish as the basis of communion and mission and as the chief locus of the spiritual formation of the laity. Some new movements were criticized for their fundamentalism and for pushing their own agendas independently of and often in competition with local diocesan and parish programs. Yet other bishops defended these movements.

Proposition 11 encouraged the renewal and adaptation of parish structures, and the establishment of small ecclesial communities. Proposition 12 recognized the effectiveness of lay associations as support groups in "a world that is secularized and marked by pluralism." The new movements "ought to have room to advance." They are instructed to collaborate with the local ordinary, but the movements that have the approval of the Holy See enjoy a great deal of autonomy (Prop. 14–16).

Lay Ministries. Some bishops found the terms lay-ministry and lay-ministers objectionable, and would reserve the title of "minister" for those who occupy a formal position in church service. Most bishops who spoke to the issue asked for greater clarity regarding ministries open to the laity. Some asked that more ministries be opened up to the laity, even that they be named as ministers of Baptism and the Anointing of the Sick, and act as official witnesses at Holy Matrimony.

The Synod acknowledged the need for participation of a greater number of laity in pastoral work, but "it does not seem opportune to set up the tasks of the laity too readily in instituted ministries" (Prop. 19). At the same time proposition 18 asked that *Ministeria quaedam*, which was the *motu proprio* of Pope Paul VI that opened ministries to the laity, be revised "taking into consideration the usage of local churches" (Prop. 18).

Women in the Church. Questions of lay ministry were closely tied to the role of women in the Church, but women's role in ministry was only one aspect of the issue. Many bishops called on the Synod to explore new ways in which women could contribute to Church life and leadership. Archbishop Weakland, speaking in the name of the American hierarchy, asked that lay women as well as lay men be permitted to function in all liturgical roles that do not require ordination; he advocated opening administrative and decision-making positions in dioceses, the Roman Curia and the diplomatic corps to them. The language of the liturgy and official Church texts should be inclusive of women. Canadian Bishop Jean-Guy Hamelin of Quebec was equally outspoken on the subject. In one way or another, most of the thirty-seven interventions that touched on women's issues said that the Church had a responsibility to respond to women's concerns about equal opportunity for jobs, wages and education, and about the value of parenting and family life. "The Church," said Archbishop Weakland, "must continue to speak out against any exploitation of women through pornography, rape, prostitution and all actions that diminish their human dignity."

Propositions 46 and 47 echoed the bishops' concerns about discrimination against women, and called for greater utilization of their talents in Church life.

FINAL ANALYSIS

The bishops at the Seventh General Assembly of the Synod of Bishops did not try to develop a new theology of the laity, but neither did they attempt to turn the clock back. In his homily at the end of the meeting Pope John Paul II said, "without distortions and sharp breaks with the past," the Church must move forward tirelessly on the path of renewal. The Synod heard much on the spiritual needs of the laity, the formation of a social conscience, and the active participation in the Church's mission and ministry. It also heard repeated warnings against the clericalization of the laity, and the need for Christians to dedicate themselves anew to the evangelization of culture.

The 1987 Synod, in the final analysis, was an episode in "a growing conflict between the action of new evangelization and the secularist movement of today's world" (Prop. 35). The interventions, papal exhortations, reports and discussions, and propositions present a drama in which the bishops can be seen as trying to mobilize the Church in defense of Christian culture. They identified threats to Christian values, human dignity and individual freedom as a tangled web of totalitarian ideologies, economic exploitation, and consummerism that even infects the Church. The theme of the Synod, however, was not *fuga mundi,* but engagement. Christians must be agents of change, involved in public life where policy decisions are made—the yeast that permeates the entire mass.

See Also: WILLIAM BAUM, JOSEPH BERNARDIN, ROGER MAHONY, OPUS DEI

Bibliography: G. CAPRILE, "Il Sinodo dei vescovi 1987," *La Civiltà Cattolica* 138, no. 4 (1987): 481–491. For the Latin text of *Christifideles laici,* see: *Acta Apostolicae Sedis* 81 (1989): 393–521. D. R. LECKEY, "The Synod of '87': A View from the Aurelian Wall," *America* 158, no. 8 (27 Feb 1988): 206–210, 222. Texts relating to the 1987 Synod published in *Origins* include the "Lineamenta," *Origins* 14, no. 38 (7 March 1985): 624–634; the "Instrumentum laboris," *Origins* 17, no. 1 (21 May 1987): 1–19; various interventions, *Origins* 17, nos. 19–22 (22 Oct 12 Nov 1987); the Synod propositions, *Origins* 17, no. 29 (31 Dec 1987): 499–509; the final "Message," *Origins* 17, no. 22 (12 Nov 1987): 387–389; and the report of Archbishop May to the American bishops, *Origins* 17, no. 25 (3 Dec 1987): 446–447. For the text of Pope John Paul's homilies in the course of the Synod and summaries of the reports submitted to the Synod and of the interventions by the participants, see the weekly English language editions of *L'Osservatore Romano* from 2 October to 9 November 1987.

[B. L. MARTHALER]

SYNOD OF BISHOPS (EIGHTH GENERAL ASSEMBLY, 1990)

The Eighth General Assembly of the Synod of Bishops met at the Vatican from 30 September to 28 October 1990. The theme, determined by Pope John Paul II after consultation with the universal episcopate, was the "Formation of Priests in the Circumstances of the Present Day," one of the Church's most pressing internal issues.

Members. Pope John Paul II appointed Lucas Cardinal Moreira Neves, OP, archbishop of São Salvador da Bahia, Brazil, as *relator* or recording secretary and Bishop Henryk Muszyński, of Włocławek, Poland, as special secretary of the Synod. The presidency of the Synod's thirty general assemblies rotated among Cardinals Simon Ignatius Pimenta, archbishop of Bombay, Christian Wiyghan Tumi, archbishop of Garoua, Cameroon, and Antonio Innocenti, prefect of the Congregation for the Clergy. The 238 participants included 169 bishops elected by the episcopal conferences, thirty-nine appointees of the pope, nineteen cardinals of the Roman Curia, ten superiors general of congregations of male religious, and one representative of the General Secretariat of the Synod. There were also seventeen experts (*auditores*), including one American and one Canadian, and forty-three observers (*auditores*), including three Americans and one Canadian. Among the *auditores* were men and women religious and laymen and laywomen. Hierarchs from the United States at the synod were the following: First, elected members Cardinals Joseph Bernardin of Chicago and James Hickey of Washington, DC; Archbishop Daniel Pilarczyk of Cincinnati, president of the National Conference of Catholic Bishops; Bishop John A. Marshall of Burlington; and John Vaughn, OFM, minister general of the Franciscans, elected by the Union of Superiors General. Second, papal appointees were Archbishop John P. Foley, president of the Pontifical Council for Social Com-

Bishops at the 1995 synod discuss the social and spiritual role of the priest. (Antonello Nusca/Liaison Agency.)

munications; Bishops Donald W. Wuerl of Pittsburgh, Harry J. Flynn of Lafayette, Louisiana, and Robert H. Brom of San Diego. Third, those with a right to attend by reason of the rules governing the synod included Cardinals William Wakefield Baum, major penitentiary of the Apostolic Penitentiary; Edmund Szoka, president of the Prefecture of the Economic Affairs of the Holy See; Myroslav Lubachivsky, major archbishop of Lviv, Ukraine; Metropolitan Archbishop Stephen Sulyk of the Ukrainian Archeparchy of Philadelphia; and Archbishop Stephen Kocisko of the Byzantine Rite, Archdiocese of Pittsburgh.

Structure. According to established procedures, the synod unfolded in three phases. During phase one (2–13 October), the participants listened to the opening and closing reports of the *relator,* Cardinal Moreira Neves, and a total of 213 interventions that dealt with the breadth of the experience of the priestly ministry in a world Church. During phase two (15–20 October), the bishops broke into thirteen smaller language groups for discussion and the drafting of recommendations from each group: three in English, three in French, three in Spanish, one in Italian, one in German, one in Latin, and, for the first time, because of the fall of various Communist re-

gimes in Eastern Europe during the previous year, one in Slavic languages. Phase three (22–27 October) was designated for the formulation of recommendations by the whole synod, the submission of amendments (*modi*), and the final voting on the recommendations (*propositiones*), together with the composition and promulgation of a closing statement by the bishops, ''Message to the People of God.''

The convocation of the synod coincided with the twenty-fifth anniversary of the establishment of the Synod of Bishops by Pope Paul VI in 1965. The first day of the assembly, 1 October, was dedicated to a series of talks detailing the history and contributions of the synods by Cardinals Jozef Tomko, prefect of the Congregation for the Evangelization of Peoples; Johannes Willebrands, president-emeritus of the Pontifical Council for Promoting Christian Unity; Aloisio Lorscheider, archbishop of Fortaleza, Brazil; Joseph Cordeiro; Paul Zoungrana; and Edward B. Clancy, archbishop of Sydney, Australia. Criticisms and recommendations for an improved structure and mode of operation that would allow for improved consultation and the hearing of other opinions, or ''prophetic'' voices, were expressed by cardinals Lorscheider and Clancy. Again, there were calls that the synod be a deliberative body in order to express better the collegiality in the Church. Other special topics outside the theme of the synod were treated on 25 October and included a progress report by Cardinal Ratzinger on the Universal Catechism (as it was then called) and a presentation by Bernardin Cardinal Gantin, prefect of the Congregation for Bishops, on the theological status of episcopal conferences. On 20 October, Archbishop Pio Laghi, pro-prefect of the Congregation for Catholic Education, reported on the state of vocations in the Church, replete with statistical charts that detailed the distribution of priests throughout the world.

Recommendations. Though the forty-one recommendations made by the delegates to the pope are confidential, the special secretary of the synod, Henryk Muszyński, offered a summary of their contents on 27 October at the closing press conference of the synod. After a review of the positive and negative conditions that impact contemporary priestly formation, Muszyński pointed to the issue of clarifying the identity of the priest that sees him in terms of being configured to Christ in such a way that he acts "in the person of Christ" and in service to the Church and the world. Such an understanding of the priest calls for a specific spirituality that is animated by pastoral charity and has a strong missionary aspect in its evangelizing service of proclaiming the Gospel. The twofold aspect of the priesthood needs to be noted here: it is a unique gift in the Church and for the Church, but it is also directed to the world and the whole of humanity for the building of the reign of God. This theory of priestly identity forms the basis for continuing to support priestly celibacy: it is a sign of the total dedication of the priest and as such a sign of the love of God for humanity. The bishops called for a reaffirmation by the papacy of the discipline of clerical celibacy in the Latin Church.

On more specific issues, the special secretary noted the following points: The synod stressed the fact that vocations to the priesthood are the responsibility of the whole Church, and especially of families, schools, parishes, and apostolic movements, which it urged to foster and accept priestly vocations and to continue to support the ordained. It saw education and formation in a seminary as the ordinary form of training for the priesthood and stressed its importance during both the early phase of discerning a vocation and in the later stages of formal training. Based on a number of successful experiments, it recommended a period of preparation or a so-called "propaedeutic year" at the very outset. This preparatory period, which could last up to two years, was seen as meeting several needs: addressing the growing lack of familiarity with the Catholic tradition, deepening the candidate's spiritual life, socialization to basic habits of living

more closely together in a seminary over many years, and continuing personal maturation, which was judged to be less developed according to the candidate's chronological age than in earlier generations for a wide variety of reasons. The synod also called for better training of seminary formation staff and the involvement of the family and of lay persons in the formation process. In this regard, the synod showed an awareness of, and continuity with, the Seventh General Assembly of 1987, which dealt with the laity.

A special point was made concerning a revision of priestly formation as a lifelong process, and hence the priesthood as demanding permanent formation. Some suggestions for advancing this creative idea included sabbaticals of varying length and intensity; workshops directed at the priest's spiritual, personal, and professional growth; and a continuing interest on the part of the bishop in his presbyterium, especially in young priests, the ailing, and priests in crisis. Finally, the bishops called for the formulation of a directory for permanent priestly formation that would offer general guidelines. The final "Message to the People of God" in the name of the synod's participants stressed most of these points, with a clear affirmation of the priesthood of the people of God. Also, it spoke of a "new clarity" on the issue of clerical celibacy and gave a forceful endorsement of ongoing formation for priests, which it called "a high priority." It urgently appealed to all in the Church to work for improving the number and quality of priestly vocations.

Other Issues. There were other points made in the course of the synod that were not mentioned in the summary. The issue of inculturation arose, particularly as it applied to local churches and their concrete circumstances, a concern especially of the bishops from South America and Africa. Also raised was the disparity between a bounty of resources in some countries and a woeful lack of even essentials in other, poorer countries, especially in many of the newly liberated countries of Eastern Europe. Many bishops appealed for solidarity. Given the current experience of widespread oppression and lack of the basic conditions for authentic human existence in many societies, many bishops called for clarification on the social role of the priest and how it relates to his spiritual identity. The benefits of smaller houses of formation in conjunction with the prevailing seminary system were extolled as a way of dealing with the problems of inculcating in the seminarian a greater sense of personal accountability and developing healthier personal relationships. Some bishops raised the possibility of ordaining so-called *viri probati*, i.e., non-celibate males of a mature age who were also of proven character and virtue, to help deal with pressing shortages of priests in certain countries. Bishops from less-developed countries cited the ordination of married clergy from other traditions who had been received into communion with the Roman Catholic Church and asked whether the solution of *viri probati* was not appropriate to the conditions in their countries. This call was interpreted, however, as impugning the discipline of clerical celibacy that the synod was in the process of reaffirming. This issue of *viri probati*, therefore, caused something of a stir at the synod. On 18 October, Cardinal Tumi responded to questions at a press conference, called to offer clarifications regarding at least three cases in Brazil where married men were ordained but were also required to separate from their wives. Some Latin American bishops could not understand why the condition of permanent continence in marriage was not imposed on churches in North America and Europe where married Anglican priests and Lutheran pastors entered into full communion with the Catholic Church and were ordained. This exchange seems to have provoked an editorial in *L'Osservatore Romano* on 21 October that stated in even greater detail the decisions of Vatican II, the Second Ordinary Synod of Bishops in 1971, and Paul VI's encyclical, *Sacerdotalis caelibatus* (1967), all of which reaffirmed the discipline of clerical celibacy in the Latin Rite.

Follow-up to the Synod. The practical results of the Eighth General Assembly of Bishops are enshrined in the document *Pastores dabo vobis* ("I Will Give You Shepherds") (PDV), the post-synodal apostolic exhortation of John Paul II, dated 25 March 1992. Of the forty-one recommendations made by the synod, reference is made to thirty-eight of them. Another result of the eighth assembly of the synod was the publication of the *Directory on the Ministry and Life of Priests*, issued by the Congregation for the Clergy (31 January 1994).

See Also: JOSEPH BERNARDIN, BERNARDIN GANTIN, DIRECTORY ON THE MINISTRY AND LIFE OF PRIESTS, EDMUND SZOKA, JAMES HICKEY, PIO LAGHI, PASTORES DABO VOBIS, JOSEPH RATZINGER, JOHANNES WILLEBRANDS

Bibliography: G. CAPRILE, "'VIII Assemblea generale ordinaria del sinodo dei vescovi," *La Civiltà Cattolica* 141, no. 4 (1990): 378–87, 486–95. Congregation for the Clergy, *Directory on the Ministry and Life of Priests* (Rome 1994). *Pastores dabo vobis,* in *Acta Apostolicae Sedis* 84 (1992): 657–804. J.P.SCHOTTE, "Perché un Sinodo sulla formazione sacerdotale?" *Seminarium,* n.s., 30 (1990): 47–68. Texts relating to the 1990 Synod published in Origins include the "Lineamenta," *Origins* 19, no. 3 (1 June 1989): 33–46; the "Instrumentum laboris," *Origins* 20, no. 10 (2 Aug 1990): 149–168; various interventions, *Origins* 20, nos. 18–21 (11 Oct–1 Nov 1990); and the final message, *Origins* 20, no. 22 (8 Nov. 1990): 349–53. For summaries of the addresses given at the Synod and full texts of selected talks and statements, see the English-language weekly edition of *L'Osservatore Romano* (8 Oct–5 Nov 1990).

[J.J. BURKHARD]

SYNOD OF BISHOPS (NINTH GENERAL ASSEMBLY, 1994)

The Ninth General Assembly of the Synod of Bishops took place from 2 to 29 October 1994. It had as its theme, "Consecrated Life and its Role in the Church and in the World," celebrated in continuity with previous assemblies on the family (1980), the laity (1987), and priesthood (1990). The synod reflected on consecrated life from its roots in the earliest centuries of Christianity and looked forward to the next century.

Archbishop Jan P. Schotte, CICM, served as secretary general of the synod. Of the 348 participants, 244 were voting members: *ex officio* members (patriarchs, major archbishops, and metropolitans of Eastern churches; the secretary general; and heads of the Roman dicasteries) numbered 38; members elected from episcopal conferences, 149; from the Union of Superiors General (USG), 10; and members appointed by the pope, 47. Of these, 130 were from the diocesan clergy and 114 from Institutes of Consecrated Life. The universality of the Church was also reflected by the membership: representatives were from Europe (94), America (69), Asia and Oceania (41), and Africa (40). In addition to growing participation from the so-called "young churches," the synod was marked by an increased presence from Central and Eastern Europe. Also participating in the 1994 Assembly were 75 auditors (51 women and 24 men) and 20 experts (12 women, 8 men), including representatives of other Christian churches. The auditors included religious (64); members of Societies of Apostolic Life (3); members of Secular Institutes (4); and four others.

Participants from the United States were present in each category. John Cardinal O'Connor of New York served as one of the three co-presidents, together with cardinals Eduardo Martínez Somalo, prefect of the Congregation for Institutes of Consecrated Life and Societies of Apostolic Life, and Edward Clancy of Sydney. Ex officio members from the U.S. were: William Cardinal Baum, major penitentiary; Edmund Cardinal Szoka, president of the prefecture for the Economic Affairs of the Holy See; Archbishop John Foley, president of the Pontifical Commission for Social Communications; and Archbishop Stephen Sulyk, Ukrainian metropolitan of Philadelphia. Elected from the NCCB were: James Cardinal Hickey of Washington, DC; Joseph Cardinal Bernardin of Chicago; Archbishop John R. Quinn of San Francisco; and Archbishop William H. Keeler of Baltimore. Elected from the USG was Abbot Primate Jerome Theisen, OSB. Papal appointees, in addition to Cardinal O'Connor, were: James Timlin, bishop of Scranton; Francis George, OMI, bishop of Yakima; and Robert Maloney, superior general of the Congregation of the Mission.

Pope John Paul II presides over the 1994 synod of bishops. (Livio Anticoli/Liaison Agency.)

Auditors from the U.S. were: Gerald Brown, SS, president of the Conference of Major Superiors of Men (CMSM), Vicent Marie Finnegan, superior general of the Carmelite Sisters of the Sacred Heart and president of the Council of Major Superiors of Women Religious (CMSWR); Doris Gottemoeller, superior general of the Sisters of Mercy of the Americas and president of the Leadership Conference of Women Religious (LCWR). U.S. religious named as experts were: Christine Born, OP, prioress general, Congregation of St. Cecilia; Paul Mankowski, SJ, Pontifical Biblical Institute; Cassian Yuhaus, CP, executive director, Ministry for Religious. John Johnston, FSC, superior general of the Brothers of the Christian Schools, served as special assistant to the secretary. At the conclusion of the Assembly, Cardinal Bernardin was elected to the new Council for the General Secretariat.

Preparation. Following the customary consultations, the theme for the ninth general assembly was announced on 30 December 1991. The *lineamenta* was published on 24 November 1992 with the two-fold purpose of promoting profound reflection on the theme in order to obtain information and directions that would assist in preparing for the assembly. Official consultations were expanded to include the International Union of Superiors General (UISG) and the World Conference of Secular Institutes (CMIS) because of the nature of the topic.

Extensive responses arrived from throughout the world; these were studied, synthesized, and used by the secretariat to prepare the *instrumentum laboris*. Statistics provided early in the text identified the 12% of the Church membership under discussion. Of the persons consecrated, 72.5% are women and 27.5% are men; 82.2% are lay, while 17.8% are priests or deacons. There are 1,425 religious institutes of women of pontifical right and 1,550 of diocesan right; 250 religious institutes of men of pontifical right and 242 of diocesan right. Secular institutes number 165 and pontifical societies of apostolic life are 39. The synod also concerned itself with consecrated virgins, widows and widowers, hermits, and groups newly developing and seeking ecclesial recognition.

The Assembly. At the beginning of the assembly, George Basil Cardinal Hume, OSB (Westminster), the general relator, offered a report further synthesizing the working document to help focus the body's task. Following some 280 interventions by members and auditors in the presence of Pope John Paul II, Hume's second *relatio* provided a further focus for phase two in discussion groups. Participants were organized into groups according to language: three in Spanish; three in French; one in Latin; one in German; two in Italian; and four in English.

Theology of Consecrated Life. The relationship between the fundamental Christian consecration of Baptism and that effected through profession of evangelical counsels (*Lumen gentium* 44; *Perfectae caritatis* 5) remains an area requiring more profound theological reflection. Inevitably the question again arose of the adequacy of two categories of persons in the Church, clergy and laity (CIC c. 207) in comparison with a tripartite formula of clergy, religious, and laity as suggested by *Lumen gentium* 31 and *Corpus canonum ecclesiarum orientalium* c. 399. Noting questions raised in the working document, Hume's first *relatio* identified the theology of charism as the category most in use and considered most apt for expressing the rich diversity and inner unity of consecrated life today. Used generically, every charism of consecrated life has its origin in the Holy Spirit, is a following of Christ, is ecclesial by nature, and involves a special consecration rooted in baptism. Used in a specific sense, the charism of a particular institute involves a further specification and unique integration of these elements.

Synodal reflections on the ecclesial nature of consecrated life frequently focused on communion and participation in the mission of the Church. The phrase *sentire cum ecclesia* was explored and numerous concrete experiences of *mutuae relationes* ("mutual relations") were shared. A positive appreciation for the role of consecrated persons in the mission of the Church was evident, as well as a mutual desire for more effective collaboration, not only between bishops and religious, but among all the baptized.

Inculturation. Synod participants recognized that consecrated life, like the Church as a whole, must become inculturated. The *instrumentum laboris* (93–94) had insisted on this point, indicating the means that would enable a true discernment of the essentials for profound inculturation rather than superficial adaptation. Without minimizing the necessity of inculturation of missionary presence in the younger churches, the synod also discussed the challenge of a right inculturation of consecrated life in the contemporary cultures of the West.

Mission. The *instrumentum laboris* challenged the synod to a reflection on consecrated life in the context of the New Evangelization of the contemporary world (2; 95). This challenge and the importance of life witness had already been given powerful impetus by the 1974 Synod [*Evangelii nuntiandi* (1975)]. Borrowing a term from the encyclical letter Redemptoris missio, much attention was given to "new areopagi." Based on the experience of St. Paul (Acts 17:22-31), the Areopagus as cultural center of the learned people of Athens became the symbol of those new sectors in which the Gospel must be proclaimed (37). Examples included the world of communications, of modern culture, of human promotion and justice, the new poor, the defense of life, and the search for God and the sacred. While participants urged the continuation of traditional works, there remained keen awareness of the need to confront these contemporary challenges in their various cultural manifestations.

Consecration and Mission. Aware of the difficulty of speaking of any single aspect of consecrated life in isolation, the closing message focused anew the essential integration of consecration and mission. As Jesus Christ was consecrated and sent out, the consecrated person "receives the grace of unifying mission and consecration" not as two unrelated moments, but "joined in deep reciprocity" (IV). Consecration is received for mission in the Church, according to the nature of each institute, but consecrated persons "have no choice but to be missionaries" (VI).

Consecration of Women in the Church. Consecrated women were among those who actively participated in the preparation of the synod through responses to the *lineamenta*. The statistics indicated the need for the synod to give particular attention to them. In his first *relatio* Cardinal Hume noted that the place of consecrated women was a challenge deserving great attention. The published summary of his speech after the interventions states: "A particular importance was attributed to the theme of consecrated women in the Church, to the need for them to have greater participation in decisions which concern them and to their contribution to the promotion of women in today's society" (II). The publication of the apostolic letter *Ordinatio sacerdotalis* (1994) may well have served to heighten sensitivity to this subject while at the same time clarifying its parameters.

Brothers in Clerical Institutes. The *instrumentum laboris* placed before the synod a request that the question of the participation of brothers in the government of "clerical and mixed" institutes be resolved in such a way that, respecting their proper nature and tradition, the matter be regulated by the proper law of each institute (32). In his intervention, Cardinal Castillo Lara, former president of the Pontifical Council for the Interpretation of Legislative Texts, set forth the state of the question, ultimately revolving around participation in the ecclesiastical power of governing.

Closure. The closing message reiterated the importance of the presence of the Eastern Catholic churches in the synod and the unique eremitic and monastic patrimony that is theirs. Once again, religious of the East were urged to be in dialogue with monks and nuns of the Orthodox churches. Likewise, in the context of the new evangelization, all consecrated persons were challenged anew to an interest in ecumenical and interreligious dialogue. The Ninth General Assembly may be seen as another stage in the Church's implementation of the Second Vatican Council and its preparation for the Third Millennium.

See Also: WILLIAM BAUM, JOSEPH BERNARDIN, EVANGELIZATION (NEW), FRANCIS GEORGE, JAMES HICKEY, BASIL HUME, WILLIAM KEELER, EDUARDO MARTÍNEZ SOMALO, JOHN O'CONNOR, ORDINATIO SACERDOTALIS, REDEMPTORIS MISSIO, JAN SCHOTTE, EDMUND SZOKA, VITA CONSECRATA

Bibliography: G. MARCHESI, "Il Sinodo dei vescovi sulla vita consacrata," *La Civiltà Cattolica* 145, no. 4 (1994): 590–599. For the Latin text of *Vita consecrata,* see: *Acta Apostolicae Sedis* 88 (1996): 377–486. Texts relating to the 1994 Synod published in *Origins* include the "Lineamenta," *Origins* 22, no. 26 (10 Dec 1992): 443–54; the "Instrumentum laboris," *Origins* 24, no. 7 (30 June 1994): 97–138; various interventions, *Origins* 24, nos. 18–22 (13 Oct–10 Nov 1994); and the final message, *Origins* 24, no. 22 (10 Nov 1994): 369–374. For various published proceedings of the synod see the English language weekly edition of *L'Osservatore Romano* (5 Oct–30 Nov 1994).

[SHARON L. HOLLAND]

SPECIAL ASSEMBLIES

SYNOD OF BISHOPS, SPECIAL ASSEMBLY FOR AFRICA

A special assembly of the Synod of Bishops for Africa met in Rome 10 April to 8 May 1994 on the general theme, "The Church in Africa and its Evangelizing Mission toward the Year 2000: You shall be my witnesses (Acts 1:8)."

The African Synod has both a prehistory and a history. The idea for a pan-African synod originated with a layman from Senegal, M. Alioune Diop, a convert to Catholicism from Islam, who at the time was the president of the Société Africaine de Culture (SAC) in Paris. A leading light in African literature, Diop was founder and director of the prestigious Présence Africaine, a review of the Black cultures, and the editor-in-chief of Présence Africaine, a publishing house based in Paris. In 1973 he proposed the idea for an African council to the Episcopal Conference of West Africa, which in turn passed it on to

Symposium of the Episcopal Conferences of Africa and Madagascar (SECAM). Nothing came of the proposal at that time, but Diop was not deterred. In November 1977 a conference organized by the SAC in Abidjan, Ivory Coast, had as its theme, "Black Civilization and the Catholic Church." During the conference, Fabian Eboussi Boulaga, from Cameroon, then a Jesuit, proposed on behalf of the Third Commission of the conference, of which he was a member, the formation of a council of the entire African Church. The assembly welcomed the idea, and a resolution was adopted. Subsequently Diop met with Pope Paul VI, who encouraged him to pray for the intention.

Meanwhile, the African bishops could not agree among themselves on what route to pursue. In 1978 Cardinal Malula of Kinshasa (Congo) raised the idea of the African Council during the meeting of SECAM in Nairobi, Kenya, but he failed to win support from his fellow bishops. A discussion at an extraordinary session of the permanent committee of SECAM in Ouagadougou, Upper-Volta (now Burkina Faso), in March 1980, showed that even the bishops who favored a meeting of bishops from all of Africa were divided. One camp favored a council, but another camp suggested that the gathering be of the nature of a synod. (A council is a deliberative body that has the authority to make binding decisions. A synod, according to the motu proprio, *Apostolica sollicitudo,* of Pope Paul VI [1965] is a consultative assembly that makes recommendations to the pope.) In 1981, in Yaoundé, Cameroon, before the opening of the SECAM general assembly some privately urged Cardinal Thiandoum, the president of SECAM, that the issue of the African Council be discussed during the meeting, but nobody raised the issue in public. Some bishops were hesitant because they were not sure whether the idea of an "African council" would please the Vatican or not and, therefore, preferred not to speak of it at all.

In May 1980, Pope John Paul II joined Catholics in celebrating a hundred years of missionary activity in Central Africa. The bishops of Zaire (now Congo) took the opportunity of the papal visit to express their desire for a meeting of African bishops. Although the Zairean bishops clearly favored a council, they asked for a "council or at least, in a first moment, a particular synod." The pope indicated a certain openness to the proposal but gave no direct answer to the request.

Meanwhile the Société Africaine de Culture continued to promote the project. With the help of some western humanitarian organizations, in 1981 SAC sent a delegation of three African theologians to Europe: O. Bimwenyi (Zaire), Jesuit Fathers Hebga and Ossama,

Opening of the African Synod at the Vatican. (Livio Anticoli/Liaison Agency)

both from the Cameroon. They toured France and Belgium in an effort to gain the support of European churches for an African council. They explained the idea of an African council as being the logical outcome of Vatican II's teaching on collegiality.

In May 1983, during their ad limina visit, the Zairean bishops renewed their proposal. Pope John Paul II agreed in principle that a consultation "under one form or another," was necessary "in order to examine the religious problems facing the entire continent." Without declaring a preference for either a synod or a council, he said it was the prerogative of the bishops to decide for themselves as to what form the meeting would take. The bishops, however, continued to be divided over the issue whether the assembly should be a council or a synod. Some looked to Rome for direction, which gave no clear signal, though one papal nuncio in Africa urged bishops to vote against the project. Vatican authorities who visited Zaire in December 1983 were clearly opposed to the project. One strategy used by opponents of an African council was to pit anglophone and francophone bishops against each other by presenting the project as typical of francophone ambition.

In 1984, Cardinal Gantin, prefect of the Roman Congregation for Bishops, a native of Benin, was sent to Kinshasa where a meeting of the SECAM was being held. Gantin explained that a council's decisions are binding and required a formal consultation of the entire episcopate. The consultation was conducted, but only one third of the churches consulted favored the idea of a council.

When the project seemed about to be buried forever, Pope John Paul II met in December 1988 with the president of SECAM and the presidents of the nine regional episcopal conferences of Africa and Madagascar, the cardinal prefect of the Congregation for the Evangelization of Peoples, and the secretary general of the Synod of Bishops. The meeting led to the pope's surprising announcement a month later that told of plans for the Special Assembly of the Synod of Bishops for Africa. In a letter dated 24 January 1989 the president of SECAM, Gabriel Gonsum Ganaka, bishop of Jos, Nigeria, responded to the papal directive. He reported on the consultation of the African episcopate about the place where the bishops would prefer the synod to take place, either Rome or an African city, the dates, and the participants. On the basis of this consultation, the pope announced in Kampala, Uganda, on 11 February 1993 that the Special Assembly of the Synod of Bishops for Africa would convene in Rome, 10 April–8 May 1994.

Planning the Synod. The preparation for the African Synod followed the general procedures in the *ordo synodi*. The planning committee (commissio antepreparatoria) included Francis Cardinal Arinze, president of the Pontifical Council for Inter-Religious Dialogue, Archbishop Albert J. Tsiahoana of Antsiranana, president of the episcopal conference of Madagascar, six other African bishops, and the presidents of the regional conferences of bishops. Pope John Paul II directed that the outline of issues to be discussed (*lineamenta*) be published in July 1990 during the ninth general assembly of SECAM. The *lineamenta* were originally printed in the three official languages of SECAM—French, English, and Portuguese—and later translated into Arabic, Swahili, Malgascio, Spanish, and Italian. The *lineamenta* consisted of eighty-one inquiries divided into two major sections. The first asked about the development of evangelization in Africa. The second examined the general theme of the synod under five headings: the proclamation of the Good News, inculturation, interreligious dialogue, justice and peace, and mass media. Though the preparatory period was not without its critics, especially from those who claimed that the African Synod had been taken over by Rome, thirty-one of the thirty-four African episcopal conferences responded to the questionnaire; the other three were in situations of war. Almost three years later in February 1993, on the basis of the responses to the *lineamenta*, the secretariat of the synod published the working paper (*instrumentum laboris*) that would be the framework for the discussions at the synod itself.

Synod Discussions. The Special Assembly of the Synod of Bishops for Africa opened 10 April 1994 with a solemn liturgy in Saint Peter's Basilica. The pope and the synodal fathers wore African liturgical vestments made in Zaire. The songs were in fourteen languages including Latin. For the first time in history, African tamtams resounded in the house of Peter. The opening eucharistic celebration was a combination of four eucharistic rites: Roman, Zairean, Ethiopian, and Coptic.

The participants numbered 317, some of whom were assistants. There were 244 members of the synod properly speaking: seventy-seven members ex officio (fourteen African cardinals, the patriarch of Alexandria, twenty-four prefects of the congregations of the Roman Curia, thirty-three presidents of episcopal conferences, and the secretary general of the Synod of Bishops); 130 elected delegates; thirty-seven members appointed by the pope; twenty periti (three sisters and seventeen priests); forty-six auditors; and seven representatives of other Christian churches.

Following the general procedures for assemblies of bishops, the first general congregation on 11 April heard reports by Cardinal Arinze whom the pope delegated to preside over the synod, and by the relator generalis of the synod, Hyacinthe Cardinal Thiandoum, archbishop of Dakar. They began two weeks of interventions by the bishops addressing the issues outlined in the working paper. Over 200 summary statements were read at the general assembly. Then, for a week, the assembly broke into small groups (*circuli minores*) to discuss the issues raised in the interventions. The fourth and final week was spent in the aula for debate and voting on the resolutions.

The Message of the Synod. The immediate result was that the synod issued a message addressed to the entire Church and in a special way to the African Churches. The assembly synod also agreed on sixty-four propositions that were submitted as recommendations to the pope. Almost all important questions facing the life and the mission of the Church in Africa were discussed at the synod. The discussions as well as the final message and recommendations echoed the five subthemes into which the general topic of the synod had been divided: proclamation, inculturation, justice and peace, interreligious dialogue, and the means of social communications, but it was the theme of inculturation that was dominant.

The final message of synod clearly affirmed "the culture which gave its identity to our people is in serious crisis" (no. 15), and baptized persons must, therefore, be able to express the gospel message in "a new dynamic of life which transforms the culture and society" (no. 17). The entire Christian life needs to be inculturated, and "special attention should be paid to liturgical and sacramental inculturation." The Bible should be translated into every African language and read "within the African context and in the spirit of [Catholic] tradition" (no. 18). The synod appealed for dialogue "within the church and among religions" (no. 20). Particular attention should be paid to the traditional religions "insofar as they constitute our cultural heritage" (no. 21), and to "the two great African Churches of Egypt and Ethiopia" as well as "our Anglican and Protestant brethren" (no. 22). The bishops assured their "Muslim brethren" of their desire "to collaborate with them everywhere on the continent in working for the peace and justice which alone can give glory to God" (no. 23).

Because African cultures are in crisis, there is a need for new models of Christian presence and witness. The synod proposed that one such model is the "Family Church." Not only does this model seem to fit more to African's deep sense of relationship, but it was also meant to inspire more people all over the world (nos. 24–25). Meeting during the International Year of the Family, the synod spoke of Christian families and the extended African family as "the sacred place where all the riches of our tradition converge'' (no. 27). The Final Statement took cognizance of the forthcoming Cairo Conference and condemned the "individualistic and permissive culture which liberalizes abortion,'' and the pressure put on the poor nations that forces them to choose options "contrary to life and morality'' (no. 30). In the name of justice the synod demand more equitable trade between the north and south. The bishops condemned political corruption, and admitted that as pastors "we have not always done what we could in order to form the laity for life in society, to a Christian vision of politics and economics'' (no. 31). Pastors are invited to encourage the laity to discover their importance in the Church and the world (no. 57). Justice and the rule of law are the basis of peace. "Democracy should become one of the principal routes along which the church travels with the people'' in working for the common good (no. 34). The synod denounced "the lust for power . . . as well as the idolatry of ethnicity, which leads to fratricidal wars'' and refugees uprooted from their homes (no. 36).

The African bishops appealed "to our Christian brothers and sisters and all people of Good Will in the Northern Hemisphere'' to intervene with their governments and international associations to stop the sale of arms, and to find a solution to the problem of debt that crushes the African continent and "renders futile every effort at economic recovery'' (nos. 40–41). They ask that African immigrants in the Northern Hemisphere be treated with respect and dignity. For their own part, the bishops propose an "examination of conscience'' for the African Churches with regard to lifestyle, self-reliance, and justice in dealing with men and women who are at their service (nos. 43–44). Toward the end of the Final Statement the bishops express their determination "to take every measure'' to see that the dignity and rights of women are fully respected (nos. 65–69).

By most accounts the Special Synod of Bishops for Africa was a success, but it had its critics. They criticized it because it focused more on the present than the future. The African Synod formulated no plan of action, nor did it establish specific goals for the African Churches. A second criticism stemmed from the location of the synod, which did not take place in Africa. Although the African bishops themselves voted to have the assembly in Rome, their decision seemed to reflect unfavorably on the ability of African countries to host such a meeting. If indeed the African Churches are to adopt "a simple lifestyle which is in keeping with the poverty, indeed the misery, of our people,'' as the bishops said in their Final Statement (no. 44), the only appropriate place for African bishops to hold an assembly is in Africa itself. In September 1995 in Yaoundé, Cameroon, Pope John Paul II promulgated the post-synodal apostolic exhortation *Ecclesia in Africa* that presented a vision of Christianity in Africa for the coming millennium.

Bibliography: G. ALBERIGO and A. M. NGINDU, eds., *"Towards the African Synod,"* Concilium 239 (London 1992). CHEZA, M. "Vers le synode continental africain,'' *Les Nouvelles Rationalités Africaines* 4 (1989): 6–22. DI MPASI, B., G. BUTTURINI, B. MAGGIONI, and P. K. SARPONG, *Teologia africana e il sinodo per l'Africa* (Bologna 1991); FACULTÉS CATHOLIQUES DE KINSHASA, *Quelle Église pour l'Afrique du troisième millénaire? Contribution au synode africain,* Actes de la XVIIIe Semaine Théologique de Kinshasa 21–27 April 1991 (Kinshasa 1992); "Final Message of the Synod for Africa,'' *Origins* 24 (19 May 1994): 1; 3–11. SYNODE DES ÉVÊQUES, *L'Eglise en Afrique et sa mission évangélisatrice vers l'an 2000. "Vous serez mes témoins'' (Actes 1,8); Lineamenta* (Vatican City 1990); *Instrumentum laboris* (Vatican City 1993).

[G. IWELE]

SYNOD OF BISHOPS, SPECIAL ASSEMBLY FOR LEBANON

The Special Assembly for Lebanon of the Synod of Bishops was held at the Vatican from 26 November to 14 December 1995. Its theme, chosen by Pope John Paul II, was: "Christ is our hope: renewed by his Spirit, in solidarity, we witness to his love.'' In response to the direction given by the Holy Father, the synodal meeting was seen as an opportunity for the six Catholic communities of Lebanon (Armenian, Melkite, Maronite, Syrian, Chaldean, and Roman) to seek spiritual renewal by rediscovering their religious roots and applying the achievements of the Second Vatican Council.

John Paul II announced the assembly in 1991. During the course of the next year the Maronite patriarch, Cardinal Nasrallah Pierre Sfeir, and the Council of Oriental Catholic Patriarchs both issued pastoral letters on the assembly. The *lineamenta* was published in Lebanon in 1993, and the *instrumentum laboris* prepared in early 1995. The 119 participants included several heads of the congregations and councils of the Roman Curia, the hierarchy of the Catholic churches in Lebanon, representative Eastern Catholic patriarchs and bishops from the Middle East, Lebanese bishops residing outside the Middle East, Greek Orthodox, Armenian Orthodox, Syriac Orthodox, and Assyrian bishops, and representatives from the Protestant, Sunni Muslim, Shiite Muslim, and Druze communities.

The synodal discussions further revealed why a special synodal assembly was convoked for a single country. The participants noted that eighteen different religious communities are to be found on Lebanese territory. Often, through the centuries, these various communities have found a way to live together in relative harmony. Therefore, the synodal assembly sought to draw up prin-

The pope opens the 1990 synod. (Livio Anticoli/Liaison Agency.)

ciples and guidelines so that Catholic churches might work together more effectively, develop closer relations with churches not in union with Rome, and foster a spirit of cooperation with Lebanese of other religions. Lebanon is the only country in the Middle East where Christians constitute a significant part of the population, and can deal with Muslims on an equal footing. The status of Christians in Lebanon has a direct impact on the future of Christian minorities in the countries of the Middle East.

At the end of their meetings the synodal participants submitted proposals for the Holy Father's consideration, which were subsequently incorporated in his post-synodal exhortation. In their closing message, the synodal fathers summarized their work and addressed some of their concerns. They noted that conversion and renewal must begin with the Catholic communities themselves. The multiplicity of the Eastern churches can be a source of divisiveness, but should be a sign of richness. Therefore, the various churches should follow the principle of complementarity and cooperation. Renewal extends not only to persons but also to all ecclesial structures so that they may better respond to their mission of service. In dealing with the notion of unity among the Catholic churches, the assembly calls for permanent structures for intra-ecclesial coordination on all levels, under the authority of the Assembly of Catholic Patriarchs and Bishops of Lebanon. The fathers spoke of a "new mentality that does not stress differences but affirms unity, while fully respecting diversity." They took note of the various initiatives for dialogue that are going on with the Orthodox churches and saw the goal of ending divisions as a special mission of the Church of Antioch. Muslim-Christian relations should be characterized by conviviality and collaboration in living and working together as fellow citizens. The assembly cited Pope John Paul II, who declared that Lebanon is "more than a country, [but] a message and model, for the East and the West" ("Message to all the Bishops of the Catholic Church concerning the situation in Lebanon" 7 Sept. 1989).

Bibliography: *L'Osservatore Romano,* English edition (29 November–20 December 1995). *Origins* 25, no. 35 (22 February 1996): 592–594.

[SEELY BEGGIANI]

The pope presides over the 1997 Synod of Bishops for America. (© Livio Anticoli/Liaison Agency.)

SYNOD OF BISHOPS, SPECIAL ASSEMBLY FOR AMERICA

During his inaugural discourse at the Fourth General Conference of the Latin American Episcopate, Pope John Paul II first approached the idea of calling a "meeting of the hierarchy in all America, perhaps synodal in nature." Subsequently, the Latin-American Episcopal Council (CELAM), the Pontifical Commission for Latin America, the National Conference of Catholic Bishops of the United States of America (NCCB) and the Canadian Conference of Catholic Bishops (CCCB), each responded positively. The Holy Father officially announced his intention to convoke a special assembly for America of the Synod of Bishops in his apostolic letter *Tertio millennio adveniente* (38). The executive meeting of CELAM and the Episcopal Conferences of the United States of America and Canada (February 1995) gave definitive confirmation to the Holy Father's initiative.

In announcing the special assembly, the Holy Father also set forth its aims: the promotion of a new evangelization in the entire continent as an expression of episcopal communion; the increase of solidarity among the particular Churches in the various fields of pastoral activity; and the highlighting of justice issues and international economic relations among the nations in all America, bearing in mind the great inequality among the northern, central, and southern regions of the continent.

Following the first meeting of the pre-synodal council, in 1985, the Holy Father chose as the synod topic *En-

counter with the Living Jesus Christ: The Way to Conversion, Communion and Solidarity in America,* thereby attempting to respond to the unique circumstance of the Church in America as well as to address the actual state of affairs affecting all the peoples and cultures on the American continent. The *Lineamenta,* made public 3 September 1996, appeared in the four official languages of the special assembly (Spanish, English, Portuguese, and French) and was distributed throughout the hemisphere. In highlighting the centrality of the living Jesus Christ as a way towards conversion, communion and solidarity, the Holy Father wished to prepare the Church in America for a more fruitful celebration of the Great Jubilee Year 2000 and more effectively to bring about the new evangelization.

The 297 participants included 233 synod fathers, 41 auditors, 18 experts, 5 fraternal delegates, and the Holy Father. The fraternal delegates represented the Greek Orthodox Church in America and the Council of Churches of the United States, Canada, Latin America, and the Caribbean. The presidents-delegate designated by the pope were Cardinal Eugênio de Araújo Sales, archbishop of São Sebastião do Rio de Janeiro (Brazil); Cardinal Roger Mahony, archbishop of Los Angeles (U.S.A.); Dario Castrillón Hoyos, archbishop emeritus of Bucaramanga (Colombia) and pro-prefect of the Congregation for the Clergy. The relator was Cardinal Juan Sandoval Iñiguez, archbishop of Guadalajara (Mexico), with Francis George, archbishop of Chicago (U.S.A.) and Estanislao Esteban Karlic, archbishop of Paraná (Argentina), as special secretaries.

The special assembly began 16 November 1997 in St. Peter's Basilica with a concelebrated Eucharistic Liturgy at which all cardinals, bishops, and priests of the assembly concelebrated with the Holy Father; the remaining synod participants were in attendance. The official languages of the synod were employed at various moments in the liturgical celebration where the some synod participants exercised roles as lectors, readers of the prayer of the faithful and bearers of gifts. The following day, after the welcoming remarks of Cardinal Araújo Sales, the General Secretary, Cardinal Jan P. Schotte, gave a report on the preparation process, and Cardinal Sandoval Iñiguez read the *Relatio ante-disceptationem.* The general congregations, in the days that followed, spoke to the themes of the assembly as set by the pope. Many of the bishops identified a need for evangelization within the Church itself; their proposals included reformation of Catholic education and a focus on small groups within parishes. The South American bishops in particular spoke repeatedly about the development of means of social communication, and urged that the Church increase her use of these means for evangelization; some of the bishops spoke of the need to engage the "new culture" produced by the technological innovations in the media. The bishops echoed the pope's call in *Tertio millennio adveniente* for a forgiveness of part or all of the international debt, but they acknowledged the practical difficulties this might involve; several bishops urged that the Church should limit its role in such matters to that of providing moral exhortation. Another matter of international relations that received considerable attention was the rights of migrants.

The synod fathers were divided into twelve small groups (*circuli minores*) on the basis of their choice of language (three English, six Spanish, and one each of Spanish- Portuguese, Spanish-Italian, and French). The groups were unanimous in their call for a focus on the importance of a personal encounter with Jesus Christ, and for improvements in religious education. They also voiced a need for the bishops to attend more directly to the needs of indigenous and African-American communities.

The final "Message to the People of God" was made public in a press conference on 11 December. The special assembly was brought to a conclusion the next day with a concelebrated Eucharistic Liturgy in honor of Our Lady of Guadalupe. Both during and after the assembly the bishops spoke enthusiastically about the new sense of solidarity they found in the assembly; though the working groups, divided by language, produced only limited mingling between bishops of different continents, the social interaction of the bishops did allow for a great deal of communication and mutual understanding of the needs of North and South.

A feature of continental or regional synods is the celebration phase of a special assembly traditionally taking place in conjunction with a papal visitation to the continent. In the case of America, this celebration phase was held 22–25 January 1998 with the visit of the Holy Father to Mexico City (Mexico) for the promulgation of the post-synodal apostolic exhortation *Ecclesia in America.* The Holy Father was principal celebrant at the Eucharistic Liturgy in the Basilica of Our Lady of Guadalupe, located at the base of Tepayac Hill, where various cardinals, bishops, priests, those in consecrated life, and the laity—many of whom participated at the synod—took part. During the homily, the Holy Father solemnly declared that the liturgical observance of Our Lady of Guadalupe, Patroness of all America, was to be raised to the category of feast in the Church's calendar for all the continent.

See Also: DARIO CASTRILLÓN HOYOS, ECCELSIA IN AMERICA, FRANCIS GEORGE, ROGER MAHONY, TERTIO MILLENNIO ADVENIENTE

[JOHN ABRUZZESE]

SYNOD OF BISHOPS, SPECIAL ASSEMBLY FOR ASIA

The Special Assembly of the Synod of Bishops for Asia, popularly known as the "Asian Synod," was held in Rome 19 April to 14 May 1998. The opening Mass in St. Peter's Basilica, presided over by Pope John Paul II, drew on the wealth and variety of faith, experience, traditions, and customs of Asia. During the liturgy, the Holy Father reminded the participants of their task: "During the Synod we would like to witness to what the Spirit of Christ says to the churches on the great Asian continent. Ours is the task of writing new chapters of Christian witness in every part of the world and in Asia [and this] calls for respectful attention to 'Asian realities' and healthy discernment in their regard."

The synod convened, taking up the call of John Paul II to face the challenge of proclaiming and bearing witness to Christ in Asia. In the sessions that followed, the 252 participants (188 synod fathers, 6 fraternal delegates, 18 experts, 40 auditors) explored the Synod's theme: "Jesus Christ the Savior and His Mission of Love and Service in Asia: ' . . . that they may have life, and have it abundantly' (John 10:10)."

Several Japanese bishops, like Bishop Nomura of Nagoya, Cardinal Shirayanagi of Tokyo, and Bishop Hamao (Yokohama) played an important role in the Synod, many spoke on the first day of the interventions, proposing questions for the Synod that set the tone and encouraged frank assessment. Other figures who made a significant contribution are Cardinal Paul Shan Kuo-Hsi (Taiwan), Archbishop Oscar Cruz (Philippines), and Cardinal Julius Darmaatmadja (Indonesia). Cardinal Shan served as the general relator for the Synod. Cruz, FABC Secretary General, was the principal redactor for the final synodal "Message to the People of God" that captured the mood and central themes of the Synod. Darmaatmadja gave the closing Synod address on 13 May.

Pope John Paul II led and guided the Synod through his presence and occasional remarks at all the plenary sessions. He noted how the Church in China remains his special concern and the focus of his first prayer each morning—two bishops from mainland China (Matthias Duan Yinming of Wanhsien [Wanxian] and his coadjutor Joseph Xu Zhixuan) were unable to travel to Rome.

Background and Preparations. Asia, a conglomerate of "continents" and giant archipelagoes, possesses a rich mosaic of cultures and subcultures; it also has a wealth of spiritual heritages. Eighty-five percent of all the world's non-Christians live in Asia. Catholics (105.2 million in 1997) represent only 2.9% of the nearly 3.5 billion Asians (over 60% of humanity). Significantly, well over

Pope John Paul II gives Holy Communion to a boy during Mass at the Jawaharlal Nehru Stadium in New Delhi. (© Reuters NewMedia Inc/CORBIS)

50% of all Asian Catholics are found in one country alone—the Philippines; thus, Catholics in many Asian nations are a small minority. Islam numbers some 700 million followers in Asia alone. The world's two largest Islamic nations are found in Asia: Indonesia and Bangladesh; each has well over 100 million Muslims. The Church in Asia faced difficult situations: riots in Indonesia, shootings in the West Bank, Muslim-Christian tensions in Bangladesh, detonation of several nuclear tests in India, the suicide-sacrifice of Pakistani Bishop John Joseph protesting Islamic blasphemy laws. The Church in Asia still faces continued persecution, and the mainland Chinese bishops were not able to attend.

The conditions in Asia and the challenges the Church faces there shaped the planning of the synod and its deliberations. The *lineamenta* for the Asian Synod were published on 3 September 1996 and circulated among Asia's episcopal conferences. The document elicited strong reaction and extensive responses, which were widely publicized in *Asia Focus* and the *East Asian Pastoral Review*. Taking a cue from these debates, the *Instrumentum Laboris* (working document) was released on 20 February 1998. By broadening the approach, it improved the struc-

ture of the *lineamenta* and proved a serviceable instrument for the synodal participants.

The actual sessions began on 20 April in the Synod Hall; Cardinal Paul Shan Kuo-Hsi, S.J. from Taiwan, the Synod's general relator, gave an extensive introduction (*relatio ante disceptationem*) that provided a comprehensive framework for discussion and elaborated the themes of an Asian vision of evangelization that set the agenda for the month-long synod: (1) a broad notion of the Church's evangelizing mission; (2) an emphasis on FABC's triple imperatives for justice, inculturation, and interreligious dialogue; (3) positive approaches to Asian religious traditions and the role of God's Spirit; (4) a central role of the local churches and the ecclesiology of communion; (5) the Church at the service of the Kingdom; (6) a humble, kenotic Church with an Asian face; (7) a recognition of the importance of Asian approaches to evangelization (e.g., emphasis on experience and witness of life).

The topics during the interventions of the days revolved around four main topics: (1) interreligious dialogue; (2) the Church becoming Asian through her dialogue with living cultures; (3) the Church learning to dialogue with the poor; and, (4) the Asian local churches as churches of the laity. The eleven discussion groups (eight English; two French; one Italian) brought insightful exchanges and comments focused on Christ and the Holy Spirit, the Church in the Asian context, and the contemporary mission of evangelization, expressed in terms of love and service. The synod approved fifty-nine proposals, none receiving fewer than 140 votes out of the maximum number of 168. Ultimately, all but seven of the propositions directly appeared in *Ecclesia in Asia,* forming nearly half of the footnoted documentation.

Pope John Paul II formally concluded the synod on 14 May with a Mass in Saint Peter's Basilica. The Asian Synod is best understood in the fuller context of the Church's celebration of the Great Jubilee Year 2000, for which the special assemblies prepared. The exhortation *Ecclesia in Asia* was intended for the Church universal as well as for the Church in Asia. The synod proved a Spirit-filled event for the whole Catholic world, but it was particularly effective in Asia, where it has engendered renewal, change, solidarity, vision, and renewed commitment to evangelization.

See Also: ECCLESIA IN ASIA

Bibliography: F. CARRERA, "Becoming an Asian Church," *World Mission* (Manila) 10, no. 5 (June 1998): 21–25. F. CLAVER, "Personal Thoughts on the Asian Synod," *East Asian Pastoral Review* 35, no. 2 (1998): 241–248. J. CUMMINS, "Synods in Contrast," *America* 179, no. 5 (29 August-5 September 1998): 9–12. J. DUPUIS, "Premier échos du Synode pour l'Asie," *Etudes* 389, no. 3 (September 1998): 215–227; "First Echoes of the Synod for Asia," *Landas* 12, no. 2 (1998): 13–28. A. GAJIWALA, "The Asian Synod of Bishops and Women: Sipping the Same Cup?" *In God's Image* 17, no. 4 (1998): 57–62. J. KROEGER, "Asia, A Continent of Emerging Missionary Hope," *Landas* 12, no. 2 (1998): 35– 56; *Verbum SVD* 40, no. 3 (1999): 329–337. J. PRIOR, "Apostles and Martyrs: Consecrated Life at the Bishops' Synod for Asia," *Review for Religious* 58, no. 1 (January-February 1999): 6–27. A. ROGERS, "Challenges for the Church in Asia in the Twenty-First Century: Reflections in the Light of the Synod of Bishops for Asia," in *Federation of Asian Bishops' Conferences: Office for Human Development, Special Assembly of the Synod of Bishops for Asia* (Manila: FABC: OHD, 1998), 22–37. L. TAGLE, "The Synod for Asia as Event," *East Asian Pastoral Review* 35, nos. 3 & 4 (1998): 366–378; "The Theological Perspectives of the Asian Synod," *Diwa* 24, no. 1 (May 1999): 2–13. J. WANG, "Sharing My First Hand Experience of the Asian Synod," *Religious Life Asia* 1, no. 1 (August 1998): 24–39.

[JAMES H. KROEGER]

SYNOD OF BISHOPS, SPECIAL ASSEMBLY FOR OCEANIA

The Synod of Bishops for Oceania, held in Rome to enable Pope John Paul II to be present, took place from 22 November to 12 December 1998. The Oceania region comprises Australia, New Zealand, Papua New Guinea, and the Pacific Islands groups that are home to the Melanesian, Polynesian, and Micronesian peoples with their rich variety of cultures and languages. The geographical area last touched by European colonization and Christian missionary activity, it is home to less than one percent of the world's Catholics. In his apostolic letter *Tertio millennio adveniente* (TMA) John Paul II explicitly declared his intention to convoke a Special Assembly for Oceania, but drew attention to only one feature of the region:

> . . . For Oceania a regional synod could be useful. In this region there arises the question, among others, of the Aboriginal People, who in a unique way evoke aspects of human prehistory. In this Synod a matter not to be overlooked, together with other problems of the region, would be the encounter of Christianity with the most ancient forms of religion, profoundly marked by a monotheistic orientation. (TMA, no. 38)

The purpose of the Oceania Synod was to consider commonly shared pastoral concerns and insights, and place them on the agenda of the universal Church or, if already there, to ensure that they received renewed attention. The theme of the synod was, "Jesus Christ and the Peoples of Oceania: Walking His Way, Telling His Truth, Living His Life." The theme invoked the image of a pilgrim people witnessing to Christ in word and action.

Participants. Given the relatively small total number of bishops in Oceania, all active bishops were invited to participate. The synod's 151 participants were made up of 117 synod fathers, 14 experts, 19 auditors, 4 fraternal delegates, and the Holy Father. With only 88 synod fathers from the Oceania region, the number of heads of dicasteries of the Roman Curia was reduced from 26 to 14 to create a better balance between synod fathers from within and outside the region. All but two bishops were Latin Rite. Disputes between Rites were not an issue within the region, but reference was made by the two eastern-rite bishops to difficulties with the Apostolic See. The 14 appointed experts, all male and nearly all from Oceania, assisted the relator and special secretary in their responsibilities. The 19 auditors came from all areas of Oceania and of church life; seven of them were women, four of whom were religious. The four fraternal delegates represented the Anglican, Presbyterian, Methodist, and Lutheran Churches in the region.

The synod was largely monolingual. While the synod had two official languages (English and French) only 12 of the 128 interventions were in languages other than English. The fact that few participants had to rely on translations contributed to an increased sense of immediacy, direct involvement and full participation.

Two Oceania native dancers acknowledge Pope John Paul II during Mass at St. Peter's Basilica. (AP/Wide World Photos. Photograph by Massimo Sambucetti)

The pope was present at all plenary sessions and, while president, his role was primarily one of listener. The actual presiding was delegated to Cardinal Pio Taofinu'u, SM, archbishop of Samoa-Apia, Cardinal Edward Idris Cassidy, president of the Pontifical Council for Promoting Christian Unity, and Cardinal Thomas Stafford Williams, archbishop of Wellington. The general relator was Archbishop Barry James Hickey of Perth (Australia), with the French-speaking Archbishop Michel-Marie-Bernard Calvet, SM, archbishop of Noumea (New Caledonia) as special secretary.

Proceedings of the Synod. The synod lasted three weeks. During the first week a total of 128 interventions were presented. The second week was taken up by discussions in small groups to draw up draft propositions. After the presentation of the draft propositions at the beginning of the third week, the small groups discussed collective amendments to the draft propositions and concluded the week by voting on the propositions.

Most of the 128 interventions made explicit reference to paragraphs in the Instrumentum Laboris, the synod's working document, which was itself a result of the lineamenta distributed for discussion in 1997. The Instrumentum Laboris set out, under each of the three elements of the synod's theme (Walking His Way, Telling His Truth, Living His Life), the major issues that had emerged from the official responses to the lineamenta. The regional response rate had been seventy percent.

Central Issues. For many of the synod fathers the fundamental question was how to guide their local Churches in responding to the many challenges confronting them in modern culture and life, many aspects of which appear to be inimical to the Christian message. Synod participants recognized several elements of a positive nature in contemporary culture, such as its concern for human rights and the environment, a deeper awareness of the role of women and a greater sensitivity to all forms of discrimination. Inculturation emerged in the synodal discussion as a key theme. Two of its aspects received particular attention: evangelization of the cultures itself and the need to communicate and celebrate the Gospel in distinctive cultural forms.

A second major theme in the interventions was linked with the first: in the task to proclaim and live the Good News the bishops of Oceania were deeply conscious that they are not alone but that many men and women have responded to the call to mission through a variety of ministries and charisms. Special mention was made of catechists who, especially in the Pacific Islands, exercise the vital role of sustaining communion in their local situations. Many synod fathers suggested that the role of catechists should be recognized as a valid and formal ministry in the Church. The importance of Catholic education was also affirmed. The synod acknowledged that the story of the Church in the whole of Oceania, and particularly Australia and New Zealand, could not be told without grateful reference to all those, and especially religious, who have contributed to the Catholic school systems. The role of teacher and model is being taken on more and more by the laity, who in doing so exercise a very real and vital ministry in the Church.

A third theme in the interventions was the call to live the faith through working for justice and peace. Synod participants mentioned that the new confidence with which indigenous people, particularly in Australia and New Zealand, are giving expression to their identity provides an important opportunity for the Church to stand in solidarity with those who have suffered greatly at the hands of the colonizing powers.

The fourth theme to emerge from the synod discussions focused on communion. The Church as communion and the image of the Church as a community of disciples speaks powerfully to peoples in the Oceania region who are isolated from one another, often on tiny islands dotted over the vast Pacific ocean. The problem of immense distances and small and isolated populations make it difficult for the eucharist to be readily available to many of the peoples of Oceania. Without the eucharist there can be no truly Christian community. In this context many of the synod fathers asked for a reexamination of the criteria for ordination to the presbyterate.

The fifth and final theme to emerge from the synod interventions was the conviction that the Church is called to present the compassionate face of Christ to the world, especially to those who suffer. Of particular concern to synod participants were those who, for a variety of reasons, find themselves in irregular marriage situations. A number of synod fathers made suggestions for change in the Church's present discipline out of concern for the people in their pastoral care.

On the final working day synod fathers voted on 50 recommendations to be submitted to the Holy Father. The 50 propositions were responses to the difficulties and challenges confronting the Church in Oceania in the call to mission and evangelization.

Special Moments of the Synod. A number of events during the synod made a deep impression on those present. First, the opening and closing Masses were stunning in the way they incorporated music, dance, costume and customs from the cultures of Oceania. The synod participants rejoiced in the particular Oceanic character that so enhanced the celebrations.

Second, the participation through suffering by one of the synod fathers. Because of heart problems before the opening of the special assembly, Max Takuira Mariu, SM, auxiliary bishop of Hamilton, New Zealand, required hospitalization and continued treatment for the duration of the working sessions of the synod. Because of this special circumstance his intervention was allowed to be read out by another synod father.

Third, the intervention by Mrs Elsie Heiss from the Office for Pastoral Care of the Aborigines in Australia. The first Aborigine to ever address a synod of bishops, she appealed with deep emotion for acknowledgment and respect for Aboriginal culture and identity. She reminded the synod that Aborigines are a deeply religious people living in Australia some thirty to forty thousand years before Abraham.

Fourth, the many stories of isolation and hardship. Stories of isolation where Catholics are unable to participate in the Eucharistic celebration because of vast distances and few priests. Stories of hardship, for example in the diocese Aitape in Papua New Guinea, which was traumatized by a tsunami killing many people in coastal villages, and in Bougainville where armed conflict has caused the death of thousands and the destruction of hospitals and clinics, schools and churches.

And lastly, the deep sorrow expressed by Bishop Tomas Camacho of the diocese of Chalan Kanoa, the northernmost diocese in Oceania. It was from one of the islands in his diocese that the planes took off carrying the atomic bombs that destroyed the Japanese cities of Hiroshima and Nagasaki. His apology to the Japanese bishop present made a profound impression.

The unique contribution of the region of Oceania merits special attention. The Church in Oceania has been founded in recent times and retains a newness that flows out of cultures that are quite different from those in the long-established churches. Made up of islands, this region is characterized by vast expanses of water where canoes, boats and planes are often more common than cars and trains. The peoples of Oceania with their strong sense of the sacred, warmth of relationships and joyful celebration, hold fast to the responsibilities of community life by sharing resources, and caring for family and community. The region has given unique cultural expression to liturgy, the use of religious symbols, and the spirit of community, and has developed lay leadership to a high degree.

[T.S. WILLIAMS]

SYNOD OF BISHOPS, SECOND SPECIAL ASSEMBLY FOR EUROPE

"Jesus Christ, Alive in His Church, the Source of Hope for Europe" was the theme of the second special assembly for Europe of the Synod of Bishops, which took place in Rome 1–23 October 1999. In the eight years following the first synod for Europe, held in December 1991, the continent had changed significantly. This second synod aimed to assess the changes of the intervening years and to discern their significance for the proclamation of the gospel in Europe. Taking as its theme "We Are Witnesses of Christ Who Has Freed Us," the 1991 synod had focused on Europe's new-found freedom as a context for the new evangelization and the living of the Christian faith. A *sui generis* event by virtue of its historical context, it was an encounter of two different ecclesial experiences: on the one hand the heroism of faith in the gulag, on the other faith in the laboratory of the pluralist and secular society. By 1999 the first synod's encouragement to continue and develop the exchange of gifts between the churches of the erstwhile communist bloc and the churches of western Europe had been carried forward at numerous levels of church life. Progress in political, economic, and social terms had also been achieved in the European Union (EU), in the non-EU states in western Europe, and in many of the new democracies of central and eastern Europe. Through the enlargement process set in motion by the EU, Europe was being reunified. Inevitably uneven, this progress was menaced by structural problems in the political, economic, and social arenas.

If by 1989 it was clear that the communist utopia had failed as a model for society, by 1999 the EU experience had demonstrated that capitalism and the free market can be managed in the direction of a social market economy and its characteristic solidarity. While this much-underappreciated dimension of European construction was the fruit of ethical options foundational to the European treaties, the European context at the turn of the millennium required a new articulation of the aims of European construction. It needed to develop a narrative discourse on European identity both *ad intra* and in terms of Europe's relations with the rest of the world. To empower the process of European construction with a capacity to promote the dignity of the human person in the face of the challenges of the twenty-first century, a public discourse reintegrating the political, economic, social, cultural, ethical, and religious dimensions of individual and societal experience was urgently needed. With the second synod on Europe the Church in Europe made a contribution to shaping that discourse.

This second synod was announced by Pope John Paul II during his apostolic visitation to Germany in June 1996. It was the fifth and last of the continental synods foreseen in the pope's 1994 apostolic letter *Tertio millenio adveniente* (21, 38). The preparatory process was facilitated by a pre-synodal council, consisting of 15 members, which held five meetings were held between March 1997 and March 1999. The theme for the synod was announced on 18 April 1997. The *Lineamenta* with an attached questionnaire was disseminated on 16 March 1998. Comments and reactions were requested for 1 November 1998 in view of the preparation of the *Instrumentum laboris,* published on 12 July 1999.

In the introduction the *Instrumentum laboris* sketches the contrasting contexts of the first and second synods for Europe: that of December 1991 was "born of a realization that a particularly historic moment was occurring in Europe" (1) where the Church needed to reaffirm that "Jesus Christ alone in the true liberator of humanity; only he can indicate the proper way to follow in Europe's new-found freedom" (ibid). Quoting Pope John Paul's homily in St. Adalbert Square, Gniezno, the introduction asks if after the collapse of one wall, another invisible wall of fear and aggressiveness is not being discovered in Europe. It asserts that "the achievements of recent years in the economic, political and social fields do not hide that this wall exists" (2). Its diagnosis of Europe's spiritual condition is that "there are signs of weariness which historical events—recent and past—have brought about deep within the hearts of its peoples" (ibid.) and that therefore the basic question to be addressed is "how to restore hope . . . in a more profound and enduring manner" (ibid.). Against this analysis the aim of the Synod is set out as being "to analyze the situation of the Church in Europe in view of the Jubilee, to indicate ways in which the immense spiritual reserves of the continent can fully develop in all areas and to foster a new proclamation of the Gospel, thus creating the basis for an authentic religious, social and economic growth" (3). Taking the encounter of the two disciples on the road to Emmaus with the Risen Lord as an icon for the human condition in contemporary Europe, part 1 of the *Instrumentum laboris* outlines the analysis of the European condition as provided by the responses to the *Lineamenta*. Part 2 affirms the Christocentricity of the new evangelization, which is the Church's message for Europe and for the world. Proclaiming Jesus Christ as the hope for Europe is the subject of part 3, which delineates the Church's proclamation of Christ in terms of *martyria, leitourgia,* and *diakonia.* Recalling the Orthodox and Catholic experience of martyrdom in Eastern Europe and noting that at the end of the second millennium the Church has one again become a Church of martyrs (*Tertio millennio adveniente* 37), the conclusion sets out the relationship of the synod on Europe to the other continental synods held in view of the

Jubilee thus: "precisely because it joins the other special assemblies of the synod of bishops—which have raised questions on the mission of the Church today in Africa, America, Asia, and Oceania, putting in relief the historic, cultural and religious moment proper to each of these parts of the world—it can be a fitting occasion to remember the bond that unites Europe to the other continents in virtue of the Gospel and its proclamation. It can also serve to rediscover the originality of the European experience and its culture by unifying the rich diversity of elements which Europe and its local Churches have in relations to the world" (90).

The Synod opened on 1 October with an opening liturgy during which Pope John Paul II proclaimed three new co-patronesses of Europe: St. Teresa Benedicta of the Cross (Edith Stein), St. Brigid of Sweden, and St. Catherine of Siena. The total of 179 synod fathers comprised 72 members ex officio, 84 elected members and 23 papal nominees. Also in attendance were 17 *adiutores,* 39 *uditores and uditrices,* 10 *delegati fraterni* and one *invitatus specialis,* Brother Roger of Taizé. The work of the Synod was carried out in the course of 19 plenary sessions and 15 sessions of the language working groups (3 Italian, 2 English, 2 French, 1 German, and 1 Spanish).

The *relatio ante disceptationem,* delivered to the opening plenary session by the *relator generalis,* Cardinal Ruoco Varela of Madrid, set out a clear, if somewhat pessimistic reading of the spiritual condition of Europe. Cardinal Ruoco emphasized more the signs of malaise in Europe than signs of hope. His diagnosis interpreted the problems of Europe as the result of an absolutist anthropocentric view of the world where God is forgotten. Europe has a fundamental choice to make about its future: either to turn back to God revealed in Jesus Christ or risk losing its historical and spiritual roots. To assist Europe in this and all regards the *relatio* called upon the Church to examine before the crucified and risen Lord its own condition so that it might give authentic witness to Christian hope in a society where hope has been eroded by progressive de-Christianization. Cardinal Ruoco's attribution of the difficulties of the Church in Europe to the crisis in regard to the truth of faith was shared by many of the synod fathers. While some spoke of a condition of apostasy, others offered a more nuanced analysis. Europe's spiritual condition was most strikingly compared to a garden where poisonous plants grow together with others that bear an antidote to their poisons.

Other contributions in the plenary sessions tried to explore the conditions of an adequate pastoral response to this European situation. The basic challenge of transmitting faith in Jesus Christ, the quality of liturgical celebration, sacramental practice (with particular reference to the sacrament of reconciliation), and the shortage of vocations to the priesthood and religious life were recurrent themes. The new religious movements were identified by many as a vital force in the Church's life and a sources of hope for society, although several bishops stressed that their activities require greater insertion in the structures and parishes of the local Churches.

Ecumenism was the subject of many interventions and it featured prominently in the discussions in the *circuli minores.* By contrast with the 1991 synod, when some Orthodox Churches did not send a fraternal delegate, the Greek, Romanian, and Russian Orthodox Churches were represented as well as the Ecumenical Patriarchate. The request for pardon in the *aula* by the representative of the Romanian Orthodox Church for the sufferings caused by his Church to the Greco-Catholic Church in Romania was a memorable moment. Notwithstanding evident difficulties between the churches both in theology and practice, numerous signs of hope were noted: significant inter-church activities in troubled regions in Europe, the positive reception of the encyclical *Ut unum sint,* the ecumenical assembly in Graz, the draft *Charta Oecumenica* for Europe being prepared by the Council of European Bishops' Conferences (CCEE) and the Conference of European Churches (KEK), and the imminent signing of the Lutheran-Roman Catholic statement on Justification (31 October 1999). It was suggested that structures for ecumenical dialogue and centers for training in ecumenism be established by bishops' conferences and synods in those regions in which they are lacking.

Contemporary socio-political issues such as family policy, migration, nationalism, and unemployment recurred frequently in the discussions. The importance of a political *diakonia* as an essential element of the new evangelization was stressed. In this regard notable appreciation of the process of European integration as carried forward by the European Union and other European institutions was evident. Peace between peoples, security, solidarity, sharing of resources between richer and poorer nations, the equal dignity of nations, and respect for the rule of law were recognized as the fruits of European construction. In a letter to the synod the newly elected President of the European Commission, Romano Prodi, described the present challenge for European construction as the Europeanization of Europe: the overcoming of nationalism and the deepening of European integration. Referring to the indelible imprint of Christianity on Europe's memory and culture, he said that Europe awaited signs of hope from the Synod. The work of Church organizations such as the Commission of the Bishops' Conferences of the European Community (COMECE), vis-à-vis these political institutions was encouraged by many of the synod fathers as a key element in evangelizing the political process of European construction.

The challenge of modernity for communicating faith in Christ and for membership of the Church was broached from numerous angles in many interventions. The ethical challenges of globalization, the role of Europe in the world, the relationship between faith and culture, developing dialogue with Islam, the role of woman in Church and society, and the relationship between law and morality were recognized as domains requiring reflection so that the Church might give a pastoral and spiritual response to the questions preoccupying contemporary Europeans.

The "Message to the People of God" details signs of hope in the Church and in Europe (3, 7). Out of their "sincere love for Europe" (6) the fathers call upon Christians to "be committed Europeans" (ibid). Likewise they appeal to those with institutional, political, and cultural responsibility to ensure that "the Christian roots of our Europe and its rich humanist tradition" will continue to promote the common good of individuals and society in Europe itself and in all countries of the world.

The second Synod for Europe was a profound expression and experience of episcopal collegiality in a Europe in the process of rebuilding its unity. It facilitated the emergence of a shared responsibility beyond the confines of national borders in the face of the pastoral, cultural, social, and political challenges in contemporary Europe. The synod testified to a Church that recognizes in the Risen Christ in her midst the source of real hope for the individual and society. It also witnessed to a Church in Europe that, listening attentively to the Word of God and celebrating faith and hope in the Risen Lord in the liturgy, seeks in the twenty-first century, together with all men and women of good will, to serve humbly in accordance with her mission the project of building a Europe firmly rooted in Christian and human values.

See Also: AMANTISSIMA PROVIDENTIA, EVANGELIZATION (NEW), EDITH STEIN, TERTIO MILLENNIO ADVENIENTE, UT UNUM SINT

Bibliography: G. MARCHESI, "Il Secondo Sinodo Speciale per l'Europa, Parte Prima: indizione, apertura, e avvio dei lavori," *La Civiltà Cattolica* 150 (1999): 4:282–91; "Il Secondo Sinodo Speciale per l'Europa, Parte seconda: dibattito, approfondimenti e messagio finale," *La Civiltà Cattolica* 150 (1999): 4:486–95. U. RUH, "Krisenphänomene und Hoffnungszeichen: Die zweite Sonderversammlung der Bischofssynode für Europa," *Herder Korrespondenz* 53, no. 12 (1999): 621–25.

[NOËL TREANOR]

PARTICULAR ASSEMBLIES

SYNOD OF BISHOPS, PARTICULAR ASSEMBLY FOR THE NETHERLANDS

The Particular Assembly for the Netherlands of the Synod of Bishops met 14–31 January 1980 in Rome. Pope John Paul II, after consultation in May 1979 with each of the seven diocesan bishops who make up the episcopal conference in the Netherlands, convened the particular assembly to address pastoral concerns that had arisen in the country. During the second half of the 1970s, it became apparent that the bishops, under the leadership of Archbishop Cardinal Johannes Willebrands, had very divergent ideas about priests and pastoral care, seminaries and theological faculties, episcopal leadership, and the role of lay persons in the church. Mutual distrust had made collegial discussion and cooperation within the episcopal conference practically impossible. In addition to the seven bishops from the Netherlands, other participants in the synod included six cardinal prefects of Roman Congregations and, on occasion, the Holy Father himself. The Dutch bishops constituted a minority.

The *Acta Apostolicae Sedis* (72 [1980]: 215–50) published in French and Dutch contain the thirty-six conclusions approved by the pope. They contain chapters on the bishops, priests, religious, lay persons (including the lay ecclesial ministers, called "pastoral workers" in the Netherlands, and dispensed priests), and various sectors of ecclesiastical life. The conclusions begin with an ecclesiology of communion, while the chapters are divided according to traditional distinctions of classes and states within the Church. The bishops are said to "unanimously subscribe to the essential distinction between ministerial or sacramental priesthood and common priesthood of the baptized, and want to safeguard the practical consequences that result from this" (no. 17). A synodal council, made up of a curia cardinal, the archbishop of Utrecht and a second Dutch bishop, was established to carry out the conclusions. The synod recommend the establishment of two commissions of Dutch bishops, one to see whether the Catholic theological faculties were suited to the task of training seminarians for the priesthood, and the other to investigate which pastoral tasks could be entrusted to professional lay pastoral workers.

In May 1981, Cardinal Willebrands stated that the opposition had become more intense, and a number of issues discussed at the synod remained unanswered. It was only in 1989 that the Dutch bishops were able to determine to some degree the tasks of the pastoral workers, on the basis of Pope John Paul's apostolic exhortation *Christifideles laici* (1988). A well- balanced judgment of this synod has not yet been written, but the intervention of this particular assembly in the ecclesiastical life of the Netherlands did not produce the necessary lessening of tensions and the much-needed trust that had been hoped for.

See Also: CHRISTIFIDELES LAICI, JOHANNES WILLEBRANDS

[RUUD HUYSMANS]

Magisterial Documents

INTRODUCTION

Pope John Paul II has issued some twenty different kinds of pronouncements, ranging from homilies and congratulatory telegrams to encyclical letters and the Code of Canon Law. Certain documents are used for teaching faith and morals; some for church governance, and others for disciplinary purposes. The Second Vatican Council recognized the diversity of texts and their particular significance when used by the pope to further his teaching. "His mind and will . . . may be known chiefly either from the character of the documents, from his frequent repetition of the same doctrine, or from his manner of speaking" (*Lumen gentium* 25). Canon 754 addresses this in legislative terms: "All Christ's faithful are obliged to observe the constitutions and decrees which lawful ecclesiastical authority issues for the purpose of proposing doctrine or of proscribing erroneous opinions; this holds particularly for those published by the Roman Pontiff or by the College of Bishops."

Papal Documents. The decretal letter is one of the most solemn forms of papal proclamations. It is presently used for the canonization of saints and is generally presumed to invoke infallibility.

An encyclical is a pastoral letter written by the pope for the entire Church. Encyclicals are used to present the moral and social teachings of the Church, or to give counsel on points of doctrine which must be made more precise or which must be taught in view of specific circumstances.

The apostolic constitution is the most solemn form of legal documents issued by the pope in his own name; it is issued only in relation to very weighty matters. For instance, the Code of Canon Law for the Latin Church was promulgated as a constitution, *Sacrae disciplinae leges* (25 January 1983); the same is true of the Code of Canons of the Eastern Churches, promulgated as *Sacri Canones* (18 October 1990). The Catechism of the Catholic Church was formally published through the constitution *Fidei depositum* (11 October 1992). Since the

pontificate of Paul VI, it is customary for constitutions to have a strong doctrinal component.

The apostolic letter *motu proprio* is the most common source of canonical legislation after the Code itself. Written on the pope's own initiative, it deals with matters that are significant, but would not merit a constitution. A *motu proprio* is legislative in nature and are directed to the Church at large. More recently, the pope has been using a more general form, simply entitled apostolic letter, to make proclamations. For instance, the letter *Ordinatio sacerdotalis* (22 May 1994) addressed the issue of admission of women to priestly ordination: "I declare that the church has no authority whatsoever to confer priestly ordination on women and that this judgment is to be definitively held by all the church's faithful." The preparations for the Jubilee Year 2000 were also announced in an apostolic letter, *Tertio millennio adveniente* (10 November 1994). What place this type of papal document will occupy in years to come is not yet totally clear. There is no doubt that it is considered to be a major papal document.

Apostolic exhortations are also a significant expression of the magisterium of the Church. As the name implies, they are exhortative, rather than legislative, in character. John Paul II has most often issued them after meetings of the synod of bishops; thus addressed to the whole world (in the case of an ordinary assembly) or a particular continent or country (in the case of a special assembly), they show the influence of the recommendations that emerged from the assembly.

Papal allocutions are the regular addresses given by the pope on the occasion of meetings with bishops, congresses, pilgrimages, and so forth. These express the ordinary papal magisterium; they are not legislative by nature. However, the repetition of a given theme in a number of allocutions gives particular insight into the personal thought of the pope on the matter. For instance, the annual addresses to the Roman Rota at the opening of the judicial year constitute a privileged opportunity for the pope to express his views of matters relating to the application of procedural law and the canons on marriage.

Curial Documents. The decree is the highest form of document issued by a department of the Roman Curia. It is a law whose interpretation is governed by the canons on laws (see canon 29). The term decree is given many practical meanings: (1) where it is used in administrative matters, it is applied to designate the decisions of the Roman dicasteries (for instance, the approval of the Constitutions of a religious institute); (2) in legislative matters, the term is applied specifically to disciplinary laws (for instance, the undated decree of the Congregation for the Doctrine of the Faith prescribing an automatic excommunication for any person who abuses the sacrament of penance by using tape recorders and similar means of social communication—*Acta Apostolicae Sedis* 80 [1988]: 1367); (3) in judicial matters, the various procedural decisions taken by the judge (as, for instance, the decisions of the Supreme Tribunal of the Apostolic Signatura).

Instructions clarify the prescriptions of laws and determine an approach to be followed in implementing them (see canon 34).

Declarations are of three types: (1) the simple declaration, which must be interpreted in the light of existing legislation (such as the Declaration of the Congregation for the Doctrine of the Faith relating to membership in Masonic organizations, November 26, 1983); (2) authentic interpretations or declarations, which have the force of law and must be promulgated (such as those issued by the Pontifical Council for the Interpretation of Legislative Texts); (3) extensive declarations, which to a certain extent modify the law, by having it apply to instances not originally covered by the legislation.

Circular letters express the intentions and policies of the Roman Curia. When accompanied by rules, these letters explain the intention, spirit, and purpose of these rules (for instance, the letter and norms governing dispensations from the obligations of priestly celibacy [18 October 1980, as revised slightly, 6 June 1997]).

Directories, such as the 1993 Directory for Ecumenism (25 March 1993) are given for the application of accepted principles and are seen as ''an instrument at the service of the whole Church . . . [whose] orientations and norms of universal application . . . provide consistency and coordination . . . with the discipline that binds Catholics together'' (no. 6). The importance of a directory is that it provides the basic principles of pastoral theology, taken from the magisterium of the Church, by which pastoral action in the ministry can be more fittingly directed and governed.

Classification. Documents can be examined from a descriptive approach, according to form and the authorities who issued them. But they can also be classified according to their juridical value or weight. Some documents are magisterial (flowing from the *munus docendi*), while others are juridical (based on the *munus regendi*). Those that are juridical can be either laws in the proper sense of the term, or administrative documents for the whole community; they can bind only the executors of the law (such as texts addressed particularly to bishops), or even be non-binding (such as guidelines).

The following section contains précis of some of the more important documents issued by John Paul II; some of the more important curial and episcopal pronouncements are treated as well.

Bibliography: J. M. HUELS, ''A Theory of Juridical Documents Based on Canons 29–34,'' *Studia canonica* 32 (1998): 337–370. E. LABANDIERA, ''Clasificación de las normas escritas canónicas,'' *Ius canonicum* 29 (1989): 679–693. F. G. MORRISEY, *Papal and Curial Pronouncements: Their Canonical Significance in Light of the ''Code of Canon Law''* (Ottawa: Saint Paul University, 1995). L. WÄCHTER, *Gesetz im kanonischem Recht: Eine rechtssprachliche une systematisch-normative Untersuchung zu Grundproblemen der Erfassung des Gesetzes im katholischen Kirchenrecht,* Müchener theologische Studien, III, Kanonistische Abteilung, Band 43 (St. Otilien: EOS Verlag, 1989).

[F. G. MORRISEY]

AD TUENDAM FIDEM

Apostolic letter, ''To Protect the Faith,'' issued *motu proprio* by Pope John Paul II, 28 May 1998, adding to the codes of canon law for the Latin and the Eastern churches. The additions add a third distinction in the levels of teaching of the Magisterium, stipulate the adherence this teaching requires and the penalties to be imposed for violation, thereby making the adjusted canons reflective of the levels of teaching set out in the Profession of Faith and Oath of Fidelity issued by the Congregation for the Doctrine of the Faith in 1989.

The first paragraph of the *motu proprio* explicitly states that it is written in response to concern for errors, especially ''from among those dedicated to the various disciplines of sacred theology'' (Introduction). Following some comments on the history of the Nicene-Constantinopolitan Creed as a summation of the faith, the document turns to an explanation of the 1989 Profession of Faith and Oath of Fidelity, which is composed of not only the Creed but also three paragraphs ''intended to describe the truths of the Catholic faith'' (no. 2). The text continues with an explanation of these three paragraphs, pointing out that while the levels of teaching described in the first and third paragraphs are provided for in the

codes of canon law, the level of teaching mentioned in the second paragraph is not. *Ad tuendam fidem* then supplies for this omission since the level of teaching omitted illustrates "the Divine Spirit's particular inspiration for the Church's deeper understanding of a truth concerning faith and morals, with which they are connected either for historical reasons or by a logical relationship" (no. 3).

The levels of teaching mentioned in the Profession of Faith and Oath of Fidelity and already provided for in the law are found in canons 750, §1, and 752 of the Latin code, and canons 598 and 599 of the Eastern code. Patterned closely on the wording of the Profession of Faith, the *motu proprio* adds the following paragraph to the law:

> Each and every thing which is proposed definitively by the magisterium of the Church concerning the doctrine of faith and morals, that is, each and every thing which is required to safeguard reverently and to expound faithfully the same deposit of faith, is also to be firmly embraces and retained; therefore, one who rejects those propositions which are to be held definitively is opposed to the doctrine of the Catholic Church. (Translation from Code of Canon Law: Latin English Edition, rev. ed. [Washington: Canon Law Society of America, 1998] 247.)

The same text is added to the Code of Canon Law for the Eastern Churches. A cross reference to canon 1371 of the Latin code stipulates that violations of this canon are met with a "just penalty."

Questions surrounding this document focus on the meaning of the word "definitive" as that is applied to official teaching, and also on which teachings fall into this second category of teaching rather than the third. When issued, the *motu proprio* was accompanied by a doctrinal commentary issued by the Congregation for the Doctrine of the Faith. The commentary states that "the correct explanation" of the three final paragraphs of the Profession of Faith and Oath of Fidelity deserve "a clear presentation, so that their authentic meaning, as given by the Church's Magisterium, will be well understood, received and integrally preserved."

Bibliography: For the text of *Ad tuendum fidem,* see: *Acta Apostolicae Sedis* 90 (1998): 457–461 (Latin); *Origins* 28, no. 8 (16 July 1998): 113–116 (English); *The Pope Speaks* 43 (1998): 327–330 (English).

[ELISSA RINERE]

AMANTISSIMA PROVIDENTIA

Pope John Paul II commemorated the sixth centenary of the death of St. Catherine of Siena, O.P., 29 April 1980, with the apostolic letter *Amantissima providentia,*

Statue of Saint Catherine of Siena in Rome, Italy. (© Karen Tweedy-Holmes/CORBIS)

addressed to the Church in Italy. Published in Italian and Latin, the opening words—the "most loving providence" of God—identify the principal theme of the letter as manifested in the life of St. Catherine. When divine providence touches and transforms the human person, it confounds the wisdom of the wise and shows how sensitive human beings can be to the influence of grace. As the first part of the apostolic letter demonstrates, St. Catherine's life (1347–1380) was a testament to the influence of grace. She lived during the chaos of the fourteenth century. The Black Death would kill about a third of the population of Europe, leading the survivors to riot, despair, and all types of irrational conduct. The decline in population also helped to cause a general depression throughout the continent. Family feuds gave rise to civil wars; and the Hundred Years War between England and France would be waged intermittently until well into the next century. The Church herself was suffering from the effects of the long stay of the popes in Avignon (1308–1378), and the ensuing Western Schism (1378–1417). Not only did these events impact on Catherine, but she became an active protagonist in them.

Catherine was the twenty-fourth of twenty-five children born to Jacopo and Lapa Benincasa at Siena. From her earliest years she was drawn to a life of prayer, and at the age of seven she made a vow of virginity. At the age of eighteen she became a member of a group of lay tertiaries, known as *Mantellate* because of the black mantle worn over the white Dominican habit. She then joined with others—laity, *Mantellate,* and members of religious orders—in adopting a life of asceticism and helping the poor and needy. At the age of twenty-one she experienced a mystical espousal to Christ, who bestowed an invisible ring upon her. In 1374 she journeyed to Florence, where the chapter of the Dominican order was in session, and she received full approbation for her style of life. In the following year, 1375, in the church of St. Christina in Pisa, the Lord bestowed on her the stigmata, but the marks did not appear on her body until after her death.

In 1376 she traveled to Avignon on a mission to restore peace between Florence and the Holy See. From that time on Catherine was intimately involved in the affairs of the papacy and the Church. She urged Pope Gregory XI to do three things: appoint worthy bishops, call a Crusade, and return the papacy to Rome. Her efforts bore fruit and on 17 January 1377 Gregory XI returned in triumph to Rome. In 1378 the Pope died and was followed by Pope Urban VI, an austere man, interested in the reform of the Church, but also given to erratic behavior. The French cardinals abandoned him and returned to Avignon to elect another pope. It was the beginning of the Western Schism, which lasted for 40 years, and did irreparable harm to the Church. In November 1378, Catherine went to live in Rome at the invitation of Pope Urban VI and spent the rest of her life in prayer and working for the unity and reform of the Church. She died on 29 April 1380, and is buried in the Dominican church, Santa Maria sopra Minerva. She had accomplished much in the thirty-three years of life and was canonized by Pope Pius II on 29 June 1461.

The second part of *Amantissima providentia* describes her writings under three headings: *Letters, Prayers,* and her masterpiece, *The Dialogue.* The 381 *Letters,* addressed to all types of people, both humble and great, are rich in spiritual doctrine as well as prudent counsel. Most of them were written between 1374 and 1380. The *Prayers* of St. Catherine were transcribed by her followers while she conversed with the Lord in ecstatic prayer. They are authentic and spontaneous expressions of a mind immersed in divine light and a heart moved by fraternal charity. *The Dialogue,* a conversation with the divine Spouse, was dictated for the most part in ecstasy between 1377 and 1378. It consists of responses made by the Eternal Truth to her queries concerning the problems in the Church and in the world.

After her death Catherine has continued to assist the Church by her luminous examples of virtue and by her marvelous teaching. For that reason numerous popes have proposed her for the admiration and imitation of the faithful. In the bull of canonization (1461) Pius II speaks of her as "a virgin of illustrious and indelible memory." Pius IX proclaimed her the second patroness of Rome and Pope St. Pius X named her the patroness of women in Catholic Action. Pope Pius XII named St. Francis of Assisi and St. Catherine of Siena the primary patrons of Italy (1939). Pope Paul VI conferred on her the title of Doctor of the Church (4 October 1970).

Nineteen years after *Amantissima providentia,* Pope John Paul II named St. Catherine as one of three co-patronnesses of Europe, along with St. Bridget of Sweden and St. Teresa Benedicta of the Cross (1 October 1999).

Bibliography: For the Latin text of *Amantissima providentia,* see: *Acta Apostolicae Sedis* 72 (1980): 569–81.

[R. J. AUMANN]

APOSTOLOS SUOS

Apostolos suos is the *motu proprio* apostolic letter issued by Pope John Paul II, 23 July 1998, that addresses the theological and juridical nature of episcopal conferences, particularly for the Latin church.

Episcopal conferences are the subject of canons 447–459 of the 1983 Code of Canon Law. The Code of Canons of the Eastern Churches organize their respective synods under the provisions of canons 110 and 152 with the exception of assemblies established in areas where several churches *sui iuris* exist and to the extent that these assemblies are comparable to episcopal conferences (See CCEO c. 322 and *Pastor bonus,* no. 58). The papal document divides itself into four sections, the last of which provides four complementary norms regarding the conference of bishops. In section one, John Paul II traces major theological-historical moments of the collegial structure or permanent assembly of the apostles as constituted by the Lord Jesus up to the call of the 1985 Synod of Bishops for a "fuller and more profound study of the theological and consequently the juridical status of episcopal conferences, and above all of the issue of their doctrinal authority in the light of no. 38 of the conciliar decree *Christus Dominus* and Canons 447 and 753 of the Code of Canon Law." This introductory section calls specific attention to pastoral cooperation, consultation, and mutual assistance in past centuries with councils, especially particular councils of both plenary and provincial types addressed in canon 281 of the 1917 Code of Canon Law as well as the nineteenth century conferences of bishops "set up for specific pastoral purposes as a means of responding to different ecclesiastical questions of common interest and finding appropriate solutions to them.'' The document repeats themes of sharing wisdom and experience as well as exchanging views to formulate a program for the common good of the church as found in Pope Paul VI's *motu proprio* entitled *Ecclesiae sanctae* of 1966, the 1973 Pastoral Directory of Bishops, and finally the canons of the 1983 code. Section two addresses collegial union among bishops as Pope John Paul II touches on the themes of unity, collegiality, and joint pastoral action as a manifestation of collegial union as it focuses in nos. 11–12 on the implications of concrete application of collegial spirit (*affectus collegialis*) with respect to the universal church. Section three sets forth Pope John Paul II's understanding of the conference of bishops as a permanent institution, the issues which currently call for the joint action of the bishops, the manner in which episcopal conferences are to organize territorially, their composition, especially with respect to deliberative or consultative voting power, and finally the authority of the episcopal conference with respect to the authority of the diocesan bishop and the requirements of a *recognitio* of the Apostolic See. Section four sets down complementary norms regarding the conference of bishops: (1) Doctrinal declarations of the conference require unanimous approval by the bishops who are members or receive the *recognitio* of the Apostolic See if approved in plenary assembly by at least two-thirds of the bishops belonging to the conference and having a deliberative vote. (2) No body of the episcopal conference outside of the plenary assembly has the power to carry out acts of authentic magisterium; nor may the conference grant such power to its commissions or other bodies set up by it. (3) For statements different from those mentioned in article two, the doctrinal commission of the conference of bishops must be authorized explicitly by the permanent council of the conference. (4) The final article required episcopal conferences to review their statutes to insure their consistency with the norms of the present document and the Code of Canon Law and to submit them to the Apostolic See for *recognitio* in accordance with canon 451 of the 1983 code.

[A. ESPELAGE]

CATECHESI TRADENDAE

Catechesi tradendae is the apostolic exhortation on Catechesis, issued by Pope John Paul II, 16 October 1979, in the wake of the 1977 Synod of Bishops which dealt with catechesis. The first draft of the exhortation, prepared by Pope Paul VI on the basis of the documentation accumulated by the Synod, was revised by Pope John Paul I, and then given final shape by John Paul II, who had himself attended the Synod. Although the text reads like the compilation that it is, *Catechesi tradendae* (CT) nonetheless reaffirms the pastoral nature of catechesis expounded in the General Directory and in *Evangelii nuntiandi* of Paul VI. Furthermore, the exhortation states that the General Catechetical Directory remains normative for catechetical renewal and the standard reference for national and regional catechisms.

Like the Synod and earlier Church documents, *Catechesi tradendae* understands catechesis to be a stage of evangelization. The central tasks of catechesis are to lead Christians to maturity of faith and to educate them to a ''deeper and more systematic knowledge of the person and message'' of Jesus Christ (CT 19). The principal source of catechesis is ''the word of God transmitted in tradition and the scriptures'' (CT 27), not, however, as a collection of abstract truths, but as ''the communication of the living mystery of God'' (CT 7).

The document stresses that catechesis is an activity for which the whole church is responsible. While *Catechesi tradendae* encourages various groups and Church organizations in their catechetical endeavors, it gives particular attention to the family's important role and responsibility. It foresees that a renewal of catechesis will lead to the renewal of the Church as a whole.

A topic of concern among the Synod participants, and consequently one discussed in some detail in *Catechesi tradendae* in some detail, is the issue of the integrity of the content of catechesis and the need for its complete and systematic presentation. In using the term ''systematic catechesis,'' the exhortation attempts to safeguard the integrity and comprehensive nature of catechesis, while at the same time it situates catechesis between the informal and improvised moments of faith sharing and the structured expressions of theological research. The emphasis on systematic catechesis, moreover, is balanced by the recognition of the relationship between catechesis and life experience. *Catechesi tradendae* underscores that the methods and content of catechesis be chosen to respond to the age and intellectual development of the learner. At the same time, it also recognizes that, as an ongoing process, catechesis at each stage builds on previous learning, arriving fully at the catechesis of adults who have ''the capacity to live the Christian message in its fully developed form'' (CT 43).

A similar balance is maintained in the discussion of the relationship between culture and catechesis. By acknowledging that the Christian message is always embodied in a particular cultural milieu, it is argued that the impact of catechesis rests on its ability to enter the heart of that culture. *Catechesi tradendae* stresses the selection of those cultural elements which are the most appropriate to help members more fully understand the gospel message.

Taken as a whole, the document strives for a balance of content and method; of established doctrinal expression and its adaptation to specific pedagogical situations; and of the presentation of the entirety of the Christian message in its suitability to the age and ability of the learner.

Bibliography: For the text of *Catechesi tradendae,* see; *Acta Apostolicae Sedis* 71 (1979): 1277–1340 (Latin); *Origins* 9, no. 21 (8 Nov 1979): 329, 331–347 (English); *The Pope Speaks* 25 (1980): 34–86 (English). For commentaries and summaries of *Catechesi tradendae,* see: CESARE BONIVENTO, *"Going, teach...": Commentary on the apostolic exhortation 'Catechesi tradendae' of John Paul II.* (Boston, Mass.: St. Paul Editions, 1980). A. S. CAMPBELL, "Toward a Systematic Catechesis: An Interpretation of *Catechesi tradendae" The Living Light* 17 (1980): 311–320. *The Living Light* 15 (1978): 1–128 (summarizes the documentation of the 1977 synod, including its thirty-four propositions).

[J.E. REGAN]

CATECHESIS, GENERAL DIRECTORY FOR

Catechetical directories are a new genre of writing in the Roman Catholic religious education that emerged at the Second Vatican Council. They furnish guidelines that delineate theological-pastoral principles, describe the nature and purpose of catechesis, set goals, outline structures, and suggest strategies for catechetical programs. The *General Directory of Catechesis* (GDC) promulgated in 1997 by the Congregation for the Clergy updates the *General Catechetical Directory* published in 1971. Composed originally in Spanish and Italian, the GDC exists in Latin (the *editio typica*), English, French, German, and other translations. The new edition reflects the orientation given to catechesis in the apostolic exhortations *Evangelii nuntiandi* of Pope Paul VI (1974) and *Catechesi tradendae* of Pope John Paul II (1979) by yoking catechesis and evangelization in the Church's mission to proclaim the Gospel. It encourages the baptismal catechumenate, restored in the *Rite of Christian Initiation of Adults* (1972), as the model for all catechesis.

The 1979 Directory, considerably longer than the earlier edition, consists of five parts. Part 1 explains the nature, object, and the duties of catechesis in the context of the Church's mission of evangelization. Part 2 recapitulates the norms and criteria for presenting the Gospel found in the 1971 edition of the Directory and explains the contents and use of the *Catechism of the Catholic Church.* Part 3 describes "the pedagogy of God" as the source and model of the pedagogy to be adopted in cate-

chesis. Part 4 focuses on the recipients of catechesis, explaining how the methods and even the message needs to be adapted according to age groups, special needs, the socio-religious context, and cultural background of those being catechized. Part 5 addresses catechesis in the local church. It outlines principles that should guide the formation of catechesis, the need to be sensitive to the surroundings where it is carried on, and the importance of coordinating catechetical and other pastoral programs for their mutual support.

The 291 numbered paragraphs of the GDC are not all of the same importance. The sections deal with divine revelation, the nature of catechesis, and the criteria governing the proclamation of the Gospel message are "universally valid." Paragraphs that refer to particular circumstances, methodology, and to the manner of adapting catechesis to diverse age groups and cultural contexts are by way of guidelines and suggestions. The immediate aim of catechetical directories is to assist in the composition of national and regional directories and the writing of catechisms.

Bibliography: *General Directory for Catechesis* (Washington, D.C.: United States Catholic Conference, 1998). C. BISSOLI, "Il Direttorio Generale per la Catechesi (1997)," *Salesianum* 60 (1998): 521–547. B. L. MARTHALER, *Sowing Seeds: Notes and Comments on the General Directory for Catechesis* (Washington, D.C.: United States Catholic Conference, 2000).

[B. L. MARTHALER]

CATECHISM OF THE CATHOLIC CHURCH

The *Catechism of the Catholic Church,* promulgated by Pope John Paul II on 8 December 1992, is a compendium of Catholic doctrine that serves as a reference text for teaching and particularly for preparing local catechisms. Modelled on the so-called "Roman Catechism," promulgated in 1566 by the Council of Trent, the Catechism of the Catholic Church is divided into four parts of unequal length: the profession of faith, the celebration of the Christian mystery, life in Christ, and Christian prayer. Part One introduces the reader to God's revelation and is organized around the tenets of the Creed. Part Two explains how God's plan for salvation is made present in the sacred actions of the Church's liturgy, especially in the sacraments. Part Three presents Catholic tradition on law and grace and the principles of Christian morality found in the Commandments. Part Four outlines the meaning and importance of prayer in Christian life and explains the petitions of the Lord's Prayer.

The Catechism of the Catholic Church consists of 2,865 numbered paragraphs, with extensive cross-references in the margins and an analytical index. The text itself is distinguished by the use of large and small print. The body of the text, in large print, presents the teaching of the Church; passages in small print offer supplementary explanations, generally historical or apologetic, and quotations from patristic, liturgical, magisterial, and hagiographic sources. Further, at the end of each thematic unit, there is a series of condensed formulas that summarize the main points of the foregoing section. The original French edition ran 676 pages; the English edition published in the United States, 803 pages.

History. The development of the *Catechism of the Catholic Church* began with a recommendation by Bernard Cardinal Law, archbishop of Boston. In the course of the proceedings of the Extraordinary Assembly of the Synod of Bishops in 1985 to celebrate the twentieth anniversary of the Second Vatican Council, Law proposed "a Commission of Cardinals to prepare a draft of a Conciliar Catechism to be promulgated by the Holy Father after consulting the bishops of the world." The proposal was endorsed by the Synod and accepted by Pope John Paul II, who, in 1986, appointed a commission of twelve cardinals to oversee the work. It was chaired by the prefect of the Congregation for the Doctrine of the Faith, Joseph Ratzinger, and included American cardinals Bernard Law and William Baum. The actual drafting of the Catechism was delegated to a committee of seven residential bishops, assisted by Christoph Schönborn, O.P., of the University of Fribourg, Switzerland, and later cardinal archbishop of Vienna.

In the initial drafts, prepared through 1987–88, the Catechism had three parts and an epilogue. The drafting of Part One, the explanation of the Creed, was entrusted to Bishops José Estepa (Spain) and Alessandro Maggiolini (Italy); Part Two on the sacraments to Bishops Jorge Medina (Chile) and Estanislao Esteban Karlic (Argentina); Part Three, the section on morals to Jean Honoré (France) and David Konstant (England). Once it was decided to make the section on prayer an integral part of the Catechism, the task of drafting Part Four was given to an Eastern theologian, Father Jean Corbon of Beirut, a member of the International Theological Commission. The seventh member of the committee, Archbishop William Levada, then of Portland, Oregon, and later of San Francisco, was charged with producing a glossary. In November 1989 the Commission sent the draft text to all the bishops of the world for their consultation. While the text received a generally positive evaluation, the Commission did examine and evaluate over 24,000 amendments suggested by the world's bishops. On 25 June 1992, John Paul II officially approved the definitive text. The formal promulgation of the Catechism came on 8 December 1992, with the publication of the apostolic constitution *Fidei depositum.*

Sister Concepción teaches a catechism class in Havana, Cuba. (AP/Wide World Photos. Photograph by Joe Cavaretta.)

The Interdicasterial Commission that supervised translations into other modern languages approved the English language text in February 1994. By 1998 the English edition published under the auspices of the National Conference of Catholic Bishops had sold two and a half million copies.

With the apostolic letter *Laetamur magnopere,* dated 15 August 1997, Pope John Paul II introduced the *editio typica,* the official version in Latin. The new edition incorporated a number of modifications in the text approved by the Pope, which bishops' conferences throughout the world were asked to include in future editions of the *Catechism.* The most notable change to the text was the section on capital punishment, which was changed to reflect Pope John Paul's arguments against the death penalty in his 1995 encyclical *Evangelium vitae.*

In March 2000, the United States bishops' conference published a second edition of the *Catechism* for the United States. This second edition incorporates the modifications promulgated in *Laetamur magnopere,* and includes an English translation of the more extensive analytical index that appeared in the Latin edition and a glossary developed by Archbishop Levada.

Nature and Purpose. The Catechism does not include pedagogical or methodological considerations. The Prologue states:

> By design, this Catechism does not set out to provide the adaptation of doctrinal presentations and catechetical methods required by the differences of culture, age, spiritual maturity, and social and ecclesial conditions among those to whom it is addressed. Such indispensable adaptations are the responsibility of particular catechisms and, even more, of those who instruct the faithful (n. 23).

The Catechism seeks to respond to an authentic need expressed by many for a clear, intelligent, and coherent presentation of the Catholic faith for the present age. According to the prologue of the Catechism:

> The Catechism of the Catholic Church is intended primarily for bishops. As teachers of the faith and pastors of the Church, they have the first responsibility in catechesis. Through the bishops, it is addressed to redactors of catechisms, priests, and catechists. It will also be useful reading for all other Christian faithful (n. 12).

Bibliography: Editorial Commission of the *Catechism of the Catholic Church, Informative Dossier* (Vatican City 1992). M. SIMON, *Un Catéchisme universel pour l'église catholique du Concile de Trente à nos jours* (Louvain 1992). J. RATZINGER, "The *Catechism* of the Catholic Church and the Optimism of the Redeemed," *Communio* 20 (Fall 1993): 469–84. BERARD L. MARTHALER, *The Catechism Yesterday & Today: The Evolution of a Genre* (Collegeville, Minn. 1995).

[J. POLLARD/D. KUTYS]

CENTESIMUS ANNUS

Pope John Paul II's ninth encyclical, issued 1 May 1991, commemorating the hundredth anniversary of Pope Leo XIII's encyclical *Rerum Novarum.* John Paul's major social encyclical is divided into six sections. Chapter one, "Characteristics of *Rerum Novarum,*" pays tribute to Leo, who faced the social problems generated by a new form of property (capital) and a new form of labor (simply for wages). Work is part of the human vocation, but when labor becomes a commodity to sell, new injustices can and did arise. In *Rerum Novarum,* Pope Leo defended the essential dignity and rights of workers, together with the principle of solidarity (under its classical name "friendship"). Criticizing both socialism and liberalism, he stated that "the defenseless and the poor have a claim to special consideration."

In chapter two, "Toward the New Things of Today," John Paul sketches the history of the last 100 years, including two world wars, the consolidation of Communist dictatorship, the arms race and the Cold War. These movements were complicated outside Europe by decolonization. He also refers to three types of response to the Communist threat: (1) the European social market economies tried to end the situations of injustice that fueled revolutionary movements by building a "democratic society inspired by social justice"; (2) others set up repressive systems of national security, which risked destroying the very freedoms they were intended to protect; and (3) affluent Western societies tried (successfully) to compete with Marxism at its own level, by demonstrating a superior ability to meet human material needs.

With this the pope comes to "The Year 1989" (chapter three), and his analysis of the fall of Communism, which he traces to the recovery and application of the principles of Catholic social teaching by Polish workers in the name of solidarity, faced with the inefficiency of the economic system and the spiritual and cultural void brought about by Communism. The consequences of 1989 apply to the Third World, in that they enable the Church to affirm "an authentic theology of integral human liberation" (no. 26), and to Europe, where a great effort is now needed "to rebuild morally and economically the countries which have abandoned Communism." Disarmament should make possible a greater "mobilization of resources" for "economic growth and common development," both in Europe and in the Third World. But development is threatened by resurgent totalitarianism, materialism, and religious fundamentalism.

The fourth chapter, "Private Property and the Universal Destination [i.e., purpose] of Material Goods," is the heart of the encyclical. An individual right to property exists but is limited by nature: it is created by human work, and since the earth as a whole was given to man in common, all possession should be subordinated to the common good. These days, the possession of "know-how, technology and skill" are just as important as material resources in the creation of wealth. This leads to new types of exclusion and poverty, especially in the Third World. To an unjust economic system where fundamental human needs remain unsatisfied and development impossible, one must oppose not socialism but a "society of free work, of enterprise and of participation," in which "the market is appropriately controlled by the forces of society and by the State." In such a system, profit is not the only regulator of the life of business, monopolies are broken down, unpayable debts are deferred or canceled, and every effort is made to create conditions under which the poorer nations may share in development (no. 35).

In advanced economies, the need for basic goods is replaced by the "demand for quality," leading to the danger of consumerism: lifestyles directed not towards "truth, beauty, goodness and communion with others for the sake of common growth" but towards acquisition for the sake of "enjoyment as an end in itself," where the definition of human needs has been distorted by a false anthropology. Consumerism alienates man from his true self, which can only be attained by self-transcendence and self-gift. It leads to the disordered consumption of natural resources and irresponsible destruction of the environment and the creation of "structures of sin" that impede human development (to which the pope opposes the structures of "human ecology," starting with the family as sanctuary of life).

Despite its advantages, the market has limits. There are "collective and qualitative needs which cannot be satisfied by market mechanisms'' and human goods which must not be bought and sold, but need to be defended by the State and society (no. 40). Marxism has failed, but marginalization, exploitation, and alienation persist. The Church endorses the ''free economy,'' but only if economic freedom is ''circumscribed within a strong juridical framework which places it at the service of human freedom in its totality,'' which is ethical and religious at its core (no. 42). She offers her social teaching, however, not as a model but as an ''indispensable and ideal orientation'' towards the common good.

In chapter five, ''State and Culture,'' the pope warns that human freedom depends on the recognition of an ultimate truth, without which ''the force of power takes over,'' and democracy slides into totalitarianism (44–45). Human rights, starting with the right to life and culminating in religious freedom, must be protected, and the security of stable currency and efficient public services assured, by the State. Families and other intermediate communities and ''networks of solidarity'' on which the culture of a nation depends should be supported. The principle of subsidiarity, however, militates against excessive State interference and control, as occurs in the ''Social Assistance State.''

The Church contributes to ''a true culture of peace'' by promoting the truth about human destiny, creation and Redemption, and about our shared responsibility for avoiding war. Peace is promoted by development, which in turn depends on ''adequate interventions on the international level'' and ''important changes in established life-styles,'' especially in the more developed economies (51–52, 58). Chapter six, ''Man Is the Way of the Church,'' emphasizes that the Church's social doctrine is inspired by her care for each human being, and forms a part of her evangelizing and salvific mission, revealing man to himself in the light of Christ. Though primarily theological, it is interdisciplinary, and rather than being merely a theory is a basis for action. With the help of grace, ''Love for others, and in the first place love for the poor, in whom the Church sees Christ himself, is made concrete in the promotion of justice'' (58).

Bibliography: For the text of *Centesimus annus,* see: *Acta Apostolicae Sedis* 83 (1991): 793–867 (Latin); *Origins* 21, no. 1 (16 May 1991): 1–23 (English); *The Pope Speaks* 36 (1991): 273–310 (English). For commentaries and summaries of *Centesimus annus,* see: RODGER CHARLES, S.J., *Christian Social Witness and Teaching,* vol. 2, *The Modern Social Teaching: Contexts: Summaries: Analysis* (Leominster: Gracewing, 1998). SAMUEL GREGG, *Challenging the Modern World: Karol Wojtyła/John Paul II and the Development of Catholic Social Teaching* (Lanham: Lexington Books, 1999). DAVID L. SCHINDLER, *Heart of the World, Center of the Church: Communio Ecclesiology, Liberalism and Liberation* (Grand Rapids: Eerdmans, 1996). GEORGE WEIGEL, ed., *A New Worldly Order: John Paul II and Human Freedom-A ''Centesimus Annus'' Reader* (Washington, D.C.: Ethics and Public Policy Center, 1992). JUDE P. DOUGHERTY, ''The Ecology of the Human Spirit,'' *L'Osservatore Romano,* English edition (16 October 1996).

[STRATFORD CALDECOTT]

CHALLENGE OF PEACE, THE

Pastoral letter of the U.S. bishops, ''The Challenge of Peace: God's Promise, Our Response,'' approved 3 May 1983. The text comprises an introduction (1–4) and conclusion (330–39) and four chapters: ''Peace in the Modern World: Religious Perspectives and Principles'' (5–121), ''War and Peace in the Modern World: Problems and Principles'' (122–99), ''The Promotion of Peace: Proposals and Policies'' (200–273), and ''The Pastoral Challenge and Response'' (274–329). Three draft texts were prepared, and the second and third in particular were widely discussed in the Catholic community and elsewhere. In an April 1983 statement, Cardinal Joseph Bernardin, the chairman of the ad hoc committee that produced the letter, and Archbishop John Roach of St. Paul and Minneapolis, the bishops' conference president, explained that changes from the second draft to the third draft represented a response to suggestions by the U.S. bishops, and were ''the product of reflection and dialogue within the Catholic community,'' of ''the exchange of views which we had with representatives of the Holy See and of several European episcopal conferences in Rome'' (18–19 January 1983), and of some helpful suggestions from government officials. The pastoral itself said that such consultations showed ''the range of strongly held opinion in the Catholic community on questions of war and peace'' (12).

The threat of nuclear war represents the greatest menace the planet has known (2). However, the necessary task of saying no to nuclear war also is complex (132); the recognition that peace is ''possible but never assured'' and that this possibility must be protected in the face of obstacles ''accounts in large measure for the complexity of Catholic teaching on warfare.'' The foundation of peace is justice, and history shows that peace and justice at times are in tension (60). There is no choice for the Christian but to defend peace against aggression, but ''it is the 'how' of defending peace which offers moral options'' (73). The church is called to be ''at the service of peace'' (23). The two purposes of Catholic teaching on peace and war are ''to help Catholics form their consciences and to contribute to the public-policy debate'' on the morality of war.

Developed at a time when deterrence strategy was at the heart of the U.S.-Soviet relationship (162), the pastoral letter adopts ''a strictly conditioned moral acceptance of nuclear deterrence'' (185). While ''deterrence of a nuclear attack may require nuclear weapons for a time,'' especially in the European theater (154), criteria for morally assessing deterrence strategy demonstrate that ''we cannot approve of every weapons system, strategic doctrine or policy initiative advanced in the name of strengthening deterrence'' (186). The intent to kill the innocent as part of a deterrence strategy is morally unacceptable (178). ''*Sufficiency* to deter is an adequate strategy; the quest for nuclear superiority must be rejected'' and nuclear deterrence should be a step toward ''progressive disarmament'' (188).

A ''new moment'' has arrived in which the nuclear age is being evaluated in terms of its ''destructive potential'' and of the stringent choices it poses ''for both politics and morals'' (126). In the past, church moral teaching sought first to prevent war and, second, to limit its consequences, but today, given the minimal possibilities of placing political and moral limits on nuclear war, the moral task is prevention: ''As a people, we must refuse to legitimate the idea of nuclear war'' (131). The bishops call for ''effective arms control leading to mutual disarmament'' (202) and urged ''negotiations to halt the testing, production and deployment of new nuclear weapons systems'' (204).

The seven criteria of a just war—''a set of rigorous conditions which must be met if the decision to go to war is to be morally permissible''—are included (80–99): just cause, competent authority, comparative justice, right intention, last resort, probability of success, and proportionality. Today, ''extraordinarily strong reasons for overriding the presumption *in favor of peace* and *against war*'' are required (83) and the principles of proportionality and discrimination have special significance. The latter principle ''prohibits directly intended attacks on noncombatants and nonmilitary targets'' (107). There are no circumstances when ''nuclear weapons or other instruments of mass slaughter may be used for the purpose of destroying population centers or other predominantly civilian targets'' (147). Furthermore, the bishops do ''not perceive any situation in which the deliberate initiation of nuclear warfare, on however restricted a scale, can be morally justified'' (150). They urge leaders ''to resist the notion that nuclear conflict can be limited, contained or won in any traditional sense'' (161).

The pastoral expresses support for ''a pacifist option'' and Christian nonviolence, and it describes just-war teaching and nonviolence as distinct, though interdependent, methods for evaluating warfare (120). It notes that the Second Vatican Council (*Gaudium et spes* 79) asked governments to enact laws protecting the rights of conscientious objectors to all wars (118). Christian non-

violence, the pastoral explains, does not adopt a passive stance toward injustice or the rights of others, but ''affirms and exemplifies what it means to resist injustice through nonviolent means'' (116).

Members of the armed services (309–317) and Catholics working in the defense industries (318) are addressed directly. Military professionals have a vocation ''to defend the peace.'' The bishops do not intend ''to create problems for Catholics in the armed forces.'' Yet, every profession ''has its specific moral questions,'' and clearly the pastoral letter's teaching ''poses a special challenge and opportunity to those in the military profession.'' The bishops say they are impressed by ''the demanding moral standards'' already observed by Catholics in military service. Military officials are reminded that ''their training and field manuals have long prohibited . . . certain actions in the conduct of war,'' especially those that harm innocent civilians. Those training others for military duties are reminded ''that the citizen does not lose his or her basic human rights by entrance into military service.'' Catholics at all levels of the defense industries, including those involved in developing and producing weapons of mass destruction, ''can and should use the moral principles of this letter to form their consciences.'' The bishops recognize the ''possibility of diverse concrete judgments being made in this complex area;'' people who decide in conscience that they no longer can be associated with defense activities ''should find support in the Catholic community,'' while those who remain in these industries or earn a profit from them ''should find in the church guidance and support for the ongoing evaluation of their work.''

The bishops note that they do ''not intend that our treatment of each of these issues carry the same moral authority as our statement of universal moral principles and formal church teaching'' (9). In the case of ''some complex social questions, the church expects a certain diversity of views even though all hold the same universal moral principles'' (12). Yet Catholics are expected to give the moral judgments in the pastoral letter serious consideration (10).

Bibliography: For the text, see: *Origins* 13, no. 1 (19 May 1983): 1–31

[DAVID GIBSON]

CHRISTIFIDELES LAICI

Apostolic exhortation of Pope John Paul II, ''The Lay Members of Christ's Faithful People,'' issued 30 December 1988, following the seventh ordinary assembly of the Synod of Bishops (1–30 October 1987), whose theme was the "Vocation and Mission of the Laity in the Church and in the World Twenty Years after the Second Vatican Council." The text comprises an introduction (nos. 1–7) and five chapters: "The Dignity of the Lay Faithful in the Church as Mystery," (nos. 8–17), "The Participation of the Lay Faithful in the Life of Church as Communion" (nos. 18–31), "The Coresponsibility of the Lay Faithful in the Church as Mission" (nos. 32–44), "Good Stewards of God's Varied Grace" (nos. 45–56), and "The Formation of the Lay Faithful in the Lay State" (nos. 57–64). The exhortation ends with an appeal to the intercession of the Virgin Mary.

Christifideles laici builds on the scriptural images of the vineyard (Mt 20:1) and of the vine and the branches (Jn 15:5). According to John Paul, the 1987 synod's significance might well consist in its recognition of the Lord's call to go into the vineyard, addressed to everyone (no. 64). The vineyard represents the whole world, which is to be transformed (no. 1). The biblical phrase, "I am the vine, you are the branches," "lends itself to a consideration of fruitfulness and life.. . . Bearing fruit is an essential demand of life in Christ and life in the church" (no. 32). The pope's intent is to promote the gift and responsibility the lay faithful have in the communion and mission of the church (no. 2). It is therefore essential to view them in the "context of the church as communion" (no. 18), in which each layperson "offers a totally unique contribution on behalf of the whole body" (no. 20).

The foundation for the dignity and mission of the lay faithful is the "radical newness of the Christian life that comes from baptism" (no. 10). Accepting the synod's call to describe the lay faithful in positive terms (rather than as those who are simply not priests and not consecrated religious), the pope insists that only by acknowledging the richness of the mystery of baptism can a basic description of the laity be achieved (no. 9). The call to holiness is universal and is rooted in baptism; in fact, "the vocation to holiness" is an essential element of the new life of baptism (no. 17). It is the also vocation and mission of the lay faithful—precisely as church members—to proclaim the gospel (no. 33), and to take an active, responsible role in the world's "re-evangelization" (no. 64).

The biblical theme of fruitfulness is re-emphasized in the pope's discussion of lay formation, the objective of which is the ongoing discovery of a person's vocation along with "the ever-greater willingness to live it" (no. 58). The pope accents the necessity of total and ongoing formation (no. 57).

The distinctive feature of the lay state is found in its "secular character" (no. 55). The vocation of the lay faithful "properly concerns their situation in the world" (no. 15). Two temptations are to be avoided: (1) being so greatly interested in "church services and tasks" that the lay faithful do not become "actively engaged in their responsibilities" in the world; (2) "legitimizing the unwarranted separation of faith from life" (no. 2). Formation of the laity should be integrated, not presenting "spiritual" life and "secular" life as two parallel lines of their existence (no. 59). The pope adds that faith is not "entirely thought out, not faithfully lived" if it does not affect a person's culture (no. 59).

Discussing women in church and society, the pope quotes a synod recommendation which said the church needs to "recognize all the gifts of men and women for her life and mission, and put them into practice" (no. 49). The many provisions of the revised Code of Canon Law on the participation of women in the church's life and mission need to be more widely known and "realized with greater timeliness and determination" (no. 51). The first step in promoting women's full participation in church and society is to openly acknowledge their personal dignity (no. 49).

The church's pastors need to "acknowledge and foster" the ministries, offices, and roles of the lay faithful "founded in baptism, confirmation and matrimony." The pope notes that in the synod "a critical judgment was voiced" about using the word "ministry" too indiscriminately so that the common priesthood and ministerial priesthood either are confused or equated (no. 23). The ministries, offices, and roles of the lay faithful in the church should be "exercised in conformity to their specific lay vocation" (ibid.). A discussion of the charisms, the gifts of the Spirit, follows the discussion of ministries, offices, and roles (no. 24).

Some other concerns discussed in the exhortation include the aged, associations and movements, culture, the family, men's roles, parishes, public and political life, small Christian communities, spirituality, work, and youth.

Bibliography: For the text of *Christifideles laici*, see: *Acta Apostolicae Sedis* 81 (1989): 393–521 (Latin); *Origins* 18, no. 35 (9 Feb. 1989): 561–595 (English); *The Pope Speaks* 34 (1989): 103–168 (English). For commentaries and summaries of *Christifideles laici*, see: ROBERT W. OLIVER, *The Vocation of the Laity to Evangelization: An Ecclesiological Inquiry into the Synod on the Laity* (1987), *Christifideles Laici* (1989), and Documents of the NCCB, 1987–96 (Rome 1997). PETER COUGHLAN, *The Hour of the Laity: Their Expanding Role* (Philadelphia: E. J. Dwyer, 1989).

[DAVID GIBSON]

COMMON GOOD AND CATHOLIC SOCIAL TEACHING, THE

This statement of the bishops of England and Wales was issued in October 1996; the release was accompanied

View of Westminster Cathedral, the see of the Catholic bishop in London, England. (© Michael Nicholson/CORBIS)

by a booklet on the use of the document in study groups. The 13,000-word document consists of two parts. The first, "Christian Citizens in Modern Britain," presents a summary explanation of the principles of the Catholic social vision. Part two applies these principles to contemporary questions. Appendices contain extracts from previous Catholic documents, and a list of relevant Catholic organizations.

The first principle and focal point of the Catholic social vision is the dignity of the human person (nos. 12–14). God became flesh as a human being, and Christ challenges us to see and serve him in our neighbor, "especially the neighbour who lacks what is essential to human flourishing" (there is a "preferential option for the poor"). Catholic social teaching develops through history (nos. 24–32), and now embraces democracy and universal human rights, while emphasizing the dependence of both on a system of common values. Observance of the Church's social teaching is not "optional"; it is part of her moral teaching in general, based both on natural law and revelation (nos. 41–47). Social and political liberation are an aspect of evangelization.

"God is a divine society of three Persons," and our social nature is an aspect of the divine image in us (nos. 16–18). Human society can be structured either to facilitate or to frustrate personal development. A well-constructed society will give priority to family life, and will integrate the "vertical" principle of subsidiarity with the "horizontal" principle of solidarity (nos. 22–23, 51–53). The former favors the dispersal of authority "as close to the grass roots as good government allows"; the latter stresses interdependence and common responsibility. These principles must be applied to Britain's relations with the European Union and participation in the international economic order (overseas aid, resolution of debt crisis, restriction of arms sales, encouragement of the poorer economies through regulation of the market; nos. 99–105). There must also be a "religious respect" for the integrity of creation and the "environmental common goods" which belong to all humanity, present and future (nos. 106–108).

The common good cannot exclude any section of the population: for example by poverty, even relative poverty (nos. 69–73). Governments must "arbitrate between the sometimes conflicting demands of a market economy and the common good" (nos. 74–85). While the "centrally commanded economies" have shown themselves to be oppressive, inefficient, wasteful, and unresponsive to human needs, the Church also "rejects belief in the automatic beneficence of market forces," which are "just as likely to lead to evil results" (to create an alienated "underclass," to encourage selfishness rather than service, to foster consumerism, etc.) unless "regulated in the name of the common good" within an ethical and legal framework. Social services "need other incentives than mere profit." The free market has undermined a sense of moral responsibility in the mass media (nos. 86–89). In the world of work, employment is more than a purely commercial contact, and the worker's rights are superior to those of capital (nos. 90–98). The Church encourages partnership in business, membership in trade unions, and a just minimum wage (nos. 109–112).

Politics is not an ignoble profession, despite the prevailing climate of suspicion and contempt among and towards politicians (nos. 57–61). Candidates in an election should be chosen for their general character and attitude, since they will have to represent the electorate in varied and unpredictable circumstances, not on the basis of a single issue such as abortion (nos. 62–65). It is true, however, that Britain has become a "culture of death," and Catholics must try to awaken the conscience of the majority against "the use or disposal of human life, as a means to another end" (nos. 66–68).

Closing on a somber note (nos. 113–120), the bishops discern a "national mood of pessimism"; a "weakening of the sense of mutual responsibility and a decline in the spirit of solidarity, thanks to the "growing priority of technology over ethics," "things over persons," and "matter over spirit." "For these threats to be resisted, the political arena has to be reclaimed in the name of the common good."

[STRATFORD CALDECOTT]

An unidentified Catholic priest blesses the congregation during the Mass before the consecration of the Our Mother of Africa Chapel at the National Shrine of the Immaculate Conception in Washington. (AP/Wide World Photos. Photograph by William Philpott.)

DIES DOMINI

On the Solemnity of Pentecost 1998, Pope John Paul II issued the apostolic letter *Dies Domini,* "Observing and Celebrating the Day of the Lord." A document of profound and deep beauty, the letter illustrates not only a firm theological grasp of the meaning of "the day of the Lord," but also a keen sense of challenges that secularized western culture poses to the traditional observance and celebration of Sunday.

John Paul II's theological analysis of Sunday is grounded by five central images highlighting the nature of Sunday as a special "day" or the "lord of days" (a title borrowed from Pseudo-Eusebius of Alexandria). In five chapters, the pope explores Sunday as *Dies Domini* ("The Day of the Lord"), *Dies Christi* ("The Day of Christ"), *Dies Ecclesiae* ("The Day of the Church"), *Dies hominis* ("The Day of Humanity"), and *Dies dierum* ("The Day of Days").

In the letter, several important themes emerge. First, Sunday itself is ultimately and intrinsically related to the biblical idea of *Shabbat* (commonly called Sabbath). This Shabbat is not simply an interruption of mundane and regular work but a celebration and thanksgiving for the work God has wrought. However, the "the Day of the Lord" is not only Sabbath with its recollection of creation, it is also the day of Christ's resurrection, the weekly Easter. Thus, within the Christian perspective, Sunday is also a celebration of the salvation that has been effected by the Paschal Mystery.

Second, "the Lord's Day," celebrating as it does the Paschal Mystery, is a day privileged by and sanctified through the gathering the church to celebrate the Eucharist. On it, precisely in the full, active, and joyful celebration of the Eucharist, the risen Christ is encountered and manifested. In this sense, Sunday is also a day of epiphany. *Dies Domini* highlights the intrinsic connection between the mystery of Church that makes the Eucharist and the Eucharist that makes the Church.

As a "Day of Humanity" the "Day of the Lord" is also a day of joy, rest, and solidarity. The subtle tones in the pope's use of the word "solidarity" should be highlighted. This solidarity involves not simply the gathering of the Christian community in its liturgical assembly; it involves also the demand for service of and solidarity with humanity so clearly implied in the Eucharist. This celebration of the Eucharist by the Christian community on the "Day of the Lord" implicates the Christian community in service to and solidarity with others.

Finally, Sunday is the "Day of Days" and in a sense the very heart of the liturgical year, the very heart of time itself, and an eschatological image of time beyond death itself (such as we can know it). In addition to the main themes, *Dies Domini* hosts a number of additional and quite pressing sub-themes that are incorporated throughout the text. For example, the relationship between the Liturgy of the Word and the Liturgy of the Eucharist is highlighted, mining the best of postconciliar liturgical theology. The need for a critical assessment of the quality of effective proclamation is readily admitted.

The pope also touches upon two controverted issues, namely the current practice in some places of Sunday assemblies without a priest and the matter of the Sunday "obligation." Regarding the first, the letter notes the problem indicating that it certainly not the norm. Regarding the Sunday obligation, *Dies Domini* affirms it within a positive context, noting the responsibility of pastors to provide ample opportunities for the fulfillment of the obligation. Also highlighted are both the need to associate with other Christians in a world that is sometimes hostile to the practice of faith as well as the necessity of creating communities of real hospitality.

Bibliography: For the text of *Dies Domini*, see: *Acta Apostolicae Sedis* 90 (1998): 713–766 (Latin); *Origins* 28, no. 9 (30 July 1998): 133, 135–151 (English); *The Pope Speaks* 43 (1998): 339–377 (English).

[MICHAEL WHALEN]

DIRECTORY FOR THE MINISTRY AND LIFE OF PRIESTS (1994)

The Second Vatican Council called for a Directory for the Ministry and Life of Priests (*Christus Dominus*, no. 44). A long time in the making, the Directory was approved by Pope John Paul II, 31 January 1994 and authorized for publication by the Congregation for the Clergy. The Directory does not replace canon law, but rather addresses the principal questions of a doctrinal, disciplinary, and pastoral nature faced by priests of the Latin rite, especially diocesan priests.

The Directory for the Ministry and Life of Priests is divided into three almost equal chapters: The Identity of the Priest, Priestly Spirituality, and Ongoing Formation. The identity of the priest is described in terms of four dimensions of his life: the Trinitarian, Christological, pneumatological, and ecclesial. These dimensions form the basis for his relationship with God, with the hierarchy, and with all the Christian faithful. The chapter on priestly spirituality is a more practical exposition of the priest's life of prayer, ministry, relationship to the Word of God and the sacraments, celibacy, and obedience. The third chapter acknowledges the rapid rate of change in the modern world and calls for a spiritual, intellectual, and pastoral education that is continuous, systematic, and personal. In addition to suggesting practical means to achieve this goal, the Directory recognizes that responsibility for those programs belongs to the entire community and that the special circumstances of new priests and those of advanced age must be taken into account.

The Directory is related to the teaching of the Second Vatican Council and relies heavily on Pope John Paul II's apostolic exhortation *Pastores dabo vobis,* published after the eighth assembly of the Synod of Bishops.

Bibliography: D. GOERGEN, ed., *Being a Priest Today* (Collegeville, Minn. 1992). R. SCHWARTZ, *Servant Leaders and the People of God* (New York 1989).

[E. PFNAUSCH]

DIVES IN MISERICORDIA

Pope John Paul II's second encyclical was issued 30 November 1980. *Dives in misericordia* (DM), "Rich in Mercy," is properly read as a continuation of the first encyclical, *Redemptor Hominis* (RH). While RH is devoted to Jesus Christ as the one who "fully reveals man to himself," DM turns to Christ as the one who makes known the Father, who reveals to humans "the countenance of the 'Father of mercies and God of all comfort'" (DM 1). Christ is at once the New Adam and the icon of the Father, fully human and fully divine. The perspectives of "anthropocentrism" and "theocentrism" are not at all antithetical; rather, "the Church, following Christ, seeks to link them up in human history, in a deep and organic way" (DM 1). For John Paul this connection is "perhaps the most important" of the teachings of Vatican II. And because "in the present phase of the Church's history we put before ourselves as our primary task the implementation of the doctrine of the great Council" (DM 1), we readily see how RH and DM, standing together at the beginning of the pontificate, signal John Paul's intent to extend the reception of the council.

DM unfolds the revelation of divine mercy in salvation history through eight chapters, beginning with the biblical message of compassion and moving toward the mission of the contemporary Church to put mercy into practice. Chapter 4 is an extended reflection upon the parable of the prodigal son, and represents perhaps the symbolic heart of the text. The younger son "in a certain sense is the man of every period'' (DM 5), and the human father of the story of course reflects the divine Father, whose ''readiness to receive the prodigal children who return to His home'' is ''infinite'' and ''inexhaustible'' (DM 13). Mary the mother of Jesus represents a special biblical manifestation of divine mercy in action, as she sings in the Magnificat of God's mercy that is ''from generation to generation.'' These words of hers ''have a prophetic content that concerns not only the past of Israel but also the whole future of the People of God on earth'' (DM 10). Mary and the other figures of salvation history all point to Christ, who ''by becoming the incarnation of the love that is manifested with particular force with regard to the suffering, the unfortunate, and sinners, makes present and thus more fully reveals the Father, who is God 'rich in mercy''' (DM 3).

Following Christ, who taught, ''Blessed are the merciful, for they shall obtain mercy,'' the Church is called to show that humans not only receive and experience the mercy of God but are likewise to practice mercy toward others. It is not enough for personal and social relationships to be governed solely by the measure of justice; ''mercy becomes an indispensable element for shaping mutual relationships between people'' (DM 14). Only through the exchange of mercy and compassion can the essential value and dignity of the person be preserved and more deeply experienced. The very mission of the Church is to be an effective sign (''sacrament,'' according to Vatican II) in the world of the compassion and love of God the Father. ''The Church herself must be constantly guided by the full consciousness that in this work it is not permissible for her, for any reason, to withdraw into herself. The reason for her existence is, in fact, to reveal God, that Father who allows us to 'see' Him in Christ'' (DM 15).

Bibliography: For the text of *Dives in misericordia,* see: *Acta Apostolicae Sedis* 72 (1980) 1176–1232 (Latin); *Origins* 10, no. 26 (11 December 1980): 401, 403–416 (English); *The Pope Speaks* 26 (1981): 20–58 (English). For a commentary on *Dives in misericordia,* see: A. DULLES, *The Splendor of Faith: The Theological Vision of Pope John Paul II* (New York: Herder & Herder, 1999).

[M. PELZEL]

DIVINUS PERFECTIONIS MAGISTER

Apostolic constitution, ''On the New Legislation for the Causes of the Saints,'' issued by Pope John Paul II on 25 January 1983. With the publication of *Divinus perfectionis magister* a new era in the process of canonization was launched. In the light of modern media of communication and more scientific notions of historical research, John Paul II took up the task begun by Pope

Paul VI to simplify the process for canonization. DPM provides norms for the structure and operation of the Congregation for the Causes of Saints (3–12) as well as procedures for dealing with each cause (13–17).

The focus of previous legislation was on the initiative and process centered in Rome under the supervision of the Congregation for the Causes of Saints. The provisions of DPM outline both a diocesan phase and a Roman phase in any cause. The text emphasizes that, at least in the early stages of a cause, it is the responsibility of the bishop of the place where the candidate died to gather all pertinent historical information regarding the ''life, virtues or martyrdom and reputation of sanctity . . . as well as, if it be the case, the ancient cult of the Servant of God, whose canonization is sought'' (1). It is now the bishop's right to introduce such a cause without first seeking the permission of the Holy See. In fact, DPM allows the initiative for a cause for canonization to come from any member or group of the Catholic faithful. A cause is considered ''recent'' if the virtue or martyrdom of the Servant of God can be proved through eyewitness accounts. Causes in which the proofs are only from written sources are considered ''ancient.'' The work of gathering information and documentation is supervised by a diocesan tribunal and local experts in matters canonical, historical, and theological.

In DPM John Paul II required the Congregation for the Causes of Saints to draw up a set of norms that would address in greater detail the general direction of the apostolic constitution. Without these ''Norms to be Observed in Inquiries Made by Bishops in the Causes of Saints,'' DPM would be incomplete. Published on 7 February 1983, they provide a necessary road map for those involved in the complexities of a canonization process. The postulator—whether a cleric, religious, or lay person—is expected to ''conduct thoroughly'' the investigations into the candidate's life to ascertain his reputation for holiness and the importance of the cause for the pastoral good of the Church. In effect, the postulator serves as advocate for the cause in both the diocesan and Roman phases. All published biographies as well as the writings of the person must be collected and examined for theological soundness. In recent causes this is often a time-consuming task.

Once the diocesan phase is completed the cause is taken to Rome, where the congregation begins its own careful study of the gathered data and makes its own judgment to be submitted to the pope for his exclusive decision to beatify or canonize the candidate. The materials gathered in the ''acts'' of the diocesan process become the basis for writing the *positio* or detailed argument supporting the eventual beatification and canonization. Often running to several volumes, the *positio* must include a critical historical biography of the candidate, a detailed exposition of the spirituality of the Servant of God, and all relevant documentation needed to support the argument for canonization. This task is entrusted to a "relator" chosen from within the congregation. The relator studies the materials of the cause, provides theological and historical expertise, and collaborates with the postulator in producing the final draft of the *positio*.

The investigation into the required miracles, governed by DPM and the Norms of the congregation, follows the same basic process as that for the reputation for holiness. One miracle is required for beatification and another for canonization. Although treated in a separate process, the formalities and structures of both the diocesan and Roman phases are required for the miracles. Since the reported miracles in many recent causes are cures from life-threatening illnesses, the role of the medical consultants is important, and the norms reflect this more contemporary awareness. These experts are expected to make a judgment regarding any possible natural or scientific explanations for the apparent cure. Miraculous cures must be instantaneous and complete. The norms are careful to define the role and scope of the medical consultant. In the case of martyrdom no miracles are required.

Bibliography: For the Latin text of *Divinus perfectionis magister*, see; *Acta Apostolicae Sedis* 75 (1983): 349–55. For more information on the process of canonization, see; "Normae servandae in inquisitionibus ab episcopis faciendis in causis sanctorum," *Acta Apostolicae Sedis* 75 (1983): 396–403. J. SARNO, *New Laws for the Causes of Saints,* Congregation for the Causes of Saints (Rome 1983).

[GABRIEL B. O'DONNELL]

DOMINUM ET VIVIFICANTEM

Pope John Paul II's fifth encyclical, issued on 18 May 1986. *Dominum et vivificantem* (DV), "The Lord and Giver of Life," dealing with the Holy Spirit "in the Life of the Church and the World." The introduction makes clear that DV stands with the first two encyclicals of John Paul, *Redemptor hominis* (RH) and *Dives in misericordia* (DM) to form a textual triptych, with each document highlighting a specific person of the Trinity. After recalling the doxology of St. Paul, "The grace of our Lord Jesus Christ and the love of God and the fellowship of the Holy Spirit be with you all" (2 Cor 3:13), John Paul continues: "In a certain sense, my previous encyclicals *Redemptor hominis* and *Dives in misericordia* took their origin and inspiration from this exhortation. . . . From this exhortation now comes the present Encyclical on the Holy Spirit" (DV 2).

DV is closely linked and makes frequent reference to the Second Vatican Council: "The Encyclical has been drawn from the heart of the heritage of the Council. For the Conciliar texts, thanks to their teaching on the Church in herself and the Church in the world, move us to penetrate ever deeper into the Trinitarian mystery of God himself . . . to the Father, through Christ, in the Holy Spirit" (DV 2). Again, as with the previous, the impending approach of the third Christian millennium forms a crucial horizon within which the present reflection on the Holy Spirit takes place. Of special importance in this context is the role of the Spirit "as the one who points out the ways leading to the union of Christians" (DV 2); Christian ecumenism is an especially prominent dimension of the millennial commemoration.

The text of DV moves in three main parts: (1) "The Spirit of the Father and the Son, Given to the Church;" (2) "The Spirit Who Convinces the World Concerning Sin;" and (3) "The Spirit Who Gives Life." Four scenes from the "Upper Room" form the framework of the encyclical's theological vision. First, there is the farewell discourse of Jesus at his final meal with his disciples (John 14 17). In this scene "the highest point of the revelation of the Trinity is reached" (DV 9). Here Jesus begins to disclose the personal role that the Spirit will play in communicating the Gospel to the world: "All that the Father has is mine; therefore I said that he [the Holy Spirit] will take what is mine and declare it to you" (Jn 16:15). John Paul then makes the obvious point: "By the very fact of taking what is 'mine', he will draw from 'what is the Father's'" (DV 7).

The second Upper Room scene takes place on the evening of the first Easter Sunday, according to John (20:19–22). Jesus breathes on his disciples and says to them, "Receive the Holy Spirit." Here "there is fulfilled the principal prediction of the farewell discourse: the Risen Christ . . . 'brings' to the Apostles the Holy Spirit" (DV 24). The further giving of the Holy Spirit to the world takes place in the third Upper Room scene, on the day of Pentecost. "This event constitutes the definitive manifestation of what had already been accomplished in the same Upper Room on Easter Sunday" (DV 25). Thus the era of the Church begins, and the Holy Spirit is precisely the soul of this new body. The fourth evocation of the Upper Room concerns the Church's fidelity to its mission, which requires it always to be attentive to the circumstances of its beginning. "While it is an historical fact that the Church came forth from the Upper Room on the day of Pentecost, in a certain sense one can say that she has never left it. Spiritually the event of Pentecost does not belong only to the past; the Church is always in the Upper Room that she bears in her heart" (DV 66).

DV explores the "double rhythm" of salvation history, the "rhythm of the mission of the Son" and the "rhythm of the mission of the Holy Spirit," both sent into the world by the Father (DV 63). The articulation of this crucial principle of Trinitarian theology reflects a recovered attention to pneumatology, especially in the self-understanding of Western Christianity. The missions of the Son and the Spirit are intimately co-related; the Spirit's role is precisely to make the Son more fully known in the world. And the role of the Son, as RH and DM had already emphasized, is itself twofold: to reveal humans to themselves and to reveal God as the Father of mercy. The Spirit helps us to ponder the total gift that Christ made of himself for our sake; on this basis, then, people are called, with the help of the same Spirit, to find themselves fully through a sincere gift of self. This idea, often cited by John Paul from *Gaudium et spes,* "can be said to sum up the whole of Christian anthropology" (DV 60). The theme of gift, of mutual giving and receiving among persons, aptly sums up Christian anthropology precisely because it is also definitive of God's very life. "It can be said that in the Holy Spirit the intimate life of the Triune God becomes totally gift, an exchange of mutual love between the divine Persons and that through the Holy Spirit God exists in the mode of gift. It is the Holy Spirit who is the personal expression of this self-giving, of this being-love" (DV 10).

Bibliography: For the text of *Dominum et vivificantem,* see: *Acta Apostolicae Sedis* 78 (1986) 809–900 (Latin); *Origins* 16, no. 4 (12 June 1986): 77, 79–102 (English); *The Pope Speaks* 31 (1986): 199 263 (English). For a commentary on *Dominum et vivificantem,* see: A. DULLES, *The Splendor of Faith: The Theological Vision of Pope John Paul II* (New York: Herder & Herder, 1999).

[M. PELZEL]

ECCLESIA DEI

Ecclesia Dei is an Apostolic letter *motu proprio* of Pope John Paul II issued 2 July 1988 at St. Peter's, that establishes a commission of collaboration and makes an appeal for a wide application of previous directives to facilitate the ecclesial communion of the members and followers of the schismatic movement of Marcel Lefebvre. The letter describes Lefebvre's actions that led to his excommunication by the Church. The pope says that the schismatic act provides a moment "for profound reflection and for a renewed pledge of fidelity to Christ and his Church" (no.2). The document explains that the root of the schism is an "incomplete and contradictory" understanding of tradition. It is incomplete because it fails to take into account the living character of tradition and contradictory because it opposes the universal magisterium of the church exercised by the bishop of Rome together with the college of bishops (no. 4). The Holy Father calls on all Catholics to reflect on their own fidelity to the

Church's tradition and on bishops in particular to exercise vigilance "full of charity and firmness" to safeguard this fidelity (no. 5).

He calls for renewed commitment and study of the teachings of the Second Vatican Council, especially points of doctrine that "perhaps because they are new, have not yet been well understood by some sections of the Church" (no. 5). In a spirit of paternal care, he urges those who have aligned themselves with the schismatic movement of Lefebvre to fulfill the "grave duty of remaining united" to the pope "in the unity Catholic Church," renewing the warning that formal adherence to the movement incurs excommunication (cf. CIC 1364). The pope expresses sympathy for with those "Catholic faithful who feel attached to some previous liturgical and disciplinary forms of the Latin tradition" (no. 6). To facilitate the ecclesial communion of these faithful, the pope calls for "a wide and generous application" of the directives in *Quattor abhinc annos,* which was issued in 1984, and which allowed use of the 1962 typical edition of the Roman Missal, the so-called Tridentine Mass.

Bibliography: For the text of *Quattor abhinc annos,* see: *Acta Apostolicae Sedis,* 76 (1984): 1088–1089). For the text of *Ecclesia Dei,* see: *Acta Apostolicae Sedis,* 80 (1988): 1495–1498; *Origins* 18, no. 10 (4 August 1988).

[EDITORS]

ECCLESIA IN AFRICA

The post-synodal apostolic exhortation issued by Pope John Paul II on his visit to Yaoundé, Cameroon, 14 September 1995, responded to the Special Assembly for Africa of the Synod of Bishops held the previous year (10 April to 8 May 1994) in Rome. The lengthy text includes an introduction, seven chapters, and a conclusion. The introduction explains the purpose of the synodal assembly and the audience to whom the exhortation is addressed. The purpose was "to promote an organic pastoral solidarity within the entire African territory and nearby islands" (5). John Paul addresses the exhortation "in the first place to pastors and lay Catholics, and then to our brothers and sisters of other Christian confessions, to those who profess the great monotheistic religions, in particular the followers of African traditional religion, and to all people of good will who . . . have at heart Africa's spiritual and material development . . ." (7).

Chapter 1 speaks of the special assembly as "a providential event of grace." John Paul describes the preparations for the synod, including his many pastoral visits to thirty six countries of Africa and Madagascar, and the carefully planned Eucharistic liturgies. He thanks the "theologians, liturgists and experts in African chants and musical instruments [who] ensured, in keeping with my wishes, that these celebrations would have a distinctly African character" (24).

Chapter 2 is subdivided. First it reviews the history of evangelization in Africa; second, it lists problems that the Church faces; and third, it urges the formation of agents of evangelization. Present-day problems include the challenge of inculturation, divisions rooted in tribalism, the shortage of vocations to the priesthood and consecrated life, political instability, and a variety of social and political difficulties. The exhortation distinguishes three phases in the evangelization of Africa: (1) the apostolic origins of the Church and the second to fourth centuries when saints and scholars flourished in North Africa; (2) the fifteenth and sixteenth centuries when the Portugese explored the African coast and missionaries evangelized Sub- Saharan Africa; and (3) the beginning of "systematic evangelization" in the nineteenth century. The pope notes the emphasis that the synod put on the formation of the lay faithful, especially lay catechists, for the task of evangelization.

Chapter 3, "Evangelization and Inculturation," is the heart of the exhortation. It affirms that the new evangelization, centered on a transforming encounter with the living person of Christ, has as its purpose the transformation of humanity from within and making it new (56, 57). The exhortation cites the "urgent priority" that the synod gave inculturation, noting "it includes theology, liturgy, the Church's life and structures" (62). The synod acknowledged the Church as God's family is an expression "particularly appropriate for Africa" (63). It called for research into African culture, especially in matters concerning marriage, the veneration of ancestors, and the spirit world (64). John Paul affirmed the synod's commitment to dialogue first among Christians and then with Muslims and African traditional religion (65–67). Evangelization must address issues of justice and peace (68), and the Church exercises it prophetic role by being the "voice of the voiceless" (70).

The first section of chapter 4 reviews "present-day challenges" and themes that had been mentioned previously. The second section explains "why the synod considered the evangelization of the African family a major priority" (80). It deplored "those African customs and practices" that deprive women of their rights, and it speaks of the dignity and role of marriage (83).

Chapters 5, 6, and 7 expand on points that early chapters had mentioned in passing. Chapter 5 returns to the formation of agents of evangelization beginning with the Christian community as a whole and then singling out laity, catechists, the family, young people, religious, sem-

inarians, deacons, priests, and bishops. In a second section it reviews the "structures of evangelization" parishes, movements and associations, schools, universities, and the need for the Church in Africa to generate its own material and financial resources. Chapter 6 speaks of the church's witness to justice, peace, and social responsibility, especially with regard to administration of public affairs and the rule of law. Among "worrisome problems" it cites restoring hope to youth, the scourge of AIDS, refugees and displaced persons, international debt, and the dignity of African women. Another section discusses the use of mass media in the cause of evangelization. Chapter 7 exhorts "all the sons and daughters of Africa" to holiness and their call to witness to Christ throughout the world. Pope John Paul emphasizes the theme of solidarity and "the positive and moral value of the growing awareness of interdependence among individuals and nations" (138).

In conclusion the Holy Father thanks all who collaborated to make the Special Assembly of the Synod for Africa a success and ends with the text of the prayer to Mary, Mother of the Church, composed by the synodal bishops.

See Also: SYNOD OF BISHOPS SPECIAL ASSEMBLY FOR AFRICA

[MAURA BROWNE]

ECCLESIA IN AMERICA

On 22 January 1999, the Holy Father made an act of visible communion and solidarity with the whole of America, from the Caribbean to the continental South and North. He journeyed to the region's symbolic center, Mexico City, to share his written reflections on the special assembly for America of the Synod of Bishops, held in Rome, from 16 November to 8 December 1998. Titled *Ecclesia in America* (EAm), the post-synodal exhortation develops the assembly's considerations, incorporating almost all of the seventy-six propositions that were recommended by the voting participants. *Encounter with the Living Jesus Christ: Way to Conversion, Communion and Solidarity* (nos. 2, 3), like the assembly, is the thematic lens for the exhortation.

To deepen an encounter with Christ, the three axial sub-themes—conversion, communion, and solidarity— should not be understood in a linear progression. Subject matter treated under each theme is not exclusive to it alone. Instead, EAm situates the gifts and challenges of America into the fusion of an integral anthropology (nos. 19, 52, 54), a deeply scriptural Christology (nos. 8–12) and an underlying ecclesiology of communion tracing the

Mexico City Cathedral at night. (© Charles O'Rear/CORBIS)

Church as the incarnate mystery of the Triune God's life. Held together by the Spirit of the Risen Lord, the Church strives through ongoing conversion to exhibit her true character (nos. 9–10, 29, 33). Drawn into a deeper intra- and interecclesial communion, the whole People of God, with both catholic lungs and a deepening fellowship with the Orthodox and our Protestant brothers and sisters will sharpen the visibility of the Christian *oikoumene* (nos.17, 38, 49). This, in turn, encourages greater cooperation with other religious traditions, especially the elder brother of Christians, the Jewish people (nos. 50–51), and propels the Church in America to witness God's grace, sign and instrument of the world's sanctification (nos. 5–6, 29, 37).

Strengthening ecclesial communion in America is a chief goal. For this reason, all members of the Body of Christ should engage fully and actively in its "living and lasting center," the Eucharist (no. 35). Through ongoing conversion of heart realized in penance and reconciliation, laity and clergy alike, faithful to their particular vocations, grow into a more visibly dynamic communion with God and each other (nos. 36, 39, 42, 43, 44). With this in mind, the pope offers pointed reflection on the lay mission. Lauding their valuable contributions in the intr-

aecclesial realm, EAm expresses the hope of the synod to recognize some of these works as specific lay ministries, grounded in baptism and confirmation. Most specific to the lay mission and pressed deeply into the exhortation is the evangelization of the world: proclaim Christ to "the various sectors of family, social, professional, cultural and political life" through a moral vision based upon human dignity, solidarity and subsidiarity (nos. 44, 55, 66). To strengthen formation in this component of the new evangelization, the pope proposes a "Catechism of Catholic Social Doctrine" that would offer general norms encouraging localized application within diverse American contexts (no. 54).

Examining fundamental aspects of the Church's social doctrine and in the trajectory of Medellín, Puebla, and Santo Domingo, EAm reaffirms the preferential love for the poor (nos. 12, 18, 58). This is manifest in its invitation to conversion from aspects of economic and cultural globalization that inhibit integral human development (no. 55). The exhortation pays particular attention to fostering an economy that includes the participation of America's poor as subjects. Noteworthy, then, is the call for substantial reduction of external debt, concern with economic "neoliberalism" that is anthropologically reductionistic, and the condemnation of activities and lifestyles that corrupt, including the crippling drug problem (nos. 22, 56, 59, 60, 61). EAm also warns against a homogenization of culture through unbridled bursts of communicative technologies, discrimination against American indigenous cultures as well as Americans of African origin, and attitudes of resistance toward new migratory flows that fester in urbanization and the denial of cultures of origin (nos. 20, 21, 64, 65, 72).

EAm describes and prescribes a diversified Christian identity in America. It bespeaks the life witness of Christians yesterday giving prominence to America's beatified and canonized, like St. Rose of Lima and the martyrs (no.15, see note 35). Today, identity is shaped in part by cultural forms of popular religion (no.16), but threatened by proselytizing activities (no.73). It is visible in a growing respect for human rights, but blinded when a moral vision crumbles (no.19). In the Jubilee Year 2000 and beyond, the Church in America is invited to an examination of conscience so that the spiritual, cultural, social, and material diversity of America can be transformed into a richer *mestizo* of communion that evangelizes the region and beyond (no. 74). As the *mestiza* image of the Virgin at Tepayac announced Christ and evangelized America (no. 11), so America's *mestizaje* encounters Christ in a new evangelization.

Bibliography: For the text of *Ecclesia in America,* see: *Acta Apostolicae Sedis* 91 (1999): 737–815 (Spanish); *Origins* 28, no. 33 (4 Feb. 1999): 565, 567–592 (English); *The Pope Speaks* 44 (1999): 204–257 (English). For commentaries and summaries, see: *The Living Light* 35, no. 4 (Summer 1999). *Medellín:Theología y pastoral para América Latina* 25, no. 99 (September 1999).

[PAUL D. MINNIHAN]

ECCLESIA IN ASIA

The Special Assembly of the Synod of Bishops for Asia, held in Rome 18 April to 14 May 1998 reflected on: "Jesus Christ the Savior and His Mission of Love and Service in Asia: 'That they may have Life and have it abundantly' (Jn 19:10)." Pope John Paul II signed the postsynodal apostolic exhortation *Ecclesia in Asia* at the Sacred Heart Cathedral, New Delhi, 6 November 1999 in the presence of more than 300 Asian bishops and large congregation.

The 140-page document published in English, French, Portuguese, and Italian has an introduction, seven chapters, and a conclusion, with different topics subdivided into fifty-one articles. Chapter 1 describes the social, political, religious, cultural, and economic realities of Asia, concluding with the Holy Father's vision in *Redemptoris missio:* "God is opening before the Church

. . . a humanity more fully prepared for the sowing of the Gospel." "This," the Holy Father adds, "I see being fulfilled in Asia" (nos.5–9).

The central issue of *Ecclesia in Asia* is "the proclamation of Jesus Christ, true God and true man, the one and only Savior for all peoples" (no.10). Chapters 2 to 4 develop christological catechesis, insisting that there is "no true evangelization without the explicit proclamation of Jesus as Lord" (no.19). The saving action of the incarnate Word, Jesus originating "in the communion of the Godhead," invites all believers in him "to enter into intimate communion with the Trinity and with one another in the Trinity." In Jesus, through the power of the Spirit, we learn that God "is very near, indeed united to every person and all humanity" in every life's situation. Even those not explicitly accepting him as the Savior receive salvation from him through the Holy Spirit (see no. 14). Christianity offers "with loving respect and esteem for her listeners" and "for the action of the Spirit in man" (no.20) this message, "of incomparable comfort and hope for all believers" (see no. 12), and "ultimate hope and strength for the people of Asia in their struggles and uncertainties" (no. 13).

The catechesis continues with pneumatology, denouncing "the tendency to separate the activity" of the Spirit from that of Jesus. The Spirit is "not an alternative to Christ." His universal presence does not excuse proclaiming "Jesus Christ explicitly as the . . . only Savior" (see no. 16). Led by the Spirit, "the prime agent of evangelization" (no. 17), in her mission of service and love, the Church offers "an encounter between Jesus Christ and the peoples of Asia" (no. 18). She evangelizes because of "Christ's command," every person's "right to hear the Good News" (see no. 20), Asians' "intense yearning for God" (no. 9) and thirst "for the fullness of life" (no. 10), which Jesus alone can give abundantly.

But, "Asia's great religions deeply intertwined with cultural values and specific word views" (no.20), some with a "clearly soteriological character" (no.2) make his proclamation as the only Savior difficult. The great question is "*how* to share" this gift "containing all gifts" (no.19).There are signs of hope (see no. 9). The "innate spiritual insight and moral wisdom in the Asian soul . . . around which a growing sense of 'being Asian' is built . . . is best discovered and affirmed . . . in the spirit of complementarity and harmony." Through this door the Church can communicate the Gospel, being "faithful both to her own Tradition and to the Asian soul" (see no.6).

Accepting "the legitimate variety of approaches to the proclamation," the Synod Fathers noted that evangelization is "both rich and dynamic," having "various as-

Iglesia Ni Cristo Church in Manilla, Philippines. (© Catherine Karnow/CORBIS)

pects and elements . . .'' (see no. 23). The exhortation deals extensively on proclamation (nos. 19–20), inculturation (nos. 21–22), witness (nos. 23,42,49), communion (nos. 24–28), mission (nos. 24,29), ecumenical and interreligious dialogue (nos. 30–31), and integral human promotion (nos. 32–41), because these have a specific relevance in Asia. Stating that the Church ''must be open to the new and surprising ways in which the face of Jesus might be presented in Asia'' (no. 20), it gives some directives/guidelines to the evangelizers in Asia: bishops, clergy, religious, missionary societies, laity, family, youth, and social communicators (nos. 43–48).

John Paul II has also insisted in his exhortation that freedom of religion is a human rights issue and appeals to governments to treat it as such. The pope observes that in some places in Asia ''explicit proclamation is forbidden and religious freedom is denied or systematically restricted'' (no. 23). Christians are forced ''to live their faith in the midst of restrictions or even the total denial of freedom'' (no. 28). He enjoins Governments to ''guarantee religious freedom for all their citizens'' (no. 28), assure ''immunity from coercion'' (no. 23) in religious matters, and recognize ''the right to freedom of conscience and religion and the other basic human rights'' (no. 34).

Bibliography: CARDINAL PAUL SHAN, ''Presentation of Ecclesia in Asia,'' *Boletin Eclesiastico de Filipinas* 76, no. 816 (January-February 2000): 145–148. H. JAMES KROEGER, ''Introducing Ecclesial in Asia,'' *Vidyajyoti—Journal of Theological Reflection* 64, no. 1 (January 2000).

[MARIO SATURNINO DIAS]

ECONOMIC JUSTICE FOR ALL

The title of a pastoral letter on the U.S. economy published by the National Conference of Catholic Bishops, November 1986. After giving a brief summary of its five chapters, this report adds a word about the controversies evoked by the consultative process that shaped the letter.

Analysis. Chapter one presents the economy as a human creation which affects human life profoundly and is therefore an important moral issue. Christians are urged to overcome the split between faith and daily life ''which Vatican II counted among the more serious errors of the modern age'' [# 21]. Three questions dominate: What does the economy do *for* people? What does it do *to* people? How do people *participate* in it? The economy is to be evaluated according to its impact on

Demonstrators march in Washington, D.C. (Catholic News Service.)

human dignity in community. This chapter indicates a brief analysis of the roots of economic problems in technological development and capital mobility and points to underlying cultural causes of economic problems: social fragmentation rooted in individualism and resulting in the loss of a common moral vision.

For help in understanding the contemporary situation, the letter turns in chapter two to the religious insights gained during Israel's Babylonian Exile. It highlights the profound dignity of every human being, a dignity that is prior to race, nationality, gender, and achievement. It is universal and bestows an equal right on each person to the resources of the earth needed for human life with dignity in community. In reflecting on the Covenant, Israel experienced the call to justice: mutual respect and care for all, especially the poor.

Jesus' teaching reflected these same values and warned against the dangers of wealth, power, prestige (parable of the rich fool), and identified himself with the poor (parable of the Last Judgment), "to reject [the poor] is to reject God made manifest in history" [# 44]. Jesus calls all to the compassionate love shown by the good Samaritan. We can trust in God to provide economic security: Jesus' Resurrection shows that God's power is greater than even death. The early Christian community followed

Jesus' guidance by sharing their resources with the poor and working to change the institutions in society responsible for poverty.

Tradition has further developed the notion of justice. The usual language used today is that of human rights. The United States needs to develop a commitment to *economic rights* to balance its commitment to political rights. Biblical justice establishes four national priorities: (1) meeting the basic needs of the poor; (2) enabling participation of the marginalized; (3) investment of wealth, talent, energy to achieve these first two; and (4) evaluation of economic policies and work life in light of their impact on families. All of society, not just the government, is responsible for seeing that the demands of justice are met. Special guidelines are offered to working people and labor unions, owners and managers, and citizens and government.

Four specific areas are selected for consideration and policy proposals are developed for each in chapter three. *Unemployment*: The document calls for a new national commitment to full employment through public and private sector jobs programs and training programs, targeted especially on the hard to employ. *Poverty*: It calls the degree of poverty a social and moral scandal and calls for its eradication through employment and through tax and welfare reform. *Food and Agriculture*: It supports measures to halt the loss of family farms and to resist the growing concentration in the ownership of agricultural resources. *U.S. in the International Economy*: It calls for the U.S. to do far more to relieve the plight of poor nations and assist their development by demilitarizing and expanding its foreign aid, establishing freer and more just trade relations, forgiving the debt of the poorest nations and restructuring the debt of the rest on more lenient terms, and promoting private investment that is sensitive to the Third World nations' own development plans.

"A New American Experiment: Partnership for the Public Good" responds to the cultural analysis and is potentially the most revolutionary material in the letter. It calls for new forms of cooperation and collaboration in the work place and at the local, regional, national, and international levels: "planning" on a participatory, community-centered model.

In chapter five the U.S. church is called to conversion. "In worship and in deeds of justice, the church becomes a 'sacrament,' a visible sign of that unity in justice and peace that God wills for the whole of humanity" [# 331]. The bishops commit the church to become a *model* of the justice proposed in the letter through its commitment to education, its support of the family, its practices as an employer, investor, property owner, charitable donor, and agent for justice, as well as through its internal policies of participation and collaboration for all.

Development. The process for developing the letter was one of its most significant and controversial elements. In November 1980, the National Conference of Catholic Bishops commissioned a pastoral letter on the U.S. economy, appointing Archbishop Rembert Weakland, OSB, of Milwaukee to head the drafting committee. After four years of study, hearings, and internal debate, the committee issued a first draft in November 1984, just days after the national presidential election. They elicited criticism and suggestions from the church and the nation at large.

Newspaper and journal articles, academic conferences, diocesan offices, discussion groups, and interested individuals fed more than 10,000 pages of response to the drafting committee. After reviewing it, they published a revised second draft in October 1985, and launched the process of public dialogue anew. A third draft appeared in June 1986, which was amended and ratified by the bishops in November 1986, by a nearly unanimous vote.

Controversy. Some European critics complained that the widely participative process watered down the bishops' authority. Cardinal Ratzinger of the Congregation for the Doctrine of the Faith took another tack, claiming that the national conferences of bishops have no teaching authority at all. Led by Archbishop Weakland, the U.S. church replied that the process was grounded in a theology that recognizes the presence of the Holy Spirit in each person and accepts the responsibility to discern the guidance of the Spirit with the help of all. In drawing upon all the gifts and inspiration of the community, they argued, its authority is greatly enhanced.

Bibliography: NATIONAL CATHOLIC CONFERENCE OF BISHOPS, *Economic Justice for All: Pastoral Letter on Catholic Social Teaching and the U.S. Economy* (Wash., D.C. 1986). J. E. HUG, *For All the People* [Two Vital Resources on the Pastoral Letter on the Economy: A Pastoral Message on *Economic Justice for All* by the Catholic Bishops of the United States and A Summary of the Pastoral Letter by James E. Hug, SJ] (Wash., D.C. 1986). Lay Commission on Catholic Social Teaching and the U.S. Economy, *Toward the Future: Catholic Social Thought and the U.S. Economy: A Lay Letter* (New York 1984). M. J. SCHULTHEIS, et al., *Our Best Kept Secret: The Rich Heritage of Catholic Social Teaching,* rev. ed. (Wash., D.C. 1987).

[J. E. HUG]

ECUMENICAL DIRECTORY

The full title of the "Ecumenical Directory" is Directory for the Application of Principles and Norms on Ecumenism. It was approved by Pope John Paul II on 25 March 1993 and published on 8 June by the Pontifical Council for Promoting Christian Unity as a general executive decree of the universal Catholic Church. It supplants the Directory for the Application of the Decisions of the Second Vatican Council Concerning Ecumenical Matters, issued during the pontificate of Pope Paul VI.

Development of the Ecumenical Directory. When the archbishop of Rouen, J. M. Martin, presented the draft of the Decree on Ecumenism (*Unitatis redintegratio*) to the Second Vatican Council, he promised that it would be followed by a directory explaining in greater detail the application of its decisions. The Secretariat for Promoting Christian Unity, charged with the task of making good on this promise, produced the Directory in stages. In 1967 Pope Paul VI ordered the publication of Part I of the Directory, and in 1970 he approved Part II. The first called for setting up ecumenical commissions in Catholic dioceses and episcopal conferences. It addressed the validity of baptism conferred in other churches and ecclesial communities, the fostering of spiritual ecumenism, and the sharing of spiritual resources (prayer, worship, and sacraments) with other Christians. The second part addressed "Ecumenism in Higher Education" and, in a particular way, in theological faculties and colleges.

The publication of the new Code of Canon Law in 1983 prompted a revision and updating of the Directory. Addressing the Roman Curia in 1985, John Paul II said:

> Every particular church, every bishop, ought to have solicitude for unity and ought to promote the ecumenical movement. The new Code of Canon Law recently promulgated recalled this in a clearer than usual fashion, because it is a matter of Christ's will (Canon 755). But the church of Rome and its bishop have to attend to this care in a quite special way. . . . It is therefore useful that in the field of ecumenism we take a look at the path which we have so far covered in the direction of unity and draw from its enlivening spirit. Among the initiatives taken within the Catholic Church I recall first of all the Ecumenical Directory. . . . This directory will need to be progressively updated in coming months, account being taken of the new Code of Canon Law and the progress of the ecumenical movement which the directory is directly intended to serve.

Once begun, it became evident that a revision of the existing directory would not be enough. A new directory that would encompass a wider scope, be more specific and concrete, and recognize the significant diversity found among the particular churches was called for. The new directory had the same aim as its predecessor, namely, the advancement of Vatican II's ecumenical vision of the Church, but it was a difficult challenge. As John Paul II remarked "it is impossible to translate perfectly into canonical language the conciliar image of the Church" though that image must always be referred to as the "primary pattern" that canonical language ought to "express insofar as it can" (*Sacrae disciplinae leges,* 1983).

Outline of the Directory. The directory is addressed first to the bishops of the Catholic Church and through them, to all the faithful, and to members of other churches and ecclesial bodies who, "it is hoped," will find it useful. The first of its five parts reaffirms the commitment of the Catholic Church to ecumenism based on the principles of the Second Vatican Council, and explains that a real and certain communion bonds the Catholic Church with other Christian churches and ecclesial communities. It emphasizes the duty of all Christians to work and pray that division be healed and overcome. Part two describes the structures, beginning with the Pontifical Council for Promoting Christianity Unity, diocesan officers, and other personnel within the Catholic Church that are charged with promoting ecumenism. Part three deals with the aims and methods of inspiring Catholics, especially those engaged in pastoral work, with an ecumenical outlook. It identifies categories of people who are to be formed as well as theological faculties, catechetical institutes, and other centers which must accept the responsibility for this formation. Part four expands on the communion that exists among Christians on the basis of their common baptism. This section describes various ways that Christians share in prayer, worship, and other spiritual activities. Part four also incorporates new guidelines on mixed marriages. Part five speaks of various forms of ecumenical cooperation, dialogue and common witness, and the principles that should guide ecumenical activities. It singles out Bible study, the adoption of common liturgical texts, ecumenical cooperation in catechesis, collaborative research, and collaboration in social and cultural programs.

Pope John Paul II has cited the Directory for the Application of Principles and Norms on Ecumenism on several occasions. It is clear from his 1995 encyclical *Ut unum sint* that he sees the directory as providing both the inspiration and framework for ecumenism in the Catholic Church.

Bibliography: "Directory for the Application of the Decisions of the Second Vatican Council concerning Ecumenical Matters, Ad Totam Ecclesiam (14 May 1967) in Vatican Council II," *The Conciliar and Postconciliar Documents,* ed. A. FLANNERY, (Northport, N.Y. 1987), 483–501. Directory for the Application of Principles and Norms on Ecumenism, 25 March 1993 (Vatican City 1993). Also U.S. Catholic Conference Publishing Services (Washington, D.C. 1993); *Origins* 23:9 (29 July 1993): 129; 131–160; *L'Osservatore Romano* (16 June 1993): i-xvii. For the text of *Ut unum sint,* see *Acta Apostolica Sedis* 87 (1995): 921–982.

[J. F. HOTCHKIN]

ECUMENICAL FORMATION

In 1998 the Pontifical Council for Promoting Christian Unity published *The Ecumenical Dimension in the Formation of Pastoral Workers.* It was intended to amplify chapter 3 of the 1993 *Directory for the Application of Principles and Norms on Ecumenism.* The text is directed to all in church leadership: "the clergy, members of institutes of consecrated life and societies of apostolic life, catechists and others formally involved in religious education, as well as leaders in new movements and ecclesial communities" (no. 3). This formation is to begin early in training programs, with a required course, and continued later with more specialized presentations. It is to be multi-leveled, adapted to the specific situation, and include spiritual, pastoral, ethical, and doctrinal formation (nos. 6–8).

The study document is divided into two parts. The first includes the elements, methodology, and practical recommendations for all areas of theological formation. The first key element to be covered is "interpretation," which touches both on the understanding of the deposit of faith and the opportunity to "understand each other and to explain [the other's] positions to each other . . . to determine whether different theological formulations are complementary rather than contradictory and so develop mutually acceptable and transparent expressions of faith" (no. 11). The second element that must permeate all formation is the "hierarchy of truths." Finally, the text emphasizes the importance of presenting the results of the dialogue and contributing to their reception so that these new insights can "enter into the life of the church, renewing in a certain way that which fosters reconciliation with other churches and ecclesial communities" (no. 13). The practical part of this first section enumerates the importance of: *(a)* integrating ecumenical dimensions in all courses, *(b)* providing for student participation, *(c)* developing interdisciplinary collaboration, *(d)* collaborating with teachers from other churches, and *(e)* working with local, diocesan, and parish priorities.

The second section provides detailed suggestions for formation programs. The introduction will focus on Catholic commitments as outlined in the directory, the role of ecumenical dialogue, and particular current and local ecumenical issues. Special emphasis is to be given to: *(a)* biblical foundations, *(b)* catholicity in time and space, *(c)* doctrinal basis of ecumenism, *(d)* history of ecumenism, *(e)* purpose and method of ecumenism, *(f)* spiritual ecumenism, *(g)* other churches and ecclesial communities, *(h)* principal areas for further dialogue, *(i)* specific ecumenical issues, *(j)* ecumenism and mission, and *(k)* contemporary challenges for ecumenism. The text ends with concrete recommendations and resources.

Bibliography: "The Ecumenical Dimension in the Formation of Pastoral Workers," *Origins* 27, no. 39 (19 March 1998): 653–651.

[J. GROS]

ESPÉRANCE NOUVELLE POUR LE LIBAN, UNE

Post-synodal apostolic exhortation, "A New Hope for Lebanon," issued by Pope John Paul II, 10 May 1997, during an historic visit to Lebanon. The Special Assembly for Lebanon of the Synod of Bishops was convoked by the pope in 1995 so that the Eastern Catholic churches of Lebanon might seek renewal and develop principles and guidelines for cooperation among themselves, between themselves and the Orthodox churches, and between Christians and Muslims. The exhortation incorporates the ideas put forth at the synod and the proposals presented to the Holy Father by the synodal participants at the end of the meeting.

The pope reiterates the theme of the synod: "Christ is our hope. Renewed in his Spirit, in solidarity, we witness his love." The exhortation begins by delineating the actual situation of the church in Lebanon. The Catholic Church is one and multiple at the same time, with an overlapping of patriarchal churches on the same territory. The assembly recommended a "new mentality" which rather than affirming differences would stress unity while respecting diversity. The Holy Father also takes note of the difficulties that have sometimes existed between Catholics and Orthodox, as well as the misunderstandings, unhappy memories, and prejudices that have sometimes colored relations between Catholics and Muslims.

The exhortation declares that starting point for renewal is in recalling that the Church is a mystery founded on Christ who is her hope and is animated by the Holy Spirit. The Church of Lebanon is to rejuvenate itself in the light of the person, life, and teaching of Christ. The synod stressed the necessity for the churches of Antioch to recover their common tradition as a basis for renewal, for communion among themselves, for ecumenical dialogue, and for their mission. It called for research, translations, and teachings faithful to the ancient sources. It also recognized the central place that the liturgy occupies in the life and perseverance of the Eastern churches. The exhortation calls for a broader role for the laity in the church and in the world, adding that the laity should be engaged in intellectual research and study, "in order that a veritable Christian culture be developed in the Arab world."

Special concern is shown regarding the state of the family in Lebanon. The present harsh economic situation has caused families to be separated as fathers or children have migrated in search of work. Family life is also being undermined by a false sense of individual autonomy. The pope calls for spiritual, moral, and material support of future couples and families. Women should be given their

proper role in the different structures of the church and in all areas of society. Youth are called to be agents of a "new evangelization."

In the search for unity, patriarchal churches are challenged to live in communion with each other and to act with co-responsibility. The synod urged the churches to pass from "a confessional mentality to a sense of authentic Church." It called upon the Assembly of Catholic Patriarchs and Bishops of Lebanon to elaborate a pastoral plan for acting conjointly wherever possible in the mission of their various churches. The Catholic Church of Lebanon should also reinforce fraternal ties with Christians of the Near and Middle East, and especially with those in Iran, Sudan, and North Africa, who are sometimes ignored. The quest for union includes a call for closer relations and mutual support between the different patriarchates in Lebanon and their corresponding communities living outside the patriarchates.

The pope notes the progress that has occurred in the dialogue with the Orthodox churches and the different theological accords that have been signed. With the synodal assembly he believes that a return to the sources and rediscovering the Antiochene tradition, which is common to a number of Catholic and Orthodox patriarchal churches, will be a productive means in the search for unity. The Council of Churches of the Middle East has become a good vehicle for ecumenical dialogue and for working towards an agreement on the date of the celebration of Easter and a common Arabic text of the Lord's Prayer and the Creed.

The pope encourages a true dialogue between believers of the great monotheist religions, conducted with mutual esteem, in order to protect and promote social justice, moral values, peace, and liberty. Lebanese are called to pardon one another and to change their mentalities so as to develop fraternity and solidarity for the reconstruction of a convivial society. Islamic-Christian dialogue should take place on many levels both in the civil sphere of everyday life and work and in the sphere of religion and moral values. Christians and Muslims should live in a spirit of openness and collaboration in a pluralistic society.

The Church is also called to the service of society. With the nation of Lebanon undergoing economic difficulties as a result of the war, the Church must especially help the poor, the marginalized, and the physically and mentally handicapped. The Church must strive to insure freedom of education and the fundamental rights of the human person in society according to the principles of equity, equality, and justice.

In his conclusion, the pope notes that because Lebanon is composed of many communities, it can be an ex-

The Cathedral of St. Sophia at Kiev, Ukraine. (Archive Photos. Reproduced by Permission)

ample of how people of different cultures and religions can live together on the same soil, and build a nation of dialogue and conviviality, while cooperating for the common good.

Bibliography: For the French text of *Une Espérance nouvelle pour le Liban,* see: *Acta Apostolicae Sedis* 89 (1997): 313–416.

[SEELY BEGGIANI]

EUNTES IN MUNDUM

Apostolic epistle of Pope John Paul II, issued 25 January 1988, commemorating the millennium of Christianity in the Russian lands. The epistle, divided into six sections, celebrates the incorporation of the East Slavic peoples—Russian, Ukrainian, and Belorussian—by baptism into the Body of Christ.

The first section of the epistle is an encomium on baptism. Using the texts from the Byzantine blessing of the baptismal water, the pope discusses the wonders of the great mystery of the baptism of Kievan Rus', the ancestor state of these modern Russian lands. He meditates on the depth of the sanctifying power which continues in these lands.

The epistle continues at length retelling how the work of Sts. Cyril and Methodius was necessary to prepare the way so that Sts. Olga and Vladimir could bring about the baptism of the people of Rus'. This all occurred in the "fullness of time" at the end of the first millennium when the Church was undivided.

The baptism of Rus' is the beginning of the Byzantine-Slav form of Christianity which in turn gives birth to the Byzantine-Slav culture. The devotion to the Passionbearers, the devotion to the mystery of the "kenosis" of Jesus, the influence of monasticism, and the art and architecture that are both part of and result of this culture are duly noted.

The pope pleads for the restoration of communion between the Orthodox and Catholic Churches. He notes that there are both Catholic and Orthodox heirs of the baptism of Kievan Rus' and he discusses the concept of sister churches and the effects of the baptismal incorporation into the Body of Christ. The epistle notes that although communion was broken between the Orthodox and Catholic Churches both Churches preserved "fundamentally intact" the deposit of the apostolic faith.

The epistle returns to the sainted brothers, Cyril and Methodius, and their mission to the Slavs. The pope notes that in 1980 he proclaimed them as patrons of Europe and that Christianity is the foundation of European peace and unity.

The final section of the epistle expresses the joy with which the Roman Church celebrates this millennium. It notes that this is the special celebration of the Russian Orthodox Church centered in Moscow and joyfully calls this Church "Sister Church" and sends the "Kiss of Peace." The pope invokes the Mother of God and cites famous icon "Znamenie" for the salvation of all Christians. He asks that we all look to her as our common Mother. He concludes with a prayer to the Trinity that the gospel and the Cross, the Resurrection and Pentecost may remain "the way, the truth, and the life" for all succeeding generations.

Bibliography: For the text of *Euntes in mundum,* see: *Acta Apostolicae Sedis* 80 (1988): 935–956 (Latin); *Origins* 17, (1988): 709–718 (English); *The Pope Speaks* 33 (1988): 244–256 (English).

[R. BRUCE MILLER]

EVANGELIUM VITAE

Pope John Paul II's eleventh encyclical letter, "The Gospel of Life," issued on the feast of the Annunciation, 25 March 1995. In 1991 an extraordinary consistory of the college of cardinals met to discuss "threats to human life in our day." The cardinals asked the pope to affirm the "value of human life and its inviolability" with the authority of the Successor of Peter. To this end, the Holy Father wrote a personal letter to each bishop, asking him to cooperate in the development of this encyclical. *Evangelium vitae* appeals to "each and every person, in the name of God: respect, protect, love and serve life, every human life" (5).

The encyclical unfolds in four chapters. Chapter one, "Present-Day Threats to Human Life," is an indictment of the growing "culture of death." By applying the story of Cain and Abel to the present-day situation, the pope shows that the fratricidal urge to take the lives of others lies at the heart of abortion and euthanasia, and of other deadly trends, such as the arms race. He shows how the exaggerated and even perverse claims of freedom from constraints in these areas are identical with Cain's self-serving question, "Am I my brother's keeper?" Underlying these claims is a mentality that "carries the concept of subjectivity to an extreme": the self no longer recognizes the equal rights of other selves, especially those less able to defend themselves. The state, even in democratic countries, risks being subverted by such claims and becoming the tool of the strong, to be used against the weak.

The "sense of God" is diminishing, along with the sense of human solidarity. The result is a "practical materialism," in which suffering has no value. What is needed is a "civilization of love and life," which cannot exist without self-sacrifice. The Church summons all people to "choose to be unconditionally pro-life," in the name of the Risen Christ, whose "blood speaks more eloquently than that of Abel."

Chapter two, "The Christian Message Concerning Life," is a meditation on the proclamation that in Jesus Christ, good is powerful enough to triumph over evil. His death, freely accepted, resulted in new life for himself and for those who believe in him. The biblical teaching on life, from the creation of the world through the Resurrection of Jesus Christ, reveals its triumphant value, without diminishing the central Christian irony that "life finds its center, its meaning and its fulfillment when it is given up."

Chapter three, "God's Holy Law," is a reflection on the Fifth Commandment, especially as it regards the death penalty, abortion, and euthanasia. The pope sets out the limits of self-defense for individuals and the state and questions the use of the death penalty: punishment "ought not go to the extreme of executing the offender except in cases of absolute necessity: in other words, when it would not be possible otherwise to defend society. Today, however, as a result of steady improvements in the organization of the penal system, such cases are very rare, if not practically non-existent." If such is the case with regard to the guilty, how much more care should be taken to protect the lives of the innocent? By "the authority which Christ conferred upon Peter and his Successors, and in communion with the Bishops of the Catholic Church, I confirm that the direct and voluntary killing of an innocent human being is always gravely immoral." The acceptance of abortion, in many areas, "in the popular mind, in behavior and even in law itself," is a "telling sign of an extremely dangerous crisis in the moral sense, which is becoming more and more incapable of distinguishing between good and evil." Considering it more necessary than ever to "to call things by their proper names," the pope, using the words of *Gaudium et spes* 51, calls abortion and infanticide "unspeakable crimes." He then reflects in some detail on the innocent victim of abortion, the child, already conceived and genetically distinct and whole. He also considers those involved in the decision to terminate the child's life, including the mother, father, doctor, nurses, and those legislatures that have legalized this "unspeakable crime" in many countries. At the other end of life's spectrum lies the question of euthanasia, "an action or omission which of itself and by intention causes death, with the purpose of eliminating all suffering." The pope condemns euthanasia as "senseless and inhumane," although it is often presented as "logical and humane." Another symptom of the culture of death, euthanasia is "a grave violation of the law of God." At the same time, the pope upholds the Church's traditional teaching that one may decide to forego "aggressive medical treatment" (extraordinary means) that "would only secure a precarious and burdensome prolongation of life," which he has elsewhere called a "prolongation of dying."

Chapter four, "For a New Culture of Human Life," is an outline of the "culture of life" based on Matthew 25: "Whatever you did for one of these least brothers of mine, you did for me." It outlines how the People of God can become a "people of life": by proclaiming, celebrating, and serving the gospel of life, by making Christian families "sanctuaries of life," and by bringing about a "transformation of culture." Such a transformation calls for a "general mobilization of consciences and a united ethical effort to activate a great campaign in support of life." This gospel of life is for the whole human family; Mary and the Church are revealed as "mothers," that is, bearers of life; and although the forces of evil may menace life, the Resurrection of Jesus Christ means that, ultimately, "death shall be no more."

Bibliography: For the text of *Evangelium vitae,* see: *Acta Apostolicae Sedis* 87 (1995): 401–522 (Latin); *Origins* 24, no. 42 (6 April 1995): 689–727 (English); *The Pope Speaks* 40 (1995): 199–281 (English). For a commentary, see: WM. KEVIN WILDES and ALAN C. MITCHELL, eds., *Choosing Life: A Dialogue on Evangelium Vitae* (Washington, D.C. : Georgetown University Press, 1997).

[DOUGLAS CLARK]

EX CORDE ECCLESIAE

Apostolic constitution issued on 15 August 1990 by John Paul II; intended to supplement the apostolic constitution on ecclesiastical faculties and universities, *Sapientia Christiana* (1979), by providing for non-ecclesiastical universities and other Catholic institutions of higher learning a description of their nature and purpose and general norms to govern their activities.

After an introduction (nos. 1–11), the text is divided into two parts. The first, "Identity and Mission" (nos. 12–49) briefly describes the nature of a university and locates Catholic identity in the Christian inspiration of individuals and the whole community, "reflection in the light of the Catholic faith upon the growing treasury of human knowledge, to which it seeks to contribute by its own research," "fidelity to the Christian message as it comes to us through the Church," and an institutional commitment to the service both of the People of God and of the whole human family (no. 13). Research undertaken at a

Catholic university should be characterized by the search for the integration of knowledge, a dialogue between faith and reason, ethical concern, and a theological perspective (nos. 15–20).

The next sections discuss the university community—teachers, students, and administrators (nos. 21–26)—and the university's place and role in the Church, both universal and local, and the responsibility of bishops to promote and assist in the preservation and strengthening of Catholic identity, with due regard to the autonomy of the sciences, including in theology, and to academic freedom (nos. 27–29).

The mission of the Catholic university is described, first, in terms of its service to Church (no. 31) and to society (nos. 32–37). For the latter the emphasis falls on the university's becoming an "instrument of cultural progress," bringing to bear Christian "ethical and religious principles," promoting social justice, and encouraging interdisciplinary research projects. The Catholic university should also be a place in which pastoral ministry assists an integration of faith and life, demonstrating this by opportunities for community worship and concern for the poor and those suffering injustice (nos. 38–42). The institution should promote the dialogue between the Gospel and culture, with special reference to local cultures and contemporary problems. It should in particular promote a dialogue between Christian thought and the modern sciences. It should encourage and contribute to ecumenical dialogue (nos. 43–47). In all these ways the Catholic university will make an indispensable contribution to the Church's primary task of evangelization (nos. 48, 49).

The second part of the document is devoted to eleven general norms to supplement other ecclesiastical legislation. Article 1 requires that they be applied locally and regionally "taking into account the statutes of each university or institute and, as far as possible and appropriate, civil law." The general norms and local or regional applications to be incorporated into governing documents and university statutes are, as necessary, to be brought into conformity with them. Article 2 legislates for the Catholic identity, which is to be made known in a public document and to be promoted by the influence of Catholic teaching and discipline over all university activities, with due regard taken for the freedom of conscience of each person and for the autonomy and freedom of the various disciplines. Article 3 lists three different ways in which a Catholic university may be established: by the Holy See, an episcopal conference, or a local bishop; by a religious institute or other public juridical person; by other ecclesiastical or lay people. Article 4 entrusts the primary responsibility for maintaining and strengthening Catholic identity to the university itself and its officials. All teachers and administrators are to be informed about this Catholic identity and expected to promote or at least respect it in ways appropriate to the different disciplines. Catholic teachers, particularly in theology, are to be faithful to Catholic doctrine and morals, and others are to respect them; non-Catholic teachers and students are to recognize and respect Catholic identity, and non-Catholic teachers are not to constitute a majority within the institution; education of all students is to include a formation in ethical and religious principles and courses in Catholic doctrine are to be made available.

Article 4 requires that the university remain in communion with the universal Church and with the local Church; bishops are to promote the good of the institution and have a right and duty to supervise the preservation and strengthening of their Catholic identity; the institution is to make periodical reports to the competent church authority on the university and its activities. Article 6 makes provisions for the pastoral ministry at the institution. Article 7 encourages cooperation among Catholic universities and between them and the programs of governments and other national and international organizations on behalf of justice, development, and progress. Articles 8 to 11 provide transitional norms for the application of these norms. The bishops of the United States in November 1999 authorized a set of norms for the application of *Ex corde ecclesiae* and sent these to Rome for approval.

Bibliography: For the text of *Ex corde ecclesiae*, see: *Acta Apostolicae Sedis* 83 (1991): 249–339 (Latin); *Origins* 20, no. 17 (4 October 1990) (English); *The Pope Speaks* 36 (1991): 21–41 (English).

[JOSEPH A. KOMONCHAK]

FAMILIARIS CONSORTIO

Apostolic exhortation of Pope John Paul II, "On the Family," issued 22 November 1981, following the fifth general assembly of the Synod of Bishops (26 September–25 October 1980), whose theme was "The Role of the Christian Family in the Modern World." The text comprises an introduction, a conclusion, and four main sections: "Bright Spots and Shadows for the Family Today" (4–10); "The Plan of God for Marriage and the Family" (11–16); "The Role of the Christian Family" (17–64); and "Pastoral Care of the Family" (65–84). To fulfill its task of serving marriage and the family, the church "ought to apply herself to understanding the situations within which marriage and the family are lived today" (4). The pope calls the 1980 synod a sign of the church's profound interest in the family (2), adding that

in this exhortation he serves as "a spokesman before humanity of the church's lively care for the family." He asks that pastoral care for the family be strengthened and developed, and treated "as a real matter of priority" (65).

The Christian family is a domestic church, "a living image and historical representation of the mystery of the church" (49). This "small-scale church," like the "large-scale church," should serve as "a sign of unity for the world," thus exercising "its prophetic role by bearing witness to the kingdom and peace of Christ" (48). Like the larger church, the domestic church needs constantly to be evangelized (51). Not closed in upon itself, "the family is by nature and vocation open to other families and to society, and undertakes its social role" (42). A fourteen-point charter of family rights (46) is included in the exhortation. They range from the family's right to exist and to progress to its right to raise children in accord with its religious and cultural values, from the right to suitable housing to the "right of the elderly to a worthy life and a worthy death," and the right "to emigrate as a family in search of a better life."

God's plan for marriage and the family is viewed here in the context of love. Created in God's image, the humanity of man and woman is inscribed with "the vocation, and thus the capacity and responsibility, of love" (11). In light of this principle, marriage and the body are envisioned in positive terms as good, as is the sexuality "by means of which man and woman give themselves to one another through the acts which are proper and exclusive to spouses." This sexuality is "realized in a truly human way only if it is an integral part of the love by which a man and a woman commit themselves totally to one another until death." Speaking of the human body, the pope insists that "man is called to love in his unified totality" as both spirit and body. "Love includes the human body, and the body is made a sharer in spiritual love." The total physical self-giving of spouses must be "the sign and fruit of a total personal self-giving in which the whole person, including the temporal dimension, is present" (11).

The sacramental marriage of the baptized is an "intimate community of conjugal life and love, founded by the Creator" (13). However, conjugal love "does not end with the couple"; it makes them capable of cooperating with God in "giving life to a new human person." Children are a reflection of the couple's love, "a permanent sign of conjugal unity" (14).

The teaching of Pope Paul VI's *Humanae vitae* against contraception is reiterated in the exhortation. Contraception overlays the spouses' total self-giving with "an objectively contradictory language"—that of "not giving oneself totally to the other." In this matter the church is both mother and teacher: remaining close to couples "who find themselves in difficulty over this important point of the moral life," but never ceasing "to exhort and encourage all to resolve whatever conjugal difficulties may arise" (32). The pope calls for "a more decisive and wide-ranging extension" of research into "the rhythms of women's fertility" as this relates to "lawful birth regulation" viewed in the context of respect for the conjugal act's "structure and finalities." This implies a greater effort "to make the natural methods of regulating fertility known, respected and applied" (35).

The exhortation's third part, on the role of the Christian family, is its longest. It recalls that the 1980 synod emphasized four general tasks for the family: "forming a community of persons; serving life; participating in the development of society; sharing in the life and mission of the church" (17).

A discussion of "the equal dignity and responsibility of women with men" is included in the third part (22). There is no doubt that this equality "fully justifies women's access to public functions." But this point must be combined harmoniously with a clear recognition of the value of women's "maternal and family role, by comparison with all other public roles and all other professions." While duly respecting women's and men's different vocations, the church in its own life must "promote as far as possible their equality of rights and dignity" (23). Men's roles, children's rights, the elderly, sex education, family prayer, liturgical prayer and other matters are among other matters discussed in part 3.

The exhortation speaks at length about the need for marriage preparation. Attention also is given in part 4 to the needs of couples in mixed marriages and to the ecumenical importance of these marriages (78). Trial marriages (80), de facto free unions ("unions without any publicly recognized institutional bond, either civil or religious") (81), and the situation of Catholics in civil marriages (82) are among other concerns discussed here. The pope takes care to distinguish the situation of divorced people who have not remarried from that of divorced persons who have remarried. The church must offer the former "continual love and assistance without there being any obstacle to admission to the sacraments" (83).

The discussion of "those who have been previously bound by sacramental marriage and who have attempted a second marriage" has been of special interest to theologians. The church should untiringly endeavor to put the "means of salvation" at the disposal of these divorced-remarried couples. The pope points to "a difference between those who have sincerely tried to save their first marriage and have been unjustly abandoned, and those who through their own grave fault have destroyed a canonically valid marriage." He notes also that some enter "a second union for the sake of the children's upbringing" and sometimes are "subjectively certain in conscience that their previous and irreparably destroyed marriage had never been valid." He reaffirms the practice of not admitting divorced people who have remarried without an annulment to Eucharistic communion. However, the church "shows motherly concern for these children of hers, especially those who through no fault of their own have been abandoned by their legitimate partner."

Bibliography: For the text of *Familiaris Consortio*, see: *Acta Apostolicae Sedis* 74 (1982): 81–191 (Latin); *Origins* 11, nos. 28–29 (24 Dec 1981): 437–468 (English); *The Pope Speaks* 27 (1982): 1–77 (English).

[DAVID GIBSON]

FIDEI DEPOSITUM

This apostolic constitution was issued by Pope John Paul II on the occasion of the publication of the *Catechism of the Catholic Church,* 11 October 1992. He begins by reminding the reader that the Lord entrusted to his Church the mission of guarding the deposit of faith ("fidei depositum").

Recognizing that the Second Vatican Council has continued to inspire the Church's life, John Paul II convoked an extraordinary assembly of the Synod of Bishops in January of 1985, to mark the 20th anniversary of the close of the council. This synod met not only to celebrate the graces and fruits of Vatican II, but also to study its teachings and promote knowledge and application of them. During this gathering, the synod Fathers expressed a desire for a compendium or catechism regarding both faith and morals which could be used as a point of reference. After the synod ended, the Holy Father responded positively to the request by initiating the process which resulted in the *Catechism of the Catholic Church.* The Holy Father is certain that, along with the renewal of the liturgy and the new codification of canon law of the Latin Church and of the Oriental Churches, this catechism will make a very important contribution to the work of renewing the whole life of the Church.

The apostolic constitution has three main parts. The first describes "The Process and Spirit of Drafting the Text" of the catechism, which began in 1986 and lasted six years. The Pope established a commission of twelve cardinals, chaired by Cardinal Joseph Ratzinger, to prepare a draft. This commission was aided by an editorial committee of seven diocesan bishops. The process involved consultation with numerous theologians, exegetes, and catechists as well as all the bishops of the world. Because of the wide consultation, the catechism that resulted received broad favorable acceptance and stands as a reflection of the collegial nature of the episcopate and the Church's catholicity.

The second part, "Arrangement of the Material," outlines the contents and explains how the four parts relate to one another. The catechism was created to present faithfully and systematically the teaching of Sacred Scripture, the living Tradition in the Church, and the authentic magisterium. It also contains much of the spiritual heritage that comes to us from the Fathers, Doctors, and saints of the Church. Thus, the catechism can be said to contain both the old and the new: the old traditional teachings of the Church presented in a new way in order to respond to the questions of the modern age.

The first part of the catechism, on the Creed, focuses on the Christian mystery as the object of faith. The second part, which deals with the sacred liturgy, explains how faith is celebrated and communicated in liturgical actions. The third and fourth parts, on the Christian way of life and Christian prayer, explain how the Christian faith also enlightens and sustains believers in their actions, and also is the basis for prayer.

The third section of *Fidei depositum* explains "The Doctrinal Value of the Text" and its purpose. The Pope declared that this catechism, as a statement of the Church's faith and catholic doctrine, is to be a sure norm for teaching the faith. He gave it to the Church's pastors and the Christian people as a sure and authentic reference for teaching the catholic doctrine and also for preparing local catechisms. The Holy Father stresses that the *Catechism of the Catholic Church* is not meant to replace local catechisms, but to encourage and assist in the writing of new local catechisms. In addition the *Catechism* is a resource for "the faithful who wish to deepen their knowledge" and those who, engaged in ecumenical work, want to be informed about the teaching of the Catholic Church.

The Holy Father closes the apostolic constitution by calling upon the intercession of the Blessed Virgin Mary, as Mother of the Word Incarnate and Mother of the Church. He asks Mary to support with her powerful intercession the catechetical work of the entire Church on every level, especially now that the Church is called to a new effort of evangelization.

Bibliography: For the text of the *Fidei depositum,* see: *Acta Apostolicae Sedis* 86 (1994): 113–118 (Latin); *Origins* 22, no. 31 (14 Jan 1993): 525, 527–529 (English).

[D. KUTYS]

FIDES ET RATIO

Pope John Paul II's thirteenth encyclical, "Faith and Reason," issued on the feast of the Triumph of the Cross (14 September 1998). Addressed to the world's bishops, it is concerned with the relation between faith and reason, especially faith and philosophy in the contemporary world. It comprises an introduction, seven chapters, and a conclusion.

In the introduction (1–6), the pope notes that both Eastern and Western thought have asked the fundamental questions of human existence. In the West, the questions have been the special focus of philosophy, which uses reason to search for ultimate truth. Modern philosophy, however, has been so absorbed in the study of human subjectivity that it has neglected the search for transcendent truth or become skeptical of its attainability. This is a matter of concern to the Church, which as the bearer of the revelation of truth in Jesus Christ, has a special mission of service (*diakonia*) of the truth.

Chapter 1 (7–15) considers revelation, basing its treatment on *Dei Filius* of Vatican I and *Dei verbum* of Vatican II. God's revelation, known through faith, is distinct from and surpasses what reason can know. It is "immersed in time and history" through Jesus Christ, the incarnate Word of God. Only in Christ is the ultimate truth about human existence to be found. Revelation does not disable reason but drives it to extend its knowledge as far as possible. Christian revelation "summons human beings to be open to the transcendent, while respecting both their autonomy as creatures and their freedom" (15).

Chapter 2, "*Credo ut intellegam* [I believe so that I might understand]" (16–23), considers biblical teaching on faith and reason. Biblical texts reflect a "conviction that there is a profound and indissoluble unity between the knowledge of reason and the knowledge of faith" (16). The Old Testament writers understood the use of applying finite reason within the context of the human relation to the mystery of God. Saint Paul holds that reason can know God, but that this capacity has been damaged by human disobedience to God. The crucifixion of Christ challenges our habitual ways of thinking and overcomes any attempt to construct an account of the meaning of existence in purely human terms.

Chapter 3, "*Intellego ut credam* [I understand so that I might believe]" (24–35), speaks of the human search for truth, which is based ultimately in the human heart's desire for God. "One may define the human being . . . as the one who seeks the truth" (28), in particular, the truth about the meaning of life and death. The search for truth is not solitary but immerses us in communities and traditions. Most of what we know, we do not experience directly but believe on the testimony of others. The search for truth requires "trusting dialogue and sincere friendship"; "a climate of suspicion and distrust" is destructive of it. Christian faith meets the human search, offering both "the concrete possibility of reaching the goal" and "a person to whom they might entrust themselves" (33).

Chapter 4 (36–48) surveys the history of the relationship of Christian faith with philosophy. The early apologists and church fathers used philosophy to express and defend Christian faith; at the same time they contributed to philosophy, purifying it of mythological elements. The medieval Scholastics continued this project, culminating in the work of Thomas Aquinas. Convinced of the harmony of faith and reason as coming from the same God, he gave reason its full scope, recognizing the autonomy of philosophy as well as its organic link to theology. But later medieval thought began an increasing separation between philosophy and faith, until in the nineteenth century much of Western philosophy explicitly opposed Christian revelation. Today, philosophy's search for truth and meaning has given way, even among many philosophers, to "instrumental reason" in the service of the market, technological power, and enjoyment. As a result, a nihilistic outlook, which claims that ultimate truth is unattainable and "everything is fleeting and provisional" (46), has gained strength. Philosophy needs faith, to recall it to its true goal, while faith needs philosophy, to temper its stress on feeling and experience and to save it from myth and superstition.

In chapter 5, "The Magisterium's Interventions in Philosophical Matters" (49–63), the pope states that the church has no official philosophy; philosophy must retain autonomy, "faithful to its own principles and methods" (49). But when philosophical opinions threaten the understanding of revealed truth, the church's magisterium must intervene. Such interventions serve right reason and are intended to stimulate philosophical inquiry. In the nineteenth century they defended reason against fideism and faith against rationalism. Today's chief problem is a "deep-seated distrust of reason" (55) and of "universal and absolute statements." Philosophers must not set "goals that are too modest"; they must not "abandon the passion for ultimate truth" (56).

Besides warning against errors, the church has also tried to promote a renewal of philosophy, as in the encyclical *Aeterni patris* of Pope Leo XIII, which sparked a revival of Thomistic philosophy. Catholic philosophers who adopted more recent methods are also commended. Although the Second Vatican Council encouraged the study of philosophy, in the years since a lack of interest in philosophy has affected many Catholic faculties and even, as "I cannot fail to note with surprise and displeasure," many theologians (61).

Chapter 6 (64–79) discusses "The Interaction between Philosophy and Theology." Theology needs philosophy in order to understand the meaning of revealed truth and the way it is proclaimed. Neither the human sciences nor the traditional wisdom of non-Western cultures can take philosophy's place. The human sciences are helpful in studying human opinions but not in arriving at the objective truth in theology. The encounter with other cultures today is something like the encounter with Greek philosophy in early Christianity, but the church cannot neglect the universality of the human spirit across cultures nor "abandon what she has gained from her inculturation in the world of Greco-Latin thought" (72).

There is a circular, mutually enhancing relationship between philosophy and theology, as can be seen in the great philosopher-theologians ancient and modern, Eastern and Western Christian. Christian philosophy is "a philosophical speculation conceived in dynamic union with faith" (76), which gives philosophy material for reflection, while purifying it and keeping it humble. Faith, in turn, "grows deeper and more authentic when it is wedded to thought and does not reject it" (79).

Chapter 7 (80–99) lays out "Current Requirements and Tasks" for philosophy and theology. Scripture affirms that "the world and human life do have a meaning" (80), which is centered in Jesus Christ. But currently we are in a "crisis of meaning" (81). We are overwhelmed with data and conflicting theories, to the point where the question of meaning may itself seem to have no sense. "To be consonant with the word of God," philosophy must recover its character as a search for the ultimate meaning of life and as "the ultimate framework for the unity of human knowledge and action" (81). It must acknowledge the human capacity to know objective truth. And it must be capable of transcending sense experience and speaking metaphysically. It must avoid eclecticism, historicism, scientism, and a democratic pragmatism that bases moral values on majority vote.

Theology requires the belief that it is possible to know universally valid truth. It needs philosophy in order to clarify the relation between historical fact and enduring meaning in Scripture and to deal with the relationship between the permanent truth of dogmatic statements and their historical and cultural conditioning. Moral theology requires "a philosophical ethics that looks to the truth of the good" and is "neither subjectivist nor utilitarian" (98).

The "Conclusion" (100–108) reiterates that philosophy and theology need one another and stresses that training in philosophy is an important part of priestly formation. The pope addresses scientists, urging them not to lose sight of the need to join science with "philosophical and ethical values" (106). He concludes by invoking Mary, who gave herself in order that "God's Word might take flesh" (108), as an image for philosophy.

Bibliography: For the text of *Fides et ratio,* see: *Acta Apostolicae Sedis* 91 (1999): 5–88 (Latin); *Origins* 28, no. 19 (22 October 98): 317–347 (English).

[WILLIAM J. COLLINGE]

INCARNATIONIS MYSTERIUM

Pope John Paul II's bull, "The Mystery of the Incarnation," announcing the Great Jubilee of the year 2000. Promulgated on the first Sunday of Advent (29 November), 1998, it announces and crowns the preparations initiated with *Tertio millennio adveniente* (1994). *Incarnationis mysterium* reiterates major themes of John Paul II's pontificate. His view of salvation history is cosmic, Christocentric, and Trinitarian. As history's culmination and ultimate meaning, Jesus Christ is the "Living One" in whom alone men discover the mystery of their lives and still their hearts' deepest desires. He reconciles humanity to the Father in the Holy Spirit. Evangelization invites all to praise the triune God, their origin and goal, while the Church acts as a leaven for transforming human society into God's family (no. 2; cf. *Gaudium et spes,* 40). She remains "the only way by which men can discover the supreme vocation to which they are destined and fulfill it in the salvation which God effected." Since all are called to Christ's grace, the Church is "the sacrament, as it were, of intimate union with God and of the unity of the whole human race," reminding men that they become more human only by being "divinized" in Christ. The only order of salvation is established in Christ, and no meaning exists outside him.

The Jubilee embraces Christianity's two historical centers: the Holy Land, the site of the Incarnation, Passion, and Resurrection of Jesus, and Rome, the see of Peter's successor. Evangelization involves "reciprocal dialogue" as well as conversion. The Jubilee invites Christian communities and Churches sharing baptism and a common faith in Christ to "grow in the unity which is the fruit of the Spirit" (no. 4). Jews and Moslems also revere the Holy Land as the place of divine revelation. Even non-believers are invited to join the Church's joy. So powerful is Jesus' death that "after it no one can be separated further from God's love (cf. Rom. 8:21–39) except by his own fault."

After recalling the Jubilee's origin in Boniface VIII's plenary indulgence and the Jubilee of 1983 (no. 5),

Pope John Paul II presents Incarnationis mysterium in a ceremony at St. Peter's Basilica. (AP/Wide World Photos. Photograph by Plinio Lepri.)

the pope designates the major feasts initiating and closing the Jubilee (Christmas, 1999–Epiphany, 2001) and specifies 18 January 2000 as the date for opening the Holy Door at St. Paul's Basilica and inaugurating the prayer week for Christian unity (no. 6).

Paragraphs 7–14 enumerate various signs attesting faith and aiding devotion in the Jubilee: first, the pilgrimage, which involves prayer, watching, and fasting, the interior preparations for reform; second, the Holy Door, symbolizing Jesus, the sole access to the Father, and inviting Christians to enter more profoundly into the Church's life; third, the indulgence, a constitutive element of the Jubilee. Perhaps because simultaneously the Pontifical Council for Promoting Christian Unity was preparing with Lutheran leaders the Joint Declaration on the Doctrine of Justification, the explanation of the indulgence encompasses two paragraphs and, continuing the personalist interpretation of Paul VI's *Indulgentiarum doctrina,* considers indulgences not in terms of a juridical application of merit but rather in terms of one's union with Christ and fellow believers. Since this union is destroyed by sin, it cannot be renewed by man alone. Conversion and penance are required for active participation in Christ's full life. Indulgences remit temporal punishment involved in purifying inordinate attachments effected by sin; their efficacy depends upon the union of love in the Body of Christ.

Two further signs of God's mercy are purification of memory and works of charity. The former recognizes the weight of errors and faults carried by the Church. Charity embraces the needy; special mention is made of international debts. Two final paragraphs recall the martyrs, who signify Christ most eloquently with their lives, and the Mother of God, who, totally faithful on her pilgrimage, became Mother of the Church, our model and intercessor.

Bibliography: For the text of *Incarnationis mysterium,* see: *Acta Apostolicae Sedis* 91 (1999): 129–143 (Latin); *Origins* 28, n. 26 (10 Dec. 1998): 445–453 (English); *The Pope Speaks* 44 (1999): 180–191 (English). For commentaries and summaries of *Incarnationis mysterium,* see: M. MARITANO, ''Il giubileo e i suoi segni nella storia del popolo cristiano,'' *Salesianum* 61 (1999): 687–740. J. MCDERMOTT, S.J., ''The Theological Significance of the Indulgence,'' *L'Osservatore Romano,* English edition (17 March 1999): 7f. E. DAL CAVOLO, ''Per una storia dell'indulgenza,'' *Salesianum* 61 (1999): 818–830. R. FISICHELLA, ''Indulgence and the Mercy of God,'' *Communio* 20 (1999): 122–133. M. MORGANTE, *Le indulgenze: Cenni storici, dottrina, norme e il giubileo dell'anno 2000* (Cinisello Balsamo: S. Paolo, 1999). L. DE MAGISTRIS, ''Il dono dell'indulgenza,'' *L'Osservatore Romano* (24 February 1999): 4.

[J. MCDERMOTT]

LABOREM EXERCENS

Pope John Paul II's encyclical on labor, dated 14 September 1981. The intermediate occasion for the encyclical was the ninetieth anniversary of *Rerum novarum,* Pope Leo XIII's social encyclical of 1891—the start of what has come to be known as ''papal social thought.'' *Laborem exercens* defined the human being as ''worker.'' Humans differ from animals because humans alone must create the conditions of their survival and wellbeing by labor. The encyclical significantly expanded the notion of work. John Paul II indicated that labor does not refer principally to industrial labor, as it tended to do in previous encyclicals, but included agriculture, clerical, scientific, service-oriented and intellectual work (nn. 1, 4).

The encyclical presented Catholic social teaching as a radical critique of communism and capitalism. Oppression and inequality in the world are caused by a disorder in the organization of labor. While capital (including the mechanical means of production and the natural resources made available for production) is ''the result of labor'' (n. 12), i.e., accumulated labor, and therefore should be united with labor and serve labor, in actual fact capital has organized itself against labor in Western society.

The encyclical formulated the fundamental principle of ''the priority of labor over capital.'' In today's world in which industries are interconnected and related to public institutions, capital is meant to serve the entire laboring society. State ownership of the industries in itself offers no guarantee that the priority of labor over capital will be respected. The encyclical defended private ownership of productive goods, but added that ownership, whether private or public, is always conditional. ''Isolating the means of production as separate property in order to set it up in the form of capital in opposition to labor—and even to practice exploitation of labor—is contrary to the very nature of these means . . . because the only legitimate title to their possessions is that they should serve labor'' (n. 14).

Laborem exercens argued that the dignity of labor is such that laborers are entitled to co-own the goods they produce and thus share in the decisions regarding the use of these goods. Workers are also entitled to share in the decisions concerning the work process. According to John Paul II, workers are meant to be ''the subjects,'' the fully responsible agents, of production. The encyclical encouraged all movements that seek to extend workers' participation in ownership and management. (At the time the encyclical appeared there was still hope that the union movement Solidarity would transform Polish society).

What strategy must be adopted to transform the economic systems of West and East so that the priority of labor be respected?

> To achieve social justice in the various parts of the world, in the various countries and in the relationship between them, there is a need for ever new movements of solidarity of the workers and with the workers. . . . The Church is firmly committed to this cause, for it considers it to be its mission, its service, a proof of its fidelity to Christ, so that it can truly be the Church of the poor (n. 8).

This radical teaching was reinstated in the ''Instruction on Christian Freedom and Liberation'' (March 1986), published by the Congregation for the Doctrine of the Faith: ''The serious socio-economic problems which occur today cannot be solved unless new fronts of solidarity are created: solidarity among themselves, solidarity with the poor to which the rich are called, solidarity among the workers and with the workers'' (n. 89).

Bibliography: For the text of *Laborem exercens,* see *Acta Apostolicae Sedis* (1981): 57–647 (Latin); *Origins* 11, no. 15 (24 Sep 1981): 225, 227–244 (English); *The Pope Speaks* 26 (1981): 289–336 (English). For commentaries and summaries of the encyclical, see: G. BAUM, *The Priority of Labor* (New York 1982). D. DORR, *Option for the Poor* (Maryknoll, N.Y. 1983). J. W. HOUCK and O. F. WILLIAMS, eds., *Co-creation and Capitalism: John Paul II's ''Laborem Exercens''* (Washington, D.C.: University Press of America, 1983).

[GREGORY BAUM]

View of the cathedral facing the Plaza de Armas in Lima, Peru. (AP/Wide World Photos)

LIMA TEXT

A statement of the Faith and Order Commission of the World Council of Churches (WCC) on "Baptism, Eucharist, and Ministry" (BEM) unanimously approved at the Commission plenary meeting at Lima, Peru, on 12 January 1982. It purports to be a statement of convergence rather than full consensus, and is submitted to the churches for their reception and response.

The very dense text cannot be adequately summarized. The language adheres closely to that of previous Faith and Order documents and, in general, that of the Bible. Where there are clear disagreements among the churches, an effort is made to give a fair statement of each position. The disagreements are explained in a running commentary which is part of the official text.

The chapter on Baptism has twenty-three paragraphs, with commentary. Baptism is described as a participation in Christ's death and Resurrection, as an event of conversion and cleansing, as a bestowal of the Holy Spirit, as incorporation into the Body of Christ, and as a sign of the Kingdom. Infant and adult ("believers") baptism are presented as "equivalent alternatives." The unusual practice of baptizing without water is noted as requiring further study.

The chapter on Eucharist contains thirty-three paragraphs, with commentary. The Eucharist (or Lord's Supper) is depicted as thanksgiving to the Father, as a memorial of Christ, as invocation of the Holy Spirit, as communion of the faithful, as an anticipation of the eschatological meal. It is described as "the sacrament of the unique sacrifice of Christ," a memorial wherein the Church intercedes in union with the great High Priest. Transubstantiation is mentioned in the commentary, with the remark that many churches do not link Christ's presence so definitely to the consecrated elements. Intercommunion is encouraged as a manifestation of "the catholicity of the Eucharist" (Comm. 19).

The chapter on Ministry (fifty-five paragraphs with commentary) begins with a treatment of the ministry of the whole people of God and states that a special or ordained ministry is constitutive of the life and witness of the Church. The ordained are described as heralds and ambassadors, as leaders and teachers, and as pastors who direct the community. Disagreements about the ordination of women are noted in the commentary.

The threefold pattern of bishop, presbyter, and deacon is recognized as ancient and as holding promise for Church unity. Bishops are portrayed as charged with preserving continuity and unity in the Church and with pastoral oversight of a given area. The apostolicity of the whole Church is held to be served and symbolized by the continuous succession of bishops. Churches that have maintained this succession are, however, urged to recognize the ''apostolic content'' of the ordained ministry in other churches.

Responses. The Lima text is preceded by a preface (not technically part of the Text) in which all churches are asked to respond officially to four questions: To what extent can you recognize in this text the faith of the Church throughout the ages? What consequences can you draw for relations with other churches? What guidance can you find in the text for your worship, life, and witness? How should Faith and Order make use of this text for its future research? The Vancouver Assembly of the WCC (1983) reaffirmed the request that the churches respond to these questions.

The official response of the the Catholic Church to BEM issued by SPUC on 21 July 1987 was basically positive, characterizing the Lima texts as ''perhaps the most significant result of the [Faith and Order] movement so far.'' ''The study of BEM,'' it asserted, ''has been for many Catholics an enriching experience.'' Noting that ''BEM demonstrates clearly that serious progress is being made in the quest for visible unity,'' the response encouraged Faith and Order ''to continue its valuable work of seeking unity in faith as a basis for visible unity.''

While observing that BEM converges with Catholic doctrine and practice on a broad range of issues, the response noted that there are occasional passages which suggest options in theology and practice not consistent with Catholic faith. Some of these may here be indicated under the headings of Baptism, Eucharist, and Ministry.

On Baptism, the SPUC found the Lima text to be ''grounded in the apostolic faith received and professed by the Catholic Church.'' The trinitarian, sacramental, and missionary dimensions of Baptism, according to the response, are well stated. But the text was faulted for its

failure to treat a number of points that Catholics consider important; e.g., the necessity of Baptism for salvation, original sin, the Baptismal character, and the completion of initiation through Confirmation (as a distinct sacrament) and the Eucharist. The SPUC response also considered that the value of infant Baptism and the importance of nurture in a Christian community should have been given more emphasis.

On the Eucharist the SPUC response praised, among other things, the strong trinitarian and christological dimensions of the text, its use of patristic and liturgical sources, and its rich ecclesiological and eschatological context. The Secretariat, however, found unfortunate ambiguities in the treatment of the Eucharist as sacrifice and in the handling of Christ's real presence through the conversion of the elements, which Catholics regard as a matter of faith. The report also objected that the problem of eucharistic sharing among churches was discussed without sufficient attention to the ecclesial significance of Holy Communion. Lima's treatment of reservation of the consecrated species was also found deficient.

On the Ministry text, SPUC was likewise positive.

> Well aware of the complexity of the ecumenical dialogue on ministry, we are grateful for the work achieved on it by the Commission and we appreciate especially the fact that its presentation goes in the direction of the major lines of what we recognize 'as the faith of the Church throughout the ages'.

On the ordination of women, SPUC took the position that this is excluded by apostolic tradition, which the Church has no authority to change. The response expressed regret that BEM is unclear as to whether the threefold ministry of bishop, presbyter, and deacon is a constitutive feature of the Church or a historically contingent disposition. It would have welcomed more emphasis on the collegiality of the bishops and on the papacy as the ''focus of unity.'' While acknowledging that ordination is in effect treated as a sacrament (without the word being used), SPUC took the position that ''ordained ministry requires sacramental ordination by a bishop standing in the apostolic succession''—a point not affirmed by BEM. For this reason SPUC considered the proposals of BEM on the mutual recognition of ministries premature.

In proposing future work for Faith and Order, SPUC called attention to three areas needing further treatment: first, sacrament and sacramentality, including (it would seem) the Church as a real and effective ''icon of the presence of God and His Kingdom in the world''; second, apostolic tradition, which should be clearly distinguished from the particular ''traditions'' that develop in the separate churches; and third, authority in the Church, including the power of definite persons and bodies to discern and make binding decisions.

On 31 August 1987, Günther Gassmann, the Director of Faith and Order, welcomed this response by SPUC as the first official response ever given by the Catholic Church to an ecumenical document. He interpreted this response as an unambiguous commitment of the Catholic Church to the one ecumenical movement. He also applauded the support given in the response to multilateral dialogue as complementary to the bilateral dialogues that the Catholic Church has vigorously sponsored since Vatican Council II.

Bibliography: *Baptism, Eucharist, and Ministry,* Faith and Order Paper 111 (Geneva 1982). J. GROS, ed., "Baptism, Eucharist, and Ministry and Its Reception in the U.S. Churches," *Journal Ecumenical Studies* 21, no. 1 (Boston 1984). SECRETARIAT FOR PROMOTING CHRISTIAN UNITY, "Baptism, Eucharist and Ministry: An Appraisal," *Origins* 17, no. 23 (Nov. 19, 1987): 401–416. M. THURIAN, ed., *Ecumenical Perspectives on Baptism, Eucharist, and Ministry,* Faith and Order Paper 116 (Geneva 1983); *Churches Respond to BEM. Official Responses to the Baptism, Eucharist and Ministry Text,* Faith and Order Paper 129, v. 1 (Geneva 1986). Faith and Order Paper 132, v. 2 (Geneva 1986); Faith and Order Paper 135, v. 3 (Geneva 1987). M. A. FAHEY, ed., *Catholic Perspectives on Baptism, Eucharist, and Ministry. A Study Commissioned by the Catholic Theological Society of America* (Lanham, Md. 1986). G. LIMOURIS & N. VAPORIS, *Orthodox Perspectives on Baptism, Eucharist and Ministry,* Faith and Order Paper 128 (Brookline, Mass. 1985); also printed in *The Greek Orthodox Theological Review* 30, no. 2 (1985).

[A. DULLES]

Assumption of the Virgin Mary *by Luca Ferrari.* (© Arte & Immagini srl/CORBIS)

MULIERIS DIGNITATEM

The Apostolic epistle, "The Dignity and Vocation of Women," was issued by Pope John Paul II on the feast of the Assumption (15 August), 1988. It was written after the seventh general assembly of the Synod of Bishops (October 1987) had recommended "further study of the anthropological and theological bases that are needed in order to solve the problems connected with the meaning and dignity of being a woman and of being a man" (MD 1). The form of the epistle is that of a meditation. The body of the text is divided into seven parts: "Woman—Mother of God," "The Image and Likeness of God," "Eve—Mary," "Jesus Christ," "Motherhood—Virginity," "The Church—The Bride of Christ," and "'The Greatest of These is Love.'"

Thematically MD builds on the encyclical *Redemptoris mater* (1987). Mary is the "archetype of the whole human race," the perfect union of the supernatural and the natural. She is also the ideal woman "of whom God was born in the fullness of time." She determines the appropriate "horizon of reflection" on the dignity and vocation of women, which is later developed around the "two dimensions of the female vocation": motherhood and vowed virginity (MD 17). The mother's physical gift of life corresponds to spiritual gifts in her role as first educator. Symbolically motherhood is tied to the new covenant which began with Mary's *fiat* "Each and every time that motherhood is repeated in human history, it is always related to the covenant which God established with the human race through the motherhood of the Mother of God" (MD 19).

Vowed virginity, the other possible vocation of women, reflects physical motherhood, but on a spiritual level. Consecrated virgins become a spousal gift for their spouse, Christ the Redeemer. "They thus give themselves to the divine Spouse, and this personal gift tends to union, which is properly spiritual in character" (MD 20). They are called to a motherhood according to the Spirit which is "open to all people, who are embraced by the love of Christ, the Spouse" (MD 21).

The Christian personalism of John Paul II is evident. Through her *fiat* Mary enters into "*interpersonal*" dialogue with God, fully personal and fully feminine as mother. The creation of human beings is essentially personal in nature, reflecting the nature of God as personal (MD 23). The spousal relationship is interpersonal, reflecting the communion of love in the Trinity (MD 7).

Contemporary discussion about women's equality is especially evident in sections that review scriptural passages central to interpreting women's roles in traditional teaching. The creation of woman as "image and likeness of God" is stressed. Genesis 2 is interpreted as a model for the essential relatedness of man and woman "in a common humanity" (MD 6), rather than as setting women in a role of subservience. The "fall" is the sin of "the first man, created by God as male and female" (MD 9). The resulting instability of men and women's relationship is disadvantageous to both. "Wives, be subject to your husbands" (Eph 5:22) is part of a larger exhortation for the "mutual subjection" of the spouses to each other out of reverence for Christ (MD 24).

The scriptural basis of feminine imagery for God is acknowledged (MD 7). "Every element of human generation which is proper to man, and every element which is proper to woman, namely human 'fatherhood' and 'motherhood,' bears within itself a likeness to, or analogy with the divine 'generating'" (MD 8).

Nearly every passage relative to Jesus' treatment of women is considered. "Christ's way of acting, the gospel of his words and deeds, is a consistent protest against whatever offends the dignity of women" (MD 15). The discipleship of women is recognized, as is Mary Magdalene's title, "the apostle of the apostles" (MD 16). Though women share in the priesthood of the faithful (MD 27 and 30), they are not called to the ministerial priesthood. "In calling only men as his apostles Christ acted in a completely free and sovereign manner" (MD 26). MD builds its case for women's roles in the church on a symbolic understanding of the nature of the sexes, which reserves certain roles for men, including leadership in the assembly and presiding at the Eucharist (MD 25 and 26). Women are warned not to "appropriate to themselves male characteristics contrary to their own feminine 'originality'" (MD 10).

Bibliography: For the text of *Mulieris dignitatem,* see: *Acta Apostolicae Sedis* no. 80 (1988) 1653–1729 (Latin); *Origins* 18, no. 7 (6 Oct 1988): 261–283 (English); *The Pope Speaks* 34 (1989): 10–47 (English).

[PAMELA KIRK]

ORDINATIO SACERDOTALIS

Apostolic letter issued by Pope John Paul II on the feast of Pentecost (22 May), 1994. In this brief letter, the pope asserts "that the Church has no authority whatsoever to confer priestly ordination on women and that this judgment is to be definitively held by all the Church's faithful" (no. 4). He confirms the constant practice and teaching of the Catholic Church regarding "a matter which pertains to the Church's divine constitution itself" (ibid.).

Ordinatio sacerdotalis first recalls that Pope Paul VI, in response to the Anglican Communion, identified some "very fundamental reasons" in support of the Catholic tradition that excludes women from sacerdotal ordination: Christ's example of choosing only men as his apostles, the Church's constant practice in fidelity to this example, and the magisterium's consistent teaching that this practice corresponds to God's plan for the Church. *Inter insigniores* (1976), a declaration of the Congregation for the Doctrine of the Faith (1976) approved by Paul VI, explains these "fundamental reasons," proposes theological reasons in support of the tradition, and denies that Christ's way of acting was dictated solely by sociological or cultural motives. Ordinatio sacerdotalis quotes Paul VI: "The real reason is that, in giving the Church her fundamental constitution, her theological anthropology-thereafter always followed by the Church's tradition—Christ established things in this way."

Ordinatio sacerdotalis develops its statement of the "fundamental reasons" by recalling the New Testament basis for linking the ministerial priesthood with Christ's call of the Twelve. John Paul repeats the position he took in *Mulieris dignitatem,* that in choosing only men Christ was not bound by cultural norms but acted with full freedom. According to the New Testament, the call of the Twelve expressed the divine plan, for Christ called "those whom he willed" only after prayer to the Father and in union with the Holy Spirit. The Church has acknowledged this way of acting as a perennial norm in granting admission to the ministerial priesthood. The Twelve were not invited to exercise a function which any member of the community might fulfill, but were intimately associated with the Lord's own mission. The apostles, in choosing fellow workers who would be their successors, followed the Lord's example. Priestly ordination continues to hand on the office Christ entrusted to the apostles, an office which includes the mission of representing Christ the Lord and Redeemer.

The pope asserts that the Church's dispensation in this matter observes the plan of God's wisdom and must not be construed as discriminating against women. The Blessed Virgin's dignity was not compromised because she was not called to apostolic office and the ministerial priesthood; neither does the non-admission of other women to priestly ordination tell against their dignity. As women saints throughout the history of the Church bear witness, women share in the apostolic mission of the whole People of God and exemplify the holiness of the faithful to which the ministerial priesthood is ordered.

Because the teaching preserved by the Church's constant and universal Tradition and firmly taught by the contemporary magisterium continues to be called into question, the pope declares—in virtue of his ministry of "confirming the brethren" (Lk 22:32)— that the Church does not have the authority to ordain women to the priesthood, and directs that this judgment is to be definitively held.

In October 1995, in response to a formal query, the Congregation for the Doctrine of the Faith said that the teaching of *Ordinatio sacerdotalis* belongs to the deposit of the faith, and that it requires definitive assent "since, founded on the written Word of God and from the beginning constantly preserved and applied in the Tradition of the Church, it has been set forth infallibly by the ordinary and universal magisterium."

Bibliography: For the text of *Ordinatio sacerdotalis,* see: *Acta Apostolicae Sedis* 86 (1994): 545–548 (Latin); *Origins* 24, no. 4 (9 June 1994): 49–52 (English); *The Pope Speaks* 39 (1994): 319–321. For commentaries and summaries of *Ordinatio sacerdotalis,* see: Congregation for the Doctrine of the Faith, *From "Inter Insigniores" to "Ordinatio Sacerdotalis"* (Washington, D.C.: United States Catholic Conference, 1998). AVERY DULLES, "Gender and Priesthood: Examining the Teaching," *Origins* 25, no. 45 (2 May 1996): 778-784.; "Pastoral Response to the Teaching on Women's Ordination," *Origins* 26, no. 11 (29 August 1996): 177–180.

[SARA BUTLER]

ORIENTALE LUMEN

Apostolic letter of 2 May 1995 of Pope John Paul II, marking the centenary of Leo XIII's letter *Orientalium dignitas,* on the Churches of the East. In the first of its two parts, *Orientale lumen* approaches the Eastern Churches through their worship, and offers elements of a liturgical ecclesiology. A principal theme is participation in Trinitarian life through the liturgy and, in a special way, through the Eucharist.

Orientale lumen identifies inculturation as one of the first great values embodied in the Christian East. Following the example of Saints Cyril and Methodius, the proclamation of the gospel should be "rooted in what is distinctive to each culture and open to convergence in universality" (no. 7). Tradition is embodied in different cultural and historical situations and conditions; it is the living memory of the Risen One articulated in the historical and cultural patrimony of each Church.

Orientale lumen looks at Eastern Christianity from the specific vantage point of monasticism, "a reference point for all the baptized . . . a symbolic synthesis of Christianity" (no. 9). Monasticism is the soul of the Eastern Churches, "an integral part of the *lumen* passed on to the West by the great Fathers of the undivided Church" (ibid.). The witness of nuns in the Christian East

is not overlooked; as a visible sign of the motherhood of God, they offer an example of the full value given in the Church to what is specifically feminine.

By contemplating the disfigured face of Christ, the man of sorrows, and the transfigured face of the risen Christ, the monk engages in a constant process of conversion. His way is not marked by personal effort alone; the spiritual father manifests God's tender and demanding fatherhood, and allows the monk to personalize the times, rhythms, and ways of seeking God.

Communion with Christ causes a love for humanity and for every creature to rise within the monk, making him a man of communion, born of the Church, and living for the Church. Communion in love is revealed first by service within the monastic community, then by such services to the Church as social assistance, itinerant preaching, and evangelization.

The second part of *Orientale lumen,* pastoral and practical in character, traces the way from knowledge to encounter. While sins of the past still burden the Churches, it is necessary to make amends for them, and seek forgiveness, so as to go beyond the degree of communion already reached. The future lies in the unity in diversity evidenced by the first councils of the Church, and in the need to make every effort toward the sharing of the same bread and the same cup.

The Eastern Churches in full communion with Rome are urged to rediscover their full identity with no diminution of their own authenticity and originality. These Catholic Churches carry the wound of being still kept from full communion with the Eastern Orthodox Churches, despite sharing in the same heritage. Conversion is required of the Latin Church that she may respect the dignity of the Eastern Churches, and how essential she considers their contribution to the full realization of the Church's universality.

John Paul II proposes knowledge of the liturgy and spiritual traditions of the Christian East. He recommends that dialogue be fostered, that specialized institutions train theologians, liturgists, historians, and canonists for the Christian East, and that appropriate teaching on these subjects be offered, especially to future priests, in seminaries and theological faculties. He further recommends regular meetings, hopes that monasteries will make a particular effort in this regard, blesses works of hospitality to Christians of the East, especially in Rome, and recommends exchanges at the parish level, joint pilgrimages to holy places, and a common recognition of the martyrs of recent decades. He decries the tensions and conflicts that marked inter-ecclesial relations in Central and Eastern Europe during the 1990s, and addresses the pastoral needs of Eastern Christians living in the mainly Latin environment of the diaspora.

Greek Orthodox bishop carries an icon of Mary. (© Hanan Isachar/CORBIS)

Invoking the Mother of God, and praying God to hasten, in the Church of the third millennium, the anticipation of communion in the fullness of the Kingdom, *Orientale lumen* gives the last word to hope.

Bibliography: For the text of *Orientalel lumen,* see: *Acta Apostolicae Sedis,* 8 (1995): 745–774 (Latin); *Origins* 25, no. 1 (18 May 1995): 1, 3–13 (English); *The Pope Speaks* 40 (1995) 357–379 (English). For commentaries and summaries of *Orientale lumen,* see: GIOVANNI MARCHESI, "La lettera apostolica di Giovanni Paolo II 'Orientale Lumen.'" *La Civiltà Cattolica* 146, no. 3 (1995): 65–74. "De sacra theologia tradenda post litteras apostolicas 'Orientale Lumen.'" *Seminarium* n.s. 36 (1996): 175–290. Proceedings of the Orientale Lumen Conferences of 1997, 1998, 1999 (Fairfax, Va.:. Eastern Christian Publications).

[M. D. KIRBY]

PASTOR BONUS

Apostolic letter, issued by Pope John Paul II on 28 June 1988. Effective 1 March 1989, *Pastor bonus* directs the first major reorganization of the Roman Curia since the 1967 promulgation by Pope Paul VI of the apostolic constitution *Regimini Ecclesiae universae. Pastor bonus* consists of a lengthy introduction followed by nine sections of norms and two appendices. The introduction is both historical and doctrinal. The historical section traces the development of the curia and the various stages of its structure and reforms. The doctrinal section provides a theological foundation for understanding the work of the curia. The curia is described as having an ecclesial character since it "as the servant of Peter's successor, looks only to help the whole church and its bishops" (no. 7). Further, the curia is given the characteristics of "instrumental," as an instrument of the Roman Pontiff; "ministerial," since it is in service to the whole church; and "vicarious," because it does not act on its own initiative (nos. 7 8).

The 193 norms of the document are organized under nine headings: General Norms (1–38), Secretariat of State (39–47), Congregations (48–116), Tribunals (117–30), Pontifical Councils (131–70), Administrative Services (171–79), Other Institutions of the Roman Curia (180–81), Advocates (183–85), Institutions Connected with the Holy See (186–93). The reorganization simplified the general structure of the curia. The number of congregations was reduced from ten to nine; councils, commissions and secretariats were reorganized into twelve pontifical councils, and the number of curial offices was reduced from six to three. The reduction in the number of congregations was accomplished by incorporating into one the Congregation for the Discipline of the Sacraments and the Congregation for Divine Worship. These two congregations were first merged in 1975, then separated in 1984. *Pastor bonus* joined them again, establishing the Congregation for Divine Worship and the Discipline of the Sacraments.

The titles of other congregations were changed, seemingly for the sake of clarity, but without any substantial adjustments in their areas of competence: the Congregation for Catholic Education became the Congregation of Seminaries and Educational Institutions, and the Congregation for Religious and Secular Institutes became the Congregation for Institutes of Consecrated Life and Societies of Apostolic Life. In other name changes, the Commission for the Authentic Interpretation of the Code of Canon Law became the Pontifical Commission for the Interpretation of Legislative Texts, and the Secretariat for Non-Christians became the Pontifical Council for Inter-Religious Dialogue. Although not explicitly named as such, the Congregation for the Doctrine of the Faith was given an oversight function with respect to work of other congregations and councils (see, e.g., 54, 94, 161).

The first appendix, "The Pastoral Significance of the Visit ad limina Apostolorum," expands on nos. 28–35 and sets out the importance and purpose of *ad limina* visits for whole church. They are said to have a threefold meaning; sacred, since the bishops make pilgrimage to the tombs of Peter and Paul, personal since each bishop meets "face to face" with the successor of Peter, and curial, since the bishops "enter into conversation with moderators of the dicasteries, councils, and offices of the Roman Curia" (6). Also, the visits are intended to enrich the curia, as its members are told of the concerns of the various particular churches.

The second appendix, "Collaborators of the Apostolic See as a Work Community," is a complement to nos. 33–36 of the apostolic constitution in which the new "Central Labor Office" is established. The appendix consists of a statement on the employment philosophy of the Vatican and a letter dated 20 November 1982, "The Meaning of Work Performed by the Apostolic See," which Pope John Paul II sent to the then Secretary of State, Agostino Cardinal Casaroli. Both these documents are intended to address, at least in part, the needs and concerns of employees of the Vatican.

Despite criticism for its lack of specificity on some points, *Pastor bonus* provided the blueprint for the reorganization of curial offices and procedures during the pontificate of John Paul II.

Bibliography: For the text of *Pastor bonus,* see: *Acta Apostolicae Sedis* 80 (1988): 841, 912 (Latin); *Code of Canon Law,* English-Latin Edition, rev.ed. (Washington: Canon Law Society of America, 1998) (English). For commentaries and summaries of *Pastor bonus,* see: JAMES H. PROVOST, "Pastor bonus: Reflections on the Reorganization of the Roman Curia." *The Jurist* 48 (1988): 499–535. "Local Church and Catholicity in the Constitution Pastor bonus." *The Jurist* 52 (1992): 299–334.

[ELISSA RINERE]

PASTORES DABO VOBIS

Post-synodal apostolic exhortation, "I Will Give You Shepherds," issued by Pope John Paul II, 25 March 1992, following the eighth general assembly of the Synod of Bishops. This lengthy exhortation elaborates on the Second Vatican Council's discussion of the priesthood, in the context of its discussion of the Church as a communion of believers. The pope begins by speaking of the gift of the priesthood; he emphasizes that the Church's first response to the crisis of priestly vocations in many parts of the world must be "a total act of faith in the Holy Spirit": trust in his care and faithfulness to his gifts. Fidelity to the divine grace already received is the main theme of the exhortation, balanced at every stage by the necessity for human cooperation with that grace (2). The pope lists the Church's efforts at implementing the council's teachings on the priesthood (3), and notes "the deep and rapid transformations in the societies and culture of our age" and "the multiplicity and diversity of contexts in which she announces the Gospel and witnesses to it" (2), which require a further aggiornamento twenty five years after the council.

Chapter 1, "The Challenges Facing Priestly Formation at the Conclusion of the Second Millennium" (5–10) gives an overview of the synodal discussion of "positive and negative elements in socio-cultural and ecclesial contexts which affect boys, adolescents and young men who throughout their lives are called to bring to maturity a project of priestly life" (5). Positive elements include "a powerful thirst for justice and peace, a more lively sense that humanity must care for creation and respect nature, a more open search for truth, a greater effort to safeguard human dignity," a growing international solidarity and a quest for meaning and for an objective standard of values. The decline of Communism, with its "violent rejection of message of spiritual and religious values" is also noted. Among the negative elements are rationalism, subjectivism, consumerism, secularism, which can involve a "practical and existential atheism," the breakup of the family, and the widening gap between affluent and indigent peoples. Within the Church, the widespread lack of due knowledge of the faith and "an incorrectly understood pluralism in theology" may have contributed to a shortage of priests in some areas, which in turn exacer-

A priest says Easter Mass in Moravee, Slovenia. The covered baskets in the aisle contain the Easter breakfast food. (© Bojan Brecelj/ CORBIS)

bates these factors. A careful discernment of these "signs of the times" is crucial in order to address the questions of the call to priesthood and the formation of those who are called.

Chapter 2, "The Nature and Mission of the Ministerial Priesthood" (11–18) addresses the "crisis of priestly identity" in the years following the council. As this crisis arose in part from a misunderstanding or misrepresentation of the council's teachings, the synod "considered it necessary to summarize the nature and mission of the ministerial priesthood" in the light of the tradition and the council's teachings. The exhortation presents this summary in terms of the Church as "mystery, communion, and mission" and the priest as "serving the Church and the world."

Chapter 3, "The Spiritual Life of the Priest" (19–34) concerns his "specific vocation to holiness" (in the context of the universal call to holiness) and his "con-

figuration to Christ, the Head and Shepherd," in "pastoral charity." This chapter then discusses, together, priestly (spiritual) life and ministry, which the council had treated somewhat separately in *Presbyterorum Ordinis*. It also discusses priestly life in terms of the "radicalism of the Gospel" (the evangelical counsels as they pertain to priests), and "membership in and dedication to the particular (diocesan) church," which does not exclude but rather should give rise to missionary zeal. The chapter ends with a call to priestly renewal "in the Spirit of Holiness."

Chapter 4, "Priestly Vocation in the Church's Pastoral Work" (35–41) concerns the encouragement of priestly vocations, which are recognized as a "mystery" within the mystery of the Church. The dialogue between God's initiative and the human response to it is treated at some length, before the practical aspects of promoting vocations are discussed. The chapter concludes with a reminder that all members of the Church are responsible for promoting vocations.

Chapter 5, "The Formation of Candidates for the Priesthood" (42–70), deals with the whole process of priestly formation, human, spiritual, intellectual, and pastoral. Its proper setting is the seminary, both major and minor, and the agents of priestly formation are the bishops, seminary authorities, professors, the community, and the candidate himself.

Chapter 6, "The Ongoing Formation of Priests" (70–81), concerns the ongoing (post-ordination) formation of priests—a rather new emphasis, much in keeping with the conciliar renewal and the Church's understanding of the development, over time, of the "priestly personality." The priest himself is the primary agent of this ongoing formation.

Because the "new evangelization" called for by the Holy Father requires "new evangelizers," the exhortation appeals to all the faithful to pray for and promote vocations, to families (especially mothers) to be generous in giving their sons to priestly service, and to young people to consider whether or not God is calling them to priesthood. *Pastores dabo vobis* concludes with prayer to Mary, Mother of Jesus Christ, Mother of the Church, and Mother of Priests.

See Also: SYNOD OF BISHOPS, EIGHTH GENERAL ASSEMBLY.

Bibliography: For the text of *Pastores dabo vobis,* see: *Acta Apostolicae Sedis* 84 (1992): 657–804 (Latin); *Origins* 21, no. 45 (16 Apr 1992): 717–59 (English); *The Pope Speaks* 35 (1992): 262–95 (English).

[DOUGLAS CLARK]

PROFESSION OF FAITH AND OATH OF FIDELITY

Canon 833 of the 1983 Code of Canon Law of the Latin Church requires a profession of faith, "in accord with a formula approved by the Apostolic See," to be made by (1) everyone who has voting rights in an ecumenical or particular council, a synod of bishops, or a diocesan synod; (2) individuals named to the college of cardinals; (3) persons promoted to the episcopacy and those equivalent to a diocesan bishop; (4) diocesan administrators; (5) vicars general, episcopal vicars and vicars judicial; (6) pastors, rectors of seminary, professors of theology and philosophy in seminaries and those promoted to the diaconate; (7) rectors of Catholic universities and university teachers who teach disciplines dealing with faith and morals; and (8) superiors in clerical reli-

PROFESSION OF FAITH

(Formula for making the Profession of Faith in those cases where it is required by law)

I, N., with firm faith believe and profess everything that is contained in the symbol of faith, namely:

I believe .... [here follows the Nicene Creed].

With firm faith I also believe everything contained in God's word, written or handed down in tradition and proposed by the Church, whether by way of solemn judgment or through the ordinary and universal magisterium, as divinely revealed and calling for faith.

I also firmly accept and hold each and everything that is proposed definitively by the Church regarding teaching on faith and morals.

Moreover, I adhere with religious submission of will and intellect to the teachings which either the Roman Pontiff or the college of bishops enunciate when they exercise the authentic magisterium, even if they proclaim those teachings by an act that is not definitive.

gious institutes and societies of apostolic life. At the end of February 1989, the Roman Congregation for the Doctrine of the Faith (CDF) issued a new formula of the profession in *L'Osservatore Romano* and at the same time introduced an oath of fidelity to be made by some, but not all, those listed in canon 833 "on assuming an office to be exercised in the name of the Church." Both the profession of faith and the oath of fidelity were to become obligatory four days later, 1 March 1989.

Although the Latin texts printed in *L'Osservatore Romano* were accompanied by a "note of presentation," the document as a whole had grave canonical defects. In addition to the inadequate interval before it was to go into effect, it lacked signatures and date. Neither did it explain the exceptional use of the newspaper for canonical promulgation, nor did it make mention of the requisite papal approval that is required for a significant innovation. Since 1917 the issuance of a such a general decree (i.e., a law) without papal delegation exceeds the power of the departments of the Roman Curia.

The question of the document's validity, however, became moot in the following October when the official *Acta Apostolicae Sedis* published a retroactive rescript dated 19 September and signed by the cardinal prefect of the CDF. The rescript stated that in an audience on 1 July 1988 Pope John Paul II had approved the action and ordered the decree promulgated. It also introduced a further norm: the approbation of vernacular versions of the two texts was reserved to the congregation.

Approved Formula. Canon 833 remained unchanged. The innovation lay in the new text itself. Prior

OATH OF FIDELITY ON ASSUMING AN OFFICE TO BE EXERCISED IN THE NAME OF THE CHURCH

(Formula to be used by the faithful mentioned in canon 833, nos. 5–8)

I, N., in assuming the office of _____, promise that both in my words and in my conduct I shall always preserve communion with the Catholic Church.

I shall carry out with the greatest care and fidelity the duties incumbent on me toward both the universal Church and the particular Church in which, according to the provisions of the law, I have been called to exercise my service.

In fulfilling the charge entrusted to me in the name of the Church, I shall hold fast to the deposit of faith in its entirety, I shall faithfully hand it on and explain it, and I shall avoid any teachings opposed to that faith.

I shall follow and foster the common discipline of the whole Church and I shall observe all ecclesiastical laws, especially those which are contained in the Code of Canon Law.

In Christian obedience I shall unite myself with what is declared by the bishops as authentic doctors and teachers of the faith or established by them as those responsible for the governance of the Church; I shall also faithfully assist the diocesan bishops, in order that the apostolic activity exercised in the name and by mandate of the Church may be carried out in the communion of the same Church.

So help me God, and God's holy Gospels, on which I place my hand.

(Changes in paragraphs four and five of the formulary, for use by those faithful indicated in CIC, canon 833, no. 8:)

I shall foster the common discipline of the Church, and I shall insist on the observance of all ecclesiastical laws, especially those which are contained in the Code of Canon Law.

In Christian obedience I shall unite myself with what is declared by the bishops as authentic doctors and teachers of the faith or established by them as those responsible for the governance of the Church; I shall also cooperate fully with the diocesan bishops, in order that, without prejudice to the character and purpose of my own institute, the apostolic activity exercised in the name and by mandate of the Church may be carried out in the communion of the same Church.

So help me God, and God's holy Gospels, on which I place my hand.

to 1967 the approved formula of the profession of faith that was canonically required (and prefixed to the 1917 code) consisted of the creed of the councils of Nicaea and Constantinople, augmented by several paragraphs that summed up the teaching of the ecumenical councils of Trent and Vatican I. The additions to the fourth-century creed were removed in 1967 in the wake of Vatican II.

Only a simple formula, with obvious references to the three modern ecumenical councils, was to be said at the end of the ancient creed:

I firmly embrace and accept all and everything which has been either defined by the Church's solemn deliberations or affirmed and declared by its ordinary magisterium concerning the doctrine of faith and morals, according as they [the teachings] are proposed by it [the Church], especially those things dealing with the mystery of the Holy Church of Christ [Vatican II], its sacraments and the sacrifice of the Mass [Trent], and the primacy of the Roman pontiff [Vatican I].

The 1989 text replaced this 1967 formula with three new paragraphs. The oblique references to the modern councils were suppressed; more important, the suggestion of the diverse levels or modes of proposal of teachings was lost, although this had evidently been derived from the 1964 dogmatic constitution on the Church (*Lumen gentium* 24). The purpose of the new text, according to the note of presentation, was to update the profession of faith "as regards style and content" and to bring it "more in line with the teaching of the Second Vatican Council and subsequent documents." The paragraph appended to the creed in the 1967 formula was modified "in order to distinguish better the types of truths and the relative assent required."

Commentary and Explanation. (For the text, see accompanying box.) In the new formula the first paragraph simply mentions matters to be believed "with firm faith," namely, matters taught "as divinely revealed and calling for faith." The wording is derived from the teaching of Vatican I, and it corresponds roughly to the norm of canon 750.

The second paragraph requires the firm acceptance and holding of Church teachings that are "definitively proposed." Nothing in the text suggests that this implicates an affirmation of divine and catholic faith. Theologians and canonists showed concern about the very nature of this "acceptance," about the ambiguity of "definitively proposed," about the distinction between truths of Christian faith infallibly defined and other teachings, about the possibility of future development or changes in such "definitive" teachings, and the like. When the text appeared, it was quickly noted that this dimension of Church teaching (unlike the first and third paragraphs) had not been touched upon in the canons of the code promulgated in 1983.

Finally, the third paragraph goes beyond matters of "divine and catholic faith." It is an assertion of adherence to other teachings of the pope and the other bishops. Not unexpectedly this corresponds to the nondefinitive, noninfallible, nonirrevocable teaching similarly characterized by canon 752, namely, teachings enunciated by the Roman pontiff or the college of bishops "when they exercise the authentic magisterium even if they do not intend to proclaim it with a definitive act." For this, the canon properly requires "not the assent of faith [like the creed and other revealed truth embraced in the first appended paragraph] but a religious *obsequium* of intellect and will."

The translation of *obsequium* is far from certain: it may mean anything from blind obedience or total submission to simple religious respect or docile reflection, even faithful, loyal dissent. The officially approved English text of the new profession of faith chooses "submission."

Oath of Fidelity. The 1989 Oath of Fidelity is distinct from the profession of faith, and different persons are canonically bound to take it "on assuming an office to be exercised in the name of the Church." The text is a promissory oath; by definition it adds to a simple promise the invocation of the name of God and obliges the oath-taker by reason of the virtue of religion. A review of the text (see accompanying box) reveals that it is not, either strictly or conventionally, an "oath of office," namely, an oath to fulfill the responsibilities of a given Church office. (Such oaths of office do exist in the Latin Church for certain officeholders, e.g., officers of tribunals required by canon 1254 to swear "that they will fulfill their function properly and faithfully.") The oath is rather a broad promise to preserve ecclesial communion and to maintain Church doctrine and discipline required of individuals on assuming of certain, but not all, ecclesiastical offices.

The note of presentation compares the new oath of fidelity to the oath of fidelity to the Apostolic See taken by bishops-elect (c.380), but the wording of the two oaths bear very little resemblance and have very different purposes. Even "fidelity" or faithfulness is not a common element: the new oath does not mention fidelity to the Roman See, and most of the promises seem concerned with the existing duties of all the Christian faithful, now to be confirmed by oath. Overall the text is a kind of pastiche of obligations, unexceptionable in themselves but without direct reference to the duties assumed by individuals appointed to Church offices.

Each of the five paragraphs deserves a word of explanation. (There are minor variants of the last two paragraphs for "superiors in clerical religious institutes and societies of apostolic life.")

Paragraph 1. The one taking the oath promises both in words and conduct always "to preserve communion with the Catholic Church." This is partially based on canon 209, §1, and binds all the Christian faithful alike. The context demands only that this obligation be sworn to and seems to imply that officeholders have a greater obligation of communion than the rest of the faithful.

Paragraph 2. This section (alone) does have aspects of an oath of office, since one promises to carry out carefully and faithfully "the duties incumbent on me toward the universal Church and the particular church in which . . . I have been called to exercise my service." The language, however, is derived from canon 209, §2, again a description of duties incumbent on all the Christian faithful. The ultimate source of the language is in *Lumen gentium* 30 and the conciliar decree on the laity, *Apostolicam actuositatem* 10, although both passages refer to lay, nonordained members of the Church without reference to any Church office.

Paragraph 3. The paragraph begins, "In fulfilling the charge entrusted to me in the name of the Church," a phrase that explicitly confirms the interpretation that the positions in question are true ecclesiastical offices to which appointments are made by Church authority, which acts officially "in the name of the Church."

The substance of the paragraph refers to doctrine; it is a promise to "hold fast to the deposit of faith in its entirety," faithfully to "hand it [the deposit of faith] on and explain it," and finally to "avoid teachings opposed to that faith." The mention of handing on the faith appears to apply to those officials who exercise the ministry of the word through preaching, catechetical formation, and other means. More important, it is the deposit of faith in the strict sense (as referred to in the profession of faith, both the credal text and the first added paragraph) that is at issue. The text is a digest of canon 750, concerning what must be believed with divine and catholic faith; the canon also requires the believer to avoid contrary doctrines and adds that revealed truth "is manifested by the common adherence of the Christian faithful under the leadership of the sacred magisterium."

Paragraph 4. As in the preceding paragraphs, it is the common duties of the faithful that are specified, with a mention of "fostering" as well as following "the common discipline of the whole Church"—presumably the greater duty for Church officials. The second clause bears no relation to Church office: "I shall observe all ecclesiastical laws, especially those which are contained in the Code of Canon Law [of the Latin Church, since the Eastern Catholics are not bound by the oath]." The oath to observe all ecclesiastical laws involves one in the graver transgression of the virtue of religion when one does not observe the canon law.

Paragraph 5. The final paragraph of the promise is somewhat repetitive and has two parts. First there is a promise "in Christian obedience" to unite oneself with the bishops, both as teachers of the faith and as those responsible for Church governance. The reference is to both doctrine and Church order. It is clearly adapted from canon 212, §1, although in that context the duties are those of the Christian faithful in general rather than those of officeholders. Second, there is a promise faithfully "to assist the diocesan bishops" in carrying out apostolic activity. While this is surely both proper and desirable, the language is somewhat ambiguous in its reference to diocesan bishops; either the local bishop or diocesan bishops in general may be meant.

Such a commentary or critique of the text of the oath of fidelity reveals no responsibilities that are unacceptable, but it does raise the grave question of binding oneself so broadly with the invocation of the Name of God in support of the oath-taker's promise.

Persons Obliged to Take the Oath. The principal question asked by canonists and especially teaching theologians is, who are obliged to take the oath of fidelity. The document specifies many named in the latter part of canon 833 (nos. 5–8), but not all the officeholders listed in the second half of the canon are included. As the title of the oath indicates, it is to be taken by individuals "on assuming an office to be exercised in the name of the Church." It is an important qualification for some of those enumerated in canon 833 do not hold Church office at all, much less one to be exercised in the name of or on behalf of the Church.

Perhaps the principal category of those simply unaffected by the new norm are teachers in colleges and universities "who teach disciplines which deal with faith or morals." Such teachers do not receive an appointment to any ecclesiastical office, unless in some exceptional case. To take another example, the president (rector) of a Catholic university may or may not be appointed to a duly established Church office; if not, he or she is bound by canon 833, no. 7 to make the profession of faith, but not bound to take the oath of fidelity.

Bibliography: F. R. MCMANUS, "Report on a Study of the Profession of Faith and Oath of Fidelity," *Proceedings (1991): Canon Law Society of America* (Washington 1992): 190–220; "Preliminary Report of the CTS [College Theology Society] Committee on Profession of Faith/Oath of Fidelity," *Horizons* 17 (1990): 103–127; *Report of the Catholic Theological Society of America Committee on the Profession of Faith and the Oath of Fidelity* (1990). L. ÖRSY *The Profession of Faith and Oath of Fidelity: A Theological and Canonical Analysis* (Wilmington, Del. 1990). H. SCHMITZ "'Professio fidei' und 'Iusiurandum fidelitatis.' Glaubenbekennis und Treueid. Widerbelebung des Antimodernisteneides?" *Archiv für katholisches Kirchenrecht* 157 (1988): 353–429.

[F. R. MCMANUS]

RECONCILIATIO ET PAENITENTIA

Apostolic exhortation of Pope John Paul II, issued 2 December 1984, bringing to completion the work of the sixth general assembly of the Synod of Bishops, which met 29 September to 29 October 1983, during the Holy Year of the Redemption. The introduction affirms that "To speak of reconciliation and penance is for men and women of our time an invitation to rediscover . . . the words with which . . . Jesus Christ began his preaching: 'Repent and believe the Gospel'." Central to this invitation is the premise that "many deep and painful divisions" are "among the various unfortunate characteristics of the world and of humanity" (1). These divisions are so pervasive that it is "not surprising if one notices in the structure of the church herself repercussions and signs of the divisions affecting human society" (2). In view of the universality of these ruptures, the pope advocates that "every institution or organization concerned with serving people and saving them . . . must closely study reconciliation in order to grasp more fully its meaning and significance and in order to draw the necessary practical conclusions" (4).

In part one, "Conversion and Reconciliation: The Church's Task and Commitment," John Paul II appeals to St. Luke's parable of the "Prodigal Son" (5) to teach that "reconciliation is a gift from God, an initiative on his part." This initiative is given "concrete form in the mystery of Christ, the redeemer, the reconciler and the liberator of man from sin in all its forms." The pope invites all to regard the *mysterium crucis* as the "loftiest drama in which Christ . . . accomplishes our reconciliation" (7). The task of reconciliation, however, is shared by "the whole community of believers" who are responsible for "doing everything possible to witness to reconciliation and to bring it about in the world." The church's "central task" is to reconcile all people "with God, with themselves, with neighbor, with the whole of creation; and this in a permanent manner." The church is reconciling when she "proclaims the message of reconciliation" and "shows man the paths and offers the means for . . . this reconciliation" (8).

The theme of part two, "The Love That Is Greater Than Sin," is that although "sin is an integral part of the truth about man" it is "countered by the truth of divine love, which is just, generous and faithful." As such, divine love "reveals itself . . . in forgiveness and redemption." The acknowledgment of one's sin "is the essential first step in returning to God." Reconciliation with God also "presupposes and includes . . . doing penance in the fullest sense of the term: repenting, showing this repentance, adopting a real attitude of repentance." In view of this end, "the church's ministry intervenes in order to bring the person to the 'knowledge of self' . . . to the rejection of evil, to the re-establishment of friendship with God, to a new interior ordering, to fresh ecclesial conversion'' (13).

In part three, ''The Pastoral Ministry of Penance and Reconciliation,'' John Paul II teaches that the ''specific mission of the church'' is ''to evoke conversion and penance in man's heart and to offer him the gift of reconciliation'' (23). Reaffirming the conclusions of the synod assembly, the pope explains that Jesus Christ entrusted the church with two principal means for promoting penance and reconciliation: catechesis and the sacraments (24). On the one hand, within the church's ''mission of operating through dialogue, the pastoral ministry of penance and reconciliation is directed to the members of the body of the church principally through an adequate catechesis'' (26). On the other hand, within the ''mysterious dynamism of the sacraments,'' each particular sacrament, ''over and above its own proper grace, is also a sign of penance and reconciliation'' (27). While the church recognizes ''many and varying forms of penance . . . none is more significant, more divinely efficacious or more lofty . . . than the sacrament of penance'' (28).

In his concluding remarks, the pope offers an ''Expression of Hope'' by appealing to the words of St. Peter: ''Have unity of spirit. . . . Do not return evil for evil. . . . Be zealous for what is right'' (1 Pt 3:8, 9, 13). He then invites all to turn to ''Christ's heart'' to draw from it ''an interior encouragement to hate sin and to be converted to God, and find in it the divine kindness, which lovingly responds to human needs.'' Likewise, he invites all to turn to the immaculate heart of Mary, ''whose fiat marked the beginning of that 'fullness of time' in which Christ accomplished the reconciliation of humanity with God'' (35).

Bibliography: For the text of *Reconciliatio et Paenitentia,* see: *Acta Apostolocae Sedis* 77 (1985): 187–275 (Latin); *Origins* 14, no. 27 (20 December 1984): 432–458; *The Pope Speaks* 30 (1985): 21–82 (English)

[KEVIN GODFREY]

REDEMPTIONIS DONUM

Pope John Paul II's apostolic exhortation, ''The Gift of Redemption,'' addressed to religious, issued 25 March 1984, the Solemnity of the Annunciation, marking the jubilee year of the Redemption, the 1,950th anniversary of the Crucifixion and Resurrection of Christ. The pope reminds religious consecrated by the profession of the evangelical counsels that their vocation is rooted in Christ's Redemption. The jubilee year presents an excel-

Annunciation *by Andrea del Sarto in Palazzo Pitti, Florence, Italy.* (© Arte & Immagini srl/CORBIS)

lent opportunity for men and women religious to renew their lives within the context of the Paschal Mystery so that their witness and service will be even more abundantly shared with humanity. The document commences with a cordial greeting to religious and concludes with a solemn entrusting of the text to the Virgin Mary, the model par excellence for consecrated men and women. The intervening sections address religious vocation, consecration, the evangelical counsels, and religious' love for the Church through their witness and service both within and beyond the context of the ecclesial community. As evident from the numerous New Testament footnotes, the text approaches religious life from a biblical model.

Religious vocation follows from a personal love encounter with Christ. He invites men and women to follow him, chaste, poor, and obedient. Christ's call respects personal freedom, since the person freely chooses a particular way of life. Through his or her affirmative response, the person offers a total gift of self in imitation of the redemptive love of the Father manifested in the Son through the Spirit. Inspired by Christ's love for humanity as reflected in his life and teachings, the person is drawn to a community of brothers or sisters in an institute approved by the Church. The total self-offering of the religious finds expression in a life of love and service in imitation of Christ. The religious becomes a witness and dispenser of good. A vocation is gift freely offered and gratefully received to be shared generously with others.

Religious consecration is rooted in and a radical expression of baptismal consecration. Through profession, religious are consecrated to God through the ministry of the Church and incorporated into their religious families. Religious consecration is inextricably bound to mission, as religious are ''sent forth'' to participate in the mission of the Church through a particular witness of life and apostolic service proper to the institute. Religious consecration deepens the religious' participation in Christ's redemption, enabling them to walk in newness of life. United with Christ in his Paschal Mystery, religious offer themselves for the salvation of the world. They become living sacrifices in imitation of him.

The evangelical counsels enable religious to live lives of charity for others. Only those to whom the grace is given can live a life of consecrated chastity. One becomes a eunuch for the sake of the kingdom and a witness to the Church's love for Christ. In renouncing the goods of marriage and family, religious witness to the eschatological Kingdom of God. Poverty, the first of the beatitudes, enables religious to comprehend more clearly the gift of divinity to humankind. Only those emptying themselves in imitation of Christ can appreciate the infinite richness of God's abundant graces. By their submission to legitimate superiors, religious imitate the obedience of Christ "even unto death," sacrificing their lives for the good of the institute and the Church. This total gift of self reflects the availability of religious for service in the Church.

Religious follow in the footsteps of the apostles through lives of witness and service. Their apostolic action proceeds from the mandate of the Church and is carried out in ecclesial communion. Dependant on a life of prayer and penance, the works of religious bear fruit throughout the numerous particular churches. Formed in the charism of the founder or foundress, religious bear witness to Christ and serve the particular needs of the people of God at different times and places and in the various cultures and particular churches. Both the contemplative and active apostolates of religious carry on the redemptive mystery of Christ. Through community life and their mutual love for one another, religious bring Christ's presence to others that "all may be one." In fine, religious are perennial witnesses to the redeeming love of Christ for all humanity.

The pope recognizes religious life as a true gift and treasure of the Church, a reality that becomes more apparent in meditating on the Redemption of Christ. Religious should invoke the Holy Spirit for assistance in pondering the depths of their identity and dignity. John Paul further pleads with religious to join with the Church in prayer for vocations, that young men and women may respond to Christ's invitation of love. He prays that the witness of religious life may be a source of support and hope for all the Christian faithful. The pope concludes by placing the exhortation in the heart of Mary, who was consecrated unreservedly to God. As model for the whole Church, Mary, chaste, poor and obedient, is a model par excellence for religious.

Bibliography: For the text of *Redemptionis donum,* see: *Acta Apostolicae Sedis* 76 (1984): 513–546 (Latin). *Origins* 13, no. 44 (12 April 1984): 721–731 (English). *The Pope Speaks* 29 (1984): 146–167 (English).

[ROSE MCDERMOTT]

REDEMPTOR HOMINIS

Pope John Paul II's sixth encyclical letter, issued on 4 March 1979. *Redemptor hominis* (RH) can be viewed, especially in the light of subsequent documents and events, as a programmatic statement revealing many of the themes that have come to define the pontificate. Foremost among these is the anticipation of the year 2000. Already in the first paragraph the Pope announces that the millennial year "will be the year of a great Jubilee." It becomes clear that John Paul envisions his papal ministry as the continued unfolding and reception of the Second Vatican Council in anticipation of the Jubilee Year 2000. The Church prepares to enter the twenty-first century precisely by deepening its understanding and implementation of the directions taken at Vatican II.

The encyclical comprises four sections: "Inheritance" (1–6), "The Mystery of the Redemption" (7–12), "Redeemed Man and His Situation in the Modern World" (13-17), and "The Church's Mission and Man's Destiny" (18–22). Although a number of the documents of Vatican II are cited, clearly it is *Gaudium et spes* that provides the encyclical with a specific point of reference.

John Paul brings his vision of Christian personalism to bear in analyzing the conditions within which men and women live in the late twentieth century. Of particular importance is a statement of *Gaudium et spes* 22: "The truth is that only in the mystery of the Incarnate Word does the mystery of man take on light" (cited in no. 8) This is coupled with the statement of *Gaudium et spes* 24 that "man can fully discover his true self only in a sincere giving of himself." The dignity of each person guides the Christian approach to the world, to economics and politics, and to an understanding of the Church itself. So John Paul emphasizes "the primacy of the person over things" (no. 16) and the welfare of the "person in the community" as "the essential criterion for all programs, systems, and regimes" (no. 17).

There is also a striking application of personalism to ecclesiology in RH 21. The Church is portrayed as the "community of disciples" in which "each member has his own special gift," which is "a personal vocation and a form of participation in the Church's saving work." Each member of the "deeply personal" society that is the Church receives a "singular, unique, and unrepeatable grace'' for the Church's communion and mission. Every human being is ''the way'' for the Church (no. 14) precisely because Christ, above all in the Incarnation and Redemption, is the way of self-discovery for each unique, ''unrepeatable'' human being (no. 13).

Another prominent theme of the pontificate is heralded in RH 6—the call to Christian unity. The Church does not have the right to risk being unfaithful to Christ's prayer ''that they may all be one.'' These words, *ut unum sint,* become the title of a groundbreaking encyclical on ecumenism published in 1995. Here again, it is a matter of extending the initiatives of the Second Vatican Council in the attempt to overcome divisions with Christians in both the East and the West.

With the publication of the subsequent encyclicals *Dives in misercordia* (1980) and *Dominum et vivificantem* (1986) it becomes evident that RH is also the first of the ''Trinitarian encyclicals'' of John Paul. The three documents focus successively on the Son, the Father, and the Spirit. A Trinitarian dimension, spelled out in the apostolic letter *Tertio millennio adveniente* (1994) likewise accrues to preparations for the Jubilee Year. John Paul draws in particular upon those scenes from the Gospels that take place in the ''Upper Room'' in order to develop this perspective. His ''theology of the Upper Room'' begins to take shape in RH and comes to fuller expression in the later documents.

Other significant themes of the pontificate also find their place in RH. For example, the importance of the saints (no. 19) and Mary (no. 22) is underscored. Elements of Catholic social teaching are also referenced. In sum, RH stands as a key that unlocks the vast treasure of documents and events comprising the pontificate of John Paul II.

Bibliography: For the text of *Redemptor hominis,* see: *Acta Apostolicae Sedis,* no. 71 (1979): 266–324 (Latin); *Origins* 8, no. 40 (22 March 1979): 625, 627–644 (English); *The Pope Speaks* 24 (1979): 97–147 (English). For commentaries and summaries of *Redemptor hominis,* see: A. DULLES, *The Splendor of Faith: The Theological Vision of Pope John Paul II* (New York: Herder & Herder, 1999). R. T. GAWRONSKI, ''Redemptor Hominis,'' in *The Thought of Pope John Paul II: A Collection of Essays and Studies,* edited by J. M. McDermott, 221–230 (Rome: Editrice Pontificia Università Gregoriana, 1993).

[MORRIS PELZEL]

REDEMPTORIS CUSTOS

Apostolic exhortation, issued on 15 August 1989, by Pope John Paul II to mark the centenary of Leo XIII's encyclical on St. Joseph, *Quamquam pluries.* Pope Leo's encyclical provided the theological basis of St. Joseph's unique and eminently supernatural mission. His vocation stemmed from his marriage to Mary, which made him her true spouse, a witness to her virginity, and a guardian, by divine appointment, of God's own Son incarnate, who paid him every honor due to parents. In *Redemptoris custos,* Pope John Paul wishes to deepen devotion to the ''Patron of the Universal Church'' (title bestowed by Pope Pius IX), to reflect upon his special place at the heart of redemption—the closest after Mary of all the redeemed—and to make clear that he was truly Mary's husband. Implicitly, at least, it seems that the Pope wishes to compensate for past omissions of giving to Joseph his rightful place in relationship to Mary.

In the first of six sections, ''The Gospel Portrait,'' the Pope follows patristic exegesis in understanding the angel's appearance to Joseph as an ''annunciation,'' parallel to Mary's. The angel introduces Joseph to the mystery of Mary's virginal motherhood by the Holy Spirit and directs him to name the child Jesus, the Father's prerogative (Matt. 1:21). Joseph's obedient faith is comparable to Mary's ''fiat.''

The second section, ''The Guardian of the Mystery of God,'' traces Joseph's journey of obedient faith. Joseph accepted his vocation to enter into the mystery of the Incarnation and Redemption precisely through his ''service of fatherhood'' (nos. 7–8). He is the first to follow Mary's ''pilgrimage of faith'' that led to Calvary and Pentecost. Although he would precede Jesus and Mary in departing this life, he was called during the hidden life to serve the person and mission of Christ directly through the exercise of his fatherhood. Besides his authority over Jesus, God also favored Joseph with a share in the love that takes its origin from the heavenly Father. The Old Testament messianic prophecies came to assume a deeper meaning and final fulfillment in this participatory fatherhood of St. Joseph.

In the birth of Jesus, his circumcision, his naming, and the flight into Egypt, Joseph fulfills the role of father in the Holy Family, in terms of both the prescriptions of Jewish law and the mission revealed by the angel. The words of the child Jesus when Mary and Joseph found him in the Temple, ''How is it that you sought me? Did you not know that I must be in my Father's house?'' (Luke 2:48–49), remind Joseph, his presumed father, of the angel's declaration concerning the child. Joseph's role as the guardian of the mystery of God would hereafter be fulfilled by his paternal duty: raising Jesus by feeding and clothing him, as well as educating him in the Law and in a trade. It is fitting that Joseph is venerated immediately after Mary in the Roman Canon since ''he fed him whom the faithful must eat as the bread of eternal life.''

In section three, ''A Just Man, A Husband,'' the Pope finds in the silence of Joseph an eloquent statement of his character and vocation. His obedience to the angel's command not to be afraid to take Mary as his wife becomes the foundation of their marriage. His gift of himself to Mary, though virginal, was nonetheless truly marital, for in its generosity, exclusivity, and covenantal character, it manifests the transformation wrought by the Holy Spirit in the natural love of man and woman. The mystery of the Church, both a spouse and a virgin, is also symbolized by the marriage of Mary and Joseph. As a consequence of the hypostatic union in which humanity has been taken up into unity of the divine Person of the Word made Flesh, all that is human, including the family and the fatherhood of Joseph, is also taken up in Christ.

The three closing sections are entitled, "Work as an Expression of Love," "The Primacy of the Interior Life," and "Patron of the Church in Our Day." In line with popes from Pius IX on, John Paul II emphasizes the Church's need to appeal to Joseph as protector and servant of the mysteries of salvation.

Bibliography: For the text of *Redemptoris custos,* see: *Acta Apostolicae Sedis* 82 (1990): 5–34 (Latin); *Origins* 19, no. 31 (4 January 1990) 507–14 (English); *The Pope Speaks* 35 (1990) 3–20 (English). For commentaries and summaries of *Redemptoris custos,* see: JAMES J. DAVIS, O. P., "Mary and Joseph in the Apostolic Exhortation *Redemptoris Custos,"Marian Studies* 42 (1991): 133–71.

[F. JELLY]

REDEMPTORIS MATER

Pope John Paul II's sixth encyclical letter, issued on the feast of the Annunciation (25 March) in 1987, presaging the Marian year (Pentecost 1987 to Assumption 1988). In the introduction (nos. 1–6), Pope John Paul emphasizes the fact that the mystery of Christ is indissolubly united with that of Mary as the God-bearer (Theotokos), solemnly defined at the Council of Ephesus in 431. This dogma is essentially and primarily a christological doctrine in which Mary is portrayed as the "spotless" and perfect archetype of the Church from the moment of her Immaculate Conception. On the threshold of the new millennium or two thousandth birthday the Son of God incarnate, the Holy Father reflects on the salvation history of the Bible in the light of a meditation on Mary's unique role in our redemption as a "New Eve" or companion of Christ.

The first of the three sections, "Mary in the Mystery of Christ," constitutes a biblical reflection upon what Vatican II aptly described as Mary's "pilgrimage of faith" (*Lumen gentium* 58). The Pope points out that this "pilgrimage" represents a constant focus for the Church and, in a sense, for all humanity. He pursues the same christocentric and ecclesiotypical Mariology as taught in

chapter 8 of *Lumen gentium.* Just as Christ cannot be contemplated apart from the redemptive activity from which his Mystical Body originated, so Mary must be considered closely connected with the Incarnation and the Redemption if she is to be viewed as the archetype of the Church uniquely redeemed by her Immaculate Conception and the consummation of the whole Body of Christ in her glorious Assumption. The Pope begins by citing the Pauline writings on the divine plan of salvation; the unique relationship between Mary and her Son in this story of grace thus becomes the focus of his meditation on the texts from the Synoptics, John, and Acts that concern Mary.

In the second section, "The Mother of God at the Center of the Pilgrim Church," the Pope speaks of Mary's indissoluble link to the mystery of the Church born on the first Pentecost, called by Christ to give apostolic witness to all nations (Matt. 28:19–20). He devotes special attention to the ecumenical issues concerning Mary, especially with respect to the East, longing for the time when both the East and the West will be the one Church again breathing with "both lungs" (no. 34). He sees this as also helping the dialogues between the Catholic Church and the Churches and ecclesial communities of the West. This will lead to the one Church of Christ singing her Magnificat, which continuously "re-echoes" in her heart as she recites the Canticle of Mary at Vespers each day.

In the third section, "Maternal Mediation," the Pope is careful to affirm Mary's salutary influence upon each one of us by her maternal mediation and intercession. He develops what Vatican II calls her spiritual motherhood, "a motherhood in the order of grace" (*Lumen gentium* 62). As in the case of the intercessory role of all the saints in heaven, it is entirely dependent upon and subordinate to the unique mediation of Christ. Mary's maternal mediation finds its origin in her "fullness of grace," embodied in her total selfgiving to God at the Annunciation. Perfected through her Assumption into glory, it extends as far as the redemptive work of her Son. Furthermore, since motherhood is always a personal relation, the maternal mediation of Mary is a way for every Christian to enter into a more intimate and immediate encounter with Christ. The special meaning of the Marian Year, beginning on Pentecost and ending on the feast of the Assumption, is that the Church should reflect on what the mystery of Mary reveals about the Church's mission and hope.

Mary's mediation is the effective maternal presence sharing in the many complex problems of our lives. She is invoked to transform the Church through her role of relating us more closely to the incarnate and saving Christ.

Bibliography: For the text of *Redemptoris mater,* see: *Acta Apostoliae Sedis* 79 (1987): 361–433 (Latin); *Origins* 16, no. 43 (9

Spanish missionary Miguel Angel Isla Lucio, seen in this undated photo with children, was found dead along with two other Spanish missionaries in Zaire on Nov. 8, 1996, where they were aiding refugees from fighting. (AP/Wide World Photos.)

April 1987) 745–766 (English); *TPS* 32 (1987): 159–197 (English). For commentaries and summaries of *Redemptoris mater,* see: *Mary. God's Yes to Man—John Paul's Encyclical "Redemptoris Mater,"* introduction by JOSEPH CARDINAL RATZINGER, commentary by HANS URS VON BALTHASAR (San Francisco: Ignatius Press, 1988). FREDERICK M. JELLY, O. P., "Ecumenical Aspects of *Redemptoris Mater,"* *Marian Studies* 39 (1988): 115–129.

[F. JELLY]

REDEMPTORIS MISSIO

John Paul II's eighth encyclical *Redemptoris missio* (RM), issued on 7 December 1990, celebrates the twenty-fifth anniversary of *Ad gentes* (Vatican II's decree on missionary activity) and the fifteenth anniversary of *Evangelii nuntiandi* (Paul VI's apostolic exhortation on evangelization). RM has the significant subtitle: "On the Permanent Validity of the Church's Missionary Mandate" the pope sounds a clarion and urgent call to all Church sectors to renew their enthusiasm and commitment to evangelize the world. Composed of eight chapters plus an introduction (nos. 1–3) and conclusion (no. 92), RM has a "doctrinal" section (nos. 4–30) and a "pastoral" section (nos. 31–91), respectively treating the "why" and "how" of contemporary mission.

The pope begins by stating his conviction about "the urgency of missionary activity" (no. 1). The pope asserts: "Missionary activity specifically directed 'to the nations' (*ad gentes*) appears to be waning . . . a fact which must arouse concern among all who believe in Christ" (no. 2). Missionary evangelization remains urgent because "it is the primary service which the Church can render to every individual and to all humanity in the modern world" (no. 2).

RM's doctrinal section of three chapters affirms the foundations of mission theology from Vatican II; it also clarifies specific "doubts and ambiguities regarding missionary activity *ad gentes*" (no. 2). Chapter one, "Jesus Christ, the Only Savior," treats core elements of dogmatic theology in relation to mission (e.g., revelation, faith, christology, and soteriology). Chapter two, "The Kingdom of God," is biblically based and describes the intimate relationship of Kingdom to Christ and the Church. Chapter three, "The Holy Spirit, the Principal Agent of Mission," examines the role of the Holy Spirit in the Church's life and its mission. In his strong reaffirmation of these basics of Church teaching, the pontiff continually links mission and faith: "Mission is an issue of faith" (no. 11); "It is only in faith that the Church's mission can be understood and only in faith that it finds its basis'' (no. 4; see also nos. 2, 36, 49).

A holistic vision of evangelization underlies all of RM, particularly its second section on concrete approaches to mission. This vision is in continuity with *Evangelii nutiandi* (nos. 17–24) and emphasizes what contemporary missiological terminology calls ''integral evangelization.'' ''Jesus came to bring integral salvation'' (no. 11); ''evangelical witness . . . is directed toward integral human development'' (no. 42); ''action on behalf of integral development and liberation . . . is most urgently needed'' (no. 58).

By viewing mission with its various complementary and mutually enriching elements, evangelizers are able to appreciate fully that ''Mission is a single but complex reality, and it develops in a variety of ways'' (no. 41). ''This mission is one and undivided, having one origin and one final purpose; but within it, there are different tasks and kinds of activity'' (no. 31). Indeed, integral evangelization is an interpretive key to linking harmoniously the numerous themes and subjects treated in RM.

Several topics are insightfully discussed in RM as they directly relate to mission: Christian family (nos. 42, 80); personal conversion (nos. 47, 59, 60, 81); missionary institutes (nos. 66, 67, 72); youth (nos. 82, 86, 89); local church (nos. 26, 39, 48–52, 62–64, 83–85); interreligious dialogue (nos. 55–57); mission vocations (nos. 32, 65, 66, 79, 84); women (nos. 70, 71); inculturation (nos. 25, 52–54, 76); basic ecclesial communities (no. 51); proclamation (nos. 44–46); mission spirituality (nos. 87–91). This enumeration is much more than a random listing of topics; underlying it is a broad, practical, integral vision for effective evangelization.

The encyclical has several strengths: RM presents solid traditional and biblical theology along with the thought of Vatican II and *Evangelii nuntiandi* and offers several trult original insights, e.g., the threefold situation of mission (nos. 32–34); mission in various ''new worlds'' (no. 37); paschal mystery and mission (nos. 6, 10, 28); and pneumatology and mission (nos. 21–30).

RM opens many avenues of theology, spirituality, mission vision, and concrete responses to contemporary problems, as the Church faces the challenge of ''bringing the Gospel, by witness and word, to all people and nations'' (no. 92). The missionary Church accomplishes its evangelizing task as it ''proceeds along *the path* already trodden by the Virgin Mary'' (no. 92).

Bibliography: For the text of *Redemptoris missio,* see: *Acta Apostolicae Sedis* 83 (1991): 249–339 (Latin); *Origins* 20, no. 34 (31 Jan.1991): 541, 543–568 (English); *The Pope Speaks* 36 (1991): 138–183 (English). For commentaries on *Redemptoris mis-*

sio, see: W. BURROWS, ed., *Redemption and Dialogue: Reading Redemptoris Missio and Dialogue and Proclamation* (Maryknoll, NY: Orbis Books, 1993). J. KROEGER, *Living Mission: Challenges in Evangelization Today* (Maryknoll, NY: Orbis Books, 1994). There are also commentaries to be found in *Omnis Terra.* They are written by Degrijse (Feb. / Mar. 1993); Kroeger (Dec. 1991 / Jan. 1995); LaVerdiere (Sep.–Oct. 1991); Odorico (Feb. 1994 / Jul.–Aug. 1994); Wolanin (Dec. 1994); Zago (Feb. 1991 / Nov. 1991 / Nov. 1992).

[J. KROEGER]

SACRAE DISCIPLINAE LEGES

Apostolic constitution (''Sacred Disciplinary Laws'') issued by Pope John Paul II, 25 January 1983, to promulgate a new code of canon law. The pope recalls that Pope John XXIII, on the same day in 1959 that he announced his intention to convoke an ecumenical council, made known his intention to reform the code that had been promulgated in 1917. *Sacrae disciplinae leges* addresses two questions. First, why did Pope John XXIII call for a reform of the existing code? Pope John Paul II points out the intuition of his predecessor anticipated the request of the Second Vatican Council and that the preparation of the new code is based on the work of the council and its focus on the renewal of Christian living. The constitution reviews the preliminary work carried out during the pontificates of Paul VI and John Paul I, and calls attention to the collegial spirit that characterizes and distinguishes the process of developing the present code. Pope John Paul II expresses his deep gratitude to everyone who collaborated in the drafting of the code and mentions several individuals by name. The pope makes it clear that the act of promulgation is ''an expression of pontifical authority and therefore invested with a primatial character,'' but at the same time he acknowledges it is a collegial work of individuals and institutions.

The second question addressed by the constitution touches on the very nature of canon law. The code derives from ''the distant patrimony'' of law contained in the Old and New Testament which in turn gave rise to the Church's juridical-legislative tradition. It is intended as legislative instrument that ''while assigning primacy to love, grace and charisms,'' contains the fundamental elements of the hierarchical and organic structure of the Church and the fundamental principles that govern the threefold office entrusted to the Church itself. In no way is it a substitute for faith, grace, charisms, and charity in the life of the Church. The image of the Church in the conciliar documents, in particular *Lumen gentium* and *Gaudium et spes,* provides the fundamental criteria that govern the entire code. Pope John Paul II emphasizes the elements that characterize this image: the Church as the people of God and hierarchical authority as service; the Church as communion determining relations between the particular churches and the universal Church, and between collegiality and the primacy; all members of the people of God, in the way suited to each, participate in the priestly, prophetic, and kingly office of Christ, to which doctrine is also linked to the duties and rights of the faithful; and finally the Church's commitment to ecumenism. The Church, organized as a social and visible structure, must have norms to guide the functions divinely entrusted to it, especially the exercise of sacred power and the administration of the sacraments. Canonical norms regulate the mutual relations of the faithful, guarantee the rights of individuals, and foster common initiatives undertaken to sustain a more perfect Christian life. The apostolic constitution decreed that the new code has the force of law in the whole Latin Church beginning from the first day of Advent (27 November), 1983.

[ART ESPELAGE]

SACRI CANONES

The decree *Sacri canones* (''Sacred Canons''), 18 October 1990, promulgated the *Code of Canons of the Eastern Churches.* As Pope John Paul II notes in the introduction, the title harkens back to the seventh ecumenical council of Nicea in 787. It spoke of the ancient canons ''that have been put forth by the divine Apostles, as tradition has it, and by the 'six holy and universal synods and local councils' as well as 'by our holy Fathers.''' As the pope points out, the authors of the sacred canons of Nicea considered them to constitute ''a single body of ecclesiastical law and confirmed it as a 'code' for all of the Eastern Churches.'' Alexandrian, Antiochene, Armenian, Chaldean, and Contantinopolitan traditions regard the sacred canons as a notable constituent of their heritage. For these churches the sacred canons constitute a single, common foundation of church order rooted in the rich variety of rites, that is, in the liturgical, theological, spiritual, and disciplinary heritage of those churches. Pope John Paul II goes on to say that ''it was always clear to each of the churches that any ordering of ecclesiastical discipline would only be firm if grounded in norms deriving from traditions recognized by the supreme authority of the Church or contained in canons promulgated by it, and that rules of particular law had to conform to the higher law in order to be valid, but that they were null if they differed from it.''

Fidelity to this heritage governed and shaped the compilation of the new code in accordance with Vatican II's decree on the Eastern Churches (*Orientalium ecclesiarum,* no. 6). The new code is presented as a help to the

ecumenical movement because ''the Eastern churches that are not yet in full communion with the Catholic Church are governed by the same and basically single heritage of canonical discipline, namely the 'sacred canons' of the first centuries of the Church.'' The decree recounts the efforts of the popes, beginning with Leo XIII at the end of the nineteenth century, to codify the canons. From the first the Roman Pontiffs planned to promulgate two codes, one for the Latin Church and the other for the Eastern Churches, in order to preserve faithfully the observance of all the Eastern rites derived from the above-mentioned five traditions. The *Code of Canons of the Eastern Churches* is careful to entrust to the particular law of individual Churches *sui iuris* whatever is not considered necessary to the common good of all the Eastern Churches. In establishing new laws the experts who labored over the Code kept uppermost in mind the best way to safeguard the economy of the salvation of souls in the richness of the life of the Eastern Churches while maintaining coherence and agreement with sound tradition.

Pope John Paul II writes: ''The *Code of Canons of the Eastern Churches* should be considered as a new complement to the teaching proposed by the Second Vatican Council. With its publication the canonical ordering for the whole Church is thus at length completed, following as it does the *Code of Canon Law* for the Latin Church, promulgated in 1983, and the 'Apostolic Constitution on the Roman Curia' of 1988, which is added to both Codes as the primary instrument of the Roman Pontiff for 'the communion that binds together, as it were, the whole Church' (ap. const. *Pastor bonus,* no. 2).'' In conclusion the pope orders that beginning 1 October 1991 the Code has the force of law for all Eastern Catholic Churches.

[ART ESPELAGE]

SALVIFICI DOLORIS

Apostolic letter, ''Salvific Suffering,'' issued by Pope John Paul II, 11 February 1984. The letter offers a reflection on the meaning of suffering, the central theme of the Holy Year of the Redemption (1983–1984), which the pope decreed to mark the 1,950th anniversary of the redeeming death of Jesus Christ. The introduction affirms that suffering forms ''part of the history of man'' and that it is ''illuminated by the word of God'' (no. 1). In view of the centrality of suffering for humanity, John Paul II explains that ''the theme of suffering in a special way demands to be faced in the context of the holy year of the Redemption . . . because the redemption was accomplished through the cross of Christ, that is, through his suffering'' (no. 3).

A depiction of the Crucifixion currently located in Aachen, Germany. (© Archivo Iconografico, S.A./CORBIS)

In the second section, "The World of Human Suffering," the pope distinguishes between "physical" and "moral" suffering. The former occurs when the "body is hurting"; the latter refers to "pain of the soul" (no. 5). Suffering is caused by the existence of evil which is "a certain lack, limitation or distortion of the good." As such, it is intertwined with both good and evil, and is related to the mystery of human freedom. Although the world of suffering exists in "dispersion," all who suffer are united in "solidarity . . . above all through the persistent question of the meaning of suffering" (no. 7).

In the third section, "The Quest for an Answer to the Question of the Meaning of Suffering," John Paul II stresses the importance of searching for answers to the question of suffering because suffering itself increases in proportion to one's lack of understanding of it (no. 9). One biblical answer is that suffering is a manner of punishment for faults that violate the transcendent moral order. On this view, suffering both "guarantees the moral order" (no. 10) and "creates the possibility of rebuilding goodness in the subject who suffers" (no. 12). The suffering of the innocent, on the other hand, exemplified in the Book of Job, demonstrates that suffering is not linked exclusively to moral order; the Lord tests Job in order "to demonstrate the latter's righteousness" (no. 11). Finally, love is the "richest source of the meaning of suffering." Ultimately, through Christ's cross humanity enters into the mystery "to discover the 'why' of suffering" (no. 13).

In the fourth section, "Jesus Christ: Suffering Conquered by Love," the pope explains that "salvation means liberation from evil," and therefore salvation and suffering are closely bound to one another. In Christ's life, "God gave his Son to 'the world' to free man from evil," an event "which bears within itself the definitive and absolute perspective on suffering." In Christ's suffering "love is manifested, the definitive love both of that only-begotten Son and of the Father who for this reason 'gives' his son. This is love for man, love for the 'world': It is salvific love.'' The opposite of salvation is not merely "temporal suffering," but "definitive suffering," which is "the loss of eternal life, being rejected by God, damnation." Thus, "the only begotten Son was given to humanity to protect man against this definitive evil and against definitive suffering" (no. 14). Confronted by the question of the meaning of suffering, Christ answers "not only by his teaching, that is, by the good news, but most of all by his suffering" (no. 18).

In the fifth section, "Sharers in the Sufferings of Christ," the pope teaches that Christ's passion effectively "raised human suffering to the level of redemption" so that each person who suffers becomes a "sharer in the redemptive suffering of Christ" (no. 19). Participation in Christ's suffering finds expression in two ways. First, Christ has become "a sharer in all human suffering." Second, each individual discovers "new content and new meaning" in his or her own sufferings through faith (no. 20). Ultimately, "to share in the suffering of Christ is at the same time to suffer for the kingdom of God" (no. 21). To such salvific suffering "is linked hope in that glory which has its beginning in the cross of Christ" (no. 22). Insofar as Christ's weakness manifested his power and his humiliation manifested his messianic greatness, so too all suffering is "an invitation to manifest the moral greatness of man" (no. 23). In view of this greatness, suffering with Christ "unleashes hope" through which the individual can "maintain the conviction that suffering will not get the better of him, that it will not deprive him of his dignity as a human being, a dignity linked to the meaning of life." Together, those who participate in the paschal mystery constitute the community of the church, which is expressed in this: "that already in the act of baptism, which brings about a configuration with Christ, and then through his sacrifice—sacramentally through the Eucharist—the church is continually being built up spiritually as the body of Christ" (no. 24). Christ wishes to be united to this sacred body, especially to those who suffer.

In the sixth section, "The Gospel of Suffering," the pope presents a meditation on the important legacy the witnesses of Christ pass on to the church and to humanity. This legacy is "a specific gospel of suffering" written by the redeemer. Together with the living word of his teaching, this suffering "became a rich resource for all those who shared in Jesus' sufferings." Beginning with the first generation of disciples and to disciples down through the ages, "Christ did not conceal from his listeners the need for suffering" (no. 25).

In the seventh section, "The Good Samaritan," the pope presents a reflection on Christ's parable of the Good Samaritan. Exemplified by the Samaritan, "'neighbor' also means the person who carried out the commandment of love of neighbor." Likewise, "it indicates what the relationship of each one of us must be toward our suffering neighbor." The person who "stops beside the suffering of another" assumes the position of the Good Samaritan. "Stopping," however, "does not mean curiosity, but availability" (no. 28). Thus, suffering is present in the world "in order to unleash love in the human person" (no. 29).

In his concluding remarks John Paul II teaches that suffering is both supernatural and human. Insofar as it is rooted in the divine mystery of the redemption of the world, it is supernatural. It is also deeply human, however, because in it the person discovers his humanity, dignity, and mission.

Bibliography: For the text of Salvifici doloris, see: *Acta Apostolicae Sedis* 76 (1984): 201–250 (Latin); *Origins* 13, no. 37 (23 Feb 1984): 609–624 (English); *The Pope Speaks* 29 (1984): 105–139 (English)

[KEVIN GODFREY]

SAPIENTIA CHRISTIANA

An apostolic constitution issued by Pope John Paul II on 15 April 1979. *Sapientia Christiana* is the canonical, academic law governing "ecclesiastical" post-secondary education.

Sapientia Christiana has two major parts: a discursive proemium or introduction in six brief sections, followed by a total of 94 normative articles, including a few transitional norms for putting the constitution into effect. The articles are both general norms for all ecclesiastical universities, faculties, and institutes and special norms for particular faculties, especially theology, philosophy, and canon law. This second main section concludes with an enumeration of the other kinds of faculties already authorized as ecclesiastical: Christian archeology, Biblical studies and ancient Christian studies, Church history, Christian and classical literature, liturgy, missiology, sacred (liturgical) music, psychology, educational science or pedagogy, religious science, social sciences, Arabic and Islamic studies, medieval studies, oriental ecclesiastical studies, *utriusque iuris* (both canon and civil law).

The general norms of the apostolic constitution (nos. 1–64) are divided into 10 sections: nature and purpose of ecclesiastical universities and faculties; the academic community and its government; teachers; students; officials and staff assistants; program of studies; academic degrees; matters relating to teaching; economic matters; and planning and cooperation of faculties. These sections are closely paralleled in the norms of application, and the same is true of the series of special norms in both documents (nos. 65–87 of *Sapientia Christiana*) concerning the particular kinds of faculties.

In dealing with the governance of ecclesiastical faculties, the constitution introduces the distinction between personal governance (by academic administrators) and collegial governance (by the teachers in their councils, committees, and the like); there is concern as well for a role for students to take part in the academic community ''in those aspects which can contribute to the common good of the faculty or university.'' In the respective sections dealing with teachers and students, it is required that the statutes safeguard rights—of the individuals, of the institution, of the ecclesial community.

The role and authority of the chancellor or *magnus cancellarius* is spelled out: he is ''the ordinary prelate on whom the university or faculty legally [i.e., canonically] depends, representing the Holy See to the university or faculty and equally the university or faculty to the Holy See.'' Commonly but not necessarily, the diocesan bishop or other local ordinary is the chancellor, except in the case of the ecclesiastical faculties of religious institutes.

An important section deals with the appointment and dismissal of teachers, with emphasis upon the kinds of academic credentials expected in a particular region and upon the probity of life and integrity of doctrine of teachers. They are to carry out their work ''in full communion with the authoritative magisterium of the Church, above all, with that of the Bishop of Rome.'' Those who teach disciplines concerning faith and morals require a canonical mission from the chancellor ''for they do not teach on their own authority but by virtue of a mission they have received from the Church.'' Teachers in other disciplines (and teachers who are not Catholics) require a permission to teach (*venia docendi*), again from the chancellor. Prior to permanent appointment (that is, with continuous tenure) and/or prior to promotion to the highest academic rank of ordinary or full professor, a teacher must also have a declaration or clearance from the Holy See, the *nihil obstat*.

Corresponding to these requirements for appointment or tenure, the norms of application spell out the steps to be taken before the suspension or dismissal of a teacher, but require that the internal statutes of each faculty determine the precise procedure. In the section treating the program of studies, the constitution attempts to define a balanced academic freedom (no. 39).

The pastoral concern of the constitution, and of the norms for application, is evident in the sections on planning and cooperation of ecclesiastical faculties. Methods of affiliation, aggregation, and broad cooperation among institutions are proposed, with special mention of the need to study the distribution of ecclesiastical faculties, a responsibility also attributed to the conferences of bishops. For the rest, the documents deal with specific requirements of persons and programs, of criteria for admission and the conferral of degrees, of support and facilities. In almost every case it is expected that the universal norms of the Roman documents are to be made effective through more detailed statutory norms enacted by the respective faculties.

As a whole *Sapientia Christiana* and the supplementary *ordinationes* may be described as a combination of principles and binding requirements, and the question of their specificity is a matter of degree. It went into effect at the beginning of the 1980–81 academic year or of the 1981 academic year, depending on the calendar in use in various places.

[F. R. MCMANUS]

SCRIPTUARUM THESAURUS

Apostolic constitution, ''The Treasury of the Scriptures,'' promulgated by Pope John Paul II on the feast of Saint Mark the Evangelist (25 April), 1979, declaring the New Vulgate edition of Scripture as ''typical.'' Issued within seven months of John Paul II's election, *Scriptuarum thesaurus* was clearly already in conceptual development for some time previous, furthering a long-standing project to provide a new critical edition of Jerome's Latin Vulgate, that edition of the Scriptures which, the document notes, ''in the regions of the West the Church has preferred.'' Indeed, states *Scriptuarum thesaurus,* the Church evidences ''such a great esteem'' for the Vulgate ''by preparing a text according to critical methodology, and precisely by means of the edition which is still being arranged along scientific guidelines by the monks of the Abbey of Saint Jerome in Rome founded for that purpose by our predecessor happy memory Pius XI (cf. apostolic constitution *Inter praecipuas,* 15 June 1933).'' This critical updating and revision of the Vulgate text in the light of more recent manuscript discoveries and other critical textual editions traces its immediate ancestry to Leo XIII's validation, in *Providentissimus Deus* (18 November 1893), of the primacy of the original languages in the understanding of the inspired text.

Scriptuarum thesaurus traces the history of the critical textual revision of the Vulgate. It was endorsed by the Second Vatican Council, and required to ''take into account the style of Christian Latinity as well as the entire tradition of the Latin Church'' (*Sacrosanctum Concilium* 91). The project had been reinvigorated by Paul VI, who, in 1965, established a special Pontifical Commission to revise all the books of Scripture for the sake of producing a Latin edition that would take account of biblical studies and that could be used in the liturgy. *Scriptuarum thesaurus* explains the ''revision'' of the Vulgate text by citing Paul VI's allocution of 23 December 1966, emphasizing the respect paid to the old text as well as to the legitimate demands of modern critical studies. The document concludes by recognizing the ''enthusiastic support'' of Paul VI and John Paul I in advancing this critical textual revision and by declaring ''the New Vulgate edition of the Holy Bible'' to be an *editio typica,* promulgated ''to be used especially in the sacred Liturgy.''

Bibliography: For the text of *Scriptuarum thesaurus,* see: *Acta Apostolicae Sedis* 71 (1979): 557–59 (Latin).

[CHRISTOPHER J. SCHRECK]

SLAVORUM APOSTOLI

Pope John Paul II's fourth encyclical letter, ''The Apostles of the Slavs,'' issued 2 June 1985, commemorating the eleventh centenary of the evangelizing work of Sts. Cyril and Methodius. In the Introduction, Pope John Paul recalls and expands on his apostolic letter *Egregiae virtutis* (1980), in which he named the brother-saints as co-patrons of Europe along with St. Benedict, as well as letters of his predecessors. In a personal note, John Paul acknowledges that he felt ''a particular obligation'' to pay tribute to Cyril and Methodius, being ''the first Pope called to the See of Peter from Poland, and thus from the midst of the Slav nations'' (3).

The encyclical looks back at the apostolic lives and work of evangelization of Cyril and Methodius. Part 2 presents a biographical sketch of the two saints. Part 3 recalls their evangelizing activity. Part 4 emphasizes their vision of the Church as one, holy, and universal. Part 5 proposes that their catechetical and pastoral method remains ''instructive for the Church today.'' Part 6 cites their work as a model of inculturation—''the incarnation of the Gospel in native culture and also the introduction of these cultures into the life of the Church'' (21). Part 7 explains the significance of the Christian millennium to the common culture of the Slavic world. Cyril and Methodius ''made a decisive contribution to the building of Europe not only in Christian religious communion but also to its civil and cultural union'' (n. 27).

Woven throughout the encyclical are reflections on the method the brothers used in evangelizing Europe and the contributions they made to Slavic culture. The words

St. Cyril of Belozersk, with scenes from his life. (© The State Russian Museum/CORBIS.)

of Christ, ''Preach the Gospel to the whole creation'' (Mk 16:15) inspired their missionary work, and they tried to adopt the customs and language of the people to whom they were preaching. Among their principal contributions were the composition of a new alphabet and their translation of the sacred literature into the Old Slavonic language. Their profound work in orthodox doctrine and their zeal gained a great deal of admiration from Roman pontiffs, patriarchs of Constantinople, and Byzantine emperors. Because of their ability to stay in touch with both the patriarch of Constantinople and the Roman See, Cyril and Methodius bridged the Eastern and Western traditions which come together in the one, universal Church.

Despite misunderstandings—the price they had to pay for their work—Cyril and Methodius served as instruments of unity in places where there was not unity between individual communities. Their approach was based on the reality that every individual and all cultures and nations have their place in God's mysterious plan of salvation.

In the conclusion of the encyclical Pope John Paul states that Cyril and Methodius by their words and life, sustained by the charism of the Holy Spirit, gave an example of a fruitful vocation not only for past time, but also for the centuries that are to come.

Bibliography: For the text of *Slavorum apostoli,* see: *Acta Apostolicae Sedis* 77 (1985): 779–813 (Latin); *Origins* 15, no. 8 (18 July 1985): 113–25; *The Pope Speaks* 30 (1985): 252–75 (English).

[DAVID CLOONEY]

SOLLICITUDO REI SOCIALIS

Pope John Paul II's seventh encyclical letter, issued 30 Dec. 1987, marking the twentieth anniversary of *Populorum progressio,* Pope Paul VI's encyclical on the development of peoples. John Paul II presents a series of reflections on the requirements of authentic human development, the international duty of solidarity, and the social responsibility of the church. In considering the relevance of the earlier document's themes for the present era, the pope aims both to pay homage to his predecessor and to set forth the tradition of Catholic social teaching (nos. 1–4).

The pope begins by characterizing *Populorum progressio* as an application of the teachings of the Second Vatican Council, and in particular the social tenets of the Pastoral Constitution *Gaudium et spes,* to the problem of the development of peoples (nos. 5–7). The encyclical, he states, is original in three respects: its bringing to bear of an authoritative ethical perspective on a problem often viewed as social and economic, its transferral of the "social question" to a global context, and its exposition of the proposition that "Development is the new name for peace" (nos. 8–10).

The next section surveys conditions in the contemporary world and comments on their implications for a renewal of the teachings of *Populorum progressio.* After discussing such indicators as world poverty; the divisions between East and West, North and South, and the First, Second, Third, and Fourth Worlds; and cultural ills such as illiteracy, social and religious oppression, and the suppression of economic initiative, the pope concludes that Paul VI's hopes for development have remained unmet and that, indeed, the situation has worsened (nos. 11–16). Because global interdependence determines that the levels of development of all nations are intertwined, even developed countries have come to manifest signs of underdevelopment, in the form of a housing crisis and burgeoning under- or unemployment. Moreover, loans to developing nations, originally intended to contribute to their development, have instead aggravated underdevelopment by producing a system of international debt (nos. 17–19). In analyzing the causes of these failures, the pope focuses on political factors, criticizing the ideological conflict between East and West and its impact, via the mechanisms of neo-colonialism, on the developing world; the "disorders" of arms production and the arms trade; and population control policies rooted in an "erroneous and perverse" concept of human development (nos. 20–25). This largely negative balance, he adds, should not overshadow hopeful signs such as increasing respect for human rights, a growing sense of international solidarity, and the spread of "ecological concern" (no. 26).

The "true nature of the development of peoples" forms the subject of the following section. This concept is distinguished from both a naive, Enlightenment belief in progress and a purely economic conception of development leading, in practice, not only to underdevelopment but to a nexus of consumerism, materialism, and anomie the pope terms "superdevelopment." Authentic human development, by contrast, retains an economic component, but subordinates the "having" of goods to the "being" of the person (nos. 27–8). Its essence, meanwhile, is moral and theological: as the pope shows in a reflection on the creation accounts in Genesis, "full" development is rooted in the human participation in the image of God and the vocation to obey the divine law, to work, and to serve others that flows from it (nos. 29–30). Christian faith, with its vision of the Kingdom, at once found a new assurance regarding the attainability of development and mandates that the church has an obligation to work toward it; this obligation, indeed, is shared by all individuals as well as the various communities including religious ones in which they find themselves, and it is mirrored in the right of all peoples or nations to full development (nos. 31–2). The moral character of authentic development is exhibited in its intrinsic commitment to the spectrum of human rights, including social, economic, political, personal, and collective rights; to the values of solidarity, freedom, and love of God and neighbor; and to respect for nature (nos. 33–4).

The pope next brings this account of development to bear on a "theological reading of modern problems." In keeping with development's primarily moral character, he asserts, the chief obstacles to development are also of a moral nature, and consist in such failings as an "all-consuming desire for profit," a widespread "thirst for power," and, building on such attitudes, "structures of sin" (nos. 35–7). In order to overcome these evils, a profound change in spiritual attitudes for Christians, a conversion is necessary, leading to the embrace of the virtue of solidarity: "a firm and persevering determination to commit oneself to the common good." The pope's exposition of the functions of solidarity both within and among societies demonstrates it to be a core value of Catholic social teaching, intimately bound up with such notions as peace, justice, the common good, the option for the poor, and the universal destination of the goods of creation. Solidarity is, he further notes, a Christian virtue, closely related to charity and, in its commitment to human unity, modeled on and symbolic of the Trinity and Christian communion (nos. 38–40).

A penultimate section presents particular guidelines for addressing the problem of development. Since the church does not profess to offer a ''third way'' between liberal capitalism and Marxist collectivism, these guidelines are not technical but moral and theological in character. Drawing on Catholic social teaching regarding the primacy of the poor, the universal destination of goods, and the ''social mortgage'' on private property, the pope calls for reforms involving the international trade and monetary systems, international organizations, and technology exchanges. Invoking the Catholic social doctrine of participation, he further counsels developing nations to promote the literacy, self-sufficiency, and political involvement of their citizens and to cooperate with one another in regional associations (nos. 41–5).

In his conclusion, the pope, making reference to Latin American liberation theology, identifies a strong link between authentic development and ''true'' liberation. Both values are manifested in the exercise of solidarity, a virtue the pope exhorts all religious people to exhibit. The letter closes with a reflection on the sacrament of the Eucharist and an appeal for the intercession of Mary (nos. 46–9).

Bibliography: For the text of *Sollicitudo rei socialis,* see: *Acta Apostolicae Sedis* 80 (1988) 513–86 (Latin); *Origins* 17, no 38 (3 Mar 1988): 642–60 (English); *The Pope Speaks* 33 (1988): 122–55 (English). For commentaries and summaries on *Sollicitudo rei socialis,* see: JEAN-YVES CALVEZ,''Sollicitudo Rei Socialis,'' in Judith A. Dwyer, ed. *The New Dictionary of Catholic Social Thought* (Collegeville, Minn.: Liturgical Press, 1994), 912–917. PETER HENRIOT, EDWARD P. DEBERRI, and MICHAEL J. SCHULTHEIS, *Catholic Social Teaching: Our Best Kept Secret* (Maryknoll, N.Y.: Orbis, 1988), 74–82.

[W. BARBIERI]

TERTIO MILLENNIO ADVENIENTE

Pope John Paul II's apostolic letter, ''As the Third Millennium Draws Near,'' dated 10 November 1994 outlines in great detail preparations to celebrate the Year of Jubilee at the beginning of the third millennium. The first of the five parts focuses on the person of Jesus Christ and explains the significance of the incarnation for salvation and redemption. Through the mediation of Christ, the Father sends the Holy Spirit who enables humans to share the inmost life of God.

Part two situates the Year of Jubilee in the history of salvation, recalling its origins and observance in the Old Testament, which included the emancipation of

Fireworks illuminate the Giza pyramids at midnight early Saturday, Jan. 1, 2000 during a millennium celebration. (AP/ Wide World Photos. Photograph by Enric Marti)

slaves, restoration of ancestral property, and the cancellation of debts. The foundations of this tradition were grounded in the theology of creation and divine providence, which holds that ''The riches of creation were to be considered as a common good of the whole of humanity.'' Individuals who possessed goods as personal property ''were really only stewards, ministers charged with working in the name of God.'' The jubilee year, meant to restore social justice, is a basis of the Church's social teaching which was reclaimed in the encyclical *Rerum novarum*. A second important aspect of ''this year of the Lord's favor'' (Isaiah's description), is that it is a time ''of remission of sins and of the punishments due them, a year of reconciliation between disputing parties, a year of manifold conversions and of sacramental and extrasacramental penance.'' In human terms jubilees mark anniversaries in the lives of individuals and institutions, and the extraordinary jubilee that marks 2,000 years since the birth of Christ is significant ''not only for Christians but indirectly for the whole of humanity, given the prominent role played by Christianity during these two [past] millennia.'' Jubilee speaks not merely of an inner joy but a jubilation that is manifested outwardly ''for the coming of God is also an outward, visible, audible and tangible event.''

Part three interprets many events of the past century, notably ''the providential event'' of the Second Vatican Council, as steps in the preparation for the celebration of the year of jubilee. The council drew much from the experiences of the immediate past, ''especially from the intellectual legacy left by Pius XII,'' and the efforts of other popes. During the council, the Church examined its own identity, reaffirmed the universal call to holiness, made provision for the reform of the liturgy, gave impetus to renewal of church life at every level, and promoted the variety of Christian vocations from laity and religious to deacons, priests, and bishops. "No council had ever spoken so clearly about Christian unity, about dialogue with non-Christian religions, about the specific meaning of the old covenant and of Israel, about the dignity of each person's conscience, about the principle of religious liberty, about the different cultural traditions within which the Church carries out her missionary mandate and about the means of social communication." The apostolic letter continues, "The best preparation for the new millennium," therefore, is a renewed commitment to the teachings and spirit of Vatican II. The series of synods, general and regional, national and diocesan, begun after the council have contributed to the preparation for the year of jubilee by promoting "evangelization, or rather the new evangelization." The popes of the past century, each in his own way, prepared for the new millennium by their efforts "to promote and defend the basic values of peace and justice in the face of contrary tendencies of our time."

John Paul II states that the theme of the Great Jubilee as "a new Advent" is "as it were a hermeneutical key to my pontificate." It is the key to understanding the importance he gives to his travels throughout the world, to visits with world leaders, and to his conversations with leaders of other churches. The Great Jubilee of the year 2000 builds on other jubilee years celebrated in the past century, notably the Marian Year and the Year of the Family.

The first three parts are prologue. The fourth and longest part of *Tertio millennio adveniente* outlines "a specific program of initiatives for the immediate preparation of the Great Jubilee," the product of consultation with the College of Cardinals and proposals made by presidents of episcopal conferences. Initiatives during the first phase of the immediate preparation (1994–96) would be designed to raise the consciousness of the faithful as to the significance of the year of jubilee and the need for repentance, conversion, and renewal. "The holy door of the Jubilee Year 2000 should be symbolically wider . . . because humanity, upon reaching this goal, will leave behind not just a century but a millennium." The Church cannot cross the threshold into a new millennium without encouraging her children to purify themselves, acknowledging their past errors, infidelities, and weaknesses. Among the sins that require repentance are those that have contributed to wound church unity in the past 1,000 years. The Great Jubilee demands fitting ecumenical initiatives so we can celebrate it, "if not completely united, at least much closer to overcoming the divisions of the second millennium." Another "painful chapter" that the Church must review in a spirit of repentance "is the acquiescence given, especially in certain centuries, to intolerance and even the use of violence in the service of truth." Above all we must examine our conscience regarding the evils of the present day: religious indifference, confusion in the ethical sphere "even about the fundamental values of respect for life and the family," erroneous theological views, and the crisis of obedience vis-à-vis the Church's magisterium. Must not Christians ask themselves about their acquiescence concerning the violation of human rights by totalitarian regimes? The examination of conscience must also consider the reception given to Vatican II. The witness of martyrs in our own century cannot be forgotten. In preparation for the year 2000 the Apostolic See would undertake to update the martyrologies for the universal Church. "In particular, there is a need to foster the recognition of the heroic virtues of men and women who have lived their Christian vocation in marriage" to encourage other Christian spouses. The cardinals and bishops emphasized the need for more regional synods in America, Oceania, and Asia, to address local problems of evangelization and other challenges.

The second phase in the preparations would take place over a span of three years (1997–99), each with its own focus and particular themes. The theme of year one is distinctly Christological, with a focus on "Jesus Christ, the one savior of the world, yesterday, today and forever." It emphasizes baptism, the gift of faith, personal renewal, and solidarity with one's neighbor, especially the most needy. The theme of year two focuses on the Holy Spirit, the principle of God's self-communication in the order of grace, who makes present in the Church and in the soul of each individual the unique revelation of Christ. It calls for a renewed appreciation of the sacraments, in particular confirmation, the variety of charisms and ministries, and the new evangelization. In view of the eschatological perspective of the kingdom of God at the end of time, this year should be a time of revitalizing the theological virtue of hope. The final stage of preparation aims at broadening horizons so that believers will see things in the perspective of Christ's revelation of the Father in heaven. Because God is Father of all, year three is a time for special emphasis on interreligious dialogue, preeminently with Jews and Muslims. The third year of preparation highlights charity, recalling its twofold aspect, love of God and love of neighbor, as summing up the moral life of the believer. In each of the three years, different aspects of Mary's role in the story of salvation receive special attention.

The actual celebration of the Great Jubilee, the focus of the three years of preparation, is a separate phase. It will take place in the Holy Land, in Rome, and the local churches throughout the world. Its aim will be "to give glory to the Trinity, from whom everything in the world and in history comes and to whom everything returns." The celebration will be "intensely Eucharistic," culminating the International Eucharistic Congress in Rome. "The ecumenical and universal character of the sacred jubilee can be fittingly reflected in a meeting of all Christians," but it must be carefully prepared in collaboration with Christians of other traditions and "a grateful openness to those religions whose representatives might wish to acknowledge the joy shared by all the disciples of Christ."

Part five concludes the apostolic letter with a reaffirmation, citing Vatican II and Pope John Paul II's own encyclicals, of the Church's missionary character. "Indeed missionary outreach is part of her very nature." It also says, "the future of the world and the Church belongs to the younger generation" who will reach maturity in the coming century. Beneath the changes in human history the Church maintains there are also many unchanging realities that "have their ultimate foundation in Christ, who is the same yesterday and today and forever."

Bibliography: For the text of *Tertio millennio adveniente*, see: *Acta Apostolicae Sedis* 82 (1995): 5–41 (Latin); *Origins* 24, no. 24 (24 Nov. 1994): 401–416 (English); *The Pope Speaks* 40 (1995): 85–113 (English).

[B. L. MARTHALER]

UNION OF BREST, APOSTOLIC LETTER ON THE FOURTH CENTENARY OF THE

Apostolic letter issued by Pope John Paul II on 12 November 1995, commemorating the fourth centenary of the union between the Greek Catholic Church in the Ukraine and the Apostolic See. Pope John Paul evokes the "often tragic and sorrowful journey of this Church" (1) and recalls that after his election to the papacy he spoke out firmly on the right of that Church to exist. He maintains that this celebration of the Union of Brest has to be seen in the context of the millennium of the baptism of Kievan Rus': it is a union rooted in the original full communion of the Byzantine Churches and the Church of Rome. The pope reflects on the historical development of the events that took place in the life of the divided Church (since 1054), and the role of Ukrainian clergy in the process of union between two sister-churches. A special stress is put on the role of the Basilian Order, as well as Metropolitans Andrii Sheptyckyi and Josyf Slipyj and their contribution to the growth of the unity between the Ukrainian Church and the Roman See in this century. The church remembers the numerous martyrs of the Ukrainian Church, and the memory of them cannot be erased.

Pope John Paul emphasizes the role of the Holy See in its assistance to the Diaspora church, particularly in the United States, Canada, Brazil, Argentina, and Australia. He praises the freedom of the Ukrainian Greek Catholic Church in these times and its active role in the universal church and world history.

Much of the letter is devoted to the significance of the Ukrainian Greek Catholic Church in the present ecumenical movement. The teaching of the Second Vatican Council on the nature and unity of the church is indispensable for understanding the celebration of the Union of Brest (5). The pope acknowledges that "there are those who see the existence of the Eastern Catholic Churches as a difficulty on the road of ecumenism" (6), and therefore wishes to emphasize the importance of charity and an appreciation of the richness shared by the Catholic and Orthodox Churches in following the path to true communion. The new-found religious freedom of the Ukrainian Greek Catholic Church is to be celebrated, but both Orthodox and Catholic Churches in the East face serious problems: "Numerous migrations and deportations have redrawn the religious geography of those lands; many years of official State atheism have profoundly affected people's minds; there is still not enough clergy to respond to the immense needs of religious and moral reconstruction: these are some of the more dramatic challenges facing all of the Churches" (7). The pope proposes the witness of the martyrs of both East and West as an inspiration for fellowship, bringing together those who reject the "violence whereby hatred for the faith violated the dignity of the human person" (8).

Reflecting on the Church and its unity, the pope refers to the words of Pope John XXIII, "What unites us is much greater than what divides us." In that manner John Paul II says that we must ask ourselves what the Union of Brest meant for us in the past, and what it will mean in the future. The pope praises the fidelity of the Catholics of Ukraine to the Successor of Peter, and at the same time he expresses his hopes that "under the action of the Holy Spirit, [the Greek Catholic Church] will understand that today this same fidelity commits it to fostering the unity of all the Churches" (12).

The letter ends by entrusting the desire for full unity to the Mother of God, who is equally honored by the East and the West and serves as a means of unity.

See Also: SLAVORUM APOSTOLI, JOSYF SLIPYJ

Bibliography: For a text of the apostolic letter, see: *Acta Apostolicae Sedis* 88 (1996): 129–40 (Ukrainian); *The Pope Speaks* 41 (1996): 150–58 (English).

[DAVID CLOONEY]

UNIVERSI DOMINICI GREGIS

Apostolic constitution issued by Pope John Paul II on 22 February 1996, establishing new norms governing the work of the cardinals and the Curia after the death of a pope and the election of a new pope. The previous legislation was set forth in Pope Paul VI's apostolic constitution *Romano pontifici eligendo,* issued in 1975. *Universi dominici gregis* contains an introduction, a promulgation, and two main parts: "The Vacancy of the Apostolic See" and "The Election of the Roman Pontiff." The first part consists of five chapters: "The Powers of the College of Cardinals during the Vacancy of the Apostolic See," "The Congregations of the Cardinals in Preparation for the Election of the Supreme Pontiff," "Concerning Certain Offices during the Vacancy of the Apostolic See," "Faculties of the Dicasteries of the Roman Curia during the Vacancy of the Apostolic See," and "The Funeral Rites of the Roman Pontiff." Part two contains seven chapters: "The Electors of the Roman Pontiff," "The Place of the Election and Those Admitted to It by Reason of Their Office," "The Beginning of the Election," "Observance of Secrecy on All Matters concerning the Election," "The Election Procedure," "Matters to be Observed or Avoided in the Election of the Roman Pontiff," and "The Acceptance and Proclamation of the New Pope and the Beginning of His Ministry."

The constitution maintains all the essential elements of *Romano pontifici eligendo*: the powers of the College of Cardinals during the vacancy of the Apostolic See are limited and well-defined; the cardinals of age remain the sole electors of the Pontiff; the election is to take place in the secrecy, under pain of excommunication, of the conclave; and two-thirds of the votes are required for election unless there is a prolonged deadlock. The introduction identifies the reason for the new document as "the awareness of the Church's changed situation . . . and the need to take into consideration the general revision of Canon Law." But at the same time it has been careful "in formulating the new discipline, not to depart in substance from the wise and venerable tradition already established."

The most significant changes introduced by the constitution concern the rules for electing the pope. The previous legislation had established that if there was a deadlock after thirty-three ballots and periods of prayer, exhortation, and consultation, the cardinals could unanimously agree to change the required two-thirds of the votes for a valid election to election by an absolute majority or else a vote in which there are only two candidates, namely, the two who received the most votes in the immediately preceding balloting. *Universi dominici gregis* changed the required unanimity to an absolute majority;

it also specified that if the cardinals agreed to hold a vote between the two previous leading vote-getters, only an absolute majority is required for election (no. 75). This last point had not been clearly specified before. The constitution also abolished two of the three methods of election: by acclamation and by compromise (in case of deadlock, allowed the cardinals to delegate their votes to a small committee of their own). Secret, paper ballot is now the only valid way to elect the Roman pontiff (no. 62). In a further, slight modification, the constitution requires two-thirds of the votes for a canonical election. Both Paul VI and Pius XII had required that one vote would be added to the traditional two-thirds established by Alexander III in his constitution *Licet de vitanda* in 1179. The reason behind the extra vote was to guarantee that the elected had obtained the traditional percentage even if he had voted for himself. The only instance in which the plus one vote will be required is if the total number of cardinals voting is not divisible by three (no. 62).

Universi dominici gregis maintains the limitation of the total number of electors to 120 and the prohibition of the cardinals who are eighty years of age from participating in the conclave, though it moves the date at which the age limit is enforced from the beginning of the conclave to the death of the previous pontiff (no. 33). The over-eighty cardinals are asked, "by virtue of the singular bond with the Apostolic See which the cardinalate represents," to lead the prayers of the faithful in Rome and elsewhere asking for divine assistance for the cardinal electors (no. 85). The only reason a cardinal elector can be excluded from voting is if he refuses to enter the conclave or abandons it with no valid cause and without the permission of the majority of the participating cardinals (no. 40).

The cardinals will be lodged in the Domus Sanctae Marthae, a new accommodation that will certainly do away with the strictures to shorten the length of the conclave as conceived by Pope Bl. Gregory X in his constitution *Ubi periculum* (1274). The cardinals will have to be transported to the traditional voting place: the Sistine Chapel. The chapel itself is to be carefully checked, by "trustworthy individuals of proven technical ability, in order to ensure that no audiovisual equipment has been secretly installed for recording and transmission to the outside" (no. 51). Finally, the coronation with the triple crown is replaced with the "solemn ceremony of the inauguration of the pontificate" (n. 92), the praxis introduced by John Paul I in 1978.

See Also: DOMUS SANCTAE MARTHAE, JOHN PAUL I, SISTINE CHAPEL (RESTORATION OF)

Bibliography: For the text of *Universi dominici gregis,* see: *Acta Apopstolicae Sedis* 88 (1996): 305–43 (Latin); *Origins* 25, no.

37 (7 Mar 1996): 617–30 (English); *The Pope Speaks* 41 (1996): 218–41 (English).

[SALVADOR MIRANDA]

UT UNUM SINT

Pope John Paul II's twelfth encyclical, issued 25 May 1995; reaffirms the "impassioned commitment" of the Second Vatican Council for the unity of the Church. In preparation for the Great Jubilee of the Incarnation, the letter recapitulates the progress the churches have made together in the last thirty years. The text lays out specific challenges for Catholics, and it offers a very concrete openness to the renewal of the papacy in service to the unity of the churches. The 103 paragraphs of the encyclical are divided into three sections.

The first section reiterates the centrality of the quest for unity in the identity of Catholics; the importance of conversion to Christ, the Church, and its unity; and the necessity of prayer. He introduces the "martyrs of our century" as "the most powerful proof that every factor of division can be transcended" (no. 1). In addition to resolving doctrinal divisions he also emphasizes the "purification of past memories" and the necessity "to acknowledge with sincere and total objectivity the mistakes made" (no. 2). The conversion and repentance are not only the duty of every Catholic, but also "of the bishop of Rome as the successor of the apostle Peter" (no. 4). The encyclical recalls that for the Catholic Church ecumenism is "not just some sort of 'appendix'" but rather it is "an organic part of her life and work, and consequently must pervade all that she is and does" (no. 20). The letter outlines the centrality of dialogue, including the dialogue of love, of truth, of conversion, and of salvation as central in Catholic relationships with other Christians and in serving the journey to full communion.

The second section recapitulates the fruits of dialogue in the last three decades, which includes both cementing the real communion that exists among Christians and among churches as well as laying the basis for the full communion for which we pray. In this section the pope discusses the solidarity in service, mission, and social action. He outlines specific developments with the churches of the East and those that have emerged from the Reformation. Pope John Paul II's own personal experience of encounters in his many trips around the globe are recounted and celebrated. In this section the pope moves beyond the conciliar designation of "separated brethren" to speak of "fellow Christians." He lifts up convergences in the sacramental life even though "it is not yet possible to celebrate together the same eucharistic liturgy." He finds it "a source of joy to note that Catholic

Pope John Paul II and Tibet's exiled spiritual leader, the Dalai Lama, meet during the closing ceremony of the Interreligious Assembly in St. Peter's Square in October 1999. (AP/ Wide World Photos. Photograph by Arturo Mari)

ministers are able . . . to administer the sacraments of the eucharist, penance and anointing of the sick to Christians who are not in full communion with the Catholic Church" (no. 45, 46).

These developments are seen not only in the context of the theological developments in the World Council of Churches and bilateral dialogues, but also in light of clarification of Catholic practice in the 1983 Code of Canon Law, the 1991 Code of Canons of the Eastern Churches, and the 1993 *Directory for the Application of Principles and Norms on Ecumenism.*

The third section outlines the future: the challenge of making the results of the dialogues "a common heritage" (no. 80, 81); the continued dialogue agenda: (1) Scripture and Tradition, (2) sacraments, (3) ordination, (4) authority and (5) Mary; prayer, collaboration, and common evangelization; and his willingness to enter into a "patient and fraternal dialogue" with ecumenical partners about how to exercise the papal office in a way to better serve the unity of the Church, even before full theological agreement is reached. He ends with an exhortation to "implore from the Lord, with renewed enthusiasm . . . the grace to prepare ourselves" for this unity (no. 102).

The Transfiguration *by Giovanni Lanfranco.* (© Araldo de Luca/CORBIS)

Bibliography: For the text of *Ut unum sint,* see: *Acta Apostolicae Sedis* 87 (1995): 921–982 (Latin). *Origins* 25, no. 4 (8 June 1995): 49–72 (English). *The Pope Speaks* 40 (1995): 295–343 (English).

[J. GROS]

VERITATIS SPLENDOR

Pope John Paul II's tenth encyclical, issued on the feast of the Transfiguration (6 August) in 1993. The purpose of the encyclical is to set forth "the principles of a moral teaching based upon Sacred Scripture and the living Apostolic Tradition" (no. 5). In the introduction, the pope notes that the Church's magisterial teaching, particularly in the past two centuries, has touched on many different questions concerning the moral life; in *Veritatis splendor* he intends rather "to reflect on the whole of the Church's moral teaching" (no. 4). The occasion for this reflection is the growth of a systematic questioning of this teaching, based on presuppositions that have "serious implications" for individual moral life, the communal life of the Church, and the just life of society. The immediate context for the encyclical is the publication of the *Catechism of the Catholic Church:* the fullness of the moral life, such as it is presented in the *Catechism* must be understood as the backdrop to the encyclical's concern with certain fundamental moral questions.

Veritatis splendor is divided into three parts. In the first, "Christ and the Answer to the Question about Morality," the pope uses the encounter between Jesus and the rich young man (Matt 19:16ff.) to show what is involved in moral teaching. The human heart naturally desires to know the full meaning of its life, and what it must do to achieve that meaning; this is why the rich young man comes to Christ. Christ's response highlights the fact that the moral life is a response to God's initiative—the "One who alone is good" alone makes the moral life possible. The commandments and the beatitudes are equally valid norms for the moral life, because they both point to the fullness of love to which every person is called. This life becomes possible in the following of Christ and the gift of the Spirit. Yet, though it is supernatural in origin, it is the norm for man in every time and place; and the role of the Church is to promote and preserve this life.

In part 2, "The Church and the Discernment of Certain Tendencies in Present-Day Moral Theology," the pope goes on to speak of a crisis in modern thought: freedom is opposed to natural law, conscience is presented as the ultimate arbiter of good and evil, and the Church's teaching on intrinsically evil acts is dismissed as irrelevant to moral evaluation. These tendencies are rooted in a denial of the dependence of freedom on truth. Rightful human autonomy does not involve the creation of one's own moral norms, but a recognition of human nature and the right order of creation through "participated theonomy," a participation in "the light of natural reason and of Divine Revelation" (no. 41). The natural law thus recognized contains both positive and negative precepts: these are equally universal, but only the latter can be formulated as norms that oblige always and everywhere because "the commandment of love of God and neighbor does not have in its dynamic any higher limit, but it does have a lower limit, beneath which the commandment is broken" (no. 52). "Conscience" also cannot be rightly understood unless it is seen as a "practical judgment", that is, a judgment that does not establish the good, but identifies the good to be done in a particular situation in light of the natural law. The pope draws particularly attention to a tendency in moral theology to separate the "fundamental option" of a person from his particular, individual acts, locating moral assessment only in the former. He notes that the fundamental option is made real only through the exercise of freedom, and therefore only through particular acts—and by the same token, it can be revoked through particular acts. Therefore, the Church's teaching that particular acts can be mortal sins must be upheld. Finally, against a "teleologistic" moral theology that locates the moral quality of acts entirely in the intention of the person and the foreseeable consequences of the act, the pope emphasizes the importance of the object of the acting person. An act can be good only when its object is, by its nature, capable of being ordered to God; if the object is incapable of being so ordered, the act is "intrinsically evil."

Part 3, "Moral Good for the Life of the Church and of the World," draws out the pastoral conclusions of the previous analysis. The Church must witness to the dependence of freedom on truth. The Crucified Christ reveals that "freedom is acquired in love" (no. 87), and the martyrs continue to exemplify this truth. Only the recognition

of certain universal moral norms guarantees just relations in society. The witness of the moral life is essential to the Church's task of evangelization and the fulfillment of her prophetic office. The pope also identifies the responsibilities of theologians and pastors for preserving and promoting this truth.

The encyclical ends with an invocation of Mary, the Mother of Mercy. Through her we learn of the possibility of the moral life lived in discipleship to Christ.

Bibliography: For the text of *Vertitatis splendor,* see: *Acta Apostolicae Sedis,* 85 (1993): 1134–1228 (Latin); *Origins* 23, no. 18 (14 Oct 1993): 297–334 (English); *The Pope Speaks* 39 (1994) 6–63 (English). For commentaries and summaries of *Vertitatis splendor,* see: J. A. DINOIA and ROMANUS CESSARIO, eds., *Veritatis Splendor and the Renewal of Moral Theology* (Chicago: Midwest Theological Forum, 1999). MICHAEL E. ALLSOPP and JOHN J. O'KEEFE, *Veritatis Splendor: American Responses* (Kansas City: Sheed and Ward, 1995). JOSEPH A. SELLING and JAN JANS, *The Splendor of Accuracy: An Examination of the Assertions Made by Veritatis Splendor* (Grand Rapids, Mich.: Eerdmans, 1995).

[G. LANAVE]

VITA CONSECRATA

Apostolic exhortation of Pope John Paul II, delivered 25 March 1996, gathering the fruits of the ninth general assembly of the Synod of Bishops. *Vita consecrata* consists of an introduction, a conclusion, and three chapters: (1) *Confessio Trinitatis,* consecrated life as an icon of Christ and the Trinity; (2) *Signum fraternitatis,* consecrated life as a sign of communion in the Church; and (3) *Servitium caritatis*, consecrated life as a manifestation of God's love in the world. The exhortation effectively captures the spirit of the interventions of the participants at the synodal session and addresses the fifty-five proposals submitted by the members of the assembly to the Pope. The chapters focus on the three essentials of the vocation: consecration, communion, and mission.

The introduction roots consecrated life in the profession of the evangelical counsels in the gospel and returns gratitude to God for this gift in the Church. The document serves as a source for reflection on consecrated life by the whole Church as well as an encouragement for those living the vocation in the midst of today's challenges.

Chapter 1 addresses the Christological and Trinitarian nature of the vocation. Those professing the counsels are configured to Christ: chaste, poor, and obedient. Through an intense living of their baptismal consecration, they enjoy an intimacy with the Trinity. Joined to Christ in his Paschal Mystery, those called to this vocation embrace his hiddenness, suffering, labors, and martyrdom in response to the Father's will. The vocation

Mother Teresa, the exemplar of the consecrated life. (© Patsy Lynch/CORBIS)

offers a vibrant witness to the life and teachings of Christ as consecrated persons live their charism and perform apostolic service within a great variety of particular churches throughout the world. Supported by the vocations of the laity and clergy, these persons renew their determination and strength through liturgical prayer and the ascetical practices of their own institutes.

Chapter 2 reflects the communal character of consecrated life in imitation of Christ within the Trinitarian community and the community of the Twelve. As communities of faith and love, institutes of consecrated life remind the Church of her own nature as a community of God's people (Acts 2: 42–47; 4: 32-35) and the world of its potential for unity and charity. Community is particularly witnessed in religious institutes and societies of apostolic life wherein members live in common, supporting one another in their life and mission. The members extend this communal dimension to persons they encounter in their various apostolates: bishops, other clerics, and laity. They labor tirelessly in the midst of selfishness, greed, hedonism, violence, ethnic cleansing, and deportation. In a word, consecrated persons witness and labor to effect the unity and reconciliation in the community of humanity for which Christ so passionately implored his Father.

Chapter 3 addresses the mission of those who profess the evangelical counsels. Consecrated persons offer a total gift of themselves; they are sent forth by the Spirit throughout the world. Imbued with their own gifts, they address all the needs of humanity: those of the poor in the forms of hunger, privation, persecution, expulsion, natural disasters, and torture; those of the affluent in the forms of loneliness, rejection, despair, moral degradation, loss of human dignity, and exploitation. Life consecrated by the profession of chastity, poverty, and obedience poses a challenge and antithesis to the false values of hedonism, materialism, and rugged individualism. The universal nature of consecrated life frees those vowed to it to serve a vast number of persons and their special needs in the many particular churches throughout the world. The evangelization of culture, social communications, education, ecumenical and interreligious dialogue, and response to those who hunger for the sacred are some of the apostolic works recommended by the Pope.

Vita consecrata ends as it begins in gratitude to God for the gift of consecrated life. Pope John Paul thanks those who pour out their lives in love and service, reminding them they "have not only a glorious history to remember and to recount, but also a great history still to be accomplished" (no. 110). He recognizes the vocation of consecrated life as belonging undeniably to the life and mission of the Church, while focused on the Kingdom. The exhortation concludes with prayers to the Holy Trinity and an invocation of the Blessed Virgin Mary.

Bibliography: For the text of *Vita consecrata,* see: *Acta Apostolicae Sedis* 88 (1996): 377–486 (Latin); *Origins* 25, no. 41 (4 April 1996): 681, 683–719 (English); *The Pope Speaks* 41 (1996): 257–338 (English).

[R. MCDERMOTT]

People and Places, Institutions and Events

INTRODUCTION

The following section contains almost 150 entries arranged, in the customary manner of encyclopedias, A–Z. It is a select list chosen not because of the intrinsic importance of the topics but because of their timeliness. Most, but not all, are linked to the entries in other sections of this volume. Most, but not all, figure prominently in the pontificate of Pope John Paul II. They present a pastiche of people, places, institutions, and events. Many are new. Others, recycled from the earlier edition of the *New Catholic Encyclopedia,* are included here because individuals have died, historical places are of current interest as sites of noteworthy events, and significant changes in the corporate life of institutions have given them new direction and purpose. Events that merited passing mention in the chronicle of Pope John Paul's pontificate and elsewhere in these pages are explained in more detail.

Almost a third of the entries in this section are taken up with short biographies of cardinals of the Catholic Church. A few are of the nature of obituaries recounting the careers and achievements of bishops who played leading roles in shaping Catholicism in the years after the Second Vatican Council. Most are simply thumbnail sketches of contemporary churchmen, intended for purposes of ready reference. They provide basic information—date of birth, educational background, ecclesiastical career, and current assignments—of prelates who are presently members of the college. Most cardinals listed in this section are from English-speaking countries, while the others, by reason of assignment and travel, have attracted attention in the English-speaking world. The fact that the majority have received the red biretta during the present pontificate is significant in assessing the caliber and qualities of the men that Pope John Paul has placed in leadership roles. That more cardinals now serve as residential bishops throughout the world than as members of the Roman curia is a result of the internationalization promoted by him and his immediate predecessors.

A handful of the cardinals named by John Paul were not bishops but theologians who, like others in this section, have enjoyed high esteem in Catholic circles because of their contributions to the intellectual and spiritual life of the Church in the postconciliar period. There are biographies of men and women who founded religious orders and promoted new religious movements. In cases where the authors were involved in the events they describe, they provide information available only to participants. Again, the selection of entries is dictated to a certain extent by timeliness and current interest. They focus on the concrete and the specific. They focus on theologians rather than theology; on biblical scholars rather advances in biblical studies. Developments in theology, the discussion of moral and ethical issues, and exploration into topics of general interest to church historians and students of religious studies are left to the appropriate volumes of the *New Catholic Encyclopedia* where space permits the comprehensive and in-depth treatment they deserve.

[EDITORS]

AD LIMINA VISIT

(Visitatio ad limina apostolorum) refers to the periodic visit to Rome required of each residential bishop (CIC c. 400; *Pastor bonus,* no. 28) and military vicar approved by apostolic authority (S.C. Consist., 28 February 1959, AAS 51:272). This visit is directly tied to the quinquennial report that is required of each residential bishop every 5 years in c. 399, as the visit is to be made the same year as that in which the report is submitted (c. 400 & sect;1). The 1983 Code of Canon Law has made the bishop's obligation to make the *ad limina* visit personally, and only if he is impeded may he satisfy the obligation through another, i.e. his coadjutor, the auxiliary, or a suitable priest who resides in the diocese (c. 400 & sect. 2). Since auxiliary and other titular bishops are not the primary pastors of a particular church and have no quin-

Pope John Paul II is welcomed by Syrian Catholic Bishop of Kerala Cyrel Mar Vasulius at Delhi's Palam Air Force Station in November 1999 at the start of a four-day visit to India. (© AFP/CORBIS)

quennial report to make, they are not held to the *ad limina* visit. This visit has a sacred meaning, since "the bishops with religious veneration pay a visit to the tombs of Peter and Paul." It has a personal meaning, "because each individual bishop meets the successor of Peter and talks to him face to face," and it has a curial meaning, that is a "hallmark of community, because the bishops enter into conversation with the moderators of the dicasteries, councils, and offices of the Roman Curia" (Appendix 1, no. 6, of *Pastor bonus*). The purpose of the visit, for the bishops, is "the strengthening of their own responsibility as successors of the Apostles and of their hierarchical communion with the Successor of Peter" (Congregation for Bishops, "Directory for the 'ad limina visit'," in *L'Osservatore Romano,* 11 July 1988). The *ad limina* visit has changed considerably under the pontificate of John Paul II from a canonical formality into a genuine exercise of the pope's care for all the Churches. As stated in the "Directory for the 'ad limina' visit," it is "an im-

portant moment in the exercise of the Holy Father's pastoral ministry," because he receives the bishops and discusses personally with them their questions concerning "their ecclesial mission." Though there is no concrete date in which the visits started, "There are, however, numerous testimonies which speak of its existence from the 4th century" (Orti, Accompanying Historico-Juridical Notes to the "Directory for the 'ad limina' visit").

[T. C. KELLY]

AMBROZIC, ALOYSIUS MATTHEW

Cardinal, archbishop of Toronto; b. 27 January 1930 in Gaberje, Slovenia, the second of the seven children of Aloysius Ambrozic and Helen Pecar. After World War II the family lived in a succession of refugee camps in

Aloysius Cardinal Ambrozic receives the ring of office from Pope John Paul II in St. Peter's Square on 2 February 1998. (Reuters/ Paolo Cocco/Archive Photos. Reproduced by Permission.)

Austria until September 1948, when they emigrated to Canada. Aloysius entered St. Augustine's seminary in Toronto and was ordained to the priesthood on 4 June 1958. After two years of pastoral work in Port Colborne, Ontario, he pursued studies in Rome, receiving a licentiate in theology from the Angelicum and a licentiate in Scripture from the Pontifical Biblical Institute. In 1960 he returned to St. Augustine's seminary as a professor of Scripture. After receiving a doctorate in theology at the University of Würzburg in Germany in 1970, he became professor of New Testament exegesis at the Toronto School of Theology and dean of studies at St. Augustine's seminary. Ambrozic was ordained auxiliary bishop of Toronto in 1976, and appointed as coadjutor archbishop in 1986, succeeding His Eminence Gerald Emmett Cardinal Carter as archbishop in 1990. On 21 February 1998 he was named cardinal by Pope John Paul II.

During his early years in academe Ambrozic earned a reputation as a biblical scholar of great promise. His study on references to the Kingdom of God in Mark was widely acclaimed. In the pastoral field his personal history and background made him especially qualified to minister to the needs of the ethnic communities in the Toronto archdiocese. He became active in the area of Catholic education, with a special interest in the archdiocesan religious education programs. He was appointed to the Christian Education Commission of the Canadian Conference of Catholic Bishops and played a significant role in the revising of the Canadian Catechism (1974). Ambrozic has been appointed to the Pontifical Council for the Pastoral Care of Migrants and Itinerant People (1990), and the Pontifical Council for Culture (1993). As cardinal he joined the Congregation for Divine Worship and Discipline of Sacraments (1999). He contributes a monthly column to *The Catholic Record,* the archdiocesan newspaper.

Bibliography: ALOYSIUS AMBROZIC, *The Hidden Kingdom: A Redaction-Critical Study of the References to the Kingdom of*

God in Mark's Gospel (Washington, D.C. 1972). MICHAEL W. HIGGINS and DOUGLAS R. LETSON, *My Father's Business* (Toronto 1990).

[D. R. LETSON]

ANNUARIO PONTIFICIO

The "pontifical yearbook" is the official directory of the Roman Catholic Church throughout the world. Published annually by the Libreria Editrice Vaticana, the *Annuario* is a reference tool that lists the members of the College of Cardinals, patriarchates, residential and titular bishoprics, abbeys and prelatures *nullius dioeceses,* apostolic administrations *ad nutum S. Sedis,* eastern rite prelates with ordinary jurisdiction, apostolic vicariates and prefectures, missions *sui juris,* and the custody of the Holy Land. It includes the Orders, Congregations and Religious and Secular Institutes, the Sacred Congregations, the tribunals and offices that make up the Roman Curia, the diplomatic representatives of the Holy See and the diplomatic corps accredited to the Holy See, as well as the members of the papal household, the administration of the Vatican State, and the vicariate of Rome. It has historical notes on many offices and agencies, addresses and telephone numbers, and a lengthy appendix containing statistics and other useful information.

Origins. Although the title, *Annuario Pontificio,* dates only from 1860 its origins are traceable to the printers Luca and Giovanni Cracas who in 1716 published *Notizie per l'anno.* Although it varied in completeness, the *Notizie* served as a directory of the hierarchy, the Curia, and the Papal court; it appeared annually with some interruptions between 1798 and 1817, until 1859. In addition, Cracas published in 1802–1803 the *Elenco degli eminentissimi signori Cardinali, delle Congregazioni e Tribunali e della Famiglia pontificia.* Beginning in 1851 the Camera Apostolica annually published the *Gerarchia della Santa Chiesa cattolica apostolica romana in tutto l'orbe ed in ogni rito con cenni storici (1851–59).* In 1860 this became the *Annuario Pontificio,* whose publication was suspended in 1870 with the loss of the papal states. In 1872, however, a new directory, which was to continue until 1911, appeared. Originally entitled *La Gerarchia Cattolica e la Famiglia Pontificia per l'anno con appendice di altre norizie riguardanti la S. Sede,* it began under the direction of a family of printers, the Monaldi brothers. In 1885 the Typographia Vaticana took over this publication. From 1899 to 1904 the annual volume was designated as the *edizione ufficiale.* In 1912 the name *Annuario Pontificio* was revived, and from 1912 to 1924 some brief notes were added on the offices of the Curia. The present format dates from 1940. Since 1967 the *Ann-uario Pontificio* has been under the direction of the Ufficio Centrale di Statistica della Chiesa. During the pontificate of John Paul II the publication has shown an increasing awareness of the importance of women in the Church's ministry and governance. Since the 1996 edition of the *Annuario,* the names of mothers general of women's orders and congregations are now included. Previously it mentioned the names of all male generals but not those of the women.

Bibliography: LARRY N. LORENZONI, "The *Annuario Pontificio:* The Vatican's Pontifical Year Book and a Recent Editorial Decision," *Review for Religious* 58, no. 3 (1999): 261–265

[R. B. MILLER]

ARCHE INTERNATIONAL, L'

L'Arche International is a federation of faith communities in which people with disabilities and their assistants choose to live and work together. The mission of L'Arche is to welcome people with disabilities and give them a valid place in society. L'Arche fosters the particular gifts and value of people with disabilities, seeking to show that people of differing intellectual capacity, social origin, religion, and culture can come together in unity, faithfulness, and reconciliation (L'Arche International, 1998). There are more than 113 L'Arche communities in thirty countries throughout the world, including 13 in the United States.

L'Arche began in France in 1964 when Jean Vanier and Father Thomas Philippe, a Dominican, invited two men with disabilities, Philippe Simi and Raphael Seux, to share a home together near Trosly-Breuil, France. Having first met Philippe and Raphael in an institution, Jean believed that a warm and loving home would have a significant impact on the lives of these two men. They all soon learned that the impact of sharing life together in a simple way lead to mutual transformation of heart.

From the desire of two people with disabilities to have a home and share life with Vanier and Father Thomas, L'Arche has grown into an international network of communities. While the founding roots of L'Arche are in the Roman Catholic tradition, it has now developed in various cultures and religious traditions throughout the world. It recognized as one of the most significant Christian ministries of the Twentieth Century.

Jean Vanier was born in Canada in 1928, the son of Georges and Pauline Vanier. He was educated in England and Canada. After serving several years in the British Navy and Canadian Royal Navy, he earned a Doctorate in Philosophy from Institut Catholique de Paris, France. He continues to live in the first L'Arche Community in

Trosly-Breuil. Vanier also inspired "Faith and Sharing" communities that meet once a month for scripture reflection, and with Marie Hélène Mathieu he founded the "Faith and Light" communities of disabled people, their families, and friends that meet regularly. Vanier received the Paul VI International Prize for his lay ministry work. Vanier has promoted L'Arche through lectures and interviews and has written more than twenty books. His Becoming Human (Mahwah, N.J., 1999) was derived from a series of lectures aired on public broadcasting in Canada. Recognizing Vanier's work, Pope John Paul II stated, "Over the past thirty years L'Arche has grown to become a dynamic and providential sign of the civilization of love."

Bibliography: JEAN VANIER, *An Ark for the Poor: The Story of L'Arche* (New York 1995).

[J. EADS]

ARGÜELLO, KIKO

Initiator of the Neocatechumenal Way; born Francisco Jose Argüello Wirtz, 9 January 1939 in Leon, Spain.

The eldest of four boys, Kiko grew up in a middle-class family. He studied arts at the Reale Academia of San Fernando in Madrid, and in 1959 won the Special National Prize for Painting. The Marxist ambiance of the sixties and the superficiality of middle-class Christian life triggered in him a deep existential crisis. This profound search for meaning eventually led him to dedicate his life to Jesus Christ and the Catholic Church. For some time he was a lecturer of the Cursillos de Cristianidad.

In 1962, together with other artists, Argüello founded a research group in Sacred Art, known as Gremio 1962. A scholarship aimed at finding common aspects of Protestant and Catholic art enabled him to tour Europe and keep in touch with the Liturgical Renewal movement. The tragic life of a maid in his home led him to a deep spiritual reflection on Christ as the Suffering Servant, and in 1964 he left everything to live among the squatters in the shanty towns of Palomeras Altas at the outskirts of Madrid. He drew from Charles de Foucauld the formula to live in silence at the feet of Jesus Christ crucified.

In the shanty towns, Argüello crossed paths with Carmen Hernandez Barrera (b. 24 November 1932 in Moncayo, Spain). After graduating in chemistry and theology, Carmen came in contact with Father Farnes Schroder, a liturgical expert, who enabled her to take cognizance of the importance of the renewal of liturgy at the Vatican Council II and the focus it placed on the celebration of the Paschal Mystery. Through their solidarity with the poor of Palomeras Altas, Kiko and Carmen developed a synthesis of the liturgical catechumenate, preaching, and kerygma, which came to be called the Neocatechumenal Way. They formed a Christian community of gypsies, illiterate people, homeless, outcasts, former inmates, and prostitutes that became a powerful sign of love of Christ crucified. With the support of the archbishop of Madrid, Casimiro Morcillo, these neocatechumenal communities were introduced into the parishes of Madrid.

In June 1968, upon the invitation of Don Dino Torreggiani, founder of the Servants of the Church, Kiko and Carmen, accompanied by a priest from Seville, traveled to Rome and started the Way in the parish of the Canadian Martyrs in Rome. Kiko lived among the poor in Borghetto Latino, a destitute suburb of Rome.

Argüello and Hernandez have attended World Youth Day celebrations and conducted several international meetings with bishops—in 1993 in Vienna for the European bishops; in 1994 in Rome for the African bishops; in 1996 for the bishops of the Middle East, and in 1997 in New York for the bishops of the United States. In 1992 Kiko was appointed consultor for the Congregation of Laity and has participated in the Sixth General Assembly of the Synod of Bishops on reconciliation, the Seventh General Assembly on the laity, and the Special Assembly for Europe. Argüello has promoted the Way, seeking to strengthen the faith of Christians in parishes by forming small communities, creating a ministry of itinerant evangelization and catechesis, and fostering vocations to ordained ministry.

[PIUS SAMMUT]

ARINZE, FRANCIS A.

Cardinal, archbishop of Onitsha, President of the Pontifical Council for Interreligious Dialogue; b. 1 November 1932, Eziowelle, Nigeria. His parents Joseph, a farmer, and Bernadette were practitioners of a traditional African religion. The family was Igbo, one of the three major ethnic groups of Nigeria. Francis was baptized at age nine by Fr. Cyprian Michael Iwene Tansi, who was beatified by Pope John Paul II in 1998. The rest of the family later followed him into the Catholic Church.

At an early age he attended a boarding school in Dunukofia where Fr. Tansi, the parish priest, was also his teacher. In 1947 he entered All Hallows Seminary in Onitsha. After completing his secondary education he taught for two years All Hallows and in 1953 entered Bigard Memorial Seminary in Enugu, Nigeria. In 1955 he went to Rome to study at the Pontifical Urban Athenaeum

Francis Cardinal Arinze. (Catholic News Service.)

"De Propaganda Fide." He was ordained a priest in the church of that athenaeum, 23 November 1958. In 1964 he earned a bachelor's degree in pedagogy at the University of London, England.

He returned to Enugu in 1960, after obtaining his doctorate in theology in Rome (his doctoral dissertation, *Ibo Sacrifice as an Introduction to the Catechesis of Holy Mass,* discusses the principles of inculturation that many years later would become norms to evangelize non-Christians). From 1961 to 1962 he taught at Bigard Memorial Seminary. Following this, he was named regional secretary for Catholic Education of Eastern Nigeria.

Pope Paul VI named Fr. Arinze titular bishop of Fissiana and appointed him coadjutor of the archbishop of Onitsha on 6 July 1965. At thirty-two he was the youngest bishop of the Church. He succeeded to the see of Onitsha in 1967. The unstable political situation that followed independence from colonial rule in 1960 was marked by power struggle among the three major tribal groups. The Biafran war claimed more than one million casualties and seriously threatened the existence of the Catholic Church in Nigeria. Archbishop Arinze worked very hard for peaceful coexistence between peoples of different religious beliefs and ethnic backgrounds. From 1979 to 1984 he was president of the Nigerian Bishop's

Conference and in 1982 was elected vice-president for Africa of the United Biblical Societies. In 1984, Pope John Paul II called him to Rome as pro-president of the Pontifical Secretariat for Non-Christians (the name of the dicastery was changed to Pontifical Council for Interreligious Dialogue by the 1988 apostolic constitution "Pastor Bonus").

In the consistory of 25 May 1985 John Paul II named Archbishop Arinze cardinal deacon of S. Giovanni della Pigna and, two days later, president of the Secretariat for Non-Christians. As president of the secretariat, he has been instrumental in developing and strengthening closer relations with Judaism, Islam, Buddhism, Hinduism, and other non-Christian religions. Cardinal Arinze has participated in all but one of the general assemblies of the Synod of Bishops and several of the special assemblies, serving as president-delegate in 1994 in the Special Assembly for Africa. The cardinal is a frequent visitor of the United States where he has a brother who is a professor at a medical college in Nashville, Tennessee.

Bibliography: Cardinal Arinze has written widely on interreligious relations; some of his books in English are: *Worship and Ritual in Christianity and Other Religions* (Rome 1974); *The Christian and Politics* (Onitsha, Nigeria 1982); *Answering God's call* (London 1983); *The Christian as Citizen* (Onitsha, Nigeria 1984); *Progress in Christian-Muslim Relations Worldwide* (Jos, Nigeria 1988); *The Church in Dialogue: Walking with Other Religions* (San Francisco 1990); *Africans and Christianity* (Nsukka, Enugu, Nigeria 1990); *Meeting Other Believers* (Huntington, Ind. 1997).

[S. MIRANDA]

ARRUPE, PEDRO

Twenty-eighth Superior General (1965–1983) of the Society of Jesus (Jesuits); b. Bilbao, Spain, 14 November 1907; d. Rome, 5 February 1991.

Early Years. The only boy among five children, Pedro Arrupe was the son of a well-to-do architect, who enabled him to receive a good education. He decided to become a physician, but in 1927, just before completing medical studies in Madrid, he felt the call to religious life and entered the Society of Jesus. When the Spanish Republic expelled all Jesuits in 1932, Arrupe studied for the priesthood in Holland and in Belgium, where he was ordained in 1936. Afterwards he continued his education in the United States.

In answer to his frequent requests Arrupe was assigned to Japan in 1938. After the Japanese attack on Pearl Harbor in 1941, he was imprisoned for thirty-three days on false charges of spying. At the time that the first atomic bomb exploded on 6 August 1945, he was director of novices in Nagatsuka, on the outskirts of Hiroshima. Arrupe rushed into the ruins to treat the wounded, and turning the Jesuit residence into a hospital, he supervised the care of more than 200 survivors for six months. In 1958 the Japanese mission was raised to a province, and Arrupe was named the first provincial superior.

Superior General. On 22 May 1965 Arrupe was elected superior general by the Thirty-first General Congregation, the legislative body of the Society of Jesus. The first Basque to lead the Jesuits since their founder, St. Ignatius of Loyola, he was eminently suited to lead the Society in the era following Vatican Council II. Arrupe was a man of international experience and vision, who could bridge East and West because he had lived and worked in both areas, spoke the languages, and appreciated different cultures. He realized that the center of gravity of worldwide Christianity was moving toward Asia and Africa. As a veteran and well-traveled missionary he had learned to adapt the Christian message and the ways of the Church to different cultures.

As superior general, Arrupe felt his mandate was to promote the renewal of Jesuit life in accord with the norms set down by Vatican II: a continuous return to the Gospel and the original inspiration of the founder and at the same time an adaptation to the changed conditions of the times. Arrupe was the first Jesuit general to travel extensively. He visited six continents, enabling him to meet and speak with thousands of Jesuits. His simplicity, warmth, vigor, candor, and obvious expertise made him an instant hit with his brother Jesuits, who referred to him affectionately as "Don Pedro."

Having come face-to-face with the dehumanizing poverty that afflicts a vast part of the human race, Arrupe had by 1970 reached a strong conviction that never left him: religious faith, to be truly evangelical, had to be vigorous in promoting justice and in opposing injustice, oppression, and social evils such as poverty, hunger, and all forms of racial discrimination. One of his earliest letters as superior general was written in 1967 to the Jesuits in the United States on racial discrimination and the interracial apostolate. The letter had wide repercussions and served the Society as a kind of "Magna Carta" for the interracial aspects of it work all over the world.

Arrupe's influence went far beyond Jesuit circles. He attended the last session of the Second Vatican Council, speaking twice before the general assembly. In 1967 he was elected to the first of five consecutive terms as president of the Union of Superior Generals, which represented some 300,000 male religious throughout the world. He participated in and spoke at all the international synods of bishops from 1967 to 1980. Arrupe took part in the great meetings of Latin American bishops in Medellín,

Father General Pedro Arrupe (left) of the Society of Jesus presents Francis Cardinal Spellman of New York with a ceramic of St. Ignatius of Loyola, founder of the Jesuit Order. (AP/Wide World Photos.)

Colombia (1968) and in Puebla, Mexico (1979), and in episcopal symposia in Europe and Africa. Quick to sense the magnitude of the worldwide refugee problem, he launched a program in 1980 throughout the Society to meet the desperate needs of millions of displaced persons, particularly in Southeast Asia and Africa.

Relations with the Holy See. Arrupe confessed that he had three great loves: Jesus Christ, the Church, and the Society of Jesus. For him the central figure in the Church was the pope, to whom he pledged himself and the Society, fostering the special bond of love and service that has linked the Society to the pope since its very beginning. He served under three popes: Paul VI, John Paul I, and John Paul II. Two of his favorite photographs showed him kneeling and receiving the blessings of Paul VI and John Paul II as he pledged the service of the Society to them.

No one was superior to Pedro Arrupe in loyalty and dedication to the Holy Father, and any meeting with the pope was a very special moment in his life. That is why moments of tension and of misunderstandings with the popes caused him so much pain. In certain Vatican circles, Arrupe was categorized as somewhat naive, an incurable optimist, and more a charismatic and inspirational leader than a strong administrator who could control his men.

During the Thirty-second General Congregation a conflict arose between Paul VI and the participants, with Arrupe in the eye of the storm. The main issue was a possible change in who would be eligible to pronounce the fourth vow of special obedience to the pope. Led by Arrupe's example, the Congregation exercised an act of obedience to the wishes of Paul VI, who was also concerned lest a spirit of social and political activism should undermine the Society's priestly ministries. Peaceful relations were restored and remained warm and friendly until Paul VI's death in 1991.

A more critical period began in April 1980 when Arrupe informed Pope John Paul II of his plans to resign as superior general and to convoke a General Congregation to elect his successor. Disconcerted by this information, the pope wrote to Arrupe on 1 May 1980 and asked him to postpone this step for the good of the Church and of the Society. The pope discussed the situation at a meeting with Arrupe in January 1981. Meanwhile the press carried reports and rumors of a rift between the Holy Father and the Society, stressing of the Holy See's apparent loss of confidence in Jesuit leadership. A second meeting took place in April 1981. The discussions were interrupted, first by the attempt to assassinate John Paul II on 13 May 1981, and then by a severe and permanently disabling stroke that Arrupe suffered when he returned 7 August 1981 from a long trip to the Philippines and the refugee camps in Bangkok. After consulting with his doctors, on 10 August Arrupe named one of his assistants vicar general for the duration of his illness, in accord with the Constitutions of the Society.

On 5 October 1981, Pope John Paul II intervened. He appointed Paolo Dezza as his personal delegate to govern the Society. At the same time the pope also appointed Giuseppe Pittau, SJ, to be Dezza's coadjutor with the right of succession. Arrupe remained the superior general but was unable to function. John Paul II clarified the unusual situation by stating that, in postponing the General Congregation and naming his own delegate, he had suspended the Jesuit Constitutions on these two points only.

Dezza convoked a meeting in Rome of all the Jesuit provincials and assistants and counsellors of the General Curia from 23 February to 3 March 1982. In a series of conferences Dezza informed the participants of the concerns and hopes of the pope for the Society. The highlight of the meeting was the audience with John Paul II and his address to the participants. The pope greeted the superior general with great affection: "To Father Arrupe, present here in the eloquent silence of his infirmity, offered to God for the good of the Society, I wish to express, on this occasion particularly solemn for the life and history of your Order, the thanks of the Pope and of the Church!" John Paul II expressed gratitude for the way his decision had been accepted, and after mentioning his concern for the order, he asked the Society to help him and all the bishops implement the Second Vatican Council, just as Paul III had asked Ignatius and his companions to help the Church to implement the Council of Trent. At the end of his address, the pope invited the order to convoke a General Congregation.

A Spiritual and Apostolic Legacy. The Thirty-third General Congregation assembled in Rome in September 1983. Arrupe offered his resignation, and Peter-Hans Kolvenbach was elected to succeed him. After his resignation as superior general, Arrupe's life was one of silent and patient prayer and suffering. In the end Arrupe left a rich spiritual and apostolic legacy in his addresses and writings. Among these are: *Challenge to Religious Life Today* (1979); *Justice With Faith Today* (1980); *Other Apostolates Today* (1981); and *In Him Alone Is Our Hope: Texts On The Heart of Christ* (1984). Always a faithful Jesuit, Arrupe articulated ideas that were developed in the Thirty-third General Congregation, which emphasized, "a spiritual doctrine at once profoundly rooted in the Gospel and our tradition and yet one which responds to the challenges of our times."

During Arrupe's final illness John Paul II came to visit him in the Jesuit Curia, regretting that Arrupe's condition prevented them from conversing. After several days in a comatose state, Pedro Arrupe died peacefully in the Jesuit infirmary, surrounded by his Jesuit brothers.

Bibliography: P. ARRUPE. *One Jesuit's Spiritual Journey. Autobiographical Conversations with Jean-Claude Dietsch, S.J.* St. Louis, 1986. JEAN-YVES CALVEZ. *Le Père Arrupe: L'Église apès le Concile.* Paris, 1997. Y.T. DEMOLA, trans. *Recollections and Reflections of Pedro Arrupe, S.J.* Wilmington, 1986. G. HUNT, ed. "Pedro Arrupe, S.J. 1907–1991." *America* 164:6 (1991): 138–188. P.M. LAMET.*Arrupe Una Explosión En La Iglesia.* Madrid, 1989.

[V.T. O'KEEFE]

ASSISI

Located in central Italy in the Umbrian valley on the slopes of Monte Subasio, Assisi gained fame as the home of SS. Francis and Clare (both of whom are buried there) and came to be a major pilgrimage center. In the twentieth century many artists and writers have made it their home. Before and after his election to the papacy, John Paul II visited Assisi several times. He joined Christian and other religious leaders for the World Day of Prayer for Peace held there 27 October 1986 and again in 1999.

History. In ancient times the site was inhabited by the *Umbri,* a local population with Etruscan ties, and later under the Romans *Assisium* it acquired the status of a municipium. Although Assisi became a diocese probably in the third century, the first recorded bishop, Aventius, was a legate of the Ostrogoths of Justinian after Totila took the town (ca. 545). The passions of SS. Victorinus, Felicianus, Sabinus, and Ruffinus (early martyr bishops) are late and unreliable. St. Ruffinus, whose cult is mentioned by St. Peter Damian, became Assisi's first patron.

From the late eighth to the twelfth century, Assisi was subject to the Lombard Duchy of Spoleto. Bishop Ugo (1036–52) was a civic leader of the newly independent Ghibelline commune. The first of Assisi's numerous wars with its belligerent Guelf neighbor Perugia occurred in 1054. Assisi was dominated by the Hohenstaufens from 1160 to 1198 when the citizens revolted against the German rulers and razed their fortress (rebuilt by Cardinal Albornoz in 1367). Under the litigious Bishop Guido II (1204–28), who approved the foundation of the first and second orders of Franciscans, the prosperous diocese owned half the area of the commune. In the fourteenth and fifteenth centuries Assisi fell under the Visconti, Montefeltro, and Sforza families, suffered internal conflicts, was sacked several times, and gradually lapsed into three relatively uneventful centuries (1535–1860) as part of the States of the Church. St. Gabriel Possenti was born there in 1838.

The communal library is rich in medieval manuscripts from religious houses suppressed in 1866. Since 1902 Assisi has been the headquarters of the International Society of Franciscan Studies and since 1939 of the pious society Pro Civitate Christiana. The First International Congress on Pastoral Liturgy met there in 1956.

Architecture and Paintings. In the center of the city there are the remains of an amphitheater from Roman times and the hexastyle Corinthian pronaos of the Temple of Minerva (first century B.C.). Among the medieval secular buildings the Piazza del Comune, the Palazzo del Capitano del Popolo (1212–1305) and the Palazzo dei Priori (1337) are notable, but Assisi's architectural glories are its major Romanesque and Gothic churches: (1) S. Maria Maggiore, or Vescovado, the first cathedral, rebuilt in 1163 by Giovanni da Gubbio, who also enlarged (2) the second cathedral, S. Rufino, with its striking Lombard Romanesque facade; (3) the Benedictine Abbey of S. Pietro, rebuilt in 1253; (4) the Basilica of S. Chiara, erected in 1257 in place of the earlier S. Giorgio over the tomb of St. Clare; and (5) the Gothic Basilica of S. Francesco (1228–53) designed by Brother Elias of Cortona which includes the single-naved upper and lower churches, the crypt tomb of St. Francis (reopened in 1818 and restored in 1925), a chapel hall rich in the saint's relics, and the vast Sacro Convento and papal residence,

A view of Assisi (Catholic News Service)

with portico (1300), cloister (1476), and eighteenth-century refectory. Outside the city are the modest eleventh century oratory of S. Damiano and the adjoining thirteenth-century convent where St. Clare lived. On the hillside above the city is the Eremo delle Carceri (Hermitage), given to St. Francis by Benedictine monks and enlarged by St. Bernardine of Siena; and in the valley below the city, the Basilica of S. Maria degli Angeli (1569–1676, rebuilt in 1836) which encloses the Portiuncula Chapel, sometimes described as the "cradle of the Franciscan Order." It was a place of retreat and prayer much favored by St. Francis.

The frescoes in the upper and lower churches of the Basilica of S. Francesco provide an invaluable record of the fresco styles of the thirteenth and fourteenth centuries in central Italy. Each level of the basilica consists of a simple nave, transept, and a sanctuary. During the fourteenth century, chapels were added to the nave of the lower church. Faded remnants of the earliest frescoes, episodes from the life of Christ and of St. Francis, are in the nave of the lower church. In the right transept, frescoes of the fourteenth century hem in an earlier painting by Cimabue depicting an enthroned Madonna with St. Francis. The juxtaposition of Christ and St. Francis occurs again in frescoes painted by Giotto's workshop and Pietro Lorenzetti in the transepts and the crossing vault. The frescoes in the St. Nicholas and the Magdalen chapels, added in the fourteenth century, are the work of pupils of Giotto. The St. Martin chapel was decorated by Simone Martini.

The walls of the upper church are divided into two registers. The upper register is covered with frescoes begun during the late thirteenth century. The earliest, in the sanctuary and transepts, are by Cimabue and assistants. On the upper half of the nave walls in two registers are stories from the Old and New Testaments. These are chiefly the work of artists of the Roman school, Torriti and Rusuti and their assistants, the anonymous Isaac Master, and the young Giotto.

The crowning decoration in the upper church are the 28 scenes from the life of St. Francis in the lower register. Framed by a painted colonnade, a *stoa pictile*, they have been variously attributed to Giotto and assistants, to the St. Cecilia Master, and to a fourteenth-century Umbrian.

Preservation and Restoration. In 1944 the Germans designated Assisi a hospital town at the request of the Holy See, and thus it escaped damage during World War II. At the end of September 1997, a series of earthquakes, the first on 27 September, devastated the city, causing extensive damage to homes and public monuments. The Basilica of San Francesco, the Church of Santa Chiara and other buildings were closed for two years and more while repairs were made and the paintings restored.

Bibliography: F. S. ATTAL, "Assisi città santa: Come fu salvata: dagli orrori della guerra," *Miscellanea francescana* 48 (1948): 3–32. A. CRISTOFANI, *Le storie di Assisi,* fourth ed. (Venice 1959). A. FORTINI, *Assisi nel media evo* (Rome 1940). WILLIAM HUGO, *Studying the Life of St Francis of Assisi* (Quincy, Ill.: Franciscan Press, 1996). B. KLEINSCHMIDT, *Die Basilika San Francesco in Assisi,* 3 vols. (Berlin 1915–28); *Die Wandmalereien der Basilika San Francesco in Assisi* (Berlin 1930). F. LANZONI, *Le diocesi d'Italia dalle origini al principio del secolo VII (an. 604),* 2 vols., second ed. (Faenza 1927), 1:461–480. F. J. MATHER, *The Isaac Master* (New York 1932). M. MEISS, *Giotto and Assisi* (New York 1960). ERNEST RYMOND, *In the Steps of Saint Francis* (Chicago: Franciscan Herald Press, 1975). I. B. SUPINO, *La Basilica di San Francesco d'Assisi* (Bologna 1924). L. TINTORI and M. MEISS, *The Painting of the Life of St. Francis in Assisi* (New York 1962). PAOLA URBANI, *Patriarchal Basilica in Assisi, Saint Francis, Artistic Testimony, Evangelical Message* (Milan: Fabri Editori, 1991). G. WEIGEL, *Witness to Hope* (New York 1999).

[R. BROWN/ E. T. DE WALD/EDS.]

BALTHASAR, HANS URS VON

Theologian, author, publisher, priest; b. 24 August 1905 of an ancient Catholic Swiss family of Lucerne; d. Basel, 26 June 1988. Balthasar received a doctorate in German literature and philosophy in 1928 following studies in Zurich, Vienna, and Berlin. He entered the Society of Jesus in 1929, studied philosophy at Pullach, near Munich, and theology (1933–37) at Lyon (Fourvière), a companion to J. Daniélou and H. Bouillard. He was ordained a priest in July 1936. For a brief time he served as an associate editor of *Stimmen der Zeit* (1937 39). In 1940, when chaplain of students in Basel, he met Adrienne von Speyr, introducing her to the Catholic Church and remaining her confessor until her death (1967). In 1945 he founded with her the secular institute *Johannesgemeinschaft.* Later he established Johannesverlag, a publishing house that issued major works on the Fathers of the Church and other "Christian masters" whom Balthasar regarded as foundational to Christian life and thought. Under his direction Johannesverlag published some 60 volumes of von Speyr's writings that she practically dictated to him in their entirety.

His departure from the Society of Jesus in 1950 dimmed his reputation for a while. He was not a *peritus* to the Second Vatican Council. Nevertheless, Pope Paul VI recognized Balthasar's brilliance, and nominated him a member of the original International Theological Commission in 1969, later reappointing him. Pope John Paul II also selected him for the commission in 1980 and 1986. In 1972 he launched in Germany and Italy the international Catholic review *Communio,* giving it both program and purpose; this review eventually appeared in 11 different languages. In 1984, Pope John Paul II recognized his achievement by personally giving him the "Pope Paul VI" prize. Although Balthasar was named a cardinal by Pope John Paul II, he died two days before receiving the red hat.

The Charism. While engaged in the spiritual exercises of St. Ignatius (1929), God unexpectedly called Balthasar to serve Him with the sole directive that he "abandon everything and follow" with a typically Ignatian indifference. This choice of God would determine his destiny, his thought, and his work. A priest who found himself at home in the Society of Jesus, Balthasar received through Adrienne von Speyr a theological and ecclesial mission, founded in the interrelated roles of Mary, John, and Peter, incarnated in the secular institute *Johannesgemeinschaft,* and founded to be an actualization of the charism of St. Ignatius under the form of a "secular institute." Obliged as a result of his activities to quit the Society, he would be broken like the eucharistic bread. Passing beyond and reformulating the Lutheran idea of Good Friday and the Hegelian notion of a speculative Friday, he received the theology of Holy Saturday through von Speyr. It gave life and strength to his mission in a secular world. The most telling sign of the power of this charism, concealed in the invisible, was the colloquium he held in Rome (1985) that assembled several hundred friends of von Speyr from around the world.

His Writings. The books of Balthasar were written from within the interior of this charism. Under the influence of Erich Przywara (1889–1972), who exercised a decisive influence on him, Balthasar wrote the *Apokalypse der deutschen Seele* (3 vols., 1937–39), in which he attempted to unveil through "the great modern spiritual figures of German history, the most recent religious attitude that, though it often remains hidden, is in a way that of 'confession'." Through Henri de Lubac, whose disciple Balthasar became at Fourvière and with whom he maintained a lifelong friendship, Balthasar's thought found its "Catholic" basis. Balthasar was responsible for the German translation of Lubac's Catholicism, a work he held in high regard, and of many other of Lubac's works. Stimulated by such a master, Balthasar studied Origen, Gregory of Nyssa, and Maximus the Confessor (he had already compiled an anthology of the works of Saint Augustine). He also learned from Karl Barth (1951), Romano Guardini (1970), Martin Buber (1958), and Gustav Siewert.

Balthasar acknowledged the lasting influence of Adrienne von Speyr on his thought and publications. "It was Adrienne von Speyr," he wrote, "who pointed out the fulfilling way from Ignatius to John, and thus laid out the foundation for most of what has been published by me since 1940. Her work and mine is neither psychologically nor philosophically separable, two halves of a whole that, as center, has but one foundation" (*Balthasar Reader,* 42). The experiences and theology of Adrienne von Speyr began to fulfill his hopes and to respond to questions, in particular, those concerning the final realities. He attributed to her his insights regarding the mystery of Holy Saturday "and hence of hell and of universal redemption as well" (ibid., 403).

Sometime about 1961, Balthasar elaborated a plan for a trilogy that he published in subsequent years as *Herrlichkeit, Theodramatik,* and *Theologik.* The multivolume work has the transcendentals—the Beautiful, the Good, and the True—as its foci; each concentrates on a different power of the human person: What can one perceive? For what should one hope? For what purpose has one intelligence? In fact, the trilogy is a theological synthesis that brings together Balthasar's vast knowledge of ancient and modern European literature and philosophy on the one hand, and the Christian tradition, including the Church fathers, scholastic and modern theology, exegesis and mysticism on the other. In Balthasar's vision of things, the theological enterprise takes as its point of departure the mystery of revelation made known in the incarnate and crucified Word of God: a glory or splendor (*Herrlichkeit*) integrating all natural beauty and surpassing all human attempts to order and shape the created universe, is made visible in Him.

The passage from "aesthetic" to "dramatic" takes place in the drama of the Incarnation and Crucifixion, whereby God gathers together and brings to perfection everything worthwhile in creation. Truth, which responds to every human question, is revealed in the kenosis of God in the Incarnation and the Crucifixion. According to Balthasar's scheme *Theologik,* which concludes the trilogy, seeks to make intelligible the inner logic that underlies God's action in history. In the Truth that is Jesus Christ, every human question and all knowing is revealed.

The Form. "To know as I am known": the vertical of Revelation and of faith traverses and gives birth to the horizontal of history and human research. Theology cannot pass over anthropology, for "man is the way of God" (John Paul II) and in Christ man is completed as God loved and created him. All converges toward and in Christ, the Son of God who is delivered up for us and united with Mary the Church. Trinity, christology, soteriology, Mariology, ecclesiology, and anthropology are united as in the *Credo*. It is the same unity. Balthasar's "catholic" theology is aided by his musical and artistic gifts. It is not systematic, but "symphonic." It finds coherence and dynamism in its "return to the center," *(Einfaltung),* which is at the same time an unfolding *(Entfaltung).*

Balthasar contemplates a God who gives Himself by revealing who He is, thereby giving life to man's free response to Him. Because of this gift of freedom that God has given man, being is essential, for following Saint Thomas (in the manner in which G. Siewert had explained him), Balthasar regarded being as the gift of God to His creatures, in which they may participate in order to receive it in their own singularity. In considering this gift (being in the transcendentals) Balthasar did not forget the giver; in God the Beautiful is divine Glory, in which human beings are called to share; in God the Good is merciful love, by which humans hope for salvation (without excluding the possibility of Hell), and in God the True is the Word of the Father, communicated by the Spirit, through whom humans know the love that is beyond all knowledge. The transcendentals, without losing their own identity, are thereby theologically transmuted.

This transformation leads to several consequences, of which we shall consider a few. That which humans may see and sense has a profundity that goes beyond what constitutes them: humans are called to contemplate the Glory of God. This intellectual act is also a sensible one, for there exist spiritual senses (cf. Origen). Correlatively Jesus is his own light; a manifestation of divine Glory in a union of spirit and body that sets aside all Platonism and demands an incarnated mystic.

The divine drama "rests in part on the notion of mission that elevates and accomplishes the psychological and Christian notion of role . . . and in part on the confrontation of a created and finite freedom with the freedom of divine infinity." The divine mission, being the economic form of the procession, "cannot be made one except with the theological notion of person." The confrontation of divine and human freedom leads, through Christ, to the abandoned state of the Son in death and to the separation of the Father and the Son, who are united without fail by the Spirit. Here Balthasar inserts a theology of Holy Saturday. These same notions of mission and person furnish the basis for an ecclesiology, wherein are illuminated the figures of Mary, John, and Peter.

Bibliography: For complete bibliography of Von Balthasar's work, see: *Hans Urs von Balthasar, Bibliographie: 1925–1990.* Einsiedeln, Switzerland, 1990. M. KEHL AND W. LOSER. *The Von Balthasar Reader.* Translated by R. J. Daly and F. Lawrence. New York, 1982. HANS URS VON BALTHASAR. "Discour du P. H. U. von Balthasar." *Hans Urs von Balthasar: Premio Internazionale Paolo VI 1984.* Brescia, 1984; *First Glance at Adrienne von Speyr.* Translated by A. Lawry and S. Englund. San Francisco, 1968; *My Work: In Retrospect.* San Francisco, 1993; *Our Task: A Report and A Plan.* Translated by John Saward. San Francisco, 1994. L..S. CHAPP. *The God Who Speaks: Hans Urs von Balthasar's Theology of Revelation.* Bethesda, Md.., 1996. E.T. OAKES. *Pattern of Redemption: The Theology of Hans Urs von Balthasar.* 2d rev. ed. New York, 1997. DAVID SCHINDLER, ed. *Hans Urs von Balthasar: His Life and Work.* Notre Dame, Ind., 1991.

[G. CHANTRAINE]

BAUM, WILLIAM WAKEFIELD

Cardinal; major penitentiary; archbishop emeritus of Washington, D.C.; b. 21 November 1926, Dallas, Texas, the son of Harold E. and Mary Leona (Hayes) White. William was still a young child when his father died and the family moved to Kansas City, Missouri; subsequently his mother married Jerome C. Baum who adopted William. He studied for the priesthood in St. Louis at Kenrick Seminary. After ordination in 1951, he did pastoral work at several parishes in Kansas City; taught at Avila College from 1954 to1956; and then pursued doctoral studies in Rome at the Pontifical Athenaeum Angelicum, 1956 to1958. Baum resumed teaching at Avila College in 1958 and continued there until 1963, at the same time engaging in pastoral ministry and serving in the diocesan chancery. He attended the Second Vatican Council as a peritus. From 1964 to 1967 he was executive director of the Commission for Ecumenical and Interreligious Affairs in the newly organized National Conference of Catholic Bish-

ops in Washington, D.C., and was a Catholic representative on working groups with the World Council of Churches and the Lutheran World Confederation. In 1967 he returned to Kansas City, where he served as chancellor of the diocese and pastor of St. James parish.

In 1970 Pope Paul VI appointed him bishop of Springfield-Cape Girardeau, and the following year he was one of the U.S. bishops elected to attend the second ordinary assembly of the Synod of Bishops in Rome. In March 1973, Paul VI appointed him to succeed Cardinal Patrick O'Boyle as archbishop of Washington, D.C. By reason of that office, Baum also served as chancellor of the Catholic University of America. His episcopal seal carried the motto "ministry of reconciliation," an expression of his enduring interest in ecumenism. The premium he put on higher education was evident in the encouragement he gave young clergy of the archdiocese to pursue advanced degrees in religious studies.

Paul VI named Archbishop Baum a cardinal in 1976 with the title of Church of the Holy Cross (in via Flaminia). He participated in the conclave that elected Pope John Paul II in 1978. When Pope John Paul called him to Rome in 1980 to serve as Prefect of the Congregation for Catholic Education, Cardinal Baum resigned as archbishop of Washington to take up the new post. Cardinal Baum was one of the twelve cardinals and bishops who formed the commission appointed by Pope John Paul in 1986 to draft the *Catechism of the Catholic Church.* He attended the special assemblies of the Synod of Bishops for Europe, Africa, and America, as well as several general assemblies of the synod. In 1990 Pope John Paul named him Major Penitentiary in charge of the Sacred Penitentiary whose jurisdiction covers matters of the internal forum and indulgences.

[RICHARD BURTON]

BERNARDIN, JOSEPH LOUIS

Cardinal, archbishop of Chicago; b. 2 April 1928, Columbia, South Carolina; d. 14 November 1996, Chicago, Illinois. Bernardin was the oldest of two children born to Joseph and Maria Simion Bernardin. His father, a stonecutter who came to America from the province of Trent in Northern Italy, died when Joseph was six. His father's death drew him closer to his mother and his sister, Elaine. He studied for the priesthood at St. Mary's College in Kentucky and at St. Mary's Seminary and University in Baltimore, where in 1948 he received an A.B. degree in philosophy before going to the Catholic University of America for a master's in education in 1952. Ordained a priest for the Diocese of Charleston on

26 April 1952, he served as vice chancellor (1954–56), chancellor (1956–66), vicar general and diocesan consultor (1962–66), and administrator (1964–65). Pope Paul VI named him auxiliary bishop of Atlanta on 9 March 1966. As auxiliary bishop Bernardin also served as pastor of Atlanta's Christ the King Cathedral from 1966 to 1968.

In 1968 Bishop Bernardin was elected general secretary of the National Conference of Catholic Bishops (NCCB) and the United States Catholic Conference (USCC) in Washington, D.C. The newly established NCCB responded to the Second Vatican Council's call for national episcopal conferences and the USCC succeeded the National Catholic Welfare Conference as the permanent secretariat of the U.S. bishops.

Bernardin was installed as archbishop of Cincinnati 19 December 1972. During his decade in Cincinnati he was host to his good friend, Karol Cardinal Wojtyła of Krakow, Poland. It is said that after Cardinal Wojtyła became Pope John Paul II he told the then-archbishop of Chicago, John Cardinal Cody, that his eventual successor would be Bernardin. Following Cody's death Bernardin was installed (25 August 1982) and the next year John Paul II named him a cardinal, with the titular church of Gesù Divin Lavoratore.

The first American cardinal created by Pope John Paul II, Bernardin became a leading spokesman for the Church in the United States, with a reputation as a conciliator and mediator. He published several books, but most of his writing took the form of pastoral letters. He was also active on the international level, serving as a member of the permanent council of the Synod of Bishops from 1974 to 1994.

In the early 1980s Bernardin chaired an ad hoc NCCB committee to examine war and peace questions. The result of the committee's work was the pastoral letter The Challenge of Peace: God's Promise and Our Response, issued by the bishops in 1983, which led to Cardinal Bernardin receiving the Albert Einstein International Peace Prize. In a lecture at Fordham University that same year, he spoke of the pastoral letter as providing a starting point for developing a "consistent ethic of life." The "dominant cultural fact" in increasing the modern awareness of the fragility of life, he said, is technology; and a consistent ethic of life is necessary to address the moral questions that arise in this context. Over the next few years Cardinal Bernardin repeatedly adverted to the theme of a "consistent ethic of life" as an essential element of the Catholic approach to a variety of moral questions, including abortion, euthanasia, capital punishment, nuclear war, poverty, and racism. In a lecture at St. Louis University in 1984, he referred to the linkage of these

William Wakefield Cardinal Baum. (© Grzegorz Galazka/ CORBIS)

ideas as a "seamless garment," an expression that quickly became the popular way to refer to the concept.

In 1993 a former seminarian charged that he had been sexually abused in the 1970s, naming Bernardin as an abuser. The cardinal strongly denied the charge. He met and prayed with his accuser, who recanted. After June 1995, when Bernardin was diagnosed with pancreatic cancer, he reached out to cancer patients and the dying in his personal ministry. Pope John Paul spoke of Bernardin's "witness of dignity and hope in the face of the mystery of suffering and death." He died in Chicago of pancreatic cancer on 14 November 1996. It was, his doctor said, a heroic death of one who loved life. He was interred in the mausoleum at Mount Carmel Cemetery in suburban Hillside. Several months later, a book of his reflections on his last years, *The Gift of Peace,* was published and quickly became a bestseller.

Bibliography: Cardinal Bernardin's extensive personal papers are in the Joseph Cardinal Bernardin Archives and Records Center, 711 W. Monroe, Chicago.

[A. F. P. WALL]

Joseph Cardinal Bernardin. (Catholic News Service.)

BEVILACQUA, ANTHONY JOSEPH

Cardinal, archbishop of Philadelphia, canon lawyer; b. 17 June 1923, Brooklyn, N.Y., one of eleven children of Luigi and Maria (Codella) Bevilacqua. The family immigrated from Italy to the United States around 1913. Bevilacqua completed seminary studies at Immaculate Conception Seminary, Huntington, New York and was ordained to the priesthood 11 June 1949. After two brief pastoral assignments he was assigned to Cathedral College in Brooklyn (1950–53), where he taught history until being sent to Rome to study canon law. In 1956 he received a J.C.D. summa cum laude from the Pontifical Gregorian University. From 1957 to 1965 he served on Brooklyn's marriage tribunal; he was then transferred to the chancery office, where he served consecutively as assistant chancellor, vice-chancellor, and chancellor until 1983. From 1968 to 1980 he taught at the diocesan seminary, during which time he earned an M.A. in political science from Columbia University (1962), and a J.D. from St. John's University Law School (1975). In 1971 he established a Catholic Migration and Refugee Office in Brooklyn, and from 1977 to 1980 taught immigration law as an adjunct professor at St. John's University Law School. A member of the bar in the states of New York (1976) and Pennsylvania (1988), he was also admitted to practice before the U.S. Supreme Court (1989).

Father Bevilacqua was ordained a bishop in November 1980. He served as an auxiliary bishop in the diocese of Brooklyn until October 1983, when Pope John Paul II named him bishop of Pittsburgh. In 1987 Pope John Paul appointed him archbishop of Philadelphia, and three years later, 29 June 1991, made him a cardinal with the titular church of SS. Redentore e S. Alfonso.

Cardinal Bevilacqua's pastoral activity is dedicated to the spiritual renewal of the faithful. He regularly visits parishes, schools, hospitals, retirement homes, and prisons. After witnessing the beatification of Philadelphian Katherine Drexel, SBS, in Rome in 1988, Archbishop Bevilacqua began the Office of Renewal to generate programs to deepen the spiritual life of Catholics. In December 1991 he inaugurated "Catholic Faith and Life 2000," a comprehensive eight-year spiritual renewal plan in preparation for the Jubilee Year 2000. Related to the spiritual renewal plans, the cardinal started two initiatives in 1994: the monthly newsletter "Voice of Your Shepherd" and a weekly call-in radio program, "Live with Cardinal Bevilacqua."

In the area of social ministry, in 1988 Archbishop Bevilacqua created the Office of AIDS Ministry. In response to racial tensions in Grays Ferry, he issued, in January 1998, "Healing through Faith and Truth," a pastoral letter on racism. Also active in ecumenical and inter-faith relations, he established the archdiocesan Office of Ecumenical and Interreligious Affairs in 1990. His expertise in canon law led to his appointment as chairman of the NCCB committee on the implementation of *Ex corde ecclesiae* (1997–99).

[MICHAEL J. MCNALLY]

BOFF, LEONARDO

University professor, theologian, writer; b. 14 December 1938 in Concordia, a small town in the state of Santa Catarina (Brazil), one of eleven children of Mansueto and Regina Fontana Boff. He was baptized Genezio Darci Boff. At age 10 he entered the minor seminary of the Franciscans, receiving the name Leonardo when he entered the novitiate of the Friars Minor (19 December 1958). He studied philosophy at Curitiba (Parana) and theology at the Franciscan school in Petrpólis (Rio de Janeiro). Following ordination to the priesthood in 1964, he continued his studies in Europe, taking courses at the University of Würzburg (Germany), the Catholic University of Louvain (Belgium), and at the University of Oxford (England). He studied under Karl Rahner 1965 to 1970 at the Ludwig-Maximilian University in Münich (Germany), where he received a doctorate in theology.

His doctoral dissertation, written in German, dealt with the sacramental nature of the Church as described in the documents of Vatican II.

In 1972 he joined the faculty of the Franciscan seminary connected with the Petroplis Institute for Philosophy and Theology and became editor of the *Revista Eclesiastica Brasileira* and the Portugese-language edition of *Concilium.* A polyglot and a prolific writer, Boff has authored and co-authored (sometimes with his brother Clodovis, a member of the Order of Servants of Mary) numerous works dealing with theology, theological anthropology, Christology, eschatology, ecclesiology, popular spirituality, and ecology. Several of his works have been translated into other languages. Among his best-known works are: *Jesus Cristo Libertador, Igreja Carisma e Poder, A Graça Libertadora no Mundo, Igreja que se Fez Povo,* and *Grito da Terra e Grito dos Pobres.* Evident throughout his works is the perspective of Latin American liberation theology, which surveys all theological approaches from the standpoint of the poor and the oppressed.

Igreja Carisma e Poder (1984), translated into English as *Church, Charism and Power,* brought a long-smouldering dispute with Church authorities into the open. The work strongly criticized the exercise of authority and power in the institutional Church from the perspective of liberation theology. As a result, in 1985 the Congregation for the Doctrine of the Faith prohibited him from speaking and publishing for a year. Boff obeyed and demonstrated his loyalty to the church by stating: "I would rather walk with the church than walk alone with my theology." Yet, he was increasingly estranged from ecclesiastical authority. In 1986 he was removed from his editorial post in *Editora Vozes,* the leading Catholic publisher in Brazil. In 1992 Boff left the Franciscan Order, resigned the priesthood, and married. He joined the faculty of the Public University of Rio de Janeiro and remains an active member of a Base Community, also located in Rio.

For the most part Boff's writings display Franciscan sensitivity, great impatience with injustice, and a very Catholic sacramental imagination. In his theological works, he incorporates the viewpoints of the poor, the role of the laity, women's issues, and ecological and environment concerns in a framework of Scholastic and modern European theology. He has written that the poor must understand that poverty is not natural, that sexism is not in the plan of God, and that the ecosystem is a gift of God and must be respected. Boff believes it is important to understand the political dimension of a liberation faith in order to alleviate the plight of the oppressed. His contribution to theology lies in the retrieval of a faith incarnat-

Anthony Joseph Cardinal Bevilacqua (at microphone). (Catholic News Service.)

ed within a social reality that is calling for justice. From Boff's standpoint it is impossible to be a Christian while at the same time being indifferent to the reality of the oppression under which two-thirds of the world's population are forced to live.

Bibliography: LEONARDO BOFF, *Jesus Cristo Libertador* (Petropólis: Vozes, 1972); *A Graça Libertadora no Mundo* (Petropólis: Vozes, 1984); *Church: Charism and Power* (New York: Crossroad, 1985); *Sacraments of Life: Life of the Sacraments,* tr. JOHN DRURY (Washington, D.C.: Pastoral Press, 1987); *Ecclesiogensis: The Base Communities Reinvent the Church,* tr. ROBERT BARR (Maryknoll, N.Y.: Orbis, 1986); *Cry of the Earth, Cry of the Poor* (New York: Orbis Books, 1997); *Ecology and Liberation: A New Paradigm* (New York: Orbis Books, 1995). HARVEY COX, *The Silencing of Leonardo Boff* (Oak Park, Ill.: Meyer-Stone Books, 1988).

[JOAQUIM PARRON MARIA]

BRADLEY, RITAMARY

Scholar, author, educator and pioneer in the Religious Formation movement; b. 30 January 1916 in Stuart, Iowa; d. Davenport, Iowa, 20 March 2000.

The daughter of James and Mary (Muldoon) Bradley, Ritamary joined the Congregation of the Humility of Mary of Ottumwa, Iowa, in 1933, and in 1972, the Sisters

Leonardo Boff (center). (AP/Wide World Photos. Reproduced by permission.)

for Christian Community. A graduate of Marygrove College in Detroit, Mich. (1938), she received a doctorate in English from St. Louis University in 1953. After teaching at Marycrest College in Davenport, Iowa, from 1940 to 1956, she joined the English department at St. Ambrose in 1965, where she was professor emerita at the time of her death.

Sister Ritamary was a powerful force in the origins and development of the Sister Formation Conference. From 1951 to 1964 she served as Associate Executive Secretary with Sister Annette Walters, C.S.J., the Executive Secretary of the Conference. She was well in advance of major superiors in grasping the changes taking place in the Church and the world, and the consequent demands upon religious-apostolic communities of sisters. Her most outstanding contribution came as founder and editor of the Sister Formation Bulletin (1954–1964). In this role, she empowered women religious of the United States by providing an open forum in which sisters could express their opinions and have them published without censorship from male editors.

With the advance of the electronic age, Bradley seized the opportunity to facilitate communication lines among all women religious and established SISTER-L, an e-mail discussion group for those interested in the history and contemporary concerns of Catholic women religious. In addition to her interest in the lives of women religious, Bradley involved herself in numerous civic and humanitarian issues. She was a member of the Davenport Civil Rights Commission; the Iowa Humanities Board program committee, and the Religion and Literature Advisory Board at the University of Notre Dame. She was a volunteer chaplain at the Scott County Jail and received the Volunteer Service Award in 1990.

Among her extensive writings are two books on the fourteenth century mystic, Julian of Norwich. She cofounded the *Fourteenth-Century English Mystics Newsletter,* now the *Mystics Quarterly.*

[MARY RODGER MADDEN]

CAMARA, HELDER PESSOA

Archbishop of Olinda and Recife; b. 7 February 1909, Fortaleza, Ceará, Brazil; d. 27 August 1999. Born into a middle-class family, the eleventh of thirteen children of Joao Eduardo—bookkeeper, journalist, committed liberal, mason—and Adelaide, primary school

Pope John Paul II meets with former Archbishop of Rio de Janeiro Dom Helder Camara at the Metropolitan cathedral, Rio de Janeiro, Brazil. (Reuters/Gregg Newton/Archive Photos. Reproduced by Permission.)

teacher and practicing Catholic. In 1923, Camara entered the diocesan seminary of St. Joseph, and was ordained as priest 15 August 1931. He took a keen interest in social movements, playing an active role in the creation of the Young Catholic Workers, the Unionizing of Catholic Women Workers, and the League of Catholic Teachers of Ceará, of which he became ecclesiastical assistant. Attracted by integralismo, a political and ideological movement in the mold of fascism, he was given permission by his archbishop to become a member of the new party. In recognition of his contribution to the Catholic Electoral League's victories in 1933–34, he was nominated Director of Public Instruction for the State of Ceará.

Disillusioned with the direction taken by State politics, he accepted an invitation to work in Rio de Janeiro in the Ministry of Education and Culture. His move to Rio coincided with his developing political consciousness and, on a much deeper level, in his self-

consciousness of his mission as a priest. His reading of Jacques Maritain's *Integral Humanism* contributed decisively to this process. Later he became the national vice-assistant to Brazilian Catholic Action. In 1952, with the support of the Vatican pro-Secretary of State, Msgr. Montini (the future Pope Paul VI), he founded the Brazilian National Conference of Bishops (CNBB), of which he became general secretary, and was ordained bishop. In 1955, he was promoted to archbishop, while remaining auxiliary to the cardinal archbishop of Rio de Janeiro. In that same year he organized, with Mgr. Larraín, bishop of Talca, Chile, the First General Conference of the Latin American Episcopate (CELAM), and served as its vice-president from 1958 to 1965.

As auxiliary bishop in Rio, Camara undertook numerous social initiatives on the local level, while as secretary of the National Conference of Bishops he was the driving force behind attempts to promote a series of "basic reforms" through the cooperation of the Church, the unions, and the governments, especially the federal government. He coordinated the preparation of the Emergency Plan—taken on officially by the Brazilian episcopacy in 1962—which eventually became the Collective Pastoral Plan of the Brazilian bishops.

In 1964 the government of Brazil was seized by a military coup; that same year, Pope Paul VI appointed Camara residential archbishop of Olinda and Recife. He continued his active pastoral ministry, quickly becoming "enemy number one" of the country's conservative forces because of his growing acclaim among the international mass media, where he was the voice of the poor and of those persecuted by the regime. He received numerous international awards during his lifetime, and was four times nominated for the Nobel Peace Prize. Among the many books he published as archbishop were *Terzo mondo defraudato* (Milan 1968), *Spirale de violence* (Paris 1970), *Pour arriver à temps* (Paris 1970), *Le désert est fertile* (Paris 1971), *Prière pour les riches* (Zurich 1972), *Cristianismo, socialismo, capitalismo* (Salamanca 1974), *Um olhar sobre a cidade* (Rio de Janeiro 1985), and *Les conversions d'un Evêque: entretiens avec José de Broucker* (Paris 1977).

He retired from his see in 1985, but continued to serve until his death in 1999, promoting the causes of peace and justice, including the world-wide campaign the Year 2000 without Misery. A brilliant orator and preacher, an efficient organizer, an indefatigable advocate of justice, a man of prayer, deeply in love with God and his creation, he became known, from the time of the council on, due to his many international conferences and sermons, as "bishop of the slums," "voice of the voiceless," "advocate of the Third World," "prophet of the Church of the Poor," "apostle of non-violence." It was for this reason he was accused by his opponents of being the "red archbishop."

Bibliography: J. DE BROUCKER, *Dom Helder Camara: The Violence of a Peacemaker,* tr. by HERMA BRIFFAULT (Maryknoll, N.Y. 1970). M. DE CASTRO, *Dom Helder: o bispo da esperança* (Rio de Janeiro 1978). J. L. GONZÁLEZ-BALADO, *Helder Camara: L'arcivescovo rosso* (Rome 1970). M. HALL, *The Impossible Dream: The Spirituality of Dom Helder Camara* (Belfast 1979). G. WEIGNER and B. MOOSBRUGGER, *A Voice of the Third World: Dom Helder Camara* (New York 1972).

[LUIZ CARLOS MARQUES]

CAMERLENGO

An Italian word that corresponds to "chamberlain" in English. In church parlance it designates the cardinal of the Holy Roman Church with specific responsibilities of treasurer and administrator during the time between the death of one pope and the election of his successor. The time period is often described as *sede vacante.* Pope John Paul II in the apostolic constitution, *Universi dominici gregis,* is the latest of five popes since St. Pius X to address this venerable office.

Appointed by the reigning pope, or elected by the College of Cardinals if the office is vacant at the pope's death, the Camerlengo continues to exercise his ordinary functions of office, submitting to the College of Cardinals matters that would have had to be referred to the supreme pontiff. Upon the death of the supreme pontiff, the Camerlengo must officially verify the pope's death and with those officials described by law draw up the official death certificate. He informs the dean of the college of cardinals who informs the cardinals and convokes them for the congregations of the college. The Camerlengo seals the deceased pope's rooms of the papal apartment and the entire apartment after the pope's funeral; he informs the cardinal vicar for Rome who informs the people of Rome of the pope's death; he notifies the cardinal archpriest of the Vatican basilica; and he takes possession of the Apostolic palace in the Vatican and the palaces of the Lateran and Castel Gandolfo for the purpose of exercising custody and administration. As a member of the College of Cardinals to whom the government of the Church is entrusted, the Camerlengo and three cardinals chosen by lot from the cardinal electors already present in Rome, form a particular congregation to deal with questions of lesser importance as compared to the general, or preparatory, congregations, which include the whole college of cardinals and which are held before the beginning of the electoral conclave.

With the consultation of the other three cardinals, the Camerlengo determines all matters of the pope's burial; and he deals, in the name of and with the consent of the College of Cardinals, with all matters that circumstances suggest for safeguarding the goods and temporal rights of the Holy See and for its proper administration. As preparation for the conclave to elect a new pope, the Camerlengo reserves quarters in the *Domus Sanctae Marthae* for the cardinal electors and the areas reserved for liturgical celebrations, in particular the Sistine chapel, making provision that a suitable number of persons be available for preparing and serving meals and for housekeeping. The Cardinal Camerlengo ensures, with the expertise of trustworthy technicians, that no violation of secrecy with regard to election events in the Sistine Chapel takes place before, during, and after the voting. During the actual voting of the cardinal electors, the Camerlengo declares the results of each session as well as disposes of ballots and any notes concerning the results of each ballot. The Carmerlengo holds office *ad bene placitum* of the Roman pontiff.

Bibliography: CIC cc. 332–335; CCEO cc. 43–48 as modified by John Paul II, "Universi Dominici Gregis," in *Acta Apostolicae Sedis* 87 (1996): 305–343.

[A. ESPELAGE]

CANON LAW, 1983 CODE

The Code of Canon Law for the Latin Church, incorporating many of the reforms of Vatican II, was promulgated on 25 January 1983, by Pope John Paul II. The apostolic constitution *Sacrae disciplinae leges* described the procedures and guiding principles of the revision. A parallel text was also proposed for the oriental Catholic Churches.

Preparation. Announced on 25 January 1959 by Pope John XXIII, and undertaken in earnest in 1966 after the conclusion of Vatican II, the task of revision spanned almost a quarter century. In 1971, the Commission began distributing draft texts for comments and observations. The draft of the *Lex ecclesiae fundamentalis* (LEF), or Fundamental Law of the Church, was the first sent out for study; it was followed by a text on administrative procedure. Later, *schemata* on crimes and penalties, sacramental law, and procedures for the protection of rights were distributed at regular intervals. In 1978, the remaining parts of the proposed Code were printed and distributed. After all the comments had been reviewed, a consolidated version of the law was prepared (1980) for the members of the Commission. Their observations were then incorporated into a *relatio* (report), distributed in 1981, which became the basis for work during the final plenary session of the Commission held in October 1981. At this meeting, a number of major issues upon which general unanimity was lacking were selected for discussion. These included norms on marriage tribunals, the sharing of jurisdiction by lay persons, and membership in Masonic societies. The Commission was also called upon to address some thirty additional issues proposed by the members.

A final version of the text was presented in 1982 to Pope John Paul II. With the assistance of a select committee, he examined the draft, invited further suggestions from Episcopal Conferences, and eventually introduced a number of additional changes in the light of suggestions received. The final text was then duly promulgated. Contrary to the norms in effect under the 1917 Code, translations of the new Code were permitted, and according to special norms issued by the Secretariat of State, 28 January 1983, such texts are to be approved by Episcopal Conferences, not by the Holy See. Only the promulgated version in Latin, however, is regarded as authentic. Translations have been published in various languages, including two different English translations; one approved by the Episcopal Conference in the United Kingdom and the other by the National Conference of Catholic Bishops in the U.S.

On 2 January 1984, Pope John Paul II, by the *motu proprio* entitled *Recognito iuris canonici codice,* established the pontifical commission for the authentic interpretation of the Code of Canon Law, under the presidency of then Archbishop (later Cardinal) Rosalio Castillo Lara, SDB. The Commission handed down its first authentic interpretation on 26 June 1984. When the Pontifical Commission for revision of the Code had completed its work and was dissolved, the Commission for Interpretation of the Code assumed responsibility for the publication of *Communicationes.*

Plan. Instead of following the plan of the 1917 Code which modeled itself closely on that of the Roman Civil Law (General Norms, Persons, Things, Trials, Crimes and Penalties), the 1983 Code follows a model based on the threefold mission of the Church: to teach, sanctify, and serve. The Code is now divided into seven books: I. General Norms; II. The People of God; III. The Function of Teaching; IV. The Function of Sanctifying; V. Temporal Goods; VI. Delicts and Penalties; VII. Procedures. While Books III and IV treat of the prophetic (Word) and priestly (Sacrament) missions of the Church, no one specific book treats of the royal mission, that of governing; rather, these norms are found in the remaining parts of the Code.

Throughout the revision process, there was question of another Book, the Fundamental Law of the Church, applying equally to Latin and Oriental rite Catholics. Opposition to such a document was strong, however, because of the risk of expressing doctrine in legislative form; it was therefore decided not to proceed at this time with the promulgation of the LEF. Because of this, a number of general norms had to be incorporated into the Code of Canon Law itself; among such were those on the rights and obligations of the faithful and many of those treating the papacy, ecumenical councils, etc.

Two particular problems regarding the plan concerned the place of personal prelatures and of institutes of consecrated life. While the drafts had placed personal prelatures within the canons on the particular Church, strong objections were raised against this on theological grounds, and prelatures were eventually moved to the first part (The Christian Faithful) of Book II, under a distinct heading. Similarly, at one point in the process it was proposed to place the canons on institutes of consecrated life alongside those treating of associations in the Church. Again, for theological reasons, Book II was divided into three parts: the Christian faithful; the hierarchical dimension of the Church; and institutes of consecrated life and societies of apostolic life, thus highlighting the charismatic dimension of consecrated life alongside the hierarchical dimension of Church structures. This new division was well received in general.

The Vision of the Church. Book II, c. 204, begins with the recognition that the Church is the people of God, comprising all the baptized. Baptism makes a person a member of the Church and the subject of rights and obligations. But the Church is not only a people; it is also a hierarchically organized community. Thus, the unifying factor is ecclesial communion with the successor of Peter and the bishops in communion with him. The Code recognizes various degrees of communion (cc. 205; 844, etc). Other Christians, who are not in full communion with the Catholic Church may nevertheless share in some of the Sacraments and sacramentals of the Church in virtue of their Baptism. The theme of "communion" is one that ties together many parts of the legislation; those who place themselves outside of ecclesial communion are known as the "ex-communicated" (c. 1331). The ecumenical dimension of the law is evident, particularly in c. 11 which no longer extends merely ecclesiastical laws to all the baptized, but limits their scope to those who have been baptized in the Catholic Church or received into it. Many other canons speak of the importance of fostering true ecumenism (cc. 383; 755, etc). The Code also recognizes that persons might leave the Church by a formal act, with certain consequences in law.

On a third level, communion leads to mission, since the Church by its nature is missionary (c. 781). This mission is threefold: to teach, sanctify, and serve. The laity, in virtue of their Baptism, are called upon to share in all these functions (c.204). The Code focuses on the Sacrament of Baptism as the unifying factor, rather than primarily on the Sacrament of Orders. These three missions are carried out through the apostolate. Canon 298 spells out seven possibilities of apostolic endeavors: promoting the perfection of Christian life, divine worship, teaching the faith, evangelization, works of piety, works of charity, and animating the world with a Christian spirit. These possibilities have been the object of further reflection in the meetings of the Synod of Bishops. For an apostolic endeavor to be truly such, however, it must be carried out in communion with the diocesan bishop (cf. c. 675).

On a fifth level, we could note that the apostolate presupposes an apostle. In various ways, the Code invites those called to the apostolate to make a whole-hearted effort to lead a holy life (c. 210), to serve the Lord with an undivided heart (cc. 277; 599), to be models of holiness (c. 387), and so forth. In other words there is no minimum; rather, there is an ideal towards which all apostles are to strive.

This vision of the Church is complemented by the recognition of the role of the Holy Spirit as soul of the Church. In seven well-chosen canons (cc. 206–879; 369–375; 573–605; 747), the action of the Holy Spirit is emphasized: the awakening of individual faith and the response, the establishment and guiding of the hierarchy, the charismatic dimension of Church life, and the unity of teaching and doctrine.

Major Features. Many factors distinguish the 1983 Code from its 1917 counterpart. In the introduction to the legislation, Pope John Paul II outlines one specific feature of the Code: not surprisingly it is "the Church's fundamental legislative document," based on the "juridical and legislative heritage of revelation and tradition." The Code, then, flows from the doctrine of the Church as a whole. Indeed, it has more doctrinal norms than did the previous law. As was the case with the LEF, however, there is a risk in applying civil law interpretative standards to the 1983 canons. The canons themselves, because they are more pastoral in outlook, are necessarily written in a particular style; expressions such as, "showing an apostolic spirit," "being a witness to all," "acting with humanity and charity" (c. 383), "showing special concern," (c. 384), being "an example of holiness," "knowing and living the paschal mystery" (c. 385), and so forth, cannot be applied literally in all instances. Rather, the Code promotes a renewed attitude of heart and mind, one that Pope Paul VI called for when he spoke of a *novus habitus mentis,* a new mentality [cf. *Acta Apostolicae Sedis* 57 (1965): 988]. Otherwise, to use his words again, the code risks becoming simply "a rigid order of injunctions" [*Origins* 3 (1973–74): 272]. The Code necessarily has a juridical characteristic, but one which is tempered by the very nature of the Church itself. Indeed, the last words of the Code to the effect that the ultimate norm is the salvation of souls—*salus animarum, suprema lex* (c. 1752), based on Cicero's *De lege* (III 3.8), express clearly the difference between this law and other codes which might at first sight be similar.

A second characteristic flows from this. Since the new Code has as one of its basic purposes to translate the teachings of Vatican II into terms of daily life for Catholics, it is not surprising to find that many of the conciliar prescriptions are repeated textually in the law. The various decrees are thus a major source of material. Since the Code implements the Council, and not the converse, it is of primary importance to return to the conciliar context as a whole for the interpretation of the law. Otherwise, there would be the danger of reducing Vatican II to those prescriptions retained for incorporation into the Code.

A third major feature of the legislation is its reliance on complementary norms. A number of the canons refer explicitly to particular norms to be elaborated by the Holy See (cf. cc. 335; 349; 569; 997;1402; 1403, etc), norms which would be too detailed or changing to be placed in a code. Many other canons refer to the decrees of Episcopal Conferences (about 100 in all), to decisions of diocesan bishops (about 300), or finally, to the proper law of institutes of consecrated life (approximately 100 canons). This means, in practice, that almost one-third of the canons allow for adaptation of some sort at the local level. A number of Episcopal Conferences have begun the task of preparing this complementary legislation (cf. c. 455). At the diocesan level, the process will usually take place within a diocesan synod; for this reason, many dioceses are presently organizing synods to prepare for the appropriate local legislation. In religious and secular institutes, although the task of revising constitutions is almost completed, many institutes are now turning their attention to complementary "codes" or specialized directories (c. 587n4) to apply the general legislation in more detail.

Some other features of the revised legislation are: inclusion of a fundamental charter of rights and obligations, the recognized importance of the particular church, the implementation of consultation on various levels, flexibility to promote the Church's mission, an increased role recognized for lay members of the Church, and accountability in regard to financial matters.

There are, however, a few weaknesses in the Code (in particular, certain norms on procedures, perhaps too great an insistence on hierarchical dimensions of Church life, and an overly cautious vision of the laity), but these are far outweighed by the advantages of the new legislation, particularly its fidelity to Vatican II and its reliance on local legislation. The Code, as a universal document, often leaves the door open for future developments (cc. 129; 1055, etc). Through this Code and the Code of Canons for the Eastern Churches the Church has completed the major task of translating Vatican II's insights into norms of practical conduct, providing a basis for healthy and orderly Church development in the years ahead.

Bibliography: *Codex Iuris Canonici auctoritate Joannis Pauli PP. II promulgatus,* in *Acta Apostolicae Sedis* 75 (1983): II, xxx–324. J. A. ALESANDRO, "Law and Renewal: A Canon Lawyer's Analysis of the Revised Code," *Canon Law Society of America Proceedings* 44 (1982): 1–40. L. CASTILLO, "La communion ecclésiale dans le nouveau Code de droit canonique," *Studia Canonica* 17 (1983): 331–355. J. A. CORIDEN, et al., *The Code of Canon Law. A Text and Commentary* (New York 1985) xxvi–1152. T. J. GREEN, "Persons and Structure in the Church: Reflections on Selected Issues in Book II," *Jurist* 45 (1985): 24–94. F. G. MORRISEY, "The New Code of Canon Law: The Importance of Particular Law," *Origins* 11 (1981–82): 421–430; "Decisions of Episcopal Conferences in Implementing the New Law," *Studia Canonica* 20 (1986): 105–121.

[F. G. MORRISEY]

CARDINALS OF THE CATHOLIC CHURCH

The prominence and role of prelates designated as cardinals is a unique feature in the Roman Catholic Church. The present (1983) Code of Canon Law assigns the cardinals three principal roles, namely, electing the Roman Pontiff; advising the pope when called together to deal with questions of special importance; and assisting the Roman Pontiff in various ways, especially in filling special offices in the Roman Curia and as papal envoys for the well being of the universal church. They wear distinctive red dress and are addressed as "Your Eminence."

By the time of Pope Gregory the Great (590–604) the term *cardinal* had acquired a technical meaning. Clergy appointed to a particular position acquired "title" to that position; other clergy assigned to a position for a time or to fill a particular function (e.g., to preside at the liturgy on a regular basis) were said to be incardinated. Thus the distinction between clerics who were "cardinal"and clerics who were "titular" "cardinal" appears in the *Liber Pontificalis* of Pope Stephen III (768–772) when the weekly liturgical celebrations in the major basilica Saint John Lateran, the cathedral of Rome, were assigned to the bishops of the suburbicarian sees (ancient sees on the outskirts of Rome). The same source reports that the Roman Synod of 769 decreed that the Roman Pontiff should be elected from among Rome's deacons and cardinal priests. In 1059, Pope Nicholas II (1058–61), continuing efforts to reform the Church, sought to free papal elections from secular influence; he published the decree *In Nomine Domine* which gave cardinal bishops the right to be the sole electors of the Roman Pontiff. The other cardinals and titular clergy of Rome were to assent to the election. The Emperor was to be informed as a courtesy.

The College of Cardinals with its three ranks of cardinal bishop, priest, and deacon had its origin under Pope Urban II (1088–99), and began to take on its present structure and duties in 1150, when Pope Eugene III appointed a dean (the bishop of the suburbicarian see of Ostia) and a *camerlengo* (chamberlain) to administer the church's resources. Initially cardinal bishops were required to reside in Rome or one of the suburbicarian sees. This custom was changed in 1163 when Pope Alexander III (1159–81) allowed the archbishop of Mainz, Conrad of Wittelsbach, to return to his see after being created a cardinal. In order to incardinate him into the Roman clergy, Alexander gave him the title of pastor of one of the churches in the city. This custom continues in practice so that each of the cardinals is titular pastor of a church in Rome. It was during the pontificate of Alexander III that the Third Lateran Council issued the decree *Licet de vi-*

CONSISTORY OF JUNE 30, 1979

Cardinal	Position	Date of Birth	Date of Death
Ballestrero, Anastasio Alberto	archbishop of Turin, Italy	Oct. 3, 1913	June 21, 1998
Caprio, Giuseppe	pro-president of the Administration of the Patrimony of the Holy See	Nov. 15, 1914	x
*Carter, Gerald Emmett	archbishop of Toronto, Canada	Mar. 1, 1912	x
*Casaroli, Agostino	pro-secretary of state	Nov. 24, 1914	June 6, 1998
Cé, Marco	patriarch of Venice, Italy	July 8, 1925	x
Civardi, Ernesto	secretary of the Congregation for Bishops and secretary of the College of Cardinals	Oct. 21, 1906	Nov. 28, 1989
Corripio Ahumada, Ernesto	archbishop of Mexico City, Mexico	June 29, 1919	x
*Etchegaray, Roger	archbishop of Marseilles, France	Sept. 25, 1922	x
*Kung Pin-mei, Ignatius	bishop of Shanghai, China	Aug. 2, 1901	Mar. 12, 2000
*Macharski, Franciszek	archbishop of Krakow, Poland	May 20, 1927	x
Ó Fiaich, Tomás	archbishop of Armagh, Northern Ireland; primate of Ireland	Nov. 3, 1923	May 8, 1990
Righi-Lambertini, Egano	papal nuncio to France and special papal envoy as permanent observer to the Council of Europe	Feb. 22, 1906	x
*Rubin, Władisław	secretary general of the Synod of Bishops	Sept. 20, 1917	Nov. 28, 1990
Satowaki, Joseph Asajiro	archbishop of Nagasaki, Japan	Feb. 1, 1904	Aug. 8, 1996
Trinh Van Can, Joseph-Marie	archbishop of Hanoi, Vietnam	Mar. 19, 1921	May 18, 1990

Cardinals marked with an asterisk are the subject of separate entries in this volume.

tanda (1179) that requires the votes of a two-thirds majority of the cardinals for a pope to be validly elected.

Since the twelfth century, cardinals have had precedence over archbishops and bishops, and since the fifteenth century, over Patriarchs (bull *Non mediocri* of Pope Eugene IV, 1431–47). Their number did not usually exceed thirty from the thirteenth to the fifteenth centuries. Pope Sixtus V fixed it at seventy on the model of the seventy elders of Israel (Num 11–16): the six cardinal bishops of the suburbicarian sees, fifty cardinal priests and fourteen cardinal deacons (*Postquam verus,* 3 Dec. 1586). The maximum number of members of the College of Cardinals remained at seventy until 1958 when Pope John XXIII set aside this rule and raised the membership to seventy-five. The number continued to grow during the pontificates of Paul VI and John Paul II, but Pope Paul VI limited the number of cardinals entitled to participate in papal elections to 120, excluding those who have reached the age of eighty (*Ingravescentem Aetatem,* 21 Nov. 1970).

Although the Council of Trent had emphasized the need to internationalize the College (''ex omnibus christianitatis nationibus,'' sess. XXIV, *dec. de ref.,* ch. 1), the cardinals from the Italian peninsula constituted an absolute majority for centuries. It was not until the pontificate of Pope Pius XII (1939–1958) in the consistory of 18 February 1946 that the Italian Cardinals lost their majority. The trend toward internationalization became even more pronounced in the pontificates of Pius's successors, especially Popes Paul VI and John Paul II.

The 1983 Code of Canon Law describes the functions, duties, and qualification of cardinals in canons 349–359. The Roman Pontiff selects clerics for the cardinalate who are outstanding for their doctrine, virtue, piety and prudence in practical matters. If they are not already bishops they must receive episcopal consecration, but Pope John Paul II has granted exceptions in the case of individuals who asked to be exempted from this requirement.

The Roman Pontiff creates cardinals by a decree published in a consistory (meeting) of the college of cardinals. From the moment of publication, they are bound by the obligations and they enjoy the rights defined by law, including that of electing a pope. Because of particular circumstance the pope sometimes promotes an individuals to the cardinalate without making the name public or, in traditional language, keeps the appointment secret *in pectore* (''in his breast''). A cardinal appointed *in pectore* is not at that time bound by the obligations nor does he enjoy the rights of the office until his name is

CONSISTORY OF FEBRUARY 2, 1983

Cardinal	Position	Date of Birth	Date of Death
*Bernardin, Joseph L.	archbishop of Chicago, USA	Apr. 2, 1928	Nov. 14, 1996
Casoria, Giuseppe	pro-prefect of the Congregation for Sacraments and Divine Worship	Oct. 1, 1908	x
*Danneels, Godfried	archbishop of Malines-Brussels, Belgium	June 4, 1933	x
Do Nascimento, Alexandre	archbishop of Lubango, Angola	Mar. 1, 1925	x
*Glemp, Józef	archbishop of Warsaw and Gniezno, Poland; primate of Poland	Dec. 18, 1929	x
Khoraiche, Antoine Pierre	Maronite patriarch of Antioch	Sept. 20, 1907	Aug. 19, 1994
Kitbunchu, Michael Michai	archbishop of Bangkok, Thailand	Jan 25, 1929	x
Kuharic, Franjo	archbishop of Zagreb, Yugoslavia	April 15, 1919	x
Lebrún Moratinos, José Ali	archbishop of Caracas, Venezuela	Mar. 19, 1919	x
*López Trujillo, Alfonso	archbishop of Medellin, Colombia	Nov. 8, 1935	x
*Lubac, Henri de	theologian (France)	Feb. 20, 1896	Sept. 4, 1991
*Lustiger, Jean-Marie Aron	archbishop of Paris, France	Sept. 17, 1926	x
*Martini, Carlo Maria, S.J.	archbishop of Milan, Italy	Feb. 15, 1927	x
Meisner, Joachim	bishop of Berlin, East Germany	Dec. 25, 1933	x
Sabbattani, Aurelio	pro-prefect of the Supreme Tribunal of the Apostolic Signature	Oct. 18, 1912	x
Vaivods, Julijans	apostolic administrator "ad nutum sanctae sedis" of Riga and Liepaja in Latvia	Aug. 18, 1895	May 23, 1990
Williams, Thomas Stafford	archbishop of Wellington, New Zealand	Mar. 20, 1930	x
Yago, Bernard	archbishop of Abidjan, Ivory Coast	July, 1916	Oct. 5, 1997

published (c. 351). This practice of reserving the name of a cardinal was started during the pontificate of Martin V (1417–1431). Pope John XXIII created three cardinals *in pectore* in 1960 and died without ever publishing their names. John Paul II reserved the names of two cardinals in the consistory of 1998 and has not yet revealed them.

The Code states that the cardinals constitute a special college (no longer calling it the ''Senate of the Roman Pontiff'' as the 1917 Code did), whose prerogative it is to elect the Roman Pontiff, advise the pope, and assist him in accordance with the norms of particular law (c. 349). The Apostolic Constitution *Universi dominici Gregis,* promulgated by Pope John Paul II (22 Feb. 1996) established the current norms for the election of a pope. It reaffirms the norm that restricts voting rights to cardinals under eighty. It belongs to the Cardinal Dean to ordain the elected Roman Pontiff a bishop, if he is not already so ordained.

The College of Cardinals is divided into three ranks: the episcopal order, to which belong those cardinals to whom the Roman Pontiff assigns the title of a suburbicarian church and Eastern-rite patriarchs who become members of the College of Cardinals; the presbyteral (priestly) order, and the diaconal order. It is possible, as circumstances require, for a cardinal to transfer, with the approval of the Holy Father, from one order to another. (c. 350) The suburbicarian churches are Ostia (reserved for the Dean of the College who unites it to his own titular church in Rome), Albano, Frascati, Palestrina, Porto-Santa Rufina, Sabina-Poggio Mirteto, and Velletri-Segni.

Cardinals have both a personal and collegial obligation of assisting the Roman Pontiff. The Holy Father assigns responsibilities to individual cardinals in the ordinary care of church matters and appoints many to head the departments and agencies in the Roman curia. For this reason, cardinals who are not diocesan bishops reside in Rome. Cardinals who head the departments and other permanent sections of the Roman curia are requested to offer their resignation from office when they have completed their seventy-fifth year.

Cardinals assist the Supreme Pastor of the Church in collegial fashion particularly in consistories, in which they are gathered by order of the Roman Pontiff and under his presidency. Consistories are either ordinary or extraordinary. In an ordinary consistory all cardinals, or at least those who are in Rome, are summoned for consul-

CONSISTORY OF MAY 25, 1985

Cardinal	Position	Date of Birth	Date of Death
*Arinze, Francis A.	pro-president of the Secretariat for Non-Christians	Nov. 1, 1932	x
Biffi, Giacomo	archbishop of Bologna, Italy	June 13, 1928	x
Castillo Lara, Rosalio José, S.D.B.	pro-president of the Pontifical Commission for the Authentic Interpretation of Canon Law	Sept. 4, 1922	x
Dadaglio, Luigi	pro-major penitentiary	Sept. 28, 1914	Aug. 22, 1990
Decourtray, Albert	archbishop of Lyon, France	Apr. 9, 1923	Sept. 16, 1994
Deskur, Andrzej Maria	president emeritus of the Pontifical Commission for Social Communications	Feb. 29, 1924	x
Fresno Larraín, Juan Francisco	archbishop of Santiago, Chile	July 26, 1914	x
*Gagnon, Edouard, P.S.S.	pro-president of the Pontifical Council on the Family	Jan 15, 1918	x
Gulbinowicz, Henryk Roman	archbishop of Wroclaw, Poland	Oct. 17, 1928	x
*Hamer, Jean Jerome, O.P.	pro-prefect of the Congregation for Religious and Secular Institutes	June 1, 1916	Dec. 2, 1996
Innocenti, Antonio	apostolic nuncio to Spain	Aug. 23, 1915	x
*Law, Bernard F.	archbishop of Boston, USA	Nov. 4, 1931	x
Lourdusamy, D. Simon	secretary of the Congregation for the Evangelization of Peoples	Feb. 5, 1924	x
*Lubachivsky, Myroslav Ivan	archbishop of Lvov of the Ukrainians	June 24, 1914	x
Mayer, Paul Augustin, O.S.B.	pro-prefect of the Congregation for the Sacraments and Divine Worship	May 23, 1911	x
*O'Connor, John J.	archbishop of New York, USA	Jan. 15, 1920	May 3, 2000
Obando Bravo, Miguel, S.D.B.	archbishop of Managua, Nicaragua	Feb. 2, 1926	x
Pavan, Pietro	theologian (Italy)	July 8, 1928	Dec. 26, 1994
Piovanelli, Silvano	archbishop of Florence, Italy	Feb. 21, 1924	x
*Poupard, Paul	pro-president of the Secretariat for Non-Believers	Aug. 30, 1930	x
Simonis, Adrianus J.	archbishop of Utrecht, Netherlands	Nov. 26, 1931	x
Stickler, Alfons, S.D.B.	pro-librarian of Holy Roman Church	Aug. 23, 1910	x
Suquía Goicoechea, Angel	archbishop of Madrid, Spain	Oct. 2, 1916	x
*Tomko, Jozef	secretary general of the Synod of Bishops; pro-prefect of the Congregation for the Evangelization of Peoples	Mar. 11, 1924	x
Tzadua, Paulus	archbishop of Addis Ababa, Ethiopia	Aug. 25, 1921	x
*Vachon, Louis-Albert	archbishop of Quebec City, Canada	Feb. 4, 1912	x
Vidal, Ricardo J.	archbishop of Cebu, Philippines	Feb. 6, 1931	x
Wetter, Friedrich	archbishop of Munich and Freising, West Germany	Feb. 20, 1928	x

tation on matters of major importance. When the pope deems that serious matters or special needs of require input from cardinals from around the world (as Pope John Paul II did on at least five occasions) he summons them to an extraordinary consistory. All cardinals, electors and non-electors, are invited to participate in these gatherings.

A third function typical of the office of cardinals that of acting as the pope's representative. The Holy Father on occasion appoints a cardinal to represent him in some solemn celebration or assembly as a *legatus a latere,* that is, as his alter ego. At times the Roman Pontiff entrusts a cardinal to act as his special envoy (*missus specialis*) with a particular pastoral task. (c. 358).

Bibliography: J. A. CORIDEN, T. J. GREEN, and D. E. HEINTS-CHEL, *The Code of Canon Law: A Text and Commentary* (New York/Mahwah: Paulist Press, 1985).

[SALVADOR MIRANDA]

CONSISTORY OF JUNE 28, 1988

Cardinal	Position	Date of Birth	Date of Death
*Balthasar, Hans Urs von	theologian (Switzerland); nominated to the cardinalate but died before the consistory	Aug. 24, 1905	June 26, 1988
*Clancy, Edward Bede	archbishop of Sydney, Australia	Dec. 13, 1923	x
*Grégoire, Paul	archbishop of Montreal, Canada	Oct. 24, 1911	Oct. 30, 1993
*Hickey, James Aloysius	archbishop of Washington, USA	Oct. 11, 1920	x
*Martínez Somalo, Eduardo	deputy Secretary of State	Mar. 31, 1927	x
*Neves, Lucas Moreira, O.P.	archbishop of Sao Salvador da Bahia, Brazil	Sept. 16, 1925	x
*Szoka, Edmund Casimir	archbishop of Detroit, USA	Sept. 14, 1927	x
Canestri, Giovanni	archbishop of Genoa-Bobbio, Italy	Sept. 30, 1918	x
Falcão, José Freire	archbishop of Brasilia, Brazil	Oct. 23, 1925	x
Felici, Angelo	apostolic nuncio to France	July 26, 1919	x
Giordano, Michele	archbishop of Naples, Italy	Sept. 26, 1930	x
Gröer, Hans Hermann, O.S.B.	archbishop of Vienna, Austria	Oct. 13, 1919	x
Hengsbach, Franz	bishop of Essen, West Germany	Sept. 10, 1910	June 24, 1991
Javierre Ortas, Antonio Maria, S.D.B.	secretary of the Congregation for Catholic Education	Feb. 21, 1921	x
Margéot, Jean	bishop of Port Louis, Mauritius	Feb. 3, 1916	x
Martin, Jacques	prefect emeritus of the papal household	Aug. 26, 1908	Sept. 27, 1992
Padiyara, Antony	archbishop (Syro-Malabarese) of Ernakulam, India	Feb. 11, 1921	Mar. 23, 2000
Paskai, László, O.F.M.	archbishop of Esztergom, Hungary	May 8, 1927	x
Pimenta, Simon Ignatius	archbishop of Bombay, India	Mar. 1, 1920	x
Revollo Bravo, Mario	archbishop of Bogota, Colombia	June 15, 1919	Nov. 3, 1995
Santos, Alexandre José Maria dos, O.F.M	archbishop of Maputo, Mozambique	Mar. 18, 1924	x
Silvestrini, Achille	secretary of the Council for the Public Affairs of the Church	Oct. 25, 1923	x
Sladkevicius, Vincentas, M.I.C.	apostolic administrator of Kaisiadorys, Lithuania	Aug. 20, 1920	May 28, 2000
Tumi, Christian Wiyghan	archbishop of Garoua, Cameroon	Oct. 15, 1930	x
Wu Cheng-chung, John Baptist	bishop of Hong Kong	Mar. 26, 1925	x

CARTER, GERALD EMMETT

Cardinal, archbishop of Toronto, Ontario, Canada; b. 1 March 1912, Montréal, Québec. Carter began his formal education at St. Patrick's Boy's School and later attended Montréal College, Grand Seminaire de Montréal, and the Université de Montréal, from which he received a Ph.D. in education in 1947. Soon after his ordination as a priest for the Archdiocese of Montréal, 22 May 1937, he was appointed ecclesiastical inspector of Montreal's English-language schools, and served from 1941 to 1956 as chaplain to the Newman Club of McGill University. As an educator, Carter made his mark on the province of Quebec in several ways: he was the first president and a charter member of the Thomas More Institute for Adult Education (1945); he was founder and principal of St. Jo-

seph's Teachers College (established in 1955); he was the rector of St. Lawrence College in Ste. Foy (1961); and he published widely on pedagogy, catechetics, religious education, educational psychology, and educational history. He published three major books on these subjects: *Catholic Public Schools of Québec* (1957), *Psychology and the Cross* (1959), and *The Modern Challenge to Religious Education* (1961).

Carter was consecrated auxiliary bishop of London, Ontario, in 1962, and succeeded to the see in 1964. He continued to intervene in educational politics in Ontario; his efforts to have full public funding extend from elementary through to the conclusion of secondary education in the Catholic schools of Ontario helped to set the stage for the decision of the government in 1984, which

CONSISTORY OF JUNE 28, 1991

Cardinal	Position	Date of Birth	Date of Death
Angelini, Fiorenzo	president of the Pontifical Council for Pastoral Assistance to Health Care Workers	Aug. 1, 1916	x
*Bevilacqua, Anthony J.	archbishop of Philadelphia, USA	June 17, 1923	x
*Cassidy, Edward Idris	president of the Pontifical Council for Promoting Christian Unity	July 5, 1924	x
Coffy, Robert	archbishop of Marseilles, France	Oct. 24, 1920	July 15, 1995
Daly, Cahal Brendan	archbishop of Armagh, Northern Ireland; primate of Ireland	Oct. 1, 1917	x
*Dezza, Paolo, S.J.	former papal delegate to head the Society of Jesus	Dec. 13, 1901	Dec. 17, 1999
Etsou-Nzabi-Bamungwabi, Frédéric, C.I.C.M	archbishop of Kinshasa, Zaire	Dec. 3, 1930	x
*Korec, Ján Chryzostom, S.J.	bishop of Nitra, Czechoslovakia	Jan. 22, 1924	x
*Laghi, Pio	pro-prefect of the Congregation for Catholic Education	May 21, 1922	x
López Rodriguez, Nicolás de Jesús	archbishop of Santo Domingo, Dominican Republic	Nov. 8, 1935	x
*Mahony, Roger M.	archbishop of Los Angeles, USA	Feb. 27, 1936	x
Mestri, Guido del	former pro–nuncio to Canada and former nuncio to Germany	Jan. 13, 1911	Aug. 2, 1993
Noè, Virgilio	coadjutor archpriest of St. Peter's Basilica	Mar. 30, 1922	x
Posadas Ocampo, Juan Jesus	archbishop of Guadalajara, Mexico	Nov. 10, 1926	May 24, 1993
Quarracino, Antonio	archbishop of Buenos Aires, Argentina	Aug. 8, 1923	Feb. 28, 1998
Ruini, Camillo	papal vicar of the Diocese of Rome	Feb. 19, 1931	x
Saldarini, Giovanni	archbishop of Turin, Italy	Dec. 11, 1924	x
Sánchez, José T.	secretary of the Congregation for the Evangelization of Peoples	Mar. 17, 1920	x
Schwery, Henri	bishop of Sion, Switzerland	June 14, 1932	x
*Sodano, Angelo	pro-secretary of state	Nov. 23, 1927	x
Sterzinsky, Georg M.	bishop of Berlin, Germany	Feb. 9, 1936	x
Todea, Alexandru	Romanian–rite archbishop of Fagaras and Alba Julia, Romania	June 5, 1912	x

ensured that the Catholic Public Schools System of Ontario would be funded at the same level as the Common School System. Bishop Carter was also involved extensively with the International Commission for English in the Liturgy, and played a critical role in the drafting of the Canadian response to *Humanae vitae,* known as the ''Winnipeg Statement'' (1969), as well as the subsequent clarification and commentary, ''Statement on the Formation of Conscience'' (1973).

Bishop Carter was a delegate to the 1974, 1977, and 1980 general assemblies of the Synod of Bishops, and was appointed to the Permanent Council of the Synod, 1977–83. In 1978 he was installed as archbishop of Toronto, and one year later was elevated to the cardinalate, receiving the titular church of Santa Maria in Traspontina. A stroke he suffered in 1981 curtailed his energetic involvement in ecclesial and political matters. Nevertheless, he took on an aggressive role in the national debate over economic policy and Catholic social doctrine. He wrote a controversial document on the Eucharist and the inadmissability of women to the ministerial priesthood (Do This in Memory of Me, 1983), and played a signal role during the papal visit to Canada in 1984. Cardinal Carter was named a Companion—the highest rank—of the Order of Canada in 1983. He relinquished his authority as ordinary to Aloysius Ambrozic in 1990.

Bibliography: RON GRAHAM, ''The Power and the Glory of Emmett Cardinal Carter,'' *Saturday Night* (1983 April). MICHAEL W. HIGGINS and DOUGLAS R. LETSON, *Portraits of Canadian Catholicism* (Toronto: Griffin House, 1986; *My Father's Business: A Biography of His Eminence G. Emmett Cardinal Carter* (Toronto: Macmillan, 1990).

[MICHAEL HIGGINS]

CONSISTORY OF NOVEMBER 26, 1994

Cardinal	Position	Date of Birth	Date of Death
Agustoni, Gilberto	pro-prefect of the Supreme Tribunal of the Apostolic Signature	July 26, 1922	x
Carles Gordó, Ricardo Maria	archbishop of Barcelona, Spain	Sept. 24, 1926	x
*Congar, Yves, O.P.	theologian (France)	Apr. 13, 1904	June 14, 1995
Darmaatmadja, Julius Riyadi, S.J.	archbishop of Semarang, Indonesia	Dec. 20, 1934	x
Echeverría Ruiz, Bernardino, O.F.M.	apostolic administrator of Ibarra, Ecuador	Nov. 12, 1912	Apr. 6, 2000
Eyt, Pierre	archbishop of Bordeaux, France	June 4, 1934	x
Fagiolo, Vincenzo	president of the Pontifical Council for the Interpretation of Legislative Texts	Feb. 5, 1918	x
Furno, Carlo	apostolic nuncio in Italy	Dec. 2, 1921	x
Grillmeier, Alois, S.J.	theologian (Germany)	Jan. 1, 1910	Sept. 13, 1998
*Keeler, William Henry	archbishop of Baltimore, USA	Mar. 4, 1931	x
Koliqi, Mikel	priest of the archdiocese of Shkodrë, Albania	Sept. 29, 1902	Jan. 28, 1997
*Maida, Adam Joseph	archbishop of Detroit, USA	Mar. 18, 1930	x
Ortega y Alamino, Jaime Lucas	archbishop of San Cristobal de la Habana, Cuba	Oct. 18, 1936	x
Oveido Cavada, Carlos, O.deM.	archbishop of Santiago, Chile	Jan. 19, 1927	x
Pham Dinh Tung, Paul Joseph	archbishop of Hanoi, Vietnam	June 15, 1919	x
Poggi, Luigi	pro–librarian and pro–archivist of the Holy Roman Church	Nov. 25, 1917	x
Puljic, Vinko	archbishop of Vhrbosna-Sarajevo, Bosnia-Herzegovina	Sept. 8, 1945	x
Razafindratandra, Armand Gaétan	archbishop of Antananarivo, Madagascar	Aug. 7, 1925	x
Sandoval Íñiguez, Juan	archbishop of Guadalajara, Mexico	Mar. 28, 1933	x
*Schotte, Jan Pieter, C.I.C.M.	secretary general of the Synod of Bishops	Apr. 29, 1928	x
Sfeir, Nasrallah Pierre	Maronite patriarch of Antioch	May 15, 1920	x
Shirayanagi, Peter Seiichi	archbishop of Tokyo, Japan	June 17, 1928	x
Suárez Rivera, Adolfo Antonio	archbishop of Monterrey, Mexico	Jan. 9, 1927	x
Swiàtek, Kazimierz	archbishop of Minsk–Mohilev, Belarus	Oct. 21, 1914	x
Tonini, Ersilio	archbishop emeritus of Ravenna-Cervia, Italy	July 20, 1914	x
*Turcotte, Jean-Claude	archbishop of Montreal, Canada	June 26, 1936	x
Vargas Alzamora, Augusto, S.J.	archbishop of Lima, Peru	Nov. 9, 1922	x
Vlk, Miloslav	archbishop of Prague, Czech Republic	May 17, 1932	x
Wamala, Emmanuel	archbishop of Kampala, Uganda	Dec. 15, 1926	x
*Winning, Thomas Joseph	archbishop of Glasgow, Scotland	June 3, 1925	x

CASAROLI, AGOSTINO

Cardinal; Vatican Secretary of State; b. 24 November 1914, Castel San Giovanni, in the province of Piacenza (Italy); d. 9 June 1998, Rome.

Agostino Casaroli was born into a pious, middle-class family and attended the minor seminary of Bedonia. He studied theology in the exclusive Alberoni College of Piacenza and canon law in Rome at the Lateran University (1936–40). Ordained a priest in 1937, he began his life-long career in the Vatican diplomatic service as an archivist in the Secretariat of State.

In February 1961 Pope John XXIII appointed Casaroli under-secretary at the Vatican Foreign Office and the Department for Extraordinary Church Affairs. Casaroli initiated a new style in dealing with the Communist bloc that came to be known as the Vatican *Ostpolitik*. The new approach situated Vatican diplomacy in the context of a policy of active neutrality between existing international blocs of nations. Although *Ostpolitik* was roundly

CONSISTORY OF FEBRUARY 21, 1998

Cardinal	Position	Date of Birth	Date of Death
*Ambrozic, Aloysius Matthew	archbishop of Toronto, Canada	Jan. 27, 1930	x
Antonetti, Lorenzo	pro–president of the Administration of the Patrimony of the Holy See	July 31, 1922	x
Araújo, Serafim Fernandes de	archbishop of Belo Horizonte, Brazil	Aug. 13, 1924	x
Balland, Jean	archbishop of Lyon, France	July 26, 1934	Mar. 1, 1998
Bovone, Alberto	pro–prefect of the Congregation for Causes of Saints	June 11, 1922	Apr. 17, 1998
*Castrillón Hoyos, Darío	pro–prefect of the Congregation for Clergy	July 4, 1929	x
Cheli, Giovanni	president of the Pontifical Council for Migrants and Itinerant People	Oct. 4, 1918	x
Colasuonno, Francesco	nuncio to Italy	Jan. 2, 1925	x
De Giorgi, Salvatore	archbishop of Palermo, Italy	Sept. 6, 1930	x
*George, Francis E., O.M.I.	archbishop of Chicago, USA	Jan. 16, 1937	x
Kozlowiecki, Adam, S.J.	archbishop emeritus of Lusaka, Zambia	Apr. 1, 1911	x
Medina Estévez, Jorge Arturo	pro–prefect of the Congregation for Divine Worship and the Discipline of the Sacraments	Dec. 23, 1926	x
Monduzzi, Dino	prefect of papal household	Apr. 2, 1922	x
Pengo, Polycarp	archbishop of Dar–es–Salaam, Tanzania	Aug. 5, 1944	x
Rivera Carrera, Norberto	archbishop of Mexico City, Mexico	June 6, 1942	x
Ruoco Verala, Antonio Maria	archbishop of Madrid, Spain	Aug. 24, 1936	x
*Schönborn, Christoph von, O.P.	archbishop of Vienna, Austria	Jan. 22, 1945	x
Shan Kuo-hsi, Paul, S.J.	bishop of Kaohsiung, Taiwan	Dec. 2, 1923	x
*Stafford, James Francis	president of the Pontifical Council for the Laity	July 26, 1932	x
Tettamanzi, Dionigi	archbishop of Genoa, Italy	Mar. 14, 1934	x
Uhac, Giuseppe	secretary of the Congregation for the Evangelization of Peoples; nominated to the cardinalate but died before the consistory	July 20, 1924	Jan. 18, 1998

criticized in some circles, it was manifestly in line with the approach of Pope John XXIII toward world problems. With patience and ingenuity he worked to insure the continued existence of the Church in hostile Communist-run countries. By accepting compromises on nonessentials, Casaroli secured conditions of passably normal life for Catholic communities, even though it was largely limited to worship and the administration of sacraments.

Casaroli's first inroads behind the Iron Curtain came about in 1963. By order of Pope John XXIII, he went to Czechoslovakia and Hungary, where the Cold War had created very complex situations for the Catholic Church. Vienna's Cardinal Franz König had done much to prepare the ground. In 1964 Casaroli signed a ''secret'' agreement with Hungary. In 1965 in Prague, he convinced the government to allow Joseph Beran, just named a cardinal by Paul VI, go to Rome to receive the red biretta. For the archbishop it meant going into exile, but it also allowed the appointment of a worthy successor, a confes-

sor of the faith and later cardinal, Frantisek Tomasek, who lived to see the end of Communism in Czechoslovakia. More dramatic was Casaroli's part in gaining the release of Hungarian Cardinal Josef Mindszenty in 1971, who fifteen years before had taken refuge in the American Embassy in Budapest. Mindszenty's deliverance ended in exile in Vienna.

In Belgrade in June 1966, Casaroli signed the first of a series of agreements that gave some degree of legality to the Catholic Church in several countries in Central and Eastern Europe. The following year he was able to visit all Catholic dioceses in Poland for an onsite analysis of the situation. In 1970 he went back in Belgrade to sign the establishment of normal diplomatic relations with a Communist country where the Catholics were a minority. By then he had been made an archbishop with the titular church of Carthage and appointed to head the Vatican Congregation for Extraordinary Church Affairs. About that time he addressed his activity toward Moscow, the center of world Communism. He went there for a week at the end of February 1971 to express the adhesion of the Holy See to the pact of non-proliferation of nuclear arms. Casaroli was given a chance to meet for the first time in half-a-century officials responsible for religious affairs in the Soviet Union. Two years later he was able to visit Czechoslovakia for a second time, where he was also allowed to ordain new Catholic bishops. The following year (March to April 1974), Casaroli was in Cuba, meeting most of the bishops and some clergy, as well as President Fidel Castro.

By 1975 Casaroli's contacts with Eastern European leaders had become routine. On 5 June, he was in East Germany, and on 26 June the Bulgarian leader Todor Zhivkov was received in the Vatican, while from 30 July to 1 August Casaroli met most of them in Helsinki on the occasion of signing the final document on security and cooperation in Europe, when he also presided over the first and final sessions of the conference. It was an event seen by observers, including Casaroli himself, as the beginning of political and military detente in Europe, leading finally to the collapse of the Iron Curtain and of Communism fifteen years later. By 1978 Cardinal Casaroli was acknowledged as a world leader in political affairs. In June he addressed the Assembly General of the United Nations in New York, reading a message from Paul VI to the world organization.

Casaroli served as Secretary of State during the short reign of John Paul I. In April 1979 Pope John Paul II confirmed him in the position, named him a cardinal on 30 June of that year, and assigned him the duties of prefect for the Council for Public (i.e., foreign) Affairs of the Church, and president of the Pontifical Commission for the Vatican City State. He continued to travel widely: to Lebanon and Hungary (1980); to Poland, just afer the attempted assassination of John Paul II (1981); and to Washington for meetings with President Ronald Reagan and other high administration officials (December 1981). On the Italian scene, he negotiated important changes and additions to the Lateran Pact, the concordat between the Holy See and Italy (February 1984), and the following year he assisted at the signing of a treaty of peace and friendship between Argentina and Chile after a year-long territorial conflict. He saw the fruits of his *Ostpolitik* when Mikhail Gorbachev initiated a policy of *glasnost* and *perestroika* in the Soviet Union (1985). In 1988 Casaroli took part in the celebrations for the Millennium of the conversion of the ancient Kievian Rus to Christianity (988–1988) and was received at the Kremlin. The following year the Secretary General of the Soviet Communist party, Mikhail Gorbachev, was in the Vatican for the "audience of the century" (1 December 1989).

Casaroli asked to be freed from his official responsibilities when he turned seventy-five, the age limit for ser-

Agostino Casaroli. (Catholic News Service)

vice in the Roman Curia; in due course his request was accepted (1 December 1990). Retirement allowed him more time for his cherished projects in the field of pastoral and humanitarian work, particularly among the youth in the Casal del Marmo (formerly Porta Portese), a school-prison for teenage detainees. He had been engaged there all his priestly life, preaching to them, hearing their confessions, preparing them for the sacraments, and following some even after they had left prison. At one point he also agreed to act as editor-in-chief of their magazine *La Tradotta*. At Casal del Marmo he was known simply as "Don Agostino." In retirement he wrote an autobiography published posthumously under the title, *Il martirio della pazienza* (*Martyrdom of Patience*). In it the cardinal evaluated with objectivity his own role in the important events in which he played a part.

At the time of his death John Paul II issued a statement praising Cardinal Casaroli for "courageous steps to improve the situation of the Church in Eastern Europe." Cararoli was buried in the Basilica of the Twelve Apostles in the center of Rome.

Bibliography: A. CASAROLI, *Il martirio della pazienza* (Torino 2000); *Nella Chiesa per il mondo. Discorsi* (Rusconi 1988); "La Santa Sede e l'Europa," *La Civiltà Cattolica* (19 Feb 1971); "Il discorso pronunciato nell'Università di Parma," in *L'Ossservatore*

Edward Idris Cardinal Cassidy. (Catholic News Service.)

Romano (18 March 1990); "La Santa Sede si è sempre impegnata per un obiettivo: affermare in concreto i diritti di Dio ed i diritti degli uomini," in *L'Osservatore Romano* (4–5 June1990); "Paolo VI e il dialogo," *Il Regno* 19 (1984); *Nella Chiesa per il mondo. Omelie e discorsi* (preface by J. GUITTON, Milano 1987); *Der Heilige Stuhl und die Völkergemeinschaft. Reden und Aufsätze* (Berlin 1981); *Glaube und Verantwortung. Ansprachen und Predigten* (Berlin 1989); *Wegbereiter zur Zeitenwende. Letzte Beitrage* (Berlin 1999). A. SANTINI, *Agostino Casaroli, hombre de dialogo* (Madrid 1993); L. DI SCHIENA, "La Segreteria di Stato: Casaroli e Silvestrini," in *Karol Wojtiła* (Roma), 81–86; G. WEIGEL, "After the Empire of Lies," chapt. in *Witness to Hope* (New York 1999), 582–627; G. ALBERIGO, "Verso la Ostpolitik," in *Papa Giovanni (1881–1963)* (Bologna 2000), 151–57; C. KRAMER VON REISSWITZ, "Rome's Kissinger," *Inside the Vatican* 7 (1998): 48–49; V. FAGIOLO, "Reciproca collaborazione. L'evoluzione dei rapporti tra Chiesa e Stato italiano dopo la revisione del Concordato firmata da Bettino Craxi e Agostino Casaroli nel 1984," *30 Giorni* 1 (2000): 40–47; "La morte del Cardinale Agostino Casaroli," in *L'Osservatore Romano* (10 June 1998) (Editorial commemoration).

[GIORGIO ELDAROV]

CASSIDY, EDWARD IDRIS

Cardinal, president of the Pontifical Council for Promoting Christian Unity; b. 5 July 1924, Sydney, Australia, the son of Harold Cassidy and Dorothy Phillips. Cassidy received his seminary training at Saint Colum-

ba's College, Springwood, and Saint Patrick's College, Manly. After ordination to the priesthood for the Diocese of Wagga Wagga, 23 July 1949, he was assigned as assistant priest to the parish of Yenda, where he worked until 1952. In 1953 he entered the Pontifical Ecclesiastical Academy in Rome to train for the diplomatic service of the Holy See; at the same time, he studied canon and civil law at the Pontifical Lateran University, receiving a J.C.D. in 1955.

Fr. Cassidy began his diplomatic service in 1955, when he was appointed to the apostolic nunciature in India, where he remained until 1962. He was then transferred to Ireland for five years, and El Salvador for three. In 1970 he was nominated apostolic pro-nuncio in Taiwan and raised to the rank of archbishop. He remained in Taiwan for almost ten years; his responsibilities also included Burma and Bangladesh. In 1979 he was appointed apostolic delegate in South Africa and Lesotho, and he remained there through years of profound political and social upheaval. His final diplomatic appointment came in 1984, when he was nominated apostolic pro-nuncio in the Netherlands, where the Church was deeply troubled by defection and division.

In 1988, Archbishop Cassidy was recalled to Rome by Pope John Paul II and was appointed substitute of the Secretariat of State in Rome, in charge of the First Section of the Secretariat of State (General Affairs), which is, in effect, the papal chancery. He was the first English-speaking substitute to be appointed to this post. The next year, he succeeded the Dutch Cardinal Johannes Willebrands as President of the Pontifical Council for Promoting Christian Unity. His experience in countries with a Catholic minority had contributed to his sense of the urgency of ecumenical and interreligious dialogue. On 28 June 1991, he was created cardinal deacon of Santa Maria in Via Lata. Cardinal Cassidy's efforts at rapprochement with Protestant denominations received particular notice with the signing of the Joint Declaration on the Doctrine of Justification, issued by the Vatican and the Lutheran World Federation in 1999.

Bibliography: Cardinal Cassidy has written a foreword to *John Paul II and Interreligous Dialogue (Faith Meets Faith),* which was published by Orbis Books in 1999.

[MARK COLERIDGE]

CASTRILLÓN HOYOS, DARÍO

Cardinal, prefect of the Congregation for the Clergy; b. 4 July 1929, in Medellín, Colombia. Castrillón studied for the priesthood in the seminaries of Antioquia, Medellín, and Santa Rosa de Osos; he was later sent to the Pontifical Gregorian University in Rome, where he earned a doctorate in canon law. He also studied in the Sociology Faculty of the University of Louvain, Belgium, specializing in religious sociology, political economics, and ethical economics. Ordained a priest 26 October 1952, in Rome, Castrillón held a variety of pastoral positions in Colombia between 1954 and 1971. He first served in parishes and then in the diocesan chancery of Santa Rosa de Osos, where his duties included the direction of the diocese's radio school and a literacy and formation program that was broadcast to rural farm families. He also served as secretary general of the Colombian bishops' conference and taught canon law at "Universidad Civil Libre."

In 1971 Castrillón was elected titular bishop of Villa del Re and appointed coadjutor, with right of succession, of Pereira, Colombia. He succeeded to the see of Pereira in 1976. From 1983 to 1987 he was the secretary general of the Latin American Episcopal Council (CELAM), and from 1987 to 1991 its president. He participated in the general conferences of the Latin American episcopate held in Medellín (1968), Puebla (1979), and Santo Domingo (1992). In 1992 he was made archbishop of Bucaramaga.

Bishop Castrillón became known in the United States especially through a trip to Washington and the United Nations in 1989, along with other CELAM officers. The bishops appealed to President George Bush to end the U.S. embargo against Nicaragua, and urged the United Nations to support dialogue in Central America. Bishop Castrillón warned about the appeal of Marxism among the poor in Latin America, emphasizing that so long as the vast gap between rich and poor remains, Marxism will continue to be "a temptation and a desire." He added that it is an "an illusion" to think that Marxism is a solution to the problems of Latin America.

In 1996 Pope John Paul II called Archbishop Castrillón to Rome as pro-prefect of the Congregation for the Clergy. In the consistory of 21 February 1998 he was created cardinal deacon of SS. Nome di Maria al Foro Traiano. Cardinal Castrillón has participated in seven assemblies of the World Synod of Bishops and was one of the president-delegates of its Special Assembly for America (1997). In 1998 he represented the pope in the signing of the Global and Definitive Agreement between Peru and Ecuador to settle their long- standing border dispute.

Bibliography: Among his published works are *América Latina hoy: Líneas para un diagnóstico* (Bogotá 1984); *Pastores para una nueva evangelización: Ejercicios Espirituales a la Conferencia Episcopal Española* (Madrid 1992) and *Santo Domingo, puerta grande hacia el tercer milenio: Desarrollo y comentarios* (Santafé de Bogotá 1994).

[SALVADOR MIRANDA]

Darío Castrillón Hoyos of Colombia holds the Italian edition of Pope John Paul II's book Gift and Mystery, *during a press conference at the Vatican in November 1996.* (AP/Wide World Photos)

CATHOLIC TRADITIONALISM

Catholic traditionalism is defined as an international movement to preserve religious, ideological, organizational, and cultic patterns of pre-Vatican II Catholic identity. Catholic traditionalism emerged in a diffuse and segmented manner. The movement was initially part of the conservative Catholic discontent with the reform initiatives of the Second Vatican Council. With the spread of conflict and polarization in the wake of the Council, and following the prohibition of the Tridentine Liturgy after November 1971, Catholic traditionalism became a more organizationally and ideologically distinct movement.

Distinguishing ideological characteristics of Catholic traditionalism include tendencies toward a literalistic and ahistorical reading of pre-Vatican II Church documents and decrees (especially those associated with the Council of Trent, Vatican I, and papal anti-modernist encyclicals and pronouncements), and a strong conspiracy orientation embued with apocalyptic imagery. The most extreme element in the movement (*sede-vacantists*) asserts that Vatican II was a "false council," that recent popes are deposed and excommunicated, and that the

Three brightly colored, traditional vestments hang in the backroom of the Cataldo Mission, built in 1848 by Jesuit missionaries in Coeur D'Alene, Idaho. (© Kevin R. Morris/ CORBIS)

Novus Ordo Mass is an intrinsically invalid rite. More moderate elements accept the authority of the Magisterium, but assert that the pope and bishops have erred in judgment. These traditionalists have also focused attention on alleged "contradictions" between the pre- and post-Vatican II Church doctrine and discipline. As a sectarian-like movement, traditionalists have openly defied Church hierarchy by establishing illicit chapels and Mass centers in a campaign to "save" the Latin Tridentine form of the Mass—the culture symbol of the traditionalist discontent with *aggiornamento*.

The first traditionalist organization, the Catholic Traditionalist Movement, Inc. was publicly launched in the United States in March 1965, when the Reverend Gommar De Pauw, a professor of theology and canon law at Mount St. Mary's Seminary in Emmitsburg, Md., issued a "Catholic Traditionalist Manifesto" warning against the Vatican II "Protestantizing" of the Roman Catholic faith. By the early 1970s, other traditionalist organizations had formed under various names in the United States. The best known are the Orthodox Roman Catholic Movement, Traditional Catholics of America, Roman Catholics of America, and St. Pius V Association; and in

Europe the Society of St. Pius X, Catholic Counter Reformation, and Association of St. Pius V. These groups, along with the support of unaffiliated traditionalist priests, established a world-wide network of traditionalist publications, schools, chapels, and Mass centers promoting pre-Vatican II theology and liturgical and sacramental practice.

The most visible figure in the traditionalist movement is the Archbishop Marcel Lefebvre. After the Second Vatican Council, the former Archbishop of Dakar (Senegal) and of Tulle (France) allied himself with those forces resisting *aggiornamento*. In 1968, he resigned as head of the Holy Ghost Fathers in a dispute over reform of the order in keeping with Vatican II directives. Lefebvre moved to Rome to retire but, by his own account, was sought out by young men desiring direction in priestly formation. In October 1970, Lefebvre opened a seminary in Econe, Switzerland. The next month, the Bishop of Fribourg canonically established Lefebvre's *Fraternité Sacerdotale de Saint Pie X* (Society of St. Pius X).

Following a canonical investigation of his seminary in 1974, the French archbishop issued an acerbic "Declaration" (November 21) repudiating the "neo-modernist" and "neo-Protestant" tendencies manifest in the documents of Vatican II. For the next several months, a series of meetings, negotiations, and an exchange of letters took place between Lefebvre and the Vatican. In June 1975, Pope Paul VI removed the canonical approval of the Society of St. Pius X and all it establishments, including the seminary at Econe. In July 1976, following public defiance of an explicit Vatican directive prohibiting new ordinations, Lefebvre was deprived of the canonical authority to exercise his priestly powers.

Subsequent negotiations failed to resolve the conflict between the French archbishop and Rome and the status of the traditionalist movement in general. Lefebvre's priestly fraternity currently operates an international network of seminaries, chapels, schools and religious foundations and remains the flagship organization in the traditionalist cause.

The number of seminarians grew from a handful in 1970 to over 350 ordained priests by the mid-1990s. In 1987, at age 82, Archbishop Lefebvre made known his intention to perpetuate the movement by consecrating episcopal successors. In order to forestall the threat of schism, the Vatican made several attempts at rapprochement, but all fell through. Finally, on 30 June 1988, Archbishop Lefebvre ordained four bishops, all members of the Society of St. Pius X, including Richard Williamson, rector of the Society's seminary in Ridgefield, Conn. Because he proceeded in defiance of papal directives, Archbishop Lefebvre and the four bishops he consecrated automatically incurred excommunication.

See Also: MARCEL LEFEBVRE

Bibliography: Y. CONGAR, *Challenges to the Church: The Case of Archbishop Lefebvre* (Huntington, Ind. 1976). MICHAEL W. CUNEO, *The Smoke of Satan: Conservative and Traditionalist Dissent in Contemporary Catholicism* (New York: Oxford University Press, 1997). M. DAVIES, *Apologia Pro Marcel Lefebvre*, v. I & II (1980, 1983). WILLIAM D. DINGES, "Roman Catholic Traditionalism," in *Fundamentalisms Observed*, edited by MARTIN E. MARTY and R. SCOTT APPLEBY (Chicago: University of Chicago Press, 1991). J. HANU, *Vatican Encounter: Conversations with Archbishop Marcel Lefebvre*, translated by E. SHOSBERGER (Kansas City 1978). MARY JO WEAVER and R. SCOTT APPLEBY, eds., "We are What You Were: Roman Catholic Traditionalism in America," in *Being Right; Conservative Catholics in America* (Bloomington: Indiana University Press, 1995).

[W.D. DINGES]

CHENU, MARIE-DOMINIQUE

Dominican theologian and medievalist; b. Soisy-sur-Seine, France, 7 January 1895; d. 1990. After entering the Dominican Order (1913) at Le Saulchoir, then in Belgium, he was forced by the outbreak of war to study in Rome (1914–20) at what is now called the Pontifical University of St. Thomas Aquinas. Assigned to teach theology at Le Saulchoir (1920), he at once set himself the task of replacing what he took to be the non-historical exposition of the Thomist system by his teacher in Rome, R. Garrigou-Lagrange with a reading of Thomas Aquinas in his historical context. His first essay in historical reconstruction of an Aquinas text (1923) was followed by many others, eventually collected in *La Parole de Dieu I—La foi dans l'intelligence* (Paris 1964). His notes toward a medieval philosophical lexicography (never completed), as well as his research on minor figures such as Robert Kilwardby, soon established him as a respected medievalist.

Having become Regent of Studies at Le Saulchoir, he published (privately) *Une école de Théologie: Le Saulchoir* (1937), little more than a pamphlet, justifying the historical emphasis in theological studies and including some caustic asides about "Baroque Scholasticism." Immediately delated to the Dominican authorities in Rome for "Modernism," it was finally placed on the Index in 1942. Chenu continued to teach and to publish the results of his research, the bulk of which appeared in his three magisterial books, *Introduction à l'étude de saint Thomas d'Aquin* (Montreal and Paris 1950), *La théologie comme science au XIIIe siècle* (Paris 1957) and *La théologie au XIIe siècle* (Paris 1957). During the occupation he became increasingly involved in projects to re-

juvenate urban Catholicism. He was in effect chief theological adviser to the nascent priest-worker movement in France. Papal anxieties about this movement emerged in the apostolic exhortation *Menti nostrae* (1950), while the encyclical *Humani generis* (1950) reaffirmed official disapproval of theologians who were dismissive of Scholasticism. By 1953 Chenu found himself relieved of all teaching duties and even exiled to Rouen for a time.

He continued to write, publishing *Saint Thomas d'Aquin et la théologie* (Paris 1959), but from this point onwards his energies went increasingly into preaching. He was theological adviser to French-speaking African bishops at Vatican II, when, not surprised at the general abandonment of Thomism, he worked behind the scenes to have his ideas about Thomas Aquinas' "evangelical humanism" incorporated into such conciliar texts as *Gaudium et spes*. His later years, back in Paris, were devoted to communicating, in lectures and sermons, his optimistic interpretation of the significance of Vatican II. He had the satisfaction of seeing *Une école de théologie* republished (Paris 1985), but he would have been the first to concede that younger theologians had almost as little interest in his work on Thomas Aquinas as in that of Garrigou-Lagrange. His unfailing optimism, as well as his historian's perspective, assured him that Aquinas would eventually return to the center of Catholic theology. While not an original thinker, and the author in his middle years of much perishable journalism, Chenu remains, with his friend Etienne Gilson, a major figure in the history of the study of Thomas Aquinas.

See Also: YVES MARIE-JOSEPH CONGAR

Bibliography: A. DUVAL, "Bibliographie du P. Marie-Dominique Chenu (1921–1965)," *Mélanges offerts à M.-D. Chenu* (Paris 1967). O. DE LA BROSSE, *Le père Chenu—La liberté dans la foi* (Paris 1969).

[F. KERR]

CLANCY, EDWARD BEDE

Cardinal, archbishop of Sydney, Australia; b. 13 December 1923, Lithgow, Australia, the son of John Bede and Ellen Lucy Clancy. He was educated at Marist Brothers' College, Parramatta, and studied for the priesthood at Saint Columba's College, Springwood, and Saint Patrick's College, Manly. He was ordained priest for the Archdiocese of Sydney on 23 July 1949. After working for a time in parishes, he pursued postgraduate studies at the Pontifical Biblical Institute in Rome (1952–54). He then returned to Sydney where he worked again in parishes from 1955–57, before being appointed lecturer in biblical studies at Saint Patrick's College, Manly, where he taught from 1958 to 1961. In 1962, he began doctoral studies at the Pontifical Urban University in Rome, where he remained through much of the Second Vatican Council. He completed his doctorate in 1964 and returned to teach biblical studies once again at Saint Patrick's College, Manly.

Pope Paul VI named Clancy auxiliary bishop of Sydney in 1974. In 1978, he was transferred to the national capital as archbishop of Canberra and Goulburn, where he showed himself an able and energetic pastor. Upon the retirement of Cardinal James Freeman in 1983, Clancy was named archbishop of Sydney. In 1986, as leader of the oldest diocese in the country, he was prominent in preparing for the pastoral visit of Pope John Paul II and in welcoming the pontiff to Australia. On 28 June 1988, he was created cardinal priest with the title of Santa Maria in Vallicella. He served as president of the Australian Catholic Bishops' Conference, and in 1992 was appointed the first chancellor of the newly founded Australian Catholic University.

In 1986 Cardinal Clancy implemented a plan to divide the Archdiocese of Sydney into three dioceses—Sydney, Parramatta, and Broken Bay; the division proved both practicable and pastorally helpful. He divided the seminary and theological faculty, moving them from North Head in Manly to Homebush and Strathfield, respectively. He brought the faculty closer to the center of Sydney in order to make theological education more available to the laity.

[MARK COLERIDGE]

COLOGNE DECLARATION

Taking its name from the place where it was issued, the Cologne Declaration is the popular label of the statement, *Wider die Entmündigung—für eine offene Katholizitate* ("Against Interdictions: For An Open Catholicism"), issued in 1989 by a group of Catholic theologians from Germany, Austria, the Netherlands, and Switzerland. The declaration identified three areas of special concern: (1) current methods of episcopal selection; (2) Roman intervention in the appointment of theology professors; and (3) theologically questionable attempts at asserting the pope's doctrinal and jurisdictional authority in an exaggerated form.

The Three Concerns. The concerns expressed in point one were prompted by the Roman Curia's unilateral filling of vacant episcopal sees around the world, in particular the appointment of Joachim Cardinal Meisner as archbishop of Cologne. Contrary to accepted tradition

Rome ignored the recommendations of the Cologne Cathedral Chapter. The Cologne declaration argued that "the autocratic methods manifest in recent episcopal appointments stand in contradiction to the Gospel spirit of brotherhood, to the positive, postconciliar experiences of freedom and to the collegiality of the bishops." With regard to point two, the Declaration asserts that Roman intervention in the appointment of theology professors "risks undermining" the local bishop's "authority and responsibility . . . to grant or withhold ecclesiastical permission to teach." The authors of the Declaration were especially concerned that in applying for positions on Catholic faculties of state universities, theologians regarded by Rome as unreliable on the birth control question had been rejected because of Roman opposition. In point three, birth control was again the point of conflict: "Recently in addresses to theologians and bishops, and without considering the differing degrees of certitude and the unequal weight of church statements, the pope has connected the teaching on birth control with fundamental truths of the faith, such as the holiness of God and salvation through Jesus Christ. As a result, critics of the papal teaching on birth control find themselves condemned for 'attacking fundamental cornerstones of Christian doctrine.'"

Among the 163 original signers of the Cologne Declaration were some of the Church's best-known theologians, including Alfons Auer, Franz Böckle, Heinrich Fries, Bernard Häring, Herbert Haag, Hans Küng, Johannes-Baptist Metz, and Edward Schillebeeckx. It attracted considerable attention and support throughout Europe in the early months of 1989. By the end of January, twenty-three Spanish theologians signed a statement of support. In February, fifty-two Dutch-speaking theologians in Flanders expressed solidarity with the Cologne signers, and in March, 130 French-speaking theologians from France, Belgium, and Switzerland issued a similar statement.

See Also: EDWARD SCHILLEBEECKX

Bibliography: "The Cologne Declaration," *Origins* 18:38 (2 March 1989): 633–34. "The Cologne Declaration," *Commonweal* 116, no. 4 (1989): 102–104. *La Documentation Catholique* 1979 (5 March 1989): 240–251.

[J. A. DICK]

COMMUNIO

Every adequate theology of the Church must begin with the proper beginning: not with Mt 16.16 (the promise of the Petrine primacy) but with 1 Tm 2.4 (the promise of universal salvation: "God our savior: he wants everyone to be saved . . .''). Traditionally the Church has been considered the Sacrament of this divine saving will, an insight revived by Vatican Council II in the Dogmatic Constitution on the Church: ''By her relationship with Christ, the Church is a kind of sacrament or sign of intimate union with God, and of the unity of all mankind'' (*Lumen gentium* 1); ''through this Spirit [Christ] has established His body, the Church, as the universal sacrament of salvation'' (ibid. 48). Accordingly the being of the Church is symbol and source of a twofold union—of God with man and of man with man. Hence, the Church is essentially a communion.

Ontology of *Communio*. Both Christ and the Church are called Sacrament, and each, analogously, is also called primal and original Sacrament (Ursakrament). The designation is not merely one among many others, equally valid; rather it is the key term in that ontology implicitly contained in the salvation history revealed in the Judaeo-Christian religious tradition. The meaning of Sacrament implies that the divine and the human are so compatible that they can be united in human experience as one event in which the human shares in and manifests the divine being to the world and invites it to participate in this sharing. Clearly, then, the Church can be understood only within the horizon of this Judaeo-Christian ontology.

Ontology of Salvation. Nowhere is the importance of philosophy more striking than in that ecclesiology which explains the Church as *communio* (koinōnia). All theology, and ecclesiology most of all, is liable to trivialize itself as soon as it forgets that it is essentially an answer to the fundamental human question (Man as the Seinsfrage), ''What is it all about?'' Generally, and unfortunately, salvation is understood too narrowly, restricted to what is called either supernatural salvation or redemption. In reality, for the Judaeo-Christian ontology, salvation includes all that is customarily parceled out as creation, grace, and glory. These three designate the three stages or degrees of created participation in uncreated being, which theologians have discerned to be implicitly revealed in the biblical account of history. Hence, the history of the world is correctly called ''salvation-history.''

If the importance of philosophy for theology is nowhere more obvious than here, likewise is the inadequacy of a ''pagan'' philosophy. Decisive for every philosophy is the perceived relation between the being of God and the being of the world. The Judaeo-Christian tradition offers the classic formulation of this mutuality in Gn 1.26–27, where the human creation is explicitly stated to be in the image and likeness of the divine creator. Although this formal insight is common to every philosophy and religion, the material content varies enormously.

Cologne Cathedral, near the banks of the Rhine. (© Patrick Ward/CORBIS)

One need only compare typical Mesopotamian, Greco-Roman, Aryan, and Judaeo-Christian theories about the originating pattern, the deity, and the originated imitation, the world.

The Divine Being, Relationship. Since the being of God is decisive for the being of whatever is not God, the being or nature of the Judaeo-Christian God must be elucidated. The first and decisive assertion is that this God is triune, three Persons in one God. Thus are avoided the inadequacies inherent in both polytheism and even certain traditional monotheisms. In Greek philosophy substance denotes a being that stands on its own, that does not inhere in nor form part of another being. It tends to connote independence and even separation, apartness, isolation. Baneful results for certain religious approaches to God are obvious, for the deity becomes not only the One, but the Alone, even the Alien. The Judaeo-Christian God, on the other hand, and precisely as triune, emphatically reveals that by virtue of his divine unicity God is not reduced to the isolated and phthisic status of a monad. In Greek philosophy substance and relation tend to be mutually hostile, so that the more one really is (substance), the less one is related (relation). The ontology implicit in the triune God simply undoes this. For this God, substantial being is being related; relation is substance. Thus, God's very being is the relationships of the Father, Son, and Holy Spirit, for God is not first Father, and then only derivatively and subsequently Son and Holy Spirit (cf. Ratzinger). Rather, the very substance of God is originally communicated Being. Hence, all being, wherever it is in being, is inescapably "being with."

Perichoresis and *Communio*. In order to describe this triune God, theologians have had recourse to many images and terms. One of the happiest has been the Greek word perichoresis, for it surpasses all others in indicating that one of the classical problems theoretical philosophy is reconciled in the triune God. Yet, it is not only a problem of theoretical philosophy, but also of practical living, namely the relation of the one and the many, of unity and diversity. Elsewhere considered contraries and even contradictories are revealed to be congenial and harmonious in the triune God. This is aptly expressed by perichoresis, which comes from Greek words meaning "to dance around with." If the anthropomorphism be permitted, perichoresis means that God is so full of being that his oneness is manyness, a manyness that in no way divides or separates, negates or isolates his oneness. Thus a term from "to dance" expresses God's being happy with himself, with his shared being—the being together of the Father, Son, and Holy Spirit. It is this kind of joyful unity in diversity that Genesis (esp. ch. 1 and 2) describes as the creation and which the Hebrew calls *shalom*.

Within this view it is perfectly "natural" that God, whose very being is communicated plenitude, should also communicate being to that which of itself is not God and, hence, which otherwise is simply not at all. To describe this communication in its various stages and degrees theologians have developed the terms creation, Christ, Church. If Christ, by his hypostatic union, is the most intense and unsurpassable instance of this theandric communication and communion of the divine with the human, then creation and Church are but the necessary antecedent and subsequent conditions: creation as the supposition and inception (protology) and Church as the consequence and completion (eschatology). Only in this context can the traditional distinction between nature and grace, the natural and the supernatural, be properly understood. It is legitimate to refer to the creation as nature and to redemption and glory as grace, but only with the understanding that all being other than the simply divine is gratuitous and, hence, grace. Thus, humanity lives in a gracious world, and always has. The distinction between natural and supernatural remains legitimate only as long as it is clearly understood that the "super" refers not to God the Creator giving the gift, but to man the creature receiving the gift. The gift is being, the full "being with" that God intends to communicate. Hence, the creature's capacity for the "supernatural" does not

demand supernatural life from a presumably reluctant God; rather, the generous God's desire to give creatures this superabundant life (Jn 1.16; 10.10) provides that there be a "nature" created to receive it.

Thus the dispute over whether the Creed's *communio sanctorum* refers to holy things or holy persons, though historically pertinent, is theologically and really otiose. All being is communion in the holy being of God, and the Church is precisely where this holy communion is celebrated. As effect and symbol of God's inward communion outwardly communicated, the Church is the Sacrament of salvation. The eternal, immanent trinity is the savingly-historical, economic Trinity.

For this reason earliest theology speaks of the Church as "a people united by the unity of the Father, Son and Holy Spirit" (Cyprian, *De Orat. Domin.* 23). Tertullian says "For the Church is itself, properly and principally, the Spirit Himself, in whom there is a trinity of one divinity, Father, Son and Holy Spirit" (*De pud.* 21). These texts can be taken as but the logical development of John's assertion that God is love (1 Jn 4.8, 16). Both really and gnoseologically the salvation-historical Trinity is the immanent Trinity.

Such lengthy Trinitarian and Christological considerations may seem excessive in a discussion of the entry on the Church as *communio*. However, as soon as such insights are even obscured, ecclesiology deteriorates into debates about lordship in the body politic of the Church, whereas it should be a *lectio divina* about the brotherhood of humanity in Christ celebrating the communion of man with God in the union of the Holy Spirit.

Being of the Church as *Communio*. If the Judaeo-Christian revelation understands that being as such is gift and communion, then it automatically follows that the being of the Church must also be gift and communion. If the divine and theandric sources of the Church are not grudging givers (Phil 2.6), then the Church must also strive for the "more" *perisseuma* that must distinguish the followers of Christ who want to enter the Kingdom of God definitively (Mt 5.20).

***Communio*, Giving and Forgiving.** In neither the institutions of its officials nor in the holiness of its members, however, does the Church expect paradisal innocence or utopian perfectionism. The true Church is not gnostic, but has always (Mt 12.36 43) known that it is, in the words of Augustine, a *corpus mixtum* of saints and sinners. The Church is aware that it is an *ecclesia reformata semper reformanda*. In the customary course of events the holiness of the Church, even as the communion of the saints, is not sinlessness, but forgiveness. For it is the Church of God, who wills not the death, but the life of the sinner (Ez 18.23); the Church of Jesus, who is the friend of sinners (Mt 11.19); and the Church of the Holy Spirit, who is the forgiveness of sins (the Postcommunion of the Roman Liturgy for Whit Tuesday, based on Jn 20.19 with Lk 20.19; 24.47 and Acts 1.8). Disastrously throughout the Church's history this precise nature of its holiness has been misunderstood, by both liberals and conservatives, reformers and integralists. The result has been presumption in those who identify the pilgrim Church with the eschatological Kingdom; despair, in those who identify the sinful Church with the Synagogue of Satan (Denz 1187). Both types are responsible for rending the seamless garment which Christ's Church is to be. Asserting their own holiness, both desert the holiness of that patient (2 Pt 3.9 with Wis 11.15–12.27), divine Wisdom which "sweetly and powerfully disposes all things" (Wis 8.1) and of whose goods and mysteries the Church is the sacramental communion. Rightly, then, the Church is most intensely Church through the Communion in the life-giving Body received at the banquet table spread by the (incarnate) divine Wisdom himself (Prv 9.1–6; Sir 24.19–22 with Lk 22:14–20 and 1 Cor 1.19–31). The gift of the Christian Church, although simultaneously sinful and holy, still the communion of saints, illuminates the fundamental insight of the Judaeo-Christian ontology, namely, that being is both divinely given and forgiven.

A Lived *Communio*. The mission of this Church is to practice this ontology. In both its structure and its life the Church is to be a communion of giving and forgiving. The officer in the Church is to be a shepherd, mindful that Jesus alone is the absolute Sacrament (Jn 10.1–10) of the Divine Shepherd (Ez 34.1). Hence, popes, bishops, pastors, and leaders of whatever kind "are not dictators over your faith, but fellow workers with you for your happiness" (2 Cor 1.24), "administrators of this new covenant" (2 Cor 3.6), who coordinate the many gifts of the one Spirit for the building up of the one Body of Christ. The members are to remember that as members they are also the fellow workers, equally responsible for the completion of the Body of Christ (Col 1.24), for it is not a monarchy, but a communion. Having been loved first by God and brought into communion with him, they are all henceforth able to love others and bring them into the same communion so that the joy of all may be complete (1 Jn 4.7, 10, 19; 1.4).

Vatican II Documents. As used in the council documents, *communio* has, amid a broad range of meaning, two major divisions: communion with God and communion among human persons. In general understanding, humanity is called to communion with God (*Gaudium et spes* 19). Specifically, humanity is called to communion with God who is Father, Son and Spirit (*Unitatis redinte-*

gratio 7, 15). Through the Eucharist, individuals are taken up into communion with Christ, and with one another (*Lumen gentium* 7). This is the communion of believers (UR 2) which has its source and center in Christ (UR 20) and was established by him as a communion of life, love and truth (LG 9), having the Holy Spirit as the principle of unity (UR 2). *Communio* is used to designate the entire mystical body of Jesus Christ (LG 50): those in glory, those being purified, and those still on pilgrimage. Thus the meaning of *communio* includes that invisible union with God and among believers, as well as the visible manifestation of that union which is membership in the Church (*Sacrosanctum concilium* 69; LG 14).

Communio is also used to designate the relationships between groups within the People of God. Religious are bound together in a fraternal communion (LG 43). There is a communion among the Catholic Eastern Churches (*Orientalium ecclesiarum* 2) and between those churches and the Pope (OE 24). There was a communion between the West and all the churches of the East before the Schism and even now there exists a communion among the separated churches themselves (UR 14). Communio refers to the relation of particular churches among themselves (*Ad gentes* 19) as well as their relationship with the universal Church (AG 38).

The Council expresses the structure of the People of God with the term "hierarchical communion" (*Presbyterorum ordinis* 15) applied in several contexts. A individual becomes a member of the episcopal college through sacramental consecration and hierarchical communion with the head of the college and its members (LG 22). He likewise exercises his ministry of teaching, sanctifying and ruling only in hierarchical communion with the head and members of the episcopal college (LG 21). *Communio* in this context is not to be understood as a vague goodwill, but as something organic which calls for a juridical structure (*Nota praevia* 2). There exists also a bond of hierarchical communion between the priests of a diocese and the bishop (PO 7). Among bishops themselves (LG 25) and among priests themselves (LG 41), the bond of *communio* should abound in every spiritual good and bear living witness of God to all.

In the area of ecumenism, the concept communio plays an important role. The most frequent designation for non-Catholic Christians is "brothers not yet in full communion" (GS 92). This use of *communio non plena* conveys a positive element, that there is communion of prayers and spiritual benefits (LG 15) between the churches, and they are joined in some real way in the Holy Spirit. The Council also recognizes that this communion is imperfect and that obstacles hinder full communion (UR 3). But terms like "excommunication," "heretic," and "schism" are never used. Communio is used in the Decree on Ecumenism to designate all Christian communities (including the Roman Church: UR 1; 4); to designate all separated churches and ecclesial communities (UR13); and to designate the Anglican communion (UR 13).

The Code and Other Church Documents. Present in the debates and in the texts of Vatican II was a tension between a "juridical ecclesiology" which describes the Church as a "perfect society" structured like a monarchy with its starting point as the primacy of the Pope, and an "ecclesiology of communion" which describes the Church as *communio,* emphasizes collegiality and has the local church as its starting point. In a commentary on the 1983 Code, James Provost makes the judgment that the ecclesiology of *communio* is "clearly more influential and provides a more consistent perspective for interpreting the council's teaching." Because the teaching of the Second Vatican Council became the foundation for the revisions in canon law, the same tensions present in the conciliar documents are evident in the Code, especially in Book II, on the People of God. The Code focuses on the external, juridically enforceable dimensions of full communion in Canon 205: "Those baptized are fully in communion with the Catholic Church on this earth who are joined with Christ in its visible structure by the bonds of profession of faith, of the Sacraments, and of ecclesiastical governance (cf. LG 14)." There is also a spiritual dimension to communion which is possessing the Spirit of Christ (LG 14). This forms the living context for the juridical aspects found in the Code and is to be seen as complementary to it.

In the apostolic constitution *Sacrae discipline leges* accompanying the promulgation of the Code, Pope John Paul II listed among those elements which characterize the true and genuine image of the Church the "doctrine in which the Church is seen as a communion." This was also a major theme in The Final Report of the Extraordinary Synod of Bishops of 1985 which celebrated the 20 year anniversary of the conclusion of the Second Vatican Council. In assessing the implementation of the teaching of the Council, the Bishops reaffirmed the ecclesiology of communion as "the central and fundamental idea of the council's documents" which is the foundation for order and a correct relationship between unity and pluriformity in the Church. In this context the bishops discussed collegiality and coresponsibility and called for continued study of the theological status and doctrinal authority of episcopal conferences; they encouraged continued ecumenical dialogue; and they acknowledged the vocation and mission of women and the emergence of "basic communities." Because the Church, as *communio* is a sacrament for the salvation of the world, the Bishops emphasized the Church's mission, particularly its preferential option for the poor and its solidarity for those who suffer. As Bishop James Malone, President of the U.S. Bishops' Conference, stated: "We are a *communio* in which the Spirit of the churches is present to each and all and in which the successor of Peter represents Christ's care for the entire Church. No Catholic can deny any of that; it is the substance of our ecclesiology" [*Origins*16 (20 Nov 1986) 394–398].

Since the Council theologians have deepened the Church's self-understanding as *communio* and sought to express more fully and clearly the connections and consequences of this many-sided concept. The community of believers throughout the world forms a communion of local churches, the bishops in communion with the Bishop of Rome whose primacy serves the unity of the whole Church. *Communio* not only expresses what the Church is, visibly and invisibly, it also expresses the Church's goal, not only among all Christian communions, but for men and women of every time and place. It is for this reason that, precisely as communion, the Church is a sacrament for the salvation of all. The clearest expression of the Trinitarian character of the Church is the Eucharist where invisible communion with God and visible communion with one another form a sacramental unity. It is a sign and instrument, possessing within itself the reality of communion with Father, Son and Spirit, but always as sign and never perfectly. Thus *communio* implies laws, rituals, apostolates and our work in building up the People of God. But at the same time, *communio* is grace and gift, for God has established his people as the Body of Christ through the power of the Holy Spirit. The *communio* that Christians receive, is their present task and future goal. It alone fulfills the human heart, for it extends beyond death.

Bibliography: H. DE LUBAC, *Catholicism: Christ and the Common Destiny of Man* (New York 1950). D. L. SCHINDLER, *Heart of the World, Center of the Church: Communio Ecclesiology, Liberalism, and Liberation* (Grand Rapids, Mich. 1996). R. KRESS, *The Church: Communion, Sacrament, Communication* (New York 1985). J. M. R. TILLARD, *Church of Churches: The Ecclesiology of Communion* (Collegeville, Minn. 1992). Y. CONGAR, *Diversity and Communion* (Mystic, Conn. 1985). J. M. MCDERMOTT, "The Biblical Doctrine of 'koinonia,'" *Biblische Zeitschrift*19 (1975): 64–77; 219–233. J. PROVOST, ed., *The Church as Communion* (Washington, D.C. 1984). E. CORECCO, *Canon Law and Communio: Writings on the Constitutional Law of the Church* (Vatican City 1999). J. RATZINGER, "The Ecclesiology of Vatican II," *Origins* 15 (1985): 370–376. G. ALBERIGO and J. PROVOST, "Synod 1985—An Evaluation," *Concilium* 188 (1986). O. SAIER, *"Communio" in der Lehre des zweiten vatikanischen Konzil* (Munich 1973).

[R. KRESS/G. MALANOWSKI]

COMMUNIO: INTERNATIONAL CATHOLIC REVIEW

Communio, an international federation of journals that now includes editions in fifteen countries (Germany, Italy, North America, France, Croatia, Belgium, Spain, Poland, Brazil, Portugal, Slovenia, Hungary, Chile, Argentina, Czech Republic), began publication in 1972. In the late 1960s, Hans Urs von Balthasar had planned a small book of essays by prominent Catholics that would address the essentials of the faith in light of the controversies following the Second Vatican Council. When it became clear that an anthology would not suffice but that a continuing conversation with different currents was necessary, he turned to the idea of a journal. The journal began to take concrete form in a conversation arranged during a session of the International Theological Commission in Rome in 1970, followed by a second meeting in Paris in 1971. Theologians called together for the first conversation were Balthasar, H. de Lubac, L. Bouyer, J. Medina, M. J. Le Guillou, and J. Ratzinger. Balthasar was made father of the joint project with special responsibility for the German branch. Le Guillou was charged with responsibility for the French. Because of Le Guillou's subsequent illness, the French edition was delayed. An Italian partner then emerged, made up partly of members of the movement Comunione e Liberazione. *Communio* thus was finally launched in 1972, with two editions, German and Italian, followed in 1974 by the North American and the French. With the help and encouragement of then archbishop of Krakow, Karol Wojtyła, a group of Polish theologians eventually secured government permission and founded an edition some ten years later (1983 1984).

In the words of Balthasar, the purpose of *Communio* is "negatively: to resist at all costs the deadly polarization brought on by the fervor of traditionalists and modernists alike; positively: to perceive the Church as a central *communio,* a community originating from communion with Christ ('given from above'); as a *communio* enabling us to share our hearts, thoughts and blessings." The journal is theological in nature, intended for specialists as well as for all those concerned with fundamental questions of the faith in its engagement with contemporary culture. In keeping with the spirit embodied in the review's title, the editors sought from the beginning to form a community among themselves and their authors that would proceed on the basis of *communio.* In North America, this has led to the formation of study circles. For the same reason, the editors chose a federated rather than centralized administration for the review, allowing for the coincidence of unity and difference among the many language areas. The different editions frequently publish translations of each other's articles.

Father Yves Congar. (Agence France Presse/Archive Photos. Reproduced by Permission.)

See Also: HANS URS VON BALTHASAR, HENRI DE LUBAC, JOSEPH RATZINGER

Bibliography: HANS URS VON BALTHASAR, "Communio: International Catholic Review," *Communio* 19 (1992): 507–8 NC; "The Mission of Communio," *Communio* 19 (1992): 509 NC. JOHN PAUL II, "Address to the Group Representing the Journal Communio," *Communio* 19 (1992): 433–435. ANTONIO SICARI, "A Reflection on the Ideals of Communio," *Communio* 16 (1989): 495–498. JOSEPH CARDINAL RATZINGER, "Communio: A Program," *Communio* 19 (1992): 436–449.

[DAVID L. SCHINDLER]

CONGAR, YVES MARIE-JOSEPH

Theologian, ecumenist, author; b. in Sedan (Ardennes), France, 13 April 1904; d. in Paris, 22 June 1995; son of Georges and Lucie (Desoye) Congar. He studied at the minor seminary in Rheims and the Institut Catholique in Paris, and in 1925 joined the Dominican Order, completing his studies and earning a doctorate in theology at the Dominican Studium of Saulchoir. He was ordained a priest in 1930, and from 1931 to 1939 he taught fundamental theology and ecclesiology at Le Saulchoir. Drafted into the army in 1939, he spent five years as a prisoner of war.

At the end of World War II, Congar returned to Le Saulchoir, where he taught until 1954, when a series of ecclesiastical decisions forced him into exile in Jerusalem, Rome, and Cambridge before being given a regular assignment in Strasbourg (1956–58). He was invited, at the express wish of Pope John XXIII, to help in the preparations for the Second Vatican Council. At Vatican II he served on the Doctrinal Commission and made major contributions to the Council's documents on the Church, ecumenism, revelation, missions, the priesthood and the Church in the modern world.

Congar contributed a running commentary on the theological discussions and events of the Council to the bi-weekly *Informations catholiques internationales* (collected in *Le concile au jour le jour* 1963–66). Vatican II represented a thorough rehabilitation of his reputation in Catholic circles; after the Council he was able to devote himself peacefully to historical and theological scholarship until a chronic bone disease made it difficult for him to write.

Writings and Thought. The list of Congar's published titles numbers more than 1,700 books and articles, among which may be found works of first-rate historical scholarship, theological exploration, contemporary ecclesial interpretation, and essays in spiritual theology. For almost fifty years he reported regularly on ecclesiology in the *Revue des sciences philosophiques et théologiques*.

On the eve of his priestly ordination, Congar received what he considered to be a divine vocation to work for the reunion of Christians. He understood that ecumenical rapprochement would require a thorough renewal in ecclesiology, and it is his research into the history of the theology of the Church and his efforts to recover a fuller ecclesial vision than had prevailed in the baroque theology of the modern era that provided the chief focus of his writings.

Congar's first major contribution, *Chrétiens desunis: Principes d'un "oecuménisme" catholique* (1937; English translation 1939), was a watershed in the Catholic Church's attitude towards ecumenism. In this work Congar offered an historical interpretation of the great schisms which have split the Church, a sympathetic presentation of the distinctive characters of Protestantism, Anglicanism, and Orthodoxy, and a statement of principles for Catholic participation in the ecumenical movement. This work also caught the attention of Roman

authorities, and it seems it was only his wartime imprisonment that enabled him to escape the condemnations which in 1942 fell upon Le Saulchoir and his colleague, Marie Dominique CHENU.

Upon his return to France after the war, Congar threw himself into the very heady atmosphere of Church life. In the late 1940s, French Catholicism was alive with the promise of Biblical, liturgical, and patristic revivals, the so-called new theology, the worker-priest experiment, and efforts to construct a new pastoral theology and practice. Congar attempted to propose principles and criteria for an authentic reform and renewal in the Church in his next great work, *Vraie et fausse reforme dans l'Église* (1950). Much of what he proposed would later be sanctioned by Vatican II, but in 1950 this was hardy stuff; and he was one of those considered to indulge in the "false irenicism" condemned that year in *Humani generis*. In 1952 all translations and re-editions of the work were forbidden by Rome.

Nonetheless in 1953 he was able to publish his very influential work, *Jalons pour une théologie du laïcat* (1953; rev. ed. 1964; English translation 1957 and 1965), which was later to find many echoes at Vatican II. The work provides a critique of the reduction of ecclesiology to "hierarchology" (a term which he seems to have coined), and a validation of the laity's participation in the threefold office of Christ.

A year later, however, the series of denunciations, warnings, and restrictive measures which he had received from Rome was crowned by an order that he desist from teaching and leave Le Saulchoir. He was ordered successively to Jerusalem, Rome, and to England. All his writings were made subject to stringent censorship. In 1956, Archbishop Weber took him under his protection at Strasbourg.

During these difficult years, Congar published, after long delays caused by the censors, a profound study of the Church under the theme, *Le mystère du Temple* (1958; English translation 1962). Unable to participate directly in ecumenical activities, he devoted himself to historical scholarship. A first fruit of this was his two-volume work, *La tradition et les traditions* (1960 and 1963; English translation 1966). This work and several lengthy essays on episcopal collegiality, on authority as service, on poverty in the Church, on the local church, and on catholicity as universal inculturation were to contribute greatly to the elaboration of the documents of the Second Vatican Council. His participation in the preparation and unfolding of the Council was to make up for the years of neglect and suspicion, and he could rightly claim the Council as the triumph of many causes for which he had been working.

Post Vatican II. After the Council, Congar continued his scholarly work and participated actively in the great debates occasioned by the remarkable changes that took place in the Church. He published two major works on the history of ecclesiology, *L'ecclésiologie du haut moyen-age* (1968) and *L'Église de Saint-Augustin à l'époque moderne* (1970). Several collections of his published works include essays on ministry, salvation, diversity and communion, the theology of Luther, and the ecclesiology of Vatican II. A three-volume work on the Holy Spirit, *Je crois en l'Esprit-Saint*(1979–80; English translation 1983), attempts to redress the neglect of pneumatology in Western theology. Many other scholarly essays remain scattered in various journals and volumes.

Congar never regarded Vatican II as an unsurpassable moment and with a remarkable openness he continued to speak and write on post-conciliar developments and problems, as for example, the challenge of Archbishop Lefebvre, political and liberation theology, and the charismatic movement.

His contribution to 20th-century theology is difficult to summarize or to synthesize. Congar's most widely acknowledged contribution is the vast work of historical recovery of the great and broad Catholic tradition before it began to be straitened by the schisms of the 11th and 16th centuries. He regarded this *ressourcement* as crucial to the life of the Church today, and all his life he has brought to the discussion of contemporary events a mind informed by a broad and deep knowledge that has enabled him to be what J.-P. Jossua calls "a prophet of tradition," that is, a theologian exercising a critical and constructive role precisely as a mediator of the achievements of the past. In all these respects, as the event of the Second Vatican Council itself illustrates, Yves Congar proved a model of a perennially necessary theological effort. Pope John Paul II named Congar to the College of Cardinals on 24 November 1994.

Bibliography: Y. CONGAR, *Le Concile se Vatican II: Son Église, Peuple de Dieu et Corps du Christ* (Paris 1984); *Dialogue Between Christians: Catholic Contributions to Ecumenism* (Westminster, Md. 1966): 1–51; *Diversity and Communion* (Mystic, Conn. 1985); *Une passion: L'unité: Réflexions souvenirs 1929–1973* (Paris 1974). E. FOUILLOUX, "Friar Yves, Cardinal Congar, Dominican: Itinerary of a Theologian," *U.S. Catholic Historian* 17 (1999): 63–90. J.-P. JOSSUA, *Le Père Congar: La théologie au service du Peuple de Dieu* (Paris 1967). T. I. MACDONALD, *The Ecclesiology of Yves Congar: Foundational Themes* (Lanham, Md. 1984). AIDAN NICHOLS, *Yves Congar* (Wilton, Conn. 1989); "An Yves Congar Bibliography 1967–1987," *Angelicum* 66 (1989): 422–66.

[J. A. KOMONCHAK]

CZĘSTOCHOWA

Capital city of province of same name in south central Poland on the Warta River in the Kraków-Częstochowa upland, 220 km from Warsaw. It is famed for its possession since 1382 of an icon of the Blessed Virgin Mary, venerated under the titles "Our Lady of Częstochowa," "Our Lady of Jasna Góra," and the "Black Madonna," the most famous icon in the country. The icon is housed in a basilica on a limestone hill known as the Jasna Góra (Bright Mountain) above the city. The complex of sacred buildings surrounding the icon constitutes one the major shrines and pilgrimage centers in Christendom. The spire of the Basilica church on Jasna Góra is the highest in Poland, 106.3 km, visible from a distance of several kilometers.

Legends abound regarding the origins of the icon of Our Lady of Częstochowa, the most popular of which attributes the painting to St. Luke, who worked on wood from the table of the Holy Family. Historians date it to the Byzantine period, sixth or seventh century, from the region around Constantinople. Measuring 122.2 cm (48.11 inches) high, 82.2cm (32.36 inches) wide, and 3.5 cm (1.38 inches) thick, the holy image was painted on wood covered by a tightly woven canvas. The Blessed Virgin Mary is represented in the *hodegetria* pose, pointing to the Christ Child, who sits erect not like a suckling infant but as the Christ-Emmanuel full of wisdom. After 500 years at the Castle of Selz in Ukraine, the icon was brought to Poland in 1382 by Prince Ladislaus of Opole, who entrusted it to the care of the Pauline Hermits at the monastery he had built for them atop Jasna Góra in Częstochowa. The same order of hermits remains its custodian today. In 1430, the icon was vandalized and desecrated by robbers, whom some historians believe were Polish nobles associated with the Hussite movement. The scars on Mary's cheek date from these events. Two large parallel scars slash vertically, while a third wider scar cuts horizontally across them. The darkened skin tone derives from a chemical reaction to fire, aging of the pigment, and centuries of votive candle smoke.

After the Swedish invasion of Poland was repulsed at Częstochowa in 1655, King Casimir proclaimed Our Lady of Częstochowa "Queen of the Realm of Poland," and from this dedication the icon attained a new status as the symbol of Polish nationalism, unity, and liberty. Through subsequent centuries of invasion, partition, Nazi occupation, and communist oppression, Poles regarded Częstochowa as the touchstone of their national identity. As part of the Great Novena of nine year's spiritual preparation for the millennium of Christianity in Poland in 1966, Cardinal Stefan Wyszyński circulated a special copy of the icon throughout Poland. In the 1980s, the

Pope John Paul II prays in front of the image of the Black Madonna in Częstochowa on 17 June 1999. (AP/Wide World Photos. Photograph by Diether Endlicher)

leaders of the Solidarity movement wore small icons of the Częstochowa Virgin on their lapels. Solidarity's founder Lech Wałęsa donated his 1983 Nobel Peace Prize to Częstochowa, where it remains enshrined.

Votive offerings fill the treasury of the Jasna Góra monastery. The icon itself is heavily decorated with bejeweled attire and crowned with diadems that date to the official papal coronation of the icon in 1717. Pope Paul VI sent a golden rose to the shrine at the conclusion of the Second Vatican Council in honor of the millennium of Poland's Christianity celebrated in 1966. Pope John Paul II sent his white sash, bloodstained from the 1981 assassination attempt. It is kept in a sealed box near the icon.

The most famous tradition associated with Częstochowa is the "Walking Pilgrimage" that dates from 1711. About fifty pilgrimage routes throughout Poland converge on Częstochowa. The walk from Warsaw takes nine days, from Kraków six days, from Gdansk thirteen days. For the feasts of the Assumption (15 August) and Our Lady of Częstochowa (26 August), more than one million pilgrims walk, and this religious Movement grew throughout the 1990s in conjunction with several visits of Pope John Paul II to the shrine. Six million visitors a year throng Częstochowa.

Bibliography: A. GIEYSZTOR, S. HERBST, and B. LESNOCORSKI, *Millenium: A Thousand Years of the Polish State* (Warsaw 1961). M. HELM PIRGO, *Virgin Mary, Queen of Poland* (New York 1957); Our Lady of Częstochowa Foundation, ed., *The Glories of Częstochowa and Jasna Góra* (Stockbridge, Mass. 1981). Z. ROZNOW and E. SMULIKOWSKA, *The Cultural heritage of Jasna Góra* (Warsaw 1974). J. ST PASIERB, J. SAMEK, *et al., The Shrine of the Black Madonna at Częstochowa* (Warsaw 1980). M. ZALECKI, *Theology of a Marian Shrine: Our Lady of Częstochowa*, Marian Library Studies, n.s. 8 (Dayton, Ohio 1976).

[JAMES E. MCCURRY]

DANNEELS, GODFRIED

Cardinal, archbishop of Mechelen-Brussels, Belgium; b. 4 June 1933, Kanegem, in the Diocese of Brugge, Belgium. The oldest of six children, Godfried Daneels studied at the major seminary of Brugge and was ordained 17 August 1957. He has a licentiate in philosophy from the Catholic University of Louvain and a doctorate in theology from the Pontifical Gregorian University, Rome. From 1959 to 1977 he was professor of liturgy and sacramental theology at the major seminary in Brugge, and from 1969 to 1977 simultaneously professor of sacramental theology at the Catholic University, Louvain. As professor in Brugge he was editor-secretary of the Flemish interdiocesan review *Collationes,* in charge of permanent diaconate in diocese of Brugge, and author of several books in theology.

Godfried Danneels. (Catholic News Service.)

Danneels was appointed bishop of Antwerp, 4 November 1977, and ordained by Leo-Jozef Cardinal Suenens, archbishop of Malines-Brussels, whom he succeeded in 1979. In 1980 he became president of the Episcopal Conference of Belgium and military ordinary for Belgium. Pope John Paul II appointed him president delegate of the Special Synod of Dutch Bishops held at Vatican City in January 1980. He was named cardinal on 2 February 1983. In 1985 he was relator at the second Extraordinary Assembly of the World Synod of Bishops.

Like his predecessors Mercier and Suenens at Malines, Cardinal Danneels has continued to promote ecumenical relations, especially between the Anglican and Roman Catholic Churches; in 1996 he hosted special commemorative observances on the occasion of the seventy-fifth anniversary of the Malines Conversations.

Bibliography: Following in a tradition well established by Mercier and Suenens, Cardinal DANNEELS has been a prolific writer especially in the areas of liturgy and contemporary spirituality. Among his best-known works are: *La liturgie dans les documents de Vatican II* (Bruges 1966); *La Priére eucharistique, formes anciennes et conception nouvelle du canon de la messe* (Paris 1967); *Qui est Dieu pour vous?: Réponses à des jeunes* (Paris 1990); *Christ or Aquarius?* (Dublin 1992); *Devenir des hommes nouveaux: Lettres d'espérance* (Paris 1993); *Messengers of Joy: How Important Is Priesthood Today?* (Dublin 1995); and *Tu n'as rien gardé pour Toi: Prières* (Paris and Brussels 1996).

[J. A. DICK]

DE MELLO, ANTHONY

Spiritual writer, retreat master, priest, member of the Society of Jesus; b. 4 September 1931; d. 2 June 1987. De Mello was raised in an old Catholic family in Bombay, India, and eventually took degrees in philosophy (Barcelona), psychology (Loyola University, Chicago), and spiritual theology (Gregorian University, Rome). He entered the Society of Jesus in Bombay in 1947. De Mello was the founder and director of the Sadhana Institute of Pastoral Counseling near Poona, India. He sought the integration of Eastern prayer methods into classical Christian forms, particularly the Ignatian Exercises. His most famous work *Sadhana* was translated into forty languages and was the distillation of scattered notes used in retreats or prayer workshops. It helped gain a wide readership for nine other books that he saw through publication in his lifetime. De Mello died while giving conferences at Fordham University.

De Mello's spirituality, while not anti-intellectual, gives priority to sensate or body-centered modes of spiritual awareness. Stillness and breathing techniques in De Mello's system are reminiscent of the hesychist. Imagination or fantasy permits a kind of self-displacement into a new historical moment. A new story emerges, such as when a person imagines walking with Jesus along the Via Dolorosa or witnessing the miracle at Cana as if at the wedding party. Feelings and intuitions are key; devotions are more secondary. Meditation is the pathway to love, not necessarily greater knowledge or cognition of some tangible reality. True cognition emerges when love is engaged. Here De Mello echoes Teresa of Avila: "The important thing is not to think much but to love." In offering spiritual counsel De Mello exhibited a self-deprecating wit and never forced his positions on his retreatants, choosing rather to teach by suggestion.

De Mello left a large body of unpublished work, some of which he edited before his death, though he never authorized their publication. Motivated in part by these later, posthumous writings, the Congregation for the Doctrine of the Faith issued a notification that some of De Mello's ideas were "incompatible with the Catholic faith and can cause harm." The principal issue was the charge of indifferentism. The Congregation called for bishops to see to the withdrawal of De Mello's works and the cessation of further reprinting. Friends and Jesuit colleagues, particularly in India, publicly protested this move, seeing it as inhibiting Christian encounters and dialogue with Eastern traditions and beliefs.

Bibliography: ANTHONY DE MELLO, *Sadhana: A Way to God: Christian Exercises in Eastern Form* (St. Louis 1978); *Praying Body and Soul: Methods and Practices of Anthony De Mello* (New York 1997). PARMANANDA DIVARKAR, "The Enigma of Anthony De Mello," *America* 179, no. 14 (1998): 8–13. WILLIAM DYCH, ed., *Anthony De Mello: Writings* (Maryknoll, N.Y. 1999).

[P. J. HAYES]

DEZZA, PAOLO

Jesuit, university rector, cardinal; b. 13 December 1901, Parma; d. 17 December 1999, Rome. His life was dedicated to higher education, teaching philosophy, administration in the Society of Jesus, and service to the Holy See. He entered the Society of Jesus in 1918, studied philosophy in Spain and theology at Naples, and was ordained a priest 25 March 1928. In 1929, Dezza began a long career at the Pontifical Gregorian University in Rome, where he taught metaphysics intermittently for more than 35 years. From 1935 to 1939 he served as provincial of the Veneto-Milanese province. He was rector at several institutions: the Jesuit philosophy scholasticate in Gallarate, Italy (1939–1941), Gregorian University (1941–1951), and St. Robert Bellarmine College (1951–1965). His *Metaphysica* became a classic textbook in many universities and seminaries. Young Karol Wojtyła attended his lectures in Rome.

In 1965 Fr. Dezza was elected assistant general of the Jesuits, and began to take on various roles within the Vatican. He was a *peritus* at the Second Vatican Council, contributing particularly to the commission that wrote the Declaration on Christian Education (*Gravissimum educationis*); he published a commentary on this document in 1965. He served as consultor at several posts of the Holy See: namely, the congregations for evangelization, religious, divine worship and sacraments, and education. He was a highly regarded adviser for the Congregation of Catholic Education, helping with the reform of the Catholic universities. He conducted the Spiritual Exercises for Popes Pius XII and John Paul I, and was confessor to Paul VI and John Paul I.

In 1981, Fr. Dezza was an assistant general when, on 7 August, Fr. General Pedro Arrupe suffered a stroke that disabled him severely. On 5 October 1981, the pope named Fr. Dezza his pontifical delegate for the Society of Jesus. This appointment suspended the Jesuit constitutions until the election of a new general. With prudence, calm, and fidelity to the pope, Fr. Dezza prepared the order for a new General Congregation. In a series of conferences and meetings, he informed the Fathers of the concerns and hopes of the pope for the Society. The special mission of Fr. Dezza lasted until 13 September 1983, when the thirty-third General Congregation elected Fr. Peter-Hans Kolvenbach as superior general.

On 28 June 1991, Fr. Dezza was created cardinal with the title of Deacon of Saint Ignatius Loyola in

Campo Marzio. It meant much for him, since the church of St. Ignatius is the church of the Gregorian University. He requested, and was granted, an exemption from the requirement of episcopal consecration. He died on 17 December 1999, at the age of 98, and was buried in the church of St. Ignatius.

[HERVÉ CARRIER]

DOMUS SANCTAE MARTHAE

The Domus Sanctae Marthae was built in 1996 to house the electors of the College of Cardinals gathered in conclave for a papal election. Pope John Paul II determined that the facilities in the Apostolic Palace, which had long been used to house the cardinals, were inadequate. Under the direction of the President of the Pontifical Commission for Vatican City, Cardinal Rosalio José Castillo Lara, the Domus Sanctae Marthae was built on the site of the old Santa Marta Hospice, which had been built by Pope Leo XIII and was a center of Allied diplomatic activity during the Second World War. It is situated in the Piazza Santa Marta opposite Saint Peter's Basilica, hard against the Vatican Wall, between the Paul VI Audience Hall and the Palazzo San Carlo. The cardinals will live, eat, and pray at the Domus Sanctae Marthae, but the voting sessions will be held twice each day in the Sistine Chapel. The new building of a basement and six floors comprises 130 apartments and a range of chapels, dining rooms, and meeting rooms. There are approximately forty permanent residents, mainly priests working in the Secretariat of State, who would be housed elsewhere during a conclave. The Domus Sanctae Marthae also accommodates groups both large and small for meetings and formal dinners on various occasions. The administration of the house is entrusted to the Daughters of Charity, whose presence in the Vatican City is of long standing.

[MARK COLERIDGE]

DRINAN, ROBERT FREDERICK

Jesuit, law professor, former U.S. congressman; b. Boston, Massachusetts, 15 November 1920, son of James J. and Ann M. (Flanagan) Drinan. In 1942, after graduating from Boston College, Drinan entered the Society of Jesus. He received an LL.M. at Georgetown University Law Center in 1950 and an S.T.L. from Weston College in Massachusetts in 1954. He was ordained to the priesthood in June 1953.

Drinan's career as a legal scholar began in 1955 when he joined the faculty of Boston College Law School as assistant dean. In 1956 he became the youngest dean

Italian bishop Paolo Dezza is seen on 26 June 1999, two days before being elevated to the dignity of cardinal by Pope John Paul II. (AP/Wide World Photos.)

in the law school's history, and held that position until 1970. During that time he published *Religion, the Courts, and Public Policy* (1963), *The Right to Be Educated* (ed. 1968), *Democracy, Dissent, and Disorder: The Issues and the Law* (1969), and *Vietnam and Armageddon: Peace, War and the Christian Conscience* (1970). In this period he also was a corresponding editor of the Jesuit weekly *America* and authored numerous articles in scholarly and popular journals. In 1966–67 he was a visiting professor at the University of Texas School of Law.

In 1970, motivated by his passionate opposition to the Vietnam War and with permission of his local Jesuit superiors, Drinan sought the Democratic nomination for Congress from a suburban Boston district (Massachusetts' Fourth Congressional District). He was elected to the Ninety-Second Congress and served five terms (1971–81). Always dressed in his clerical collar, Drinan most famously served on the House Judiciary Committee during the Nixon impeachment hearings in 1974. In these years he also published Honor the Promise: America's Commitment to Israel (1977). He left Congress in 1981 after Pope John Paul II directed priests to withdraw from politics.

After leaving Congress Drinan joined the faculty of the Georgetown University Law Center, where he created

Robert F. Drinan at a press conference, announcing he will not run for re-election to Congress in 1980. (AP/Wide World Photos. Reproduced by permission.)

courses in human rights and founded the *Georgetown Journal of Legal Ethics,* the first journal dedicated to legal ethics, which became the premier voice on professional responsibility in the legal academy. He published *Beyond the Nuclear Freeze* (1983), *God and Caesar on the Potomac: A Pilgrimage of Conscience* (1985), *Cry of the Oppressed: The History and Hope of the Human Rights Revolution* (1987), *Stories from the American Soul: A Reader in Ethics and American Policy for the 1990s* (1990), and *The Fractured Dream: America's Divisive Moral Choices* (1991). In his nearly two decades at Georgetown, Drinan became an internationally renowned expert in human rights and legal ethics.

Over the years, Drinan's publicly expressed views on abortion aroused much controversy. In the mid-1960s, he offered a "novel analysis that from his anti-abortion perspective, repeal of abortion statutes would be preferable to reform since it would remove the subject from governmental review rather than place the state in the position of expressly approving some abortions while disapproving others" (Garrow, 341). He later publicly defended Roe v. Wade—the 1973 Supreme Court decision finding a constitutional right to abortion—judging it flawed but on the whole balanced. While morally op-

posed to abortion, and fully accepting Catholic teaching on the subject, Drinan often expressed doubts as to the proper way to oppose it, and consistently advocated legal abortion as the way to deal with the practice on terms that permit a woman to make a private choice, guided by personal conscience and judgment.

Bibliography: SHERMAN L. COHN, "A Tribute to Robert F. Drinan, S.J.: Honoring a Lifetime of Public Service," *Georgetown Journal of Legal Ethics* 8 (1995): 745–748. DAVID J. GARROW, *Liberty & Sexuality: The Right to Privacy and the Making of "Roe v. Wade"* (New York: MacMillan Publishing Co., 1994). VINCENT A. LAPOMARDA, "A Jesuit Runs for Congress: The Rev. Robert F. Drinan, S.J. and His 1970 Campaign," *Journal of Church and State* 15 (1973): 205–222.

[KEVIN P. QUINN]

DULLES, AVERY

Jesuit priest, theologian; b. 24 August 1918, Auburn, New York. Dulles was the son of John Foster Dulles, U.S. secretary of state (1953–59), and Janet Avery. His serious attention to the faith, begun through his study of classical and modern philosophers (e.g., Aristotle, Plato, Jacques Maritain, Etienne Gilson) at Harvard University, was definitively marked by an experience he had during a walk one February day along the Charles River in Boston—a conversion experience he later described in *A Testimonial to Grace*: "Never, since the eventful day . . . have I doubted the existence of an all-good and omnipotent God." In 1940 he both graduated from Harvard and was received into the Roman Catholic Church. The following year, he entered law school at Harvard and also co- founded the nearby St. Benedict Center, whose director, Fr. Leonard Feeney, later became involved in a lengthy controversy about salvation outside the Roman Catholic Church.

During World War II, Dulles served as an officer in the U.S. Navy (1942–46), where he managed to continue reading philosophy and theology on his own. After completing military service, for which was awarded the Croix de Guerre, he entered the Society of Jesus (14 August 1946). After his novitiate, he studied philosophy at Woodstock College and received a Ph.L. in 1951. After teaching philosophy for two years at Fordham University, he returned to Woodstock to study theology under such noted theologians as Gustave Weigel and John Courtney Murray. He also began reading the writings of the Protestant theologian Paul Tillich, whose emphasis on the importance of symbol for the theology of revelation would later become evident in Dulles's own writings about revelation. On 16 June 1956, he was ordained to the priesthood.

After receiving an S.T.L. at Woodstock in 1957, Dulles made his Jesuit tertianship at Munich. In 1960 he

Avery Dulles shakes hands with his father, John Foster Dulles, following the former's ordination. Watching are Mrs. Dulles and Francis Cardinal Spellman. (AP/Wide World Photos)

received a doctorate from the Gregorian University, in Rome, writing a dissertation on *"Vestigia ecclesiae" outside the True Church* under the direction of the Dutch Jesuit ecumenist Jan Witte. He returned to Woodstock and taught courses on apologetics, revelation, and biblical inspiration (1960–74). Early in his career at Woodstock, he published *Apologetics and the Biblical Christ* (1963), a short but influential book in which he reexamined traditional approaches to apologetics in light of modern understandings of revelation, faith, and inspiration. This early work displays many characteristics found in Dulles's later writings: a respectful yet critical examination of the Catholic theological tradition along with perceptive proposals about contemporizing this heritage in light of current biblical and theological scholarship.

For Dulles, 1974 was a year of transition and accomplishment. The transition was occasioned by the decision of the Jesuit provincials in the United States to close Woodstock College; consequently, Dulles accepted a professorship in systematic theology at the Catholic University of America, where he remained on the faculty until he reached mandatory retirement age in 1988. The accomplishment was the publication of his widely influential *Models of the Church,* which looked at the Church from five (later six) different perspectives or "models." This approach, which resonated with similar methodologies in philosophy and science, provided both theologians and pastoral ministers with multiple insights into the different and sometimes conflicting aspects and agenda of the Church.

Nine years later, Dulles used a similar approach in his *Models of Revelation* (1983), where he described five different "models" of revelation, before proposing "symbolic mediation" as a perspective that both emphasizes the strengths and minimizes the weakness of the individual models. After retiring from Catholic University,

Dulles was named the Laurence J. McGinley Professor of Religion and Society at Fordham University. In that position, he published a companion piece to his work on revelation, *The Assurance of Things Hoped For* (1994), which presents both a historical overview of the theology of faith and a discussion of various "models" of faith.

In addition to his many books and numerous other writings, Dulles has served as the president of both the Catholic Theological Society of America (1975–76) and the American Theological Society (1978–79). He has also been active in many ecumenical conversations, including the Lutheran-Roman Catholic Dialogue in the United States and the Lima meeting of the Faith and Order Commission of the World Council of Churches, which produced a significant consensus statement on *Baptism, Eucharist, and Ministry* (1983). He has served as a consultant to many bodies, including the Papal Secretariat for Dialogue with Non-Believers (1966–73) and the International Theological Commission. His scholarly contributions have been recognized by the conferral of some twenty honorary doctorates.

Dulles's theological writing is consistently careful and critical, well researched, and precisely but clearly articulated. Yet it is difficult to place him in any one theological school. The undergirding of his work is usually provided by the Aristotelian and Thomistic traditions. Yet his employment of these traditions is amplified by a broad spectrum of thinkers, ranging from Catholic scholars like John Henry Newman to philosopher-scientists like Michael Polanyi. Like both Newman and Polanyi, Dulles is a collector of historical data, which he creatively analyzes and systematically organizes into syntheses that are enlightening, thought-provoking, and useful, both theologically and pastorally. He examined his theological methodology in *The Craft of Theology* (1992; expanded edition, 1995) and in a more personal vein in the fiftieth- anniversary edition of *A Testimonial to Grace* (1996). Other major writings include *The Survival of Dogma* (1971), *The Resilient Church* (1977), and *A Church to Believe In* (1982). Since the Second Vatican Council, Dulles has often been regarded as the preeminent Catholic systematic theologian in the United States.

[JOHN FORD]

DZIWISZ, STANISŁAW

Bishop, papal secretary, historian of liturgy; b. 27 April 1939 in Raba Wyżna near Nowy Targ, Poland, son of a railway worker. In 1957 he began theological studies at the Kraków Archdiocesan Seminary, and was ordained a priest by Archbishop Karol Wojtyła in 1963. After several years of pastoral work in a parish, he becam a chaplain of Archbishop Wojtyła in Kraków. In Kraków, he pursued his studies at the Papal Faculty of Theology, finishing a licentiate in Theology as well as doctorate in the history of liturgy (1982). His dissertation, a study in the development of the cult of St. Stanislaus in Poland through the sixteenth century was published as a book in 1984. He served with distinction on Archdiocesan commissions concerned with liturgy and pastoral care in the 1970s.

After Karol Wojtyła's election as Pope John Paul II in 1978, Fr. Dziwisz was named his personal secretary, and editor of the Polish versions of all his papal documents. He discharged these duties with energy, discretion, and tact, accompanying the pope tirelessly on his many foreign travels. In 1996 he was named Pronotary Apostolic *De Numero,* and in 1998, he was consecrated by John Paul II Titular Bishop of San Leone, and was appointed Adjunct Prefect of the Papal House.

[PAUL RADZILOWSKI]

ENDO, SHUSAKU

Novelist; b. 27 March 1923, Tokyo, Japan, the son of Tsunehisa Endo, an employee of Yasuda Bank, and Ikuko Endo; d. 29 September 1996. The family moved to Manchuria in 1929 when his father was transferred there. After his parents' marital separation he returned with his mother to the Kobe area of Japan, where they lived with an aunt who was Catholic. His mother became a Catholic, and at her insistence Endo was baptized, receiving the name Paul.

Endo studied French literature at Keio Preparatory School, graduating in 1948. Two years later he went to France and studied modern Catholic literature; he was greatly influenced in methodology by François Mauriac, especially *Thérèse Desqueyroux* and its probing of the depth of human evil, but also Mauriac's break with the Versailles Garden formula of French psychological novels in favor of the realism of Dostoevsky. Existentialism in its myriad forms dominated the philosophical and literary expression of Endo's French world.

His novel *Chinmoku* (Silence) appeared in 1966 and established his reputation as a major author. Its story centers on the sixteenth and seventeenth century contact of the Jesuit mission with Japan and the subsequent persecution. It was an economic, political, and religious clash of East and West. His Life of Jesus was first published in magazine articles designed to introduce Christ to non-Christians; the book enjoyed phenomenal success, yet he felt that it needed continual revision to express his new faith insights.

Endo achieved a reputation as one of Japan's foremost and most prolific writers. His Catholic faith underscored his portrayal of life, the depths of evil together with the aspirations towards divine union. His greatest novel, Deep River, traces the religious journey of five Japanese to the Ganges River where God is symbolized with the name "Onion." Otsu, who reflects Endo himself speaks, "My trust is in the life of the Onion who endured genuine torment for the sake of love . . . as time passes, I feel that trust strengthening within me. I haven't been able to adapt to the thinking and the theology of Europe, but when I suffer all alone I can feel the smiling presence of my Onion, who knows all my trials." Endo spent his literary life delving into the unconscious of his characters. There was an East-West contrast throughout, a Buddhist-Christian dialogue, the encounter of world religions, and in it all there was his personal growth in Catholic faith reaching out to all cultures. Endo felt the basic human unity at the unconscious level seeking the ultimate in art, music, language, and culture.

He died 29 September 1996 in the embrace of his Church, receiving the last sacraments from his intimate priest friend Fr. William Johnston, S.J. His influence and the paths he has opened into interreligious dialogue remain a major legacy to be pursued as the Church continues to interact with the great religious traditions of Asia.

Bibliography: The Complete Literary Works of Shusaku Endo in fifteen volumes is under way at Shincho Publishing Company. Important works now translated into English include *Silence* (Kodansha International 1982); *Life of Jesus* (Tokyo: Tuttle, 1979); *Deep River* (Tokyo: Tuttle, 1994), *Foreign Studies* (Tokyo: Tuttle, 1989); *Golden Country* (Tokyo: Tuttle, 1970); *The Final Martyrs* (Tokyo: Tuttle, 1993); *Scandal* (Tokyo: Tuttle, 1988); *The Sea and Poison* (New York: Taplinger, 1972); *Volcano* (Tokyo: Tuttle, 1979); *When I Whistle* (Tokyo: Tuttle, 1974).

[PATRICK O'DONOGHUE]

EPISCOPAL CONFERENCES

Episcopal conferences embody the collegial (conciliar or synodal) exercise of church authority by the bishops of a region or a nation, arising from the recognition in *Lumen gentium,* no. 23, of subsidiarity on one hand and the personal responsibility of archdioceses and dioceses to collaborate on the other. Contemporary determinations about episcopal conferences flow from three historical items: the revision of the Code of Canon Law in 1983; the 1985 Synod of Bishops, held to celebrate the twentieth anniversary of the end of the Second Vatican Council; and *Apostolos suos,* the *motu proprio* of Pope John Paul II on 21 May 1998 that addresses the theological and juridical nature of episcopal conferences.

Conferences of bishops, or national episcopal conferences, originate during the nineteenth century in Eu-

Children dressed as the Dalmation dogs from the Disney film "101 Dalmatians" are greeted by Pope John Paul II and Stanisław Dziwisz in St. Peter's Square. (AP/Wide World Photos. Photograph by Plinio Lepri.)

rope—for example, Belgium (1830), Germany (1848), Austria (1849), and regional meetings in Italy—but they have deeper roots in the ancient practice of the Church to organize assemblies of bishops at the level of ecclesiastical provinces. In the Eastern Church, these provinces comprise metropolitan and suffragan dioceses; in the Latin Church, the archdioceses and dioceses of a particular geographic region form provinces. The latter have long standing ecclesiastical recognition according to canon 292 of the 1917 Code of Canon Law, while the former received definitive canonical status in 1965 at Vatican Council II with the decree *Christus Dominus,* nos. 37–38, and the specifications set forth by Pope Paul VI in his apostolic letter, *Ecclesiae sanctae* of 5 August 1966 (section 1, no. 41).

European assemblies of bishops had their importance recognized as akin to ecclesiastical provinces, but these meeting took place in a historical context of rising European nationalism that often cast liberalism and democracy as oppressors to institutional Catholicism, specifically to the Holy See. In the United States of America, the first national conference of bishops took place in September 1919, although annual meetings of the metropolitan archbishops took place in the final decades of the previous century. In subsequent years, the American episcopate met in annual conference and transacted business first as the National Catholic Welfare Conference and then after Vatican II under two titles: the National

Shusaku Endo. (AP/Wide World Photos. Reproduced by permission.)

Conference of Catholic Bishops and the United States Catholic Conference. In 2000, the episcopate reorganized again as the United States Conference of Catholic Bishops.

1983 Code of Canon Law. Chapter 4 of book 2, "The People of God," of the 1983 Code includes thirteen canons (447–59) dealing with the general nature and responsibility of episcopal conferences. The canons are largely derived from the conciliar decree *Christus Dominus* on the pastoral office of bishops in the Church. The canons on national conferences constitute a fourth illustration of the groupings of particular churches, or dioceses, in the organizational structure of the Catholic Church.

The canons embody two aspects of conferences in which they differ from the ancient tradition of particular councils: They are permanent bodies (c. 447), not occasional assemblies, and they have the canonical character of juridic persons in the Church (c. 449, §2). Canons 448 and 450 establish the membership of national conferences, respecting the competence of the Holy See sated in canon 449, §1. Canons 451–59 set the composition and operating procedures of the conference. Canon 455 merits particular notice. The canon deals with a great number of practical applications, but it also raises serious theo-

logical implications, precisely because it touches the autonomy of individual bishops and the relationship of diocesan bishops with each other and the Holy See. Early recognition of this difficulty appeared in an 8 November 1983 letter of the Cardinal Secretary of State to each national episcopal conference indicating where the conference (a) *may* and (b) *must* issue local norms (see *Communicationes* 15 (1983):135–39.)

1985 Synod of Bishops. With respect to conferences of bishops, the synod members wrestled with two tendencies: one seeing episcopal conferences as a centralizing influence in a nation or region and the other seeing the responsibility and innate power of the bishop of the individual, particular church. A 1988 letter from the Congregation of bishops focused on the theological and the juridic status of national conferences.

On the theological status, the letter repeatedly draws a sharp line between episcopal collegiality (itself the expression of the communion of the local churches) in the full or strict sense and in the partial or limited sense. They are judged collegial only in an analogical and inexact sense. Admitting that the remote foundation of conferences is in the particular (provincial or regional) councils held since the end of the second century, the text sharply distinguishes councils and conferences and dwells upon the pastoral utility of the conferences. The latter are said to lack any proper magisterial office, although their teachings are to be received with a "religious submission of mind" in accord with canon 753.

On the juridic status, the Roman letter dealt with the conferences in three sections: (1) restraints on teaching, conceived merely as "applying pronouncements of the magisterium of the universal Church"; (2) the distinction between the authority of the individual diocesan bishop and the conferences, with the actions of the conferences limited to "moral authority" in most instances; and (3) proposals for consensus for nonbinding decisions, with special attention to the danger of a conference's subsidiary organs, commissions, or offices being confused with the conference itself.

Critique of the Roman letter saw many of the concerns as matters of ecclesiastical polity rather than theology and church law. Challenges were made for more precision in terminology and a thorough grounding of both the theological and juridical status of national conferences in conciliar, canonical, papal, historical, and liturgical references. The response of the bishops of the United States was that a new draft should be prepared with the collaboration of representative bishops, canonists, theologians, and historians.

Apostolos suos. The *motu proprio* of 21 May 1998 represents the response to request of the 1988 synod of bishops and subsequent consultations. The document contains four sections. Section 1 traces major theological-historical moments of the collegial structure or permanent assembly of the apostles as constituted by the Lord Jesus. Section 2 addresses collegial union among bishops as it touches on the themes of unity, collegiality, and joint pastoral action. Section 3 sets forth Pope John Paul II's understanding of the conference of bishops as a permanent institution, the issues that currently call for the joint action of the bishops, the manner in which episcopal conferences are to organize territorially, their composition, especially with respect to deliberative or consultative voting power, and finally the authority of the episcopal conference with respect to the authority of the diocesan bishop and the requirements of a *recognitio* of the Apostolic See. Section 4 sets down complementary norms regarding the conference of bishops.

See Also: APOSTOLOS SUOS

[ARTHUR ESPELAGE]

ETCHEGARAY, ROGER

Cardinal, archbishop of Marseilles, president of Central Committee for the Jubilee of the Holy Year 2000; b. 25 September 1922, in Espelette, Basque region of France, to Jean-Baptiste Etchegaray and Aurélie Dufau. Studied for the priesthood first in the Petit Séminaire of Ustaritz and later in the Grand Séminaire of Bayonne. He was sent to Rome and studied in the Pontifical Gregorian University where he earned a licentiate in theology and a doctorate in canon law and civil law with a dissertation entitled "The baptism of the children of non-practicing Catholic parents." Ordained to the priesthood 13 July 1947, he did pastoral work in his diocese and was secretary to Bishop Léon-Albert Terrier who also appointed him secretary general of diocesan works of the Catholic Action. Bishop Paul Guyon, successor of Bishop Terrier and later cardinal, named Fr. Etchegaray vicar general and director of diocesan works of Catholic Action. From 1961 to 1966 he served as secretary adjunct of the Episcopal Conference of France. In 1962, Pope John XXIII appointed him domestic prelate. He became secretary of the Committee for relations between European Episcopal Conferences in 1965. This committee was the precursor of the Council of European Episcopal Conferences of which Msgr. Etchegaray was the first president from 1971 to 1979. He occupied the post of general secretary of the Episcopal Conference of France from 1966 until 1970.

Pope Paul VI named him titular bishop of Gemelle di Numidia and auxiliary of Paris in 1969. The following

Roger Etchegaray. (Catholic News Service.)

year he was promoted the archbishopric of Marseille. In 1975 Archbishop Etchegaray was elected president of the French Episcopal Conference and later that same year was named prelate of the *Mission de France,* a position he retained until 1983. He has been very active in the Synod of Bishops: he participated in twelve of its assemblies and was a member of the general secretariat from 1983 to 1987.

Pope John Paul II created Archbishop Etchegaray a cardinal priest in the consistory of 30 June 1979; he received the titular church of S. Leo I. He continued as archbishop of Marseilles till 1985. He was appointed president of the Pontifical Councils of Justice and Peace (1984–1998) and *Cor Unum* (1984–1995). Under instructions from Pope John Paul, Cardinal Etchegaray and Bishop Jorge Mejía, secretary of the Pontifical Council for Justice and Peace, prepared the outline and initial draft of the encyclical *Sollicitudo rei socialis.* Cardinal Etchegaray was also given responsibility for arranging the World Day of Prayer for Peace which brought religious leaders from around the world to Assisi in 1986. In 1994 he was named president of the Committee for the Grand Jubilee of the Holy Year 2000, thus being responsible for the organization of the Jubilee celebrations. In 1998, he was elevated to the order of cardinal bishops receiving the title of the suburbicarian see of Porto-Santa

Rufina, previously held by Cardinal Agostino Casaroli. Cardinal Etchegaray has been one of the most significant papal emissaries, undertaking diplomatic missions to Russia, China, Indonesia, Iran, and Iraq, as well as helping to arrange the papal visit to Cuba.

See Also: ASSISI, EUROPEAN SYNOD OF BISHOPS, SOLLICITUDO REI SOCIALIS

[SALVADOR MIRANDA]

ETERNAL WORD TELEVISION NETWORK (EWTN)

The Eternal Word Television Network (EWTN) transmits religious programming around the clock throughout the world. Its studios are located on the grounds of Our Lady of the Angels Monastery in Birmingham, Alabama. Under Catholic auspices, EWTN uses up-to-date technology to offer services that include television (wired and wireless cable, direct broadcast satellite), short-wave and AM/FM radio, news publishing, and online services (www.etwn.com).

The founder and supervisor of EWTN is Mother Angelica, a Franciscan nun. Born Rita Frances Rizzo on 20 April 1923 in Canton, Ohio, she joined the Poor Clares of Perpetual Adoration (PCPA) in Cleveland on 15 August 1944. From 1946 to 1961 she lived at the Santa Clara Monastery in Canton. With an intense desire to found a new convent, Mother Angelica began exploring possibilities. In 1961 an invitation came from Archbishop Thomas Toolan of the Mobile-Birmingham Diocese to establish a new convent in his diocese. In 1962, the monastery of Our Lady of the Angels was dedicated. During the early years of the Birmingham community, they found a number of ways to raise funds to keep the monastery going. They moved from making fishing lures to roasting peanuts and in 1973 decided to begin a book apostolate based on presentations given by Mother Angelica.

Mother Angelica's involvement in television ministry began in March 1978 when she was interviewed by a Chicago station. Following that interview she began videotaping programs for the Christian Broadcasting Network (CBN). By 1978, Mother Angelica had begun making plans for her own production studio to spread the Word and called it the Eternal Word Television Studio. Mother Angelica's dream was to reach common persons, teach them the various types of spirituality, provide family programming for children and adults, be a vehicle of expression for various Catholic organizations, and provide inexpensive but high quality programming for dioceses that could not afford to make their own programs. On 18 September 1980, she applied for a license from the Federal Communications Commission to activate the Eternal Word Television Network (EWTN).

When EWTN began transmission on 15 August 1981, the network reached sixty thousand homes; nineteen years later, the program could be seen in more than fifty-nine million homes around the world. In 1983, EWTN launched its flagship series "Mother Angelica Live." Cablecast live three nights each week, this program combined a Bible lesson taught by Mother Angelica with a talk show featuring prominent Catholic theologians, clergy, and lay persons, as well as entertainers and sports figures. Topics discussed ranged from the traditions of the Catholic faith to current church issues.

What began as a beam of faith has evolved into an international network transmitting Christian programs with a Catholic point of view. EWTN, marketed as the global Catholic network, reaches Europe, Africa, and the Pacific Rim. In 1996 EWTN expanded with Spanish television and radio services in the USA market. In 1999 EWTN announced La Red Global Catolica, the twenty-four-hour Spanish cable network, and Radio Catolica Mundial, EWTN Spanish radio network, which are available not only within the United States but in Central and South America. Hispanic programming originates from over a dozen countries and reflects the diversity of the Hispanic community.

A state-of-the-art web site (www.ewtn.com) reflects a diversity of services and select information concerning the Catholic Church. It offers a library of select church documents, recent statements by the pope and church leaders, a gallery of religious art, catalogue for purchasing Catholic publications and religious art, Catholic Headlines News from Catholic World News, Vatican Information Services and Zenit, as well as "Life on the Rock," which is directed toward young people in their search for networking into Catholic youth groups, Catholic colleges, and religious communities. Visitors to the web site can download video and audio programs and clips to their computers.

In 1984, EWTN became the first religious network to receive one of the cable industries' ACE (Award for Cable Excellence) nominations for a series targeted to a specific audience (the family). In the same year, Mother Angelica received the Gabriel Award for Personal Achievement with EWTN from the National Catholic Association of Communicators (Unda-USA).

Bibliography: "The Electronic Church Spreads the Word," *U.S. News & World Report* (23 April 1984). "Determination," *Cablevision* (30 Jan. 1984). "Satellites that Serve Us," *National Geographic* (Sept. 1983). "A New Cable-TV Network with a Difference," *New York Times* (15 Aug. 1981). SISTER M. RAPHAEL, *My Life with Mother Angelica* (Our Lady of the Angels Monastery 1982). "The Broadcasting Nun," *New Covenant* (Nov. 1984). D. O'NEIL, *Mother Angelica: Her Life Story* (New York 1986).

[A. A. ZUKOWSKI]

EVANGELIZATION, NEW

"New evangelization" designates a renewed approach adopted by the Church, in the spirit of Vatican II, for announcing Jesus Christ to the secularized minds and cultures of our times. Used notably by Pope John Paul II, the term has become common in the Church and was described as an effort "new in its ardor, new in its method, new in its expression" [speech to CELAM, 9 March 1983].

Characteristics. The characteristics of new evangelization—also called second evangelization, or re-evangelization—come to light when compared to "first" evangelization. The aim of first evangelization is to reveal the newness of Christ the Redeemer to peoples who do not know him, in order to convert, baptize them, and implant the Church in their midst. Over the centuries, whole nations and traditional cultures have thus been evangelized by a slow process that progressively transformed attitudes, behaviors, and all aspects of individual and social life. Key figures of the first evangelization are well known: Saints Paul, Irenaeus, Patrick, Willibrod, Boniface, Cyril and Methodius, and Francis Xavier. The first evangelization is far from being finished; the mission of the Church "is still only beginning," wrote John Paul II in *Redemptoris missio*, noting that "the number of those who do not know Christ and do not belong to the Church is constantly on the increase" [no. 1; 3]. The current epoch has even made the first evangelization more complex: in China, in India, in Japan, in Muslim and Buddhist regions, and also in many sectors of modern societies apparently closed to the message of Christ.

In contrast, the second evangelization tries to reach populations that were Christianized in the past, but are now living in a secularized culture that depreciates Christian values, diffuses religious indifference, confines religion to the private sphere, and even at times persecutes or marginalizes believers and their communities.

Obstacles to the New Evangelization. The meaning of the new evangelization is further discovered by identifying the people to whom it is destined. In general, they are those whose faith has been so weakened and dissolved that they are effectively in need of a new discovery of Jesus Christ. These persons are most difficult to reach: their faith has faded into a vague sentiment, a residual interest that verges on indifference or practical agnosticism. Religion does not seem to be significant for them anymore. Christian behavior has been reduced to a cultural routine, as is witnessed by the secularized celebration of Christmas and Easter.

For some people, faith has been uprooted because the first evangelization never penetrated beyond the surface: religious convictions were never interiorized because of a lack of ongoing Christian formation shared in a faithful community. For others, faith has been repressed and rejected as a fearful reminiscence of moral alienation. Because of scarce, superficial, or even unbalanced teaching, they confuse faith with an unbearable imposition of moral interdictions. Faith really never grew beyond an infantile sentiment later rejected as an apparently liberating step toward adulthood.

Worshipers in Kinshasa, Zaire. (AP/Wide World Photos. Photograph by David Guttenfelder.)

Still one of the most disturbing situations is the spread of an attitude of moral autarky, whereby a person retreats into a purely subjective morality, rejects all objective norms, mistrusts all authority and doctrine, and refuses any transcendent commitment. This is one of the most formidable obstacles the evangelizer must overcome in order to announce Jesus Christ to modern culture.

In all the situations described above, the evangelizer should never assume that faith is totally dead. It may remain as a dormant faith, substituted by other interests, such as worldly prestige, success, money, and pleasure. However, the evangelizer must be convinced that in every human heart there is ultimately a thirst for peace, enlightenment, and happiness, which can reveal an unconscious sign of hope in Christ the Redeemer.

Evangelization of Cultures. What emerges as a central problem for evangelizers is the growing impact of today's cultures on people's moral and religious life, as Vatican II had clearly foreseen. With the advance of modernity in all countries, there is no longer a "support culture" as in past societies, where Christian traditions, lifestyles, and institutions used to sustain one another. Now all can feel the pervading influence of a secularized attitudes; all are immersed in a "culture of indifference," leading to the devaluation or even the elimination of Christian faith. The Church, attentive to this fact, has entered into a new pastoral strategy aiming at evangelizing cultures themselves, which entails converting together "the personal and collective conscience of people" [Evangelii nuntiandi, no. 18]. This is one of the newest aspects of the new evangelization, which requires a practical redefinition of pastoral work and a reconversion of all evangelizers.

The leading assumption is that cultures themselves, as well as persons, have to be evangelized. Culture is to be viewed as a typical human reality and, therefore, the object of mercy and redemption on the part of Christ, whose death and resurrection extends salvation to all that is human: persons and their creations and cultures. What is indispensable is a renewed pastoral approach including, first, the ability to perceive the cultural dimension of evangelization; and, second, the readiness of all evangelizers, from the bishops to the laity, to join forces in such a complex but rewarding task. Cultural analysis must lead to cultural evangelization. It is less a question for experts than a new kind of sensitivity. When Christians look at cultures with the eyes of the Redeemer, they are inspired by their faith to discern in their milieu the dominant values, the current attitudes, the modes of behavior that exert an often decisive influence for both good and evil. They have to discern the cultural traits that contradict the gospel and are destructive of human dignity. Together they promote the liberation, purification, and elevation of cultures by announcing their salvation in Christ. They invite all sectors of society to adopt a Christian way of living in family, school, hospital, work, leisure, the university, the media, and economic and political life.

In a pluralistic world, evangelizing culture cannot be construed as imposing a Christian social system, or attempting to restore Christendom. Rather, it is a free call to hear the message of the gospel, addressed to those who wish to hear it willingly. While freely proclaiming the full message of the gospel, the Church enters into an open dialogue with all people of good will who can share such evangelical values as love, peace, justice, compassion for the poor, the dignity of the person and the family, solidarity of all men and women, respect for nature and its development, and the moral accountability of everyone before the divine Creator and Lawgiver. An ecumenical and interreligious dialogue is necessary for reaching all men and women who are seeking what moral and spiritual force is capable of guaranteeing the humanum. Evangelizing cultures starts from the theological conviction that the Holy Spirit is at work in all human hearts, inspiring the evangelizers as well as the evangelized, predisposing every single conscience and each culture to accept the redemption achieved through the mystery of the death and resurrection of Jesus Christ.

The new evangelization refers to the penetration of the gospel in mindsets more than to its geographical diffusion, as Paul VI vividly expressed in *Evangelii nuntiandi:*

> For the Church it is not simply a matter of preaching the gospel message in ever wider geographical areas or to ever larger populations. It is also a matter of reaching and overturning, by the force of the gospel message, the criteria of judgement, the ruling values, the points of interest, the lines of thinking, the sources of inspiration, and the patterns of living among human beings that are contrary to God's message and salvation plan [no. 19].

This approach is now being called inculturation, that is "the intimate transformation of authentic cultural values through their integration in Christianity and the insertion of Christianity in the various human cultures" [*Remptoris missio*, no. 52].

The Church is now strongly committed to the task of the new evangelization on all continents, notably with synods held in Africa, Asia, America, Europe, and Oceania. In Western countries, Catholics have been generous in supporting missions abroad, but many remain hesitant to attempt the evangelization of their compatriots who still ignore Christ. Some of them fear that "evangelizing" could be confused with the "proselytizing" of fundamentalist groups or might infringe on private beliefs and convictions. This cultural barrier is now being overcome, as shown in the more frequent use of the terms "inculturation," "re-evangelization," and "evangelization of culture" by Catholics in North America and other Western countries. They are all ways of expressing the need for the new evangelization.

Bibliography: H. CARRIER, *Evangelizing the Culture of Modernity* (Maryknoll 1993); *Guide pour the l'inculturation de l'Évangile* (Rome: Editrice Pontifica Università Gregoriana, 1997).

[H. CARRIER]

FOCOLARE MOVEMENT

The worldwide Focolare Movement (Work of Mary) embodies a specific form of spirituality best described as the Gospel seen from the perspective of unity; the aim is to strive for the unity Jesus prayed for on the night before he died; "Father, may they all be one" (see Jn 17:21). Focolare had its origin in 1943 in Trent, Italy, when a young schoolteacher, Chiara Lubich, together with a few young women, amid the devastation of World War II, came to see that there is but one ideal that can never fail.

This "ideal" is God, who is love. They focused their lives on the gospel and many others followed. Within a few months, over 500 people had joined them in living what was emerging as a new spirituality in the Church: the "spirituality of unity," which is based on the mutual love inherent in Jesus' new commandment. It is a way of going to God together, which brings about a change in individuals, in groups and society, uniting people beyond all their differences.

In 1962 Focolare was initially approved by Pope John XXIII, and received the continued blessing of Pope Paul VI, who on 8 February 1978, said to a group of its members: "Be faithful to your inspiration which is so modern and so fruitful." The movement spread to every continent and came into special prominence in 1977 when its foundress, Chiara Lubich, was awarded the Templeton Prize for progress in religion.

The spirituality of the Focolare Movement bears striking kinship with the spirit of the Second Vatican Council. The council frequently recalls the promise of Jesus to be present wherever two or more are united in his name (Mt 18.20). The council's stress on unity is well known. "For the promotion of unity belongs to the innermost nature of the Church" (*Gaudium et spes* 42). These are only two of the fundamental points of the spirituality of the movement.

The Focolare Movement has many branches, including five that are movements in their own right, though animated by an identical spirituality and represented in the General Coordinating Council of Focolare in Rome and locally. At the core are the focolarini, lay men and women living in separate communities called Focolare houses. Following the evangelical counsels of poverty, chastity, and obedience, the focolarini work as other lay persons in regular jobs and professions. Their goal is to maintain unity and hence the presence of the risen Lord. Some married persons, while continuing to live in their families, participate fully in the life of the Focolare houses.

Also part of the Focolare Movement are the Volunteers, who emerged in the wake of the Hungarian Revolution of 1956. They are lay people wholly committed to living the spirituality of unity and, through it, to renewing society.

The young generations make up three Movements known as the Gen (New Generation), first formed in 1966. They are divided according to their age into the Gen II for teenagers and young adults; Gen III for children; and the Gen IV for the little ones.

The priests' movement is made up of diocesan priests committed to living the Focolare spirituality.

Often the life of unity of these priests brings about a transformation of parish life. Seminarians living this spirit make up the GenS (Gen Seminarians).

There are also bishops who share in the spirituality of the Focolare, as well as men and women religious, who are associated with Focolare while continuing to live in their own communities. Focolare spirituality helps them to see how the specific charism of their founders can be lived in the present time. They also cultivate a rapport of unity with other religious orders and congregations. Young religious living this spirit form the GenR (Gen Religious).

Between 1966 and 1984, a further development saw the emergence of large-scale but less formally organized bodies within the Focolare: New Humanity, New Families, Youth for a United World, Young for Unity, Parish Movement; all of these aim to bring a spirit of unity into their respective environments and fields of endeavor.

At the international headquarters of the Focolare, the president (who according to its statutes will always be a lay woman) is helped by a council in which all branches of the Focolare and all aspects of the life of its members are represented. The Focolare throughout the world is organized in seventy-five "zones" (i.e., geographical territories), each with its own council acting in unity with the international headquarters.

Wherever the Focolare Movement exists various ecumenical activities take place. Of particular interest is the Ecumenical Center of Ottmaring, Germany, where Lutherans and Catholics work together, though they live in separate communities. Over the years, the Focolare has built relationships with many ecclesial movements and associations within the Catholic Church. The movement is present throughout the Christian world and has also spread, particularly since 1977, among non-Christian religions.

The Focolare carries on social, cultural, and economic activities in many countries. Every year summer meetings called Mariapolis (City of Mary), are held for those who wish to come into contact with Focolare. The goal of the Mariapolis is to generate the presence of Christ in the community through the practice of mutual and constant charity. Permanent Mariapolises exist in Italy, Africa, Argentina, and Brazil. The movement operates "New City" publishing houses in many countries. The Focolare monthly magazine New/Living City, is devoted to the spirituality of the movement, and is published in twenty-four languages. In the United States the Mariapolis Luminosa, New City Press, and Living City magazine are located in Hyde Park, N.Y. In 1991 the movement launched the "Economy of Sharing," a set of guidelines intended to reconcile the often conflicting worlds of economics and solidarity.

On the vigil of Pentecost 1998, during the meeting of ecclesial movements and new communities with Pope John Paul II, Chiara Lubich described the essence of that something new the Focolare offers. "Holy Father, you identified love as the 'inspiring spark' of all that is done under the name of Focolare, and it is really true. It is the driving force of our movement. Being love and spreading love is our general aim. In fact, the Focolare Movement is called to bring an invasion of love into the world."

See Also: CHIARA LUBICH

Bibliography: JIM GALLAGHER, *A Woman's Work: A Biography of the Focolare Movement and Its Founder* (New York, 1990).C. LUBICH, *May They All Be One* (New York, 1997); *Unity and Jesus Forsaken* (New York, 1997).

[R. D. TETREAU/GARY BRANDL/ANNE LINGLEY]

FUCHS, JOSEF

Moral theologian; b. Bergisch Gladbach, Germany, 5 July 1912. Fuchs entered the diocesan seminary of Cologne in 1931 and was ordained a priest of that diocese in 1937. He studied at the Gregorian University, receiving licentiates in philosophy and theology. In 1938 he entered the German province of the Society of Jesus and received an S.T.D. from the Jesuit theologate at Falkenberg, Holland, in 1940. After four years in parish work, he returned to study, receiving a Th.D. from the University of Münster in 1946. Having taught moral theology at St. George Hochschüle from 1947, Fuchs was appointed to the faculty of the Gregorian University in Rome in 1954. Although he reached the mandatory retirement age of seventy in 1982, he remained active, providing consultation to faculty and students of the Gregorian.

A prolific author, Fuchs's writings include fourteen books, several of which are collections of essays, as well as more than fifty other articles. Over the years, he gave extended attention to a wide variety of issues. His early writings focus on the theology of sexuality and marriage in St. Thomas Aquinas. Between 1958 and 1960 he published four textbooks on various areas of moral theology patterned on the classic "manualist" tradition but introducing new insights, which he used in his teaching at the Gregorian University and which were exported by his multinational student population. The early 1960s were especially fruitful, resulting in articles on new issues in sexual ethics, the place of law in human society, and a sundry other topics. In 1965 he published *Natural Law: A Theological Investigation,* a major work in the field of Catholic moral theology and a pivotal document in Fuchs's own intellectual history. It coincided with a long series of publications exploring the implications for moral theology of the vision of Vatican II, particularly as that vision is articulated in *Gaudium et spes.*

A major turning point in his career was Fuchs's membership on the Papal Commission on Family, Births, and Population of 1965–68. He is alleged to have been an author of the so-called "majority report" that Pope Paul VI ultimately rejected in the writing of *Humanae Vitae.* In any case, Fuchs's views on the permanence, universality, and exceptionlessness of concrete moral norms changed as a result of his reflections during these years.

Though Fuchs has addressed a variety of specific questions, his abiding focus, particularly in the years since Vatican II, has been the core commitments on which a Christian morality is based. He discussed the character of the natural law, the relationship of human morality and Christian life, the identity of the moral person, the shape and limits of moral norms, the role of conscience, issues of secularism and religious commitment, and the significance of moral community, especially the Catholic Church as an institution, for personal moral decision making. In many of these areas, Fuchs gives evidence of being deeply influenced by the theological anthropology of Karl Rahner.

Fuchs's influence has been worldwide, thanks to his role at the Gregorian University. That influence is greater yet because he taught in the ecclesiastical period prior to, during, and since the Second Vatican Council. Indeed, he is both a commentator on and a major contributor to the renewal of moral theology occurring in this period. Along with his colleague at the Alphonsianum University, Bernard Häring (also born in 1912), Fuchs has been described as a "revisionist" and associated with the methodology of proportionalism.

Bibliography: F. FUCHS, *Natural Law: A Theological Investigation* (New York 1965); *Human Values and Christian Morality* (Dublin 1970); *Personal Responsibility and Christian Morality* (Washington 1983); *Christian Ethics in a Secular Arena* (Washington 1984); *Christian Morality: The Word Becomes Flesh* (Washington 1987); *Moral Demands & Personal Obligations* (Washington 1993). T. O'CONNELL, *Changing Roman Catholic Moral Theology: A Study in Josef Fuchs* (Ann Arbor 1974).

[T. E. O'CONNELL]

GAGNON, EDOUARD

Cardinal, president of the Pontifical Council for the Family; b. 15 January 1918, Port-Daniel, Québec. From a family of eleven children, Gagnon was educated at Collège de L'Assomption, Universite de Montréal, graduating with a B.A. in 1936. He was ordained a priest of the Society of Saint Sulpice (a congregation committed to the education of priests) in Montréal in 1940 and received a D.Th. from the Université de Montréal in 1941. He went on to do graduate work in canon law and received a

J.C.D. from Laval University, Québec City, in 1945. Gagnon served as a professor at the Université de Montréal from 1945 to 1954 and then as rector of the Grand Seminary, St. Boniface, Manitoba, from 1954 to 1961. From 1961 to 1964 he assumed new duties in the same capacity at a seminary in Manizales, Columbia. Thus began an extensive familiarity with South America, ensuring both his rich fluency in Spanish and Portuguese and a life-long interest in the social and ecclesiastical issues on the continent, particularly in the area of family planning.

Gagnon attended the Second Vatican Council as a peritus with responsibility for lay auditors, and served as a provincial of the Society of Saint-Suplice in Canada, Japan, and Latin America in the late 1960s. In 1969 he was consecrated bishop of the Diocese of Saint-Paul, Alberta, but resigned his pastoral duties in 1972 because of ill health. In the same year he became rector of the Pontifical Canadian College in Rome and began what was to become a permanent residency in the city.

His association with the Pontifical Council for the Family dates from 1973, when he was appointed its first vice-president. In 1983 he was named archbishop of Giustiniana Prima and appointed pro-president of the council. Two years later he was created a cardinal deacon with the deaconry of S. Elena fuori Porta Prenestina and duly appointed president of the council, a position he retained until 1990. He has been a prolific writer in the areas of moral theology, canon law, and the sociology of the family.

Cardinal Gagnon, although no longer resident in Canada, retained a strong interest in his homeland, and enthusiastically promoted the cause for canonization of the first Canadian-born saint, Marguerite d'Youville, founder of the Sisters of Charity in the early 1700s in Quebec.

See Also: ST MARGUERITE D'YOUVILLE

[MICHAEL HIGGINS]

GANTIN, BERNARDIN

Cardinal, dean of the College of Cardinals; b. 8 May 1922, Toffo, Dahomey (now Benin), the son of a railroad employee. His last name means "iron tree" (Gan=tree and tin=iron) and this is reflected in his coat of arms. In 1936 he entered the minor seminary of his country and later continued his priestly studies in the Seminary of Ouidah, being ordained a priest on 14 January 1951 in Cotonou. After teaching languages in the seminary for two years, he was sent to the Pontifical Urbanian Athe-

Bernardin Cardinal Gantin. (Catholic News Service.)

naeum and the Pontifical Lateran University in Rome, obtaining licentiates in theology and canon law. When he was preparing his doctoral dissertation, Pope Pius XII named him titular bishop of Tipasa di Mauritania and auxiliary of Cotonou. Gantin was consecrated bishop in 1957 in St. Peter's basilica by Cardinal Eugène Tisserant, dean of the College of Cardinals. In 1960, Bishop Gantin was promoted to the metropolitan see of Cotonou. As archbishop, Gantin promoted educational institutions and the formation of catechists and also supported and fomented autochthonous vocations to the priesthood and the religious life. During those years he also was president of the regional episcopal conference which included Dahomey, Togo, Ivory Coast, Upper Volta, Sénégal, Nigeria and New Guinea. He was one of the fathers of the Second Vatican Council.

Pope Paul VI called Gantin to Rome and successively appointed him secretary-adjunct of the Sacred Congregation for the Evangelization of Peoples (1971), secretary of the same congregation (1973), vice-president of the Pontifical Commission for Justice and Peace (1975), and then its pro-president (1976). In 1977 the pope created him cardinal deacon of the Sacro Cuore di Cristo Re, and two days later he became president of the Justice and Peace commission. He took part in the two conclaves of 1978, and Pope John Paul I named him president of the Pontifical Council "Cor Unum."

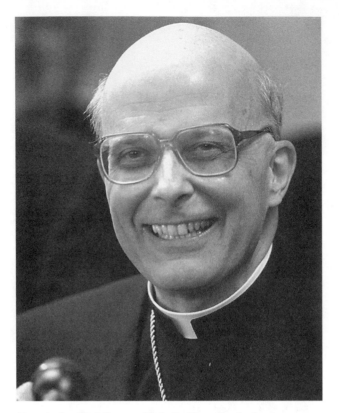

Francis Cardinal George. (Catholic News Service.)

Cardinal Gantin has attended 14 of the assemblies of the Synod of Bishops and was a president-delegate to the assembly of 1980. In 1982, he accompanied Pope John Paul II in his papal visit to Benin; he was the only one to upstage the pontiff, receiving the most enthusiastic cheers from the crowd. In the change of leadership of the Curia in 1984, John Paul II appointed Cardinal Gantin prefect of the Congregation for Bishops and, as such, president of the Pontifical Commission for Latin America. He occupied both posts for fourteen years before resigning them when he reached the mandatory retirement age. At the time of his appointment he opted for order of cardinal priests and his deaconry was elevated *pro illa vice* to a title. Two years later, the pope elevated him to cardinal bishop of the title of the suburbicarian see of Palestrina. In 1993 the cardinal bishops elected him dean of the College of Cardinals and as such he also assumed the title of the see of Ostia.

[SALVADOR MIRANDA]

GEORGE, FRANCIS E.

Cardinal, archbishop of Chicago; b. 16 January 1937, Chicago, Ill., to Francis J. George and Julia R. McCarthy. George enrolled at Saint Henry Preparatory Seminary, Belleville, Illinois, where he entered the Missionary Oblates of Mary Immaculate (OMI) 14 August 1957. He studied theology at the University of Ottawa, Canada, and was ordained a priest 21 December 1963. After ordination he earned a master's degree in philosophy at the Catholic University of America in 1965, a doctorate in American philosophy at Tulane University in 1970, and a master's in theology from the University of Ottawa. During those years, he taught philosophy at the Oblate Seminary, Pass Christian, Mississippi (1964–69); Tulane University (1968); and Creighton University (1969–1973). From 1973 to 1974 he was provincial superior of the Midwestern province, headquartered in St Paul, Minnesota, and from 1974 to 1986 he served in Rome as vicar general of the Oblates of Mary Immaculate. Upon his return to the United States he was named coordinator of the Circles of Fellow for the Cambridge Center for the Study of Faith and Culture in Cambridge, Massachusetts (1987–90). During that time he obtained a doctorate in sacred theology from the Pontifical University Urbaniana in Rome (1988).

Pope John Paul II named George bishop of Yakima, Washington, in 1990, and in 1996 made him archbishop of Portland, Oregon. Less than a year later, on 8 April 1997, John Paul II appointed him archbishop of Chicago, the first native son to be named to the see. By reason of this office Archbishop George became Chancellor of the Catholic Church Extension Society and the University of Saint Mary of the Lake, Mundelein, Illinois. In January 1998 Pope John Paul announced Archbishop George's elevation to the College of Cardinals with the titular church of San Bartolomeo all'Isola. The pope appointed him as a member of the General Assembly of the Synod of Bishops on Consecrated Life, and named him a delegate and one of two special secretaries at the Synod for America in 1997. Cardinal George serves on several committees of the National Conference of Catholic Bishops, and since 1990 has been episcopal moderator and member of the board of the National Catholic Office for Persons with Disabilities. He brings personal experience to this latter role because a bout with polio in his youth left him with permanent damage to his legs. Since his arrival in Chicago, Cardinal George's background has shaped his vision and priorities for the Archdiocese. His experience with the disability community has made him a forceful advocate for all life issues. His teaching and higher education experiences have led him to accept frequent invitations to speak at universities and to describe the relationship between Faith and Culture. His membership in a missionary congregation supports his strong interest in evangelization, the subject of his first pastoral letter in Chicago. His publications include several books and many articles on religious life, inculturation, and pastoral issues.

Bibliography: Among his many publications are: *Incultura-tion and Ecclesial Communion* (Rome: Urbaniana Press, 1990); ''Evangelizing American Culture,'' in *The New Catholic Evangelization,* ed. K. BOYACK, Mahwah, N.Y.: Paulist Press, 1992), 42–55; ''Bishops and the Splendor of the Truth,'' in *The Splendor of the Truth and Health Care,* ed. RUSSELL E. SMITH, Braintree, Mass.: The Pope John XXIII Medical-Moral Research and Education Center, 1995), 17–28; ''Institutional Conversion at the Turn of the Millennium,'' *Seminarium,* (1999): 135–47.

[LOUIS J. CAMELI]

GLEMP, JÓZEF E.

Cardinal and archbishop of Warsaw, Poland; b. 18 December, 1929 in Inowrocław, Poland. As a teenager Józef Glemp was a forced laborer on a German farm. He was ordained a priest at Gniezno in 1956, and after two years of pastoral work in parishes, he studied Civil and Canon law at the Gregorian University in Rome, earning his doctorate in 1964. He soon proved a talented canon lawyer and administrator, serving from 1967 to 1979 as a member of the secretariat of Stefan Cardinal Wyszyński, Archbishop of Gniezno and Warsaw, and Primate of Poland.

He was named Bishop of Warmia in 1979 and was consecrated 21 April of that year. After the death of Cardinal Wyszyński, he was named Archbishop Metropolitan of Gniezno and Warsaw, and Primate of Poland on 7 July 1981. On 2 February 1983 Pope John Paul II appointed him Cardinal-Presbyter of Sancta Maria trans Tiberim. In 1992 he gave up the office of Archbishop of Gniezno when it was separated from personal unions with the Warsaw Archdiocese, but he retained the title of Primate of Poland, which had traditionally been attached to the Gniezno see.

[PAUL RADZILOWSKI]

GRAY, GORDON JOSEPH

Cardinal, archbishop of St. Andrews and Edinburgh; b. 10 August 1910, Leith, Edinburgh, Scotland; d. 19 July 1993, Edinburgh, Scotland. Gray began studying for the priesthood at St. Joseph's College in Mark Cross and continued at St. John's Seminary, Wonersh. Following his ordination to the priesthood, 15 June 1935, he served as assistant in St. Andrews (1935–41), where his uncle was parish priest. He received an M.A. from the University of St. Andrews in 1939, becoming the first Catholic priest to graduate from that school in modern times. After parish duty in the Scottish Borders (1941–47), he was appointed rector of the junior seminary at St. Mary's College, Blairs.

In 1951 Fr. Gray was nominated archbishop of St. Andrews and Edinburgh. During his thirty-four years of service in that position, he opened thirty new parishes, and oversaw the building of thirty-seven new churches. He founded St. Andrew's College, Drygrange, Melrose, enabling students for the priesthood to be formed and educated within the archdiocese. The growth of the church in these years coincided with prospering ecumenical relations; in 1968 Archbishop Gray became the first Catholic since the Reformation to preach from John Knox's pulpit in St. Andrews. The next year he preached in St. Mary's Episcopal Cathedral. Archbishop Gray was the first bishop in the world to respond to Pope Pius XII's appeal to dioceses to send priests to the missions (encyclical *Fldei donum* [1957]). He sent priests first to Uganda and Nto Edino (Nigeria), and later to Bauchi in Northern Nigeria. The relationship with Bauchi was to continue for many years, and became the focus of missionary activity in the archdiocese. After the Second Vatican Council, he served for six years as chairman of the International Commission for English in the Liturgy

Pope Paul VI created him cardinal with the title Santa Clara a Vigna Clara in 1969, the first resident cardinal in Scotland since the Reformation. This event was welcomed with joy within the Catholic community, and generally within the wider Scottish community. He participated in the conclaves that elected John Paul I and John Paul II, and welcomed the latter on his visit to Scotland in 1982. He retired as archbishop in 1985, and spent nine years in Edinburgh before his death on 19 July 1993.

[MICHAEL PURCELL]

GRÉGOIRE, PAUL

Cardinal, archbishop of Montreal; b. 24 October 1911 in Verdun, Montreal south; d. 30 October 1990; the eldest in a family of three boys until the onset of the Great Depression when his parents adopted another nine children. Grégoire entered the Grand Séminaire de Montréal and was ordained to the priesthood on 22 May 1937.

After ordination Grégoire pursued doctoral studies at the University of Montreal, writing a dissertation on John Dewey's philosophy of education; he also earned a licentiate in sacred letters, a masters degree in history, and a diploma in pedagogy from the University of Montreal. In 1942 Grégoire was appointed director of students at the Séminaire de Saint-Thérèse, Blainville, as well as instructor in the philosophy of education at l'École normale secondaire and l'Institut pédagogique, teacher training schools he would replace with the Institut Catholique de Montréal in 1979. In 1950 Grégoire's involvement in education took yet another turn when Archbishop Paul Émile Léger asked him to accept the chaplain's position at the University of Montreal, a position he cherished until his advancement to the episcopacy.

Pope John XXIII named Grégoire auxiliary bishop of Montreal in 1961. He was appointed apostolic administrator in 1967, and archbishop the following year, after Léger's resignation.

Although Grégoire's more unassuming, self-effacing, and reflective bearing was a marked contrast to that of his predecessor, Grégoire and Léger did share a common commitment to the preferential option for the poor: Léger resigned his position as archbishop to live among the lepers of Africa and Grégoire demonstrated his own concern for the disadvantaged by waiting tables at the Accueil Bonneau soup kitchen for homeless men in Montreal, by founding the Maison du Père as a men's refuge from the streets (the Maison du Père is generally considered to be Grégoire's proudest accomplishment), and by establishing the Résidence du Vieux Port for alcoholic and dysfunctional men. By way of implementing the directives of Vatican II, Grégoire established consultative councils and augmented the active role of his auxiliaries.

On his seventy-fifth birthday, Grégoire dutifully submitted his resignation, but rather than accepting it John Paul II elevated him to the college of cardinals on 28 June 1988. In the summer of 1990, Grégoire was diagnosed with the stomach cancer that claimed his life on 30 October of that year. He was laid to rest in the episcopal crypt at Mary Queen of the World Cathedral in Montreal.

Bibliography: PAUL GRÉGOIRE, "The Church in Montreal on the Eve of the Olympics," *L'Osservatore Romano,* English edition, no. 32 (5 August 1976): 7–8. "Son Excellence Monseigneur Paul Grégoire, archevêque de Montréal." *L'Église de Montréal* 45 (4 December 1986): 935–951.

[D. R. LETSON]

GRIFFITHS, BEDE

Benedictine monk, writer; b. Walton-on-Thames, England, 1906; d. Shantivanam Ashram, Tamil Nadu, India, 13 May 1993. In 1932 Bede Griffiths entered the Roman Catholic Church; a few months later, he joined the Benedictine Abbey of Prinknash. For fifteen years he hardly left the cloister and relished the order and peace of monastic life. However, his study of Indian religion and philosophy stirred another level of his search for wholeness, and, in 1955, he left for India "to find the other half of my soul." There he learned Sanskrit and in 1968 took over direction of the Benedictine ashram of Shantivanam, which had been founded by the two great pioneers of an Indianized Christianity, Jules Monchanin and Henri le Saux (Abhishiktananda).

In India Griffiths formed a small, fragile community of great international influence that symbolized his deepest beliefs and intuitions. Among these were the need for a truly Asian Christianity reexpressing its faith through the terms of its own philosophy and scriptures. He saw modern Christianity at a crossroads comparable to that faced in the primitive Church when a Jewish framework of ideas and symbols struggled with those of the Gentile world. In his early days in India he met with official and semi-official opposition to his ideas and to his new form of ashramic-monastic life, but toward the end of his life he received official approval. He was always quick to confront and debate the reactionary forces of a eurocentric Christianity, either in India or in the West, and to point out what he saw as general inherent tendencies of all Semitic religions. For him these were the centrality of the dualistic model of seeing God, the domination of male symbolism and leadership, and the intolerance of exclusive claims to truth and salvation. In this spirit, for example, his revision of the psalter for ashram worship excised curses and denunciatory verses.

An anthology of world scriptures published posthumously illustrated Griffiths's belief that all religions originate in an intuition or experience of *advaita* or nonduality. They then decline into excessive rationalism, with its consequent rigidities of dualism and exclusivism, before ascending back through their contemplative traditions to a vision of simplicity and universalism. This latter belief underlies the importance he attributed to the influence of his fellow Benedictine John Main in restoring a method of contemplative meditation to Christianity from within the Christian monastic tradition. Griffiths's last book, *The New Creation in Christ,* takes Main's ideas on contemplation and the modern pursuit of community and personal wholeness as its inspiration for affirming a renewed tradition of lay monasticism. This book dispels any idea that Griffiths's universalist vision of religion resulted in any ultimate syncretism or dilution of Christian specificity.

With characteristic lucidity and elegance of literary style, Bede Griffiths wrote on Indian Christianity, modern Church controversies, Indian scripture, the meeting of East and West, and the encounter of modern science and religious mysticism. Despite his prophetic contemporaneity and inclusivity of vision, Griffiths harbored a deep distrust of modern technological civilization. He believed in the evolutionary movement toward global unity but saw irreconcilable self-contradictions at the core of modern society. He lived and taught from this tension without personal dogmatism and with a growing sweetness of nature that touched the hearts of his listeners around the world during the extensive travels of his last years.

After his stroke in 1990, Griffiths described a personal transformation and affective liberation that he attributed to the awakening of the *muladara chakra.* At Oxford he had struggled through an intellectual journey that took him from fin de siècle aestheticism to twentieth century Romanticism. In this he was accompanied by C.S. Lewis, a friend for forty years, who described him as "one of the toughest dialecticians of my acquaintance." Yet, it was only after a battle with religious faith and an experiment with utopian living that he accepted the fully spiritual context of his pursuit for truth and wholeness.

Bede Griffiths, in his life and teaching, symbolized the meeting between Christianity and the other world religions, which he considered the most significant event of the twentieth century. As such a symbol (don and sannyasi), he and his writings have continued to inspire the interfaith movement since his death.

Bibliography: BEDE GRIFFITHS was the author of a number of books, more than 300 articles, and several audio and video recordings. His books include an autobiography entitled *The Golden String* (London 1954); *Christian Ashram* (London 1966); *Vedanta and Christian Faith* (London 1973); *Return to the Centre* (London 1978); *The Marriage of East and West* (London 1982); *The Cosmic Revelation* (London 1983); *The River of Compassion* (Warwick NY 1987); *A New Vision of Reality* (London 1991); *The New Creation in Christ* (London 1992); *Psalms for Christian Prayer* (Shantivanam 1993); *Pathways to the Supreme* (Shantivanam 1994); *Universal Wisdom* (London 1994). SHIRLEY DU BOULAY, *Beyond the Darkness: A Biography of Bede Griffiths* (New York: Doubleday, 1998).

[I. FREEMAN]

HAMER, JEAN JÉROME

Cardinal, theologian, Dominican friar; b. 1 June 1916, Brussels, Belgium; d. 2 December 1996, Rome. Upon joining the Order of Preachers in 1934, Hamer took the name of Jérôme and began his studies at the Dominican Studium Generale, La Sarte, at Louvain; he received a doctorate in theology from University of Fribourg, Switzerland. At the beginning of the Second World War he entered the military, and in 1940 spent three months in a prisoner-of-war camp. Following his ordination to the priesthood, 3 August 1941, he continued his theological studies. In 1944 he joined the faculty of theology at the University of Fribourg; he taught at the Pontifical Angelicum Athenaeum, in Rome (1952–53), and served as rector of the Studium Generale of Saulchoir, France (1956–62). His most influential works from this period were his books *Karl Barth*, a major study of Barth's dogmatic method, and *The Church Is a Communion*, prompted by Pius XII's encyclical *Mystici corporis*. In 1962 he was appointed secretary general of studies for his order and general assistant for the French Dominican provinces, a position he held till 1966.

Hamer was an expert at the Second Vatican Council for the Secretariat for Christian Unity; in 1966 he was made secretary adjunct for the secretariat, and in 1969 appointed secretary. Shortly after the council he published a commentary on the declaration *Dignitatis humanae* in *La liberté religieuse* (Paris 1967). In 1973 he was named titular archbishop of Lorium and appointed secretary of the Congregation for Doctrine of Faith, receiving his episcopal ordination from Pope Paul VI in Vatican City.

Hamer was appointed pro-prefect of the Congregation for Religious and Secular Institutes in 1984 and was elevated to prefect after being made cardinal deacon, with the deaconry of St. Saba, the following year. He attended several assemblies of the Synod of Bishops, including the first special assembly for Europe (1991), before resigning his prefecture in 1992. He died 2 December 1996, in Rome, and is buried in Rome's Campo Verano Cemetery.

[J. A. DICK]

HÄRING, BERNARD

Moral theologian; professor; Redemptorist priest; b. Böttingen, Germany, 10 November 1912; d. 3 July 1998. It is commonly acknowledged that Häring had a crucial role in the reshaping of moral theology in this century. From 1941 to 1945, having been conscripted into the German army, he served as a medical orderly in France, Poland, and Russia. From 1949 to 1953 and from 1957 until his retirement in 1988, he was a professor at the Alphonsian Academy in Rome.

In 1964, Paul VI named a papal commission on birth control, of which Häring was a member. The pope issued the encyclical *Humanae vitae* in 1968. Responding to what he saw as an urgent pastoral need, Häring spoke out on the role of conscience. On other occasions also he expressed controversial views that did not escape the attention of ecclesiastical authorities. However, he was never formally censured.

Contribution to Moral Theology. Häring engaged in a critical discussion with Rudolf Otto, Max Scheler, and others. He developed a personalist religious ethic based on experience, feeling, and value, rather than on abstract rational analysis. The role of such an ethic is to evoke dispositions and form character, rather than enunciate principles and deduce norms.

In Häring's place in the history of moral theology depends primarily on his early work, *Das Gesetz Christi* [ET *The Law of Christ* (1961)]. Instead of a legalistic system of precepts and sanctions, Häring offered a Christian moral message founded on the Bible. The moral life is empowered by grace, that is, by a new being in Christ. Moral theology, therefore, must be integrated with a theology of the sacraments as historical events of grace. Biblical leitmotifs provide the vision, and Christian virtues the framework. Although subordinate to the Bible, the natural law is still normative. Much of the content of *The Law of Christ* is similar to that of the earlier manuals. What is new is the vision and the openness to dialogue with the secular sciences, sociology, and psychology. The biblical orientation provided an opening for ecumenical dialogue, which the author cultivated assiduously. His medical ethics, rather than solving dilemmas, provided a distinctive theological interpretation of life and death.

A major work, *Free and Faithful in Christ* (1978–1981) developed the themes of Christian freedom and the liberty and creativity of conscience. In saying that conscience is creative he did not mean that it is autonomous or arbitrary; it is bound by fidelity to Christ. While affirming the historicity of natural law, he rejected relativism. This book contributed to developing and popularizing the idea of the fundamental option. Always alert to contemporary issues, the author discussed the ethics of ecology, the media, and peace. Häring's thinking on peace and war continued to develop. By 1986 he was arguing that we must move toward abandoning the just-war theory and replacing it with an ethic of nonviolence. Responsibility is fundamental. The "goal-commandment," as distinct from a negative limit or mere ideal, expresses a summons to organized action toward an end. "Reciprocity of consciences" indicates the way in which Christians ought to seek truth, namely through a community endeavor, governed by mutual respect. Responding to recent controversy, Häring held that there is an intimate connection rather than a dichotomy between a "faith-ethic" and an "autonomous ethic." For him, the deontological dimension of ethics means God's call to a loving response, and the teleological, a movement toward sanctity. Moral theology is to be pastoral, personalist, and communitarian; an embodiment of the healing role of faith rather than a system of control by law.

Bibliography: Häring has published over eighty books and hundreds of articles. The following are some of the more significant: *Das Heilige und das Gute: Religion und Sittlichkeit in ihrem gegenseitigen Bezug* (Krailling/Munich 1950); *Das Gesetz Christi* (Freiburg im Breisgau 1954; 8th. ed. 1967); ET *The Law of Christ* (Westminster 1961–1966); *Medical Ethics* (Slough 1972); *Ethics of Manipulation: Issues in Medicine, Behavior Control and Genetics* (New York 1975; *Free and Faithful in Christ* (New York 1978–1981); *The Healing Power of Peace and Nonviolence* (Mahwah 1986); *No Way Out? Pastoral Care of the Divorced and Remarried* (Slough 1990); *My Witness for the Church* (Mahwah 1992).

[B. V. JOHNSTONE]

HESBURGH, THEODORE MARTIN

Holy Cross priest, president of the University of Notre Dame; b. 25 May 1917, Syracuse, New York. Hesburgh was the second of five children of Theodore Bernard and Anne Marie (Murphy) Hesburgh. His father worked his way up to a management position with the Pittsburgh Plate Glass company and provided comfortable middle-class circumstances for his family.

Hesburgh decided to enter the Congregation of Holy Cross upon his graduation from high school and began studies at the University of Notre Dame in the fall of 1934. After completing initial philosophy studies and a novitiate year, he was sent to study at the Gregorian University in Rome (1937–40), where he developed a facility in languages (including Latin, French, German, and Italian).

With the outbreak of the Second World War he returned to the United States, completing his theological studies at Holy Cross College seminary in Washington, D.C. Following ordination to the priesthood on 24 June 1943, Hesburgh pursued advanced theological studies at the Catholic University of America where he obtained his S.T.L. in 1944 and his S.T.D. in 1945. His thesis, concerned with the nature of the lay apostolate, was published by the University of Notre Dame Press as *The Theology of Catholic Action*.

Despite his request to be assigned as a military chaplain in the Pacific, Hesburgh's superiors ordered him to return to Notre Dame where he lived and worked for the rest of his life. He taught in the religion department, wrote a widely used theology textbook, *God and the World of Man*, and served notably as chaplain to married veterans and their families. After a brief term as chair of the religion department (1948–49) he served for three years (1949–52) as executive vice president, and at age thirty-five succeeded John Cavanaugh, C.S.C., as Notre Dame's fifteenth president.

Hesburgh's dynamic leadership transformed Notre Dame from a mainly undergraduate and somewhat provincial institution known best for its winning football program to the leading American Catholic university and an important national teaching and research institution. He proved an extraordinary fund-raiser and effectively used the support of foundations and private individuals to almost double student enrollment and to dramatically enhance not only faculty size and quality but also the physical facilities, financial resources, graduate programs, and academic prestige of the institution. He guided Notre Dame through years of student unrest with a minimum of campus disruption, and introduced study-abroad programs in England, France, Austria, Israel,

Japan, China, and Mexico. He aimed to shape Notre Dame as a beacon, bridge, and crossroads "where all the vital intellectual currents of our time meet in dialogue." Guided by the spirit of the Second Vatican Council, he prompted the 1967 shared governance measures which transferred ownership and juridical control of Notre Dame from the Congregation of Holy Cross to a predominantly lay board of trustees and a board of fellows equally divided between Holy Cross and lay members. In 1972 he oversaw the admission of undergraduate women to the formerly all-male student body.

Concern for institutional autonomy and academic freedom guided Hesburgh's important involvements in the leadership of American Catholic universities and in the International Federation of Catholic Universities (IFCU). He helped frame and eagerly promoted the landmark 1967 Land O'Lakes statement and the 1972 IFCU document, "The Catholic University in the Modern World," which argued against any interference by authorities external to the university.

Hesburgh ably served both Church and nation and maintained involvements in an extraordinary number of national and international associations and organizations. He represented the Vatican on the International Atomic Energy Agency from 1957 to 1970 and led IFCU from 1963 to 1970.

In 1954 President Dwight Eisenhower appointed him to the National Science Board, the first of fifteen presidential appointments. Most important of these was his membership on the United States Commission on Civil Rights, which he joined at its foundation in 1957 and on which he served until 1972, including three years as its chair (1969–72). During the Carter administration Hesburgh held the rank of ambassador and led the American delegation to the U.N. Conference on Science and Technology for Development. He also served on the Presidential Clemency Board in 1974–75 and chaired the Select Commission on Immigration and Refugee Policy in 1979–81.

Hesburgh's broad interests in development, human rights, world peace, and higher education guided his extensive work in private bodies such as the Rockefeller Foundation, the Overseas Development Council, the American Council on Education and the Council on Foreign Relations.

Hesburgh retired as president of Notre Dame in 1987, and in 1990 published a memoir, *God, Country, Notre Dame,* which became a national bestseller. Accorded widespread recognition throughout his career, Hesburgh has received numerous awards and honors including the Medal of Freedom from President Lyndon

Father Theodore M. Hesburgh. (Archive Photos, Inc. Reproduced by permission.)

Johnson in 1964, the Charles Evans Hughes Award from the National Conference on Christians and Jews (1970), the Meikeljohn Award from the American Association of University Professors (1970), and the Congressional Gold Medal in 2000.

Bibliography: THEODORE M. HESBURGH and JERRY REEDY.*God, Country, Notre Dame.* New York: Doubleday, 1990. THEODORE M. HESBURGH, *The Humane Imperative: A Challenge for the Year 2000. The Terry Lectures.* New Haven: Yale University Press, 1974.MICHAEL O'BRIEN,*Hesburgh: A Biography.* Washington, D.C.: The Catholic University of American Press, 1998.CHARLOTTE A. AMES,*Theodore M. Hesburgh: A Bio-Bibliography.* Westport, Conn.: Greenwood Press, 1989.

[WILSON MISCAMBLE]

HICKEY, JAMES ALOYSIUS

Cardinal, archbishop of Washington, D.C.; b. 11 October 1920, Midland, Michigan. Hickey studied at St. Joseph's Seminary, Sacred Heart Seminary College in Detroit, and Theological College in Washington, D.C. He also earned an S.T.L. in theology from the Catholic University of America. Ordained a priest for the Diocese of Saginaw, 15 June 1942, Father Hickey served (1946–47) as assistant pastor of St. Joseph's Church in that city be-

James A. Hickey. (Catholic News Service.)

fore leaving for graduate studies in Rome where he earned a doctorate in canon law from the Pontifical Lateran University and a doctorate in moral theology at the Pontifical Angelicum University.

Father Hickey returned to Saginaw in 1951 to become secretary to Bishop Stephen S. Woznicki. By that time two of the future cardinal's life-long interests—the welfare of minority Catholics and the training of seminarians—had emerged. An article he had published as a seminarian on the plight of Hispanic migrants came to the attention of his superiors and led to his being asked to organize Saginaw's first Hispanic apostolate. He learned Spanish so that he might better respond to the many concerns of this rapidly growing Catholic community in his diocese. He served as director of vocations in Saginaw and managed the building of St. Paul's Seminary, becoming its first rector in 1959. Bishop Woznicki sent him to the Second Vatican Council as his *peritus* and proxy, where he worked on the commission drafting the document on the formation of seminarians.

Hickey was elected titular bishop of Taraqua and consecrated auxiliary bishop of Saginaw in 1967, serving as diocesan administrator after Bishop Woznicki's retirement in 1968. Service as chairman of the National Conference of Catholic Bishops' committee on priestly

formation and as consultor to the Vatican's Congregation for Catholic Education led to his appointment in 1969 as rector of the Pontifical North American College in Rome. He established of one of the first intensive programs for the continuing education of priests.

In 1974 Pope Paul VI named Hickey bishop of Cleveland. In addition to establishing an Office for Black Catholics he strengthened the sister-parish program between individual churches in Cleveland and in El Salvador begun by his predecessors, authorizing assistance to the Archdiocese of San Salvador. He began to appear frequently before congressional committees and other public forums to demand more humanitarian aid and less military assistance for Central America.

Pope John Paul II named Hickey Archbishop of Washington in 1980, and elevated him to the rank of cardinal, with the title of S. Maria Madre del Redentore a Tor Bella Monaca, in 1988. He attended the eighth and ninth general assemblies of the Synod of Bishops, and was a member of its general secretariat from 1990 to 1994. He continued to have a strong and effective concern for minority Catholics and for education, establishing a Secretariat for Black Catholics and an Office of Hispanic Pastoral Affairs and strongly promoting the permanent diaconate program. As archbishop of Washington he served as chancellor of the Catholic University of America, and during much of his tenure chaired the board of governors of his beloved North American College.

[MORRIS MACGREGOR]

HOMOSEXUALS, PASTORAL CARE OF

A letter addressed to the worldwide Catholic episcopate by the Congregation for the Doctrine of the Faith (CDF), ''On the Pastoral Care of Homosexual Persons'' (1 October 1986), effectively confirmed the position of the U.S. National Conference of Catholic Bishops (NCCB) that homosexual persons are entitled to ''a special degree of understanding and care'' from the Christian community (pastoral letter, ''To Live in Christ Jesus,'' 11 November 1976).

The essential requisites of this special pastoral care, as indicated in the CDF letter and in previous statements of the Holy See and local/regional episcopates, can be discussed under the following headings: 1) a realistic and compassionate understanding of the homosexual orientation or condition; 2) the avoidance of permissive approaches to the moral evaluation of homosexual genital activity; and 3) positive initiatives to facilitate the harmonious integration of homosexual persons into the Christian community and wider society.

Homosexual Orientation. In its earlier "Declaration on Certain Questions Concerning Sexual Ethics" (29 December 1975), CDF acknowledged the homosexual orientation as follows:

> A distinction is drawn, and it seems with some reason, between homosexuals whose tendency comes from a false education, from a lack of normal sexual development, from habit, from bad example, or from other similar causes, and is transitory or at least not incurable; and homosexuals who are definitively such because of some kind of innate instinct or a pathological constitution judged to be incurable (n. 8).

Consistent with this acknowledgment, the NCCB stated in 1976 that "some persons" discover that they have a homosexual orientation "through no fault of their own," and the 1986 CDF letter reaffirms that this orientation, in and of itself, "is not a sin" (n. 3). On the contrary, it is sinful to subject anyone to opprobrium or discrimination on account of his/her sexual orientation [Washington State Catholic Conference, "The Prejudice Against Homosexuals and the Ministry of the Church" (28 April 1983)]. Persons so oriented, "like everyone else, . . . have a right to respect, friendship and justice, . . . [and] should have an active role in the Christian community" (NCCB 1976). Moreover, especially where a homosexual orientation is perceived as unalterable so as to exclude all prospect of marriage, it is precisely this fact which gives the person a special claim on the Church's "pastoral understanding and care" (*ibid.*).

Considerable difficulties still beset efforts to reach a sound understanding of the homosexual orientation itself from an authentically Christian perspective. Behavioral and social scientists offer no clear or uniform account of this orientation in terms of its genesis, exclusivity, permanence, or other related questions. Confronted with obscure data and often conflicting interpretations from within the scientific community, the Church disowns any pretense at "an exhaustive treatment" of the "complex" homosexual question, remaining open to enlightenment from the human sciences while confident of its own "more global vision . . . [of] the rich reality of the human person" (CDF 1986, n. 2).

In line with its mandate to uphold "the Catholic moral perspective" (*ibid.*), CDF indicates some concern lest a duly compassionate regard for persons with a homosexual orientation be misconstrued as license for the genital activity to which that orientation inclines. This is the evident sense of the Congregation's statement that the homosexual "inclination," understood as "a more or less strong tendency ordered toward an intrinsic moral evil"—i.e., seen under the precise aspect of an inclination toward sinful sexual acts—is itself "an objective dis-order" (n. 3). Whatever legitimate difficulties may be raised concerning this last phrase, two points should be made clear: the phrase does not signify that the homosexual orientation itself is in any sense sinful (indeed, as noted above, the exact opposite is stated); and it refers only to "a particular inclination" toward sin inherent in the homosexual orientation, not globally to all aspects of the sexual affectivity of persons so oriented—nor, even less, to the overall personality or character of such persons.

Reactions to the 1986 CDF letter, however, indicated that pastors find it extremely difficult to dissuade homosexual people from the notion that the Church views them as fundamentally flawed persons on account of their sexual orientation. This misperception may reflect the proneness of many homosexual people to over-identify with their sexual orientation, viewing any criticism of any aspect of that orientation as a profound assault on their personal dignity. While such over-identification is surely inappropriate (CDF 1986, n. 16), it is often an understandable overreaction to the unjust rejection which these persons suffer [Bp. Francis Mugavero (Brooklyn), pastoral letter, "Sexuality: God's Gift" (11 Feb. 1976)]. Hence the foremost pastoral imperative—even prior to offering moral instruction—is for the Church to convince homosexuals in practical terms that it accepts them fully as persons whom it is ready to serve with genuine love and respect.

Homosexual Activity. Inasmuch as pastoral care must also include moral instruction, the magisterium adheres to the traditional Judeo-Christian teaching that "homosexual activity, . . . as distinguished from homosexual orientation, is morally wrong" (NCCB 1976). Pope John Paul II, confirming this stand in an address to the U.S. hierarchy (Chicago 5 Oct. 1979), stressed the obligation of bishops to maintain this teaching as "compassionate pastors" and "not betray [any homosexual] brother or sister" by holding out "false hope" that the teaching could change. The 1986 CDF letter echoes this approach (n. 15).

By contrast with the 1975 CDF Declaration and also much earlier tradition centered on natural law reasoning with reference to the procreative meaning of sexuality, the 1986 letter articulates the Church's rejection of homosexual genital activity in terms of a theological anthropology emphasizing the unitive equally with the procreative dimension, as seen in the Genesis teaching on creation:

> God . . . fashions mankind male and female, in his own image and likeness. Human beings, . . . in the complementarity of the sexes, . . . are called to reflect the inner reality of the Creator.

They do this in a striking way in their cooperation with Him in the transmission of life by a mutual donation of the self to the other. . . . Homosexual activity is not a complementary union, able to transmit life; and so it thwarts the call to a life of that form of self-giving which the Gospel says is the essence of Christian living (nn. 5–7).

Although the same CDF document (n. 6) also cites various other Biblical texts which comment adversely on homosexual practices—the Sodom story (Gn 19), the Levitical condemnations (Lv 18:22; 20:13), and Pauline writings (Rom 1:26–27; 1 Cor 6:9; 1 Tm 1:10)—these references are preceded by a stipulation that the Church's position is not based "on isolated phrases for facile theological argument" (n. 5). In any case the relevance of this material is subordinate to that of the Genesis creation theology which provides "the basic plan for understanding this entire discussion of homosexuality" (n. 6). Hence, in accord with sound theology as well as pastoral sensitivity, the presentation of the Church's moral teaching should avoid an exaggerated emphasis on the condemnation of homosexual activity (such as would result from simplistic Biblical prooftexting) but should concentrate on articulating the positive "spousal significance" of human sexuality as the basis for recognizing the deficiency of any genital activity that does not do full justice to that significance.

The Church's pastoral strategy is less developed as regards the positive guidance of those believers whose homosexual orientation precludes marriage—perhaps permanently, if this orientation resists change—and who meanwhile seem unprepared to live a celibate life. The dilemma of such persons is a very difficult one demanding special support and help from pastors and from the entire Christian community, instead of the contempt or rejection which has too often been the response.

The authoritative teaching (CDF 1975) indicates a general negative norm, *viz.,* that "no pastoral method can be employed which would give moral approval to these [homosexual] acts on the grounds that they would be consonant with the condition of such people," but positive alternatives remain unspecified. Some local and regional episcopates (England and Wales 1979; San Francisco 1983), without recognizing committed homosexual relationships as an acceptable equivalent of marriage or morally endorsing homogenital acts within such relationships, have suggested the appropriateness of welcoming homosexuals thus situated into the full sacramental life of the Church if their relationship is prudently deemed the only present alternative to the incomparably worse evil of promiscuity (a particularly acute danger in face of the AIDS peril), and if there is reasonable hope that through prayer and the support of the Sacraments

they may progressively grow into chastity. This approach emphasizes the need to respect the believer's sincere and upright conscience, as well as the principle of gradualism as enunciated by John Paul II [*Familiaris consortio,* n. 34; cf. application to homosexuality by B. Kiely in *L'Osservatore Romano* (14 Nov. 1986) n. 7].

Positive Initiatives. The process of growth toward chastity itself requires support from pastors and the whole Church community. The Church cannot be effective in insisting upon rigorous moral standards for homosexual persons as regards chastity, or in discouraging their participation in permissive homophile communities, as long as it does not make wholesome friendship available to such persons within its own body. Ironically the deprivation of such friendship is itself a major provocation (often unconsciously) toward the very unchastity which the Church condemns; if the basic human need for companionship, affection, and intimacy is not met in wholesome ways, its fulfillment will be sought in disordered ways including inappropriate sexual conduct. The 1986 CDF letter includes a guarded but unmistakably clear acknowledgment that all Catholics must take every reasonable opportunity to help their homosexual fellow believers replace their lonely isolation with healthy interpersonal relationships (n. 15).

The same document contains other noteworthy progressive elements, e.g., the identification of "violent malice in speech or in action"—now often called homophobia—as a continuing evil which "deserves condemnation from the Church's pastors wherever it occurs," and likewise a strong affirmation that homosexual people share in "the intrinsic dignity of each person [which] must always be respected in word, in action and in law" (n. 10). Inclusion of the homosexual question in catechetical programs on sexuality is now encouraged, and particular concern is also to be shown for the families of homosexual persons (n. 17).

It is the responsibility of diocesan bishops, individually and/or in regional conference, to implement such initiatives according to conditions in their respective territories (CDF 1986, nn. 13, 15, 17). During the 1990s a growing number of U.S. dioceses developed programs of outreach and support for gay and lesbian Catholics; and the NCCB officially recognizes the National Association of Catholic Diocesan lesbian and Gay Ministries (NACDLGM). In 1997 the NCCB Committee on Marriage and Family issued a warmly positive pastoral letter titled "Always Our Children" that was directed primarily to parents of homosexual persons but was also addressed to gay and lesbian Catholic themselves; it was slightly revised in 1998, following input from the CDF.

The tendency of the CDF has been to stress the cautionary points of its 1986 letter. In a June 1997 memorandum, the Congregation again advised bishops to be wary of civil-rights initiatives regarding homosexual persons, even suggesting that some instances of social discrimination against these persons would not be unjust. In July 1999, after years of investigation by various church agencies, the CDF ordered Sr. Jeannine Gramick, SSND, and Father Robert Nugent, SDS, the co-founders of New Ways Ministry in the U.S., to cease their nearly three decades of nationwide ministry to homosexual persons and their families; the two had not satisfied the Congregation's demand for an "unequivocal" declaration of their "personal assent" to the condemnations articulated in its 1975 and 1986 documents with regard to homosexual activity. NCCB president Bishop Joseph Fiorenza (of Houston, Texas) sought at once to assure gay Catholics and their families that the CDF action against Gramick and Nugent would not weaken the U.S. hierarchy's commitment to promote a caring and compassionate ministry to the homosexual community.

The Catechism of the Catholic Church reiterates that homosexual acts can "under no circumstances . . .be approved" (no. 2357), and adds that the homosexual orientation itself is "objectively disordered" (no. 2358, in the *editio typica*). The same text also states, however, that the number of homosexually oriented men and women "is not negligible," that these persons "must be accepted with respect, compassion and sensitivity," and that any sign of "unjust discrimination" against them should be avoided. Even the summons to chastity is couched in terms of a confident expectation that homosexual people are capable of "Christian perfection" (no. 2359).

In presenting the full range of church teaching as summarized in these Catechism references, the more benign and positive elements of this teaching (which are less well known) need to be better highlighted and more broadly applied in practice, whereas the more severe and cautionary elements should be treated as subordinate though not ignored. These latter actually indicate problems which can be effectively addressed only by a full and unambiguous commitment of the Church to a multi-dimensional effort of positive pastoral support for homosexual persons. If the attraction of such persons to homophile movements opposed to Catholic moral teaching is cause for concern, it must also be admitted that such movements have provided at least a modicum of the needed personal acceptance and understanding which homosexuals have not often found in the Church or elsewhere. Hence the Church must provide an alternative for these men and women which clearly offers a more adequate and genuine affirmation of their personal worth. In sum, the commitment to uphold authentic Christian standards of sexual morality must be seen as an integral part of wider pastoral efforts to promote charity and justice.

George Basil Cardinal Hume. (Catholic News Service.)

Bibliography: J. GALLAGHER, ed., *Homosexuality and the Magisterium: Documents from the Vatican and the U.S. Bishops* (Mt. Rainier, Md. 1986). USCC., *Human Sexuality: A Catholic Perspective for Education and Lifelong Learning* (Washington, D.C. 1990). L. S. CAHILL, *Sex, Gender, and Christian Ethics* (Cambridge 1996). S. M. OLYAN, and M. C. NUSSBAUM, eds., *Sexual Orientation and Human Rights in American Religious Discourse* (Oxford 1998).

[B. WILLIAMS]

HUME, GEORGE BASIL

Cardinal Archbishop of Westminster, 1976–1999; b. Newcastle-upon-Tyne, England, 1923; novitiate at Ampleforth Abbey 1941; studied at Ampleforth, Oxford (history), and Fribourg University (theology); ordained priest 1950; elected *Magister Scholarum* for the English Benedictine Congregation 1957, 1961; Abbot of Ampleforth 1963–1976; appointed by Pope Paul VI to the Metropolitan See of Westminster on 17 February 1976; created cardinal 24 May 1976; d. Westminster, 17 June 1999.

Hume was widely regarded as the spiritual leader in Britain at the end of the twentieth century. Part of the legacy he left is the acceptance of the Roman Catholic Church as a native (and not foreign) Church, alongside the Established and Free Churches, thus signaling the demise of any lingering effects of the Penal Laws in Britain.

As abbot of a large monastery at the time of the Second Vatican Council and as archbishop of the premier see in Britain, he was able to maintain peace, stability, and unity within the communities he served. Hume could do this because he listened with great honesty and openness and recognized that whatever tensions there might be, all involved shared a common faith. The last talk he prepared on this theme, under the auspices of the Catholic Common Ground initiative, was called "One in Christ, Unity and Diversity in the Church Today."

His episcopate was marked by a number of significant events. Among these was the National Pastoral Congress (1980), which elicited *The Easter People,* the bishops' accompanying response. His tenure also saw the publication of *The Common Good,* which articulated Catholic social teaching for contemporary society (1996), and the publication of *One Bread, One Body* (1998), which set out teaching on the Eucharist. This latter document was to be useful in making decisions about the admission of non-Catholic Christians to communion, reconciliation, and the anointing of the sick.

Hume served the Church in England and the world in a number of roles. From 1979 to 1999 he was president of the Bishops' Conference of England and Wales. From 1979 to 1987 he served as president of the Council of European Bishops' Conferences, which was established to deal with social and ethical problems within the European Economic Community. He was also co-chair of the Council of European Churches (Orthodox, Reformed and Anglican Churches). He was a member of the Secretariat for Christian Unity, Congregation of Religious and Secular Institutes, Pontifical Commission for the Revision of the Code of Canon Law, and the Joint Commission set up by the Holy See and the Orthodox Church to promote theological dialogue between their Churches. He also attended the synods of bishops in 1977, 1980, 1983, 1987, 1990, 1994 (serving as relator general); and the Extraordinary Synod in 1985.

Ecumenism and Social Justice. Hume played an important role in ecumenism. He began to dialogue with the Orthodox while he was abbot of Ampleforth. Recognizing the special position of the Anglican communion in ecumenical affairs, he made particular efforts to ensure close and developing relationships with the Church of England. His first act as archbishop of Westminster was to lead a group of Benedictine monks to Westminster Abbey to sing Vespers there for the first time since the Reformation. Pope John Paul II's visit in 1982 was both a celebration for Catholics in Britain and an occasion of great ecumenical significance. During this visit the pope met Queen Elizabeth II at Buckingham Palace and the archbishop of Canterbury at the shrine of St. Thomas à Becket.

In 1987 at an important ecumenical gathering at which plans for new ecumenical instruments were being discussed, Hume urged Catholics to move from "cooperation to commitment" in the search for Christian unity. He subsequently became joint president both of Churches Together in England and of the Council of Churches for Britain and Ireland.

After the decision of the Church of England to ordain women as priests, large numbers of Anglican clergy petitioned to join the Catholic Church. Rome gave permission for married convert clergy, under certain conditions, to be ordained priests. In his most public initiative (encouraged by the Holy See), Hume managed to ensure that individuals whose conscience led them to the Catholic Church were duly welcomed, but without the cordial relationships with the Church of England being spoiled. At the same time Catholic sensitivities to the introduction of married clergy, and anxieties there might be over priestly celibacy were largely overcome.

A reconciler and bridge-builder, Hume did much to heal wounds between the Jewish and Catholic communities. He was active in promoting understanding with people of other faiths. He was with Pope John Paul II at the gathering of world religious leaders at Assisi to pray for peace (1986).

Hume was deeply committed to matters of justice. His initiative in highlighting certain serious miscarriages of justice in England led to the release of a number of prisoners and to a new system of investigation of such cases. By other initiatives he gave clear guidance on a wide variety of public moral and social issues: life issues, marriage and family life, global poverty and international debt, human rights, homelessness, refugees and asylum seekers, the arms trade and nuclear disarmament, homosexuality, and education. Hume was instrumental in mounting significant seminars in London that discussed topics like business and moral standards in post-communist Europe (1992), the arms trade (1995), and world debt (1996).

Two weeks prior to Hume's death Queen Elizabeth II presented him with the Order of Merit—awarded to individuals of exceptional merit, in the personal gift of the Queen. The Chief Rabbi in England (Dr. Jonathan Sacks) wrote of him in *The Times:* "He spoke of God in a secular age and was listened to. He articulated clear moral values and his words shone through the relativistic mist. He took principled political stands and was respected for it. He showed that humility has a power and presence of its own."

At the time of Cardinal Hume's death, Pope John Paul II commented on his devoted service, thanking God for ''having given the Church a shepherd of great spiritual and moral character, of sensitive and unflinching ecumenical commitment and firm leadership in helping people of all beliefs to face the challenges of the last part of this difficult century.''

George Basil Hume was an outstanding figure in the Catholic Church in the latter part of the twentieth century, with an influence far beyond his own country and his own family of faith. He was a leader, a profoundly spiritual, impressively intelligent, a man of great authority. His loyalty to the Church was complete and came from his childlike faith in Christ. Hume always kept in touch with his Benedictine roots; he was described as ''someone who turns strangers into friends.''

Bibliography: GEORGE BASIL HUME, *Searching for God* (London: Hodder and Stoughton, 1977); *In Praise of Benedict* (London: Hodder and Stoughton, 1981); *To Be A Pilgrim* (London: St Paul, 1984), *Towards a Civilisation of Love* (London: Hodder and Stoughton, 1988); *Light in the Lord* (London: St Paul Publications, 1991); *Remaking Europe: the Gospel in a Divided World* (London: SPCK, 1994); *Footprints of the Northern Saints* (London: Darton, Longman and Todd, 1996); *Basil in Blunderland* (London: Darton, Longman and Todd, 1997); *The Mystery of the Cross* (London: Darton, Longman and Todd, 1998). *Mystery of the Incarnation* (London: Darton, Longman and Todd, 1999). ''Basil Hume, Archbishop of Westminster'' in *Oremus* (Magazine of Westminster Cathedral, Special Edition, July 1999). Bishops' Conference of England and Wales. *Briefing* 29 (July 1999). CAROLYN BUTLER. *Basil Hume by his Friends* (1999). TONY CASTLE, ed., *Basil Hume, A Portrait* (1986). PETER STANFORD, *Cardinal Hume and the Changing Face of English Catholicism* (1993).

[D. KONSTANT]

INCULTURATION, LITURGICAL

A hallmark of Pope John Paul II's pontificate has been his extensive travels to the local churches on nearly every continent. Central to these visits are major liturgical celebrations that draw upon local culture to express the genius of the local churches. At the opening and closing of the special assemblies of the Synod of Bishops the Eucharistic liturgies took up the particular cultural expressions, at the pope's expressed wishes (*Ecclesia in Africa,* no. 25). At the opening of the Holy Door to commence the Jubilee Year, African horns and signs of reverence from Asia and Oceania emphasized the universality of the salvation and the mission of the Church to the whole world.

Throughout the history of Christian worship, liturgy and culture have always been intricately entwined: the culture of a given group of people yielded great influence on the forms, symbols, language, time, and place of their worship. With the documents of the Second Vatican Council, the imperative of liturgical inculturation gained unparalleled impetus and theological articulation. This entry first takes up the issue of terminology surrounding the notion of liturgical inculturation. After considering historical evidence of the interaction of liturgy and culture, it presents the documents of Vatican II and the instruction on inculturation and liturgy. Then, it examines recent attempts at liturgical adaptation throughout the world.

Problem of Terminology. The term ''inculturation'' is an ambiguous neologism that arose in the 1960s. When one examines conciliar texts, one observes that the terms *aptatio* (''adaptation'') and *accomodatio* (''accommodation'') are used interchangeably to refer to the Church's task of aggiornamento and the whole process of liturgical change. After the council, the term *aptatio* came to refer to the task of the local bishops, part of the revitalization envisioned by the council, and *accomodatio* came to refer to the provisions in the typical editions of the Roman liturgical books for the minister to select alternatives in the local celebration of the liturgy.

Following A. Chupungco, adaptation is a culturally neutral term that refers to the Church's whole renewal. Different terms have been coined to speak of the methods of that renewal. The term ''inculturation'' was coined to refer to the need to keep the Christian message intact through the process of cultural exchange. In 1975 at the Thirty-second General Congregation of the Society of Jesus, the Latin word *inculturatio* was adopted in the discussions, probably the equivalent of the English ''enculturation'' (Roest-Crollius 1978). As A. Shorter explains, ''enculturation'' is a technical anthropological term for the socialization of a person, the way that the person is inserted into her or his culture (1988). ''Inculturation'' soon replaced ''enculturation'' in missiological, theological, and liturgical discourse and took on an entirely different meaning. Pope John Paul II introduced the term into Church documents in a 1979 address to the Pontifical Biblical Commission and later that year elaborated on it in *Catechesi tradendae,* no. 53.

In current liturgical discourse, the following principle terms are used to name the levels of interaction of liturgy and culture: acculturation, inculturation, and creativity. The term ''acculturation'' refers to the interaction that ensues from the juxtaposition of two cultures (Shorter 1988; Chupungco 1989). Acculturation names the initial stage of the encounter of the Roman liturgy with the local culture. The liturgy of the Roman Latin typical editions is placed side by side with elements from the culture where they interact but neither the liturgy nor the culture is assimilated into the other. The initial interaction of the liturgy and the local culture could then lead to inculturation, that is, the liturgy is so inserted into the culture that it would absorb the genius of the culture and the culture would be affected by the liturgy. Yet, the liturgy would not become the culture nor culture the liturgy; rather, both would undergo a process of internal transformation to shape something new (Chupungco 1993). Neither the liturgy nor the culture would lose their identities, but they would no longer be what they were before. The liturgy would be so inserted into the cultural frame that might speak, sing, and move according to the people's language, thought, rites, symbols, gestures, and arts. Liturgy would thus ritualize according to the local cultural pattern. Some scholars go on to name a third phase, that of creativity. Here, the liturgical rites are fashioned independent of the Roman *ordo* and euchology. At this stage, the Christian faith might be embodied in the local culture in such a way that new forms of expressing it emerge and so enrich the Church universal. The task of inculturation is ongoing: in the process of mutual assimilation, dimensions of the culture will undergo transformation in light of the memories, values, and hopes negotiated by the liturgy ordered in the typical editions and by the proclamation of the Gospel. Likewise, the culture will more authentically embody the Christian faith.

Liturgy and Local Church in History. Christian worship has always interacted with cultures, adapting cultural elements, transforming them, and even rejecting them. Christian worship originated in the culturally plural matrix of Palestinian Judaism, Hellenism, and Roman imperialism. As Christianity quickly spread through the Mediterranean basin into Asia Minor, Africa, and east to Syria, the regional styles of worship, already influenced by Jewish forms, developed according to the cultural genius of the local churches. The local churches of Alexandria, Antioch, Edessa, Milan, Jerusalem, Rome, and Constantinople generated distinctive liturgical usages that could be classified as families of rites. The content and rhetoric of euchology, the anaphoral structure, the order of worship at eucharist and initiation, the times and seasons of prayer each varied according to the different churches.

The Roman rite itself bears the marks of cultural adaptation. While the locus of imperial power shifted to Constantinople, the influence of pagan Roman culture on Christian worship and ministry in the church at Rome was considerable. With the invasion of the northern peoples, Rome was obliged to open itself to their cultures. At the same time, the liturgy of Rome came to hold a preeminent, if not idealized, position vis-á-vis other legitimate and integral usages in the northern territories. Roman liturgical books were exported to the Germanic and Gallican churches in the interest of unifying liturgical praxis. The editors charged with preparing the books found themselves confronted with the daunting task of conforming local usage to distinctly Roman practices that were celebrated in the geographical coordinates of the *Urbs* and suppressing that which did not conform. However, the hallmarks of Roman liturgy—its terse prayers, its sober ritual, and its juridical reserve—were foreign to the Germano-Gallican spirit. Thus, significant adaptations were required, and the Franco-Germanic culture was intertwined with the Roman liturgy. The popes adopted this liturgy after systematic abbreviation, and it was passed throughout Europe.

Tridentine Uniformity. With the Council of Trent, the liturgy of the Roman church became carefully regulated. The Missal of Pius V (1570) was binding on all churches of the west except those that could trace their usages back two hundred years. The use of the vernacular, called for by the reformers, was rejected, and the Latin language required. Trent sought to preserve and guarantee the venerable Roman tradition, as it was then perceived. The printing press made the dissemination of the uniform and codified liturgical books in Latin, or *editiones typicae,* facile. It is important to note that while the codified and uniform Roman liturgy became hegemonic, the relationship between cultic praxis of Christian faith and local culture survived and in many instances flourished on the "unofficial" level of popular devotions, pious practices, pilgrimages, and the myriad local feasts and observances.

Missionary encounters with non-western European cultures prompted a reconsideration of the obligation to use the Tridentine forms. The Chinese Rites controversy (1603–1742), errupting around Matteo Ricci's (1552–1610) efforts of looking within the culture for authentic ways of expressing Christian faith, marks a significant point for the relationship of Roman liturgy and culture. Ricci made allowances for the Chinese Christians to participate in ancestral and Confucian rites. Rome became concerned and in 1742 definitively condemned these usages. The Chinese Rites controversy revealed two crucial developments: first, the imperative of discerning what is essential within the dominant sociocultural matrix and endeavoring to accommodate it in the Christian tradition. Second, it demonstrated how a thoroughly western, classicist perspective misapprehends the difference of an eastern approach to religion and culture (Luttio 1994).

In the nineteenth century, the issue of the relationship between local usages, the prevailing cultural scene, and the codified Roman liturgy arose. In the instance of the revival of "neo-Gallican" usages in France, liturgists, like P. Guéranger, argued that diversion from the pure Roman liturgy was aberrant and needed to be suppressed. The Roman liturgy, which had the approbation of papal authority, was a means to reckon with the prevailing cultural forces: nationalism, liberal bourgeois culture, and the irrationality of romanticism. With the stirrings of the liturgical movement, the study of Christian liturgy and concern for participation in worship gave impetus to explore how to make the liturgy an authentic celebration of the people. The discussions at the Assisi Congress of Pastoral Liturgy in 1956 witnessed to missionary interest in the relationship between liturgy and culture.

Vatican II. The interaction of the movements in the decades preceding prevailed upon the formulations of Vatican II. As K. Rahner observed, Vatican II promised the actualization of the Church as a world Church, not a western European Church. The relationship between the Church and world is reciprocal: the Church acts on the world and the world on the Church. It is this spirit that permeates the documents of Vatican II. The first document issued by the council, *Sacrosanctum concilium* (SC), is a watershed moment for the relationship between liturgy and culture, but it must also be read in the context of later conciliar decrees.

SC no. 21 states that there are both "unchangeable elements" and "elements subject to change" in the liturgy. Nos. 22–23 take up issues of authority and method. SC posits the authority for change with the Apostolic See and local bishops and insists on the preservation of "sound tradition." Careful investigation through theological, historical, and pastoral study must guide revision. Most significantly, if the good of the Church requires, "new forms adopted should in some way grow organically (*organice crescant)* from forms already existing" (no. 23). SC nos. 37–40 has been called the "Magna Carta" of liturgical flexibility (Chupungco 1982). In this section, a Eurocentric perspective is attenuated: "Even in liturgy the Church has no wish to impose a rigid uniformity in matters which do not involve faith or the good of the whole community. Rather, she respects and fosters the spiritual adornments and gifts of the various races and peoples." In no. 38, given that "the substantial unity of the Roman rite is maintained," provision is made for legitimate local variations, and adaptations (*aptationes)* may be made even for the structuring of rites. No. 39 specifies that it is the task of the territorial ecclesiastical authority (i.e., the bishops) and that the "limits of the typical editions of the liturgical books" are to be observed. However, no. 40 provides for a "even more radical adaptation (*profundior aptatio)*" that, developed by competent local authorities, will need the approbation of the Apostolic See.

These texts need to be read in light of other later conciliar documents. *Gaudium et spes* acknowledges the plurality of cultures (no. 53) and the fact that culture is a human product (no. 55). Most importantly, no. 58 states that the Church and the transmission of the Gospel are not tied exclusively to any one culture or any one way of life, but rather the Church can "enter into communion with various cultural modes, to her own enrichment and theirs, too." While Western culture has been the mediating form of evangelization, other cultures might be capable of handing on the Gospel as well. *Lumen gentium* no. 26 presents the understanding of the local realization of the universal Church. *Ad gentes* no. 15 calls for the assemblies of the faithful, "endowed with the riches of its own nation's culture," to be "deeply rooted in the people." Number 19 speaks of the phases of building a community of the faithful, and number 22 relates the nascent churches to the incarnation.

Recent Roman Documents. The *Catechism of the Catholic Church* (CCC) speaks of the context and need for inculturation, echoing contemporary theological and liturgical discourse on the relationship and between faith, liturgy, and culture. The theme of diversity and the need for the Church to engage the variety of human cultures peppers the CCC. For example, CCC no. 814, in the context of Church unity, affirms that the Church "from the beginning" has been marked by "a great diversity," different gifts, and "multiplicity of peoples and cultures." CCC no. 1075 explains that the Church "aims to serve the whole Church in all the diversity of her rites and cultures." It acknowledges that sacramental signs and symbols are rooted in creation and human culture (no. 1145), and the Church is able to integrate "all the authentic riches of cultures" (no. 1202). "Liturgy requires," it emphasizes, "adaptation to the genius and culture of different people" (no. 1204). In its sensitivity to diversity, the CCC states, "each Church proposes . . . according to its historic, social, and cultural context, a language of prayer: words, melodies, gestures, iconography" (no. 2663). The need for critique and conversion is also noted (no. 1206; 2820).

In the midst of pastoral initiative and critical theological discourse, the Congregation for Divine Worship and the Discipline of the Sacraments issued the fourth instruction on the implementation of *Sacrosanctum Concilium,* "Inculturation of the Liturgy within the Roman Rite," (ILRR). The instruction sets down norms regarding the interpretation and implementation of SC nos. 37–40. ILRR has five sections: an introduction with preliminary observations; part one on the process of inculturation throughout salvation history; part two, theological and ecclesiological bases and preliminary conditions for inculturation; part three, principles and practical norms with regard to the Roman rite; and part four, areas open to adaptation in the Roman rite.

In the introduction the document notes the use and meaning of the term "inculturation," explaining that it has a double movement of the Church's introducing the Gospel in the culture and at the same time assimilating the culture's values (no. 4). In number 7, ILRR acknowledges the coexistence of many cultures in the western churches of which the Church must take account, in addition to missionary churches on other continents. After discussing the encounter of Christian faith with various cultures, the instruction offers several theological and ecclesiological precepts concerning relationship between liturgy and the local churches. ILRR emphasizes the need for the proclamation of the scriptures in the local language as the first step of inculturation (no. 28). Only then, after study by scholars, by "wise people" who live the culture, and by pastors of the area, can any adaptations be made (no. 29–30). In the third section ILRR explains that the governing principle of liturgical inculturation is the maintenance of "the substantial unity of the Roman rite. This is currently expressed in the typical editions of liturgical books published by the authority of the supreme pontiff and in the liturgical books approved by the episcopal conferences for their areas and confirmed by the Apostolic See" (no. 36). It posits the authority for adaptations of the Roman rite first "to the Apostolic See, which exercises it through the Congregation for Divine Worship and Discipline of the Sacraments" (no. 37). In the fourth section, after elaborating areas for legitimate adaptation in the liturgy of the sacraments, blessings, and liturgical year, ILRR lays down the procedure for the bishops' conferences to ask for the Apostolic See's approval. With regard to the "more profound adaptations" mentioned by SC no. 40, ILRR indicates that "adaptations of this kind do not envisage a transformation of the Roman rite" and "are made within the context of the Roman rite" (no. 63).

Contemporary Attempts. Since the promulgation of the typical editions of the Roman liturgical books, there have been several attempts at inculturating the Roman liturgy. India was one of the first countries to move on the program of cultural adaptation of the Roman liturgy. The task was daunting: India is an extremely culturally diverse country, and Christians are a minority. As soon as 1965, a national liturgical center was set up. First, elements of Indian culture were juxtaposed with the Roman liturgical setting. Then, the liturgical books were not only translated into the vernacular, but new texts were composed. Third, non-Christian scriptures were introduced into the liturgy. On 15 April 1969 they enumerated twelve points of liturgical inculturation, concerning gestures and postures, forms of homage, and objects and elements used in worship [see *Notitiae* 5 (1969): 365–374]. Later, a new order for the Eucharist, new Eucharistic

prayers, and Catholic celebrations of Indian festivals were introduced. While only one revised Eucharistic prayer later received local approval, the task of liturgical adaptation continues, more so in the north than in the south. Also, it seems to be more evident on the "unofficial level" of popular devotion than in the official Latin rite liturgy [Chengalikavil 1993]. Critical reflection by scholars and authorities continues.

The impetus toward indigenous liturgical expressions of the faith has marked the Catholic Church in Africa, Oceania, and Asia. Relatively successful examples have taken place on an official level in the dioceses of the former Zaire, Malawi, Cameroon, Kenya, and Ghana. In Polynesia, Melanesia, and Oceania the local churches have sought to wed traditional island culture with liturgical celebration. Progress is also being made in the churches of Asia. Among liturgical scholars these local celebrations have raised questions concerning the methods and agency of the process of inculturation. Foreign authorities face thousands of cultures and languages and the fact that the very symbols of western Christian liturgy are foreign to non- western cultures. The people in the local churches, experts in their own culture, grapple with the forms and content of Christian faith. For example, debate has taken place with regard to the use of imported wheat bread and grape wine for the Eucharist in African and Asian cultures where rice, millet, or palm wine are indigenous.

United States. The whole project of liturgical adaptation of the Roman liturgy heralded by the council touches not only Africa and Asia, but North and South America and Europe as well. With regard to contemporary western, Euro-American culture, some liturgists have questioned the premise of adapting the Roman liturgy to what they perceive as a dominant culture that cannot authentically incarnate the Christian gospel. Less pessimistic critics speak of the need to attenuate the counter-cultural notion of liturgy and stress the imperative of mutual interaction and critique so that the liturgy can most authentically express the given community's faith. In many ways, the liturgy is a cultural event because the liturgy is western European, so that the issues faced in Africa and Asia of foreign symbols, gestures, and language are not so pronounced.

But many cultures make the face of the American church quite complex. Liturgical books have been translated into some of the Native American languages, and Asian-American assemblies have begun to explore the question of the relationship between their cultures and liturgy. The question of inculturation is also alive for African-American and Hispanic assemblies and their desire to develop adequate forms for liturgical worship. Yet, even the terms "African-American," "Hispanic," or "Asian-American" cannot be used monolithically as if uniform African-American, Hispanic or Asian-American cultures existed. Hispanic liturgy is making great strides with regard to weaving the religious experience of Hispanic communities, popular religiosity, and the liturgy. Hispanic liturgists have realized that it is through study of the particular values and practices of Hispanic pieties and popular devotions that the liturgy can be incarnated in the various assemblies. Hispanic composers have fashioned diverse liturgical music, and official liturgical texts have been translated into Spanish. The efforts of the Mexican American Cultural Center, the Hispanic subcommittee of the Bishops' Committee on the Liturgy, and the Instituto de Liturgia Hispana have greatly aided the assimilation of Hispanic culture and liturgy. Much work has also been done with regard to African-American communities. Through the publication of *In Spirit and Truth* (1987) and *Plenty Good Room* (1990), liturgical acculturation has taken root in most predominately African-American assemblies. These documents explore the ways that elements of the African-American religious experience and spirituality can be assimilated into the Roman Liturgy. The publication of *Lead Me, Guide Me* (Chicago 1987) offers a corpus of music for African-American Catholic assemblies.

The acculturation of Asian, Hispanic, and African-American liturgy affords the Church in the United States a means of transforming its received notions of spirituality and worship. The work in these communities enables the rest of the Church to be aware of its own cultural patterns and see the Christian faith embodied in a plurality of ways. The mutual transformation enriches the Church's catholicity.

Conclusion. Consideration of historical and contemporary attempts at the program of liturgical adaptation demonstrate the importance of taking the concrete local culture and situation of the churches seriously. The process of liturgical inculturation presupposes a proclamation of the Gospel within the culture itself in order that the ritual celebration might be an authentic celebration of the people's paschal faith. Liturgical inculturation is a complex issue that raises serious theological, ecclesiological, hermeneutical, and liturgical questions. Yet, it remains a pivotal issue as the Church enters the next millennium.

See Also: CATECHESI TRADENDAE, CATECHISM OF THE CATHOLIC CHURCH, ECCLESIA IN AFRICA, ECCLESIA IN AMERICA, ECCLESIA IN ASIA, KARL RAHNER

Bibliography: The literature on liturgical inculturation is extensive. The reader is directed to S. A. STAUFFER, "Bibliography on Worship and Culture," in *Christian Worship: Unity and Cultural Diversity,* LWF Studies 1 (Geneva, 1996), 113–142. In particular the work of Anscar Chupungco figures prominently. A bibliography of his work can be found in *Liturgy for the New Millennium: A Commentary on the Revised Sacramentary. Essays in Honor of Anscar Chupungco,* ed., M. FRANCIS and K. PECKLERS (Collegeville, Minn., 2000), 165–168. See also S. BEVANS, *Models of Contextual Theology* (Maryknoll 1992). M. FRANCIS, *Shape a Circle Ever Wider: Liturgical Inculturation in the United States* (Chicago, Ill., 2000). D. POWER, "Liturgy and Culture Revisited," *Worship* 69 (1995): 225–243. A. SHORTER, *Toward a Theology of Inculturation* (Maryknoll 1988). R. SCHREITER, *Constructing Local Theologies* (Maryknoll 1985); *The New Catholicity: Theology Between the Global and the Local* (Maryknoll 1997).A. PEREZ, "The History of Hispanic Liturgy since 1965" in *Hispanic Catholic Culture in the U.S.: Issues and Concerns,* ed. J. P. DOLAN and A. F. DECK (Notre Dame 1994) 360–408; Articles cited here include: L. CHENGALIKAVIL, "Indigenous Liturgy: An Indian Perspective," in *L'Adattamento culturale della liturgia: metodi e modelli,* ed. I. SCICOLONE, *Analecta Liturgica* 19 (Rome 1993) 205–221. CONGREGATION FOR DIVINE WORSHIP AND DISCIPLINE OF THE SACRAMENTS, "De Liturgia romana et inculturatione. Instructio quarta ad exsecutionem Constitutionis Concilii Vaticani Secundi de Sacra Liturgia recte ordinandam (ad Const. art 37–40)," *Notitiae* 30 (1994): 80–115; English trans. *Inculturation of the Liturgy within the Roman Rite* (Vatican City 1994). G. DE NAPOLI, "Inculturation as Communication," *Inculturation* 9 (1987): 71–98. M. D. LUTTIO, "The Chinese Rites Controversy (1603–1742): A Diachronic and Synchronic Approach," *Worship* 68 (1994): 290–312. K. RAHNER, "Toward a Fundamental Theological Interpretation of Vatican II," *Theological Studies* 40 (1979): 44–56. A. ROEST- CROLLIUS, "What's So New About Inculturation? A Concept and its Implications," *Gregorianum* 59 (1978): 721–738; *Lead Me, Guide Me: The African American Hymnal* (Chicago 1987). *In Spirit and Truth: Black Catholic Reflections on the Order of Mass,* The Secretariat of the Bishop's Committee on the Liturgy of the National Conference of Catholic Bishops (Washington DC 1987). *Plenty Good Room: The Spirit and Truth of African American Worship,* statement of the Black Liturgy Subcommittee of the Committee on the Liturgy of the National Conference of Catholic Bishops (Washington, D.C. 1990).

[R. E. MCCARRON]

INCULTURATION, THEOLOGY OF

The term "inculturation," as applied to Christianity, denotes the presentation and re-expression of the Gospel in forms and terms proper to a culture. It results in the creative reinterpretation of both, without being unfaithful to either. Evangelization respects culture as part of the human phenomenon and as a human right. The manipulation or oppression of culture is, therefore, an abuse. Culture is a coherent system of meanings embodied in images and symbols that enables the individual to relate cognitively, emotionally, and behaviorally to the world and to communicate this understanding to others. It is the prism through which a human society views the whole of its experience, domestic, political, social, economic, and political. Culture is learned by the human being through socialization and is developed throughout life. It gives identity to a human group and controls its perception of reality. For the purposes of theology, it is at once more positive and more precise than the term ''context.'' Syncretism denotes an anomalous conflict of meaning when, in the process of evangelization, cultures ''domesticate'' the Gospel and distort its meaning. No culture is deemed to be unfailingly Christian, since inculturation is a constant call to conversion and renewal.

Evangelization must enter into dialogue with cultures if it is to produce any effect on human beings. Cultures are empirically diverse; therefore, evangelization leads to culturally diverse ways of living the Gospel. Inculturation, opposed to uniformity, demands the legitimization of diversity. There can be no monopoly of cultural forms in a truly Catholic communion. This is true in spite of the mutual influence of evangelizing and evangelized cultures (''interculturation'') and of the accumulation by the Church of current, but contingent, cultural elements as an inherited patrimony. Until the realization in the twentieth century that culture is a plural phenomenon, the Church took it for granted that there was a single, universal culture of humanity, the perfection of which was deemed to be Christianity in its western, Latin form. No allowance was made for factors of cultural diversity in theological controversy, and the Church was unable to accommodate the initiatives of early Jesuit missionaries, such as Mateo Ricci, Roberto de Nobili, and Pedro Paez, when they tried to evangelize foreign cultures from within. In the twentieth century, particularly at the Second Vatican Council, and in the subsequent assemblies of the Synod of Bishops, cultural pluralism has been accepted, together with inculturation as a demand of evangelization. However, an influential minority in the Church still claims that western culture possesses a universal significance for evangelization, in spite of its technocratic nature, its secularizing influence, and its tendency to undermine the religious values of indigenous cultures.

Christological Basis for Inculturation. Among the Christological bases for inculturation, the doctrine of the world-seeding Logos as God's agent in creation goes back to Justin Martyr and the second century apologists, typified by Clement of Alexandria. It has reappeared in the missionary decree of the Second Vatican Council, *Ad gentes,* and in modern creation theology. The Logos, the Divine Truth or Divine Reason, exists in disseminated form throughout creation, and every human tradition perceives it darkly, before it is enlightened for them by the proclamation of the Word incarnate. This proclamation does not outmode these traditions, but gladly recognizes the elements of truth they contain. Another Christological approach is the analogy with the incarnation of Jesus Christ and the parallel between his cultural education in

Palestine and modern missionary evangelization. The parallel demonstrates that Christ is the subject of inculturation and that the incarnation inserted him into the intercultural dynamic of human history. However, it plays down the challenge that Christ offered to his own culture, and suggests that the Gospel, like the divine pre-existence, comes to a culture in a culturally disembodied form. The most fruitful Christological approach is to compare inculturation with the Paschal Mystery, to which it is linked causally as well as analogically. Through his passion, death and resurrection, Christ became universal Lord and made himself available to people of every culture. The Paschal Mystery also offers an analogy for the conversion of culture, which dies and rises under the impact of evangelization, thus becoming more authentic and more faithful to its underlying truth.

Ecclesiological Approaches to Inculturation. Ecclesiological approaches to inculturation include first the logic of the Church's universal mission. That mission is the continuation of the *missio Dei,* God's loving dialogue with the world, and the fulfilment of the great commandment of universal love that is logically prior to the great commission to teach all nations. This love is a perfect communion of differences and, therefore, liberating. In this area the theology of inculturation encounters the theology of liberation. The second ecclesiological basis of inculturation is the authentic tradition of the Church and the role of the Church's magisterium. The primary reality of the Church is local: the particular church and the sociocultural region within which its witness takes place. Its primary task is to reconcile local culture to the Church's tradition, which is centered on the interpretation of the Christ event. This interpretation is based on a trajectory of meaning that ascends to the outlooks of the New Testament. Sacred tradition, with its growth of insight, passes organically from culture to culture and from clarity to clarity throughout history. Although the Bible occupies a privileged position in this tradition, together with the sacramental and hierarchical ministry that derives from the actions and commands of Christ witnessed by the New Testament, and although the meaning of faith-statements made by the Church's magisterium is not open to contradiction, all these can only be understood today with reference to their historical and cultural contexts. Reformulation in accordance with the Church's lived cultural plurality is strictly necessary, if they are to be taken seriously.

The concept of inculturation seems to carry certain consequences for the shape of the Church to come, among them the abandonment of a preference for western culture and a greater diversification in Christian life and practice. The fields of inculturation include: theology, catechesis, liturgy, religious life, marriage and family life, health and healing, secondary ecclesial ministries and structures. Inculturation would therefore assume a relative pluralism in all these fields. Since inculturation cannot be imposed, but depends on the experience and initiatives of the local community, the concept seems to envisage ecclesial structures that favor increased participation and collaboration.

Bibliography: D. AMALORPAVADASS, "Réflexions théologiques sur l'inculturation," *La Maison Dieu* 179 (1989): 58–66. G. A. ARBUCKLE, *Earthing the Gospel* (London 1990). M. DE C. AZEVEDO, *Inculturation and the Challenges of Modernity* (Rome 1982). R. O. COSTA, *One Faith-Many Cultures* (New York 1988). J. B. METZ, "Unity and Diversity: Problems and Prospects for Inculturation," *Concilium* 204 (1989): 79–87. E. J. PÉNOUKOU, *Eglises d'Afrique: Propositions pour l'Avenir* (Paris 1984). P. SCHINELLER, "Inculturation as the Pilgrimage to Catholicity," *Concilium* 204 (1989): 98–106. A. E. SHORTER, *Toward a Theology of Inculturation* (New York 1988); *Evangelization and Culture* (London 1994).

[A. E. SHORTER]

INTERNATIONAL COUNCIL FOR CATECHESIS (COINCAT)

The International Council for Catechesis (COINCAT) was established by Pope Paul VI on 7 June 1973 as a consultative body within the Congregation for the Clergy. The general purpose of COINCAT as explained in the *Annuario Pontificio* is "to study the more important catechetical themes for the service of the Apostolic See and the episcopal conferences and to present proposals and suggestions." Specifically, it investigates concrete themes and important catechetical problems for the universal Church, suggesting solutions and proposals for pastoral action; it provides information on the necessity of catechesis and new approaches being taken in various parts of the world; and it facilitates the exchange of catechetical experiences between the Holy See and the diverse areas in the Church and among the members themselves.

Since its inception COINCAT has provided valuable service both to the Apostolic See and episcopal conferences, especially through its biannual plenary sessions. In the past it has studied such issues as catechesis as an ecclesial act (1976), the settings for catechesis (1977), catechesis and youth (1978), the formation of catechists for the 1980s (1979), catechesis and reconciliation (1983), adult catechesis in the Christian community (1988), catechesis for life in a pluralistic and secularized world (1990), and inculturation of faith and the language of catechesis (1992). The 1988 session resulted in the publication of *Adult Catechesis in the Christian Community,* a document that became a landmark within the body of the Holy See's catechetical works.

From the beginning COINCAT has been an international group. The first twenty-four permanent members appointed for five-year terms in 1976 included the patriarch of the Melkites and archbishops, bishops, priests, sisters, and lay people from Asia, Europe, Africa, Australia, North, Central, and South America. Among the initial appointees were two from the United States, Bishop John B. McDowell of Pittsburgh and Sister Maria de la Cruz Aymes of San Francisco. McDowell was succeeded by Msgr. Wilfrid H. Paradis, then of the USCC Department of Education, who in turn was succeeded by Msgr. Francis Kelly of the National Catholic Education Association. Sister Maria de la Cruz was reappointed twice and for a time served as president of COINCAT. By 1992 the membership had grown to thirty.

In 1994 the International Council was reorganized. The cardinal prefect of the Congregation for the Clergy became the president, and the secretary of the congregation served as vice-president. The number of permanent members, appointed to six-year terms, was set at ten. The new structure allows for the appointment of *periti* whose areas of expertise are suited to a particular project. These *periti* further enhance COINCAT's international character and competence. The newly constituted COINCAT met for the first time in Rome in September 1994. The members and *periti* formulated general principles and drew up an outline for the revised edition of the *General Directory for Catechesis* published in 1997.

Bibliography: *Annuario Pontificio per l'Anno 2000* (Vatican City 2000). W. H. PARADIS, "Report on the Fifth Meeting of the International Catechetical Council, Rome, April 11–17, 1983," *The Living Light* 20 (1984): 159–70.

[J. POLLARD]

INTERNATIONAL THEOLOGICAL COMMISSION

Pope Paul VI, in response to a recommendation made during Vatican Council II and the specific proposal of the 1967 Synod of Bishops, established the International Theological Commission, 28 April 1969 (*Acta Apostolicae Sedis* 61 [1969] 431–432; cf. 713–716). The function of the ITC is "to study doctrinal questions of major importance in order to offer advisory assistance to the Holy See and, in particular, the Congregation for the Doctrine of the Faith" (Statutes, ibid. 540–541). It has only a consultative and not a deliberative voice in the functioning of the ordinary magisterium of the Church.

Format. The Commission consists of thirty members chosen by the pope from names recommended by the cardinal prefect of the Congregation for the Doctrine of the Faith after consultation with the national episcopal conferences. The members, representing various nations and diverse schools of theology, are chosen for their proficiency in one or another of the theological disciplines and for their fidelity to the magisterium. The initial appointment is for five years and may be renewed for another quinquennium. The cardinal prefect of the CDF presides over the commission and is assisted in the administration by a secretary general.

When the commission was first established in 1969, it had among its members many of the most prestigious Catholic theologians of the time. Several had been *periti* at the Second Vatican Council: Hans Urs von Balthasar, Louis Bouyer, Yves Congar, O.P., Philippe Delhaye, André Feuillet, P.S.S., Henri De Lubac, S.J., Gerard Philips, Karl Rahner, S.J., Joseph Ratzinger, and Rudolf Schnackenburg. The English-speaking theological community was represented by Barnabas Ahern, C.P., Walter Burghhardt, S.J., and Bernard Lonergan, S.J. Several of these were reappointed for the second quinquennium (1974), and they were joined by Edouard Hamel, S.J., and Jean-Marie Tillard, O.P., of Canada, and John Mahoney, S.J., from Great Britain. Half the appointees named to the commission in 1980 by Pope John Paul II were holdovers; new members included Michael Ledwith of Ireland, Carl Peter of the U.S., Walter Principe, C.S.B., of Canada, John Thornhill, S.M., of Australia, and Christophe von Schönborn of Switzerland.

In 1986 a new term of the Commission began. Among the members were the distinguished theologians Hans Urs von Balthasar and Georges Cottier, O.P., of Switzerland, Giuseppe Colombo (Italy), Jean Corbon (Lebanon), Philippe Delhaye and Jan Walgrave, O.P., of Belgium, and Joachim Gnilka and Walter Kasper of West Germany. At the time of their appointment in 1986, Bonaventura Kloppenburg, O.F.M. (Brazil), and Franc Perko (Yugoslavia) were auxiliary bishops. The English-speaking world was represented by John Finnis of England, Gilles Langevin of Canada, Michael Ledwith of Ireland, Carl Peter and William May of the U.S., Francis Moloney, S.D.B., of Australia, and Felix Wilfred of India. Professors Finnis (Oxford University) and May (The Catholic University of America) were the first laymen to be appointed to the commission. By the end of the quinquennium in 1991 several members had been named diocesan bishops and were no longer eligible to serve on the commission, whose function is to offer informed advice to the magisterium. By reason of their position as residential bishops Walter Kasper, André-Jean Léonard (who had been appointed to the commission to replace the deceased Walgrave), Jorge Medina Estevez of Chile, a member from the beginning, and Franc Perko belonged to the magisterium.

Among internationally significant theologians appointed to the commission in 1992, Colombo, Corbon, and Gnilka continued to give their prestigious service. They were joined by Joseph Doré, S.S. (France), Adolphe Gesché (Belgium), Hermann Pottmeyer (Germany), and Max Thurian (Switzerland-Italy). Langevin, Ledwith, May, and Moloney, joined by Avery Dulles, S.J., of the U.S., Charles Acton of England, Sebastian Karotemprel, S.D.B., of India, Joseph Osei-Bonsu of Ghana, represented the English-speaking theological community. A long-standing member of the Commission, Christoph von Schönborn, O.P., and three first-time members, Joseph Doré, S.S., Norbert Strotmann Hoppe, M.S.C. (Peru), and Joseph Osei-Bonsu were appointed bishops during the course of the quinquennium. Professor Gösta Hallonsten of Sweden was a new lay member of the commission, replacing Professor Finnis. During the course of the quinquennium, Max Thurian passed away and was not replaced.

Appointees in 1997 for a new quinquennium included holdovers Pottmeyer and Gesché, as well as three-termers Francis Moloney, S.D.B., Jean-Louis Bruguès, O.P., and Henrique Noronha Galvão. They were joined by new members: Roland Minnerath (France), Bruno Forte (Italy), Gerhard Müller (Germany), and several lesser known theologians. The Anglophone world was represented by Charles Acton (England), Christopher Begg (USA), Joseph Di Noia, OP (USA), George Karakunnel (India), Sebastian Karotemprel, S.D.B. (India), Thomas Norris (Ireland), Anthony Ojo (Nigeria), and Luis Tagle (Philippines). An obvious effort was made to internationalize the commission further with appointment Tanios Bou Mansour, O.L.M., of Lebanon, Fadel Sidarouss, S.J., of Egypt, and Rafael Salzar Cardenas, M.Sp.S., of Mexico. The increased internationalization of the commission has had the unintended result of a diminution of the representation of the European centers of theological learning and to some extent a lessening of the expertise of the group as a whole. It has also made communication more difficult, especially in the subcommissions where instantaneous translation is not generally available.

In the first 30 years the commission had only two presidents. Cardinal Franjo Seper, prefect of the Congregation for the Doctrine of the Faith during the latter part of Pope Paul VI's pontificate, presided 1969–81. Cardinal Josef Ratzinger became president in 1981 when Pope John Paul II appointed him as prefect of the CDF. Monsignor Philippe Delhaye of Belgium served as secretary general of the commission from 1972 until ill health forced him to resign in 1989. Cardinal Ratzinger appointed Georges Cottier, O.P., of Switzerland to replace him in 1990.

Procedures and Themes. The commission begins each quinquennium with a wide-ranging discussion of a number of theological issues that the members regard as worthy of the Holy See's attention. The themes that are chosen for examination become the focal points of the commission in the following four years. In its early years the commission examined and published documents dealing with sacerdotal ministry (1971); the unity of faith and theological pluralism (1972); the apostolicity of the Church and apostolic succession (1973); criteria for the knowledge of Christian morality (1974); the relation between the magisterium and theologians (1975); Christian salvation and human progress (1976); and the sacrament of marriage (1977). These were followed by published statements dealing with the selected questions in christology (1979); theology, christology, and anthropology (1981); reconciliation and penance (1982); and the dignity and rights of the human person (1983). In commemoration of the twentieth anniversary of the close of Vatican II, the commission published a document on selected items in ecclesiology (1984); and in 1985, it published a commentary on four propositions dealing with Jesus' self-consciousness and His awareness of His mission.

The four themes selected by the commission for study during the quinquennium beginning in 1986 were: faith and inculturation; interpretation of dogma; fundamental moral theology; and current questions in eschatology. The commission established in 1992 devoted itself to an examination of contemporary soteriology; Christianity in relation to other religions; a contemporary presentation of the mystery of God; and the Eucharist. The commission established in 1997 directed its attention to the Church and the sins of the past; the permanent diaconate; the inculturation of revelation; and the theology of creation.

The procedures of the commission follow a routine. After the selection of the themes to be studied during the quinquennium, the president of the ITC appoints sub-commissions to examine them and draft a working paper, the *instrumentum laboris,* that serves as the basis for discussion and debate by the commission as a whole. When the members agree upon and approve a final text, the document is submitted to a plenary session of the commission for formal approval. The Congregation for the Doctrine of the Faith receives the finished documents, and decides how best to use the work of the Theological Commission. Some documents have been used as a resource for the CDF and others have been published. The commission's study that resulted in the document *Memory and Reconciliation: The Church and the Sins of the Past* (2000) took on a particular significance. On the Second Sunday of Lent 2000, Pope John Paul II made the presentation of the document a highlight with his own memorable comments at an event marking the celebration of the Jubilee Year.

Bibliography: International Theological Commission, *International Theological Commission: Texts and Documents 1969–1985,* ed. M. SHARKEY, (San Francisco 1989). A collection of the Commission's documents from 1985–1996, most of which have appeared in a number of languages in various international scholarly journals, is in preparation.

[B. M. AHERN/W. E. MAY/F. J. MOLONEY]

JOHN PAUL I, POPE

Pontificate 26 August–28 September 1978; b. Albino Luciani, 17 October 1912, Forno di Canale, Italy. He was born into a poor family. His father, a Socialist Party organizer, was at one point forced to migrate to Switzerland for work. After studies in the minor seminary at Feltre and the major seminary at Belluno, young Luciani was ordained a priest, 7 July 1935. Fr. Luciani earned a doctorate in theology at the Gregorianum in Rome in 1937, and served briefly as a parish priest at Forno di Canale and Agerdo. From 1937–47 he was professor of theology, canon law, and history of sacred art at the Belluno seminary, for a time serving also as vice rector. Popular as a preacher and a catechist, his book *Catechism Crumbs* went through several editions. While continuing to teach, he also became in 1947 pro-chancellor of the diocese, then named vicar-general. In 1958 he was named to the see of Vittorio-Veneto and ordained bishop by John XXIII at St. Peter's. He participated in Vatican Council II, and his commitment to its spirit of renewal was expressed in a pastoral letter to his diocese in 1967, ''Notes on the Council.''

Bishop Luciani, named Patriarch of Venice in 1969, was created cardinal by Pope Paul VI at the consistory of 5 March 1973, with San Marco, Piazza Venezia, as his titular church. In 1976 he published *Illustrissimi,* an imaginative book of letters he addressed to famous literary and historical figures, including Jesus. In the conclave that met in August 1978 to elect a successor to Paul VI, Cardinal Luciani was elected the first day, on the fourth ballot. His election was surprising because of its swiftness and was welcomed because of his warmth and simplicity. He did away with the traditional papal coronation and was installed as the supreme pastor by receiving the archiepiscopal pallium on 3 September 1978; the pope referred to the ceremony as the inauguration of his pastoral ministry. The program Pope John Paul outlined the day after his election proposed the following: to continue to put into effect the heritage of Vatican II; to preserve the integrity of church discipline in the lives of priests and faithful; to remind the entire Church that the first duty is evangelization; to continue the ecumenical thrust, without compromising doctrine but without hesitancy; to pursue with patience but firmness the serene and constructive dialogue of Paul VI for pastoral action; to support every laudable and worthy initiative for world peace.

The pope did not live carry out this program; the Church and the world were shocked by his sudden death after barely a month in office. But John Paul I had long suffered from poor health, although illness was kept secret and not revealed until after his death. His physical condition and the pressures of the office, not a fanciful assassination plot, joined to bring his pontificate to an abrupt end. The ''September Papacy'' had brought fulfilment to the longing in people's hearts for a person and a leader who radiated joy, holiness, and simple goodness. His passing left the hope that the response to his brief pontificate would be remembered by his successors and by every pastor in the Church.

Bibliography: JOHN CORNWELL, *A Thief in the Night: The Mysterious Death of Pope John Paul I* (New York: Simon & Schuster, 1989). PETER HEBBLETHWAITE, *The Year of Three Popes* (Cleveland: Collins, 1979).

[T. C. O'BRIEN]

JOHN PAUL II CULTURAL CENTER

The cultural center that takes its name and inspiration from Pope John Paul II is located in Washington, D.C. The center features state-of-the-art exhibits and interactive media activities designed to provide visitors an experience that inspires faith, promotes religious values, and fosters respect for diverse cultural backgrounds. The five main galleries explore (1) the history of the Church and the papacy; (2) how faith is celebrated around the world; (3) the relationship between the human and the physical world; (4) ways that God's presence is expressed in art; and (5) world cultures and their relationship to the Catholic Church.

Works by Christian artists from around the world and from the collection of the Vatican Museum are displayed. The permanent collection highlights Marian themes. Another component integral to the center is the Intercultural Forum. Scholars research and study themes related to the impact of the papacy on world cultures and the promotion of values relating to the dignity of the human person. Facilities included a library, auditorium and conference rooms. The inspiration for the center is Pope John Paul's call for renewed evangelization in the new millennium.

The multi-million dollar project initiated by Cardinal Adam Maida, archbishop of Detroit, and designed by Leo A. Daly, architect, engineer, and interior designer, and Edwin Schlossberg, Inc., exhibit designer. It opened during the Jubilee Year 2000 on a fourteen-acre site adjacent to the Basilica of the National Shrine of the Immaculate Conception and the Catholic University of America in northeast Washington, D.C.

[G. MICHAEL BUGARIN]

JOHN PAUL II INSTITUTE ON MARRIAGE AND FAMILY

The John Paul II Institute for Studies on Marriage and Family, with headquarters at the Pontifical Lateran University in Rome, has as its purpose study and research that highlight the uniqueness and importance of the Church's mission to the family. The Synod of Bishops (Fifth General Assembly, 1980) had called for the creation of theological centers devoted to the study of the Church's teaching on marriage and the family. Pope John Paul II responded in October 1982 by issuing *Magnum Matrimonii Sacramentum,* an apostolic constitution that serves as the charter of the Institute. The Institute is empowered to grant degrees, and its president is appointed by the Holy Father.

It was Pope John Paul II's stated intention that the work of the Institute be spread throughout the world, and thus it established extensions in Spain (Valencia), Mexico (Mexico City-Guadalajara), and the United States (Washington, D.C.). The last was founded by the invitation of James Cardinal Hickey, archbishop of Washington, and the request of Virgil C. Dechant, supreme knight of the Knights of Columbus, to serve American and other English- speaking students. The Congregation for Catholic Education gave it the status of a pontifical faculty 22 August 1988.

The curricula of the John Paul II Institute encompass the full range of studies required for a complete theological education in the areas of marriage and family: philosophy, theological method, systematic and spiritual theology, Christian ethics and moral theology, public policy, canon law, biblical theology, and the life sciences. The programs of study seek to foster in students the theological competency necessary for the exercise of a variety of Christian ministries, including counseling, pastoral and missionary work in the specialized areas of marriage and family, and for religious leadership positions, especially in family life bureaus. In particular, the Institute prepares its students for work in Christian education, research, and publication, especially as members of the faculties of seminaries, theological schools, and departments of religious studies. In addition, the Institute enables per-

John Paul II Cultural Center. (Leo A. Daly. Photograph by Michael Fischer.)

sons anticipating professional service in education, health care, social work, community and public interest organizations, law, and public life to understand more fully the theological basis of their vocations.

The American extension is located at 487 Michigan Avenue, NE, Washington, DC 20017.

[C. A. ANDERSON]

JOHN XXIII, POPE

Pontificate, 28 October 1958 to 3 June 1963; b. Angelo Giuseppe Roncalli, 25 November 1881, Sotto il Monte, Bergamo, Italy; d. 3 June 1963, Rome. He was the third of 13 children, the first son, of pious peasants, Giovanni Battista and Marianna Giulia (Mazzola) Roncalli, who were sharecroppers (*mezzadri*). At 12 he entered the diocesan minor seminary at Bergamo. After taking the doctorate in theology from the Roman Seminary (Apollinare), he was ordained on 10 August 1904.

As he was beginning graduate studies in Canon Law, he was appointed secretary of the new bishop of Bergamo, Count Giacomo Radini-Tedeschi, whom Roncalli served faithfully for more than 9 years, gaining experience in Catholic action and an understanding of the problems of the working class. At the same time he taught at the diocesan seminary. In 1915, when Italy entered World War I, he was called to the army and was assigned to military hospitals in Bergamo.

In 1925 Roncalli was appointed titular archbishop of Areopolis and apostolic visitor to Bulgaria. He promptly took up residence in the politically troubled capital, Sofia, and concerned himself with the problems of the Eastern rite Catholics, who constituted a small, scattered minority of about 4,000 among the predominantly Orthodox population. He had fewer anxieties over the 40,000 Catholics of the Latin rite, who were better organized but were dependent on the political and ecclesiastical support of France.

In 1934, Roncalli was named apostolic delegate to Turkey and Greece, and took up residence in Istanbul. He succeeded in closing the breach that existed between the delegation and the local clergy of the Latin rite. Amid trying circumstances he fostered harmony among the different national colonies in the city. To show his respect for the government and people of Turkey, he introduced the use of the Turkish language into divine worship and official documents. During World War II, when Istanbul became a center of international espionage and intrigue, Roncalli provided the Holy See with much valuable information that he obtained from diplomats as well as public sources. He also helped many persecuted Jews fleeing from central and eastern Europe.

In Greece, where he was confronted with the confusion existing among the 50,000 Catholics of the country, he eventually succeeded in bringing about greater unity of action among the bishops of the Latin, Byzantine, and Armenian rites.

In 1944 Pius XII chose Roncalli for the difficult position of nuncio to Charles de Gaulle's new provisional government in Paris. Unobtrusively he labored to repair the spiritual divisions that had been exacerbated by the war and its consequences. He traveled widely, made a pilgrimage to Lourdes almost every year and in 1950 journeyed to Algeria and other parts of North Africa. In his dealings with the French bishops, he was tolerant of discussion in the intellectual sphere and patient with innovations in the pastoral ministry. Thus he viewed Cardinal Emanuel Suhard's novel plan to evangelize the dechristianized masses (Mission de France) hopefully, and he attentively observed the activities of the worker-priests.

Roncalli was made a cardinal on 12 January 1953, and a short time later named the patriarch of Venice. During his five years in Venice, he wrote brief, frequent circular letters on topics of current importance; increased the number of parishes and showed his concern for the working class; and developed various forms of Catholic action.

After Pius XII's death on 9 October 1958, Roncalli was elected pope on 28 October. In the consistory of 25 January 1959 he proposed to the cardinals three major undertakings: a diocesan synod for Rome, an ecumenical council for the universal Church, and a revision of the Code of Canon Law (preceded by the promulgation of the Code of Oriental Law). The synod, the first in the history of Rome, was solemnly opened by the pope in the Basilica of St. John Lateran on 24 January 1960. Its decrees, promulgated by the apostolic constitution *Sollicitudo omnium ecclesiarum,* were designed to remedy the ills of the Church in a city that had grown from 400,000 inhabitants in 1900 to more than 2 million in 1960 and that had only 220 secular and 360 religious priests.

Although he died after the first session, the ecumenical council, which he decided to call the Second Vatican Council, is undoubtedly the major achievement of John's pontificate. Attributing the idea of convoking such an assembly to a sudden inspiration from the Holy Spirit, he prescribed as its immediate task the renewal of the religious life of Catholics and the bringing up to date of the teaching, discipline, and organization of the Church, with the ultimate goal being the unity of Christians.

Pope John appeared in public for the last time at his window in the Vatican on 22 May 1963. Shortly thereafter he began to succumb to a gastric cancer from which he had suffered for about a year. Having endured a prolonged agony, he died on 3 June (Pentecost Monday). As the world mourned, his body was buried in a simple tomb in the crypt of St. Peter's.

A man of evangelical simplicity and unaffected humility, John XXIII was never ashamed of his lowly origins and always remained closely attached to his native soil and his rustic family. His diary, *Journey of a Soul* [tr. by D. White (New York 1965)], published posthumously, reveals a profound interior life and an unwavering trust in Divine Providence. One of his favorite apothegms was *Voluntas Dei, pax nostra* (God's will, our peace), a phrase he borrowed from St Gregory Nazianzen. He was a highly cultured man, versed in history, archeology, and architecture, fond of literature (especially Manzoni), art, and music; he could speak French, Bulgarian, Russian, Turkish, and modern Greek, besides Italian and Latin. Gifted with an agreeable disposition and a ready wit, he was characteristically open and affable, understanding and compassionate, jovial and calm, familiar in audiences, hospitable, and a lively conversationalist. Throughout his life he valued the care of souls above any other occupation. He disliked the bureaucracy of the Roman Curia, demythologized the papacy, and diminished the cult of the pontifical personality. He allowed as much freedom of thought and action as possible to others and recognized the limitations of his own knowledge and ability. He perceived the need of reform and his pontificate is regarded as a turning point in the history of the Catholic Church. Considered by some, because of his advanced age and ambiguous reputation at the time of his election, to be merely a transitional pontiff, John XXIII instead initiated a new age. As part of the Jubilee Year 2000 events, his beatification by Pope John Paul II was scheduled for 3 September together with Pope Pius IX.

Bibliography: V. BRANCA and S. ROSSO-MAZZINGHI, ed. *Angelo Giuseppe Roncalli : dal patriarcato di Venezia alla cattedra di San Pietro* (Florence 1984). G. ALBERIGO, ed. *Giovanni XXIII : transizione del papato e della Chiesa* (Rome 1988). P. HEBBLETHWAITE, *Pope John XXIII, Shepherd of the Modern World* (Garden City, NY 1985).

[R. TRISCO]

KASPER, WALTER

Theologian, secretary of the Pontifical Council for Promoting Christian Unity, bishop emeritus of Rottenburg-Stuttgart; b. 5 March 1933, Heidenheim, Germany. Kasper was the oldest of the three children of Franz Josef and Theresia (Bacher) Kasper. From 1952 to 1956 he studied philosophy and Catholic theology at the universities of Tübingen and Münich. In 1954 he brought attention to himself with the work, "The Doctrine of Human Knowledge in the *Quaestiones Disputatae De Veritate* of Thomas Aquinas." After ordination to the priesthood, 6 April 1957, Kasper served the vicarate in Stuttgart and Tätigkeit as instructor at the Tübingen seminary "Wilhelmsstift" (1958–1961). He received a doctorate in theology from Tübingen in 1961 with his work entitled "The Doctrine of Tradition in the Roman School."

From 1961 to 1964 Kasper was an academic assistant for Leo Scheffczyk and Hans Küng at Tübingen. In 1964 he completed his *Habilitationsschrift*, "Philosophy and Theology of History in Schelling's Late Philosophy," and was appointed to the chair for Dogmatics at the University of Münster. In 1970 he joined the Catholic theological faculty of Tübingen University. He became known in the English- speaking world through his work in Christology and the doctrine of God. His best-known book, *Jesus the Christ*, was published in 1974 (Eng. trans., New York, 1976), followed eight years later by *The God of Jesus Christ* (Eng. trans., New York, 1984). In 1983–1984 he was a guest lecturer at The Catholic University of America in Washington, DC.

During this same period Kasper assumed several tasks in the ecclesial realm. In 1974 he was appointed to the International Theological Commission by Pope Paul VI. In 1979 he became a consultant for the Pontifical Council for Promoting Christian Unity and a representative of the Catholic Church on the Faith and Order Commission of the World Council of Churches (WCC). As consultant and member of the faith commission of the German Bishops' Conference Kasper was the primary author of the first volume of the 1985 German bishops' "Catholic Adult Catechism." He was appointed special secretary of the extraordinary assembly of the Synod of Bishops (1985).

Pope John Paul II appointed Kasper bishop of the diocese of Rottenburg-Stuttgart in 1989. He took the motto "veritatem in caritate" whereby he made it clear that he understood the bishop's responsibility as that of serving the truth in love. From the beginning, Bishop Kasper made the focus of his diocesan leadership the task of the new evangelization, which he understood as the imperative question of the church and society in Europe. New evangelization as a new inculturation of the gospel, requires, according to Kasper, renewal and deepening of the belief of the church in line with Scripture and Tradition as well as dialogue and a profound engagement with the surrounding culture, reflection on Christian identity as well as the realization of an appropriate form of the Church in the present moment. Kasper showed himself to be open to innovations that could be reconciled with the theological essence of the church; this underscored his reputation as a circumspect theologian and bishop, regarded on balance as being a reformer. He regarded the *communio* ecclesiology of the Second Vatican Council as decisive. The search for appropriate method of the transmission of faith, particularly through marriage and family, reform of the liturgy, the cooperation of priests and the laity in the pastoral community and the community at large, and the overcoming the "schism between faith and modern culture" (Pope Paul VI) were the emphases of his work as bishop.

Bishop Kasper was the chief author of many theological, ethical, and sociopolitical pronouncements that issued from the German bishops' conference. His pastoral letter, written jointly with Archbishop Oskar Saier (Freiburg im Breisgau) and Bishop Karl Lehmann (Mainz), entitled, "To the Troubled Souls of Persons from Broken Marriages, Separated and/or the Remarried" (1993), aroused international attention, though it was not well received in Rome.

In 1994 Kasper became co-president of the Joint Roman Catholic-Evangelical Lutheran Commission of the Pontifical Council for Promoting Christian Unity. In 1998 Pope John Paul appointed him a consultant for the Congregation for the Doctrine of the Faith. The following year, the pope called him to Rome to serve as secretary of the Pontifical Council for Promoting Christian Unity. The first high point in the exercise of his new office was witnessed in the Joint Declaration on the Doctrine of Justification of the Lutheran World Federation and the Roman Catholic Church 1999 in Augsburg.

[JOACHIM DRUMM]

KEELER, WILLIAM HENRY

Cardinal, archbishop of Baltimore; b. 4 March 1931, San Antonio, Texas, the son of Thomas and Margaret (Conway) Keeler. The family soon moved to Lebanon, Pennsylvania, where William attended Catholic elementary and high schools before he entered St. Charles Seminary, Overbrook, Philadelphia, where he received a B.A. in 1952. He was sent for further studies to the Pontifical Gregorian University and was ordained to the priesthood in Rome on 17 July 1955. After receiving an S.T.L. in

William Henry Cardinal Keeler. (© Grzegorz Galazka/CORBIS.)

original thirteen states. The same year Keeler was elected vice-president of the National Conference of Catholic Bishops, and later served as its president (1992–1995). He was elevated to the college of cardinals in 1994, with the titular church of St. Mary of the Angels.

Cardinal Keeler took part in a number of ecumenical and interreligious initiatives on the national and international levels. From 1984 to 1987 he served as chairman of the NCCB's Committee for Ecumenical and Interreligious Affairs; in 1987 he arranged for Pope John Paul II's meeting with national Jewish leaders in Columbia, North Carolina. He helped to arrange a meeting between Imam W. D. Mohammad, of the Muslim American Society, and Pope John Paul II, and attended an historical meeting of Catholic bishops and leaders with the Grand Mufti of Syria. After being made a cardinal, he was appointed to the Congregation for the Oriental Churches and the Pontifical Council for Promoting Christian Unity; in 1997 he welcomed Ecumenical Patriarch Bartholomew to Baltimore.

Bibliography: THOMAS W. SPALDING, *The Premier See: The History of the Archdiocese of Baltimore 1789–1994.* 2d ed. Baltimore: Johns Hopkins University Press, 1995.

[C. J. KAUFFMAN]

1956 he returned to the U.S. and spent two years in parish ministry in the diocese of Harrisburg and as secretary of the diocesan tribunal. In 1958 he was sent back to Gregorian University to study canon law, where he received a J.C.D. in 1961. After another year in pastoral duty, he returned to Rome as secretary to the bishop of Harrisburg for the Second Vatican Council. Father Keeler was officially appointed a *peritus* to the council by Pope John XXIII, and served on the staff of the *Council Digest,* a daily communication service sponsored by the bishops of the United States.

Appointed vice chancellor of Harrisburg in 1965, he later became chancellor and vicar general. In 1979 he was ordained bishop, with the titular see of Ulcinium, and appointed auxiliary bishop of Harrisburg. Bishop Keeler was elected administrator of the diocese by the college of consultors in 1983, and the next year Pope John Paul II appointed him ordinary of the diocese. He was installed by Cardinal John Krol, archbishop of Philadelphia.

Pope John Paul appointed Keeler archbishop of Baltimore in 1989, following the resignation of Archbishop William Borders. Archbishops Keeler and Borders presided together at the 1989 Bicentennial of the hierarchy in the United States honoring the 1789 appointment of John Carroll as the first bishop of the first diocese in the

KÖNIG, FRANZ BORGIA

Cardinal, archbishop of Vienna; b. 3 August 1905, Rabenstein, Lower Austria into a farmer's family, the eldest of 10 children. He attended the grammar school of the Benedictine Monastery of Melk, and in 1927 went on to Collegium Germanicum-Hungaricum in Rome, where he studied philosophy (Ph.D., 1930) and theology (Ph.D., 1936) and was ordained to the priesthood on 29 October 1933. During his stay in Rome he also studied old Persian religions and languages at the Pontifical Institute Biblicum. After his return to his home diocese of Sankt Pölten, Lower Austria, he served as chaplain in smaller parishes and then as curate to the cathedral. His teaching career began in 1945 with an appointment to lecture in religious studies at the University of Vienna; from 1948 to 1952 he taught moral theology at the University of Salzburg. He published widely in the field of comparative religion, his chief work being the three-volume *Christus und die Religionen der Erde* (1948). In 1952 he was elected titular bishop of Liviade and appointed coadjutor of Sankt Pölten, with right of succession. Continuing his work in religious studies he compiled his *Religionswissenschaftliches Wörterbuch* (1956) and was appointed editor for the second edition of the *Lexikon für Theologie und Kirche* (10 vols). Pope Pius XII appointed him archbishop of Vienna in 1956, and two years later he was created cardinal, with the title of S. Eusebio, by Pope John XXIII. He was also the ordinary for Greek-rite Catholics living in Austria and, from 1959 to 1968, military vicar of Austria. In 1959 Cardinal König founded the Afro-Asian-Institute in Vienna as a platform for intercultural and interreligious exchange between the Christian West and the newly emancipated Afro-Asian countries. This spontaneous experiment gave him a clear vision and firm attitude at the Second Vatican Council regarding religious freedom (declaration *Dignitatis Humanae,* 1965) and interreligious dialogue (declaration *Nostra Aetate,* 1965). König was appointed to the Central Preparatory Commission of the Second Vatican Council and for the first session served in the Theological Commission. Karl Rahner was his *peritus* at the council.

In 1965 Pope Paul VI appointed Cardinal König president of the Secretariat for Non-Believers, a position he held until 1980. A concern for dialogue—ecumenical, interreligious, church-state—was the hallmark of his public activity. In Austria he tried to heal the wounds of civil war and the dissent of pre-war Austria (Austrofascism vs. Austro-Marxism) by reconciling trade unions and socialists with the church. A breakthrough was achieved by his lecture at the General Assembly of the Austrian Trade Unions 1973, "Kirche und Gesellschaft." His first diplomatic contacts with eastern churches under communist oppression resulted in a profound ecumenical engagement with Orthodoxy and Old Oriental Churches from which the foundation "Pro Oriente" took its origin (1964). The resulting mutual visits and free theological exchange bore rich fruit, including the "Vienna Formula" (1993), which cleared old misunderstandings in Christology by a commonly accepted definition of the natures and person of Christ with a large impact on interecclesial relationships. The global dimension of the gospel's message led Cardinal König to cooperate with the Congregation of World Mission in Rome (1968). He also made notable attempts to engage in dialogue with scholars. In 1968 he offered an attempt to reconcile natural sciences and Christian faith with "Der Fall Galilei." He also helped to found the "Institut für die Wissenschaften vom Menschen" (1983), which since that time has held biennial seminars with the pope at Castel Gandolfo. In 1985 Cardinal König resigned his archbishopric. For the next five years he served as president of "Pax Christi International."

It is widely held that Cardinal König took the lead in advancing the candidacy of Karol Wojtyła in the 1978 conclave that elected him as Pope John Paul II.

Bibliography: ALOIS SCHIFFERLE, *Geduld und Vertrauen: Franz Kardinal König—Texte und Gespräche,* Paulusverlag, 1995. ANNEMARIE FENZL, and REGINALD FÖLDY, eds. *Franz Kardinal König. Haus auf festem Grund.* Amalthea, 1994. FRANZ KÖNIG, *Appelle an Gewissen und Vernunft.* Tyrolia, 1996. JOHANNES KUNZ, ed. *Kardinal Franz König: Ansichten eines engagierten Kirchenmannes.* Edition S 1991.

[PETRUS BSTEH]

Franz Cardinal König c. 1963. (Express Newspapers/Archive Photos. Reproduced by Permission.)

KOREC, JÁN CHRYZOSTOM

Cardinal, bishop of Nitra, Slovakia; b. 22 January 1924, Bosany, Czechoslovakia. Joined Society of Jesus 15 Sept. 1939. In 1950 he had to interrupt his studies of philosophy when the Communist regime suppressed religious orders. Because of the religious persecution, Korec was ordained to the priesthood (1 October 1950) before completing his studies. Towards the end of that year, the organization and activities of the Church were paralyzed: the bishops jailed or placed under house arrest; 3000 diocesan priests sent to jail; religious, nuns and seminarians deported; and monasteries, convents and ten of the twelve seminaries closed. In the face of this persecution, Pope

Pius XII wrote to the Jesuit provincial of Czechoslovakia authorizing the ordination of six new bishops. Fr. Korec, together with 5 other priests, was secretly ordained a bishop in 1951 by Pavel Hnilica, S.J., himself an underground bishop. The ordination took place in a hospital and lasted only one hour. At 27 he was youngest bishop in the world. Because the government refused him the licence it required all priests to have, he had to perform his episcopal ministry in secret.

Bishop Korec worked in a factory from 1951 to1958 and later was librarian at Institute of Labor Hygiene. Arrested in 1960, he was sentenced to twelve years in prison because of his pastoral activities. In jail he developed an intense spiritual program: daily celebration of the Mass, prayer, meditation, and study (reviewing his studies in philosophy and theology by heart). In his request from release from jail he affirmed that he had never knowingly done anything against the constitution of his country, and said, ''The accusation of being loyal to the pope, I consider an honor. This loyalty does not need the approval of anybody. Jail has not absolutely diminished this loyalty. On the contrary, this loyalty to the pope has been precisely what has allowed me to endure imprisonment.''

Rehabilitated in 1968 because of a general amnesty, he was released from jail seriously ill. The following year, after another judicial process, he was totally rehabilitated. Because of ill health, he had to be admitted in a hospital, and when he was released, he worked as street sweeper in Bratislava and later in a tar factory. In 1974 his rehabilitation was annulled and he was sent to prison for four more years to complete the sentence. Later he was freed because of poor health. He lost his job of street sweeper and was placed in the unemployment list until he found a job in a chemical factory unloading packages, work that he had until 1984. After the Velvet Revolution succeeded in Czechoslovakia and the status of the Church was normalized, he was appointed rector of the Seminary of Bratislava (1990) and nominated to the diocese of Nitra later the same year. Later he was elected president of the Regional Episcopal Conference of Slovakia. In remembrance of his days as a street sweeper, his pastoral staff is a broom.

In the consistory of 28 June 1991 Bishop Korec was created cardinal by Pope John Paul II, with the titular church of Ss. Fabiano e Venanzio a Villa Fiorelli. He participated in the second special assembly for Europe of the World Synod of Bishops, October 1999.

Bibliography: He has written profusely, more than 60 volumes, 20 of which have been published in Austria, Italy, and Canada. Some of them are: *Jezis zídaleka a zblizka* (Bratislava, 1990); *Kriz vo svetle pravdy Korespondencie Jana Chryzostoma Korca zostavil Peter Tibensky* (Bratislava 1991); *Od barbarskej noci* (Bratislava 1992, c1976); *Bratislavsky Ve'lky Piatok : zbierka autentickych dokumentov o zhromazdeni veriacich 25. marca 1988* (Bratislava 1994); *Cirkev v dejinach Slovenska* (Bratislava, 1994); *Clovek na cestach Zeme* (Martin 1997); *Svedectva pravdy o Slovensku* (Radosina 1997); *Gesu Cristo ora e sempre: Esercizi spirituali predicati a papa Giovanni Paolo II* (Cinisello Balsamo 1998).

[SALVADOR MIRANDA]

KROL, JOHN JOSEPH

Cardinal, archbishop of Philadelphia; b. Cleveland, Ohio, 26 October 1910; d. Philadelphia, Pa., 3 March 1996. The fifth child of John Krol Sr., a stone cutter by trade, and Anna Pietruszka, Krol received his early education at St. Hyacinth's elementary school and the Cathedral Latin School in Cleveland. Upon graduation from high school in 1927 he found employment as a meat cutter in a local market. He eventually answered God's call to the priesthood, began his studies at St. Mary's College, Orchard Lake, Michigan, and completed them at St. Mary's Seminary in Cleveland. He was ordained on 20 February 1937 at Cleveland's St. John's Cathedral by Bishop Joseph Schrembs. His first and only parochial assignment followed at Immaculate Heart of Mary Parish in Cleveland. The following year he was sent to Rome for studies in canon law. With the outbreak of World War II he was recalled to the United States and assigned to the Catholic University of America where he completed the doctorate in canon law.

In 1942 Krol returned to Cleveland and the chair of canon law at St. Mary's Seminary. At the same time, he functioned as defender of the bond, vice-chancellor, and eventually chancellor of the diocese. In 1948 he was elected president of the Canon Law Society of America. Pope Pius XII created him Papal Chamberlain in 1945 and Domestic Prelate in 1951. In 1953 Monsignor Krol was named auxiliary bishop of Cleveland and titular bishop of Cadi. He chose as his episcopal motto *Deus Rex Meus,* a heraldic pun on his own name (*krol* is Polish for ''king'').

In 1960 Pope John XXIII announced his intention of summoning an ecumenical council. Bishop Krol was named to the preparatory commission on bishops and the government of dioceses. As the council years unfolded he would go on to be appointed one of the five undersecretaries of the council. He was also a member of the central coordinating committee of the council. Before the council convened, Krol was named to succeed Cardinal O'Hara as tenth ordinary of the Archdiocese of Philadelphia. He was installed on 22 March 1961. On the same day as his appointment to Philadelphia, the archdiocese was split to create the diocese of Allentown.

Archbishop Krol arrived in Philadelphia at a time of social and demographic change. Of the thirty-nine parishes he founded, all but five were in the suburbs; of sixteen parishes closed or consolidated, all but two were within the city of Philadelphia. One of Archbishop Krol's chief priorities was Catholic education. During his tenure St. Charles Borromeo Seminary received full accreditation for its college program. A student apostolate program was introduced, and a school of religious studies for religious and laity was founded. Despite the decline in enrollment during the 1970s, Krol maintained a viable archdiocesan school system. One of his most successful efforts to raise funds for the schools was the foundation of BLOCS (Business Leaders Organized for Catholic Schools). This was a non-sectarian community business effort to raise money for Catholic schools as a recognition of their value to the whole community. In 1963 Archbishop Krol was named chairman of the Education Department of the National Catholic Welfare Conference (NCWC). In 1965 he was elected vice-chairman of the administrative board of the NCWC. When the NCWC gave way to the newly organized NCCB/USCC, he was elected vice-president of the NCCB and president of the same body in 1971. As spokesman for the Catholic bishops he testified against nuclear arms and the arms race before Congress during the deliberations on the SALT Treaty of 1979.

Archbishop Krol was a strict constructionist with regard to the liturgical reforms of the Second Vatican Council. One innovation he consistently opposed was that of Saturday evening Mass. To the end of his life he battled for the sanctity of Sunday observance. In matters ecumenical he was among the leaders of the American hierarchy. In 1964 he founded the Archbishop's Commission on Human Relations with a twofold mandate of directing the archdiocesan ecumenical movement and of promoting racial harmony in cooperation with other faith groups. His ecumenical efforts brought him recognition from the Mason's Golden Slipper Square Club in 1966 when they granted him their Brotherhood Award. In 1967 he received the first John Wesley Ecumenical Award. In 1968 he was given the Human Relations Award of the National Conference of Christians and Jews.

On 26 June 1967 Pope Paul VI named Krol to the College of Cardinals, the same day that Archbishop Karol Wojtyła received the red biretta. Krols' titular church was Santa Maria della Mercede e Sant' Adriano. He was appointed to the Congregation for the Evangelization of Peoples and the Congregation for Oriental Churches. He also served on the Prefecture of Economic Affairs of the Holy See.

In 1976 Cardinal Krol and the archdiocese hosted the Forty-first International Eucharistic Congress. During his tenure the cardinal diligently pursued the causes of Phila-

John Cardinal Krol. (Catholic News Service.)

delphia's local heroes of the faith. He saw the canonization of St. John Neumann, CSSR, fourth bishop of Philadelphia, in June 1977. In 1964 he opened the cause of Mother Katherine Drexel, foundress of the Sisters of the Blessed Sacrament, which ultimately led to her canonization in October 2000.

Cardinal Krol participated in the two historic conclaves of 1978 that elected Popes John Paul I and John Paul II. In October 1979 he welcomed John Paul II to Philadelphia on the journey that would take the pontiff to New York, Boston, Chicago, Des Moines, and Washington D.C.

Much still remains to be known about the historic collaboration between Pope John Paul II and President Ronald Reagan in the downfall of Communism in Poland the 1980s, but there have been credible reports that the line from the Vatican to the White House ran through Philadelphia and Cardinal Krol.

The Cardinal retired from his archdiocesan duties on 11 February 1988. During his retirement years he was a moving force behind the Papal Foundation that was set up in 1988 to ease the financial burdens of the Holy See in the wake of the Banco Ambrosiano collapse. Cardinal Krol died at the archepiscopal residence on the feast day of Mother Katherine Drexel. He is interred in the crypt

Bishop Ignatius Kung, who was imprisoned by Chinese Communist authorities for decades for refusing to renounce allegiance to Rome. (AP/Wide World Photos.)

of Philadelphia's Cathedral Basilica of Sts. Peter and Paul.

Bibliography: J. F. CONNOLLY, *The History of the Archdiocese of Philadelphia* (Philadelphia 1976).*The Catholic Standard and Times* vol. 100 (March 1996). *The American Catholic Who's Who* (Washington 1980).

[THOMAS J. MCMANUS]

KUNG PIN-MEI, IGNATIUS

Cardinal, bishop of Shanghai and apostolic administrator of Suzhou and Nanking; b. 2 August 1901 in P'outong, China; d. 12 March 2000 in Stamford, Connecticut. He was the oldest of four children in a family that had been Catholic for several generations. He entered the Shanghai diocesan seminary in 1919. After nine years of seminary training and two years of pastoral work he was ordained a priest, 28 May 1930. During the next twenty years he served as chaplain and headmaster at schools in Siongkang and Shanghai.

Consecrated as bishop of Suzhou in 1949, he was transferred the next year to Shanghai and appointed apostolic administrator of Suzhou and Nanking. For the next five years Bishop Kung oversaw a church that suffered from increasing persecution by the newly established communist government, refusing to join the government-supported Chinese Catholic Patriotic Association. In 1955 he was arrested along with a number of priests and lay people, and five years later he was sentenced to life imprisonment. Though repeatedly pressured to abandon his allegiance to the pope and to join the Patriotic Church, he never yielded, becoming a symbol of fidelity to the persecuted church.

Kung was released from prison for health reasons in 1985, but was kept under house arrest. In 1988 he was granted permission to travel to the United States for medical treatment, and spent the last twelve years of his life living with his nephew in Connecticut and giving interviews and homilies about the condition of the church in China.

In the consistory of 1979, Pope John Paul II created Bishop Kung a cardinal *in pectore,* keeping his identity secret. The bishop himself did not know of his elevation until 1989, when he had a private audience with the Pope in Rome, and it was made public only at the consistory of 1991. The Pope said that Bishop Kung had "given witness by word and deed, through long suffering and trials, to what constitutes the very essence of life in the Church: participation in the divine life through the apostolic faith and evangelical love."

Bibliography: *L'Osservatore Romano,* English edition (8 July 1991).

[EDITORS]

LAGHI, PIO

Cardinal, papal representative in Jerusalem, Argentina, and the United States, prefect of the Congregation for Catholic Education; b. 21 May 1922, Castiglione (Forlì), Italy. Laghi completed his primary and secondary education at the Salesian institute in Faenza, and then entered the diocesan seminary for philosophy. He was assigned to study theology at the Pontifical Lateran University in Rome, while continuing his priestly formation at the Roman Seminary. On 20 April 1946, he was ordained to the priesthood for the diocese of Faenza. After a brief parochial assignment in Porto Garibaldi (Ferrara), he was sent back to Rome, again to the Lateran University, where he completed doctorates in theology (1947) and canon law (1950). At the request of the secretariat of state, he was assigned to the Pontifical Ecclesiastical Academy in the fall of 1950, there to prepare for service to the diplomatic mission of the Holy See.

In 1952 Laghi was appointed as secretary to the apostolic nunciature in Managua, Nicaragua, where he mastered Spanish. Three years later he was posted to the apostolic delegation in Washington, D.C. In addition to the duties of the nunciature, he learned English, engaged in pastoral work, and began a lifelong fascination with American culture and the Catholic Church in the United States. After six years in Washington, he was transferred to the nunciature in India, working there until his recall to Rome in 1964, where he served five years in the Council for Public Affairs of the Secretariat of State. It was while here that he successfully convinced his somewhat apprehensive superiors that it would be timely to open the archives of the Holy See from the period of World War II to the scrutiny of scholars.

Pio Cardinal Laghi. (Catholic News Service.)

In 1969, he was ordained a bishop, with the titular see of Mauriana, and nominated by Pope Paul VI as apostolic delegate in Jerusalem and Palestine. During his five years there, he was particularly vocal in defense of the rights of the Church and the Palestinian people. His diplomatic duties extended as well to Cyprus, where he was pro-nuncio, and to Greece, as apostolic visitor.

His skills were such that Paul VI appointed him apostolic nuncio to Argentina in 1974, and for six years he attempted to protect the prerogatives of the Church and the rights of the people under a hostile military government. His service there has been criticized as too accommodating to the junta, but both those who observed him there, and subsequent research, have shown him effectively engaged in the more discrete advocacy proper to diplomats, and regularly prodding the sometimes apprehensive hierarchy of the country to take a more aggressive role in defense of human rights.

Pope John Paul II appointed Archbishop Laghi apostolic delegate to the United States in 1980. For nine-and-a-half years his own personal manner, knowledge of America, and style of collaboration with the bishops made him a very visible and popular papal representative. His tenure coincided with controversies, such as those involving Raymond Hunthausen, the archbishop of Seattle,

Charles Curran, professor of moral theology at the Catholic University of America. In 1984, diplomatic relations between the Holy See and the United States were established, so that he became the first apostolic pro-nuncio in America, with responsibilities then extending to representing the interests of the Holy See to the White House, the State department, and Congress. The U.S. bishops especially noted his annual address to the conference each November, on such topics as seminaries, vocations, and Catholic schools, and appreciated his extensive travel throughout the country.

His near decade in America came to an end in 1990, when he was appointed (pro-)prefect of the Congregation for Catholic Education; he was created a cardinal in the consistory of 28 June 1991, with the title of S. Maria Ausiliatrice in Via Tuscolana. As prefect he showed special interest in seminaries, particularly after the post-synodal exhortation *Pastores dabo vobis* (1992), and in Catholic universities, especially in the implementation of the apostolic letter *Ex corde Ecclesiae*. Beginning in 1992 he also served as president of the Pontifical Oratory of St. Peter, and since 1993 as Protector of the Sovereign Order of Malta. In November 1999, his resignation as prefect was accepted.

[TIMOTHY M. DOLAN]

LATERAN PACTS 1985

On 3 June 1985, with the exchange of ratifications between the Holy See and the Italian government, the Concordat of 18 February 1984, went into effect. This agreement between the Vatican and the Italian State amounts to a revision of the original Concordat which formed a part of the Lateran Pacts of 11 February 1929. Over the course of time it had become outdated in several areas. The Concordat of 1985, which probably will be referred to commonly as the ''Revised Lateran Pacts,'' retained some of the fundamental provisions of the earlier agreement.

The revised Concordat consists of a Preamble, 14 Articles and an Additional Protocol which is to be regarded as an integral part of the agreement. There is also a Protocol of Approval to which both parties affixed their signatures on 15 November 1984, and which regulates the norms governing ecclesiastical goods.

Outline of the Pact. The Preamble explains why the Holy See and the Government of the Italian Republic thought it necessary and opportune to modify the old Concordat. Since 1929, many changes had occurred in the political and social order which dictated such a modification. Additionally, developments brought about by the Second Vatican Council on the subject of relations between Church and State likewise demanded change. There has been for several decades in Italy a political regime vastly different from that of the period of the original Pacts. After the Second World War, the nation had adopted a new Constitution and it was therefore both necessary and desirable to revise the Concordat in order to bring it into closer harmony with the Italian Constitution. The Constitution of 1948 included the principle, from the original Lateran Pacts, that ''modifications of the [Lateran] Pacts, accepted by both parties, do not require a revision of the Constitution.'' This principle was important to both the Italian government and the Holy See in reaching their decision to revise the Lateran Pacts rather than simply abolish them completely. Such radical action would have required a change in the Constitution which, quite understandably, would have entailed a far more complex process. The new Concordat retains throughout its text the above-mentioned principle.

In the very first article of the Concordat, the Government of the Italian Republic and the Holy See reaffirm that the State and the Catholic Church are, each in its proper order, independent and sovereign. Furthermore, each party commits itself to respect fully that principle in their mutual relations and they pledge reciprocal cooperation in promoting the good of citizens and the country. The Church, for its part, acknowledges the independence and sovereignty of the State in temporal affairs and binds itself not to interfere in those matters which are proper to the State. On the other hand, the State concedes that the Church is truly independent and sovereign in the spiritual and religious order.

In its Pastoral Constitution on the Church in the Modern World, *Gaudium et spes,* the Second Vatican Council dealt with the question of relations between the Church and the political community. The Council document stated:

> The political community and the Church are autonomous and independent of each other in their own fields. Nevertheless, both are devoted to the personal vocation of man, though under different titles. This service will redound the more effectively to the welfare of all insofar as both institutions practice better cooperation according to the local and prevailing situation.. . . For man's horizons are not bounded only by the temporal order; living on the level of human history he preserves the integrity of his eternal destiny (n. 76).

While the State refrains from expressing judgments of a religious, spiritual or moral value, it does recognize that man has certain needs which lie beyond its scope and which the State, of itself, cannot adequately meet. At the same time, the State acknowledges that the Church can

The Cathedral of St. John Lateran in Rome. (© Ruggero Vanni/CORBIS)

accomplish much for the good of the country. This occurs, for example, whenever the Church contributes to the uplifting of the moral tone of the citizenry, or through its acts of charity towards the impoverished in society. The Concordat makes it improbable to think of the Church and State as completely distinct one from the other. Reciprocal ignorance and mutual disinterest have been replaced by a healthy harmony which requires each party to meet with each other and to work together for the common good.

It is highly significant that in the Concordat's Additional Protocol both sides agreed that "the Catholic Church is no longer to be regarded as the only State religion." Such was the arrangement sanctioned by the original Lateran Pacts, but now the concept of a State religion implies that there exists a confessional State which is Catholic. This would be inconsistent with the teaching of the Second Vatican Council where it is declared that the

Church does not desire any privileged position vis-à-vis the political community (cf. *Gaudium et spes,* n. 76).

In the second article of the Concordat, the Italian Republic recognizes that the Church enjoys ample freedom in carrying out its pastoral, educational and charitable mission of evangelization and sanctification. This Article takes into account the broad scope of the Church's mission which is not confined merely to worship but includes, among others, the tasks of educating its members and performing charitable acts. When the Church establishes its own schools, whether for the formation of its clergy or for the education of young people, it does so to fulfill its own proper mission and not to supplement the State's educational system.

In regard to the appointment of bishops, article three abrogates the practice previously in force whereby candidates for episcopal appointment had to be presented by the Holy See to the government for notification, in case it had some objection. The requirement of bishops to take an oath of fidelity to the State before the President of the Republic has also been dropped. The fourth article exempts priests, deacons and religious in vows from military service, allowing them to select some form of civil service instead in times of national emergency.

The revised Concordat, in its fifth article, assures that houses of worship cannot be occupied, expropriated or demolished by the State except for grave cause and only with the prior consent of the competent ecclesiastical authority. Additionally, in this article, the right of sanctuary is upheld.

Sundays and other religious feasts determined by both parties are officially recognized holidays according to article six. Article seven guarantees that ecclesiastical institutions and associations receive treatment identical to any other association, without discrimination or privilege. The State acknowledges that institutions established or approved according to Canon Law possess a true juridical personality within society.

The most profound innovations of the Revised Concordat can be found in article eight which treats of marriage. In contrast to the original Concordat, no mention is made here of marriage as a sacrament. This is consistent with the fact that the State no longer holds that the Catholic religion is the religion of the State. The Concordat states only that the State recognizes the civil effects of marriage contracted according to the norms of Canon Law, provided that certain conditions are met. Whereas in the 1929 Concordat, sentences of nullity of marriage and dispensations from *ratum et non consummatum* marriages received ratification by the State, the Revised Concordat stipulates that only nullity cases will have this effect when one of the parties to the marriage formally requests it. At this point in the Concordat, the Holy See sought to reaffirm its teaching on marriage and wished to emphasize the solicitude which the Church has in safeguarding the dignity and the values of the family. Such a declaration is understandable in the context of legislation which had been passed in recent years that permitted divorce and abortion in Italy.

Article nine guarantees the Church the right to establish its own schools. An important element of this article is the norm governing the teaching of religion in the public schools. "The Italian government, acknowledging the value of religious culture and taking into consideration the fact that Catholicism forms a part of the historical patrimony of the Italian people, will continue to permit the teaching of religion in the public schools at every level except at the university level." The right to choose whether a pupil will receive religious training in the public school is left to the parents or the students at the time of their enrollment.

Although recognized by the State, those institutions of formation in ecclesiastical disciplines that have been established in accord with Canon Law fall under the sole competency of the ecclesiastical authority. Article eleven guarantees the exercise of religious freedom to those whose personal liberty is in some way restricted, as in the case of people in hospitals, nursing homes, prisons, the armed forces, etc. The State will appoint ecclesiastics for this service upon presentation by competent Church authority. The Holy See and the Italian Republic have also agreed to collaborate in preserving the historical and artistic patrimony which they share. The final two articles of the Concordat reiterate a constant theme, that of collaboration between the two parties. These articles call for a spirit of collaboration and conclude that not every single situation can be foreseen by the present agreement. Thus, the door is left open for further negotiations, always in a collaborative way, should these prove necessary in the future.

Relevance. Finally, we may ask what is the importance of this Concordat for the Church in Italy? First, it does allow the Church greater freedom. The Church in Italy is now able to exercise that *libertas ecclesiae* it has received from Christ. This is the ultimate purpose of establishing an agreement between Church and State. Secondly, the Church reaches out to the State and obligates itself to collaborate to a greater extent in the promotion of the well-being of the citizenry. In the words of *Gaudium et spes,* "whatever truth, goodness, and justice is to be found in past or present human institutions is held in high esteem by the Church . . ." (n. 42). Thirdly, the Church cannot be dependent on the State as it strives to fulfill its own mission. Thus, there is an urgent need to involve the laity in a far greater way and to make the Catholic community understand that it must support its clergy and institutions. The important matter of the teaching of religion in the schools can no longer be taken for granted. Parents and children are now called upon to make an active choice for this institution.

For the Church in Italy, the Revised Concordat signifies greater freedom but at the same time it implies on the part of the Church a greater effort to collaborate with the Italian government. Of particular importance is the notion that the Church must now rely more and more on itself for its own mission.

In addressing Mr. Bettino Craxi, then President of the Italian Republic, Pope John Paul II referred to the Revised Concordat as "an instrument of harmony and collaboration." The Concordat, he noted, "is situated now in a society characterized by free competition of ideas and by pluralistic articulation of the various social components. It can and must constitute an element of promotion and growth, fostering the profound unity of ideals and sentiments by which all Italians feel themselves to be brothers in the same homeland.''

Bibliography: Text of the Revised Concordat *La Civiltaà Cattolica* I (1984) 470–478 [Italian]. F. LOMBARDI, ''I nuovi rapporti tra la Chiesa e lo Stato in Italia,'' *ibid.*, 479–494. G. DE ROSA, ''Che cosa cambia in Italia dopo la revisione del Concordato?'' *ibid.*, 176–187. address in *L'Osservatore Romano,* English edition (19 August 1985): 6–7 (contains addresses in English on the concordat by A. CASSOROLI, B. CRAXI, and JOHN PAUL II.

[P. LAGHI]

LAW, BERNARD FRANCIS

Cardinal, archbishop of Boston; b. Torreon, Mexico, 4 November 1931; son of United States Army Air Corps Col. Bernard A. and Helen (Stubblefield) Law. Law received a B.A. from Harvard University in 1953 before beginning studies for the priesthood at St Joseph Seminary, St. Benedict, Louisiana, and the Pontifical College Josephinum, Worthington, Ohio. After being ordained to the priesthood on 21 May 1961, he served in a variety of pastoral capacities in the diocese of Natchez-Jackson, Mississippi, including editor of the diocesan newspaper. From 1968 to 1973, he served as secretary of the U.S. Bishops' Committee of Ecumenical and Religious Affairs. Pope Paul VI appointed Fr. Law bishop of Springfield-Cape Girardeau, Missouri, in 1973. On 24 January 1984, Pope John Paul II appointed him archbishop of Boston, succeeding the late Cardinal Humberto S. Medeiros. The following year, the pope named him cardinal and assigned him the title of Santa Susanna, the parish church for Americans living in Rome.

In Boston, Cardinal Law thoroughly reorganized the church's central administration into a cabinet structure, drawing on clergy and laity to oversee the many departments of the archdiocese. An archdiocesan synod was celebrated to provide for pastoral planning. Cardinal Law instituted a cluster system of small groups of parishes throughout the archdiocese to implement the reconfiguration of parishes and to provide shared pastoral services and resources. He championed the cause of Catholic education and fostered close ties with the Eastern Orthodox Churches. He provided leadership on race issues in the Boston area, forging effective ecumenical cooperation. He promoted closer Catholic-Jewish relations, leading joint pilgrimages to Nazi-era death camps as well as to the Holy Land and Rome. Major archdiocesan institutions, such as the seminary and the cathedral, were renovated for renewed service in the third millennium.

Pope John Paul appointed Cardinal Law a member of the second extraordinary assembly of the Synod of

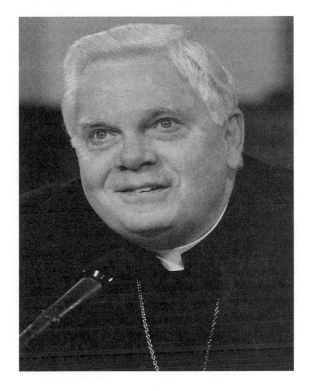

Bernard Cardinal Law (Catholic News Service.)

Bishops, 24 November to 8 December 1985. His proposal that the Holy See prepare a catechism or ''compendium of all Catholic Doctrine regarding both faith and morals'' for the universal church was adopted in the Synod's final report. The pope appointed him to the twelve-member Commission of Cardinals charged with overseeing the development of the text of the *Catechism of the Catholic Church.* His pursuit of direct, personal contacts with the bishops of Mexico, Cuba, Vietnam, China and elsewhere strengthened the Catholic Church in those countries. His meetings with Cuban President Fidel Castro helped prepare the way for John Paul's historic visit to Cuba in 1998. In 1997, Law attended the Special Assembly of the Synod of Bishops for the Americas. In the National Conference of Catholic Bishops, Cardinal Law chaired the Pro-Life, Migrants and Refugees, and International Affairs Committees.

[DOUGLAS K. CLARK]

LECTIONARY FOR MASSES WITH CHILDREN

The *Lectionary for Masses with Children* (LMC) adapts the Roman Lectionary for Mass (1981) to the needs and capacities of pre-adolescent children. The aim

Young girls light votive candles in New York's St. Patrick's Cathedral on Christmas night. (AP/Wide World Photos. Photograph by Scott Braut.)

of the LMC is to nourish the faith of children and lead them to full participation in the worship of the whole assembly. The translation of the scriptures used is the Contemporary English Version (CEV), a translation from the original languages prepared specifically for children by the American Bible Society.

The publication of a LMC follows the recommendation of the Directory for Masses with Children published by the Congregation for Divine Worship (no. 43) and approved by Pope Paul VI in 1973. The National Conference of Catholic Bishops of the United States approved the Lectionary for Masses with Children in November 1991 and the Apostolic See granted permission for an experimental use of the lectionary in 1992. The LMC is best understood within the broader context of the Directory, the General Instruction of the Roman Missal, and the Introduction to the Lectionary for Mass.

Principles and Directives. Part One of the Introduction of the LMC reflects on the importance of the celebration of the word of God for the formation of the community. Part Two provides basic principles for liturgies of the word with children: 1) the Gospel is always read; 2) a liturgical dismissal is used when children occasionally celebrate a separate liturgy of the word; 3) and a homily by the priest or an explanation of the readings by one of the adults is given at Masses with children.

Part Three discusses the purpose and provides foundational principles. This section also underlines some basic principles of liturgical catechesis such as the formative influence of liturgy; the need to involve children in the actions of the liturgy as well as to appeal to the intuitive nature of children through the use of ritual elements and symbols; and the liturgy of the word is ritual prayer and not an instructional session. The final section of part three includes catechetical notes on the relationship of the lectionary to the liturgical year and on the way in which the Church's calendar expresses and shapes Christian identity.

Part Four treats ''Particular Issues'' connected with the liturgy of the word celebrated with children. It examines the place of celebration, objects used in celebration, the importance of the use of music, and the need to preserve the common format of the full assembly in the liturgies for children.

The LMC may be used at Sunday Masses when there are large numbers of children present along with adults (although proper balance and consideration for the entire assembly requires that LMC should not be used exclusively or even preferentially), at a separate liturgy of the word with children, or at other liturgical celebrations within the context of the liturgical year. On Christmas Day, Epiphany, Sundays of Lent, Easter Sunday, Ascension, and Pentecost, the universal lectionary takes precedence. The readings from the children's lectionary may be used only when the celebration of the liturgy of the word for the children is held in a place apart from the main assembly.

The Content of the Lectionary. The LMC follows the content and arrangement of readings for the three cycles of Sundays, the proper of seasons, solemnities, and feasts of the Lord in the Roman Lectionary. All three readings for Sunday are included when they are suitable for use with children. At least one reading is always given in addition to the Gospel and common texts for sung responsorial psalms are included.

Sets of readings that reflect the liturgical and theological motifs of the major seasons are provided for weekdays of the year (seasons and Ordinary Time). The final section of the lectionary is comprised of Gospel acclamations for weekdays in Ordinary Time, the Proper of the Saints, Common of the Saints, ritual Masses and Masses for special occasions.

Bibliography: C. DOOLEY, *To Listen and Tell: Introduction to the Lectionary for Masses with Children with Commentary* (Washington, DC 1993). PETER MAZAR and ROBERT PIERCY, *A Guide to* the *Lectionary for Masses with Children* (Chicago: Liturgy Training Publications, 1993).

[CATHERINE DOOLEY]

LEFEBVRE, MARCEL

Missionary, bishop of Tulle (France), titular archbishop and superior general of the Holy Ghost Fathers; b. Tourcoing, France, 29 November 1905; d. Martigny, Switzerland, 25 March 1991. Marcel Lefebvre was one of eight children of René and Gabrielle Lefebvre. Madame Lefebvre, a pious but demanding mother who predicted that her son Marcel would play a "great role" in the church, died in 1938. Marcel's father, a rigid disciplinarian with monarchist political views, was active in the French underground during World War II. Captured by the Nazis, he died in Sonnenburg Prison at age sixty-two in 1944.

Marcel studied for the priesthood at the French seminary in Rome. After receiving degrees in philosophy and theology, he was ordained on 21 September 1929 and subsequently appointed to the working-class parish of Marias-de-Lomme, an industrial suburb of Lille, France. Three years later, through the influence of his older brother René, a priest member of the Holy Ghost Fathers, Marcel joined the same congregation. He was sent to Gabon, where he served as rector of a seminary and in various missionary apostolates in French Equatorial Africa.

Lefebvre returned to France in 1945 to head the training school of the Holy Ghost Fathers at Mortain. Two years later he returned to Africa, was ordained a bishop, and named vicar-apostolic of Dakar by Pope Pius XII. In September 1948, Lefebvre was appointed apostolic delegate for the whole of French-speaking Africa, a position he held for the next eleven years. He returned again to France in 1959 and was appointed bishop of the diocese of Tulle by Pope John XXIII. In 1962, when he was elected superior general of the Holy Ghost Fathers, the pope named him titular archbishop of Synnada in Phrygia.

Between 1960 and 1962, Archbishop Lefebvre served on the Central Preparatory Commission charged with producing the schemata presented at the Second Vatican Council. Although he later professed that he approached Vatican II with high hopes and an open mind, his work on the Preparatory Commission quickly led to disillusionment. During the Council debates, Lefebvre's opposition to the new theological currents intensified. He was a founder of the International Group of Fathers (Coetus Internationalis Patrum) an organization of conservative prelates who maneuvered to uphold tradition against

Archbishop Marcel Lefebvre acknowledges the crowd attending the public mass marking the fiftieth anniversary of his ordination. (AP/Wide World Photos.)

the liberal-progressive elements pressing for change. Lefebvre sided with the conservatives in all the major Council debates and refused to sign the conciliar documents on the Church in the Modern World (*Gaudium et Spes*) and the Declaration on Religious Liberty (*Dignitatis Humanae*).

Seminary at Econe. In 1968 Lefebvre resigned as head of the Holy Ghost Fathers in a dispute with members of the Chapter General over reform of the order in keeping with the Council directives. He then moved to Rome to retire but, by his own account, was sought out by a group of young men who were looking for someone to direct them in traditional priestly formation. Lefebvre, who had previously directed a small group of conservative seminarians to the French seminary in Rome, subsequently encouraged them to pursue their studies at the University of Fribourg in Switzerland. He abandoned this course of action when he became convinced that the university—like the Church itself—was "infected" with modernism. In June 1969 he gained permission from Bishop Charriere of Fribourg to establish a house for seminarians and with the approval of Bishop Adam of Sion, Lefebvre obtained a large house belonging to the canons of Saint Bernard in the canton of Valias, Switzerland. This property became the Econe seminary, opening formally on 7 October 1970. The following month, Bishop Charriere canonically established Lefebvre's priestly fraternity as the *Fraternité Sacredotale de Pie X* (the Society of Saint Pius X)—named after the Pope known as the "scourge of modernists."

Lefebvre's seminary quickly developed a reputation as a traditionalist stronghold committed to the Tridentine rite, to Thomistic theology, and to a general repudiation of the reforms of Vatican II. In the fall of 1974, in response to Lefebvre's escalating critique of the Council and continuing use of the (then prohibited) Tridentine Mass, and in response to pressures from French bishops who opposed Lefebvre's "rebel seminary," the Vatican announced an investigation of Econe. On 21 November, in reaction to the "scandal" occasioned by remarks made by the two Belgian priests who carried out the visitation, Lefebvre issued an acerbic declaration denouncing the neo-modernist and neo-Protestant tendencies that were contributing to the "demolition of the Church, to the ruin of the priesthood, to the destruction of the Holy Sacrifice of the Mass and the sacraments, to the disappearance of religious life, and to naturalist and Teilhardian teaching in universities, seminaries, and catechetics. . . ." Lefebvre renounced the new Mass as the pre-eminent symbol of all postconciliar trends opposed to "orthodoxy and the never-changing Magisterium." He pronounced Vatican II "entirely corrupt" and asserted that fidelity to the true Church could only be assured by a "categorical refusal" of the Council.

In February 1975, Lefebvre was asked to go to Rome for a "discussion" with curia officials. Shortly after the meeting, his Declaration was condemned as "unacceptable on all points." In spite of this reprimand, a public rebuke by Pope Paul VI, and an order to close his seminary, Lefebvre continued his traditionalist initiatives. On 22 July 1976 he was officially suspended *a divinis* for refusing a direct Vatican order prohibiting ordinations. Defying the suspension in August, the "rebel archbishop" gave a controversial and emotional sermon during a public and previously planned Mass at Lille. He denounced the "bastard sacraments," the "adulterous union of the Church with the Revolution," and the ecumenical dialogues with Protestants—while reiterating the call for the re-establishment of the temporal power of the Church wherever possible.

For the next twelve years, communication between Lefebvre and the Vatican remained open. The archbishop corresponded with Pope Paul VI and his successors and answered various doctrinal queries from the Vatican. While these discussions proceeded without resolve, Lefebvre's priestly fraternity steadily expanded its international network of traditionalist publishing enterprises, chapels, schools, priories, and seminaries. Lefebvre traveled extensively on behalf of the Society, giving spiritual conferences to his priests and supporters and bringing the traditional sacraments to beleaguered groups of traditionalist Catholics.

Excommunication and Death. Following the election of Pope John Paul II (1978) the atmosphere in Rome regarding the "Econe affair" turned more conciliatory. Lefebvre met personally with John Paul II on 18 November 1978. Although the expectation of rapprochement was high, negotiations between Lefebvre and the Vatican remained at an impasse throughout the 1980s. In 1983, Lefebvre retired as superior general of the Society and chose Father Franz Schmidberger, a German priest, as his successor.

While appearing publicly irenic and willing to reach some accommodation with Church officialdom, Lefebvre continued to equivocate on his position on Vatican II and on the doctrinal integrity of the new (Novus Ordo) Mass. In October 1983, he increased pressure on the Vatican by intimating that he would ordain an episcopal successor, with or without papal permission.

Aging and in ill health, Lefebvre renewed this threat again in 1987 during the June ordinations at Econe when he announced his "Operation Survival" for tradition. A new round of Vatican negotiations ensued, culminating the following year in the archbishop's signing a 5 May 1988 protocol granting him much of the substance of his previous demands: official recognition of the Society, semi-independence from diocesan bishops, and permission to continue to use the Tridentine liturgy. On the critical issue of a successor, Lefebvre received permission to ordain one bishop.

The long-sought solution to the "Econe problem" proved short-lived, however. Lefebvre promptly withdrew his assent to the protocol the following day. Insisting that the Vatican was stalling and had not collaborated effectively, he demanded a 30 June date for the ordinations and the right to ordain more than one episcopal successor. These demands were refused. Lefebvre, in turn, proceeded with his plans to "perpetuate tradition" in spite of a flurry of last minute Vatican pleas. On 30 June 1988, under a tent church constructed in the shadow of his flagship seminary in Econe, he ordained four of his priests as bishops. Lefebvre and his new bishops incurred immediate excommunication—along with Bishop Antonio de Castro Mayer of Campos, Brazil, a longtime supporter of Lefebvre's, who attended the ordinations.

Following his excommunication, Lefebvre's contact with the Vatican diminished, although several overtures were undertaken from Rome to reopen the conversation. Through his writing and public pronouncements, Lefebvre maintained that his excommunication was "absolutely null and void." His denunciations of Vatican II, the conciliar Church, the de-Christianization of society, and the subversion of Catholicism by a cabal of Freemasons, communists, and liberal and modernist forces within it continued unabated.

In the early hours of 25 March 1991, following surgery for the removal of an abdominal tumor, Marcel Lefebvre died in Martigny in the Canton of Valais near Econe, Switzerland.

Archbishop Lefebvre's serene and tranquil public demeanor and deep personal piety belied a resolute and doctrinaire mind. His many years of seminary and episcopal experience sharpened his administrative acumen and political sagacity in dealing with the internal affairs of his expanding priestly fraternity and with Vatican officials. To his opponents and detractors he was an incorrigible reactionary whose conservative religious views and rigid ecclesiology paralleled the ancien regime political thinking of France's extreme rightwing elements. From the magisterial perspective Lefebvre became a recalcitrant and disobedient servant who refused to recognize an ecumenical council, broke the bonds of ecclesial unity, and led his followers into a schism because of his "incomplete and contradictory" notion of the Church's living tradition.

To many of his supporters, however, the French archbishop was a "saint," a modern day Athanasius, an instrument of Providence who heroically exposed the "false spirit" of Vatican II and who acted to save the Church from its betrayal by a modernist bureaucracy and the forces of subversion that had long conspired against it.

Throughout his controversy with the Vatican, the "rebel archbishop" presented his actions in the rhetoric of classical sectarianism: as pristine and uncorrupted initiatives through which he and his supporters alone maintained continuity with the true faith. He died professing that he had done no more than "hand down" what he had received by his own training and ecclesial mandate.

Bibliography: Y. CONGAR. *Challenge to the Church: The Case of Archbishop Lefebvre* (Huntington IN 1976). J. HANU, *Vatican Encounter: Conversations with Archbishop Lefebvre,* trans. E. Shosberger (Kansas City KS 1978). M. DAVIES, *Apologia Pro Marcel Lefebvre,* Vols. I, II, III (Dickinson TX 1980, 1984, 1988). M. LEFEBVRE, *A Bishop Speaks: Writings and Addresses, 1963-1975* (Edinburgh n.d.); *I Accuse the Council* (Dickinson TX 1982); *An Open Letter to Confused Catholics* (Herefordshire, England 1986). F. LAISNEY, *Archbishop Lefebvre and the Vatican, 1987-1988* (Dickinson TX 1989). W. DINGES, "Roman Catholic Traditionalism," in M.E. MARTY and R.S. APPLEBY, eds., *Fundamentalisms Observed,* Vol. I (Chicago 1991): 66-101. *The Angelus* XI:7 (July 1988); XIV:5/6 (May/June 1991).

[W. D. DINGES]

LEGIONARIES OF CHRIST

A clerical congregation established in Mexico City in 1941 by Marcial Maciel, a priest from Cotija, Michoacán. During the religious persecution in Mexico in 1936, Maciel, then a 16-year-old seminarian, felt called to start a religious congregation of priests. On 3 January 1941 under the auspices of Francisco Gonzáles Arias, bishop of Cuernavaca, he founded the Legion of Christ and opened the Sacred Heart Apostolic School with a group of thirteen boys.

In 1946 Maciel opened a second Apostolic School and the first novitiate in Comillas, Santander, Spain. On 25 May 1948, the Holy See granted the Legion the nihil obstat necessary for the canonical establishment of a diocesan congregation. The Holy See elevated it to pontifical status with the Decree of Praise (Decretum laudis) on 6 February 1965 and gave definitive approval of its Constitutions on 29 June 1983.

Regnum Christi. Meanwhile in 1949 Father Maciel founded Regnum Christi, an apostolic movement dedicated to the service of humanity and the world. It includes laity, men and women, deacons and priests. The association reminds its members of their responsibility, rooted in baptism, to make faith the driving force in their daily lives and to undertake organized apostolic activity. The Regnum Christi Movement is inspired by the charism of its founder and is closely allied with the Legionaries of Christ.

In 1950 the Legion of Christ moved its general headquarters to Rome and established a Center for Higher Studies. In 1958 the Legionaries, with the support of Mexican Catholics, built the church of Our Lady of Guadalupe adjacent to the Generalate. The Legion has centers of formation in Mexico, Spain, Italy, Ireland, and the United States. Its U.S. headquarters are in Cheshire, Conn.

Bibliography: J. GARCIA, "Legionari di Cristo" and "Marcial Maciel," *Dizionario degli Isituti di Perfezione,* 5 vols. (Rome 1978). MARCIAL MACIEL, *Integral Formation of Catholic Priests* (Hamden, Conn.: Legion of Christ, Inc. 1998).

[J. GARCIA]

LONERGAN, BERNARD

Theologian, university professor, author, member of the Society of Jesus; b. 17 December 1904, Buckingham,

Quebec (Canada); d. Pickering, Ontario, 26 November 1984. The eldest of three sons born to Gerald J., a land surveyor, and Josephine Helen (Wood) Lonergan, Bernard showed himself a precocious youngster. He was educated by the Christian Brothers at the elementary level in his hometown, and later acquired a solid grounding in classical languages, the humanities, and mathematics at Loyola High and Loyola College in Montreal. He entered the Society of Jesus at age 17 (1922), received his philosophic training at Heythrop College in England (1926–29), and earned an external Bachelor of Arts in classics at London University (1929–30). By his own account, it was the basic honesty and modesty of his Jesuit professors in philosophy that made the greatest impact on him at the time. He was especially influenced by the genial instruction in mathematics he received from his tutor, Charles O'Hara, S.J., and seriousness with which Lewis Watt, S.J. approached questions about economics and morality in the social encyclicals. He confessed that Newman's *An Essay in Aid of a Grammar of Assent,* "made (him) something of an existentialist" (*Second Collection,* 271). Letters of the period attest to Lonergan's fascination with methodology; and one can discern his budding interest in cognitional theory from the titles of three of his works from this period: *Blandyke Papers:* "The Form of Mathematical Inference" (1928); "The Syllogism" (1928); "True Judgment and Science" [on Newman's illative sense] (1929).

Early Career and Insight. After a three-year period teaching at Loyola College in Montreal, Lonergan attained a licentiate in theology at the Gregorian University in Rome (1937), where he had been ordained a priest in 1936. There he went on to do doctoral work on Thomas Aquinas's theory of grace and human freedom (1938–40), though he was not actually awarded the doctorate until after World War II (1946). The next 13 years were evenly split as professor of theology at Jesuit theologates in Montreal and Toronto. His intensive research on the thought of Aquinas gave rise to an impressive flow of publications in theological journals, principally of his reworked doctoral thesis, "St. Thomas's Thought on *Gratia Operans,*" which appeared in installments in *Theological Studies* (1941–1942); and "The Concept of *Verbum* in the Writings of St. Thomas," in five parts in the same journal between 1946 and 1949.

During these years Lonergan labored to find in economics, sociology, and history the theoretic basis that might underpin a concrete realization of the conditions required to achieve the ends envisioned in the great social encyclicals of Leo XIII and Pius XI. This work is documented in unpublished manuscripts, including the final version of an "Essay on Circulation Analysis" (c.

1943–44), a topic to which Lonergan returned in his later works.

In a series of courses taught during the late 1940s at the Thomas More Institute for Adult Education in Montreal (founded by his life-long friend and collaborator, R. Eric O'Connor, S.J.), Lonergan attempted to transpose what he had learned from Aquinas about human understanding and knowledge into the world of the twentieth century, addressing issues in mathematics and sciences undreamt of by St. Thomas. The result was *Insight: A Study of Human Understanding* (1957).

Method in Theology and Post-Method Interests. In 1953 Lonergan had taken up duties as professor of dogmatic theology at the Gregorian University in Rome during which time he published several works in Latin related to his courses on Christology and the Trinity. He characterized them as products of teaching in a situation that "was hopelessly antiquated" (*Second Collection,* 212). These maps for the 650 students attending his lectures include *De constitutione Christi ontologica et psychologica supplementum* (1956), *Divinarum personarum conceptionem analogicam* (1957), *De Verbo incarnato* (1961, with later revisions), and *De Deo trino* (1964).

The main challenge to which Lonergan responded in his Roman years "came from the *Geisteswissenschaften,* from the problems of hermeneutics and critical history" (*Second Collection,* 277). His concern to take seriously the 19th-century emergence of scholarship and to think out the implications of human being as constituted by meaning in history is most explicitly documented in the notes from his *exercitatio* courses (graduate seminars devoted to specialized topics)—*De intellectu et methodo, De systemate et historia,* and *De methodo theologiae*—as well as in summer courses on topics such as mathematical logic, existentialism, philosophy of education, and method in theology.

After 12 years in Rome, he returned to Toronto to be treated for cancer in 1965. Following his recovery from the surgical removal of one of his lungs, his superiors at Regis College made it possible for him to complete his *Method in Theology.* The period after 1964–65 witnessed the reformulation of *Insight*'s preoccupation with experience, direct understanding, and reflective understanding in terms of "intentionality analysis" (*Method,* ch. 1), blossoming into what Lonergon would at last affirm to be the primacy of the practical and existential level of human consciousness on which we evaluate, decide, act and love. This change supplements his sensibility for historical mindedness cultivated in Rome with new developments regarding the role of the dynamic unconscious, feelings, images and symbols, and religious experience.

The sweep of these developments permit Lonergan in *Method* to situate his intentionality analysis of the fourfold cognitional structure of attentiveness, intelligence, reasonableness, and responsibility into ever more concrete and complex contexts. Accordingly, *Insight*'s chapter 18, in which "the good was the intelligent and the reasonable" (*Second Collection*, 277), shifts into the context of "The Human Good" (*Method*, ch. 2) with its elaboration of feelings as intentional responses to vital, social, cultural, religious, and personal values. Again, *Insight*'s idea of meaning as "a relation between sign and signified (x)" gets plunged into "Meaning" (*Method*, ch. 3), with its types, elements, functions, realms, and stages. Similarly, *Insight*'s account of mystery and myth and of God's existence and nature (ch. 19) are shifted into the context of "Religion" (*Method*, ch. 4) where "the question of God is considered more important than the precise manner in which an answer is formulated, and our basic awareness of God comes to us not through our arguments or choices but primarily through God's gift of . . . love" (*Second Collection*, 277).

Both on the way to *Method* and after its publication Lonergan published a series of essays and lectures clarifying, applying, drawing the implications of, and further working out the implications of the 1964–65 shift to the primacy of the practical and existential (*Second Collection* and *Third Collection*). In the academic year of 1971–72 Lonergan was the Stillman Professor at Harvard Divinity School in Cambridge, Mass., where he put the finishing touches on *Method*, which finally came out in 1972. From 1975 until 1983 he taught at Boston College, alternating each year between courses having to do with issues in *Method* and those devoted to the last great preoccupation of his productive years, economics and the dynamics of history.

Of his post-*Method* work most students of Lonergan would probably agree with Frederick E. Crowe, S.J., that the chief fruit is his ever sharper elucidation of the two complementary rhythms of human development with the healing vector moving from above downwards (i.e., of being-in-love with God [with love's eyes of faith],believing, evaluating, judging, understanding, experiencing); and the creative vector moving from below upwards (i.e., experiencing, understanding, reflecting, deliberating, believing, loving). Next in importance would probably be his analysis of the "pure cycle" of the rhythms of money circulation within and between economic factors producing things for producers (surplus circuit of capital formation) and those producing goods and services for consumers (basic circuit). This analysis lays bare the normative intelligibility of exigencies underlying people's free and moral accommodations to the anti-egalitarian and egalitarian flows of money, goods, and services required by industrial exchange economies. Lonergan saw the intelligibility of the economy as depen-

dent upon people's intelligence, reasonableness, responsibility—and so convertedness—in a way unsuspected by and unaccounted for by either Marxist or "supply-side/demand-side" conventions in economic theory.

Achievement. The Christian faith is now undergoing a hermeneutical crisis diagnosed by Lonergan as rooted in Christianity's inability to make the transition to modern society and culture. As a Roman Catholic theologian he was critical of the failure of Catholic philosophy and theology to pass from the fixist norms espoused by a mentality he named 'classicist' towards a transcultural normativity compatible with historical consciousness. To be sure, he was no less critical of the historicist or positivist drift towards relativism on the part of those who more or less renounced any kind of normativity along with the heritage of scholasticism. Lonergan's life was dedicated chiefly to helping Christian theology meet this hermeneutical crisis and make the transition to modernity without losing its integrity.

Both Lonergan's execution of this task and the results of his work are profoundly and uniquely hermeneutical, especially in the way his lifework pivots on his nuanced historical relationship to the paradigm-figure of the Middle Ages, Thomas Aquinas. He concluded that "in the practice of Aquinas (theology) was . . . the principle for the molding and the transformation of a culture." The lesson Lonergan learned from St. Thomas' practice was that besides "reflecting on revelation" by "investigating, ordering, expounding, communicating divine revelation" theology "has somehow to mediate God's meaning into the whole of human affairs" *Second Collection*, 62).

One thing that makes the meaning of 'method' for Lonergan so profound and so unprecedented, therefore, is the manner in which his project of method flows out of the way he paid attention to, understood, judged, and appreciated the practice of Aquinas as a theologian. As he insisted in *Method*, such "encounter is the one way in which self-understanding and horizon can be put to the test" (247). Whereas ordinary ideas about method tend to be technical in the Enlightenment vein of Descartes or Bacon, and so are focussed on "a set of verbal propositions enunciating rules to be followed in a scientific investigation" (*Second Collection*, 64), Lonergan placed method in the context of Aquinas's dictum that "it is characteristic of the wise person to bring about order in all things." By reconceiving the Thomist viewpoint of highest wisdom in terms of the phenomenological notion of horizon, Lonergan makes method in the most serious sense a matter of at once utmost radicality and complete concreteness. To do method for Lonergan comes down to appropriating and articulating the grounds of theological (and *any*) practice in one's own total and basic horizon.

Hence, on account of his engagement with the thought of Aquinas, method in its plainer but quite important sense of "distinguishing different tasks, and thereby eliminating totalitarian ambitions" (*Second Collection,* 212) was realized by Lonergan to be anchored in the human subject's appropriation of method as 'transcendental'—i.e., the thematization of our own ultimate (and so transcultural) set of operations of experiencing, understanding, reflecting, deliberating, deciding, and loving. Thus, at root, 'method' means 1) appropriating the structures of one's own conscious intentionality that specify our horizon as total and basic; and 2) consciously living in accord with one's horizon by following the transcendental precepts: Be attentive. Be intelligent. Be reasonable. Be responsible. Be loving.

The cognitive dimension of consciousness became most clear to Lonergan while writing the *Verbum* articles, especially the implications of the dependency of that dimension of consciousness upon the practical and existential levels. Deliberation, decision, and loving action presuppose and complement knowing, but the way knowing presupposes and complements those operations is even more crucial. Lonergan was increasingly able to express in terms of the notion of intentionality the metaphysical explanation of human freedom and divine grace that he had earlier retrieved in the 1930s and 1940s from St. Thomas.

In *Insight* Lonergan had tended to equate the breakthrough to the total and basic horizon with the appropriation of rational consciousness in one's affirmation of oneself as a knower (ch. 11) (fourth-level rational *self*—consciousness takes center-stage only at ch. 18); with one's clear recognition that knowing is a compound dynamic structure of experiencing, understanding, and judging; and especially with one's ability "to discriminate with ease and from personal conviction between one's purely intellectual activities and the manifold of other 'existential' concerns that invade and mix and blend with the operations of intellect to render it ambivalent and its pronouncements ambiguous" (intro., xix). Already in his lectures on "Intelligence and Reality" (1950–51) he had indicated that the key to *Insight*'s breakthrough was "radical intellectual conversion" (27) because it involved a revolution in oneself and a purification of oneself from what he there calls "inhibiting and reinforcing (i.e., reductively utilitarian) desires" (19) in order to liberate the pure, disinterested, and unrestricted desire to know being, and to make this desire normative in one's actual living. By the time of writing *Method,* however, what was implicit before was fully explicated: on account of the primacy of the practical and existential levels of conscious intentionality intellectual conversion (as uncovery of one's horizon as total and basic) presupposes both moral conversion (from one's spontaneous likes to the truly good or right) and religious conversion (from stupid self-centeredness to being-in-love with God).

But, as was already altogether clear in *Grace and Freedom,* religious conversion is the result of the gift of God's self-communication, beyond the horizon of finite human knowing and choosing. God's Spirit and Word are sent to make moral and intellectual conversion possible. Those conversions in turn demand the exercise of our liberty by which we reorient ourselves and bring the horizon of our day-to-day living into ever closer attunement with the infinite potentiality of our total and basic horizon. Openness as Gift heals us to transform our sinful closedness and elevates us to the factual, healing and creative openness of divine adoption.

Bibliography: The Lonergan Research Institute, Toronto, has a complete archive of Lonergan's works. The *Collected Works of Bernard Lonergan* is being published by the Lonergan Research Institute and the University of Toronto Press. B. LONERGAN. "Insight Revisited." In *Second Collection* (London 1974). P. BYRNE. "The Fabric of Lonergan's Thought." *Lonergan Workshop* 6 (Atlanta 1986). F. E. CROWE, *Lonergan* (Collegeville, Minn. 1992). J. FLANAGAN. *Quest for Self-Knowledge: An Essay in Lonergan's Philosophy* (Toronto 1997). V. GREGSON. *The Desires of the Human Heart: An Introduction to the Theology of Bernard Lonergan* (New York 1988). R. LIDDY. *Transforming Light: Intellectual Conversion in the Early Lonergan* (Collegeville, Minn. 1993).

[F. G. LAWRENCE]

LÓPEZ TRUJILLO, ALFONSO

Cardinal, president of the Pontifical Council for the Family; b. 8 November 1935, Villahermosa, Colombia, of a prominent family of Antioquia. His father was in charge of the General Accounting Office of the State, one of his brothers was a minister of state and a relative was Bishop of Socorro and San Gil until 1975. López Trujillo studied sociology at the National University of Colombia in Bogotá; theology at the Grand Seminary of Bogotá; philosophy at the Pontifical Angelicum Athenaeum in Rome (receiving a Ph.D.); and spiritual theology at the Pontifical Theological Faculty and Pontifical Institute of Spirituality "Theresianum." He was ordained a priest in Rome, 13 November 1960. For the next two years he furthered his studies with courses in psychology, sociology, and Marxism.

Returning to Bogotá, he was named a professor of philosophy, psychology, and patrology at the Grand Seminary and also taught at the National University, the Institute for Social Development (IDES), and the Pedagogical University of Bogotá. He was charged with the preparatory work for the 39th International Eucharistic Congress that was held in Bogotá in 1968, presided over by Pope Paul VI during the first papal trip ever to Latin America. From 1968 to 1971 Fr. López Trujillo was pastor of the Epiphany parish and from 1969 to 1973 vicar general of the archdiocese. In 1970, he was assigned to coordinate theological and pastoral reflection for the Latin American Episcopal Council (CELAM).

Paul VI named him titular bishop of Boseta and auxiliary of Bogotá in 1971. He received the episcopal ordination in that city. Bishop López Trujillo was elected secretary general of CELAM in 1972 and from 1979 to 1982 served as its president. He has participated in three of the General Assemblies of the Latin American Episcopate, first as an expert (Medellín, 1968) and later as a bishop (Puebla, 1979, where he was secretary general of the meeting; and Santo Domingo, 1992). He has also taken part in twelve assemblies of the Synod of Bishops and was a member of its general secretariat from 1983 until 1987.

In 1978, Bishop López Trujillo was appointed coadjutor archbishop, with right of succession, of Medellín. He succeeded to that see the following year. Pope John Paul II created him a cardinal priest with the title of S. Prisca in 1983; at 47, he was then the youngest member of the College of Cardinals. In addition to his intense activities in CELAM he showed great pastoral dynamism in his archdiocese, establishing new parishes, paying special attention to the poor and marginalized people and founding theological and philosophical faculties in the Pontifical Bolivarian University. He criticized the terrorist tactics of drug traffickers and guerrillas in Colombia, surviving several attempts on his life. He wrote widely on the themes of liberation and Marxism, criticizing some theologians for relying too much on Marxist principles. He resigned the pastoral government of the archdiocese after being called to Rome as president of the Pontifical Council for the Family in 1990. He has written several books on the place of the family in evangelization.

[SALVADOR MIRANDA]

LUBAC, HENRI DE

Theologian, cardinal; b. Cambrai, 20 February 1896. After the study of law, Henri Marie- Joseph Sonier de Lubac entered the Society of Jesus in 1913 at the novitiate of Saint Leonard (Great Britain). During his study of letters (Canterbury 1919–20), philosophy (Jersey 1920–23), and theology (Ore Place, Hastings 1924–26; Lyon-Fourviere 1926–28) he had as fellow students Yves de Montcheuil (1899–1944) and Gaston Fessard (1897–1978). De Lubac published many of their works

Alfonso Cardinal López Trujillo (Catholic News Service.)

after their deaths. Stimulated by their friendship, his thought developed through contact with such great masters as the philosopher Maurice Blondel (1861–1949), whose more important correspondence he would later publish, and Léonce de Grandmaison (1868–1927), Pierre Rousselot (1878–1915), Joseph Maréchal (1878–1944), and Joseph Huby (1878–1949).

After ordination to the priesthood (1927), and following his tertianship (Paray-le-Monial, 1928–29), de Lubac taught fundamental theology at the Catholic Faculty of Lyon (not at Fourvière, as legend has it), where he succeeded Albert Valensin, brother of Auguste, many of whose works de Lubac also published posthumously [notably *Auguste Valensin: Textes et documents inédits* (Paris 1961)].

The following year, de Lubac founded the chair of the history of religion at Lyon and become acquainted with Jules Monchanin (1895–1957) who initiated him to "Mahayanasutralamkara" and who had a decisive influence over his thought [cf. *Images de l'abbé Monchanin* (Paris 1967)]. While in residence at the Jesuit theologate at Fourvière (Lyons), he founded in 1940, with J. Daniélou the collection *Sources chrétiennes*, which would become famous. Having fought during World War I and been seriously wounded in 1917, he nurtured and enliv-

Henri de Lubac shown at a symposium on atheism held in Rome. (AP/Wide World Photos.)

ened a spiritual resistance movement against Nazism during World War II with his confreres Pierre Chaillet and Gaston Fessard, publishing the journal *Témiognage chrétien* [cf. R. Bedarida, *Les armes de l'espirit: Témiognage chrétien, 1941–1944* (Paris 1977)]. From its inception he collaborated as advisor and author on the collection of monographs *Théologie* published at Fourvière. From 1947 to 1950, he was director of *Recherches de Science religieuse,* a review founded by P. L. de Grandmaison. In 1950, the authorities of his order barred him from teaching (until 1959) and theological research (a measure that would be progressively relaxed). They were not, however, implementing the directive of the encyclical *Humani generis* (1950), but the "mots d'ordre" of a small group of theologians who prosecuted the so-called *Ecole de Fourvière* and *Nouvelle Théologie.* Later this same group attempted to have his theology condemned by the Council. Pope Pius XII, who did not condemn de Lubac or his ideas, sent him words of encouragement through a letter dictated to his confessor, P. A. Bea, S.J.

In August 1960, Pope John XXIII, who knew of the affair as nuncio at Paris, named him consultor of the preparatory commission to the Ecumenical Council of Vatican II. As a *peritus* on the theological commission, de Lubac participated thereafter in all the work of the coun-

cil (1962–65). And the same superior general who had prohibited de Lubac from teaching asked him to defend the thought of his friend and confrere, Pierre Teilhard de Chardin (1881–1955), fearing that it might be condemned by the council. Lubac defense of Teilhard, which demonstrated an exact understanding of his thought, was decisive to his exoneration.

Named as a member of the International Theological Commission (1969–74), de Lubac became a consultor to the Pontifical Secretariats for Non-Christians and for Non-Believers. He sought to understand the true sense of the conciliar teachings, and to guard against a "para-council" which would make Vatican II an absolute point of departure for drawing the Church in an unjustified direction. During this period he traveled through North and South America and received numerous doctorates *honoris causa.* A founding member of the review *Concilium,* from which he retired in November 1965, he also contributed to the foundation of the international Catholic review *Communio,* with the later Cardinal J. Ratzinger, and Louis Bouyer, M. J. Le Guillou, and H. U. von Balthasar and served as a member o the French editorial committee until May 1977. John Paul II, who developed ties of friendship with de Lubac during the Council, created him cardinal in 1983.

Works. Like the opening of an opera, de Lubac's *Catholicisme* (1938; Eng. 1950) brings to our understanding nearly every theme of his truly "organic" theology. He considers in this book how the Spirit of God works through society and history in order to make humanity the Body of Christ according to the design of the Father, Who has created humanity in His image as persons and who has loved them, from that time on, as they are in themselves. The created and incarnated spirit which is man is henceforward an impulse toward God, who is his origin and calls him to Himself, while the Church, as the Body of Christ, is missionary. Moved by "the natural desire for God," the primordial act of the human spirit is the fundamental "certitude" of the original "faith," which in other words is "the knowledge of God" which envelops and critiques (*via negativa*) affirmations of God.

Correlatively, atheism merits theological reflection. De Lubac treats of oriental and occidental atheism, as well as both the atheism that is anterior to Christ, that of Buddhism, and that which is posterior to Christ and specifically anti-Christian, that of Feuerbach, Nietzsche, and Comte, which he distinguishes from that of Proudhon: this latter is formed through a reaction against a Church dominated by an "unsupportable reactionary narrowness of a certain kind of Catholicism found during the Restoration" (H. U. von Balthazar, *Henri de Lubac,* 65). Concerning anti-Christian atheism, de Lubac discerns the shadow of Joachim of Flora of the twelfth century. The theory of Abbot Joachim, according to which the spirit realizes the design of God apart from the incarnated Word, in effect inspired Lessing and the Enlightenment which would secularize it, as well the progressive movements up to our day. It risks contaminating the Church when it admits an "atheistic hermeneutic of Christianity" (*Athéism et sens de l'homme*, 23 ff.).

With a capacity for both affirming and denying God, the human spirit has a history- determining destiny that he beyond at the same time that it belongs to him. According, in effect, as the human spirit considers itself called to filial adoption by God, as rising to the center of the cosmic becoming, or as receiving the revelation of God through Jesus Christ, the created spirit of man is moved by an identical movement in its own depths: it directs itself and is guided toward an end which is gratuitous. This is respectively, elevation to the supernatural life; the Spirit; and Jesus, the Son of God. This end is prepared: with regard to supernatural elevation, it is the natural desire of God; with regard to the spirit, the world; and with regard to Jesus Christ, it is Israel and the chosen people. But because it is gratuitous, this end goes beyond all that has been prepared: the desire for God, the world, Israel, and all that transforms within.

It is well suited to de Lubac's purpose to consider separately the problematic of the spiritual, treated in *Surnaturel* (1946) and *Mystére du surnaturel* (1956), that of anthropogenesis, undertaken during his studies of Teilhard de Chardin, and that of the connection between the old and the new covenant, developed in *Histoire et Espirit* (1950) and in *Exégèse Médiéval* (1959–65). These three problematics clarify one another without ever recurring, though de Lubac treated all three together in his *Pic de la Mirandole* (1974).

This kind of analogy between movement and structure finds its principle and its end in the Lord Jesus. The universe is Christ-like by its constitution and destination, for man finds his final reality in Christ and knows of no movement of the Spirit that could go beyond Christ (*contra* Joachim of Flora). Furthermore, as in clear in *Corpus Mysticum* (1944, 1968), one part of de Lubac's Christology is implicitly eucharistic: in His singular Body through which He places Himself into human history and becomes cosmic, Jesus fulfills the destiny of humanity thanks to the eucharistic offering of Himself through which he is united to the Church, His spouse and body. Consequently, the ecclesiology of de Lubac is also eucharistic. Thence its Marian dimension, the reciprocal interiority of the particular churches within the universal Church is also the human subject who believes in the God of the Trinity, bringing to completion the primordial consciousness of God and the movement of the human spirit toward God; it is in this sense that all believe and become persons [cf. *La Foi chrétienne* (1969, 1970)].

Influence. Henri de Lubac never defended his work as an original theological contribution. He only gave, he said, his voice to the tradition. As a matter of fact, he showed it to be living. The originality of his work is that of the tradition itself. His influence is both discrete and diffuse—not that of a school, but more that of a master. One can see it in the ecclesiology of Vatican II which is eucharistic (J. Ratzinger), and in the dogmatic perspective—not rationalistic—of *Dei verbum*. Instead of imposing from outside the ideas of theological reflection, the apologetic of de Lubac is dogmatic, inviting the scientific study of religion to leave its methodological neutrality, which is fallacious, to abandon the idea of a "transcendent unity of religions," as well as that of a diffraction of the religious into the cultural, and to raise in their proper relief and contrast the great spiritual options, which lead the Christian to better perceive the absolute novelty of Christ. In brief, de Lubac's apologetic is dogmatic in being historic [cf. M. Sales in his admirable *Der Gott Jesu Christi* (Mainz 1982)]. Just as he has overcome the opposition, born in the sixteenth century, between the natural and supernatural ends of the human spirit, de Lubac has also overcome the division between positive and speculative theology, which had appeared in the same century.

Correlatively, all historical questions have been renewed. In effect, de Lubac observes a unity between history and the Spirit everywhere. Exegesis should also become a renewed being [cf. M. van Esbroeck, *Herméneutique, structuralisme et exégèse. Essai de logique kérygmatique* (Paris 1978); P. Pirct, *Exégèse et Philosophie* (Brussels 1987)], as should moral theology, which can depart from its positivism and its Kantian transcendentalism thanks to his doctrine of the supernatural. For all of these reasons and in diverse manners it is clear that the Modernist crisis is overcome from within and in principle: history and Spirit are reconciled. If one agrees that this crisis recovered vigor after Vatican II and has not since ceased to rage (cf. G. Chantraine, *Vraie et fausse liberté du théologien* 1969), one will know that de Lubac's work has not ceased to be fertile.

Bibliography: K. N. NEUFELD and M. SALES, *Bibliographie Henri de Lubac, S. J. 1925–1974* (Einsiedeln: Johannes Verlag, 1974); "Bibliographie de Henri de Lubac (corrections et compléments) 1942–1989," H. de Lubac, *Théologie dans l'histoire*, 2:408–416. J. P. WAGNER, *La théologie fondamentale selon Henri de Lubac* (Paris: Cerf, 1997). H. DE LUBAC, *At the Service of the Church: Henri de Lubac Reflects on the Circumstances That Occasioned His Writings* (San Francisco: Communio Books, 1993); *Théologie dans l'histoire* (Paris: Desclée de Brouwer, 1990). H. U.

VON BALTHASAR, *The Theology of Henri de Lubac: An Overview* (San Francisco: Ignatius Press, 1991). J. A. KOMONCHAK, "Theology and Culture at Mid-Century: The Example of Henri de Lubac," *Theological Studies* 51 (1990): 579–602. S. WOOD, *Spiritual Exegesis and the Church in the Theology of Henri de Lubac* (Grand Rapids, Mich.: Eerdmans, 1998). *L'homme devant Dieu: Mélanges offerts au père Henri de Lubac*, 3 vols. (Paris: Aubier, 1963–64). D. L. SCHINDLER, ed., "The Theology of Henri de Lubac: Communio at Twenty Years," *Communio* 19 (1992): 332–509.

[G. CHANTRAINE]

LUBACHIVSKY, MYROSLAV IVAN

Cardinal, major-archbishop of the Ukranian see of Lviv; b. 24 June 1914, in Dolyna, Western Ukraine, the son of Eustachius and Anna (née Olijnyk). Lubachivsky studied philosophy and theology first at the Ukrainian Catholic Seminary in Lviv, and then in Innsbruck, Austria. After ordination to the priesthood on 21 September 1938 he did doctoral studies in theology, earning a degree in biblical studies from the Pontifical Biblical Institute; he also studied philosophy at the Gregorianum, and spent two years in the study of medicine. Father Lubachivsky immigrated to the United States in 1947, and after fulfilling the residency requirements he became a naturalized citizen. He served as secretary for the Ukrainian Catholic Committee for Refugees and at the same time taught in the Preparatory Seminary in Stamford, Connecticut. In addition to pastoral work in a number of parishes he published a collection of sermons for Sundays and feast days in both Ukrainian and English, and translated the *Catechism of the Council of Trent*. In 1968 he was named spiritual director of St. Josephat's Ukrainian Catholic Seminary in Washington, D.C. From 1971 to 1977 he was chaplain to the Sisters of St Basil in Philadelphia, taught theology at Manor College and St Basil's Academy, and administered Sacred Heart Mission. In 1977 he was appointed spiritual director at St Basil's Seminary in Stamford.

In September 1979, Pope John Paul II appointed Lubachivsky metropolitan-archbishop of Philadelphia. A few months later (27 March 1980), John Paul II, following the recommendation of the Synod of the Ukrainian hierarchy held in Rome, nominated him archbishop coadjutor with right of succession to the see of the major-archbishopric of Lviv. Upon the death of Cardinal Slipyj, 7 September 1984, Lubachivsky assumed the position of archbishop-major of Lviv. In 1985 Pope John Paul installed him as a cardinal, only the fifth prelate of the Ukrainian Church to be so honored, and assigned him the titular church of S. Sophia a via Boccea. His Beatitude Lubachivsky was able to take up residence in Lviv only with the dissolution of the Soviet Union. When in 1988 the Russian Orthodox church excluded the Greek Catholics of the Ukraine from the millennial celebration of Christianity in Russia, Pope John Paul addressed a letter, *Magnum baptismi donum,* to His Beatitude Lubachivsky and all the Catholics of the Ukraine. The pope commended their heroic witness to the faith and said he looked forward to the day when Greek Catholics in the Ukraine could practice their faith in freedom.

[ANN LASZOK]

LUBICH, CHIARA

Founder of the Focolare Movement; b. 22 January 1920, in Trent, Italy, the first of four children. Lubich's family experienced extreme poverty in the years of the fascist regime when her father was jobless because of his socialist leanings. To support herself while studying she did private tutoring, and in 1939 took a position as an elementary school teacher. Faced with the destruction and violence of World War II, she and a small group of friends chose God-Love as the only ideal worth living for. Soon the meaning of their lives became clear: to bring the human family together in unity by working for the fulfillment of Jesus' prayer to the Father, "May they all be one" (Jn 17:21). From their daily commitment to the Gospel, the "spirituality of unity" came to life and gave rise to the Focolare, a movement of spiritual and social renewal of worldwide dimensions (and which over the years would generate publishing houses, model towns of witness, the Economy of Sharing business system, study centers, among others). It soon attracted the attention of Igino Giordani, a journalist and member of parliament, who ultimately came to be considered a cofounder.

In 1977 Lubich was awarded the prestigious Templeton Prize for Progress in Religion. In their press release the Templeton Committee praised her work saying, "By stressing love, Chiara Lubich has contributed much to the spiritual development of many people of various denominations. Her work of building unity is one of the most important contributions to the relationships among churches and religions today." In 1981 the founder of a Buddhist lay movement invited her to Tokyo to share the principles of the Focolare Movement with 10,000 Buddhists. In May, 1997, Imam W. D. Mohammed, of the Muslim American Society, invited her to address his followers in a Harlem mosque dedicated to Malcolm X. In the light of her experience as a Christian, she stressed love as the element capable of bringing humanity together as one family. In 1988 she received the coveted UNESCO Prize for Peace Education.

Lubich's direction of the Focolare Movement continues through her life example and writings, especially

"Word of Life," a monthly newsletter that reaches over three million people in eighty languages. Her spirituality inspires a following in countries throughout the world.

See Also: FOCOLARE MOVEMENT

[GARY BRANDL/ANNE LINGLEY]

LUBLIN, CATHOLIC UNIVERSITY OF

Founded with the approval of the Polish Catholic hierarchy in 1918, the Catholic University of Lublin (Katolicki Uniwersystet Lubelski or KUL for short), has as its motto *Deo et Patriae*—"for God and country." The founder and first rector, the Rev. Dr. Idzi Radziszewski modeled the statutes on those of the Catholic University of Louvain. In 1920, KUL received a state charter and recognition by the Holy See. The university flourished until the outbreak of World War II in 1939, when it was forced to close. During the war, the university's property was pillaged, many faculty members imprisoned, and some executed. As elsewhere in Poland, teaching went underground for the duration of the war, but it reopened in 1944 and began anew.

The University's main mission is integral understanding of the human person. The University is organized into six faculties: theology, philosophy, civil and canon law, humanities, social sciences, mathematics and natural sciences. These are subdivided into institutes and smaller units, organized around chairs occupied by a senior professor. The university encourages a network of interdisciplinary institutes in order to understand better the mystery of the human person in all its aspects. The basic degree offered by most programs is the Masters' degree, and many programs also offer doctorates and postdoctoral studies.

After World War II, KUL, in spite of obstruction by government authorities, established contacts with many international academic centers, first in the West and after 1989, with the collapse of the Communist regime, with the East as well. The University has an international enrollment with many students from the former USSR and its satellites. Its professors have been invited to teach in Western Europe and the United States, and the university cites its geographic location and history in consciously fostering academic ties to the East.

KUL has one of the better university libraries in Poland, possessing close to 1.3 million volumes in the year 2000, with its largest holdings in the humanities and social sciences. It holds many rare books and manuscripts as well.

KUL is probably best known for the school of philosophy in which it has nurtured since the Second World

Jean-Marie Cardinal Lustiger. (Catholic News Service.)

War, the so-called "Lublin School." In one of its aspects, this school takes Thomist metaphysics as its starting point, especially emphasizing St. Thomas's postulate that being has a certain priority of importance over essence, and using this as a basis to critique the radical essentialism of modern Idealist philosophy from the standpoint of a balanced metaphysical realism, rather than various fashionable nihilisms from which it is more usually criticized. In another of its aspects, the Lublin school seeks to apply philosophy to understanding the nature and dilemmas of the human person, and to this end it uses the methods of phenomenology (i.e. description of human consciousness without reference to external realities). The most prominent representatives of this school are Mieczysław Krąpiec, O.P., and Karol Wojtyła (John Paul II), who was a faculty member at KUL for twenty-five years.

[PAUL RADZILOWSKI/K. TUROWSKI]

LUSTIGER, JEAN-MARIE

Cardinal, archbishop of Paris; b. Aaron Lustiger, 17 September 1926, Paris, France. He was born to a Jewish immigrant family of Polish descent. His parents were nonreligious members of the Jewish Socialist movement of Poland and the Soviet Union. As the threat of German occupation grew at the beginning of the Second World War, the family moved from Paris to Orléans. Lustiger's father escaped the Holocaust by going into hiding; his mother was deported to Auschwitz, where she died in 1943. Lustiger lived with a Roman Catholic family in Orléans and, in August of 1940, was baptized there. At that point, he adopted the Christian name Jean-Marie. Even after his baptism, he wore the yellow Star of David that Jews were obligated to wear by the German forces of occupation. His sister Arlette also converted.

Lustiger did lycée studies in Paris and in Orléans and superior studies in Letters at the Sorbonne. He pursued his ecclesiastical formation at the Seminary "des Carmes" of the Institut Catholique de Paris. After being ordained a priest, 17 April 1954, he exercised his pastoral ministry as a chaplain of the Paris university parish, chaplain to the students of La Sorbonne and of "Grandes Ecoles" (E.N.S.de Saint-Cloud, Fontenay). From 1959 to 1979 he was director of the Centre Richelieu, responsible for chaplains of the new universities of the Parisian region, and in 1969 was appointed pastor of the busy parish of Sainte-Jeanne-de-Chantal in Paris.

Pope John Paul II named Fr. Lustiger bishop of Orléans on 10 November 1979; he received his episcopal ordination from François Marty, archbishop of Paris. When a Paris synagogue was bombed in 1980, Bishop Lustiger urged Christians to remember their connections to Judaism, reminding them that the founder of their faith was also a Jew, and affirming his own Jewish identity. The next year he was promoted to the metropolitan see of Paris.

John Paul II created him cardinal priest of Ss. Marcellino e Pietro in 1983. He is the first Jewish convert to be named to the College of Cardinals in modern times. Cardinal Lustiger has participated in five assemblies of the Synod of Bishops, was president-delegate to the synod of 1991, and served as a member of its general secretariat from 1990 to 1994. By papal bull, he was transferred to the title of S. Luigi dei Francesi in 1994. In 1995, the prestigious Académie Française elected him as one of its members. He has published numerous collections of homilies, interviews, and conversations, several of which have been translated into English.

Bibliography: Works by Jean-Marie Cardinal Lustiger include: *Dare to Believe: Addresses, Sermons and Interviews, 1981–1984* (Slough, 1986); *First Steps in Prayer* (New York, 1987); *The Lord's Prayer* (Huntington, Ind., 1988); *Dare to Rejoice: A Celebration of Christian Life* (Huntington, Ind. 1990); *The Mass* (London 1990); *Choosing God, Chosen by God: Conversations with Jean-Marie Cardinal Lustiger* (San Francisco 1991).

[SALVADOR MIRANDA]

MACHARSKI, FRACISZEK

Cardinal and archbishop of Kraków, Poland, b. 20 May 1927 in Kraków, Poland. After studying at the Kraków Archdiocesan Seminary, he was ordained a priest in Kraków in 1950. After several years of pastoral work in a parish, he did his graduate studies at the University of Freiburg, Switzerland, finishing a doctorate in theology there in 1960. Upon his return to Poland he became a professor at the Kraków seminary, and eventually its rector, in 1970. From 1972 to 1977 he was chairman of the Archdiocesan Commission for Pastoral and Sociological Affairs, and was a member of several other archdiocesan commissions.

He was named Archbishop of Kraków by John Paul II, his friend and predecessor in the see, who consecrated him in Rome 6 December 1979. On 30 June 1979, he was named Cardinal-presbyter of Sanctus Joannes ante Portam Latinam. In the next year he became vice-chairman of the Polish Episcopal Conference, and in 1981 the first grand-chancellor of the newly created Papal Academy of Theology in Kraków.

[PAUL RADZILOWSKI]

MAHONY, ROGER MICHAEL

Cardinal, archbishop of Los Angeles; b. 27 February 1936, North Hollywood, California, to Victor, a poultry farmer, and Loretta (Baron) Mahony. Mahony was one of the very first students to enroll at Our Lady of the Angels Preparatory Seminary in Mission Hills, California; he then attended Saint John's Provincial Seminary in Camarillo and was ordained to the priesthood for the diocese of Fresno, 1 May 1962, by Bishop Timothy Manning. After ordination, he attended the Catholic University of America in Washington, D.C., where he received a doctorate in social work. He returned to Fresno to serve as diocesan director of Catholic Charities and Social Services (1964–70), chancellor (1970–80), and pastor of Saint John's Cathedral (1973–80). In addition, he taught at California State University at Fresno and at Coalinga College. His intense interest in the ministry to the Hispanic population gained him a position on the Administrative Council of the Episcopal Committee for Hispanics, and the position of secretary of the ad hoc Committee for Farm Workers of the National Conference of Catholic Bishops.

In 1975, Mahony was ordained auxiliary bishop of Fresno. While auxiliary bishop, he held the position of assistant secretary of labor for farm workers in the administration of California governor Jerry Brown. Pope John Paul II transferred Bishop Mahony to the see of Stockton in 1980, and promoted him to the metropolitan see of Los Angeles in 1985. Pope John Paul named him a cardinal on 28 June 1991 with the title of Ss. Quattro Coronati.

Cardinal Mahony's active and highly visible leadership put him at the center of some controversies and at the same time enabled him to reach to the farthest outposts of the most populous diocese in the country. Early in his tenure as archbishop of Los Angeles, despite his long-standing reputation as a labor priest, he found himself at odds with cemetery workers. He met with criticism when local businessmen provided him with a helicopter that he piloted himself. His relationship with Los Angeles's powerful media and film industry, initially testy and filled with mutual suspicion, led him to found "Catholics in Media," an organization to influence, shape, and reward the entertainment industry. Cardinal Mahony has been a frequent caller on local talk radio, and has used his skill as a ham radio operator to keep contact with ordinary people all around the world. He was quick to grasp the power of the Internet and frequently uses it to hold chat sessions with his people.

The cardinal's ties with the rich and powerful in Los Angeles led to a unique coalition between the Church and the city when his close friend and advisor Richard Riordan was elected mayor of Los Angeles. A high priority in Mahony's tenure as archbishop was to erect a new cathedral for the City of the Angels. When in 1994 the Northridge earthquake so undermined the Cathedral of Saint Vibiana that repairing it was not an option, Cardinal Mahony obtained a prime location in the Los Angeles Civic Center on which to build the Cathedral Center of Our Lady of the Angels in grand contemporary style.

Cardinal Mahony's ministry changed in style and substance over the years. His struggle with prostate cancer gave him a deeper appreciation of his own vulnerability and limitations, and drew him close to another cancer victim, Joseph Cardinal Bernardin of Chicago. Mahony's friendship with Bernardin and his participation in the latter's "Common Ground" project expanded his view of the Church's need to interact with contemporary society. His personal friendships with other religious leaders in Los Angeles led to a signed covenant among Catholics, Lutherans, and Episcopalians.

Cardinal Mahony increased lay involvement in the administration of the archdiocese. He expanded the services of the archdiocese while simplifying archdiocesan structures. A pastoral letter on the liturgy, *Gather Faithfully Together,* published on the feast of Our Lady of the Angels, 4 September 1997, served as a call to renewal for the parishes in the archdiocese. The later years of Cardinal Mahony's ministry have returned him to his roots in Catholic social activism. He has fostered free and open

Roger Cardinal Mahony. (Catholic News Service.)

dialogue in the archdiocese—especially through the expansion of the Los Angeles Religious Education Congress, an annual event that draws thirty thousand participants from all over the world. With funds and friendship he has supported churches in the developing world, especially in Central and South America.

[C. SCHIPPE]

MAIDA, ADAM

Cardinal, archbishop of Detroit; b. 18 March 1930, East Vandergrift, Pennsylvania. Adam Joseph Maida was the first of three sons born to Adam Maida and Sophie Cieslak Maida. His father came to the United States from a rural area near Warsaw, Poland; his mother was born in the United States. He graduated from St. Vincent's College, Latrobe, Pennsylvania, in 1952, with a B.A. in Philosophy. In 1956 he received a licentiate in Sacred Theology from St. Mary's University in Baltimore. After ordination as a priest the same year, he was assigned to pastoral work in the Diocese of Pittsburgh. He obtained a licentiate in Canon Law from the Pontifical Lateran University in Rome in 1960 and a doctorate in Civil Law from Duquesne Law School in 1964, where he subsequently became an adjunct professor. He also taught the-

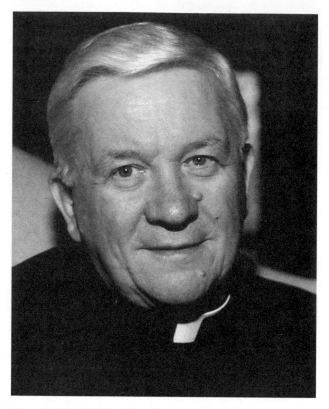

Adam Cardinal Maida. (Catholic News Service.)

ology at La Roche College and served as vice chancellor and general counsel for the diocese.

In 1984, Fr. Maida was ordained and installed as bishop of Green Bay, Wisconsin. In 1990, Pope John Paul II named him archbishop of Detroit, and four years later made him a cardinal, with the titular church of Sts. Vitalis, Valeria, Gervase, and Protase.

Since being elevated to the College of Cardinals, Cardinal Maida has served the Church in a variety of capacities. In May 1996, Pope John Paul II appointed Cardinal Maida as a papal legate to the nineteenth International Marian Congress, held in Częstochowa, Poland. In 1997, Cardinal Maida participated in the Special Synod for America at the Vatican, and in 1999, Pope John Paul II appointed him a member of the Second Special Assembly for Europe of the Synod of Bishops. As the episcopal moderator and president of the Pope John Paul II Cultural Foundation in the United States, Cardinal Maida took the lead in establishing the Pope John Paul II Cultural Center in Washington, D.C.

Bibliography: Maida's earliest published works deal chiefly with canon law: *The Tribunal Reporter: A Casebook and Commentary on the Grounds for Annulment in the Catholic Church* (1970); *Ownership, Control and Sponsorship of Catholic Institutions* (1975); *Issues in the Labor-Management Dialogue: Church Perspectives* (1982); and *Church Property, Church Finances and Church-Related Corporations: A Canon Law Handbook,* with Nicholas P. Cafardi (1983).

[G. MICHAEL BUGARIN]

MARCINKUS, PAUL CASIMIR

Archbishop, Vatican official; b. 15 January 1922, Cicero, Ill. The son of Lithuanian immigrants Michael Marcinkus and Helen Lenart, he grew up in Cicero, a working-class suburb of Chicago. After completing philosophical and theological studies at St Mary of the Lake Seminary, Mundelein, Ill., he was ordained a priest 3 May 1947 by Cardinal Samuel A. Stritch. After ordination he served as an assistant at St. Christina Parish on Chicago's south side, a rapidly growing neighborhood with many parishioners of Lithuanian descent. After working for a year on the metropolitan tribunal, he was sent to Rome to earn a doctorate in canon law at the Pontifical Gregorian University. While finishing his degree he also worked in the Secretariat of State and in 1954 completed the course at the Pontifical Ecclesiastical Academy. After entering the Holy See's diplomatic service, he was first posted to Bolivia (1955–56), and then to Canada (1956–59). From 1959 to 1969 he worked in the Secretariat of State.

At the end of the Second Vatican Council, the American bishops decided to open a house in Rome for their own accommodation during visits to the Eternal City and to serve as a residence for U.S. diocesan clergy working for the Holy See. Working with officials of the Bishops' Conference, Marcinkus oversaw the purchase and refurbishing of two apartment buildings which were opened in 1968 as Villa Stritch. He also served as the first director of the residence. His organizational skills came to the attention of Pope Paul VI, who entrusted him with arranging the logistical details of his various trips abroad. Starting with the visit to the Holy Land in 1964, he continued to coordinate papal trips outside Italy until the autumn of 1982. During the height of the U.S. bombing campaign in North Vietnam, he brought President Lyndon B. Johnson a letter from Paul VI urging a cease-fire. Johnson in turn asked the pope to help nudge the Vietnamese to the negotiating table.

In 1968 Marcinkus was appointed secretary of the Institute for Religious Works (IOR), an institution providing savings, lending, and currency exchange services for Vatican employees, religious institutes, and missionary projects. Consecrated titular bishop of Horta in 1969, in 1971 he was promoted to president of the same institute, a post he held until 1989. He was responsible for modernizing accounting procedures, diversifying investments, and improving the overall organization. His tenure at the institute was marred, however, by the Banco Ambrosiano scandal in the 1980s. Although the Vatican denied any wrongdoing, a settlement was negotiated with the Italian government in which IOR paid $244 million to Ambrosiano's creditors against any present or future claims, an action which Marcinkus opposed.

In 1981 he was also appointed pro-president of the Pontifical Commission for Vatican City State and promoted to archbishop. The commission is responsible for the administration of Vatican City's temporalities. Among other projects, he was responsible for organizing and financing the restoration of the Sistine Chapel. Upon his retirement in 1990 he returned to the United States.

[ROBERT DEMPSEY]

MARTÍNEZ SOMALO, EDUARDO

Cardinal, Camerlengo of the Holy Roman Church, prefect of the Congregation for Institutes of Consecrated Life; b. 31 March 1927, in Baños de Río Tobía, Spain, to a family of ten children. Martínez Somalo began his studies for the priesthood at the Seminary of Logroño and later was sent to the Pontifical Gregorian University in Rome where he obtained licentiates in theology and in canon law. After his ordination as a priest in Rome, 19 March 1950, he returned to pastoral ministry in his native diocese. He later returned to Rome to study at the Pontifical Ecclesiastical Academy, the Vatican school of diplomacy, and at the same time attended the Pontifical Lateran University, earning a doctorate in canon law with a thesis entitled "Il Concordato spagnolo del 1953 alla luce dei suoi due primi articoli" (The Spanish Concordat in the Light of its First Two Articles). In 1956 he joined the Vatican Secretariat of State; in 1970 he was sent to London as counselor of the apostolic delegation. During those years he also taught the future Church diplomats at the Academy. He accompanied Pope Paul VI on his visit to Bogotá, Colombia, in 1968, the first time a pope had traveled to Latin America. Recalled from England after a few months, he became assessor of the Secretariat of State (1970–75) and at the same time did pastoral work in Roman hospitals.

Pope Paul VI elected Msgr. Martínez Somalo titular archbishop of Tagora and appointed him nuncio in Colombia in 1975. He received the episcopal ordination at St. Peter's basilica from Cardinal Jean Villot. Pope John Paul II appointed him substitute of the Secretariat of State, the second ranking position in that Roman dicastery, in 1979. Archbishop Martínez Somalo was created cardinal deacon of SS. Nome di Gesù in the consistory of 28 June 1988; three days later, he was named prefect

Pope John Paul II greets Archbishop Paul Marcinkus as he arrives in the Clementine Hall, Rome. (Reuters/Archive Photos. Reproduced by Permission.)

of the Congregation for Divine Worship and the Discipline of the Sacraments. He has participated in eight assemblies of the Synod of Bishops and was a president-delegate of two of them. In 1992 he was named prefect of the Congregation for Institutes of Consecrated Life and Societies of Apostolic Life, and the following year Camerlengo of the Holy Roman Church (administrator of the property and the revenues of the Holy See). As such, he also directs the preparations for the conclave, and takes charge of the same.

See Also: CAMERLENGO

[SALVADOR MIRANDA]

MARTINI, CARLO MARIA

Jesuit, cardinal, archbishop of Milan; b. 15 February 1927, Turin, Italy. Martini entered the Society of Jesus in 1944 and was ordained a priest 13 July 1952, in Chieri (Torino). After completing his studies in the Jesuit houses at Cuneo, Gallarate, and Chieri, he earned a doctorate in fundamental theology in 1959 at the Pontifical Gregorian University. He took his final vows as a Jesuit in 1962. That same year he was named professor of textual criti-

Carlo Maria Cardinal Martini. (Sestiny Agency/Liaison Agency.)

cism of Sacred Scripture at the Pontifical Biblical Institute in Rome, and later became dean of the faculty. In 1969 Pope Paul VI appointed him rector of the Biblicum and in 1978 rector of the Pontifical Gregorian University.

In 1979 Pope John Paul II appointed Martini archbishop of Milan, ordaining him bishop in St. Peter's basilica. In 1983 the pope named him cardinal priest with the titular church of St. Cecilia. From 1987 until 1993 he served as president of the Council of the European Episcopal Conference. A regular participant in the assemblies of the Synod of Bishops, he was a member of the council of the general secretariat from 1980 to 1990.

An eminent New Testament scholar, Martini reads several languages, ancient and modern, and has authored numerous books and countless journal articles. His interest in Scripture was already evidenced in his doctoral dissertation, ''Il problema storico della Risurrezione negli studi recenti.'' In 1964 he prepared a new edition of A. Merk's ''Novum Testamentum graece et latine'' and be-

came one of the five editors (the only Catholic) of the Ecumenical Committee for the publication of ''The Greek New Testament.'' The second edition, which constitutes the basis of the more than 800 translations world-wide, appeared in 1969. His important study of the Dead Sea Scrolls, *Notes on the Papyri of Qumran Cave 7* appeared in an English translation (Missoula, Mont. 1972). His more recent works deal with pastoral themes and spiritual advice. His popular works draw heavily on Scripture for their inspiration and content. Several have been translated into English including the widely circulated *Through Moses to Jesus: The Way of the Paschal Mystery, The Testimony of St Paul: Meditations on the Life and Letters of St. Paul,* and *The Pastoral Practice of Lectio Divina.* Cardinal Martini has expressed more than once his desire to retire to the Holy Land when he reaches the mandatory age, to continue his scriptural studies and research.

As archbishop of Milan his approach to pastoral ministry is characterized by openness and dialogue. His Friday evening sessions in the cathedral with the young people of the archdiocese have become legendary. In 1980, he started the ''Scuola della Parola'' to help the faithful approach Scripture according to the method of *lectio divina.* In 1987, he began a series of encounters on the ''demands of faith'' also known as the ''Cathedra of the non-believers'' addressed to persons in search of the faith.

Bibliography: Some other titles by this most prolific author are: *Ministers of the Gospel: Meditations on St. Luke's Gospel* (1989), *Jacob's Dream: Setting out on a Spiritual Journey* (1992), *Perseverance in Trials: Reflections on Job* (1992), *Letting God Free Us: Meditations on Ignatian Spiritual Exercises* (1994), *Once More from Emmaus* (1995), *A Prophetic Voice in the City: Meditations on the Prophet Jeremiah* (1997), *Belief or Non-Belief: A Confrontation,* with Umberto Eco (2000).

[SALVADOR MIRANDA]

MCCORMICK, RICHARD A.

Jesuit, moral theologian, writer; b. 3 October 1922, Toledo, Ohio; d. 12 February 2000, Clarkston, Michigan, the son of Edward J. McCormick, a distinguished physician and sometime president of the American Medical Association, and Josephine Beck McCormick. McCormick entered the Society of Jesus in 1940; studied philosophy at the Jesuit seminary in West Baden Indiana; beginning in 1947 he taught English and Greek at St Ignatius High School in Cleveland before returning to West Baden in 1950 to study theology. McCormick was ordained a priest in 1953. He attended the Pontifical Gregorian University in Rome from 1955 to1957, where he earned a doctorate in moral theology. From 1957 to 1973, he taught moral theology at the Jesuit theologate that during those years moved from West Baden to Chicago. In 1974, he was named the Rose F. Kennedy Professor of Christian Ethics at the Kennedy Institute of Ethics at Georgetown University and in 1986 he became the John A. O'Brien Professor of Christian Ethics at the University of Notre Dame.

McCormick's numerous articles in theological and medical journals as well as in Catholic intellectual journals of opinion, especially the Jesuit magazine *America* where he once served as an associate editor, gained him an international reputation. McCormick's most important publications were the "Notes on Moral Theology" he published annually in Theological Studies from 1965 to 1984. These notes were subsequently collected in two volumes—*Notes on Moral Theology 1965–80* (Washington 1981) and *Notes on Moral Theology 1981–84* (Lanham, Md.,1984). He authored *How Brave a New World? Dilemmas in Bioethics* (Garden City, N.Y. 1981) and *Health and Medicine in the Catholic Tradition* (New York, 1984). The volume he edited with Paul Ramsey, *Doing Evil to Achieve Good: Moral Choice in Conflict Situations* (Chicago: Loyola University Press, 1978), brings together theologians from different churches and philosophers discussing McCormick's theory of proportionalism. McCormick was co-editor with Charles E. Curran of eleven volumes in the series *Readings in Moral Theology* (Paulist Press). His last two books were collections of essays: *The Critical Calling: Moral Dilemmas Since Vatican II* (Washington, 1989) and *Corrective Vision: Explorations in Moral Theology* (Kansas City 1994).

The time frame in which McCormick wrote witnessed a significant change toward a more academic understanding of the discipline itself. Prior to the 1960s moral theology was associated with the seminary and the manuals of moral theology had as their purpose the training of confessors. The Second Vatican Council specifically called for a life-oriented moral theology that would reflect on the totality of the Christian life including the vocation to perfection and holiness. Vatican II urged new methodological approaches that would give more prominence to role of the Scriptures, seek to bridge the gulf between faith and daily life as well as the separation between the supernatural and the natural, recognize the importance of historicity, and engage in dialogue with other theological disciplines. The post-conciliar period was a time of great ferment in the theological disciplines. Pope Paul VI's encyclical *Humanae vitae* in 1968 reiterated the condemnation of artificial contraception for spouses and raised the two issues that dominated much of Catholic moral theology in succeeding decades, namely, the existence and grounding of absolute moral norms such as the condemnation of contraception, and practical

questions of ecclesiology regarding the role and function of hierarchical teaching on moral matters and the proper response of Catholics. With his characteristic clarity and incisiveness, McCormick insisted on the [progresssive?] processive nature of the search for moral truth by all in the church and pointed out that the hierarchical church has a learning function as well as a teaching function. He firmly defended the possibility and even the need to dissent from some non-infallible church teaching. McCormick's early training and extensive knowledge of the manualist tradition continued to influence him, but over the years he modified his position on a number of significant issues. He himself listed ten areas in which his theological views changed—the nature of the church, the importance of lay witness, ecumenism and the search for moral truth, the role of dissent, the changeable and the unchangeable in the church, certainty and uncertainty, effective teaching in the church, the imperative of honesty, and the dynamic nature of faith.

In the course of his academic career, McCormick challenged and disagreed with the hierarchy's positions on specific points of sexual and marital ethics and some conflict situations, but he staunchly defended the very early beginning of the truly human life of the fetus and the condemnation of active euthanasia. In dealing with the question of absolute norms in moral theology, McCormick developed a theory of proportionalism by which he sought to establish a middle position between the traditional neoscholastic natural law approach, on the one hand, and a utilitarianism or consequentialism, on the other hand. The natural law with its theological acceptance of human sources of moral wisdom and knowledge and its philosophical emphasis on a realistic epistemology formed the basis for his understanding of moral theology. He proposed an understanding of natural law that involved a shift from classicism to historical consciousness with a greater emphasis on human experience, a move to the person and the subject away from the emphasis on the natural and the given, a development away from the teaching of the manuals that tended to identify the human and the moral with the physical structure of the act, and a change from the deontological or law model of the manuals of moral theology. While he recognized the need to incorporate both Scripture and systematic theology into moral theology, these two aspects are more implicit than explicit in his work.

McCormick served as a president of the Catholic Theological Society of America and was the recipient of its Cardinal Spellman Award as "Outstanding Theologian of the Year" in 1969. In addition to his service in many Catholic institutions and societies, he was the recipient of numerous honorary degrees. A member of the Ethics Advisory Board of the Department of Health, Edu-

A sister of the Missionaries of Charity order helps a patient at a missionary home in Calcutta. (Reuters/Kamal Kishore/Archive Photos. Reproduced by Permission.)

cation, and Welfare, he served on ethics committees of the American Hospital Association, the National Hospice Organization, and the American Fertility Society. In 1990, he was elected to membership in the prestigious American Academy of Arts and Sciences.

McCormick never fully recovered from the stroke he suffered in June 1999 and he died at the Jesuit Healthcare Community at Colombiere Center in Clarkston, Michigan. The funeral liturgy was celebrated at Gesù Jesuit Church in Toledo, 17 February 2000, with burial in the Jesuit cemetery next door. His papers are at Loyola University of Chicago.

[CHARLES E. CURRAN]

MISSIONARIES OF CHARITY

An international congregation of religious women, the Missionaries of Charity (abbreviated M.C.) have as their primary ministry the service of "the poorest of the poor" irrespective of caste, creed, and nationality. Their headquarters are located in Calcutta, India where the congregation was founded by Mother Teresa Bojaxhiu. The

foundation was approved as a diocesan congregation in 1950 and made a pontifical institute in 1965. The distinctive habit of the Missionaries of Charity, made famous by Mother Teresa, consists of a white cotton sari with a blue border that covers the head, a cincture made of rope, sandals, a crucifix, and rosary. The sisters nurse sick and dying destitutes, including victims of AIDS, teach street children, visit and care for beggars, lepers, and their children, and provide shelter for the abandoned and homeless. They foster special devotion to Jesus in the Blessed Sacrament, and proclaim the Word of God to the spiritually destitute by their presence and the spiritual works of mercy.

In March, 1997 the congregation elected Sister Nirmala and a council of four sisters to succeed Mother Teresa, who had asked to be relieved of administrative duties because of her poor health. At the time of Sister Nirmala's election, the order had some 4500 nuns working in more than 100 countries.

See Also: MOTHER TERESA OF CALCUTTA

Bibliography: DESMOND DOIG, *Mother Teresa: Her People and Her Work* (San Francisco: Harper & Row, 1976). MALCOLM

MUGGERIDGE, *Something Beautiful for God,* 2d ed. (San Francisco: HarperSan Francisco, 1986).

[B.L. MARTHALER]

MOTHER TERESA OF CALCUTTA

Founder of Missionaries of Charity, teacher, social worker, Nobel Peace Prize Laureate; b. 26 August 1910, Shkup, Albania, in the Ottoman Empire (now Skopje, the capital of the Republic of Macedonia); d. 5 September 1997, Calcutta, India. Baptized Gonxha (in English, Agnes) Bojaxhiu, she was one of five children of a middle-class family. Her father Nikola, a grocer, died in 1919, and her mother, Dronda, in 1968. At the age of 18, Gonxha joined the Sisters of Loreto with the intention of serving in the missions. En route to India she spent two months in Ireland, studying English. When she entered the novitiate in 1929 at Darjeeling in the foothills of the Himalayas, she became known as Sister Teresa. Professed in 1931, she was sent to teach at St Mary's School for Girls in Calcutta. On 10 September 1946, while riding the train to Darjeeling, Sister Teresa experienced "a second calling," a vocation to serve the poor of Calcutta. In August 1948, she left the sisters of Loreto with the blessing of her superiors and the permission of the archbishop of Calcutta to live in the slums of Matizhil. She donned the sari and applied for citizenship in her adopted country. Teresa's initial effort was to organize dispensaries and outdoor schools where she fed, clothed, and taught poor children. The women, including some of her former students, whom she enlisted as volunteers to assist in the work became the nucleus of the Missionaries of Charity. In 1950 the order received canonical approval from church authorities.

In 1952 Mother Teresa opened the first of many hospices for the dying. In 1957 she founded a leper colony called Shanti Nagar (Town of Peace) near Asansol, India. Under her guidance the Missionaries of Charity established numerous centers where they ministered to the aged, lepers, cripples, AIDS victims, and the dying. In 1963 the Indian government awarded her the Padmashri ("Lord of the Lotus") for her services. As the Missionaries of Charity expanded their ministry to other countries, Mother Teresa's reputation spread throughout the world. In recognition of her work Pope Paul VI awarded her the first Pope John XXIII Peace Prize in 1971, and she received the Nobel Prize for Peace in 1979. Upon accepting the Nobel honor she said, "I choose the poverty of our poor people. But I am grateful to receive [the Nobel] in the name of the hungry, the naked, the homeless, of the crippled, of the blind, of the lepers, of all those people who feel unwanted, unloved, uncared-for throughout society, people that have become a burden to society and are shunned by everyone."

Mother Teresa. (AP/Wide World Photos. Reproduced by permission.)

The sisters continued every six years to reelect her as major superior until early 1997 when, because of her rapidly failing health, they acceded to her wish to step down. In March they elected Nepal-born Sister Nirmala to head the order. Surrounded by sisters of the community Mother Teresa died peacefully on 5 September 1997. On 13 September they buried her in a simple white marble tomb in the mother house of the Missionaries of Charity. In reminiscing about Mother Teresa some weeks after her death Pope John Paul II who had met with her on several occasions said, "I hope she will be a saint." Eighteen months later, he dispensed with the normal five-year waiting period and allowed the archbishop of Calcutta to initiate the formal process for beatification.

See Also: MISSIONARIES OF CHARITY

Bibliography: EILEEN EGAN, and KATHLEEN EGAN, eds., *Mother Teresa and the Beatitudes* (San Francisco: Ignatius Press, 1992). CHRISTIAN FELDMAN, *Mother Teresa: Love Stays,* translated by PETER HEINEGG (New York: Crossroad, 1998). MALCOLM MUGGERIDGE, *Something Beautiful for God,* 2d ed. (San Francisco: HarperSan Francisco, 1986).

[B. L. MARTHALER]

Joaquin Navarro-Valls. (Catholic News Service)

NAVARRO-VALLS, JOAQUIN

Vatican press spokesman, correspondent, medical doctor, member of *Opus Dei*; b. 16 November 1936, Cartagena, Spain.

Navarro-Valls was born into a family of six children; his father was a lawyer. He began his professional life as a doctor, receiving a doctorate in medicine from the University of Granada in 1961 and teaching in the faculty of medicine at the same university until 1964. At the same time, he pursued an interest in journalism. He founded the Barcelona magazine *Diagonal* in 1964, before becoming a foreign correspondent for the newspaper *Nuestro Tiempo* and receiving a degree in journalism (1968). In 1977, he became foreign correspondent for the Madrid daily *ABC,* covering Italy, the Vatican, and the eastern Mediterranean, as well as serving on special assignments in Equatorial Africa, Japan, and the Philippines. In 1980 he received a Ph.D. in communications from the University of Navarra, and in 1983–84 he served as president of the Foreign Press Association in Italy.

Navarro-Valls became a ''numerary'' member of *Opus Dei* as a university student in Granada, where he also participated in an experimental theater program. In the 1970s he published four books: *La manipulacíon publicitaria* (Barcelona 1970), *La familia y el mundo ac-* *tual* (Barcelona 1976), *La familia y la educacíon* (Caracas 1978) and *Fumata blanca* (Madrid 1978.)

In 1984, as he was about to return to Spain to resume an earlier career of teaching medicine and psychiatry, Navarro-Valls was named by Pope John Paul as Vatican spokesman. His appointment was an effort by the pope to respond to the increasing demands and challenges of the international news media, which had begun to follow the pope's activities at the Vatican and abroad with unprecedented attention. Navarro-Valls directed the Vatican Press Office, increasing its staff to about eighteen and strengthening its autonomy as an office operating under the wing of the secretariat of state. In 1990, Navarro-Valls pushed for the creation of the Vatican Information Service, an appendage to the press office, which sends official information in story form to nunciatures and bishops around the world. He convinced Vatican budget officials to finance an expensive renovation of the press office, whose facilities dated to the time of the Second Vatican Council. When the Vatican entered the online age in the late 1990s, the press office led the way, providing Internet access to its daily output of information.

For the more than 300 journalists permanently accredited to the Vatican, Navarro-Valls changed the style of information gathering. He gave background briefings on sensitive issues, arranged numerous press conferences when official documents were unveiled and responded quickly, by Vatican standards, to breaking news. He kept close tabs on what the media were reporting about the pope and the Vatican, instituting the compilation of a daily world press review that was sometimes passed on to the pope. From time to time he met with the pope to discuss the impact of church actions in the global media.

Fluent in five languages, Navarro-Valls was most prominently in the public eye during moments of crisis: when Panamanian dictator Manuel Noriega took refuge in the Vatican nunciature in Panama City; when a disgruntled member of the Swiss Guard murdered his commander and the commander's wife inside Vatican grounds; or when Pope John Paul went into the hospital. In a break with longstanding Vatican tradition, Navarro-Valls gave detailed briefings on the pope's medical operations.

Recognizing the increasing importance of media and public relations in modern diplomacy, John Paul occasionally used Navarro-Valls in a quasi-diplomatic role. He was a key man on Vatican delegations to major U.N. conferences: on population (Cairo, 1994); on social development (Copenhagen, 1995); on women (Beijing, 1995); and on global housing (Istanbul, 1996). When the pope prepared to visit Cuba in 1998, he sent Navarro-Valls to Havana for talks with Fidel Castro, to iron out disagreements on media issues; the two reportedly got along well, and the pope's trip was a success for the church. In the Holy Year 2000, Navarro-Valls cooperated with Rome city officials to offer greatly expanded services to visiting journalists.

[JOHN THAVIS]

NEOCATECHUMENAL WAY

The Neocatechumenal Way, or the Neocatechumenate, is a loosely organized Catholic renewal and catechetical apostolate founded in 1962 in the Palomeras slums of Madrid by Kiko Argüello, who serves as a chief catechist of the movement and is currently a consultor to the Pontifical Council on the Laity. From the start, the Neocatechumenate received the approval and support of the bishop of Madrid at the time, Casimiro Morcillo.

In 1974 Pope Paul VI welcomed members of Neocatechumenal communities in a general audience and declared that this "way" after baptism would "renew in today's Christian communities those effects of maturity and deepening that, in the primitive Church, were realized by the period of preparation for baptism." Twenty-five years later, in 1990, Pope John Paul II officially recognized the Neocatechumenal Way as "an itinerary of catholic formation, valid for our society and for our times" and encouraged bishops and priests in the Church to "value and support this work for the new evangelization." Again in 1994, Pope John Paul II praised the Neocatechumenal Way for showing that "the small community, sustained by the Word of God and by the dominical Eucharist, becomes a place of communion, where the family recovers the sense and the joy of its fundamental mission to transmit both natural and supernatural life." In 1997 Pope John Paul II encouraged members of the Neocatechumenal Way in their effort to draft statutes for ecclesiastical recognition.

With the encouragement of Pope Paul VI and Pope John Paul II, the Neocatechumenal Way has spread to dioceses whose bishops welcome it and in parishes whose pastors are committed to it. There are about 200,000 members in more than one hundred countries, organized in 300 small communities in 80 dioceses. Giuseppe Gennarini brought the Neocatechumenal Way to the United States in 1975; they are represented in the archdioceses of Denver, Newark, New York, and Washington, as well as on the West Coast and Texas.

Explicitly avoiding the appellations "movement" or "association," the Neocatechumenal Way is a self-styled program or apostolate of Christian formation. With its stress on exclusive fellowship, intense personal commitment, simplicity of life, communal sharing, and apostolic zeal, the Neocatechumenal Way takes its inspiration from the structure and ethos of the first Christian communities who were known as adherents of "the Way." The program seeks to recover and replicate the early Christian catechumenal pattern of kerygma, conversion, and liturgy as a phased or progressive formation of new Christians: the announcement of salvation that calls for moral decision and thus changes the lives of its hearers and is sealed by participation in the sacramental life of the Church. Proponents of the Neocatechumenal program offer it to Christians who are already baptized but who lack adequate formation in the faith and are thus "quasi-catechumens." It appeals to committed Catholics who want to deepen their faith and to fallen-away Catholics who want to rediscover it.

Service to Local Church. Although the Neocatechumenate is fundamentally a lay movement, the commitment and leadership of the diocesan bishop and the local pastors are crucial to its organization and activities. The founders and leaders of the Neocatechumenate stress its role as a service to the local church. The Eucharist, celebrated by the pastor with great reverence in homes or in small groups, is the anchor of the Neocatechumenal Way. Participants in the seven-year long formation program are called "catechumens" in order to signal the fact that even the baptized person may not yet have attained a sufficient level of conversion and knowledge in the life of the faith. While continuing to live at home, catechumens participate in this formation as members of communities of fifteen to thirty members who meet at least twice a week for catechesis and to celebrate the Eucharist. Day-long meetings are held monthly, as well as occasional social gatherings and regular "scrutinies" and liturgies to mark the transition to a new stage of formation. Eventually, some members become "itinerants" and move on in order to establish Neocatechumenal communities elsewhere.

Another important aspect of the Neocatechumenate is its dedication to the cultivation of religious and priestly vocations and to the foundation of "missionary seminaries" with formation programs patterned on the principles of the Neocatechumenal Way. The best known of these seminaries is the Redemptoris Mater in Rome. Others have been founded in Madrid, Warsaw, Bangalore, Newark, Medellín, Bogotá, Callao (Peru), and Takamatsu (Japan). The seminaries are distinguished by their combination of Christian initiation and formation for the presbyterate.

In 1990 Pope John Paul II assigned to Bishop Paul Josef Cordes, now president of the Pontifical Council "Cor Unum," responsibility *ad personam* for the apostolate of the Way.

Lucas Moreira Cardinal Neves. (Catholic News Service.)

Bibliography: G. GENNARINI, "The Role of the Christian Family in Announcing the Gospel in Today's World," *L'Osservatore Romano,* English edition (19 October 1987):18–19. JOHN PAUL II, "Address to Itinerant Catechists," *L'Osservatore Romano,* English edition (2 February 1994): 10–11. Ibid., "Address to Members of the Neocatechumenal Way," *L'Osservatore Romano,* English edition (5 February 1997): 9. "Epistola R.P.D. Paulo Iosepho Cordes, episcopo tit. Naissitano, Delegato *in persona* ad Communitates Novi Catechumenatus," *Acta Apostolicae Sedis* 82 (1990): 1513–1515. PAUL VI, "Address to Neocatechumenal Communities," *Notitiae* 95–96, (1974): 230.

[J.A. DINOIA]

NEVES, LUCAS MOREIRA

Cardinal, prefect of the Congregation for Bishops; b. 16 September 1925, São João del Rey, Brazil. Neves was the eldest of ten children. His father was a shoemaker whose ancestors were African slaves from Benin, and his mother a school teacher. At an early age he entered the Order of Preachers and, having completed his philosophical studies, he took solemn vows on 7 March 1948. He then was sent to St. Maximin Theological School in Var, France, where he was ordained a priest on 9 July 1950. Fr. Neves continued his studies for two years and then returned to Brazil for a period of intense pastoral activity: vice-master of novices and students (1952–53); ecclesi-astical assistant of the Catholic University Youth Organization in São Paulo (1952–53); director of the journal "Mensageiro do Santo Rosario" in Rio de Janeiro (1954–62); ecclesiastical assistant of the Catholic University Youth Organization in Rio de Janeiro (1954–59); spiritual counselor and later national vice-assistant of the Christian Family Movement (1959–65); official in the Conference of Catholic Bishops of Brazil (1966–67) and spiritual counselor to intellectuals and artists, especially in the theater, in Rio de Janeiro and São Paulo (1962–67).

Pope Paul VI elected Fr. Neves titular bishop of Feradi Maggiore and appointed him auxiliary of the archbishop of São Paulo in 1967, a position he filled until being called to Rome in 1974 as vice-president of Council for the Laity. In 1979, Pope John Paul II named him secretary of the Congregation for Bishops and of the College of Cardinals, promoting him to the rank of archbishop. Archbishop Neves played an important role in discussions between the Vatican and the Brazilian bishops about liberation theology, helping to set up a series of meetings between Brazilian bishops, the curia, and the pope in 1986.

In 1987, Neves was transferred to the metropolitan and primatial see of São Salvador da Bahia in Brazil; the next year, John Paul II created him cardinal priest of the title of Ss. Bonifacio ed Alessio (a church that has been assigned to Brazilian cardinals since 1905). Cardinal Neves was appointed relator for the 1990 general assembly of the synod of bishops; in preparation for the synod he highlighted the need for the bishops to emphasize spiritual formation in seminaries. From 1990 to 1994 he served as a member of the general secretariat of the synod of bishops. He was an active member of the Latin American episcopate, participating in the general conferences in Medellín (1968), Puebla (1979) and Santo Domingo (1992), and serving as president of the Episcopal Conference of Brazil (1995–98).

In 1998, the pope called Cardinal Neves to the Vatican again as prefect of Congregation for Bishops and president of Pontifical Commission for Latin America. At the same time, he was elevated to the rank of cardinal bishop of the suburbicarian see of Sabina-Poggio Mireto, while retaining *in commendam* his titular church of Ss. Bonifacio ed Alessio. As prefect, Cardinal Neves wrote a letter to bishops' conferences throughout the world identifying the changes the conferences would have to make in order to conform to the pope's *motu proprio* on the theological and juridical nature of episcopal conferences (*Apostolos suos*).

See Also: APOSTOLOS SUOS

[SALVADOR MIRANDA]

NEW AGE MOVEMENT

The New Age (NA) Movement is a variegated cultural phenomenon. In its broadest sense, the term refers to a configuration of Eastern and Western esoteric psychologies, philosophies, and religious traditions that have been brought into convergence with new paradigms in science and modern psychology. The New Age Movement has links with the Eastern and Western occult and mystical/metaphysical traditions. In the United States, the movement is the inheritor of the Aquarian "new religious consciousness" of the 1960s and 1970s.

New Age cultural referents include health food stores, parapsychology research organizations, psychic development groups; interest in reincarnation, astrology, witchcraft, tarot cards, the I Ching, out-of-body experience, channeling, and in the "healing powers" of crystals and pyramids; "transformational" techniques ranging from meditation to martial arts; alternative or "holistic" medicine, body therapies, and a melange of other "consciousness raising" techniques.

While there is no hard-line NA gospel *per se*, nor unanimity of NA beliefs, the conviction that humanity is on the threshold of a radical spiritual transformation is a central motif. New Age thinking also embraces eclectic and syncretistic healing strategies and spiritual disciplines, reasserts various forms of supernaturalism and sacramentalism, and promotes the full realization of human potential. Themes of "transformation," "consciousness raising," "self-realization," "higher self," the "god within," and "global unity" are standard NA parlance. New Age thinking also animates elements of the contemporary environmental movement, notably in relation to eco-feminism and creation theology.

Growth of the Movement. The spread of NA thinking in modern society has been propagated through movement literature and through a multitude of seminars and training programs focused on human potential and self improvement. Various teachers, empowerment practitioners, and assorted shamans have facilitated such programs. These include cultural celebrities as diverse as Baba Ram Dass (Richard Alpert), a former professor of psychology at Harvard; the actress Shirley MacLaine; and David Spangler, formerly a co-director of a Scottish community at Findhorn and author of *Revelation, The Birth of a New Age* (1976). New Age perspectives have also been popularized by Marilyn Ferguson's book, *The Aquarian Conspiracy: Personal and Social Transformation in the 1980s,* an impassioned discussion of the need to create a new society based on a "turnabout in consciousness" and a vastly enlarged concept of human potential.

Cultural historians have emphasized the continuity between current NA ideas and earlier American interest

New Age Visionary. (© Catherine Karnow/CORBIS)

in metaphysical, occult, and non-Western spiritual traditions (viz., Transcendentalism, Spiritualism, Theosophy, New Thought). They have also pointed to NA affinities with the long-standing American utopian tradition and the quintessential American dream of transcending one's background by reinventing one's self.

Social and behavioral science perspectives link the appeal of the NA to the cultural crisis of post-1950s America. From this perspective, the NA is a cultural response to the weakening of structures and institutions that integrate society. The contradictions of late capitalism's commodity culture and the spiritual poverty of the technocratic state, characterized by massive bureaucracy, depersonalization, aesthetic sterility, and the dominance of instrumental rationality compounded this crisis. Other factors facilitating the spread of NA thinking include the decline of mainline religions, the expansion of comparative religion courses, the increase in Asian immigration, and mass marketing techniques by NA spiritual entrepreneurs. The high media visibility of Hollywood celebrities promoting NA concepts and theories also contributed to the cultural visibility of the movement.

During the last four decades, a large part of the recruiting ground for religious and spiritual experiment has been among the relatively privileged and social elites. In this context, the spread of the NA Movement is attributable, in part, to structural characteristics of demographic and generational shifts associated with an emerging cohort of ''baby boomers'' whose affluence and greater discretionary time have freed them for diverse spiritual and cultural pursuits.

Criticism of the Movement. Criticism of NA therapies and philosophies comes from two main sources: left-leaning cultural critics and academics and conservative Christians. Cultural critics and academics censure the movement for its assault on the heritage of the Enlightenment and for sowing doubt about the trustworthiness of rational thought. Accordingly, NA devotees promote alchemist-like spirituality, superstition, pseudoscience, incipient totalitarianism, a dangerous ahistoricism, and, in some cases, outright fraud.

Cultural critics also asserted that exotic NA interests such as crystal gazing and ''harmonic convergence'' are contrived, artificial phenomena that actually point to the triviality of spiritual matters in modern society. From a psychological perspective, some NA devotees manifest narcissistic and obsessive self-fixation traits that mirror the powerlessness, alienation, and atomistic individualism endemic in society. New Age ''higher consciousness'' is, therefore, little more than a misguided initiative to rescue the modern American ''minimal self.'' In addition, NA practitioners have been accused of mimicking liberalism's idioms of globalism, cooperation, and tolerance. However, because some currents in the movement reject or minimize reformist political struggle, they implicitly promote apolitical escapism and reinforce the status quo.

The most aggressive assault on NA thinking comes from fundamentalist and conservative Christians who link NA spiritual effervescence with exotic ''cults,'' with secular humanism, and with the emergence of a ''false'' and ''one world'' religion. ''Bible believing'' Christians denounce NA apologists for distorting and/or rejecting the Bible's message of sin and salvation, for promoting the ''occult'' and ''demonic,'' and for contaminating the Christian tradition with false spiritual ideas. The New Age Movement is construed as the shadow of the anti-Christ and another cultural barometer of the apostate age.

More moderate Christian critics point to the latent gnosticism in much NA thought and to the movement's promotion of magic-like ritualization and its cooption of traditional religious symbolism. These critics have also reproached the NA Movement for failing to address the reality of evil (or for viewing social and structural oppression as merely a state of mind), for failing to link ''self-realization'' with moral guidance, and for extolling forms of self-exploration that too readily degenerate into self-

promotion. In addition, both secular and religious critics criticize certain NA currents for amoralism, for the degradation and blatant commercialization of piety, and for the tendency to reduce religion to psychology.

The spread of New Age thinking has also been interpreted in more positive ways. First, the phenomenon shows that people do not respond to new social and cultural problems by abandoning religion as much as by developing new religious innovations and orientations on the ruins of the old. What is ''new'' about much NA thinking is not the content, *per se*, but the unexpected spread of such ideas in the face of assumptions regarding the alleged inexorable triumph of secularization.

Second, the NA Movement points to the continuing problem of the bifurcation of religious and scientific orientations that has long afflicted Western civilization. In response to this situation, people often compartmentalize their meaning systems. The privatization of religion is one aspect of this; the idolatry of technique another. New Age thinking with its call for ''holistic'' and ''integrated'' living is both symptomatic of this cultural problem and a creative and contemporary response to it.

Third, while the spread of NA theories and practices can be seen as an indictment of organized religion's failure to respond in creative and dynamic ways to new cultural trends, the movement has also stimulated a renewed interest in mysticism, meditation, and spiritual renewal within the Christian tradition. New Age ideals have also converged with a new stress on eclectic approaches to spirituality in many mainline churches.

The most positive aspects of NA ideals are those that encourage consensus decision making, integrated living, the emphasis on freedom for positive growth, creative action, and the call for human solidarity. Certain NA motifs are also highly relevant to aspects of the emerging ecological ethos and for the need for a new cosmology relevant to environmental concerns.

In its overall composition and visibility, the NA Movement gives expression to the dynamic and ongoing realignment of religion and culture. In reference to the Christian tradition, the NA Movement provides another opportunity for both spiritual revitalization within the tradition and for a new and creative discernment of the vibrant relationship between the Gospel and culture.

Bibliography: JOHN A. SALIBA, *Christian Responses to the New Age Movement* (London, 1999). F. M. BORDEWICH, ''Colorado's Thriving Cults,'' *The New York Times Magazine* (1 May 1988): 37–44. W. D. DINGES, ''Aquarian Spirituality: The New Age Movement in America,'' *The Catholic World* (May/June 1989): 137–142. M. FERGUSON, *The Aquarian Conspiracy: Personal and Social Transformation in the 1980s* (Los Angeles 1980). C. LASCH, *The Minimal Self; Psychic Survival in Troubled Times* (New York

A Hare Krishna sits on a blanket and chants. The words to the chant are printed on a nearby sign. (© Vince Streano/CORBIS)

1984). J. R. LEWIS and J. G. MELTON, *Perspectives on the New Age* (Albany 1992). T. PETERS, *The Cosmic Self* (San Francisco 1991).

[W. D. DINGES]

NEW RELIGIOUS MOVEMENTS

New Religious Movements is a label covering a broad spectrum of world-wide spiritual ferment that has been especially pronounced since the 1960s. Use of the expression has partially superceded the terms ''sect'' or ''cult'' in reference to non-mainline religious movements—although the latter (more pejorative) terms are still widely used in public discourse.

The discussion of new religious movement (NRMs) in this article is restricted to North America. However, NRMs are a world-wide phenomena by no means confined to the United States. A wide variety of both indigenous and imported NRMs have flourished globally in the

post–World War II era, especially in Latin America, Africa, and Japan. While it is not possible to gage accurately the total number of individuals involved in these movements, the scale on which they have emerged since the 1960s is unique.

NRMs in North America vary considerably in size, in theological and organizational characteristics, and in their spiritual techniques, therapies and rituals. They can be grouped into three broad categories:

1. Movements of a non-Christian, non-Western derivation: Buddhist groups (Zen, Nichiren Shoshu, Tantrism), Hare Krishna (International Society for Krishna Consciousness), Transcendental Meditation (Science of Creative Intelligence), Meher Baba, and other Hindu- derived guru groups.

2. Christian or Neo-Christian groups: Charismatics/ neo-Pentecostals, the Unification Church (Moonies), groups associated with the Jesus Movement (Alamo

Foundation, Children of God), the Way Ministry, the conservative/fundamentalism New Religious Right, televangelist ministries, Roman Catholic Traditionalists.

3. Religio-therapeutic self-help groups derivative of transpersonal psychology and the human potential movement that syncretistically combine traditional and eclectic elements of religious language, symbolism, and discipline (Scientology, est, Arica, Eckankar and various ''New Age'' groups).

Aside from the above categories, NRMs have also been grouped according to leadership style, organizational characteristics, and whether or not their theologies are monistic or dualistic; world rejecting, world affirming, or world accommodating.

Although it has been common practice to refer to the above groups as ''new'' religious movements, many were neither new as religious phenomenon nor new to the American culture. The Hare Krishna movement was brought to the United States in 1965 by A. C. Bhaktivedanta Swami Prabhupada. The beliefs of the movement, however, derive from a *bhakti* tradition founded by Sri Caitanya in Bengal, India, in the sixteenth century. Other Buddhist and Hindu-derived movements popularized in the 1960s had earlier penetrated American culture through the initiatives of individuals such as Swami Vivekananda, Madame Blavatsky, Soyen Shaku, Shigetsu Sasaki, Paranahansa Yogananda, and others. Ethnic-based Eastern religions had also taken root in American society long before popular interest in these traditions surfaced during the 1960s and 1970s. The New Religious Right also had clear historical lineage in early 20th century Protestant fundamentalism.

The ''new'' aspects of NRMs in the 1960s and 1970s applied to their unexpected growth in the face of secularization (especially the assumption that supernaturalism was outmoded and dying); the fact that many such movements—especially the counter-culture and quasi-therapeutic groups—appealed to a youthful constituency, which was predominantly middle-class, affluent, college-educated and which had not been traditionally associated with marginal religious movements; the manner in which NRMs offered religious cosmologies with unique combinations of theological or cultural elements that in themselves were familiar; and where NRMs were based on religious forms of another culture or where they expressed a radical shift in American cultural values.

Two aspects of NRMS have received widespread attention. The first concerns assessment of the social and historical factors that facilitate the rise of such movements. The second concerns explicating the dynamics of recruitment and commitment by which NRMs form and sustain their membership.

The Rise of New Religious Movements. Religious movements seem to arise where dominant religious institutions are internally unstable, where theological innovation is possible, where charismatic leadership is present, where the socio- political climate fosters religious liberty and expressiveness, and where the normative meaning and plausibility structures of a society have been weakened.

Historians generally interpreted the proliferation of NRMs in the 1960s and 1970s as a manifestation of the religious enthusiasm that periodically alters the American religious landscape. These outbreaks of religious effervescence (''Great Awakenings'') give expression to the realignment of religion and culture brought about by revitalization tendencies within religious traditions themselves, and by socio-cultural adjustments attending modernization.

The rise of NRMs has also been linked to the dynamics of secularization. According to this view, religious history is dominated by cycles rather than by a linear trend toward increasing secularity. The staying power of religion lies in the fact that individuals continue to need supernaturally based ''compensators'' for rewards that are scarce, inequitably distributed, or materially unattainable. Thus, most individuals do not respond to new social and cultural problems by abandoning religion, but by developing religious innovations or new religions on the ruins of the old, especially where mainline religions have moved in the direction of secularization and cultural accommodation. Viewed from this perspective, secularization is a self-limiting process that actually stimulates the rise of NRMs.

A different interpretation, more in keeping with the traditional assessment that secularization has a corrosive effect on religion, holds that NRMs are a manifestation of, rather than a response to, secularization. Counter culture and religio-therapeutic groups in particular are derided as contrived, artificial, and bizarre phenomena that point to the triviality of religion in modern society. These movements give expression to the structural differentiation of religion and to its reduction to the status of a packaged and marketed consumer item in contemporary culture. Such groups are said to manifest ritualized traits of narcissistic and obsessive self-fixation. In so doing, they mirror the powerlessness and alienation endemic in modern society. They have no formative influence on the larger culture, either because their sources of inspiration are esoteric and highly subjective, or because participants see themselves in exclusive terms and withdraw from ''worldly pursuits'' in an individualized quest for salvation—thus reinforcing the status quo and testifying to the waning social significance of religion in modern society.

This interpretation of the rise of NRMs vis-à-vis secularization theory is not applicable, however, to movements that stress moral constraints, self-discipline, and social altruism.

Cultural Crisis. A widely accepted perspective on the rise of NRMs is the cultural crisis hypothesis. This interpretive framework focuses on the socio-cultural conditions conducive to religious change. It does not explain the appeal of particular NRMs nor differential growth rates among them.

The culture crisis hypothesis holds that NRMs flourish in response to fundamental alterations in the social and meaning structures that integrate a society. Because religious values and forms are enmeshed with the historical, cultural, and social structures through which religious self-understanding is expressed, strains and alterations in these dimensions of social reality necessarily produce strains and alterations in the religious sphere. According to this hypothesis, the rise of NRMs in the United States was functionally related to a broad value crisis and mass disaffection from the common understanding of American culture that occurred between the election of President John F. Kennedy and the collapse of the American regime in Vietnam in 1975. The trauma of the Civil Rights Movement, the atrocities in Vietnam, assassinations, and the spread of post-Watergate political cynicism, eroded core American cultural values and the structures by which they were upheld, including institutions responsible for conveying moral and spiritual values. These cultural shocks polarized Americans, delegitimized institutional authority, eroded the politico-moral ideology of American civil religion, and brought about a decisive break with the meaning of the past, especially among many idealist youth.

NRMs grew fruitfully in this cultural vacuum. In one manner or another, most NRMs emphasized the primacy of experience over creed and dogma, access to spiritual and personal empowerment, unifying values in the form of a pragmatic, success-oriented, or a syncretistic theology proposed as a new revelation, and more meaningful expressions of social solidarity and community-oriented life styles.

Movements such as the Unification Church and the New Religious Right responded to the culture crisis with a revitalized synthesis of political and religious themes. The "Moral Majority" and kindred groups, such as Christian Voice, Religious Roundtable, and National Christian Action Coalition, called for a restoration of moral traditionalism, a renewed sense of national order and purpose, and a reassertion of values and myths associated with the gospel of wealth, patriotic idealism, and the messianic understanding of American life and national identity.

The rapid proliferation of NRMs during the 1960s has also been interpreted as a consequence of social experimentation (not directly related to a cultural crisis) stemming from demographic and generational shifts and the new life styles and social arrangement flamboyantly popularized by the "hippie" counter-culture. By the 1960s, the "baby boom" and the post–World War II transformation of the American class structure had produced a burgeoning youth population whose affluence, social posture, and greater discretionary time facilitated experimentation with a wide variety of living arrangements and life styles. Widespread psychedelic drug experimentation provided an important link between the youth-oriented counter-culture and the rise of NRMs. In some instances, drug experimentation altered spiritual frames of reference and/or broke down normative perceptions of everyday reality, thereby facilitating movement into NRMs that emphasized meditative or "mystical" religious experience. In other instances (especially the Jesus Movement of the late 1960s), NRMs provided participants with a therapeutic means of kicking a drug habit.

While the precise relationship between the presence of cultural fragmentation and crisis and the rise of NRMs remains subject to debate, it is clear that the proliferation of NRMs is both stimulated and facilitated by strain in value, meaning, and plausibility structures that undergird a social order. The presence of outmoded or discredited myths, ideologies, and institutional arrangements, and the absence of meaningful community experience are key factors conducive to religious ferment.

Conversion Recruitment. Prior to the 1960s, social and behavioral science theories about participation in "sects" and "cults" focused almost exclusively on the lower-class origins of such movements and on the psycho-economic relationship between their ideology and alleged deprivations of neophytes. Sociological and anthropological studies consistently linked the rise of "sects," "revitalization movements," "cargo," and "crisis" cults to severe social and cultural dislocation. Participation in such movements was viewed as compensatory behavior that arose in response to unrest, privation, and maladjustment. Although the concept of deprivation was broadened to include social, organismic, ethical, and psychical tensions, the operating assumption continued to hold that converts to "sects" and "cults" were individuals who experienced some form of personal or cultural trauma. This assumption animates the culture crisis hypothesis discussed earlier.

Although deprivation/motivation theory remains an important insight into religious affiliation, the understanding of conversion/recruitment on the basis of the analysis of NRMs is now more nuanced, interactive, and process oriented. Deprivation/motivation has come under serious criticism because of its conceptual vagueness, reductionism, and failure to give adequate attention to the active role played by religious groups and organizations in the conversion/recruitment process. While it is true that some people will find a particular world- view more appealing than another because of their psychological or emotional state, closer attention has been drawn to issues of structural availability, to how conversion/recruitment works as a funneling process, to the role of social interaction and interpersonal bonds, to the role of participants as active seekers, and to the specific strategies by which groups mobilize resources and seek participants to achieve their objectives.

Conversion/recruitment dynamics vary across groups and among individuals. However, most studies of conversion/recruitment vis-à-vis NRMs have focused on two levels of analysis: predispositional and situational factors.

Predispositional factors are internal variables related to a convert's motivational state and prior socialization. They include the presence of ''felt needs'' and/or tensions in the individual, the holding of a religious problem-solving perspective, and religious-seeking incentives.

Many participants in NRMs were geographically unsettled, subjectively dissatisfied with their lives, alienated from dominant institutions, and lacking strong communal ties. Many had participated in or experimented with several NRMs before actually joining a specific one. Participants also tended to be drawn from the ranks of young adults previously socialized in mainline (and more liberal) religious traditions, but who were unchurched at the time of their NRM affiliation.

Situational factors are external variables related to the individual's interaction with the proselytizing organization. They include encountering the NRM at a ''turning point'' in one's life, the development (or pre-existence) of affective bonds, intensive encapsulation, and the weakening or neutralization of affective ties outside the movement.

Studies have consistently shown that NRMs that employed the establishment of affective bonds in the service of proselytizing grew more rapidly than those that did not. Movements that recruited individuals who were social isolates before joining had slower growth rates because their members failed to provide a new network for movement growth. NRMs that isolated their participants from society, or that required the severance of non-movement interpersonal ties, also grew less rapidly than those that were more fluid and open.

Studies of conversion/recruitment dynamics in NRMs also suggest that some individuals assume move-ment roles and participate in group activities prior to actual commitment to or knowledgeable understanding of the specific belief system. Social pressures and group encapsulation then work to intensify commitment. Conversion/recruitment under these circumstances is a socially structured event arising out of role relationships and the necessity of legitimating behavior at variance with the individual's normal social intercourse. The fact that some individuals joined NRMs quickly and with only sketchy knowledge about the group gave rise to questions about group manipulation and deception.

Other theories explain conversion to NRMs as rational choice process in which individuals assess their needs at the time and determine the balance of rewards and costs associated with a particular movement. Ambiguities over gender role identity and relationships have also been linked with NRMs involvement.

Deprogramming Controversy. Not unlike controversies surrounding new religions in earlier eras, contemporary NRMs have met with varying degrees of public hostility and opposition. Conflicts over groups such as the Children of God (The Family), the Unification Church, and the Hare Krishna movement have generally focused on allegations of financial exploitation, misrepresentation, political intrigue, authoritarian leadership, sexual impropriety, and charges that such groups utilize ''brainwashing'' and ''mind-control'' techniques both as strategies for recruitment and as a means of retaining individuals against their will. The tragic mass murder/suicide of over 900 followers of the Rev. Jim Jones in Guyana in 1978—along with other well-publicized controversies surrounding NRM leaders—stimulated anti-cult initiatives at the time.

In response to the above factors, and to youth behavior that violated parental perceptions and expectations and the cultural values of materialism, occupation competition, and achievement, anti-cult groups, such as the American Freedom Foundation, the Citizens Freedom Foundation, and the Spiritual Counterfeit Program, began forming in the early 1970s. These organizations consisted primarily of parents, NRM apostates, and professional ''deprogrammers'' who viewed many NRMs as dangerous expressions of intense religious commitment, zealotry, or dogmatic sectarianism.

To secure the goal of freeing individuals from ''destructive cults,'' anti-cult organizations established informational networks, monitored NRMs, sought to educate the public through published and media material, and lobbied to gain support for their activities and legislation to curb NRM activity.

Coercive action against NRM participants was initiated under the aegis of seeking temporary guardianships and conservatorships through the legal system. More controversial extra-legal initiatives included forcible abductions and intense "deprogramming" sessions. Courts have generally been reluctant to prosecute coercive deprogramming on the grounds that such episodes involve family or parental matters.

Although anti-cult groups have had only limited success in mobilizing other institutions against new religions, they have been more successful at achieving symbolic degradation of NRMs. However, there has been little empirical evidence to show that the vast majority of NRM participants are recruited through "brainwashing" or coercive tactics, or that they were kept in movements by Orwellian-like mind-control techniques. The perception that NRMs engage in "brainwashing" has repeatedly been called in question by scholarly research and by many religious leaders. The small number of actual recruits relative to contacts and the extremely high dropout rates among groups against which such charges have been directed belie such allegations.

Religious Response to NRMs. The attitude of mainline religious bodies toward NRMs varied from active opposition, to indifference, to qualified endorsement.

Protestant conservative/fundamentalist groups took the most active role in developing a coherent and largely negative response. Literature published by these organizations assert Christian claims of exclusivism and alert individuals to the "dangers" of cults as the work of the anti-Christ.

A second approach is a more benign rejection of NRMs as a resurgence of gnosticism—especially those groups that emphasize "knowledge," mystical experiences, and freeing the divine within. These NRMs are held to be incompatible with Christianity and, in the case of those Eastern derived religions, unlikely to become socially significant outside their own cultural milieu.

A third approach looks positively on NRMs as legitimate religious phenomena, as presenting new opportunities for inter-religious dialogue, as a challenge for self-evaluation, and as a stimulus for spiritual and ecclesial renewal within mainline religions.

On 4 May 4 1986, the Vatican released a report on "Sects or New Religious Movements: Pastoral Challenge" in response to mounting episcopal concern over the dramatic growth of NRMs among Catholic populations. According to the document, the spread of NRMs is not to be viewed as a threat but as a stimulus for spiritual and ecclesial renewal. Such movements are to be approached with an attitude of openness and understanding reflecting the principles of respect for the person and religious liberty laid down by Vatican II. At the same time,

Catholics are cautioned against being "naively irenical." The Church's response to NRMs is acknowledged to extend beyond the "spiritual" to the social, cultural, political, and economic conditions from which NRMs draw their constituents. Community and parish patterns that are more caring and relevant are encouraged. Special attention is to be paid to the role of Holy Scripture, catechesis and evangelization. Forms of worship and ministry are to be relevant to cultural environments and life situations. Creativity in the liturgy, diversified ministries, and lay leadership are also called for in response to NRMs.

See Also: NEW AGE MOVEMENT

Bibliography: S. E. AHLSTROM, "National Trauma and Changing Religious Values," *Daedalus* (Winter 1978): 13–29. E. BAKER, ed., *Of God and Men: New Religious Movements in the West* (Macon, Ga. 1983). D. G. BROMLEY and P. E. HAMMOND, *The Future of New Religious Movements* (Macon, Ga. 1987). J. A. BECKFORD, *Cult Controversies: The Societal Response to New Religious Movements* (New York 1985). D. BROMLEY and J. T. RICHARDSON, eds., *The Brainwashing/Deprogramming Controversy* (Toronto 1983). R. S. ELLWOOD, *Religious and Spiritual Groups in Modern America* (Englewood Cliffs, N.J. 1973). L. P. GERLACH and V. HINE, "Five Factors Crucial to the Growth and Spread of a Modern Religious Movement," *Journal for The Scientific Study of Religion* 7 (1966) 23–40. B. WILSON, ed., *The Social Impact of the New Religions* (New York 1981). C. GLOCK and R. BELLAH, eds., *The New Religious Consciousness* (Berkeley 1976). J. NEEDLEMAN and G. BARKER, eds., *Understanding the New Religions* (New York 1978). J. T. RICHARDSON, *Conversion Careers: In and Out of the New Religions* (Beverly Hills, Calif. 1978). T. ROBBINS and D. ANTHONY, eds., *In Gods We Trust: New Patterns of Religious Pluralism in America* (New Brunswick 1981). A. D SHUPE and D. G. BROMLEY, *The New Vigilantes: De Programmers, Anti-Cultists and the New Religions* (Beverly Hills, Calif. 1980). R. STARK and W. S. BAINBRIDGE, *The Future of Religion: Secularization and Cult Formation* (Berkeley 1985). R. WUTHNOW, *The Consciousness Reformation* (Berkeley 1976). MICHAEL FUSS, et al., *Rethinking New Religious Movements* (Rome: Pontifical Gregorian University, 1998). MARC GALANTER, *Cults: Faith, Healing, and Coercion*, 2d. ed. (New York: Oxford University Press, 1999). LORNE L. DAWSON, *Comprehending Cults: The Sociology of New Religious Movements*. (Toronto: Oxford University Press, 1998).

[W. D. DINGES]

NOUWEN, HENRI JOZEF MACHIEL

Spiritual writer, priest, pastoral theologian, clinical psychologist; b. 24 January 1932, Nijkerk, Holland; d. 21 September 1996, Hilversum, Holland. Nouwen was the eldest of the four children of Laurent Jean Marie Nouwen and Maria Huberta Helena Ramselaar; his uncle, Msgr. A. C. Ramselaar, was a Vatican adviser on Jewish-Christian relations. After ordination to the priesthood in Utrecht, 21 July 1957, he studied psychology at the Catholic University of Nijmegen, Holland, graduating in 1964. He spent the next four years in the United States, with two years as a fellow in the program for religion and psychiatry at the Menninger Foundation in Topeka, Kansas, and two years teaching psychology at the University of Notre Dame. Upon returning to the Netherlands he continued his studies in theology, receiving an M.A. from the University of Nijmegen in 1971. From 1971 to 1981 he taught pastoral theology at Yale Divinity School. A growing concern with the plight of the poor in Central and South America led him to leave Yale for Bolivia and Peru, where he lived and worked for two years. He returned to the United States in 1983 as a part-time lecturer at Harvard Divinity School and became a well-known speaker on the conditions in South America. After a chance meeting with Jean Vanier, the founder of L'Arche, Nouwen resigned from Harvard and spent a year-long sabbatical with the original L'Arche community in Trosly-Breuil, France. The following year he became the pastor of the L'Arche community of Daybreak at Richmond Hill in Ontario, Canada, a position he held until his death in 1996. Nouwen is buried in King City, close to Daybreak. The Henri Nouwen Literary Centre, housed in Nouwen's former office at L'Arche Daybreak, has collected his letters, papers, and manuscripts.

The author of more than forty books and the originator of numerous articles on subjects as varied as disability, monasticism, peacemaking, and AIDS, Nouwen was an internationally renowned speaker and preacher whose charismatic style of witness won him a large following. Weaving his clinical psychological insights and theological knowledge, he articulated a spirituality of the heart for a generation disillusioned with traditional religion. For Nouwen, the heart was "that intimate core of our experience," the center of all relational life. His skill lay in reinterpreting theology for a contemporary audience within a modern Catholic framework. Much of his thinking developed from one of his earliest and most important texts, *The Wounded Healer*, written for people in ministry. Wounds, he wrote, were a source of healing for others and should be shared, though not self-indulgently. Nouwen wrote extensively about loneliness, alienation, intimacy and love, connecting ministry with spirituality, social compassion with contemplation. His universal approach to spirituality and sense of personal engagement with readers enabled him to cross denominational and religious divides as few Catholic writers had done before.

Bibliography: HENRI J. M. NOUWEN, *Intimacy* (Notre Dame, Ind. 1969); *Creative Ministry* (Garden City, N.Y., 1971); *The Wounded Healer* (Garden City, N.Y. 1972); *Reaching Out* (Garden City, N.Y. 1975); *The Genesee Diary* (Garden City, N.Y. 1976); *The Living Reminder* (New York 1977); *Clowning in Rome* (Garden City, N.Y. 1979); *The Way of the Heart* (New York 1981); *Compassion* (Garden City, N.Y. 1982); *¡Gracias!* (San Francisco 1983); *Lifesigns* (Garden City, N.Y. 1986); *The Road to Daybreak* (New York 1988); *In the Name of Jesus* (New York 1989); *The Return of the Prodigal Son* (New York, 1994); *Life of the Beloved* (New York, 1992); *Our Greatest Gift* (San Francisco 1994); *With Burning Hearts* (Maryknoll, N.Y. 1994); *The Inner Voice of Love* (New York 1996); *Adam* (Maryknoll, N.Y. 1997); *Sabbatical Journey* (New York 1998). MICHAEL FORD, *Wounded Prophet: A Portrait of Henri J. M. Nouwen* (New York 1999).

[MICHAEL FORD]

O'CONNOR, JOHN JOSEPH

Cardinal, archbishop of New York; b. 15 January 1920, Philadelphia; d. 3 May 2000, New York. The fourth child of Thomas and Dorothy Gomple O'Connor, he grew up in a working-class neighborhood in southwest Philadelphia, where he attended local public elementary and junior high schools and West Catholic High School for Boys before entering St. Charles Borromeo Seminary in 1936. Ordained a priest of the Archdiocese of Philadelphia on 15 December 1945, he spent the next seven years as a teacher and guidance counselor in archdiocesan high schools while also serving as a parish priest.

O'Connor began a twenty-seven year career as a navy chaplain in 1952. His service with the Marines in the Vietnam War earned him the Legion of Merit. He strongly defended American involvement in the Vietnam War in *A Chaplain Looks at Vietnam* (Cleveland, 1968), but later he expressed regret for having done so. In 1972 O'Connor was appointed the first Catholic senior chaplain at the U.S. Naval Academy, and in 1975 he attained the highest position available to him when he became the U.S. Navy Chief of Chaplains with the rank of Rear Admiral. He retired in 1979. During his military career, he also earned a doctorate in political science from Georgetown University.

In 1979 O'Connor was appointed titular bishop of Curzola and auxiliary to the Military Vicar, Terence Cardinal Cooke. O'Connor first became well-known nationally when he was appointed to the five-member episcopal committee that prepared "The Challenge of Peace," the pastoral letter issued by the U.S. hierarchy in 1983. One week after the publication of the pastoral letter, he was appointed the bishop of Scranton, Pennsylvania. He was installed in June, 1983, but remained in Scranton for only another seven months; on 31 January 1984, he was appointed archbishop of New York in succession to Cardinal Cooke, who had died the previous October. One year later, Pope John Paul II made him cardinal, with the titular church of Ss. Giovanni e Paolo. On the same day as his elevation it was announced that the Military Ordinariate had been reorganized as the Archdiocese for the Military Services, U.S.A., severing the connection between the archbishop of New York and the Military Ordinariate that had existed since its inception in 1917.

Cardinal Cooke, a shy man who disliked confrontation, made no attempt to fill the national role of his predecessor, Francis Cardinal Spellman. By contrast, O'Connor seemed to welcome confrontation and clearly aimed at assuming a prominent role in the U.S. hierarchy. He liked to be compared to the feisty John Hughes, New York's first archbishop, and he favored a style of leadership that seemed to be modeled on that of John Paul II. Although he was sixty-four years old when he became archbishop, O'Connor adopted a grueling schedule with heavy emphasis on preaching and public appearances, the frequent use of both the press and television, and numerous pastoral visits to parishes and institutions. He also enjoyed occupying center stage at large-scale special events such as the annual Mass for the Disabled in St. Patrick's cathedral and a youth rally at Yankee Stadium that drew 40,000 people. In deference to New York's large Hispanic population, he mastered Spanish sufficiently well to celebrate Mass and preach in their language.

As in Scranton, O'Connor gave high priority to right-to-life issues. At a press conference in June 1984, he answered a question about Catholic politicians and abortion legislation with the statement: "I do not see how a Catholic in good conscience can vote for an individual expressing himself or herself as favoring abortion." The comment was widely interpreted as a criticism of Congresswoman Geraldine Ferraro, the Democratic candidate for vice-president, and led to public sparring between O'Connor and Governor Mario Cuomo of New York.

O'Connor's well-attended weekly press conferences after Sunday Mass in St. Patrick's cathedral gave him a forum to comment on public issues. He relished the publicity, but he discontinued the press conferences in 1990, candidly admitting that he had said "some dumb things."

Two groups with whom O'Connor established particularly warm relationships were organized labor and New York's large and influential Jewish community. The Service Employees International Union, grateful for his support of labor unions, publicly hailed him as "the patron saint of working people." Commenting on the award, Msgr. George G. Higgins said, "Few bishops in U.S. history have been as consistently supportive as Cardinal O'Connor of labor's basic rights." Dr. Ronald Sobel, senior rabbi of Temple Emanuel-El, said: "I know of no member of the American Catholic hierarchy who has been more consistently sensitive to the interests of the Jewish people." At the time of the Persian Gulf War in 1991, the former admiral tried to restrain widespread pro-war enthusiasm by declaring: "No war is good. Every war is at best the lesser of evils." Mario Cuomo, with whom he often clashed, paid tribute to O'Connor's com-

John Cardinal O'Connor. (Catholic News Service.)

mitment to social justice by saying, "His work should have earned the cardinal a reputation as one of the Vatican's favorite social progressives as well as one of its premier conservative dogmatists."

O'Connor committed the archdiocese to maintaining its network of parochial schools, especially in poor neighborhoods, despite the sharp decline in the number of teaching sisters and brothers. The Catholic Church also remained a major provider of health care and social services to the poor in New York City. However, the staffing of parishes became increasingly difficult since O'Connor was reluctant to close or consolidate parishes even as the number of active diocesan priests fell from 777 in 1983 to 585 in 1999. The number of diocesan seminarians decreased even more precipitously, from 221 to 84, despite O'Connor's persistent personal efforts to promote vocations.

Cardinal O'Connor offered his resignation to Pope John Paul II on reaching the mandatory retirement age of 75, but the pope allowed him to remain in office. In October of that year O'Connor welcomed the pontiff to New York for a successful papal visit that included a Mass before 125,000 people in Central Park. In late August 1999 O'Connor underwent surgery for a brain tumor from which he never fully recovered, although he continued to

A starving ten-year-old Sudanese girl lies with her mother and brother inside a compound in south Sudan. (AP/Wide World Photos. Photograph by Brennan Linsley.)

make limited public appearances until the following March. On the occasion of his 80th birthday, the U.S. Congress bestowed upon him its highest civilian award, the Congressional Gold Medal. He died on 3 May 2000. He was buried in the crypt of St. Patrick's Cathedral, next to Pierre Toussaint, a Haitian born into slavery who worked as a barber in New York and whom John Paul II had declared "Venerable" in 1996. O'Connor had brought Toussaint's remains to St. Patrick's from an abandoned cemetery for blacks in lower Manhattan, and requested that he be buried next to him.

Bibliography: JOHN O'CONNOR, and EDWARD KOCH, *His Eminence and Hizzoner* (New York 1989). NAT HENTOFF, *John Cardinal O'Connor: At the Storm Center of a Changing Catholic Church* (New York 1988).

[THOMAS J. SHELLEY]

OPTION FOR THE POOR

The meaning and intent of the phrase "option for the poor" is found in *Octogesimo adveniens* (1971), an apostolic letter of Pope Paul VI, which stated, "In teaching us charity, the gospel instructs us in the preferential respect due to the poor and the special situation they have in society: the more fortunate should renounce some of their rights so as to place their goods more generously at the service of others" (n. 23; cf. n. 42). The voluntary commitment to the cause of the socially deprived and solidarity with them in their problems and struggles was first given formal expression by the Latin American bishops at Medellin (1968), and was reaffirmed at their Conference in Puebla (Mexico), attended by Pope John Paul II in 1979.

In the Latin American framework the "preferential option for the poor" is inextricably associated with themes of liberation theology, and the struggle against oppression of every kind. During the period between Medellin and Puebla, considerable controversy surrounded the struggle for social justice that Medellin had affirmed and accelerated. As base communities began to organize and contend for the rights of the poor, individuals and groups with vested interests in the establishment used repressive methods to defend their power bases and privileges. Advocates of a new, more just social order were subjected to torture, imprisonment, murder and exile.

The document published by the Latin American bishops at the close of the Puebla meeting contains a chapter titled, "A Preferential Option for the Poor" (nn. 1134–1165). Although the document does not present a systematic analysis of the phrase, it clearly describes what is involved.

> . . . we are going to take up once again the position of . . . Medellin, which adopted a clear and prophetic option expressing preference for, and solidarity with, the poor.. . . We affirm the need for conversion on the part of the whole Church to a preferential option for the poor, an option aimed at their integral liberation (n. 1134).

> This option, demanded by the scandalous reality of economic imbalances in Latin America, should lead us to establish a dignified, fraternal way of life together as human beings and to construct a just and free society (n. 1154).

> We will make every effort to understand and denounce the mechanisms that generate this poverty (n. 1160).

The Puebla Document (DP) identifies the poor as the indigenous peoples (DP 34), the peasants (DP 35), the workers (DP 29, 36), the marginalized urban dwellers (DP 38), the underemployed and the unemployed (DP 37, 50, 576, 838), children (DP 32) and the elderly (DP 39). It concerned the bishops that the marginalized were looked upon as second-class citizens whose rights could be crushed underfoot with impunity (DP 1291, DP 18). In a "Message to the Peoples of Latin America" the Puebla Conference stated very clearly that to opt for the poor means to take up their cause (n. 3).

Although Pope John Paul II in his address to the bishops at Puebla did not use the phrase "option for the poor," he expressed a similar idea when he stated, the Church "is prompted by an authentically evangelical commitment which, like that of Christ, is primarily (*sobre todo*) a commitment to those most in need." On other occasions during his visit to Mexico he expressed a preferential, though, he took pains to make it clear, not an exclusive love for the poor.

The option for the poor has been adopted as a formal principle by the Canadian and U.S. bishops in recent statements on the economies of their respective nations. This is an important acknowledgment by these hierarchies that the program of social reform that this axiom implies is relevant also in first-world contexts. The Canadian Conference of Catholic Bishops in its statement on the socioeconomic order mentioned ''the preferential option for the poor,'' and then added:

> In a given economic order, the needs of the poor take priority over the wants of the rich. This does not, in turn, simply mean more handouts for the poor. It calls, instead, for an equitable redistribution of wealth and power among peoples and regions.

The U.S. bishops in their pastoral message *Economic Justice for All* (1986) do not speak of a *preferential*, but of a *fundamental* option for the poor.

> This ''option for the poor'' does not mean pitting one group against another, but rather, strengthening the whole community by assisting those who are most vulnerable. As Christians, we are called to respond to the needs of *all* our brothers and sisters, but those with the greatest needs require the greatest response (n. 16).

The American bishops introduce their reflection on the option for the poor with the assertion, ''the justice of a society is tested by the treatment of the poor.''

In his encyclical *Sollicitudo rei socialis* (On Social Concern, 1987) Pope John Paul II spoke of the ''*option or love of preference* for the poor'' and explained, ''This is an option, or *special form* of primacy in the exercise of Christian charity, to which the whole tradition of the Church bears witness'' (SRS 42). The pope goes on to emphasize the global dimensions of the social question and says:

> this love of preference for the poor, and the decisions which it inspires in us, cannot but embrace the immense multitudes of the hungry, the needy, the homeless, those without medical care and, above all, those without hope of a better future. It is impossible not to take account of these realities (SRS 42).

This same terminology, ''a preferential love'' for people oppressed by poverty, appears in the Catechism of the Catholic Church (2448). The CCC also quotes the Vatican II decree *Apostolicam actuositatem,* which makes the point that ''the demands of justice'' requires that we share our goods with the poor, and ''that which is already due in justice is not to be offered as an act of charity'' (2446). The Catechism, like *Sollicitudo rei socialis,* calls for structural reform at all levels to redress the inequitable distribution of the world's goods and the international economic imbalance.

In the years since the axiom was first formulated, the preferential option for the victims of social injustice has come to represent a short-hand description for a new kind of program aiming at integral liberation of all powerless, marginalized, economically deprived, despised and outcast persons. The elimination of starvation, disease, unemployment, unjust wages, homelessness, illiteracy, impoverishment, in brief, all manifestations of institutionalized violence or social sin is seen as a prophetic challenge to all people who yearn for peace founded on justice. And this agenda which uses a variety of descriptions to illustrate a sociology of oppression is seen as an inescapable consequence of fidelity to the gospel message which, according to the pastoral statements of bishops across several continents, itself gives priority to service of the poor and disadvantaged.

Bibliography: R. ANTONCICH, *Christians in the Face of Injustice. A Latin American Reading of Catholic Social Teaching* (Maryknoll, N.Y. 1987). G. BAUM, *The Priority of Labor: A Commentary on Laborem exercens Encyclical Letter of Pope John Paul II* (New York 1982). G. BAUM and D. CAMERON, *Ethics and Economics: Canada's Catholic Bishops on the Economic Crisis* (Toronto 1984). L. BOFF and V. ELIZONDO, eds., *Option for the Poor: Challenge to the Rich Countries* (Edinburgh 1986). L. BOFF,, *Cry of the Earth, Cry of the Poor* (Maryknoll, N.Y. 1997). M. BYERS, ed., *Justice in the Marketplace: Collected Statements of the Vatican the United States Catholic Bishops on Economic Policy, 1891–1984* (Wash., D.C. 1985). D. DORR, *Option for the Poor: A Hundred Years of Vatican Social Teaching,* rev. ed. (Maryknoll, N.Y. 1992). I. ELLACURIA and J. SODRINO, eds. *Mysterium Liberationis. Fundamental Concepts of Liberation Theology* (Maryknoll, N,Y, 1993), J. EAGLESON and P. SCHARPER, eds., *Puebla and Beyond: Documentation and Commentary* (New York 1979). G. GUTIERREZ, *The Power of the Poor in History* (New York 1983) NATIONAL CONFERENCE OF CATHOLIC BISHOPS, *Economic Justice For All: Pastoral Letter on Catholic Social Teaching and the U.S. Economy* (Wash., D.C. 1986).

[P. SURLIS]

OPUS DEI

The Prelature of the Holy Cross and Opus Dei is a personal prelature of the Roman Catholic Church, with its central offices located in Rome. The Second Vatican Council made provisions for the juridical format of personal prelatures to facilitate the carrying out of ''specific apostolic tasks.'' Prelatures form part of the pastoral and hierarchical structure of the Church. They are dependent on the Congregation for Bishops.

The aim of the prelature of Opus Dei is to promote among Christians an awareness that all are called to seek holiness and to contribute to the evangelization of every sphere of society. The prelature provides for the pastoral and spiritual care of its members, extending this help to many other people, in accord with each one's situation and profession (cf. *Statutes of Opus Dei,* 2:1). The faithful of the prelature strive to put into practice the teachings of the Gospel by exercising the Christian virtues and sanctifying their ordinary work (cf. *Statutes of Opus Dei,* 2).

Msgr. Josemaría Escrivá founded Opus Dei on 2 October 1928. On 14 February 1930, Blessed Josemaría understood by God's grace that Opus Dei was meant to develop its apostolate among women as well. From 1946 on, he resided in Rome. He died on 26 June1975 and was beatified on 26 June 1992. From Rome he oversaw Opus Dei's apostolic expansion throughout the world, beginning with Portugal, England, Italy, France, Ireland, the United States, and Mexico. From the outset, he relied on the encouragement and stimulus of the episcopal hierarchy. From 1943, Opus Dei received all of the necessary approvals from the Holy See, culminating in its establishment as a personal prelature by Pope John Paul II on 28 November 1982.

The prelature of Opus Dei spread throughout every continent, comprises the prelate, currently Bishop Javier Echevarría, 1,700 priests, and 90,000 laity who, with a divine vocation, are freely incorporated into the prelature. The clergy incardinated in the prelature come from among the laymen. "The laity incorporated in the Prelature do not alter their personal situation, either canonically or theologically. They continue to be ordinary lay faithful, and act accordingly in everything they do, specifically in their apostolate (Congregation for Bishops, Declaration concerning Opus Dei, 23 August 1982, 2b).

The lay faithful of the prelature enjoy the same freedom as other Catholic citizens, their equals, in all professional, family, social, political, and financial activities. These activities do not fall under the prelature's jurisdiction, which extends only to the ascetical and apostolic commitments that each one freely assumes by means of a contractual bond. The prelature's lay faithful remain under the diocesan bishop's jurisdiction in everything established by common Church law for the Catholic faithful.

The Priestly Society of the Holy Cross, inseparably united to the Prelature of Opus Dei is governed by the prelate of Opus Dei as its president general. The prelature's priests belong to the Priestly Society of the Holy Cross. In addition, diocesan priests who wish to seek holiness in the exercise of their ministry may be associated as well. Their tie to the priestly society in no way compromises their loyalty to their own bishop, who continues to be their only superior. The prelature of Opus Dei also relies on cooperators, some of whom are non-Catholics or even non-Christians. Although not incorporated into the prelature, cooperators collaborate in its apostolate by their prayer, work, and alms.

The prelature of Opus Dei directs the Pontifical University of the Holy Cross in Rome, as well as the University of Navarre in Spain. Other apostolic undertakings, including universities in Latin America, Italy, and the Philippines, student residences, cultural centers, technical and agricultural institutes, medical clinics, and a variety of centers for the development of disadvantaged areas, have the pastoral assistance of the prelature which takes on responsibility for their Christian orientation.

Opus Dei's most important contribution to the Church's mission, however, is not its corporate apostolates but rather the effort of each member to sanctify his or her ordinary, daily work and to bring those around them closer to God. The process for beatification is underway for several members of Opus Dei, among them the Argentine engineer Isidoro Zorzano (1902–1943) and the young Spanish woman Montserrat Grases (1941–1959).

Bibliography: P. BERGLAR, *Opus Dei. Life and Work of its Founder Josemaría Escrivá* (Princeton: Scepter Publishers, 1993). A. FUENMAYOR, F. OCARIZ, and J. L. ILLANES, *The Canonical Path of Opus Dei* (Princeton and Chicago: Scepter Publishers and Midwest Theological Forum, 1994). J. L. ILLANES, *On the Theology of Work* (Dublin: Four Courts Press, 1982). A. DEL PORTILLO, *Immersed in God: Blessed Josemaría Escrivá, Founder of Opus Dei* (Princeton: Scepter Publishers, 1996). P. RODRIGUEZ, *Particular Churches and Personal Prelatures* (Dublin: Four Courts, 1986). P. RODRIGUEZ, F. OCARIZ, and J. L. ILLANES, *Opus Dei in the Church: An Ecclesiological Study of the Life and Apostolate of Opus Dei* (Dublin and Princeton: Four Courts Press and Scepter Publishers, 1994).

[R. PELLITERO]

PIUS IX, POPE

Pontificate, 16 June 1846 to 7 February 1878; b. Giovanni Maria Mastai Ferretti, 13 May 1792, Senigallia (Ancona), Italy; d. 7 February 1878, Rome.

Pius IX's family was of the lower nobility, known for moderate reform tendencies. The future pope studied (1802–09) in Volterra at the college run by the Piarists until he suffered an epileptic attack. His health restored, he studied theology at the Roman College and was ordained 10 April 1819. He was initiated into Ignatian spirituality by the saintly Cardinal Carlo Odescalchi, and for a short time thought of joining the Jesuits. He spent his first priestly years at the Roman orphanage of Tata Giovanni. He accompanied (1823–25) Msgr. Giovanni Muzi, apostolic delegate to Chile and Peru, where his interest in the missions was roused. After returning to Italy, he declined a diplomatic career and took charge of the Roman hospice of San Michele. As archbishop of Spoleto (1827–32) he confronted the revolutionary troubles of

1831 mildly yet firmly. He was transferred to Imola in 1832 and made cardinal in 1840. After the death of Gregory XVI, he was elected pope 16 June 1846. He took the name Pius IX in remembrance of Pius VII, who had aided him in his youth.

Politically, the most significant events of his thirty-two-year pontificate were the unification of Italy and the consequent loss of the States of the Church. Although Pius was merciless in his judgment of the manner in which Italy realized its unification under the lead of anti-clerical Piedmont, he was never disinterested in the national cause; and to the astonishment of many of his counselors, he had to be restrained from publicly manifesting sympathy with certain aspirations of the heroes of the *Risorgimento*. Yet early in his pontificate he also made it clear that he would never agree to participate actively in a war for Italian independence against Austria, because this would be incompatible with his role as common father of all the faithful. After the assassination of the papal prime minister in 1848, the pope fled the uprising and took refuge in Gaëta in the kingdom of Naples. He returned to Rome in 1850, but in 1859 the papal states began to fall to Piedmont, culminating in the occupation of Rome itself in 1870. Pius IX, who regarded himself less as a dethroned sovereign than as the custodian of a property for which he was responsible to all Catholics, refused to bow to the fait accompli. After refusing to accept the Law of Guarantees, proposed by Italy, he made himself a prisoner in the Vatican.

The Roman Question and the bitter politicoreligious conflicts with Italy that resulted from the official world's incomprehension of the Holy See's preoccupations by no means absorbed all Pius IX's energies. The essential part of his pontificate was on another plane, i.e., the internal guidance of the Church. He concluded concordats with Russia (1847), Spain (1851), Austria (1855), and several Latin American states. Further, he promoted Catholic reinvigoration in Germany, where the *Kulturkampf* highlighted the new vitality of this Church, so weak only a half-century previously. He reestablished the hierarchy in England (1850) and in the Netherlands (1853), and erected 206 new dioceses and vicariates apostolic, notably in the U.S. and in British colonies. With his urging missionary work expanded vigorously throughout the world.

Pius IX's teaching had great doctrinal significance. He published numerous encyclicals and allocutions, playing an important role in the revival of neoscholasticism. He also took frequent occasion to recall the principles that should guide the restoration of society, particularly in the encyclical *Quanta cura* and the accompanying Syllabus of Errors, both of which were the objects of passionate discussions. In 1849 he began to canvass the bishops on the subject of the Immaculate Conception, and in 1854 solemnly defined it as a dogma of the Church, promoting a flowering of Marian devotion. He consecrated the whole Catholic world to the Sacred Heart in 1875, and he issued more beatifications and canonizations than any previous pope. Above all he convoked Vatican Council I (1869–70), important for its definition of papal primacy and infallibility, on which most contemporary attention concentrated, and also for its constitution *De fide catholica,* which was characteristic of Pius IX's positive contribution and marked a strong effort to eliminate the last traces of the naturalistic Deism of the Enlightenment and to refocus Catholic thought on the fundamental data of revelation.

This vast doctrinal effort had its counterpart in Pius IX's parallel effort to deepen the clergy's spiritual life and to stimulate the devotion of the faithful. The greatest of the many changes in the Church during his pontificate was the deepening spiritual quality of average Catholic life. Among the many factors contributing to this development, the pope's personal role was important, because he appeared to all as an exemplar of piety, and still more because he consecrated a good part of his efforts to activate and sometimes to hasten the evolution that followed the great revolutionary crisis.

Notable among his many good qualities and merits were his touching simplicity, his great goodness, his serene courage in adversity, his lively practical intelligence, and his fervor that aroused the admiration of all who saw him at prayer and corresponded with his intimate sentiments. Still more remarkable were his pastoral virtues, his care to act always as a priest, and even under the torment of the Roman question to comport himself not as a sovereign defending his throne, but as a man of the Church cognizant of his responsibility before God for the defense of Christian values menaced by the rise of laicism, rationalism, and impiety. His admirers soon after his death introduced his cause for beatification. He was declared venerable in 1985. As part of the Jubilee Year 2000 events, his beatification by Pope John Paul II was scheduled for 3 September together with Pope John XXIII.

Bibliography: G. MARTINA, *Pio IX (1851–1866).*(Rome 1986). L. BOGLIOLO, *Pio IX : profilo spirituale* (Vatican City 1989). A. SERAFINI, *Pio Nono: Giovanni Maria Mastai Ferretti, dalla giovinezza alla morte nei suoi scritti e discorsi editi e inediti* (Vatican City 1958–). A. POLVERARI, *Vita di Pio IX* (Vatican City 1986–1988).

[R. AUBERT]

POLAND

Poland, the largest of the West Slavic States, has exercised a marked influence on the history of Eastern Europe. Under the Piast dynasty (960–1386), it was comprised of Great Poland (with its chief centers at Gniezno, Poznań, and Kruszwica), Little Poland (Cracovia), Mazovia, and Silesia. Under the Jagiellonian dynasty (1386–1572) Poland spread far to the east and became a great power. In the period of the Elective Monarchy (1572–1795) and of foreign rule (1795–1916) the Poles had a checkered history. Then, following the restoration of an independent Polish State (1919–39), came a new division of Polish territory in the wake of World War II and ultimately the formation of the Polish People's Republic (Polska Rzeczpospolita Ludowa), a Communist regime. Although Poland once had a mixed population of Poles, Germans, Lithuanians, Ukrainians, Russians, and White Russians, after World War II its inhabitants were overwhelmingly of Polish origin. The ecclesiastical history of Poland, which is the main concern of this section of the article, may be divided conveniently into five major periods. The main features in the history of the Church are presented systematically under each period.

Middle Ages

The first traces of Christianity are found in the area of Cracovia during the second half of the ninth century and are connected with the missionary activity of Methodius, the Apostle of the Slavs, in Moravia. The spread of Christianity in Poland, however, really began under the Piast Prince Mieszko I (ca. 960–992). In 965 he married the Czech princess Dobrava (Dabrówka) and was baptized the following year. In 968 a missionary bishopric was established for Poland, and Jordan, the first bishop, carried on his work from Poznań. To counteract the efforts of the German Church and of the first two Ottonian emperors to put the Polish bishopric under the jurisdiction of the archbishopric of Magdeburg, Mieszko placed his land in a kind of vassal status under the protection of the pope (990).

Establishment of the Polish Hierarchy. In the year 1000, the archbishopric of Gniezno was erected with Kolobrzeg, Wrocław, and Cracow as its suffragans. Pope Sylvester II, Emperor Otto III, and Bolesław Chrobry, the son and successor of Mieszko (992–1025), all had an active part in this foundation. Chrobry continued his father's policy as a vigorous and successful promoter of Christianity in Poland, and a year before his death he received the royal crown from Rome. The boundaries of the archdiocese of Gniezno at first corresponded to those of the Piast realm. The archbishop was responsible for the care of souls in Great Poland. His suffragan bishops had the task of spreading and solidifying the Christian faith in the border areas: the bishop of Kolobrzeg, in Pomerania; the bishop of Cracow, in Little Poland and the adjacent territories acquired in the North and East; and the

bishop of Wrocław, in Silesia. The establishment of the Polish hierarchy in the year 1000 was decisive for the incorporation of Poland into Western Christendom.

Growth in the 11th, 12th, and 13th Centuries. Among the missionaries at the end of tenth century and the beginning of the eleventh were the martyrs St. Adalbert of Prague (d. 997), St. Benedict of Benevento, John and companions (d. 1003), and Bruno of Querfurt (d. 1009). The spread of the Church was threatened temporarily by a pagan reaction in 1046–47. In the eleventh and twelfth centuries Gniezno acquired new suffragans: Poznań, Włocławek, which replaced the shortlived bishopric of Kruschwitz, in Kujavia, Płock in Mazovia, Lebus on the Middle Oder, and later Wilna (Vilna), Lutsk, and Chełmno. Bishops, such as St. Stanislaus of Cracow (d. 1079), defended the rights of the Church against the encroachments of the state, and in the period of the division of inheritances among the Piasts, they maintained the consciousness of Polish unity. The metropolitans of Gniezno and other ecclesiastical princes emphasized the importance of the Polish language in the light of the threat of the German colonists whose immigration resulted in Polish decline in the western lands of the Piasts, especially in Silesia. The idea of Polish unity was kept alive also in the Polish kingship, and enjoyed the full support of the Church.

The monastic and cathedral schools, which were the vehicles for all education and culture, the cathedral chapters, the development of parish organizations, and the spread of the religious orders (Benedictines, Cistercians, Premonstratensians, Franciscans, Dominicans, Carmelites, Augustinians, Hospitallers, and Templars) all contributed to the solid establishment and growth of Christianity. The Order of Knights, the Fratres Militiae Christi, or Knights of the Sword, founded by Duke Conrad of Mazovia in 1228, which because of its location was also called the Knights of Dobrin, passed in 1237 into the Order of the Teutonic Knights, which established a state of its own in Prussia. The interior growth of the Church in the age of the Piasts is evidenced by the number of saints and blesseds. Among them are: Bp. Wincenty Kadłubek of Cracow (d. 1223), author of the *Chronica de gestis (illustrium) principum ac regum Poloniae;* Bp. Jan Prandota of Cracow (1242–66), who represented in his person the ideal bishop of his time; the Dominicans, Czesław (d. 1222), who defended Wrocław during the great attack of the Mongols, and Hyacinth (Jaczko Odrowąż, d. 1257), who was active as a missionlary in Prussia and South Russia; duchess Hedwig (Jadwiga, d. 1243), mother of duke Henry II of Silesia who fell in battle against the Mongols at Liegnitz; in 1241, a woman equally honored by Germans and Poles as a patroness of Christian charity; the Premonstratensian nun Bronisława

(d. 1259); and the Poor Clares, Salomea (d. 1268), Kinga (d. 1292), and Jolanta (d. 1298).

Under the First Kings of the Jagiellonian Dynasty. In the middle of the fourteenth century Poland had again become a closely knit state. King Casimir III the Great (1333–70), the last famous Piast, extended its territory by the incorporation of the principalities of Halicz (Galicia) and Volhynia. To serve the spiritual needs of his Orthodox subjects, he brought about the restoration of the Galician metropolitanate, with Przemyśl, Chełmno, and Vladimir as its eparchies. Roman Catholic bishoptics arose also in these places. In 1367 he recognized the Armenian bishop of Lvov, so that three Christian confessions existed side by side in his realm. Shortly before 1364 he founded the *Studium generale* or University of Cracow. The marriage in 1386 of Casimir's granddaughter Hedwig (Jadwiga), the youngest daughter of King Louis of Hungary (1342–82) and Poland (1370–82) with the grandduke Jagiełło of Lithuania, who became King of Poland as Władysław II (1386–1434), inaugurated the union of Poland and Lithuania under the Jagiellonians. This union was more strongly established in the course of the fifteenth and sixteenth centuries and was sealed by the union of Lublin in 1569.

Władysław II, in 1387, founded the bishopric of Vilna, through which Roman Christianity was spread in Lithuania. This missionary work was aided very much by the establishment of the faculty of theology at the University of Cracow in 1397. Several Polish bishops and professors, among them the rector of the University of Cracow, Paul Vladimiri (Paweł Włodkowicz), were present at the Council of Constance. Paul in his tractate *De potestate papae et imperatoris respectu infidelium* condemned all conversion of pagans by force. Through this work he involved himself in the diplomatic battle between Poland and the Teutonic Order that took place after the military defeat of the German knights at Tannenberg (1410).

Under Casimir IV (1447–92) a thirteen-year war (1454–66) weakened the political independence of the Teutonic Order, and the bishopric of Ermland passed under the protection of the Polish king. The marriage of the king to Elizabeth of Hapsburg made possible the expansion of the power of the Jagiellonian house to Bohemia and Hungary. During Casimir's long reign the Orthodox population in Poland-Lithuania continued to enjoy toleration, but through the development of the Archbishopric of Lvov tensions arose between the Latin hierarchy and the Orthodox eparchs, and between those who went over to Catholicism and the majority of the population who were adherents of Orthodoxy. Bishop Zbigniew Oleśnicki of Cracow (1423–55, cardinal from 1449) exercised, as an adviser for many years, a strong influence on the internal and foreign policies of the three first kings of the Jagiellonian dynasty. He suppressed the Hussite movement, which entered Poland from Bohemia, and his secretary Jan Długosz (1415–80) was the preceptor of the royal princes and the author of several historical works (among them *Historiae Polonicae libri XII*).

Spiritual Life In the Late Middle Ages. Polish bishops and professors who had participated in the reform councils spread Humanism in Poland-Lithuania, and in the second half of the fifteenth century the *Devotio Moderna* also made its influence felt. In the midst of the breakup of the rather circumscribed medieval outlook and of criticism against high ecclesiastics, benefices multiplied and churchmen devoted themselves more to political activities than to the care of souls. Yet, one should not overlook the contributions of outstanding pastors, especially the archbishops of Gniezno, such as Jakób Świnka (1283–1314) and Jarosław Bogorja Skotnicki (1342–74, d. 1376), or the first bishop of Vilna, the Franciscan Andrzej (d. 1398), or the holy and fruitful activity of provincial and diocesan synods. Besides the new monasteries erected by the orders already mentioned, foundations were made by Hieronymites, Bernardines, Minims, Brethren of the Common Life, and others.

Worthy of particular note also are the several distinguished saints and blesseds, among them Abp. Jakob Strepa of Halicz-Lvov (d. 1409); Jan Kanty (d. 1473), who was well known as a professor at the University of Cracow and as a friend and helper of needy students; the Bernardine Simon of Lipnica (d. 1482) a promoter of the veneration of the Holy Name of Jesus; the Jagiellonian prince Casimir (d. 1484), who was distinguished for his veneration of the Blessed Virgin Mary; the Bernardines Bl. Jan of Dukla (d. 1484), who despite his long blindness was famous as a preacher and confessor; and Władysław of Gielniów (d. 1505), who was active as a missionary in Lithuania and who as a writer of religious poems promoted the veneration of the Passion of Christ and devotion to the Mother of God.

The Jagiellonians defended the West against the Turks, who flooded southeastern Europe after their capture of Constantinople (1453), and in 1529 they penetrated as far as Vienna. Against them and the Orthodox Russians, Poland-Lithuania served as a bulwark of Christendom (*antemurale christianitatis, przedmurze chrześciaństwa*).

Reformation to the Final Partitions

Numerous young nobles who had studied at foreign universities, for example, at Wittenberg, Geneva, and Strassburg, and the German burghers, who played a very important role in some cities, were favorably disposed to the ideas of Luther, Calvin, and the other leading personalities of the Reformation. Following the secularization of the State of the Teutonic Order into a duchy (1525) and the conversion to Protestantism of the grandmaster Albrecht of Brandenburg-Ansbach, who became the first duke of Prussia (1525–68), Königsberg developed rapidly as a Protestant center from which the new teaching was channeled into Poland and Lithuania, where it was quickly absorbed.

Spread of the Reformation Into Poland. The rapid spread of the Reformation is to be explained by the shortcomings of the higher clergy, by abuses in the lower clergy and numerous monastic establishments, and by the quarrels between the higher and lower nobility over the extent of ecclesiastical jurisdiction. Royal officials, men of learning, and politicians, such as Andrzej Frycz-Modrzewski (1503–72), and poets, such as Mikołaj Rej (1505–69) prepared the way for Protestantism in Poland. As early as 1520, King Sigismund I (1506–48) issued an edict against Luther's writings, but he did not succeed in halting the spread of Protestantism. After his death the adherents of the Reformation put their hopes in Sigismund II Augustus (1548–72), who was in communication by letter with Melanchthon and Calvin. He did not abandon Catholicism, but the Protestant movement in Poland reached its zenith during his reign. At the imperial diet held at Piotrków in 1565, a constitution was drawn up and put into effect by which ecclesiastical courts were deprived of the jurisdiction they formerly enjoyed. The nobles could then establish Protestantism in their own properties and territories.

The Protestants in Poland at that time fell into three groups: the Lutherans, the Reformed, who were headed by Jan Łaski (1499–1560), and the Bohemian Brethren. From 1555 they carried on negotiations among them with the object of establishing an independent Polish national church. At the convention held at Sandomierz in 1570 they reached agreement on the fundamental elements of belief. This *consensus Sandomirensis* has been called the first attempt at realizing the idea of Protestant universality. At any rate, it made it possible, following the death of Sigismund Augustus, for the dissenters to become politically united at the Warsaw Confederation of 1573. Temporarily, Stancarism, which stemmed from Francesco Stancaro (1501–74), and Socinianism, which took its name from Fausto Sozzini (Socinius, 1539–1604), played important roles. This anti-Trinitarian movement, whose adherents were also called Arians or Polish Brethren, was suppressed in 1658.

The Beginnings of the Counter Reformation. Sharp disputes among the various Protestant groups,

Catholic reforms, and the Counter Reformation weakened the position of Protestantism, which had gained its chief support in the noble classes and in the higher levels among the burghers. Faced with the political threat to Poland-Lithuania of the Swedes in the north, of the advancing Russians in the east, and of Turkish attacks in the south, Polish political leaders and bishops emphasized the necessity of the abolishment of all ecclesiastical division and of return to the Catholic Church as a matter that was absolutely vital to the national interest. Catholicism had already taken on new strength.

Numerous diocesan and provincial synods issued decrees against the abuses that had become widespread in the Late Middle Ages, and they also came to grips with the Protestant religious views. The Archbishops Jan Łaski of Gniezno (1510–31) and Andrzej Krzycki (1535–37), who as bishop of Przemyśl (1523–27) had written against Luther, sought to check Protestantism. The polemical works of John Eck, Johannes Cochlaeus, and Georg Witzel (Wicelius) were disseminated throughout Poland. Stanislaus Hosius (1504–79) was especially zealous in defending the Church through his polemical and systematic writings (for example, his *Confessio catholicae fidei*) and his pastoral and ecclesiastico-political measures. As bishop of Chełmno from 1549, of Ermland from 1551, and as cardinal from 1561, he succeeded in bringing about a renewal of the life of the Church.

Work of Papal Nuncios and Jesuits. Polish Catholicism received essential help from Rome through admonitory papal briefs to the Polish kings and through the work of the nuncios, who by political means and visitations strove to put into effect the decrees of the Council of Trent. The nuncio Giovanni Francesco Commendone (1563–65) persuaded King Sigismund II Augustus to give the Jesuits the protection of the crown; the nuncio Alberto Bolognetti (1581–85) through his letters and sermons contributed to the return of many nobles to Catholicism; and the nuncio Germanico Malaspina (1593–97) made the preparations for the Union of Brest (1596), through which most of the Orthodox bishops of Poland-Lithuania were united with Rome. The Union of Brest was a great victory in the struggle for the unity of the Church. However, the national tensions between Poles and Ukrainians and the political altercations involving Poland-Lithuania, the Cossacks, and Russia hindered the development of the Union. The Basilian St. Josaphat Kuncevyč (1580–1623, archbishop of Płock from 1618) and the Jesuit St. Andrew Bobola (1592–1657) were murdered by fanatical Cossacks.

The nuncios were strongly supported by Cardinal Hosius and other members of the Polish episcopate. It will suffice to mention: Martin Kromer of Ermland (1579–89); Marcin Białobrzecki of Kamieniec (1577–86); Stanisław Karnkowski of Włocławek (1567–81), and later archbishop of Gniezno (1581–1603), who as preacher, writer, and diplomat opposed Protestantism, and by synods, the erecting of seminaries, and patronage of the Jesuit order, hastened the re-Catholization of Poland; and Jan Dymitr Solikowski, archbishop of Lvov (1583–1603). In the religious strife of the age the Jesuits Melchior Grodziecki (1584–1619) and St. John Sarkander (1576–1620) died as martyrs.

Success of the Counter Reformation in Poland. Sigismund III Vasa, king of Poland (1587–1632), and also king of Sweden (1594–1604), whom Rubens glorified as the "Tamer of Heresy," completed the Counter Reformation in Poland-Lithuania. The Jesuits were its acknowledged champions. They were active as teachers and leaders in new educational institutions and as diplomats, preachers, missionaries, confessors, writers, and publicists. Typical representatives were Benedict Herbest (1530–93), Jakób Wujek (1540–97), Piotr Skarga (1536–1611), Maciej Kazimierz Sarbiewski (1595–1640), and Gaspar Druzbicki (1590–1662). The older orders, the Dominicans, Franciscans, Bernardines, Paulites, Augustinians, and Carmelites played an important role beside the Jesuits. The new orders or congregations as, for example, the Reformati (OFM Ref), Piarists, Capuchins, Trinitarians, Vincentians, and others, spread rapidly. Orders and congregations of women engaged actively in education, in the care of the sick, and in other works of charity. Among the mystics of the age, the Carmelite Teresa Marchocka (1603–52) deserves mention.

When Swedes, Russians, and Turks poured into Polish territory, the Church gathered all her forces to drive out these enemies of her religion. The heroic defense of the Paulite monastery on the Jasna Góra at Częstochowa in 1655 was the occasion for raising this place of pilgrimage with its icon of the "Black Mother of God" to the status of a Polish national shrine. In 1666 King John II Casimir (1648–68) proclaimed Mary Queen of Poland (*regina Poloniae, królowa Korony Polskiej*). Pope Alexander VII bestowed the title of *rex orthodoxus* on John and his successors. Marian devotion, which had struck deep roots in Poland in the Middle Ages, flourished anew. Catholicism was officially recognized as the religion of the State.

Political Decline and Repressive Religious Policy. In the period of the Elective Monarchy (1572–1795) Poland-Lithuania lost the position as a great power that it had attained under the Jagiellonians. Because King John III Sobieski (1674–1696) won victories against the Turks and played a major role in freeing Vienna from the Turk-

ish siege in 1683, he received from Pope Innocent XII the title of *defensor fidei*. In the eighteenth century, Poland-Lithuania faced the catastrophe of partitions under the Saxon electors, Augustus II (1697–1733) and Augustus III (1733–63), who were forced upon it as kings by its neighbors.

The victory of the Counter Reformation led to measures that went beyond the solid establishment of Catholicism. Protestantism was suppressed, and in 1717 the erection of new Protestant churches was forbidden. Following an attack by the Protestant population on the Jesuit *Gymnasium* in Toruń in 1724, the burgomaster and nine other Protestants were executed. The United Catholics, or adherents of the Union, who even in the preceding century had to overcome external and internal difficulties, were now treated as Catholics of "the second class;" they were forced to accept certain forms and practices of the Roman Catholic State Church. The rights of the Orthodox were also curtailed. The kings of Prussia and the Russian czars took action to protect the Protestants and Orthodox respectively under Polish rule. Catherine II (the Great) set her favorite Stanisław August Poniatowski (1764–95) upon the Polish throne. Through Gen. N. V. Repnin, her ambassador in Warsaw, she interfered in ecclesiastical affairs, e.g., in 1767 she had Bp. Kajetan Sołtyk of Cracow (1759–88) and Bp. Józef Andrzej Zaluski of Kiev (1759–74) arrested and deported to Russia. The patriotic Catholic opposition, under the leadership of Bp. Adam Stanisław Krasiński (1759–95, d. 1800), formed the Confederation of Bar. Jan Dołowicz, the Carmelite prior of Bar (d. 1801), even founded an "Order of the Holy Cross" to protect the faith, but after a four-year struggle the confederates were wiped out by the Russians.

The Partitions of Poland (1772–1815). In the first partition (1772) carried out by Russia, Austria, and Prussia, Poland lost about thirty percent of its territory and thirty-five percent of its inhabitants. In the attempts to stabilize conditions by reforms, several ecclesiastics took a prominent part. Among them should be mentioned as preacher, educational reformer, and statesman the famous Piarist Stanisław Konarski (1700–73), Abp. Michał Jerzy Poniatowski of Gniezno (1785–94), Bp. Adam Stanisław Naruszewicz of Lutsk (1790–96), the founder of modern Polish historiography, and Canon Hugo Kołłątej (1750–1812), who carried out important curricular reforms. They participated actively also in the formation of the Constitution of 3 May 1791, in which the Catholic religion was recognized as the official religion of the State, but in which also the free practice of religion was guaranteed for all dissenters.

The second partition of Poland by Russia and Prussia in 1793, and the third in 1795, by which the three neighboring Great Powers seized the rest of Poland, brought an abrupt end to the efforts at internal reform. The papal nuncio in Warsaw, Lorenzo Litta (1793–95), registered a solemn protest against the injustice done to Poland-Lithuania, but his protest died away unheard. Russia seized two-thirds, and Prussia and Austria the remaining third between them. The name of Poland vanished from the map. The Church was seriously weakened materially by the confiscations and secularization of her possessions. The grand-duchy of Warsaw, established by Napoleon (1807–09), was abolished in 1813 and its territory divided between Prussia and Russia. The Congress of Vienna, which is rightly charged with the fourth partition of Poland, delivered the final blow in 1815: Russia received eighty-two percent, Austria ten percent, and Prussia eight percent of the former Polish kingdom.

Foreign Domination, 1815–1918

The Poles did not meekly accept the loss of independent statehood, but held tenaciously to their national consciousness and to their language. As in earlier crises, the Catholic Church in this period also was a bond that united the Polish-speaking population at home and abroad. In the Congregation of the Resurrectionists, whose first members made their vows in Rome in 1842 *(Congregatio a Resurrectione Domini Nostri Jesu Christi;* in Polish, *Zmartwychstancy)*, belief in the Resurrection of Christ and the firm conviction that Poland would be restored were combined in a special way.

Polish Catholics under Russian Rule. In the parts of Poland annexed by Russia, the oppression of the Poles and of Catholicism, which was regarded as a foreign body, was especially severe. The Russian government conducted a continual campaign against the United, or adherents of the Union, in particular. Already under Catherine II eight million United were incorporated into the Orthodox Church by force. The eparchies, which had not been abolished earlier, comprising 1.5 million faithful and 1,500 parish churches, were placed under the control of the United-Greek College in St. Petersburg in 1829. Nicholas I (1825–55) granted the request of the Synod of Płock that the adherents of the Union should be reunited with the "Old Orthodox Mother Church." Those who did not abandon the Union with Rome voluntarily were forced to do so. In 1875 the Diocese of Chełmno in Congress Poland (Russian Poland) was declared to be an Orthodox bishopric, and thus the Union was abolished in the whole territory under Russian rule. Small groups of faithful continued in secret to be loyal to the Union. The Edict of Toleration of 17 April 1905 permitted them to become Roman Catholics, but a return to their old United status was forbidden.

Dependent Status of the Roman Catholic Church. The Roman Catholic ecclesiastical administration was reduced to a condition of severe dependence under Russian rule. In Stanisław Sienstreńcewicz-Bohusz, whom she appointed to head her newly erected archbishopric of Mogilev (1782–1826), Catherine II found a willing helper. Alexander I (1801–25) established (1801) the Roman Catholic Ecclesiastical College in St. Petersburg in order to control the Church. In the grand-duchy of Warsaw, Polish Catholics had a short breathing spell. But in the period of the "Kingdom of Poland," which from 1815 to 1830 was governed in personal union with Russia, it was soon evident that any cooperation with the Church was to be based purely on considerations of public policy. In order to break the influence of the bishop of Gniezno, who as primate of Poland possessed a measure of authority that extended beyond the boundaries of his own jurisdiction proper, Alexander I had Warsaw, which had been made a bishopric in the Prussian partition territory in 1798, raised to the status of an archbishopric in 1817. In the following year seven bishops were placed under its jurisdiction as suffragans.

The expulsion of the Jesuits from Russia in 1820, the dissolution of the numerous monasteries, the possibility of divorce from a Catholic partner on the occasion of the other partner's conversion to the Orthodox faith, were all threatening portents. After the failure of the Polish revolution of 1830–31, they were followed by harsh measures against the Church. The government refused to give official approval to episcopal candidates (the archiepiscopal See of Warsaw, for example, was vacant from 1829 to 1836, and from 1838 to 1856), in 1832 it suppressed 200 monasteries; in 1834 it restricted freedom of movement on the part of the clergy; and in 1841 it confiscated the major portion of ecclesiastical property. In 1846 the priest Piotr Ściegienny, who advocated the freeing of the peasants and national revolt, was arrested in Kielce and condemned to hard labor in Siberia, from which he was not permitted to return before 1871. The convention of 1847 made between Nicholas I and Pope Pius IX was never really implemented.

Tensions mounted under the government of Alexander II (1855–81), when the Poles rose in revolution against the Russian terror in 1863–1864, only to be crushed with much bloodshed. Archbishop Zygmunt Szczęsny Feliński of Warsaw (1862–83, d. 1895), Bishops Adam Krasiński of Vilna (d. 1891), Wincenty Chościak-Popiel of Płock (archbishop of Warsaw 1883–1912), and Konstanty Lubieński of Sejny (1863–69), along with 400 clerics, were banished to Siberia. Almost all monasteries and Catholic societies were abolished, and processions outside churches and May devotions were forbidden. In 1866 the government repudiated the convention made with Rome in 1847. In 1869–1870 it ordered the use of the Russian language in divine worship and punished numerous bishops and clerics who opposed the new regulations with banishment to Siberia. No permission was given the bishops to attend Vatican Council I.

Improvement after 1882. It was only after 1882, when Pope Leo XIII and Alexander III (1881–94) had worked out an agreement, that some alleviation of the oppressive conditions was introduced. The use of the Russian language in sermons and devotions was limited to communities with a Russian population. The use of Polish was permitted in Polish cities and Polish rural areas. In 1884 Leo XIII was able to fill the vacant sees. The Edict of Toleration of 1905 under Nicholas II (1894–1918) brought further alleviations, but restrictions were again imposed only two years later (1907). The government recognized and supported the Mariavites, whose leading personalities were excommunicated by Rome in 1906.

The Poles under Austria. In Galicia the situation for Polish Catholics was better. The government in Vienna was the only one of the three partition powers to give them assistance and support, although in the first half of the nineteenth century the influence of the State Church of Josephinism was still active. The Concordat of 1855 and the autonomy granted to the Poles in 1867, with their own diet, were fruitful for the life of the Church. Education at all levels was conducted in Polish. The Academy of Cracow was founded in 1872. Cracow and Lvov with their universities and theological faculties were outstanding Catholic centers. From 1884 the Jesuits in Cracow published the monthly, *Przegląd Powszechny,* which became a vehicle for leading Catholics. Distinguished bishops were active as ecclesiastical statesmen, theological writers, and preachers. Special mention should be made of the Prince-Bishops of Cracow, Albin Dunajewski (1879–94) and Jan Kozielko Puzyna (1895–1911, cardinal from 1901), Abp. Józef Bilczewski of Lvov (Lemberg, 1900–23), and Bp. Józef Sebastian Pelczar of Przemyśl (d. 1924).

Between the Roman Catholic hierarchy and the United, who had acquired a separate archbishopric of Lvov in 1807, relations became strained, resulting essentially from the national opposition between Poles and Ukrainians. After long negotiations a formula of agreement was worked out at Rome in 1863, which dealt with disputed questions but did not clarify all points. The United, under the leadership of their metropolitans, especially Sylvester Sambrytovyč (1885–98, cardinal from 1895) and Andreas Count Szeptyckyj (1900–44), strove to gain political and ecclesiastical independence.

Polish Catholicism under German Rule. During the Prussian partition area the differences between the Protestant government and the Catholic, and especially the Polish-speaking, population became worse decade by decade, although the bull of Pope Pius VII, *De salute animarum,* issued in 1821 had regulated anew ecclesiastical affairs in the eastern parts of Prussia. The bishopric of Posen (Poznań) was raised to an archbishopric and was united in a personal union with the archbishopric of Gnesen (Gniezno), which retained the greatly extended diocese of Kulm (Chełmno) as a suffragan. The dioceses of Ermland and Breslau (Wrocław), which meantime had been freed from their dependence on Riga and Gniezno respectively, were placed directly under the Holy See. Following the Polish revolution of 1830–1831, the Prussian Lord Lieutenant Eduard von Flottwell (1830–41) promoted German institutions and culture and Protestantism in order to restrict the influence of the Polish nobility and clergy. In 1839 the demands of the government on the question of mixed marriages led to the internment of Abp. Martin von Dunin of Gniezno (1831–42) in the fortress of Kolberg. His successor Leo Przyłuski (1845–65) in 1848 demanded the restoration of the national rights of the Poles.

The quarrel between the German government and the Poles reached its zenith in the period of the *Kulturkampf.* Through his policy Bismarck wished, among other things, to deprive the growing Polish nationalism of its spiritual leaders. Abp. Mieczysław Halka Ledóchowski (1865–86) of Gniezno-Poznań (Gnesen-Posen), two auxiliary bishops, and numerous clergy were arrested, and their parishes left vacant. The pressure of the *Kulturkampf,* which slackened after some years, and other government measures, for example, the suppression of the Polish language in schools and in public life, did not have the success expected. Archbishop Julius Dinder (1886–90) tried in vain to bring about a settlement. After long negotiations, Abp. Florian Oksza-Stablewski (1891–1906) succeeded in obtaining permission for the use of Polish in religious instruction in the schools. An expropriation law was passed against Polish landed property in 1908, against which Cardinal Georg Kopp of Breslau protested in the Upper House of the German Parliament. This law enkindled a general outburst of anger that had repercussions beyond the borders of Germany. The condition of tension remained, as was evidenced by the vacancy in the archiepiscopal See of Gniezno-Poznań during the years 1906 to 1914.

Along with the Polish bishops, who during the period of the domination of Poland by the partition powers defended the Catholic tradition, one must praise the old orders and new congregations for their splendid service in maintaining Catholicism and in spreading and deepening the knowledge of the Catholic religion. Mention should be made of the Jesuit writer and missionary Karol

Antoniewicz (d. 1852), the Salesian August Czartoryski (d. 1893), the Carmelite Rafal Kalinowski (d. 1907), and the Redemptorist Bernard Lubienski (d. 1933). Several new Polish communities were founded in the second half of the nineteenth century. In 1855 Edmund Bojanowski (d. 1871) founded the Little Servant Sisters of the Immaculate Conception, and Sofja Truszkowska founded the Felician Sisters (Felicjanki); in 1857 Jozefa Karska (d. 1860) and Marcelina Darowska, the Sisters of the Immaculate Conception of Mary (Niepokalanki); in 1875 Franciszka Siedliska (d. 1902), the Sisters of the Holy Family of Nazareth (Nazaretanki); in 1891–92 Brother Albert, ''the Polish Francis'' (Adam Chmielowski, d. 1916), the Albertines, including both men and women; in 1893 Bronislaw Markiewicz (d. 1912), the Sisters of St. Michael the Archangel (Michaelitki).

The Church in the Republic of Poland, 1918–39

When the Polish Republic was created in November 1918, the bishops, who had cared for the faithful in the three partition areas, were faced with difficult problems of organization. In the rebuilding of Polish Catholicism, the leaders were the Archbishops Edmund Dalbor of Gniezno (1915–26) and Aleksander Kakowski of Warsaw (1913–38), who were made cardinals in 1919, and the nuncio Achille Ratti (1919–21), the later Pope Pius XI The Concordat of 10 February 1925, and the bull *Vixdum Poloniae* of Pope Pius XI, issued 28 October of the same year, constituted the foundation for the new ecclesiastical order in Poland. Two new archbishoprics, Cracow and Vilna, were erected beside the existing archiepiscopal sees of Gniezno-Poznań (Gnesen-Posen), Warsaw, and Lvov, and four new dioceses were established: Częstochowa, Katowice, Lomza, and Pinsk. The new organization comprised five ecclesiastical provinces with a total of fifteen suffragan sees.

The Polish census of 1936 indicated that Catholics comprised 75 percent of the population (Roman Catholics 63.8 percent, and adherents of the Union 11.2 percent), the Orthodox and Jews, 10 percent each, and Protestants, 3 percent. Catholicism, which was the acknowledged religion of the great majority of the Polish population, was respected even by religiously indifferent statesmen, as Józef Piłsudski (d. 1935) who as chief of state headed the Republic from 1918 to 1922 and guided it in the years 1926 to 1935 under several authoritarian governments. The generally harmonious relations between Church and State were seriously impaired by the new marriage legislation, the proposed penal code, and, above all, in the summer of 1938, by the expropriation and destruction of Orthodox churches in the Lublin area with governmental authority and support. The papal nuncio in Poland Filippo Cortesi (1936–47) and the Polish episcopate disassociated themselves definitely from this harsh action on the part of the government. Under the leadership of the bishops, at whose regularly held conferences the Primate Augustyn Hlond (1926–48) served as president, the Church, through an effective consolidation of its forces, exercised a strong influence on public life.

Flourishing Catholic Life. The number of bishops in the period from 1918 to 1938 rose from twenty-three to fifty-one, and the number of diocesan and regular clergy increased by about forty-three percent, reaching a total of nearly 13,000. The religious orders enjoyed a marked growth in this same period. At the outbreak of World War II there were about 2,000 monastic foundations, 1,600 priests, 4,500 lay brothers, and 17,000 sisters. The numerous pilgrimages to the shrines of the Blessed Virgin at Częstochowa, Piekary, and Ostra Brama in Vilna and the increasing participation in the foreign missions and in religious congresses bore witness to a flourishing religious life. The Church intensified the care of souls by the multiplication of parishes, by the development of its social work in its organized charities and in its St. Vincent de Paul societies, by Catholic Action, which furnished a more solid adult education program, and by the apostolate of the press. In 1939 there were more than 250 Catholic periodical publications, 38 of these being organs of the United Church. Every diocese had its own Sunday paper. The religious orders also exhibited marked zeal in the field of the Catholic press. The scholarly life of the Church, which had a solid foundation in obligatory religious education, was promoted through the theological faculties of Warsaw, Cracow, Lvov, and Vilna, by the Catholic University of Lublin, founded in 1918, and by the diocesan seminaries. This scholarly activity was reflected in a series of important theological journals.

The United Catholic Church of Poland was composed of the Armenian Bishopric of Lvov, which had 4,000 faithful, as well as the 3,500,000 members of the Greek-Catholic rite in East Galicia, and some parishes of the Eastern Slavic rite totaling about 25,000 faithful. They in common were opposed to the Polish government, which wished to restrict their separate status within the Church in favor of the Latin rite. The government hoped that Latinization would lead to the complete assimilation of the United faithful into the main stream of Polish life and culture.

The Church in Poland, 1939–65

Until the end of World War I, Polish Catholicism led a different kind of existence in the eastern provinces of Prussia, in the Russian Vistula area, and in Austrian Galicia, but within two decades an abrupt standardization was put into effect. The German-Soviet Pact and the German Polish campaign of September 1939 created a new political situation for the Church. The incorporation of the eastern Polish territory into the Soviet Union entailed the prohibition of religious propaganda, persecutions, and deportations of clergy and laity.

The Poles under the National Socialist Regime. The German National Socialist regime seized the territory of the ecclesiastical province of Gniezno-Poznań (Gnesen-Posen) and parts of the archbishoprics of Warsaw and Cracow, which it designated "the incorporated eastern territories" and it established a general government that included the main parts of the ecclesiastical provinces of Warsaw and Cracow and the western border areas of the ecclesiastical provinces of Lvov and Vilna. Following the outbreak of the German-Soviet War, East Galicia, with the major portion of the ecclesiastical province of Lvov was added to the general government also. The harsh measures of the German authorities, the ideological outlook of Alfred Rosenberg, race theory, and Jewish persecutions threatened the Church, which was reduced to a slave status in the Warta District and was heavily oppressed in the general government.

In the Warta District members of the hierarchy were brutally beaten; the clergy was decimated in a frightful manner; seminaries, numerous establishments of religious orders, and all Catholic schools and associations were abolished; ecclesiastical property was expropriated; sisters were driven from their convents; churches in large part were closed (in Poznań, for example, of thirty churches only two were left open for Polish-speaking Catholics and one for German-speaking faithful); wayside crosses and shrines were destroyed; Polish inscriptions on gravestones were effaced; and loyalty to religion was made extremely difficult and was ridiculed in every conceivable manner. More than three million Polish Catholics were left completely outside the pale of the law and were at the mercy of the despotic whims of the National Socialists.

The Archbishop of Cracow, Adam Sapieha (1925–51, cardinal from 1946), served as spokesman for all the Polish bishops, making repeated representations to the administration of the general government in order to obtain alleviations in the treatment of priests under arrest and sent into exile, to provide for the recruitment and theological training of seminarians, and to maintain the charitable activities of the Church. Following the systematic elimination of the Church from public life, and especially after the liquidation of the Catholic press and of higher Catholic education, the spiritual activity of the Church under the general government was confined to divine worship, the care of souls, and religious instruction. The youth organizations and societies of men under the leadership of Catholic Action were forbidden, but in the underground they served in part as assistance organizations for persecuted clerics and Jews. The German occupation officials were bent on depriving the Church of her age-old function of being a protective shield for all that was characteristic in Polish life and culture. Their anti-ecclesiastical attack paralyzed Catholic life and widely destroyed it.

In all, thirteen Polish bishops were exiled or arrested and put in concentration camps. Of these the following died: Auxiliary Bishop Leo Wetmanski of Płock on 10 May 1941, and Archbishop Antoni Nowowiejski of Plock on 20 June 1941 in Soldau (Działdowo); Auxiliary Bishop Michał Kozal of Włocławek on 26 January 1943 in Dachau; Auxiliary Bishop Wladyslaw Goral of Lublin at the beginning of 1945 in a hospital bunker in Berlin. There were 3,647 priests, 389 clerics, 341 brothers, and 1,117 sisters put in concentration camps, in which 1,996 priests, 113 clerics, and 238 sisters perished. On 14 August 1941, Maximilian Kolbe met his death in the concentration camp at Auschwitz (Oświecim). He offered his life in substitution for that of a father of a family who had been condemned to die. The diocesan clergy of the Polish Church, who at the beginning of World War II numbered 10,017, lost 25 percent (2,647). The National Socialist terror raged against leading Catholic laymen as well as against the clergy, and many laymen were put to death. The concentration camps of Auschwitz, Bojanowo, Dachau, Majdanek, Oranienburg, Ravensbrück, Stutthof, Treblinka, and others were sites of Polish martyrdoms.

Reorganization of the Polish Church. The collapse of the German East Front and the end of World War II introduced a new chapter in Polish history. The Polish Committee for National Liberation, the so-called Lublin Committee, in a manifesto of 22 July 1944 guaranteed, among other things, freedom of conscience and respect for the rights of the Catholic Church. Clergy and faithful devoted their efforts to healing the material and mental wounds caused by the occupation and the effects of the war. The Primate, Cardinal Augustyn Hlond—from 1946 also archbishop of Warsaw—undertook the rebuilding of ecclesiastical organization. He consecrated several bishops; restored the seminaries; made provisions for religious instruction, for the restoration of Catholic schools, and for the redevelopment of the ecclesiastical press; and revived the activity of the religious orders. Owing to the political territorial changes, modifications in the Polish ecclesiastical organization were necessary. In the East the largest part of the archdiocese of Vilna and Lemberg (Lvov) were lost. In the West, the new organization was fitted into the structure of the ecclesiastical province of

East Germany. In the occupied German eastern territories, the so-called Polish West and North territories, five apostolic administrations were established in 1945 with their centers at Oppeln (Opole), Breslau (Wrocław), Allenstein (Olsztyn), Landsberg (Gorzów Wielkopolski), and Danzig (Gdańsk).

Difficulties of the Church under a Communist Government. On 12 September 1945 the Polish government abrogated the Concordat of 1925. The nationalization of Catholic presses and the censorship of Catholic publications marked the beginning of restrictions on the freedom of the Church. They were followed (1948–50) by the censorship of all ecclesiastical publications, by the elimination of Catholic youth associations and broadcasts, by the dissolution of the Caritas Association, the nationalization of hospitals, and by the expropriation of the largest portion of ecclesiastical property. Primate Stefan Wyszyński, took over direction of the archdioceses of Gniezno and Warsaw after the death of Cardinal Hlond (16 December 1948). (He was made a cardinal in 1953.) He made an agreement with the government on 14 April 1950. The bishops obtained the recognition of their dogmatic, liturgical, and catechetical demands, but the normalization of the relations between Church and State, which they expected, did not take place.

Out of the latent battle between Church and State a more open conflict broke out (1952–55). The government decree of 9 February 1953, on the filling of ecclesiastical offices, subordinated episcopal jurisdiction to the supervision of the State. Bishop Czeslaw Mieczyslaw Kaczmarek of Kielce (1938–63) was already arrested in 1951. In 1953 Cardinal Wyszyñiski, and, in 1954, Auxiliary Bishop Antoni Baraniak of Poznań (archbishop from 1957) were likewise deprived of their freedom. The absolute authority of the governmental office for ecclesiastical affairs; the dissolution of some major and minor seminaries, including seminaries of religious orders; the measures directed against the Catholic University of Lublin; the abolition of the Catholic faculties at the beginning of the winter semester of 1954 to 1955; the prohibition of January 1955 against the imparting of religious instruction in the elementary schools; the arrest and imprisonment of priests; the frequent search of private domiciles by the police; and the expropriation of monasteries all endangered most seriously the independence of the Church. In addition to pressures from the outside, attempts were made to split the interior unity of Catholicism by means of the so-called "patriotic priests," who were pushed into key positions in the Church by the office of ecclesiastical affairs, and of "progressive Catholics" who organized themselves as the Pax-Movement and were supported by the government. These Catholics of leftist orientation developed the Pax Press and presented themselves as the true representatives of Polish Catholicism. The Church was pushed very much into the background in public life. The number of churches and chapels declined about thirty percent; the monasteries for men, forty percent; and convents for women, about forty-five percent. Because of the arrests, imprisonments, and banishments of priests, many parish posts could be filled in a temporary fashion only. On 8 December 1955 concern for the unity of the Church in Poland moved Pope Pius XII to address a letter to the Polish episcopate. He not only dealt with the persecution of the Church, but he emphasized, among other points, the danger of the "Progressive Catholics."

Church-State Relations 1956–57. In the fall of 1956 Władysław Gomułka, after the thaw (odwilz) that freed Poland from Stalinism, took over the political leadership and the situation of the Church improved. Cardinal Wyszyński was freed and returned to Warsaw, 28 October 1956. A commission made up of representatives of both Church and state was established to remove the existing tensions. The government decree of 9 February 1953, was withdrawn. Imprisoned bishops and clergy were given their freedom, the vicars capitular who had been appointed in the Polish west and north territories by the office for religious affairs in 1951 were now selected from loyal supporters of the cardinal. Religious instruction was permitted as an elective subject in schools before and after the hours set for obligatory studies. The Catholic laity obtained influence in internal political affairs, the press, and journalism. In May 1957, Gomułka declared that he saw the necessity of a coexistence between believers and nonbelievers, between the Church and socialism, and between the people's sovereignty and the hierarchy of the Church.

Polish Catholicism, 1956–1965. The Church utilized the alleviations that had been granted in 1956 to make itself heard. Through a carefully prepared and successfully conducted nine-year Novena (1957–66) the Church injected itself into the celebration of the millennium of Poland (Millennium Poloniae). The ideological reaction of communism was hesitant at first but soon became clearer. In the preparations for the Sejm (Parliament) elections of 16 April 1961 the watchword went out that Polish atheism must fight with the Catholic hierarchy, and that the domination of the souls of the whole nation was the issue at stake. On 15 June 1961 a law again abrogated the teaching of religion in the schools. The Church replied by constructing a thick network of catechetical support points, that the ministry of education tried in vain to bring under its control. The State applied the screw of taxation against the Church; used the pretense of paper shortages against ecclesiastical papers and periodicals; attacked Cardinal Wyszyński and other bishops, charging them with demagoguery and fanaticism; and restricted the freedom of the Church in systematic fashion.

In 1965, the Church was seeking to overcome these threats through a concentration of her forces. Her interior development was evidenced by the sound training of numerous seminarians in the major seminaries (4,000 seminarians in 1965); by the further development of the Catholic University of Lublin and of the Catholic Academy in Bielany near Warsaw; by appropriate methods of pastoral care; by the zealous activity of numerous religious orders and congregations; by courageous argumentation against dialectic and practical materialism; by the publication of several theological journals of high standing, as, for example, the *Ateneum kapłańskie* (Włocławek), the *Collectanea theologica* (Warsaw), and the *Homo Dei* (Warsaw); by cooperation in the Ecumenical Movement; by close contact with Rome as the center of the Church; and by the implementation of the decrees and suggestions of Vatican Council II. There was a flourishing religious life that was evidenced by zealous attendance at divine worship, the reception of the Sacraments, the intense devotion to the Blessed Virgin, and the restoration of old churches and erection of new ones. It was reflected also in the appearance of weekly Church papers like *Przewodnik Katolicky* (Poznań) and *Gość Niedzielny* (Katowice), in the sociocultural weekly *Tygodnik Powzechny* (Cracow), as well as in the monthly paper *Znak* (Cracow).

[B. STASIEWSKI]

The Church in Poland, 1965–2000

The Failure of the Five-Year Plan. The five-year plan introduced by the Władyslaw Gomułka regime ended in failure, further reducing living standards. It worsened shortages in consumer goods, stoked hidden inflation, and widened the gap between the Polish Peoples' Republic (PRL) and the West. The still-unsettled question of Poland's western borders on the Oder and Neisse Rivers continued to impede relations with West Germany (which did not recognize those frontiers) while heightening Polish dependence on the Soviet Union. In 1965 the Treaty of Friendship, Cooperation and Mutual Assistance between the PRL and the USSR was extended a further twenty years. Conflict with the Church grew over ecclesiastical preparations to mark the millennium of Christianity in Poland in 1966; the PRL wanted to treat the occasion as merely the thousandth anniversary of the Polish State. The Polish episcopate addressed a letter to its German counterpart, "forgiving and seeking forgiveness" between Poles and Germans. This effort at mutual reconciliation resulted in Gomułka, first secretary of the

Polish United Workers' Party (PZPR) accusing Primate Wyszyński of interfering in the prerogatives of the State. Within the PZPR itself, dissidents succeeded for the first time in expanding civil rights, particularly in the area of culture.

In reaction to the conservatism of Gomułka and hard-line communists ("partisans"), a liberal dissident wing emerged within the PZPR, made up primarily of the party's intelligentsia, which enjoyed some support from youth and students. Gomułka and other hard-liners would seize upon events following the 1967 Arab-Israeli Six Day War and anti-Russian student protests in early 1968 following performances of Mickiewicz's play *Dziady* ("Forefathers' Eve") to purge those "revisionists" in the name of "anti-Zionism." This internecine party warfare, inspired from Moscow, resulted in the migration of about 10,000 Jews from Poland (not all of them party members) at the time.

The Gomułka regime lost further public credibility after the 1968 Soviet-led invasion of Czechoslovakia and the worsening economic situation in Poland. The ongoing failure of communist central planning only deepened Poland's dependence on the Soviet Union. Although the Gomulka regime sought to maintain control of the situation, it found itself increasingly isolated, distrusting even its closest collaborators; party and government purges continued.

Departing from its traditional anti-West German stance, however, the PRL signed a treaty in December 1970 with Chancellor Willy Brandt's government, normalizing Polish-West German relations and recognizing Poland's postwar western borders. This resulted in the normalization of ecclesiastical government in those so-called "Recovered Lands" through the creation of dioceses and the appointment of ordinaries in lieu of apostolic administrators.

The economic crisis of 1968 to 1970 resulted, in part, in a weak supply of basic goods. Steep price increases announced just before Christmas 1970 spurred protests by workers in Gdańsk, Sopot, Gdynia, and Szczecin. The protests were put down bloodily, with 45 dead and about 1,200 wounded. In the wake of those protests, the Central Committee forced Gomułka and his coterie to resign. Edward Gierek became first secretary of the PZPR; Piotr Jarosiewicz replaced Józef Cyrankiewicz as premier. Gierek, who had begun his career as a communist activist in Belgium and France, gave the impression of a technocrat who promised to raise living standards and improve the economy, thereby buying a certain measure of social confidence ("Help us?" "We'll help!" was a contemporary slogan). Gierek fostered the illusion of liberalization in the areas of culture (censorship became more elastic), social control (travel abroad became easier) and toward the Church. At the same time, persecution of the opposition in fact intensified, e.g., a 1971 law provided for convictions in the absence of court decisions. These efforts went in tandem with slogans about patriotism and the building of socialism in close alliance with the USSR. One outcome of these campaigns was the approval by Parliament (Sejm) 3 February 1976 of constitutional changes previously adopted by the Seventh Congress of the PZPR that acknowledged the leading role of the party in the building of socialism and pledging Poland's indissoluble friendship with the USSR. Both the Church and dissident circles protested that decision, emphasizing that they conflicted with provisions of the 1975 Helsinki Final Act signed by Poland at the Conference on Security and Cooperation in Europe. Despite increased diplomatic contacts with the West, Polish dependence on the Soviets grew in the Gierek-Brezhnev era.

In the sphere of Church affairs, the government's authority grew as direct talks between the PRL and the Vatican took place and efforts were made to repair relations with Cardinal Wyszyński. A new internal administrative division of the country into 49 voivodships occurred, although it served to intensify centralized party leadership while reducing the significance of the local party apparatus.

Economically, a boom in investments, overextension of western credit, and growth in consumerism in the period 1971 to 1975 were all passed off as evidence that Poland was growing closer to Western affluence. The lifestyle bought by over-indebtedness to western credit eventually destabilized the economy by increasing the money supply even as the availability of real goods continued to decline. Starting in 1974, a new economic crisis (which, in socialist states also meant a new political crisis) began. Price increases announced by Premier Jarosiewicz on 24 June 1976 resulted in workers' protests in Radom, Ursus, and Plock. The militia suppressed the protests, resulting in about 1,000 arrests and 100 jailings.

Solidarnoś. The opposition acquired a new lease on life. On 23 September 1976 the Committee for the Defense of Workers (KOR) was founded. The Church came out on the side of workers, providing shelter and succor for members of the opposition, irrespective of their religious convictions (or lack thereof). The government backed down from the price hikes, which simply hastened economic collapse. The majority of those convicted in the 1976 protests were ''pardoned'' in the amnesty of 19 July 1977, which still punished opposition activities with short-term punishments or punishment by time served.

Opposition labor organizing continued. On 26 March 1977 the Movement in Defense of Human and Civil Rights (ROPCiO) was formed. In 1978 some free trade unions, the Self- Defense Committee of Farmers and the Trade Union of Farmers were all founded on local levels. Contacts were also formed with opposition movements in the other satellite countries. The Church, particularly through Primate Wyszyński, criticized the situation in Poland with the aim of fostering its improvement.

The election of Cardinal Karol Wojtyła as Pope John Paul II in 1978 and his first pilgrimage to Poland 2–10 June 1979 emboldened society to take initiatives apart from party and government direction. Malaise in the PRL, in turn, led to half-hearted prosecution of independent opposition organizations. The politico-economic crisis in the USSR was also slowly deepening.

One of the repercussions of this situation was the foundation in 1979 of a radical pro- independence organization led by Leszek Moczulski, the Confederation of Independent Poland (KPN). Independent trade unions also began asserting themselves more vigorously and the first strikes broke out in Lublin. Against this setting, the Eighth Congress of the PZPR in February 1980 resulted in nothing new. The only changes were at the level of personnel, e.g., Edward Babiuch replaced Jarosiewicz as premier.

Spring 1980 saw more shortages and price increases announced in July ushered in a wave of strikes in Lublin and Swidnik that spread on 14 August to the Gdańsk Shipyards and all along the Polish seacoast. An Interfactory Strike Committee was formed in August in various production centers throughout the country. In contrast to 1970, this time the PRL did not use force. Instead, it negotiated with the strikers, under the proviso that permitting independent trade unions would not be allowed to undermine the ''leading role'' of the party in society nor seek changes to the Constitution. That process led the way to the formation in the Gdansk Shipyards of the independent trade union *Solidarność* (Solidarity) under Lech Wałęsa's leadership. Solidarity soon encompassed the whole country as regional trade unions were founded (the first in the Mazowsze region on 4 September 1980). A ''National Committee for Understanding'' was set up in early September with Wałęsa as its head. The struggle to register Solidarity as an independent trade union went on until 10 November 1980, when the Supreme Court confirmed the union's constitution.

Gierek was removed from office on 6 September 1980 by the Sixth Plenum of the Central Committee of the PZPR. Stanisław Kania replaced him as first secretary. Kania advocated finding a political solution to the Polish crisis. But neither the party nor the government could constrain independent union organizing of diverse sectors of society: students, artists and scholars, farmers. Having begun with about 3.5 million members, Solidarity reached more than 9 million by the end of August 1981. The regime grew confused and fearful of a Soviet invasion. But the governing apparatchiks had no intention of giving up power and, under the leadership of General Wojciech Jaruzelski preparations for martial law began. Conflict between Solidarity and the PRL increased in 1981 as the regime took an increasingly hard line. Militia-initiated provocations (in Bydgoszcz, for example, Solidarity activists were beaten up in the local voivodship council's chamber) and efforts by the PZPR to limit Solidarity's local influence further fueled distrust and propelled events towards conflict. Ongoing Soviet pressure (e.g., the Letter of the Central Committee of the Communist Party of the Soviet Union to the Central Committee of the PZPR), the radicalization of attitudes in the party and in Solidarity, and the death of Primate Wyszyński in May 1981 (who had exercised a moderating influence) all brought confrontation closer.

The second half of 1981 saw an increase in mutual accusations between the party and Solidarity and a growing wave of strikes. During Solidarity's General Congress on 5 September 1981, a "Message to the Working People of Eastern Europe" was adopted, expressing an interest in expanding the ideals of Solidarity to other satellite countries. Absent from the document were any traces of the postulates of socialist ideology or adherence to the doctrine of the party's "leading role" in society.

General Jaruzelski's assumption of the role of First Secretary of the PZPR in October 1981 signaled the beginning of a reckoning with Solidarity, which had already been suggested by the use of the army in quelling strikes. Solidarity sought to call a national strike. Its National Commission assembled on 11–12 December 1981 in Gdańsk. On the night of 12–13 December martial law was declared in Poland and the majority of Solidarity activists interned. The Church, through the Primate's Committee for Assistance to Persons Deprived of Liberty intervened in the name of human rights. Armed reserve militias (ZOMO) and army took over Solidarity-controlled factories. At the Wujek Mine in Silesia nine miners were killed 16 December. The regime transformed itself into the "Military Council of National Salvation" (WRON), with the "Council for the Defense of the Nation" acting as its shadow. The party nevertheless lost members, with about 700,000 quitting. Solidarity went underground, although opportunists and proponents of the regime left it. Military commissars assumed control over the direction of all spheres of life, including the economy. Instead of the "normalization" that the WRON promised, however, chaos and acute shortages of basic goods afflicted the population.

The regime intended to liquidate Solidarity. The Trade Unions Act of 8 October 1982 adopted by the Sejm sought to regulate the union without its consent. A "Patriotic Front for the Rebirth of the Nation" (PRON) was created, intended to facilitate the party's "dialogue" with society. That dialogue included gestures of reconciliation like the release of Wałęsa in November 1982, the gradual freeing of other internees, and finally the suspension of martial law 18 December 1982. At the same time, more intense repression of the opposition meant losses for the underground Solidarity movement, now led by its Temporary Coordinating Commission (TKK) with offices in Brussels. Although Pope John Paul II's second pilgrimage in June 1983 and the formal lifting of martial law on 22 July were further reconciliatory gestures on the regime's part, repression of the opposition continued. The Church paid for its public encouragement of Solidarity with the murder of several priests, including the Rev. Jerzy Popiełuszko. Popiełuszko, murdered on 19 October 1984, organized monthly "Masses for the Fatherland" in a Warsaw church that combined patriotic hymns with sermons of encouragement rooted in Catholic social teaching. But even harsher punishments (the Criminal Code was updated on 1 July 1985, and there were 386 political prisoners by the end of 1986) could not staunch the hemorrhage of the regime's authority. The creation of an All-Poland Understanding of Trade Unions (OPZZ), which was pro-regime, further polarized labor.

On 6 November 1985 Jaruzelski further took over the Office of Chairman of the Council of State. The amnesty of 17 July 1986 did not eliminate political repression, although the regime sought to reach some understanding with society by establishing a Consultative Council on 6 December. Although limited participation in the Council by the opposition was permitted, it refused to take part.

Pope John Paul II's third pilgrimage to Poland on 8–14 June 1987 took place amid an atmosphere of the regime's weakening grip and the reappearance of active, though weakened, structures of Solidarity. On 25 October 1987 the National Executive Commission of Solidarity was founded but, at the core of the union, permanent divisions in ideology and tactics had already occurred. In December 1987 regional structures of Solidarity reappeared publicly. Throughout 1987 and 1988, it was apparent that the government's economic program had failed. Following a wave of strikes General Kiszczak, the interior minister, met with Wałęsa on 31 August 1988. On 27 September Mieczysław Rakowski became premier.

The End of the PRL/PZPR. The regime, while still displaying strength, called for "roundtable" dialogue with the opposition. The "Roundtable" discussions took place on 6 February 5 April 1989. They guaranteed immunity to the departing regime. On 7 April the Sejm adopted a new electoral law and established a presidency and senate. The semi-free elections of 4 June 1989 manifested social support for Solidarity and utterly discredited the regime. On 19 July General Jaruzelski was chosen by a majority of three votes in a joint session of Parliament to become president. On 24 August 1989 Tadeusz Mazowiecki became premier.

The PZPR was given the interior and defense ministries in the new government. Parliament adopted changes to the Constitution heralding the end of the PRL, although Mazowiecki's "broad line" policy refusing to address the PRL/PZPR past guaranteed ongoing communist influence in practice. The PZPR formally ceased to exist in January 1990, although part of that grouping formed the Social Democracy of the Republic of Poland (SdRP) party, which included Aleksander Kwasniewski. Multiple other parties arose.

Solidarity, which had at first entered Parliament as the "Citizens' Parliamentary Club" (OKP) soon broke up into several political groupings of varying orientations. The "Centrist Understanding" (PC), formed in January 1991, eventually became a Christian-Democratic type party. Another faction that broke off in January 1991 later named itself (in May) the "Democratic Union," taking the name "Freedom Union" in 1994.

Liberals and the left frequently found a coincidence of interests on various subjects, e.g., the exclusion of the Church from public life. *Gazeta Wyborcza,* at first the only independent daily newspaper independent of the communist regime, dominated public opinion. Public disorientation in political matters manifested itself in the 1990 presidential elections. The finalists were Walęsa and Stanisław Tyminski, a candidate of indeterminate provenance who had outpolled Mazowiecki in the first round. Walesa won.

Jan Krzysztof Bielecki of the Liberal-Democratic Congress became premier. The electoral ordinance fostered Parliamentary fracturing (there were twenty-nine parties) and made it difficult for the government to function. In 1991 Parliamentary elections eight parties and twenty-nine smaller groups competed. The Democratic Union won 12.3 percent of the vote, followed by the "Democratic Left Alliance" (SLD), the "former" communists assembled from various smaller groups, also polling 12 percent. Solidarity won 5 percent. The government of Jan Olszewski (PC) lasted from December 1991 to 4 June 1992; Walęsa's own ambivalence was decisive in Olszewski's fall, since that government had promised to undertake de-communization and lustration. The next government, from Waldemar Pawlak's leftist Polish

Farmers' Front (PSL) lasted from 5 June 7 July 1992. Hanna Suchocka's (UD) government endured until the end of May 1993.

The difficulties of successive governments were caused by the economic reforms of Finance Minister Leszek Balcerowicz, whose "shock therapy" was acutely felt by the public at large, by the lack of a decisive break with the legacy of the PRL (the consequence of Mazowiecki's "broad line" politics) and by the contradictory interests among different parties and actors. A growing anticlericalism could also be felt, especially in the SLD, UW, the Union of Labor (UP) and parts of the PSL. One expression of this anticlericalism was the fight over the concordat between Poland and the Vatican, signed at the end of July 1993 but entering into force only in early 1998. In 1992 a new ecclesiastical reorganization of Poland took place, dividing the country into thirteen metropolitan and forty suffragan sees. Liberal circles, represented by journals like *Gazeta Wyborcza* and *Tygodnik Powszechny,* sought to divide Polish Catholicism into two camps: "fundamentalist" (i.e., those acknowledging traditional Catholic truths) and "open" (i.e., subordinating Catholicism to secularized ideology).

Political Division, Social Reform, and an Uncertain Future. On 17 November 1992 Walesa signed the so-called "Little Constitution" that was to remain in force until adoption of a new fundamental law. A leftist alliance won the 19 November 1993 parliamentary elections. Their victory was caused by divisions in the political landscape, discontent with the pain of economic reforms, and popular hopes fueled by the former Communists that they would spur economic growth. The SLD and PSL together won 45 percent of the vote. The decline of Walęsa's and Solidarity's influence was the consequence of political conflicts, economic scandals, the communist past of various high-ranking officials, and the growing disparity between the generally poor (and growing poorer) public-at-large and the *nouveau riche* of the former communist *nomenklatura.* The SLD-PSL formed a new government under PSL leader Waldemar Pawlak, which lasted until February 1995 when he was replaced by SLD premier Jozef Oleksy.

Economic growth (7 percent in 1997) did not go hand-in-hand with growth in per capita income ($5,600). Unemployment (2.2 million in 1997) remained high and 15 percent of the population lived below the poverty line. In 1996, however, the Organization for Economic Cooperation and Development (OECD) added Poland to the list of the 28 most dynamically growing economies in the world.

Amid a field of thirteen candidates, Aleksander Kwasniewski (SLD) defeated Lech Walęsa for the Polish presidency in 1995. Oleksy resigned as premier in January 1996, succeeded by Włodzimierz Cimoszewicz (SLD). On 27 April 1997 Parliament adopted a new constitution, subsequently approved by 53.75 percent of the voters in a May referendum; it went into force on 17 October.

An alliance of rightist groups led by Solidarity leader Marian Krzaklewski formed "Solidarity Electoral Action" (AS), which took first place (33.8 percent) in September 1997 parliamentary elections. The SLD came in second (27.13 percent), followed by UW (13.37 percent) Solidarity Action formed a coalition with the UW under AS premier Jerzy Buzek.

Buzek's government undertook reforms put off by previous governments. On 7 May 1998 it adopted reforms of Poland's internal administrative divisions, introducing the notion of counties but reducing the number of voivodships. On 13 October 1998 a new system of social security was adopted and on 1 January 1999 school reforms became law.

On 12 March 1999 Poland became a member of NATO. Within the framework of preparing for accession to the European Union (which appears to have only about 50 percent support in public opinion polls) the government has begun economic reforms one consequence of which is the pauperization of villages and a rise in unemployment (caused by the sale of Polish factories that are then downsized or closed by their new owners). These reforms, in turn, generated opposition to the government, particularly among farmers. Reforms of the health service also struck hard at the poorest, especially in terms of price increases for drugs. Fractures within the governing coalition itself deepened while the left prepared for a populist campaign.

The lack of political stabilization in Poland, unchanged since 1989, effected social morality, particularly in a growing crime rate and the continual legal sanctions. Sentimentality for the PRL also manifests itself in some social opinion. The future course for Poland rests with the outcome of presidential elections scheduled for 2000 and parliamentary elections likely in 2001.

See Also: EDMUND BOJANOWSKI, ALBERT CHMIELOWSKI, CZĘSTOCHOWA, JOHN OF DUKLA, RAPHAEL KALINOWSKI, ST. KINGA, MAXIMILLIAN KOLBE, MARTYRS OF POLAND, JERZY POPIEŁUSZKO, ADAM SAPIEHA, JAN SARKANDER, FRANCISZKA SIEDLISKA, ANGELA MARIA TRUSZKOWSKA

Bibliography: NORMAN DAVIES, *God's Playground: A History of Poland,* vol. 2, *1795 to the Present* (New York 1982). H. SLABEK, *Historia spoleczna Polski (1944–1970)* (A Social History of Poland: 1944–1970) (Warsaw 1988). J. HOLZER, *Solidarność* (Solidarity) (Warsaw 1990). T. MOLDAWA, *Ludzie władzy 1944–1991* (The People in the Government, 1944–1991) (Warsaw 1991). G. LONGWORTH, *The Making of Eastern Europe* (London 1991). I. PRIZEL and A. MICHTA, eds., *Polish Foreign Policy Reconsidered: The Challenges of Independence* (London 1995). W. ROSZKOWSKI, *Historia Polski, 1914–1991* (The History of Poland: 1914–1991) (Warsaw 1995). J. POPIELUSZKO, *The Way of My Cross: Masses at Warsaw* (Chicago 1986).

[ZYGMUNT ZIELINSKI]

PONTIFICAL ACADEMIES

Pontifical academies are loose networks of scholars and representatives of various professions organized by the Holy See for the advancement of the arts, science, and culture. Each has its own by-laws and, in most cases, the members are appointed by the Roman pontiff. The *Annuario Pontificio* for the year 2000 lists the following pontifical academies: (1) the Pontifical Academy of Sciences; (2) the Pontifical Academy of Social Science; (3) the Pontifical Academy for Life; (4) the Pontifical Academy of St. Thomas Aquinas (formerly the Pontifical Academy of St. Thomas and Catholic Doctrine, founded in October, 1879); (5) the Pontifical Academy of Theology; (6) the Pontifical Academy of Our Lady Immaculate, founded in 1835; (7) the Pontifical International Marian Academy, founded in 1946; (8) the Distinguished Pontifical Academy of Arts and Letters of the Pantheon Virtuosi, founded in 1543; (9) the Pontifical Roman Academy of Archeology, founded in 1810; and (10) the Pontifical Academy of the "Cult of the Martyrs," founded in 1879. There have been other pontifical academies in the course of the centuries. Those listed here represent true pontifical academies. Additionally, institutions such as the Pontifical Ecclesiastical Academy, formerly known as the Academy of Noble Ecclesiastics, founded in 1701, enjoy the prerogatives of a pontifical academy, but are entrusted with special duties in service to the Church's diplomatic corps.

The most prominent pontifical academy is the Pontifical Academy of Science, the *senatus scientificus,* according to Pope Pius XI, dedicated to the mathematical, physical, and natural sciences. It attempts "to pay honor to pure science, wherever it is found, and to assure its freedom and to promote its research, which constitute the indispensable basis for progress in science." At its full complement the membership stands at 80, a number established by Pope John Paul II in 1986. This academy is directly responsible to the Holy Father, who appoints the members, and its expenses are met through the Patrimony of the Holy See. Members, regardless of religious confession, are drawn from different countries, and they are appointed for life. By reason of their office, the directors of the Vatican Observatory and its Astrophysical Laboratory and the prefects of the Vatican Library and the Secret Archives of the Vatican are appointed "Academicians *pro tempore.*"

The Pontifical Academy of Sciences has its roots in the Academy of the Lincei (*Academia Linceorum,* from its emblem, a lynx) which was founded in Rome in 1603 by Federico Cesi, Giovanni Heck, Francesco Stelluti and Anastasio de Filiis, all contemporaries and sometime rivals of Galileo. In 1847 Pope Pius IX reestablished the Academy as the Pontifical Academy of the New Lincei. Pope Pius XI renewed and reconstituted the Academy in 1936, and bestowed upon it its present name. The Academy's activities range from a traditional interest in pure research to a concern with the ethical and environmental responsibility of the scientific community. The premises of the Academy are in the Casina Pio IV, built in 1561, and it is there that members gather in plenary session.

The Pontifical Academy of Social Sciences was founded by Pope John Paul II on 1 January 1994, with the *motu proprio* called *Socialum scientiarum.* Its statutes indicate that its objective to promote "the study and progress of the social, economic, political and juridical sciences, and of thus offering the Church the elements which she can use in the study and development of her social doctrine." The academy is autonomous and at the same time, maintains a very close relationship with the Pontifical Council for Justice and Peace, with which it coordinates the planning of various initiatives. Its academicians are named by the pope and their number cannot be fewer than 20 nor more than 40. They are chosen because of their high level of competence without distinction to religious denomination. In its early years, the Academy centered its plenary sessions and workshops on three themes: work and employment, in 1996, 1997 and 1999; democracy in 1996, 1998, and 2000; and social dimensions of globalization in 2000 and 2001. The headquarters of the academy are in the Casina Pio IV, in the Vatican Gardens. The Pontifical Academy for the Social Sciences has its own foundation to provide for its financial needs.

With the *motu proprio* entitled *Vitae mysterium* of 11 February 1994, John Paul II instituted the Pontifical Academy for Life. Its primary objective is to study problems of bio-medicine and law, especially as they relate to the promotion and defense of life, in accord with Christian morality and the directives of the Church's magisterium. The Vitae Mysterium Foundation, instituted in October 1994, finances this academy which is linked to the Pontifical Council for Pastoral Assistance to Health Care Workers and various other dicasteries of the Roman Curia committed to the service of life. Seven-

ty members are named by the pope and represent different branches of the biomedical sciences. The academy's activities focus on issues related to the Human Genome Project and specifically on the identity, localization, heterogeneity, and the mutability of those genes which constitute the hereditary patrimony of humanity. Further, because of the substantial unity of the body with the spirit—*corpore et anima unus: una summa*—the human genome has not only a biological significance, but is the bearer of an anthropological dignity, which has its foundation in the spiritual soul which pervades it and vivifies it (cf. Discourse of His Holiness John Paul II to Members of the Academy, 24 February 1998).

The Pontifical Academy of St. Thomas took on renewed significance in view of Pope John Paul's encyclical *Fides et ratio* (1999), in which the pontiff made a sustained plea for the value of the Angelic Doctor's work among moderns (see especially no. 57). Similarly, *Fides et Ratio* (nos. 92–99) would have the Pontifical Academy of Theology assist in the promotion of the sacred sciences, but always in dialogue with and in light of contemporary culture.

The Pontifical Academy of Our Lady Immaculate grew out of a small circle of students at the Gregorian University in Rome and became recognized by the Sacred Congregation for Studies, as it was then called, in 1847. One of its traditions has been presenting a "floral homage" before the statue of Mary Immaculate in the Piazza di Spagna on 8 December. Pope John Paul II approved the new statutes for the Academy in 1988 and 1995. Another Marian academy, the Pontifical International Marian Academy, founded by Carlo Balić, O.F.M., in 1946, promotes historical studies related to the Virgin Mary. In this connection (and largely through Balić's own scholarship), the academy has helped sponsor the herculean effort to develop a critical edition of the works of John Duns Scotus. It was also charged with the organization of various Marian congresses throughout the world. Raised to the status of a pontifical academy by Pope John XXIII in 1959 through the *motu proprio* called *Maiora in dies,* the Academy enjoys a continued working relationship with the Friars Minor at the Antonianum in Rome.

Of the three remaining pontifical academies, the Academy of the Arts is the oldest, with a history stretching back to Pope Paul III in 1542. Its statutes were revised and approved by Pope John Paul II in 1995. The Academy seeks to support sculptors, writers, architects, film makers, musicians, poets, and painters. The Academy works cooperatively with the Pontifical Council for Culture, and its virtuosi are nominated by the Holy Father. The Pontifical Academy of Roman Archaeology (formerly the Academy of Roman Antiquities) was founded in 1810, becoming a pontifical academy in 1829 under Pius VIII. It seeks to promote the study of archaeology and the history of ancient and medieval art. The Cardinal Secretary of State is its protector. Finally, the Pontifical Academy of the Cult of the Martyrs was founded as the Collegium Cultorum Martyrum in 1879 and collaborates with the Congregation for Divine Worship and the Discipline of Sacraments. Its work involves liturgical studies, archeology, and hagiography. Its statutes were revised and approved in 1995. The Academy is historically based at the German College in Rome.

See Also: ANNUARIO PONTIFICO

Bibliography: *Annuario Pontificio per l'Anno 2000* (Vatican City: Libreria Editrice Vaticana, 2000), 1876–1893, 2018–2024. RÉGIS LADOUS, *Des Nobel au Vatican: La fondation de l'académie pontificale des sciences* (Paris: Cerf, 1994). MARINI-BETTELO and GIOVANNI BATISTA, *Activity of the Pontifical Academy of Sciences, 1936–1986* (Vatican City: Pontificio Academia Scientiarum, 1987); *Historical Aspects of the Pontifical Academy of Sciences,* 28 October 1986 (Vatican City: Pontificio Academia Scientiarum, 1986). ''Inter Munera Academiarum,'' *Acta Apostolicae Sedis* 91:9 (September 1999): 849–853.

[PATRICK J. HAYES]

PONTIFICAL BIBLICAL COMMISSION

This article reports on the significant activities of the Pontifical Biblical Commission (PBC) during the reign of Pope John Paul; in particular it concentrates on the document *The Interpretation of the Bible in the Church* that was issued in 1993.

In 1972 Pope Paul VI appointed the PBC, a group of scholars who were to discuss the use of Scripture in the writings on liberation theology. They met for the last time in 1977 without, however, publishing a statement on the subject. There was no plenary session in 1978 (nor for that matter in 1984 and 1990).

Themes from 1979 to 1993. In 1979 a second group of scholars was established with Bishop A.-L. Descamps again serving as secretary. After Descamps' death in October 1980, he was replaced as secretary by H. Cazelles in 1981. The theme of the 1979 plenary session was acculturation in Sacred Scripture itself. The majority of the discussion papers were published in revised form in *Fede e cultura alla luce della Bibbia—Foi et culture à la lumière de la Bible* (1981). The four successive sessions (1980, 1981, 1982, and 1983) were devoted to recent questions concerning christology, and they resulted in the publication of *Bible et christologie* (1984), consisting of two main parts: the official document of the Commission in Latin and French and nine discussion papers by individual members in the original languages.

Cazelles was again named secretary of the Commission's third group in 1984. Four sessions (1985, 1986, 1987, and 1988) investigated the relation between the local churches and the universal, unique People of God. This investigation led to the publication of the volume *Unité et diversité dans l'Église* (1989). The book contains the official French text of the Commission and twenty contributions by individual members in different languages. For the last session (1989) a new theme, the interpretation of the Bible in the Church, was raised, and a first discussion of it took place.

Biblical Interpretation. In 1990 A. Vanhoye was appointed secretary of the fourth group. In three sessions (1991, 1992, and 1993) the interpretation of the Bible in the Church was studied further and a document redacted. On 24 April 1993, during a solemn audience at the Vatican, a double anniversary was celebrated: the centenary of the encyclical *Providentissimus Deus* (Leo XIII, 1893) and the fiftieth anniversary of the encyclical *Divino afflante spiritu* (Pius XII, 1943). During the audience the Pontifical Biblical Commission submitted to Pope John Paul II its new document, *The Interpretation of the Bible in the Church.* In his address the pope explained why he had approved this text and wished a wide circulation of it. The original French text was translated into many languages and published. At a press conference on 18 March 1994, the president of the Commission, Joseph Cardinal Ratzinger, its secretary, Albert Vanhoye, and four members presented the text to the media and answered questions raised by the journalists.

In the document's introduction the Commission sought to alleviate the fear caused in some quarters by the scientific study of the bible by stressing the positive contributions of scientific investigation:

> Biblical studies have made great progress in the Catholic Church and the academic value of these studies has been acknowledged more and more in the scholarly world and among the faithful. This has greatly smoothed the path of ecumenical dialogue. The deepening of the Bible's influence upon theology has contributed to theological renewal. Interest in the Bible has grown among Catholics, with resultant progress in the Christian life. All those who have acquired a solid formation in this area consider it quite impossible to return to a pre-critical level of interpretation, a level which they now rightly judge to be quite inadequate. (no. 30)

The document raises several questions. Is the historical-critical method the only valid exegetical approach, and is this method the exclusive domain of specialists? Moreover, the historical-critical method is often attacked because of its so-called sterility; it is often said that doubt, if not unbelief, arises from it. What about new and seemingly more promising approaches? The Pontifical Biblical Commission was asked to reflect on this malaise. Could the Commission "indicate the paths most appropriate for arriving at an interpretation of the Bible as faithful to its character both human and divine?" (no. 32)

Structure of the Document. The Commission presented its considerations in four main parts. First, there is a discussion of the different methods and approaches: thirteen of them are analyzed and carefully evaluated (e.g., rhetorical analysis, the sociological approach, the liberationist approach, the feminist approach). Then, the document investigates the philosophical question of what hermeneutics actually involves, and it deals with the question of the meaning or meanings of inspired Scripture (the literal, spiritual, and fuller senses). In the third part the characteristics of a Catholic interpretation of the Bible are considered: what has exegesis done during the long tradition of the Church and how can the task of the exegete be defined today? The last part is concerned with the interpretation of Scripture in the life of the Church: how can the Bible be actualized? What kind of attention must be given to inculturation? What are the different uses of the Bible (in liturgy, in individual or communal reading, in pastoral ministry, and in ecumenism)? The first reactions from both scholars and religious leaders underline the importance of this document.

Throughout his pontificate Pope John Paul II emphasized that the results of biblical scholarship should be in service to the Church's integral mission of proclaiming the Word of God to the world today. (Address to Pontifical Biblical Commission, *Acta Apostolicae Sedis,* no. 77 [1985]: 972 ff.) He echoed this call in a 1989 address, where he spoke of the intimate connection of the task of biblical scholarship to the believing community. The goal of biblical scholarship, the pope explained, should be the transformation of the people of God, a deepening of the call to conversion, and the proclamation of the good news of salvation, ordered to the communion of all in God (*Acta Apostolicae Sedis,* no. 81 [1989]: 1224).

See Also: JOSEPH RATZINGER

Bibliography: Pontifical Biblical Commission, *Fede e cultura alla luce della Bibbia—Foi et culture à la lumière de la Bible,* Atti della sessione plenaria 1979, ed.J.D. BARTHÉLEMY (Turin 1981); *Bible et christologie* (Paris 1984); *Unité et diversité dans l'Église* (Vatican City 1989); *The Interpretation of the Bible in the Church.* (Address of Pope John Paul II and Document of the P.B.C.) (Vatican City 1993). J. A. FITZMYER, *Scripture and Christology: A Statement of the Biblical Commission with a Commentary* (New York 1986).

[J. LAMBRECHT/ EDS]

PONTIFICAL COUNCIL FOR CULTURE

In 1982 Pope John Paul II created the Pontifical Council for Culture and with a sense of symbolism signed the letter on the feast of the Ascension. This new body was to serve at the crossroads between faith and lived realities, as an organization of encounter and of research; it was to deepen "the relations of the Holy See with every manifestation of culture." Similar to other Vatican dicasteries involved with dialogue, this Council was intended to communicate *ad extra,* and especially with those places where the meanings and values of humanity are being formed. Its very existence was to witness to the desire of the Church to collaborate with people of culture everywhere.

Three principal factors lay behind this papal initiative. At the Second Vatican Council, *Gaudium et spes* devoted a substantial chapter to the topic of culture, noting that the concept had widened from an older meaning of conscious development and creativity to include various ways of life in society. Second, the pastoral relevance of different cultural contexts came to the fore during the seventies, especially through the 1975 call of Pope Paul VI for an in-depth "evangelization of cultures" (*Evangelii nutiandi*). Third, Pope John Paul II had shown a personal interest in the whole field of culture and had often spoken of it as the key to what makes us human and as a crucial dimension for the very future of humanity, most notably visiting UNESCO on 2 June 1980.

In the letter of foundation the pope expressed his vision thus: "The synthesis between culture and faith is not just a demand of culture but also of faith. A faith that does not become culture is a faith which has not been fully received, not thoroughly thought through, not faithfully lived out." Gradually the Pontifical Council entered into collaboration with international organizations and cultural institutions throughout the world. It organized many international conferences, such as a symposium on "Christianity and Culture in Europe" to prepare for the 1991 Synod of Bishops. It worked, in cooperation with other Vatican organizations, on a document on the presence of the Church in university culture. It is actively involved with Catholic Cultural Centers in many countries, seeking to be a channel of contact and communication between them.

In 1993 Pope John Paul II issued the *motu proprio* entitled *Inde a Pontificatus,* which merged the previous pontifical councils for culture and for dialogue with nonbelievers under the title of Pontifical Council for Culture. With this refoundation the aims of the Council are further clarified. It has two sections: (1.) faith and culture and

(2.) dialogue with cultures. Its aims are fourfold: to foster meeting places between the gospel and contemporary cultures; to help toward evangelizing cultures and inculturating the Gospel; to build up contacts with cultural institutions at the local level and to further intercultural dialogue; to promote dialogue with unbelievers and reflection on this issue.

The Council's publications include books arising from the various congresses organized over the years, and a quarterly review entitled, *Cultures and Faith.* Since its inception it has had only one president, Paul Cardinal Poupard.

[M. P. GALLAGHER]

PONTIFICAL COUNCILS

Operate on the fourth tier of the Holy See's governing structure. Pontifical councils have within their competence special functions in connection to ecclesial life that the pope deems to be of primary importance. As such, they carry out their duties in an official capacity in the pope's name and by his authority (CIC, c. 360). At the end of the twentieth century there are eleven pontifical councils, all of which fall under the regulations of *Pastor bonus,* the 1988 apostolic constitution of Pope John Paul II that reorganized the Roman Curia. These include the Pontifical Council for the Laity, the Pontifical Council for the Promotion of Christian Unity, the Pontifical Council for the Family, the Pontifical Council for Justice and Peace, the Pontifical Council "Cor Unum," the Pontifical Council for the Pastoral Care of Migrants and Itinerant People, the Pontifical Council for the Pastoral Assistance of Health Care Workers, the Pontifical Council for the Interpretation of Legislative Texts, the Pontifical Council for Inter-religious Dialogue, the Pontifical Council for Culture (which subsumed the Pontifical Council for Dialogue with Non-Believers in 1993), and the Pontifical Council for Social Communications.

Structures

All the pontifical councils are led by a cardinal or archbishop who takes title of the office of president (*Pastor bonus* I, a. 3, §§1). They are assisted typically by a secretary and undersecretary. Members are usually selected from the episcopate; consultors and professional staff are employed to assist in the work of each council. Lay participation is permitted on all councils, though clerics continue to dominate. Each dicastery may issue norms relative to its field of competence or may join with other curial bodies in issuing joint statements of mutual concern. The councils meet on a regular basis, sometimes

in plenary assembly. Membership on each of the councils is by term appointment or at the pleasure of the Holy Father. Many of the pontifical councils are housed in offices located in the St. Callixtus complex in Rome's Trastevere neighborhood.

History and Aims

The history of pontifical councils varies, though they all sink their roots in the twentieth century. Some, such as the Pontifical Council for the Laity and the Pontifical Council for the Promotion of Christian Unity, emerged directly from commissions established to participate in the Second Vatican Council. Other dicasteries were shaped by Pope Paul's apostolic constitution *Regimini Ecclesiae universae* (15 August 1967) which established norms for the implementation of the conciliar decrees during an "experimental period" in which the local churches would seek ways to adapt to the new situation created by the Second Vatican Council. Pope John Paul II has established several pontifical councils either as entirely new entities (Health Care, Legislative Texts, Culture) or by raising already established secretariats or commissions to the dignity of a pontifical council (Christian Unity, Family, Justice and Peace, Migrants and Itinerant Peoples, Social Communications). What follows here is a brief history of each of the pontifical councils, together with a short description of their fundamental purposes.

Pontifical Council for the Laity. The Pontifical Council for the Laity seeks to engage the lay apostolate on all levels through sustained interaction with international lay groups, national laity councils, and institutions participating in Catholic Action. It promotes the lay apostolate under the guidance of the relevant texts of the Second Vatican Council as well as the post-synodal apostolic exhortation *Christifideles laici* (1988). The council's history may be traced as far back as 1908 when Pope Pius X issued the apostolic constitution *Sapienti consilio.* That text reformed the Roman Curia and was later made part of the universal law of the Church (1917), making the Sacred Congregation of the Council competent for "the discipline of the secular clergy and of the Christian people." The importance of Catholic Action in the years preceding the Second Vatican Council provided the impetus for a more formal recognition of the lay apostolate in the council itself. The conciliar decree *Apostolicam actuositatem* proposed that a secretariat for the laity form part of the Roman Curia (AA 26), and this was formally constituted "ad experimentum" for five years by the *motu proprio Catholicam Christi ecclesiam* of Pope Paul VI (6 January 1967). Pope Paul gave both recognition and definition to this secretariat. With *Regimini,* the "Consilium de Laicis" was given general and particular norms, the latter of which were altered with only minor changes in *Pastor bonus*. Nearly ten years after the creation of the "Consilium de Laicis," Paul VI's *motu proprio Apostolatus peragendi* (10 December 1976) further solidified this dicastery by making it a pontifical council. The current council comprises sections pertaining to youth, Catholic international organizations, and (in conjunction with the Congregation for the Clergy) new ecclesial ministries within parishes and other contexts, as well as emerging associations of the lay faithful.

Pontifical Council for the Promotion of Christian Unity. In 1966, after the council had ended, Pope Paul VI confirmed the Secretariat for Promoting Christian Unity as a permanent dicastery of the Holy See. In *Pastor bonus* Pope John Paul II changed the secretariat into the Pontifical Council for Promoting Christian Unity (effective 1 March 1989). The council exercises a double role. First of all, it is entrusted with the promotion, within the Catholic Church, of an authentic ecumenical spirit according to the conciliar decree *Unitatis redintegratio.* It was for this purpose that an Ecumenical Directory was published in 1967–70 and a revised edition issued in 1993 entitled "Directory for the Application of Principles and Norms on Ecumenism." The council also aims to develop dialogue and collaboration with other churches and world communions. Since its creation, it has established a cordial cooperation with the World Council of Churches; twelve Catholic theologians have been members of the Faith and Order Commission, the theological department of the WCC. The work of this dicastery is divided between an Eastern section, dealing with Orthodox churches of Byzantine tradition and the Oriental Orthodox Churches (Coptic, Syrian, Armenian, Ethiopian, and Malankara), as well as the Assyrian Church of the East; and a Western section, dealing with the different churches and ecclesial communities of the West and the World Council of Churches. This dicastery also maintains the Commission for Religious Relations with the Jews that Pope Paul VI established on 22 October 1974. Although it is an autonomous unit, it is largely staffed by members of the pontifical council.

Pontifical Council for the Family. This dicastery was instituted by John Paul II with the *motu proprio Familia a Deo instituta* (9 May 1981), replacing the Committee for the Family created by Paul VI in 1973. The committee had remained closely linked to the "Consilium de Laicis" and was governed by *Catholicam Christi Ecclesiam.* There are still links between the two pontifical councils, such as the presence of the two secretaries in each of the presidential committees. The council is responsible for the promotion of the pastoral ministry of and apostolate to the family, assisting in all dimensions of family life and encompassing such issues as responsi-

ble procreation, theology and catechesis of the family, marital and family spirituality, the rights of the family and the child, lay formation, and marriage preparation courses. Due to the influence that issues such as pornography, prostitution, and drugs can have on the family, these topics also fall under the council's purview.

Pontifical Council for Justice and Peace. Pope Paul VI created the Pontifical Commission "Iustitia et Pax" in 1967 as an experiment (together with the Pontifical Council for the Laity) but made it a definitive dicastery of the Holy See with the *motu proprio Iustitiam et pacem* (1976). It became a pontifical council with *Pastor bonus.* The council's raison d'etre is to promote peace and justice in the world according to the gospel and the social doctrine of the Church. It is principally concerned with labor and human rights and frequently collaborates with other organizations, not necessarily affiliated with the Church, who share common goals.

Pontifical Council "Cor Unum." The Pontifical Council "Cor Unum" was created by Paul VI who described it, in his *lettera autografa* (hand-written letter) *Amoris officio* (15 July 1971), as a dicastery at the level of the universal Church "for human and Christian promotion." The council is concerned with understanding the demands of solidarity and development and enacting them according to the principles of the gospel. The council promotes the catechesis of charity and stimulates the faithful to bear witness to it, coordinates initiatives of those Catholic institutions that help the less fortunate, helps promote a more just distribution of aid in times of disasters, and acts as a go-between with Catholic charitable and humanitarian organizations. Half of the council's members are bishops and representatives from developing countries, while the other half represent Catholic aid organizations. "Cor Unum" is also responsible for the Holy Father's charitable donations. From the World Council of Churches (Unit IV), the council receives information on aid programs for those countries that have been struck by natural calamities, ethnic conflicts, or civil wars. In 1984, Pope John Paul established the John Paul II Foundation for the Sahel, providing drought relief and and programs against desertification. In 1992, the Holy Father also founded the Populorum Progressio Foundation, which is at the service of indigenous, racially mixed, Afro-American, and campesinos of Latin America and the Caribbean.

Pontifical Council for the Pastoral Care of Migrants and Itinerant Peoples. Pope Pius XII drew attention in 1952 to a pressing pastoral need that had been fomenting throughout the aftermath of the Second World War, namely, the plight of the emigrant. The apostolic constitution *Exsul familia* (1952) established both the Superior Council for Emigration and the Work of the Apostleship of the Sea within the Consistorial Congregation, now known as the Congregation for Bishops. Six years later Pope Pius broadened the scope of the congregation's duties to include air travelers through an institution called ''Opera dell'Apostolatus Coeli o Aeris.'' In 1969, at the request of the Congregation for Bishops, Paul VI updated his predecessor's creations and the following year established a single entity with his *motu proprio Apostolicae caritatis* (19 March 1970), calling it the Pontifical Commission for the Spiritual Care of Migrants and Travelers. This commission embraced all those pastoral ministries regarding human mobility: migrants, exiles, refugees, seafarers, air travel personnel and passengers, nomads, pilgrims, and tourists. To these were later added gypsies and ''circus people.'' With *Pastor bonus* the commission was raised to the dignity of a pontifical council.

Pontifical Council for Pastoral Assistance to Health Care Workers. With the *motu proprio Dolentium hominum* (11 February 1985), John Paul II instituted the Pontifical Commission for the Pastoral Assistance to Health Care Workers, which with *Pastor bonus* became a pontifical council. It stimulates and promotes the work of formation, study, and action carried out by the diverse international Catholic organizations in the health care field. The council coordinates the activities of different dicasteries of the Roman Curia as they relate to the health care sector and its problems. It spreads, explains, and defends the teachings of the Church on health issues and favors its involvement in health care practice. It also maintains contacts with the local Churches and especially with bishops' commissions related to health care.

Pontifical Council for the Interpretation of Legislative Texts. With his *motu proprio Cum iuris canonici* (15 September 1917), Pope Benedict XV inaugurated a pontifical commission for the authentic interpretation of the Code of Canon Law, promulgated the previous May. At the time of the Second Vatican Council the commission became an instrument by which the council's legislation was prepared. In the post-conciliar era, the commission was responsible for delivering authentic interpretations of the conciliar texts as well as working toward a revised code of canons in light of the new legislation. That code was approved by Pope John Paul II in 1983. He later charged the commission with the task of interpreting the new code through his *motu proprio Recognito iuris canonici codice* (2 January 1984). *Pastor bonus* raised the commission to the dignity of a pontifical council, and placed it council in charge of all authentic interpretations of both singular and inter-dicastoral documents.

Pontifical Council for Culture. Dating back to the Second Vatican Council, this pontifical council's roots are grounded in *Gaudium et spes* 53–62. It did not emerge as a distinct entity until John Paul II founded it in 1982 (personal letter to the Cardinal Secretary of State, 20 May 1982). In his *motu proprio Inde a Pontificatus* (25 March 1993), John Paul II merged the Pontifical Council for Dialogue with Non-Believers (founded in 1965 by Paul VI) with the Pontifical Council for Culture. The council's main tasks are to bring the gospel into diverse cultures and seek ways to enliven those in the sciences, letters, and arts through the Church's sustained interest in their work ''in the service of truth, goodness, and beauty.'' As such, this dicastery coordinates the activities of the pontifical academies and cooperates on a regular basis with the Pontifical Commission for the Cultural Heritage of the Church.

Pontifical Council for Social Communications. This dicastery has undergone a number of incarnations since the secretariat of state of Pope Pius XII first ordered that a Pontifical Commission for the Study and Ecclesiastical Evaluation of Films on Religious or Moral Subjects be established (30 January 1948, by letter, protocol no. 153.561). On 17 September 1948, Pius XII approved the statutes of this new office and renamed it the Pontifical Commission for Educational and Religious Films, later to become the Pontifical Commission for Cinema, the statutes of which were approved 1 January 1952. After consultation with bishops and Catholic film organizations, the name of the commission was once more changed, this time to the Pontifical Commission for the Cinema, Radio, and Television (31 December 1954). Pope John XXIII entrusted the commission with developing the Vatican Film Library. Pope John also added the responsibility of coordinating the communications media needed for the Second Vatican Council. Pope Paul VI transformed it into the Pontifical Commission for Social Communications (*motu proprio In fructibus multis,* 2 April 1964). It was responsible for dealing with the all the problems raised by cinema, radio, television, and the daily and periodical press in relation to the interests of the Catholic religion. With *Pastor bonus,* the commission became a pontifical council.

See Also: CHRISTIFIDELES LAICI

Bibliography: *Annuario Pontificio: 2000* (Rome: Libreria Editrice Vaticana, 2000). THOMAS J. REESE, *Inside the Vatican: The Politics and Organization of the Catholic Church* (Cambridge: Harvard University Press, 1996). *Canon Law Digest,* vols. 5–8.

[PATRICK HAYES]

POPIEŁUSZKO, JERZY

Priest, Polish patriot; b. 14 September 1947, Okopy, Poland; d. 20 October 1984, Warsaw, Poland. Jerzy was

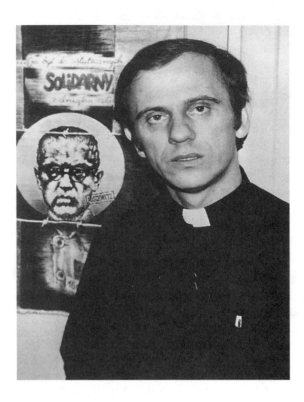

Jerzy Popiełuszko. (Catholic News Service.)

second youngest of the five children born to Marianna and Wladyslaw Popiełusko. When Jerzy was baptized in the parish church in Suchowola his peasant parents named him Alfons, after his godfather, and it was only later when he entered the seminary in Warsaw that he adopted the name Jerzy. After he was ordained a priest by Cardinal Stefan Wyszyński, 28 May 1972, he ministered in a number of parishes on the outskirts of Warsaw. In addition to parish duties and despite his own fragile health Fr. Popiełuszko served as a chaplain to nurses, medical students, and retired medical personnel in Warsaw. In the summer of 1980 he visited relatives in America, returning to Poland at the end of July in time to join the formation of the Solidarity movement in Gdansk in August, 1980. When government declared martial law in December, 1981, Popiełuszko visited prisoners and organized support for their families. About the same time his ''patriotic sermons'' in the parish church of St Stanislaw Kostka in the Zoliborz district of Warsaw drew large crowds and attracted the attention of Communist authorities. Popiełuszko expounded the moral and spiritual dimension of the Solidarity cause, underlining the need for both nonviolence and resistance. The government sought to silence him by harassment and intimidation. In July 1984, Popiełuszko was in indicted on the charge of ''abusing freedom of conscience and religion to the detri-

ment of the Polish People's Republic.'' During the night of 19 October, members of the security police abducted Fr. Popiełuszko, savagely beat him, weighted his body with stones, and threw him into a reservoir near Wloclawek. To save face the government launched an investigation. Four members of the security policy confessed the crime and led investigators to Fr. Popiełuzko's body. He is buried in the churchyard of St Stanislaw Kostka.

Bibliography: GRAZYNA SIKORSKA, *Jerzy Popiełuszko: A Martyr for the Truth* (Grand Rapids, Mich.: Eerdmans, 1985).

[EDITORS]

POUPARD, PAUL

Cardinal, president of Pontifical Council for Culture; b. 30 August 1930, Bouzillé, France. Poupard started his ecclesiastical studies at the minor seminary of Beaupréau. Later he went to the University Seminary of Angers, and finally attended the Ecole des Hautes Etudes at the Sorbonne, Paris, where he earned doctorates in theology and history. The subject of his dissertation was the relation between reason and faith and Church and state. After ordination to the priesthood on 18 December 1954, he taught for four years at Mongazon School in Paris and spent one year was an adjunct at the National Scientific Research Center. From 1959 to 1971 Fr. Poupard worked in the French section of the Vatican Secretariat of State and served as chaplain of the Institute San Domenico in Rome. In 1972, Msgr. Poupard returned to Paris as rector of the Institute Catholique, a position he occupied until 1980. During these years he was also vice-president of the Society of French Ecclesiastical History and was awarded the Cardinal Grente grand prize of the Academie Française.

On 2 February 1979, Pope John Paul II elected Msgr. Poupard titular bishop of Usula and appointed him auxiliary of Paris. He was promoted to archbishop and appointed pro-president of the Vatican Secretariat for Non-Believers the following year. In 1982, he was appointed to the council of presidency and president of the executive committee of the Pontifical Council for Culture. He was one of the overseers of the commission that reopened the case of Galileo Galilei, and in 1992 presented the commission's findings at a meeting of the Pontifical Academy of Sciences.

John Paul II created Archbishop Poupard cardinal deacon of S. Eugenio in the consistory of 25 May 1985. Two days later, he was named president of the Secretariat for Non-Believers. The pope transferred him to the presidency of the Pontifical Council for Culture in 1988; the council was merged with the Pontifical Council for Dialogue with Non-Believers in 1993, and cardinal Poupard continued as its president. In 1996, after the mandatory decade as a cardinal deacon, he opted for the order of priests and the title of S. Prassede.

Cardinal Poupard has participated in eleven assemblies of the Synod of Bishops and was a president delegate of the second special assembly for Europe (1999). He has frequently represented the pope as his special envoy in France. Some of his writings stemming from his work on the Pontifical Council for Culture have been translated into English, including *Galileo Galilei: Toward a Resolution of 350 Years of Debate: 1633–1983* (ed.; Pittsburgh, 1987), *The Church and Culture: Challenge and Confrontation: Inculturation and Evangelization* (St. Louis, 1994), and *Science in the Context of Human Culture* (2 vols.; Vatican City, 1994–1997).

[SALVADOR MIRANDA]

Paul Cardinal Poupard with Pope John Paul II. (©Grzegorz Galazka/CORBIS)

PUEBLA

The Third General Conference of the Latin American Episcopate (CELAM III), took place in Puebla, Mexico, in January 1979. The meeting, originally intended to mark the tenth anniversary of CELAM II at Medellín, had to be postponed because of the deaths of Pope Paul VI and Pope John Paul I. Paul VI's apostolic exhortation *Evangelii nuntiandi* provided the theological background. The presence of John Paul II, especially his remarks in three major homilies, set the tone.

Meeting Overview. The CELAM Secretariat, strongly influenced by Bishop Alphonso Lopez Trujillo, prepared a preliminary document which concentrated on the problem of secularization and the role of the Church in Latin America's transition from a rural-agrarian society to an urban-industrial society. At the outset divisions emerged among the voting bishops and non-voting participants. Many felt that the preliminary document was a betrayal of the program established at Medellín. Gradually a consensus emerged. CELAM president, Cardinal Aloisio Lorsheider of Brazil was instrumental in bringing the perspective of the meeting closer to the social analysis, methodology, and human rights concerns of Medellín. Unofficial *periti*, mainly Latin American liberation theologians, also influenced the process leading to the final document.

The bishops recognized that the social, economic, and political problems of 1968, not only remained, but had become more serious. Secularization was not the principal obstacle to spreading the gospel. Evangelization in Latin America meant that the Church had to address once again the problems of poverty, structural injustice

and social sin. Once this situation was faced, the discussions took on more of a liberationist perspective. The final document, to some degree, reflects this perspective, "... a cry is rising to heaven, growing louder and more alarming all the time. It is the cry of a suffering people who demand justice, freedom and respect for the basic rights of human beings and peoples" (par. 87).

Final Document. The final document is divided into five parts: Pastoral Overview of the Reality That is Latin America; God's Saving Plan for Latin America; Evangelization in the Latin American Church; Communion and Participation; A Missionary Church Serving Evangelization in Latin America; Under the Dynamism of the Spirit: Pastoral Options. The conference's view of Jesus is significant for its attempt to hold a middle ground within the contemporary Latin American theological context. It lamented the attempt to distort the message of Jesus and use it for ideological purposes. "That can be done in one of two ways: either by turning him into a politician, a leader, a revolutionary, or a simple prophet on the one hand; or on the other hand, by restricting him, the Lord of history, to the merely private realm" (par 178).

Two dominant themes emerged: "Communion and Participation" and "A Preferential Option for the Poor" On the one hand the central motif of communion and participation appeared to try to replace liberation as the dominant theological message. The preferential option for the poor, however, recalled and reinforced the message of liberation. "We affirm the need for conversion on the part of the whole Church to a preferential option for the poor, an option aimed at their integral liberation" (par. 1134). The text continues, "The vast majority of our fellow humans continue to live in a situation of poverty and even wretchedness that has grown more acute" (par

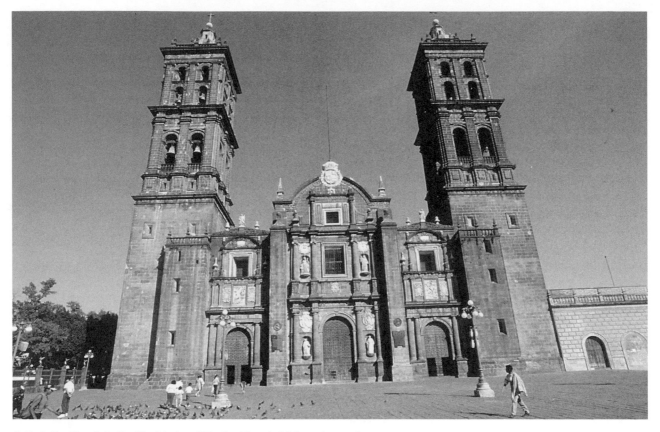

A Catholic Church in Puebla, Mexico. (Wernher Krutein/Liaison Agency.)

1135). "Hence service to the poor is the privileged, though not exclusive, gauge of our following of Christ" (par. 1145).

In spite of some repetition and contrast, the final document clearly understands evangelization as liberating from personal and social sin and as fostering communion and participation both in the Church and in society at large. CELAM III endorsed a centrist position but further committed the Church to social pastoral planning, solidarity with basic Christian communities and defense of the poor.

See Also: OPTION FOR THE POOR, ALFONSO LOPEZ TRUJILLO

Bibliography: CELAM III, *La Evangelizacion en el Presente y en el Futuro de America Latina: Puebla, Documento Aprobado* (Mexico 1979); J. EAGLESON and P. SCHARPER, eds., *Puebla and Beyond: Documentation and Commentary,* translated by J. DRURY (Maryknoll 1979) (References in text to paragraph numbers are the same in Spanish and English versions). P. BERRYMAN, "What Happened at Puebla," *Churches and Politics in Latin America,* ed. D. H LEVINE (Beverly Hills, Calif. 1979). E. DUSSEL, *The History of the Church in Latin America: Colonialism to Liberation,* translated by A. NEELY (Grand Rapids 1981). G. GUTIERREZ, *The Power of the Poor in History* (Maryknoll 1983). P. LERNOUX, *Cry of the People* (New York 1980). G. MACEOIN, *Puebla, a Church Being Born* (New York 1980).

[J. P. HOGAN]

RAHNER, KARL

German theologian; b. Freiburg im Breisgau, Germany, 5 March 1904; d. Innsbruck, Austria, 30 March 1984. One of seven children of Karl Rahner, Gymnasium Professor, and Luise Trescher. After concluding his secondary education he entered the Society of Jesus' novitiate at Feldkirch in Vorarlberg, Austria, on 20 April 1922, three years after his brother Hugo. During his philosophical studies from 1924 to 1927, first at Feldkirch, then at Pullach near Munich, he was influenced especially by Joseph Maréchal's (1878–1944) Thomistic response to the thought of Immanuel Kant. After teaching Latin at the Feldkirch Novitiate, where Alfred Delp was one of his students, Rahner studied theology at Valkenburg in the Netherlands (1929–33). There his earlier reading of Christian spirituality was deepened through study of the Apostolic Fathers, the patristic period, and medieval thinkers such as Bonaventure. He was ordained a priest on 26 July 1932, and pursued his Jesuit tertianship at Saint Andrea in Carinthia, Austria (1933–34).

Early Foundations. Intended by his Jesuit superiors to be a professor of the history of philosophy, Rahner was sent to the University of Freiburg im Breisgau to prepare a doctorate. He attended Martin Heidegger's seminars with other Catholic students such as Max Müller, Gustav Siewerth, Bernard Welte, and Johannes B. Lotz. When his doctoral director, Martin Honecker, rejected his interpretation of Saint Thomas' epistemology, Rahner returned to Innsbruck. In the course of the academic year 1936–37, he was able to satisfy the doctoral and postdoctoral requirements for teaching in the University's faculty of theology and began to lecture the following year. After the Nazis abolished the theology faculty (July 1938) and the Jesuit college (October 1939), Rahner moved to Vienna to work under Karl Rudolph at the Pastoral Institute. For five years he served as a consultant there, also offering courses and occasional lectures. In the final year of World War II he became a pastor at Mariakirchen in Lower Bavaria.

For three years after the war he taught dogmatic theology at Berchmanskolleg in Pullach and then, in August 1948, returned to Innsbruck's faculty of theology, which had just been reopened. Named an *Ordinarius* the following summer, he remained at Innsbruck through the winter semester of 1964, teaching a cycle of courses on the doctrines of creation and original sin; grace and justification; faith, hope and charity; and the Sacraments of Penance, Anointing of the Sick, and Orders. In the early 1950s his doctoral students included Adolf Darlap, Walter Kern, Herbert Vorgrimler, and Johann Baptist Metz.

In these foundational years of Rahner's theological career his interests ranged from the primary philosophical studies elaborated in his doctoral dissertation and his Salzburg lectures on the philosophy of religion, through classic early publications on prayer and the Christian life, to highly technical re-examinations of questions long considered settled by the neo-scholastic theology that dominated most of Catholic thought at the time, and certainly its major official pronouncements. His Freiburg thesis *Geist in Welt* (1939) sought a contemporary retrieval of the Thomistic insight into sense experience as the enduring ground for human knowledge. Heidegger's question of Being also helped to guide his understanding of religion in its historical dependence on the transcendent self-disclosure of a personal God (*Hörer des Wortes* 1941). His first years in Innsbruck saw the publication of the meditations collected in *Encounters with Silence* (1938) and his Lenten sermons in postwar Munich appeared in an eloquent book *On Prayer* (1949).

But it was his probing analyses of human existence in a world permeated by divine grace that gave Rahner's early writings their explosive force. Emphasizing the dy-

Karl Rahner. (UPI/Corbis-Bettmann. Reproduced by permission.)

namics of knowledge and freedom yet guided most deeply by the mystery of God's own gift of self, he reconceived the terms of the relationship between nature and grace, took the conciliar definitions as a starting point rather than an end for christological reflection, and renewed ecclesiology by examining the Church in its origin, its sacramental actualization, and its pastoral practice. When his early theological essays were gathered in the first three volumes of the *Schriften zur Theologie* in 1954, 1955, and 1956 (English translation, *Theological Investigations*), it was clear that a wholly original dialectical mind had appeared on the Catholic scene. During this period his prodigious editorial labors began as well, and he was responsible for four editions of Denzinger's *Enchiridion Symbolorum* (1952–57) and seven editions of *Der Glaube der Kirche in den Urkunden der Lehrverkündigung* (1948–65).

Programmatic Years. A second, programmatic phase coincided roughly with Rahner's work as coeditor for the second edition of *Lexikon für Theologie und Kirche* (1957–65) and his contributions to the preparation and course of the Second Vatican Council. Continuing to teach at Innsbruck, he also lectured extensively, undertook new editorial responsibilities, and for a year (1962–63) was subject to a preliminary censorship regulation from Rome. When the University of Munich in 1963 invited him to become Romano Guardini's successor in the Chair of Christian World View and Philosophy of Religion, he received permission from his Order to accept the call and began teaching in Munich in the summer semester of 1964. In that year also, a monumental two-volume Festschrift, *Gott in Welt,* appeared in honor of his sixtieth birthday.

In view of urgent contemporary questions, Rahner had previously sought to re-appropriate Catholic tradition through a dialectical discussion with scholastic theology and the dogmatic tradition. He probed the implication of these studies and began to write more programmatically on the correlation between theology and anthropology within the historical process. In a world that is always and everywhere invited to union with God (the ''supernatural existential,'') he argued, responsible theology must conduct a continuing transcendental reflection on the structural conditions of possibility for salvation. In *Schriften IV* (1960) he published seminal essays on mystery, the Incarnation, the theology of symbol, and the hermeneutics of eschatological assertions. An analogy of transcendence unifies these essays materially, envisaging history as a response to the Holy Mystery that draws the world toward eternity through self-communication in Word and Spirit. In the essays of *Schriften V* (1962), the analogy was significantly broadened by his discussion of evolutionary science, world religions, and utopian views of the future. *Schriften VI* (1966) continued his effort to express the Church's new self-understanding in a secularized, pluralistic world.

In these same years Rahner published major essays in pastoral theology (*Sendung und Gnade* 1959; English translation, *Mission and Grace* 1963) and gathered a new collection of essays in spirituality (*Schriften VII* 1967). In 1962 he helped to draft a plan for the *Handbuch der Pastoraltheologie,* which subsequently appeared in five volumes (1964–72) with Rahner as one of its editors. With Heinrich Schlier he conceived the series of *Questiones Disputatae* (1958 ff.) in which appeared some of his own most original contributions on the inspiration of Scripture, the theology of death, the prophetic mission of the Church, the relation between episcopacy and papal primacy, and the renewal of the diaconate. Rahner was a founding member of the editorial committee that planned *Concilium,* chaired its section on pastoral theology, and with Edward Schillebeeckx edited its first issue in 1965. With Adolf Darlap he planned *Sacramentum Mundi* and then supervised its German edition (4 v. 1967–69).

Late Development. When it appeared that Rahner would be unable to direct doctoral students in theology at Munich and also that there were hopes for collaborating on serious reform of theological education elsewhere, he accepted the University of Münster's invitation to become Ordinary Professor of Dogmatics and the History of Dogma and moved to the Westphalian capital in the summer semester of 1967. His years at Münster were fruitful ones during which he continued to reflect on Roman Catholicism's efforts to appropriate Vatican II and developed his response to critics who found his own theological anthropology reductionistic (Hans Urs von Balthasar) or politically impractical (Johann Baptist Metz). Reflecting on the historical concreteness of Christianity and its social responsibility, three further volumes of the *Schriften* (1967, 1970, 1972) offer important insights on theology's place in the human search for meaning; careful situational analysis as a requirement for religious authenticity; the need for a contemporary introduction (mystagogy) to the experience of God; a new understanding of Jesus as humanity's way to God (Christology from below); and reform of the Church as a declericalized, more democratic and socially critical community of service to the world.

Retiring to Munich in 1971, Rahner first lived at the Jesuit writers' residence near Nymphenburg. His major project there was the preparation of his *Grundkurs* or ''Introduction to the Idea of Christianity'' (1976; English translation, *Foundations of Christian Faith* 1978). Though not an adequate synthesis of his thought, the book does present his typical approach to central topics of Christian doctrine. In the years immediately before it, he published several briefer works on Church reform (1972) and on an ecumenical understanding of Church office (1974), as well as *Schriften XI* (1973), which gathers his early studies on the practice and theology of penance, and Schriften XII (1975), which centers on the doctrine of the Holy Spirit. Having participated in the first planning of *Mysterium Salutis* (5 v. 1965–76), he continued to contribute major articles to that new, historically conceived dogmatic theology.

Final Dialectic. After moving to the Berchmanskolleg in Munich and living there for several years, Rahner returned again to Innsbruck and made it his final residence (1981–84). Between 1976 and 1984 he lectured and wrote vigorously, publishing four more volumes of the *Schriften* (v. XII–XVI: 1978, 1980, 1983, 1984); a new edition of his *Dictionary of Theology* (1976); moving essays on prayer (1977), love of neighbor and love of Jesus (1981, 1982); and a dialogical apology for contemporary faith, co-authored with Karl-Heinz Weger (1979). He was also represented by several anthologies, one of which, *The Practice of Faith* (1982), also serves well as a general introduction to his thought. He continued his editorial involvements and, fortunately, allowed himself a new candor in his autobiographical reflections.

Although his final years are remarkably consistent with his previous career, significant developments nevertheless do occur in his consolidation of a thoroughly historical Christology; in his proposal for a "universal pneumatology" that might precede Christology in the future; in his arguments for a truly world church and his pleas for ecumenical seriousness; in a series of moral essays on the virtues required of late twentieth-century Christians. Throughout the writings of this last phase, Rahner noted the deepening relativism and skepticism in European culture and attempted to address it. "The old schoolmaster," as he styled himself, also became disturbingly frank about the climate of the Catholic Church, which he had served all his life and would serve to the end.

Systematic theologian though he was, Rahner's thought may be better characterized as a lifelong meditation on the correlation between human experience and God's self-communication. Because of his insistence that theology analyze the conditions of possibility for divine salvific action, he is most often described as a transcendental theologian. Even from the beginning, however, his method required historical research and reflection, since the dynamics of grace always unfold in an unfinished, temporal world where servitude and suffering are all too obvious. In fact, it may be even more exact to see Rahner as a Catholic dialectical theologian. His career presents a personal response to the religious issues of his day and an enduring effort to conceive human history as destined for an eternal communion with God that can only be achieved through the course of time. Thus, a concrete dialectic of transcendence in history characterized his life as well as his thought and influence.

Bibliography: The Theology Department at the University of Innsbruck in Austria maintains the collection of Rahner's manuscripts and papers at the Karl Rahner Archive. For a complete, chronological listing of Rahner's publications *see:* R. BLEISTEIN, ed., *Bibliographie Karl Rahner 1969–1974* (Freiburg 1974). R. BLEISTEIN and E. KLINGER, eds., *Bibliographie Karl Rahner 1924–1969* (Freiburg 1969). A. E. CARR, "Karl Rahner," in D. G. PEERMAN and M. E. MARTY, eds., *A Handbook of Christian Theologians* (Nashville 1984): 519–542. W. V. DYCH, *Karl Rahner* (Collegeville, Minn. 1992). H. D. EGAN, *Karl Rahner: The Mystic of Everyday Life* (New York 1998). P. IMHOF and E. MEUSER, "Bibliographie Karl Rahner 1979–1984," in E. KLINGER and K. WITTSTADT, eds., *Glaube im Prozess* (Freiburg 1984): 854–871. P. IMHOF and H. TREZIAK, "Bibliographie Karl Rahner 1974–1979," in H. VORGRIMLER, ed.,*Wagnis Theologie* (Freiburg 1979): 579–597.L. J. O'DONOVAN, ed., *A World of Grace: An Introduction to the Themes and Foundations of Karl Rahner's Theology* (New York 1980). C. D. PEDLEY, "An English Biographical Aid to Karl Rahner," *Heythrop Journal* 15 (1984): 319–365. H. VORGRIMLER, *Understanding Karl Rahner: An Introduction to His Life and Thought* (New York 1986).

[L. J. O'DONOVAN]

Joseph Cardinal Ratzinger. (Catholic News Service.)

RATZINGER, JOSEPH

Cardinal, Prefect of the Vatican Congregation for the Doctrine of the Faith and theologian; b. Marktl am Inn, Germany, 16 April 1927.

Joseph Ratzinger, the youngest of three children born to Joseph and Maria Ratzinger, grew up in rural Bavaria in a period of great political chaos for Germany as the Weimar Republic was in decline and the Nazis were rising to power. He began his education at the primary school in the village of Aschau. From there he went on to the gymnasium in the town of Traunstein. In 1939 as Europe was moving into the opening phase of World War II, Ratzinger began seminary studies in Traunstein, but in 1943, he was called to service. At the end of the war he found himself in an American prisoner-of-war camp near the city of Ulm.

After his release from the camp he studied philosophy in the seminary at Freising and theology at the University of Munich. During these years Ratzinger became familiar with the work of a number of Roman Catholic authors whose writings would have a lasting effect in the development of his personal theological vision. These included especially Michael Schmaus, Romano Guardini, Joseph Pieper, Odo Casel, and Henri de Lubac. For the youthful student, these authors opened new worlds such as the history of doctrine, the significance of humanism, the possibility of richer interpretations of Scholasticism than that found in the dominant form of neo-Thomism, and the deeper meaning of the reform of the liturgy. Two books of De Lubac, *Catholicism* and *Corpus Mysticum,* opened insights into the mystery of the Church that would eventually help Ratzinger shape his own ecclesiology. In the summer of 1951 he was ordained to the priesthood by Cardinal Faulhaber in the cathedral of Freising.

In the year prior to his ordination, Ratzinger worked on a study of St. Augustine's ecclesiology, (*People and House of God in Augustine's Doctrine of the Church*) that was later accepted as his dissertation for the doctoral degree in theology. In working on this project, he came under the influence of Gottlieb Söhngen who was well-known for his interest in Augustinian theology. After about a year of pastoral ministry, Ratzinger was assigned to lecture on theology in the seminary at Freising, while completing studies for the doctorate in theology, awarded him in 1953.

During his time as lecturer at the seminary at Freising, Ratzinger began working on his second major historical study, again with the encouragement of Söhngen. This took the form of a study of a medieval theologian, St. Bonaventure. This research was completed in the summer of 1955 and the draft corrected in 1956 and 1957. It was published in 1959 under the title: *The Theology of History in St. Bonaventure.* Within a year of the completion of this study Ratzinger was appointed as a lecturer at the University of Munich and as professor of fundamental theology and dogma at the College of Philosophy and Theology in Freising.

In spring 1959 Ratzinger began lecturing as ordinary professor of fundamental theology at the University of Bonn. His courses included topics such as revelation, basic questions in the philosophy of religion, and ecclesiology. During his years at Bonn, he came to know Cardinal Frings of Cologne who at that time was a member of the Central Preparatory Commission for Vatican Council II. Ratzinger accompanied the cardinal to Rome as a theological adviser and was eventually named a *peritus* of the Council.

In 1963 he moved to the University of Münster to take over the chair of dogmatic theology. His work at the Council continued even as he developed his courses in theology at the university. But by the summer of 1966 he had moved to Tübingen and joined the Catholic theological faculty there, and was present in the late 1960s when a Marxist movement on the campus led to a revolt that shook the university. During his time at Tübingen he was able to write a commentary on the Apostles' Creed, published in English with the title *Introduction to Christianity* (1969).

In 1969 he accepted an invitation from the recently opened university at Regensburg. At Regensburg, he joined in a collaborative project with Johann Auer, one of his colleagues on the faculty, that took the form of a nine-volume study of Christian doctrine entitled *Kleine Katholische Dogmatik.* Ratzinger's most important contribution to this project is the volume that treats the major themes of eschatology (*ET Eschatology, Death and Eternal Life* [1988]). During his time at Regensburg he was appointed to the newly established International Papal Theological Commission.

On the vigil of Pentecost in 1977 Ratzinger was ordained archbishop of Munich-Freising and soon thereafter was named cardinal. As he took up these new duties, he chose as his motto a text from the third epistle of St. John: "Coworkers of the Truth" (3 Jn 1:8). As he himself explains, this text expresses two of his persistent concerns. The first of these is the understanding of the Church as a communion of faith and of the body of bishops not as isolated individuals but as a group or a collegium whose function consists in service to the Church community. The second is a concern for the reality of truth and an awareness of the feeling of emptiness that follows when one loses the sense that there is some truth by which to guide human life. Both of these concerns played a basic role in his work as archbishop and continue to motivate much of his understanding in his present work. In November 1981 Cardinal Ratzinger was appointed Prefect of the Sacred Congregation for the Doctrine of the Faith, and he continues to exercise that office up to the present.

Ratzinger's study of Augustine's ecclesiology and of Bonaventure's theology of history stand as major studies in the history of doctrine. Beyond this, his Introduction to Christianity can be described as a contemporary classic. He has contributed numerous articles to lexicons and periodicals over many years. In 1985 a lengthy interview with the cardinal, published under the title *The Ratzinger Report,* offers helpful understandings of his vision of Vatican Council II and its aftermath. He has published *Called to Communion* and *Salt of the Earth,* both of which present key insights into his theological understanding of the Church. The latter is in the form of an extensive interview. In 1998 he published *Milestones: Memoirs 1927–77.* This takes the reader through the first fifty years of his life up to the time of his appointment as archbishop of Munich.

Ratzinger's writings cover a wide range of topics including the theology of history, revelation, ecclesiology, preaching, catechesis, liturgical reform, and eschatology. His work presents a theology of remarkable depth and power reflecting the cardinal's abiding conviction concerning the importance of objective truth. He offers especially a theology of revelation arrived at largely by his study of the medieval work of St. Bonaventure but still significant in dealing with problems such as those raised by historical criticism of the Scriptures today. Beyond this he offers a penetrating theology of Church that retrieves key insights of Scripture and of patristic ecclesiology and echoes themes found in the theology of J. A. Möhler of the nineteenth-century school of Tübingen. This dimension of the cardinal's work offers a vision of the Church that is far richer than that of the centuries of post-Tridentine Catholic theology and provides a basis for the his discussion of issues such as Christian brotherhood, the Church and the world, and Christianity in relation to the other religions of the world. The ecclesiology helps clarify the positive possibilities together with the limits that the cardinal would place on all these areas of discussion. Independently of his work at the Congregation of the Doctrine of the Faith that has become more controversial over the years, Cardinal Ratzinger stands out as a major Catholic theologian whose work represents an important contribution to Roman Catholic theology in the modern era.

Bibliography: AIDAN NICHOLS, *The Theology of Joseph Ratzinger: An Introductory Study* (Edinburgh 1988). JOSEPH RATZINGER, *Principles of Catholic Theology: Building Stones for a Fundamental Theology* (San Francisco 1987); *Called to Communion: Understanding the Church Today* (San Francisco 1996); *Salt of the Earth: The Church at the End of the Millennium* (San Francisco 1997); *Milestones: Memoirs 1927 1977* (San Francisco 1999); *Eschatology, Death and Eternal Life,* trans. M. WALDSTEIN, ed. A. NICHOLS (Washington, D.C. 1988).

[ZACHARY HAYES]

ROMERO, OSCAR A.

Archbishop of San Salvador, El Salvador (1977–80); b. Ciudad Barrios, 15 August 1917; d. San Salvador, 24 March 1980. Romero is remembered for his courageous preaching and leadership of the San Salvador archdiocese. His efforts toward the creation of a more just society led to his assassination.

Ordained to the priesthood in 1942, Romero returned to his native El Salvador, where he served as pastor to a church in the city of San Miguel and earned a reputation as a radio preacher. In 1967 he was appointed secretary of the Salvadoran bishops' conference, and in 1970 he was made an auxiliary bishop of San Salvador. He became bishop of the rural diocese of Santiago de María in late 1974 and archbishop of San Salvador on 22 February 1977.

At the time of his elevation to the rank of archbishop, wealthy landowners were attacking the Church's pastoral

Oscar Romero. (Catholic News Service.)

practice in the countryside. Peasants were forming small ecclesial communities in which they learned to discuss the gospel and apply it to the unjust social conditions that dominated their own lives. Many of them joined peasant organizations to seek social and political change. Controlling the mass media and the government, the oligarchy kept Romero under constant pressure and frequent attack. During his years as archbishop, six priests and numerous lay ministers were assassinated, but the archbishop was never intimidated. A compelling preacher, Romero reached large audiences through his use of the archdiocesan radio station, where he worked for Church by defending the poor and calling for social justice.

Foreseeing his own assassination, he intensified his message in his final weeks. On 23 March 1980, he pleaded with the government to stop the repression of dissent, calling on soldiers not to obey orders to murder peasants. The next day, an assassin's bullet felled him while he preached in the chapel of the cancer hospital that also served as his residence. He is widely venerated as a martyr, and his tomb in the San Salvador cathedral is a popular shrine.

Bibliography: O. A. ROMERO, *Mons. Oscar A. Romero: Su Pensamiento,* extant homilies in eight projected volumes (San Salvador 1980). *La Voz de los Sin Voz: La Palabra Viva de Monseñor Romero* (San Salvador 1980); English translation: *Voice of the*

Voiceless: The Four Pastoral Letters and Other Statements (Maryknoll, N.Y; 1985). *The Church Is All of You,* ed. J. R. Brockman (Minneapolis 1984). J. R. BROCKMAN, *Romero: A Life* (New York 1990). J. SOBRINO, *Archbishop Romero: Memories and Reflections* (Maryknoll, N.Y. 1990).

[J. R. BROCKMAN]

RUBIN, WŁADYSŁAW A.

Cardinal, prefect of Sacred Congregation for Oriental Churches; b. 20 September 1917 in the village of Toki near Tarnopol (then in Austrian Galicia, between the World Wars in Poland, since 1945, in Ukraine) to a prosperous peasant family of the Latin Rite; d. 28 November 1990, Vatican City.

After finishing his secondary education, he began theological studies at the Lwów (L'viv) seminary in 1935, but left at the end of 1937, uncertain of his vocation to the priesthood. He briefly studied law, and then attended a military academy in Tarnopol. In World War II, he served in the Polish army during the September 1939 campaign in the course of which Poland was partitioned between Nazi Germany and the Soviet Union. Rubin was captured by Soviet border guards trying to escape abroad to join Polish forces in the West, and was sent to a labor camp, from which he was released to join a Polish Army forming from Soviet deportees after the Nazi invasion of the Soviet Union.

Rubin passed with this army through the Middle East, where, now certain of his calling, he resumed his theological studies at the Jesuit University in Beirut, Lebanon, meeting there clerics of several different Eastern Rites. He was ordained a priest in Beirut 30 June 1946, and from 1946 to 1949 he was involved with ministry to Polish refugees in Lebanon. Thereafter he took a doctorate in canon law at the Gregorian University in Rome. In 1953, he was named a pastor of Poles living in Italy, and in 1959 became rector of the Polish College at the Gregorian University.

He was made a Papal Chamberlain in 1959, and in April 1963 a Domestic Prelate of John XXIII. In 1964 he became rector of the *hospicium* in Rome for Polish pilgrims, and on 29 November of that same year, was consecrated titular bishop of Serta and suffragan bishop to the Archepiscopal See of Gniezno by Stefan Wyszyński, Primate of Poland, with a special mission to the Polish emigration and Poles living abroad. In this last capacity Bishop Rubin traveled tirelessly, visiting various Polish and Polish-descended communities on all continents except Antartica.

On 24 February 1967, he was appointed Secretary General of the Synod of Bishops by Pope Paul VI, and played an important role in the development, organizing, and practical operation of this young institution. He was made Cardinal-Bishop of Sancta Maria in Via Lata in June, 1979. From 1980 to 1985 he was Prefect of the Congregation for Eastern Rite Churches, making major pastoral visits to the Eastern Rite communities in India and North America.

Bibliography: WACLAW SZETELNICKI, *Lwowianin na Drogach Świata. Władysław Kardynał Rubin.* Rome: Gregorian Pontifical University, 1985.

[PAUL RADZILOWSKI]

SANT'EGIDIO, COMMUNITY OF

The Community of Sant'Egidio is a public association of lay people dedicated to evangelization and charity in more than 35 countries of world. The community has as its center the Roman Church of Sant'Egidio, from which the community takes its name. The community began in Rome in 1968 in the period following the Second Vatican Council at the initiative of Andrea Riccardi, a young man who was then less than twenty. Riccardi gathered a group of high-school students to listen to and to put the Gospel into practice. The first Christian communities of the Acts of the Apostles and Francis of Assisi served as reference points. Thus, the small group of women and men began visiting the crowded slums on the outskirts of Rome and started an afternoon school (*Scuola Popolare* [''People's School''] now known as ''Schools of Peace'') providing tutoring for drop-out children.

From its very beginnings, the Community has maintained a continuous presence of prayer and welcome for the poor and for pilgrims in the area of Trastevere and in Rome as it spread throughout the world. The different communities share the following principles: prayer, evangelization, solidarity with the poor, ecumenism and dialogue. The first work of the Community is prayer, which is an essential part of the life of the community in Rome and communities throughout the world and central to the overall direction of the community's search for a more authentic Christian living. The communities gather frequently to pray together, and in many cities there is a common prayer open to everybody. The second pillar is communicating the Gospel. The members take personal responsibility to communicate the Good News to others, leading them to a ''missionary fraternity'' in many parts of the world.

The third fundamental and daily commitment typical of Sant'Egidio that flows from this commitment to the Gospel is the service to the poor, lived as friendship. This friendship widened to other poor people—the physically and mentally disabled, homeless, immigrants, the terminally ill—and to different situations: prisons, homes for the elderly, gypsy camps, and refugee camps. The communities' love for the poor has become work for peace and reconcilation, taking the view that war is the greated of all poverties. Through prayer, meetings, dialogues, and stress on common humanity, the Community tries to resolve conflicts and facilitate humanitarian aid to the civil populations who most suffer from war.

The evangelically rooted commitment to work with poor people is at the base of other humanitarian initiatives, addressed to all people of good will, with no regard to their religious belief. These include a campaign against anti-personnel mines, aid to refugees, war, famine victims; working against slavery and capital punishment. These activities, rooted in the struggle to affirm the value of life without exceptions, involves the members of Sant'Egidio all over the world.

The Community is also committed to serving ecumenical and interfaith dialogue. Since 1987 Sant'Egidio has been committed both at grassroots and international level to host meetings and prayer gatherings in the spirit of the 1986 World Day of Prayer for Peace in Assisi. In 1998 the community promoted the twelfth International meeting *Uomini e Religioni*, which brought together representative of all the major religions in Bucharest to pray and work together for peace. As Pope John Paul II said in Sant'Egidio on its twenty-fifth anniversary in 1993 they have no other limit "but charity."

Bibliography: COMUNITÀ DI SANT'EGIDIO, *Stranieri nostri fratelli; verso una società multirazziale* (Brescia 1989). A. MONTONATI, Il sapore dell'utopia: La Comunità di Sant'Egidio (Rome 1999). A. RICCARDI, *Sant'Egidio, Roma e il Mondo,* Colloquio con J.D. Durand e R. Ladous (Rome 1997).

[EDITORS]

SANTO DOMINGO (1992)

Santo Domingo in the Dominican Republic was the site of the Fourth General Meeting of the Consejo Episcopal Latino Americano or Latin American Bishops' Conference held 12–28 October 1992. Nine years previously, at a gathering of bishops in Haiti, Pope John Paul II announced that the topic for CELAM IV would be New Evangelization and that its opening would coincide with the five hundredth anniversary of the landing of Columbus in the Western hemisphere, 12 October 1492, and the beginning of the first evangelization.

CELAM IV brought together Catholic bishops from twenty-two nations in South and Central America. It was

The Cathedral Santa Maria la Menor in Santo Domingo, Dominican Republic, was constructed between 1521 and 1544. It was the first cathedral built in the Americas. (© Jeremy Horner/ CORBIS)

chaired by the Vatican secretary of state, Angelo Cardinal Sodano. Much of the preparatory work for the meeting, including the drafting of the "working document," was in the hands of the secretary general of CELAM, Bishop Raymundo Damasceno Assis, who also served as co-secretary general of the meeting. The other co- secretary, Bishop Jorge Medina Estévez, was appointed by the Holy See. In addition to a number of lay observers, there were also five Protestant observers from traditional Protestant groups (but no representatives of newer Pentecostal movements).

Preparations. During the nine years between the pope's speech and the CELAM conference, an enormous amount of time and energy was devoted throughout Latin America to meetings, study and research, discussions with laity, and working drafts (that soon became good-sized books). The most important of the drafts was a document entitled *Secunda Relatio* ("Second Report"), which provided an excellent synthesis of the ideas of all the national bishops' conferences of Latin America, thus providing a panorama of the Church in the entire continent. This *relatio* was not accepted, however, by conservative leaders of the conference. Another document, the

Documento de Trabajo (''Working Document''), was also rejected on the very first day of the conference. The proceedings then were entrusted to small working groups, thirty in all, which were not open to plenary sessions. They discussed and produced drafts on a wide range of topics and issues that were synthesized by a powerful drafting committee and then presented for discussion and voting in the plenary sessions.

Up to the last few days of the meeting in Santo Domingo, there were serious forebodings that the seventeen-day meeting would not be able to produce a final document. In the end, however, a staff under the direction of Archbishop Luciano Mendes de Almeida of Brazil, working around the clock, was able to produce a final document during the last frantic days of the conference. In places it displays signs of haste and poor organization and has been criticized because of its lack of prophetic vision. Although there were serious differences of opinion among the bishops, the document was approved by 201 of the 206 voting delegates, with five abstentions and no opposing votes.

Results of the Conference. Pope John Paul II inaugurated the meeting with a lengthy ''Opening Address'' to the bishops. The general interpretation of the speech is that it did not open new avenues, but neither did it close any doors. The pope's outline included (1) a ''new evangelization,'' with Jesus as the model; (2) ''human development,'' which appeared to be a euphemism for the struggle for justice and liberation; and (3) ''Christian culture,'' that is, the inculturation of evangelization and social justice in the nations of Latin America and the Caribbean. These three chapters became the major building blocks of the final documents.

Chapter One was concerned largely with the diverse ministries and charisms for the new evangelization, including approbation of the base ecclesial communities and the crucial role of all lay persons, especially women and the young. Evangelization was envisioned not only as essential catechesis (a huge task), but also as a vigorous outreach to lapsed and indifferent Catholics and as dialogue with non-Christian religions, non-believers, and members of Christian ''fundamentalist'' sects.

The subject of women was treated in seven carefully crafted paragraphs (nos. 104–111) of Chapter One. This is the most substantive and profound statement on women to be found in the writings of the Latin American bishops. A less successful statement, however, is to be found in the ecumenical arena (nos. 139–146). The first sentence on this topic does not bode well for authentic dialogue: ''The problem of the sects has reached dramatic proportions and has become truly worrisome, particularly due to increasing proselytism.''

In Chapter Two, the bishops achieved a consensus regarding nine ''new signs of the times.'' Each sign was elaborated by a brief social analysis, followed by pastoral reflections and plans for action. These signs for Latin America are (1) human rights, (2) ecology, (3) the earth as God's gift, (4) impoverishment, (5) human labor, unemployment, and underemployment, (6) migration, (7) democracy, (8) foreign debt, and (9) the integration of Latin American economies.

Chapter Three, on ''Christian culture,'' is the shortest part of the document and appears to have taken approaches and concepts from both of the previous chapters, resulting in a kind of mélange. From the beginning a great deal of attention is devoted to inculturation toward the indigenous or Amerindians, the African Americans, and the *mestizos,* i.e., those of mixed blood. (The new interest in ethnicity and women's issues was dramatically highlighted by the presence at the meeting of Rigoberta Menchú, a Guatemalan Indian woman who had been awarded the Nobel Prize for Peace.)

Santo Domingo also emphasized the culture of the city. Everywhere on the continent there is a ''passage from rural culture to urban culture, which is the location and driving force of the new universal civilization'' (no. 155). On the other hand, the bishops showed themselves quite aware of the belts of poverty and misery that surround the cities. Finally, the Santo Domingo documents make a strong appeal for Catholic education, from the lowest grades to the universities, and plea for much more expertise in the use of the social media of communication.

Bibliography: A. T. HENNELLY, ed., *Santo Domingo and Beyond: Documents and Commentaries from the Fourth General Conference of Latin American Bishops* (Maryknoll, N.Y. 1993).

[A. T. HENNELLY]

SAPIEHA, ADAM STEFAN

Cardinal, archbishop of Kraków, Poland; b. 14 May 1867 in Krasiczyn near Przemysl, Poland (then in Austrian Galicia), d. 27 July 1951, in Kraków; buried in the Wawel Cathedral in Krakow.

Adam Sapieha was born into an Polish-Lithuanian aristocratic family, and from an early age was taught the values of patiotism an public service. He took a degree in law from the Jagiellonian University in Kraków (1890), in theology from the University of Innsbruck (1894), and finally a doctorate in law from the Gregorian University in Rome (1896), in addition to which he received training in diplomacy. He was ordained a priest of the diocese of Lwow (L'viv) 1 October 1893

After his ordination, he quickly distinguished himself in pastoral work, most notably in his service to the sick during a cholera epidemic. He served as vice-rector of the Metropolitan Seminary in Lwów in the years 1897–1901. In 1906 he was made chamberlain to Pope Pius X, and had considerable influence on his policies toward the church in historically Polish lands.

He was named Bishop of Kraków in 1911 and was consecrated by Pius on 17 December of that year, taking up his diocese 3 March 1912. In 1925 he was made the first Archbishop-Metropolitan of Kraków. His interests and activities as a bishop were many, ranging from a strong concern for the intellectual and moral formation of the clergy, to education, to youth ministry, to the charitable activities which were so especially needed in the wake of the two world wars, their aftermath, the Great Depression of the 1930s.

Sapieha was always a strong proponent of Poland's independence, and during the Nazi occupation (1939–45), his support for the Polish underground in the face of Nazi attempts to liquidate all vestiges of Polish nationhood and national leadership (including many members of the clergy) was notable and courageous. He also encouraged the provision of baptismal papers to Jews to save them from extermination.

On 18 February 1946, he was named Cardinal Presbyter of Sancta Maria Nova by Pius XII. Cardinal Sapieha spent the last years of his life rebuilding and stabilizing the church in his archdiocese after the cataclysm of the Second World War. From 1945 he was head of Caritas in Poland, until the Communist authorities put it under state control in 1950. He ordained Karol Wojtyła (the future John Paul II), and acted as his mentor both when Wojtyła was a seminarian and when he was a young priest.

Bibliography: *Ksiega sapieżynska,* vols. 1-2. JERZY WOLNY, ed. Kraków: 1982–1986.JACEK CZAJKOWSKI, *Kardynał Adam Stefan Sapieha.* Wrocław: Ossolineum, 1997.

[PAUL RADZILOWSKI]

SCHILLEBEECKX, EDWARD

Dominican priest, theologian; b. Antwerp, 12 November 1914. Edward Schillebeeckx, the sixth of fourteen children, has roots in the ancient Flemish Catholic culture of northwest Belgium. He entered the Order of Preachers in 1934 (being given the religious name Henricus, after Henry Suso), studied in Ghent and Louvain, and, after brief military service, was ordained a priest in 1941. He was sent to Paris in 1946, chiefly to work with M. D. Chenu, but he also attended the lectures of Maurice Merleau-Ponty. Schillebeeckx intended to write his doctoral thesis on nature and grace, but he was recalled after

Edward Schillebeeckx, 1979, Vatican City. (AP/Wide World Photos, Inc. Reproduced by permission.)

a year to teach theology in the Dominican study house in Louvain. His first book (the product of his teaching) appeared in 1952: a massively detailed study (running to 690 pages) of the patristic background and medieval context of Thomas Aquinas's concept of sacramentality. Because it has never been translated, the fundamental importance of this magnificent book has not been generally recognized. In 1959 Schillebeeckx brought out a non-technical version of his principal conclusions (*Christ the Sacrament of Encounter with God*). The individual sacraments should be related to the ''primordial sacrament,'' which is the glorified humanity of Christ himself. The historical approach to Aquinas associated with Chenu, together with Merleau-Ponty's phenomenology of personal encounter, uncovered a rich conception of the sacraments as encounter with God.

In 1957 Schillebeeckx accepted the chair of dogmatic theology in the Catholic University of Nijmegen (which he was to occupy until his retirement in 1982). The unexpected convening of the second Vatican Council in 1959 soon involved him in preparatory work for the Dutch bishops. He drafted the pastoral letter that the Dutch episcopate published at Christmas, 1960, about what to expect from the Council: renewal of the liturgy and reform of structures of church government. During the Council Schillebeeckx was active in Rome as personal theologian to Bernard Cardinal Alfrink. There is reason to believe that he had influence on the development of the constitutions *Lumen gentium* and *Gaudium et spes* (particularly on the section on marriage in the latter). In 1965 he was a co-founder of the international journal *Concilium.* In countless essays and lectures he sought to disseminate the ideas of the Council. By 1970, however, he believed that the ''spirit of Vatican II'' (as he understood it) had been stifled.

Postconciliar Development of his Thought. Meanwhile, concern about a crisis of faith that he perceived among North American and European believers led Schillebeeckx to reconsider basic theological concepts in the light of recent philosophical work (neo-Heideggerian hermeneutics, Anglo-American analytic philosophy, and especially the critical theory of the Frankfurt school). He hoped to make Christian faith more intelligible to people at home in a pluralistic and secularized society. Much struck by the Anglican Bishop John Robinson's book *Honest to God* (1963) and (on his first visit to the United States in 1966) by the ''death of God'' theology, he began to reconsider his assumptions about the possibility of knowing God. In his Louvain days, he published a study of ''the non- conceptual cognitive elements in our knowledge of God,'' which he believed to be crucial in Aquinas's religious epistemology. He now sought to widen this into a sense of the mystery at the heart of all human experience, and particularly of suffering, which no concepts can ever fully grasp. The essays on revelation, tradition, interpretation, experience, truth, and so on, although only ''soundings'' (*peilingen*), introduced themes that would reappear in his three-volume Christology, the major work of his years at Nijmegen.

Prompted by invitations to address various problems in the postconciliar Church, particularly in Holland, Schillebeeckx continued to advocate reform of certain ecclesiastical institutions. An essay on the celibacy of the clergy (1966) was followed by a stream of articles, culminating in a book on the ministry (1980), reissued with revisions to meet criticisms (1985). In 1970, however, he set himself the task of absorbing the results of modern biblical studies, a rare and risky step for a systematic theologian trained in pre-Vatican II Thomism. In 1974 Schillebeeckx published a massive survey (nearly 700 pages) of recent exegesis of the synoptic gospels (*Jesus: An Experiment in Christology*). His enthusiasm made him vulnerable to the charm of the most adventurous theories (such as the three-stage tradition of the Q community). But the very idea of reconstructing the significance of the figure of Jesus on the basis of the synoptic gospels immediately alarmed theologians for whom the Chalcedonian dogma offered the only viable starting point for

orthodox Christianity. A second, even longer volume appeared in 1977, incorporating monographs on Paul and John as well as detailed accounts of the rest of the New Testament (*Christ: The Experience of Jesus as Lord*). Apart from digesting a library of recent exegesis, the two volumes offer what is in effect a liberation Christology, based as far as possible on the New Testament as read by critical-historical exegesis, and appealing to an audience for whom post-Enlightenment philosophical anthropology marks out the conditions of meaningful experience.

The promised third volume on ecclesiology was postponed while Schillebeeckx replied in an ''interim report'' (1978) to critics of his exegesis and readers who suspected his orthodoxy. He also engaged in an exchange of letters with the Congregation for the Doctrine of the Faith, culminating in a conversation in Rome in 1979 that exonerated him. Apart from one chapter on ''democratic rule in the Church,'' the last volume of the trilogy (*Church: The Human Story of God*), running only 250 pages, turns away from reflection on the Church as an institution to sketch an account of the liberation of humanity as the ''story of God.''

Audience is important. Schillebeeckx's first great book develops a rich doctrine of the sacraments on the basis of the hypostatic union for students who are already devout Catholics. The trilogy, by contrast, seeks to bring those who are aware of a sacred dimension to life, in the midst of a thoroughly secularized society, nearer the possibility of accepting the message of salvation from God in Jesus that is attested in the New Testament.

Bibliography: R. J. SCHREITER, ed.,*The Schillebeeckx Reader* (New York 1984); with complete bibliography (1945-1983).T. M. SCHOOF, ed., *The Schillebeeckx Case: Official Exchange of Letters and Documents* (New York 1984). R. J. SCHREITER AND M. C. HILKERT, eds., *The Praxis of Christian Experience: An Introduction to the Theology of Edward Schillebeeckx* (San Francisco 1989). P. KENNEDY, *Schillebeeckx* (Collegeville, Minn. 1993).

[F. KERR]

SCHÖNBORN, CHRISTOPH

Cardinal, archbishop of Vienna; b. 22 Jan. 1945, Skalná (now in the Czech Republic). The political turmoil that divided Europe after World War II forced the von Schönborns to leave their native Bohemia in September 1945 and to take up residence in Austria, signaling a change of fortunes for a family whose several branches had occupied for centuries a high place among European aristocracy. Young Christoph pursued his elementary and secondary studies in the rural region of Austrian Vorarlberg. In 1963, Schönborn entered the novitiate of the Dominican Order in Austria, and was then sent to

Walberberg near Bonn to study philosophy and theology. After his priestly ordination in 1970 by Cardinal Franz König—whom he would later succeed as archbishop of Vienna—Schönborn pursued the study of Byzantine and Slavic Christianity in France both at the Sorbonne and Le Saulchoir, and was awarded a doctorate in 1974. He was ordained bishop in 1991. He served as auxiliary to the archbishop of Vienna until 1995 when he was first appointed coadjutor on 13 April; he was appointed archbishop a few months later, on 14 September. In the consistory of 1998, Pope John Paul II named him to the College of Cardinals, assigning Cardinal Schönborn the titular Roman church of Gesù Divin Lavoratore.

In the mid to late 1960s, Schönborn encountered the prevailing currents of theological unrest in Regensburg, Vienna, and Paris. Two main directions of theological inquiry had emerged from the post-conciliar critique of Leonine-revival Thomism: one encouraged updating through Christian encounter with actual political and social realities; the other focused on a retrieval and re-presentation of early Christian writings and historical forms of theological thought. Schönborn's mentors, including Dominican Father Marie-Joseph Le Guillou, directed him to the figures and traditions of Eastern Christianity and the importance they held for renewal of the Church. His 1972 study of the celebrated opponent of Monothelitism, Sophronius of Jerusalem (d. 638), illustrated Schönborn's early allegiance to the *ressourcement* school, which during the immediate postwar period had developed its spiritual center in Paris. His doctoral thesis, *L'Icone du Christ* (Eng. trans. God's Human Face) established him as an authority on Maximus the Confessor (d. 662). While completing his thesis, Father Schönborn served as student chaplain in Graz (Austria). In 1975, he assumed the chair of dogmatic theology at the University of Fribourg in Switzerland. His university teaching and research owed much to the directions set by his intellectual mentor Joseph Ratzinger, and in 1980 Schönborn was named to the International Theological Commission. Schönborn, who speaks the major European languages fluently, acquired worldwide prominence in 1987 when he was named secretary to the Commission of Cardinals and Bishops charged with drafting the Catechism of the Catholic Church.

In a relatively brief time Schönborn emerged as leader of the Church in Austria, assuming the office of President of the Austrian Bishops' Conference in June 1998. Obliged to confront serious difficulties in both Church and nation, Schönborn unstintingly promoted the renewal inaugurated at the Second Vatican Council. His native intelligence and personal charm contribute to the success of his efforts. Sponsorship of an international school of theology at Gaming (Austria) and direction of a new se-

Christoph Schönborn. (Catholic News Service.)

ries of theology manuals (AMATECA) rank among his noteworthy accomplishments. Serving on a number of Vatican congregations, he is well known for his leadership in Orthodox-Roman Catholic dialogue. He has continued his intellectual work, publishing several books and articles in scientific and popular journals aimed at expounding the truth of the Catholic religion. English translations of his writings and frequent lectures have gained him a wide following in the United States and other Anglophone countries. The land of his birth formally recognized his achievements when the Catholic Theology Faculty at the University of Prague awarded him an honorary doctorate in 1999.

Bibliography: Works by Cardinal Schönborn include: *The Mystery of the Incarnation* (1992); *From Death to Life: The Christian Journey* (1995); *Living the Catechism of the Catholic Church: The Creed,* with David Kipp (1995); *Loving the Church: Spiritual Exercises Preached in the Presence of Pope John Paul II* (1998); *A Basket of Flowers: A Young Girl's Fight Against Injustice* (1999); *The Essential Catholic Catechism: A Readable, Comprehensive Catechism of the Catholic Faith,* with Alan Schreck (2000); *Living the Catechism of the Catholic Church: The Sacraments* (2000).

[ROMANUS CESSARIO]

SCHOTTE, JAN PIETER

Cardinal, secretary general of the World Synod of Bishops; b. 29 April 1928, Beveren-Leie, Belgium. He was one of five children, son of Marcel and Rhia Schotte. His father and his grandfather were school teachers. He joined the Congregation of the Immaculate Heart of Mary (Missionaries of Scheut), in Brussels in 1946 and was ordained a priest on 3 August 1952; he intended to become a missionary in China. He did further study in his community's houses at the Catholic University of Louvain (1953–1956) and the Catholic University of America (1962–1963). From 1963 to 1967 he was a faculty member at his congregation's seminary in Louvain and an assistant in the Superior Institute of Religious Sciences, Catholic University of Louvain. He later served as rector of Immaculate Heart Mission Seminary in Washington, D.C.

From 1967 to 1972 Fr. Schotte was secretary general of his congregation in Rome and vice-president of the Commission of Superiors General. In 1980 he was named secretary of the Pontifical Council for Justice and Peace. His synthesis report of discussions between Vatican officials and U.S. bishops in 1983 on the bishops' proposed pastoral letter The Challenge of Peace became an important point of reference for the final revision of that letter. At the particular synod for Holland (1980) he was called on to act as a translator for the curial officials; he attended the sixth general assembly of the Synod of Bishops, in 1983, as assistant to the French-language group.

He was named titular bishop of Silli and vice-president of the Pontifical Council for Justice and Peace in 1983. In 1984 he was the chief delegate of the Vatican to the International Population Conference in Mexico City. He was promoted to archbishop and appointed secretary general of the World Synod of Bishops in 1985, acting in that capacity at the second Extraordinary Assembly of the World Synod of Bishops. During labor disputes at the Vatican in the mid-1980s, Bishop Schotte became the Vatican's chief negotiator; he was appointed President of the Office of Labor of the Apostolic See in 1989. In 1992 he attended the fourth General Conference of the Latin American Episcopate, in Santo Domingo, Dominican Republic.

Pope John Paul II created him cardinal deacon, 26 November 1994; he received the red biretta and deaconry of St. Giuliano dei Fiamminghi. As secretary general of the Synod of Bishops he has attended not only the general and extraordinary assemblies, but also the special assemblies for America, Asia, Oceania, and the second special assembly for Europe.

See Also: SANTO DOMINGO (1992), SYNOD OF BISHOPS (SECOND EXTRAORDINARY ASSEMBLY), SYNOD OF BISHOPS (SIXTH GENERAL ASSEMBLY)

[J. A. DICK/EDITORS]

SIN, JAIME LACHICA

Cardinal Archbishop of Manila, Philippines; b. 31 August 1928 in New Washington, Aklan, on the province of Panay, part of the Visayas group of islands in central Philippines; the child of Juan Sin, a Chinese merchant from Amoy, South China, and Maxima Lachica, a native of Kalibo, Aklan, and a member of the landed gentry. He is the seventh among nine siblings of five boys and four girls.

Although Sin's uncle, Gabriel Reyes, was the first Filipino archbishop of Manila, his father initially resisted his entering the seminary. His mother who insisted that young Jaime be allowed to study for priesthood. On 3 April 1954 he was ordained priest at the Cathedral of the Immaculate Conception in Roxas City, Capiz.

After ministering from 1954 to 1957 to the *barrios* in the mountains, Sin was appointed as the first rector of St. Pius X Seminary in Roxas City. Sin gained government- recognition of the seminary program. On 18 March 1967, Sin was appointed auxiliary to the archbishop of Jaro and was named coadjutor archbishop with right of succession on 18 March 1972.

Premier Prelate. Two years later Pope Paul VI appointed Sin archbishop of Manila. Pope Paul VI named him a cardinal of the Church 24 May 1976. He was the third Filipino to attain such honor. Among the significant positions held by Cardinal Sin in his 46-year career include a two-time presidency of the influential Catholic Bishops' Conference of the Philippines (CBCP) in the 1970's, and membership in the following congregations and councils of the Holy See: Synod of Bishops in Rome (Oct. 1977), Sacred Congregation for the Evangelization of Peoples (1978, 1983), Sacred Congregation for Catholic Education (1978, 1983), Pontifical Council for Social Communications (1978, 1984), Secretariat for Non-Christians (1978, 1983), Council of Cardinals for the Study of Organization and Economic Questions relating to the Holy See (June 1981), Prefecture of Economic Affairs of the Holy See (May 1982), Sacred Congregation for Bishops (6 December 1983), Council for Public Affairs of the Church (5 January 1984), Sacred Congregation for the Clergy (7 March 1984), Sacred Congregation for the Sacraments (5 December 1984), and the Sacred Congregation for the Divine Worship (15 December 1984).

Champion of Justice and Morality. Cardinal Sin is a brilliant and prolific writer of pastoral letters, homilies and reflections, only a few of which have been collected in book form. One such pastoral letter protested the raid of a Jesuit seminary in Novaliches (north of Manila) in 1974 allegedly because the latter were hiding the leftist leader Jose Maria Sison. The letter was the very first attack on martial law by any Philippine institution. His writings dwell on various aspects of human existence and struggle, with emphasis on man's dignity and rights. Sin has been very vocal about Church and State relations. For him, the separation of the two, as Philippine laws state, should not necessarily mean isolation, nor should it connote the absence of collaboration. Furthermore, he is outspoken against conduct that erodes the morals of society and has consistently opposed gambling and related forms. Sin's strong advocacy of freedom—freedom to do good, to express one's ideas without restraint, and to involve oneself in nation building—made him a champion of democracy during the dark era of martial law in the Philippines

Cardinal Sin has received so far 26 honorary doctorate degrees from such institutions as Georgetown and Yale in the U.S., Ateneo, La Salle, and UST in the Philippines, and Fu-Jen University in Taipei. In 1992, President Corazon C. Aquino bestowed upon him the Philippine Legion of Honor.

Cardinal Sin's sensitivity to the temporal needs of his flock was manifested in various civic endeavors, such as two housing projects in Metro Manila in the 1980s, hospitalization and pension benefits for bishops and priests, the establishment of Caritas Manila, the social welfare arm of the archdiocese, and the financial assistance extended to poor dioceses in the country through the sale of hundreds of shares of the then Archdiocese of Manila-owned Philtrust Bank. Sin's comments on the political scene have earned him fierce criticism. Many of his detractors would like him to avoid political controversy, confining his homilies and pronouncements to ''Church'' issues. But the cardinal is adamant. To reflect on politics ''is a duty,'' he maintains. For him, politics ''has its moral dimension and cannot just be left to the politician.''

Bibliography: FELIX B. BAUTISTA, *Cardinal Sin and the Miracle of Asia: A Biography* (Manila 1987). NICK JOAQUIN, *The Book of Sin* (Manila 1992). MSGR. JOSEFINO S. RAMIREZ, ed., *A Decade of Sin* (Manila 1995).

[ZANDRO G. RAPADAS]

SISTINE CHAPEL, RESTORATION OF

On 11 December 1999, Pope John Paul II presided at a prayer service to mark the completion of the restora-

Jaime Cardinal Sin. (Catholic News Service.)

tion of the Sistine Chapel. The fifteenth century chapel takes its name from Pope Sixtus IV (1471–1484) who commissioned it, and engaged notable Italian artists of the day to decorate it Rosselli, Botticelli, Ghirlandaio, and Perugino. Early in the sixteenth century Pope Julius II persuaded Michelangelo to redo the vaulted ceiling, a project that was finished in 1513. Over the centuries, the elements, dust, and candle-smoke dimmed the colors of the frescoes and caused them to deteriorate.

An ambitious restoration program, begun in 1964, went through several phases during the pontificates of Paul VI, John Paul I, and John Paul II, including the cleaning and repair of the fifteenth-century frescoes, which depicted scenes from the lives of Moses and Christ, the roof and battlements, and the frescoes on the entrance wall that continued the fifteenth-century cycle. In 1980 the project turned to the portraits of the popes and of Michelangelo's frescoes, successively the lunettes, the ceiling frescoes, and the *Last Judgment*. The final phase of the work, completed in 1999, repaired the cycle of murals by artists of the Florentine and Umbrian schools.

Means and Method of Restoration. The climax of the work was reached in April 1994 with the ceremonial unveiling of the *Last Judgment*. Pope John Paul II celebrated a Mass in the chapel in honor of the event (8 April

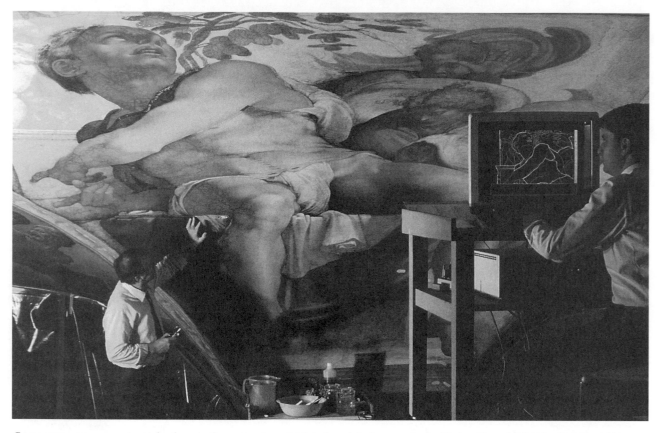

Conservators use computer technology in the restoration of Michelangelo's frescoes in the Sistine Chapel. (© Vittoriano Rastelli/ CORBIS)

1994), using the opportunity to highlight the theology enshrined in Michelangelo's frescoes.

The decision to clean Michelangelo's paintings was taken after examination of the lunette of Eleazar and Nathan detected tiny cracks in the color fabric of the whole ceiling. They were caused by the shrinking of the covering of glue that pulled away the layers of originally luminous color. Previous restorers had used the glue to revive the frescoes darkened by dust and soot. After research, experiment, and a trial cleaning in June 1980 on the figure of Eleazar, the frescoed surfaces of the ceiling in the Sistine were cleaned by a method using the solvent known as AB57, applied briefly and removed with a sponge soaked in distilled water. The few parts retouched by Michelangelo *a secco* (after the plaster had set, thus sensitive to water) were cleaned last with specific organic water solvents fixed with a solution of Paraloid B72. Watercolor was used for some modest pictorial restorations. Because Michelangelo had used the delicate lapis lazuli in coloring and a more *a secco* technique for the *Last Judgment,* it called for different cleaning methods, including washings with distilled water and treatments with a solution of water and ammonium carbonate. All the stages of the work were scrupulously filmed. The Chapel was kept open for the public to see the progress of the enterprise since the scaffolding covered the ceiling frescoes only partially at any one time.

The program of cleaning rid the frescoes in the Sistine of the polluting conditions chiefly responsible for their deterioration. To counter continuing pollution, however, experts decided to eschew use of resinous or other protective substances on the frescoes, to install a conditioning system with a monitored annual cycle for air filtration, and to lay dust-retaining carpeting on the stairs leading to the Chapel from the Vatican Museums.

Michelangelo's Genius Rediscovered. During the cleaning, a photogrammetic survey of the ceiling and the *Last Judgment* revealed fresh details about their state of preservation and shed new light on Michelangelo's technical procedures and virtuosity. About six thousand specialists and scholars from the fields of art and culture examined the outcome of the restoration carefully. Many of them approved the astonishing results, but some art historians reacted with strong criticism.

The cleaning of the frescoes in the Sistine, originally both Chapel and fortress, revealed long-lost or unobserved details of Michelangelo's work. The architectural design of the ceiling, which ingeniously divided one dramatic scene from another, became powerfully evident. Because the myriad of figures from the family scenes in the lunettes to the protesting saints in the *Last Judgment* was more clearly delineated, the emotions of tenderness, fear, and fury registered in their gestures and expressions became more apparent. The meticulous painting of the ceiling histories from the first scene of the Creation to the Drunkenness of Noah was found to contrast sharply with the rapid execution of the lunettes, some of which had been left almost as studies. This discovery led scholars to deduce that for the lunettes, Michelangelo did not use cartoons and did the painting without using his assistants. Michelangelo's skilled use of traditional Tuscan *buon fresco* for the vault and the lunettes also became manifest. This demanding technique requires the painting of complete details of entire sections of the work onto fresh plaster. Art scholars could detect his sudden decisions to make changes in his figures by noting where he removed the frescoed plaster and applied a new layer on which to paint. The restored clarity of the *Last Judgment* revealed the strength and audacity of Michelangelo's brushstrokes, the mastery of his composition, the intellectual and pictorial brilliance of his balancing of mass and space, and the detailed expression of his mischievous or macabre humor.

The restoration and cleaning of the Sistine Chapel opened the way for many years of further study and appreciation. Worldwide attention focused on the need to reassess Michelangelo's place in the development of Renaissance painting and of his aims and achievements as a colorist and draftsman. He was perceived as well situated in the lineage of Tuscan painting, beginning in the studio of Ghirlandaio in Florence and influencing younger Florentine painters such as Rosso and Pontormo. Michelangelo used colors on the ceiling of the Sistine Chapel to model his figures. His varied shades created immense light and startling shimmering effects: gleaming white, flesh tints, yellows, and greens. His use of abrupt juxtapositions of violets, greens, and yellows in the lunettes produced wonderful impressions of light and shade. After veils of grime were removed from the Last Judgment, the colors appeared incandescent, with the figures rising and falling in a space of blue so luminous that the wall on which they were painted seemed to have dissolved.

The 'rediscovery' of Michelangelo as a painter vastly different from the somber artist previously perceived was accompanied by scholarly reappraisals of other aspects of his life, his complex personality, and his always surprising art: spiritually resonant poetry, original architecture, and expressive sculpture in stone.

Bibliography: Detailed bibliographies on the cleaning of the Sistine Chapel have been published in the *Monumenti, Musei e Gal-*

lerie Pontificie series. Other recent publications on Michelangelo and/or the cleaning of the Sistine Chapel include: G. COLALUCCI, ''Brevi considerazioni sulla tecnica pittorica e la problematica di restauro degli affreschi michelangioeschi della volta Sistina'' in *Problemi del restauro in Italia,* ed. CAMPANOTTO (Udine 1988); ''The Frescoes of Michelangelo on the Vault of the Sistine Chapel. Original Technique and Conservation,'' in *The Conservation of Wall Paintings,* Proceedings of a Symposium organised by the Courtauld Institute of Art and the Getty Conservation Institute, London, July 13–16, 1987, ed. S. CATHER (Singapore 1991). DE MAIO, *Michelangelo e la Controriforma* (Roma-Bari 1981). M. HALL, *Michelangelo—The Sistine Ceiling Restored* (New York 1993). F. HARTT, G. COLALUCCI, F. MANCINELLI, (and D. SCHLESAK in the German edition), *La Cappella Sistina,* 3 vols. Vol. 1, *La preistoria della Bibbia;* vol. 2, *Gli antenati di Cristo;* vol. 3, *La storia della Creazione* (Milan 1989–90; Paris, 1989–90; Luzern 1989–91; Anversa 1990–91; Tokyo 1990–91; New York 1991; Warsaw 1991). R. HATFIELD, *Trust in God: The Sources of Michelangelo's Frescoes on the Sistine Ceiling* (Florence 1991). F. MANCINELLI, ''La pulitura degli affreschi di Michelangelo nella Cappella Sistina,'' in *Il problema della Cappella Sistina,* ed. ISTITUTO SUPERIORE DI ARTE SACRA (Rome 1987). J. D. OREMLAND, *Michelangelo's Sistine Ceiling: A Study of Creativity* (Madison, Conn. 1989); *The Sistine Chapel: Michelangelo Rediscovered,* Eng. ed. (Great Britain 1986). ''All Salvation History Leads to Christ,'' *L'Osservatore Romano,* English edition (15 December 1999).

[G. A. BULL]

SLIPYJ, JOSYF

Cardinal, archbishop, leader of Ukranian Catholics; b. Zazdrist in the Ukraine, 17 Feb. 1892; d. Rome, 7 Sept. 1984. Josyf Kobernyckyj-Dyckowskyj Slipyj (also spelled Slipyi) was born in the Western Ukraine (Galicia) when it was still a part of the Austrio-Hungarian Empire. He received his theological education and seminary training in Lvov (Lviv, Lemberg), Innsbruck and Rome. Ordained a priest in 1917, in 1922 he was appointed to the faculty of the Major Seminary in Lvov (now part of Poland), and became president of the newly founded Theological Academy. He started a respected theological quarterly *Bohoslovia* that he later (1963) revived in Rome, after a long lapse, as a yearly publication.

In 1939 Slipyj was made coadjutor to Metropolitan Szeptyckyj of Lvov, whom he succeeded as head of the Uniate Ukrainian Church in 1944. The difficulties he had with the Nazi occupation during the first few months of his tenure were nothing in comparison to what he suffered at the hands of the Bolsheviks who took over the next year (1945), annexing the Western Ukraine to the Soviet Union. Arrested and condemned for unspecific crimes, Slipyj spent 18 years in prison, labor camps and exile in Siberia (1945–63). His church was officially annihilated through forced union with the Russian Orthodox Church (Synod of Lvov 1946).

Slipyj was allowed to leave the Soviet Union in 1963 as a result of initiatives that had been set in motion by

Archbishop Josyf Slipyj celebrates the Divine Liturgy at the Cathedral of the Holy Name in Bombay. (AP/Wide World Photos.)

Pope John XXIII. He spent the rest of his life in Rome as a witness to the vitality of the Church in the Ukraine, notwithstanding the long years of repression. He spoke of a "church in the catacombs" in terms which, to some, sounded exaggerated, but later were found to be quite accurate.

Role in the West. Pope Paul VI gave Slipyj the title *Major Archbishop* of the Ukrainian Church, with right and privileges similar to those of a patriarch. The title, newly created by Vatican II, was the source of misunderstanding and much friction between the Holy See and Ukrainians in the West. Many thought that *patriarch* was the more rightful title for the head of the large and long-suffering Ukrainian Church. The appointment of Slipyj as a cardinal in 1965 did not satisfy pressure groups within the Ukrainian community, and at times Slipyj himself seemed to speak and act as an opponent of the Vatican's *OstPolitik*. Although his actions and movements were restricted, Slipyj visited most Ukrainian communities in Europe and America, and held two Synods of Ukrainian bishops in Rome (1971, 1980). He was also outspoken on behalf of his persecuted people. Some of his strong statements caused an exchange of letters between Patriarch Pimen of Moscow and Pope John Paul II (1980–81).

The cultural activity of the Ukrainian cardinal was also remarkable. He played a principal part in the establishment of the faculty of St. Clement of Rome, a Ukrainian Catholic University (1963), and the construction of St. Sophia, the Ukrainian Catholic Cathedral (1969), modeled in part on that of Kiev. Both are located in the Eternal City. He wrote highly speculative treatises on the doctrine of the Holy Trinity, and he appeared as quite an expert on problems of Unionism, Ukrainian church history and liturgy. Shortly before his death at the age of 92, a new edition of his *Omnia Opera* appeared.

Bibliography: J. SLIPYJ, *Omnia Opera Card, Josephi (Slipyj Kobernyckyj-Dyckovskyj) Archiepiscopi Majoris*, 13 v. (Rome 1968–83) [Volume 14, with contributions by a number of authors, was added after his death (Rome 1984)]. M. MARUSYN, *Mitropolit Josif Slipyj* [in Ukrainian], (Rome-Brussels 1972); *Cristiani d'Ucraina. Un popolo dilaniato ma non domato* (Rome 1983). G. CHOMA, "La vita e le opere del Cardinale Slipyj," *Euntes Docete* 38 (1985): 217–236. G. CAPRILE, "Il Card: Josif Slipyj Pastore e Studioso," *La Civilta Cattolica* (1985): 400–404. J. PELIKAN, *Confessor between East and West: A Portrait of Ukrainian Cardinal Josyf Slipyj* (Grand Rapids, Mich. 1990).

[G. ELDAROV]

SODANO, ANGELO

Cardinal, secretary of State; b. 23 Nov. 1927, Isola d'Asti, Italy, the second of Giovanni and Delfina Sodano's six children. Giovanni was a Christian Democrat

Angelo Cardinal Sodano receives gifts during the consecration of the Immaculate Conception Church in Moscow in December 1999. (AP/Wide World Photos. Photograph by Ivan Sekretarev.)

deputy in the Italian Parliament from 1948 to 1963. Sodano entered the seminary of Asti and was sent to Rome, where he earned doctorates in theology at the Pontifical Gregorian University and in canon law at the Pontifical Lateran University. After ordination to the priesthood in Asti, 23 Sept. 1950, he taught dogmatic theology at the diocesan seminary and exercised his pastoral ministry among young students. In 1959 he entered the Pontifical Ecclesiastical Academy, the diplomatic school of the Holy See. He served as secretary of the nunciatures in Ecuador, Uruguay, and Chile. In 1962 he was named privy chamberlain supernumerary, and the following year chaplain of the pope. From 1968 until 1977, he was an official in the Council for Public Affairs of the Church. During this period, he visited Romania, Hungary, and East Germany as a member of missions of the Holy See to those governments.

Because of his organizational skills and his tact as a mediator, in 1977 Pope Paul VI named him titular archbishop of Nova di Cesare and apostolic nuncio in Chile. Cardinal Antonio Samorè, librarian and archivist of the Holy Roman Church, ordained him a bishop in Asti. In Chile, he visited almost all the dioceses of the country, repeatedly asked Augusto Pinochet to respect human rights, and was instrumental in the successful Vatican mediation between Chile and Argentina in a territorial dispute over several islands and the waters off their Southern coasts in the Beagle channel.

Pope John Paul II recalled Archbishop Sodano to the Vatican in 1988 and named him secretary of the Council for Public Affairs of the Church. The next year, after the reorganization of the Curia mandated in the constitution *Pastor Bonus,* he became secretary of the section for relations with the United States, in the secretariat of state. He also gave special attention to the Pontifical Commission for Russia, of which he was the president, and was the Vatican representative to the meeting of ministers of foreign affairs of the Conference on European Security and Cooperation held in Vienna, Copenhagen, New York, and Paris. In 1990, when the pope accepted the resignation of Cardinal Agostino Casaroli as secretary of state, the engineer of the Vatican "Ostpolitik," Archbishop Sodano, was named to replace him as pro-secretary. A few months later, on 28 June 1991, John Paul II created him cardinal priest with the title of S. Maria Nuova and the following day named him secretary of state.

Cardinal Sodano has participated in seven assemblies of the Synod of Bishops and was one of the president-delegates of the Fourth General Conference of the Latin American Episcopate held in Santo Domingo, Dominican Republic, in 1992. In 1994, the pope promoted him to the order of the cardinal bishops with the title of the suburbicarian see of Albano, while retaining *in commendam* his titular church of S. Maria Nuova.

[SALVADOR MIRANDA]

SOLIDARITY

Solidarity, as defined by Pope John Paul II, represents "a firm and persevering determination to commit oneself to the common good; that is to say for the good of all and of each individual, because we are all really responsible for all" (*Sollicitudo rei socialis,* no. 38). Solidarity is a recurring theme in the writings of John Paul II. In the encyclical *Centesimus annus* he says that the term describes "one of the fundamental principles of the Christian view of social and political organization," and notes that previous popes have identified the same principle under the name "friendship" (Leo XIII), "social charity" (Pius XI), and "the civilization of love" (Paul VI) (no. 3). John Paul II's repeated appeal to this principle in a variety of contexts makes it clear that solidarity is neither a vague feeling of compassion or commiseration, nor the union of one group in society over against another. Though the pope uses the word to describe the union of workers against the degradation of their work (*Laborem exercens,* no. 8), he insists that solidarity "aims at the good of social justice," and is not undertaken "for the sake of 'struggle' or in order to eliminate the opponent" (ibid., no. 20). It is a human and Christian virtue, describing the commitment to the common good. It has three principal manifestations, according to whether the common good is taken to refer to goods, activities, or the communion of persons. This same division is found in the treatment of solidarity in the Catechism of the Catholic Church, nos. 1940–1942.

According to John Paul II, the common good can consist of goods, realized in individuals, that share a common species. Because of our common humanity we can say that we share a common status, in the sense that no person is more or less human than another; that there are perfections common to us all, such as health, knowledge, and religious devotion; and that there are things whose use is inherently common, such as money, food, and technology. Each of these can be the ground of moral and legal rights, and thus can express a reason for solidarity. In *Sollicitudo rei socialis* the "virtue" of solidarity is described initially as the willingness to make a moral response to common goods described in this way (no. 38). Likewise the Catechism says, "Solidarity is manifested in the first place by the distribution of goods and remuneration for work" (no. 1940). Solidarity thus described recognizes and is committed to the virtue of distributive justice, not only on the part of the state, but also on the part of other social groups: families, unions, business enterprises.

The common good can also be realized in the common activity of individuals. John Paul applies this idea to the domestic political order, international relations, the initiatives of intermediate societies, and economic life (cf. CCC 1941). In *Centesimus annus* he writes:

> By means of his work a person commits himself, not only for his own sake but also for others and with others. Each person collaborates in the work of others and for their good. One works in order to provide for the needs of one's family, one's community, one's nation, and ultimately all humanity. Moreover, a person collaborates in the work of his fellow employees, as well as in the work of suppliers and in the customers' use of goods, in a progressively expanding chain of solidarity. (No. 43; cf. *Laborem exercens,* no. 8)

Insofar as the common good is constituted by common activity, having its own inherent perfection and value, the supplanting of that activity through the intervention of "higher" powers results in the loss of the good itself. The good is not simply the external result (e.g., the just distribution of goods), but the collaborative activity whereby the external result is produced. Pope John Paul speaks also, in the same vein, of the "subjectivity" of society, constituted by "structures of participation and shared responsibility" (*Centesimus annus,* no. 46); totalitarian societies invariably bring about "the destruction of the true subjectivity of society and of the individual citizens"—not because the State does a poor job of distributing common goods equitably, but because in such a society the individual and the people as a whole are reduced to objects.

The principal meaning of "common good" is found in the theological concept of communion: the greatest

The leaders of Poland's Solidarity trade union, including its leader Lech Wałęsa (center), during a press conference in Paris during the 1980s. (Imapress/Archive Photos. Reproduced by Permission.)

common good is the communion of persons. Papal and conciliar documents speak of "communion" typically in reference to those means by which the individual becomes part of, or grows in, the body of Christ (e.g., marriage, Eucharistic fellowship, baptism). It is this understanding of "common" that governs the others. In *Sollicitudo rei socialis* John Paul says:

> Beyond human and natural bonds, already so close and strong, there is discerned in the light of faith a new model of the unity of the human race, which must ultimately inspire our solidarity. This supreme model of unity, which is a reflection of the intimate life of God, one God in three Persons, is what we Christians mean by the word "communion." (No. 40)

The Catechism (no. 1942) likewise speaks of solidarity involving the communication of spiritual goods. This communion has often, throughout Christian history, been the inspiration for the fostering of solidarity in temporal goods, impelling souls then and now to the heroic charity of monastic farmers, liberators of slaves, healers of the sick, and messengers of faith, civilization, and science to all generations and all peoples for the sake of creating the social conditions capable of offer-

ing to everyone possible a life worthy of man and of a Christian. (Ibid., quoting a discourse of Pius XII).

Solidarity therefore involves charity as well as justice: communion in common goods and activities finds a root in the common nature of man, but it is ultimately secured by the recognition that every person is called to share in the communal life of the Trinity.

With this notion of solidarity, John Paul II has marked out the basis for an understanding of social and political life that challenges the distinctively modern notion of the political good. The revolutions of the nineteenth century produced an aggressively secularist and monistic notion of solidarity achieved by, or exemplified in, the state; in certain species of liberalism, on the other hand, a mechanistic notion of the market is given primacy. In *Centesimus annus* John Paul II criticizes any system that would "suffocate" the human person "between two poles represented by the State and the marketplace" (no. 49); in *Evangelium vitae* he warns that authentic solidarity is not compatible with the way the democracies understand themselves today. Contrary to their own constitutions, some human lives are deemed unworthy of

James Francis Cardinal Stafford. (Catholic News Service.)

protection. The "civilization of love" bases the social good on solidarity: the authentic interdependence of persons, leading to communion.

Bibliography: RUSSELL HITTINGER, "Making Sense of the Civilization of Love," *In The Legacy of Pope John Paul II: His Contribution to Catholic Thought* (New York: Herder & Herder, 1999).

[RUSSELL HITTINGER]

STAFFORD, JAMES FRANCIS

Cardinal, president of the Pontifical Council for the Laity, archbishop emeritus of Denver, Colorado; b. 26 July 1932, Baltimore, Maryland, the only child of businessman Francis Emmett and Mary Dorothy (Stanton) Stafford. Always studious and an achiever, Stafford entered Loyola College in Baltimore in 1950 with the intention of pursuing a career in medicine, but in 1952 the violent death of a friend caused him to rethink his future and to enter St. Mary's Seminary in Baltimore. In 1954 he was sent to the Pontifical Gregorian University in Rome, where he received a licentiate in sacred theology in 1958. He was ordained to the priesthood on 15 December 1957 at the North American College.

After serving as a parish priest until 1962, Fr. Stafford earned a master's degree at the Catholic University of America (1964). He matriculated at Rutgers University in alcohol studies and the University of Wisconsin in management. In 1964 he was chosen assistant director and in 1969 director of the Baltimore archdiocesan Associated Catholic Charities, which, from 1969 on, ran most of the inner-city programs. In 1969 he was also named chairman of a committee to reorganize the central services of the archdiocese and in 1971 was made head of a committee to create its collegial structures, pastoral councils at three levels. In 1971 he was also elected by his fellow priests president of the priests' senate. When in 1976 Fr. Stafford was ordained auxiliary bishop, Archbishop William Borders appointed him urban vicar for the city of Baltimore.

In 1982, Pope John Paul II named Bishop Stafford the second bishop of Memphis, Tennessee. There he openly opposed the prevailing racism, defended the rights of workers, and opened new avenues of ecumenism. In 1986 he was named archbishop of Denver, Colorado. The most memorable event of his ten years there was Pope John Paul's visit on the occasion of World Youth Day (1993). In Denver Archbishop Stafford wrote and spoke increasingly on the importance of doctrine, ecumenical relations, marriage, family life, and other matters of current concern. In a 1994 pastoral letter he warned against land development in Colorado that displaced the poor and elderly.

In 1996, Pope John Paul called Archbishop Stafford to Rome to head the Pontifical Council for the Laity. In December 1996 he convened a Vatican conference on women. In 1997 he organized a World Youth Day for a papal visit to Paris along the lines of that in Denver as well as the first congress of lay Catholics in the Middle East, at Beirut, Lebanon. He also worked with a small group of American archbishops on a lectionary for the Mass to resolve the problem of inclusive language and was one of eight curial heads to sign an instruction approved by the pope that warned against assigning priestly roles to lay ministers. Pope John Paul elevated him to cardinal in 1998, assigning him the titular church of Gesù Buon Pastore alla Montagnola For the Jubilee Year Cardinal Stafford planned another World Youth Day and an international congress on the elderly, both in Rome.

Bibliography: THOMAS W. SPALDING, *The Premier See: A History of the Archdiocese of Baltimore, 1789-1989.* Baltimore, 1989.

[THOMAS W. SPALDING]

SUENENS, LEON-JOSEPH

Ecumenist and cardinal archbishop of Mechelen-Brussels, Belgium; b. Brussels, 16 July 1904; d. Brussels,

6 May 1996; studied at the Gregorian University in Rome (1921–1929) and was ordained a priest for the Mechelen (Malines) archdiocese in 1927.

In 1930 Suenens was appointed professor of philosophy at the seminary of Mechelen and then vice-rector of the Catholic University of Louvain in 1940, and in 1945 he became auxiliary bishop to Cardinal Van Roey, whom he succeeded as archbishop of Mechelen and primate of Belgium (1961). Suenens was responsible for the division that resulted in the creation of the new diocese of Antwerp. Pope John XXIII named him a cardinal in 1962, and soon after a member of the Central Commission for Vatican II. Suenens then presented the pope an outline of the themes he felt had to be dealt with at the Council. This outline was endorsed by Pope John and warmly supported by a number of influential cardinals, including G. B. Montini, the future Pope Paul VI. There no doubt that it decisively influenced the further proceedings of Vatican II.

Vatican II. Pope Paul VI appointed Suenens as one of the four moderators who guided the proceedings of the Council. His three main interventions promoted the ideas of a permanent diaconate, proposed an age limit of 75 for bishops, and stressed the value of charisms conferred upon the laity. Friendly contacts with non-Catholic observers at the Council resulted in Suenens' deep and personal involvement in ecumenical relationships. Year after year he was invited to the U.S. and to Britain by a wide diversity of ecclesiastical organizations as a leading figure of the post-conciliar Church. Meanwhile he pursued his efforts to defend the legacy of Vatican II, "keeping guard at the doors opened by the Council" (Methodist Bishop Corson). At the first Synod of Bishops (1967) Suenens recommended the creation of an International Theological Commission, which was established soon thereafter. This same concern prompted him to publish his book *Co-responsibility in the Church* (1968), which made a considerable impact. He later raised the same issue in two interviews which appeared in the French press. There ensued a heated controversy, in which Suenens had to vindicate his loyalty to the Holy See in the face of public criticism from high ranking prelates. His ideas on collegiality received, however, a wide support in the Second Synod of Bishops.

No less controversial was his proposal in the Third Synod (1971) that the ordination of married men be considered in regions where celibate priests were lacking. Throughout his episcopacy, Suenens has been constantly on the look-out for "signs of the times" and seeds of spiritual renewal for the Church. Hence interest in and support of the Legion of Mary, Marriage Encounter, and since the early 70s, the Charismatic Renewal. At the request of Pope Paul VI, he became the unofficial but very efficient shepherd of Catholic charismatic groups and communities throughout the world, which contributed in a decisive way both to their acceptance by the hierarchy and to the preservation of their Catholic identity. He also stressed the value of a spiritual renewal for ecumenical rapprochement. Suenens' wide range of interests and untiring pastoral zeal is best evidenced in the impressive series of books he authored: *Theology of the Legion of Mary* (1954); *The Right View of Moral Rearmament* (1954); *The Gospel to Every Creature* (1957); *Mary, the Mother of God* (1959); *The Nun in the World* (1962); *Love and Self-Control* (1962); *Christian Life Day by Day* (1964); *Co-Responsibility in the Church* (1968); (with Archbishop M. Ramsey) *The Future of the Christian Church* (1970); *A New Pentecost?* (1975); *Ecumenism and Charismatic Renewal* (1978) (with D.H. Camara); *Charismatic Renewal and Social Action* (1979); *Renewal and the Powers of Darkness* (1982).

When Cardinal Suenens reached the age of retirement in 1979, he resigned his see, but continued to promote charismatic renewal, always faithful to the motto on his coat of arms: *In Spiritu Sancto*. When he died at the age of 91, Pope John Paul II recalled the important role Suenens played at the Second Vatican Council.

Bibliography: L.-J. SUENENS, ''Aux origines du Concile Vatican II,'' *Nouvelle revue thé'ologique* 107 (1985): 3–21, with first-publication of original documents. E. HAMILTON, *Cardinal Suenens: A Portrait* (London 1975). P. WEBER, ''Le Cardinal Suenens,'' *la foi et le temps* 16 (1985–6): 400–422.

[P. LEBEAU]

SZOKA, EDMUND CASIMIR

Cardinal, president of Prefecture for the Economic Affairs of the Holy See, archbishop of Detroit; b. 14 September 1927, Grand Rapids, Michigan. Szoka's parents, Casimir and Mary (Wolgat), were immigrants from Poland. He earned a B.A. at St. John's Interdiocesan Seminary, Plymouth, Michigan, and then studied theology at Sacred Heart Seminary, Detroit, being ordained to the priesthood 5 June 1954. For the next seventeen years he served in several pastoral assignments, and was secretary to Bishop Thomas Noa of Marquette, Michigan, from 1955 to 1962, accompanying him to the first session of the Second Vatican Council. During those years he also pursued degrees in canon law (J.C.B. and J.C.L.) at the Pontifical Lateran University in Rome. He was appointed the first bishop of Gaylord when the diocese was created in 1971, and from 1972 to 1977 served as president of the National Conference of Catholic Bishops. In 1981 Pope John Paul II appointed him to succeed Cardinal John De-

Edmund Cardinal Szoka. (Catholic News Service.)

arden as archbishop of Detroit. In Detroit he was known as a more than competent administrator, who reached out to the laity by establishing groups such as the Friends of the Cardinal, which would meet regularly with him and voice their concerns. On 28 June 1988, the pope named him cardinal with the title of Ss. Andrea and Gregorio al Monte Celio, a church that is closely associated with Pope Gregory the Great.

In his time as archbishop of Detroit Cardinal Szoka gained a reputation as an efficient manager of finances and resources. In 1989 Pope John Paul II made him a member of the Council of Cardinals for the Study of Organizational and Economic Problems of the Holy See. When, the following year, John Paul appointed him President of the Prefecture of Economic Affairs of the Holy See, Cardinal Szoka resigned as archbishop of Detroit to take up residence in Rome. He is credited with introducing the use of computers into the Vatican on a large scale and modernizing its budgetary and accounting practices. He balanced the Vatican's budget, which for many years was operating at a sizable deficit. In fact, by the end of his fourth year as prefect the Holy See began to record modest surpluses. In 1997 the pope named him President of the Pontifical Commission for Vatican City State—in effect, governor of Vatican City. Pope John Paul has appointed Cardinal Szoka as legate to several assemblies of the Synod of Bishops and as special papal envoy on a number of occasions to Japan, Poland, and other countries throughout the world.

[THOMAS CARSON]

TISCHNER, JÓZEF CASIMIR

Priest, philosopher; b. 12 March 1931, Stary Sącz, in the southern mountain region of Poland; d. 28 June 2000 in Krakow. Ordained a priest in 1978. Studied philosophy at the Jagiellonian University in Kraków, where Karol Wojtyła (the future John Paul II) and the phenomenologist Roman Ingarden were among his teachers. Beginning in the 1950s Tischner contributed to the Catholic weekly *Tygodnik Powszechny,* which was at one time during the Communist era the only opposition newspaper in Poland, providing a forum for many of Poland's intellectuals. Using his position as head of the Papal Theological Academy in Kraków Tischner brought academics and other intellectuals together for discussions that Archbishop Wojtyła hosted in the archbishop's palace. In 1983, Tischner was instrumental, with the financial support of Cardinal Franz König of Vienna, in organizing the first of the biennial seminars at Castel Gandolfo that provided Pope John Paul an opportunity for conversation with intellectual leaders and academics in various disciplines.

An early supporter of the Solidarity movement, Tischner served as chaplain to its first congress in Gdańsk, September 1981. The sermon he delivered at the Mass anticipated by two weeks John Paul's social encyclical ''On Human Work'' (*Laborem exercens*) and touched on many of the same themes. Later that year, when the communist regime imposed martial law, he wrote *The Spirit of Solidarity,* which endeavored to expound philosophically the motive spirit behind this extraordinary social and political movement. This work set out to subtly demonstrate the errors underlying the ideology and practice of the Communist regime as concerns democracy, work, progress, and human dignity. The regime, he argued, had serious undermined the meaning of these important concepts in the public discourse, and so Solidarity must, building on the common bonds between people, and their common concerns (which Communism sought to obscure), restore them to their proper sense, that is, to show their full ethical dimension. In 1993, in another one of his works, *The Unfortunate Gift of Freedom,* Tischner chided people who, dissatisfied with the rapid changes underway, blamed the nation's newly won freedom for the threat of consumerism, abortion, pornography, and other social evils.

Like his teacher and friend, Karol Wojtyła, Tischner is notable as philosopher and academic who never lost the ability to speak to ordinary people. Many of his nine books were widely read and well received by a broader public.

Bibliography: JÓZEF TICHNER, *The Spirit of Solidarity*. Cambridge, Mass: Harper and Row, 1982. JÓZEF TICHNER and JACEK ŻAKOWSKI, *Tischner czyta Katechizm*. Kraków: Znak, 1997.

[PAUL RADZILOWSKI]

TOMÁŠEK, FRANTIŠEK

Cardinal, archbishop of Prague; b. 30 June 1899, Studénka, Moravia; d. 4 Aug. 1992, Prague, Czechoslovakia. Tomášek's father was a teacher and director of the local school; he died in 1906 at the age of forty. To be able to provide a good education for her six children, his mother moved the family to Olomouc. There Tomášek did his elementary and secondary studies with a stint in the army during the First World War. He entered the seminary of Olomouc in 1918 and was ordained to the priesthood 5 July 1922. For the following twenty-seven years he exercised his pastoral ministry in the archdiocese of Olomouc, joining the Cyril-Methodius theological faculty in 1934; he obtained a doctorate from the faculty in 1938. The Nazi occupation of the country and the closing of all the universities in Moravia and Bohemia interrupted his priestly and teaching activities. At the end of the war in 1945, he was able to continue teaching until 1950 when the Communist authorities closed the faculty. During these years he published his most important work, the best-selling *Katolicky katechismus*.

On 12 October 1949, Tomášek was elected titular bishop of Buto and appointed auxiliary of Olomouc. His election and consecration were kept secret because of the religious persecution of the Church by the Communist regime. Bishop Tomášek was imprisoned in the concentration camp of Zeliv from 1951 to 1954. After his release, he resumed his pastoral work as a parish priest in Moravaska Huzova. He was the only Czech bishop allowed to go to Rome to participate in the Second Vatican Council. When the Communist authorities sent Archbishop Josef Beran to exile in Rome in 1965, Bishop Tomášek was named apostolic administrator of Prague. He embraced the reforms of the "Prague Spring" of 1968, establishing a Movement for Conciliar Renewal; this was repressed when the state suppression of the Church was reasserted, following the Soviet invasion later that year.

Pope Paul VI created him a cardinal in the consistory of 1976 but reserved his name in pectore until 27 June 1977 when his name was published and he received the titular church of Ss. Vitale, Gervasio e Protasio. Later that year he was promoted to the metropolitan see of Prague. His cautious approach to the "Charter 77" movement that was trying to gain concessions from the government produced dismay among Catholic intellectuals. He later took a firmer stand towards the regime and the dissatisfaction faded.

Cardinal Tomášek participated in the two conclaves of 1978 as well as in four assemblies of the Synod of Bishops. In 1985, he led the Church in Czechoslovakia in the celebration of the 1,100th anniversary of the death of St. Methodius, even as Pope John Paul II issued the encyclical *Slavorum apostoli* to celebrate the evangelization of the elebrate the evangelization of the Slavic nations by Sts. Cyril and Methodius. He supported the "Velvet Revolution" of 1988, insisting on the use of non-violent methods to peacefully oust the Communist government. He hosted Pope John Paul II's visit to Czechoslovakia in 1990; the following year, the pope accepted his resignation of the pastoral government of the archdiocese. He died on 4 August 1992 in Prague and was buried in the crypt of the metropolitan cathedral of St. Vitus.

See Also: SLAVORUM APOSTOLI

[SALVADOR MIRANDA]

TOMKO, JOZEF

Cardinal, prefect of Congregation for the Evangelization of Peoples; b. 11 March 1924, Udavské, Czechoslovakia. Tomko started his priestly studies at the Theological Faculty of Bratislava and later was sent to Rome where he attended the Pontifical Lateran Athenaeum and the Pontifical Gregorian University, earning doctorates in theology, canon law, and social sciences. After ordination to the priesthood, 12 March 1949, in Rome, he became vice-rector and rector of the Pontifical Nepomucenus College and residence for priests from mission and Latin American countries (1950–65). During the same time he was active in pastoral work in the dioceses of Rome and Porto e Santa Rufina. In 1962 he entered the service of the Holy See as adjunct in the Book Censorship Section of the Congregation for the Doctrine of the Faith and four years later was promoted to "capo ufficio" of the doctrinal section. He was appointed special secretary of the first general assembly of the Synod of Bishops (1967). In 1970 he started an eight-year teaching career at the Pontifical Gregorian University; later, he cofounded the journal of the Institute of Sts. Cyril and Methodius in Rome. In 1974 he was appointed undersecretary of the Congregation for Bishops.

Pope John Paul II elected Msgr. Tomko titular archbishop of Doclea and appointed him secretary general of

Jozef Cardinal Tomko, protected by Burundian soldiers, walks through a crowd on his way to a requiem mass for Archbishop Joachim Ruhuna, who was murdered on 17 September 1996. (Reuers/Corinne Dufka/Archive Photos. Reproduced by Permission.)

the Synod of Bishops in 1979. At the consistory of 25 May 1985, Pope John Paul created Archbishop Tomko a cardinal, assigning him the deaconry of Gesù Buon Pastore alla Montagnola. He thus became, after the division of Czechoslovakia, the first Slovakian cardinal in modern times. Two days later he was named prefect of the Congregation for the Evangelization of Peoples and grand chancellor of Pontifical Urbanian University, posts he still occupied at the beginning of the Jubilee Year 2000. In 1996, Cardinal Tomko opted for the order of priests and the title of S. Sabina. He has participated in thirteen assemblies of the Synod of Bishops and was president-delegate of the Special Assembly for Asia (1998). His positions, both with the Synod and with the congregation for evangelization, have brought him in touch with the situation of the church throughout the world; he has represented the pope as his special envoy in twelve occasions, chiefly in Africa and South America.

[SALVADOR MIRANDA]

TRIDENTINE MASS

Named for the Council of Trent *(Concilium Tridentinum),* the Roman-Rite form of celebrating the Eucharist

had been in obligatory use from 1570 until the 1969 publication of the Order of Mass reformed by decree of Vatican Council II. In its 25th and final session in 1562 Trent left it to the Roman Pontiff to reform the Missal. Beginning in 1564, a commission under Pius IV and St. Pius V worked on the *Missale Romanum ex decreto SS. Concilii Tridentini restitutum, Pii V Pont. Max. iussu editum,* published in 1570 (last *editio typica,* 1962). A more accurate designation of the form of celebration proper to this Missal would be ''the Mass of Pius V.''

In current usage the designation ''Tridentine Mass'' may simply connote an Order distinct from that of the 1969 Order of Mass. Once the latter was promulgated, its use obligatorily replaced, first in Latin and then in the vernacular, the former Order of Mass. This was made clear by the Apostolic Constitution *Missale Romanum* (3 April 1969) of Pope Paul VI, and implemented by the Congregation for Divine Worship in the Instruction *Constitutione Apostolica* (20 Oct. 1969). The same document (no. 19) authorized Ordinaries to allow elderly priests to retain the 1962 Missal and its Order of Mass when celebrating without a congregation. These dispositions were repeated in the Notifications of the same Congregation

Instructione de Constitutione of 1971 and *Conferentiarum Episcoporum* of 1974.

Controversy. The opponents of Vatican Council II intend by the name ''Tridentine Mass'' an orthodox continuity with the Eucharistic teaching of Trent alleged to be missing from the 1969 Order of Mass, which they impugn as invalid, even heretical. In a letter to Archbishop Marcel Lefebvre, leader of the most publicized recalcitrance, Pope Paul VI expressed the reason for the obligatory adoption of the new Order of Mass: the unity of the whole ecclesial community, of which the Order of Mass is a singular sign. Paul VI also stated and rejected the key point of the Lefebvre opposition that only the Tridentine Mass preserved the authentic sacrifice of the Mass and ministerial priesthood.

The issue of the Tridentine Mass took a new turn in 1984. A survey of all the bishops of the Church, reported in *Notitiae* in 1981, indicated little dissatisfaction with the reformed Missal and a minuscule interest in a return to the Latin liturgy. Apparently, however, there were some loyalists who wished to celebrate the Tridentine Mass. In their favor the Congregation for Divine Worship announced in 1984 an indult allowing petitioners to celebrate a Tridentine Mass in the letter ''Quattor Abhinc Annos'' (*Acta Apostolicae Sedis* no. 76 [1984]: 1088–1089). The concession can be made by the diocesan bishop to those known to have no ties with the opponents of the 1970 Roman Missal. The celebration must be in Latin, follow the *Missale Romanum* of 1962, without intermingling elements of the 1970 *Missale Romanum*. The bishop determines the day and place of celebration and limits participation to the petitioning priest and faithful.

In 1988 John Paul II issued the apostolic letter *Ecclesia Dei,* which called for a wider and more generous application of the directives for the Tridentine Mass. The Pontifical Commission *Ecclesia Dei* issued guidelines implementing the apostolic letter in 1991. The guidelines indicate that the celebration of the Tridentine Mass may be celebrated in parish churches, the regularity and frequency of which depends on the needs of the faithful. The guidelines grant faculties to the local ordinary to give permission for the use of the 1962 Missal. It calls for the celebrants of these Masses to emphasize their adherence to legislation of the universal Church and the juridical value of the liturgy of Vatican II in their preaching and contacts. It does grant, however, that the new lectionary in the vernacular could be used at these Masses, but cautions that pastors should take care not to impose it and thus impede the return of those who maintain the integrity of the former tradition.

See Also: ECCLESIA DEI, MARCEL LEFEBVRE

Bibliography: International Commission on English in the Liturgy, *Documents on the Liturgy,* Collegeville, Minn. 1982, Documents 59, 61 (on the Lefebvre case) 202, 313 (promulgation of the new Order of Mass), 209, 216 (on the use of the new Roman Missal). J. J. JUNGMANN, translated by F. A. BRUNNER, *The Mass of the Roman Rite,* Reprint (Westminster, Md., 1986). ''La Messe du toujours,'' *Notitiae* 6 (1970): 231–232. Pontifical Commission *Ecclesia Dei,* ''Guidelines on the Tridentine Mass,'' *Origins* 21 (18 July 1991): 144–145. For the inquiry on the use of Latin and of the so-called Tridentine Mass, see *Notitiae* 7 (1981): 589–609. For the 1984 indult, see *Notitiae* 11 (1985): 9–10.

[T. O'BRIEN/EDS.]

TURCOTTE, JEAN-CLAUDE

Cardinal, archbishop of Montreal; b. 26 June 1936 in Montreal, the second of four surviving sons and two daughters (a seventh child died in infancy). Despite the family's modest means, all six children were well educated and all pursued professional careers. Turcotte attended the Sulpician André-Grasset classical college (1947–55) with the assistance of a vocational scholarship and the generosity of two maternal uncles, both priests. Turcotte pursued his studies at the Grand Séminaire de Montréal where he completed his licentiate in theology and was ordained to the priesthood, 24 May 1959. He was influenced in his early ministry by the Quiet Revolution. After two years as curate to Saint Matthias Parish (1959–61), Turcotte was appointed chaplain to the Young Christian Workers in 1961, and to the Christian Worker Movement and the Young Independent Catholic Women's Movement in 1964. He received a certificate in Social Pastoral Sciences from the Catholic University of Lille in France in 1964.

Archbishop Grégoire appointed Turcotte vicar-general and general coordinator for pastoral activities of the archdiocese in 1981 and John Paul II elevated him to auxiliary bishop of Montreal in 1982; he was installed as archbishop of Montreal on 17 March 1990, succeeding Paul Grégoire. The pope made him a cardinal in 1994, with the title of Nostra Signora del SS. Sacramento e Santi Martiri Canadesi, and that same year appointed him to the ninth general assembly of the synod of bishops, on religious and consecrated life. In 1997 the pope appointed him one of the presidents of the Synod for America.

Bibliography: PIERRE MAISONNEUVE and JEAN-CLAUDE TURCOTTE, *Jean-Claude Turcotte: L'homme derriere le cardinal* (Ottawa: Novalis, 1998).

[D. R. LETSON]

VACHON, LOUIS-ALBERT

Cardinal, archbishop of Québec City, and primate of Canada; b. 4 Feb. 1912, Saint-Frédéric-de-Beauce, Québec. Vachon's formal education began in the Minor Seminary of Québec, followed by the Grand Seminary of Québec, from which he graduated with a B.A. in 1934. He was ordained a priest of the Archdiocese of Québec on 11 June 1938. In 1947 he received a D.Ph. in philosophy from Laval University, Québec City, and in 1949 a D.Th. in theology from the Pontifical Angelicum Athenaeum, Rome. He taught at Laval from 1949 to 1955, and later served as the university's vice-rector (1958–59) and rector (1960–72); his years of service were interrupted by a three-year term as rector of the Seminary of Québec (1955–58). He wrote numerous works during his years in education in Quebec including: *Unité de l'Université* (1962), *Apostolat de l'universitaire catholique* (1963); *Progrès de l'université et consentement populaire* (1964); *Les humanités, aujourd'hui* (1966); and *Excellence et loyauté des universitaires* (1969). During the Quiet Revolution in Québec—which began in 1959 and continued through most of the sixties—the Church found itself either stripped or voluntarily divested of most of its responsibilities in the areas of health, social services, and higher education. Vachon presided over Laval's own transition in status and self-definition from a Roman Catholic university to a nonconfessional one.

Vachon was ordained an auxiliary bishop of the Archdiocese of Québec in 1977 and promoted to archbishop in 1981 following the resignation of Maurice Cardinal Roy. He was created a cardinal priest in 1985, with the title of S. Paolo della Croce a "Corviale." He was Prèsident de l'Assemblée des évêques du Québec from 1981 to 1984 and a delegate to the 1983 general assembly of the Synod of Bishops. It was at this synod that Vachon delivered a nuanced intervention, "Male and Female Reconciliation in the Church," in which he proclaimed, "let us recognize the ravages of sexism, and our own male appropriation of Church institutions and numerous aspects of the Christian life. Need I mention the example of the masculine language of our official-and even liturgical texts? . . . Our recognition, as Church, of our own cultural deformation will allow us to overcome the archaic concepts of womanhood which have been inculcated in us for centuries." The intervention caused the Canadian bishops, and more specifically the Québec bishops, to be identified as "progressives" on the issue of women in the church. Vachon resigned his see in 1990 and was succeeded by Maurice Couture.

[MICHAEL HIGGINS]

WEST, MORRIS L.

Novelist; b. 26 April 1916, Melbourne, Australia; d. 9 October 1999, Sydney, Australia. At age fourteen West entered the order of the Christian Brothers, leaving nine years later on the eve of his scheduled final vows. As a Christian Brother he completed an undergraduate degree and taught for six years in the Australian schools of the order, both lower grades and high school. World War II drew him into military intelligence, where he also wrote and published his first novel, notable especially for its autobiographical detail.

By 1954, having left the military and worked successfully for ten years in Australian radio, West had suffered a failed marriage and an emotional collapse. A year of total bed-rest left him recovered and committed to a life of letters. In 1959, following a period of European travel, a second marriage, and the publication of a handful of undistinguished novels, West gained world attention and a prodigious readership with *The Devil's Advocate.* The surface story of the Church's investigation into the possible sainthood of a villager in wartime Italy is thickened by the political and procedural intricacies of Vatican bureaucracy and subtle psychological layering of moral discernment. Thereafter, for nearly forty years, West's almost annual publications commanded wide critical and popular interest, interest centered within but not confined to denominational boundaries.

The Shoes of the Fisherman, written in 1963, projects much of the euphoric spirit of the Second Vatican Council while following the early papal career of an Eastern-bloc prelate. Kiril I spent years of his young life in a Soviet gulag, an experience that both toughened and humanized him in ways quite different from the usual clerical career path. His jailor, his personal persecutor, eventually becomes the Soviet premier; together they form a secret partnership to moderate East-West tensions. Both of these novels were immensely popular and both were recreated in film. Although West chafed at the label "Catholic novelist," which he carried throughout his publishing career, these two works, like many other novels he wrote, are fully immersed in a Catholic ecclesial context. Two titles with a similar intramural accent are *The Clowns of God* (1981), a futurist novel of a pope forced into abdication whose visions of the end of the world are feared as potential incitement to world crisis; and *Eminence* (1998), his final published work, which explores the possible direction of the papacy and Church after Pope John Paul II.

Equally characteristic of West's fictional style are his use of highly topical settings, which bring often powerful thrusts to his narrative momentum. In addition to Rome and the council, he uses, for example, Saigon during the Vietnam War (*The Ambassador* [1963]), and the Middle East in the midst of Jewish-Arab tensions (*The Tower of Babel* [1968]). The former title claimed wide interest for its insider's depiction of American complicity in the ouster and murder of a fictional President Diem. Students of West found in the novel a deepening interest in Eastern religion, especially Buddhism.

West's abiding interest in deeply spiritual encounters, explored within an explicitly Catholic context and idiom, combined with an ability to project his stories onto a stage framed by global ideological strife, caused him to be compared with Graham Greene. A half-generation younger than Greene and the other heroes of the Catholic literary revival, West differs most significantly for having caught the wave of hope released by Vatican II. Thus although his moral landscapes project shadowy, often ambiguous pathways toward awareness and the good, they are far less bleak, their protagonists far less abject. Instead one finds West's stories imbued with a powerfully rising tone of personal renewal and spiritual possibility.

The comparison with Greene was costly to his critical reputation. But there were other reasons why West was considered an author of the second level. His plots are masterfully crafted and instantly engaging, but they often crowded the border of melodrama. And the chronic complaint about religious literature that the penetration of the divine into the secular is achieved more by ''magic'' than by a sure sacramentalism haunted the reviews of his novels. Nevertheless, even his critics honored him for his dogged persistence in searching out those narrow passages in life when the challenge of the cross is faced.

In 1996 West wrote a loosely connected but engaging retrospective of his life, *A View from the Ridge.* In it he reflected upon the refusal of the marriage court of his Australian archdiocese to annul his first marriage in 1951, and he declared that the spiritual crisis it provoked was a decisive moment for both his life and his art. ''It forced me,'' he wrote, ''to examine the roots and meaning of my unexamined beliefs I had held and taught for so long.'' Thereafter and to the end of his life, West remained outside the sacramental gates of the Church. But many vestiges of his public and professional life testify to a profound loyalty and commitment to the faith community of his birth. And his literary interpretation of Catholic Christianity during the latter half of the twentieth century will serve the interests of historians for many years to come. He died in his home in Sydney Australia on 9 Oct. 1999.

Bibliography: M. L. WEST,*The Devil's Advocate* (New York 1959); *The Shoes of the Fisherman* (New York 1963); *The Ambassador* (New York 1965); *A View from the Ridge* (San Francisco 1996); ''Testimony of a Twentieth Century Catholic,'' *America* 117 (2 Dec. 1967): 678–681.

[PAUL MESSBARGER]

Morris L. West. (AP/Wide World Photos. Reproduced by permission.)

WILLEBRANDS, JOHANNES GERARDUS MARIA

Cardinal, president of the Pontifical Council for Promoting Christian Unity, archbishop of Utrecht and primate of Holland; b. 4 Sept. 1909, Bovenkarspel, Netherlands. Willebrands studied in the seminary of Warmond and was ordained a priest 26 May 1934. He earned a doctorate in philosophy at the University of St. Thomas Aquinas (Angelicum), Rome, in 1937 with a dissertation entitled ''The Illative Sense in the Thought of John Henry Newman.'' Back in Holland he taught at Warmond, becoming rector of the seminary in 1945.

In 1946 Willebrands accepted the presidency of the St. Willebrord Association, a group devoted to promoting Catholic apologetics. Through his efforts it developed into an instrument for promoting ecumenism in the Netherlands. Even more significant was his cooperation with a priest friend, Frans Thijssen, in founding the Catholic Conference for Ecumenical Questions. This unofficial group of Catholic scholars became, with the knowledge of the Dutch bishops and the Holy See, a kind of informal contact from within the Catholic Church with Orthodox, Anglican, and Protestant ecumenists and leaders. It contributed notably to the coming into being and operation of the Pontifical Council for Promoting Christian Unity.

Johannes Cardinal Willebrands. (© Bettmann/CORBIS)

In 1960 Pope John XXIII chose Monsignor Willebrands to be the secretary of the preparatory commission on ecumenism for the Second Vatican Council, under the presidency of Cardinal Augustin Bea, S.J. In 1962 Willebrands visited Orthodox leaders, secretaries of world confessional families (e.g. Lutheran World Federation, World Alliance of Reformed Churches, etc.), and the World Council of Churches to explain the new ecumenical outreach on the part of the Catholic Church. This prepared the ground for other confessions to send observers to the council and, in the long run, led to the bilateral theological dialogues that began after the council and were to be central in the Catholic ecumenical enterprise.

Working with a number of scholars who had been in the Catholic Conference, Willebrands produced the text that was the basis for the conciliar Decree on Ecumenism, *Unitatis Redintegratio.* Willebrands also had major responsibility for the Declaration on Religious Liberty (*Dignitatis humanae*), the Declaration on the Relations of the Church to Non-Christian Religions (*Nostra Aetate*), and a substantial part of the Constitution on Divine Revelation (*Dei Verbum*).

Pope Paul VI consecrated Monsignor Willebrands titular bishop of Mauritania in 1964. Before the council ended, the preparatory commission for ecumenism was declared a permanent organ of the Roman Curia with the title of Secretariat for Promoting Christian Unity. (In 1988 it was renamed the Pontifical Council for Promoting Christian Unity.) After Cardinal Bea died in 1968 Willebrands was named president of the new dicastery and created cardinal deacon of Saints Cosmas and Damian. Under his guidance the secretariat produced a Directory on Ecumenism and initiated a series of international bilateral theological dialogues with major Christian confessions (as of the year 2000 there are nine of these) as well as a cooperative relationship with the World Council of Churches, especially its Faith and Order Commission. To promote reception of the ecumenical stance of Vatican II within the Catholic Church Willebrands encouraged the establishment of ecumenical commissions in bishops' conferences and began to have occasional meetings of their representatives in Rome. In 1974 Willebrands established within the secretariat the Commission for Religious Relations with Judaism, based on Vatican II's *Nostra Aetate 4.* He guided it carefully to focus on questions of doctrine, pastoral practice, and religious formation, avoiding complicated political questions. This approach bore visible and striking results with the visit of Pope John Paul II to the Rome synagogue in 1986 and ultimately to the more spectacular papal visit to Israel in 2000.

In 1975 Pope Paul VI asked Cardinal Willebrands to become archbishop of Utrecht and primate of Holland while remaining president of the secretariat. This meant living in Utrecht but coming to Rome at regular intervals. These visits became less frequent as he dealt with a Church whose institutions had been deconstructed by postconciliar polarization and by secularization. Using his sympathetic style and human relations skills he was able to win respect for his leadership and establish some sort of equilibrium without being able fully to recuperate the forces of the Church. It was a relief in 1983 to hand over the archdiocese to a successor whose way he had prepared. He returned to Rome at an important moment as several of the relationships and ecumenical dialogues were reaching new maturity. His collaboration with Pope John Paul II became closer and ever more fruitful. He provided leadership in such events as the 1986 Assisi World Day of Prayer for Peace and responded to the crisis in relations with the Anglican Communion and with the Orthodox Churches, as well as encouraged the ever-more promising theological developments with the Lutheran World Federation and with the Faith and Order Commission of the World Council of Churches.

When Willebrands reached the statutory age of retirement at seventy-five, John Paul asked him to continue in office; he did so until his eightieth birthday in 1989, at which time he became president emeritus of the Pontifical Council for Promoting Christian Unity and the Commission for Religious Relations with the Jews. Willem Visser't Hooft, the founding secretary of the World Council of Churches, described Cardinal Willebrands as "a man with a fine combination of vision and realism." That quality enabled him to give a stamp and direction to Catholic participation in the ecumenical movement. For the communications media, he never became the iconic figure that Cardinal Bea was. Yet Willebrands has been the architect of the current Catholic official ecumenical engagement, which has had Pope John Paul II as its immensely talented entrepreneur.

Bibliography: The Pontifical Council for Promoting Christian Unity: Information Service, nos: 1–101 (1966 to 2000) contains most major addresses, letters and articles by Cardinal Willebrands. Number 101 is devoted to him and includes biographical material, a selection of his writings and speeches and an evaluation of the present ecumenical situation. JAN GROOTAERS, "Jan Cardinal Willebrands: The Recognition of Ecumenism in the Roman Catholic Church," *One in Christ* 6, no. 1 (1970): 23–44. CARDINAL JOHANNES WILLEBRANDS, "The Future of Ecumenism," *One in Christ* 11, no. 4 (1975): 310–323.

[BASIL MEEKING]

WINNING, THOMAS JOSEPH

Cardinal, archbishop of Glasgow, Scotland; b. 3 June 1925, Wishaw, Lanarkshire, Scotland. Winning was the only son of Thomas Winning and Agnes (née Canning). He began his studies for the priesthood at St. Mary's College, Blairs (1941–43), where he studied philosophy. His theological studies started at St. Peter's College Glasgow, and continued, once peace was restored in Europe, at the newly reopened Pontifical Scots College in Rome and the Gregorian University, from which he obtained his licence in Sacred Theology. Although he had been accepted as a student for the archdiocese of Glasgow, he was ordained to the priesthood on 18 December 1948 for the newly created suffragan diocese of Motherwell. Following a brief curacy at Chapelhall (1949–50), he returned to the Scots College in Rome and received a doctorate cum laude in canon law at the Gregorian University in 1953.

Following his return to Scotland, he served in several pastoral assignments, and was diocesan secretary from 1956 to 1961. In 1961, he was appointed as spiritual director at the Scots College, and returned to Rome (1961–66). While there, he was appointed an advocate of the Sacred Roman Rota (1965). On his return to Scotland, he became parish priest at St. Luke's, Motherwell, and also *Officialis* and Vicar Episcopal of the Motherwell diocese. In 1970, the Scottish hierarchy established a National Scottish Marriage Tribunal, and Thomas Winning was appointed its first president.

On 22 October 1971 Winning was nominated titular bishop of Louth and appointed auxiliary bishop of Glasgow, receiving, receiving episcopal ordination from the archbishop of Glasgow on 30th November, the Feast of St. Andrew. Following the death of Archbishop Scanlan, he was translated to Glasgow as Archbishop in 1974. Twenty years later, Pope John Paul II created him cardinal priest (26 November 1994), with the title of S Andrea delle Fratte. The only Scottish cardinal, he has been a prominent spokesman for the church. In 1997 he attracted national attention for offering spiritual, personal, and financial help to any woman faced with the possibility of an unwanted pregnancy; those who felt that abortion was the only option would receive financial support from the Church to enable them to have their child. The same year, he was appointed special papal envoy to the celebration of the fourteenth centenary of the death of St. Columba.

[MICHAEL PURCELL]

WORLD YOUTH DAY

The observance of a World Youth Day grew out of the United Nations International Youth Year in 1985. Pope John Paul II encouraged its annual observance by Roman Catholics. In most countries of the Catholic world, the observance is held on Palm Sunday, but in the United States it is customarily set for the last Sunday in October. Every second year, at the bidding of Pope John Paul, the Vatican Council for the Laity in collaboration with the bishops of the host country has organized an international gathering. Young adults and youth, thirteen to thirty, from all over the world come together to witness, proclaim, and celebrate their Christian faith. The 1987 assembly met in Buenos Aires, Argentina; in 1989 in Santiago de Compostela, Spain; in 1991, in Częstochowa, Poland; in 1993, in Denver, Colorado; and in 1995, in Manila, Philippines. John Paul II was present at these gatherings, attended in each case by several hundred thousand young people. The international celebration of World Youth Day in 1997 was held in Paris. In the interim period between 1997 and World Youth Day 2000, regional events were held throughout the world. For example, Chile hosted the celebration for North, Central, and South America. World Youth Day 2000 is a Jubilee event in Rome, taking as its theme "The Word Became Flesh and Dwelt Among Us."

Bibliography: C. VAN DER PLANCKE "La rencontre mondiale des jeunes à Częstochowa et la construction de l'Europe," *Lumen Vitae* 47 (1992): 61–66.

[B. L. MARTHALER]

World Youth Day. (Catholic News Service.)

WYSZYŃSKI, STEFAN

Cardinal, archbishop of Gniezno and Warsaw, Poland; b. 3 August 1901 in the village of Zuzela on the River Bug (then in the Russian Empire, now in Poland), son of a church organist; d. in Warsaw, 28 May 1981.

Wyszyński's mother died when he was nine, and her last words were taken to mean that Stefan should become a priest, a vocation he remained certain of throughout his young adulthood. After finishing his secondary education at several different schools due to the adverse conditions of World War I, he studied theology and philosophy at the Włocławek Major Seminary and, despite ill-health, was ordained priest 5 August 1926.

After his recovery, he was appointed priest of the Włocławek Cathedral and editor of the diocesan newspaper. From 1925 to 1929, he studied law and Catholic social theory at the Catholic University of Lublin, writing a doctoral thesis on church-state relations and family rights as concerns education. He published prolifically on the subject of Catholic social teachings and their application in concrete social reform throughout the 1930s, and became actively involved in ministry to working-class youths, as well as in supporting the Christian trade union movement.

Targeted for arrest by the Gestapo after the Nazi invasion of Poland in 1939, he spent most of the years of World War II in hiding, during which time he variously ministered to the blind and served as a chaplain to the Polish underground resistance movement.

On 25 March 1946, he was named bishop of Lublin, and consecrated in Częstochowa on 5 May of that year. On 12 November 1948 he was named archbishop of Gniezno and Warsaw, and Primate of Poland; he was named cardinal of Sancta Maria trans Tiberim by Pius XII on 12 January 1953. It thus fell to him to lead the Polish church through the difficult years in which Poland was subjected to intense Stalinization. Wyszyński prudentially saw that although the church could not compromise its basic independence, it should also avoid, whenever possible, open confrontation with the Communist authorities. This did not stop the regime from imprisoning many priest, nuns, and bishops, or even Wyszyński himself (from 25 September 1953 to 26 October 1956), but it did spare the Polish clergy, already depleted by Nazi persecution, from another potential bloodbath. As a result of the ''Polish October'' civil disturbances of 1956, he was released from prison by the Communist authorities and appealed for public calm, thus helping to avoid a possible Soviet invasion of Poland.

In the next decade he devoted himself to encouraging the faithful to prepare spiritually for the great celebration marking the 1000th anniversary of Poland baptism in 1966, which, among other things, promoted Poland's strong tradition of Marian devotion, all as a way of strengthening the Polish church in the face of continuing attempts by the authorities to undermine it. He also took part in the Second Vatican Council.

Although in 1980 he proved slow to recognize at first the importance of the Solidarity workers' movement, in the last months of his life he gave it important and judicious moral support. A man of impressive charisma and charity, he was widely mourned at his passing. His case for beatification was begun in 1989.

Bibliography: ANDRZEJ MICEWSKI, *Cardinal Wyszyński: A Biography*. San Diego: Harcourt, Brace, Jovanovich, 1984. *Człowiek niezwykłej miary. OjciecŚwiety Jan Paweł II o Kardynale Stefanie Wyszyńskim, Kardynał Wyszyński o sobie, Kardynał Józef Glemp o Kardynale Stefanie Wyszyńskim.* MIROSŁAW PLASKARZ, et al, eds. Warsaw: Wydawnictwo Archidiecezji Warsawskiej, 1984). STEFAN CARDINAL WYSZYŃSKI, *A Freedom Within: the Prison Notes of Stefan Cardinal Wyszyński*. San Diego: Harcourt, Brace, Jovanovich, 1982. STEFAN CARDINAL WYSZYŃSKI, *All You Who Labor: Work and the Sanctification of Daily Life*. Manchester, N.H.: Sophia Institute, 1985.

[PAUL RADZILOWSKI]

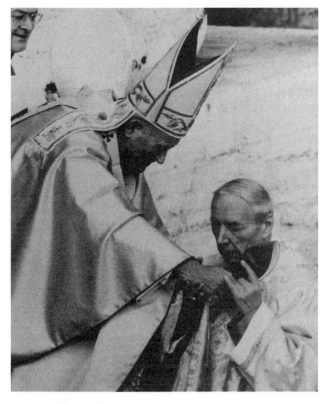

Cardinal Wyszyński kisses the pope's hands during the papal investiture ceremony in St. Peter's Square. (© Bettmann/ CORBIS.)

Cloud of Witnesses: Saints and *Beati*

INTRODUCTION

The veneration of saints, beginning with the cult of martyrs, has been a hallmark of the Catholic tradition from the earliest days of the Church. Between the sixth and tenth centuries, the number of deceased who received honor as saints notably increased. A reputation for a holy life, a great spirit of charity, and especially a report of miracles were the only requirements for sainthood in those early days. New names were added to the calendars and martyrologies; the number of feasts rapidly grew; and lives of the saints, often legendary, were written.

In the early medieval period popular fame or the *vox populi* proved to be an inadequate criterion for sanctity. Abuses crept in, and ecclesiastical authorities gradually introduced more formal procedures, first by local bishops, later by Roman pontiffs. The first papal canonization for which there is documentary evidence was that of St. Udalricus in 973. Pope Gregory IX formulated procedural norms (1234) that guided inquiries into a person's reputation for sanctity. In the sixteenth century when Pope Sixtus V reorganized the Roman curia with the constitution *Immensa aeterni Dei* (1588), he entrusted the task of overseeing the canonization process to the Congregation of Rites. The congregation developed procedures and norms that lasted into the pontificate of Pope Urban VIII. In 1642 Pope Urban codified the decrees governing the canonization of saints in a single volume under the title *Urbani VIII Pont. O.M. decreta servanda in canonizatione et beatificatione sanctorum.* In the following century Pope Benedict XIV wrote a masterful treatise that set the norms for centuries to come. *De Servorum Dei beatificatione et Beatorum canonizatione* explained in a clear and definitive manner the principles and methods governing the processes of beatification and canonization and clarified the fundamental concept of the heroic degree of virtue.

The 1918 Code of Canon Law summarized the juridical and administrative procedures in the beatification and canonization of saints (cc. 1999–2141). The 1983 Code says simply, "The causes of the canonization of the servants of God are regulated by special pontifical law"(c. 1403). Pope Paul VI issued two documents on the subject. *Sanctitas clarior* (1969) was a step in implementing Vatican II's constitution *Lumen gentium* (nos. 40, 47, 50). It clarified the competencies and procedures of bishops with regard to the introduction of causes of servants of God for beatification. *Sacra rituum congregatio* divided the Congregation of Rites into two congregations, one for Divine Worship and the other for the Causes of Saints. The new Congregation for the Causes of Saints included an office with historiographic and hagiographic functions.

Pope John Paul II's apostolic constitution *Divinus perfectionis magister* (25 January 1983) and the respective *Normae servandae in inquisitionibus ab episcopis faciendis in causis sanctorum* (7 February 1983) reformed the procedures for promoting the cause of a saint and restructured the congregation. The constitution enlarged the role of local ordinaries in saints' causes by giving them the right to initiate investigations into the lives, virtues, martyrdom, veneration, and asserted miracles for the candidate. It also assigned to the congregation a college of relators whose task is to assist with the drafting of the *Positiones super vita et virtutibus (o super martyrio)* of the servant of God.

The importance that Pope John Paul II accords the saints as witnesses to Christian values may be seen in the number and variety of individuals that he has beatified and canonized. Between 1903 and 1978 there were a total of seventy-nine beatifications and ninety-eight canonizations celebrated under seven pontiffs. As of 30 June 2000 Pope John Paul II has canonized 324 saints in thirty-nine ceremonies and a formal confirmation of cult. Eleven of the ceremonies were held outside the Vatican in such diverse sites as (in order of occurrence): Seoul, Korea; Asunción, Paraguay; Messina, Italy; Santo Domingo, Dominican Republic; Madrid, Spain; Riga, Latvia; Olomouc, Czech Republic; Košice, Slovakia; and three sites in Poland. The saints recognized include 96 Vietnamese (martyrs), 93 Korean (martyrs), 32 Spanish, 29 French, 27 Mexicans, 17 Italians, 9 Japanese (martyrs), 7 Polish, 4 Czech (martyrs), and one each from Germany, Belgium, Hungary, Latvia, Croatia, Paraguay, Ecuador, the Philippines, Canada, and Chile.

During that same period Pope John Paul has beatified 993 individuals in 122 ceremonies, four confirmations of cult, and three liturgical confirmations. Forty-six of the beatifications were celebrated during papal visits outside the Vatican in Australia (Sydney), Austria (Vienna), Belgium (Brussels), Brazil (São Paulo), Canada (Montréal), Chile (Santiago), Congo (Kinshasa), Croatia (Zagreb), Ecuador (Guayaquil), France (Lyons, Paris), Germany (Berlin, Cologne, Münich), India (Kottayam, Kerala), Italy (Asti, Bologna, Brescia, Caravaggio, Colle Don Bosco, Florence, Genoa, Susa, Trent, Turin, Vercelli), Lesotho (Maseru), Malagasy Republic (Tananarive), Mexico (Mexico City), Nigeria (Onitsha), Papua New Guinea (Port Moresby), Peru (Arequipa), Poland (Białystok, Kraków, Poznán, Rzeszow, Toruñ, Warsaw, Zakopane), Slovenia (Maribor), Spain (Seville), Sri Lanka (Colombo).

John Paul II has called on the Church ''to foster the recognition of the heroic virtues of men and women who have lived their Christian vocation in marriage'' and to honor Christ by acknowledging his ''presence through the fruits of faith, hope and charity present in men and women of many different tongues and races who have followed Christ in various forms of Christian vocation'' (*Tertio millennio adveniente*, no. 37). The new saints and blesseds represent all walks of life from peasant to royalty; laity, religious, and the ordained; artists, children, farmers, founders, scientists, scholars—in short, the whole gamut of human experience.

Announcing the Jubilee 2000, John Paul II placed special emphasis on the person of the martyr, noting that at the end of the second millennium, ''The Church has once again become a Church of the martyrs'' (ibid.). The majority of those raised to the altars are martyrs who died primarily in the twentieth century during periods of civil unrest and religious persecution, including World War II, the Spanish Civil War, and the Mexican Revolution. The increased number of beatification and canonizations in last century manifests the vitality of the local Churches (ibid.). The pope sees these canonizations and beatifications as an instrument for the evangelization of local churches and as a sign of the universal call to salvation and holiness.

[K. RABENSTEIN/EDS.]

AGNES OF BOHEMIA, ST.

A.k.a. Agnes of Prague; princess; Poor Clare abbess; b. Prague, Bohemia, c. 1200–1205?; d. Prague, Bohemia, 2 March 1281 or 1282; canonized by Pope John Paul II, 12 November 1989.

Agnes was the daughter of Ottokar I, King of Bohemia, and Constance of Hungary, the sister of King Andreas II of Hungary, and also the cousin of St. Elizabeth of Hungary (1207–1231). Although she was betrothed at the age of three to Boleslaus, son of Duke Henry of Silesia, she received her early education from the Cistercian nuns of Trebnitz and was attracted to religious life. In order to free herself from her obligation to marry, she appealed to Pope Gregory IX, who intervened on her behalf and allowed her to consecrate herself to virginity.

Agnes constructed two hospitals for the poor and persuaded members of the Military Order of Crusaders of the Red Star (Bethlehemites) to staff them. In 1232, Agnes built a Franciscan friary and the Poor Clare convent of Saint Savior in Prague. Saint Clare sent her five nuns from Assisi to help establish the convent, where Agnes received the veil in 1234 or 1236 and was later elected abbess. Four letters from St. Clare addressed to Agnes are extant.

Agnes is known for her humility and loving service to others. She enjoyed cooking for the sisters and mending the clothes of lepers. She is said to have performed miracles and to have possessed the power to see the future (prescience). She predicted the victory of her brother Wenceslaus I, the King of Bohemia, over the Duke of Austria. Before her peaceful death, Agnes obtained permission to give up all revenues and property held in common.

Agnes was buried near her convent. About 1322, her body was exhumed and transferred to a special coffin that was lost during the Hussite uprising. At the time of her canonization, Pope John Paul II praised the new saint:

> She is an example of courage and spiritual help for the young people who generously consecrate themselves to the religious life; for all those who follow Christ, she is a stimulus of charity practiced toward everyone with total dedication, overcoming every barrier of race, nation or mentality.

Feast: 2 March (Franciscans).

Bibliography: I. BRADY, ed. *The Legend and Writings of St Clare of Assisi.* New York, 1953. M. FASSBINDER. *Die selige Agnes von Prag, eine königliche Klarissin.* Werl, 1957. T. JOHNSON. ''To Her Who Is Half of Her Soul: Clare of Assisi and the Medieval Epistolary Tradition [analysis of Clare's letters to Agnes of Prague].'' *Magistra: A Journal of Women's Spirituality in History* 2, no.1 (Summer 1996): 24–50. W.W. SETON. *Some New Sources for the Life of Bl. Agnes of Bohemia.* 1915. Reprint. Aberdeen, Scotland, 1966.

[K. RABENSTEIN]

AGOSTINI, ZEFERINO, BL.

Founder of the Ursuline Daughters of Mary Immaculate; b. 24 Sept. 1813,Verona, Venetia, Italy; d. there, 6 April 1896; beatified 25 Oct. 1998.

The elder child of a doctor, Antonio Agostini, and Angela Frattini, Agostini's father died while he was still young. His mother ensured that her two sons received a Christian education at local schools. He entered the seminary as a day student and was distinguished by his piety, concern for contemporary problems, discipline, and success in his studies. Agostini was ordained on 11 March 1837. Assigned to parish work, he took charge of catechesis and the recreational program for boys. In 1845, he was named pastor of a large, poor parish, a position he maintained until his death 50 years later. He started many social and pastoral initiatives in this very populated district of the city, but his special concern was the education of women and girls. He founded the Pious Union of Sisters, dedicated to St. Angela Merici, in response to three young women who were volunteering themselves as religious to serve the poor. The rule received episcopal approbation in 1856. That same year he founded a school for destitute girls and the congregation of the Ursuline Daughters of Mary Immaculate primarily for those assistants in the school who wished to live in community. The first 12 Ursulines professed their vows in 1869.

His spirituality is marked by long periods of daily prayer and a particular devotion to Angela Merici, in whom he found a model for the education of girls.

During the beatification Mass in Rome on 25 Oct. 1998, John Paul II described Agostini as "a humble and sure witness of the Gospel, in Verona, during the second half of the nineteenth century, at a very fruitful time for the Italian Church. His faith was strong, his charitable action efficacious, and his priestly spirit a burning flame."

Bibliography: *Acta Apostolicae Sedis,* no. 21 (1998): 1049. *L'Osservatore Romano,* English edition, no. 43 (1998): 3.

[K. RABENSTEIN]

ALBERT, FEDERICO, BL.

Priest, founder of the Congregation of Vincentian Sisters of the Immaculate Conception (Albertines); b. 16 October 1820, Turin, Piedmont, Italy; d. 30 September 1876, Lanzo Torinese, Italy; beatified by John Paul II, 30 September 1984.

Although Federico Albert recognized his vocation to the priesthood early in life, he could not afford to attend the seminary. As an adult he passed the required examinations for candidates to the priesthood and was ordained. Albert was an able pastor of souls in several Torinese parishes, as well as a spiritual guide for other priests. He was a friend and early collaborator of John Bosco, and himself served the young and old with special zeal. To provide the needy with further assistance, Albert founded and directed the Albertines.

Pope John Paul II said of Father Albert: "His spirit of faith, his unconditional obedience to the Pope and his bishop, and his priestly charity made him an element of balance among the members of the priesthood and a zealous pastor, particularly attentive to youth and the poor" (beatification homily).

Feast: 30 September.

Bibliography: *Acta Apostolicae Sedis* 77 (1985): 1020–1023. *L'Osservatore Romano,* English edition, no. 44 (1984): 6–7.

[K. RABENSTEIN]

ALLAMANO, GIUSEPPE, BL.

Priest; founder of the Consolata Society for Foreign Missions and the Missionary Sisters of the Consolata; b. Castelnuovo d'Asti, Piedmont, Italy, 21 January 1851; d. Turin, Piedmont, Italy, 16 February 1926; beatified by Pope John Paul II, 7 October 1990.

Giuseppe Allamano was the fourth of the five children of Joseph and Marianna Allamano. He was baptized in the same church as his great-uncle, Joseph Cafasso, and John Bosco. While a secondary school student at Valdocco, John Bosco served as his spiritual mentor. After completing his studies in Turin, he was ordained (1873). Thereafter he was a professor of theology and director of the Ecclesiastical College in Turin. In 1880 Allamano became rector of the Sanctuario della Consolata, a Marian shrine in Turin, which houses what is reputed to be one of the earliest known icons of the Blessed Mother (4th century). A residence for priests was attached to the shrine. Under his direction the Consolata again became an important center of Marian piety. He promoted many charitable works, won wide popularity as a preacher and confessor, and promoted Catholic Action, labor unions, and the Catholic press. Hemoptysis (coughing up blood) prevented him from following his dream of evangelizing abroad, but he founded the Institute of the Consolata for Foreign Missions (1901) and its companion Missionary Sisters of the Consolata (1910). He directed both congregations, as well as the shrine, until his death. In 1902 Allamano sent two priests and two lay missionaries to the Kikuyus of Kenya (Zanzibar). They baptized the king and opened 12 mission stations. Thereafter Consolata missionaries were dispatched to Mozambique

(1905), Ethiopia (1913), Tanganyika (Tanzania) (1922), Somalia (1924), and Brazil (1946). By the end of the century, about 1,000 Consolata Missionaries and 1,100 sisters were to be found in 26 countries. Allamano's spirituality is best characterized as trusting in God's guidance of and provision for his work. He also had a deep devotion to the Blessed Virgin Mary, who originally brought the Word of God into the world. He died peacefully in Turin, where his relics are enshrined in a chapel dedicated to him at the motherhouse of the Consolata Missionaries.

During the beatification ceremony Pope John Paul II said of Fr. Allamano: ''He reminds us that in order to stay faithful to our Christian vocation we must know how to share the gifts we received from God.''

Feast: 16 February.

Bibliography: *Acta Apostolicae Sedis,* 82 (1990): 1020. *L'Osservatore Romano,* English edition, nos. 41, 42 (1990). L SALES. *Il servo di Dio Giuseppe Allamano.* 3d. ed. Turin, 1944; *La dottrina spirituale del servo di Dio Can. G. Allamano.* Turin, 1949.

[K. RABENSTEIN]

ALMERÍA, MARTYRS OF, BB.

d. 29 August to 12 September 1936, Almería, Andalucia, Spain; beatified by John Paul II, 10 October 1993.

At the outbreak of the three-year Spanish Civil War, 19 Lasallian Brothers of the Christian Schools (Christian Brothers) ran a free school and St. Joseph's College in Almería in the southeastern-most corner of the Iberian Peninsula. On 22 July 1936, members of the Popular Front arrested and confined in makeshift prisons the local religious as enemies of the revolution. Although some survived the privation and mistreatment, two bishops and seven Christian Brothers did not. Each of these martyrs was shot to death without a trial for the crime of professing and teaching the faith.

Herrero, Valerio Bernardo, Bl., baptized Marciano Herrero Martínez, brother; b. 11 July 1909, Porquera de los Infantes, Spain; entered the novitiate 1 February 1926; d. 30 August 1936 near Tabernas. Together with Brother Edmigio and Amalio, he was transferred on 3 August 1936 to the crowded Astoy Mendi prison, where their names were added to a list of religious. At the end of August the trio was loaded on a truck, presumably bound for Cartagena, but they were executed en route, and their bodies thrown in a well or mine shaft.

Medina Olmos, Emmanuel (Manuel), Bl., bishop of Guadix (Spain), the diocese just west of Almería; d. 29 August 1936. Bishops Medina and Ventaja were the first of this group to suffer. They were taken to an isolated spot with fifteen other prisoners and executed.

Mendoza, Amalio, Bl., baptized Justo Zariquiegui Mendoza, brother; b. 6 August 1886, Salinas de Oro, Spain; entered the novitiate 13 September 1902; d. 30 August 1936 near Tabernas.

Rodríguez, Edmigio, Bl., baptized Isidoro Primo Rodríguez González, brother; b. 4 April 1881, Adalia, Spain; entered the novitiate 8 October 1898; d. 30 August 1936 with Brs. Amalio and Valerio near Tabernas.

Rodríguez, José Cecilio, Bl., baptized Bonifacio Rodríguez González, brother; b. 14 May 1885, La Molina de Ubierna, Spain; entered the novitiate 21 November 1901; d. 12 September 1936, Almería. Brothers José Cecilio and Aurelio María were the last to die. They were briefly detained in a convent, then transferred to Capitan Segarra prison. They were among 28 prisoners executed by a firing squad. Their bodies were thrown into a mine shaft.

Säiz, Teodomiro Joaquín, Bl., baptized Adrián Säiz Säiz, brother; b. 8 September 1907, Puentedey, Spain; entered the novitiate 15 August 1923; d. 8 September 1936, Almería. Like three others of this group, Brothers Teodomiro Joaquín and Evencio Ricardo were transferred to Astoy Mendi prison. They were shot on the roadside. Their discarded bodies were never found.

Uyarra, Evencio Ricardo, Bl., baptized Eusebio Alonso Uyarra, brother; b. 5 March 1907, Viloria de Rioja, Spain; entered the novitiate 2 February 1923; d. 8 September 1936, Almería.

Ventaja Milan, Diego (James) Bl., bishop of Almería; d. 29 August 1936. Bishop Ventaja was given several opportunities to flee the war zone, but insisted upon remaining with his flock. He died with Bishop Medina and 15 other prisoners. A monument to his courage stands in Almería.

Villalón, Aurelio María, Bl., baptized Bienvenido Villalón Acebrón, brother; b. 22 March 1890, Zafra de Záncara, Spain; entered the novitiate 22 August 1906; d. 12 September 1936, Almería. Brother Aurelio María was director of St. Joseph's College. When he was shot, his prayer of several years was heard: ''What happiness for us if we could shed our blood for the lofty ideal of Christian education. Let us double our fervor and thus become worthy of such an honor.'' *See* José Cecilio Rodríguez above.

Feast: 16 November.

Bibliography: J. PÉREZ DE URBEL, *Catholic martyrs of the Spanish Civil War,* tr. M. F. INGRAMS (Kansas City, Mo. 1993).

[K. RABENSTEIN]

ALVARADO CARDOZO, LAURA ELENA, BL.

Baptized on 3 Oct. 1875, as Laura Evangelista, called in religion María of San José; is also known as María of Venezuela; co-foundress of the Augustinian Recollects of the Heart of Jesus; b. 25 April 1875, at Choroní, Girardot District, Aragua (then called Estado Guzmán Blanco), Venezuela; d. 2 April 1967, at Maracay, Venezuela; beatified 7 May 1995.

Laura Evangelista was the eldest of the four children of Clemente Alvarado and his then common-law wife Margarita Alvarado Cardozo. When Laura was three, the family moved to Maracay, where she received her early Christian education at home. From ages five to sixteen, she attended a private school, where she earned the esteem of her teachers and classmates. At her first communion she promised to serve God. Four years later on that feast she made a private vow of her virginity to Christ.

Shortly thereafter, she began instructing poor children at home, supporting the project financially with her own labor. Together with her spiritual director Fr. Vicente López Aveledo she worked to found the first hospital in Maracay, Saint Joseph's. She devoted herself to the care of the sick in spite of the difficulty of the work, the opposition of her parents, and the demoralizing poverty that surrounded her. In 1896, she was named director of the hospital.

Together with Fr. López she founded the Congregation of the Sisters of the Poor of Saint Augustine (1901), better known as the Augustinian Recollects of the Heart of Jesus. They assumed the rule of Saint Augustine and the habit of Santa Rita. Laura was named superior general and confirmed her vow of virginity in 1902. The following year she made her perpetual vows and took the name María of San José. Until 1960 when she was succeeded by Sister Lourdes Sanchez, Mother María guided the congregation's work of caring for the sick in thirteen hospitals, the elderly, and orphans in thirty-seven houses throughout Venezuela. After a long illness patiently borne, Mother María died at the age ninety-two. She was buried with her wooden cross in her hands in the chapel of the Immaculate Conception Home in Maracay.

At the beatification Mass, John Paul II said of the first Venezuelan blessed: "This extremely important event is like a new beginning in the life [of the Venezuelan Church]. In a certain sense the saints and blesseds confirm the maturity of the Christian community. . . . Her boundless love of Christ in the Eucharist led her to dedicate herself to the service of the neediest, in whom she saw the suffering Jesus."

Feast: 25 April.

José de Anchieta. (The Library of Congress.)

Bibliography: *Acta Apostolicae Sedis* (1995): 564. *L'Osservatore Romano,* English edition, no. 19 (1995): 1, 2, 4; no. 20 (1995): 2–3.

[K. RABENSTEIN]

ANCHIETA, JOSÉ (JOSEPH) DE, BL.

Jesuit priest, "Apostle of Brazil"; b. 19 March 1534, at San Cristóbal de la Laguna, northern end of Tenerife, Canary Islands, Spain; d. 9 June 1597, at Reitiba (now Anchieta), Espíritu Santo, Brazil. On 22 June 1980, shortly before his pastoral visit to Brazil, Pope John Paul II beatified José de Anchieta, one of the founders of São Paolo and Rio de Janeiro.

Anchieta was born into a noble family related to St. Ignatius of Loyola. After studying for a year in the Jesuit college at Coimbra, Portugal, he entered the Society of Jesus on 1 May 1551. Following his novitiate the 19-year-old Anchieta was sent to Brazil (1553) where he worked in the missions until his death 44 years later.

At first he was in the captaincy of São Vicente and was one of the founders of the village of São Paulo de Piratininga and the Jesuit school there. He learned Tupi, the language in general use on the coast and prepared a grammar for it that was published 10 years later. He also wrote catechetical texts and many canticles, dialogues and religious plays in Tupi and in Portugese for teaching the faith to the Indians.

In 1567, Anchieta was appointed superior of the Jesuits in the captaincy of São Vicente. During his 10 years (1577–1587) as the fifth provincial of Brazil, he was the major architect of a plan later used elsewhere to liberate the indigenous people from brutal slavery under the colonists. He gathered the natives into *aldeias,* communities similar to the *pueblas* in Mexico and *reducciones* in the Spanish colonies of South America, where they could be instructed in the faith, protected from exploitation, and taught the arts and letters. Much of the indigenous culture was preserved because he encouraged native crafts and music. He also possessed a fair knowledge of medicine, which he employed to help the natives. The last years of his life he spent in the captaincy of Espíritu Santo.

Above all, Anchieta was a man of action, a missionary of the first rank. During his life he was the object of popular veneration because of his apostolic work, his lofty ideals, and a certain untenable and unsubstantiated reputation for heroic deeds. He was said to have suppressed cannibalism practiced on enemy captives, who were eaten at ritual banquets, and to have protected the chastity of Christian Indian women, who were often raped in local wars. His fame as a miracle-worker added to his effectiveness as a missionary. No one has been so openly termed a saint, apostle, and father of Christianity in colonial Brazil as has Anchieta. Two biographers, Sebastián Beretario, who wrote in Latin, and Simão de Vasconcellos, who wrote in Portuguese, reflected in their writings the sincere feeling of veneration toward him then current in seventeenth-century Brazil. This devotion continues to be strong today among Brazilian Catholics. Pilgrimages are still made to the house of his birth in Tenerife and a bronze statue of him was erected in La Laguna in 1960. It is said that he baptized 2 million Indians. Although so high a number may be apocryphal, it assuredly testifies to his reputation for numerous baptisms.

Anchieta was an excellent writer, using both Portuguese and Tupi-Guaraní. In addition to two catechetical texts, he attempted to teach the faith to the Indians by composing many canticles, dialogues, and religious plays. One of his morality plays, the three-hour *Auto de Pregacão Universal,* performed in the open-air at Bahia, may have been the first acted in the New World. His other important theatrical venture was the allegorical *Na Festa de S. Lourenco* or *Misterio de Jesus.* He also compiled the first Tupi-Guaraní grammar (1555) and later a Tupi dictionary. His medieval-style poetry combined religious images with native customs.

After his death his body was buried in the Jesuit chapel at Espírito Santo The local tribes came in vast numbers to honor him. The bishop of Bahia preached at his funeral and named Anchieta the "Apostle of Brazil." Although Anchieta's cause was introduced by the petition of the Brazilian Jesuits in 1615, and he was declared venerable on 10 Aug. 1736, it had been forgotten during the suppression of the Society of Jesus in the second half of the eighteenth century. Pope John Paul II praised Anchieta for his pioneering missionary spirit sustained through his profound union with God.

Feast: 9 June (Jesuits).

Bibliography: *Acta Apostolicae Sedis* 73 (1981): 253–258. *Compendio de la vida del apóstol de el Brazil, V.P. J. de Anchieta,* tr. B. ANCHIETA (Xeres de la Fr. 1677). *L'Osservatore Romano,* English edition 26 (1980): 10–11. S. BERETARIO, *Josephi Anchietae Societatis Jesu sacerdotis . . . vita* (Lyons 1617). CRÉTINEAU-JOLLY, *History of the Society of Jesus,* II, 119 (Paris 1851). H. G. DOMINIAN, *Apostle of Brazil: The Biography of Padre José de Anchieta, S.J. 1534–1597* (New York 1958). S. DE VASCONCELLOS, *Vida do veneravel padre José de Anchieta,* 2 v. (Rio de Janeiro 1943). C. VIEIRA, *El padre Anchieta* (Buenos Aires 1945).

[F. MATEOS]

ANDREW THE CATECHIST, BL.

A.k.a. André de Phú Yên, lay catechist, protomartyr of Vietnam; b. 1625, Ran Ran, Annam (Vietnam); d. 27 July 1644, at Ke Cham, Annam.

A fervent Vietnamese Christian woman named Joanne convinced the Jesuit missionary Alexandre de Rhodes to accept her sickly, youngest son Andrew as his student. Rhodes later baptized Andrew at age 15 or 16. About 1641 Andrew joined the *Maison Dieu* (God's House) association of catechists and, in 1643, vowed with other catechists to serve the Church throughout his life. Despite a prohibition against Christianity, Andrew continued to spread the Gospel and as a result was beaten, tortured, and placed under house arrest in July 1644.

Mandarin Ong Nghè Bo offered Andrew an opportunity to recant the faith but he refused. Condemned to death, Andrew was publicly hanged and then decapitated. Fr. de Rhodes retrieved the body, and Andrew's remains were taken to Macao for burial. Fr. de Rhodes, an eyewitness to Andrew's martyrdom, recorded the circumstances of his death. Although many other Vietnamese martyrs, including 125 from the nineteenth century, were previously beatified, Andrew has been remembered by Vietnamese Catholics as the country's first martyr.

During the beatification Mass in St. Peter's Square on 5 March 2000, Pope John Paul II said: ''Today Bl. Andrew, protomartyr of Viet Nam, is given as a model to the Church of his country. May all Christ's disciples find in him strength and support in trial, and be concerned to strengthen their intimacy with the Lord, their knowledge of the Christian mystery, their fidelity to the Church and their sense of mission!''

Feast: 27 July.

Bibliography: *L'Osservatore Romano*, English edition, no. 10 (8 March 2000). PHAM DINH KHIEM, *The First Witness*. Saigon, 1959.

[K. RABENSTEIN]

APOR, VILMOS, BL.

Martyr, bishop of Györ in northwest Hungary; b. 29 February 1892, Segesvar, Hungary (now Romania); d. 2 April 1945, Györ; beatified in St. Peter's Square by John Paul II, 9 November 1997.

By birth, Apor was a baron, the sixth child of a noble family. Receiving his early education from the Jesuits, he began his theological studies at their college in Innsbruck, Austria (1910), where he earned a doctorate. After his ordination (24 August 1915), he was incardinated in the diocese of Nagyvárad, becoming a parish priest in Gyula. He served as a military chaplain during World War I and then returned to Hungary to assume the duties of prefect of Nagyvárad's seminary and curate in Gyula. He also founded a theological college. In 1941 Pope Pius XII appointed him bishop to the diocese of Györ because of his zeal for catechesis, his charity toward the poor, his ecumenical sensitivity, and his encouragement of fellow priests.

He condemned racist laws introduced in Hungary (May 1939) in writing and his sermons. Through his efforts and those of others such as Blessed Jósef Mindszenty, the majority of the Jews in Budapest were spared Nazi extermination camps. He was shot by Soviet soldiers on Good Friday 1945 while trying to protect about 100 women to whom he had given refuge in the episcopal residence, and died of his wounds on Easter Monday. He was originally buried in the Carmelite church, but is now enshrined in the cathedral of Györ.

During the beatification homily, Pope John Paul II called Apor: ''the 'parish priest of the poor,' a ministry which he continued as bishop during the dark years of the Second World War.''

Feast: 13 July (Györ); 23 May (Knights of Malta for whom he was conventual chaplain)

Bibliography: L. BALÁSSY, *Apor Vilmos, a vértanú püspök* (Budapest 1989). S. CSEH, *Apor püspök vértanúhalála: ahogy a*

Tapestry hanging from the central balcony on the facade of St. Peter's Basilica bearing effigy of Vilmos Apor. (AP/Wide World Photos)

szemtanú átélte (Budapest 1997). E. HULESCH, *Gyóori nagypéntek 1945: a koronatanú így látta* (Györ 1990). *L'Osservatore Romano*, English edition, no. 37 (1996): 6; no. 46 (1997): 1–2. E. SZOLNOKY, *Fellebbezés helyett: Apor Vilmos püspök élete és vértanúsága* (Szeged, Hungary 1990).

[K. RABENSTEIN]

ARMENIA, MARTYRS OF, BB.

A.k.a. Salvatore Lilli of Cappadocia and companions, martyrs; d. 22 November 1895, near Mujuk-Deresi, Cappadocia, Armenia (now eastern Turkey); beatified at Rome by Pope John Paul II 3 October 1982.

Among the 100,000 civilians of Armenia slaughtered by the Turkish Army in 1895–96 were Franciscan Father Salvatore Lilli and seven of his parishioners. Salvatore of Cappadocia (b. 19 June 1853 in Cappadocia) was the son of Vincenzo and Annunziata Lilli. He joined the Franciscans (1870), completed his studies in Bethlehem following the suppression of religious orders in Italy (1873), received presbyteral ordination in Jerusalem (16 April 1878), and was sent to Marasco, Lesser Armenia (1880), where he was named pastor (1890). He diligently cared for the sick during a cholera epidemic (1890). In an effort to improve living conditions, Lilli established schools, clinics, and other social services.

In 1894, he was transferred to the mission at Mujuk-Deresi. When the violent persecution of Christians began the following year, Lilli's superiors twice urged him to leave, but he refused to abandon his flock. The following month Turkish soldiers invaded the convent, injuring many including Lilli as he tried to help others. The Christians were confined to a convent cell, where they were alternately abused and cajoled in an effort to convert them to Islam. Lilli urged the farmers imprisoned with him to remain steadfast. En route under guard to Marasco, they were ordered to apostatize; they refused and were killed.

Killed with Father Salvatore were seven of his parishioners: Jeremias (Ieremias) Ouglou Boghos, Lilli's assistant; David Oghlou David and his brother Toros Oghlou David; Khodianin Oghlou Kadir (Khodeanin Khadjir); Baldji (or Baldju) Oghlu Ohannès; Dimbalac Ouglou Wartavar; and Kouradji Oghlou Zirou (also spelled Tzeroum, Ziroun, Zirun).

The ordinary process for their beatification was begun in 1930–32 and initiated in Rome in 1959 by Pope John XXIII. The apostolic process in Aleppo, Syria, (1962–64) investigated the veracity of the claim of martyrdom, which was testified by an eyewitness, an eleven-year-old girl who survived.

Feast: 19 November.

Bibliography: *L'Osservatore Romano,* English edition, no. 42 (1982): 9–10.

[K. RABENSTEIN]

ARNÁIZ BARÓN, RAFAEL, BL.

Trappist Oblate mystic; b. 9 April 1911, Burgos, Spain; d. 26 April 1938, San Isidro de Dueños, Palencia, Spain; beatified by John Paul II in Rome, 27 September 1992.

Rafael Arnáiz, the eldest of four children in a socially prominent family, was educated by the Jesuits, then studied architecture in Madrid. Following the completion of military service, he joined the Trappists (Ordo Cisterciensium Reformatorum seu Strictioris Observantiae) at San Isidro de Dueños in Palencia (1933). Almost immediately diabetes mellitus forced him to return home. Once he was better, Rafael returned to San Isidro, but was never able to become a monk because of his health. Another attack brought about his death at age twenty-seven. He is remembered for his continual search for unity with God and for his spiritual writings, which attracted pilgrims to his grave at San Isidro.

According to Pope John Paul II, during Blessed Rafael's brief but intense monastic life, he provided an example "of a loving and unconditional response to the divine call" (Beatification homily).

Bibliography: R. ARNÁIZ BARÓN, *Vida y escritos de Fray María Rafael Arnáiz Barón,* ed. M. BARÓN, 10th ed. (Madrid 1974). J. ALVAREZ, *Rafael* (Burgos 1952). A. COBOS SOTO, *La "pintura mensaje" del hermano Rafael: estudio crítico de la obra pictórica del venerable Rafael Arnáiz Barón, "monje trapense"* (Burgos 1989). L. MAQUEDA, *Un secreto de la Trapa,* 2d. ed. (Burgos 1993).

[K. RABENSTEIN]

ASENSIO BARROSO, FLORENTINO, BL.

Bishop of Barbastro (Spain), martyr; b. 16 October 1877, Villasexmir, Valladolid, Spain; d. 9 August 1936, near Barbastro in the central Pyrenees, Spain; beatified by John Paul II, 4 May 1997.

Born into a poor family, Florentino was able to go to seminary and was ordained in 1901. After earning the licentiate and doctorate in theology from the Pontifical University of Valladolid, he taught there. Illness forced him to leave teaching. Upon recovery Asensio was assigned to Valladolid cathedral. His serenity and piety resulted from his devotion to the Blessed Sacrament and inspired his homilies. He gained renown as a zealous preacher and spiritual director. He was consecrated bishop of Barbastro on 26 January 1936 despite civil disturbance. While he had initially hesitated to accept the position, he ministered with fervor, introducing reform, caring for the poor and the sick, and writing a pastoral letter that appealed for unity in Christ.

Soon after his consecration, he was watched by the Communist authorities. On 20 July 1936, he was placed under house arrest. Later he was imprisoned, then placed in solitary confinement, tortured, and mutilated for "collaborating with the enemies of the people." He was shot to death in a cemetery. His mortal remains were recovered from the common grave of the twelve shot with him, and placed in cathedral crypt.

During Bishop Asensio's beatification, Pope John Paul II related that the martyr proclaimed his staunch faith in Christ by serenely telling his executions: 'I am going to heaven.'

Feast: 2 August.

Bibliography: V. CÁRCEL ORTÍ, *Martires españoles del siglo XX* (Madrid 1995). W. H. CARROLL, *The Last Crusade* (Front Royal, Va. 1996).

[K. RABENSTEIN]

ASTORCH, MARÍA ANGELA, BL.

Mystic, virgin of the Poor Clare Capuchins; b. 1 September 1592, Barcelona, Spain; d. 2 December 1665, Murcia, Spain; beatified by John Paul II, 23 May 1982.

María Angela was professed with the Poor Clares in Barcelona. She was appointed novice mistress and formation director for her sisters because of her spiritual maturity. She had great care for her charges and was later elected abbess of the community. María Angela is often called the ''Mystic of the Breviary'' because her identification with the liturgical life of the Church led her to mystical union with God.

Pope John Paul II remarked at her beatification that ''she was able to respect the individuality of each person, helping the one concerned 'to keep in step with God' which means something different for each one. In this way her profound understanding did not become inert tolerance'' (beatification homily).

Feast: 9 December (Capuchins).

Bibliography: M. A. ASTORCH, *Mi camino interior*, ed. L. IRIARTE (Madrid 1985). L. DE ASPURZ, *Beata María Angela Astorch, Clarisa Capuchina, (1592–1665): la mística del breviario* (Valencia 1982). *Acta Apostolicae Sedis* (1982): 607. *L'Osservatore Romano*, English edition, no. 24 (1982): 6–7

[K. RABENSTEIN]

AVIAT, FRANCESCA SALESIA, BL.

Baptized Leonie (Leonia), educator, co-founder of the Sister Oblates of Saint Francis de Sales; b. 16 September 1844, Sezanne, France; d. 10 January 1914, Perugia, Umbria, Italy; beatified by John Paul II, 27 September 1992.

Leonie wanted to join the Visitation Nuns, but her family opposed her vocation. Her spiritual director, Father Louis Alexander Alphonse Brisson suggested that she found a women's religious congregation. Thus, in Troyes, France (1866), animated by the spirit of Saint Francis de Sales, the Oblates began providing Christian education to young women working in the mills that sprang up with the Industrial Revolution. The first sisters took their vows in 1871. Due to anti-Church legislation adopted in France at the turn of the 20th century, Mother Aviat moved (1903) to Perugia, Italy, where she began the order anew, wrote the order's constitution, received the approval of Pope Saint Pius X (1911). She died at age 69. She was declared venerable in 1978.

At her beatification, Pope John Paul II declared Mother Aviat ''dedicated her life to educating young working women.''

Alexander Palmieri, chancellor of the archdiocese of Philadelphia, speaks during a press conference in March 2000. Behind him are two sketches of Mother Aviat. (AP/Wide World Photos. Photograph by Chris Gardner.)

Bibliography: M.-A. D'ESMAUGES, *Leonie Aviat, Mutter Franziska Salesia, die Gründerin der Oblatinnen des hl. Franz von Sales* (Eichstatt 1993), tr. from Italian *Leonie Aviat Madre Francesca di Sales* (Padua 1992).

[K. RABENSTEIN]

BACCILIERI, FERDINANDO MARIA, BL.

Diocesan priest, tertiary of the Servants of Mary, founder of the Servants of Mary of Galeazza; b. 14 May 1821, Campodoso di Reno Finalese near Modena, Emilia-Romagna, Italy; d. 13 July 1893 in Galeazza, Bologna, Italy; beatified by John Paul II, 3 October 1999.

Ferdinando Maria Baccilieri was temporarily assigned as administrator of Santa Maria de Galeazza parish in Bologna, but stayed for forty-one years. In his youth he had attended the Bolognese school of the Barnabites and the Jesuit school at Ferrara, then joined the Jesuits at Rome (1838). Poor health forced him to return home. Upon recovering, Baccilieri studied for the priesthood at Ferrara and was ordained (1844). He dedicated himself to missions and to preaching (until he lost his voice in 1867). He also taught Latin and Italian at the seminary in Finale Emilia, and gave spiritual direction. He began (1848) doctoral studies in canon and civil law at the Pontifical University of Bologna. In 1851, Cardinal Archbishop Oppizzoni of Bologna asked him to administer the troubled Santa Maria parish, where he became pastor. He served with a deep affection for the poor, a strong devotion to the Virgin Mary, and a commitment to sacramental ministry.

Father Baccilieri founded a women's religious order, the Servants of Mary, to provide education for poor girls of the parish. The order started as the Confraternity of the Sorrows of Mary but became a more formal congregation as the members were clothed in the mantellate of the Servite Third Order (1856), began to live in community (1862), and adopted the constitution and rule of the Mantellate Servite Sisters in Rome (1866). The congregation, which was recognized by the archbishop of Bologna in 1899 and approved by the Vatican in 1919, now has members in Italy, Germany, Brazil, South Korea, and the Czech Republic.

On 6 April 1995, Baccilieri was declared venerable. A miracle attributed to his intercession was approved by the Vatican, 3 July 1998. In his beatification homily, Pope John Paul II called Father Baccilieri: "A poor 'country priest,' as he liked to describe himself, who cultivated souls with vigorous preaching, in which he expressed his deep inner conviction."

Feast: 1 July (Bologna).

Bibliography: M. G. LUCCHETTA, *Ferdinando Baccilieri* (St. Ottilien 1993).

[K. RABENSTEIN]

BAKANJA, ISIDORE, BL.

Lay martyr; b. ca. 1885 in the Boangi area of the Belgian Congo; baptized 6 May 1906, Mbandaka (Coquilhatville); d. 8 or 15 August 1909, Busirá, Congo; beatified by John Paul II, 24 April 1994.

Isidore Bakanja was baptized about age 18. He was working as a mason's assistant when he was evangelized by Trappist missionaries from Westmalle Abbey, Belgium. Isidore wore a scapular to attest to his new faith and so often shared his faith with others that many thought he was a catechist. Isidore migrated to Ikile in search of other Christians. There he was employed as a domestic servant by A. van Cauter, the agent of the Belgium Anonymous Society that controlled the regional rubber plantations and ivory trade. Finding that many of

the agents hated the missionaries, Isidore tried to return home, but was detained. On 2 February 1909, Bakanja was scourged, beaten, and incarcerated in chains for refusing to remove his scapular. Later, he was banished from the village so that the company inspector would not discover the cruelty inflicted on him. En route Isidore met the inspector, who was horrified at the festering wounds and cared for him until Isidore died about six months later. A canonical inquiry was begun for Isidore's cause (1913–14), but dropped for political reasons. In 1976, the cause was reopened at the request of a Zairean lay group, known as the Catechists.

During the beatification ceremony, Pope John Paul II declared Isidore a 'true catechist' who toiled generously for "the Church in Africa and for her evangelizing mission."

Feast: 15 August.

Bibliography: *Je meurs parce que je suis chrétien: le Conseil des laïcs catholiques médite sur la vie et le message qu'Isidore Bakanja adresse à ses frères zaïrois* (Kinshasa n.d.). C. DJUNGU-SIMBA K., *Bakanja Isidore: vrai zaïrois, vrai chrétien* (Kinshasa 1994). I. MATONDO KWA NZAMBI, *Le bienheureux Isidore Bakanja: la voix qui crie dans la forêt* (Limete, Kinshasa 1994). D. VAN GROENWEGHE, *Bakanja Isidore, martyr du Zaïre: récit biographique* (Brussels 1989). H. VINCK, *Bakanja Isidore: dossier pastoral* (Mbandaka, Zaire 1983).

[K. RABENSTEIN]

BAKHITA, GIUSEPPINA, BL.

A.k.a. *Madre Moretta* (Black Mother), emancipated slave, Daughter of Charity of Canossa (*Istituto delle Figlie della Carità*); b. *c.* 1869–70, Darfur, the Sudan, North Africa; d. 8 February 1947, at Schio near Vicenza, Venezia, Italy; beatified at Rome by John Paul II, 17 May 1992.

Although "Bakhita," meaning "lucky one," is treated as her surname, it was the name given to Giuseppina by the slave traders, who kidnapped the young Islamic girl. She was sold to various owners in the markets of El Obeid and Khartoum, where her fifth master, the Italian Consul Callisto Legnani, purchased her at about age twelve. When Legnani returned to Genoa (Liguria) with Bakhita, the wife of his friend Augusto Michieli asked and received permission to keep the slave with her. Bakhita became the nanny to Mimmina Michieli and moved with the family to Zianigo in Venezia. The Michielis returned to Africa to manage a new hotel, but entrusted their daughter and Bakhita to the Canossian Sisters in Venice. There she was formally introduced to the faith. A few months later (9 January 1890) Bakhita was baptized Giuseppina, confirmed, and received her first Communion. Upon the return of the Michielis, Bakhita adamantly expressed her desire to remain with the Canossians. Signora Michieli claimed ownership but the cardinal archbishop of Venice and the king's procurator intervened to declare her a free woman. She entered the novitiate, 7 December 1893, and was consecrated, 8 December 1896. Sister Giuseppina served her sisters for twenty-five years as cook, seamstress, and portress at the houses of Venice, Verona (1896–1902), and Schio (1902–47). She was especially beloved by the students for her sweet nature and musical voice. Before her final illness, Giuseppina traveled throughout Italy to raise money for the missions. The portrait of the former slave now hangs in the cathedral at Khartoum, Sudan.

The process for her beatification began twelve years after her death. She was declared venerable, 1 December 1978. After the required post-beatification miracle at Mother Giuseppina's intercession was approved, 21 December 1998, the consistory for her canonization was held 2 July 1999. Her canonization as the first Sudanese saint is scheduled for 1 October 2000, in Rome. Pope John Paul II beatified Giuseppina as a witness to evangelical reconciliation.

Feast: 8 February.

Bibliography: *M. Bakhita: Saintly Daughter of Africa Tells Her Story* (Harere 1997). *Bakhita*, (Kinshasa: Editions St. Paul Afrique, 1983).

[K. RABENSTEIN]

A tapestry depicting Giuseppina Bakhita. (AP/Wide World Photos)

BALDO, GIUSEPPE, BL.

Priest, founder of the Little Daughters of Saint Joseph; b. 19 February 1843, Puegnago (near Brescia), Lombardy, Italy; d. 24 October 1915, Ronco all'Adige near Verona; beatified by John Paul II, 31 October 1989.

Son of the farmers Angelo Baldo and his wife Hippolita Casa, Baldo entered the seminary of Verona (1859) and was ordained with papl indult for the Diocese of Verona in 1865 at age twenty-two. After serving as a parish priest for a time, he was appointed vice-rector of the seminary. During his decade of teaching, Baldo wrote books on spirituality and pedagogy. In 1877, he asked for and received a parochial position at Ronco all'Adige. Although he was contemplative and devoted to the Eucharist, he was also active in social work for the poor and marginalized. He established a mutual benefit society, schools for adults and children, a nursery, and a farm loan bank. He organized the Servants of Charity of Our Lady of Succor to care for the homebound sick, then founded a hospital (1888) and the Little Daughters of St. Joseph to staff it (1894). Baldo also established an Archconfra-

ternity of Christian Mothers, a Blessed Sacrament Confraternity, and a Society of the Forty Hours devotion. Baldo's holiness was especially evident in his patient endurance of illness during his last two years. In 1950, his mortal remains were enshrined in his parish chapel.

At Baldo's beatification, Pope John Paul II encouraged the faithful to invoke the new blessed "in order to imitate his example of faith, charity, and holiness."

Bibliography: F. MALGERI, *Don Giuseppe Baldo Prete di Ronco all'Adige* (Turin 1995). E. VALENTINI, *Il messaggio pedagogico sociale del servo di Dio, Don Giuseppe Baldo* (Verona 1956).

[K. RABENSTEIN]

BANDRÉS Y ELÓSEGUI, MARÍA ANTONIA, BL.

Religious; b. 6 March 1898, at Tolosa, Guipúzcoa, Spain; d. 27 April 1919, at Salamanca, Spain; beatified in Rome by John Paul II, 12 May 1996.

María Antonia, born into a well-to-do family in the Basque country of north central Spain near the border with France, was the second of the fifteen children of the lawyer Ramón Bandrés and his wife Teresa Elósegui. She attended the local school run by the Daughters of Jesus, the congregation founded by Cándida María Cipitria (who was beatified with María Antonia). Despite her family's position in society, María Antonia provided assistance and catechesis to working women in the suburbs. Seeking greater perfection, she joined Mother Cándida's order at Salamanca (8 December 1915) and professed her religious vows (31 May 1918). María Antonia's health failed when she was twenty years old. Her agnostic doctor, Filiberto Villalobos, and his friends Miguel de Unamuno and Indalecio Prieto testified that her serenity and patient endurance inspired their conversion to faith.

Pope John Paul II said of María Antonia: "United to Christ in her sickness, she left us an eloquent example of participation in the saving work of the Cross" (Beatification homily).

Bibliography: E. ITÚRBIDE, *Antoñita Bandrés Elósegui, religiosa de Hijas de Jesús: fuego de holocausto que redime* (Pamplona 1960).

[K. RABENSTEIN]

BAOUARDY, MARÍAM, BL.

In religion, Marie de Jésus Crucifié, a.k.a. Marie of Pau, Discalced Carmelite; b. 5 January 1846, at Abellin (Zabulon, between Nazareth and Haifa), Cheffa-Amar, Galilee, Palestine (now Israel); d. 26 August 1878, at Bethlehem; beatified by John Paul II, 13 November 1983, at Rome.

Miríam was born into a poor, Lebanese, Greek Melchite Catholic family headed by Giries (George) Baouardy and Maríam Chahyn. Her parents died when she was very young. When she was three, an uncle in Alexandria, Egypt, took in the orphaned Maríam and her brother Boulos (Paul). At age 13, she refused an arranged marriage in order to consecrate her virginity to God and entered domestic service. She had never learned to read or write. While working for families in Alexandria, Jerusalem, Beirut, then Marseilles, she discerned her vocation. In 1865, she entered the Sisters of Compassion but was forced to leave due to ill health. For the next two years (May 1865 to June 1867) she was a postulant of the Institute of the Sisters of St. Joseph of the Apparition until she was judged unsuited for the cloister because of the unusual manifestations of her spiritual life, which included levitation, ectasies, and stimagtization (1867–76). Together with her former novice mistress, Miríam joined the Discalced Carmelites at Pau, France (14 June 1867). In 1870, she was sent with a group of founding sisters to Mangalore, India, where she made her profession (21 November

1871). Her spiritual director, Apostolic Vicar Ephrem M. Garrelon, believing her mystical experiences were a sign of demonic obsession, obliged her to return to France in 1872. In August 1875, she traveled to Palestine to build a carmel at Bethlehem and to plan another for Nazareth.

Marie de Jésus Crucifié is best remembered for her humility and devotion to the Holy Spirit. Her cause was officially introduced in Rome on 18 May 1927. She is the patron of prisoners.

Feast: 25 August (Carmelites)

Bibliography: *Acta Apostolicae Sedis* 77 (1985): 5–8. *L'Osservatore Romano,* English edition, no. 48 (1983): 10.

[K. RABENSTEIN]

BARBAL COSAN, JAIME HILARIO, ST.

Baptized Manuel, a.k.a. Diego Barbal, Lasallian Christian Brother martyr; b. 2 January 1898, Enviny (Diocese of Urgel), Lérida Province, northern Spain; d. 18 January 1937, Tarragona, Spain; beatified on 29 April 1990 and canonized, 21 November 1999, by John Paul II in Rome, Italy.

At age twelve Manuel Barbal Cosan began his studies for the priesthood in the minor seminary at La Seo de Urgel. When he developed a hearing loss and was advised to return home, he feared that he would be unable to fulfill his religious vocation. He attended the De la Salle training center at Mollerusa for seven months, then the brothers of the Christian Schools at Irun, Spain, accepted him into their novitiate (24 February 1917). For sixteen years (1918–34) he taught at De la Salle schools (Mollerusa, 1918–23, 1924–25; Manresa, 1923–24; Oliana, 1925–26; Pibrac near Toulouse, 1926–34), and became known for his professional competence as a teacher and catechist, as well as for his piety and adherence to the rule. When his hearing loss became too profound to continue teaching, he worked as cook in the school at Calaf (1934) and in the garden of Saint Joseph's novitiate at Cambrils, Tarragona (from December 1934), while he continued to write about French, Castillan, and Catalonian literature.

Upon hearing of the martyrdom of his religious brothers at Turón (with whom he was canonized), he expressed to his family his desire to die likewise. En route to visit them, he was recognized as a religious, arrested at Mollerusa (18 July 1936), and imprisoned locally, then at Lérida (24 August). He was transferred to the prison ship *Mahon* at Tarragona (5 December). Refusing to win his release by denying his religious identity during the summary trial(15 January 1937), Jaime Hilario was taken to Monte de los Olivos cemetery for execution by firing squad. He was the first of ninety-seven Lasallian brothers of the District of Catalunia to die during the Spanish Civil War and in the first group of martyrs of the period to be canonized. His cause was joined with that of the Martyrs of Turón, who had died three years before Barbal.

Pope John Paul II said of the Lasallians: "They all prepared for death as they had lived: with persevering prayer in a spirit of brotherhood, without hiding their religious state."

Feast: 18 January (Lasallian Brothers)

Bibliography: V. CÁRCEL ORTÍ, *Martires españoles del siglo XX* (Madrid 1995). L. SALM, *The martyrs of Turón and Tarragona: the De La Salle Brothers in Spain* (Romeoville, Ill. 1990).

[K. RABENSTEIN]

BARBANTINI, MARÍA DOMENICA BRUN, BL.

Widow, foundress of the Pious Union of the Sisters of Charity and the Sister Servants of the Sick of St. Camillus; b. 17 January 1789, Lucca, Tuscany, Italy; d. there 22 May 1868. Pope John Paul II beatified Maria Domenica on 7 May 1995.

Maria Domenica's husband, Salvatore Barbantini, died six months after they were married in 1811, and a short time later she gave birth to a son. A woman of boundless energy, she balanced motherhood and care for her deceased husband's business while caring for those in need. Her own dedication and example attracted other women to the same work, and together they formed the Pious Union of the Sisters of Charity (1817). Following the death of her 8-year-old son, she abandoned herself completely to God. She lived for a time with the Sisters of the Visitation as she tested a contemplative vocation. Fr. Antonio Scalabrini, later superior general of the Order of St. Camillus, encouraged her to found the Sister Servants of the Sick of St. Camillus (1829). The archbishop of Lucca's approved of the rule in 1841 authorized the organization as a diocesan religious institute.

Bibliography: *Acta Apostolicae Sedis* (1995): 564. *L'Osservatore Romano,* English edition, no. 19 (1995): 2, 4.

[K. RABENSTEIN]

BARBASTRO, MARTYRS OF

Felipe de Jesús Munárriz Azcona and fifty companions; martyrs; members of the Congregation of Missionary Sons of the Immaculate Heart of the Blessed Virgin Mary (Claretian Missionaries); b. 4 February 1875 at Allo (Navarre), Spain; d. 2 August 1936, Barbastro (Huesca), Spain; beatified by John Paul II, 25 October 1992.

The first decades of the twentieth century found Spain mired in political upheaval and social unrest. Violent religious persecutions unfolded following the establishment of the Republic in 1931. During the civil war (1936–39) there was a massive elimination of priests, nuns, and Catholic lay leaders throughout Spain. Fifty-one of those killed were Claretians, mostly young seminarians who had recently arrived at the Claretian house in Barbastro to complete the last year of their theological studies.

On 20 July 1936, the students, their professors and superiors, and some Claretian brothers were arrested and accused of harboring weapons. They were taken to the auditorium of the Piarist seminary where they were subjected to various forms of psychological and physical abuse. Between 2 August and 18 August, all fifty-one were executed.

In addition to the superior, Father Felipe Munárriz, the following were also martyred on 2 August 1936: Father Juan Díaz Nosti (b. 18 February 1880 at Quinta de los Catalanes, Asturias); Father Leoncio Pérez Ramos (b. 12 September 1875 at Muro de Aguas, Rioja).

The martyrs of 12 August 1936 include: Father Sebastián Calvo Martínez (b. 20 January 1903 at Gumiel de Izán, Burgos); Wenceslao María Clarís Vilaregut (b. 3 January 1907 at Olost de Llusanés, Barcelona); Father Pedro Cunill Padrós (b. 17 March 1903 at Vic, Catalonia); Brother Gregorio Chirivás Lacambra (b. 24 April 1880 at Siétamo, Huesca); Father José Pavón Bueno (b. 19 January 1901 at Peral, Cartegena); Father Nicasio Sierra Ucar (b. 11 October 1890 at Cascante, Navarre).

The martyrs of 13 August 1936 include: Javier Luis Bandrés Jiménez (b. 3 December 1912 at Sangüesa, Navarre); José Brengaret Pujol (b. 18 January 1913 at Sant Jordi Desvalls, Gerona); Brother Manuel Buil Lalueza (b. 31 August 1914 at Abizanda, Huesca); Antolín María Calvo y Calvo at Gumiel del Mercado, Burgos); Tomás Capdevila Miró (b. 5 May 1914 at Maldá, Catalonia); Esteban Casadevall Puig (b. 18 March 1913 at Argelaguer, Gerona); Eusebio María Codina Millá (b. 7 December 1914 at Albesa, Lérida); Juan Codinachs Tuneu (b. 12 February 1914 at Santa Eugenia de Berga, Vic); Antonio María Dalmau Rosich (b. 4 October 1912 at Urgell, Lérida); Juan Echarri Vique (b. 30 March 1913 at Olite, Navarre); Pedro García Bernal (b. 27 April 1911 at Santa Cruz de Salceda, Burgos); Hilario María Llorente Martín

(b. 14 January 1911 at Vadocondes, Burgos); Brother Alfonso Miquel Garriga (b. 24 February 1914 at Prades de Molsosa); Ramón Novich Rabionet (b. 8 April 1913 at Sellera del Ter, Gerona); José María Ormo Seró (b. 18 August 1913 at Almatret, Lérida); Father Secundino María Ortega García (b. 20 May 1912 at Santa Cruz de la Salceda, Burgos); Salvador Pigem Serra (b. 15 December 1912 at Viloví de Onyar, Gerona); Teodoro Ruiz de Larrinaga García (b. 9 November 1912 at Bargota, Navarre); Juan Sánchez Munárriz (b. 15 June 1913 at Malón, Zaragoza); Manuel Torras Saez (b. 12 February 1915 at Sant Martí Vell, Gerona).

The martyrs of 15 August 1936 include: José María Amorós Hernández (b. 14 January 1913 at Puebla Larga, Valencia); José María Badía Mateu (b. 30 September 1912 at Puigpelat, Tarragona); Juan Baixeras Berenguer (b. 21 November 1913 at Castelltersol, Barcelona); José María Blasco Juan (b. 2 January 1912 at Játiva, Valencia); Rafael Briega Morales (b. 24 October 1912 at Zaragoza); Brother Francisco Castán Messeguer (b. 1 February 1911 at Fonz, Huesca); Luis Binefa Escalé (b. 18 September 1912 at Fondarella, Lérida); José Figuero Beltrán (b. 14 August 1911 at Gumiel del Mercado, Burgos); Ramón Illa Salvía (b. 12 February 1914 at Bellvís, Lérida); Luis Lladó Teixidor (b. 12 May 1912 at Viladesens, Gerona); Brother Manuel Martínez Jarauta (b. 22 December 1912 at Murchante, Navarre); Father Luis Masferrer Vila (b. 9 July 1912 at Torelló, Barcelona); Miguel Massip González (b. 8 June 1913 at Llardecans, Lérida); Faustino Pérez García (b. 30 July 1911 at Baríndano, Navarre); Sebastián Riera Coromina (b. 13 October 1913 at Ribas de Fresser, Gerona); Eduardo Ripoll Diego (b. 9 January 1912 at Játiva, Valencia); Francisco Roura Farró (b. 13 January 1913 at Sors, Gerona); José María Ros Florensa (b. 30 October 1914 at Torms, Lérida); Alfonso Sorribes Teixidó (b. 17 December 1912 at Rocafort de Vallbona, Lérida); Agustín Viela Ezcurdia (b. 4 April 1914 at Oteiza de la Solana, Navarre).

The martyrs of 18 August 1936 include: Jaime Falgarona Vilanova (b. 6 January 1912 at Argelaguer, Gerona); Atanasio Vidaurreta Labra (b. 2 May 1911 at Adiós, Navarre).

Numerous testimonies remain that witness to the events, including those of two Argentinean Claretians who were spared. The martyrs' own testimony is found in the writings they left on scraps of paper, on bits of chocolate wrappers, and in the inscriptions they made on the back of a piano stool. To the end, they sang, forgave their persecutors, and proclaimed their faith with enthusiasm.

The cause of beatification of the fifty-one Claretians of Barbastro was introduced shortly after the end of the Spanish civil war. Pope Paul VI put a moratorium on beatifications of Spanish Civil War victims that remained in effect until Pope John Paul II considered the situation in Spain changed and reopened the processes.

Speaking at the beatification in Rome, Pope John Paul II affirmed that "these Claretians died because they were disciples of Christ, because they would not deny their faith and their religious vows . . . with their blood they challenge us to live and die for the Word of God which we all have been called to announce."

Feast: 13 August

Bibliography: GABRIEL CAMPO VILLEGAS, *The Claretian Martyrs of Barbastro, August 1936,* trans. J. DARIES (Rome 1992).

[LEN BROWN]

BARBIERI, CLELIA MARIA RACHEL, ST.

Virgin, co-foundress of the Congregation of Minims of the Sorrowful Mother; b. 13 Feb. 1847, in Le Budrie, San Giovanni, Persiceto (diocese of Bologna), Emilia, Italy; d. there on 13 July 1870; canonized 9 April 1989.

Clelia was born into a working class family; the death of her father Joseph in 1855 left the family in poverty. Clelia assumed many responsibilities for the household so that her mother, Hyacintha (née Nanett), could support them. At age 14, Clelia became a catechist for her parish. Her pastor, Gaetano Guidi, suggested that she and Teodora Baraldi begin teaching young women secular subjects as well. Barbieri and Baraldi lived with two other friends in a small community called the Retreat of Providence. When she and Orsola Donati founded the Minims (Little Sisters) of Our Lady of Sorrows (1868) under the patronage of St. Francis of Paola, Clelia became the youngest founder in the history of the Church. Clelia's spirituality centered around contemplation of the Blessed Sacrament, which was her "glorious inspiration" (John Paul II). She was subject to mystical experiences and possessed the gift of reading hearts.

Following her sudden death from tuberculosis at age 23, she was buried in the Church of Santa Maria Annunziata in her hometown, where she was venerated almost immediately. The Congregation of Minims of the Sorrowful Mother, which was given pontifical status in 1949 and attached to the Servites, has spread throughout Italy and into Tanzania and India, where they operate hospitals, nursing homes, and elementary schools, and serve as catechists and catalysts of parochial charitable ministries. She is patroness of those ridiculed for their piety.

At her canonization Pope John Paul II declared that Clelia "is not the fruit of a particular school of spirituality but the genuine product of that first and fundamental school of holiness which was the parish church of her village.''

Feast: 13 July.

Bibliography: *Acta Apostolicae Sedis* 60 (1968): 680–684.*L'Osservatore Romano,* English edition, no. 32 (1968): 2, 8. P. BERTI, *Santa Clelia Barbieri* (Milan 1991). L. GHERARDI, *Il sole sugli argini. Testimonianza evangelica della b. Clelia Barbieri* (Bologna 1970). G. GUSMINI, *Beata Clelia Barbieri*, 4th. ed. (Bari, Italy 1968). C. ZAPPULLI, *The Power of Goodness: The Life of Blessed Clelia Barbieri* (Boston 1980).

[K. RABENSTEIN]

BARRÉ, NICHOLAS, BL.

Pedagogue, founder of the Schools of Charity, the Congregation of Sisters of the Holy Infant Jesus (a.k.a. the Ladies of St. Maur), and the Sisters of the Holy Infant Jesus of Providence of Rouen (France); b. 21 October 1621, Amiens, France; d. 31 May 1686, Paris; beatified by John Paul II, 7 March 1999, at Rome.

Born into a well-to-do family, Nicholas chose to enter the Order of the Minims of St. Francis de Paul at age 18 and was professed at Amiens in 1641. Even before his ordination Barré was given the chair of theology at Paris, which he held with honor for 20 years. At the convent of the Royal Square (Paris), he had as confreres illustrious men of science, of wide knowledge, and profound spirituality. Although he trained many students in scholastic as well as spiritual matters, he spent the major part of his ministry in preaching, spiritual direction, and the great work of instituting free popular teaching. In Rouen first (1662) and later in Paris, he founded and directed those Schools of Charity of the Holy Infant Jesus that became models throughout France. To these schools he gave program, method, and teachers whose religious, cultural, and didactic preparation he had scrupulously supervised. The Institute of the Sisters of the Holy Infant Jesus had two distinct branches: one in Rouen, also called the ''Institute of Providence''; the other at Paris, called the ''Institute of the Dames of St. Maur,'' from the house of its foundation. Barré considered also a male branch of the Congregation: the ''Teachers.'' This, however, was accomplished in the foundation of the Brothers of the Christian Schools by St. John de la Salle, whom Barré had directed, advised, and encouraged.

Barré had a solid base of Thomistic theology and a sense of equilibrium that enabled him to avoid the excesses of rigorism and laxism. He fought both Jansenism and Quietism. Humility, faith, charity, mortification, and personal encounter with Jesus in the Eucharist are the pillars of his spiritual doctrine. He was an advocate of frequent Communion, and often affirmed that Holy Communion is the best disposition for Holy Communion. His extant spiritual works are *Lettres spirituelles* (Rouen 1697; Toulouse 1876) and *Maximes spirituelles* (Paris 1694).

His cause for beatification was introduced before the Sacred Congregation of Rites in 1931. On 6 April 1998, a miracle attributed to his intercession was approved. During the beatification Mass, Pope John Paul II said, Barré worked tirelessly as the apostle of free education because he feared that ''spiritually thirsty people living in the desert of religious ignorance, ran the risk of drinking from the corrupt fount of some ideas of their time.''

Feast: 21 October.

Bibliography: *Œuvres complètes*, ed. T. DARRAS, M. T. FLOUREZ, and M. F. TOULOUSE (Paris 1994). *Acta Apostolicae Sedis* no. 7 (1999): 310–312. *L'Osservatore Romano*, English edition, no. 8 (1999): 2; no. 10 (1999): 1, 3, 6. C. FARCY, *Le Révérend Père Barré, religieux minime* (Paris 1942). B. FLOUREZ, *Marcheur dans la nuit: Nicolas Barré, 1621–1686*, 2d. ed. (Paris 1994). H. DE GRÈZES, *Vie du R. P. Barré . . .* (Barle-Duc 1892). G. MORETTI, *Un pedagogista santo* (Rome 1929). G. PAPÀSOGLI, *Nicola Barré, educatore di anime* (Rome 1975).

[A. BELLANTONIO]

BAYS, MARGUERITE, BL.

Seamstress, member of the Third Order of Franciscans; b. 8 September 1815, La Pierraz, Siviriez, Fribourg Canton, Switzerland; d. 27 June 1879, Siviriez, Switzerland; beatified by John Paul II in Rome 29 October 1995.

Marguerite, born into a farming family, led a simple life, working as a dressmaker. Active in her parish, she catechized children, established the Association for the Holy Childhood there, and helped to found a Catholic newspaper. Beyond the parish, she visited the sick and dying. She received the stigmata after being miraculously cured of intestinal cancer (8 December 1954). For the next twenty-five years, she mystically relived Christ's Passion each Friday. She died on the octave of the Feast of the Sacred Heart. Despite Rome's refusal of her cause, her mortal remains were exhumed in 1929 and enshrined in the convent of la Fille-Dieu at Romont, which was governed by Marguerite's goddaughter and great-niece, Mother Marie-Lutgarde Fasel.

Finally her cause was accepted in 1953. Pope John Paul II remarked during her beatification that through Marguerite, ''We discover the importance of prayer in lay life. . . . She devoted herself without reserve to the poor and sick.''

Feast 27 June.

Bibliography: R. LOUP, *Marguerite Bays*, 3d. ed. (Fribourg, Switzerland 1969).

[K. RABENSTEIN]

BÉLANGER, DINA, BL.

Known in religion as Marie Sainte-Cecile de Rome or Sister Cecilia, musician, mystic, religious of the Sisters of Jesus-Marie; b. 30 April 1897, Québec, Canada; d. 4 September 1929, Sillery, Québec, Canada; beatified in Rome by John Paul II, 20 March 1993.

Dina Bélanger was an accomplished pianist who received special training in Canada and New York, but unable to find satisfaction in the secular world, she desired to become totally united with God. When Dina joined the Sisters of Jesus-Marie (1920), she took the name of the Roman martyr who was the patroness of musicians, St. Cecilia. During the course of her life as a religious, Dina's devotion to the Blessed Sacrament transformed her into a woman of infectious joy, despite an illness that was contracted soon after her profession. Her sanctity was also marked by a devotion to the Blessed Mother and saints, and she respected those in authority as representatives of God. Under obedience to her superiors, Dina wrote her compelling autobiography the *Canticle of Love.*

Pope John Paul II, who beatified Dina Bélanger because of her devotion to Jesus in the Blessed Sacrament, remarked during the beatification homily that "she reached such a high degree of intimacy with God . . . that her whole being was overwhelmed by Him."

Feast: 4 September (Canada).

Bibliography: DINA BÉLANGER, *Canticle of love* English tr. by MARY SAINT STEPHEN (1945; reprint, Québec1984). B. GHE-RARDINI, *Negli abissi dell'amore: Dina Bélanger e la sua esperienza mistica; una valutazione teologica* (Rome 1991).

[K. RABENSTEIN]

BERTONI, GASPARE LUIGI DIONIGI, ST.

(Caspar); Diocesan priest of Verona, founder of the Congregation of the Priests of the Holy Stigmata of Our Lord; b. 9 October 1777, Verona, Venetia, Italy; d. there, 12 June 1853; canonized by John Paul II, 1 November 1989, Rome.

The son of a prosperous lawyer, Francesco Bertoni, and his wife Brunora Ravelli, Gaspare was educated at home with his sister, who died in childhood. Later he at-

tended St. Sebastian's, where he became acquainted with the then suppressed Jesuits. The first of his many mystical experiences occurred on the day of his first communion, when he also discerned his vocation. He entered the seminary (1795), joined the Gospel Fraternity for Hospitals during the French occupation to care for war victims, and was ordained in 1800. His early years in the priesthood were divided between teaching in the seminary and working as a parish priest.

Aware of the need to salvage youth from the moral breakdown of society, he began to devote his energies to education. Gradually other priests joined him, and on 4 November 1816, the group adopted a rule of life under the leadership of Bertoni. This was the foundation of the Stigmatine Congregation, which took its name from their residence, *Le Stimate*, formerly owned by a pious confraternity but given to Bertoni for his work.

In addition to founding the Stigmatines, Bertoni acted as spiritual director to the Daughters of Charity of Canossa, established Marian oratories, and promoted devotion to the Espousal of Mary and Joseph and to the Five Wounds of Christ. From 1812, following an ecstasy, he endured physical troubles that entailed numerous operations prior to his death. His grave is in the Stigmatine church at Verona.

During his canonization ceremony Pope John Paul II declared that Bertoni "drew up a project of Christian life which foresaw for all people, regardless of their state in life, the call to holiness; not only for priests, but also for husbands and wives, following the example of the Holy Couple of Nazareth."

Feast: 12 June.

Bibliography: *Epistolario del Venerabile servo di Dio Don Gaspare Bertoni*, G. STOFELLA (Verona 1954); "Memoriale privato" in *Collectanea Stigmatina 4*, ed. G. STOFELLA (Rome 1962). *Acta Apostolicae Sedis* 68 (1976): 486–489. *L'Osservatore Romano*, English edition, no. 45 (1975): 1–4; no. 45 (1989): 1–2. I. BONETTI, *La grammatica di Don Gaspare: meditazioni quotidiane dagli scritti di San Gaspare Bertoni* (Bologna 1993). G. CERESATTO, *Il volto e l'anima del venerabile Gaspare Bertoni* (Verona 1951). G. FIORIO, *Lo spirito del venerabile servo di Dio Don Gaspare Bertoni* (Verona 1914); *Vita del venerabile servo di Dio Don Gaspare Bertoni* (Verona 1922). G. GIACOBBE, *Vita del Servo di Dio Don Gaspare Bertoni* (Verona 1858). L. MALAMOCCO, *Quando senti il grillo cantare* (Udine 1996). G. MATTEI, *Il venerabile Gaspare Bertoni* (Verona 1924). L. MUZII, *Voglia di santità* (Rome 1989). E. RADIUS, *Gaspare Bertoni* (Verona 1975). G. STOFELLA, *Enciclopdia Cattolica*, 9:1988; *Il diario spirituale di Leopoldina Naudet e il venerabile Don Gaspare Bertoni* (Verona 1930); *Pagine di vita cristiana del venerabile Gaspare Bertoni* (Vicenza 1947); *Il Venerabile Gaspare Bertoni* (Verona 1952). N. DALLE VEDOVE, *Il venerabile Don Bertoni*, 2 v. (Rome 1962); *La giovinezza del venerabile Gaspare Bertoni e l'ambiente veronese dell'ultimo '700* (Rome 1971); *San Gaspare Bertoni, Fondatore degli Stimmatini* (Verona 1989); *Un modello di santo abbandono* (Verona 1951);

Vita e pensiero del beato Gaspare Bertoni agli albori dell '800 veronese (Rome 1975). L. ZAUPA, *Gaspare Bertoni: un santo per il nostro tempo* (Verona 1994).

[J. E. MULLEN/EDS.]

BESSETTE, ANDRÉ, BL.

Baptized Alfred; thaumaturgist, member of the Brotherhood of the Holy Cross; b. 9 August 1845, at Saint-Gregoire d'Iberville (southeast of Montréal), Québec, Canada; d. 6 January 1937, Montréal; beatified in Rome by John Paul II, 23 May 1982.

Alfred, the eighth of the twelve children of Isaac Bessette and Clothilde Foisy, was left sickly and orphaned by age twelve. He unsuccessfully attempted various occupations as a smith, cobbler, and baker. During the U.S. Civil War he did manual labor in mills and on farms in New England, where he learned English. He returned to Montréal in 1867 and was accepted as a Holy Cross postulant despite his precarious health and illiteracy. With the help of Bishop Bouget of Montréal, Brother André professed his vows 27 December 1870. He gained a reputation as a healer during his many decades as porter of Notre Dame College. His devotion to St. Joseph, patron of the Universal Church, led him to build St. Joseph's Oratory atop Mont Royal in Montréal. The first small chapel (15' X 18') erected in 1904, was enlarged in 1908 and 1910. The cornerstone for a new crypt church—to hold 1,000 people—was laid in 1917, but the roof was not added until 1936. The oratory, where Blessed André served as guardian for thirty years and is buried, was solemnly dedicated as a minor basilica in 1955.

John Paul II called Brother André a radiant man of prayer who daily gave those wounded by life "a welcoming ear, comfort and faith in God, confidence in the intercession of St. Joseph" (Beatification homily).

Feast: 6 January (U.S.A.).

Bibliography: K. BURTON, *Brother André of Mount Royal* (Notre Dame, Ind. 1952). J. G. DUBUC, *Le frère André* (Saint-Laurent, Québec 1996).H. GRENON, *Le frère André* (Montréal 1981).A. HATCH, *The Miracle of the Mountain: The Story of Brother André and the Shrine on Mount Royal* (New York 1959). M. LACHANCE, *Le frère André* (Montréal 1979). C. B. RUFFIN, *The Life of Brother André: The Miracle Worker of St. Joseph* (Huntington, Ind. 1988). S. T. STEIN, *The Tapestry of Saint Joseph: Chronological History of St. Joseph and His Apostle, Blessed Brother André* (Philadelphia, Pa. 1991). *Acta Apostolicae Sedis* 75 (1983): 14–16. *L'Osservatore Romano,* English edition, no. 24 (1982): 6–7.

[K. RABENSTEIN]

BETANCUR (BETHANCOURT), PEDRO DE SAN JOSÉ (PETER OF ST. JOSEPH), BL.

Franciscan tertiary, missionary, founder of charitable institutions and the Hospitaler Bethlehemites; b. 16 May 1619, at Villaflores, Chasna, Tenerife Island, Spain; d. 25 April 1667, Guatemala City, Guatemala. On 22 June 1980, in Rome, John Paul II honored Pedro's joyful service and humility by beatifying him.

Although he was descended from Juan de Bethancourt, one of the Norman conquerors (1404) of the Canary Islands, his immediate family was very poor and his first employment was shepherd of the small family flock. In 1650, he left for Guatemala, where a relative had preceded him as secretary to the governor general. His funds ran out in Havana and Pedro had to pay for his passage from that point by working on a ship. He landed in Honduras and walked to Guatemala City, arriving there on 18 Feb. 1651. He was so poor that he had to join the daily bread line at the Franciscan friary. In this way he met Fray Fernando Espino, a famous missionary, who befriended him and remained his lifelong counselor. Through Fray Fernando, Pedro was given work at a local textile factory, which that enabled him to support himself, but which also employed culprits condemned by the court. In 1653, he entered the local Jesuit college of San Borja in the hopes of becoming a priest. But he lacked the ability to study and was soon forced to give up this dream. In the college, however, he had met Manuel Lobo, SJ, who was his confessor throughout his life.

Fray Fernando invited him to join the Franciscan Order as a lay brother, but Pedro felt that God called him to remain in the world. Hence, in 1655, he joined the Third Order of St. Francis and took the tertiary habit as his garb. By this time his virtues were widely recognized in the city. In 1658, María de Esquivel's hut was given to him and Pedro, remembering the experiences of his first desperate days in Guatemala, immediately began a hospital (Nuestra Señora de Belén) for the convalescent poor, a hostel for the homeless, a school, an oratory, and a nursing community known as the Bethlehemites. From then on all his time was spent in alleviating the sufferings of the less fortunate. He begged alms with which to endow Masses to be celebrated by poor priests; he also endowed Masses that were to be celebrated at unusually early hours so that the poor might not have occasion to miss Mass because of their dress. He also had small chapels erected in the poorer sections where instruction was given also to the children. On August 18, he would gather the children and have them sing the Seven Joys of the Franciscan Rosary in honor of the Blessed Mother, a custom that passed to Spain but today remains only in Guatemala. On Christmas Eve he inaugurated the custom of imitating St. Joseph in search of lodgings for the Blessed Mother.

The gentle, kind man known as "St. Francis of the Americas" died peacefully in his hospital, hoping that his companions would carry on the many works he had begun. He is entombed in the Church of San Francisco in the old section of Guatemala City. Interest in his cause was renewed by the 1962 publication of his biography by Vázquez de Herrera.

Feast: 25 April (Franciscan).

Bibliography: *Acta Apostolicae Sedis* 73 (1981): 253–258. *Gracias, Matiox, Thanks, Hermano Pedro: A Trilingual Anthology of Guatemalan Oral Tradition,* ed. & tr. M. C. CANALES and J. F. MORRISSEY (New York 1996). *L'Osservatore Romano,* English edition, no. 26 (1980): 10–11. J. ARRIOLA C., *Los milagros del venerable siervo de Dios, hermano Pedro de San José de Betancourt, efectuados en su vida y después de su muerto py su digno sucesor fray Rodrigo de la Cruz* (Guatemala 1983). A. ESTRADA MONROY, *Breve relación de la ejemplar vida del venerable siervo de Dios, Pedro de San Joseph Betancur* (Guatemala 1968). T. F. HALL DE ARÉVALO, *El apóstol de la campanilla* (Guatemala 1980). F. A. DE MONTALVO, *Vida admirable y muerte preciosa del venerable hermano Pedro de San José Betancur . . .* (Guatemala 1974). M. SOTO-HALL, *Pedro de San José Bethencourt, el San Francisco de Asís americano,* 3d. ed. (Guatemala 1981). F. VÁZQUEZ DE HERRERA, *Vida y virtudes del V. Hermano Pedro de San José de Betancur,* ed. L. LAMARDRID (Guatemala City 1962). D. DE VELA, *El Hermano Pedro (en la vida y en las letras)* (Guatemala City 1935 & 1961).

[L. LAMADRID]

BOCCARDO, GIOVANNI MARIA, BL.

Diocesan priest, founder of the Congregation of the Poor Daughters of Saint Cajetan; b. 20 November 1848, Testona di Moncalieri (near Turin), Italy; d. 30 December 1913, Pancalieri, Italy; beatified in Milan, by John Paul II, 24 May 1998.

Giovanni Boccardo studied at the diocesan seminary of Turin and was ordained (1871). For the next eleven years he provided spiritual direction to seminarians in Chieri and Turin. His first parochial appointment was to Pancalieri in 1882 and remained there until his death. Although he enjoyed the seminary, he viewed his parochial assignment as an opportunity for evangelization. When cholera struck the village (1884), he personally tended the sick. Afterwards he established the Hospice of Charity to care for those left abandoned or homeless by the epidemic, including orphans and the poor elderly. He founded the Poor Daughters of St. Cajetan to continue the work of the hospice. Within a few years the congregation spread throughout Italy.

Pope John Paul II considered Boccardo as "a man of deep spirituality and, at the same time, a dynamic apostle, a promoter of the religious life and the laity, ever attentive to discerning the signs of the times" (Beatification homily).

Bibliography: G. COSTA, *Ma chi è stato Giovanni M. Boccardo?* (Pinerolo 1976).

[K. RABENSTEIN]

BOJANOWSKI, EDMUND, BL.

Layman, founder of the Sister Servants of the Mary Immaculate (S.S.M.I.); b. 14 November 1814, Grabonóg (near Poznán), northwestern Poland; d. 7 August 1871, Gorka Duchowna, Poland; beatified in Warsaw, Poland, by John Paul II, 13 June 1999.

Born into a landed family of nobility, Bojanowski studied literature at the universities of Breslau (Wrocław) and Berlin. Although he contracted tuberculosis in his 20s, he walked more than a mile daily to attend Mass and personally responded to the misery he encountered by teaching literacy and opening reading rooms for the poor, particularly in rural areas. During the cholera epidemic of 1849, he not only founded an orphanage and hospital, but he also tended to the victims of the disease himself in these institutions and in their country homes. Bojanowski also founded a daycare nursery in Gostyn. In 1850, three young girls and a widow committed themselves to running the nursery. In 1855 they became the nucleus of the Sister Servants of Mary Immaculate (originally called the Little Servants of the Mother of God), which had branches in Europe, Africa, and America working in a variety of apostolates, including daycare centers for children. Bojanowski also organized a passive resistance to Prussian repression. He entered the seminary in 1869, but he was forced to leave because of ill health and died two years later.

He was declared venerable 3 July 1998; a miracle attributed to his intercession was approved 21 December 1998. During the beatification homily, Pope John Paul II said that Bojanowski "anticipated much of what the Second Vatican Council said about the apostolate of the laity."

Feast: 7 August.

Bibliography: M. WINOWSKA, *Edmond Bojanowski: précurseur de Vatican II* (Paris 1979).

[K. RABENSTEIN]

BONILLI, PIETRO, BL.

Parish priest, founder of the Sisters of the Holy Family of Spoleto; b. 15 March 1841, San Lorenzo (di Trevi), Umbria, Italy; d. 5 January 1935, at Spoleto, Umbria; beatified in Rome by John Paul II, 24 April 1988.

Pietro, son of Sebastian Bonilli and Maria Allegretti, attended the diocesan seminary and was ordained priest in 1863. From 1863–98 he served San Michele Arcangelo Parish in Cannaiola di Trevi (near Spoleto). There he founded the ''Little Orphanage of Nazareth'' (1884) and the Congregation of Sisters of the Holy Family (1888) to staff it and expand his ministry to the poor. He also opened (1893) a hospice for the deaf and blind, which the sisters moved to Spoleto. He followed them and was appointed canon of Spoleto cathedral and rector of the regional seminary. Before his death he was honored (1908) by Pope St. Pius X. Bonilli's tomb is in his church of San Michele Arcangelo.

In beatifying Bonilli, Pope John Paul II said: ''He remained for thirty-five years in a parish in the most depressed area of the Diocese of Spoleto, where religious and moral conditions were exceptionally poor and disheartening. . . . Father Bonilli lavished his charity on all who needed assistance.''

Bibliography: *L'Osservatore Romano,* English edition, no. 16 (1988): 12.

[K. RABENSTEIN]

BONINO, GIUSEPPINA GABRIELLA, BL.

Foundress of the Sisters of the Holy Family of Savigliano; b. 5 Sept. 1843, Savigliano, Piedmont, Italy; d. 8 Feb. 1906, Savona, Liguria, Italy; beatified 7 May 1995.

Raised in a religious family, Bonino moved to Turin when she was 12. Her spiritual director, discerning her true vocation, encouraged her to make a temporary vow of virginity when she was 18. In 1869 she moved back to Savigliano to care for her ailing father until his death. During a pilgrimage to Lourdes in 1877 in thanksgiving for a successful back surgery, she was given to understand that her vocation was to return God's gift of a good family by becoming a mother to numerous infants and children with no family. Twice she sampled the cloistered life before realizing that her service would be better undertaken in an active religious community. She founded and became the superior of the Sisters of the Holy Family, an institute dedicated to serving orphans and the elderly poor (1881). She founded four other houses before her death.

During his homily at her beatification, John Paul II proclaimed: ''Her charism was family love, learned and practiced above all while living with her parents until adulthood and then by following the Lord's call in conse-crated life. From the family as the domestic church to the religious community as a spiritual family: this is the summary of her humble journey, hidden but of incalculable value, that of the family, the environment of extraordinary love in ordinary things.'' She is one of the patronesses of families.

Feast: 8 February.

Bibliography: *L'Osservatore Romano,* English edition, no. 19 (1995): 2, 4. G. MINA, *Quando l'amore chiama: una vita presente nell'oggi: Madre Giuseppina Gabriella Bonino, fondatrice delle Suore della Sacra Famiglia di Savigliano* (Cavallermaggiore 1993).

[K. RABENSTEIN]

BOSATTA, CHIARA DINA, BL.

Baptized Dina, a.k.a. Chiara de Pianello, religious of the Daughters of St. Mary of Providence; b. 27 May 1858, at Pianello Lario near Como, Lombardy, Italy; d. there 20 April 1887; beatified by John Paul II, 21 April 1991.

Dina and her sister Marcellina Bosatta were among the first to support the work of Blessed Luigi Guanella. Living as a religious at home, Dina served the poor of her parish from whom she contracted a disease that afflicted her the rest of her life. In 1886, she formally joined the congregation Guanella had founded, taking the name Chiara (Clara), and she served as superior of the community for a time. A contemplative, she offered God her own life to protect, raise, and educate children and young people in difficulty. Chiara died at the age of twenty-nine. At Chiara's beatification, Pope John Paul II honored her vocation.

Feast: 20 April.

Bibliography: *Acta Apostolicae Sedis* 83 (1991): 369–71. *L'Osservatore Romano,* English edition, no. 16 (22 April 1991): 10.

[K. RABENSTEIN]

BOSSILKOV, EVGENIJ, BL.

Bishop; first blessed of Bulgaria; first martyr of the Communist era; b. 16 November 1900, Belene, Bulgaria; d. 11 November 1952 in Sofia, Bulgaria; beatified 15 March 1988 by Pope John Paul II.

Given the name Vincent at birth by his Latin-rite family, he took the name Evgenij (Eugene), after receiving the habit of the Passionist congregation in Ere (Belgium) in 1919, where he had gone for novitiate and further seminary studies after his minor seminary years in Oresh and Rousse in Bulgaria. He was ordained to the presbyterate in 1926 and sent to Rome for further education at the Pontifical Institute for Eastern Church Studies (P.I.O.S.), where he received a doctorate after defending the thesis, "The Union of the Bulgarians with the Church of Rome at the beginning of XIII Century" (1931). Bossilkov returned to Bulgaria, where he was assigned first to the office of Bishop Damian Theelen of Nicopolis (Rousse), but later put in charge of St. Joseph's parish in the large Catholic village of Bardarski Gheran (1934). Bossilkov initiated a new style in dealing with parishioners, often going well beyond strictly spiritual needs, reaching out toward non-Catholics, especially among the intellectual and professional leaders throughout the country. He played soccer with the youth and hunted in the countryside with the adults.

After the Communist takeover in September 1944, Bossilkov suffered the limitations imposed by the atheistic regime on the country and on the Church in particular. Documents indicate that he was shadowed by the intelligence service of the Communist underground long before the end of the war. When Bishop Theelen died in 1946, Bossilkov was appointed an administrator of the diocese. The following year he was named bishop. During this period, he worked closely with the apostolic delegate, Francesco Galloni, until the latter's expulsion from the country in December 1948. At that point, persecution of the Church was escalated; all Catholic institutions were separated from the Church, religious orders were disbanded, and many priests and religious were arrested, questioned, and sent to prison. In 1952 a series of trials, some behind closed doors, deprived the Church of practically all able clergy.

In one of the trials, held 30 September to 4 October, 37 ecclesiastics were sentenced to prison, while four—Kamen Vichev, Pavel Djidjov, Josaphat Shishkov, and Bishop Bossilkov—received death sentences. The evidence brought up during the examination of Bossilkov's cause shows that real ground for the harsh sentence was rather his refusal to head a schismatic National Church. Half a century elapsed before documents could be produced (1992) that proved the execution had been carried out late in the night of 11 November 1952. Bossilkov's grave is unknown, though his blood-stained shirt and pectoral cross were later returned to his family.

The canonization process was initiated in the West by the order of the Passionist Fathers in 1985. However the regime in Bulgaria, not having recovered from the international uproar over their alleged connection with the attempt on the life of the pope (13 May 1981), put great pressure on the Bulgarian bishops in the country. They

in turn convinced church authorities in Rome to suspend the process (December 1985). When the political climate changed and normal diplomatic relations were established between Bulgaria and the Holy See in the summer of 1991, Bishop Samuil Djoundrin of Bossilkov's native diocese made formal petition that the process be resumed.

When John Paul II beatified Bossilkov in 1998, he called him the "brightest glory" of Bulgaria's church.

Bibliography: *Canonizationis seu Declarationis Martyrii Servi Dei Eugenii Bossilkov, C.P. Positio super Martyrio* (Rome 1993). PIERLUIGI DI EUGENIO, *Beato Eugenio Bossilkov. Morire per la fede* (Teramo1998). GIORGIO ELDAROV, *Bossilkov.* Collection of articles in: *Abagar* (*Bulgarian Catholic Journal*) 3 and 4 (1998) (in Bulgarian).

[GIORGIO ELDAROV]

BOURGEOYS, MARGUERITE, ST.

Foundress and first superior of the Sisters of the Congregation de Notre Dame; b. Troyes, France, 17 April 1620; d. Montreal, Canada, 12 Jan. 1700; canonized 2 April 1982 by Pope John Paul II.

The daughter of a prosperous merchant, Marguerite grew up in a quiet corner of Champagne. In 1653, after several unsuccessful attempts to enter the cloister, she sailed for Canada with Paul de C. Maisonneuve, Governor of Montreal, a frontier garrison in New France, founded only 12 years before. There in 1658 she opened the first school in Montreal in an abandoned stone stable. Within a few years she had established a school for Indians, an Indian mission, a boarding school for the daughters of merchants, and a training school for the poor. As the scope of her work grew, she brought assistants from France; later, Canadian-born girls and two Indians joined her in her work. The group developed into a new kind of religious community, not bound to the cloister, but free to go, dressed in the costume of the poor, wherever their zeal and the needs of the people demanded. In 1698, 2 years before her death, the Congregation de Notre Dame won ecclesiastical approval.

The foundress consistently refused endowments, dowries for her companions, and gifts of money that would have made her life less directly dependent on God. She and her religious supported themselves by sewing, living frugally so that they could give alms to the poor. They began needed buildings without the money to complete them and offered the work of their hands in exchange for the services of carpenters and masons. After a disastrous fire in December 1683, the community was left destitute. As soon as the ground thawed in the spring, they began, totally without resources, the construction of a new school. With alms, Marguerite built a chapel as a place of pilgrimage to Our Lady, Notre Dame de Bon Secours; she and her companions carried stones and poured mortar for the masons. Marguerite spent her last years writing an autobiography.

Feast: 12 January (Canada).

Bibliography: CM. BOURGEOYS, *Les Écrits de Mère Bourgeoys. Autobiographie et testament spirituel* (Montreal 1964). E. MONTGOLFIER, *La vie de la vénérable Marguerite Bourgeoys dite du Saint-Sacrement, institutrice, fondatrice* (Montreal 1818). É. M. FAILLON, *Vie de la soeur Bourgeoys*, 2 v. (Villemarie 1853). A. JAMET, *Marguerite Bourgeoys*, 2 v. (Montreal 1942). Y. CHARRON, *Mère Bourgeoys*, tr. SISTER ST. GODELIVA (Montreal 1950). K. BURTON, *Vahant Voyager* (Milwaukee 1964). PATRICIA SIMPSON, *Marguerite Bourgeoys and Montreal 1640–1665* (Montreal: McGill-Queen's University Press, 1997).

[V. M. COTTER]

BOUTEILLER, MARTHE LE, BL.

Baptized Aimée Adèle, nicknamed "Soeur Cidre" or "Sister Cider," religious; b. 2 December 1816, La Henrière (near Percy), Manche, France; d. 18 March 1883, at the Abbey of Saint-Sauveur-le-Vicomte, France; beatified in Rome by John Paul II, 4 November 1990.

Aimée, the third of the four children of André and Marie-Françoise le Bouteiller, was raised on a small farm. Aimée attended a local religious school. Her school mistress, Sister Marie-Françoise Farcy inspired the young girl's religious vocation. She joined the Sisters of St. Madeleine Postel (1842) and served the Abbey of Saint-Sauveur-le-Vicomte in the kitchen, fields, and laundry for the rest of her life. Her constant cheerfulness and devoted service radiated the love of God through ordinary tasks.

In beatifying Sister Marthe, Pope John Paul II said: "The extreme simplicity of her life did not prevent the other sisters from recognizing her true spiritual authority."

Bibliography: M. CLÉVENOT, *Adèle l'obscure: soeur Marthe* (Paris 1989).

[K. RABENSTEIN]

BRACCO, TERESA, BL.

Lay woman; martyr; b. 24 February 1924, Santa Giulia in Sanvarezzo (diocese of Acqui), Savona, Italy; d. 28 August 1944, Zerbi (near Sanvarezzo); beatified by Pope John Paul II, 24 May 1998, in the Piazza Vittorio, Turin, Italy.

The formation of Teresa Bracco began under the tutelage of her parents, Giacomo Bracco and Anna Pera,

Marguerite Bourgeoys. (Archive Photos, Inc. Reproduced by permission.)

who were humble farmers with a strong devotion to the Eucharist and the Blessed Mother. Throughout her short life she attended daily Mass and had great devotion for the Eucharist. Teresa became known for her modesty in dress and speech. Her spiritual maturity prepared her to resist the threat of rape by the Nazi soldier, who shot her twice then crushed her skull. Her death was declared a martyrdom on 7 July 1997.

During her beatification, Pope John Paul II proclaimed that in Teresa Bracco "the virtue of chastity shines out . . . she was its champion and witness to the point of martyrdom."

Feast: 28 August (Italy).

Bibliography: C. SICCARDI, *Martire a vent'anni* (Rome 1998).

[K. RABENSTEIN]

BRANDSMA, TITUS, BL.

Carmelite priest, martyr for the freedom of the Catholic press, philosopher, historian of mysticism; b. 23 February 1881, Oegeklooster in Bolsward, Friesland, The Netherlands; d. 26 July 1942, Dachau Concentration

Camp near Munich, Germany. Beatified 3 November 1985 by Pope John Paul II.

One of 6 children of Tjitsje Postma and her husband Titus, Brandsma was baptized Anno Sjoerd and took the name Titus when he entered the Carmelite Order in 1898. His activities in the novitiate served as the foundation for much of his later work: he published a Dutch translation of selected writings of works of St. Teresa of Avila (1901), acted as literary agent for his religious brothers, and began an in-house magazine that was eventually available to all Dutch Catholics.

Ordained in 1905, Brandsma earned the doctorate in philosophy at the Gregorian University in Rome (1909). Returning to The Netherlands, he lectured in the Carmelite major seminary at Oss founded *Carmelrozen*, a journal of Carmelite spirituality and organized scholars to translate the works of St. Teresa. Meanwhile he promoted the study of Frisian language and culture, engaged in various civic and religious projects such as editing the local paper and establishing an apostolate for the reunification of the Oriental Churches.

In 1923, he took up a post as professor of philosophy and the history of mysticism at the newly founded Catholic University of Nijmegen and in 1932 became rector. In addition to distinguishing himself in the study of medieval Dutch mysticism, he wrote on sociology and gained a reputation as a journalist. In 1935, he lectured in the U.S. In that same year he was appointed spiritual director of the union of Dutch Catholic journalists and began his campaign to denounce the anti-Semitic laws passed in Germany. After the Nazis occupied Holland in 1940, he vigorously defended the Catholic schools and refused to dismiss Jewish children from them. In the name of the Dutch bishops and with full knowledge of the likely consequence for himself, Brandsma induced Catholic newspaper editors to reject Nazi propaganda.

On 19 Jan. 1942 Brandsma was imprisoned at Scheveningen where he composed poetry, meditations on the Way of the Cross, and two booklets (*My Cell* and *Letters from Prison*). Beginning in April he was transfered from prison to prison, arriving at Dachau 19 June. A month later Brandsma was taken to the camp hospital, where he became the subject of medical experiments. He was injected with carbolic acid, giving his Rosary to the nursing aid who prepared it and died ten minutes later. His body was cremated and the ashes deposited in a common grave.

Feast: 27 July (Carmelites).

Bibliography: *Acta Apostolicae Sedis* (1985): 1151. J. ALZIN, *A Dangerous Little Friar* (Dublin 1957). H. W. F. AUKES, *Het leven van Titus Brandsma* (Utrecht 1963). R. M. VALABEK, ed., *Essays on Titus Brandsma: Carmelite, Educator, Journalist, Martyr* (Rome 1985). B. HANLEY, *No Strangers to Violence, No Strangers to Love* (Notre Dame, Ind. 1983). H. KLEIN, *Liebender ohne Mass. Titus Brandsma* (Trier 1967). B. MEIJER, *Titus Brandsma* (Bussum 1951). F. MILLAN ROMERAL, "Carmelitas en Dachau: las cartas del P. A. Urbanski, desde el lager, en el 50 aniversario de la liberación," *Carmelus* 42 (1995): 22–43. *L'Osservatore Romano,* English edition, nos. 44 & 46 (1985). J. REES, *Titus Brandsma: A Modern Martyr* (London 1971). E. RHODES, *His Memory Shall Not Pass* (New York 1958). S. SCAPIN, *Tito Brandsma: maestro di umanitá, martire della libertá* (Milan 1990). R. TIJHUIS, "Met Pater Titus Brandsma in Dachau," *Carmelrozen* nos.31–32 (1945/46): 18–21, 53–58, 80–85. English translation: Dachau Eye-witness, in: AA.VV., Essays on Titus Brandsma, edited by R. Valabek (Rome 1985): 58–67.

[A. STARING/K. RABENSTEIN]

BRAZIL, MARTYRS OF, BB.

A.k.a. André de Soveral (b. ca. 1572, Sao Vicente, Brazil), Ambrósio Francisco Ferro, and twenty-eight companions, or the Martyrs of Rio Grande do Norte, protomartyrs of Brazil; d. 1645 in northern Brazil, 16 July 1645 in Cunhaú and 3 October 1645 in Uruaçu (both near Natal); beatified in Rome by John Paul II, 5 March 2000.

The martyrdom of André, Ambrósio, and their companions took place in the context of anti-Catholic persecution by Dutch Calvinists who had invaded the Rio Grande do Norte region of Brazil in 1630. The Gospel had been brought to Natal, Brazil, by two Portuguese Jesuits and two Franciscans on 25 December 1597, who catechized the Indios. The following century the Dutch Calvinists overtook the region and restricted Catholic practice.

The Massacre at Cunhaú occurred on Sunday, 16 July 1645. Sixty-nine parishioners were worshiping together in the Chapel of Our Lady of the Candles. Dutch soldiers barred the church doors and launched an attack against unresisting civilians. The Massacre at Uruaçu (3 October 1645) was led by a convert to Calvinism. Dutch troops and armed natives attacked Father Ambrósio Francisco Ferro and some of his parishioners. One of them, Mateus Moreira, was particularly remembered by Pope John Paul II, both at the at the closing of the National Eucharistic Congress in Natal (1991) and during the beatification homily for refusing to deny the Real Presence of Jesus in the Eucharist.

The martyrs include André de Soveral, native Brazilian priest, and Ambrósio Francisco Ferro, Portuguese priest; and the laymen Antônio Baracho; the Spaniard Antônio Vilela Cid; Antônio Vilela and his son, slaves; Diogo (James) Pereira; Estêvao Machado de Miranda and his two children; Francisco de Bastos; the son of Francisco Dias, a young slave; Francisco Mendes Pereira; Joao da Silveira; the Frenchman Joao Lostau Navarro; Joao Martins, a youth, and his seven young friends; José do Porto; Manuel Rodrigues de Moura and his wife; Mateus (Matthew) Moreira; Simao Correia; and Vicente de Souza Pereira.

On 21 December 1998, John Paul II declared that the thirty died as martyrs for the faith, and at their beatification he prayed: "Let us ask God that the example of faith of these first Christians, especially those families of martyrs . . . may bring us to renew our commitment to a fruitful and bold evangelization at all levels of society."

Bibliography: P. HERONCIO, *Os holandêses no Rio Grande* (Rio de Janeiro 1937). *L'Osservatore Romano,* English edition, no. 10 (2000): 2.

[K. RABENSTEIN]

BROTTIER, DANIEL, BL.

Priest of the Congregation of the Holy Spirit and the Immaculate Heart of Mary; b. 7 September 1876, La Ferté-Saint-Cyr (near Beaugency), Diocese of Blois, France; d. 28 February 1936, Paris, France; beatified at Rome by John Paul II, 25 November 1984.

Brottier felt called to the priesthood from his childhood. In 1887 he entered the minor seminary of Blois, where he proved to be a brilliant student and an entertaining friend. In 1892, he began his study of philosophy at Blois's major seminary. After his ordination as a diocesan priest (22 October 1899), he taught at the college of Pontlevoy. Feeling a call to the missions, he joined the Holy Ghost Fathers at Grignon-Orly (26 September 1902), professed his temporary vows (30 September 1903), and was sent to Saint-Louis, Senegal, Africa. During his time in Senegal (1903–11), he demonstrated a special concern for orphans, helped found an organization for the education of girls, and in 1906 published the first Catholic monthly in West Africa, which ceased when he returned to France in 1911. In France, he raised the money to build Dakar's cathedral (consecrated 2 February 1936) in honor of those who had died in Africa for France. His bravery as a military chaplain in the twenty-sixth Infantry during World War I was rewarded with five citations, the *Croix de Guerre,* and the Legion of Honor medal. Brottier attributed his survival to St. Thérèse de Lisieux in whose honor he built a chapel at Auteil (1925). In 1923, the archbishop of Paris chose Brottier to administer the Orphan Apprentices of Auteuil, founded by Abbot Roussel in 1866. He undertook this work with zeal, and the number of orphans in his care rose from 175 to 1,408. He died at St. Joseph Hospital in 1936.

Feast: 28 February

Bibliography: *Acta Apostolicae Sedis* 78 (1986): 486–89. *Au Sénégal: sûr les traces du père Brottier: jubilé de la Cathédrale du Souvenir Africain, 1936/1986* (Paris 1986). G. G. BESLIER, *Le Père Brottier* (Paris 1946). P. CROIDYS, *Le père Brottier, serviteur ardent de la charité* (Paris 1945). C. GARNIER, *Ce père avait deux ames* (Paris 1956); *Le père Brottier: hier, aujourd'hui, demain* (Paris 1981). J. GOSSELIN, *Daniel Brottier: visages et reflets* (Paris 1989). *L'Osservatore Romano,* Englsh edition, no. 50 (1984): 2,12.

[K. RABENSTEIN]

BÜTLER, MARÍA BERNARDA, BL.

Baptized Verena; missionary; foundress of the Franciscan Missionary Sisters of Maria Help of Christians; b. 28 May 1848, at Auw, Aargau, Switzerland; d. 19 May 1924, at Cartagena, Colombia; beatified by John Paul II in Rome, Italy, 29 October 1995.

Verena, born into a Swiss peasant family, joined the Franciscan Missionary Sisters of Maria Hilf at Altstätten, where she was professed as Maria Bernarda (1869) and served as novice mistress. While superior of the convent, she was invited by Bishop Schumacher of Portoviejo to establish a presence in Ecuador. Maria Bernarda left Switzerland with six sisters, 19 June 1888. In Ecuador she founded communities of the Franciscan Missionaries of Mary Help of Christians (*María Ausiliatrice*) in Chone, Santana, and Canoa Ben. Persecution in 1895 forced her community into exile in Bahia, Brazil. From there fifteen sisters traveled to Colombia, where they were welcomed by Bishop Eugenio Biffi of Cartagena. He gave the sisters a wing of the *Obra Pia* women's hospital from where Mother Maria Bernarda founded communities in Austria and Brazil. She died after serving the poor and sick for fifty-six years as a religious.

A miracle attributed to her intercession was approved 26 March 1994. Pope John Paul II remarked that Mother Maria Bernarda "was convinced that the principal virtue is charity, the soul of all other virtues" (Beatification homily).

Feast Day: 19 May (Franciscans).

Bibliography: *L'Osservatore Romano,* English edition, no. 44 (1995): 1–2, 4.

[K. RABENSTEIN]

CAIANI, MARIA MARGHERITA DEL SACRO CUORE, BL.

Baptized Marianna Rosa Caiani, foundress of the Franciscan Minims of the Sacred Heart; b. 2 November 1863, Poggio a Caiano, Diocese of Pistoia, Tuscany, Italy; d. 8 August 1921, Montughi (near Florence), Italy; beatified by John Paul II, 23 April 1989.

Main altar inside St. Peter's Basilica during Daniel Brottier's beatification ceremony. At the top is a tapestry depicting him. (AP/Wide World Photos)

Marianna Rosa worked in her family's store until after the deaths of her father Giacomo (1184) and mother Luisa (1890). In 1893, she tested her vocation at the Benedictine convent in Pistoia, but returned to Poggio a Caiano. There she founded a school (1894) and, with two companions who had left other convents, a community (1896). They formed (1905) the Minims of the Sacred Heart, who aided the wounded, sick, elderly, poor, and children of Tuscany. Maria Margherita was elected mother superior in 1915 for a term to last the rest of her life. She revised the congregation's constitution in 1920 to meet new needs and attach it to the Franciscans.

Pope John Paul II (1986) declared at her beatification that she "made an option for Christ Crucified, whom she loved in the symbol of the divine Heart. She loved him in the needy, the least, and the smallest." Patroness of Tuscany.

Bibliography: ISTITUTO MINIME SUORE S. CUORE, *Madre Maria Margherita Caiani* (Poggio a Caiano 1969). *Acta Apostolicae Sedis* (1989): 563.

[K. RABENSTEIN]

CALABRIA, GIOVANNI, ST.

St. Giovanni (John); founder of the Poor Servants of Divine Providence and Poor Women Servants of the Divine Providence (PSDP); b. 8 Oct. 1873, at Verona, Italy; d. 4 Dec. 1954, at San Zeno, Italy; canonized by Pope John Paul II, 18 April 1999.

When the financial situation of his nearly destitute family worsened at the death of his father, 12-year-old Giovanni found employment as an errand boy. Despite his poverty and other difficulties, he pursued his priestly vocation. His seminary studies were interrupted by a mandatory 2 years of military service during which he founded an association to care for the convalescent poor. He was ordained in 1901.

Calabria's work with the poor began while he was still in the seminary when he volunteered to care for typhus victims. As a parish priest he found a young, abused runaway shivering in the cold. Taking the boy into his home, he gave him his bed. Thus began a career that earned him the title, "the apostle of the street children." St. Giovanni built the (*Casa Buoni Fanciulli*) in 1907, the first in a series of shelters for abandoned adolescents throughout Italy. He also constructed others for the elderly and ill. His spirituality, based on Matthew 25, taught him to see the face of Christ in the suffering. It led him to found congregations for both men and women as well as to acts of charity like the care of chimney sweeps during the winter, and the integration of the disabled into the working world. His longing for Christian unity caused him to correspond frequently with the author C. S. Lewis and others of like mind. Upon his death his remains were buried in his congregation's motherhouse at Verona.

Divine Providence brothers and sisters live in communities in Italy, Brazil, Argentina, Uruguay, Paraguay, Chile, Angola, Colombia, the Philippines, Russia, Rumania, and India. In addition to those in consecrated religious life, Don Calabria's spirituality imbues several lay associations, including the Associazione ex Allievi (for former students of Don Calabria centers), Spazio Fiorito (young people and families involved in educational, spiritual, and social activities), Unione Medico Missionaria Italiana (doctors who work in lesser developed countries to train indigenous doctors and nurses, and raise funds to assist children), and Association Francesco Perez (coordinates activities of volunteers). Don Calabria's work continues through these organizations in hospitals, prisons, technical schools, drug-addiction centers, parishes, and social service centers.

At his canonization Pope John Paul II called Calabria "an exemplary witness to the Resurrection." He continued: "He radiated an ardent faith, genuine charity, a readiness to sacrifice himself, love for the poor, an eagerness for souls, and loyalty to the Church. In the Year of the Father, leading up to the Great Jubilee Year 2000, we are called to emphasize the virtue of love of neighbor."

Feast: 4 December.

Bibliography: *L'Osservatore Romano,* English edition 15 (1988): 2, 5. E. BESOZZI, *Carisma e processi organizzativi* (Milan 1984). G. GECCHELE, *Biografia spirituale del servo di Dio don Giovanni Calabria* (Rome 1966). C. S. LEWIS, *The Latin Letters of C.S. Lewis,* tr. M. MOYNIHAN (South Bend, Ind. 1998). I. SCHUSTER, *L'epistolario card. Schuster-don Calabria (1945–1954)* (Milan 1989). Vatican Information Service (April 18, 1999).

[K. RABENSTEIN]

CALAFATO, EUSTOCHIA, ST.

Poor Clare abbess; b. 25 March 1434, Annunziata near Messina, Sicily, Italy; d. 20 January 1468 (or 1491?), Montevergine, Italy; beatified by John Paul II on 11 June 1988, Messina.

The daughter of Bernard Calafato, a wealthy merchant, and his wife Macalda Romano Colonna, known for her holiness, she was named Smeralda (Smaragda, "emerald") because of her beauty. She overcame the opposition of her brothers and joined the Poor Clares at S. Maria di Basicò ca. 1446, taking the name Eustochia. After eleven years she received permission from Callistus III to found a community of more rigorous discipline under the Franciscan Observants. Established first at S. Maria Accomodata (1458), the community was transferred to Montevergine (1463) to house increased membership. Outstanding were Eustochia's love of penance and poverty, her endurance of many great interior and exterior sufferings, the miraculous efficacy of her prayers, and her devotion to the Passion, on which she wrote a tract no longer extant. She was elected abbess at 30, and died at 35. Her body is venerated in the church of Montevergine. In iconography, she is commonly portrayed kneeling before the Blessed Sacrament.

At her canonization Pope John Paul II said: "From her cell in the monastery of Montevergine she extended her prayer and the value of her penances to the whole world . . . [to] alleviate every suffering, ask pardon for the sins of all." Patron of Messina, especially during earthquakes.

Feast: 20 January (formerly 16 February).

Bibliography: *Acta Apostolicae Sedis* (1988): 715. *Bullarium Franciscanum,* new series, 2:221. M. CATALANO, ed., *La leggenda della beata Eustochia da Messina,* 2d. ed. (Messina 1950). G. MILIGI, *Francescanesimo al femminile: Chiara d'Assisi ed Eustochia da Messina* (Messina 1994).

[M. F. LAUGHLIN]

CALLO, MARCEL, BL.

Lay man, martyr; b. 6 December 1921, Rennes, France; d. 19 March 1945, Mauthhausen concentration camp, near Linz, Austria; beatified at Rome, Italy, by John Paul II, 4 October 1987.

Marcel Callo, one of nine children from a working class family, attended school in Rennes until he was apprenticed to a typographer at age twelve. He became an active member and leader of the Young Christian Workers (*Jeunesse Ouvriere Chretienne* (JOC) or the "Jocistes"). He had just become engaged to marry (August 1942) when the Nazis occupied France. Marcel and his friends helped many escape the Nazis by giving them their Red Cross armbands. When the Nazis forced Marcel into labor at the Walther arms factory in Zella-Mehlis, Thuringia, Germany, he regarded it as an opportunity to evangelize. Within the labor camp he organized the JOC. He was arrested by the Gestapo (19 April 1944) for excessive Catholic activity after arranging for a Mass in French. At first he was held at Gotha prison, Germany. Marcel was then sent to Flossenbürg concentration camp, and finally, on to the Mauthausen concentration camp (26 October 1944). For a time he sorted rivets for Messerschmitt aircraft at the outlying Gusen I camp, but before long (7 November) he was moved to the Gusen II, where prisoners built airplanes underground in terrible conditions with little food. There Marcel continued to encourage his fellow prisoners until he was hospitalized in the Revier at Gusen (5 January 1945). He died of malnutrition and exhaustion in the deplorable *Sanitäts-Lager* just beyond the walls of Mauthausen.

Pope John Paul II remarked that Marcel's "entire life became an offering of thanksgiving to God" (beatification homily).

Feast: 19 April.

Bibliography: M. FIÉVET, *Martyrs du nazisme: Marcel Callo, jociste de Rennes (1921–45), mort en martyr au camp de Mauthausen, béatifié à l'occasion du synode des évêques sur l'apostolat des laïcs, Rome, Octobre 1987 et les autres!* (Paris 1987). P. GOUYON, *Marcel Callo, témoin d'une génération* (Paris 1981); *Marcel Callo* (Salzburg 1988). A. MATT, *Einer aus dem Dunkel—Die Befreiung . . .* (Zürich 1988). R. PABEL, *Marcel Callo—Dokumentation* (Eichstaedt-Wien 1991). *L'Osservatore Romano,* English edition, no. 40 (1987): 20.

[K. RABENSTEIN]

CALUNGSOD, PEDRO, BL.

A.k.a. "El Visayo," lay catechist, martyr; b. ca. 1654–58 in the Visayas region of the Philippines; d. 2 April 1672 in Tomhon on San Juan, Ladrones Islands (now Guam, Marianas Islands); beatified by John Paul II, 5 March 2000.

The only documentation concerning Calungsod's life is found in the materials about his companion in martyrdom, Blessed Fr. Diego Luis de San Vitores. Calungsod received his education in minor seminary of Loboc, Bohol, where he learned doctrine, Spanish, and Latin. Arriving on Guam with the first Jesuit missionaries (16 June 1668), fourteen-year-old Pedro assisted San Vitores in the evangelization the Marianas Islands, which were then under the Filipino Diocese of Cebu. In the first six months, the missionaries counted 13,000 baptisms; another 20,000 natives were under instruction. For four years Pedro assisted by teaching Christian hymns and the catechism and serving at Mass until the day the priest and catechist encountered the local chieftain, Matapang and his friend Hirao. Matapang was enraged that San Vitores, at the request of the chief's wife, had baptized his daughter against his will. Pedro had an opportunity to escape, but threw himself in the path of Hirao's spear, offering himself in a fruitless effort to save the priest. San Vitores's and Calungsod's bodies were stripped, tied together to a large rock, and thrown into the Tomhon Bay. Calungsod's cause was initiated following the beatification (6 October 1985) of San Vitores, whom he was shielding. His decree of martyrdom was read 27 January 2000.

John Paul II urged youth to follow the Pedro's example because his "love of Jesus inspired him to devote his teenage years to teaching the faith as a lay catechist" (Beatification homily).He is the patron of Filipino youth.

Feast: 1 April (Philippines).

Bibliography: *Father San Vitores, His Life, Times, and Martyrdom,* ed. E. G. JOHNSTON (Agana, Guam 1979). C. G. AREVALO, *Pedro Calungsod* (Manila 1999). F. GARCÍA, *Sanvitores in the Marianas,* tr. F. PLAZA (Mangilao, Guam 1980). A. DEL LEDESMA, *Mission in the Marianas: An Account of Father Diego Luis de Sanvítores and His Companions, 1669–1670,* tr. WARD BARRETT of *Noticia de los progressos de nuestra Santa Fe, en las Islas Marianas . . . desde 15 de mayo de 1669* (Minneapolis 1975). I. LEYSON, *Pedro Calungsod: Prospects of a Teenage Filipino* (Cebu, Philippines 1999). P. MURILLO VELARDE, *The "Reducción" of the Islands of the Ladrones, the Discovery of the Islands of the Palaos, and Other Happenings,* tr. F. E. PLAZA (Mangilao, Guam 1987). J. N. TYLENDA, *Jesuit Saints & Martyrs* (Chicago 1998), 337–39.

[K. RABENSTEIN]

CAMPIDELLI, PIUS (PIO), BL.

Baptized Luigi, known in religion as Pius of St. Aloysius, Passionist brother; b. 29 April 1868, Trebbio di Poggio Berni (near Rimini), Italy; d. 2 November 1889, San Vito di Romagna, Casale, Italy; beatified by John Paul II, 17 November 1985.

Gigino, as he was called by his family, was the fourth of the six children of poor farmers. After his father, Giuseppe Campidelli, died in 1874, an uncle came to help Gigino's mother, Filomena Belpani, with the farm. In 1877 the Campidellis became acquainted with the Passionists during a mission. Gigino entered the Passionist novitiate in the province of the Pieta (eastern Italy), which had been closed in 1866 shortly after the death of (Saint) Gabriel Possenti and reopened by (Blessed) Bernard Silvestrelli in 1882. Campidelli made his profession on 30 April 1884 and received the name Pio di San Luigi. He became known for the depth of his prayer life and fidelity to his vows while studying for the priesthood. He received minor orders at San Entizio (Viterbo) prior to being diagnosed with tuberculosis in 1889. He offered his suffering for the Church and died at age twenty-one.

At Campidelli's beatification, Pope John Paul II remarked that "it is fitting that this year [the International Year of Youth] should see him honored and put before all young people as a model and an inspiration."

Bibliography: L. ALUNNO, *Pio Campidelli* (Isola 1985).G. CINGOLANI,*Pio Campidelli: la rivincita dell'anonimato* (Turin 1989). *Acta Apostolicae Sedis* (1985): 141. *L'Osservatore Romano,* English edition, no. 47 (1985): 3–4.

[K. RABENSTEIN]

CANORI-MORA, ELISABETTA, BL.

Married mystic, Trinitarian Tertiary; b. 21 November 1774, Rome, Italy; d. there 5 February 1825; beatified by John Paul II, 24 April 1994.

Elisabetta was the daughter of a wealthy, Christian family headed by Tommaso Canori and Teresa Primoli. Under the tutelage of the Augustinian Nuns of Cascia (1785–88), she grew spiritually. In 1796, she wedded Cristoforo Mora (d. 1845), a lawyer who abused her and eventually abandoned her and their two children (Marianna and Luciana; two others had died in infancy), reducing the family to poverty. Elisabetta provided for her children and paid her husband's debts by working as a maid, laundress, and seamstress. While earning a living and raising her family, Elisabetta ministered generously to the poor and sick. Following a grave illness in 1801, she was favored with many spiritual gifts, and she became a member of the secular third order of the Most Holy Trinity in 1807. Her home was always open to those in need of spiritual or material comfort. She offered the sufferings of her life for the conversion of her husband, who, after her death, became a Trinitarian tertiary and Conventual Franciscan priest. Her body rests in the Trinitarian San Carlino alle Quattro Fontane Church in Rome. A miracle attributed to Elisabetta's intercession was approved, 6 July 1993.

During her beatification, Pope John Paul II said that Elisabetta "in the midst of numerous conjugal difficulties, showed her total fidelity to the commitment assumed in the sacrament of marriage and responsibilities deriving from it." Patroness of abused spouses.

Feast: 4 February.

Bibliography: *La mia vita nel cuore della Trinità. Diario della Beata Elisabetta Canori Mora, sposa e madre* (Vatican City 1996). P. GIOVETTI, *Madri e mistiche: Anna Maria Taigi ed Elisabetta Canori Mora* (Milan 1991); *Elisabetta Canori Mora: Sposa, madre e mistica romana* (Milan 2000). P. REDI, *Elisabetta Canori Mora: un amore fedele tra le mura di casa* (Rome 1994). *Acta Apostolicae Sedis* (1994): 501–503.

[K. RABENSTEIN]

CANOSSA, MADDALENA GABRIELLA, ST.

Foundress of the Daughters of Charity of Canossa; b. 2 March 1774, Verona, Italy; d. Verona, Italy 10 April 1835; canonized by John Paul II in Rome, 2 October 1888.

After the death in 1779 of her father, a wealthy marquis, Ottavio of Canossa, her mother Marchesa Teresa

Szluha remarried in 1781. Maddalena, who was then raised by an uncle, was given a private education. In 1799 she dedicated herself to caring for poor girls, and in 1800 she began to house some of them. In 1803 she opened a charity school, but when she attempted, in 1805, to dwell there herself she was constrained to return to her family. In 1808 she founded her religious congregation, dedicated to educational and hospital work. By the time of her death the Canossian Sisters had five houses. Her remains are housed in a marble sarcophagus in Verona.

Maddalena was beatified by Pius XII, 7 December 1941. During her canonization, Pope John Paul II related that when she saw the material and moral misery around her ''she saw that she could not love her neighbor 'as a lady,' that is by continuing to enjoy the privileges of her social class, and merely sharing her possessions without giving herself.''

Feast: 8 May (formerly 14 May).

Bibliography: D. BARSOTTI, *Dio solo e Gesù crocifisso: teologia di un carisma* (Milan 1985). M. FARINA and F. RISPOLI, *Maddalena di Canossa* (Turin 1995). I. GIORDANI, *Maddalena di Canossa,* 4th ed. (Brescia 1957). L. LIBERA, *Lettere di direzione spirituale alla marchesina Maddalena Gabriella di Canossa,* supplement to A. CATTARI, *Maddalena Gabriella di Canossa, gli anni decisivi di un itinerario spirituale* (Milan 1982). G. STOFELLA, *Enciclopedia Cattolica,* 3:610–611. A. BUTLER, *The Lives of the Saints,* rev. ed. (New York 1956), 2:309–311. T. PICCARI, *Sola con Dio* (Milan 1965).

[A. MENATO]

CARAVARIO, CALLISTO (KALIKST), BL.

Missionary priest, Salesian martyr; b. 8 June 1903, Cuorgne near Turin, Piedmont, Italy; d. 25 February 1930, Lin-Chow Tsieu, southern China; beatified by John Paul II, 15 May 1983.

Callisto was educated by the Salesians, including Vicenzo Cimatti (1879–1965), who inspired his missionary spirit. Callisto entered the order in 1918, was professed in 1919, and fulfilled his dream of evangelizing foreign lands when he was sent to the mission in Macao (1924), then to Shanghai (China), and Timor (Indonesia), where he labored for two years. He returned to Shiu Chow, China, in March 1929, and was ordained two months later in Shanghai by Luigi Versiglia (1873–1930). Thereafter he was assigned to the growing mission at Lin Chow. Six months later he returned to Shiu Chow to report his progress to Bishop Versiglia, who decided to visit the mission. The party, including the Salesians and several young Chinese, was ambushed en route. One of the female catechists earlier had rebuffed an attacker's marriage proposal. When he showed his determination to take the aspiring nun by force, the priests intervened, were beaten, and shot. The bodies of the martyrs were recovered and buried at the door of the church of Saint Joseph in Lin Kong How.

Pope John Paul II honored the martyrs for their self-oblation ''for the salvation and the moral integrity of their neighbors'' (beatification homily).

Feast: 13 November (Salesians).

Bibliography: G. BOSIO, *Monsignor Versiglia e Don Caravario* (Turin 1935). T. LEWICKI, *''Ten kielich mam wypełnić krwią'': opowieść o pierwszych meczennikach salezjanskich* (Warsaw 1985). *Acta Apostolicae Sedis* 78 (1986): 140–42. *L'Osservatore Romano,* English edition, no. 21 (1983): 11.

[K. RABENSTEIN]

CASANI, PIETRO, BL.

Priest, assistant to founder of Pious Schools, educator, preacher; b. 8 September 1572, Lucca, Italy; d. 17 October 1647, Rome, Italy; beatified by Pope John Paul II, 1 October 1995.

Of noble birth, Pietro was 20 years old when he decided to dedicate himself completely to the service of God and entered the Congregation of the Mother of God in Lucca, founded by St. John Leonardi, for whom Casani served as secretary. After Casani was ordained a priest, he centered his services especially on hearing the confessions of and doing pastoral work with youth. In Lucca, he established a congregation of Our Lady of the Snows. His way of life was marked by his enthusiasm for priestly and religious vocations, which he fostered by word and example.

In the union of the Luccan Congregation with the Pious Schools founded by St Joseph Calasanctius in 1614, Casani served as secretary general and recotr of St Pantaleon in Rome. When the union was dissolved in 1617, Casani remained a Piarist and dedicated himself to the Christian education of poor children and the life of poverty. Casani worked closely with Joseph Calasanz, who appointed him the first rector of the motherhouse of St Pantaleon in Rome, first assistant general, first novice master, and first provincial of Genoa and Naples and commissioner general for the foundations in Central Europe. Casani traveled throughout Tuscany, Lombardy, Liguria, Germany, and Poland where he founded schools and novitiates. A theologian, he wrote fluently in both Latin and Italian, and he left manuscripts that credit him as a writer and mathematician. His last few years were spent in Rome at the side of the Calasanz, bearing with him the suffering and troubles of the order. He died at the motherhouse, where his body was interred. His cause was opened shortly after his death by Calasanz, but Calasanz's death and loss of significant documents delayed the process until 1995, when Pope John Paul II—born in the land where Casani once labored—beatified him.

Bibliography: *Epistolario di Calsanzio,* ed. L. PICANYOL, 9 vols. (Rome 1950–1956). G. SÁTHA, *San José de Calasanz, su obra . . . ,* tr. C. AGUILERA and J. CENTELLES (Madrid 1956). *Memorie storiche . . . P. Casani* by an anon. Piarist (Rome 1904); *Acta Apostolicae Sedis* (1995): 721–22.

[LOUIS MESKO/R.P. MATEO]

CATANOSO, GAETANO, BL.

Priest of Reggio Calabria, founder of the Congregation of the Sisters of St Veronica of the Holy Face (*Congregazione delle Suore Veroniche del Volto Santo*); b. 14 February 1879, Chorio di San Lorenzo, Reggio Calabria, Italy; d. 4 April 1963, Reggio Calabria; beatified by John Paul II, 4 May 1997.

Gaetano's parents were landowners who encouraged his faith and vocation. Ordained in 1902, he gained a reputation for holiness while serving as a parish priest. In 1920, he founded a parish confraternity and newsletter devoted to the Holy Father. He also used the bulletin to promote the Poor Clerics Association and to encourage vocations. Catanoso was appointed pastor of Santa Maria della Candelora, Reggio Calabria (1921), where he founded the Missionaries of the Holy Face and built a shrine in honor of the Holy Face. The first members of the congregation—dedicated to charity, prayer for reparation, and catechesis—were clothed in 1935 and their constitutions were approved by the diocese in 1958. To renew spirituality among his flock, Catanoso promoted eucharistic and Marian devotions, catechesis, and parish missions. He organized teams of priests to conduct these missions in the region. In addition to his parish work (1921–50), Catanoso served as chaplain to religious institutes, a prison, a hospital, and the archdiocesan seminary. He was immediately venerated after his death.

An inexplicable healing at his intercession, approved as a miracle 25 June 1996, led to his beatification. During that ceremony Pope John Paul II said Gaetano Catanoso "worked tirelessly for the good of the flock entrusted to him by the Lord."

Bibliography: A. SORRENTINO, *Il Tuo Volto, Signore, io cerco* (Reggio Calabria 1996). *Acta Apostolicae Sedis,* no. 12 (1997): 599.

[K. RABENSTEIN]

CENTURIONE BRACELLI, VIRGINIA, BL.

Widow, foundress of the Brignoline Sisters; b. 2 April 1587, Genoa, Italy; d. there 15 December 1651; beatified at Genoa by John Paul II, 22 September 1985.

At age 15, Virginia complied with the wish of her father, the doge of Genoa, and married Gasparo Grimaldi Bracelli (d. 1625). She was left a widow with two daughters at age 20. During a famine she opened her palace, which she called *Santa Maria del Refugio dei Tribolati,* to abandoned children and those in distress. In 1619, the women who worked with her in the apostolate bound themselves by a solemn promise of perseverance to a common life under the Franciscan Rule. The Daughters of Our Lady of Mount Calvary, known as the Brignoline Sisters, opened their second house (1641) through the munificence of the Marquess Emmanuele Brignole and soon spread throughout northern Italy. The sisters were invited to Rome in 1815 and moved the motherhouse to the Esquiline Hill near St. Norbert's Church in 1833. In addition to founding the Brignolines, Mother Virginia organized a group to maintain Genoa's *Madonnette,* about 900 sacred images of the Virgin Mary recessed into the outer walls of guild halls and houses throughout the city.

Feast: 15 December.

Bibliography: R. MAGAGLIO, *Una patrizia genovese antesignana della moderna assistenza sociale: cenni biografici sulla serva di Dio Virginia Centurione Bracelli (1587–1651) nel centenario della sua traslazione dal Convento di Brignole alla Chiesa del conservatorio di Marassi (1872–1972)* (Genoa 1972). *Acta Apostolicae Sedis* (1986): 968–971. *L'Osservatore Romano,* Eng. ed. 40 (1985): 5,8.

[K. RABENSTEIN]

CEVOLI, FLORIDA, BL.

Baptized Lucrezia Elena, Poor Clare mystic; b. 11 November 1685, Pisa, Italy; d. 12 June 1767, Città di Castello (Perugia), Umbria, Italy; beatified by John Paul II, 16 May 1993.

As the daughter of Curzio Cevoli and his wife, Countess Laura della Seta, Lucrezia was born into a life of privilege. During her schooling under the Poor Clares of San Martin Convent, Pisa (1780–85), she discerned a call to religious life and contemplation. On 7 June 1703, despite opposition from her family, Lucrezia became Florida upon entering the Poor Clares at Città di Castello, where Saint Veronica Giuliani was her novice mistress. Following her profession (10 June 1704), Sister Florida held various offices, including cook, novice mistress, pharmacist, and vicaress. She succeeded Veronica as abbess in 1727 and was re-elected to that office for the next thirty years with some breaks. Mother Florida was distinguished by her spirit of prayer and fidelity to the Rule. As abbess she is remembered for reforming the community and encouraging her sisters to receive the Eucharist weekly.

Pope John Paul II remarked at her beatification that her enclosure and desire for recollection did not stop her from sharing in the problems of contemporary society. ''On the contrary, her spiritual intimacy made her interest agreeable and efficacious, as attested by the correspondence she maintained with some influential individuals of her time and her authoritative mediation for peace.''

Feast: 12 June.

Bibliography: L. DE ASPURZ IRIARTE, *Beata Florida Cevoli, discepola di santa Veronica Giuliani* (Siena 1993).

[K. RABENSTEIN]

CHAMINADE, JOSEPH GUILLAUME, BL.

Founder of the Marianists and the Marianist Sisters; b. 8 April 1761, Périgueux (Dordogne), France; d. 22 January 1850, Bordeaux. Chaminade was the youngest of the 15 children of a textile merchant. After ecclesiastical studies in Périgueux, Bordeaux, and Paris, he was ordained (1784) and earned a doctorate in theology (1785). He then joined his two brothers as a teacher in the seminary of Mussidan. During the French Revolution he refused to take the oath in support of the Civil Constitution of the Clergy. As a nonjuring priest he exercised his ministry in disguise at Bordeaux until forced into exile in Spain (1797–1800). At the shrine of Our Lady of the Pillar in Saragossa he was inspired to found sodalities and religious societies. Upon his return to France he centered his activities in Bordeaux for the remainder of his life. He acted as administrator of the diocese of Bazas (1800–1802) before his appointment as canon of the Bordeaux cathedral (1803). Chaminade was responsible for the return of many of the constitutional clergy and for the reestablishment of various religious societies. In 1816 he founded the Marianist Sisters; and in 1817, the Marianists. The origins of almost all pious works and benevolent institutions in Bordeaux during the first half of the nineteenth century have been traced to Chaminade's efforts. The *Manuel du Serviteur de Marie* (Bordeaux 1801) was Chaminade's sole published work, but his numerous writings are extant in MS form, together with the notes taken by those attending his conferences, supply a complete picture of his spirituality. A monument, topped by a statue of Mary Immaculate, marks his grave in Bordeaux. His cause was opened in 1909 and his beatification was approved by Pope John Paul II, 20 December 1999.

Bibliography: H. ROUSSEAU, *William Joseph Chaminade* (Dayton 1914). G. ANGELI, *Dottrina mariana del p. Chaminade* (Subiaco 1976). K. BURTON, *Chaminade, Apostle of Mary* (Milwaukee 1949). M. CHAMINADE, *Our Lady's tinker* (St. Meinrad, Ind. 1950). M. DARBON, *Guillaume-Joseph Chaminade* (Paris 1946). G. DOIG KLINGE, *Dos maestros espirituales: Guillermo José Chaminade y Fray Luis de Granada*, 2d. ed. (Lima 1990). G. GOYAU, *Chaminade, fondateur des Marianistes, son action religieuse et scolaire* (Paris 1914). H. LEBON, *Dictionnaire de Spiritualité Ascétique et Mystique*, 2:454–459. A. L. SEEBOLD, *Social-Moral Reconstruction according to the Writings and Works of William Joseph Chaminade* (Washington 1948). A. M. WINDISCH, *The Marianist Social System according to the Writings of William Joseph Chaminade* (Fribourg, Switz. 1964).

[G. J. RUPPEL]

CHAMPAGNAT, MARCELLIN JOSEPH BENOÎT, ST.

Priest, founder of the Marist Teaching Brothers (Little Brothers of Mary); b. 20 May 1789, in the hamlet of Le Rosey (Loire), France; d. 6 June 1840, Notre Dame de l'Hermitage, Loire.

The ninth of ten children born to Jean-Baptiste, a miller, and Marie-Thérèse, An older sister, Louise, a nun, returned home when her convent was destroyed during the French Revolution

He had no formal education until he was fifteen and was tutored by his teacher brother-in-law Benedict Arnaud in order to enter the junior seminary of Verrieres. At the major seminary in Lyons his fellow seminarians included St. Jean Baptiste Vianney (the Cure of Ars), St. Peter Chanel, and Ven. Jean Claude Colin. Champagnat was one of the original group of seminarians at Lyons who discussed with Colin the foundation of the Marist Fathers. They envisioned teaching brothers, who would be organized by Champagnat, as well as priests in this planned Society of Mary. After ordination (1816) Champagnat was assigned as a curate in LaValla (Loire). An encounter there with a dying boy who was totally ignorant of Catholic teachings convinced him of the need for teachers who could provide excellent education in rural areas. This incident expedited the foundation of the Marist Brothers (2 Jan. 1817) with Jean Marie Granjon and Jean-Baptiste Audras as its first members. They opened their first school in Marlhes (1818). The archbishop of Lyons blessed their work and gave it financial support. In 1824, Champagnat was relieved of parish duties to devote himself to organizing and directing his institute.

Meanwhile Champagnat continued to collaborate with Colin in establishing the Marist Fathers. He pronounced his vows as a member in 1836 when Rome approved the congregation. Champagnat was inclined to have the brothers subject to the superior of the Marist Fathers, but Colin, superior of the society, overruled him, making him the superior of the brothers. Champagnat published his pedagogical ideas in *Guide des Écoles* (1853), a work that has been reprinted many times and that serves as a norm for the Marist Brothers. In addition to instilling in students a sense of the transcendent, the need for social values, and commitment to fraternal and divine service, his principals stressed new methods of teaching literacy. In addition to this work, many of his letters to his brothers survive. He died about six weeks later, after dictating his ''spiritual testament,'' and was buried in the cemetery at Notre Dame de l'Hermitage.

Pope John Paul II canonized Champagnat, 18 April 1999, in St. Peter's Square. During the homily the Holy Father praised his sensitivity to the spiritual and educational needs of his time and his efforts to overcome the prevailing religious ignorance, and the abandonment that youth were experiencing. John Paul held him up as ''a model for all parents and educators to help them look upon youth with hope, to encourage them with total love, which will make a true human, moral and spiritual, formation possible.''

Feast: 6 June.

Bibliography: *Acta Apostolicae Sedis,* 10 (1999): 459–461. *L'Osservatore Romano,* English edition, no. 16, (1999). *Vatican Information Service* (19 April 1999). BR. JEAN BAPTISTE, *Life and Spirit of J. B. M. Champagnat* (Paris 1947). G. CHASTEL, *Marcellin Champagnat* (Paris 1939). J. COSTE and G. LESSARD, eds., *Origines maristes,* 4 v. (Rome 1960–66). M. A. DORADO SOTO, *El pensamiento educativo de la Institución Marista* (Valencia 1984). J. ÉMILE, *Dictionnaire de spiritualité ascétique et mystique,* 2:459–461. BR. IGNACE, *Le Bx. Marcellin Champagnat* (Paris 1955). S. D. SAMMON, *A Heart that Knew No Bounds: The Life and Mission of Saint Marcellin Champagnat* (New York 2000). J. VIGON, *Le Père Champagnat* (Paris 1952).

[L. A. VOEGTLE/EDS.]

CHAVARA, KURIAKOSE (CYRIAC) ELIAS, BL.

Priest, cofounder of the Syro-Malabar Carmelites of Mary Immaculate and the Congregation of the Mother of Carmel, and a pioneer figure in the Catholic Press in India; b. 10 February 1805, at Kainakary, Kerala (Malabar), India; d. 3 January 1871, in Changanacherry, Koonammavu, Kerala; beatified by John Paul II, 8 February 1986, in Kerala together with Blessed Alphonsa Muttathupandatu.

Ordained in 1829, he founded an institute, which was canonically erected as a Carmelite congregation in 1855, when he was confirmed as its superior. He was appointed vicar-general of the Vicariate Apostolic of Verapoly in 1861. Two printing presses set up by early Portuguese missionaries to Kerala in South India had disappeared, and in 1844 Chavara was determined to reactivate this apostolate. Designing his own press and using type made by a local blacksmith, he was able in a few years to send to the Congregation of the Propagation of the Faith in Rome copies of 10 devotional and catechetical books that he had published. He also edited the liturgical books of the Syro-Malabar rite. In 1887, his press first issued *Deepika,* now the oldest daily paper in Malayalam, and in 1902 the *Flower of Carmel,* the most widely circulated Catholic magazine in Kerala. In 1963, the Church in Kerala maintained some 20 publishing establishments issuing four Catholic dailies, 12 weeklies or monthlies, and a great volume of other Catholic literature. The diocesan process for Chavara's beatification was inaugurated by the archbishop of Changanacherry on 3 January 1958. This man, praised during his beatification by Pope John Paul II for his heroic service, died after a long illness. In 1889, his body was transferred to Mannanam.

Feast: 3 January (Carmelites).

Bibliography: *Chavara carama'sathabdi,* ed. H. PERUMALIL (Alleppey 1971). *Acta Apostolicae Sedis* 78 (1986): 1076–1078. *L'Osservatore Romano,* English edition, no. 7 (1986): 6–7. W. HERBSTRITH, *Begegnung mit Indien und einem seiner grossen christlichen Pioniere Kuriackos Elias Chavara* (Trier 1969). J. KANJIRAMATTATHIL, *The Pastoral Vision of Kuriakos Elias Chavara* (Bangalore, India 1986). K. MATHOTHU, *Blessed Father Kuriakose Elias Chavara* (Palai, India 1988).

[F. MAURILIUS/K. RABENSTEIN]

CHÁVEZ OROZCO, MARÍA VICENTA OF SANTA DOROTEA, BL.

Baptized Dorotea (Dorothy), a.k.a. Mother Vicentita, foundress of the Servants of the Poor (now called the Servants of the Holy Trinity and the Poor); b. 6 February 1867, Cotija, Michoacán, Mexico; d. 30 July 1949, Santísima Trinidad Hospital, at Guadalajara, Jalisco, Mexico; beatified 9 November 1997 by John Paul II.

The fourth and youngest child of a family that lived amid poverty, Dorotea was drawn to caring for the sick through the work of her parish priest, Fr. Agustín Beas, who established a six-bed infirmary in the rectory tended by members of the St. Vincent de Paul Society. She became his patient when she fell ill with pleurisy in 1892. At that time she discerned her vocation for ministering to the sick and poor, and began her service in the infirmary immediately upon her recovery later that year. She took private vows with Catalina Velasco and Juana Martin del Campo (1895). When her nursing companions abandoned her and their patients in 1898, she conceived the idea of a congregation. It was realized 12 May 1905 with the first sisters professing canonical vows in 1911. Beginning in 1913 she wisely guided her spiritual daughters for thirty years as superior general. She refused to discontinue her work in spite of dangers and calamities. Mother Vicentitia was threatened by revolutionaries (1910–20), and harassment by anti-clerical soldiers in 1926 forced the closure of the motherhouse chapel. In addition, a major earthquake rocked San Vicente Hospital (Zapotlán). She is lauded not only for her charity, but also for her heroic obedience, a virtue that she considered the highest form of sacrifice. Prior to the heart attack that caused her death, Mother Vicentita saw her congregation grow into an important charitable institution that supported eighteen hospitals, clinics, and nurseries.

At her beatification John Paul II proclaimed that she "built her work on the foundation of the suffering Christ, caring with the balm of charity and the medicine of comfort for the wounded bodies and afflicted souls of Christ's favorite ones: the destitute, the poor, and the needy."

Feast: 30 July.

Bibliography: *Acta Apostolicae Sedis* 21 (1997): 1049. *L'Osservatore Romano,* English edition, no. 46 (1997): 1–3.

[K. RABENSTEIN]

CHEVRIER, ANTOINE MARIE, BL.

Priest, Franciscan tertiary, founder of the priests and sisters of the Institute of the Prado; b. 16 April 1825, Lyons, France; d. there 2 October 1879; beatified by John Paul II 4 October 1986 in Lyons.

The son of silk industry workers in Lyons, Chevrier's was ordained in 1850 and immediately began serving the poor in Saint-André parish in the Guillotière, a working class suburb of Lyons. His ministry was transformed in 1856 when he discerned a call to help victims of the Rhône flood and share in their disinheritance. In 1857, he consulted with John Vianney, who encouraged him to become chaplain of the "Ville de Jesus Infant," a massive charitable organization founded by Camille Rambaud. In 1860, Chevrier acquired the infamous dance hall called "The Prado" and converted it into "the Providence of the Prado," lodgings and classrooms for poor children and adolescents, as well as a clinic for the sick. While continuing to live at the Prado, Chevrier was assigned to the parish of Moulin-à-Vent nearby (1867), but was relieved of this duty in 1871 in order to devote him-

self full time to establishing a congregation to continue the Prado. He wrote thousands of pages of commentary, including treatises and a training manual, to assist those who followed him. The Society of the Priests of the Prado came to fruition in 1877, when the first four men had completed their studies in Rome and received ordination. The Institute consists of priests, religious, and lay collaborators. Chevrier died at age fifty-four and was buried in the chapel of the Prado.

Pope John Paul II called Chevrier "the apostle of the poorest working class neighbors outside Lyons at the moment in which great industry was born" (beatification homily).

Feast: 2 October.

Bibliography: M. ALLIOD, *Un fondateur d'action sociale, Antoine Chevrier* (Paris 1992). A. ANCEL, *Le Prado: la spiritualité apostolique du Père Chevrier* (Paris 1982). A. C. B. ARTS, *De eerbeid waardige Père Antoine Chevrier* (Bussum 1946). P. BERTHELON, *Le message du père Chevrier* (Le Puy 1960); *A. Chevrier, un carisma per evangelitzar els pobres* (Montserrat 1986); *Antoine Chevrier: prêtre selon l'Evangile* (Paris 1986). A. LESTRA, *Le maréchal Pétain chez le père Chevrier. . . .* (Lyon 1941); *Le père Chevrier, avec lettres de Son éminence le cardinal Pacelli et de Son éminence le cardinal Maurin* (Paris 1944). *L'Osservatore Romano,* English edition, no. 42 (1986): 2–4. J. F. SIX, *Vie du père Chevrier, prêtre selon l'Evangile* (Paris 1986). H. WALTZ, *Un pauvre parmi nous, le Père Chevrier* (Lyon 1941). *Acta Apostolicae Sedis* 79 (1987): 301–10.

[K. RABENSTEIN]

CHMIELOWSKI, ALBERT, ST.

Baptized Adam, artist, founder of the Brothers (and Sisters) of the Third Order of St. Francis Servants of the Poor; b. 20 August 1845, Igolomia (near Krakow), Miechów District of southern Poland; d. 25 December 1916, Krakow, Poland; both beatified (22 June 1983 at Krakow) and canonized (12 November 1989 at Rome) by John Paul II.

In 1863, the aristocratic Adam Chmielowski abandoned his study of agriculture to join an uprising against the Russian occupation. Wounded and taken prisoner, Adam's left leg was amputated. He escaped prison and fled to France, where he studied engineering for a year, then art, before a general amnesty permitted his return to Poland as an artist (1874). Adam's paintings increasingly turned to religious themes; one of his most famous works, "Ecce Homo" (Jesus before Pontius Pilate), led Adam to a spiritual metamorphosis. After a decade as a successful artist, he entered the Jesuits (1880), though he left to become a Franciscan tertiary. He worked first in the countryside and then in Krakow, gradually abandoning his painting and turning his studio into a homeless shelter. Inspired by another former freedom fighter, St. Rafał Kalinowski, Adam took the name Albert (1887), donned a simple grey habit, and pledged religious vows (1888) before Cardinal Archbishop Albin Dunajewski. Thereafter the former socialite lived a life of poverty and organized shelters, soup kitchens, and other charitable institutions. Chmielowski's work and personality attracted followers who formed the nucleus of the Albertine Brothers (1888) and Sisters (1891), congregations that now serve the poor of Poland, Argentina, Italy, and the United States. In 1938, Brother Albert, who had founded twenty-one refuges in Poland, was posthumously awarded Poland's highest honor for his work among the destitute.

John Paul II wrote a play (1949), released as a motion picture in 1998, about Saint Albert, whom he called "Our God's Brother." During the canonization homily, the holy father said that Albert understood the necessity of "giving one's soul."

Feast: 17 June.

Bibliography: A. CASIERI, *Fratel Alberto, al secolo Adamo Chmielowski* (Rome 1989). W. KLUZ, *Adam Chmielowski, Brat Albert*, 2d. ed. (Krakow 1982). K. MICHALSKI, *Brat Albert*, 4th ed. (Krakow 1986). AL. OKOŃSKA, *Adam Chmielowski: Brat Albert*, 2d. ed. (Warsaw 1999). *Acta Apostolicae Sedis* 77 (1985): 461–463.

[K. RABENSTEIN]

CHYLINSKI, RAFAŁ MELCHOIR, BL.

Baptized Melchoir, Conventual Franciscan priest, musician; b. 8 January 1694, Buk in Wysoczka near Poznán, Poland; d. 2 December 1741, Łagiewniki near Łodz, Poland; beatified by John Paul II, 9 June 1991, in Warsaw, Poland.

Melchoir completed three years of military service and exited as an officer. Although he had studied with the Jesuits, he entered the Conventual Franciscans at Krakow (1715). He received the name Rafał (Raphael) and studied theology and philosophy. Because of a shortage of priests, his studies were cut short, and he was ordained in 1717. After being assigned to nine parishes in different cities, he was appointed to Łagiewniki, Poland, where he remained, except for a short period, until his death thirteen years later. Chylinski's simple, powerful preaching, commitment to the Sacrament of Reconciliation, and life of self-sacrifice drew people of all classes. He enhanced liturgical worship by playing the harp, lute, and mandolin. For twenty months (1736–37) he ministered to victims of a Warsaw flood and resultant epidemic without considering the risk to his own health. Before his death at age forty-seven, he became known as the patron of the poor whom he would supply from his own need. His body rests in the Franciscan church at Łagiewniki, which became a pilgrimage site.

Pope John Paul II called Father Rafał: "a man of much prayer and, simultaneously, of a great heart for the poor" (beatification homily).

Feast: 2 December (Franciscans).

Bibliography: L. J. BERNATEK, *Rafał Chylinski: studium z dziejów zycia religijnego w epoce saskiej* (Warsaw 1971); *Błogosławiony Rafał Chylinski z Łagiewnik* (Niepokalanów 1991).

[K. RABENSTEIN]

CIMATTI, MARIA RAFFAELLA, BL.

Baptized Santa Cimatti, virgin of the Congregation of Hospital Sisters of Mercy; b. 6 June 1861, Celle di Faenza near Ravenna, Emilia-Romagna, Italy; d. 23 June 1945, Alatri, Italy; beatified at Rome by John Paul II, 12 May 1996.

Santina, as she was called by her family of modest means, was the eldest of six children, three of whom died in childhood. When her mother was widowed (1882), Santina helped to raise and educate her younger brothers, Venerable Vincenzo Cimatti (1879–1965), who became the first Salesian missionary in Japan (1925), and another who also became a Salesian priest. Until her brothers and mother were safely settled, she responded to her vocation by teaching catechism and working with children. Then, she joined the Hospital Sisters of Mercy in Rome (1889), professed her initial vows (1891), and received the name Sister Maria Raffaella. Thereafter she devoted herself to the care of the sick and poor, first as a pharmacy assistant at Alatri and later at Frosinone. She was elected superior of the house at Frosinone (1921–28), then superior of Alatri (1928–40). Renouncing her position in 1940 after fifty years of religious life, she spent the majority of her time in prayer. At the age of eighty-three, she became known as the "Angel of the Sick" for the comfort she gave the wounded of the Second World War. Her courage in personally confronting the German Field Marshal Kesselring prevented massive bombing of Alatri. Her cause for canonization was opened in 1962.

Pope John Paul II spoke of Maria Raffaella "as a humble religious who constitutes a shining example of femininity plainly realized in self-giving."

Feast: 23 June.

Bibliography: *Acta Apostolicae Sedis*, no. 12 (1996): 551–53. *L'Osservatore Romano*, no. 20 (1996): 1; no. 21 (1996): 4–5.

[K. RABENSTEIN]

CIPITRIA Y BARRIOLA, CÁNDIDA MARÍA DE JESÚS, BL.

Baptized Juana Josefa, foundress of the Daughters of Jesus (Hijas de Jesús); b. 31 May 1845, Berrospe, Andoáin, Guipúzcoa, Spain; d. 9 August 1912, Salamanca, Spain; beatified at Rome by John Paul II, 12 May 1996 (with María Antonia Bandrés y Elosegui, one of her religious sisters).

As the daughter of a weaver, Juana Cipitria was virtually uneducated, yet in Salamanca she founded the Daughters of Jesus for the purpose of educating girls (8 December 1871). The congregation began after Juana (later Mother Cándida María de Jesús) had gathered like-minded women to assist with a series of charitable and educational programs she had started under the guidance of Jesuit Father Miguel Herranz. His influence can also be seen in the order's constitution (approved by Leo XIII, 1902), which is based on that of St. Ignatius of Loyola. Her various foundations share her commitment to incarnating social justice and appreciation of contemplation. The Daughters of Jesus now operate schools, medical dispensaries, retreat houses, and social service centers around the globe, including in Argentina, Colombia, Japan, the Philippines, Spain, and the United States. Mother Cándida was declared venerable 6 July 1993.

At her beatification Pope John Paul II observed: "The attention she showered on her sisters, the benefactors of her works, priests, students, the needy, to the point of becoming universal, are a visible expression of her love for God, of the radical way she followed Jesus and her total commitment to the cause of his kingdom" (beatification homily).

Bibliography: M. MARCOS, *Del Tormes al río Azul* (Salamanca 1932).

[K. RABENSTEIN]

CIRER CARBONNEL, FRANCINAINA, BL.

Known in religion as Francinaina de los Dolores de María, a.k.a. Francinaina de Sencelles, foundress of the Sisters of Charity; b. 1 June 1781, Sencelles, Mallorca, Balearic Islands, Spain; d. there 27 February 1855; beatified by John Paul II, 1 October 1989.

When Cirer's wealthy family refused her permission to become a nun, she led a life of poverty, consecration to prayer, and obedience to the will of God as a lay woman. Even after the deaths of all her family members, she remained in her home, caring for the sick, engaging in spiritual exercises, and offering her possessions for the work of her parish and the relief of the poor. Nevertheless her holiness drew others to her. On 23 December 1850 at age 70, she provided her home and the funds to found the Sisters of Charity in Sencelles. She pronounced her vows with two companions on 7 December 1951 and continued her works of charity and evangelization until her death. Today her tomb in the Sisters of Charity convent in Sencelles is a place of pilgrimage.

Pope John Paul II, who declared Francinaina venerable in 1983, said at her beatification that throughout her life she "obeyed God's will—a divine will that was sometimes difficult to discern . . . a life full of uncertainty, but a life in which there was no obstacle to serving God in everything."

Feast: 27 February.

Bibliography: J. LLABRÉS I MARTORELL, *La beata Francinaina de Sencelles* (Mallorca 1989, 2d ed. Mallorca 1990). B. C. LLULL, *Francisca Ana Cirer. Una vida evangélica* (Mallorca 1971). B. OLIVER, *Sor Francina-Aina dels Dolors (La Tia Xiroia de Sencelles)* (Mallorca 1970). T. SUAU PUIG, *Sor Francinaina Cirer, una vida para los demas* (Mallorca 1992). *Acta Apostolicae Sedis* (1989): 1030.

[K. RABENSTEIN]

COCCHETTI, ANNUNCIATA, BL.

Religious, foundress of the Sisters of St. Dorothy of Cemmo; b. 9 May 1800, at Rovato, Lombardy, Italy; d. 23 March 1882, Cemmo, Val Camonica, Lombardy, Italy; beatified by John Paul II, 21 April 1991.

After the death of her parents, Annunciata was raised by her devout grandmother, a noblewoman. She received her education from the Ursulines until their suppression by Napoleon, then from tutors in her home. Annunciata lived with her uncle in Milan for six years following the death of her grandmother in 1823. In 1831, she joined Erminia Panzerini at Cemmo, where they taught girls. With the help of Bishop Girolamo Verzeri, Annunciata founded the Sisters of Saint Dorothy of Cemmo (1840). After receiving training as a religious in Venice, she returned to Cemmo to govern the community until her death.

In his beatification homily, Pope John Paul II praised her "strong asceticism which helped her overcome the difficulties she met throughout her daily life."

Bibliography: A. ZUCCHETTI, *Il pane sul muricciolo: beata Annunciata Cocchetti, fondatrice delle Suore Dorotee di Cemmo* (Milan 1990). *Acta Apostolicae Sedis* (1991): 564.

[K. RABENSTEIN]

COLL GUITART, FRANCISCO, BL.

Dominican priest, founder of the Dominican Sisters of the Annunciation; b. 18 May 1812, Gombreny (Gombrèn) near Gerona (Catalonian Pyrenees), Spain; d. 2 April 1875, Barcelona, Spain; beatified in the first ceremony presided over by John Paul II, 29 April 1979.

Coll was the youngest of ten children of a wool carder who died when Coll was four. Even while studying at the seminary of Vich (1823–30), he devoted himself to the catechesis of children. He also taught grammar to pay for his education. He joined the Dominicans at Gerona (1830), where he was professed and ordained to the diaconate. When the friars were exclaustrated by the government (1835), Coll continued to live as a Dominican and was ordained priest (28 March 1836) with the consent of his superiors. After serving as a parish priest (1836–39), Coll preached throughout Catalonia for several decades, giving popular missions and offering spiritual direction, like his friend St. Anthony Mary Claret, whom he aided in forming the Apostolic Fraternity of priests. Named director of the secular order of Dominicans (1850), Coll reopened the former Dominican friary, cared for the cholera victims during the 1854 outbreak, and founded the Dominican Sisters of the Annunciation (1856) to provide for the religious formation of youth in poor and neglected regions. From 1869 until his death, Coll suffered from increasing physical problems caused by a stroke, including blindness and the loss of mental acuity. Nevertheless, the Dominicans, upon returning to Spain in 1872, found that Coll had carefully maintained the order's spirit and work throughout its suppression. Coll's mortal remains are venerated in the motherhouse of La Annunciata (Vich), which had grown to 300 members in 50 houses by the time of his death.

At Coll's beatification Pope John Paul II reflected on the glory of his heritage, saying that it "takes on concrete form in a magnificent and tireless work of evangelical preaching, which culminates in the foundation of the Institute known today as that of the Dominican Sisters of La Anunciata."

Feast: 19 May (Dominicans).

Bibliography: L. GALMÉS MÁS, *Francisco Coll y Guitart, O.P., vida y obra* (Barcelona 1976). *Acta Apostolicae Sedis* (1979) 1505–08. *L'Osservatore Romano,* Eng. Ed. 19 (1979): 6–7.

[K. RABENSTEIN]

COLOMBIÈRE, CLAUDE DE LA, ST.

Missionary priest of the Society of Jesus; ascetical writer; b. 2 February 1641, Saint-Symphorien d'Ozen (near Grenoble, between Lyons and Vienne), Dauphiné, France; d. 15 February 1682, at Paray-le-Monial, France; canonized by John Paul II in Rome, 31 May 1992.

Born of noble parentage, Claude entered the Society of Jesus at Avignon (25 October 1659). Thereafter he taught grammar and literature at Trinity College, Lyons (1661–66), then took up theological studies in Paris at Clermont College. The year after his ordination (6 April 1669), he returned to Lyons to teach rhetoric (1670–73). He began his tertianship (final year of spiritual formation for the Jesuits) following a year-long assignment as preacher in the Jesuit church of Lyons. Having taken final vows, in 1675 Colombière was named superior of the Jesuit house at Paray-le-Monial, where he demonstrated academic brilliance and became the spiritual director of St. Margaret Mary Alacoque. Thereafter he was a zealous apostle of devotion to the Sacred Heart of Jesus, first celebrated privately by the two saints on 21 June 1675. This devotion, centered on the humanity of Christ, was aimed at countering Jansenism. In October 1676 Colombière was sent to London, England, as chaplain to the Mary Beatrice d'Este, the duchess of York, wife of the future King James II. From England he continued his spiritual direction of St. Margaret Mary by letter. Imprisoned as a conspirator in the fictitious Titus Oates Plot to overthrow King Charles II, Colombière was spared death because of his position in the household of the duchess of York and the protection of King Louis XIV; however, Colombière was banished (1679). He returned to Lyons where he was spiritual director to the young Jesuits, then repaired to Paray-le-Monial, where he died. He was buried in the Jesuit chapel at Paray-le-Monial; a church was built over the same spot in 1685.

During the canonization homily, Pope John Paul II called Colombière "a true companion of St. Ignatius" and said he "attained the perfect freedom of one who gives himself unreservedly to the will of God." Patron of toy makers and turners.

Feast: 15 February.

Bibliography: C. DE LA COLOMBIÈRE, *Escritos espirituales del Beato Claudio de la Colombière, S.J.* (Bilbao, Spain 1979); *Oeuvres du R. P. Claude de la Colombiáre* (Avignon 1832; Paris 1864), which includes "Pious Reflections," "Meditations on the Passion," and "Retreat and Spiritual Letters." G. GUITTON, *Le bienheureux Claude La Colombière: apôtre du Sacré-Cœur, 1641–1682: d'après ses œuvres (sermons et correspondance) et de nombreux documents inédits . . .* (Paris 1981); *Perfect Friend: The Life of Blessed Claude La Colombière, SJ,* tr. W. J. YOUNG (St. Louis 1956). R. H. LAVIGNE, *The Life of St. Claude de la Colombiere: Spiritual director of St. Margaret Mary* (Boston 1992); *Special messenger* (Boston 1978). W. LÜBEN, *Der ehrwürdige diener Gottes p. Claudius de la Colombière* (New York 1884).

[K. RABENSTEIN]

COMBONI, DANIELE, BL.

Missionary bishop in Africa; founder of Comboni Missionaries of the Sacred Heart and the Missionary Sisters Pie Madri della Nigrizia; b. Limone del Garda (near Lake Garda), northern Italy, 15 March 1831; d. Khartoum, Sudan, 10 Oct. 1881; beatified by Pope John Paul II, 17 March 1996.

Daniele was the only one of the eight children of his farmer parents to live. With a view to dedicating his life to evangelizing Africa, he studied languages and medicine as well as theology at the diocesan seminary and Verona Institute for missionary preparation before his ordination to priesthood.

In 1857 he went to Khartoum with four other priests via the Holy Land. The five labored along the White Nile, suffering deplorable shortages of food and water in an unfamiliar climate and a hostile environment that left three dead within a short time. The failed mission was aborted by the Propaganda Fide, and Comboni and his companion returned to Italy (1859) to train more missionaries.

On 15 September 1864 Comboni conceived of a plan for the evangelization of Africa that involved "saving Africa with Africans." Europeans would establish missions along the coast and make expeditions inland to educate Africans to evangelize others. The plan included the use of female missionaries. In 1867, with papal approval, he founded the Verona Fathers because the new bishop of Verona no longer allowed the Institute for missionary preparation to have its own seminarians or priests. The first group left before the end of the year to establish a mission post at Cairo.

Returning to Europe to seek funding, he also established the Missionary Sisters of Verona or Pie Madri della Nigrizia (1872). He prepared a document for Vatican Council I that included his plan, which received approval on 18 July 1870, from Pope Pius IX. Comboni was appointed provicar apostolic (1872) and then vicar apostolic (1877) of the Vicariate Apostolic of Central Africa embracing Sudan, Nubia, and territories south of the great lakes. The following year he was involved in famine relief in Khartoum. Besides traveling widely in his vicariate and establishing missions at Khartoum, El-Obeid, Berber, Delen, and Malbes, Comboni sought to end the widespread slave trade and its abuses, which led to his abduction by a Freemason in Paris during one of his fundraising trips.

Comboni was also a linguist, geographer, and ethnologist, and contributed extensively to scientific journals. He compiled a dictionary of the Nubian language, and published studies on the Dinka and Bari tongues. His reports, such as *Un passo al giorno sulla via della mis-sione* (Bologna, 1997) and *Gli scritti* (Bologna, 1991), and correspondence provide much information on the history of African civilization. Comboni succumbed to malaria during his journey from El-Obeid to Khartoum in July 1881. Nevertheless, he continued to work for several months before he died.

On the day of beatification, Pope John Paul II said that the example of Comboni (and Guido Maria Conforti) should lead us to "apostolic fervor and a commitment to conversion," through more "active charity towards the poor. . . . we cannot pretend not to see the suffering of so many brothers."

Feast: 10 October.

Bibliography: D. AGASSO, *Un profeta per l'Africa* (Milan 1993). O. BRANCHESI, *Safari for Souls* (Cincinnati 1951). A. CAPOVILLA, *Daniele Comboni,* 6th ed. (Verona 1923). C. FUSERO, *Daniele Comboni,* 3rd ed. (Bologna 1961). L. FRANCESCHINI, "Il Comboni e lo schiavismo," in *Archivo Comboniano* (Verona 1961): 27–65. MONS. M. GRANCELLI, *Daniele Comboni e la missione dell'Africa Centrale* (Verona 1923). A. MONTONATI, *Il Nilo scorre ancora* (Bologna 1995).

[K. RABENSTEIN]

COMENSOLI, GERTRUDE CATERINA, BL.

Known in religion as Gertrude of the Blessed Sacrament, foundress of the Sacramentine Sisters of Bergamo; b. 18 January 1857, Biennio, Brescia, Lombardy, Italy; d. 18 February 1903, Bergamo, Lombardy; beatified by John Paul II, 1 October 1989.

Gertrude, the fifth of ten children in a poor family, learned to love and revere the Blessed Sacrament from her parents' example. She was a Maria Bambino Sister of Charity until ill health forced her from the convent. Upon her recovery, she taught in association with the Company of Angela Merici while serving as a lady's companion to a countess. After meeting Francesco Spinelli (1879), founder of the Sisters of Perpetual Adoration of the Blessed Sacrament, she founded the Sacramentine Sisters of Bergamo (1882), dedicated to Christian education and adoration. The first sisters received the religious habit in 1884. From Bergamo, where they had started, the sisters moved to Lodi, where they received episcopal approval in 1891. They returned to Bergamo the following year, expanded the congregation's ministries, and received papal approval 1908. When financial difficulties beset the Sacramentine Sisters, Spinelli was removed from their direction by the bishop. The beatification process for Gertrude Comensoli was opened in 1928. She was declared venerable by John XXIII.

Pope John Paul II remarked at her beatification that it was the "example of the poor and humble Christ, contemplated especially in the Eucharistic mystery, which guides the commitment of Gertrude Comensoli on the difficult spiritual journey and the distressing events of the foundation of the Blessed Sacrament Sisters.''

Bibliography: C. COMENSOLI, *Un'anima eucaristica, madre Gertrude Comensoli* (Monza 1936). *La Suora Sacramentina alla scuola della Serva di Dio Madre Gertrude Comensoli* (Bergamo 1960). *Acta Apostolicae Sedis* (1989): 1030.

[K. RABENSTEIN]

CONFORTI, GUIDO MARIA, BL.

Founder of the Xaverian Missionary Fathers; archbishop. b. 30 Mar. 1865, Casalora di Ravadese (near Parma), Italy; d. 5 Nov. 1931, Parma, Italy.

Son of Rinaldo and Antonia Conforti, Guido attended the Christian Brothers' school at Parma. Fascinated by a biography of St. Francis Xavier, he desired to become a missionary to foreign lands. In 1872 he entered the diocesan seminary and was ordained on 22 Sept. 1888. He aided Paul Manna, PIME, in founding the Pontifical Missionary Union of the Clergy, of which he later became the first national president (1918). Missionary activity *ad gentes* was still his great ideal, although his precarious health prevented him from undertaking such a strenuous activity. On the feast of St. Francis Xavier, 3 Dec. 1895, he established a seminary for training missionaries, and in 1898 he founded the Pious Congregation of St. Xavier for Foreign Missions. In 1902, he was named archbishop of Ravenna, but resigned the see in 1904 because of serious illness. In 1907, after Conforti's health improved, Pope Pius X personally asked him to accept an appointment as archbishop of Parma. For the next twenty-four years he worked with admirable zeal and prudence for the flock entrusted to his care. In addition, he continued to oversee the Xavieran Fathers, visiting their missions three years before his death. In 1941, ten years after his demise, the diocesan process for his beatification began.

At the time of Blessed Guido's beatification, 17 March 1996, Pope John Paul II praised him as ''a model of genuine pastoral charity who knew how to invite believers to open their hearts to those who were distant without forgetting the needs of local communities.''

Feast: 5 November.

Bibliography: L. BALLARIN, *L'anima missionaria di G. M. Conforti* (Parma 1962). G. BARSOTTI, *Il servo di Dio G. M. Conforti* (Rome 1953). G. BONARDI, *Guido Maria Conforti* (Parma 1936). V. C. VANZIN, *Un pastore, due greggi* (Parma 1950).

[K. RABENSTEIN]

CORMIER, HYACINTHE-MARIE, BL.

Baptismal name Henri Marie; master general of the Order of Preachers (Dominicans) and spiritual writer; b. 8 December 1832, at Orleans, France; d. 17 December 1916, at Rome, Italy; beatified 20 November 1994 at Rome.

After the early death of Cormier's father, his mother took him and his brother Eugene to live near their uncle who was a priest. Both boys entered the junior seminary at Orleans, but Eugene died the following year. Shortly after he was ordained a priest of the diocese of Orleans in 1856, he entered the novitiate of the Order of Preachers at Flavigny by Father Henri Lacordaire and given the name Hyacinthe. The Dominican community hesitated to profess him because of his health but in 1859 when Cormier fell seriously ill, he was anointed and allowed to make his profession in the belief he had only days to live. He recovered and served the Dominicans for another 50 years.

As a professor of theology, he demonstrated a firm grasp of the faith. During the years 1866–74 he was the first provincial of the restored province of Toulouse and again in1878–82, serving intermittently as prior in various convents. Cormier's administrative competence helped solidify the Dominican restoration begun by Henri Lacordaire.

Beginning in 1891 he served in generalate of the Order, first as *socius* to Master General Frühwirth (1891–96), then as procurator general until 1904 when he was elected the 76th master general. As master general (1904–1916), Cormier restored many suppressed provinces and erected new ones, including one in Canada and another in California. His time as master general coincided with the difficult period of modernism in the Church, and he promulgated a new *ratio studiorum* for the Order. In 1909 he established the international Angelicum University (now the Pontifical University of St. Thomas) in Rome and lent his support to the theological faculty of the University of Fribourg in Switzerland. A noted spiritual director, Cormier was an esteemed confidant of St. Pius X, prized for his intellectual honesty and compelling moral judgment.

Cormier practiced strict conformity to the Dominican Rule. Because he had been born on the Feast of the Immaculate Conception, he had a strong devotion to the Blessed Virgin Mary and the Rosary. Despite his heavy schedule of teaching, writing, administering, and spiritual direction, he spent hours daily before the Blessed Sacrament.

Cormier had written his doctoral thesis on the biblical rationalism of David Straus. Among his 171 printed writings examined during the beatification process were encyclical letters, biographies, and spiritual books, including *Instruction des Novices* (Paris 1880) and *Quinze entretiens sur la liturgie dominicaine* (Rome 1913).

Cormier died quietly in Rome at the age of 84 and was buried in the church adjacent to the Pontifical University of St. Thomas. At Cormier's beatification in 1994, Pope John Paul II declared:

> Truth is not an abstract notion. For us it is one person, the person of Christ, King of the universe. In his life, Father Cormier never ceased to live the truth and he passed it on to all his Dominican brothers with humility and perseverance. Did he not combine truth with charity in his motto, *Caritas veritatis?* Indeed, the founder of the Angelicum University reminds us that God requires us to use the faculties of our spirit, a reflection of his own, to glorify him.

Feast: 21 May, the anniversary of his election as master general.

Bibliography: *Acta Capituli Generalis Ordinis Praedicatorum 1920* (Rome 1920): 60–67. S. SZABÓ, *Hyacinth Marie Cormier,* translated by C. G. Moore (New York 1938).

[A.B. WILLIAMS/K. RABENSTEIN]

CRISPIN OF VITERBO, ST.

A.k.a. *Il Santorello* in Viterbo, Capuchin lay brother, questor, and apostle of the poor; b. 13 November 1668, Viterbo, Italy; d. 19 May 1750, at Rome; canonized 20 June 1982, by Pope John Paul II at Rome.

After receiving his early education from the Jesuits, Pietro Fioretti followed the trade of shoemaker until he joined the Roman province of the Capuchins on 22 July 1693, and became Brother Crispin. He was cook, gardener, and placed in charge of the infirmary. For forty-six years he acted as questor, the chief financial officer. From his early days as a Capuchin until his death, he was blessed with the gift of miracles and an infectious joy and cheerfulness. Both laity and ecclesiastics sought him for encouragement. In his many years of questing in Orvieto, he not only became the provider for his Capuchin family, but begged for all the poor. Throughout his life Crispin's spirituality was based on his trust in Mary Immaculate. In 1748, because of ill health, Crispin was sent to the infirmary in Rome, where he died of pneumonia two years later. His incorrupt body now rests under a side altar in the Capuchin church at Rome.

Presiding at his first canonization ceremony, Pope John Paul II praised Crispin as a "humble brother without any history, who simply accomplished his mission and understood the true value of our earthly pilgrimage."

Feast: 21 May (Capuchins).

Bibliography: *Acta Apostolicae Sedis* 75 (1983): 789–795. *Analecta Ordinis Fratrum Minorum Cappucinorum,* v. 1–70, see general index. "Epistola exhortativa nunc primum edita," *Analecta Ordinis Fratrum Minorum Cappuccinorum* 27 (1911): 19 ff. *Bibliotheca Sanctorum IV* (Rome 1964) 312 f. *Bullarium Ordinis Fratrum Minorum Capuccinorum,* v. 1–7 (Rome 1740–52), v. 8–10, (Innsbruck 1883–84) v. 10. R. BRANCA, *Un frate allegro* (Cagliari 1971). C. HAMMER, "Our Lady's Favorite," *Round Table of Franciscan Research* 23 (1958): 17–21. *L'Osservatore Romano,* English edition, no. 26 (1982): 1–2. GIORGIO DA RIANO, ed., *Massime e preghiere,* 3d. ed. (Rome 1950).

[T. O'ROURKE]

CUSMANO, GIACOMO, BL.

Physician, priest, founder of the Servants of the Poor and the Congregation of the Missionary Servants of the Poor (MSP); b. 15 March 1834, Palermo, Italy; d. there 14 March 1888; beatified at Rome by John Paul II, 30 October 1983.

Giacomo was born into a bourgeois family. Following the death of his mother, Maddalena Patti, in 1837, her older sister Vincenzina Patti cared for the Cusmano children. His pious aunt instilled in Giacomo the sense of charity for which he became known, and his Jesuit teachers at Palermo reinforced this virtue. Although he contemplated becoming a missionary, he studied and practiced medicine at Palermo, offering his services to the poor free of charge. Under the spiritual direction of Monsignor Turano, he followed his vocation to the priesthood and was ordained on 22 December 1860. Cusmano used his wealth to buy land, buildings, and factories to provide employment, housing, and training. With the blessing of Archbishop Naselli and the approval of Pope Pius IX, Cusmano founded (5 August 1868) the first *Boccone del Povero* ("Morsels of the Poor"), which spread throughout Sicily to provide for orphans, the aged, and the sick. He also founded two congregations to serve these people. The first Servants of the Poor brothers received their habit on 4 October 1884; the Missionary Servants, 21 November 1887. When the first Sister Servants were veiled (23 May 1880), his aunt Vincenzina Patti was appointed superior. After exhausting his own resources, he begged in the streets of Palermo and relied on God to provide the rest. Many miracles are attributed to his intercession. He is noted for his courage in working among the impoverished during a cholera epidemic in 1888, which led to his death at age 54.

During his beatification Pope John Paul II reflected that Cusmano's love for God and neighbor translated into "the gift of himself to the most needy and suffering in a service pushed to the point of heroic sacrifice." Patron of the poor.

Feast: 13 March.

Bibliography: *Lettere del servo di Dio p. Giacomo Cusmano fondatore del Boccone del povero* (Palermo 1970). F. CONIGLIARO, L'evento-Cristo nell'esistenza del povero: la profezia ecclesiale di Giacomo Cusmano, in AA. VV., La ''Chiesa'' del Cusmano (Palermo 1995) 50–178. M. T. FALZONE, *Giacomo Cusmano: poveri chiesa e societ&agrave* (Palermo 1986). G. LENTINI, *Un santo a Palermo* (Rome 1985); *Beato Giacomo Cusmano: medico e prete dei poveri* (Turin 1989). *Acta Apostolicae Sedis* 77 (1985): 112–14. *L'Osservatore Romano,* Eng. ed. 47 (1983): 6–7.

[K. RABENSTEIN]

DAIMIEL, THE MARTYRS OF, BB.

A.k.a. Nicéforo Diez Tejerina and Companions, 26 religious from the Passionist house of studies, Christ of the Light, outside the city of Daimiel, about 80 miles south of Madrid, Spain; they were Nicefero Diez Tejerina, 43; Ildefonso García Nozal, 38; Pedro Largo Redondo, 29; Justiniano Cuesta Redondo, 26; Eufrasio de Celis Santos, 21; Maurilio Macho Rodríquez, 21; Jose Estalayo García, 21; Julio Mediavilla Concejero, 21; Fulgencio Calvo Sánchez,19; Honorino Carracedo Ramos, 19; Laurino Proaño Cuesta, 20; Epifanio Sierra Conde, 20; Abilio Ramos Ramos, 19; Anacario Benito Nozal,30; Felipe Ruiz Fraile, 21; Jose Osés Sáinz, 21; Felix Ugalde Irurzun, 21; Jose Maria Ruiz Martínez, 20; Zacarias Fernández Crespo, 19; Pablo Maria Lopez Portillo, 54; Benito Solana Ruiz, 38; Tomas Cuartero Gascón, 21; Jose Maria Cuartero Gascón, 18; German Pérez Jiménez, 38; Juan Pedro Bengoa Aranguren, 46; Felipe Valcobado Granado, 62; beatified 1 Oct.1989 by John Paul II.

Born in 1893 in Spain, Nicéfero Tejerina responded to God's call to embrace religious life in the Passionist Congregation. He studied in Toluca, Mexico, but because of the persecution of the Church there during the presidency of Plutarco Calles, he was arrested and later exiled to the United States, where he finished his studies in Chicago. He was ordained by Archbishop George Mundelein in 1916. After ministering in the U.S., Mexico, and Cuba, he returned to Spain in 1932 to assume responsibilities as provincial superior of the order there. An antireligious climate swept Spain after the proclamation of the republic in 1931.

In 1936 Nicéforo went to visit the young religious studying for ordination and missionary work, the priests who taught them, and the brothers who served in the community at Daimiel. On the night of 21 July 1936, militiamen entered the Passionist house and ordered the thirty-one religious to leave in one hour. The militiamen ordered the group to the cemetery and told them to flee. At the same time, they alerted companions in the surrounding areas to shoot the religious on sight. The Passionists split into five groups. The first group of nine was captured and shot to death outside the train station of Carabanchel in Madrid on 22 July 1936.

The second group of twelve, Father Nicéforo among them, was taken at the station at Manzanares and shot by a firing squad. Nicéforo and four others died immediately; seven were taken to the hospital where one later died. Six of them recovered, only to be shot to death later on 23 October 1936. Three other religious, traveling together, were executed at the train station of Urda (Toledo) on 25 July. Two gave their lives at Carrion de Calatrave on 25 September. Only five of the thirty-one religious were spared. Numerous eyewitnesses testified afterwards to the brave faith and courage shown by the Daimiel community in their final moments, especially the signs of forgiveness they gave their executioners. Today their bodies are interred in the Passionist house at Daimiel.

At their beatification John Paul II said of them: ''None of the religious of the community of Daimiel was involved in political matters. Nonetheless, within the climate of the historical period in which they lived, they were arrested because of the tempest of religious persecution, generously shedding their blood, faithful to their religious state of life, and emulating, in the twentieth century, the heroism of the Church's first martyrs'' (Homily, 1 Oct. 1989).

Feast: 23 July.

[VICTOR HOAGLAND]

DAROWSKA, MARCELINA KOTOWICZ, BL.

In religion Maria Marcelina; widow, co-foundress of the Sisters of the Immaculate Conception of Mary (*Niepokalanki*); b. 16 January 1827, Szulaki, Podolia, Ukraine; d. 5 January 1911, Jazłowiec, Ukraine; beatified in Rome, Italy, by John Paul II, 6 October 1996.

Although Marcelina Kotowicz expressed a desire to enter religious life, her dying father made her promise that she would marry. She fulfilled her pledge in 1849 by marrying Karol Darowski and bore him two children before his death three years later. Her son died the next year. In 1854, Marcelina traveled to Rome, where she met Resurrectionist Father Hieronim Kajsiewicz, who became her spiritual director, and through him met Josephine Karska, with whom she founded (1857) the Congregation of the Sisters of the Immaculate Conception of the Blessed Virgin Mary. After Josephine's death in 1860, Marcelina moved her four sisters to Jazłowiec

(Archdiocese of Lviv [now Ukraine]), where the congregation opened its first school for girls (1 November 1863) without the approbation of the state. Dissatisfied with the quality of available textbooks, Mother Marcelina purchased a printing press in 1901 and began publishing books written by the sisters. When government authorities attempted to regulate the subjects taught, Marcelina threatened to close the schools and alter the 1867 constitutions to create a contemplative order. Despite these problems and other difficulties with governmental authorities, at the time of her death the Sisters of the Immaculate Conception had seven convents, each of which ran a school for girls. In 1882, Marcelina commissioned Tomasz Oskar Sosnowski to sculpt an image of the Immaculate Conception, which became famous as "Our Lady of Jazłowiec," an object of national veneration. More than 200 sisters continue Marcelina's work of forming Christian women in Poland, the Ukraine, and Belarus.

She was beatified by Pope John Paul II, who said that Mother Marcelina "is an example of an apostolic faith that creates new ways for the Church to be present in the world and forms a more just and human society. . . ."

Feast: 6 January (Lviv).

Bibliography: E. JABLONSKA-DEPTULA, *Marcelina Darowska niepokalanka* (Lublin 1996). M. A. SOLTAN, *Czlowiek wielkich pragnien: matka Marcelina Darowska* (Szymanów 1978).

[K. RABENSTEIN]

DELANQUE, JOAN, ST.

Known in religion as Joan of the Cross (Jeanne de la Croix); foundress of the Sisters of Saint Anne of the Providence of Samur; b. 18 June 1666 at Samur, Anjou, France; d. 17 August 1736 at Fencet, France.

The youngest of 12 children, Joan's early years were not edifying: she was small, coquettish, avaricious, and quick tempered. When her widowed mother's death left her proprietress of the family's religious goods store, Jeanne planned to enrich herself on pilgrims to the shrine of Our Lady of Ardilliers. Intent upon making money, she scandalized her neighbors by keeping the shop open on Sundays. Her miserly nature is revealed in her refusal to keep food on hand so that she could tell beggars that she had nothing to give them. The Holy Spirit spoke to her through two different individuals in 1698. One was a dubious visionary named Françoise Suchet, whose pious exhortation stirred Joan. The other was Abbé Genetau, whose conversations caused her to reform her life. After performing severe penance she was granted an ecstasy in which her vocation to help the poor was revealed. She began this at once by giving away her goods to the poor

and living a life of austerity and penance. Her home, known as "Providence House," in which she cared for orphans, was destroyed in an earthquake in 1703. She started over, closed her shop in order to devote herself full-time to charity, and gathered like-minded women, including her niece, to found formally the Sisters of St. Anne (later called the Sisters of Providence) in 1704. The sisters cared for single mothers, prostitutes—anyone in distress. Jeanne had a devotion to the Christ Child, which led her to her particular work with orphans. Her rigorous personal life drew criticism from the local bishop, from Jansenists, and from Louis de Montfort until her sincerity was proved. The congregation received diocesan approval in 1709. When she died peacefully at the age of 70, the people of Saumur praised her goodness.

At the canonization of this "great prodigy of charity" on 31 October 1982, Pope John Paul II declared: "The Holy Spirit himself led her to see Christ in the poor, the Christ Child in their children. . . . And with Christ she wished to show to the poor the tenderness of the Father. To this God she had recourse with the audacity of a child, expecting everything from him, from his Providence. . . ."

Feast: 17 August.

Bibliography: *Acta Apostolicae Sedis* 40 (1948): 314–19; 79 (1987): 233–37. BAUDOT-CHAUSSIN. 8:311–317. *L'Osservatore Romano,* English edition, no. 45 (1982):1, 2, 12. F. TROCHU. *La Bienheureuse Jeanne Delanoue,* new ed. (Paris 1950).

[K. RABENSTEIN]

DELUIL-MARTINY, MARIE OF JÉSUS, BL.

Baptized Marie Caroline Philomène; foundress of the Daughters of the Sacred Heart of Jesus; b. 28 May 1841, Marseilles, France; d. 27 February 1884, La Servianne Convent, Marseilles; beatified by Pope John Paul II in Rome, 22 October 1898.

Educated by the Visitation nuns in Lyons, Marie became a member of the Guard of Honor of the Sacred Heart of Jesus. Under the guidance of Jean Colage, S.J., she founded in 1873 in Belgium a contemplative congregation of women to make reparation to the Sacred Hearts of Jesus and Mary and to pray for priests. She took the name Marie de Jésus. The Institute's constitutions were definitively approved by the Holy See in 1902. As a model for the institute the foundress chose the Blessed Virgin under the aspect of victim and associate of Christ in the Passion. She adopted from Msgr. O. Van den Berghe the devotion to Mary as "virgin and priest." In 1916, the Holy Office published a decree forbidding representations of Mary in priestly vestments; and in 1927 it prohibited the spread of this devotion among the faithful, but permitted the daughters to practice the devotion within the confines of the congregation. During the lifetime of the foundress, the congregation spread in France and into Belgium. It has since established houses in Austria, Italy, Switzerland, and the Netherlands. Marie Deluil-Martiny was shot to death by an anarchist employed at the motherhouse. Her remains rest in the Basilica of the Sacred Heart at Berschem (near Antwerp), Belgium.

At the beatification rite, Pope John Paul II declared that when she founded the order ''she put eucharistic adoration at the center of their religious life. With her deep understanding of Christ's sacrifice, she wanted to unite herself with Him continually in the offering of the Blood of Christ to the Blessed Trinity.''

Feast: 27 October.

Bibliography: *Acta Apostolicae Sedis* (1989): 1079. L. LAPLACE, *Immolation: Life of Mother Mary of Jesus,* tr. J. F. NEWCOMB (New York 1926). R. GARRIGOU-LAGRANGE, *La Vita interióre della Madre Maria di Gesù* (Milan 1939). On the cult of the ''Virgin and priest,'' see: R. LAURENTIN, *Marie, l'église et le sacerdoce,* 2 v. (Paris 1952–53). A. DE BONHOME, ''*Dévotions prohibées,*'' *Dictionnaire de Spiritualité Ascétique et Mystique,* 3:786–788.

[M. H. QUINLAN]

DIEZ Y BUSTOS DE MOLINA, VITORIA, BL.

Martyr, teacher, Carmelite of the Teresian Institute; b. 11 November 1903, Seville, Spain; d. 12 August 1936, Rincón at Hornachuelos near Cordoba, Spain; beatified by John Paul II on 10 October 1993.

Vitoria, the only child of a devout, middle-class couple, wanted to become a missionary and an artist, but bowed to her parents' wish that she teach. She studied pedagogy while also taking art classes in her hometown. Seeing an opportunity to combine teaching with evangelization, she became a member of the Teresian Institute, founded by Blessed Pedro Poveda Castroverde (1874–1936). Vitoria was assigned to teach first in Cheles near the Portuguese border. The following year she was transferred to an Andalusian country school in Hornachuelos. There she was active in the life of the parish and in charitable ministries. In addition to the charism of teaching, Vitoria possessed a profound joy that attracted others to her words. At the start of the Spanish Civil War, when many abandoned the faith, Vitoria used her position to influence her charges and their families to remain faithful. She was arrested by the revolutionaries with seventeen men on 11 August 1936. The next day they were executed and their bodies thrown into a mine shaft. The declaration of her martyrdom was signed on 6 July 1993.

Speaking of Blessed Vitoria at her beatification, Pope John Paul II said: ''She was able to sanctify herself in her work as a teacher in a rural community. . . . The happiness she transmitted to all was a faithful reflection of that unconditional surrender to Jesus.''

Feast: 10 October.

Bibliography: G. MARTINA, ''To Become a Saint,'' *Sanctity Today* (Rome 1998-1999).

[K. RABENSTEIN]

DOMINGO Y SOL, MANUEL, BL.

Priest, founder of the Fraternity of Diocesan Worker Priests; b. 1 April 1836, Tortosa, Tarragona, Spain; d. there 25 January 1909; beatified by John Paul II, 29 March 1987.

Son of Francisco Domingo Ferré and Josefa Sol Cid, Manuel received his early education at local schools and from a tutor before undertaking the study of philosophy in the diocesan minor seminary (1851–52) and theology in the major seminary. He was ordained deacon by the bishop of Vich (1859) and priest at Tortosa (1860).

After another year of study, he began his ministry by concentrating on catechesis and giving missions in towns surrounding Tortosa. On 7 March 1862, he took possession of the parish at La Aldea, thirteen kilometers from Tortosa. While serving his parish he completed further study in theology at the University of Valencia and began teaching at Tortosa's seminary. Among his many pastoral works were the founding of Catholic Youth of Tortosa (1869), an evening school for workers and artisans, the publication *El Congregante* to foster Christian ideals among youth, a theater complex, and a recreational center. He became known as a great confessor and a spiritual director for the discernment of vocations. In 1872 to 1873, Domingo established the College of Church Vocations of St. Joseph in Tortosa in order to allow poor seminarians to continue their study of philosophy and theology. Later he founded similar schools at Almería, Burgos, Lisbon, Murcia, Orihuela, Plasencia, Rome (Pontifical Spanish College), Toledo, and Valencia. With six other priests, Domingo founded the Fraternity of Diocesan Worker Priests (1883) to further foster vocations. Manuel Domingo, whose cause was opened in 1946, was declared venerable by Paul VI (4 May 1970).

He was beatified by John Paul II, who called him ''the holy apostle of priestly vocations.''

Bibliography: J. M. JAVIERRE, *Reportaje a Mosén Sol: un hombre bueno y audaz* (Madrid 1987). F. MARTÍN HERNÁNDEZ, *Mosen Sol: vida de Manuel Domingo y Sol, fundador de la Her-*

mandad de Sacerdotes Operarios Diocesanos (Salamanca 1978). *L'Osservatore Romano,* English. edition, no. 14 (1987): 1–2.

[K. RABENSTEIN]

DONDERS, PETER, BL.

Redemptorist missionary priest; b. 27 Oct. 1809, Tilburg, the Netherlands; d. 14 Jan. 1887, Batavia, Suriname (formerly Dutch Guiana), South America; beatified 23 May 1982.

Born into a poor family, headed by Arnold Denis Donders and Petronella van den Brekel, he received little schooling and had to delay his vocation in order to help support the family by working in a factory. He was accepted as a domestic in the minor seminary of St. Michiels-Gestel, Holland, in the autumn of 1831 and the following year was admitted as a student. Having unsuccessfully sought entry into the Franciscans, Jesuits, and Redemptorists, he made his major seminary studies at Oegstgeest, South Holland, and was ordained 5 June 1841. On 1 Aug. 1842, he departed for Surinam, arriving 16 Sept., labored there on the missions until his death. His first duties entailed preaching and ministering the sacraments to plantation slaves. In the course of 8 years, he instructed and baptized 1,200.

The mission was ceded to the Dutch Redemptorists in 1865, and Donders entered that congregation on 1 Nov. 1866, making his profession to the first Redemptorist apostolic vicar (Johan Baptist Swinkels) on 24 June 1867 (age 57), at Paramaribo. He was dedicated particularly to the care of the 600 inmates of the leprosarium at Batavia, and he labored there for many years (1856–66, 1867–83, 1885–87) as priest and nurse. Endowed with a spirit of prayer and charity, he exhibited mercy to the most miserable and abandoned of all classes. In 1868 and 1869, he also learned the languages of and worked among the Indians (Arrowaks, Warros, and Caribs) and Bush Negroes (Maroons). In 1883, when his health began to fail, he was transferred to Paramaribo, then to Coronie, but he returned to Batavia in Nov. 1885 to resume his previous work. He died in the leprosarium, was buried in Batavia, and later placed in a vault in the Cathedral in Paramaribo (1921).

Pope John Paul II praised Donders as "an incentive for the renewal and flourishing of the missionary thrust which in the last century and in this one has made an exceptional contribution to the carrying out of the Church's missionary duty."

Feast: 14 January (Redemptorists).

Bibliography: *Acta Apostolicae Sedis* 74 (1982): 1205–7. *L'Osservatore Romano,* English edition, no. 24 (1982): 6–7. C. J. ANTONELLIS, *The Story of Peter Donders* (Boston 1982). J. CARR, *A Fisher of Men* (Dublin 1952). J. L. F. DANKELMAN, *Peerke Donders: schering en inslag van zijn leven* (Hilversum 1982). J. KRONENBURG, *An Apostle of the Lepers* (London 1930). B. L. J. RADEMAKER, *Petrus Donders* (Bussum, Neth. 1956).

[A. SAMPERS]

DREXEL, KATHARINE MARIE, BL.

Foundress of the Blessed Sacrament for Indians and Colored People (later Sisters of the Blessed Sacrament); b. 26 Nov. 1858, Philadelphia, Pa.; d. 3 March 1955, Cornwell Heights, Pa.; beatified 20 Nov. 1988; canonization scheduled for 1 Oct. 2000, when she will become the second U.S.-born saint after Elizabeth Seton.

Granddaughter of Francis Martin Drexel, founder of a Philadelphia banking house, Katharine's Protestant mother, Hannah Jane (Langstreth) Drexel, died when Katharine was an infant; two years later her father Francis Anthony Drexel married Emma M. Bouvier, who became a devoted mother to Katharine, her elder sister Elizabeth, and their stepsister Louise. Katharine was educated at home by private governesses, traveled in Europe and the U.S., was a Philadelphia debutante in 1879, and took part in many social activities.

The Church called upon the wealthy Drexel family to help implement the decrees of the Third Plenary Council of Baltimore (1884), which legislated for missionary activity among Indians and African Americans. Katharine had inherited a fortune at the death of her stepmother (1883) and father (1885). While recovering from an illness in a German spa in 1886, she recruited many priests and nuns for the Native American missions. During a visit to Rome she asked Leo XIII to recommend a religious order to which she could give her fortune on condition that it be used only for African- and Native-Americans. When the pope challenged her to be their missionary herself, her vocation was decided. On 7 Nov. 1889 she began her novitiate with the Sisters of Mercy of Pittsburgh, Pa., and in 1891 she and a few companions founded the Sisters of the Blessed Sacrament for Indians and Colored People in a convent made over from the old Drexel summer home at Torresdale, Pa. Within a year there were twenty-one sisters.

Requests for help soon came from Southern centers for Blacks and from Indian missions in the Southwest. Mother Katharine built and maintained missions and staffed them with sisters. Later she opened schools and convents in Columbus, Ohio; Chicago, Ill.; Boston, Mass.; and Harlem, New York City. In 1915 she established Xavier University in New Orleans, La., which has been the only predominantly African American Catholic institution of higher learning in the United States since its founding. By 1927 the university's growth led Mother Drexel to plan larger quarters. The new site and buildings, costing $600,000, were dedicated by Cardinal Dennis Dougherty in 1932. In 1935 Mother Drexel suffered a heart attack, but she continued her work, which included long day-coach trips to her 49 foundations in the Northeast, Midwest, and Deep South. At her golden jubilee in 1941, a letter from Pius XII described her work as ''a glorious page in the annals of the Church.'' Although an invalid during her last years, she devoted herself to prayer until her death at 96. Her body is enshrined in the Philadelphia suburb of Bensalem, Pa.

At her death there were more than 500 sisters teaching in sixty-three schools throughout the country. She had spent more than $12 million of her inheritance on work for the disadvantaged minorities of the U.S. and the advancement of human rights. In 2000, her work continues at forty-eight sites in twelve states and Haiti. Katharine's cause, introduced in 1964 by John Cardinal Krol of Philadelphia, culminated 27 Jan. 2000, when the restoration of hearing to seventeen-month-old Robert Gutherman (May 1994) was declared a miracle wrought through her intercession.

During the beatification Mass, John Paul II explained that Drexel ''constantly listened to Christ's voice. . . . In her life of exceptional apostolic service, God has shown forth the riches of his mercy and grace, and his power to achieve great things in human weakness. . . . In a remarkable way Bl. Katharine imitated Jesus. . . .'' Patron of Native Americans and African-Americans.

Feast: 3 March (U.S.A.).

Bibliography: K. BURTON, *The Golden Door: The Life of Katharine Drexel* (New York 1957). C. M. DUFFY, *Katharine Drexel* (Philadelphia 1966). G. D. KITTLER, *Profiles in Faith* (New York 1962). P. LYNCH, *Sharing the Bread in Service: Sisters of the Blessed Sacrament* (Bensalem, Pa. 1998). E. TARRY, *Katharine Drexel, Friend of the Neglected.* (New York 1958).

[K. BURTON]

DUCHESNE, ROSE PHILIPPINE, ST.

Missionary, foundress of the U.S. branch of the Society of the Sacred Heart; b. Grenoble, France, 29 Aug. 1769; d. St. Charles, Mo., 18 Nov. 1852. Her father, Pierre François Duchesne, was active in the legal and political life of Grenoble, and in national life after 1797. Her mother, Rose (Perier) Duchesne, was from Dauphiné. In 1780 Philippine was sent to study at the Convent of the Visitation, Sainte Marie d'en Haut, where she was attracted to religious life. Despite her father's opposition,

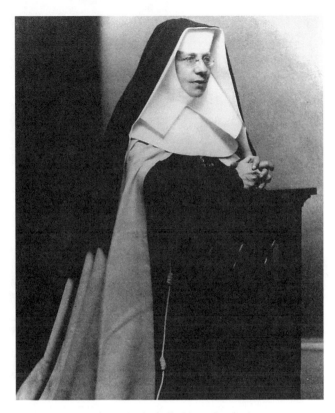

Katharine Marie Drexel. (Catholic News Service.)

she entered the Visitation Order on 10 September 1788, but returned home in 1792 when, as a result of the French Revolution, religious were expelled from their convents. For 10 years she devoted herself to charity, often sheltering priests persecuted by the revolutionary government, nursing the sick, and teaching the neglected children of Grenoble. When peace returned to France, she obtained possession of the convent of Sainte-Maried'en-Haut, which had been confiscated by the revolutionary government for a prison. In 1804, having failed in her efforts to bring the scattered Visitandine nuns back to their home, she and a few companions joined the Society of the Sacred Heart (founded in 1800 by St. Madeleine Sophie Barat) and Sainte-Marie-d'en-Haut became the second convent of the new order.

In 1815 Mother Duchesne was transferred to Paris and founded the first convent of her order there. Three years later, she and four companions left France for the U.S., arriving at New Orleans, La., on 29 May 1818. Bp. William Du Bourg of Louisiana commissioned Mother Duchesne to open a school in St. Charles, Missouri, the first free school west of the Mississippi River for Catholic and non-Catholic children. In 1819 she built a convent at Florissant, Missouri, and operated a free parish school, a small orphanage, a short lived school for Indian girls, and an academy for boarding pupils, along with a novi-

John Duns Scotus, lithograph by J. Faber. (Library of Congress.)

tiate for U.S. members of the Sacred Heart Society. In 1827 Bishop Joseph Rosati welcomed her to St. Louis, Missouri, where John Mullanphy provided a house and 24 acres of land for an orphanage, academy, and parish school. At 72, she founded a mission school for Potawatomi Indian girls at Sugar Creek, Kansas. She did not teach the children, for she could not learn their language, but she nursed the sick among the Potawatomi, who called her Quah-kah-ka-num-ad, Woman-who-prays-always. In 1842, she was recalled to St. Charles, where she spent the remaining years of her life. She was canonized by John Paul II on 3 July 1988.

Feast Day: 18 November.

Bibliography: L. CALLAN, *Philippine Duchesne* (Westminster, Md. 1957); *The Society of the Sacred Heart in North America* (New York 1937). C. M. MOONEY, *Philippine Duchesne: A Woman With the Poor* (New York 1990).

[L. CALLAN]

DUNS SCOTUS, JOHN, BL.

Franciscan philosopher and theologian; b. ca. 1266, Duns, Scotland; d. 8 November 1308, Cologne. He is known by the scholastic titles of *Doctor subtilis, Doctor maximus,* and *Doctor Marianus*; beatified by John Paul II on 20 March 1993.

As a boy Scotus was trained by his paternal uncle, Elias Duns, at the Franciscan friary in Dumfries, Scotland. At the age of 15 he joined the Friars Minor and was sent to Oxford shortly before 1290. After his ordination in 1291, he was sent to Paris to study theology. From 1293 to 1296 he studied under Gonsalvo of Balboa (Gonsalvus Hispanus), and then returned to work on the *Sentences* from 1297 to 1301. In 1302 he returned to Paris to complete the requirements for the degree, but in the following year he was forced to leave the university because he refused to subscribe to Philip the Fair's appeal to a General Council against Boniface VIII. He finally received the degree in 1305 and lectured at the University of Paris as a regent master in the Franciscan chair until 1307. Toward the end of 1307 he was sent to Cologne, where he lectured until his death.

The most important of Scotus's writings are the commentaries on the *Sentences* of Peter Lombard, of which there are many versions (five of bk. 1, three of bk. 2, five of bk. 3, and two of bk. 4). The original lecture notes used at Oxford (*Lectura prima*) were definitively arranged by Scotus in an *Ordinatio* (commonly known as the *Opus Oxoniense*). Basically the same notes were used by Scotus in his Paris lectures (*Reportatio Parisiensis*). It is probable that Scotus also lectured on the *Sentences* at Cambridge before 1300 (*Reportatio Cantabrigiensis*). Some of the published commentaries on Aristotle can be considered authentic, particularly *Quaestiones super universalia* of Porphyry, *De praedicamentis, Super Perihermeneias, Super libros elenchorum, De anima,* and *Metaphysica* (lib. 1–9). To these must be added the *Tractatus de primo principio, Theoremata,* and certain *Quaestiones disputatae, Quodlibeta,* etc.

An attentive study of Scotus's doctrine reveals the intimate unity of his philosophy and theology. Although his philosophical doctrines cannot be considered corollaries of Christian faith, it would be a mistake to think that his philosophy was developed independently of the faith. The primacy of being constitutes the basis of his epistemology and metaphysics; the primacy of will characterizes his ethics; and the notion of Infinite Being who is Love dominates his entire theology.

The basic intuition of Scotus's theological speculation is the perception of God as the Infinite Being who is Love. Scotus made first a distinction between the knowledge God has of Himself (*theologia Dei*) and the knowledge man has of Him through revelation and theological speculation (*theologia nostra*). Consonant with the Franciscan tradition, Scotus emphasized the affective and practical role of theology rather than the abstract and speculative. For Scotus the purpose of theology is to love God above all things.

One of the most distinguished English thinkers of the late Middle Ages, John Duns Scotus was formed in the Augustinian-Franciscan tradition at Oxford and Paris. Although only 42 when he died, he created a new school of scholastic thought that had considerable influence on later thinkers even outside the Franciscan school.

His body was originally buried in the Franciscan church in Cologne, near the altar of the Three Kings. Toward the end of the 16th century it was moved to the middle of the choir near the main altar. His remains were frequently authenticated in the sixteenth and seventeenth centuries, and as recently as 1954. Veneration of his remains has existed from ''time immemorial'' and canonical proceedings for his beatification were held in Cologne in 1706 and in Nola in 1710 and 1905–06. In 1906, the bishop of Nola declared that the cult given to Bl. Duns Scotus was from time immemorial. The Order of Friars Minor requested the Congregation of Rites to confirm this for the universal Church, but nothing resulted until 1993, at which time Pope John Paul II praised him as a model for this age and ''an example of fidelity to the revealed truth, of effective, priestly, and serious dialogue in search for unity.''

Feast: 8 November (Franciscans).

Bibliography: Works by John Duns Scotus: *Opera omnia:* ed. L. WADDING et al, 12 v. (Lyon 1639); 26 v. (Vivès; Paris 1891–95); critical ed. C. BALIĆ (Vatican City 1950-). *The De Primo Principio of John Duns Scotus,* ed. and tr. E. ROCHE (St. Bonaventure, N.Y. 1949). *Philosophical Writings,* ed. and tr. A. B. WOLTER (New York 1962). Literature about John Duns Scotus: É. H. GILSON, *Jean Duns Scot: Introduction à ses positions fondamentales* (Paris 1952). O. SCHÄFER, *Bibliographia de vita, operibus et doctrina Iohannis Duns Scoti doctoris subtilis ac mariani, saec. XIX–XX* (Rome 1955); *Johannes Duns Scotus,* v.22 (1953) of *Bibliographische Einführungen in das Studium der Philosophie,* ed. I. M. BOCHEŃSKI (Bern 1948-). B. DE SAINT-MAURICE, *John Duns Scot: A Teacher for Our Times,* tr. C. DUFFY (St. Bonaventure, N.Y. 1955). J. K. RYAN and B. M. BONANSEA, eds., *John Duns Scotus 1265–1965,* Studies in Philosophy and the History of Philosophy (Washington 1965).

[C. BALIĆ]

DUROCHER, MARIE ROSE, BL.

Foundress of the Congregation of the Sisters of the Holy Names of Jesus and Mary in Canada; b. St. Antoine, Quebec, Canada, 6 Oct. 1811; d. Longueuil, Quebec, Canada, 6 Oct. 1849; beatified by Pope John Paul II, 23 May 1982.

The tenth of eleven children, Eulalie Mélanie Durocher was educated by the Sisters of the Congregation of Notre Dame at their convents in St. Denis and Montreal. From the age of 18, shortly after the death of her mother, she served as hostess, parish worker, nurse and homemaker in the Beloeil parish where her brother, Theophile, was pastor. For 13 years Durocher coordinated activities in the rectory, organized programs in religious education for children and young women of the parish, and cared for the poor and sick of the surrounding village. During the latter part of this period, with the assistance of the Oblates of Mary Immaculate who had recently arrived from France, Eulalie established the first Canadian parish Sodality.

In October 1843, at the request of Bishop Ignace Bourget, bishop of Montreal, Durocher, together with two companions, Mélodie Dufresne and Henriette Céré, founded the Congregation of the Sisters of the Holy Names of Jesus and Mary, at Longueuil. The purpose of the congregation, as stated in the 1850 *Chronicles,* was ''to give religious education to the poorest and most abandoned children.'' The Oblates of Mary Immaculate helped the three women with the new foundation, offering spiritual guidance as well as financial and moral support. The new congregation adopted the habit and a modified form of the Constitutions of a Marseilles community of the same name, a group whom the Oblates had directed in France, and who were unable to send sisters to Canada to begin a new foundation. The Marseilles community later ceased to exist because of political upheaval in France. On 8 December 1844, during the pontificate of Gregory XVI, the Canadian congregation was canonically established, with Eulalie (Sister Marie Rose) as its first superior.

A woman of deep faith, practical wisdom and singleness of purpose, Sister Marie Rose overcame many obstacles to commit her congregation to its work with the poor and illiterate. Poor living conditions, misunderstanding from an Oblate pastor who had been a main source of support, and false reports about the congregation spread by a discontented priest of the diocese were the greatest challenges during these early years. Undaunted, Sister Marie Rose particularly addressed the needs of young women, whose religious education as well as overall education was sorely neglected in Quebec at this time. Using the congregation's limited resources to provide them with the best quality of education available, she even sent some sisters away for professional training to insure their thorough preparation for teaching. Through her numerous letters and frequent visits, Sister Marie Rose fostered a sense of unity among the sisters which enabled them to stay focused on their mission despite the hardships they endured.

When Sister Marie Rose died at 38 years of age, six years after its foundation, the community had 30 sisters teaching 384 students in four schools. In 1859 the first distant mission of the congregation was founded in Oregon. From 1931 on, the congregation spread beyond North America to Basutoland (Lesotho), Japan, Brazil, Peru, and Haiti.

Feast: 6 October.

Bibliography: "Sister Marie Rose Durocher," Archives, Sisters of the Holy Names of Jesus and Mary (Longueuil). F. ALLISON, *She Who Believed in Tomorrow* (Montreal 1981). J. BEAUDET, *Braise au coeur du pays* (Montreal 1982). C. MARIE, tr., *Beatificationis et Canonizationis Servae Dei Mariae Rosae Durocher*, 10 v., *Positio* (Vatican City 1975). P. DUCHAUSSOIS, *Rose of Canada* (Outremont 1934). G. DUVAL, *Par le chemin du roi: une femme est venue* (Montreal 1982). E. TERESA, *So Short a Day* (New York 1954). M. THERIAULT, "Foundress of the Sisters of the Holy Names of Jesus and Mary," *Vita Evangelica* (Ottawa 1975).

[P.A. PARACHINI]

DUSMET, GIUSEPPE BENEDETTO, BL.

Cardinal, archbishop of Catania; b. 15 August 1818, Palermo, Sicily, Italy; d. 4 April 1894, Catania, Sicily; beatified by John Paul II, 25 September 1988.

Giuseppe, the son of the Marquis Luigi Dusmet and his noble wife Maria Dragonetti, was taught by the Benedictines of San Martino delle Scale at Badia from age five, then stayed to pronounce his vows (10 August 1840). He was ordained priest in 1842. After his election as prior in 1858, he reformed San Nicoló Abbey in Catania. He left the abbey in protest of government interference before it was closed like those of all religious orders. Although he was consecrated archbishop of Catania (10 March 1861) and received the cardinal's red hat (1888), he remained a humble Benedictine monk at heart. Thereafter he was even more devoted to the poor, the suffering, and his order. During a cholera epidemic, he provided for those in need, and he ministered to victims of earthquake and epidemic in the streets. He played a large role in reforming the Roman Benedictine College of Sant'Anselmo and the Confederation of Benedictine Congregations. The cardinal's remains rest in Catania's cathedral. His cause was introduced by Archbishop Carmelo Patanè (7 January 1931), and he was declared venerable by Pope Paul VI (15 July 1965).

In his beatification homily, Pope John Paul II praised Dusmet, saying "he literally stripped himself of everything in order to put on poverty, whose humble servant he was." Patron of evangelical charity.

Bibliography: A BENEDICTINE OF STANBROOK ABBEY, *A Sicilian Borromeo, the servant of God, Joseph Benedict Dusmet, Archbishop of Catania and Cardinal of the Holy Roman Church* (London 1938). *Acta Apostolicae Sedis* (1988): 1092.

[K. RABENSTEIN]

EBNER, MARGARETHA, BL.

Mystic, Dominican virgin; b. ca. 1291, Donauwörth (near Nuremberg), Bavaria, Germany; d. 20 June 1351, Medingen, Bavaria, Germany; beatified by John Paul II, 24 February 1979.

A child of the nobility, Margaretha received a classical education at home. She was solemnly professed (1306) at the Dominican convent at Maria-Medingen near Dillingen. Dangerously ill for many years, Ebner offered penances—abstinence from wine, fruit, and the bath—for those who had died in the war devastating the countryside. She was suddenly cured, but then forced with the other sisters to the leave the convent during the campaign of Ludwig the Bavarian. Shortly thereafter the death of her nurse, to whom she was emotionally attached, caused Margaretha to grieve inconsolably. But in 1332 she regained her composure through the efforts of Henry of Nördlingen, who then assumed her spiritual direction. The correspondence between them is the first collection of this kind in German. Under his tutelage, she wrote with her own hand a full account of all her revelations and conversations with the Infant Jesus, including the answers she received from him, even in her sleep. This diary is preserved at Medingen in a manuscript that dates to 1353. From her letters and diary we learn that she remained loyal to the excommunicated Ludwig the Bavarian, whose soul she learned in a vision had been saved. Among her other correspondents were many contemporary spiritual leaders, including Johannes Tauler. She is considered one of the leaders of the Friends of God. Her body now rests in a chapel built in 1755 in the Maria-Medingen Convent church. Pope John Paul II praised Ebner, the first person he beatified, for her perseverance.

Feast: 20 June (Dominicans).

Bibliography: M. EBNER, *Major Works*, tr. & ed. L. P. HINDSLEY (New York 1993). M. GRABMANN, *Neuaufgefundene lateinische Werke deutscher Mystiker* (Munich 1922). P. STRAUCH, *Margeretha Ebner und Heinrich von Nördlingen* (Amsterdam 1966). A. WALZ, "Gottesfreunde und Margarete Ebner," in *Historisches Jahrbuch* (1953), 72:253–265. L. ZOEPF, *Die mystikerin Margaretha Ebner* (Berlin 1914).

[K. RABENSTEIN]

ELIZABETH OF THE TRINITY, BL.

Carmelite mystic; (name in the world, Elisabeth Catez) b. 18 July 1880, Camp d'Avor, Bourges, France; d. 9 November 1906, Dijon, France; beatified in Rome 25 November 1984 by Pope John Paul II.

Elizabeth Catez is to be distinguished from two other Carmelites of the same name: Elizabeth of the Trinity of the Carmel of Tours (de Quatrebarbes, 1506 to 1660), and Elizabeth of the Trinity of Nantes (E. Duterte de la Coudre, 1881 to 1919). When Elizabeth was seven, her father, a military officer, died; but Elizabeth and her sister Marguerite received an excellent Christian education from their mother, who was much devoted to the writings of St. Teresa of Avila. Her mother also encouraged the development of her musical talent by sending her to the Dijon Conservatory. At the age of fourteen, Elizabeth made a vow of virginity. She entered the Carmel at Dijon 2 Aug. 1901; received the Carmelite habit from Bishop Le Nordez of Dijon on 8 Dec. 1901; and was professed 11 Jan. 1903. On 21 Nov. 1904, she composed her celebrated prayer, "Oh My God, Trinity Whom I Adore" (see M. Amabel du Coeur de Jésus; bibliography). About Easter 1905 she discovered in St. Paul her vocation, which was the praising of the glory of the Trinity. She twice received the grace of transforming union, first on the Feast of the Ascension (1906), and again a little later.

At nineteen, reading the *Way of Perfection* of Teresa of Avila, Elizabeth's attention was drawn to a formula that is the key to the understanding of her interior life and her spiritual doctrine: "in the heaven of my soul." Her personal existence came to be spent entirely in the presence of God, where she wanted nothing to distract her or prevent her life from becoming a continuous prayer. She desired to retire within herself and live in the little cell God had built in her heart, in that little corner of herself where she could see Him and have the feeling of His presence.

Two steps mark the rapid spiritual ascension of Elizabeth. In the first she appears in great purity of soul, reaching out to the enjoyment of the presence within her of the Three Divine Persons: "I have found my heaven upon earth, for heaven is God, and God is in my soul" (letter to Mme. de Sourdon, June 1902). In the second and more sublime stage she appears passing beyond herself in order to give herself more to the praise of the glory of the Trinity, just as Jesus had no thought but for the glory of the Father: "Since my soul is a heaven wherein I dwell while awaiting the heavenly Jerusalem, this heaven, too, must sing of the glory of the Eternal, nothing but the glory of the Eternal" (*Last Retreat*, seventh day). The holy soul devoted to the divine indwelling thus became an apostle of the praise of the glory of the Trinity. The indwelling of the Trinity in the soul was the center of her doctrine as it was of her life. At the root of her teaching, as a condition fundamental to all spiritual life, is inner silence, i.e., a withdrawal from all that is created and a stilling even of the soul in the presence of God. All within should be quieted that the soul may hear the Word and be instructed by Him. In this silence the contemplative soul finds the fullness of God. The essential acts of this intimacy with the Guest within consist in a continual exercise of faith and love. Love proves itself by these acts and leads to an absolute fidelity to the will of God even in the slightest matters. The supreme model of this divine life is the Word, perfect praise of the glory of the Father, who wishes to prolong in each of us the mystery of His adoration and redemptive immolation. "O my Christ . . . crucified for love, I beseech You to identify my soul with all the movements of Your soul, to immerse me, to possess me wholly and to substitute Yourself for me, so that my life is nothing but a ray beaming out from Your life" (Prayer to the Trinity). Elizabeth saw in the Virgin of the Incarnation all the concentration upon God within her that was her own ideal of holiness. It seemed to her that the attitude of the Virgin during the months between the Annunciation and the Nativity is a model for all interior souls. The issue of this spiritual life is the unceasing praise of the blessed in heaven that is described in the last chapters of Revelations, which became Elizabeth's favorite reading.

This spiritual doctrine concerning what is, in effect, the ultimate unfolding and development of the Christian's baptismal vocation was gathered together in two retreats composed at the end of her life: *How to find Heaven upon Earth* and the *Last Retreat on the Praise of Glory,* which she left as a spiritual last testament.

At the age of twenty-two she displayed the first signs of Addison's disease, which led to her death at twenty-six. Her last words: "I go to the light, to love, to life."

During the beatification Mass in Rome, Pope John Paul II remarked that Elizabeth "gives witness to an openness to the Word of God . . . nourishing with it her prayer and reflection, to the point of finding therein all her reasons for living and of consecrating herself to the praise of the glory of this Word."

Feast: 8 November (Carmelites).

Bibliography: Works by St. Elizabeth: The Archives of the Dijon Carmel contain nearly all her original writings. *Souvenirs* (Dijon 1909); Eng., *The "Praise of Glory:" Reminiscences . . .* (London 1913; repr.Westminster, Md. 1962); *Spiritual Writings,* ed. M. M. PHILIPON, tr. MOTHER ST. AUGUSTINE OF THE SACRED HEART (New York 1962). Complete Works Of Elizabeth Of The Trinity, v. 1: *Major Spiritual Writings,* v. 1, tr. A. KANE (repr. Washington, DC 1996); *Letters From Carmel,* v. 2, tr. A. E. NASH (San Diego 1984); *Light Love Life: A Look at a Face and a Heart,* ed. C. DE MEESTER, tr. A. KANE (Washington 1987). Literature. *Acta Apostolicae Sedis* 79 (1987): 1268–73. *L'Osservatore Romano,* English edition, no. 50 (1984). 12, 2. AMABEL DU CŒUR DE JÉSUS, *The Doctrine of the Divine Indwelling: A Commentary on the Prayer of Sister Elizabeth of the Trinity* (Westminster, Md. 1950); *À la lumiére, à l'amour, à la vie* (Paris 1933). H. U. VON BALTHASAR, *Elizabeth of Dijon, An Interpretation of Her Spiritual Mission,* tr. A. V. LITTLEDALE (New York 1956); *Two Sisters in the Spirit: Thérèse of Lisieux & Elizabeth of the Trinity,* tr. D. MARTIN (Fort Collins,

Col.: Ignatius, 1997). L. BOUYER, *Women Mystics: Hadewijch of Antwerp, Teresa of Avila, Thérèse of Lisieux, Elizabeth of the Trinity, Edith Stein*, tr. A. E. NASH (Fort Collins, Col. 1993) 155–72. L. BORRIELLO, *The Spiritual Doctrine of Blessed Elizabeth of the Trinity: Apostolic Contemplative*, tr. J. AUMANN (Staten Island, N.Y. 1986). P. M. FÉVOTTE, *Aimer la Bible avec Elisabeth de la Trinité* (Paris 1991); *Virginité, chemin d'amour: à l'école d'Elizabeth de la Trinité* (Paris 1993). M. M. PHILIPON, *The Spiritual Doctrine of Sister Elizabeth of the Trinity* (Westminster, Md. 1947). J. RÉMY, *Ce que croyait Elisabeth de la Trinité* (Paris 1984). E. VANDEUR, *Trinity Whom I Adore: Prayer of Sister Elizabeth of the Trinity* (New York 1953); *Pledge of glory; meditations on the Eucharist and the Trinity* (Westminster, Md. 1958).

[M. M. PHILIPON]

ENGLAND, SCOTLAND, AND WALES, MARTYRS OF, BB.

A.k.a. George Haydock and Companions, d. 1584–1679. On 22 November 1987, Pope John Paul II beatified 85 Roman Catholics who were executed in England because of their religion. The group included 30 Yorkshiremen, 11 from Lancashire, 4 from Durham, 3 from Gloucestershire, 3 Londoners, and others from counties throughout England, as well as 3 Welshmen, a Scot, and an Irishman. Fifty-six were secular priests, 4 Franciscans, 2 Jesuits, 1 Dominican, and 22 laymen. Of the 85 in this group, 67 were executed during the reign of Elizabeth I, 9 under James I, 6 under Charles I, and 3 under Charles II. The dates of their deaths range from 1584, when William Carter, a London printer, was executed under Elizabeth I, to 1679, when the priest, Charles Meehan, an Irish Franciscan, was executed under Charles II.

The beatification of these victims of the English penal laws is especially noteworthy because it was a protracted process that led to the official recognition of their martyrdom, and because it took place at a time when the Church of Rome and the Church of England were being drawn closer together in ecumenical dialogue and mutual recognition.

The Beatification Process. The martyrs who had suffered for their Catholic faith during penal times were long the object of veneration, but it was only after the 1850 restoration of the Roman Catholic hierarchy in England that the cause of beatification and canonization began in earnest. Over the years, the cases of more than 350 "servants of God" were investigated. It was necessary in each case to untangle the juridical reasons for their execution from the concrete circumstances in order to establish whether an individual was truly a martyr for the faith or a political activist. Fifty-four were beatified in 1886, including John Fisher, bishop of Rochester, and

Thomas More, sometime Lord Chancellor (both of whom were canonized in 1935). Nine were beatified in 1895, and 136 more in 1929.

In 1970 Pope Paul VI canonized 40 more of the blessed martyrs. Their canonization was accompanied by renewed interest in recusant history and the introduction of the causes of martyrs who had not yet been beatified were resumed in 1978. New documentary evidence substantiating the constancy of their confession of faith and the circumstances of martyrdom moved the cases of George Haydock and 83 others forward. Later the cause of the Scottish priest, George Douglas, was joined to the group bringing the number to 85.

Seventy-five of the group were sentenced under the Elizabethan statute [27 Eliz. c. 2] of 1585 "against Jesuits, seminary priests and such other like disobedient persons." According to this law, Catholic priests, ordained abroad, were charged with high treason when they returned to England, liable to the brutal punishment of being hanged, drawn, and quartered (HDQ). Anyone assisting Catholic priests in any way was guilty of a felony, punishable by hanging. The 10 others were tried under other statutes. Haydock the priest and Carter the layman, executed before the above statute was enacted, were tried for high treason under a statute of 1352. A priest and six laymen were tried for being reconciled or persuading others to be reconciled to the ancient faith: treasonable acts under the Elizabethan statute of 1581. The layman, John Bretton, was condemned for allegedly uttering "seditious words and rumors against the Queen's Majesty."

Ecumenical Implications. One reason for the delay in promoting the cult of the Anglo-Welsh martyrs was the time taken to weigh the impact that their beatification and canonization might have on ecumenical relations between the Anglican and Roman Catholic Churches. On the eve of the canonization of the Forty Martyrs in 1970, the British Council of Churches, issued an irenic statement that recognized the importance of these witnesses to the faith for Roman Catholics. The BCC declared that the different Christian denominations all acknowledge "the martyr tradition as one in which all have shared and from which all may draw strength, even across denominational boundaries."

In announcing the intention of Pope John Paul II to beatify the group of 85 Anglo-Welsh martyrs in 1987, Cardinal Basil Hume, Roman Catholic archbishop of Westminster, noted that "martyrs make the best ecumenists" because "dialogue between the Churches has to be carried forward by people who are secure in their faith and dedicated to the pursuit of truth." For his part, Anglican Archbishop of Canterbury, Robert Runcie, responded, "whereas in the past this announcement would have fueled controversy and communal rivalry, today we can celebrate their heroic Christian witness and together deplore the intolerance of the age which flawed Christian convictions.''

The 85 Blessed Martyrs. The following inventory is based on the list published by the Catholic Truth Society supplemented by other material. The coporate feast day for the 85 blessed martyrs, listed alphabetically, is 22 November. Unless indicated otherwise the martyr was executed under Elizabeth I.

Adams, John, priest; b. ca. 1543 at Winterbourne or Martin's Town, Dorsetshire; d. 8 October 1586, HDQ at Tyburn (outside London), England. He had been a Protestant minister. Upon his conversion to Catholicism, he went to Rheims, where he was ordained a priest (1580). He returned to England in March 1581, where he labored at Winchester and in Hampshire, helping many, especially of the poorer classes. He was also a noted exorcist. Adams was imprisoned in 1584 and banished the following year with seventy-two other priests. He returned, was again arrested for high treason, and executed, with two others, BB. John Lowe and Robert Dibdale. According to Anthony Tyrrell's *Confessions,* Adams and Lowe were specifically selected for execution by Justice Young on the advice of Tyrrell, who was chagrined by his failure to implicate the Jesuit William Weston in the Babington Plot and knew they exercised the greatest influence over imprisoned Catholics. William Warford, who knew Adams, described him as a man of ''average height, with a dark beard, a sprightly look and black eyes. He was a very good apologist, straightforward, very pious, and preeminently a man of hard work.''

Atkinson, Thomas, priest; b. ca. 1546 in the East Riding, Yorkshire, England; d. 11 March 1616, HDQ at York under James I. After his studies and ordination to the priesthood at Rheims (1588), he immediately returned to his native England. For twenty-eight years he went about mostly on foot, ministering to his flock, especially the poor, and became so well known that he could not safely travel by day. At age seventy he was betrayed and taken to York with his host, Mr. Vavasour of Willitoft, and some members of the family. A pair of beads and the form of an indulgence found upon him confirmed his religion. He suffered ''with wonderful patience, courage, and constancy, and signs of great comfort.''

Bamber, Edward (*alias* Helmes, Reding, Reading), priest; b. ca. 1600 at the Moor, Poulton-le-Fylde or at Carlton, Blackpool, Lancashire; d. 7 August 1646, HDQ at Lancaster under Charles I. Many of the details of Bl. Edward's life are uncertain. He was educated abroad (Valladolid, Douai, or Seville and St. Omer). Following his ordination (1626), he was sent to England, where the governor of the castle observed him kneel down to thank God upon disembarkation at Dover. He was imprisoned, but soon released into exile. He was probably chaplain at Standish Hall, near which he was arrested soon after his second return. En route to Lancaster Castle he was lodged at the Old-Green-Man Inn near Claughton-on-Brock, and managed to escape from his drunken keepers. A Mr. Singleton of Broughton Tower (who had been warned in a dream to help him), sheltered and assisted him during the next 16 years. Arrested the third time (1643), Bamber was committed to Lancaster Castle, where he remained in close confinement for three years, escaped once, and was recaptured. At his trial with two other priests, BB. Whitaker and Woodcock, two former Catholics testified that Bamber had administered the sacraments, and he was condemned to die. Bamber, who was known for his zeal and courage in pastoral work, instruction, and disputation, suffered with great constancy. He reconciled to the Church a felon executed with him, and encouraged his fellow martyrs to die bravely. An ode composed on his death is still extant.

Beesley (Bisley), George, priest; b. ca. 1563 at The Hill in Goosnargh (Goosenoor) parish, Lancashire, England; d. 2 July 1591, HDQ on Fleet Street in London. As with the scions of many ancient Catholic families of England, he was sent to Rheims, where he was ordained in 1587. On 1 November 1588, he returned to his native land, where he labored primarily in London and in the north of England. He was a strong, robust young man when captured by Topcliffe late in 1590, but reduced to a skeleton by torture. He endured all with invincible courage and could not be induced to betray his fellow Catholics. His last words were *''Absit mihi gloriari nisi in cruce Domini nostri Jesu Christi''* and, after a pause, ''Good people, I beseech God to send all felicity.''

Bell, Arthur (*alias* Francis Bell), Franciscan priest; b. 13 January 1590, at Temple- Broughton (near Worcester), England; d. 11 December 1643, HDQ at Tyburn (London) under Charles I. When Arthur was eight his father died and his mother put him in the care of her brother Francis Daniel who sent Bell abroad to study at age twenty-four. After completing the course at the English College in Valladolid, Spain, he was ordained a priest at Salamanca. He received the Franciscan habit at Segovia, 8 August 1618. He was one of the first members of the Franciscan community at Douai, where he subsequently fulfilled the offices of guardian and professor of Hebrew. Called to Scotland in 1632 as the first Franciscan provincial, his efforts to restore the order there proved unsuccessful, and he returned to England, where he labored until his arrest (6 November 1643) as a spy and committed to Newgate Prison. The record of his trial show a man of singular devotion, who did not shrink from suffering.

When the death sentence was declared, he praised God and thanked his judges for allowing him to die for Christ. Bell wrote *The History, Life, and Miracles of Joane of the Cross* (St. Omer 1625) and translated from the Spanish Andrew a Soto's *A brief instruction on how we ought to hear Mass* (Brussels 1624).

Belson, Thomas, gentleman; b. ca. 1565 at Brill, Aylesbury, Buckinghamshire, England; d. 5 July 1589, hanged at Oxford. He studied at Oxford, then for a time at the English College in Rheims (1584). On a visit to Oxford he was arrested with his confessor Bl. George Nichols, Fr. Richard Yaxley, and Bl. Humphrey Pritchard, a servant. They were sent to London for examination before Walsingham and repeated tortures in Bridewell and the Tower and then returned to Oxford for trial. Belson was found guilty of felony for assisting the priests. Feast: 12 February.

Bickerdike, Robert, gentleman; b. at Low Hall (near Knaresborough), Farnham, Yorkshire, England; 8 October 1586, HDQ at York. He was arrested for giving a priest, St. John Boste, a glass of ale, but at his trial he was also accused of using treasonable words. He was acquitted, but Judge Rhodes, determined to have his blood, had him removed from the city jail to York Castle and retried and condemned for being reconciled to Rome and for treasonable opinions.

Blake, Alexander, hostler (stableman), d. 4 March 1590, hanged at Gray's Inn Lane (London). He was arrested, sentenced, and died with Bl. Nicholas Horner for having harbored Fr. Christopher Bales.

Bowes, Marmaduke, married gentleman; b. possibly at Ingram Grange (near Appleton), Welbury, Cleveland in Yorkshire; d. 26 November 1585, hanged at York. Marmaduke and his wife were imprisoned at York and released, but required under bond to appear in York at the assizes beginning 23 November 1585. Upon his arrival, he found that Bl. Hugh Taylor was about to be arraigned. Previously Bowes had offered food and drink in his home to Fr. Taylor, which had been observed by his children's former tutor, an apostate Catholic. Bowes, though always a Catholic at heart, had outwardly conformed to the Anglican Church; the tutor provided the sole evidence against Bowes, leading to his condemnation for harboring and assisting an unlawful priest. Bowes boldly confessed his faith as a Catholic before his death.

Bretton (Britton), John, married gentleman; b. ca. 1529 in West Bretton (near Barnsley), Yorkshire, England; d. 1 April 1598, hanged at York. Born into an old Catholic family, Bretton was the father of a daughter and 4 sons, one of whom was probably Dr. Matthew Britton, prefect and professor at Douai in 1599. An ardent Catholic, John was often separated from his wife and family, owing to the constant persecution that he suffered for his faith. He was convicted and fined several times for recusancy. In later life he was maliciously and falsely accused of traitorous speeches against the queen and condemned to death. Upon refusing to renounce his faith he was executed for high treason against Elizabeth I.

Bullaker, Thomas, in religion John Baptist Bullaker, Franciscan priest; b. ca. 1602–1604 at Midhurst, Chichester, Sussex, England; d. 12 October 1642, HDQ at Tyburn, London, or at Dorchester under Charles I; the only son of a successful physician. His Catholic parents sent him to the English College at St. Omer at an early age and later to Valladolid, Spain. After a period of discernment he received the Franciscan habit at Abrojo (1622), and a few years later (1627–28) was ordained priest. In returning to England (1630), he was betrayed by the ship's captain upon their landing at Plymouth, immediately seized, and cast into prison. Upon his liberation he began his twelve-year ministry among the poor and sick Catholics of London. On 11 September 1642 Bullaker was arrested while celebrating Mass in the house of his benefactress. He has left a partial but touching account of his arrest and trial.

Burden, Edward, priest; b. ca. 1540 in Co. Durham, England; d. 29 November 1588, HDQ at York, England. He studied at Trinity College, Oxford, before completing his theological studies on the Continent. He was ordained (1584) at Douai and returned to England in 1586 to work in Yorkshire. He was condemned for his priesthood and suffered with Fr. John Hewett (beatified 1929).

Cadwallador, Roger (*alias* Rogers), priest; b. 1562–1568 at Stretton Sugwas, Herefordshire, England; d. 27 August 1610, HDQ at Leominster under James I. After completing his studies at the English College at Valladolid, he was ordained priest (1593). Returning to England in 1594, he labored zealously in Herefordshire for about 16 years. He and Bl. Robert Drury were among the priests signing the loyal address of 21 January 1603, in response to which the Government issued the Oath of Allegiance, which was problematic for Catholics. Cadwallador translated Theodoret's *Philotheus, or the lives of the Fathers of the Syrian deserts.* Pursuivants began searching for him in June 1605, but he was not found until Easter Day 1610, when he was arrested in the home of the widow Winefride Scroope. A full account of his torture and martyrdom is given by Challoner.

Carter, William, printer; b. 1548 in London, England; d. 11 January 1584, HDQ at Tyburn (London). Son of Agnes and John Carter, a draper, he began a ten-year apprenticeship under the queen's printer, John Cawood, in 1563, and later served as secretary to the imprisoned Nicholas Harpsfield, the last Catholic archdeacon of Canterbury. Upon the Harpsfield's death, Carter married and set up a press on Tower Hill. Among the "lewd" or Catholic books he printed was a new edition (1,000 copies) of Dr. Gregory Martin's A *Treatise of Schism* (1578), which discouraged Catholics from attending Protestant churches. The book also contained a paragraph expressing confidence in the triumph of the Catholic Faith through the metaphor of pious Judith slaying Holofernes. Because this was maliciously interpreted as an incitement to slay the queen, Carter was arrested and later charged with sedition and inciting Catholics to murder the queen. In 1582, he was transferred to the Tower, and following torture on the rack, he was indicted at the Old Bailey, 10 January 1584.

Crow(e), Alexander, priest; b. ca. 1550 at Howden, Yorkshire, England; d. 30 (or 13) November 1586, HDQ at York. He followed a trade for some years before beginning his seminary studies at Rheims, where he was ordained ca. 1583. He returned to the English Mission in 1584 to begin his work in Yorkshire, where he was arrested at Duffield on his way to a baptism and condemned for priesthood.

Davies, William, priest; b. in North Wales, possibly in Crois in Yris, Denbighshire, or at Colwyn Bay, Wales; d. 21 July 1593, HDQ at Beaumaris, Anglesey, North Wales. He arrived at the English College in Rheims, 6 April 1582, just in time to assist the first Mass of the Bl. Nicholas Garlick. Following his own ordination in April 1585, he labored zealously in Wales and reclaimed many Catholics. In 1591–92, he was arrested at Holyhead with four students whom he was sending via Ireland to the English College at Valladolid, he was thrown into the dungeon in Beaumaris Castle, and separated from his companions. Later he was able to join the students for an hour daily and even to celebrate Mass. An indulgent judge allowed Catholics from all parts to consult him, and Protestant ministers came to dispute with him. When the death sentence was pronounced at the assizes, Davies intoned the *Te Deum,* which the others took up. To still the murmurs of the people against the injustice of the sentence, the judge reprieved the condemned until the queen's pleasure be known. Davies was sent to Ludlow to be examined by the Council of the Marches. He was transferred to various prisons until he was sent back to Beaumaris, where his young companions were being held. For some six months they lived the life of a religious community, dividing their time between prayer and study, "with so much comfort to themselves that they seemed to be rather in heaven than in prison." At the summer assizes it was decided that the priest must die as a traitor. Eventually his young companions escaped from prison and the youngest made his way to Valladolid,

where he recounted the whole story to Bishop Yepes, who recorded it in his *Historia particular de la Persecución en Inglaterra.* There is now a chapel in Anglesey, built as a memorial to the martyr. Feast: 27 July.

Dibdale, Robert (Richard), priest; b. ca. 1558 at Shottery, Warwickshire (or Worcestershire); d. 8 October 1586, HDQ at Tyburn. He studied and was ordained at Douai or Rheims (1584), then returned to England to work in the London area. He practiced exorcisms at the home of Sir George Peckham in Denham, where he had been chaplain until a raid in June 1586. He then served as chaplain to Richard Bold, who had just settled at Harlesford in order to withdraw from the anti-Catholic life at Elizabeth's Court. Dibdale was tracked down, arrested, tried in the company of Bl. John Amias (beatified 1929), and condemned for his priesthood. Anthony (Dean) Champney, an eyewitness to his execution, has left an account in his history.

Douglas, George, priest; b. at Edinburgh, Scotland; d. 9 September 1587, HDQ at York, England, under Charles II. He was a schoolmaster at Rutland before his ordination at Paris, ca. 1574. Ten years later he entered the English mission field, where he was arrested, but released. He was arrested again at Ripton, Yorkshire, and condemned for "persuading to popery."

Drury, Robert, priest; b. 1567 in Buckinghamshire, England; d. 26 February 1607, HDQ at Tyburn (London) under James I. He began his seminary studies at Rheims in 1588 and completed them at the English College at Valladolid, Spain, where he was ordained (1593). Upon his return to England, he worked chiefly in London. His name is affixed to the appeal against archpriest Blackwell, which is dated 17 November 1600, from Wisbeach Prison. An invitation from the government to the appellant priests to acknowledge their allegiance and duty to the queen (dated 5 November 1602) led to the famous loyal address of 21 January 1603, which was drafted by Dr. William Bishop and signed by thirteen leading priests, including Drury and Bl. Roger Cadwallader. In this address they acknowledged the queen as their lawful sovereign, repudiated the claim of the pope to release them from their duty of allegiance to her, and expressed their abhorrence of the forcible attempts already made to restore the Catholic religion and their determination to reveal any further conspiracies against the government which should come to their knowledge. In return they ingenuously stated that as they were ready to render to Caesar the things that were Caesar's, so they should be permitted to yield to the successor of Peter that obedience which Peter himself might have claimed under Christ's commission. Thus they hoped to distinguish between their several duties and obligations as to be ready on the one hand "to spend their blood in defence of her Majesty," but on the other they would be willing "to lose their lives than infringe the lawful authority of Christ's Catholic Church." Although the theological faculty of Louvain condemned their repudiation of papal power to depose the sovereign, the pope himself selected Dr. Bishop to revive episcopal authority in England in 1623.

The results of the address were disappointing; Elizabeth died within 3 months of its signature, and James I soon proved that he would not be satisfied with purely civil allegiance. He thirsted for spiritual authority. With the assistance of an apostate Jesuit, a new oath of allegiance was crafted with a subtlety designed to trouble the conscience of Catholics and divide them on the lawfulness of taking it. It was imposed 5 July 1606, about the time of Drury's arrest.

Drury was condemned for his priesthood, but offered his life if he would take the new oath. A letter from Jesuit Father Persons against its lawfulness was found on him. The oath declared that the "damnable doctrine" of the deposing power was "impious and heretical," and it was condemned by Pope Paul V, 22 September 1606, "as containing many things contrary to the Faith and Salvation." This brief, however, was suppressed by the archpriest, and Drury probably did not know of it. He died because his conscience would not permit him to take the oath.

A pious contemporary account of his martyrdom, entitled "A true Report of the Arraignment . . . of a Popish Priest named Robert Drewrie" (London, 1607; reprinted in the *Harleian Miscellany*) calls him a Benedictine, and says he wore his monastic habit at the execution. He may have been a Benedictine oblate.

Edmund, priest; b. in Kent, England; d. 27 May 1590, HDQ at Durham. He studied at Rheims and Rome, where he was ordained (1589). The following March 22, he was sent to the English Mission, but was soon arrested with BB. Richard Hill, John Hogg, and Richard Holiday in the north of England soon after they landed at Tynemouth. They were caught during the hysteria following the defeat of the Spanish Armada.

Errington, George, gentleman; b. ca. 1554 at Hirst (or Herst), Northumberland; d. 29 November 1596, HDQ at York, England. He served as a courier and escort for Catholics traveling between the northeast of England and the Continent, which had to be accomplished furtively. He was imprisoned in the Tower of London from 1585–87 and at York Castle in 1591 and 1593–94, but released. When Errington was again arrested for recusancy and imprisoned at York, a Protestant minister came to him, feigning an interest in Catholicism. Errington was

tricked into attempting to persuade the minister to convert. For this reason he was condemned with BB. William Knight and William Gibson for "persuading to popery."

Filcock, Roger (*alias* Nayler, Arthur), Jesuit priest; b. ca. 1570 at Sandwich, Kent, England; d. 27 February 1601, HDQ at Tyburn (London). He studied at Rheims (1588–90) and at St. Alban's Seminary, Valladolid, where he was ordained (ca. 1597). He applied to enter the Jesuits in Spain but was sent instead to the English Mission. En route he was captured at sea by the Dutch, but escaped to Kent in early 1598. Under the *alias* Roger Arthur he began his two-year ministry. Shortly after being admitted to the Society of Jesus by Fr. Henry Garnet, Filcock was betrayed by someone who had known him as a student at Valladolid, arrested (summer 1600), and imprisoned at Newgate before he could undertake his novitiate in Flanders. He was charged with being a priest on 23 February 1601, indicted three days later. The judge directed the jury to find him guilty of high treason although there was no evidence against him. When he and his former classmate at Valladolid, St. Mark Barkworth were taken to the gallows for execution, they found that St. Anne Line, for whom Filcock had acted as confessor, had just been executed. At the gallows Filcock denied treason, but admitted that he was "a Catholic, a priest, and a member of the Society of Jesus." Feast: December 1 (Jesuits).

Fingley (Finglow), John, priest; b. at Barmby-in-the-Marsh (or Barneby near Howden), Yorkshire, England; d. Aug. 8, 1586, HDQ at York. He studied at Cambridge and at Rheims, where he was ordained to the priesthood, 25 March 1581. The following month he entered the mission field in northern England. He was arrested, tried, and condemned for being a Catholic priest and reconciling English subjects to the ancient Church.

Flathers, Matthew (*alias* Matthew Major), priest; b. ca. 1580 at Weston, Otley, Yorkshire, England; d. 21 March 1608, HDQ at York under James I. Three months after his ordination at Arras on 25 March 1606, he was sent to English mission. He was discovered almost immediately by government emissaries, who, after the Gunpowder Plot, had redoubled their vigilance. He was brought to trial on the charge of receiving orders abroad, i.e., from the Vatican, and condemned to death. By an act of unusual clemency, the sentence was commuted to banishment for life. Undaunted, Flathers returned to England in order to fulfill his mission, and, after ministering for a brief time to oppressed Catholics in Yorkshire, was again apprehended. Flathers was offered his life on condition that he take the recently enacted Oath of Allegiance. On his refusal, he was condemned to death and taken to the common place of execution outside Micklegate Bar, York.

Flower, Richard (*vere* Floyd or Lloyd; *alias* Graye, Fludd), gentleman; b. ca. 1567 in Anglesey (diocese of Bangor), North Wales; d. 30 August 1588, hanged at Tyburn (London). Flower, the younger brother of Fr. Owen Lloyd, was arrested in London (1588) and condemned for assisting Fr. William Horner, a seminary priest. He suffered with Bl. Fr. Richard Leigh and the blessed laymen Edward Shelley, Richard Martin, John Roche (all beatified in 1929), and St. Margaret Ward. He is frequently confused with Fr. William Way, who used the *alias* Flower.

Garlick, Nicholas, priest; b. ca. 1555 at Dinting, Glossop, Derbyshire; d. 24 July 1588, HDQ on St. Mary's Bridge at Derby. He studied at Gloucester Hall, now Worcester College, Oxford. He finished his studies, but did not take a degree, perhaps because it required taking the Oath of Supremacy. For the next 7 years he was schoolmaster at Tideswell in the Peak (Derbyshire), where his personal holiness so influenced his pupils that three of them, including Bl. Christopher Buxton (beatified 1929), followed him to Rheims in June 1581. He was ordained in 1582 and returned to England the following January. After working for a year in the Midlands, he was arrested and sent into exile (1585). Although he knew that he would be shown no mercy should he be found again in England, he was soon back at work in the same neighborhood. In 1588, he was apprehended with Bl. Robert Ludlam by the infamous Topcliffe at Padley Hall, the home of John Fitzherbert, whose son betrayed the priests. They were confined in the verminous Derby Gaol with Bl. Richard Simpson.

Gibson, William, servant; b. near Ripon, Yorkshire, England; d. 29 November 1596, HDQ at York. Arrested for his involvement in an uprising in the North, he spent many years imprisoned at York Castle where gained a reputation for piety. He was sentenced with BB. George Errington and William Knight for trying to "persuade to popery" a Protestant prisoner, who indicated an interest in Catholicism, but used it as a tool to gain freedom for himself and intelligence for the authorities.

Grimston (Grimstow), Ralph, married gentleman; b. Nidd, Knaresborough, Yorkshire, England; d. 15 June 1598, hanged at York. Arrested with Fr. Peter Snow with whom he was traveling to York about 1 May 1598. He was charged with felony for having aided a priest and having attempted to prevent Snow's apprehension.

Grissold, Robert, a.k.a. Robert Greswold or Griswold, farm laborer; b. at Rowington, Warwickshire; d. 16 July 1604, hanged at Warwick under James I. Grissold, who was in the service of Mr. Sheldon of Broadway, was attending Bl. John Sugar, when they were arrested in his hometown on 8 July 1603. The two martyrs shared a

year's captivity before Grissold was charged with refusing to attend church and for assisting Sugar, a seminary priest.

Hambley, John, priest; b. ca. 1560 at St. Mabyn, Bodmin, Cornwall; d. 20 (?) July 1587, HDQ at Salisbury. He was a Protestant who was converted by reading one of Fr. Persons' books in 1582. He took up seminary studies at Rheims, and was ordained at Laon (22 September 1584). The following year he returned home and worked in the Western Counties. On his way to witness a wedding, he was betrayed and captured around Easter 1586. He was tried and condemned at Taunton, but saved his life for the moment by denying his faith, then managed to break prison, and fled to Salisbury. The following August, however, Hambley was found during a methodical search of Catholic homes on the eve of the Assumption. Again his resolve wavered; he offered conformity and the names of most of his Catholic friends, and was released. Around Easter 1587 he was apprehended a third time and pledged conformity, but recovered quickly, confessed his faith, and suffered "manfully, and inveighing much against his former fault." In this final test, encouragement came from his fellow inmate, Bl. Thomas Pilchard.

Hardesty, Robert, layman; b. in Yorkshire; d. 24 September 1589, hanged at York. He was arrested for harboring and aiding a seminary priest, Bl. William Spenser, with whom he was executed following internment at York Castle.

Haydock, George, priest; b. ca. 1556 at Cottam Hall, Preston, Lancashire; d. 12 February 1584, HDQ at Tyburn (London). He was the youngest son of devout Catholics: Evan Haydock of Cottam Hall and Helen, daughter of William Westby of Mowbreck Hall, Lancashire. About 1574 or 1575, he followed his father and brother to Douai, then continued his studies at the English Colleges in Rome and Rheims. Following his ordination at Rheims, 21 December 1581, he returned to England. In February 1582 he was arrested in London and spent fifteen months in the Tower. Within the Tower he was able to administer the Sacraments to his fellow-prisoners. He was indicted with BB. Wm. Dean, James Fenn, Thomas Hemerford, John Munden, John Nutter (all beatified 1929), and two other priests on 5 February 1583, on charges of conspiracy against the queen at Rheims. They were found guilty on 7 February and sentenced to death. The other four were shackled to "the pit" in the Tower, but Haydock, still weak from malaria, was sent back to his quarters lest he cheat the executioner by dying in prison. He said Mass early on Wednesday 12 February, before being drawn in hurdles to Tyburn. Haydock was alive when he was disemboweled. An eyewitness account of the execution, which is included in Pollen's *Unpublished Documents relating to the English Martyrs* (London, Catholic Record Society, 1908, v. 5), describes Haydock as ''a man of complexion fayre, of countenance milde, and in professing of his faith passing stoute.''

Heath, Henry, in religion Paul of St. Magdalen, Franciscan (OFM) priest; b. ca. 1599 near Peterborough, Northamptonshire; d. 17 April 1643, HDQ at Tyburn (London) under Charles I. He was the son of the Protestant John Heath. After receiving his degree at Corpus Christi College, Cambridge (1617), he became the college librarian. In 1622, he was received into the Church by George Muscott. After a short stay at the English College at Douai, he entered St. Bonaventure's convent there ca. 1624–25, where he led a frugal and scholarly existence for many years. Upon obtaining permission to join the English Mission in early 1643, he crossed from Dunkirk to Dover disguised as a sailor. On the night of his arrival in London, he was arrested as a shoplifter. When papers found in his cap betrayed his religion, he was taken to Compter Prison. The next day he was brought before the lord mayor, and, on confessing he was a priest, was sent to Newgate. Examined by a Parliamentary committee, he was indicted for being a priest. At his place of execution, Heath reconciled one of the criminals that was to die with him. In an unusual act of mercy, he was allowed to hang until he was dead.

Hill, Richard, priest; b. in Yorkshire; d. 27 May 1590, HDQ at Durham. He studied at Rheims and was ordained at Laon (1589). He traveled with BB. Edmund Duke, John Hogg, and Richard Holiday to England, where they were soon arrested, arraigned, and condemned together. Two Protestants, Robert and Grace Maire, impressed with the courage of the martyrs, were converted.

Hogg, John, priest; b. at Cleveland, North Riding, Yorkshire, England; d. 27 May 1590, HDQ at Durham. He studied at Rheims from 15 October 1587, and was ordained with his fellow martyrs BB. Richard Holiday and Richard Hill on 23 September 1589. They were all arrested while taking up their posts in the north of England and condemned for treason as seminary priests.

Holiday, Richard, priest; b. in Yorkshire, England; d. 27 May 1590, HDQ at Durham. He went to Rheims to study at the English College on 6 September 1584, but was not ordained priest until 1589. He was arrested and condemned for his priesthood with Bl. Edmund Duke, Richard Hill, and John Hogg almost immediately upon arrival in England.

Horner, Nicholas, tailor; b. at Grantley, Yorkshire, England; d. 4 March 1590, HDQ at Smithfield, London. Arrested in London on the charge of assisting Catholic priests, he was released. Charged a second time with assisting Bl. Christopher Bales (beatified 1929), a seminary priest, he refused to conform religiously in exchange for his life. On the eve of his execution, according to a letter from Horner's friend to St. Robert Southwell, he had a vision of a crown of glory hanging over his head, which filled him with courage to face the impending ordeal.

Hunt, Thomas (*vere* Benstead), priest; b. ca. 1574 in Norfolk, England; d. ca. 11 July 1600, HDQ at Lincoln. He studied at the English Colleges of Valladolid and Seville, Spain, where he was ordained (ca. 1599). He was not in England long before he was arrested. Imprisoned at Wisbeach, Hunt escaped with 5 others and remained free for several months. He was with Bl. Thomas Sprott at Saracen's Head Inn, Lincoln, when he was arrested a second time. They were convicted of treason for being priests. Feast: 12 February.

Hunt, Thurstan (*alias* Greenlow), priest; b. ca. 1555 at Carlton Hall (near Leeds), Yorkshire, England; d. ca. 3 April 1601, HDQ at Lancaster; ordained at Rheims by Cardinal de Guise after he completed study there in 1584. Thereafter he worked in Lancashire, Yorkshire, and Cheshire for fifteen years. On 30 September 1600, he was captured near Preston by the authorities while trying to rescue Bl. Robert Middleton as he was being taken to prison. They were imprisoned in London, but returned to Lancaster for sentencing and execution. Following their execution, their relics were eagerly gathered and venerated. Hunt's ''haughty courage stout'' was commemorated in a contemporary song. Feast: 12 February.

Ingleby (Ingolby), Francis, priest; b. ca. 1551 at Ripley, Yorkshire, England; d. 3 June 1586 (old calendar), HDQ at York, England. The fourth son of Sir William Ingleby and his wife Anne, Ingleby studied at Brasenose College, Oxford (before 1565), and was a student of the Inner Temple in 1576. He began seminary studies at Rheims in 1582 and ordained priest at Laon in 1583. About three months later he left France to join the English Mission, where he labored in Yorkshire until he was arrested in the spring of 1586. He was one of the priests to whom St. Margaret Clitherow offered refuge in her home. Feast: 8 Aug.

Knight, William, gentleman; b. ca. 1572 at South Duffield, Hemingbrough, Yorkshire, England; d. 29 November 1596, HDQ at York. On coming of age he claimed from his Protestant uncle property left to him by his father, Leonard Knight. When his uncle denounced him to the authorities for being a Catholic, he was immediately arrested. In October 1593, Knight was remanded to York Castle, where BB. William Gibson and George Errington were already confined. A certain Protestant clergyman, also a prisoner, arranged to gain his freedom by feigning a desire to become a Catholic. He won the confidence of Knight and his two companions, who explained the faith to him. With the connivance of the authorities, he was directed to Bl. Henry Abbot (beatified 1929), then at liberty, who endeavored to find a priest to reconcile him to the Church. Thereupon Abbot was arrested and, together with Knight and his two comrades, sentenced to death for persuading the clergyman to embrace Catholicism—an act of treason under the penal laws.

Lambton (Lampton), Joseph, priest; b. 1569 at Malton, Yorkshire; d. 24 July 1592 (?), HDQ at Newcastle-on-Tyne. This second son of Thomas Lambton and his wife Katharine Birkhead of West Brandon, Durham, studied at the English College in Rheims (1584–1589) and in Rome. Ordained at age twenty-three in 1592, he was sent to the English Mission and was arrested upon landing at Newcastle with Bl. Edward Waterson (beatified 1929). Feast: 27 July.

Lampley, William, glover; b. probably at Gloucester; d. HDQ there, 12 February 1588. He was tried for persuading some of his relatives to "popery," but offered leniency if he would conform to the new religion. Upon his refusal he was sentenced to be HDQ, an unusual punishment for a layman.

Lowe, John, priest; b. ca. 1553 at London, England; d. 8 October 1586, HDQ at Tyburn. He was a Protestant minister who was converted to Catholicism and then studied for the priesthood at Douai and at Rome, where he was ordained in 1582. He ministered in the London area, where he was a well-known exorcist. He was condemned for his priesthood and executed with BB. Robert Bickerdike, John Adams, and Robert Dibdale.

Ludlam (Ludham), Robert, priest; b. ca. 1551 at Radbourne (near Sheffield), Derbyshire; d. 24 July 1588, HDQ on St. Mary's Bridge at Derby. Like Bl. Nicholas Garlick with whom he died, Ludlam studied at Oxford, taught for a time, then engaged in seminary studies at Rheims, where he was ordained (May 1581). After a six-year apostolate in his homeland, he was arrested with Garlick in the home of an ancient Catholic family through the treachery of one of the sons. He and Garlick fortified the flagging faith of their fellow-prisoner, Bl. Richard Simpson. All three were tried, condemned for their priesthood, and executed together.

Meehan, Charles, Franciscan priest; b. ca. 1640 in Ireland; d. 12 August 1679, HDQ at Ruthin, Denbighshire, Wales, under Charles II. A member of the Irish Province of the Franciscans, he was ordained ca. 1672. In 1678, he was arrested in Denbigh, North Wales, en route from the Continent to Ireland, where penal laws were also in effect. Feast: 12 February.

Middleton, Robert, Jesuit priest; b. 1571, at York; d. ca. 3 April 1601, HDQ at Derby. Born into a Catholic family, he appears to have practiced as an Anglican for a time, but he was reconciled to the Church, perhaps because of the martyrdom of St. Margaret Clitherow, née Middleton (d. 1586). In 1594, he began seminary studies at Rheims and then Seville before transferring to the English College in Rome (1597), where he was ordained (1598). He labored in Lancaster for two years. In 1599, Middleton wrote a letter to Jesuit superior Henry Garnet requesting admittance into the Society of Jesus; it is unknown whether Middleton ever received the response informing him of his acceptance, for 30 September 1600, he was arrested while riding from Preston to Fulde in Lancashire. A rescue attempt was made but failed, leading to the apprehension of Bl. Thurston Hunt also. During questioning Middleton acknowledged the authority of the queen in temporal matters and said that he prayed God would one day make her a Catholic. Middleton and Hunt were condemned in March 1601 for their priesthood. Feast: 1 December (Jesuits).

Nichols (Nicolls, Nicholas), George, priest; b. ca. 1550 at Oxford, England; d. there 5 July 1589, HDQ. He studied at Brasenose College, Oxford, then was assistant master (usher) at St. Paul's School, London. He arrived at Rheims with Bl. Thomas Pilchard, 20 November 1581; he went on to Rome and was ordained priest (1583) at Rheims by Cardinal Louis de Guise. During his six year ministry in and around Oxford, he was responsible for many conversions, including that of a celebrated highwayman during his confinement at Oxford Castle. After his arrest at Catherine Wheel Inn by the university officers he proved to be a stout controversialist. Nichols was sent to Bridewell Prison, London, together with BB. Richard Yaxley, Thomas Belson, and Humphrey Pritchard. On 30 June all four were sent to Oxford for trial and were condemned. The heads of the priests were set up on the castle, and their quarters on the four city gates.

Norton, John, gentleman; b. in Yorkshire; d. 9 August 1600, hanged at Durham. He was the second son of Richard Norton, who had been attainted with rebellion in 1569, and his second wife Margaret Redshaw. John Norton and his wife were arrested in their home at Laymsley, Co. Durham, for harboring an illegal priest, Bl. Thomas Palaser. They were condemned to death, but Mrs. Norton was reprieved because she was pregnant. Palaser and Norton died with their companion Bl. John Talbot.

Nutter, Robert (alias Askew, Rowley), secular, then Dominican priest, b. ca. 1555 at Burnley, Lancashire, England; d. 26 July 1600, HDQ at Lancaster. Born into a wealthy family, he and his brother Bl. John Nutter (beatified 1929) studied at Brasenose College, Oxford, before being smuggled across the English Channel to enter the English College at Rheims. Robert was ordained there 21 December 1581. He returned to England with Bl. George Haydock using forged names and passports. The next eighteen years were divided between ministerial work and imprisonment. Sentenced into exile at Boulogne with twenty other priests, but using the alias Rowley returned to England, where he was again committed to prison at Newgate on 30 November 1585. In 1587, he was transferred to the Marshalsea, then to Wisbeach Castle, Cambridgeshire (1589–90). He and several other fervent prisoners established and followed a monastic rule of life. From prison Nutter wrote to the French provincial requesting that he be admitted to the Dominican Order as a tertiary. According to the report of attorney Thomas Hesketh, he was professed a Dominican in the presence of secular priests at Wisbeach, which was certified to the provincial at Lisbon.

Osbaldeston (Osbaldston), Edward, priest; b. ca. 1560 at Osbaldeston, Lancashire, England; d. 16 November 1594, HDQ at York. Studied at Douai, then at Rheims, where he was ordained (21 September 1585). He worked on the Continent until he was sent to Yorkshire in April 1589. He was betrayed by an apostate priest in 1594 and tried at York and convicted with high treason for being a priest. Challoner prints a portion of a still extant letter from Osbaldeston to his fellow-prisoners in York Castle, which reveals the martyr's humility and the serene trust in God with which he anticipated his death.

Page, Anthony, priest; b. ca. 1563 at Harrow-on-the-Hill, Middlesex, England; d. 20 April 1593, HDQ at York. Attended Oxford (1581–1584) and the English College at Rheims where he was ordained in 1591. He was sent on the English Mission, but immediately arrested and condemned for being a priest.

Palaser (Palasor, Palliser, Palaster, or Pallicer), Thomas, priest; b. ca. 1570 at Ellerton-upon-Swale (near Boulton), North Riding, Yorkshire, England; d. 9 August 1600, HDQ at Durham. He studied in the English College at Valladolid where he was ordained (1596). Upon returning to England, he was arrested almost immediately in the home of Bl. John Norton with Norton, his wife, and Bl. John Talbot. All four were tried at Durham and sentenced to death: Palaser for his priesthood and the others for assisting him. Another gentleman was condemned at the same time but released when he apostatized. The attempted poisoning of Palaser and his companions by the jailer's wife resulted in the conversion of Mary Day, her servant.

Pike (Pikes), William, carpenter, probably married; b. in Dorset; d. December 1591, HDQ at Dorchester. He lived on the Moors, near Christchurch, Hampshire, and

was an Anglican. On his way home from Dorchester one day, probably in 1586, he met Bl. Thomas Pilcher who convinced him of the truth of Catholicism. Thereafter he was reconciled to the Roman Church, and it was for this that he was arrested. At his trial he was asked to apostatize in order to save his life and that of his family, but refused, saying that it did not become a son of Mr. Pilcher to do so. Feast: 12 February.

Pilcher (Pilchard), Thomas, priest; b. ca. 1557 at Battle, Sussex; d. 1587, HDQ at Tyburn or Dorchester. A fellow of Balliol College, Oxford, in 1576, he earned his master's (1579), and resigned his fellowship the following year. In November 1581, he began study in Rheims and was ordained priest at Laon in March 1583. That same year he went back to England to work in Hampshire and Dorset. In 1585, he was arrested and banished, but returned almost immediately to serve another two years before being apprehended in March 1587.

Pormort (Portmot), Thomas (alias Whitgift, Price, Meres), priest; b. ca. 1560 at Little Limber, Lincolnshire; d. 20 February 1592, HDQ in St. Paul's churchyard, London. He was probably related to the Pormort family of Great Grimsby, and was the godson of Protestant Archbishop Whitgift. He studied at Cambridge for a short time, then at Rheims, and Rome. After his ordination, he entered the household of Bishop Owen Lewis of Cassano (March 1587) and served as prefect of studies in the Swiss College at Milan for a time before starting off for England. Upon reaching Brussels around 29 November 1590, he used the name Whitgift to obtain a job as manservant to Mrs. Geoffrey Pole, traveling with her via Antwerp to England, where he was arrested in London on 25 July 1591. He managed to escape, but was arrested again and convicted on high treason for having ''persuaded to popery'' a haberdasher named John Burrows. Archbishop Whitgift endeavored to delay the execution in order to persuade his godson to conform but without success.

Postgate (Posket), Nicholas (alias Watson, Whitmore), priest; b. ca. 1596–59 at Kirkdale House, Egton (Eyton) Bridge, Yorkshire; d. 7 Aug. 1679, HDQ at York under Charles II. He studied at Douai (1621–1628), where he was ordained priest in 1628. On 29 June 1630, he began his fruitful, 49-year apostolate in Yorkshire. He was apprehended by the exciseman Reeves at the house of Matthew Lyth of Sleights, Little Beck (near Whitby), and was condemned for his priesthood. Following his execution, his remains were given to his friends and interred. One of his hands was sent to Douai College. His portable altar-stone is now venerated at Dodding Green, Westmoreland.

Pritchard (or ap Richard), Humphrey, servant; b. in Wales; d. 5 July 1589, hanged at Oxford, England. While the pious Humphrey worked at St. Catherine's Wheel Inn, opposite the east end of St. Mary Magdalen's Church, Oxford, he covertly assisted hunted Catholics for twelve years. He was arrested and sent to Bridewell Prison, London, with BB. Richard Yaxley, Thomas Belson, and George Nichols for assisting unlawful seminary priests. When told during his trial in Oxford that he did not know what it was to be a Catholic, he replied that he knew what he was to believe and that he would willingly die for so good a cause.

Robinson, Christopher, priest; b. at Woodside (near Carlisle), Cumberland, England; d. 19 August 1598, HDQ at Carlisle. Studied at Rheims, where he was ordained (1592) before entering the English Mission. In 1594, he witnessed the condemnation and execution of St. John Boste at Durham, of which he has left a graphic account (*Catholic Record Society's Publications,* v. 1, London 1905). He labored primarily in Westmorland and Cumberland until his arrest and imprisonment at Carlisle. During his confinement, the Protestant Bishop Robinson of Carlisle engaged him in several disputations in an effort to persuade him to save his life by conforming to the new faith.

Rowsham (Rousham), Stephen, priest; b. ca. 1555 in Oxfordshire; d. March(?) 1587, HDQ at Gloucester. Upon completing his studies at Oriel College, Oxford, in 1572, he began a ministry in the Church of England. While serving at St. Mary's Church, Oxford, ca. 1578, he became convinced of Catholicism. He made his way to Rheims in April 1581, where he was ordained a Catholic priest (1582). He returned to England on 30 April 1582, but was recognized and arrested within days of his arrival. He spent half of the next three years confined to the "Little Ease" dungeon in the Tower of London, before being sent into exile. He stayed at Rheims from 8 October 1585 to 7 February 1586, then made his way back to his field of labor in the west of England. After a year's activity, he was apprehended in the home of the widow Strange at Gloucester, tried, and executed for his priesthood.

Sandys, John, priest; b. in the diocese of Chester or Lancashire; d. 11 August 1586, HDQ at Gloucester. He studied at Oxford and Rheims, where he was ordained priest (1584). On 2 October that year, he was sent to Gloucestershire, where he labored until his arrest and conviction as an unlawful priest.

Scott, Montford (Monford Scot), priest; b. ca. 1550 at Hawkestead, diocese of Norwich; d. 2 July 1591, HDQ in Fleet Street, London. He was one of the earliest theology students at the English College of Douai, having arrived there in 1574. In 1575, while still a subdeacon, he accompanied Dominic Vaughan to England, where they fell into the hands of the authorities in December 1576.

Vaughan betrayed the names of Catholics in London and Essex. Scott returned to Douai for presbyteral ordination at Brussels in 1577 then set out for the English Mission. He worked primarily in East Anglia and is mentioned as having labored in Kent (1580), Norfolk, Suffolk (1583), Lincolnshire, and Yorkshire (1584). In 1584, he was arrested at York with his cousin, Bl. Brian Lacey (beatified 1929), who served as his assistant and whose brother had betrayed them. He was taken to London and imprisoned for seven years until his release was secured by a monetary payment on the condition that he leave the country. He went to visit the prisoners at Wisbeach Castle, where he was again apprehended. Scott was brought to trial (30 June 1591) at Newgate in the company of Bl. George Beesley, condemned for being in the country illegally, and executed the following day.

Sergeant, Richard (*alias* Lee, Lea, or Long[e]), priest; b. in Gloucestershire; d. 20 April 1586, HDQ at Tyburn. He was the son of Thomas Sergeant of Stone and his wife Katherine Tyre of Hardwick. After earning his baccalaureate at Oxford (ca. 1570–71), he entered the English College at Rheims and was ordained priest at Laon (1583). He left for England on 10 September, working for several years in the mission prior to his indictment at the Old Bailey on 17 April 1586, as Richard Lea, *alias* Longe. He suffered with Bl. William Thomson, who was also executed as an unlawful priest.

Simpson (Sympson), Richard, priest; b. ca. 1553 at Well, Ripon, Yorkshire, England; d. 24 July 1588, HDQ at Derby. After a short time as a Protestant minister, his journey to the Catholic Church caused him to be imprisoned. Released (or exiled) he began his studies for the priesthood at Douai in 1577, was ordained a priest, and was sent back to England. He labored in the mission field for almost ten years prior to his arrest and banishment. He returned furtively, but was caught passing from Lancashire to Derbyshire. He was reprieved at the Lenten assizes of 1588, and almost conformed. His fellow inmates, Nicholas Garlick and Bl. Robert Ludlam, comforted and encouraged him to hold fast to the faith. He repented of his inconstancy and was condemned for high treason because he was an unlawful priest.

Snow, Peter, priest; b. at Ripon, Yorkshire, England; d. 15 June 1598, HDQ at York. He entered the seminary at Rheims in 1589 and was ordained at Soissons, France, 1591. After working in Yorkshire for about seven years, he was arrested about 1 May 1598, while traveling to York with Bl. Ralph Grimston. Snow was condemned and executed for his priesthood.

Southerne, William, priest; b. ca. 1579 at Ketton, Co. Durham; d. 30 April 1618 at Newcastle-under-Lyme under James I. Following his studies at Douai and Valladolid, he was ordained and returned to England. There he worked for fourteen years primarily among the poor of Staffordshire, particularly at Baswich, which then belonged to a branch of the Fowler family. He was arrested while saying Mass and sentenced in his vestments for being a priest and refusing the Oath of Supremacy. He remained in Stafford prison for six days after his condemnation because no one was willing to hang him. Finally he was strangled, then drawn and quartered. His head was stuck on one of the gates of Stafford.

Spenser, William, priest; b. ca. 1555 at Gisburn, Yorkshire, England; d. 24 September 1589, HDQ at York. His maternal uncle, Bl. William Horn, sent him (1573) to Trinity College, Oxford, where he earned his master's degree in 1580. He used his position at Oxford to influence his pupils regarding the truth of Catholicism, but delayed his formal reconciliation with the Church until 1582 when he was received into communion at Rheims. He then began his seminary studies. After presbyter ordination (1583). On 29 August 1584, he was sent to England, where he worked in Yorkshire. One of his greatest accomplishments was the reconciliation of his parents and uncle, who later became a priest. Spenser voluntarily gave himself up to authorities at York Castle in order to assist those imprisoned there. He was condemned for his priesthood and was executed with Bl. Robert Hardesty.

Sprott (Spratt), Thomas, b. ca. 1571 at Skelsmergh (near Kendal), Westmorland, England; d. 11 July 1600, HDQ at Lincoln, England. After studying at Douai, he was ordained in 1596 and sent on the English Mission that same year. During a search for robbers in a Lincoln inn, authorities found holy oils and breviaries among the possessions of Sprott and his companion Bl. Thomas Hunt. They were arrested. During the trial Judge John Glanville directed the jury to find them guilty, though they neither confessed nor were proven to be priests.

Sugar (Suker), John (*alias* Cox), priest; b. ca. 1558 at Wombourne, Staffordshire, England; d. 16 July 1604, HDQ at Warwick under James I. Sugar, described as *clerici filius* (son of a clergyman), studied at Merton College, Oxford; however, he did not received his degree because he objected to swearing the Oath of Supremacy. Nevertheless, he became a Protestant minister at Cannock (Cank), Staffordshire. After converting to Catholicism, he studied at Douai, was ordained there in 1601, and immediately returned to England. He worked in Warwickshire, Staffordshire, and Worcestershire. On 8 July 1603, he was arrested with Bl. Robert Grissold at Rowington, Warwickshire. After a year's imprisonment at Warwick, Sugar was condemned on 14 July for his priesthood.

Sutton, Robert, priest; b. ca. 1545 at Burton-on-Trent, Staffordshire, England; d. 27 July 1588, HDQ at Stafford. He received his master's degree from Christ Church, Oxford (1567). In 1571, he was the Anglican rector of Lutterworth, Leicestershire, but was converted to Catholicism by his younger brother William, who later became a Jesuit. The thirty-year-old Robert and his twenty-five-year-old brother Abraham arrived together at the English College of Douai on 23 March 1575. They were ordained priests at Douai and left for England on 19 March 1578. Robert labored in Staffordshire until his arrest and banishment in 1585. Upon his return, he was apprehended, tried, and condemned for high treason because he was a seminary priest. Catholics were able to secure part of his remains as relics. His thumb is now at Stonyhurst College. This *beatus* is the second English martyr of this name; the other, the companion of Bl. William Hartley, was beatified in 1929. Feast: 27 July.

Sykes, Edmund, priest; b. at Leeds, Yorkshire, England; d. 23 March 1587, HDQ at Tyburn in York. He completed his seminary studies at Rheims, where he was ordained in 1581. He labored in his native Yorkshire until 1585 when he was betrayed by an apostate, Arthur Webster. He was captured, and imprisoned for about six months. Banished to the continent, he made his way to Rome. He made his way back to England in June 1586 and six months later, he was betrayed by his brother in whose home he was apprehended. He was held as prisoner at York Castle until arraignment at the Lenten assizes, when he was condemned for his priesthood.

Talbot, John, married gentleman; b. at Thornton-le-Street (in the North Riding), Yorkshire, England; d. 9 August 1600, hanged at Durham. He was arrested for being in the company of Bl. Thomas Palaser in the home of Bl. John Norton, condemned for assisting a priest and refusing to attend the state church.

Taylor, Hugh, priest; b. ca. 1560 at Durham, northeast England; d. 25 November 1585, HDQ at York. He was ordained priest in 1584 at Rheims (or possibly Douai). On 27 March 1585, he was sent on the English Mission and immediately arrested together with Bl. Marmaduke Bowes. Taylor was the first martyr condemned under the recently enacted Statute 27 Eliz. c. 2. He was immediately executed.

Thomson (Thompson), William (*alias* Blackburn), priest; b. ca. 1560 at Blackburn, Lancashire, England; d. 20 April 1586, HDQ at Tyburn. He was ordained at Rheims in 1584. Returning to England, he worked in and around London until his arrest in the home of Roger Line, the husband of Bl. Anne Line (beatified 1929), while saying Mass. He was indicted on 17 April 1586, at the Old Bailey with Bl. Richard Sergeant and condemned for his priesthood.

Thorp(e), Robert, priest; b. in Yorkshire; d. 15 May 1591, HDQ at York. He studied at the English College in Rheims, where he was ordained in April 1585. He worked for about ten years in Yorkshire, renowned for his devotion and constancy. He was in bed very early on Palm Sunday 1595 when authorities came to arrest him in the Menthorpe home of Bl. Thomas Watkinson. Someone supposedly observed him gathering palms the night before and reported his actions to the local justice of the peace. Thorpe was condemned as a traitor for being a priest.

Thules (Thulis), John, priest; b. ca. 1568 at Whalley, Upholland, Lancashire, England; d. 18 March 1616, HDQ at Lancaster under James I. He began his studies at Rheims and then completed them at Rome, where he was ordained (April 1592). He immediately returned to his homeland to begin a twenty-year apostolate. He was a prisoner at Wisbeach Castle, Cambridgeshire, for some years and later escaped. He labored in Lancashire, until he was arrested by Earl William of Derby and was committed to Lancaster Castle, where fellow-martyr Roger Wrenno was confined. A curious metrical account of the martyrdom of Thules and Wrenno, as well as portions of a poem composed by Thules, are included in Pollen's *Acts of the English Martyrs*, 194–207.

Thwing (Thweng), Edward, priest; b. ca. 1565 at Heworth or Hurs (near York); d. 26 July 1600, HDQ at Lancaster. He was the son of Thomas Thwing and his wife Jane Kellet of York, and may have been related to Bl. Thomas Thwing (d. 1680, beatified 1929), also of Yorkshire. He studied at Rheims and with an interval spent with the Jesuits at Pont-à-Mousson. At Rheims he was a reader in Greek and Hebrew and a professor of rhetoric and logic. He was ordained priest at Laon, 20 December 1590. In 1597, he was sent on the English Mission and immediately was arrested and imprisoned at Wisbeach, whence he escaped with Bl. Robert Nutter to Lancashire. They were arrested in May 1600, tried at the next assizes, and condemned for being priests.

Watkinson, Thomas, gentleman; b. at Hemingborough or Menthrope, Yorkshire; d. 31 May 1591, hanged at York. He was a Catholic of the lesser nobility, who is described as a widower with a family and as cleric; he may have been in minor orders. He lived a solitary life and assisted the seminary priests out of his devotion to Christ. He was arrested when Bl. Robert Thorpe was discovered in his home on Palm Sunday 1595. He was charged with harboring a priest, but was offered clemency if he would worship in the state church. He refused and was executed.

Webley, Henry, layman; b. ca. 1558 at Gloucester, England; d. 28 August 1588, hanged at Mile's End Green, London. He was arrested at Chichester Harbour in 1586 and condemned for assisting Bl. William Dean (beatified 1929), a seminary priest.

Wharton, Christopher, priest; b. ca. 1540 at Middleton, Yorkshire, England; d. 28 November 1600, HDQ at York. The second son of Henry Wharton and Agnes Warcop of Wharton he received the master's degree from Trinity College, Oxford (1564), then became a fellow. In February 1583, he began seminary studies at Rheims. He continued his studies for two years after ordination (1584) before returning to England in the company of Bl. Edward Burden. After thirteen years of labor in difficult circumstances, he was arrested with the widow Eleanor Hunt in her home and incarcerated in York Castle. They were tried at the Lenten assizes in 1600, condemned, refused life in exchange for conformity to the state church. Hunt died in prison, while Wharton heroically suffered the fate of those convicted of treason. Wharton was known for his humility and charity.

Whitaker, Thomas (*alias* Starkie), priest; b. ca. 1611–14 at Burnley, Lancashire; d. 7 August 1646, at Lancaster under Charles I. He received his first education at the school where his father, Thomas Whitaker, was master. Through the influence of the Towneley family, he received his seminary education at the English College at Valladolid, Spain. Following his ordination (1638), he returned to England, where he ministered in Lancashire for five years. He was arrested once during this period, but escaped while being transferred to Lancaster Castle. On 7 August 1643, he was seized at Place Hall, Goosenargh, and confined to Lancaster Castle. During his three-year imprisonment he became known for his spirit of continual prayer and his charity to fellow inmates. Before his trial he made a month's retreat in preparation for death.

Woodcock, John (alias John Faringdon or Thompson), in religion, Martin of St. Felix, Franciscan priest; b. 1603 at Clayton-le-Woods (near Preston), Lancashire; d. 7 August 1646, HDQ at Lancaster under Charles I. He was born into a middle class family headed by his Protestant father Thomas and his Catholic mother Dorothy. He himself confessed Catholicism ca. 1622. Thereafter he studied for a year at St. Omer, then entered the English College at Rome (Oct. 1629). In May 1630, he entered the Capuchin friary in Paris, but the following year he joined the exiled English Franciscans at St. Bonaventure, Douai. There he received the habit from Bl. Henry Heath (1631), was professed by Bl. Arthur Bell (1632), and was ordained (1634). He served as chaplain at Arras, Flanders, until he was sent to England in 1640. After working zealously for two years, he retired to a friary on the Continent. Late in 1643 or early 1644, he returned to England via Newcastle-on-Tyne and was arrested his first night in

Lancashire. After a two-year imprisonment, he was tried with BB. Edward Bamber and Thomas Whitaker. All confessed to their priesthood and were therefore condemned. The Franciscan nuns at Taunton possess an armbone of the martyr.

Woodfen, Nicholas (*alias* Nicholas Wheeler; arraigned as Nicholas Devereux), priest; b. ca. 1550 at Leominster, Herefordshire; d. 21 Jan. 1586, HDQ at Tyburn (London). He studied at Douai and Rheims, where he was ordained (1581). Thereafter he immediately began his ministry in London, especially among the barristers of the Inns of Court. He was caught by pursuivants and convicted for his priesthood.

Wrenno (Worren), Roger, weaver; b. ca. 1576 at Chorley, Lancashire, England; d. 18 March 1616, hanged at Lancaster under James I. A devout layman, Wrenno was imprisoned with other Catholics in Lancaster Castle but escaped with Bl. John Thules one evening before the Lenten assizes. They were recaptured the following day. Wrenno refused to exchange the oath of supremacy for his life and was hanged just after Fr. Thules.

Yaxley, Richard, priest; b. ca. 1560 at Boston, Lincolnshire; d. 5 July 1589, HDQ at Oxford. Richard, the third son of William Yaxley and his wife Rose Langton, went to Rheims in 1582 to study for the priesthood. Ordained to the priesthood in 1585, he began his labors in and around Oxford in February 1586. Arrested with Bl. George Nichols and two others, they were interrogated at Oxford. Sent to London for further questioning, they were imprisoned at Bridewell. Yaxley was sent to the Tower of London as a close prisoner on 25 May 1589, and appears to have been racked frequently until sent back to Oxford on 30 June to stand trial for treason. Following his execution, his head was placed on a pike at Oxford Castle and his other remains on the four gates of the city.

Bibliography: *The Catholic Martyrs of England and Wales* (London 1985). *L'Osservatore Romano,* English edition, no. 44, (1987): 6–7; no. 48, (1987): 6. J. GIBBONS, *Concertatio Ecclesiae Catholicae in Anglia adversus Calvinpapistas et Puritanos,* ed., M. ROGERS (1588, reprint, Farnborough 1970). M. L. CARRAFIELLO, *Robert Parsons and English Catholicism, 1580–1610* (London 1998); *The Catholic Martyrs of England and Wales* (London 1985). R. CHALLONER, *Memoirs of Missionary Priests,* 2 v. (London, 1741–42 and Edinburgh 1877–78). P. COLLINSON and J. CRAIG, eds., *The Reformation in English Towns, 1500–1640* (New York 1998). *Acts of the Privy Council* (London 1890–1907). S. DORAN, *Princes, Pastors, and People: The Church and Religion in England, 1529–1689* (London 1991). M. J. DORCY, "Ven. Robert Nutter," *St. Dominic's Family* (Dubuque, Iowa: Priory Press, 1964), 341–342. T. P. ELLIS, *The Catholic Martyrs of Wales, 1535–1680* (London 1933). G. R. ELTON, *Policy and Police: The Enforcement of the Reformation in the Age of Thomas Cromwell* (Cambridge 1972). D. FLYNN, *John Donne and the Ancient Catholic Nobility* (Bloomington, Ind. 1995). H. FOLEY, *Records of the English Province of the Society of Jesus,* 7 vols. (London 1878–83). J. FOSTER, *Alumni Oxonienses* (Oxford 1892); *Glover's Visitation of Yorkshire* (London (privately printed), 1875). GILLOW, *Biblical Dictictionary of English Catholicism,* 5 v. (London and New York 1885–1902). C. HAIGH, *Reformation and Resistance in Tudor Lancashire* (London 1975). F. HEAL & R. O'DAY, eds. *Church and Society in England: Henry VIII to James I,* (London 1977). KNOX, *First and Second Diaries of English College, Douai* (London 1878). D. M. LOADES, *The Oxford Martyrs,* 2 ed. (Bangor, Gwynedd 1992). P. MARSHALL, *The Catholic Priesthood and the English Reformation* (Oxford 1994). T. M. MCCOOG, *The Society of Jesus in Ireland, Scotland, and England: 1541–1588* (New York 1996). J. MORRIS, *The Troubles of Our Catholic Forefathers* (London 1872); *The Catholics of York under Elizabeth* (London 1891). J. H. POLLEN, *Acts of the English Martyrs* (London, 1891); *English Martyrs 1584–1683 in Catholic Record Society,* 5 v. (London, 1908); *The English Catholics in the Reign of Queen Elizabeth . . .,* 2nd ed. (New York 1971). M. STANTON, *Menology of England and Wales* (London, 1887). J. THADDEUS, *The Franciscans in England 1600–1859,*15 v. (London, 1898). M. TODD, ed., *Reformation to Revolution: Politics and Religion in Early Modern England* (London 1995). J. N. TYLENDA, *Jesuit Saints & Martyrs* (Loyola Press, Chicago 1998), 65–66, 87–88. S. UNDSET, *Stages on the Road,* translated by A. G. CHATER (Freeport, NY 1934). A. WALSHAM, *Church Papists: Catholicism, Conformity, and Confessional Polemic in Early Modern England* (Rochester, NY 1993). WATSON, *Decacordon of Ten Quodlibet Questions* (1602). W. WESTON, *An Autobiography from the Jesuit Underground,* translated by P. CARAMAN (New York 1955). R. WHITING, *Local Responses to the English Reformation* (New York 1998). D. DE YEPES, *Historia Particular de la persecución de Inglaterra* (Madrid 1599).

[J. JUKES/K. RABENSTEIN]

ESCRIVÁ DE BALAGUER Y ALBÁS, JOSEMARÍA, BL.

Founder of the Prelature of the Holy Cross and Opus Dei; b. 9 January 1902, Barbastro, Spain; d. 26 June 1975, Villa Trevere, Rome, Italy.

One of 6 children of José Escriva and Dolores Balaguer, Escrivá studied at the School of Law of the Univ. of Saragossa after High School, subsequently receiving the doctorate in law from the Univ. of Madrid (1939). Once his seminary studies were completed in Saragossa, he was ordained on 28 March 1925. Later he received a doctorate in theology from the Pontifical Lateran University, Rome. His priestly work began in rural parishes and was continued among university students and people from a wide variety of backgrounds in the slums of Saragossa and Madrid.

On 2 October 1928 he founded Opus Dei, an association whose object is to spread Christian doctrine and virtues in all environments of social and professional life. It provides a spiritual life style for those who want to follow Christ more closely, but who choose to remain in secular society. In 1946, Msgr. Escrivá de Balaguer moved his residence to Rome and traveled throughout Europe to prepare and consolidate the apostolic work of Opus Dei. Between 1970 and 1975, he carried out an extensive work of preaching and catechetical instruction in practically every country of Latin America and in various European nations. In addition to historical, juridical, and theological writings, he is the author of widely read spiritual books, most of which have been translated into several languages, including *The Way* (Chicago 1954), *Holy Rosary* (Chicago 1953), *Conversations with Msgr. Escrivá de Balaguer* (Shannon 1968), *Christ Is Passing By* (Chicago 1974), *Friends of God* (Madrid 1977), and *La Abadesa de las Huelgas* (Madrid 1944). *The Way*, first published in 1934 under the title *Consideraciones espirituales*, by 1999 had sold 4,721,000 copies in 42 languages.

Addressing a crowd of 300,000 faithful gathered on 17 May 1992 in St. Peter's Square for Escrivá's beatification, Pope John Paul II said, ''With supernatural intuition, Bl. Josemaría untiringly preached the universal call to holiness and apostolate. Christ calls everyone to become holy in the realities of everyday life. Hence work, too, is a means of personal holiness and apostolate, when it is done in union with Jesus Christ.'' Escrivá's body is entombed in the Prelatic Church of Our Lady of Peace at Viale Bruno Buozzi in Rome.

Feast: 26 June.

See Also: OPUS DEI

Bibliography: Works by Blessed Josemaría Escrivá: *Children of God: The Life of Spiritual Childhood* (Princeton, N.J. 1998). *Friends of God,* Eng. tr. (Princeton, N.J. 1977). *Furrow* (Princeton, N.J. 1986). *The Forge* (Princeton, N.J. 1987). *The Way of the Cross* (Princeton, N.J. 1981). *The Way,* reprint (Princeton, N.J. 1985). Works about Blessed Josemaría Escrivá: *Así le vieron: testimonios sobre monseñor Escrivá de Balaguer*, ed. R. SERRANO (Madrid 1992). J. H. BENET, *Josemaria Escrivá de Balaguer: un hombre de Dios* (Madrid 1992). P. BERGLAR, *Opus Dei: Life and Work of its Founder* (Princeton, N.J. 1995). S. BERNAL, *Msgr. Josemaría Escrivá de Balaguer* (New York 1977). F. O. BRAÑA, *Vivir como hijos de dios: estudios sobre el Beato Josemaría Escrivá* 4th ed. (Pamplona 1999). A. BYRNE, *Sanctifying Ordinary Work* (New York 1975). L. CARANDELL, *Vida y milagros de monseñor Escrivá de Balaguer* (Barcelona 1992). C. CAVALLERI, *Immersed in God: Blessed Josemaria Escriva* (Princeton, N.J. 1996). *Estudios sobre Camino: colección de estudios*, ed. J. MORALES (Madrid 1988). F. GONDRAND, *At God's Pace* (Princeton, N.J. 1982). *Hombre de Dios: testimonios sobre el fundador del Opus Dei* (Madrid 1994). F. OCARIZ, *Canonical Path of Opus Dei* (Princeton, N.J. 1994). R. G. PÉREZ, *Trabajando junto al beato Josemaría* (Madrid 1994). *La personalidad del Beato Josemaría Escrivá de Balaguer* (Pamplona 1994). A. DEL PORTILLO, *Immersed in God: Blessed Josemaría Escrivá* (Princeton 1996). J. YNFANTE, *Opus Dei: así en la tierra como en el cielo* (Barcelona 1996).

[M. M. KENNEDY]

Portrait of Josemaría Escrivá. (AP/Wide World Photos)

EUSE HOYOS, MARIANO DE JESÚS, BL.

A.k.a. Fr. Marianito, diocesan priest; b. 14 October 1845, Yarumal (Diocese of Antioquia), northwestern Colombia; d. 12 July 1926, Angostura, Colombia; beatified as the first Colombian-born blessed, 9 April 2000 by John Paul II.

The eldest of the seven children of Pedro Euse (of Norman heritage) and Rosalía de Hoyos, Mariano was educated at home in order to ensure a Christian formation. Even as a child he took time from his farming duties to teach other children the catechism. When he decided to become a priest (age 16), he was entrusted to the care of his uncle, Fr. Fermín Hoyos. On 3 February 1869, Mariano entered the Medellín seminary. He was ordained (14 July 1872), assigned as assistant to his uncle at San Pedro, then to Yarumal (1876–78) and Angostura (1878). As assistant to his ailing pastor, Rudesindo Correa, he supervised the completion of the church edifice. Upon Correa's death, Fr. Marianito became pastor and committed himself to caring for the needy during civil war. When his own safety was threatened, several times he was forced into hiding. He was known for his poverty, his selfless charity, his simple but effective preaching, and his pastoral zeal, particularly in his ministry to farmers and children. He died after a long illness. Marianito was buried in the chapel of the Virgin of Carmen, which he had constructed.

During Euse Hoyos's beatification, Pope John Paul II noted that civil conflict started in Colombia 52 years prior and continues today. He expressed the hope that Hoyos's ''shining testimony of charity, understanding, service, solidarity, and pardon are an example in Colombia and also a valuable aid to continue working for peace.''

Feast: 13 July.

[K. RABENSTEIN]

FAÀ DI BRUNO, FRANCESCO, BL.

Mathematician, scientist, inventor, composer, founder of the Sisters of Our Lady of Suffrage, and the Pious Works of Saint Zita, priest; b. 29 March 1825, Alessandria, Piedmont, northern Italy; d. 27 March 1888, Turin, Italy; beatified by John Paul II, 25 September 1988.

Francesco Faà di Bruno, the youngest of the twelve children of Marquis Louis Faà di Bruno, was a remarkable man of great talent and deep faith imbued from his infancy in the ancestral castle at Bruno. Following the death (1834) of his mother, Carolina Sappa, Francesco studied at the Collegio San Giorgio di Novi Ligure until his entrance (1840) into the Royal Military Academy at Turin. He completed his training, proved his valor in the War of Independence (1848), and rose to the rank of captain-of-staff in the Sardinian Army (1849).

Faà di Bruno was assigned to Paris (1849), but resigned his commission (1853) to study at the Sorbonne under Augustin Louis Cauchy and Urbain Leverrier. There he also became aquainted with Abbé Moigno and Charles Hermite. Upon his return to Turin, he was a professor of Mathematics at the university for the rest of his life. In recognition of his achievements as a mathematician, the degree of Doctor of Science was conferred on him by the Universities of Paris and Turin. In addition to some ascetical writings, the composition of some sacred melodies, and the invention of some scientific apparatuses, Faà di Bruno made numerous and important contributions to mathematics. In 1858, he published a series of seven articles on the religious and pedagogical function of music, as well as a small volume on the topic.

He joined (1850) the Saint Vincent de Paul Society with Cauchy and Adolphe Baudon, and later (1853) established a chapter in Turin. Faà di Bruno founded (2 February 1859) the charitable Opera Pia Santa Zita in the San Donato district of Turin to aid house servants and ensure their right to participate in festival liturgies. The society was placed under the patronage of Saint Zita and had Saint John Bosco as its vice president. In addition to this major accomplishment, Faà di Bruno established Saint Joseph's Hospital for the sick and convalescent (1860), a home for aged priests (1862), classes for the vocational education of poor youth (1864), a women's branch of the Opere known as the Congregazione delle Suore Minime di Nostra Signora del Suffragio (1868), as well as other foundations.

He accomplished all the above as a dedicated layman. On 22 October 1876 (age 51), he was ordained priest. The following month he opened (30 October) the church he founded (Chiesa del Suffragio) to the public and celebrated (1 November) his first Mass as Father Francesco.

John Paul II praised Faà di Bruno for his ability ''to find positive responses to the needs of his time'' (beatification homily).

Bibliography: Not only was Blessed Francesco a prolific author in both science and music, but his life and works have generated a formidable number of scholarly studies. Below is a sample of some of the more recent titles. L. CONDIO, Francesco Faà di Bruno (Turin 1932). Facoltà di Teologia dell'Ateneo Romano della Santa Croce, Il Beato Francesco Faà di Bruno e la donna (Rome 1991). Istituto Superiore di Scienze Religiose di Torino, Francesco Faà di Bruno e l'Eucaristia (Turin 1996). R. LANZAVECCHIA, Francesco Faà di Bruno (Alessandria, Italy 1980). V. DEL MAZZA, Il Coraggio della Carità (Turin 1988). V. MESSORI, Un italiano serio: il beato Francesco Faà di Bruno (Milan 1990); Ser Cristiano en un mundo hostil, tr. J. ROUCO and A. MONTERO (Madrid 1997); Il beato Faà di Bruno—Un cristiano in un mondo ostile (Milan 1998). P. PALAZZINI, Francesco Faà di Bruno scienziato e prete (Rome 1980). Pontificia Università Lateranense, La Spiritualità di Francesco Faà di Bruno nell'esperienza francese (Rome 1983). P. RISSO, Un genio per Cristo: profilo biografico del beato Francesco Faà di Bruno (Padua 1992). C. TRABUCCO, Francesco Faà di Bruno, pioniere dell'assistenza sociale (Rome 1957). Università degli Studi di Torino-Facoltà di Lettere e Filosofia, Francesco Faà di Bruno e la musica (Turin 1992). Acta Apostolicae Sedis (1988): 1092.

[K. RABENSTEIN]

FASANI, FRANCESCO ANTONIO, ST.

Baptized Donato Antonio Giovanni Nicolò, known in religion as Francis Antony of Lucera, also called ''Padre Maestro,'' Franciscan priest; b. 6 August 1681, Lucera, Apulia, Italy; d. there 29 November 1742; canonized by John Paul II, 13 April 1986, at Rome.

The son of Giuseppe Fasani, a farmer, and Isabella della Monica. After Giuseppe's death (ca. 1691), Isabella married a man who provided for 'Giovanniello's' education. He entered the Conventual Franciscan novitiate at Monte Sant'Angelo Gargano (Foggia), 23 August 1695, and made his solemn profession one year later. Thereafter he studied literature and philosophy at Venafro (Isernia), Alvito (Frosinone), Montella (Avellino), and Aversa (Caserta), and theology at Agnone (Isernia). Following his ordination at the tomb of St. Francis of Assisi in 1705, he earned a doctorate in theology in Rome (1709), taught theology at the College of St. Bonaventure, then philosophy at St. Francis Convent, Lucera. In addition to his renown as a teacher, Fasani gained a reputation as a lucid preacher, spiritual director, and minister, especially among prisoners and the poor. He served in many offices: guardian at S. Rocco ad Alberona (Foggia, 1709–12) and Lucera (1712–15; 1739–42), and master of novices (Lucera, 1723–29), as well as provincial of Sant'Angelo Province (1720–23). He was known for his simplicity, humility, charity, fidelity to the Franciscan Rule and the spirit of its founder, and devotion to the Immaculate Conception. He composed novenas, including some of the first to the Immaculate Conception, meditations, sermons, Marian hymns, and a pamphlet on the attributes of God. The body of the saint is enshrined under the altar of Lucera's church dedicated to St. Francis.

During the canonization rite, Pope John Paul said: "Francesco made the love taught us by Christ the fundamental characteristic of his existence, the basic criterion of his thought and activity, the supreme summit of his aspirations."

Feast: 27 November (Franciscans).

Bibliography: Works by St Francesco Fasani: *Le 7 Novene Mariane*, ed. F. COSTA (Padua 1986). *Mariale, interpretazione allegorico-spirituale del Cantico dei Cantici*, ed. F. COSTA (Padua 1986). *Il Padre Nostro (Expositio brevis)*, ed. E. GALIGNANO, tr. A. TOLVE and V. PERGOLA (Italian tr. of Fasani's commentary on the Our Father) (Lucera 1996). Literature about St Francesco Fasani: *Compendium vitae virtum et miraculorum necnon actorum in causa canonizationis beati Francisci A. Fasani, sacerdotis ordinis fratrum minorum conventualium* (Rome 1985). *L'Osservatore Romano*, English edition, no. 16 (1986): 3. A. ANGELINI, *Predestinata!* (Terni, Italy 1968). G. DE ANGELIS, *Prodigio di un sorriso* (Lucera 1991). L. M. BERARDINI, *Il Beato Francesco Antonio Fasani* (Rome 1951). R. COLAPIETRA, *Da Masaniello a Carlo di Borbone, I Convegno Nazionale di Studi su San Francesco A. Fasani* (Lucera 1989). L. DI FONZO, *L'immagine di S. Francesco nei Sermoni e nella vita del Fasani* (Bari 1986); *Santo di Lucera, Profilo cronologico di S. Francesco A. Fasani* (Bari 1986). I. DI GIOVINE, *San Francesco A. Fasani* (Lucera 1989). G. GUASTAMACCHIA, *Il bel San Francesco. La Chiesa del Padre Maestro*, ed. G. PREZIUSO (Lucera 1973). M. MARSICO, *Profilo storico e spirituale di San Francesco A. Fasani* (Rome 1986). B. NONNI, *Francesco Antonio Fasani dei Frati Minori Conventuali* (Lucera 1985). A. ORSITTO, *Il Santo dei poveri* (Lucera 1986). G. STANO, *La stella di Lucera* (Frigento, Italy 1986). T. TOLVE, *Padre Maestro: il cammino dell'amore* (Lucera 1987). G. TRINCUCCI, *Un Santo e la sua città* (Foggia 1988). R. ZAVALLONI, "San Francesco educatore," in *Pedagogia e vita* (Rome 1980). P. ZOLLA, *San Francesco A. Fasani* (Lucera 1986).

[K. RABENSTEIN]

FASCE, MARIA TERESA, BL.

Abbess of the Order of Saint Augustine; baptized Marietta; b. 27 December 1881, Torriglia (near Genoa), Italy; d. 18 January 1947, Cascia (near Perugia), Italy; beatified 12 October 1997.

Born into a wealthy family, Teresa served as a catechist in the Augustinian parish of Our Lady of Consolation, Genoa, where she became acquainted with the order's spirituality and captivated by the life of St. Rita of Cascia (canonized 1900 when Teresa was 19) Fasce joined the community in June 1906 and professed her vows the following year. She received permission for exclaustration (right to live outside the community) to reflect on her vocation. After 10 months with her family, she returned (1911) with a determination to renew the community. Thereafter she professed her solemn vows (1912) and served St. Rita's as novice mistress (1914–17), vicar (1917–20), and abbess (1920–47). She took in orphaned girls whom she called her little bees, which thus gave rise to the name of the orphanage, St. Rita's Hive, which is located next to the church. Fasce worked to relieve suffering in the area. Additionally, she helped to build a new church and nearby an Augustinian seminary, a hospital, and a retreat house. During the Second World War she courageously and repeatedly opposed the Nazis by denying them access to the convent and those under her protection. Her activity obscures her deeply contemplative vocation, which she encouraged within the community. She wrote the bulletin *Dalle api alle rose* (*From Bees to Roses* (from 1923) in order to spread devotion to St. Rita. Thereafter many pilgrims visited St. Rita's tomb. Mother Maria Teresa died peacefully after suffering for years from a breast tumor, diabetes, and various cardiac and circulatory problems, and was buried in the crypt of St. Rita's Basilica next to her patroness.

At the time of her beatification, John Paul II said of Mother Maria Teresa: "The Church holds her up today as a radiant example of the living synthesis between contemplative life and a humble witness of solidarity to men and women, especially to the poorest, the humble, the abandoned, and the suffering."

Feast: 18 January.

Bibliography: *Acta Apostolicae Sedis,* no. 20 (1997): 999. *L'Osservatore Romano,* English edition, no. 29 (1995): 5; no. 42 (1997):1, 2, 11. A. ANGELINI, *Predestinata!* (Terni, Italy 1968).

[K. RABENSTEIN]

FEBRES CORDERO MUÑOZ, MIGUEL FRANCISCO, ST.

Baptized Francisco, a.k.a. Miguel of Ecuador, scholar, author, philologist, poet, member of the Lasallian Institute of the Brothers of Christian Instruction, first Ecuadorian saint; b. 7 November 1854, Cuenca, Ecuador; d. 9 February 1910, Premia del Mar (near Barcelona), Spain; canonized by John Paul II, 21 October 1984.

The scion of a politically prominent family of Cuenca headed by Francisco Febres Cordero Montoya and Ana Muñoz, Francisco was among the first students of the Lasallian Brothers at Cuenca (1863). Franciso joined the Lasallian Brothers, in spite of the initial resistance of his family and a physical deformity that made walking difficult. He took the habit at Cuenca, 24 March 1868 at age thirteen, and took the name Brother Miguel, the first native Ecuadorian in the Institute. Following his formation, he became a beloved teacher of languages (Spanish, French, and English) at the order's schools at Cuenca, then Quito. His pedagogical skills led to his appointment as public examiner and inspector of Quito's schools. His passion, however, was teaching the catechism to boys preparing for the sacraments. Miguel published the first of his many textbooks, a Spanish grammar, when he was seventeen. His work in the fields of linguistics and literature won him acclaim as a scholar and membership in the National Academies of Ecuador (1892, which included membership in the Royal Academy of Spain), France (1900), and Venezuela (1906). He also authored a catechism and other pious works, including hymns. At a time boding civil unrest and religious persecution in France, he was assigned first to Paris (March 1907), then to the motherhouse at Lembecq-lez-Hal (near Brussels), Belgium (July 1907) to translate the Institute's documents into Spanish from French. Because the less temperate climate affected his health, he was transferred (1908) to the juniorate at Premia de Mar near Barcelona, where he was noted for his heroic efforts on behalf of his charges and the church during the July 1909 anarchist riots. Shortly thereafter, he contracted pneumonia and died. His body was returned to Quito at the start of the Spanish Civil War. The Ecuadorean government dedicated a monument to his honor in 1955. Miguel of Ecuador was beatified by Pope Paul VI 30 October 1977.

At Miguel's canonization, Pope John Paul II said: "He never hesitated to present and exacting and demanding Christianity to the young men sent to him." He is the patron of crippled children.

Feast: 9 February (Lasallian Brothers).

Bibliography: *Un religieux équatorien, frère Miguel de l'Institut des Frères des écoles chrétiennes, 1854–1910* (Lembecq-lez-Hal, Belgium 1913). G. CEVALLOS GARCÍA, *Salí tras tí, clamando, y eras ido* (Cuenca, Ecuador 1962). R. CRESPO TORAL, *El hermano Miguel de las escuelas cristiana* (Cuenca, Ecuador 1937). R. L. GUIDI, *Un cuore per la scuola: vita di fratel Miguel delle Scuole cristiane* (Vicenza 1977). E. MUÑOZ BORRERO, *Antología acerca del Hermano Miguel* (Cuenca, Ecuador 1967); *Un académico en los altares: el beato hermano Miguel de las Escuelas Cristianas* (Quito 1977). M. OLIVÉ, *San Miguel Febres Cordero—ese hermano: 21 de octubre de 1984, fiestas de la canonización* (Caracas, Venezuela 1984). L. PÁEZ FUENTES, *El hermano Miguel, maestro ejemplar* (Quito 1977); *Labor pedagógica, científica y literaria del hermano Miguel* (Quito 1991). L. SALM, *Brother Miguel Febres Cordero, F.S.C.: Teacher, Scholar, Saint* (Romeoville, Ill. 1984). *Acta Apostolicae Sedis* 78 (1986): 5–12. *L'Osservatore Romano*, English edition, no. 45 (1977): 3–9; no. 46 (1984): 6–7.

[K. RABENSTEIN]

FERNÁNDEZ SOLAR, TERESA DE LOS ANDES, ST.

Baptized Juana Enriquita Josefina de la Corazón Sagrada, known in religion as Teresa of Jesus, Discalced Carmelite mystic, victim soul; b. 13 July 1900, Santiago, Chile; d. 12 April 1920, Los Andes Carmel, Chile; both beatified (3 April 1987, Santiago) and canonized (21 March 1993, Rome) by Pope John Paul II.

Juana was one of seven children of Miguel Fernández Jaraquemada and Lucía Solar Armstrong. She vowed perpetual virginity at age fifteen (1915). Although she was often sick, upon completing her education at the finest schools in Santiago, Juana entered the Carmel of Los Andes and received the name Teresa of Jesus (7 May 1919) and began her novitiate five months later. At the beginning of March 1920, she predicted her impending death. After she fell gravely ill with typhus on Good Friday, 2 April 1920, arrangements were made for her to make her profession *in articulo mortis* on 6 April. She died six days later. She left behind numerous letters and a diary (*Historia de la vida de una de sus hijas,* 1917–20) filled with spiritual wisdom, the fruit of her intense prayer life and mystical gifts. Miracles began to occur at her tomb in Los Andes soon after her death.

When Pope John Paul II canonized Teresa as the first Chilean saint, he proposed her as a model for youth, saying that she is a shining witness to the precept "that it is in the loving, adoring, and serving God that the human creature finds greatness, joy, freedom, and fulfillment . . . particularly to the young people who hunger for the truth." She is a patroness of the sick.

Feast: 13 July.

Bibliography: *L'Osservatore Romano,* English edition, no. 18 (1987): 8–9.

[K. RABENSTEIN]

FERRARI, ANDREA CARLO, BL.

Cardinal; archbishop of Milan; founder of the Company of Saint Paul (*Compagnia di San Paolo*); b. 13 August 1850, Lalatta di Protopiano (diocese of Parma), Emilia-Romagna, Italy; d. 2 February 1921, Milan, Lombardy, Italy; beatified by John Paul II, 10 May 1987.

Son of Giuseppe Ferrari and Maddalena Langarine, Andrea received both his early education and seminary training at Parma, where he was ordained to the priesthood on 20 December 1873. Thereafter he was appointed vice-rector of Parma's seminary (1873), rector (1876), and cathedral canon (1878). He was named bishop of Guastalla (1890), then transferred to the diocese of Como, Lombardy (1891), where he proved himself a true "Father of Souls." Three years later he was made archbishop of Milan (1894) and created a cardinal. He founded the Company of Saint Paul for pastoral work, many churches, the Catholic University of the Sacred Heart, and charitable institutions. During World War I, Ferrari organized a group to care for soldiers and prisoners, for which he received the Grand Cross of Saints Maurizio and Lazarro (1919). He continued his pastoral work until death, even when bedridden.

At his beatification Pope John Paul II likened Ferrari's pastoral heart to that of the Good Shepherd and praised his fervent charity.

Feast: 1 February (Archdiocese of Milan)

Bibliography: G. CARACCIOLO, *La fede e le opere: la figura del cristiano nella pastorale del cardinal Ferrari e nella Compagnia di San Paolo* (Milan 1994). A. MAJO, *A. C. Ferrari: uomo di Dio, uomo di tutti* (Milan 1994); *Il Card. Ferrari, i cattolici e il catechismo nella scuola* (Milan 1995). L. MONTAGNA, *Il cardinale Andrea Carlo Ferrari e l'ora presente* (Milan 1969). G. PONZINI, *Il cardinale A.C. Ferrari a Milano, 1894–1921: fondamenti e linee del suo ministero episcopale* (Milan 1981). G. ROSSI, *Il cardinal Ferrari* (Assisi 1956). C. SNIDER, *L'episcopato del cardinale Andrea C. Ferrari* (Vicenza 1982). *Acta Apostolicae Sedis* (1987): 690. *L'Osservatore Romano*, English edition, no. 21 (1987): 18–19.

[K. RABENSTEIN]

FIESOLE, GUIDO DA (FRA ANGELICO), BL.

Known in history as Fra Angelico; baptised Guido di Pietro (his father's name was Pietro); also known as Guido da Fiesole and Giovanni da Fiesole (John Faesulanus); Dominican priest, Florentine painter; b. ca. 1386–87, near Vicchio di Mugello, Tuscany, Italy; d. 18 February 1455, La Minerva Friary, Rome.

Guido was already a recognized artist at age twenty, when he entered the Dominican monastery at Fiesole with his brother Benedetto. He took the religious name John of the Angels. Shortly thereafter, because of the Great Western Schism, Fra Giovanni and his brother (adherents to the Avignon claimant, Gregory XII) left Fiesole for the Dominican convent in Foligno, Umbria. The brothers moved to Cortonna to escape the pestilence that ravaged Foligno, and four years later made their way back to Fiesole where Giovanni remained the next sixteen years.

As a young friar he worked at illuminating manuscripts such as the *Dominican Diurnal 3* (Laurentian Library, Florence), while his brother completed an exquisite set of choir books. From 1409, he continued his studies and was ordained priest at Fiesole in 1418. In the 1440s, he was appointed prior of San Marco (Florence), which he decorated with his paintings, and held that office for three years. Pope Eugene IV wished to appoint him archbishop of Florence, but he declined in favor of Saint Antoninus.

Among his works are "Coronation of the Virgin" (Uffizi, Florence); "Last Judgment"; and "Deposition from the Cross" (1433, S. Marco Museum, Florence). He also painted the the frescoes in the cloister and cells of the remodeled monastery of S. Marco (1437), Florence.

During the last ten years of his life, Angelico was much in demand. In 1445, Eugene IV summoned him to the Vatican to work on the frescoes in the chapel of the Sacrament. These frescoes were later destroyed. In 1447, he began the "Last Judgment" frescoes in the S. Brixio Chapel, Orvieto cathedral (finished years later by Signorelli), but was summoned again to the Vatican by Nicholas V to paint scenes from the lives of SS. Stephen and Lawrence in the Nicholas Chapel. In 1449, he returned to Fiesole to become prior of San Domenico. He returned to Rome to finish work there, and it was there he died. The body of Bl. Fra Angelico now rests in S. Maria sopra Minerva, Rome.

John Paul II issued a *motu proprio,* 3 October 1982, granting a liturgical cultus to the Dominicans for Fra Angelico, long known as *il beato Angelico* because of his "angelic" moral virtues. The Holy Father wrote: "[E]ven today his art makes the way to God more accessible for us. And this is the purpose of sacred art. . . . the time has arrived to place him in his proper light in Church of God, to which he still continues to speak through his heavenly art." In 1984, he was declared patron of artists by Pope John Paul II.

Feast: 18 February (Dominicans)

Bibliography: *Acta Apostolicae Sedis* 75 (1983) 796–99. V. ALCE, *Angelicus pictor: vita, opere e teologia del Beato Angelico* (Bologna 1993). U. BALDINI, *Beato Angelico* (Florence 1986). K.

BERING, *Fra Angelico: Mittelalterlicher Mystiker oder Maler der Renaissance?* (Essen 1984). G. DIDI-HUBERMAN, *Fra Angelico: Dissemblance & Figuration*, tr. J. M. TODD (Chicago 1995). G. FALLANI, *Vita e opere di fra Giovanni Angelico* (Florence 1984). J. & M. GUILLAUD, *Fra Angelico: The Light of the Soul* (New York 1986). A. HERTZ, *Fra Angelico* (Freiburg im Breisgau 1981). J. W. POPE-HENNESSY, *Fra Angelico* (Riverside, N.Y. 1990). M. SALMI, *Il beato Angelico* (Spoleto 1958). J. T. SPIKE, *Fra Angelico* (New York 1996). C. B. STREHLKE, *Angelico* (Milan 1998). G. VASARI, *Lives of the Artists; biographies of the Most Eminent Painters, Sculptors and Architects of Italy,* abridged and edited by BETTY BURROUGHS (New York 1946).

[E. T. DE WALD/EDS.]

FRANCIA, ANNIBALE MARIA DI, BL.

Founder of the Rogationist Fathers of the Heart of Jesus and the Daughters of Divine Zeal, known as "the father of orphans and the poor"; b. 5 July 1851, Messina, Sicily, Italy; d. there 1 June 1927; beatified by John Paul II, 7 October 1990.

Annibale was the son of a noble family headed by Francis di Francia, Marquis of Santa Catarina, and his wife Anna Toscano. When Annibale was two, his father, who was papal vice-counsel to Pius IX, died. Stories about Annibale's days in a Cistercian boarding school (1858–66) describe acts of the heroic compassion which characterized his entire life. When the school was closed during the Revolution of 1866, the Sicilian poet Felice Bisazza tutored him. Annibale used his writing skills to compose articles for his uncle's periodical, *La Parola Catolica*, poetry (*The Hymns of July First*), prayers, and pamphlets.

At eighteen Annibale recognized his call to the priesthood. A month before his ordination (16 March 1878), he encountered a blind youth, Francis Zancone, who introduced him to the need for charity. Thereafter he joyfully dedicated himself to the spiritual and temporal relief of the most neglected, beginning in the neighborhood of Avignone in Messina. He established evening and boarding schools for boys, a kindergarten for girls, and orphanages dedicated to Saint Anthony of Padua (to whom Annibale later built a shrine in Messina). Like others who heroically give of themselves he encountered opposition, but received the support of his archbishop, Giacomo Cusmano, and John Bosco. For the physically poor, especially children in the Anthonian orphanages, he begged from door to door. For the spiritually poor he prayed "to the harvest master to send workers to the field" (Mt 9:38).

For the purpose of praying for vocations to the priesthood and religious life and for caring for needy children and the poor, Francia formed the Rogationists Fathers and Daughters of Divine Zeal. Melanie Calvat, one of the visionaries of La Salette, spent a year at the female institute (1897–98) helping Francia firmly establish it following some setbacks. Orphanages run by the sisters multiplied quickly after 1902 to meet each new crisis in Italy (e.g., earthquake, cholera, war). The Rogationists have expanded beyond the borders of Italy to other countries in Europe, Argentina, Brazil, India, the Philippines, Rwanda, and the United States. Additionally, to invite others to unite spiritually to pray for vocations, he established a Holy Alliance for bishops, prelates, and priests, as well as the Pious Union of Evangelical Prayer for laity.

For many years Annibale was the spiritual director for the writings of the Luisa Piccarreta (1865–1947; cause opened February 1994), who recorded private revelations on the Divine Will. Among the nineteen volumes to which he gave the *nihil obstat* were *The Virgin Mary in the Kingdom of the Divine Will* and *The Hours of the Passion of Our Lord Jesus Christ*.

Throughout his life Blessed Annibale conscientiously fulfilled his priestly obligations, showed Christ-like love to the most vulnerable, and trusted completely in Divine Providence. In beatifying Annibale di Francia, Pope John Paul II held him up to the Church as the "authentic precursor and zealous teacher of the modern pastoral ministry of vocations."

Feast: 31 May (Rogationists).

Bibliography: L. PICCARRETA, *The Clock of Passion*, ed. A. DI FRANCIA (Oria, Italy 1921). *Insegnamenti* 13, no. 2 (1990): 830. *L'Osservatore Romano,* English edition, no. 28 (1997): 9; no. 31 (1997): 1.

[K. RABENSTEIN]

FRASSATI, PIER GIORGIO, BL.

Lay youth, member of the Dominican Laity; b. 6 April 1901, Turin, Italy; d. there 4 July 1925; beatified by John Paul II, 20 May 1990.

Pier Giorgio Frassati, marked by youthful vitality, optimism, and charity, combined a love of politics, sports, outdoor life, study, and piety. His agnostic father, Alfredo Frassati, founder and owner of the liberal Turin daily *La Stampa*, was appointed senator of the Kingdom (1913). His mother, Adelaide Amelia, saw that her children received religious training. Pier Giorgio began his studies (1910) in the state school in Turin with his younger sister Luciana, but was later sent to the Jesuit school in 1913. The following year, he enrolled in the Apostleship of Prayer and the Company of the Most Blessed Sacrament. After graduating from high school (1918), he studied mineralogy in the Faculty of Industrial Mechanical Engineering at the Royal Polytechnic of Turin in order to ''serve Christ among the miners.'' At the university, he became active in many Christian groups. He joined the Italian Catholic Students Federation (1919), the St. Vincent de Paul Society (1919), the university Nocturnal Adoration Group (1920), the newly founded Popular Party (1921) that promoted Catholic teaching based on *Rerum Novarum*, and the *Milites Mariae* of the Young Catholic Workers (1922). He became a member of the Dominican Laity (1922), taking the name Girolama in honor of the Dominican Savanarola to the surprise of many who thought of him as a sportsman or political activist. During his father's tenure as Italian ambassador to Berlin (1920), Pier Giorgio worked with Father Karl Sonnenschein to seek out and assist the poor, just as he did in Turin. There he also became friendly with Karl Rahner and his family.

At the age of twenty-four, Frassati was stricken with acute poliomyelitis of which he died after five days of terrible suffering. On his deathbed he gave money and instructions to his sister to continue to see to the needs of the families dependent upon his charity. Thousands of the poor he had helped without public knowledge attended his funeral. His cause for beatification was opened in 1932 but suffered delays. On 16 July 1989, Pope John Paul II prayed at Frassati's tomb in Pollone. It has since been translated to Turin's cathedral.

Pope John Paul II beatified ''the man of the eight beatitudes'' saying: ''The secret of his apostolic zeal and holiness is . . . in prayer, in persevering adoration, even at night, of the Blessed Sacrament, in his thirst for the Word of God, which he sought in Biblical texts; in the peaceful acceptance of life's difficulties, in family life as well; in chastity lived as a cheerful, uncompromising discipline; in his daily love of silence and life's 'ordinariness.''' Patron of youth.

Feast: 4 July (Turin).

Bibliography: F. ANTONIOLI, *Pier Giorgio Frassati* (Rome 1985). C. CASALEGNO, *Una vita di carità* (Casale Monferrato 1990). R. CLAUDE, *Le rayonnement de Pier-Giorgio Frassati, d'après les ''Testimonianze'' de don Cojazzi* (Tournai 1946). A. COJAZZI, *Pier Giorgio Frassati*, tr. H. L. HUGHES (London 1933); *Pier Giorgio Frassati: testimonianze* (Turin 1977). R. FECHTER, *Frassati; leben eines jungen katholiken in dieser zeit* (Munich 1935). L. FRASSATI, *La carità di Pier Giorgio* (Rome 1951); *Mon frère Pier Giorgio; les dernières heures* (Paris 1952); *L'impegno social, e giudizi sul carattere* (Rome 1953); *Mio fratello Pier Giorgio; vita e immagini* (Genoa 1959); *Mio fratello Pier Giorgio; la morte* (Turin 1960); *Pier Giorgio Frassati, i giorni della sua vita* (Rome 1975); *Il cammino di Pier Giorgio* (Milan 1990). G. A. SCALTRITI, *Pier Giorgio Frassati e il suo Savonarola* (Rome 1979).

[K. RABENSTEIN]

FRASSINELLO, BENEDETTA CAMBIAGIO, BL.

Married woman, foundress of the Benedictine Sisters of Providence *(Benedettine della Provvidenza);* b. 2 October 1791, Langasco (near Genoa), Italy; d. 21 March 1858, Ronco Scrivia, Italy; beatified at Rome by John Paul II, 10 May 1987.

She was the daughter of Giuseppe and Francesca Cambiagio, who moved to Pavia while Benedetta was still young. Following a mystical experience in 1811, Benedetta wanted to devote herself to prayer in a convent, but instead she complied with her family's wishes and married Giovanni Battista Frassinello (7 February 1816). In 1818, the couple agreed to live together in perpetual continence while caring for Benedetta's younger sister Maria, who suffered from intestinal cancer. Following her death (1825), they both chose to enter religious life: Giovanni joined the Somachi, while Benedetta took the habit of the Ursulines. Illness forced Benedetta to leave the convent and return to Pavia, where she decided to help abandoned girls. Giovanni left his monastery also to assist her in this task. Although Benedetta was appointed ''Promoter of Public Instruction'' and they publicly vowed perfect chastity, the couple suffered criticism for their unusual relationship. That impelled them to turn over their work to the bishop (1838) and retire to the village of Ronco Scrivia. In 1833, with her husband and five companions, Benedetta founded the educational Institute of Benedictine Sisters of Providence, which continues its work in Italy and Peru.

Feast: 10 May.

Bibliography: G. GUDERZO, I problemi socioeconomici di Pavia 'restaurata' e la risposta religiosa di Benedetta Cambiagio Frassinello, *Studi e fonti di Storia lombarda. Quaderni milanesi* 17–18 (1989) 56–73. *ActApS* (1987) 690. *OssRomEng* 21 (1987) 18–19.

[K. RABENSTEIN]

FRASSINETTI, PAOLA ANGELA MARIA, ST.

Also Paula; foundress of the Congregation of Sisters of St. Dorotea (Dorotheans); b. 3 March 1809, Genoa, Italy; d. 11 June 1882, Rome; canonized 11 March 1984.

The only daughter of the five children of John and Angela Frassinetti, Paola's four brothers became priests. When her mother died in 1818, her aunt took charge of the family until her own death in 1821. After that, Paola cared for the household. She was educated at home by her father and brothers. Bronchial problems caused her to go to Quinto al Mare (Genova) in 1830, where she lived with her brother (Ven.) Giuseppe Frassinetti, a priest. She served as the parish housekeeper and taught the local girls. When Paola's ill health frustrated her attempts to join a religious congregation, she founded her own institute, the Dorotheans, at St. Clara's (12 Aug. 1834), which was dedicated to the education of girls from all walks of life. After difficult early years, the institute received papal approval in 1863. Paola remained superior general until her death; after 1841 she resided in Rome. She saw the Dorotheans spread through Italy and abroad to Portugal and Brazil.

In 1876, Frassinetti suffered the first of several paralyzing strokes. She died peacefully of pneumonia at the mother house, St. Onofrio in Rome, where she is buried. She is patroness of the sick.

During her canonization Mass Pope John Paul II declared: "She was convinced that whoever wants to undertake a path to perfection cannot renounce the Cross, mortification, humiliation, and suffering, which assimilate the Christian to the divine model, who is Crucified."

Feast: 11 June.

Bibliography: *Acta Apostolicae Sedis* 77 (1985): 923–928. *L'Osservatore Romano,* English edition, no. 13 (1984): 3. H. CASHIN, *A Great Servant of God, Mother Paola Frassinetti . . .* (Staten Island, N.Y. 1951). H. TRINKLER, *Die andere Möglichkeit* (Freiburg, Switzerland 1977). J. UNFREVILLE, *A Foundress in 19th Century Italy: Blessed Paula Frassinetti and the Congregation of the Sisters of St. Dorothy* (New York 1944).

[F. G. SOTTOCORNOLA]

FRELICHOWSKI, STEFAN WINCENTY, BL.

Diocesan priest, martyr; b. 22 January 1913, Chelmza, Poland; d. 23 February 1945 in the concentration camp at Dachau (near Munich), Germany; beatified at Torun, Poland, by John Paul II, 7 June 1999.

As a Polish Scout prior to his entry into the seminary, Stefan "acquired a particular sensitivity to the needs of others" (John Paul II, beatification homily). He was ordained a priest in 1937. He was working at his first assignment as a parish priest at Torun when he was arrested with several other priests by the Gestapo and soon released after a few days. On 18 October 1939, he was again stopped and sent to Oranienburg-Sachsenhauusen. Over the course of the next fourteen months, he was transferred successively to "Fort Seven," Stutthof, Grenzdorf, Oranienburg-Sachsenhausen, and finally Dachau (13 December 1940). At each stop along the way, Frelichowski witnessed to the love of Christ through his

humble service to others. During the typhus epidemics at Dachau (1944–45), he risked his life to bring forbidden material and spiritual comfort to the afflicted and dying until he himself contracted the disease, then developed pneumonia. He died in the camp hospital at age thirty-two—just two months before the end of the war. The decree of Frelichowski's martyrdom was signed on 26 March 1999.

Pope John Paul II chose to beatify Frelichowski in the city where two peace treaties were signed and a colloquium was held between Catholics and Calvinists because he was a peacemaker. The pope said: "He generously shared peace with others because his soul drew strength from the peace of Christ. And that strength was so great that not even death as a martyr was able to crush it" (beatification homily).

Bibliography: *Acta Apostolicae Sedis* (1999): 639–40.

[K. RABENSTEIN]

FRIEDHOFEN, PETER, BL.

Chimney-sweep; founder of the Brothers of Charity of Mary Help of Christians; b. 25 February 1819, Weitersburg (near Koblenz am Rhein), Germany; d. 21 December 1860, Koblenz; beatified by John Paul II, 23 June 1985.

A year after Peter's birth, his father died leaving his wife to provide for seven children. Each of the children had to begin earning money for the family as soon as they were able. Peter, next to the youngest, and his older brother Jacob traveled around the region sweeping chimneys. Jacob died leaving a wife and eleven children whom Peter tried to assist financially. While continuing his work, Peter began to engage in his vocation—caring for the helpless, especially children. He established charitable projects in Adenau, Cochem, and Wittlich. From these charities evolved the Order of Brothers of Mercy of Mary the Helper (founded 1849) for the service of the poor, the sick, and the aged. Once Peter and his companion Karl Marchand were trained by the Alexian Brothers, adapted their Rule, and had the order's constitution approved by Bishop Arnoldi of Trier (2 July 1848), the Brothers of Mercy opened their first house (21 June 1850). The first brothers received the religous habit in 1851. The bishop of Trier and president of the Rheinland patronized the order and assisted in its work. At the time of Friedhofen's death from tuberculosis, the congregation had spread throughout Europe and into Brazil, China, and Malaysia. His body was interred at Trier am Mosel.

Pope John Paul II said that Peter Friedhofen demonstrated "a love that knew no limits in its universal sacrifice of self" (beatification homily).

Bibliography: *Acta Apostolicae Sedis* (1985) 784. *L'Osservatore Romano,* Eng. ed. 29 (1985): 6–7.

[K. RABENSTEIN]

GABRIEL, COLOMBA JOANNA, BL.

Baptized Joanna Matylda (Matilda) Gabriel; Benedictine nun; foundress of the Oblates of Saint Benedict and the Benedictine Sisters of Charity (*Sororum Ord. S. Benedicti a Caritate*); b. 3 May 1858, Stanislawow, Poland (now Ivano-Frankivsk, Ukraine); d. 24 September 1926, Centacelle (suburb of Rome), Italy; beatified by John Paul II, 16 May 1993.

Joanna, born into the Polish nobility, was known in her time as "a woman born for love." She received her education locally and at Leopoldi, where she joined the Benedictines and became Sister Colomba. Called to serve poor working girls, she transferred to Rome (1900), spent time at Subiaco (1902), then returned to Rome (1903). Under the spiritual direction of Dominican Hyacinth Cormier, Sister Colomba taught catechism and began visiting the sick and poor of the Roman Prati district. She gathered lay people to assist in her ministry, who became the Benedictine Oblates. In 1908, Colomba established the religious Benedictine Sisters of Charity to open homes and operate charitable programs for the needy of Rome. With the patronage of Italian Queen Elena, Pope Saint Pius X and Pope Benedict XV, the congregation expanded throughout Italy, to Romania and Madagascar.

Pope John Paul II recalled at her beatification: "On the path of suffering the Holy Spirit uprooted [Colomba] from her homeland, led her to leave everything and begin all over."

Bibliography: *Acta Apostolicae Sedis* (1993): 601–03.

[K. RABENSTEIN]

GALAND, AGNÈS OF JESUS, BL.

A.k.a. Agnès de Langeac; Dominican nun; mystic; b. 17 November 1602, Puy-en-Velay (near Langeac), France; d. 19 October 1634, Langeac; beatified by John Paul II, 20 November 1994.

Agnès, a vivacious and generous child, was educated by the Sisters of the Holy Virgin. She entered the Domin-

ican convent at Langeac (1623) and, displaying the enthusiam that characterized her early life, was elected prioress in 1627. In accordance with her understanding of God's will revealed through a vision of the Virgin Mary (1631), Sister Agnès used her gift of prayer and her hidden penances for the good of Jean Jacques Olier, abbot of Prébrac, who was then a young priest living irresponsibly and whom she had never met. She is said to have bilocated (1634) to the Church where Father Olier was praying during a retreat under the direction of Saint Vincent de Paul. She met Olier just before her death. Twenty years later he founded the Sulpicians.

Pope John Paul II said during her beatification that Agnès de Langeac "was able, without the slightest reservation, to enter into God's plan for her, offering her intellect, will, and freedom to the Son of Man, that he might transform them and harmonize them totally with his own!"

Feast: 19 October (Dominicans).

Bibliography: *Mère Agnès de Langeac et son temps: une mystique dominicaine au grand siècle des âmes: actes du colloque du Puy* (Le Puy, France 1986). J. BOUFLET, *Petite vie de Agnès de Langeac* (Paris 1994). M. J. DORCY, *Saint Dominic's Family* (Dubuque, Iowa 1964) 386–87. E. PANASSIÈRE, *Mémoires sur la vie d'Agnès de Langeac* (Paris 1994). R. DE TRYON-MONTALEMBERT, *Agnès de Langeac: "Qui a Dieu a tout"* (Paris 1994).

[K. RABENSTEIN]

GALVÃO DE FRANÇA, ANTÔNIO DE SANT'ANA, BL.

Franciscan priest; founder; b. 1739, Guaratinguetá, São Paulo, Brazil; d. 23 December 1822, São Paulo; beatified at Rome, Italy, 25 October 1998, the first Brazilian native *beatus*.

Antonio's socially prominent, devout father encouraged his son's religious vocation by sending him to study (1752–56) at the Jesuit seminary of Belém. Eventually, Antonio entered novitiate of the Alcantarine Franciscans at Macacu near Rio de Janeiro (1760), professed his solemn vows (1761), and was ordained priest (1762). Upon completing his studies (1768), he was appointed porter at St. Francis Friary in São Paulo and engaged in priestly ministry. While serving as chaplain to the Recollects of St. Teresa (1769–70), Father Galvão met the mystic Sister Helena Maria Espirito Santo. With her he founded the convent of Our Lady of the Conception of the Divine Providence in 1774, a women's religious community that initially required no vows. Following Helena's death (1775), he continued to nurture the community—the *Recolhimento de Nossa Senhora da Luz* (Recollects of Our

Lady of Light)—by writing its rule, ensuring the completion of its convent and church (dedicated in 1802), and guiding its incorporation into the Order of the Immaculate Conception (1929). In addition to this work, Galvão served as novice master in Macacu (1781), guardian of St. Francis Friary in São Paulo (1798, 1801), definitor (1802), visitator general, and chapter president (1808); he founded St. Clara Friary in Sorocaba (1811). Above all, he responded to his religious vocation by caring for the poor, sick, afflicted, and enslaved. In his declining years the priest lived at the Recolhimento da Luz, where his mortal remains are enshrined in its church. On 8 March 1997, he was declared venerable.

Pope John Paul II called Galvão "a fervent worshiper of the Eucharist, a teacher and defender of Christian charity, a prudent counselor for the spiritual life, and a defender of the poor" (beatification homily).

Feast: 25 October.

Bibliography: C. E. MARCONDES DE MOURA, *Os Galvao de França no povoamento de Santo Antonio de Guaratinguetá* (Sao Paulo 1993). V. WILLEKE, *Franciscanos na história do Brasil* (Petrópolis, Brazil 1977). *L'Osservatore Romano,* English edition, no. 43 (1998): 3

[K. RABENSTEIN]

GAPP, JAKOB, BL.

Priest of the Society of Mary (SM); b.Wattens, Tyrol, western Austria, 26 July 1897; d. Plötzensee Prison, Berlin, Germany, 13 August 1943; beatified by Pope John Paul II on 24 November 1996; feast: 13 August (Society of Mary); Beatified 24 November 1996, in St. Peter's Basilica.

Jakob Gapp, the seventh child of Martin Gapp and Antonia Wach, completed secondary school under the tutelage of the Franciscans at Hall, Tyrol. During World War I Gapp served in the military on the Italian front; received the silver medal of Courage Second Class after being wounded in 1916; and was a prisoner of war at in the Italian Piedmont from 4 Nov. 1918 to 18 Aug. 1919.

After, Gapp made his vows as a Marianist at Greisinghof, Upper Austria, he worked for four years in Graz. He entered the seminary at Fribourg, Switzerland, where he was ordained on 5 April 1930. His first eight years as a priest, Gapp worked as a primary school teacher, director of religious education, and chaplain in Marianist schools in Austria.

During the depression following World War I, he collected and distributed food and funds to those in need, and helped the unemployed to find jobs. He refused to heat his own room in winter in order to give his allotment of coal to poor families. This sense of justice led to his final demise.

Gapp came to recognize the incompatibility of National Socialism and Christianity after reading Nazi publications, particularly Alfred Rosenberg's *Myth of the Twentieth Century,* the statements of the Austrian bishops, and Pius XI's encyclical *Mit brennender Sorge.* He boldly denounced the "abhorrent and totally irreconcilable" ideology when German troops occupied Austria in March 1938. Because of his notoriety as an enemy of Nazism, in October 1938, the Gestapo forbade him to teach. Despite the ban, he continued to advise parishioners to ignore German propaganda and defended Pope Pius XI against Nazi slander in a sermon on 11 Dec. 1938. Advised to leave Austria, Gappe served as librarian and chaplain at the Marianist motherhouse in Bordeaux for several months before being reassigned to Spain (May 1939). In Spain Gapp found himself isolated among the Marianists because his confrères could not understand his insistence that Catholics must vocally oppose injustice in all forms, particularly that of the Nazis. During his three years in Spain, Gapp was transferred to San Sebastián, Cádiz, Lequeitio, and finally Valencia.

In August 1942 Gapp received messages from two German agents posing as refugee Jews from Berlin in need of his help. They were living just across the border at Hendaye in southern France. When he drove over the border to meet them on 9 November, Gapp was immediately arrested by the Gestapo. He was detained at several French prisons before being taken to Berlin. There he was tried before the infamous *Volksgerichtshof* and condemned to death on 2 July 1943 on the charge of high treason. The sentence specified that his remains were not to be returned to his family for burial because Gapp had "defended his conduct on expressly religious grounds. For a religious people Fr. Gapp would be considered a martyr for the faith, and his burial could be used by the Catholic population as an opportunity for a silent demonstration in support of an already judged traitor. . . .''

In the six hours between being informed of his execution and his decapitation by guillotine, Gapp wrote moving letters to his superior and his family. Gapp's body was sent to the Anatomical-Biological Institute of the Univ. of Berlin on the grounds that it would be used for research. The only known relic is the ring Gapp received upon his religious profession, which is kept in the Marianist novitiate at Greisinghof, Austria. Gapp was respected even by his enemies. Himmler had remarked to Gapp's judge that Germany would easily win if there were more party members as committed to the cause as Gapp was to his Christian faith.

Feast: 13 August (Society of Mary).

Bibliography: *Blessed Jakob Gapp, Marianist* (Dayton, Ohio: North American Center for Marianist Studies, 1999).

L'Osservatore Romano, English edition, no. 48 (1996). J. M. SALAVERRI, *Jakob Gapp Martyr de la Foi* (Saint-Augustin 1997).

[K. RABENSTEIN]

GÁRATE, FRANCISCO, BL.

Jesuit brother, affectionately called "Brother Courtesy"; b. 3 February 1857, Azpeitia (near Loyola Castle), Spain; d. 9 September 1929, Bilboa, Spain; beatified by John Paul II, 6 October 1985.

Francisco Gárate, the second of eleven siblings, was raised in a devout farming family in which three sons became Jesuits. He entered domestic service (1871) as a house servant at the new Jesuit College of Nuestra Señora de la Antigua at Orduña. Because the Jesuits had been expelled from Spain (1868), Francisco sought entrance into the Society of Jesus (1874) at the novitiate in Poyanne in southern France. After professing his initial vows in 1876 and spending another another year in Poyanne, he was assigned as infirmarian and sacristan (1877–87) at the College of Santiago Apostolo in La Guardia, Pontevedra in western Spain, where he was known for his extreme kindness. He professed his final vows in August 1887. In March 1888, he was transferred to Bilbao in northern Spain because his service in the infirmary was affecting his health. For the next forty-one years, Brother Francisco was doorkeeper at the Jesuit university in Duesto Bilbao. There he became renowned for the evangelizing power of his humble, joyful service to all he encountered.

In beatifying Gárate, Pope John Paul II honored Brother Francisco's Christian perfection in the way of humble service.

Feast: 10 September (Jesuits).

Bibliography: J. ITURRIOZ, *H. Francisco Garate, S.I.: "Portero" de Deusto* (Bilbao 1985). J. A. DE SOBRINO, *Tres que dijeron 'si'* (Madrid 1985). *Acta Apostolicae Sedis* 79 (1987): 7–10. *L'Osservatore Romano,* English edition, no. 42 (1985): 6–7.

[K. RABENSTEIN]

GATTORNO, ROSA MARIA BENEDETTA, BL.

A.k.a. Anna Rosa Gattorno, widow, mother, founder of the Institute of Daughters of St. Anne; b. 14 October 1841, Genoa, Italy; d. 6 May 1900, Rome; beatified by Pope John Paul II, 9 April 2000.

One of six children born to Francesco Gattorno and Adelaide Campanella, Rosa was educated at home. She married her cousin Gerolamo Custo (5 November 1852) and gave birth to three children (1853–57). Gerolamo's death from tuberculosis (1858) left her with continued financial problems and a sickly, deaf-mute eldest daughter. Her youngest child died the same year. Though grief-stricken, Rosa offered herself in charitable service and care of her two surviving children. She privately vowed perpetual chastity and obedience (1858), then added a vow of poverty (1861). Even during her marriage, Rosa grew spiritually through daily communion and the gift of a hidden stigmata. As her reputation for holiness increased, she was chosen president of the Pious Union of the New Ursulines Daughters of Mary Immaculate and revised its rule (1864).

This revision led her to consider founding a new religious order, but she was torn between her duty to her children and her new heightened sense of religious vocation. She sought advice from her confessor, the archbishop of Genoa, St. Francis of Camporosso and Pope Pius IX (1866), and then decided to establish the Institute of Daughters of St. Anne. The new foundation was made in Piacenza, 8 December 1866, with the help of Giovanni Battista Tornatore, C.M. Rosa received the habit in 1867 and was professed with eleven other sisters in 1870. The institute, dedicated to working with disadvantaged youth, received approval in 1879, as did the rule in 1892. She collaborated with Bl. Giovanni Battista Scalabrini in ministering to the speech- and hearing-impaired. She contracted a virulent influenza in February 1900, died the following month, and was buried in the church adjoining the generalate.

The institute expanded before and after Mother Rosa's death throughout Europe to South America, Africa, the Middle East, Asia and Oceania, where the sisters have been engaging in evangelization, catechesis, and assistance to the poor including drug rehabilitation centers, schools, daycare centers, and homes for the elderly. Her charism has expanded to include contemplative sisters, an association of priests (Sons of St. Anne), a secular institute, and a lay association (Movement of Hope).

At her beatification, John Paul II said Rosa "transformed her life in one continuous immolation for the conversion of sinners and the sanctification of all. Trusting providence totally, and inspired by a courageous impulse of charity, she had only one end: to serve Jesus in his suffering members, and in the wounds of her neighbor, with sensitivity and maternal attention."

Feast: 6 May.

Bibliography: *L'Osservatore Romano,* English edition, no. 16 (2000): 3.

[K. RABENSTEIN]

GÉRARD, JOSEF VALENCIA, BL.

Oblate missionary priest; b. 12 March 1831, Boux-ières-aux-Chênes (near Nancy), France; d. 29 May 1914, Roma, Lesotho, Africa; beatified at Maseru, Lesotho, by John Paul II, 15 September 1988.

Josef, son of the peasants Jean Gérard and Ursula Stofflet, studied at Pont-à-Mousson and Nancy seminary (1851–52) before pronouncing his final vows as an oblate of Mary Immaculate (1852). After completing his studies at Marseilles, he left for Natal (1853), South Africa, where he was ordained nearby at Pietermaritzburg (February 1854). His first efforts as a missionary among the Zulus was unsuccessful. In 1862, he travelled on horse-back to establish a mission in Basutoland (now Lesotho) at the "Village de la Mère de Jésus" (also known as Roma). There he won the heart of the great warrior king Moshoeshoe, baptized his first converts (1865), and established a flourishing school and convent. He labored alone to found St. Monica's Mission in the northern part of the country (1876), before returning to Roma in 1898. The Basuthos remember Gérard as a man whose prayer led him to care for the sick and weak.

After praying at Gérard's tomb in Maseru, Pope John Paul II described this "servant of reconciliation and peace" as "a missionary eager to understand souls" (beatification homily).

Bibliography: *Father Joseph Gérard, O.M.I., Speaks to Us from South Africa and Lesotho, 1854–1914*, ed. M. FERRAGNE, tr. G. BROSSARD (Maseru, Lesotho 1980). J. MORABITO, *Jamais plus comme lui! : vie et vertus du serviteur de Dieu, le père Joseph Gérard* (Rome 1980). *Acta Apostolicae Sedis* (1988): 961.

[K. RABENSTEIN]

GERHARDINGER, KAROLINA ELIZABETH FRANCES, BL.

In religious life, Maria Theresia of Jesus, Theresa of Jesus, foundress of the School Sisters of Notre Dame; b. 20 June 1797, Stadtamhof (near Regensburg), Bavaria, Germany; d. 9 May 1879, Munich, Bavaria, Germany.

Karolina was the only child of Willibald Gerhardinger, a ship-master on the Danube, and Frances Huber. She attended the cloister school of the Congregation de Notre Dame until they were forced to disband by government order in 1809. Michael Wittmann, cathedral pastor and later bishop of Regensburg, continued the King's School for Girls with three apprentice teachers, including Karolina. At 15 she received her government certificate and began teaching in the parish school at Stadtamhof. At 18 she told the bishop she would like to become a nun.

Only then did he reveal his wish to see founded the kind of religious institute that St. Peter Fourier had planned but that the Church and the world of the 17th century had been unready to accept—a community of teaching sisters who would not be confined to monasteries and thus could teach in poor villages.

Rev. Matthias Siegert, who was commissioned by Bishop Wittmann to study the new pedagogy pioneered by Pestalozzi, became educational and spiritual director of the new congregation, in which Karolina's "Teresian spirit" flowered and her teaching genius matured. Only in 1833 was she allowed to take her vows, after the state and ecclesiastical authorities were convinced her community could maintain itself. Gerhardinger opened the first house in Neunburg vom Wald (Oberpfalz) joined by two other women, Maria Blass and Barbara Weinzierl. They lived a common life in poverty dedicated to the Blessed Virgin Mary, the model for her sisters and young girls. The congregation received episcopal sanction in 1834 and spread quickly to small towns and villages throughout Germany, 13 other European countries, and abroad. In 1843 the mother house was established at Munich in a convent given to them by King Louis Philippe. In 1847, Mother Gerhardinger and 5 sisters migrated to the mountains of Pennsylvania to teach children of German immigrants. Although they were unwelcome there, St. John Neumann paved the way for a better reception in Baltimore. In America they endured hunger and other hardships, but nevertheless spread throughout the eastern U.S. After 2 years in the U.S. Gerhardinger returned to Bavaria.

Gerhardinger pioneered a new form of religious life. The sisters were sent out in twos or threes so that they could serve in many small communities. Mother Maria Theresia insisted that the sisters be allowed to direct themselves under a central government, rather than being placed under the control of the local bishop, in order to maintain a common spirituality without a physical community life. Although the sisters found opposition to the new concept, the institute was formally recognized by the Vatican in 1854. Pope Pius IX in 1865 approved the constitution which was the first to allow a sister to govern the members of the women's congregation. For the rest of her life she actively fostered the education of girls and oversaw the growth of her community. Pope John Paul II beatified her 17 November 1985 and named her patron of Christian educators.

Feast: 9 May.

Bibliography: *Acta Apostolicae Sedis* 79 (1987): 243–247. *L'Osservatore Romano,* English edition, no. 47 (1985). F. FRIESS, *Life of Reverend Mother Mary Teresa of Jesus Gerhardinger* (Baltimore 1921). C. GRÖN, *Eine Frau steht am Steuer* (Munich 1962).

M. D. MAST, *Through Caroline's Consent* (Baltimore 1958). *Mother Caroline and the School Sisters of Notre Dame in North America*, 2 v. (St. Louis 1928). T. SCHMIDKONZ, *Du Gott. Gebets-Meditationen zu Worten von M. Theresia von Jesu Gerhardinger* (St. Ottilien, Germany, 1985). *Selige Theresia von Jesu Gerhardinger (1797–1879): ein Leben für Kirche und Schule zum 200. Geburtstag . . .* (Regensburg 1997).

[M. D. MAST]

GIACCARDO, TIMOTEO GIUSEPPE DOMENICO VICENZO ANTONIO, BL.

Baptized Giuseppe Domenico Vicenzo Antonio (Joseph Dominic Vincent Anthony) Giaccardo, publisher, Pauline priest, founder of the Pious Disciples of the Divine Master; b. 13 June 1896, Narzole (diocese of Alba), Cuneo, Italy; d. 24 January 1948, at Rome; beatified 22 October 1989.

His parents were peasant farmers who began instilling in their son a strong spirit of prayer from infancy. Giaccardo met Fr. James Alberione, founder of the Society of St. Paul, while serving Mass at St. Bernard's Church in Narzole in 1908. Giaccardo entered the diocesan seminary in Alba (1917), but he received his bishop's permission to join the Paulines, despite the bishop's initial caution about the new society. Giaccardo was ordained in 1919 as the first priest of the new order, taking the name Timothy upon his profession in 1920.

Giaccardo's ministry consisted of writing, editing, and distributing religious material. In addition, he helped in the formation of younger members of the order as a teacher of theology and served as vocation director. In 1926, he was entrusted with founding the society's first house in Rome. There he edited the weekly *The Voice of Rome* and managed the pressroom. He was recalled to Alba to direct the motherhouse, but sent back to Rome in 1946 as provincial superior of the Society of St. Paul and vicar general of the congregation. Recognizing the importance of prayer to support the active ministries of the Pauline Family, he established the nucleus of the contemplative branch, the Sister Disciples of the Divine Master. When the Holy See opposed the division of the Daughters of St. Paul, Giaccardo was given the delicate task of persuading Vatican authorities to approve the community, which happened in 1948.

Although Giaccardo was Alberione's chosen successor, he died shortly after the approbation of the new contemplative order. His body was laid to rest in the lower crypt of the Basilica of Mary, Queen of Apostles, next to the house he founded.

During the beatification Mass, John Paul II declared: "Timothy Giaccardo, the first disciple of Father Alber-

ione, interpreted fidelity to his own priestly vocation as proclaiming the Gospel through the press, thereby having an even broader and deeper effect on his brothers and sisters. Thus he proposed to spread the Gospel and the Church's teaching through the modern means of social communication, which he saw as the principal and typical apostolate of the modern world.'' He is the patron of publishers.

Feast: 22 October.

Bibliography: E. FORNASARI, *Bl. Timothy Giaccardo: An Obedient Prophet*, tr. K. D. WHITEHEAD (New York 1991). G. PAPÀSOGLI, *Il beato Timoteo Giaccardo della Società San Paolo* (Turin 1989).

[K. RABENSTEIN]

GIMÉNEZ MALLA, CEFERINO, BL.

A.k.a. "El Pele," married gypsy, martyr, lay Franciscan; b. 26(?) August 1861, Fraga, Huesca, Catalonia, Spain; d. 9 August 1936, in the cemetery of Barbastro, Spain; beatified by John Paul II, 4 May 1997, as the first gypsy and second lay martyr of the Spanish Civil War.

Ceferino (Zeferino) was one of over 500,000 gypsies to suffer racial and religious persecution in the 20th century. Following his marriage to Teresa Giménez Castro of Lérida, Ceferino moved with his new wife to Barbastro. The marriage, a gypsy union that was regularized in 1912 in the Catholic Church, resulted in no children of their own, but the couple adopted Teresa's niece Pepita. A successful horse trader, Giménez used his negotiating skills to settled disputes and gained a reputation for fairness. He was also known for his charity and piety. Ceferino's illiteracy and humility belied his great wisdom, which led even his bishop, Blessed Florentino ASENSIO BARROSO, who was martyred hours after Ceferino and beatified with him, to seek his counsel. He was a member of the city council of Barbastro and, as one of the first 159 Franciscan tertiaries of Barbastro (initiated by the Capuchins in 1926), elected to the advisory council of the society. Ceferino was arrested for defending a young priest who was being harassed. During his 15-day imprisonment in the Capuchin friary with 350 other detainees, Ceferino incited the guards by daily praying the Rosary. Despite the intervention of Eugenio Sopena, an influential member of the revolutionary committee and Ceferino's neighbor, he was shot by a Republican firing squad for refusing to renounce his faith. Eighteen others, mainly priests and religious, died with him and were buried in unmarked graves. Ceferino's cause was opened in Barbastro in 1993, and the decree of martyrdom was issued in Rome on 17 December 1996.

When Pope John Paul II beatified Ceferino, he noted that his life "shows the presence of Christ in diverse people and races and that all are called to holiness'' (beatification homily). Patron of gypsies.

Feast: 4 May.

Bibliography: *L'Osservatore Romano,* Eng. ed. 42 (1995): 8.

[K. RABENSTEIN]

GRANDE ROMÁN, JUAN, ST.

In religion Juan (Grande) Pecador (John the (Great) Sinner), religious of the Hospitaller Brothers of St. John of God; b. 6 March 1546, Carmona (near Seville), Andalusia, Spain; d. 3 June 1600, Jerez de la Frontera (near Cadiz), Spain; canonized in Rome by Pope John Paul II, 2 June 1996.

Like his father before him, Juan Grande was a cloth merchant in Carmona until he left home to discern his vocation in solitude near Marcena. Upon discovering God's will for his life, Grande moved to Jerez de la Frontera (1566). He tended prisoners and the elderly poor, first in a room off the chapel of La Virgen de los Remedios, then in a hospital (Nuestra Señora de la Candelaria) that he established next to the Church of San Sebastian. He became known for his extreme austerity, intense prayer life, and service to anyone in need including prisoners, prostitutes, and even 300 fugitive Spanish soldiers after the English stormed Cadiz. During an epidemic in 1574, he successfully mounted a campaign to help victims that involved many people, even the city council. That same year he adopted the rule of the Hospitallers of St. John of God and gathered others to assist in his apostolate. In 1576, he took the habit of the Hospitallers and transferred Candelaria into their hands. At the request of Bishop Rodrigo de Castro of Seville, he reorganized the local hospital system to provide better care to the poor. He contracted the plague ravaging Jerez in 1600 and offered himself to God in atonement. The epidemic ended with his death in Candelaria Hospital. He was originally buried in the hospital courtyard, but later translated to his titular shrine in the hospital of the Brothers of St. John of God in Jerez.

During the canonization Mass, John Paul II said Grande's prayer nourished him: "[He] found God, loved him, felt himself loved, and in the heart of God, the Father of all, he loved all the needy . . . begging for all, knocking at doors, saying that it is impossible to be indifferent to the fate of the poor and that serving them is 'a question of conscience.'" He is patron of Jerez.

Feast: 3 June.

Bibliography: *L'Osservatore Romano,* English edition, no. 29 (1995): 5; no. 23 (1996): 1–2, 5, 12. J. L. REPETTO BETES, *El her-*

mano Juan Pecador: biografía crítica del beato Juan Grande O. H., fundador del Hospital Jerezano de la Candelaria (Jerez de la Frontera 1984). H. SANCHO DE SOPRANIS, *Biografía documentada del beato Juan Grande, O.H., fundador del Hospital de Candelaria de Jerez de la Frontera* (Jerez de la Frontera 1960).

[K. RABENSTEIN]

GRANZOTTO, CLAUDIO, BL.

Baptized Riccardo, Franciscan friar; sculptor; b. 23 August 1900, Santa Lucia di Piave, Treviso, Italy; d. 15 August 1947, Padua, Italy; beatified by John Paul II 20 November 1994.

Riccardo was the youngest of nine children in a family of modest means. After the death of his father (1909), he worked in the field and as a carpenter and bricklayer to help support his family. He developed a passion for art at age fifteen, but had to set it aside to complete his military service (1918–22). Upon discharge, he studied at the Academy of Fine Art in Venice, where he earned a diploma in sculpture (1929). He was a moderately successful artist with his own studio when he joined the Franciscans in Venice (7 December 1933) and received the name Claudio. Thereafter he combined prayer and sculpture, completing four grottos of Lourdes, one of which in Chiampo is identical in proportion to that in Massabielle, France. The man dedicated to prayer, beauty, and compassion died of a brain tumor in the hospital at Padua and was buried at the foot of the Grotto of Lourdes in Chiampo. Bishop Albino Luciani, the future Pope John Paul I, opened the diocesan process for Claudio's beatification (16 December 1959).

During the beatification homily, Pope John Paul II said Claudio "knew how to express the infinite beauty of divine contemplation in sculpture, . . . transforming it into a privileged instrument of apostolate and evangelization."

Feast: 2 September (Franciscans).

[K. RABENSTEIN]

GUÉRIN, MOTHER THEODORE, BL.

Foundress of the Sisters of Providence of Saint Mary-of-the-Woods, Indiana; b. 2 October 1798 at Etables-sur-mer, Brittany, France; d. 14 May 1856 at Saint Mary-of-the-Woods, Ind.; beatified 25 October 1998 by Pope John Paul II.

Christened Anne-Thérèse by her parents, Laurent, a lieutenant in Napoleon's navy, and Isabelle Guérin, she was one of four children, two of whom died tragically by fire in early childhood. Her father was attacked and killed by brigands in 1813 as he was returning home from military service. Taught by her mother as a young child, Anne Thérèse later attended a local primary school for a brief period. A young seminarian cousin, who lived for some time in the Guérin household, tutored her in theology, history, and philosophy.

At the age of sixteen, Anne Thérèse became both the caretaker of her invalid mother and the teacher and guardian of her younger sister Marie Jeanne. After ten years of devoted service to her family, Anne Thérèse was able to fulfill her cherished desire to enter the Congregation of the Sisters of Providence at Ruillé-sur Loir where she received the religious name Sister St. Theodore. Having pronounced her vows on 8 September 1825, she was appointed the following year as superior of a school in the industrial town of Rennes, where she remained for eight years. After being transferred to Soulaines, Sister St. Theodore, in addition to teaching and administering the local school, studied pharmacy and medicine with a local doctor. At this time the Academy of Angers (Université de France) awarded her a medal for excellent teaching methods, especially in the field of mathematics.

In the summer of 1839, the bishop of Vincennes, Indiana, Celestine de Hailandière came to the sisters' motherhouse in Ruillé seeking volunteers to bring, as he said, "the French religious spirit" to the United States. The superior general, Mother Mary Lecor, agreed to send sisters should any volunteer for this mission. There were five, and Sister St. Theodore was asked to be their leader. She accepted the call and with two professed sisters and three novices left France in July 1840. On 22 October 1840, the six French sisters arrived at the little clearing in the forest already named Saint Mary-of-the-Woods. There they established an academy for girls, the first in Indiana, and began the foundation of a new religious congregation modeled on the one they had left in France. During her sixteen years in America, Mother Theodore as she was now called, founded sixteen schools, both academies and free schools for the poor as well as two homes for orphans. Mother Theodore Guerin was the sixth citizen of the United States and the first in Indiana to be designated as blessed.

Feast: 3 October.

Bibliography: *Mother Theodore Guerin, Journals and Letters,* ed. M. T. MUG (Saint Mary-of-the-Woods, Ind. 1937). M. B. BROWN, *History of the Sisters of Providence.* Vol. 1:1806–1856 (New York 1949). K. BURTON, *Faith Is the Substance* (New York 1959). P. B. MITCHELL, *Mother Theodore Guerin: A Woman for Our Time* (Saint Mary-of-the-Woods, Ind. 1998). M. T. MUG, *Life and Life-Work of Mother Theodore Guérin* (New York 1904). J. E. RYAN, *Positio Super Virtutibus ex officio Concinnata* (Rome 1987).

[M. R. MADDEN]

GUERRERO GONZÁLEZ, ANGELA DE LA CRUZ, BL.

Foundress of the Sisters of the Cross; b. 30 January 1846, Seville, Spain; d. there 2 March 1932; beatified at Seville by John Paul II, 5 November 1982.

The growing sanctity of Angela, the uneducated daughter of a simple family, was recognized by Father Torres Padilla as she was working in a shoe factory in Seville. After she was initially rejected by the Carmelites of Seville, accepted, then forced to leave because of illness, Torres suggested in 1871 that she adopt a rule of life to live as a religious in the secular world. Thereafter she professed a private annual religious vow and recruited peasants as sisters in the Company of the Cross to serve the sick and needy in rural areas. Shortly after the founding of the congregation (2 August 1875), the sisters heroically ministered to victims of an epidemic in Seville (1876). Angela is remembered as a servant to the poorest of the poor, and for her spirituality of the Cross in a life of poverty, detachment, and humility.

Feast: 2 March.

Bibliography: *Escritos íntimos,* ed. by J. M. JAVIERRE (Madrid 1974). J. M. JAVIERRE, *Madre dei poveri* (Rome 1969); *Sor Angela de la Cruz* (Madrid 1982).

[K. RABENSTEIN]

GUÍZAR, RAFAEL VALENCIA, BL.

Bishop of Veracruz, Mexico; b. 27 April 1878, Cotija, Michoacán, Mexico; d. 6 June 1938, Mexico City; beatified in Rome by John Paul II on 29 June 1995.

Rafael was one of eleven children born to the wealthy hacendados Prudencio Guízar González and Natividad Valencia Vargas. A brother, Antonio, became bishop of Chihuahua. Rafael's studies were begun at home and completed in the seminary of his native Diocese of Zamora; he was ordained on 1 June 1901.

Missionary Work. From the first, the future bishop felt an overwhelming impulse to work as a home missionary. He had physical and spiritual gifts that fitted him for this work, and eight days after his ordination he began his first missionary journey, which lasted almost two years. While assigned to the diocesan seminary as spiritual director, Rafael continued his mission work by founding with his own funds a school for poor girls and on 3 June 1903, a Congregation of Missionaries of Our Lady of Hope with a special college in Jacona, Michoacán, as well as another college for boys in Tulancingo, whose graduates he hoped would enlist in large numbers in his missionary congregation. The missionaries were to dedicate themselves to work in Mexico and the neighboring nations. In June 1910 Guízar was forced to order the dissolution of his foundation of missionaries. Neither the disappointment of the failure of his personal foundation nor the honors that he received dimmed the zeal of this priest for the missions, and by 1910 he had preached innumerable missions in six Mexican states, especially in southeastern Mexico.

The chaos in Mexico consequent on the fall of Porfirio Díaz ended the home missions but opened for the young priest new opportunities to serve the souls of his fellows. Disguised as a peddler, a homeopathic physician, or an accordion player, he traveled with the armies of the revolution, ministering to the wounded and preaching whenever the opportunity presented itself. Often he returned from these missions of mercy with his hat and clothes pierced with bullet holes. Often too, his priestly ministrations would rouse the anger of the revolutionary leaders and on numerous occasions he was condemned to death. His success in escaping this supreme penalty made him a marked man in so many areas that he finally fled to Guatemala in 1916. Under the name of Rafael Ruíz he was able to take up again his life as a home missionary and in one year married 7,000 couples. In 1917 Guízar landed in Cuba and until the end of 1919 he preached 143 missions there. While preaching a mission in the cathedral of Havana in August 1919, Guízar was told that he had been named bishop of Veracruz. His first reaction was to flee to Colombia where he preached for about four months. But on 30 November 1919, he was consecrated bishop in Havana, and on 4 January 1920, he arrived in Veracruz. His arrival coincided with a disastrous earthquake in a number of cities of his diocese and the new bishop immediately went to help his stricken people. With the permission of his brothers, he sold the beautiful pectoral cross of gold set with precious stones that they had given him, used the money for the poor, and thenceforth wore a cross made of brass.

Reaction to Persecution. During his episcopate, Guízar had to suffer persecution, as did his brother bishops, especially after Plutarco Elías Calles came to power. Guízar had his own particular cross in the person of the governor of Veracruz, Adalberto Tejada, who on 17 June 1931 decreed that he would permit only one priest for each 100,000 inhabitants. Guízar, recognizing that this decree made it physically impossible for the priests to carry out their duties, closed all the churches in the state in order to force the situation on the attention of the people. Tejada answered with a decree ordering that the bishop should be shot wherever he was found in the state. Guízar at the time was in Mexico City but he ordered his secretary to drive as rapidly as possible to the governor's

palace in Jalapa. Guízar boldly walked into the governor's office, stating that he respected authority and that he wished to spare the governor's lieutenants the trouble of shooting him. The daring move paid off because the surprised governor did not dare shoot the bishop. Thus, Guízar was free to organize more than 300 Eucharistic centers, where his priests could minister to the people in ever-increasing numbers while the churches were closed. He was even able to maintain a seminary with more than 100 seminarians, who, though forced to move from place to place, were able to complete their studies and be ordained. In this way the diocese counted more priests at the end of the persecution than at its beginning. Worn out with his work, the bishop died in Mexico City. In 1950 his body was exhumed and found to be incorrupt. Thereafter his remains were translated to his titular chapel in the cathedral of Veracruz.

The cause for his beatification was introduced in Rome 11 August 1958. At Bishop Guízar's beatification Pope John Paul II said that "no difficulty prevented him from fulfilling his missionary tasks."

Bibliography: E. J. CORREA, *Mons. Rafael Guízar Valencia: El obispo santo 1878–1938* (Mexico City 1951). J. DE LA MORA, *Breves apuntes biográficos del Excmo. y Rvmo. Sr. Dr. D. Rafael Guízar Valencia, obispo de Veracruz* (Mexico City 1955). J. A. PEÑALOSA, *Rafael Guízar, a sus órdenes* (Mexico City 1990). E. VALVERDE TÉLLEZ, *Bio-bibliografía eclesiástica mexicana, 1821–1943*, 3 v. (Mexico City 1949).

[E. J. CORREA]

HAZE, MARIA THERESIA, BL.

Baptized Jeanne, known in religion as Marie-Thérèse du Sacré-Coeur de Jésus, foundress of the Daughters of the Holy Cross of Liège; b. 27 February 1782, Liège, Belgium; d. there 7 January 1876; beatified by John Paul II, 21 April 1991.

Haze experienced considerable hardship in her early life because the French Revolution forced her parents into exile and caused the loss of their property. With the guidance of Canon Jean-Guillaume Habets (d. 1876), the co-founder, Maria founded her religious congregation in Lüttich (1833) with five companions using the Rule of the Jesuits. The sisters conducted schools, nursed the sick, took care of women who were penitents or prisoners, and tended the destitute in public poorhouses. During Maria's lifetime the congregation, which was recognized by the Vatican 1 October 1845 and approved 9 May 1851, spread to Germany, India, and England. Her cause for beatification, introduced by Pope Pius IX (1851) and formally opened with the *commissio introductionis causae* by Pope Pius X (1911), was concluded by Pope John Paul

II, who said that Haze "invites [the Daughters of the Cross] to put into action the Gospel call to serve Christ in the person of the frailest and most suffering members of his body."

Bibliography: L. HUMBLET, *La Vénérable Mère Marie-Thérèse Haze* (Liège 1924). J. DE MARCHI, *The Venerable Mother Marie Thérèse Haze* (no site 1928). M. E. PIETROMARCHI, *La venerabile Maria Teresa Haze, fondatrice delle Figlie delle Croce* (Rome 1946). A. VÄTH, *Unter dem Kreuzesbanner* (2d ed. Düsseldorf 1929).

[M. B. BLISS]

HEDWIG OF ANJOU, ST.

(Polish: Jadwiga; a.k.a. Hedwig of Lithuania), queen of Poland, married woman; b. 1374 in Buda (now part of Budapest), Hungary; d. 17 July 1399, at Krakow, Poland; canonized on Blonia Esplanade in Krakow, Poland, 8 June 1997.

Hedwig was the younger daughter of King Louis I of Hungary and Poland and Elizabeth, princess of Bosnia. At age 9 she was betrothed to Duke William of Austria, whom she came to love; however, the Polish parliament vetoed this alliance. She demonstrated her obedience in refusing to elope with the young duke. Upon the death of her father and with the consent of the Polish nobility, 10-year-old Hedwig ascended to the throne of Poland in 1384. Her marriage at age 12 to Grand Duke Władysław Jagiello of Lithuania (thereafter King Ladislaus II of Poland) began a 400-year alliance between Poland and Lithuania and contributed to the growth of Christianity throughout the region. As part of the marriage contract, Jagiello became a Christian, destroyed pagan temples, and required the baptism of the Lithuanian people. The queen used her position to further evangelization by urging a moral reform upon her subjects. In 1397, she received permission from Pope Boniface IX to establish the Theology Faculty of the Jagiellonian University of Krakow, where Pope John Paul II studied theology and philosophy before and after World War II. She founded several hospitals at Biecz, Sandomierz, Sacz, and Stradom, and she defended the rights of peasants against the Polish nobility. Queen Hedwig combined contemplation and action. She was a woman of extraordinary piety, personal asceticism, and charity, especially to the poor. Often she would kneel in meditation at the feet of the Crucified Christ on the Black Cross in Wawel cathedral to learn God's generous love from Christ himself. At age 25, she died giving birth to her first child, who did not survive. In 1896 Hedwig was beatified by Pope Leo XIII. In his impassioned homily at her canonization in 1997, Pope John Paul II praised Hedwig for her evangelization of Lithuania, the Ukraine, and Belarus, her heroic charity, and sense of justice rooted in Gospel values:

St. Hedwig. (© Francis G. Mayer/CORBIS)

The most profound characteristic of her short life and, at the same time the measure of her greatness, was her spirit of service. Her social position, her talents, her whole private life she offered completely to the service of Christ and, when it was her time to reign, she also devoted her life to the service of the people entrusted to her. . . . and her sensitivity to social wrongs was often praised by her subjects.

The body of this patroness of Poland is now venerated in the cathedral of Krakow, Poland.

Feast: 17 July (formerly 28 Feb. in Poland).

Bibliography: *L'Osservatore Romano,* English edition, no. 26 (1997): 3–5, 7.

[K. RABENSTEIN]

HESSELBLAD, ELISABETH, BL.

A.k.a. Maria Hesselblad, apostle of ecumenism, nurse, foundress of the Order of the Most Holy Savior of Saint Brigit; b. 4 June 1870, Fåglavik (near Hundene), Alvsborg, Sweden; d. 24 April 1957, Rome; beatified by John Paul II, 9 April 2000 at Rome.

Elisabeth was the fifth of the thirteen children born to Swedish Lutherans, Augusto Roberto Hesselblad and

Cajsa Pettesdotter Dag. She immigrated to the U.S. (1888) to help support her family. She earned a nursing diploma at Roosevelt Hospital, N.Y., where she tended the sick, caring not only for their physical needs but their spiritual needs as well. Here she came in contact with Catholics for the first time. After experiencing a call during a Eucharistic procession in Brussels, she was later received into the Catholic Church in Washington, D.C., in 1902. She noted in her memoirs how significant her devotion to the Eucharist was. Two days later she left for Rome, where she discerned a vocation to promote Christian unity, but then returned to the U.S., where her health deteriorated. Now gravely ill, she went to Rome to the the *Casa di S. Brigida* to die. However, her health improved, and she joined the Carmelites (25 March 1904), who were established in that very house of St. Bridget, whose writings Maria Elisabeth long admired.

In 1906, Pope Pius X gave Hesselblad special permission to take the habit of the Bridgettines. She was unsuccessful in reestablishing a Bridgettine community in Rome with members of existing communities in Europe. On 9 September 1911, she began a new branch of the Brigettines with three English postulants, using the original order's Augustinian Rule. The order received canonical approval in 1920. She exhorted her sisters to work tirelessly for Christian unity throughout the world.

During World War I and especially World War II, Mother Elisabeth worked tirelessly to aid those who needed assistance. She cared for the poor and offered hospitality and a hiding place to Jews and others persecuted by racist laws. In 1947 Mother Elisabeth's longing to build bridges to those of other faiths became reality when she became an enthusiastic collaborator with Fr. Boyer, a worker in the ecumenical field.

At a Vatican ceremony (13 November 1999) shortly after the signing of a joint Catholic-Lutheran declaration (Augsburg, 31 October 1999), the pope dedicated a statue of St. Bridget, Europe's co-patroness, in the presence of the highest Lutheran representatives of Sweden and Finland, as well as the Swedish king and queen. John Paul II recalled that Bridget's "passion for Christian unity sustained her entire life. And, thanks to her witness and the witness of Mother Elisabeth Hesselblad, this commitment has come down to us through the mysterious stream of grace which overflows the bounds of time and space." At Hesselblad's beatification he reiterated: "By constantly meditating on God's word, Sister Elisabeth was confirmed in her resolve to work and pray that all Christians would be one."

Feast: 4 July.

Bibliography: *L'Osservatore Romano,* English edition, no. 15 (2000): 2. M. TJADER, *Mother Elisabeth: The Resurgence of the Order of Saint Birgitta* (New York 1972).

[K. RABENSTEIN]

HOSPITALLERS OF ST. JOHN OF GOD, MARTYRS OF THE, BB.

A.k.a. Blessed Braulio María Corres, Federico Rubio, and companions; d. 1936–37, Spain; beatified at Rome by John Paul II, 25 October 1992.

The seventy-one Hospitallers of St. John of God assumed under this title died at various times and places during the infamous persecution of the Church during the Spanish Civil War. At the outbreak of violence, the prior general, Father Narcissus Durchschein, urged the brothers to continue their sacred duty to the sick, unless the civil authorities took over the work or "until such time as a *force majeure* obliges them to leave" (letter dated 4 April 1936). The martyrs were all brothers serving in different capacities, ranging in age from eighteen to seventy-five years old, and were Spaniards except seven young Colombians.

Apostolic School of Talavera de la Reina (d. 25 July 1936, Toledo). The first four martyrs ran the order's new Juniorate (opened 1935) in Talavera near Toledo:

Federico Rubio Alvarez, baptized Carlos, brother and priest; b. 1862, Benavides, Léon.

Jerónimo Ochoa Urdangarín, brother; b. 1904, Goñi, Navarre.

Juan de la Cruz Delgado Pastor, baptized Eloy, brother; b. 10 December 1914, Puebla de Alcocer, Badajoz.

Primo Martínez de S Vicente Castillo, superior; b. 1869, San Román de Campezo, Alaya.

At the outbreak of civil unrest, they sent their twenty-two youngest charges home. The brothers' house was searched twice for weapons (23 and 25 July 1936). Following the second raid the brothers were arrested, interrogated, and taken to a site near the *Virgen del Prado*, where they were shot. All four were buried in a common grave in Talavera's cemetery, but re-interred in separate tombs (November 1936). On 22 November 1946, their bodies were translated to Ciempozuelos (Madrid), where they were buried in the Pantheon Chapel (14 January 1937).

San Juan de Dios Sanitarium at Calafell (d. 30 July 1936, Tarragona). About the same time as the house of the Hospitallers was searched in Toledo, the Communist authorities began harassing the brothers in Tarragona (23–29 July 1936). On 25 July, the militia took charge of the institute. They stripped the brothers of their habits and removed any sign of religion. The brothers continued their work for the next several days, while increasing the time spent in prayer. The brothers were provided documentation to travel to France, but warned that their safety could not be guaranteed. Nevertheless, nineteen of the twenty-seven Hospitallers left for Barcelona the morning of 30 July. They were picked up by the militia en route. The truck stopped within the border of the Calafell District and four youths were removed from the group. A firing squad of nineteen militiamen shot the others:

Antonio Llauradó Parisi, novice; b. 13 June 1920, Reus, Tarragona.

Antonio Sanchiz Silvestre, novice; b. 6 December 1910, Villamarchante, Valencia.

Benito José Labre Mañoso González, baptized Arsenio, brother; 19 July 1879, Lomoviejo near Valladolid.

Braulio María Corres Díaz de Cerio, baptized Pablo, brother and priest; b. 1897, Torralba de Rio, Navarre.

Constancio Roca Huguet, baptized Saturnino, brother; b. 12 August 1895, Sant Sadurni d'Anoia near Barcelona.

Domingo Pitarch Gurrea, novice; b. 12 February 1909, Villareal, Castellón.

Enrique Beltrán Llorca, novice; b. 14 November 1899, Villareal, Castellón.

Eusebio Forcades Ferraté, baptized Antonio, brother; b. 28 September, Reus, Tarragona.

Ignacio Tejero Molina, novice; b. 31 July 1916, Monzalbarba near Zaragoza (shot the day before his twentieth birthday).

Julián Carrasquer Fos, baptized Miguel, superior; b. 1881, Sueca, Valencia.

Manuel Jiménez Salado, brother; b. 29 October 1907, Jerez de la Frontera near Cadiz.

Manuel López Orbara, novice; b. 5 February 1913, Puente de la Reina, Navarre.

Rafael Flamarique Salinas, novice; b. 24 October 1903, Mendívil, Navarre.

Tomás Urdanoz Aldaz, novice; b. 7 March 1903, Echarri, Navarre.

Vicente de Paúl Canelles Vives, brother; b. 25 June 1894, Onda, Castellón.

Colombian Martyrs (d. 9 August 1936, Barcelona). These seven Colombians became the first of their homeland to be beatified. They were sent from the Colombian mission (opened 1920) to the San José Psychiatric Institute in Ciempozuelos (near Madrid) for training. When the Spanish brothers of the community were taken into custody on 7 August, Br. Guillermo Llop arranged with the Colombian ambassador, Dr. Uribe Echeverry, for their safe passage and repatriation and with the Claretian Sisters for money to cover travel expenses. The seven young brothers were taken off the train from Madrid to Barcelona, incarcerated overnight, and kept incommunicado with the embassy. Embassy officials found their bodies at the hospital mortuary the following morning, together with more than 100 others killed that day in Barcelona. The first Colombian *beati* are:

Arturo Ayala Niño, baptized Luis, brother; b. 7 April 1909, Paipa, Boyacá, Colombia. Brother Arturo joined the Hospitallers (1928) and joined the community at Ciempozuelos, Spain, in 1930.

Esteban Maya Gutiérrez, baptized Gabriel, brother; b. 19 March 1907, Pácora Calda, Antioquia, Colombia. In 1932, he joined the order, where he was known for his humility, intelligence, and obedience.

Eugenio Ramírez Salazar, baptized Alfonso Antonio, brother; b. 2 September 1913, La Ceja, Antioquia, Colombia. He entered the order (1932), professed his vows (1935), then was transferred to Spain.

Gaspar Páez Perdomo, baptized Luis Modesto, brother; b. 15 June 1913, La Unión, Huila, Colombia. Shortly after joining the Hospitallers (1933) and professing his solemn vows, he was sent to Spain to finish his religious and professional formation.

Juan Bautista Velázquez Peláez, baptized Juan José, brother; b. 9 July 1909, Antioquía, Colombia. He was a teacher prior to joining (1932) the Hospitallers, who characterized him as joyful and pious. After traveling to Spain (1934), he lived with the communities at Córdoba, Granada, and Ciempozuelos.

Melquíades Ramírez Zuloaga, baptized Ramón, brother; b. 13 February 1909, Sonsón, Antioquia, Colombia. Ramón entered the order at age 21. In April 1935 he traveled to Spain to complete his professional and religious formation at the community of Ciempozuelos, where he was known for his simplicity and patience.

Rubén de Jesús López Aguilar, brother; b. 12 April 1908, Concepción, Antioquia, Colombia. He was known for his spirit of prayer and obedience. During the armed conflict between Colombia and Peru (1933), he volunteered to work in the hospital at Pasto in the militarized zone. In 1936, he joined the community at Cimpozuelos, Spain.

Institute San José de Carabanchel Alto (d. 1 September 1936, Madrid). The isolated hospital for epileptics was relatively untouched by the violence of early July. On 29 July 1936, militia searched the institute for three hours and forbade the brothers to engage in any further "worship or religious expression." Undeterred, the brothers continued to pray together in secret for the next month. The mayor of Carbanchel arrived (29 August) with an armed escort, confiscated administrative records and money, and appropriated the hospital. Three days later (1 September) the brothers were herded into vehicles and taken to the "Charco Cabrera," where they were executed for being the servants of God. The mortal remains of the following martyrs were solemnly translated, 18 June 1942, to the church crypt in the Institute of San José:

Benjamín Cobos Celada, baptized Alejandro, brother; b. 9 July 1887, Palencia.

Canuto Franco Gómez, baptized José, brother; b. 23 December 1871, Aljucer, Murcia.

Carmelo Gil Arano, baptized Isidro, brother; b. 15 May 1879, Tudela, Navarre.

Cecilio López López, baptized Enrique, brother; b. 25 June 1901, Fondón, Almeria.

Cesáreo Niño Pérez, baptized Maríano, brother; b. 15 September 1878, Torregutiérrez near Segovia.

Cosme Brun Arará, baptized Simon, brother; b. 12 November 1894, Santa Coloma de Farners, Girona.

Cristino Roca Huguet, baptized Miguel, priest, director of the juniorate; b. 6 June 1899, Mollins de Rei, Barcelona.

Dositeo Rubio Alonso, baptized Guillermo, brother; b. 10 February 1869, Madrigalejo near Burgos.

Eutimio Aramendía García, baptized Nicolás, assistant superior; b. 23 December 1878, Oteiza de la Solanna, Navarre.

Faustino Villanueva Igual, baptized Antonio, brother; b. 23 January 1913, Sarrión, Teruel.

Proceso Ruiz Cascales, baptized Joaquín, superior; b. 4 October 1887, Beniel, Murcia.

Rufino Lasheras Aizcorbe, baptized Crescencio, brother; b. 15 June 1900, Arandigoyen, Navarre.

Martyrs at Barcelona (d. 1936). The Hospitallers of St. John of God ran two institutions in Barcelona. All but one of the fifty-two brothers who staffed the Psychiatric Hospital of Our Lady of Monserrat of San Baudilio de Llobregat made it safely to Marseilles, France, after a period of physical and psychological harm.

Protasio Cubells Minguell, (baptized Antonio, provincial councillor and secretary; b. 1880, Coll de Nargó near Lleida; d. 14 December 1936) was arrested while giving music lessons to two children. His body was found in the street the next day.

The others martyred in Barcelona were attached to the Children's Hospital, whose institute was the residence of the Brother Provincial of Aragon. The twenty-two brothers were subjected to various threats and indignities, including the confiscation of the hospital and all its goods, 20–26 July. The brothers scattered to find refuge in various parts of the city, but five were killed:

Acisclo Piña Piazuelo, baptized Joaquín, brother; b. 1878, Caspe, Zaragoza; d. 10 November 1936. He was arrested in the home of his superior's relative on 5 November and killed with forty other people after suffering in St. Elia Prison.

Francisco Javier Ponsa Casallach, brother; b. 1916, Moiá near Barcelona; d. 28 September 1936. He was arrested at his family's country home (27 September), taken to San Feliu de Codinas, Barcelona, by truck, and shot.

Juan Antonio Burró Más, brother; b. 28 June 1914, Barcelona; d. 5 November 1936. Although attached to the institute at Barcelona, Juan Antonio was completing his military service at the time of the Revolution. He was betrayed as a brother and killed.

Juan Bautista Egozcuezábal Aldaz, brother; b. 13 March 1882, Nuin, Navarre; d. 29 July 1936. Juan Bautista was captured near Esplugas de Llobregat and shot. He died in the hospital the following day.

Pedro de Alcántara Villanueva Larráyoz, baptized Lorenzo, brother; b. 1881, Navarre; d. 11 September 1936. He was arrested (4 September) with the family who gave him refuge.

Hospital of San Rafael (d. Madrid). The thirty-five member community at San Rafael's were harassed from the middle of July 1936. The situation was made more difficult because the hospital depended on charity personally collected by the brothers, who could no longer walk safely through the streets. The hospital was confiscated by the government 20 August and the brothers force to leave by 24 October. Although there were members of the community who were missing after 1939, only three were known to have been martyred:

Gonzalo Gonzalo Gonzalo, brother; b. 24 February 1909, Conquezuela, Soria; d. 4 August 1936. He was killed while dressed as a peasant to collect alms to support the hospital and institute.

Jacinto Hoyuelos Gonzalo, brother; b. 11 September 1914, Matarrepudio near Santander; d. 19 September 1936.

Nicéforo Salvador del Río, brother; b. 9 February 1913, Villamorco near Palencia; d. 30 November 1936.

Psychiatric Hospital of San José, Ciempozuelos (Madrid). As in the other hospitals, the government took over the hospital (31 July 1936) at Ciempozuelos (about eighteen miles from Madrid), posted militiamen around the perimeter, removed all religious symbols, and suppressed worship. The brothers continued to nurse the sick and to gather early in the morning for worship. On 7 August each brother was searched, imprisoned, and told he would die the following day. Brother Guillermo Llop asked the chief of general security to spare the brothers. The chief responded by having all fifty-three religious taken to an underground prison for the night and transferred on 9 August to San Antonio Prison in the former Scolopian College on the Calle Hortaleza. They were temporarily separated on 28 November when fifteen were assassinated; another six died on 30 November, and the last, on 11 February.

Angel Sastre Corporales, novice; b. 16 August 1916, Vallaralbo del Vino near Zamora; d. 28 November 1936.

Antonio Martínez Gil-Leonis, novice; b. 2 November 1916, Montellano near Seville; d. 30 November 1936.

Arturo Donoso Murillo, brother; b. 31 March 1917, Puebla de Alcocer near Badajoz; d. 30 November 1936.

Clemente Díez Sahagún, brother; b. 23 November 1861, Fuentes de Nava, Palencia; d. 28 November 1936.

Diego de Cádiz García Molina, baptized Santiago, provincial secretary; b. 14 December 1892, Moral de Calatrava near Ciudad Real; d. 30 November 1936.

Eduardo Bautista Jiménez, brother; b. 5 January 1885, La Gineta, Albacete; d. 28 November 1936.

Flavio Argüeso González, baptized Atilano, brother; b. 1877, Mazuecos, Palencia; d. 12 December 1936.

Francisco Arias Martín, priest, novice; b. 26 April 1884, Granada; d. 18 August 1936.

Guillermo Llop Gayá, baptized Vicente, brother, superior; b. 10 November 1880, Villareal, Castellón; d. 28 November 1936. Brother Guillermo had a distinguished career among the Hospitallers. He entered the order in 1898. From 1912–22, he served as novice master for the Roman province, where he tended the wounded during World War I, and later he became prior of the house at Frascati. He helped reinvigorate the order in Chile (1922–28). He returned to Spain in 1928 to serve as prior of community running the Psychiatric Hospital in Ciempozuelos near Madrid.

Hilario Delgado Vilchez, baptized Antonio, brother; b. 18 April 1918, Cañar near Granada; d. 28 November 1936.

Isidoro Martínez Izquierdo, novice; b. 9 April 1918, Madrid; d. 28 November 1936.

Jesús Gesta de Piquer, brother; b. 19 January 1915, Madrid; d. 30 November 1936.

José Mora Velasco, priest, postulant; b. 18 August 1886, Córdoba; d. 28 November 1936.

José Ruiz Cuesta, postulant; b. 6 November 1907, Dílar near Granada; d. 28 November 1936.

Juan Alcalde Alcalde, novice; b. 20 October 1911, Zuzones near Burgos; d. 28 November 1936.

Juan Jesús Adradas Gonzalo, baptized Maríano, priest and brother; b. 15 August 1978, Conquezuela, Soria; d. 28 November 1936.

Julián Plazaola Artola, brother; b. 12 September 1915, San Sebastián, Guipúzcoa; d. 28 November 1936.

Lázaro Mújica Goiburu, baptized Juan María, brother; b. 5 April 1867, Ideazábal, Guipúzcoa; d. 28 November 1936.

Martiniano Meléndez Sánchez, baptized Antonio, brother; b. 15 January 1878, Malaga, Costa del Sol; d. 28 November 1936.

Miguel Rueda Mejías, baptized Francisco, brother; b. 19 January 1902, Motril near Granada; d. 30 November 1936.

Pedro de Alcántara Bernalte Calzado, novice; b. 4 August 1910, Moral de Calatrava near Ciudad Real; d. 28 November 1936.

Pedro María Alcalde Negredo, brother; b. 26 November 1878, Ledesma near Soria; d. 28 November 1936.

Román Touceda Fernández, baptized Rafael, assistant superior; b. 22 January 1904, Madrid; d. 30 November 1936.

Tobías Borrás Román, baptized Francisco, brother; b. 14 April 1861, San Jorge, Castellón; d. 11 February 1937.

Feast: 30 July (Hospitallers).

Bibliography: V. CÁRCEL ORTÍ, *Martires españoles del siglo XX* (Madrid 1995). F. GÓMEZ CATÓN, *La Iglesia de los mártires en la provincia eclesiástica tarraconense* (Barcelona 1989). J. PÉREZ DE URBEL, *Catholic martyrs of the Spanish Civil War*, tr. M. F. INGRAMS (Kansas City, Mo. 1993). *Acta Apostolicae Sedis*, no. 21 (1992): 1064.

[K. RABENSTEIN]

HOUBEN, CHARLES OF MOUNT ARGUS, BL.

Baptized Johannes Andreas, Passionist missionary priest; b. 11 December 1821, Munstergeleen, the Netherlands; d. 5 January 1893, Dublin, Ireland; beatified by John Paul II, 16 October 1988.

The fourth of the eleven children of Peter Joseph and Elizabeth Houben, Johannes had difficulties with his studies, yet persevered and realized his religious vocation. While serving five years in the military reserves (1840–45), Houben worked in his uncle's mill. He entered the Passionist novitiate (1845), took his vows (1846) and the name Charles of St. Andrew, and was ordained (1850). Thereafter he worked among the poor and humble in England. In July 1857 he was assigned to the Mount Argus Retreat House, Dublin, Ireland, where he distinguished himself through his apostolate as a confessor. He remained in Dublin the remainder of his life, except for a short return to England in 1866. Houben suffered patiently in his later years. Since 1949 his relics have been interred in the Passionist church at Mount Argus.

Pope John Paul II praised Houben during his beatification ceremony for his ecumenical effects and ministry of reconciliation, saying he was "daily concerned with the difficulties of others."

Bibliography: P. F. SPENCER, *To Heal the Broken-Hearted* (Dublin 1988).

[K. RABENSTEIN]

HURTADO CRUCHAGA, ALBERTO, BL.

Jesuit priest; b. 22 January 1901, Viña del Mar, Chile; d. 18 August 1952, Santiago de Chile; beatified by Pope John Paul II, 16 October 1994.

Hurtado, known as "the Apostle of the Poor," experienced poverty himself following the death of his aristocratic father when he was four. While attending the Jesuit Colegio San Ignacio (1909–17) in Santiago, he spent his Sunday afternoons tending the city's poor. He postponed entering the Jesuit novitiate until 14 August 1923, in order to support his family, complete his military service, and earn a law degree (August 1923) at the Catholic University of Santiago. His entered the Jesuit novitiate at Chillán (1923–24) and Córdoba, Argentina (1925). After professing his first vows (15 August 1925), he continued his studies in the humanities, philosophy, and theology in Spain (1927–32), Ireland, and finally Belgium, where he was ordained at Louvain in 1933. After completing his final year of training at Drongen, he returned to Santiago de Chile (1936) to teach theology at the Colegio San Ignacio and pedagogy at Catholic University of Santiago. As a frequent retreat master he affected the lives of many young men: He fostered more than 100 priestly vocations and led others to committed service as laymen. In 1941, he undertook the chaplaincy of Catholic Action's youth movement in Santiago, and later nationally. In 1944, the charismatic priest challenged female retreatants to assist the city's poor. Their response resulted in the founding El Hogar de Cristo (Christ's Hearth), family-like housing first for homeless children, then for adults, that provided vocational training and/or rehabilitation. In 1945–46, while studying sociology at the Catholic University of America and residing with the Jesuit community at Georgetown University, Washington, D.C., Fr. Hurtado visited Fr. Flanagan's Boys Town to adapt the concept to Chile. Returning to Chile he founded (1947) the Chilean Trade Union Association (ASICH) based on the social teachings of the Church. His last years were spent extending his work and the social teachings of the Church. He died in 1952 of pancreatic cancer. His most famous composition is *Is Chile a Catholic country?* (Santiago 1941); however, between 1947 and 1950 he wrote on Church's social teaching, including *Social Humanism, On Unions,* and *The Christian Social Order.* In 1951 he founded the journal *Mensaje (Messages)* to further explain magisterial teaching on social justice.

John Paul II, who visited Hurtado's tomb in 1987, called him "the friend of God and man." During the beatification ceremony, the pope praised him for his use of modern communications methods to spread the Gospel.

Feast: 18 August (Jesuits).

Bibliography: *Alberto Hurtado: cómo lo vimos,* ed. H. M. BRUNET (Santiago, Chile 1994). *El padre Hurtado: quién fue?: qué haría hoy?* (Santiago, Chile 1994). *Padre Alberto Hurtado: "contento, señor, contento,"* vida, obra y testimonios (Santiago, Chile 1990). A. MAGNET, *El Padre Hurtado* (Santiago, Chile 1990). O. MARFÁN J., *Alberto Hurtado: Cristo estaba en él* (Santiago, Chile 1993). L. E. MARIUS, *Mensaje y compromiso del Padre Alberto Hurtado* (Caracas 1994). J. L. RUIZ-TAGLE IBAÑEZ, *Alberto Hurtado: un hombre, un santo* (Santiago, Chile 1992). J. VADELL, *Bienaventurados los pobres* (Santiago, Chile 1978).

[K. RABENSTEIN]

IRELAND, MARTYRS OF, BB.

A.k.a. Dermot O'Hurley and 16 Companions; d. 1579–1654; beatified 27 September 1992 by Pope John Paul II.

These seventeen martyrs were intended represent the hundreds of Irish martyrs who suffered in the period beginning with Henry VIII of England's severance of communion with the Holy See in 1535 and the Irish Parliament's abolishing papal jurisdiction in 1537 through the first half of the seventeenth century. In 1560, the Irish Parliament recognized Queen Elizabeth I as the supreme head of the Church of Ireland and declared Anglicanism to be the official religion of the country. Elizabeth's excommunication by Pope St. Pius V in 1570 sparked a new persecution in England, while an uprising of nobles spurred reprisals of the same ilk in Ireland. Penal laws, similar to those in England were soon enacted; however, they were irregularly enforced in some areas. The Irish refused to surrender their faith even during the terrible era of Oliver Cromwell's protectorship (1653–58).

The causes for 259 Irish martyrs were introduced on 16 March 1915. Oliver Plunkett has been canonized and several others were beatified in 1929 among the English martyrs, for example John Roche, John Cornelius (O'Mahony), John Carey, Patrick Salmon, and Ralph Corby. While thousands were killed, only a few hundred causes have been submitted. There were few records since many documents and much property were destroyed. Conflicting oral reports and the clergy's use of pseudonyms made the investigation difficult. The *Decretum super martyrio* has been issued for the following:

Ball, Margaret (Eleanor) Birmingham, widow; b. County Meath, Ireland; d. 1584 at Dublin. This housewife, the widow of Bartholomew Ball, was arrested by her own apostate son, Walter Ball, who was the mayor of Dublin. Bl. Margaret died in the dungeon of Dublin Castle from the abuse and torment she suffered. She was the only Irish woman who is recorded as suffering for the faith during the persecutions of Henry VIII and Elizabeth I.

Cavanagh (Canavan), Patrick, sailor; d. 5 July 1581 at Wexford. Patrick was hanged, drawn, and quartered for conveying Catholic priests and laymen to safety in France. He was the last of the Wexford Martyrs to die with Matthew Lambert. John O'Lahy, who was martyred with Cheevers, Meyler. Yet Cavanagh, was not beatified. They are celebrated as the Wexford Martyrs on 5 July (Wexford).

Cheevers, Edward, sailor; d. 5 July 1581 at Wexford. Hanged with Cavanagh, Meyler, and O'Lahy for conveying priests to France.

Feast: 5 July (Wexford).

Collins, Dominic, Jesuit lay brother; ca. 1566, at Youghal, County Cork, Ireland; d. 31 October 1602, Cork. Both Dominic's father and brother were mayor of his hometown. The penal laws in Ireland made it so difficult for Catholics that many, including Collins, fled to the Continent. From 1586 to 1589, Collins worked as a servant in various inns in Nantes, Brittany (northern France). Thereafter he enlisted in the army of Duke Philip Emmanuel of Mercoeur, to fight against the Huguenots of Brittany. During his nine-year military career, he attained the rank of captain of the calvary and was made military governor of Lapena. Discontented with his continued military service, Collins confided to the visiting Irish Jesuit Thomas White. The priest introduced the thirty-two-year-old soldier to the Jesuit superiors in the area. Collins finally entered the novitiate at Santiago de Compostela on 8 December 1598, and took his first vows on in 1601. Seven months later he was assigned to the Irish mission as assistant to James Archer, who was notorious among English authorities in Ireland. Collins was imprisoned in Cork and offered various inducements, including a high military commission and ecclesiastical preferments within the Church of Ireland, to provide information on the Spanish plans to invade England and to agree to serve the queen. Upon his continued refusal to deny allegiance to the Holy See, he was condemned on 9 July. Accounts of his death vary, but all agree that he was hanged. Some say he was left on the gallows; others that he was drawn and quartered. His body was buried in secret by Catholics near the site of his execution.

Feast: 30 October (Jesuits).

Higgins, Peter, sometimes rendered O'Higgin, Dominican priest, prior of Naas; b. 1600, at Dublin, Ireland; d. there on March 24, ca. 1642. The thousands of Dominicans in Ireland were reduced to four friars by the end of the reign of Elizabeth I. Fr. Higgins, prior of Naas Priory in County Kildare, was well-liked by people of all faiths. He was arrested following the Insurrection of 1641. Dublin was wracked by rumors that Protestants had been massacred in Ulster at the instigation of priests. His martyrdom was poorly recorded. Death dates range from 1641 to 1643. Hanged at Dublin.

Feast: 30 October (Dominicans).

Kearney, John, Franciscan priest; b. Cashel; d. 11 March (or 13 May) 1653, Clonmel, County Tipperary, Ireland. He defied the ban on priests issued by Cromwell. Arrested and hanged.

Lambert (Lamport), Matthew, baker of Wexford, d. 5 July 1581, Wexford. He is sometimes described as a parish priest (pastor) of the Dublin Diocese, but was more probably a baker (pistor). Arrested for harboring a Jesuit priest. He was hanged on the same day as the sailors Cavanagh, Cheevers, and Meyler, known as the Wexford Martyrs.

Feast: 5 July (Wexford).

MacKenraghty, Maurice, a.k.a. Murtagh Kenraghty (Kimracha, Kinrechtin, Makenrachtus, Macionn-rachtaigh, or O'Kenraghty in Gaelic which is Anglicized as Hanratty or Enright), priest; b. Kilmallock, Co. Limerick; d. 20 April 1585, Clonmel, Co. Tipperary. Son of a silversmith, Maurice was chaplain to Gerald, 16th Earl of Desmond, following his return from abroad as a priest who had attained a degree in theology. He was arrested by the Earl of Ormond, following an uprising led by the Desmond against the English tyranny. MacKenraghty remained steadfast and so he was hanged as a traitor.

Meyler (Myler), Robert, sailor, d. 5 July 1581, Wexford. Meyler was hanged with Cheevers and Cavanagh for conveying priests to France.

Feast: 5 July (Wexford).

O'Brien, Terence Albert, Dominican bishop of Emly; b. 1600 at Tower Hill Castle, Cappamore, Co. Limerick, Ireland; d. 31 October 1651, at Ball Bridge, Limerick. As the son of Murtagh O'Brien and Catherine Galwey, he was related to many of the public figures of the day. His paternal uncle, Maurice O'Brien (d. 1613), was the Protestant bishop of Killaloe; his grandfather, Sir Geoffrey Galwey, was recusant mayor of Limerick early in the century. Terence, educated at St. Peter Martyr priory in Toledo, Spain, was ordained there ca. 1628. After returning to Limerick, he labored in Ireland until 1643, when he was elected provincial of the Irish Dominicans. While attending a general chapter in Rome (1644), he sought assistance for the Irish Confederation, then in revolt against the English. A strong supporter of Papal Nuncio Giovanni Rinuccini in the internal and factional struggles within Irish Catholicism, O'Brien was consecrated bishop of Emly at Waterford at Rinuccini's recommendation on 2 April 1648. Bishop Terence was visiting Limerick when the town was captured by Cromwell's son-in-law, Ireton. He was arrested, condemned to death "as an original incendiary of the rebellion," and hanged for encouraging the Irish defense. The pectoral cross, which he took off and handed to his mother at the gallows is still preserved in the Dominican priory at Limerick.

Feast: 13 and 30 October (Dominicans).

O'Devany, Conor (Cornelius), Franciscan bishop of Down and Connor; b. ca. 1553; d. 1 February 1612, Dublin. He entered the Franciscan friary of Donegal at an unknown date and was consecrated bishop of Down and Connor, 1 Feb. 1583. In 1587, O'Devany was one of the Irish prelates who met in the Diocese of Clogher, where the decrees of the Council of Trent were promulgated. In 1588, he was arrested and confined in Dublin Castle, but two years later he was released by W. Fitzwilliam, the lord deputy. In 1591, he was granted special ecclesiasti-cal faculties by Cardinal William Allen because of his piety and zeal. Bishop O'Devany picked up the story of Ireland's martyrs at about the point where Jesuit Fr. John Houling left off in his preparation of an abstract for the canonization process of 11 bishops, 11 priests, and 44 laypeople. O'Devany gathered information on more martyrs until the time of his own death. Fortunately, he had forwarded a copy of his work to Fr. Holywood, SJ, which Bishop David Rothe of Ossory used in preparing the 1619 publication of *Processus Martyrialis* and the later *Analecta nova et mira* (ed. P. Moran, Dublin 1884). In 1605, O'Devany was accused by spies of visiting the pope and the king of Spain at the request of Hugh O'Neill, and was arrested with Patrick O'Loughbrain, a secular priest. The two were tortured. He remained in prison until his trial for high treason in 1611, during which he was found guilty and sentenced to death. Hanged and quartered.

O'Healy (O'Hely), Patrick, Franciscan bishop of Mayo, Co. Leitrim, Ireland; b. in west Ireland (probably Connaught); d. 1579 (date given variously as 13 or 22 August or September 1579), Kilmallock, Co. Limerick. Little is known with certainty of his early career beyond his education in Spain and Italy by the Franciscans, his ordination, and his consecration as bishop of Mayo, ca. 1576. In this period of Irish history, the Celtic clergy, and especially the hierarchy on the continent, were barred from relieving Irish Catholics at home of their shortage of priests, and the Tudor government kept a constant vigil on all Irish harbors to prevent European-ordained clerics from returning. But Bishop O'Hely, with a number of clerical companions, slipped into Ireland by following a circuitous course through Dingle Bay into Kerry, not far from Tralee. Although he eluded the royal guards who were assigned to search ships, he was turned over to the royal authorities by an informer a few weeks after his arrival. Following his arrest he was summoned before Sir William Drury, the king's representative at Kilmallock, Co. Limerick. O'Healy refused to deny his faith or recognize Queen Elizabeth I as head of the Church, saying that he could not barter his faith for life or honors. He and his close companion Cornelius O'Rourke were tortured for several days, hanged, and their bodies suspended on the gallows for more than two weeks.

O'Hurley, Dermot, a.k.a. Dermond O'Hurly, archbishop of Cashel; b. 1519 at Lickadoon (near Limerick), Ireland; d. June 19–30, 1584, near Stephen's Green in Dublin. As the son of the landed aristocrat William O'Hurley, Bl. Dermot received his education at Rheims, Louvain, and Rome. His brilliance as a student developed into a faculty for eloquent defense of the Catholic faith. He taught at many of Europe's finest universities after earning his doctorate. In Rome on 11 September 1581, he was consecrated archbishop of Cashel by Pope Gregory XIII. En route to his see, Bishop O'Hurley was intercepted and held at Dublin Castle. The English authorities believed the bishop had knowledge of the military plans of the rebelling Irish nobility, among whom were numbered his kinsmen. In an attempt to persuade the bishop to reveal military secrets, he was tortured but refused to provide any information or to deny his faith. After four days of excruciating pain, he was thrown into prison. A political storm broke out over his torture. English jurists, horrified as details of his sufferings spread throughout the land, announced that there was no legal reason for the bishop to endure further imprisonment. The representatives of the Crown ignored the outrage of their supporters and hanged the archbishop. The exact date is unknown because of the secrecy with which the act was accomplished to avoid a further outcry. His body was buried by some friends in St. Kevin's churchyard.

O'Loughbrain (O'Lochran, O'Loughran), Patrick, secular priest from County Tyrone (some mention him as a Franciscan); d. 1 February 1612, Dublin. Hanged with Bishop O'Devany.

O'Rourke, Conn, a.k.a. Cornelius O'Rorke, Franciscan priest; d. 1579 at Kilmallock. He descended from an old Gaelic aristocratic family: Breifne, and was a companion to Bishop O'Healy in his martyrdom. O'Rourke was tortured and hanged for protesting the English attempts to repress the Church in Ireland.

Taylor (Tailler), Francis, lord mayor of Dublin; d. 30 January 1621. He was the son of a wealthy, landed family of Swords. Bl. Francis, a merchant, became lord mayor of Dublin in 1595. Later he was elected to Parliament, but the election was overturned and he was thrown into prison instead. For seven years he was imprisoned at Dublin Castle before he died of his tortures.

Tirry (Tirrey), William, Augustinian priest from Cork; b. 1608–9, Cork; d. 12 (or 2) May 1654, in the Market Square at Clonmel, County Tipperary, Ireland. He became an Augustinian ca. 1627, and studied at Valladolid and Paris, where he qualified for admission to the faculty of theology in 1635. He returned to Ireland before 1640, and was probably prior of Fethard when in 1646 he was appointed provincial secretary. He became prior of Skryne in 1649, but because of the Cromwellian persecution he remained at Fethard. He was a man of great holiness, and miracles were attributed to his intercession by his contemporaries. Tirry was arrested while vesting for Mass on Holy Saturday (4 April) 1654. He was condemned under the anti-Catholic law of 6 January 1653. William urged the Irish to endure all things and remain steadfast in the faith as he was hanged.

Feast: 12 May (Augustinians).

At their beatification Pope John Paul invoked their memory with thanksgiving: "We thank [these martyrs] for the example of their fidelity . . . it is a heritage of the Irish people and a responsibility to be lived in every age. In a decisive hour, a whole people chose to stand firmly by its covenant with God. . . . The religious and political turmoil through which these witnesses lived was marked by grave intolerance on every side. Their victory lay precisely in going to death with no hatred in their hearts. They lived and died for love. Many of them publicly forgave all those who had contributed in any way to their martyrdom."

Bibliography: R. BAGWELL, *Dictionary of National Biography,* 14:773–774. BOURCHIER, *De Martyrio Fratrum Ord. Min.* (Ingolstadt 1583). W. M. BRADY, *The Episcopal Succession in England, Scotland, and Ireland, A.D. 1400 to 1875,* 3 v. (Rome 1876–77). A. BRUODIN, *Propugnaculum Catholicæ Veritatis* (Prague 1669). T. DE BURGO, *Hibernia Dominicana* (Cologne 1762). J. S. CRONE, *Concise Dictionary of Irish Biography,* rev. ed. (Dublin 1937). M. R. D'ARCY, *The Saints of Ireland* (St. Paul, Minn. 1985), 190–209. M. J. DORCY, *Saint Dominic's Family* (Dubuque, Iowa 1964), 412–414. J. T. GILBERT, *Dictionary of National Biography,* 14:864–865. GONZAGA, *De Origine Seraphic Religionis* (Rome 1587). M. B. HACKETT, "The Tirry Documents in the Augustinian General Archives," *Archivium Hibernicum* 20 (1957): 98–122. M. J. HYNES, *The Mission of Rinuccini . . .* (Dublin 1932). W. J. LOCKINGTON, *The Soul of Ireland* (New York 1920), 123–136. F. X. MARTIN, "The Tirry Documents in the Archives of France, Paris," *Archivium Hibernicum* 20 (1957): 69–97. M. MCALEESE, *The Irish Martyrs* (Ravensgate 1995). S. MCMANUS, *Story of the Irish Race* (New York 1944). H. P. MONTAGUE, *The Saints and Martyrs of Ireland* (Gerrards Cross, Ireland 1981): 78–88. CARDINAL MORAN, *Spicilegium Ossoriense* (Dublin 1874). D. MURPHY, *Our Martyrs* (Dublin 1896). S. Ó MURTHUILE, *A Martyred Archbishop of Cashel* (Dublin 1935). J. O'HEYN & A. COLEMAN, *Irish Dominicans of the 17th Century* (Dundalk 1902). M. O'REILLY, *Memorials of Those Who Suffered for the Catholic Faith* (London 1868), *Memoires of the Irish Martyrs* (New York 1869). O'SULLEVAN BEARR, *Patriciana Decas* (Madrid 1629). A. F. POLLARD, *Dictionary of National Biography,* 14:959. J. N. TYLENDA, *Jesuit Saints & Martyrs* (Chicago 1998) 357–59. A. J. WEBB, *Compendium of Irish Biography* (Dublin 1878).

[K. RABENSTEIN]

ITURRATE ZUBERO, DOMINGO, BL.

Known in religion as Dominic of the Most Holy Sacrament, Trinitarian priest; b. 11 May 1901, Dima (Basque region), Spain; d. 8 April 1927, Belmonte, Spain; beatified by John Paul II, 30 October 1983.

Domingo evidenced a religious vocation from an early age, joined the Trinitarians, and was ordained priest. During his short life, he became known for the devotion with which he celebrated Mass and his obedience.

John Paul II praised Domingo, saying: "He strove to live according to two central principles of the spirituality of his order: the mystery of the Holy Trinity and the work of the Redemption, which lead to a life of intense charity" (beatification homily).

Feast: 7 April.

Bibliography: *L'Osservatore Romano,* English edition, no. 46 (1983): 6–7.

[K. RABENSTEIN]

JABLONSKA, BERNARDINA, BL.

Known in religion as Maria Bernardina, virgin, co-foundress of the Congregation of the Sisters of the Third Order of St. Francis of Assisi, Servants of the Poor (Albertines); b. 5 August 1878, Pizuny-Lukawica, Poland; d. 23 September 1940, Krakow; beatified 6 June 1997, at Wielka Krokiew Arena, Zakopane, Poland, near John Paul II's former archdiocese.

Bernardina, the fourth child of the landed farmers Gregory Jablonski and Maria Romanow, received her education from private tutors and from books borrowed from her pastor's library. When she was eight years old she met and was impressed by Saint Albert CHMIE-LOWSKI. She assuaged her sorrow at her mother's death in 1893 by turning increasingly to prayer. On 13 September 1896, she left home to begin her postulancy in the new congregation being founded by Chmielowski despite her father's opposition and without the approval of her pastor. The following year she was among the first seven Albertine sisters to receive the habit. Her initial decade of religious life was spent doing household chores and tending the sick, as her faith grew. In 1907, Chmielowski named her superior, a position she maintained until her death. Together with Saint Albert she founded hospices for those who were sick and homeless as a result of war. Bernardina is remembered not only for her charity, but also for the way in which she helped the suffering regain their human dignity. Mother Maria Bernardina was declared venerable on 17 December 1996. On 8 March 1997, a miracle attributed to her intercession was approved.

Pope John Paul II said during her beatification: "She wanted to satisfy her neighbor's every request, to dry every tear, to console at least with a word every suffering soul. She always wanted to be good to everyone, but even better to those most tried by fate. She used to say: 'My neighbor's suffering is my suffering.'" Patron of the poor and handicapped.

Feast: 23 September.

[K. RABENSTEIN]

JAMET, PIERRE-FRANÇOIS, BL.

Priest, b. 13 September 1762, Fresnes, France; d. 12 January 1845, Caen, France; beatified by John Paul II, 10 May 1987.

Following Jamet's ordination (1787), he was assigned as chaplain to the Sisters of the Good Savior. He was forced into hiding in order to continue his ministry after refusing to take the oath of allegiance to civil authorities that was demanded by the revolutionaries. During this period he wrote a sign-language dictionary for the deaf-mutes under his care. After the French Revolution Jamet restored and expanded the Good Saviors, continued to devote himself to the care of the mentally and physically disabled, and served as rector of Caen University (1822–30).

Because Jamet is the patron of the deaf, his beatification ceremony, during which Pope John Paul II praised him as a father of the needy, was signed.

Feast: 7 May.

Bibliography: G. A. SIMON, *Une belle figure de prêtre et d'homme d'oeuvres a la fin du XVIIIe et au commencement du XIXe siecle. L'abbe Pierre-Francois Jamet, second fondateur de l'Institut du Bon-Sauveur, recteur de l'Academie de Caen* (Caen 1935). *Acta Apostolicae Sedis* (1987): 690. *L'Osservatore Romano,* English edition, no. 21 (1987): 18–19.

[K. RABENSTEIN]

JANSSOONE, FRÉDÉRIC CORNIL, BL.

Franciscan missionary; b. 19 November 1838, Ghyvelde (near Dunkirk), Flanders, Belgium; d. 4 August 1916, Montréal, Québec, Canada; beatified by John Paul II, 25 September 1988.

Although Frédéric was the youngest of thirteen children from a wealthy farm family, he had to quit school to help his mother after his father's death (ca. 1848). He soon discovered that his love for others made him a great saleman—this talent later served him well as a preacher. After his mother's death in 1861, he discerned his vocation. He entered the Franciscan novitiate (June 1864), was ordained (17 August 1870), served as a military chaplain during the Franco-Prussian War (1870–71), and was custodian for a time at the Bordeaux monastery. In 1876, he was sent to the Holy Land, where he raised funds to maintain two ancient churches, built a new one at Bethlehem, and revived the custom of pilgrims praying the Stations of the Cross in the streets of Jerusalem. He traveled to Canada (1881–82) to collect alms for the Holy Land and returned there six years later (1888). The rest of his life was spent preaching, evangelizing, and establishing the Canadian province of the Franciscans from his base at the shrine of Our Lady of Cap-de-la-Madeleine. Janssoone also composed about thirty popular monographs, most of which are spiritual descriptions of the Holy Land and hagiography. His deep spirituality and ministerial zeal drew many through him to Christ.

At Janssoone's beatification Pope John Paul II noted the Franciscan "gives us the example of contemplative prayer that is able to embrace the works of creation, the events of daily life, and encounters with each other."

Feast: 5 August.

Bibliography: Works: *Vie de saint François d' Assise* (Montréal 1894); *Vie de notre Seigneur Jésus-Christ, écrite avec les paroles mêmes des quatre évangélistes* (Québec 1894); *La bonne sainte Anne. Sa vie, ses miracles, ses sanctuaires* (Montréal 1896); *Saint Joseph. Sa vie, son culte* (Québec 1902); *Le ciel, séjour des élus* (Montréal 1912). Literature: O. LAMONTAGNE, *Un témoin de l'autre monde: le père Frédéric dans l'intimité* (Trois-Riviáres, Québec 1960). R. LÉGARÉ, *An Apostle of Two Worlds*, tr. R. BROWN (Chicago 1958) tr. of *Un apôtre des deux mondes: le père Frédéric Janssoone* (Montréal 1953); *Un grand serviteur de la Terre Sainte, le père Frédéric Janssoone* (Trois Rivières, Québec 1965). H. LEMAY, *Bibliographie et iconographie du Serviteur de Dieu le R. P. Frédéric Janssoone* (Québec 1932). THOMAS F. MURPHY, *Our Lady's Herald. A short Account of the Life of Father Frederick Janssoone.* (Trois Rivières 1965). *Acta Apostolicae Sedis* 32 (1940): 516ff.

[K. RABENSTEIN]

JARRIGE, CATHERINE, BL.

A.k.a Catinon Menette, lay Dominican tertiary; b. 4 October 1754, Doumis near Cantal and Mauriac, Diocese of Saint-Flour, France; d. 4 July 1836, Mauriac, France; beatified by John Paul II, 24 November 1996.

The youngest of seven children in a poor family, Catinon Menette ("Catherine the Little Nun") entered domestic service at age nine. About 1774, she moved to Mauriac, became a Dominican tertiary, and rearranged her priorities so that she could live the Rule of the menettes in its entirety. By this time she was employed as a lace-maker to rent the garret room she shared with her sister. In her free time Catherine responded to the needs of the less fortunate, often by begging on their behalf. During the French Revolution, she established and supplied a covert network of safe houses to protect refuge priests and deliver them to safety. Though she was arrested several times, the authorities were never able to convict her of any offense. Following the Reign of Terror, Catherine continued her charity, assisted in repairing the hospital, supervised the renovation of her parish church, and urged the lapsed to return to the Church. Her cause for beatification was not opened until 1929. She was declared venerable in 1953 and a miracle attributed to her intercession was approved 25 June 1996.

On the day of her beatification, Pope John Paul II said that she "aided numerous material and spiritual forms of poverty." He continued his praise: "Her humble yet shining life makes us immediately think of Mary of Nazareth, whose example inspired the new blessed's generous dedication in serving her neighbor."

Feast: 4 July.

Bibliography: M. C. DE GANAY, *La Menette des prêtres, Catherine Jarrige* (S. Maximin, France 1923). V. MARMOITON, *La vie héroique de Catherine Jarrige* (Toulouse 1956). J. B. SERRES, *Catherine Jarrige, dite Catinon Menette* (Paris 1864, 3d ed. 1910). *L'Osservatore Romano,* Eng. ed. 48 (1996): 1–3.

[K. RABENSTEIN]

JOHN OF DUKLA, ST.

(Polish: Jan); Observant Franciscan priest; b. ca. 1414 in Dukla in the Central Beskid Mountains of Galicia in the southeastern extremity of Poland; d. 29 September 1484, at Lviv (Lvov), now in the western Ukraine; canonized 10 June 1997.

John of Dukla was born into a middle-class family. He studied at the Jagiellonian University of Krakow, which had been founded by Queen St. Hedwig. After living as a hermit in Dukla, John became a Franciscan at Lemberg (1440), where he was ordained and served as guardian. About this time he realized that he must share the fruit of his contemplation with others. At the instigation of John of Capistrano, he became a member of the Observant Franciscans (Bernardines) in 1463. Thereafter John was a successful missioner in Galicia, especially among the Ruthenian schismatics and the German burghers of Lviv. Impassioned preaching, pastoral zeal, ardent prayer, patience, and charity were hallmarks of his sanctity. Blinded in old age, he continued to hear confessions, and he preached by having others read his sermons. Originally his remains were buried in the cemetery of Lviv. In 1945 the body was translated to Rzeszow, then to the church of the Franciscans at Dukla. Although John was beatified in 1733 by Pope Clement XII, his canonization had been delayed because of the partition of Poland. He is one of the patrons of Poland and Lithuania.

The day before the canonization Mass, the Pope John Paul II venerated John's relics, saying: "Blessed John earned fame as a wise preacher and zealous confessor. Crowded around him were people hungry for sound doctrine of God, to hear his preaching or, at the confessional grill, to seek comfort and counsel."

Feast: 10 July (formerly 28 September and 1 October).

Bibliography: *L'Osservatore Romano,* English edition, no. 26 (1997): 8, 11; no. 27 (1997): 6–8, 11.

[K. RABENSTEIN]

JOUBERT, EUGÉNIE, BL.

Religious of the Holy Family of the Sacred Heart; b. 11 February 1876, Ysingeaux, France; d. 2 July 1904,

Pilgrims on their knees in front of the shrine of Our Lady of Guadalupe, Hidalgo, Mexico. (© Hulton Getty/Liaison Agency)

Liège, Belgium; beatified by John Paul II, 20 November 1994.

In 1895, Joubert joined the new congregation of the *Soeurs de la Sainte-Famille de Sacré-Coeur*, founded at Puy by Mère Marie Ignace Melin. She taught catechism to small children at Saint-Denis and Aubervilliers until her health failed. From that time she was assigned to Liège, where she died at age twenty-eight after a two-year illness. She is known for her devotion to the Sacred Heart and her practice of the "Little Way."

At her beatification, Pope John Paul II related that Eugénie "took care in preparing the little ones for their First Confession and First Communion. . . . for she knew that no human child, however poor or humble he might be, is indifferent to God."

Bibliography: J. BOUFLET, *Le charisme et la catéchèse* (Paris 1998).

[K. RABENSTEIN]

JUAN DIEGO, BL.

According to tradition, the name of the Indian to whom the Virgin Mary appeared at Tepeyac, a hill out-side of Mexico City, on 9 December 1531. According to this same tradition, Juan Diego's given name was Cuauhtlatoatzin, and he was born around 1474 in Cuautitlán, about twenty kilometers north of Tenochtitlán (Mexico City). He was married but had no children. When he and his wife were baptized in 1524, he took the name Juan Diego, and his wife the name María Lucía. The earliest written account (1649) of the apparitions, the *Nican Mopohua,* calls him a *macehualli* (poor Indian). In 1666 when a formal ecclesiastical inquiry was made into the apparitions, Juan Diego was described as being devout and religious even before his conversion. After this, he was said to have walked weekly to Tenochtitlán to attend Mass and receive catechetical instruction. When his wife died in 1529, he went to live with his uncle, Juan Bernardino. Juan Diego was 57 at the time of the apparitions and from then on he lived in a small room attached to the chapel that housed the image of Our Lady of Guadalupe, as its custodian. He is said to have received special permission from the bishop to receive communion three times a week. He died on 30 May 1548 at 78 years of age.

Juan Diego was recognized as blessed by means of an equivalent beatification on 6 May 1990 at the Basilica of Our Lady of Guadalupe in the presence of Pope John Paul II with the reading of a decree from the Sacred Congregation for the Causes of Saints. It recognized that public devotion to Juan Diego was a long tradition, approved an obligatory memorial for the archdiocese of Mexico City and an optional memorial for other dioceses. The decree set 9 December, the date of the first apparition, as the day for the memorial.

Although there are written accounts from the sixteenth century that mention both the shrine and devotion to the Virgin of Guadalupe, the first written mention of Juan Diego is in the above cited *Nican Mopohua*. This so called *silencio guadalupano* of over a century has led some, including the abbot of the Basilica of Guadalupe, Msgr. Guillermo Shulemberg Prado, and the Vincentian historian Stafford Poole, to question the historicity of Juan Diego. This view caused a certain amount of controversy in 1996 and led to the resignation of the abbot.

Bibliography: VIRGIL ELIZONDO, *Guadalupe: Mother of the New Creation* (Maryknoll, N.Y.: Orbis Books, 1997). RICHARD NEBEL, *Santa María Tonantzin Virgen de Guadalupe: Continuidad y transformación religiosa en México.* translated by CARLOS WARNHOLTZ BUSTILLOS (Mexico City: Fondo de Cultura Económica, 1995). STAFFORD POOLE, C.M., *Our Lady of Guadalupe: The Origins and Sources of a Mexican National Symbol, 1531–1797* (Tucson: University of Arizona Press, 1995). *The Story of Guadalupe: Luis Laso de la Vega's Huei tlamahuicoltica of 1649,* edited and translated by LISA SOUSA, STAFFORD POOLE, C.M., and JAMES LOCKHART (Stanford: Stanford University Press; Los Angeles: UCLA Latin American Center Publications, 1998).

[JOSE ANTONIO RUBIO]

JUGAN, JEANNE, BL.

Known in religion as Marie of the Cross, foundress of the Little Sisters of the Poor; b. 25 October 1792, Petites-Croix (near Cancale), Brittany, France; d. 29 August 1879, Pern, France; beatified by John Paul II, 3 October 1982.

After the death of her fisherman father, Joseph Joucan, when she was four, her mother, Marie Horel, supported the six children as a farm laborer and taught them the faith. At sixteen, Jeanne, the youngest child, became a kitchen maid to a charitable family. The mistress, Viscountess de la Choue, took her on visits to the sick and poor. At twenty-five, Jugan joined the third order of the Heart of the Admirable Mother (founded by St. John Eudes), gave away her meager possessions, and began working in a hospital, but after six years of exhausting work she returned to domestic service. Realizing that she could do more, she then devoted herself entirely to the poor, especially widows.

Hospital work and domestic service had prepared Jugan for giving hospitality to the aged in Saint-Servan. She was aided by two other women, Virginie Tredaniel and Marie Jamet, to whom Abbé Augustin Marie Le Pailleur had given a rule and a charge to care for an elderly blind woman, Anne Chauvin. All four women lived together in Jugan's home and elected her superior, 29 May 1842. Eventually a benefactor purchased an abandoned convent for the Little Sisters. These women, and others who assisted them, begged daily for the needs of the elderly in their care. The sisters ate what was left after feeding their guests. Houses were soon established in Rennes, Dinan, Tours, and Angers. Although Jugan was reelected superior (8 December 1843), she was suddenly replaced (23 December 1843) by twenty-three-year-old Marie Jamet through the action of Le Pailleur. No recognition of her role as foundress came during her lifetime. After receiving a petition from the people of Saint-Servan, the French Academy made her recipient of one of its annual awards for virtue (December 1845) in appreciation of her heroic charity in caring for the poor. In 1852, the congregation was officially recognized, and she was sent to the motherhouse for the remaining twenty-seven years of her life, without an active role in the growth of the community.

Her contemporary Charles Dickens wrote: "There is in this woman something so calm, and so holy, that in seeing her I know myself to be in the presence of a superior being. Her words went straight to my heart, so that my eyes, I know not how, filled with tears."

It was not until 1893 that Jugan was recognized as the founder of the congregation whose rule was approved by Pius X in 1907. In beatifying Jugan Pope John Paul II said: "I give thanks to the Lord for bringing about what Pope John XXIII had so rightly hoped for and Paul IV so ardently desired" the beatification of Jugan.

Feast: 30 August.

Bibliography: G. M. GARRONE, *Poor in spirit*, tr. A. NEAME (London 1975). A. HELLEU, *Jeanne Jugan, Foundress of the Little Sisters of the Poor*, tr. M. A. GREY (St. Louis 1942). P. MILCENT, *Jeanne Jugan: Humble So As to Love More*, tr. A. NEAME (London 1980). F. TROCHU, *Jeanne Jugan*, tr. H. MONTGOMERY (Westminster, Md. 1950). *Acta Apostolicae Sedis* (1984) 346–49. *L'Osservatore Romano,* Eng. ed. 42 (1982): 9–10.

[T. F. CASEY/K. RABENSTEIN]

KAFKA, MARIA RESTITUTA, BL.

Baptized Helena, nurse, martyr of the Franciscan Sisters of Christian Charity ("Hartmannschwestern"); b. 10 May 1894, Hussowitz-Brunn, Moravia (now Brno, Czech Republic); d. 30 March 1943, Vienna, Austria; beatified by John Paul II, 21 June 1998, in the Plaza of Heroes in Vienna, Austria.

Helena Kafka was the sixth daughter of a cobbler who moved the family to Vienna while she was still a child. While in her teens she began working as a sales clerk, then as a nurse, which put her into contact with the nursing Hartmannschwestern. She took the name "Restituta" upon entering the congregation (1914). Sr. Restituta was a skilled surgical nurse (1919–39), but also gained a reputation for championing the cause of those in need: the poor, the oppressed, and the unjustly accused—even a Nazi doctor.

Following the Anschluss (March 1938), she was an outspoken opponent of Adolf Hilter. She was arrested on Ash Wednesday 1942 for replacing the pictures of Hitler in each room of a new hospital wing with crucifixes and refusing to remove them. On 28 October 1942, she received the death sentence for treason. Upon being offered her freedom in exchange for leaving the order, she refused. For the next five months, until the order of decapitation was executed, Sr. Restituta nursed other prisoners without regard to political affiliation.

On 6 April 1998, her martyrdom was declared. Standing before the balcony where Hilter announced the Anschluss of Austria, Pope John Paul II beatified Kafka saying: "She did not wish to be silent even in the face of the National Socialist regime. . . . She risked her life for her witness to the Cross."

Feast Day: 29 October (Franciscans).

Bibliography: P. RONAI, *Schwester Maria Restituta Kafka* (Innsbruck 1998).

[K. RABENSTEIN]

KALINOWSKI, RAFAŁ OF ST. JÓZEF, ST.

Baptized Józef (Joseph), engineer, freedom fighter, Discalced Carmelite (OCD) priest, "martyr of the confessional"; b. 1 Sept. 1835, at Vilna, Lithuania; d. 15 Nov. 1907, at the Carmel in Wadowice, Poland; canonized 17 Nov. 1991 by Pope John Paul II.

Born in Lithuania to an aristocratic Polish family, Kalinowski entered the military in 1853 and studied civil engineering at the Academy of Military Sciences, St. Petersburg. Thereafter he was appointed to the fortress at Brest Litowski, Belarus, where he was charged with overseeing the building of the railway line between Kurst and Odessa. His success in that task led to his promotion to captain about the time the Russian Army occupied Poland (1863). Although he desired to devote himself to charity, as a Polish patriot, he accepted the position of minister of war in Vilna and participated in the uprising (1863) against the Russian occupation. He was captured in 1864 and condemned to death. Later his sentence was commuted to 10 years' exile in Siberia. The first four years were spent in a desolate labor camp, where he became known as a man of boundless charity and serenity. Fellow prisoners sought him out for spiritual advice. He was freed in 1874, but since he was forbidden to live in any major Polish city, he went to Paris, where he became tutor to Prince August Czartoryski, who later became a Salesian priest.

In 1877, he was received into the Austrian Carmelites, taking the name Rafał of St. Józef and was ordained priest in 1882. Thereafter he began his work of restoring the Discalced Carmelites in Poland, especially in Czerna, Krakow, and Wadowice, where he a founded a monastery (1892) and served as its prior. His primary apostolate centered on the confessional. His gift of charity made him a much sought spiritual director, but he also taught novices and served in other capacities. Among his spiritual sons is St. Albert Chmielowski.

His spiritual life is marked by continual prayer fed by austerity and silence. He also longed and worked for Christian unity. He also wrote several books on Carmelite spirituality. Kalinowski is buried at Czerna.

Pope John Paul II, who was born in Wadowice and tried to become a Carmelite, beatified Kalinowski in 1983 at Krakow, Poland. When Kalinowski was canonized in 1991, he was the first Carmelite friar to be so honored since John of the Cross in 1726. At the canonization Mass, the pope said: "He was an esteemed confessor and spiritual director. He guided souls in the sublime knowledge of the love of God, Christ, and Our Lady, the Church and neighbor. . . ."

Feast: 19 November (Carmelites).

Bibliography: *Acta Apostolicae Sedis* 76 (1984): 1045–1047. *L'Osservatore Romano,* English edition, no. 28 (1983): 9–10. S. ADAMCZYK, *Niespokojne serce* (Krakow 1983). R. BENDER, *Powstaniec-zakonnik [ojciec] Rafał Kalinowski* (Warsaw 1977). J. GALOFARO, *Al Carmelo attraverso la Siberia* (Rome 1960). C. GIL, *O. Rafał Kalinowski* (Krakow 1979). R. KALINOWSKI, *Listy* (Lublin 1978). S. T. PRASKIEWICZ, *St. Raphael Kalinowski: An Introduction to His Life and Spirituality,* tr. T. COONAN, M. GRIFFIN, and L. SULLIVAN (Washington 1999).

[K. RABENSTEIN]

KARLOWSKA, MARIA, BL.

Foundress of the Sisters of the Good Shepherd of Divine Providence; b. 4 September 1865, Stupówka (now Karlowo near Gziezno), Poland; d. 24 March 1935, Pniewita, Poland; beatified by John Paul II, 6 June 1997, at Wielka Krokiew Arena, Zakopane (near Krakow), Poland.

The eleventh child of Matthew Karlowska and Eugenia Dembinski, Maria attended school in Poznán, where her family had moved after her birth. Following the death of her parents (1882), Maria worked in her sister's tailor shop, where she met a prostitute. Maria came to understand that her mission was to work for the moral and social rehabilitation of prostitutes and to tend to those suffering from venereal diseases. Her ministry attracted a number of like-minded women. Together they founded the Good Shepherd Sisters in 1894. That same year, with financial help from Duchess Aniela Poluticka, Maria established the Good Shepherd Institute in Winiary (near Poznán) to care for prostitutes. Both Prussian and Polish civil authorities commended Karlowska's work, which continues today in seven Polish educational institutions for girls and women, three homes for single mothers, and a rehabilitation center. Karlowska's cause for beatification started in 1965. She was declared venerable 11 July 1995, and on 8 March 1997, a miracle attributed to her intercession was approved.

During her beatification on the Feast of the Sacred Heart, Pope John Paul II said: "Her devotion to the Saviour's Sacred Heart bore fruit in a great love for people . . . a love [that] will never say 'enough.'"

Feast: 5 June.

Bibliography: M. KARLOWSKA, *Wybór pism Marii Karlowskiej,* ed. J. R. BAR (Warsaw 1981). *L'Osservatore Romano,* English edition, no. 29 (1995): 5.

[K. RABENSTEIN]

KASSAB, NIMATULLAH AL-HARDINI YOUSEF, BL.

Baptized Youssef Girgis (Joseph George) Kassab, scholar, priest of the Maronite Rite; b. 1808 at Hardine, Caza de Batroun, northern Lebanon; d. 14 December 1858, at Kfifan Monastery, Lebanon; beatified by John Paul II, 10 May 1998.

Son of Girgis Kassab and Maryam Raad, Youssef attended the monastery school of Saint Antony Abbot at Houb (1816–22). On 1 November 1828, he joined the Lebanese Maronite Order of Monks at Saint Antony at Qozhaya. He took the name Brother Nimatullah (''Grace from God''). Following a two-year probation and profession at Qozhaya (14 November 1830), he studied theology at the Monastery of Keprianos and Yustina in Kfifane.

From the time of his ordination by Bishop Semaan Zouein (Christmas Day 1835) until his death, Nimatullah was involved in the formation of new priests as director of the scholasticate (1938–45) and a professor of moral theology at Bharsof (1847–50) and Kfifan (1835–38, 1853–56), where one of his students was Sharbel Maklouf (canonized by Pope Paul VI, 9 October 1977). Nimatullah served as administrator of the monastery of Our Lady of Tamiche (1847–50) and as assistant general for three terms (1845–48, 1850–53,1856–58). He refused appointment to the office of abbot general, although he was the recognized master of spirituality in the order. Despite suffering through two civil wars (1840 and 1845), Nimatullah remained unshaken in faith and invariably charitable in his interactions with others until his death from pleurisy aggravated by the cold. Saint Sharbel was among the brothers who attended his deathbed.

Nimatullah's body was reburied in his monastery church at Kfifan (18 May 1996), where many miracles occurred. He was declared venerable by John Paul II on 7 September 1989.

At Nimtullah's beatification, John Paul praised him: ''Through his rigorous asceticism, his long periods of prayer before the Blessed Sacrament, his concern for theological research, and his merciful attention to his brothers, Blessed Hardini is a model of Christian and monastic life for the Maronite community and for all Christ followers in our time.''

Feast: 14 December (Maronites).

Bibliography: D. ATTWATER, *Saints of the East* (New York 1963) 180–84. O. ELIAS, *The Blessed Nimatullah Kassab Al-Hardini* (Beirut 1998). *Acta Apostolicae Sedis* 12 (1998) 599.

[K. RABENSTEIN]

KAZIMIERCZYK, STANISLAW, BL.

Augustinian canon regular of the Lateran of Corpus Christi; b. 1433 at Casimiria, near Krakow, Poland; d. there 3 May 1489; John Paul II recognized his ancient cultus, 18 April 1993, following the issuance of the *decretum* 21 December 1992.

Stanislas, son of Soltyn Matthias and Jadwiga, attended the local schools before studying at the Jagiellonian University of Krakow. After joining the canons regular of the Lateran of Corpus Christi (1456), professing his vows, and completing his studies for the priesthood, he was ordained. Thereafter he served the community in many roles, including novice master and subprior. But he is remembered for his defense of the faith against John Hus and John Wyclif, his devotion to the Blessed Sacrament, concern for the poor and sick, and preaching. Some of his written sermons and lectures have survived the destruction of World War II. His body now rests in the church of the Corpus Christi.

Bibliography: *Acta Apostolicae Sedis* (1993): 549.

[K. RABENSTEIN]

KERN, JAKOB FRANZ, BL.

Baptized Franz (Francis) Alexander Kern, Norbertine priest; b. 11 April 1897, Vienna; d. there, 20 October 1924 beatified in the *Heldenplatz* at Vienna, 21 June 1998.

One of three children of a working-class family, Kern discerned a call to the priesthood at an early age. He was in the minor seminary at Hollabrunn hoping to become a diocesan priest, when his studies were interrupted by the outset of World War I. He was drafted (1915) and sent Völklabruck for officer training. As an officer in the Austrian Army with the Fourth Tyrolean Imperial Fusiliers, he was severely wounded on the Italian Front (11 September 1916). After recuperating in Salzburg for nearly a year, he resumed his seminary studies, but was recalled to military duty until the end of the war. Thereafter he recommenced with his training for the archdiocesan priesthood. Upon hearing that Father Isidor Bogdan Zahrodnik, a Norbertine, had left his monastery for the schismatic Czech National Church, Jakob felt an inward compulsion to make vicarious satisfaction. He entered the Premonstratensian Abbey of Geras, northwest of Vienna near the Czech border, to begin his novitiate (1920). On 23 July 1922, with a dispensation because he had not taken his final vows, Brother Jakob was ordained in Saint Stephen's Cathedral, Vienna. He developed complications from his war injuries that debilitated him. On the day he was to make his solemn profession, he died during a second surgery. Kern's mortal remain are preserved in a small silver casket in a chapel adjacent to the Norbertine abbey church at Geras.

At his beatification Pope John Paul II called Kern "a witness of fidelity to the priesthood," who united "his own life with the sacrifice of Christ on the Cross to offer it vicariously for the salvation of others."

Feast: 20 October.

Bibliography: P. VOGEL, *Drei Aarauer Pioniere* (Zurich 1980). H. J. WELDINGER *Jakob Kern*, tr. H. S. SZANTO (Silverado, Calif. 1998); *Sühnepriester Jakob Kern* (Graz 1960) *L'Osservatore Romano*, Eng. ed. 29 (1995) 5; 25 (1998) 2.

[K. RABENSTEIN]

KINGA, ST.

A.k.a. Cunegund or Kunigunde, princess (sometimes referred to as "queen") of Malopolska (Little Poland), widow, consecrated virgin of the Poor Clares; b. 1224, Hungary; d. 24 July 1292, Stary Sacz (also Sandeck, Sandecz, or Sandez), Poland; canonized at Stary Sacz, Poland, by John Paul II, 16 June 1999.

Kinga was the daughter of King Bela IV of Hungary, Arpad Dynasty, and his wife, Maria, daughter of Emperor Theodorus Lascharis of Constantinople. Among the religious luminaries of her lineage are her sisters Saint Margaret of Hungary (d. 1270) and Blessed Jolenta of Hungary (d. 1299), her great-aunt Queen Saint Hedwig of Silesia (d. 1243), her aunt Saint Elizabeth of Hungary (1207–31), her uncle Blessed Ludwig IV of Thuringia (1200–27), and her cousin Blessed Gertrude of Altenberg (d. 1297). Kinga's position required her to marry (1239) Boleslaw II, sovereign of Lesser Poland (Krakow, Sandomire, and Lublin). Tradition relates that by mutual consent the couple pledged vows of perpetual continence before their bishop and their marriage was never consummated. Throughout her married life, Kinga continued to engage in prayer, mortification, and personal charity. Her spirituality was influenced by her contemporaries, the Dominican Saint Hyacinth (d. 1257) and the Blessed Bronisława (d. 1259), Sadok (d. 1260), and Salomea (d. 1268). At Boleslaw's death (1279), Kinga sold her possessions to relieve the poor, then took the veil at Stary Sacz Abbey, which she had built for the Poor Clares.

While Pope Alexander VIII approved Kinga's cultus as a beata in 1690, her cause for canonization required reintroduction and her heroic virtues were declared on 3 July 1998.

Speaking during Kinga's canonization, Pope John Paul II said: "As a princess she knew how to be about her Father's business even in this world. At her husband's side she shared in his rule, showing firmness and courage, generosity and concern for the good of the country and her subjects."

Patroness of Poland and Lithuania (declared 1695). Feast: 24 July (Poland); 27 July (Franciscans).

Bibliography: *Blogoslawiona Kinga: zyciorys, zbiór modlitw*, ed. J. R. BAR (Warsaw 1985). R. PICO, *Vita della venerabile Cunegonde, reina di Polonia*, based on data collected by A. BZOWSKI (Rome 1633) *Vita sanctae Kyngae ducissae Cracoviensis* (Tarnów 1997).

[K. RABENSTEIN]

KITBAMRUNG, NICHOLAS BUNKERD, BL.

Baptized Benedictus, priest, martyr; b. ca. 31 January to 28 February, 1895, on a sampan in the Nakhon Chaisri district (mission of Bangkok), Thailand; d. 12 January 1944, near Ban Han, Thailand; beatified at Rome by John Paul II, 5 March 2000.

One of six children of converts to the faith, Joseph Poxang and Agnes Thiang Kitbamrung, Nicholas entered the minor seminary of Hang Xan at thirteen. He completed his studies at Penang (Malaysia) Seminary and was ordained in Assumption Cathedral, Bangkok, by Bishop René Perros (24 January 1926). He began his pastoral work as assistant at Bang Nok Kheuk, Samut Songkhram province, where he also taught catechesis to Salesian seminarians and Thai to the priests establishing a mission in Thailand. He was transferred to Phitsanulok (1928), where he taught the language to his newly arrived pastor and learned a Chinese dialect (Hakka) himself. In 1930, he was sent as a missionary to North Vietnam and Chiang Mai (northern Thailand) to strengthen the faith of those who had left the Church due to privation. At the end of that mission, he was assigned to the Khorat District to engage in catechesis and re-evangelization of lapsed Catholics. He began evangelizing virtually unexplored lands along the border of Laos in 1937. He was arrested as a French spy (1941) during the war between France and Indochina and sentenced to ten years' imprisonment. While incarcerated Nicholas contracted tuberculosis, which was aggravated by maltreatment. Nevertheless, he continued to minister to his fellow inmates and baptized many of them before his death. When his illness became severe he was left in a hospital to die because he was a Catholic. The decree of martyrdom in his cause was promulgated, 27 January 2000. He was beatified with forty-three other martyrs from the young churches.

At that time Pope John Paul II declared Fr. Nicholas of Thailand: "outstanding in teaching the faith, in seeking out the lapsed, and in his charity towards the poor. Constantly seeking to make Christ known to those who had never heard his name, Father Nicolas undertook the difficulties of a mission through the mountains and into Burma. The strength of his faith was made clear to all when he forgave those who falsely accused him, deprived him of his freedom and made him suffer much.'' Patron of Thailand.

Bibliography: *L'Osservatore Romano,* Eng. ed. (8 March 2000): 1, 2–3.

[K. RABENSTEIN]

KOLBE, MAXIMILIAN, ST.

Franciscan priest, evangelizer, ''martyr of charity''; b. 8 January 1894, Zdunska Wola, Poland; d. 14 August 1941, in Oświęcim (Auschwitz), Poland. Baptized Raymond Kolbe, he took the religious name Maximilian when he entered the Conventual Franciscan Order's novitiate on 4 September 1910. Having professed simple vows as a friar on 5 September 1911 and solemn vows on 1 November 1914, he was ordained a priest in Rome, Italy, on 28 April 1918. While still a seminarian in Rome, on 16 Octobrer 1917 he founded the *Militia Immaculatae,* a movement promoting evangelization through Marian consecration. Returning to Poland in 1919, he soon initiated a mass media apostolate to further the work of evangelization. In 1922, he launched the publication *Rycerz Niepokalanej* (Knight of the Immaculate), whose monthly circulation would grow to one million issues by 1939. His publishing apostolate expanded to include three additional journals and one daily newspaper.

Though debilitated by tuberculosis, Kolbe founded a massive Franciscan friary and evangelization center, *Niepokalanów* (City of the Immaculate) near Warsaw in 1927 and a similar one in Nagasaki, Japan, in 1930. He labored at the Japanese mission for six years. He was regarded as an innovator in religious life, entrusting key responsibilities to nonordained friars trained in various specialties of the apostolate.

As guardian of Niepokalanów during the Nazi occupation of Poland, Kolbe welcomed more than 1,500 displaced Jewish refugees, ministering to them with such sensitivity that he even provided for their celebration of Jewish religious feasts. He was arrested by the Gestapo on 17 February 1941 after publishing an article entitled ''Truth.'' First imprisoned at Pawlak jail in Warsaw, he was transported to Oświęcim (Auschwitz) concentration camp on 28 May 1941. Though beaten, tortured, and subjected to extra punishment because he was a priest, Kolbe constantly encouraged his fellow prisoners to love their enemies: ''Hatred destroys; love alone creates.'' In late July 1941, a prisoner escaped from his barracks. In retaliation, the Nazis selected ten individuals for execution. One of the condemned, Franciszek Gajcwniczek, cried aloud that he had a wife and children. Moved by the plight of this family man, Kolbe stepped forward to take Gajowniczek's place. The Nazi commandant Fritsch allowed the substitution. Consigned with the other nine to a subterranean cell, Kolbe survived without food or water for nearly two weeks, until the Nazis dispatched him and the other survivors with lethal injection on 14 August. On 17 October 1971 Pope Paul VI beatified him, and on 10 October 1982 Pope John Paul II canonized him with the title ''Martyr of Charity.''

Bibliography: J. DOMANSKI, *I dati storici della vita del P. Massimiliano M. Kolbe* (Rome 1973); *For the Life of the World: Saint Maximilian and the Eucharist* (Libertyville, Ill. 1993). A. FROSSARD, *''Forget Not Love'': The Passion of Maximilian Kolbe* (Kenosha, Wisc. 1977). A. RICCIARDI, *St. Maximilian Kolbe: Apostle of Our Difficult Age* (Boston 1982). A. ROMB, ed., *The Kolbe Reader: The Writings of St Maximilian M. Kolbe, OFMConv.* (Libertyville, Ill. 1987). P. TREECE, *A Man for Others: Maximilian Kolbe Saint of Auschwitz, In the Words of Those Who Knew Him* (San Francisco 1982).

[JAMES E. MCCURRY]

KOLPING, ADOLF, BL.

Pioneer German Catholic social leader; Founder of the Kolping Societies *(Gesellenvereine)*; b. Kerpen, near Cologne, 8 December 1813; d. Cologne, 4 December 1865. Kolping was the son of a shepherd, Peter Kolping, and Anna Maria Zurheyden. He apprenticed as a shoemaker. While working twelve hours a day he prepared himself for institutions of higher learning by teaching himself. He was graduated from the Marzellengymnasium at the age of twenty-four, and then studied at the Universities of Munich and Bonn (1841–44). After his ordination at Cologne in 1845, he was assigned to the struggling industrial city of Elberfeld, where he was impressed by the effects of the new capitalism. He joined a youth organization founded by a teacher, Johann Gregor Breuer, became its president in 1847, and after two years of successful effort began to be called ''father of the journeymen.'' This organization was his model when, in 1849, he was transferred to the Cologne cathedral and founded there a Catholic association of journeymen. Even in his lifetime his ''Kolping Families'' *(Kolpingwerke)* spread throughout Europe and to America; at his death he was mourned by some 26,000 members in 400 different branches.

Kolping's spiritual character was formed by his family, his early sacrifices, and hard work. On the intellectual level he encountered at Munich the heritage of Johann Michael Sailer (1751–1832), for whom religion was the basis of all education. The social teachings of Franz von Baader (1765–1841) likewise left their mark upon his program. Professors who influenced him especially were Josef Görres, Ignaz Döllinger, and Friedrich Windischmann. Kolping deliberately opposed the intellectual tendencies of his age. He was a leader against the rationalism and antisocial individualism then found in the social and political spheres as liberalism among the upper classes and socialism among the lower. Nevertheless, he developed no system, but became a man of action.

Kolping recognized the new value of work and achievement in the transition from the feudal to the modern social order, as well as the importance of the education of the individual for the attainment of this value. He furthered the education of the young people in his association, which he wanted to have recognized as ''a people's academy in the people's style.'' At the same time, he demanded occupational efficiency, saying, ''Religion and work are the golden foundation of the people.''

Kolping's strength as an educator lay in his fostering of those attitudes that enable individuals to achieve something by their own power and to improve their social position. His purpose extended to raising the intellectual and spiritual status of the whole working class. In 1849, Kolping was appointed vicar of Cologne cathedral and began to write and speak extensively to promulgate the ideas of the Gesellenverein, defend the rights of workers, and awakened Catholics to their socio-political responsibilities. Kolping used the money generated by his writings to found several periodicals: *Rheinische Kirchenblatt, Feierstunde*, and *Vereinsorgan* (1850–54), *Rheinischen Volksblätter für Haus, Familie, und Handwerk* (from 1854), the *Katholischer Volkskalender* (1850–53), *Kalender für das katholische Volk* (1853-66). The so-called German ''John Bosco'' or ''Journeymen's Father'' died at age fifty-one and was buried in the Minoritenkirche, Cologne.

At his beatification, Pope John Paul II called Kolping the ''precursor of the great social encyclicals.'' He described the blessed as a man who ''stood with both feet planted firmly on the ground, and was oriented toward heaven.''

Bibliography: *Schriften. Kölner Ausgabe*, Vol. I: Documents, Diary, Poems, ed. H. J. KRACHT (Cologne 1975; 2d ed. 1981); Vol. II: Letters, ed. M. HANKE (Cologne 1976); Vol. III-V: Social Statements and the Gesellenverein, ed. R. COPELOVICI et al. (Cologne 1985–87); Vol. VI: Pictures from Rome, ed. H. J. KRACHT (Cologne 1986). *Briefe*, ed. M. HANKE and R. COPELOVICI (Cologne 1991). *Kolping und sein Werk*, ed. Generalsekretariat der kath. Gesellenvereine (Cologne 1920). Literature. T. BRAUER, *Kolping* (Freiburg 1923, Kevelaer 1935). A. BUETTNER, *Kolping Der Mann Gottes: Priester des Volkes* (Cologne 1937). V. CONZEMIUS, *Kolping Der Gesellenvater aktuell, damals und heute* (Fribourg-Hamburg 1982). C. FELDMANN, *Adolf Kolping: Für ein soziales Christentum* (Freiburg 1991). H. FESTING, *Kolping und sein Werk. Ein Überblick über Leben und Wirken des großen Sozialreformers sowie über die Entwicklung seines Werkes bis heute* (Freiburg 1981); *Was Kolping für uns bedeutet* (Freiburg 1985). H. GRANVOGL, *Kolping und die christliche-soziale Bewegung* (Augsburg 1987). M HANKE, *Sozialer Wandel durch Veränderung des Menschen. Leben, Wirken und Werk des Sozialpädagogen Kolping* (Mülheim 1974). H. J. KRACHT, *Kolping: Ein Mann von gestern mit Ideen für morgen* (2d. ed. Essen 1972); *Kolping: Sozialpädagoge und Erwachsenenbildner* (Cologne 1977). R. MÜLLER, *Adolf Kolping: Visionär und Reformer* (Freiburg 1991). L. PERRIDON, *Gesellschaftspolit. Bedingungen der Arbeit Kolpings* (Augsburg-Munich 1978). T. REMPE, *Kolping: Grundsätze zur Pädagogik und Organisation seines Werkes* (Cologne 1975). B. RIDDER, *Person und Leben Kolpings in Urkunden und im Urteil von Zeitgenossen* (Cologne 1960). G. RITZERFELD, *Kolping* (Cologne 1963). S. G. SCHÄFFER, *Kolping, der Gesellenvater. Ein Lebensbild* (Münster 1880, 1882, reprinted Paderborn 1894, Cologne 1927, 1947, 1952, 1961). *Acta Apostolicae Sedis* (1991) 1064.

[H. FISCHER]

KOREA, MARTYRS OF, SS.

A.k.a. Andrew Kim Tae-gon and Companions, and Paul Chong Hasang and Companions; d. in Korea, 1839, 1846, 1866, and 1867. During his 21st international pastoral visit, Pope John Paul II canonized 103 of the estimated 8,000-10,000 martyrs of Korea on 6 May 1984, in its capital Seoul. This marked the bicentennial of Christianity in Korea and the first canonization ceremony held outside the Vatican. After noting the uniqueness of the Korean Catholic community in the history of the Church, he said: ''The death of the martyrs is similar to the death of Christ on the Cross, because, like his, theirs has become the beginning of new life.''

The canonized Korean Martyrs are 103 Catholics first beatified in two groups: 79 martyrs who died during the Choson Dynasty (1839–46) were beatified in 1925; 24 martyred in 1866–67 were raised to the altar in 1968. Among the group were 10 French missionaries (3 bishops and 7 Paris Society of Foreign Missions (MEP), 46 Korean men (1 priest, 1 seminarian, 25 lay catechists, and 19 other laymen), and 47 Korean women (15 virgins, 11 married women, 18 widows, 3 of unknown marital status, 3 of them were catechists). They ranged in age from 13 to 78. Most of the canonized saints were beheaded, but 17 were hanged or strangled, 10 expired in prison, and 7 died under torture. Their common feast is 20 September on the General Roman Liturgical Calendar.

The names of the two martyrs listed in the liturgical calendar are Andrew Kim Te-gon, the first Korean priest, and Paul Chong Pasang, a renowned lay leader.

Andrew Kim Te-gon, b. Tchoung-tcheng Province, Korea, 21 August 1821; d. near Seoul, Korea, 16 September 1846, was born into Korean nobility. Kim's father Ignatius Kim, and grandfather, In-He Kim (d. 1814) died for the faith. After his baptism (1836) Andrew went with two other Korean youths to seminary in Macao, China, where he remained until 1842. He then set out for his native land, but not until his third attempt and after many difficulties did he succeed in entering closely guarded Hermit Kingdom by way of Manchuria (1845). In 1844 he was ordained a deacon, and in 1845 he crossed the Yellow Sea and was ordained a priest in Shanghai, becoming the first native Korean priest. He returned to Korea in company with Bp Jean Ferréol, the vicar apostolic, and Fr. A. Daveluy. In 1846 Kim was assigned to arrange for the entrance of more missionaries by some water routes that would elude the border patrol. During this process he was arrested, imprisoned, tortured, and finally beheaded at the Han River near Seoul, the capital. The body was exposed publicly for three days, according to the custom, before burial at the site of execution. After forty days the Catholics were able to obtain the remains and bury them on Mi-ri nai Mountain about thirty-five miles distant. In 1949 the Holy See designated him the principal patron of the clergy of Korea.

Paul Chong Hasang (Cheong), seminarian, lay catechist, d. 22 Sept. 1839 (age 45), hanged outside the small west gate in Seoul. Paul was one of the lay leaders of the early Korean Church. His father, leader of the confraternity of Christian doctrine, and his uncle were martyred in the Shin-Yu persecution of 1801. Following in their footsteps, Paul gathered the scattered Christians and labored to strengthen the infant Korean Church. He traveled nine times to Beijing as a servant to the Korean diplomatic mission in order to petition the bishop of Beijing to send priests to Korea. Because his plea fell on deaf ears, he appealed directly to Rome in 1925, which led to the dispatch of French missionaries. He also wrote to the prime minister a short apologetic (Sang-Je-Sang-Su) on Christian doctrine and its harmony with national values in the hope of ending the persecution of Christians. Paul was one of the three men sent by Maubant to Macao for seminary training; however, he was martyred prior to ordination. His mother Cecilia and sister died for their faith shortly thereafter.

The earliest missionaries to Korea are also included among the martyrs canonized: Laurent Joseph Marius Imbert, bishop; b. 1786, Marignane (Bouches-du-Rhône), France; Pierre Philibert Maubant, b.1803 in Vaussy (Calvados); Jacques Honoré Chastan, b. 1803 in Marcoux (Basses-Alpes). Imbert entered the MEP in 1818, was ordained in 1819, and went to China (1820) after ordination, where he labored as a missionary until he became the second vicar apostolic of Korea (1837) and the first one to enter the country. Preceding him were two French confreres, Maubant and Chastan. Maubant was ordained in 1829, joined the MEP in 1831, and set out for Korea in 1832. He entered the country in 1836, the same year as Chastan, who was ordained in 1826, joined the MEP in 1827, and went to Thailand before his assignment to Korea (1832). Since the Hermit Kingdom, as Korea was known, did not admit foreigners and did not tolerate Christians, the three men, the only priests then in the country, could not engage openly in their apostolate. An edict, issued in April 1839 was followed by fierce persecution. Bishop Imbert (whose Korean name was Bom) found it necessary to flee from Seoul, the capital, in June. He remained in hiding until betrayed by a renegade Christian and seized by the authorities (11 August). From his prison in Seoul he sent to his two priests a controversial letter that directed them to come forward. Maubant (Ra in Korean) and Chastan (Cheong) came as directed. The three were tried, tortured, and sentenced to military execution. After they had been beheaded at state expense at a public and solemn ceremony in Sae Nam Do near Seoul (21 Sept. 1839), their heads were suspended in public to terrify Christians. There mortal remains are enshrined at Samsong-san, near Seoul.

Besides these men, the following other marytrs were canonized. They listed by their given name together with their date of death and age at the time of death.

Agatha Chon Kyong-hyob (Kyung-Hyun Jeon, Tiyen), virgin; d. 26 Sept. 1839 (52), beheaded outside the small west gate.

Agatha Kim A-gi (Up-Yi Kim), widow; d. 24 May 1839 (65); beatified 1925.

Agatha Kwon Chin-i (Jin-Yi Kwon), housewife; d. 31 Jan. 1840 (21), beheaded at Dang-Gogae.

Agatha Yi (Lee), virgin; d. 9 Jan. 1840 (17), hanged at Po Chung Ok.

Agatha Yi Kan-nan (Gan-Nan Lee), widow; d. 20 Sept. 1846 (32), hanged at Po Chung Ok.

Agatha Yi Kyong-i (Kyung-Yi Lee), virgin; d. 31 Jan. 1840 (27), beheaded at Dang-Gogae.

Agatha So-Sa Lee, widow; d. 24 May 1839 (55), beheaded outside small west gate

Agnes Kim Hyo-ju (Hyo-Joo Kim), virgin; d. 3 Sept. 1839 (23), beheaded outside the small west gate. She was imprisoned with her sister Columba Kim.

Alexius U Se-yong (Se-Young Woo); d. 21 March 1866 (21), beheaded at Saenam-To, then was displayed.

Andrew Chong Hwa-gyong (Hwa-Kyung Jung; Cheong; Tjyeng), lay catechist; d. 23 Jan. 1840 (33), hanged at Po Chung Ok.

Anna Kim Chang-gum (Jang-Keum Kim), widow; d. 20 July 1839 (50), beheaded outside small west gate.

Anna Pak A-gi (Ah-Ki Park), housewife, 24 May 1839 (56), beheaded outside small west gate.

Antoine Daveluy, French bishop; d. 30 March 1866 (49) beheaded at Kalmaemot, then the head was displayed as a warning to other Christians. He entered Korea with Andrew Kim Tae-gon and Bp. Ferréol in 1845. In 1862, he baptized forty catechumens in the Christian refuge now called Han-Ti (meaning "mass grave") in the Palgong Mountains. Later all the Christians of the village were massacred in a surprise attack and buried together. Daveluy was responsible for establishing a press to print catechisms and for collecting and preserving information on those martyred. He edited the first Korean-French dictionary, which authorities burnt together with other Christian books. In an attempt to spare other Christians, Daveluy turned himself in. From jail he wrote to Aumaitre and Martin Huin suggesting the same course of action. He was consecrated auxiliary to Bp. Berneux (1856) and martyred with Aumaitre, Huin, and Joseph Chang Chu-gi just three weeks after becoming the 5th apostolic vicar of Korea.

Anthony Kim Song-u (Sung-Woo Kim), lay catechist, d. 29 April 1841 (46), strangled in prison at Dang-Gogae for harboring foreign priests in his home. Two of his brothers were also martyred.

Augustine Pak Chong-won (Jong-Won Park), lay catechist; d. 31 Jan. 1840 (48), beheaded at Dang-GoGae.

Augustine Yi Kwang-hon (Kwang-Hun Lee, Ni), lay catechist; d. 24 May 1839 (52), beheaded outside small west gate.

Augustine Yu Chin-kil (Jin-Kil Yoo, Ryou, Nyou); d. 22 Sept. 1839 (48), beheaded outside small west gate.

Barbara Cho Chung-i (Zung-Yi Cho), housewife; d. 29 Dec. 1839 (57), beheaded outside the small west gate.

Barbara Ch'oe Yong-i (Young-Yi Choi), housewife; d. 1 Feb. 1840 (22), hanged at Dang-Gogae.

Barbara Han A-gi (Ah-Ki Han), widow; d. 24 May 1839 (47), beheaded outside the small west gate.

Barbara Kim, widow; d. 27 May 1839 (34) in prison.

Barbara Ko Sun-i (Soon-Yi Ko), housewife; d. 29 Dec. 1839 (41), beheaded outside the small west gate.

Barbara Kwon Hui (Hee Kwon), housewife; d. 3 Sept. 1839 (45), beheaded outside the small west gate.

Barbara Yi (Jung-Hee Lee, Yong-h'ui), widow; d. 3 Sept. 1839 (40), beheaded outside the small west gate. She is the aunt of Barbara Yi Chong-hui (infra) and sister of Magdalene Yi Yong- h'ui.

Barbara Yi Chong-hui (Jung-Hee Lee), virgin; d. 27 May 1839 (14) in prison. Her aunts Barbara Jung-Hee Lee and Magdalene Yi Yong-h'ui were martyred several months later.

Bartholomew Chong Mun-ho (Moon-Ho Jung), county governor; d. 23 Dec. 1866 (65), beheaded at Jun Joo (ChonHo), where he is buried.

Benedicta Hyon Kyong-nyon (Kyung-Ryung Han; Hyen), lay catechist; d. 29 Dec. 1839 (45), beheaded outside the small west gate.

Catherine Chong Ch'ol-yom (Chul-Yom Jung; Cheong), housewife; d. 20 Sept. 1846 (29), hanged at Po Chung Ok.

Catherine Yi (Lee), widow; d. 26 Sept. 1839 (56) in prison.

Charles Cho Shin-ch'ol (Shin-Chul Cho, Tjyo); d. 26 Sept. 1839 (46), beheaded outside the small west gate.

Charles Hyon Sok-mun (Seok-Moon Hyun, Hyen), lay catechist; d. 19 Sept. 1846 (49), decapitated and head displayed at Seoul. Bishop Imbert entrusted the care of the Korean Christians to Charles before the deaths of the three priests.

Cecilia Yu So-sa (Ryou), widow and mother of Paul Chong Hasang and Elizabeth Chong Ch'ong-hye; d. 23 Nov. 1839 (78) in prison.

Columba Kim Hyo-im, virgin; d. 26 Sept. 1839 (25), imprisoned, pierced with red hot awls scorched with burning coals, then beheaded outside the small west gate.

Damian Nam Myong-hyok, lay catechist; d. 24 May 1839 (37) beheaded outside small west gate. He was a model husband and father.

Elizabeth Chong Ch'ong-hye (Jung-Hye Jung; Cheong), virgin, younger sister of Paul Chong Hasang; d. 29 Dec. 1839 (42), beheaded outside small west gate.

Francis Ch'oe Kyong-hwan (Kyung-Hwan Choi, Tchoi), lay catechist; d. 12 Sept. 1839 (34) in prison. Francis is the father of Korea's second native priest, Thomas Yang-Up Choi. During the Gihae persecution his family was arrested. His youngest son starved to death in his mother's arms in prison; however, four of his sons survived to witness the beheading of Francis' wife, Maria Song-Rye Yi, the year following his death (1840). Although his sons did not die for the faith, they suffered becoming exiled beggars. In 1849, Fr Yang-Up Choi returned to his homeland to pray at his father's grave near AnYang in the village of DamBae-Gol.

Ignatius Kim Che-jun (Je-Joon Kim), father of Andrew Kim and lay catechist; d. 26 Sept. 1839 (43), beheaded outside the small west gate.

John Baptist Chon Chang-un (Jang-Woon Jeon), vendor and publisher; d. 9 March 1866 (55), beheaded outside the small west gate.

John Baptist Nam Chong-sam (Jong-Sam Nam), regional governor; d. 7 March 1866 (49), beheaded outside the small west gate of Seoul. Chong-sam was renowned as a just government official. Before his arrest and martyrdom he resigned his position and retired to Myojae because he could not offer sacrifice to his ancestors in good conscience. He is remembered as a model of chastity, charity, and poverty.

John Baptist Yi Kwang-nyol (Kwang-Ryul Lee), technician; d. 20 July 1839 (44), beheaded outside the small west gate.

John Pak Hu-jae (Hoo-Jae Park), merchant; d. 3 Sept. 1839 (40), beheaded outside the small west gate.

John Ri Mun-u (Moon-Woo Lee), lay catechist; d. 1 Feb. 1839 (31), hanged at Dang-Gogae. He was a Korean layman who wrote a still extant letter from prison; beatified 1925.

John Yi Yun-il (Yoon-Il Lee), lay catechist; d. 21 Jan. 1867 (43), beheaded at Kwan-Duk Jung in TaeKu. In 1987, his body was translated to the Lourdes Grotto at TaeKu, where Pope John Paul II stopped to pray in 1984.

Joseph Chang Chu-gi (Joo-Ki Jang), lay catechist and teacher of Chinese literature; d. 30 March 1866 (63). The first Korean seminary was established in his home in 1856. One room was used as a classroom and dormitory; the other as a rectory. He was decapitated and head displayed at Kalmaemot for trying to protect the Christians hidden in his pottery kiln, which had been used by the Christians as a place of worship and to support themselves once they were dispossessed of family and property for their religion.

Joseph Chang Song-jib (Sung-Jip Jang, Tjyang), brother of Anthony Sung-Woo Kim; d. 26 May 1839 (53), strangled in prison at Po Chung Ok.

Joseph Cho Yun-ho (Yoon-Ho Cho), farmer; d. 23 Dec. 1866 (18) died at JunJoo.

Joseph Im Ch'i-baek (Chi-Baek Im, Rim), Seoul boatman; d. 20 Sept. 1846 (42) hanged at Po Chung Ok.

Julietta Kim, virgin; d. 26 Sept. 1839 (55), beheaded outside the small west gate.

Just Ranfer de Bretennières, French priest; d. 7 March 1866 (28), decapitated, head displayed at Seoul.

Lawrence Han I-hyong (Yi-Hyung Han), lay catechist; d. 20 Sept. 1846 (47), hanged Po Chung Ok.

Lucy Kim, virgin; d. 20 July 1839 (21) outside the small west gate.

Lucy Kim (II), widow; d. 26 Sept. 1839 (70) in prison.

Lucy Pak Hui-sun (Hee-Soon Park), virgin; d. 5 May 1839 (38), beheaded outside the small west gate.

Louis Beaulieu, French priest; d. 7 March 1866 (26), decapitated and head displayed at Seoul.

Luke Hwang Sok-tu (Seok-Du Hwang), lay catechist; d. 30 March 1866 (53), beheaded then displayed at Kalmaemot. Luke was the brilliant co-worker of Bishop Daveluy. He translated the Bible into Korean and wrote catechetical material for publication.

Magdalena Cho, virgin; d. 26 Sept. 1839 (32) in prison.

Magdalena Han Yong-i (Young-Yi Han), widow; d. 29 Dec. 1839 (55), beheaded outside the small west gate.

Magdalena Ho Kye-im (Gye-Im Her; He Kye-im, Ho), housewife; d. 26 Sept. 1839 (66), beheaded outside the small west gate.

Magdalena Kim Ob-i (Ah-Ki Lee), widow; d. 24 May 1839 (52), hanged outside the small west gate.

Magdalena Pak Pong-son (Bong-Son Park), widow; d. 26 Sept. 1839 (43), beheaded outside the small west gate.

Magdalena Son So-byok (So-Byuk Son), housewife; d. 31 Jan. 1840 (39), hanged at Dang-GoGae.

Magdalena Yi Yong-dok (Young-Duk Lee), virgin; d. 29 Dec. 1839 (27), beheaded outside the small west gate.

Magdalena Yi Yong-h'ui (Young-Hee Lee), virgin; d. 20 July 1839 (30) outside small west gate. She is the sister of Barbara Yi.

Maria Pak K'un-agi (Keum-AhKi Park), housewife; d. 3 Sept. 1839 (53), beheaded outside the small west gate. Her husband, Philip Kim, was also martyred but is not numbered among these saints.

Maria Won Kwi-im (Gui-Im Won, Ouen), virgin; d. 20 July 1839 (21), beheaded outside the small west gate.

Maria Yi In-dok (In-Duk Lee), virgin; d. 31 Jan. 1840 (22), hanged at Dang-GoGae.

Maria Yi Y'on-hui (Yeon-Hee Lee), wife, mother, member of a simple form of religious sisterhood; d. 3 Sept. 1839 (35), beheaded outside the small west gate.

Mark Chong Ui-bae (Eui-Bae Jung), lay catechist; d. 11 March 1866 (71), decapitated and head displayed at Seoul.

Martha Kim Song-im (Sung-Im Kim), widow; d. 20 July 1839 (49), outside the small west gate.

Martin Luc (Luke) Huin, French priest; d. 30 March 1866 (30), beheaded and head displayed at Kalmaemot.

Paul Ho Hyop (Im Her, He, Heo), soldier; d. 30 Jan. 1840 (45), hanged at Po Chung Ok.

Paul Hong Yong-ju (Young-Joo Hong), lay catechist; d. 1 Feb. 1840 (39), beheaded at Dang-GoGae.

Perpetua Hong Kum-ju (Keum-Joo Hong), widow; d. 29 Sept. 1839 (35), beheaded outside the small west gate.

Pierre Aumaitre, French priest of MEP; d. 30 March 1866 (29), beheaded at Kalmaemot.

Peter Cho Hwa-so (Hwa-Seo Cho), farmer; d. 13 Dec. 1866 (51), beheaded at Jun Joo.

Peter Ch'oe Ch'ang-hup (Chang-Hoop Choi), lay catechist; d. 29 Dec. 1839 (52), beheaded outside the small west gate.

Peter Ch'oe Hyong (Hyung Choi), lay catechist; d. 9 March 1866 (52), beheaded outside the small west gate.

Peter Chong Won-ji (Won-Ji Jung), farmer; d. 13 Dec. 1866 (20), beheaded at JunJoo.

Peter Hong Pyong-ju (Byung-Joo Hong, Kong), lay catechist; d. 31 Jan. 1840 (42), hanged at Dang-GoGae.

Peter Kwon Tug-in (Deuk-In Kwon, Kouen), producer of religious goods; d. 24 May 1839 (34) in prison outside small west gate.

Peter Nam Kyong-mun (Kyung-Moon Nam), soldier, lay catechist; d. 20 Sept. 1846 (50), hanged at Po Chung Ok.

Peter Son Son-ji (Seon-Ji Son), lay catechist; d. 13 Dec. 1866 (46), beheaded at SupJungYi with Bartholomew Chong Mun-ho. Their bodies rest at Chon Ho in the north Cholla Province.

Peter Ho-Young Lee, lay catechist; d. 25 Nov. 1838 (35) in prison.

Peter Won-Seo Han, lay catechist; d. 13 Dec. 1866 (20), beheaded at Jun Joo.

Peter Yi Myong-so (Myung-Seo Lee), farmer; d. 13 Dec. 1866 (45), beheaded at Jun Joo.

Peter Yi Tae-ch'ol (Dae-Chul Yoo, Ryou, Ryau), youth; d. 31 Oct. 1839 (13) at Po Chung Ok. Little Peter had presented himself to the magistrates, proclaiming that he was a Christian. The judges were horrified at his tortures. Fearing the popular opinion would turn again the authorities, his executioners strangled him after his return to prison.

Peter Yu Chong-nyul (Jung-Ryung Yoo), lay catechist; d. 17 Feb. 1866 (29) at PyungYang (now in North Korea).

Pierre-Henri Dorie, French priest; d. 7 March 1866 (27), beheaded at SaeNamTo and head displayed.

Protasius Chong Kuk-bo (Kook-Bo Jung, Cheong), noble and maker of musical instruments; d. 20 May 1839 (40) in prison at Po Chung Ok. He apostatized under torture and was released. Later he regretted his weakness, gave himself up to the authorities, and died from his torments.

Rosa Kim, widow; d. 20 July 1839 (55), beheaded outside the small west gate.

Sebastian Nam I-gwan (Yi-Kwan Nam), lay catechist; d. 26 Sept. 1839 (59), beheaded outside the small west gate.

Simeon Berneux, French bishop; d. 7 March 1866 (52), beheaded.

Stephen Min Kuk-ka (Geuk-Ga Min), lay catechist; d. 30 Jan. 1840 (53), hanged at Po Chung Ok.

Susanna U Sul-im (Sul-Im Woo), widow; d. 20 Sept. 1846 (43), hanged at Po Chung Ok.

Teresa Kim, widow; d. 9 Jan. 1940 (44) hanged at Po Chung Ok.

Teresa Kim Im-i (Yim-Yi Kim), virgin; d. 20 Sept. 1846 (35), hanged at Po Chung Ok.

Teresa Yi Mae-im (Mae-Im Lee), housewife; d. 20 July 1839 (51), outside small west gate.

Thomas Son Cha-son (Ja-Sun Son), farmer; d. 30 March 1866 (22), hanged at Gong Joo.

Bibliography: *Acta Apostolicae Sedis* 17 (1925): 366–69. *L'Osservatore Romano,* English edition, no. 20 (1984): 5–6, 20. C. DALLET, *L'Histoire de l'Eglise de Corée* (1874), 118–85. *Documents relatifs au martyrs de Corée,* 2. v. (Hong Kong 1924). C. A. HERBST, ''Unless the Grain of Wheat First Die . . . ,'' *American Ecclesiastical Revue* 139 (1958): 331–37; ''The Bishop Dies,'' ibid. 138 (1958): 149–57; ''Korea's Martyr-Patron,'' ibid. 137 (1957): 330–41. K. D. KIM, *Life of Kim Dae Kun* (Seoul 1960), in Korean. A. LAUNAY, *Martyrs français et coréens* (1925). S. A. MOFFETT, *The Christians of Korea* (New York 1962). M. W. NOBLE, *Victorious Lives of Early Christians* (Seoul 1933).

[C. A. HERBST/K. RABENSTEIN]

KOŠICE, MARTYRS OF, SS.

Melichar Grodziecký, Marek Križín, and Stefan Pongrácz; priests, martyrs; d. 7 and 8 Sept. 1619 at Košice in the far eastern portion of Slovakia; beatified 1905; canonized by Pope John Paul II, 2 July 1995 at the airport of Košice.

Košice was a Calvinist stronghold in the early seventeenth century. These martyrs came from three countries in order to offer the sacraments to Catholics who were otherwise without priests. The king's deputy petitioned the Jesuits to send priests to tend to the minority population and gratefully housed the two respondents in his official residence outside the city. Protestant antipathy toward Catholicism increased. Upon hearing that the Calvinist prince of Transylvania was approaching Košice under Georg I Rákóczi, the Jesuits hurried back to the city to be with their flock and were joined by the canon Križín. On the morning of 7 September, soldiers tried to force them into apostasy. Upon their refusal, the priests were brutally beaten and killed. Their bodies were thrown into a sewage ditch, where they remained for 6 months before a pious countess was given permission to bury them. Immediately after death, they became the objects of veneration. Their relics are now housed in the Ursuline church at Trnava, Croatia.

Melichar Grodziecký, a.k.a. Melchior Grodech or Grodecz, Jesuit priest; b. ca. 1584, in Grodziec (a village between Biesko and Cieszyn), Silesia, Poland. Melichar was born into a noble family and had Bishop John of Olomouc as an uncle. Melichar was educated by the Jesuits at Vienna, Austria. After joining the Society of Jesus at Brno, Moravia (1603), which was founded by his uncle John, he studied philosophy and theology, was ordained (1614), and worked as a teacher in Prague. At the outbreak of the Thirty Years War, he passed through Moravia and Slovakia, finally settling in Košice. Following the initial beating, Fr. Melichar was stripped, tortured, and finally he was mercifully beheaded.

Marek Križín a.k.a. Mark Crisin, Korosy, or Križevčanin, diocesan priest, administrator of Széplak Abbey; b. 1588 at Križevči, Croatia. Born into a noble Croatian family, he was educated by the Jesuits in Vienna and Graz, where he earned a doctorate in philosophy, and at the Germanicum (1611–1615) in Rome. Following ordination in Rome, he ministered for two years in his homeland. Then his former professor in Graz, Cardinal Pázmány, appointed him head of the Trnava seminary and a canon of the Esztergom Cathedral (Hungary). In 1619, he accepted assignment as administrator of the property of the former Benedictine abbey of Krásna near Košice in the hope of stimulating the faith there. In the face of persecution he remained at the service of his flock, offering an example of fidelity to Christ. Križín, to whom the attention of the soldiers had first turned, suffered the same tortures as Grodziecký. When Križín fainted from the pain, he was beheaded.

Stefan (Stephen) Pongrácz, Jesuit priest; b. ca. 1582 at Alvincz Castle, Transylvania, Hungary. Born into a noble family, he studied classics in his homeland, then attended the Jesuit College at Cluj, Romania, and abandoned the prospect of a brilliant, secular career in order to enter the Society of Jesus at Brno, Moravia (1602), where he first met Grodziecký. Following his studies in philosophy at Prague (Bohemia) and theology at Graz (Austria), he was ordained in 1615. He taught for a time at the Jesuit college at Humenné, Slovakia, before accepting the invitation to minister in troubled Košice. Despite savage and prolonged torture, Pongrácz' was alive when the soldiers threw him into the sewage ditch with his dead companions. He suffered in pain for another 20 hours before giving up his spirit.

During the canonization ceremony the Holy Father noted: "This canonization was also an important ecumenical event, as was evident both at my meeting with representatives of the Protestant denominations and during my visit to the place that commemorates the death of a group of the faithful of the Reformation." He prayed at the monument commemorating their death.

On first glance it is difficult to reconcile the Pope John Paul II's efforts toward Christian unity and this canonization of three martyrs of the Reformation. But as he explained it in his homily:

> Today's liturgy invites us to reflect on the tragic events of the early seventeenth century, emphasizing, on the one hand, the senselessness of violence relentlessly visited upon innocent victims and, on the other, the splendid example of so many followers of Christ who were able to face sufferings of every kind without going against their own consciences. Besides the three Martyrs of Košice many other people, also belonging to Christian confessions, were subjected to torture and suffered heavy punishment; some were even put to death. How can we fail to acknowledge, for example, the spiritual greatness of the 24 members of the Evangelical Churches who were killed at Presov? To them and to all who accepted suffering and death out of fidelity to the dictates of their conscience the Church gives praise and expresses admiration. . . . May [the example of the three new saints] renew in their fellow citizens of today a commitment to mutual understanding. . . .

Feast: 7 September (Jesuit calendar).

Bibliography: *L'Osservatore Romano,* English edition, no. 27 (1995): 1–3; no. 28 (1995): 6, 11; no. 29 (1995): 9. J. N. TYLENDA, *Jesuit Saints and Martyrs* (Chicago 1998): 290–292.

[K. RABENSTEIN]

KOSTISTK, GEREMIA OF VALACHIA, BL.

Also known as Jeremiah or Jeremy of Valachia, and Ieremia Stoica, Capuchin; b. 29 June 1556, Zaro, Romania; d. 5 March 1625, Naples, Italy; beatified by John Paul II, 30 October 1983, as the first Romanian officially beatified.

Leaving his friary in Romania to travel to Naples, Geremia startled the locals by living in imitation of Christ for forty years. He was known for his spiritual wisdom and fraternal love for the poor and sick to whom he ministered selflessly. He fell ill while tending the sick and died at age sixty-eight.

At his beatification Pope John Paul II said: "The glorification of this faithful servant of the Lord, after three centuries of concealment, is reserved to our time, marked by the search for ecumenism and solidarity among peoples on an international level."

Feast: 8 May.

Bibliography: F. S. TOPPI, *Spirito francescano nel beato Geremia Stoica da Valacchia, Studi e Ricerche Francescane* (1984) 127–42. *Acta Apostolicae Sedis* 76 (1984): 550–53. *L'Osservatore Romano,* Eng. ed. 46 (1983): 6–7.

[K. RABENSTEIN]

KOWALSKA, FAUSTINA, ST.

Baptized Elena, in religion Maria Faustina, visionary, virgin of the Congregation of the Blessed Virgin Mary of Mercy; b. 25 August 1905, at Głogowiec (west of Łodz), Poland; d. 5 October 1938, at Kraków; both beatified (18 April 1993) and canonized (30 April 2000) in Rome by John Paul II.

Known as the apostle of Divine Mercy, Faustina was the third of ten children (six survived infancy) in a poor family. Although she had only two years of formal education, her diaries exhibit profound insight. She was baptized at St. Casimir's, Swinice Warckie; at age seven (1912), she first heard Jesus in an inner locution inviting her to strive for perfection. In 1922, she expressed a desire to enter the convent, but, because her parents needed her financial help, she worked as a housekeeper in Aleksandrów, Łodz, and Ostrówek. At age twenty-nine, she first attempted to enter a convent in Warsaw, but was turned away. Following a vision of the suffering Christ, she entered the Sisters of the Blessed Virgin Mary of Mercy (1 August 1925) and changed her name. After her postulancy at a vacation house and novitiate in Kraków, she made her temporary vows, 30 April 1928. Faustina professed her final vows in 1933 before Bishop Stanislaus Rospond of Kraków. Thereafter, she served her sisters as an unassuming cook, gardener, and porter in the congregation's houses at Kraków, Płock, and Vilnius.

On 22 February 1931 in Płock, Faustina had a vision of Jesus, asking her to promote the Second Sunday of Easter as a celebration of Divine Mercy and spread the devotion throughout the world. After a psychiatric assessment certified Faustina's mental health, Father Michael Sopocko, her spiritual director, arranged for artist Kazimierowski to render a painting of her vision of Jesus as the merciful savior with streams of red and white light shining from his heart. Faustina kept a journal of her mystical experiences. Only a few of her superiors, her confessor, and spiritual director knew of her visions, revelations, hidden stigmata, and gifts of ubiquity, reading souls, and prophecy. A poor translation of her nearly 700-page diary was condemned by the Vatican in 1958. However, when popular veneration of Faustina continued, Cardinal Karol Wojtyła had it re-translated, which resulted in the ban's removal, 15 April 1978, six months before his election to the papacy. In visions Christ also asked the humble sister to propagate the Chaplet of Divine Mercy, veneration of the Divine Mercy image inscribed "Jesus, I trust in You," and the remembrance of his death each day at 3:00 P.M.

Faustina, the inspiration for the Polish Apostles of Divine Mercy, died from tuberculosis. The movement comprised of priests, religious, and laity has spread to twenty-nine countries. Pope John Paul II made a pilgrimage to Faustina's tomb at the Sanctuary of Divine Mercy in Kraków-Łagiewniki (7 June 1997), where she died and which the young Wojtyła visited daily before work at the Solvay factory.

Her cause for beatification was reopened in Rome, 30 January 1968. Pope John Paul II culminated his life-long efforts to propagate devotion to the Divine Mercy (see *Dives in Misericordia*, 1980) by canonizing Sister Faustina and officially declaring (30 April 2000) that the Second Sunday of Easter would also be designated "Divine Mercy Sunday" throughout the Church.

At both Faustina's beatification and canonization ceremonies, the Holy Father linked Christ's message through Faustina as the antidote to the misery of the twentieth century. At her beatification, he spoke of the "testimony given by all those who were encouraged by this message in the cruel experiences of the Second World War, in the concentration camps, and in the bombings."

Feast: 5 October.

Bibliography: Writings by St. Faustina: *Divine Mercy in My Soul: The Diary of the Servant of God, Sister M. Faustina Kowalska.* (Stockbridge, Mass. 1987). *Revelations of Divine Mercy: Daily Readings from the Diary of Blessed Faustina Kowalska,* ed. G. W. KOSICKI (Ann Arbor, Mich. 1996). Literature about St. Faustina: J. BURKUS, *Gaila minios* (Hot Springs, Ark. 1983). G. W. KOSICKI, *Now is the Time for Mercy* (Stockbridge, Mass. 1991). MARIAN FATHERS, *The Promise* (Stockbridge, Mass. 1987). S. MICHALENKO, *The Life of Faustina Kowalska* (Ann Arbor, Mich. 1999). C. M.

ODELL, *Faustina: Apostle of Divine Mercy* (Huntington, Ind. 1998). S. URBANSKI, *Zycie mistyczne błogoslawionej Faustyny Kowalskiej* (Warsaw 1997).

[K. RABENSTEIN]

KOZAL, MICHAŁ, BL.

Bishop, martyr of Dachau; b. 27 September 1893, Ligota (now Nowy Folwark near Poznán), Poland; d. 26 January 1943, Dachau Concentration Camp; beatified at Warsaw, Poland, by John Paul II, 14 June 1987.

Kozal was born into a devout peasant family. Following his ordination to the priesthood (1918), he held parish assignments while teaching in Catholic secondary schools. In August 1939, Kozal was appointed by Pope Pius XII auxilary bishop of Wloclawek, Poland, then named bishop. During the short time between his consecration and arrest in which he could celebrate only a single Mass, Kozal was responsible for sending to safety Stefan Wyszynski. Kozal was arrested by the Gestapo on 7 November 1939 as part of the Nazi drive to eradicate the Polish intelligentsia and elite. He was held for a time in a Wloclawek prison, then sent to a convent in Lad. Following stops in Szczeglin and Berlin, Kozal was interned at Dachau (25 April 1941). For the next two years he secretly celebrated Mass whenever possible and ministered to his fellow prisoners. He was killed with an injection of carbolic acid.

Feast: 14 June.

Bibliography: S. BISKUPSKI, *Meczénskie biskupstwo ksiedza Michala Kozala; bararzynstwo hitlerowskie w walce z Kósciolem Katolickim w Polsce* (2d. ed. Warsaw 1955). T. BOJARSKA, *Cierniowa mitra* (Warsaw 1971). W. FRATCZAK, *Biskup Michal Kozal: zycie-meczénstwo-kult* (Warsaw 1987). F. KORSZYNSKI, *Un vescovo polacco a Dachau* (Brescia 1963). Nuremberg War Crimes Trial Proceedings, v. 4, 511. *L'Osservatore Romano,* Eng. ed. 23 (1987): 12.

[K. RABENSTEIN]

KOZKA, KAROLINA, BL.

Virgin martyr for purity, lay woman; b. 2 August 1898, Wal-Ruda, Poland; d. there 18 November 1914; beatified at Tarnów, Poland, by John Paul II, 10 June 1987.

The fourth of the eleven children of the farmers Jan Kozka and Maria Borzecka, vivacious Karolina developed an intense prayer life at an early age. She was dragged into the woods and killed by one of the occupying Russian soldiers after rejecting his advances. When her body was found nearly three weeks later, it was interred in the churchyard at Zabawa (6 December 1914). Her relics were translated in November 1917 and a cross erected at the execution site.

The embroidered drapery with an image of sister Faustina Kowalska hangs on the facade of St. Peter's Basilica. Pope John Paul II made her his first canonization of the Jubilee year. (© AFP/CORBIS)

Bibliography: *Acta Apostolicae Sedis* (1987) 739. *L'Osservatore Romano,* Eng. ed. 29 (1987) 3–5.

[K. RABENSTEIN]

KÓZMÍNSKI, HONORAT, BL.

Baptized Florence Wenceslaus John Kózmínski, a.k.a. Honorat a Biala, architect, Capuchin, founder; b. 16 October 1829, Biala Podlaska, Poland; d. 16 December 1916, Noew Miasto, Poland; beatified by John Paul II, 16 October 16, 1988.

Kózmínski was the second of four children of an affluent architect and his pious spouse. Following in his father's footsteps, he studied architecture at the Warsaw School of Fine Arts. Kózmínski's faith failed at his father's death (1845), but was reinvigorated during his internment (1846–47) on a false charge of treason against the Russian occupation and subsequent illness. He became a Capuchin (December 1848), received the name Honorat, and was ordained 8 December 1852. Thereafter he preached and served as spiritual director in Warsaw. Under the Russian occupation, he founded more than twenty associations and congregations, including the Circles of the Living Rosary and the Sister Servants of Mary Immaculate (1878). Most of these groups were reorganized by the Polish hierarchy in 1908. Among the surviving organizations is the Franciscan Sisters of Saint Felix of Cantalice (Felicians), founded by Mother Angela Truszkowska under the spiritual direction of Blessed Honorat, who witnessed the dedication of the initial Felician sisters on 21 November 1855. Although Honorat was placed under house arrest at Zakroczym monastery during the Russian period of suppression, he continued to provide spiritual direction. From 1892 to 1895, Kózmínski ministered at Nowe Miasto until he was appointed commissary for the Polish Capuchins. He died following a painful illness.

Pope John Paul II beatified Honorat saying that he was ''a man of constant prayer, especially of adoration of the Blessed Sacrament, immersed in God and at the same time open to earthly reality. . . . He shows us . . . how to persevere according to God's Will, and work in difficult times.''

Bibliography: *Dziedzictwo bl. Honorata Kózmínskiego*, ed. H. I. SZUMIL & G. BARTOSZEWSKIEGO (Sandomierz 1998). C. C. BILLOT, *Honorat Kozminski* (Blois, France 1982). W. KLUZ, *Ziarnko gorczycy: o Honorat Kózmínski OFMCap* (Warsaw 1987). F. DA RIESE PIO X, *Onorato Kózmínski da Biala Podlaska: un polacco che visse sempre in piedi* (Rome 1976). M. SZYMULA, *Duchowóśc zakonna: duchowóśc zakonna wedlug nauczania bl. Honorata Kózmínskiego* (2d. ed. Warsaw 1999). M. A. WERNER, *O. Honorat Kózmínski, kapucyn* (Poznan 1972). *Acta Apostolicae Sedis* (1988): 1173.

[K. RABENSTEIN]

LAMENT, BOLESLAWA MARIA, BL.

Foundress of the Missionary Sisters of the Holy Family; b. 3 July 1862, Lowicz, Poland; d. 29 January 1946, Bialystak, Poland; beatified at Boleslawa, Poland by John Paul II, 5 June 1991.

Lament is remembered for persevering in charity during difficult times. She began her work by establishing organizations in her home town to care for the ill and abandoned, which led to the founding of the Missionary Sisters of the Holy Family (1905). The sisters soon spread to St. Petersburg, Mohilev, and Zytomierz. The turmoil of World War I and subsequent civil unrest forced Lament to reestablish her missions three times. Before her death the congregation extended to Pinsk, Vilnius, and Bialystak. Long before the Second Vatican Council, Lament labored for Christian unity.

At her beatification Pope John Paul II declared that Boleslawa ''set herself apart by showing sensitivity to human misfortune.''

Bibliography: B. LAMENT, *Wybór pism Boleslawy Lament*, ed. R. J. BAR (Warsaw 1976).

[K. RABENSTEIN]

LAVAL, FRANÇOIS DE MONTMORENCY, BL.

First bishop of Québec, Canada; b. 30 April 1623, Montigny-sur-Avre, France; d. 6 May 1708, Québec, Canada; beatified by John Paul II, 22 June 1980.

François Laval was the third son of Hughes de Laval, knight and Lord of Montigny, and of Michelle de Péricard. As a younger branch of the Montmorency, his family bore its arms as well as those of the Lavals on its blazon. The coat of arms, engraved on a stone in the old church of Montigny-sur-Avre, is still extant, as is the lordly manor of the family. At age nine, Laval entered the royal college of La Flèche, a renowned Jesuit institution, where he began preliminary studies for the priesthood. Ten years later he transferred to the Jesuit Collège de Clermont in Paris for theological courses. While there he also frequented the Caen Hermitage, a house for closed retreats founded by Jean de Bernières-Louvigny, famous mystic and spiritual director who influenced his spiritual development. During Laval's prolonged studies, his father and two older brothers in turn were killed in 1645 while pursuing their military careers. Despite these trials and the material responsibility for his family, he was ordained (1647) before renouncing his patrimonial rights. Already canon in the cathedral of Évreux from the age of twelve, he became its archdeacon soon after his ordination and diligently performed the functions of these offices until his resignation in 1654 to enter a hermitage in Caen.

His candidacy for the office of first bishop of New France was supported by the Jesuits and the French court, and on 3 June 1658, Rome named him vicar apostolic with the title of bishop of Petrea, *in partibus infidelium.* Despite the intrigues of some French bishops he finally received episcopal consecration 8 December 1658, feast of the Immaculate Conception, to which he later consecrated his cathedral. The young bishop departed from La Rochelle on 13 April 1659, and after a brief stop at Percé, landed on 16 June at Québec, where the small colony received him with great joy. He immediately set about organizing the Canadian Church, until then without a real leader. Leaving the apostolate of the Indians to the Jesuits, he entrusted the care of the French colonists to the few secular priests. To guarantee a supply of diocesan priests, both from the colony and from his mother country, he founded the Seminary of Québec (1663), a community designed not only to form priests but to provide lodgings for those worn out by their ministry. He soon associated this seminary to that of the Paris Foreign Mission Society and added a minor seminary (1668). Laval undertook pastoral visits in his huge diocese, traveling great distances on snowshoes in winter and by canoe when the rivers were free of ice. Despite obstacles and infringements of the civil authority on the ecclesiastical domain, the Canadian Church grew rapidly and became firmly united. In 1674, after prolonged negotiations, made difficult by the Gallicanism of the French episcopacy, Laval secured the erection of the Diocese of Québec. It was immediately subject to Rome and had jurisdiction over all the lands discovered by the French in North America.

From the beginning the bishop was aware of the disorders caused by the traffic in alcohol in the colony, particularly of its tragic consequences among the Indians. He energetically fought the abuses of the traders, who were often protected by the governor and his counselors, and even by the French court, and on three different occasions he went directly to the king to plead for the spiritual and temporal interests of the colony. He supported existing religious communities, helped in new foundations in the cities and countryside, and tried to manage the Recollect Franciscans, who returned to Canada through the intervention of the civil authorities. His great concern for education led him to consolidate the Seminary of Québec, which was already providing several Canadian priests. After securing for it a beautiful plot of land, he generously contributed to the construction of its buildings, one of which, dating from 1678, still exists. To ensure its future he acquired vast *seigneuries* and ceded to it all their goods. He also founded the School of Arts, Trades, and Agriculture of St. Joachim, 8 leagues from Québec, and helped to open primary schools. On orders from the court he even tried instructing natives in his minor seminary.

By visits and ordinances he stimulated individual and community piety. Devotions to the Virgin and Ste. Anne de Beaupré (the well-known pilgrimage spot dates from his time) flourished, as well as to the Holy Angels and the Holy Family, whose confraternity and feast were instituted by his mandate. New France was the first country in the world to have an Office of the Holy Family. The fervor of the French establishments was remarkable and was imitated by some of the natives, among whom high mysticism was discovered, as with the young Iroquois maid Kateri Tekakwitha. Laval himself solemnly baptized Daniel Garakonthie, Onondaga chief. In 1688, weakened by cares, labors, and infirmities, Laval resigned and was replaced by Bp. J. B. de Saint-Vallier. The "old bishop" retired to his seminary, spending his time in prayer, works of mercy, and, frequently, at pontifical functions during his successor's long absences. Their differences over policy was a hard trial for the older man.

François de Montmorency Laval, engraving. (Archive Photos, Inc. Reproduced by permission.)

After Laval's death his reputation for sanctity kindled piety, and extraordinary favors were granted through his intercession. His cause of canonization was begun in 1878, introduced in Rome in 1890, and reached a decisive stage in the 1960 decree proclaiming the heroic nature of his virtues. His remains lie in a funeral chapel in the Seminary of Québec, a pilgrimage site.

At his beatification Pope John Paul II reflected that Laval "could have aspired to the most promising human careers, but he preferred to respond generously to the invitation of Christ. . . .He settled in Québec and dedicated himself with indefatigable zeal to the expansion of the Kingdom of God, realizing in himself the ideal figure of the bishop."

Feast: 6 May (Canada).

Bibliography: *La positio de la cause* (Rome 1956), a collection of known letters. *Quebecen. beatificationis et canonizationis ven. servi Dei Francisci de Montmorency-Laval Episcopi Quebecensis 1708: altera nova positio super virtutibus ex officio critice disposita* (Rome 1956). N. BAILLARGEON, *Le séminaire de Québec sous l'épiscopat de Mgr de Laval* (Québec 1972). É. BÉGIN, *François de Laval* (Québec 1959). G. E. DEMERS, *Mgr. de Laval* (Montréal 1951). É. GERVAIS, *Le Vén. François de Montmorency-Laval* (Montréal 1952). A. H. GOSSELIN, *Vie de Monseigneur de Laval*, 2 v. (Québec 1890; new ed. 1906); *Au pays de Mgr de Laval: letters de voyage* (Québec 1910). H. HOUSSART, *Mgr. de Laval vu par son* *serviteur* (Québec 1961). C. DE LA ROCHEMONTEIX, *Les Jésuites et la Nouvelle-France au XVIIme siècle,* 3 v. (Paris 1895–96). A. VACHON, *François de Laval* (Montréal 1980). *Acta Apostolicae Sedis* (1981): 235–58. *L'Osservatore Romano,* Eng. ed. 26 (1980): 10–11.

[H. PROVOST/ K. RABENSTEIN]

LAVAL, JACQUES DÉSIRÉ, BL.

Doctor, priest of the Congregation of the Holy Heart of Mary (now merged with the Holy Ghost Fathers); apostle of Mauritius; b. 18 September 1803, Croth, Diocese of Évreux, Normandy, France; d. 9 September 1864, Port-Louis, Mauritius; beatified in the first beatification ceremony presided over by John Paul II, 29 April 1979.

Laval, the son of a lawyer with extensive land holdings and a pious mother who tended the needy, owned his own farm by age thirteen. After attending local schools, he completed his secondary studies at Évreux, then studied the humanities in Paris, theology at Saint Stanislaus College in Évreux, and medicine in Paris, where he earned a doctorate at the Sorbonne (21 August 1830). He opened a successful medical practice in Saint-André near Évreux, while serving as captain of the national guard and maintaining a large household. He returned to the practice of the faith following a riding accident (1835). That summer he decided to continue his theological studies at Saint-Sulpice Seminary in Paris, where he became acquainted with François Libermann. Laval was ordained priest in 1838 and decided to join Libermann in a single mission for the welfare of Black slaves. Until they established their mission, Laval administered the parish of Pinterville, Évreux Diocese. During the summer of 1841, Laval donated his entire wealth to Libermann, joined the Congregation of the Holy Heart of Mary, and accompanied the newly appointed bishop to the island of Mauritius. Thus, on 11 September 1841, Father Laval, whose companions remembered him as ''the saint who always says he does nothing,'' began his twenty-three year ministry to a parish of 80,000. He is responsible for baptizing 67,000 emancipated slaves and instituting works for economic, social, and technical development on the island. His cause for canonization was opened in 1918.

Pope John Paul II praised Laval for his missionary efforts: ''He has all the kindness of a father, all the pity of a pastor, for these people. One by one they come towards him. He receives them with respect, sweetness, and cordiality'' (beatification homily). Patron of slaves.

Bibliography: Works: J. D. LAVAL, *Extraits de sa correspondance,* ed. J. LÉCUYER (Paris 1978); *Le Serviteur de Dieu, Jacques-Désiré Laval, de la Congr. du St. Espirit et du St. Coeur de Marie*

(Paris 1912). Literature: J. ACKING, *Père Laval* (Port Louis 1986). B. BOCAGE, *Le Père Jacques Laval: un saint de chez nous* (Pacy-sur-Eure, France 1989). F. DELAPLACE and M. PIVAULT, *Le Père Jacques-Desirè Laval, Apôtre de L'ile Maurice* (Paris 1932). J. FITZSIMMONS, *Father Laval* (London 1973). J. MICHEL, *Les auxiliaires laïcs du bienheureux Jacques Laval, apôtre de l'île Maurice* (Paris 1988). J. T. RATH, *Jakob Laval, der Apostel von Mauritius* (Dormagen 1978). *Acta Apostolicae Sedis* 72 (1980): 154–57. *L'Osservatore Romano,* Eng. ed. 19 (1979): 6–7.

[K. RABENSTEIN]

LEDÓCHOWSKA, URSZULA (URSULA), BL.

Baptized Julia Maria, founder of the Ursuline Sisters of the Agony of Jesus in Gethsemane; b. 17 April 1865, Loosdorf, Austria (now Lipnica Murowana near Tarnów, Poland); d. 29 May 1939, Rome, Italy; beatified by John Paul II, 20 June 1983, at Poznán, Poland.

Urszula was born into a privileged family of Count Antonius Halka-Ledóchowski and his Swiss wife; the sister of Maria Teresa Ledóchowska and Wladimir Ledóchowski, superior general of the Jesuits; and niece of Cardinal Miecysław Ledóchowski. Following financial setbacks the family moved to Saint Poelten (1873), where her father died two years later. Urszula founded a congregation of Ursulines, known as the Gray Ursulines, at Pniewy (near Poznán). She shared the benefits of her privileged family life by caring for and teaching young people. In 1907, she left Krakow to work in St. Petersburg, Russia. Three years later she moved the boarding school for Polish girls from St. Petersburg to Karelia, Finland, until she herself left Russia for Scandinavia (1914). After receiving papal approbation from Benedict XV following the war, the Gray Ursulines spread throughout Poland and beyond. Urszula was called to Rome by the Holy See, where she inspired many Catholic institutions.

Feast: 29 May.

Bibliography: T. BOJARSKA, *W imie trzech krzyzy: opowiesc o Julii Urszuli Ledóchowskiej i jej zgromadzeniu* (Warsaw 1981). J. LEDÓCHOWSKA, *Zycie dla innych: blogoslawiona Urszula Ledóchowska* (Poznán 1984). *Acta Apostolicae Sedis* (1987) 1264–68. *L'Osservatore Romano,* Eng. ed. 27 (1983) 10–11.

[K. RABENSTEIN]

LEISNER, KARL FRIEDRICH WILHELM MARIA, BL.

Priest, martyr; b. 28 February 1915, Rees am Niederrhein, Westphalia, Germany; d. 12 August 1945, Planegg (near Munich); beatified 23 June 1996 by John Paul II during his third pastoral visit to Germany.

Karl's parents, Wilhelm Leisner and Amalie Falkenstein, moved to Kleve in 1921, where he attended the local public school. He studied philosophy and theology at the Borromeo College in Munster (1934–36); theology at Freiburg in Breisgau (1936–37) and Munster (1937–39). While at the university, his bishop commissioned him as diocesan (1934–36) leader of youth groups. To circumvent Nazi control, Karl taught his charges the catechism on excursions. His education was interrupted for six months in 1937 by mandatory national agricultural service in Sachsen and Emsland. During this period he again opposed Nazi regulations by organizing Sunday Mass for fellow workers. Leisner entered Munster's diocesan seminary (1938) and was ordained deacon (25 March 1939) by Bishop Clemens Augustinus Graf von Galen.

While recuperating from tuberculosis in the sanitarium at St. Blasien, Schwarzwald, he was arrested (8 November 1939) for offhandedly expressing regret that an assassination attempt against Hitler had failed. He was held in the prison of Freiburg (1939–40), then taken Mannheim's prison. After Mannheim, he was taken to the concentration camps at Sachsenhausen and Dachau (24 December 1940). On 17 December 1944, French Bishop Gabriel Piguet of Clermont-Ferrand secretly ordained Leisner to the priesthood at Dachau. Fr. Leisner furtively celebrated Mass for the first and only time on 26 December in the barrack's chapel. Dachau was liberated by Allied troops on 4 May 1945. Leisner, suffering the effects of tuberculosis and imprisonment, died a few months later at the age of thirty in a sanitarium at Planegg near Munich.

In 1966 his body was exhumed from his grave in Kleve and placed in the Martyrs Crypt in Xanten cathedral. His cause was opened in Rome, 15 March 1980. Among the documents examined were his diary with entries from 23 March 1927 through 25 July 1945, and about 130 substantial letters, which provide insight into his spirituality.

Pope John Paul II said that Leisner "was very early to recognize the anti-Christian nature of the ruling party" and that he felt called "to show people the way to God and to make no concessions to the so-called 'popular world view'" (Beatification homily).

Bibliography: *Christus meine Leidenschaft, Karl Leisner, sein Leben in Bildern und Dokumenten*, ed. W. HAAS (Kevelaer 1985); *Karl Leisner: Mit Christus leben. Gedanken für jeden Tag*, ed. W. HAAS (Kevelaer 1979). O. CESCA, *Castelo no tormenta, Carlos Leisner* (Santa Maria, Brazil 1963). C. FELDMANN, *Wer glaubt, muss widerstehen: Bernhard Lichtenberg-Karl Leisner*, 3d ed. (Freiburg 1996). R. LEJEUNE, *K. Leisner: Wie Gold geläutert im Feuer* (Strassburg 1988). O. PIES, *Stephanus heute, Karl Leisner, Priester und Opfer.* (Kevelaer 1951). J. SCHMIEDL, *Karl Leisner: Leben für die Jugend* (Vallendar-Schönstatt 1996). *L'Osservatore Romano,* English edition, no. 26 (1996): 1–3.

[K. RABENSTEIN]

LENTINI, DOMENICO, BL.

(Dominic); Priest of the Diocese of Tursi-Lagonegro (formerly Policastro); b. 20 November 1770, at Lauria, Potenza, Italy; d. there 25 February 1828; beatified 12 October 1997 by Pope John Paul II.

The youngest of the five children of Macario Lentini and Rosalia Vitarella, Lentini studied in the seminary at Salerno and was ordained in 1794. In addition to his ministry in Lauria, he taught literature, philosophy, and theology to young people in his home without monetary compensation. He preached and catechized throughout the diocese and spread the devotion to Our Lady of Sorrows. He is called the "precursor to the Curé d'Ars" (St. John Vianney) because of his willingness to make himself available to hear confessions and his gift of reading hearts. He practiced personal austerity in order to provide charity to the poor, and frequent penances in the spirit of reparation.

Pope John Paul II praised Lentini during his beatification homily as a priest rich in his priesthood "who in his itinerant preaching never tired of inviting to conversion and return to God. For this reason his apostolic activity was accompanied by the diligent ministry of the confessional."

Feast: 25 February.

Bibliography: *Acta Apostolicae Sedis* 20 (1997): 999. *L'Osservatore Romano,* English edition, no. 42 (1997): 1–2. G. REALE, *Domenico Lentini, santo di paese* (Reggio Calabria 1977).

[K. RABENSTEIN]

LICHTENBERG, BERNHARD, BL.

Priest, martyr, provost of Berlin; b. 3 December 1875, Ohlau, Silesia, Poland (then Germany); d. 5 November 1943, Hof, Upper Franconia, Germany; beatified with Karl Leisner, 23 June 1996, during Pope John Paul II's third pastoral visit to Germany in Berlin's Olympic Stadium.

One of five children of the devout Catholic grocer August Lichtenberg and his wife Emilie, Bernhard was raised in the predominantly Protestant town of Ohlau. After studying in Prague, Munich, and Innsbruck, he completed his theological studies in Breslau (now Wrocław, Poland), where he was ordained in 1899. He held various parish assignments in Berlin, then served as military chaplain (1914). In 1931 he joined St. Hedwig's cathedral chapter in Berlin, where he was appointed to the parish the following year and named provost in January 1938. He was a tireless promoter of the apostolate for priestly vocations. As early as 1935, Lichtenberg protested from St. Hedwig's pulpit and to the government leaders against the atrocities in the concentration camps. Lichtenberg condemned the elimination of religious instruction in the schools, the secularization of marriage, and the euthanasia practiced against the innocent. Beginning in November 1938, he prayed publicly every day "for the oppressed non-Aryan Christians, for the persecuted Jews, and for prisoners in the concentration camps." Arrested in October 1941 but released shortly thereafter, he continued his prayers and protests. On 22 May 1942, he was sentenced to two years' imprisonment for treason and "misuse of his official position." While in prison Lichtenberg, who was 68 years old, suffered a heart attack. The Gestapo, fearing he would die in Berlin in their custody, put him in a cattlecar en route to Dachau concentration camp. At Hof he was so sick that he was unloaded and taken to the city hospital, where he died.

John Paul II declared Lichtenberg a martyr on 2 July 1994. Following the beatification rite, during which the pope said Lichtenberg knew that martyrdom was "final and inevitable consequence of a life lived in following Christ," John Paul II prayed at the martyr's tomb in the crypt of St. Hedwig's Cathedral.

Feast: 5 November (Archdiocese of Berlin).

Bibliography: W. ADOLPH, *Im Schatten des Galgens* (Berlin 1953). A. ERB, *Bernhard Lichtenberg: Dompropst von St. Hedwig zu Berlin,* 5th ed. (Berlin 1968). C. FELDMANN, *Wer glaubt, muss widerstehen: Bernhard Lichtenberg-Karl Leisner,* 3d. ed. (Freiburg 1996). D. HANKY, *Bernhard Lichtenberg. Priester. Bekenner. Martyrer* (Berlin 1994). B. M. KEMPER, *Priester vor Hitlers Tribunalen* (Munich 1996). E. KOCK, *Er widerstand* (Berlin 1996). H. KÜHN, *Blutzeugen des Bistums Berlin* (Berlin 1952). K. MAGIERA, *Bernhard Lichtenberg* (Berlin 1963). O. OGIERMANN, *Bis zum letzten Atemzug* (Leipzig 1983).

[K. RABENSTEIN]

LONGO, BARTOLO, BL.

A.k.a. the "Man of Mary" and "Brother Rosario," Dominican tertiary, founder of the shrine of Our Lady of Pompeii, and of the Daughters of Saint Rosario of Pompeii; b. 11 February 1841, Latiano, Apulia, southern Italy; d. 5 October 1926, Pompeii, Italy; beatified by John Paul II, 26 October 1980.

Son of a prosperous physician named Bartolomeo Longo and his wife Antonietta Luparelli, Bartolo Longo received a good education from the Piarists at Francavilla Fontana and Lecce, then studied law at the University of Naples, where he received his degree (1864). During his university years Bartolo was influenced by the anticlericalism of the time, involved himself in popular occult spiritism. After a severe depression, Dominican Father Alberto Radente led him to conversion (29 May 1865). Thereafter he devoted himself to charitable works. Bartolo became a Dominican Tertiary with the name Brother Rosario (25 March 1871).

In 1872, Longo went to Pompeii valley on business for the Countess Marianna Farnararo de Fusco (d. 9 February 1924), whom he married in 1885. Observing the despair and lack of faith in the region and recalling Father Alberto's devotion to the Rosary, Bartolo decided to encourage it there, while continuing his works of mercy and teaching the catechism. With much difficulty he established a Confraternity of the Holy Rosary and sought to build a shrine of the Blessed Mother. After several unsuccessful attempts to raise funds, he took up Bishop Formisano of Nola's suggestion to collect a "soldo" (penny) a month from each of 300 donors. The cornerstone was laid in 1876. Fortuna Agrelli provided a major contribution after her miraculous healing in 1884, which led to the consecration of the Shrine of Our Lady of the Rosary (7 May 1891). Pope Saint Pius X raised it to the status of a pontifical basilica in 1894. About 1900, Bartolo was falsely accused of financial mismanagement, but he was later cleared of the charge.

Longo promoted a unique "Rosary of the Fifteen Saturdays" and 54-day Novena Rosary of Our Lady of Pompeii. He also advocated the definition of the Assumption of Mary as dogma and founded the Dominican Daughters of Saint Rosario. He and his wife built an orphanage for girls (1887), hospices for the children of prisoners (1892 and 1922), a typesetting workshop and printing press to publish pamphlets, a hospital, music school, and two houses for Dominican tertiaries near the shrine. Other charities have grown up in the "City of Mary" around the shrine where hundreds of miraculous cures are alleged to have occurred. Before his death, Bartolo also wrote *The Fifteen Saturdays, Petition* (1883), and began the magazine *The Rosary and the New Pompeii* (founded 1884). His mortal remains now rest in the basilica of Pompeii under the throne of Our Lady's shrine (1983).

Pope John Paul II, during his beatification of Longo, called him the "herald of the Blessed Virgin Mary's Rosary" and said he was "a layman who had lived his ecclesial pledge to the full."

Feast: 6 October (Dominicans).

Bibliography: *Bartolo Longo e il suo tempo: atti del convegno storico promosso dalla Delegazione pontificia per il Sant-*

uario di Pompei sotto l'alto patronato del Presidente della Repubblica, ed. F. VOLPE. P. M. FRASCONI, *Don Barolo Longo* (Alba 1941). A. ILLIBATO, *L'archivio Bartolo Longo: guida-inventario* (Naples 1986). I. LÜTHOLD-MINDER, *Die Rosenkranzkönigin von Pompei und ihr Advokat Bartolo Longo* (Hauteville, Switz. 1981). N. TAMBURRO, *Bartolo Longo, pioniere di civiltà: nel centenario di Pompei* (2nd ed. Pompei 1975). *Acta Apostolicae Sedis* (1981) 529–32. *L'Osservatore Romano* (English edition) 44 (1980) 10–11.

[K. RABENSTEIN]

LOOR, ISIDORE OF SAINT JOSEPH DE, BL.

Passionist priest; b. 18 April 1881, Vrasene, eastern Flanders, the Netherlands; d. 6 October 1916, Kortrijk (Courtrai) Monastery, Belgium; beatified by John Paul II, 30 September 1984.

As the eldest of three children of subsistence farmers, Isidore received six years of elementary education at the local school. At the suggestion of a Passionist missionary, Isidore joined the Passionists at Ere, Belgium (7 April 1907) and became brother Isidore of Saint Joseph. After his religious profession in 1908, he served the community as cook, gardener, custodian of the preparatory school, and later (1914) as porter. Intense penitential prayer helped Brother Isidore to cope with several crises: cancer that required the removal of his right eye (1911); the conversion of the monastery into a German military hospital and its abandonment by all but five brothers and three priests during World War I; and the metastasis of cancer to his intestines (1916). This simple, diligent "Brother of the Will of God" suffered his final illness with great fortitude. He was buried next to the Passionist Church, where those remembering him came to pray for his intercession and received his help.

The official process for his beatification was opened in 1950. Pope John Paul II offered the world obsessed with personal freedom the example of Brother Isidore's "growing conformity to the Will of the heavenly Father in following Jesus Christ" (beatification homily).

Bibliography: n.a., *Isidore of St. Joseph* (Kortrijk 1960). M. CLAYES, *The Life of Brother Isidore de Loor* (Chicago 1976). H. GIELEN, *Het diepste lied zingt binnenin: de zalige broeder Isidoor de Loor* (Tielt, Netherlands 1984). C. VAN HEMELEN, *Blessed Isidore De Loor Passionist* (Dublin 1984). *Acta Apostolicae Sedis* 78 (1986): 965–968. *L'Osservatore Romano*, Eng. ed. 44 (1984): 6–7.

[K. RABENSTEIN]

LUCCI, ANTONIO, BL.

Baptized Angelo Nicola; Conventual Franciscan, bishop; b. 2 August 1682, Agnone, Isernia (near Naples), Italy; d. 25 July 1752, Bovino, Italy; beatified at Rome by John Paul II, 18 June 1989.

Angelo was the fifth of the seven children of Francesco Lucci and Angela Paolantonio. The family owned two vineyards and a copper firm, but Francesco worked as a cobbler. Francesco's unexpected death in 1604 led to some financial difficulties, but he had provided for Angelo's education under the Conventual Friars Minor at Agnone until the age of 15. Despite his mother's objections, Angelo entered the order at Isernia (1697), professed his vows (1698), and took the name Antonio. He continued his studies at Venafro, Alvito, Aversa, Agnone, and Assisi, and was ordained priest in 1705.

After receiving his doctorate in theology (1709), he assigned to San Lorenzo (Naples), where he taught and ministered. The profundity of his theological insight gained him several positions, including provincial superior of Sant'Angelo (1718), rector of San Bonaventura, Rome (1719–29), theological advisor for two Roman synods, consultor to the Holy See (1725), and spiritual director to Princess Maria Clementina Sobieski. He was consecrated bishop of Bovino (7 February 1729) by Pope Benedict XIII. Even after his episcopal consecration, Lucci continued to conduct his life according to the Franciscan Rule in poverty, humility, and charity. He emptied his treasury to provide for the poor and was known to give away even the clothes off his back. As bishop, he was known for his pastoral zeal, even to teaching children's catechism classes to prepare them for the sacraments. In addition to reforming the clergy and religious and building schools, Bishop Lucci defended the rights of the poor and the vulnerable in response to the problems of the era. He died in the odor of sanctity after 23 years as bishop and was buried in his cathedral at Bovino.

Lucci's cause was initiated shortly after his death: informative process (1758–60), official introduction (1764), apostolic process (1769–70), and publication of the *positios* (1793 and 1835). Pope Pius IX declared Lucci venerable (1847). His cause was reopened recently when a number of miracles were attributed to his intercession. After one was approved (18 June 1989), Lucci was beatified by Pope John Paul II, who noted that the new blessed was "attentive to the signs of the times."

Bibliography: *Acta Apostolicae Sedis* (1989): 764.

[K. RABENSTEIN]

MACKILLOP, MARY HELEN, BL.

Known in religion as Mary of the Cross, a.k.a. Maria Ellen MacKillop, educator, foundress of the Josephite Sisters; b. 15 January 1842, Fitzroy (near Melbourne), Australia; d. 8 August 1909, Sydney, New South Wales. At her beatification by John Paul II, 19 January 1995, at Randwick Racecourse in Sydney, she became the first Australian beata.

Mary MacKillop. (Catholic News Service.)

The daughter of Highland Scottish immigrants, she was working as a governess when in 1861 she met Fr. Julian Tenison Woods, a missionary from England and one of the chief architects of Australia's Catholic education system. He inspired her to dedicate her life to teaching the children of the bush. In 1865, Mary and two younger sisters began teaching in an abandoned stable at Penola, South Australia. Moving to Adelaide, Mary MacKillop and Fr. Woods founded the Institute of the Sisters of St. Joseph of the Sacred Heart. Together with her companions Mary pronounced the vows of religion (15 August 1866) and took the name of Mother Mary of the Cross. Her efforts to adapt the new community to a colonial environment encountered a decade of lay and clerical misunderstanding and opposition. In 1871, the bishop of Adelaide excommunicated her and disbanded the sisterhood. A Jewish person gave the homeless nuns a house rent free, until their restoration in 1872. In 1874, Mother Mary traveled to Rome and submitted her rule to Pope Pius IX. Rome's eventual decision was a compromise but the foundress won her principal point of central government for the sisters throughout the Australian colonies. She established 160 Josephite houses and 117 schools attended by more than 12,000 children. When she died after a long illness, her congregation numbered about 1,000. Her tomb is in a vault donated by a Presbyterian woman in front of Our Lady's Altar in the Mount Street Josephite Chapel, North Sydney.

During the beatification homily Pope John Paul II said that MacKillop ''did not just free people from ignorance through schooling or alleviate their suffering through compassionate care. She worked to satisfy their deeper, though sometimes unconscious longing for 'the unsearchable riches of Christ.''' Patron of Australia.

Feast: 7 August.

Bibliography: M. MACKILLOP, *Julian Tension Woods, A Life* (Blackburn, Vic., 1997). Australian Catholic Truth Society, *Mother Mary of the Cross: Her Personality, Her Spirit* (Melbourne 1973). C. DUNNE, *Mary MacKillop: No Plaster Saint* (Sydney 1994). P. GARDINER, *Mary MacKillop: An Extraordinary Australian* (Newtown, N.S.W. 1993). A. HENDERSON, *Mary MacKillop's Sisters: A Life Unveiled* (Sydney 1997). D. LYNE, *Mary MacKillop, Spirituality and Charisma* (Sydney 1983). W. MODYSTACK, *Mary MacKillop: A Woman Before Her Time* (New York 1982). F. O'BRIEN, *Called to Love* (Homebush, NSW 1993). L. O'BRIEN, *Mary MacKillop Unveiled* (N. Blackburn, Vic. 1994). L. STAUB-STAUDE, *The Anatomy of A Saint* (Naracoorte, S. Aust. 1993). O. THORPE, *Mary McKillop*, 3d. ed. (Sydney 1994).

[J.G. MURTAGH/EDS.]

MALLINCKRODT, PAULINE VON, BL.

Foundress of the Sisters of CHRISTIAN CHARITY; b. 3 June 1817, Minden, Westphalia, Germany; d. 30 April 1881, Paderborn (near Münster), Germany; beatified in Rome by John Paul II, 14 April 1985.

Her mother was a devout Catholic; her father, a high-ranking civil servant, was a Protestant of tolerant views. Her brother Hermann became a Catholic leader in public life. In Aachen, where she spent her earlier years, Pauline frequented the circle of the poet Louise Hensel (1798–1876), who became a Catholic in 1818. When she was 18, she declined to marry a well-to-do Protestant. In Paderborn, where she lived from 1839, Pauline dedicated herself to works of charity, founded an association of women to help the impoverished sick (1839), and established a day nursery (1840). In 1842, Pauline opened a school for blind children. She persuaded St. Madeleine Sophie Barat to have her institute take charge of this school, but the Prussian government would not grant admittance to the French religious congregation.

As a result Pauline founded her own congregation (21 August 1849) and served as its first superior general. During her lifetime the institute extended its apostolate to include teaching in elementary and secondary schools. When the Kulturkampf caused the closing of seventeen houses in Germany, Pauline moved the motherhouse to

Mont-Saint-Guibert near Brussels, Belgium, and also began to establish houses abroad. She visited the U.S. (1873) shortly after the first group of her sisters arrived in New Orleans, and again in 1879 after journeying to her foundation in Chile. She traveled also to England, where houses were started. By the time of her death from pneumonia in 1881, the Sisters of Christian Charity had 492 members in 45 houses. Mother Pauline is buried in the Motherhouse in Paderborn.

The decree introducing her cause for beatification was issued in 1958. At her beatification in 1985, Pope John Paul II called her ''a gigantic figure of a woman in the history of the Church. . . . The style of her sanctity and of her apostolate is more of today than of yesterday.''

Feast: 30 April.

Bibliography: PAULINE VON MALLINCKRODT, *Kurzer Lebensabriß unserer teuren Würdigen Mutter und Stifterin Pauline v. Mallinckrodt, von ihr selbst verfaßt* (Paderborn 1889). T. BARKEY, *Damit ihr Leben gelingen kann* (Paderborn 1984). A. BUNGERT, *Pauline v. Mallinckrodt,* (Würzburg 1980). K. BURTON, *Whom Love Impels: The Life of Mother Pauline von Mallinckrodt, Foundress of the Sisters of Christian Charity* (New York 1952). J. J. DEGENHARDT, *Dienstbereit in der Liebe Christi* (Paderborn 1985). BR. ERNEST, *A Happy Heart: A Story of Mother Pauline von Mallinckrodt* (Notre Dame, Ind. 1956). C. FRENKE, *Pauline v. Mallinckrodt in ihrer Zeit* (Paderborn 1984). A. HÜFFER, *Pauline von Mallinckrodt* 2d. ed. (Münster 1902). *The Life of Mother Pauline von Mallinckrodt, Foundress of the Sisters of Christian Charity* (New York 1917). A. METTE, *Die Liebe zählt nicht—nur die Liebe zählt* (Paderborn 1985). *L'Osservatore Romano,* English edition, no. 19 (1985): 6–8. K. SANDER-WIETFELD, *Pauline von Mallinckrodt: Ein Lebensbild nach ihrer Briefen und Aufzeichnungen* (Paderborn 1985). A. SCHMITTDIEL, *Pauline von Mallinckrodt* (Paderborn 1949). SISTERS OF CHRISTIAN CHARITY (U.S.), *Enriching Many* (Mendham, N.J. 1942). D. WEDMORE, *The Woman Who Couldn't Be Stopped* (Mendham, N.J. 1986).

[N. BACKMUND]

MANDIČ, LEOPOLD BOGDAN, ST.

Baptized Bogdan (Adeodato in Italian); a.k.a. Leopold da Castelnovo (Castronovo); Capuchin priest; b. 12 May 1866, Castelnuovo of Càttaro (Herceg Novi, Kotor Bay in Croatian), southern Dalmatia, Bosnia-Hercegovina; d. 30 July 1942, Padua, Venetia, Italy; canonized by John Paul II, 16 October 1983.

Bogdan was the eleventh of 12 children in a noble but poor family headed by Peter Mandič, who owned a fishing fleet, and Carlotta Zarevič, daughter of Countess Elena Bujovič. Bogdan began his seminary studies at Udine, Venetia, Italy (16 November 1882) with the desire to work for the unification of Orthodox and Catholic Christians in foreign lands, but his Capuchin superiors knew that his frail health could not withstand the hardships. He received the habit and took the name Leopold at Bassano del Grappa, Vicenza (1884). After pronouncing his vows (1885), Leopold studied for the priesthood at Padua, where he made his solemn profession (1888), and Venice, where he was ordained (1890). Following assignments in various friaries, he was transferred to Padua (1906), where he remained for the rest of his life, except for one year's incarceration during World War I because he would not renounce his Croat nationality. In Padua, he was known for his cheerfulness, modesty, care for the sick, and his patient compassion in the confessional, where he heard confessions extended hours every day, and his penances and prayer.

At Leopold's canonization, Pope John Paul II called him ''an heroic servant of reconciliation and penance,'' who offered himself daily ''for the full reunification of the separated Oriental and Latin Churches.''

Feast: 12 May (Capuchins).

Bibliography: L. MANDIČ, *Spisi Svetoga Leopolda Bogdana Mandiča,* ed. O. H. BORAK (Zagreb 1992). *ActApS* 68 (1976) 548–550; 76 (1984) 937–944. *OssRomEng* 1976, n. 20, 6–7; 1983, n. 43, 1, 3. T. CATTAROSSI, *Leopoldo Mandić: valori umani nell'azione pastorale* (Rome 1980). L. GUTWENGER, *Pater Leopold Mandič, der Heilige zwischen Ost und West: ein charismatischer Beichtvater* (Stein am Rhein 1983). F. DA RIESE, PIO X, *Beato Leopoldo Mandič da Castelnovo: servì i peccatori per l'unità della Chiesa* (Rome 1976). U. SUMAN, *C'era una volta padre Leopoldo: la bontà di un santo in 50 racconti* (Padua 1993).

[K. RABENSTEIN]

MANETTI, TERESA MARIA DELLA CROCE, BL.

Baptized Teresa Adelaida Cesina, a.k.a. Teresa di Firenze (Teresa of Florence), foundress of the Third Order Carmelite Sisters of Saint Teresa (Congregazione delle Carmelitane di S. Teresa); b. 2 March 1846, San Martino a Campi Bisenzio (near Florence), Tuscany, Italy; d. there 23 April 1910; beatified at Florence, Italy, by John Paul II, 19 October 1986.

Daughter of Salvatore Manetti and Rosa Bigali, Teresa sought to alleviate the difficulties of others. In 1872, she retired with a few friends to the countryside, where they could pray, work together, and provide a Christian education to local children. Their formal religious community, founded 15 July 1874 with the arrival of other young women, combined the contemplative Carmelite spirituality of prayer and Eucharistic Adoration with apostolic work in parishes, schools, and mission fields. On 16 July 1876, Teresa was admitted to the Third Order of Discalced Carmelites and changed her name to Teresa della Croce. In 1877, the sisters opened their home to orphans. The first twenty-seven sisters were veiled in the Discalced Carmelite habit, 12 July 1888. In 1902, her special desire to have perpetual adoration was granted. Before her death, Teresa saw the institute receive approbation by Pope Saint Pius X (27 February 1904) and the first sisters leave to establish missions in Lebanon (1904) and Palestine (1907). The woman of fervent devotion and ''angelic innocence'' died at age sixty-four. Her writings were approved 27 November 1937, and the beatification process opened in Rome in 1944. She was declared venerable in 1975 and a decree issued on the approval of a miracle in November 1985.

Feast: 23 April (Carmelites).

Bibliography: *Acta Apostolicae Sedis* (1986) 1144. *L'Osservatore Romano,* Eng. Ed. 39 (1986) 9.

[K. RABENSTEIN]

MANKIDIYAN, MARIAM THRESIA CHIRAMEL, BL.

Baptized Thresia, virgin, mystic, founder of the Congregation of the Sisters of the Holy Family; b. 26 April 1876, Trichur, Puthenchira, Kerala, India; d. 8 June 1926, Kuzhikattusery; beatified in Rome by John Paul II, 9 April 2000.

When Thresia was twelve, her once-wealthy mother (Thanda) died leaving her with a father (Thoma) and elder brother who were alcoholics, along with three other siblings. Even as a child Thresia fasted four times weekly, kept all-night vigils, and, at age ten, consecrated her life to God, the poor, sick, lonely, and orphaned. Beginning in 1909, Thresia experienced many mystical phenomena. She joined the Carmelite tertiaries in 1910. Three years later she received long-awaited permission from her bishop, Apostolic Vicar Mar John Menachery, to enter consecrated community life with three friends, who also dedicated themselves to prayer and penance. They defied convention by venturing into the streets unaccompanied to serve those in need. The Congregation of the Holy Family was canonically established 14 May 1914 with Mariam Thresia as superior and the Rule of the Holy Family Sisters of Bordeaux. In 1915, she founded a girls school in Puthenchira. At the time of her death 11 years later, the congregation had 55 sisters in three convents running four schools, a study home, and an orphanage. By 2000, the congregation had grown to more than 1,500 members serving the poor in Germany, Ghana, India, and Italy.

When Pope John Paul II beatified Thresia, considered the forerunner of Mother Teresa of Calcutta, he said that her ''willingness to embrace the Cross of Christ enabled her to remain steadfast in the face of frequent misunderstandings and difficult spiritual trials.''

Feast: 6 June.

[K. RABENSTEIN]

MANYANET Y VIVES, JOSÉ, BL.

Priest, founder of the Congregation of the Sons of the Holy Family and the Institute of the Missionary Daughters of the Holy Family of Nazareth; b. 7 January 1833, Tremp, Pallars Jussá, Catalonia, Spain; d. 17 December 1901, San Andres de Palomar, Barcelona, Spain; beatified by John Paul II, 25 November 1984.

José Manyanet, the youngest of nine children born to farmers Antonio Manyanet and Bonaventura Vives, was baptized on the day of his birth. Following the death of his father in 1834, José informally became the ward of Father Valentín Lledós, who influenced his future vocation, as did his mother Bonaventura's piety. At age twelve, he left home to begin his education in the Piarist school at Barbastro (1845–50). He continued his study of philosophy at the seminary of Lleida (1850–53) and theology at Seu d'Urgell (1853–59), where he was mentored by Bishop José Caixal and ordained as priest (9 April 1859).

From his ordination until 1865, Manyanet successfully served Bishop Caixal in several offices while engaging in pastoral ministry as confessor, spiritual director, preacher, catechist, and promoter of several associations. Because he had a heroic concern for the family, which he recognized was threatened by divorce and personal independence, he founded two institutions: *Hijos de la Sagrada Familia* (1864 in Tremp) and *Hijas de la Sagrada Familia* (1874 in Talarn). Manyanet and his first companions made their religious profession in Barcelona, 2 February 1870, and received pontifical approval 22 June 1901. The order operates schools for the Christian education of children and promotes devotion to the Holy Family in Argentina, Brazil, Colombia, Italy, Mexico, Spain, the United States (from 1920), and Venezuela. They also publish the periodical *Revista La Sagrada Familia.*

The founding of the female branch was more difficult. Bishop Caixal placed a new community of women founded by Ana María Janer (1859) under the direction of Manyanet. The order was consumed by crisis until it was again recognized by Bishop José Morgades of Vich (1892) under the direction of the cofoundress, Mother Encarnación Colomina. She gave the order its new name *Misioneras Hijas de la Sagrada Familia de Nazaret,* which was approved by the Vatican, 10 May 1958.

In addition to writing the constitutions of both the orders he founded, Manyanet contributed several books:

Meditaciones: El espíritu de la Sagrada Familia (Meditations: The Spirit of the Holy Family); *La Escuela de Nazaret* (The School of Nazareth); and *Preciosa joya de familia* (The Precious Jewel of Family). He also advocated for the liturgical celebration of the Feast of the Holy Family, which was instituted by Pope Leo XII (1892). For many years before his death Father Manyanet secretly bore the stigmatization of Jesus.

His mortal remains are enshrined in a bronze urn in the Beato José Manyanet Chapel in the School of Jesus, Mary, and Joseph of Saint Andrew of Palomar (Barcelona). The ordinary informative process for his beatification began in 1931, and his cause was formally introduced by Pope Pius XII in 1951.

Pope John Paul II, who declared Manyanet venerable (12 July 1982), praised him during the beatification for looking at "the examples of Nazarene sanctity which the Holy Family teaches. From here was born his apostolic commitment to try to bring that message to the world and to make every home a Nazareth."

Bibliography: D. MORERA, *Among the Stars: The Life of Father Joseph Manyanet* (New York 1957). *Acta Apostolicae Sedis* 77 (1985) 935–39. *L'Osservatore Romano,* Eng. ed. 50 (1984): 2,12.

[K. RABENSTEIN]

MARCH MESA, NAZARÍA IGNACIA, BL.

In religion, Nazaría Ignacia of Santa Teresa of Jesús; foundress of the Missionary Crusaders of the Church (*Las Misioneras Cruzadas de la Iglesia*); b. 10 January 1889, Madrid, Spain; d. 6 July 1943, Buenos Aires, Argentina; beatified by John Paul II, 27 September 1992.

Nazaría was the fourth of the ten children of José March y Reus, a sailor and later businessman, and his wife Nazaría Mesa Ramos. She first sensed a call to religious life while she was preparing for her first communion (1898) and made a vow of perpetual virginity at age 11. Desiring to be a Jesuit missionary like Saint Francis Xavier, she formed her young friends into a secret missionary society of the Sacred Heart; they prayed and offered sacrifices for the missions. Her family moved to Mexico due to economic reasons in 1906. En route, Nazaría became acquainted with two members of the *Hermanitas de los Ancianos Desamparados* (Little Sisters of the Abandoned Elderly) with whom she began her religious life (1908). In 1912, she went to Bolivia, where with the approval of the nuncio, the Bolivian Church hierarchy, and 40 centavos, she founded at Oruro the Missionary Crusaders. Nazaría was soon joined by others,

elected superior general, and began to evangelize workers in cities, mines, and the countryside. Among other works she organized the first syndicate for female workers in Latin America, opened soup kitchens for the unemployed, and advocated for the advancement of women. Her foundation with houses in Argentina, Bolivia, Spain, and Uruguay, received definitive approval, 9 June 1947, four years after her death. Her mortal remains were enshrined in her community at Oruro in 1972.

Pope John Paul II, at Nazaría's beatification, said she founded the Missionary Crusaders to " 'go out into the streets' to meet people, to be in solidarity with them, to help them, especially if these people were covered with sores of material need . . . but primarily to bring them to God." Patroness of Mexican barrios.

Bibliography: *Acta Apostolicae Sedis* (1992): 919.

[K. RABENSTEIN]

MARCHISIO, CLEMENTE, BL.

Priest, founder of the Institute of the Daughters of Saint Joseph; b. 1 March 1833, Racconigi, Italy; d. 16 December 1903, Rivalba, Italy; beatified by John Paul II, 30 September 1984.

Father Marchisio is known for his assiduous attention to duty, his devotion to the Holy Eucharist, and his concern for the poor. He found the Daughters of Saint Joseph to extend his care of the needy, but also stressed the necessity of prayer to support the congregation's apostolate. Pope John Paul II, in his beatification homily, described Marchisio as "the image of Christ the Good Shepherd."

Feast: 20 September.

Bibliography: N. SARALE, *Teologia della semplicità: biografia di don Clemente Marchisio. . . .* (Rome 1975). *Acta Apostolicae Sedis* 77 (1985) 931–35. *L'Osservatore Romano,* Eng. ed. 44 (1984): 6–7.

[K. RABENSTEIN]

MARELLO, GIUSEPPE, BL.

Bishop of Asti, Piedmont, Italy, founder of the Oblates of Saint Joseph; b. 26 December 1844, Turin, Italy; d. 30 May 1895, in the bishop's residence at Savona, Italy; beatified by John Paul II, 26 September 1993, in the Campo del Palio at Asti, Italy.

While still a child Giuseppe (Joseph) moved from Turin to Santi Martino Alfieri with his father Vincenzo after the death of his mother, Anna Maria. He entered the minor seminary at age twelve and was ordained priest in 1868. In his capacity as secretary to Bishop Carlo Savio of Asti, Father Marello attended Vatican Council I. During this time he also assumed responsibility for a retirement home, served as spiritual director, and taught catechism. He founded the Oblates of St. Joseph in 1878 to be "hermits at home" in order to be "effective apostles away from home." Marello wanted his followers to be humble servants of the Church, ready to serve the bishops in whatever tasks were assigned them. The congregation was approved in 1909 by the Vatican after Marello's death. They opened their first mission in the United States in 1929. Following his episcopal consecration (17 February 1889), Bishop Marello dedicated his work especially to youth and the abandoned. His remains were enshrined at Asti. Pope John Paul II, in his beatification homily, called Bishop Marello a model "pastor of the People of God."

Bibliography: G. MARELLO, *Los escritos y las enseñanzas del bienaventurado José Marello,* ed. M. PASETTI (Santa Cruz, Calif. 1993). J. B. CORTONA, *Brief Memories of the Life of Joseph Marello, Bishop of Acqui, and of the Congregation He Founded . . .* (Santa Cruz, Calif. 1993). G. SISTO, *I, the Undersigned Poor Sinner: The Life of Blessed Joseph Marello* (Santa Cruz, Calif. 1993). L. M. TOSCHI, *Holiness in the Ordinary: Three Essays on the Spirituality of Blessed Joseph Marello* (Santa Cruz, Calif. 1993).

[K. RABENSTEIN]

MARIE DE L'INCARNATION MARTIN, BL.

First woman missionary to the New World, foundress of the Ursuline Sisters in Canada; b. 28 October 1599, Tours, France; d. 30 April 1672, Quebec, Canada; beatified by John Paul II in Rome, 22 June 1980. The daughter of middle-class parents, Florent and Jeanne (Michelet) Guyart, Marie acceded to her father's wishes and in 1617 married Claude Martin, despite her own attraction to religious life. When her husband died less than three years later, she became housekeeper for her sister, Madame Paul Buisson. Shortly after, Marie received revelations concerning the Incarnation, the Sacred Heart, and the Blessed Trinity. Influenced by the unusual caliber of Marie's interior life, her spiritual director, Dom Raymond of St. Bernard, agreed to her desire for religious consecration. On 25 January 1632, she entered the Ursuline monastery at Tours, leaving her 12-year-old son to the care of her sister. During her novitiate, Marie wrote a full account of her spiritual life in obedience to her Jesuit director. This work, the *Relation of 1633,* was supplemented by another, the *Relation of 1654,* which was written in Canada, and together they provide the most important documents for a study of her mystical life.

In 1635 Marie received in a dream the first hint of her missionary vocation. Four years later she finally set sail, accompanied by two other Ursulines and Mme. Madeleine de la Peltrie (1603–71), their lay foundress and chief financial supporter. Arriving in Quebec on 1 August 1639, the missionaries immediately opened their first school in the Lower City. Despite sickness, poverty, and Indian persecution, the school grew, and in 1642 the Ursulines moved to a larger monastery. In 1648, when Iroquois hostilities endangered Quebec, Marie was advised to return to Europe, but she and her nuns chose to remain in New France. Her letters to her son Claude, a Benedictine monk, were collected and published by him in 1681 (2d ed., 2 v. Paris 1876, 3d ed. by Albert Jamet, 4 v. Paris 1929–39) and provide a valuable source for seventeenth-century Canadian history. She also composed catechisms in Huron and Algonquian and a dictionary of French and Algonquian. When Pope John Paul II beatified Marie de l'Incarnation, he praised her contemplative gifts and her service to the Church.

Feast: 30 April (Canada).

Bibliography: *Écrits spirituels et historiques,* ed. A. JAMET, 4 v. (Paris 1929–39); *The Autobiography of Venerable Marie of the Incarnation,* tr. J. J. SULLIVAN (Chicago 1964). *Marie of the Incarnation: Selected Writings,* ed. I. MAHONEY (New York 1989). *Marie de l'Incarnation, relation autobiographique de 1654* (Solesmes 1976). Acta Apostolicae Sedis 73 (1981): 253–258. *L'Osservatore Romano,* English edition, no. 26 (1980):10–11. M.-P. DEL ROSARIO ADRIAZOLA, *La connaissance spirituelle chez Marie de l'Incarnation: la "Thérèse de France et du Nouveau Monde"* (Paris 1989). J. L. BEAUMIER, *Le reliquaire de la Grande Ursuline: ou, Histoire de la chapelle Saint-Michel à Tours, France* (Trois-Rivières 1972). G. BOUCHER, *Du centre à la croix: Marie de l'Incarnation* (Sillery, Québec 1976). M.-F. BRUNEAU, *Women Mystics Confront the Modern World: Marie de l'Incarnation and Madame Guyon* (Albany, New York 1998). H. R. CASGRAIN, *Histoire de la vénérable mère Marie de l'Incarnation, première supérieure des Ursulines de la Nouvelle-France* (Quebec 1882). P. F. X. CHARLEVOIX, *La vie de la mere Marie de l'Incarnations, institutrice & premiere superieure des ursulines de la Nouvelle France* (Paris 1724). N. Z. DAVIS, *Women on the Margins: Three Seventeenth-Century Lives* (Cambridge, Mass. 1995). F. DEROY-PINEAU, *Marie de l'Incarnation: Marie Guyart, femme d'affaires, mystique, mère de la Nouvelle-France* (Paris 1989). C. GOURDEAU, *Les délices de nos coeurs: Marie de l'Incarnation et ses pensionnaires amérindiennes* (Sillery, Québec 1994). A. G. L'HEUREUX, *The mystical vocabulary of Venerable Mère Maria de l'Incarnation* (New York 1969). F. JETTÉ, *The Spiritual Teaching of Mary of the Incarnation,* translated by M. HERMAN (Montreal 1963). D. MAHONEY, *Marie of the Incarnation, Mystic and Missionary* (Garden City, N.Y. 1964). A. MALI, *Mystic in the New World: Marie de l'Incarnation* (New York 1996). G. M. OURY, *Ce que croyait Marie de l'Incarnation* (Tours 1972); *Dom Claude Martin: le fils de Marie de l'Incarnation* (Sablé-sur-Sarthe 1983); *Marie de l'Incarnation* (Québec 1973); *Physionomie spirituelle de Marie de l'Incarnation* (Solesmes 1980); *Les saints de Touraine* (Chambray-les-Tours 1985): 180–191. A. THIRY, *Marie de l'Incarnation; itinéraire spirituel* (Paris 1973). J.-N. VUARNET, *L'aigle-mère: récit* (Paris 1995).

[D. MAHONEY]

MARMION, JOSEPH COLUMBA, BL.

Abbot of Maredsous and spiritual writer; b. 1 April 1858, Dublin, Ireland; d. 30 January 1923, Maredsous, Belgium. Born of an Irish father and a French mother, Joseph studied at Belvedere College in Dublin and at Holy Cross seminary of Clonliffe. He was then sent to the Irish College in Rome and studied at the College of Propaganda Fide. In the year following his ordination (16 June 1881), he returned to Ireland, where he was assigned to the parish of Dundrum. Soon afterward he became professor of philosophy at Holy Cross seminary. In 1886, with the permission of Cardinal Edward MacCabe, he entered the Benedictine monastery at Maredsous in Belgium. In 1899 he became prior and then professor at Mont-Cesar in Louvain, and in 1909 was made abbot at Maredsous.

Marmion became recognized as a master of the spiritual life, and his reputation further increased after his death. His books have gone through numerous editions in ten languages and are considered classics on the spiritual life. His teaching was drawn essentially from the Gospels, the Epistles of St. Paul, and the Rule of St. Benedict. Emphasizing the doctrine of the adoption of the children of God, Marmion exalts the person of Christ, the center of the whole interior life.

Along with his writing, Marmion carried on an extensive apostolate. He occupied himself by giving fatherly guidance to a large Benedictine monastery; hearing confessions and preaching retreats especially to priests and religious in Belgium, England, and Ireland; and keeping up an enormous correspondence. He was the close friend and spiritual director of Cardinal D. S. Mercier, Archbishop of Malines, who held the abbot in highest esteem.

Veneration of Dom Marmion began immediately after his death, and his reputation for sanctity gave rise to the opening of the process of his beatification in 1954. Pope John Paul II has scheduled his beatification ceremony for 3 September 2000. Two Benedictine monasteries have been placed under his patronage: Marmion Abbey in Aurora, Ill., and Glenstall Abbey in Eire.

Bibliography: His writings (in Eng. tr.) include:*Christ the Life of the Soul* (London 1925), *Christ in His Mysteries* (London 1925), *Christ the Ideal of the Monk* (London 1926), *Sponsa Verbi* (London 1939), *Union with God* (London 1949), *Words of Life on the Margin of the Missal* (London 1940), *Come to Christ, All You Who Labour* (London 1946), and *Christ the Ideal of the Priest* (London 1953). Works about Blessed Joseph Columba Marmion include: T. DELFORGE, *Columba Marmion: Servant of God*, tr. R. L. STEWART (London & St. Louis 1965). M. M. PHILIPON, *The Spiritual Doctrine of Dom Marmion*, tr. M. DILLON (Westminster, Md. 1956). R. THIBAUT, *Abbot Columba Marmion*, tr. M. ST. THOMAS (St. Louis 1949). M. TIERNEY, *Dom Columba Marmion* (Blackrock, Co. Dublin 1994).

[J. C. WILLKE]

MARTILLO MORÁN, NARCISA DE JESÚS, BL.

Lay mystic; b. 1832, at Daule (Nobol) near Guayaquil, Ecuador; d. 8 December 1869, Lima, Peru; beatified by John Paul II, 25 October 1992.

Narcisa's parents, Pedro Martillo Mosquera and Josefina Morán, were peasant farmers who died while Narcisa was very young. The middle child of nine, Narcisa moved to Guayaquil to find work as a seamstress to help support her siblings. For more than fifteen years, with a short break (ca. 1865) in Cuenca, she dedicated her life to manual labor, prayer, teaching catechism, and caring for the neediest residents of the capital. In Cuenca, she was invited by the bishop to enter the Carmelites, but discerned that her vocation was in the world. In 1868, she travelled to Lima, Peru, where she lived as a lay woman in the Dominican convent. A pious woman, Narcisa did penances and was devoted to the Cross of Christ. Soon after her death pilgrims began praying at her tomb in Lima. Her cause for beatification was opened in 1889.

In 1955, her body was translated to Guayaquil and now rests in her native town of Nobol under the altar of the Santuario de la Beata Narcisa de Jesús. Pope John Paul II praised her as the glory of Ecuador.

Feast: 30 August.

Bibliography: *Acta Apostolicae Sedis* 21 (1992): 1017.

[K. RABENSTEIN]

MATULAITIS, JURGIS, BL.

In Polish his name is Jerzy Matulewicz; superior general of the Marian Fathers; b. 13 April 1871, Lugine, Lithuania; d. 24 January 1927, Kaunas, Lithuania; beatified at Rome by John Paul II, 28 June 1987, the six hundredth anniversary of the ''baptism'' of Lithuania (Apostolic Letter, 5 June 1987).

Matulaitis completed his philosophical and theological studies at Kielce and Warsaw seminaries and at the Catholic Academy in St. Petersburg, Russia, where he was ordained 25 November 1898. He continued his studies at the University of Fribourg (Switzerland), where in 1902 he earned the doctorate in sacred theology ''praeclarissime'' for his dissertation *Doctrina russorum de iustitia originali*. After two years as professor of Latin and Canon Law at the Kielce seminary, he went to Warsaw, where he pioneered the Catholic movement for social betterment among the workers. In 1907 he was nominated to the faculty of the Catholic Academy of St. Petersburg as professor of sociology and later of dogmatic theology.

In 1909, while still professor and vice rector of the Academy, with the permission of Pope St. Pius X, he undertook the clandestine reform of the Order of Marians of the Immaculate Conception (Marian Fathers), which had been founded in 1673 by Stanislaus Papczýnski. It was suppressed in 1864 by the Russian Czarist Government, and reduced in 1909 to a single member. Dispensed from the required novitiate, Matulaitis secretly entered the order and adapted it to the needs of the Church in modern times. He composed new constitutions and instructions to govern and direct the life and activity of the congregation, which he served as superior general from 1911 until his death. In 1913 he visited the United States and established the first Marian house at Chicago.

In 1918 he was nominated by Pope Benedict XV to the vast and troubled Diocese of Vilnius, which he governed for seven years. In 1925 he was elevated to the rank of titular archbishop and named by Pius XI as apostolic visitator to Lithuania in order to establish an ecclesiastical province and to negotiate a concordat between the Lithuanian government and the Holy See. In addition to being responsible for the renewal of the Congregation of Marian Fathers, he wrote constitutions for some seven religious congregations. In Lithuania he founded the Congregation of Sisters of the Immaculate Conception, and in Byelorussia, the Congregation of Servants of the Sacred Heart. He died in 1927, and in 1934, his body was translated from Kaunas cathedral to the Marianist church of Marijampolér (where he had been baptized), now a national shrine.

Pope John Paul II hailed Bishop Matulaitis as "the far-sighted and caring Pastor of all his children, even the most remote . . . [who was] faithful to his episcopal motto: 'Conquer Evil with Good'" (Apostolic Letter, 5 June 1987).

Feast: 27 January (Marianists); 12 July (Lithuania).

Bibliography: V. CUSUMANO, *Innamorato della Chiesa* (Milan 1962). T. GÓRSKI & Z. PROCZEK, *Rozmilowany w Kosciele: błogoslawiony arcybiskup Jerzy Matulewicz* (Warsaw 1987). A. KUCAS, *Archbishop George Matulaitis*, tr. and ed. S. C. GAUCIAS (Chicago 1981). C. A. MATULAITIS, *A Modern Apostle* (Chicago 1955). S. MATULIS, *Lexikon für Theologie und Kirche,* 2d. ed., 7:183. *L'Osservatore Romano,* English edition, no. 27 (1987): 6–7.

[W. FOGARTY]

MAYER, RUPERT, BL.

Blessed, priest, member of Society of Jesus, noted for his anti-Nazi activities; b. Stuttgart, 23 January 1876; d. Munich, 1 November 1945. The son of Kolumban, a prosperous merchant, and Maria (Schäurer) Mayer, Ru-

pert studied in the universities of Fribourg, Munich, and Tubingen before entering the seminary at Rottenburg. He was ordained a priest 2 May 1899, and the following year entered the Jesuits, making his novitiate in Lichtenstein and taking further theological studies at Valkenburg in the Netherlands. Mayer gained a reputation as a preacher of parish missions in Germany, Switzerland, and the Netherlands. During World War I he volunteered to be a chaplain, was wounded and lost his left leg.

In 1921 Mayer was appointed chaplain of the Men's Sodality, a position he held until his death. He cofounded and was spiritual director of the Sisters of the Holy Family, a community that works among the very poor. In 1925, he inaugurated the *Banhofsmission*, a ministry to travelers.

Mayer was one of the first to recognize the incompatibility of Nazism and Christianity. The Nazi rejection of the Old Testament and the Jewish element in Christianity seemed to him intolerable and absurd. He regarded Hitler as "hysterical." These views made him an object of police attention after the Nazi accession to power in 1933. The Ministry of Justice gave him a warning because of his anti-Nazi position. In April 1936 Mayer was forbidden to preach throughout Germany and later arrested, but released on the condition that he should confine himself to the sacramental ministry and service of the poor. Although he accepted the condition under duress or "obedience," on 3 November 1939, Mayer was again arrested. Confined first to the concentration camp at Sachsenhausen, he spent the duration of the war in Ettal Abbey. On 11 May 1945, he returned to Munich, only days after World War II ended in Germany and began to preach again, but he died six months later at the age of 69. His tomb in the crypt of the Sodality Chapel on Neuhauserstrasse in Munich soon became a place of pilgrimage. Pope John Paul II beatified Mayer on 3 May 1987, in the Olympic Stadium in Munich.

Feast: 3 November (Jesuits).

Bibliography: A. KÖBLING, ed., *Father Rupert Mayer: A Modern Priest and Witness for Christ* (Munich: Schnell and Steiner, 1950; 1975). OTTO GRITTSCHNEDER, ed., *Ich Predige Weiter: Pater Rupert Mayer und das Dritte Reich* (Rosenheim, Germany 1987). LAPOMARDA, V. A. *The Jesuits and the Third Reich* (n.p.: Edwin Mellen, 1989). *L'Osservatore Romano,* English edition, no. 22 (1987): 2, 3. TYLENDA, *J. N. Jesuit Saints And Martyrs* (Chicago: Loyola University Press, 1998).

[P. HEBBLETHWAITE]

MAZENOD, CHARLES JOSEPH EUGÈNE DE, ST.

A.k.a. Eugène de Mazenod, bishop, founder of the Oblates of Mary Immaculate; b. 1 August 1782, Aix-en-

Provence, France; d. 21 May 1861, Marseilles, France; canonized in Rome by John Paul II, 3 December 1995.

Mazenod was the son of the president of the Board of Excise in Provence, who belonged to the nobility of the robe. During the French Revolution, he immigrated with his family (April 1791) to Nice, Turin, Venice, and Palermo without being able to undertake regular studies. He returned to France in 1802 and decided, after a grave personal religious crisis, to become a priest. During his three years at Saint-Sulpice seminary, he was profoundly influenced by Msgr. Emery and participated in the Catholic resistance in favor of Pius VII and the black cardinals. Upon returning to Aix after ordination (1811), the young priest devoted himself to ministering to the poor and to an association for youths. In 1817, he became interested in popular missions. To promote them he founded a community that was the germ of the Oblates of Mary Immaculate. When his uncle, Fortuné de Mazenod, became bishop of Marseilles in 1823, he made Charles his vicar-general. Mazenod became a titular bishop in 1832 and succeeded his uncle as bishop in 1837. During these years Mazenod devoted himself to the restoration and reorganization of the diocese, while acting as superior general of his missionary institute, which received the approval of the Holy See in 1826. Mazenod played a very active role also in the religious affairs of France and in 1856 became a senator of the Second Empire. In Marseilles he confronted difficult spiritual and material problems created by the changed economic and social situation in the city, whose population had doubled. The bishop established the structures used in the diocese for the next half-century and more. He created twenty-two parishes, rebuilt the cathedral, Notre-Dame de la Garde, and twenty-five other churches, increased clerical recruitment, and promoted religious congregations. The most celebrated of the societies inaugurated by him was that of Timon David for young workers. Membership in the Oblates remained small until 1843, and then grew rapidly when Mazenod began to accept missions in Canada, U.S., Ceylon, and South Africa. In these lands the Oblate apostolate bore remarkable results. Mazenod was an ardent ultramontane but displayed moderation in the controversies concerning the classics, the liturgy, Gallicanism, and Liberalism. He supported Hugues Félicité de Lamennais in Rome to the end. On the other had, he was intransigent and resolute concerning educational freedom and the Roman Question. Upon his death in 1861 he was buried in the cathedral of Marseilles. Mazenod's cause was introduced in Rome in 1936; he was beatified on 19 October 1975.

During Mazenod's canonization, Pope John Paul II said the saint "had a profound awareness of the universality of the Church's mission . . . [and] devoted particular attention to the evangelization of the poor, wherever they were found." Patron of troubled marriages, dysfunctional families, broken homes, families in crisis.

Feast: 21 May (Oblates of Mary Immaculate).

Bibliography: *Lettres aux correspondants d'Amérique* (Rome 1977). *Acta Apostolicae Sedis* 68 (1976): 241–243. *Beatificationis et canonizationis servi Dei Caroli Iosephi Eugenii de Mazenod* (Rome 1968). L. N. BOUTIN, *Le double charisme du bienheureux Joseph-Eugène de Mazenod* (Montréal 1978). R. ETCHEGARAY, *Petite vie de Eugène de Mazenod* (Paris 1995). A. HUBENIG, *Living in the Spirit's Fire* (Toronto 1995). J. LEFLON, *Eugène de Mazenod, évêque de Marseille, fondateur des missionaires oblats de Marie Immaculée*, 3 v. (Paris 1957–65), Eng. tr. F. D. FLANAGAN (Washington, D.C. 1994). S. C. LORIT, *La scelta dei poveri: vita di Eugenio de Mazenod* (Rome 1975). *L'Osservatore Romano*, English edition, no. 44 (1975): 6–7; no. 49 (1995): 1–2. A. ROCHE, *Le Bienheureux Eugène de Mazenod: évêque de Marseille, fondateur des missionnaires oblats de Marie-Immaculée* (Lyon 1975).

[J. LEFLON/EDS]

MAZZARELLA, MODESTINO, BL.

Baptized Domenico, known in religion as Modestino of Jesus and Mary, Franciscan Alcantarine priest; b. 5 September 1802, Frattamaggiore, Naples, Italy; died 24 July 1854, Naples; beatified by John Paul II, 29 January 1995.

Domenico was the fourth child in a pious, working-class family headed by Nicolà Mazzarella, a cordmaker, and his wife Teresa Espósito, a weaver. In his youth Domenico showed such devotion as an altar boy and as patron of Our Lady of Good Counsel that Bishop Agostino Tommasi sponsored his seminary studies at Aversa (1820–21). After Tommasi's death (1821), Domenico continued his education at home. In 1822, he joined the Franciscans at Grumo Nevano and received the habit and name Modestino at Piedimonte Matese in Caserta (3 November 1822). Following his novitiate at Santa Lucia del Monte, Naples, he was professed (27 November 1824), completed his studies at the convents of Grumo Nevano, Portici, and Santa Lucia, and was ordained priest at Aversa cathedral (22 December 1827). Thereafter he served in various roles within the order, including guardian of the friaries of Mirabella Eclano (Avellino) and Pignataro Maggiore (Caserta). In 1839, he was transferred to Santa Maria della Sanità in a populous Neopolitan slum, where he distinguished himself through his defense of life. He worked among the poor until his death from cholera, contracted while ministering to other victims of the epidemic. A miracle attributed to Modestino's intercession was approved 23 December 1993.

Pope John Paul II beatified Modestino, saying that he "was able to share fully the expectations and anxieties of the weakest, responding to the deep need for God found in his brothers and sisters who thirsted for justice and love. . . . [He was] a minister of mercy and comfort to every social class, especially through his diligent, patient celebration of the sacrament of Reconciliation.''

Feast: 24 July.

Bibliography: *Acta Apostolicae Sedis* (1995): 249.

[K. RABENSTEIN]

MAZZUCCONI, GIOVANNI BATTISTA, BL.

Missionary priest, martyr of the Pontifical Institute for Foreign Missions (PIME); b. 1 March 1826, Rancio di Lecco (near Milan), Italy; d. 7 September 1855, Woodlark Bay, Papua New Guinea; beatified by John Paul II, 19 February 1984.

The ninth of the twelve children of Giacomo Mazzucconi and Anna Maria Scuri, Mazzucconi studied in the seminaries of Monza and Milan. In the summer of 1845, he and his friend Carlo Salerio met the prior of the Certosa of Pavia, who had been a missionary in India. This sparked an interest in the young men, who maintained correspondence with the priest. In the meantime Giovanni was ordained (25 May 1850) and the Pontifical Institute for Foreign Missions (PIME) was established with apostolic approval. Two months later (July 1850), Mazzucconi received an invitation from Monsignor Angelo Ramazzotti to become a charter member of the PIME, together with Father Salerio, three other clergymen (Timoleone Raimondi, Angelo Ambrosoli, and Paolo Reina), and two catechists (Giuseppe Corti and Luigi Tacchini). They intended to go first to Oceania. Following a three-month journey, the missionaries arrived (25 July 1852) in Australia, where they studied the language and customs of New Guinea under the tutelage of a Marist for two months. Upon their arrival at Woodlark Island (28 October 1852), the mission was divided into three groups with Mazzucconi, Reina, a catechist, and their Marist mentor continuing to Rook Island, where they worked for two years under difficult conditions. The missionaries attempted to gain the trust of the natives by helping and teaching them new agricultural methods.

After the attempts failed, Mazzuconi returned to Sydney (January 1855), where he became seriously ill. Upon his recovery he sailed (18 August 1855) back to Woodlark not knowing that his companions had abandoned the mission stations at Woodlark and Rook. When his schooner ran aground on a coral reef, he was killed with an axe by one of the locals. Eight months later Father Raimondi led an expedition to find Mazzucconi and learned of his martyrdom.

Feast: 10 September (Archdiocese of Milan).

Bibliography: P. GHEDDO, *Mazzucconi di Woodlark: un martire per il nostro tempo* (Bologna 1983); *Missione i Oceania: Giovanni Mazzucconi, martire a Woodlark* (Turin 1984). N. MAESTRINI, *Mazzucconi of Woodlark: Biography of Blessed John Mazzucconi* (Detroit 1983). *Acta Apostolicae Sedis* (1984) 300. *L'Osservatore Romano,* Eng. ed. 12 (1984): 3–4.

[K. RABENSTEIN]

MEINHARD OF LIVONIA, ST.

A.k.a. Meinrad, Augustinian missionary, bishop; b. ca. 1130 in Germany; d. 14 August 1196, Yxkill, Livonia (near Riga, Latvia); canonized by John Paul II at Riga, Latvia, 8 September 1993.

Meinhard entered religious life at the monastery of Segelberg, Germany. Following his profession as an Augustinian canon regular and ordination as a priest, he left the safety of his monastery to preach in pagan lands. He was consecrated the first bishop of Livonia (c.1184) and fixed his see at Yxkill on the Düna. He brought monks from his former convent to form a community of canons regular at his castle. Christianity found firm footing in the region due to his efforts to form a native clergy and establish standards for their training. Originally he was buried at his castle in Livona. The see was transferred to Riga (1201) following his death, and his relics translated later that century to Riga's cathedral.

Feast: 12 April.

Bibliography: S. KUCINSKIS, *Svetais Meinards: Ikskiles biskaps, 1186-1196: Latvijas apustulis* (Riga 1993).

[K. RABENSTEIN]

MENNI FIGINI, BENEDETTO, ST.

Baptized Angelo Ercole Menni, priest of the Hospitallers of Saint John of God, founder of the Hospitaller Sisters of the Sacred Heart of Jesus; b. 11 March 1841, Milan, Italy; d. 24 April 1914, Dinan, northern France; canonized 21 November 1999 in Rome by John Paul II.

As one of the fifteen children of Luigi Menni and Luisa Figini, Angelo learned charity at home. He gave up his job as a bank clerk to serve the soldiers wounded in the Battle of Magenta. He joined the Brothers of St. John of God (1860) and was ordained priest in Rome (1866). In 1867, he was sent to Spain to revitalize the order, following its suppression by anticlerical laws. Despite threats to his life and temporary expulsion, he founded a children's hospital in Barcelona (1867). His work with the elderly, abandoned children, polio victims, and the mentally ill over the next thirty-six years attracted many other vocations allowing him to open and staff twenty-two hospitals in Spain, Portugal, and Mexico, thus restoring the Hospitallers' work in Latin America. In 1880, Menni founded the Hospitaller Sisters of the Sacred Heart of Jesus in Ciempozuelos (near Madrid, Spain) with María Josefa Recio and María Angustias Gimenez, who established a psychiatric hospital in Granada (1881). The female branch of the Hospitallers spread throughout Europe and to Africa, Asia, and Latin America. Menni later served as apostolic visitor (1909–11) and prior general (1911), before resigning due to ill health in 1912. His body rests in the motherhouse chapel of the Hospitaller Sisters in Madrid.

In the canonization homily, Pope John Paul II praised Menni for carrying out his service "with a humility based on hospitality and blameless integrity."

Feast: 24 April.

Bibliography: *Acta Apostolicae Sedis* 78 (1986): 710–713. *L'Osservatore Romano,* English edition, no. 29 (1985): 6–7. M. SOROLDONI, *Santità alla sbarra: la vita contestata di Benedetto Menni* (Rome 1981). E. ZUÑEDA SALAZAR, *Benito Menni, testigo de la caridad* (Madrid 1985).

[K. RABENSTEIN]

MERTEN, BLANDINA, BL.

Baptized Maria Magdalena, virgin of the Ursuline Sisters of Mount Calvary, Ahrweiler; b. 10 July 1883, Düppenweiler, Saarland, Germany; d. 18 May 1918, Trier, Rhineland Palatinate, Germany; beatified by John Paul II, 1 November 1987.

Maria Magdalena was the ninth child of a peasant family. After she completed grammar school, a tutor helped her prepare (1898–99) for entrance to the teachers' college of Marienau bei Vallendar, where she studied from 1899 to 1902. After passing the licensing examination, she was a teacher in Oberthal, Saarland, then taught in Morscheid, Hunsrück (1903–07) and Großrosseln an der Saar (1907–08). A chance meeting with the Ursuline superior of Kalvarienberg, Ahrweiler, led to her entry into the order (22 April 1908) and profession of temporary vows (3 November 1910). Thereafter she taught children in the order's schools at Saarbrücken and Trier. She professed her final vows in 1913 and contracted tuberculosis shortly thereafter. She endured her illness with resolute patience and remained committed to her teaching obligations until her death. On 18 May 1990, Sister Blandina's mortal remains were transferred to her new titular chapel, designed by Karl P. Böhr, in Trier's Saint Paulin cemetery.

At her beatification, Pope John Paul II praised Blandina's heroism in performing the little things with and for love.

Feast: 18 May.

Bibliography: *L'Osservatore Romano,* Eng. ed. 47 (1987): 7–8. M. H. VISARIUS, *A Hidden Spouse of Our Lord: The Life of Sister Blandine Merten, Ursuline, compiled from recollections, letters and her notes* (New York 1938).

[K. RABENSTEIN]

MESINA, ANTONIA, BL.

Lay virgin martyr, member of Catholic Action; b. 21 June 1919, Orgosolo (near Nuora), Sardina, Italy; d. there 17 May 1935; beatified by John Paul II, 4 October 1987.

Antonia Mesina, born into a poor and pious family in a small village, joined Catholic Action in 1934. While gathering wood with a companion near her home in May 1935, Antonia was assaulted by a youth, Giovanni-Ignacio Catgui. Her friend ran for help as Catgui tried to rape Antonia. Enraged he attacked her with stones, brutally killing her. Pope John Paul II beatified her for her fidelity to purity and piety.

Feast: 17 May.

Bibliography: V. SCHAUBER, *Pattloch Namenstagskalender,* ed. H. M. SCHINDLER (Augsburg 1994): 127. *Acta Apostolicae Sedis* (1987): 983. *L'Osservatore Romano,* English. edition, no. 40 (1987): 20.

[K. RABENSTEIN]

MEXICO (GUADALAJARA), MARTYRS OF, SS.

A.k.a. Martyrs of the Cristero Movement, or Cristobal Magallanes and 24 Companions; d. 1915–1937, Mexico; both beatified, 22 November 1992, and canonized, 21 May 2000 by John Paul II.

Jubilee 2000 was a watershed year for Catholicism in Mexico. In 1992, after 150 years of antireligious laws that forced the Church into near obscurity, laws such as those forbidding the wearing of a religious habit in public were rescinded. In 2000, the first National Eucharistic Congress was convened since just before the latest government persecution (1924–34), which sparked the uprising of the Cristero Rebellion. Most of the twenty-two priests and three lay martyrs included in this group were victims of that persecution in the area around Guadalajara; however, a few testify to the sufferings of earlier periods. The causes of martyrs from other areas of Mexico

1928, Guadalajara. Justino was the son of an extremely poor family. He completed his initial studies at Zapotlán, then entered Guadalajara's seminary (1894). After his ordination (1904), he served as a parish priest at Poncitlán, Encarnación, Jalisco, and Cuquío. Despite an atmosphere of anticlericalism and religious indifference, he was an exemplary priest. While he was pastor of Cuquío (Archdiocese of Guadalajara), he founded the Congregation of Claretian Brothers of the Sacred Heart to care for orphans and poor children. When the persecution intensified, he and his pastor, Atilano Cruz, decided to remain with their flock despite the danger, but hid themselves on the nearby ranch of Las Cruces with Justino's brother José María and Toribio Ayala (28 June 1928). Federal forces arrived there at dawn with the mayor of Cuquío. Justino opened the door, shouted ''Viva Cristo Rey!,'' and was shot. His body was deposited in the Cuquío's town square. His mortal remains were moved to San Felipe Church in Cuquío.

Luis Batiz Sainz, pastor; b. 13 September 1870, San Miguel del Mezquital, Zacatecas, Archdiocese of Durango; d. 15 August 1926, Puerto de Santa Teresa, near Zacatecas. At 12 he entered the seminary of Durango, where he was known for his piety. From his ordination (1 January 1894) until his death, he served as spiritual director of the seminary and parish priest at San Pedro Chalchihuites. His involvement with Catholic Action led him to found elementary and technical schools. After convening a meeting of the National League in defense of religious freedom before the bishops closed the churches, Batiz was denounced as a conspirator plotting to overthrow the government and forced into hiding. He was arrested 14 August. When the townspeople demanded his release, he was transferred to Zacatecas. En route he was executed together with three members of Catholic Action (Manuel Morales, Salvador Lara, and David Roldán).

Manuel Morales, married layman; b. 8 February 1898, Mesillas near Sombrerete, Zacatecas, Diocese of Durango; d. 15 August 1926, Puerto de Santa Teresa near Zacatecas. After Manuel's birth, his family moved to Chalchihuites, where he later met Luis Batiz. He attend the Durango seminary but left to support his poor family, married, and sired three children. Known for his piety, he was secretary to the Circle of Catholic Workers and a member of the Mexican Youth for Catholic Action. As president of the National League, he announced at its first meeting that its mission was to peacefully petition the government to repeal laws suppressing religious liberty. After Batiz's arrest, he organized the locals to secure the priest's freedom. Instead he was himself arrested, totured, then shot near Zacatecas.

Margarito Flores García, priest; b. 22 February 1899, Taxco, Guerrero, Diocese of Chilapa; d. 12 November 1927, Tulimán, between Chilapa and Chilpancingo. From the age of 12, Margarito dedicated himself to God's service, while working in the fields the help support his poor family. He entered the seminary at Chilapa and was ordained priest (1924). Soon thereafter he was appointed professor in the seminary. He took refuge in Mexico City during the persecution and attended the academy of San Carlos. After he was arrested, then released, there, he decided to return to Chilapa, where the vicar general had named him pastor of the parish at Atenango del Rio, Guerrero. He was captured upon his arrival, humiliated, and led to Tulimán where he was shot.

Mateo Correa Magallanes, pastor; b. 22 or 23 July 1866, Tepechitlán, Zacatecas, Diocese of Zacatecas; d. 6 February 1927, Durango, Jalisco, Diocese of Zacatecas. He was ministering in the parish at Valparaíso, Zacatecas, during the persecution. Correa administered First Communion to Miguel Agustin Pro He faithfully executed his sacerdotal duties, including evangelizing and serving the poor. He was continually harassed by the authorities, arrested and released. The last time he was administering the last rites. He was detained for several days at Fresnillo, Zacatecas, then taken to Durango. There General Eulogio Ortiz asked him hear the confessions of some prisoners. Later he asked the priest to reveal the content of those confessions or be killed. When he refused, he was martyred outside Durango, where his relics are enshrined in the cathedral in the Chapel of Saint George the Martyr.

Miguel de la Mora, priest; b. 19 June 1878, Tecalitlán, Jalisco, Diocese of Colima; d. 7 August 1927, Colima, Colima. He was chaplain of Colima cathedral, a simple, charitable priest, who was always ready to serve. Colima was the first state to require priests to register in order to exercise their sacradotal ministries. When the bishop and priests protested, the government exiled them. Miguel was one of those who were hidden to ensure the faithful were not left untended. He was discovered and threatened with imprisonment. Unwilling to disobey the instructions of his bishop, Miguel attempted to leave the city, but was apprehended and condemned to execution. Upon reaching the appointed place at noon, he declared his faith and his love of the Blessed Mother. Miguel was felled by bullets as he prayed the rosary.

Pedro de Jesús Maldonado Lucero, priest; b. 15 June 1892, Sacramento, Chihuahua; d. 11 February 1937, Chihuahua. At seventeen he entered the Archdiocesan seminary at Chihuahua. When political upheaval interrupted his schooling (1914), he studied music. Following his ordination (1918) in El Paso, Texas, he dedicated himself to catechizing children, and promoting all-night vigils and Marian associations at S. Isabel, Chihuahua. In 1934,

Pedro was imprisoned, maltreated, and exiled to El Paso, but soon returned. A group of drunk soldiers apprehended him after Ash Wednesday liturgy, beat him and shot him. He died later from the injuries he sustained.

Pedro Esqueda Ramírez, priest; b. 29 April 1887, San Juan de Los Lago, Jalisco; d. 22 November 1927, San Miguel el Alto, near Teocaltitlán. Pedro Esqueda, a precocious child, began his formal education at age four. He entered the seminary of Guadalajara (1902), which was seized and closed before he completed his studies. Returning to his home parish, he served as a deacon until his ordination was arranged in 1916 at which time he was named pastor. His passion for catechesis inspired Pedro to found several centers for training catechists. When the persecution of the Church worsened in 1926, Pedro went into hiding, moving from house to house until he was captured in hiding by *federales* on 18 November 1927. They beat the priest, held him incommunicado in the abbey, tortured him for the next few days, and shot him in Teocaltitlán.

Rodrigo Aguilar Alemán, pastor; b. 13 March 1875, Sayula, Jalisco, Diocese of Ciudad Guzmán; d. 28 October 1927, Unión de Tula, Jalisco, Diocese of Autlán. He studied at the auxiliary seminary of Ciudad Guzmán, where he showed exceptional literary talent. Following his ordination to the priesthood (1905), he served in various parishes. He was serving as interim pastor of the Unión de Tula when he was persecuted for his priesthood. He took refuge on a farm from where he continued to minister to the faithful and direct spiritual exercises. He was betrayed by one of his flock and arrested by troops under the command of Brigadier General Juan Izaguirre. He was hanged from a mango tree in the town square the following day. His body was translated to the parish church at Tula.

Román Adame Rosales, priest; b. 27 February 1859, Teocaltiche, Jalisco, Diocese of Aguascalientes; d. 21 April 1927, Yahualica, Guadalajara. After completing his seminary studies at Guadalajara, Román was ordained priest (30 November 1890) and assigned to various parishes. He concentrated his energies on catechesis, popular missions, the construction of chapels in the surrounding areas (and St. Joseph's Church), the care of the sick, and the education of children. He founded an association of the Daughters of Mary and encouraged nocturnal adoration of the Blessed Sacrament. As pastor of Nochistlán, Zacatecas, Archdiocese of Guadalajara, this profoundly humble priest secretly administered the sacraments during the persecution until his hiding place was betrayed. He was arrested at night and tortured. Later he was imprisoned at Yahualica, where he was deprived of food and water for several days. On the day of his execution,

he was taken to the church cemetery, where a grave had already been opened for him and shot. Román's body was exhumed and returned to Nochistlán.

Sabás Reyes Salazar, priest; b. 5 December *c.* 1879-83, at Cocula, Jalisco, Archdiocese of Guadalajara; d. 13 April 1927 (Wednesday of Holy Week), Tototlán, Guadalajara, Diocese of San Juan de los Lagos. He came from a poor family, studied in Guadalajara's seminary, then transferred to the diocese of Tamaulipas and was ordained (1911). At the beginning of the revolution, he returned to Guadalajara to minister in various parishes, primarily forming catechists. Despite the outbreak of anti-clerical persecution, he continued working in Tototlán. When federal troops attacked as he was returning from a baptism, he found refuge for two days before he was discovered by Izaguirre's troops. In vain they tortured him with fire to elicit the hiding places of Francisco Vizcarra and other priests, then riddled his body with bullets. His body rests in the church at Tototlán.

Salvador Lara Puente, lay youth; b. 13 August 1905, Berlin, Súchil, Archdiocese of Durango; d. 15 August 1926, Puerto de Santa Teresa near Zacatecas. Like his cousin David Roldán, he abandoned his studies at Durango seminary in order to assist his family financially. While working for a mining company, he remained active in pastoral work, Mexican Youth for Catholic Action (president), and the National League (secretary). He was arrested and shot with his cousin, after witnessing the assassination of their pastor, Batiz, and Manuel Morales.

Toribio Romo González, priest; b. 16 April 1900, at Santa Ana de Guadalupe, near Jalostotitlán, Jalisco, Diocese of San Juan de los Lagos; d. 25 February 1928, Tequila, Jalisco, Archdiocese of Guadalajara. At thirteen he began studying at the minor seminary of San Juan de los Lagos. He participated in Catholic Action while attending Guadalajara's seminary (1920–22), and was ordained 1922. His ministry in various parishes (Sayula, Tuxpan, Yahualica, Cuquío, and Tequila) concentrated on preparing catechesis, assisting workers, and promoting Eucharistic devotion. Forced into hiding with Justino Orona, he made his headquarters in an abandoned factory and conducted his ministry in Tequila at night. Soldiers broke in and shot him. In 1948, his body was enshrined in a chapel built for it at Jalostotitlán.

Tranquilino Ubiarco Robles, priest; b. 8 July 1899, Zapotlán el Grande, Jalisco, Diocese of Ciudad Guzmán; d. 5 October 1928, Guadalajara. During the Carrancista Revolution his seminary was closed and its buildings seized, but Tranquilino continued his studies in private while undertaking pastoral work. In 1920. At the invitation of the bishop, he went to Sinaloa, but returned when the bishop died soon after his arrival. He resumed his studies at Guadalajara's seminary and was ordained (August 1923). Thereafter Tranquilino taught catechism in study circles and founded a Christian newspaper. At the height of the persecution, he was named pastor of Tepatitlán's parish (Diocese of San Juan de los Lagos). For fifteen months he ministered in private homes and established a public feeding center. While preparing to celebrate a nuptial Mass in a private home in Guadalajara on 5 October 1928, soldiers arrived to arrest him. He was sentenced to death by hanging on the outskirts of the city. Tranquilino's mortal remains were transferred to the parish church.

Bibliography: J. CARDOSO, *Los mártires mexicanos* (Mexico City 1953). R. HARO LLAMAS, *El padre Galván: una vida sacerdotal en el marco histórico de su tiempo* (Guadalajara, Jalisco 1977).

[K. RABENSTEIN]

MICHEL, TERESA GRILLO, BL.

Baptized Maddalena Grillo, widow, foundress of the Congregation of the Little Sisters of Divine Providence; b. 25 September 1855, Spinetta Marengo, Alessandria, Italy; d. there 25 January 1944; beatified in the Piazza Vittorio, Turin, Piedmont, Italy, by John Paul II, 24 May 1988.

Maddalena, the youngest of the five children, was born into a life of privilege. Her mother, Maria Antonietta Parvopassau, had been born into the local aristocracy, while her father, Giuseppe Grillo, was chief physician at Alessandria's hospital. Her mother moved the family to Turin following her husband's death. Maddalena attended grammar school in Turin, before being sent to the Ladies of Loretto boarding school in Lodi (Lombardy). Having completed school (1873), Maddalena returned to Alessandria for her debut into society. She married (2 August 1877) Giovanni Battista Michel, a captain of the Bersaglieri. During 14 years of marriage, the couple lived in Acireale, Catania, Portici, and Naples. Her sorrow at the death of Giovanni from sunstroke might have turned to despair had she not read the life of Saint Joseph Cottolengo. His life inspired her to share the grief of the abandoned: orphans, the elderly, the sick. She turned her home into a shelter for those in need. As the numbers grew, she sold her home in order to buy and renovate a large building on the Via Faa di Bruno (1893), which became the "Little Shelter of Divine Providence." She continued her work despite opposition and enlisted the aid of others. On 8 January 1899, Maddalena and eight co-workers received the religious habit and new names in the shelter's chapel, becoming the Congregation of the Little Sisters of Divine Providence. Almost immediately the institute grew exponentially: houses were established

in Apulia, Liguria, Lombardy, Lucania, the Piedmont, and Veneto. Eighteen months after the institute's foundation, a house was opened in Brazil (13 June 1900) and, at the request of Blessed Luigi ORIONE (1872–1940), houses in Argentina (1927). Thereafter, Teresa crossed the Atlantic eight times to establish homes for the aged, hospitals, nurseries, orphanages, and schools and in Latin America.

At her beatification, Pope John Paul II said that Teresa "was called by the Lord to spread love especially among the very poor" (beatification homily).

Bibliography: V. CÁRCEL ORTÍ, *Martires españoles del siglo XX* (Madrid 1995). J. PÉREZ DE URBEL, *Catholic Martyrs of the Spanish Civil War, 1936-1939*, tr. M. F. INGRAMS (Kansas City, Mo. 1993). A. PRONZATO, *Una donna per sperare: madre Teresa Michel fondatrice delle Piccole suore della Divina Provvidenza* (Turin 1978).

[K. RABENSTEIN]

MÍGUEZ, FAUSTINO, BL.

Baptized Manuel, a.k.a. Faustino of the Incarnation, educator, scientist, Piarist priest, founder of the Daughters of the Divine Shepherdess (Calasanctian Sisters); b. 25 March 1831, Xamirás, Acebedodel Rio, Celanova, Orense, Galicia, Spain; d. 8 March 1925, at Getafe near Madrid, Spain; beatified by John Paul II, 25 October 1998.

Manuel, the fourth child of Christian farmers, studied Latin and the humanities in Orense. There, Manuel was inspired by the life of Saint Joseph Calasanz (1556–1648) and entered the novitiate of Calasanz's order, Poor Clerics Regular of the Mother of God of the Pious Schools (Piarists), at Saint Ferdinand's in Madrid (1850), professed his vows, and was later ordained. He taught for nearly fifty years in Piarist schools, including those at Celanova, El Escorial, Getafe, Guanaboacoa, Monforte de Lemos, San Fernando, and Sanlúcar de Barameda, while continuing to improve his own education. His genuine love for children exhibited itself in his kindness and his dedication to teaching them the love of truth. At the invitation of St. Anthony Mary Claret, Faustino travelled to Cuba to teach in various colleges. Returning to Spain, he used his study of botany to uncover the healing power of plants and manufactured medicines for the sick, poor people of the region. His legacy in this area is the Míguez Laboratory in Getafe.

Míguez was particularly sensitive to the dignity of women, whom he regarded as the soul of the family. Appalled by the illiteracy and marginalization of women in Sanlúcar de Barrameda, he founded the Calasanctian Sisters (2 January 1885) with the support of the bishop of Seville. The congregation, recognized by the Holy See in 1910, is dedicated to the education and formation of children, especially poor girls. This congregation has continued to endure and prosper in Spain and Latin America.

Míguez, who was also known as a patient, wise confessor, died at the age of ninety-four. In beatifying Father Faustino, Pope John Paul II pointed out that "In school and on the street, in the confessional and in the laboratory, Father Faustino Míguez was a transparency of Christ, who welcomes, forgives, and encourages" (beatification homily).

[K. RABENSTEIN]

MOGAS FONTCUBERTA, MARÍA ANA, BL.

Co-foundress of the Capuchin Congregation of Franciscan Missionaries of the Mother of the Divine Shepherd; b. 13 January 1827, Corró de Vall-Granollers (near Barcelona), Catalonia, Spain; d. 3 July 1886, Fuencarral (north of Madrid), Spain; beatified by John Paul II, 6 October 1996.

Raised in Barcelona by her widowed aunt/godmother María Mogas following the deaths of her father Lorenzo Mogas (d. 1834) and mother Magdalena Fontcuberta (d. 1841). María Ana was provided with all the benefits of high social standing, as well as faith. She searched for her vocation under the spiritual direction and met the exclaustrated Capuchin Father José Tous Soler. He introduced her to two former Capuchin nuns, María Valdés and Isabel Yubal. All had been given permission to minister outside the convent. Together they founded at Ripoll (near Gerona) the third order regular sisters of the Mother of the Divine Shepherd (13 June 1850) for the education of children. With the permission of bishop of Vic the sisters were veiled. He gave them charge over a school at Ripoll, and María was elected superior (September 1950). Mother María Ana professed her vows, 25 June 1851. When the two former Capuchin nuns returned to their cloister, María fulfilled the legal requirements to administer a school, then recruited new members. The congregation grew rapidly thereafter and a second group was established in Barcelona. At the request of Bishop Benito Serra, María Ana began to work with the noblewoman María Antonia Oviedo to establish (December 1865) a ministry for the regeneration of prostitutes in Ciempozuelos (Madrid). She later abandoned the project and accepted instead the direction of another school. Following her death her body was buried in Santa Ana cemetery. After miracles occurred at her grave, it was exhumed (1893) and translated to the college chapel. Her relics were lost during the Spanish civil war (1936), but recovered in 1967 and placed in the motherhouse at Madrid. A miracle attributed to her intercession was approved in 1996.

Pope John Paul II in beatifying Mother María Ana said: "Faithful to the Franciscan ideal, she showed her preference for the poor, an ability to forgive and forget ingratitude and insult, as well as a dedication to the education of children, care for the sick and for those who suffered any kind of need."

Feast: 6 October.

Bibliography: I. PAZ GONZÁLEZ, *Las Terciarias Franciscanas de la Madre del Divino Pastor: (contribución al estudio de la vida religiosa en España durante el último cuarto del siglo XIX)* (Madrid 1978). *Acta Apostolicae Sedis* (1996): 999.

[K. RABENSTEIN]

MOLAS Y VALLVÉ, MARÍA ROSA DOLORIBUS FRANCISCA, ST.

Foundress of the Sisters of Our Lady of Consolation (*Hermanas de Nuestra Señora de la Consolación*); b. 24 March 1815, Reus (near Tarragona), northeastern Spain; d. 11 June 1876, Tortosa, Spain; canonized by John Paul II, 11 December 1988.

María Rosa, the daughter of craftsmen who owned a small shop, postponed her entry into religious life to tend her father's household after her mother's death from cholera. As Sister María Rosa she joined an association of pious workers at the hospital in Reus (1841). Because of her practical intelligence, she was sent (1849) to Tortosa as superior of the House of Mercy. She reorganized and updated the facility and procedures to improve the care given to its 300 mentally ill patients. When she discovered that her congregation had no ties to any ecclesiastical authority, she placed herself and her eleven sisters under the jurisdiction of the local bishop in 1857. Her spirit of communion and ecclesiastical obedience led to a new congregation: the Sisters of Our Lady of Consolation. The sisters, formally constituted as a congregation in 1868, dedicated themselves to providing health and educational services; however, María Rosa wrote the Rule to allow the order to respond to other needs of the Church. She herself mediated disputes and even crossed a battle line to negotiate a cease-fire during an attack on Reus. She established in Tortosa ten houses, seventeen hospitals, schools, and shelters for the poor before her death. María Rosa was beatified on 8 May 1977 by Pope Paul VI.

At her canonization Pope John Paul II praised her spirit of charity, saying: "Mother María Rosa is one of those chosen by God to proclaim to the world the mercy of the Father. She had the charism to be an instrument of reconciliation and of spiritual development.''

Feast: 11 June.

Bibliography: J. M. JAVIERRE, *María Rosa Molas, una mujer misericordiosa* (Madrid 1975). M. T. SALES, *Fiamme sull'Ebro: vita della m. Maria Rosa Molas* (Milan 1969). *Acta Apostolicae Sedis* (1977): 606; (1989): 98. *L'Osservatore Romano,* English edition, no. 20 (1977): 2–5.

[K. RABENSTEIN]

MOLINA, MERCEDES DE JESÚS, BL.

Also known as the ''Rose of Baba and Guayaquil,'' foundress of the *Congregación de Santa Mariana de Jesús* or *Marianitas;* b. 1828 Baba (Los Rios), Ecuador; d. there 12 June 1883; beatified on the Las Samenes Esplanade in Guayaquil by John Paul II, 1 February 1985.

Mercedes began her life's work as a laywoman with the motto: ''As much love for as many sufferings as there are in the world.'' She set her hand to the task by teaching orphans and aiding the abandoned, and ministering to the poor in Guayaquil. Eventually her world expanded to include the ill-treated native Jibaros and abandoned children at Cuenca. On Easter Monday 1873, the bishop of Riobamba gave episcopal approval to her formation of the *Marianitas,* named after Saint Maríana de Jesús Paredes y Flores, the ''Lily of Quito.'' The Marianitas continued her apostolate after Mercedes' death at age fifty-five.

Pope John Paul II declared Mother Mercedes de Jesús ''a model for living'' and praised her practice of ''charity toward all those who, in poverty, suffering, and abandonment, reflected the mystery of the poor child of Bethlehem or of Christ suffering on Calvary'' (beatification homily).

Bibliography: C. E. MESA, *Mercedes Molina, fundadora de las Marianitas* (Quito 1973). *Acta Apostolicae Sedis* (1985): 327.

[K. RABENSTEIN]

MOLLA, GIANNA BERETTA, BL.

Physician, mother, ''Martyr for Life''; b. 4 October 1922, Magenta near Milan, Lombardy, northern Italy; d. there 28 April 1962; beatified by John Paul II, 24 April 1994, the Year of the Family.

Gianna was the tenth of thirteen children of Alberta Beretta and Maria de Micheli—who ensured that she received a Catholic education. Gianna began her apostolate of caring for the sick and elderly as a member of the Saint Vincent de Paul Society while still in school. Gianna was also a leader in the Catholic Action Movement, organizing retreats and spiritual exercises. Upon graduating from the University of Pavia with degrees in medicine and surgery (1949), she practiced medicine with her brother Ferdinando Beretta at Merero (near Magenta) and studied pediatric medicine at the University of Milan (1950–52). After completing her education she devoted more time to providing medical attention to the indigent. She married engineer Pietro Molla (24 September 1955) with whom she had three children: Pierluigi (b. September 1955), Mariolina (b. December 1957), and Laura (b. July 1959). In the second month of her fourth pregnancy, Gianna was diagnosed with a large uterine fibroma that required surgical removal. As a doctor she knew that her best chance for survival would mean the killing the baby in her womb; nevertheless, she pleaded with the surgeon to save the life of her child regardless of the risk to her own life. Her daughter Gianna Emanuela was born, 21 April 1962. Gianna Beretta Molla, however, died one week later. Her body lies in the cemetery of Mesero (near Magenta). Her process for beatification was opened in Rome, 15 March 1980. She was declared venerable in 1991.

Her husband and three children attended Gianna's beatification, during which Pope John Paul II said:''After an exemplary existence as a student, as a girl fully engaged in the ecclesiastical community, as a wife and a happy mother, she offered and sacrificed her life in order that the child she was carrying could live.'' Patroness of healthcare workers, mothers, professional women, the prolife movement, spouses, and unborn children.

Feast: 28 April (Archdiocese of Milan).

Bibliography: *Gianna Beretta Molla, Il tuo grande amore mi aiuterà a essere forte. Lettere al marito* (Cinisello Balsamo, Italy 1999). G. PELUCCHI, *Una vita per la vita* (Turin 1989). F. DA RIESE, *Per amore della vita. Gianna Beretta Molla medico e madre* (Rome 1994).

[K. RABENSTEIN]

MONTAIGNAC DE CHAUVANCE, LOUISE-THÉRÈSE DE, BL.

Foundress of the Oblates of the Sacred Heart of Jesus; b. 14 May 1820, Le- Havre-de-Grace, France; d. 22 June 1885, Moulins, France; beatified by John Paul II, 4 November 1990.

As the daughter of a wealthy financier—Aimé Montaignac de Chauvance and his wife Anne de Ruffin— Louise-Thérèse was educated at a boarding school from age seven. Although she did not pursue a Carmelite vocation, she made a private vow of perpetual chastity (8 September 1843), founded the Guild of the Tabernacle for Perpetual Adoration (1848) and an orphanage at Montluçon. With the help of her aunt, she formed (1852) an association of Christian women at Montluçon with the mission of restoring the faith in France. This became the Pious Union of the Oblates of the Sacred Heart (21 December 1874) dedicated to "renewing society by their example and their holy lives." Montaignac was elected superior general on 17 May 1880 and held that office until her death. The oblates live in community or secular life in Europe, Africa, and Central America and continue her work of operating orphanages, providing religious education, financing poor parishes, and directing retreats. Montaignac also founded the "Samuels" for the formation of young Christians discerning religious vocations.

Pope John Paul II praised Montaignac during her beatification for her recognition that "serving the Lord and serving the Church are the same thing" and for ceaselessly reminding others of the love of the Heart of Jesus.

Feast: 22 June.

Bibliography: P. FERLAY, *La force de la foi: itinéraire spirituel de Louise-Thérèse de Montaignac* (Paris 1990). *Acta Apostolicae Sedis* (1990): 1090–91.

[K. RABENSTEIN]

MONTAL FORNÉS, PAULA, BL.

Known in religion as Paula of St. Joseph Calasanz, foundress of the Daughters of Mary (*Hijas de Maria, Religiosas de las Escuelas Pias*); b. 11 October 1799, Arenys de Mar (near Barcelona), Spain; d. 26 February 1889, Olesa de Montserrat near Barcelona, Spain; beatified by John Paul II, 18 April 1993.

Born into a large family of artisans, Paula began working to help support the family after her father's death (1789). Paula grew especially concerned about the formation of Christian women while teaching in schools. In 1829 she opened a school in Figueras near Gerona and dedicated herself "to bring families to eternal salvation by teaching children the fear of God." She opened an additional seven schools. Montal was aided in her effort by the Piarists, especially Augustín Casanovas, who is considered the cofounder. Both sought to instill in the new institute the spirit of Joseph Calasanctius, by adapting to women the constitutions that he wrote for the Piarists. By the time of her death, the order had more than 300 sisters operating nineteen schools throughout Spain. Her cause was introduced in 1959 and she was declared venerable in 1988. A second miracle attributed to her intercession was approved 1 July 2000, leading the way to her canonization.

Feast: 26 February (Archdiocese of Barcelona).

Bibliography: *Acta Apostolicae Sedis* (1993): 549.

[K. RABENSTEIN]

MONTE, BARTOLOMEO MARIA DAL, BL.

Diocesan priest, missionary, preacher; b. 3 November 1726, Bologna, Italy; d. 24 December 1778, at Bologna; beatified 27 September 1997 at Bologna by John Paul II.

The son of Orazio dal Monte and Anna Maria Bassani, Bartolomeo was confirmed (1733) by Cardinal Prospero Lambertini of Bologna, the future Pope Benedict XIV. Bartolomeo studied at the Jesuit Santa Lucia College for a future career as a banker. Leonard of Port Maurice, himself later canonized, encouraged Bartolomeo to ignore his father's opposition to a priestly vocation; Bartolomeo was ordained in 1749 and completed his seminary studies in theology (1750–51). He then undertook his life's work: preaching missions and retreats not only in Bologna, but also in sixty-two other dioceses. His powerful preaching led many to reconciliation and conversion of life. According to the citation issued 16 March 1777, Father dal Monte's charity, the purity of his doctrine at a time when Jansenism was spreading, and holiness of his life won for him honorary citizenship in the principality of San Marino. His body is enshrined in Our Lady of Peace Chapel in Bologna's Basilica of Saint Petronius. The decree approving a miracle wrought at his intercession was promulgated on 11 July 1995.

Pope John Paul II said: "Blessed dal Monte shines brightly before us as a witness to Christ who was particularly sensitive to the demands of the modern age" (beatification homily).

Bibliography: L. MIRRI, *Un apostolo delle missioni popolari: Bartolomeo Maria Dal Monte (1726–1778) e la sua "Operetta"* (Bologna 1995). *L'Osservatore Romano*, Eng. ed. 29 (1995): 5.

[K. RABENSTEIN]

MONTEAGUDO, ANA DE LOS ANGELES, BL.

Dominican mystic; b. ca. 1600, Arequipa, Peru; d. there 10 January 1686; beatified by John Paul II, 2 February 1985, at Arequipa, Peru, while on a pastoral visit to Latin America.

Ana, the daughter of the Spaniard Sebastián Monteagudo de la Jara and his Peruvian wife Francisca Ponce de León, was entrusted to the care of the Dominican sisters of Santa Catalina de Siena until she reached marriageable age. She returned home at her parents' request and eventually overcame their objections to her religious vocation. In 1618, she began her novitiate at Santa Catalina and appended the name "de los Angeles." She served as novice mistress. After she was chosen as prioress (1647), she reformed the community of nearly 300 sisters. The entire life of Blessed Ana was spent in prayer and apostolic work.

Feast: 10 January (Dominicans).

Bibliography: *Acta Apostolicae Sedis* (1986): 909–12. *L'Osservatore Romano,* Eng. ed. 11 (1985): 8–9.

[K. RABENSTEIN]

MORAGAS CANTARERO, MARÍA SAGRARIO OF SAN LUIS GONZAGA, BL.

Baptized Elvira Moragas Cantarero; pharmacist, Discalced Carmelite martyr; b. 8 January 1881, at Lillo (near Toledo), Spain; d. 15 August 1936, at the Pradera of San Isidro near Madrid; beatified by John Paul II, 10 May 1998.

Elvira was the third of the four children of Isabel Cantarero and Ricardo Moragas, who was appointed pharmacist to the royal household and moved his family to Madrid in 1886. One of the first Spanish women to earn a degree in pharmacy, Elvira was planning a secular career until she felt called to religious life. Nevertheless, she delayed her response to raise her younger brother Ricardo after the deaths of their father (1909) and mother (1911) and run the family pharmacy until he could take it over. She was a capable, just, and charitable professional; she entered the Discalced Carmelite convent of Saints Anne and Joseph in Madrid (1915). There she began her postulancy (21 June 1915), then took the habit and the name María Sagrario de San Luis Gonzaga upon beginning her novitiate (21 December 1915). She professed her solemn vows in 1920. She was appointed mistress of novices (April 1927), then was elected prioress (1930–33), and was again elected as prioress (1 July 1936) just before the outbreak of violence in Madrid (18 July 1936). When the convent was attacked (20 July 1936), she sent her sisters to safety and hid herself with another sister in the city rather than taking refuge in her brother's house at Pinto. The two were found and arrested in the Ruiz home, 14 August. The following day she was executed by firing squad for refusing to denounce others. Her body was exhumed and translated to the convent chapel after the war. On 8 March 1997, the decree of martyrdom was signed for Mother María Sagrario.

During her beatification Pope John Paul II pointed to María Sagrario as a model for pharmacists, then referred to her martyrdom: "She found the strength not to betray priests and friends of the community, facing death with integrity for her state as a Carmelite and to save others."

Bibliography: *Acta Apostolicae Sedis* (1998): 559.

[K. RABENSTEIN]

MORANO, MADDALENA CATERINA, BL.

Religious of the Daughters of Mary Help of Christians; b. 15 November 1847, Chieri (near Turin), Piedmont, Italy; d. 26 March 1908, at Catania, Sicily; beatified at Catania by John Paul II, 5 November 1994.

Although Maddalena was forced from age eight to help support her family following the deaths of her elder sister and father, she also continued her studies. In 1866, she received her teaching diploma and began her career in a rural school in Montaldo while serving as a catechist in her parish. By 1878, she had saved enough money to provide for her mother's needs. No longer bound to supporting her family financially, she entered the Daughters of Mary Help of Christians, founded by John Bosco (1872). In 1881, he sent her to Trecastagni (Catania) to oversee an existing institute and instill Salesian methods in its work. From there Maddalena founded new houses and established new services for the poor on the island. She also coordinated catechetical instruction in eighteen parishes and trained catechists. During her twenty-five years in Sicily, Morano served as local and provincial superior. Her remains now rest in the crypt of the institute at Messina. In 1935, the archdiocesan investigation of Maddalena's cause began.

At her beatification, Pope John Paul II called Morano "a born teacher" with an "outstanding pedagogical talent and love for God and neighbor."

Feast: 15 November.

Bibliography: M. L. MAZZARELLO, ed., *Sulle frontiere dell'educazione: Maddalena Morano in Sicilia* [Papers presented at various meetings organized by Pontificia Facoltà di scienze dell'educazione "Auxilium"] (Rome 1995).

[K. RABENSTEIN]

MOREAU, LOUIS-ZÉPHYRIN, BL.

Bishop of St. Hyacinthe, Québec, Canada; b. 1 April 1824, Bécancour, Canada; d. 24 May 1901, St. Hyacinthe; beatified by John Paul II, 10 May 1987.

Born and raised in a Catholic community in Québec, Louis-Zéphyrin was ordained priest in 1846 after completing his seminary studies locally. Following a variety of pastoral assignments, he was appointed secretary to his bishop (1852). On 16 January 1876, he was consecrated the fourth bishop of Saint-Hyacinthe. During his twenty-five years as bishop, Moreau oversaw the building of the new cathedral and promoted charitable, educational, and religious organizations. Additionally, he founded two religious communities: one dedicated to Saint Joseph; the other to the Sisters of Saint Hyacinthe. The latter, with the unique apostolate of administration to relieve the burden from priests and other religious, spread to the United States in 1929.

Feast: 24 May (Canada).

Bibliography: J. HOUPERT, *Monseigneur Moreau, quatrième Évêque de Saint-Hyacinthe* (Montréal 1986). R. LITALIEN, *Prêtre québécois à la fin du XIXe siècle: style de vie et spiritualité d'après Mgr Louis-Zéphryn Moreau* (Montréal 1970). *Acta Apostolicae Sedis* (1987): 690. *L'Osservatore Romano,* Eng. ed. 21 (1987): 18–19.

[K. RABENSTEIN]

MORELLO, BRIGIDA DI GESÙ, BL.

Widow, founder of the Ursuline Sisters of Mary Immaculate; b. 17 June 1610, San Michelle di Pagana di Rapallo (near Genoa), Liguria, Italy; d. 3 September 1679, Piacenza, Emilia-Romagna, Italy; beatified by John Paul II, 15 March 1998.

The daughter of the nobles Nicolo Morello and Lavinia Borgese, Brigida had to care for her sibilings when her mother fell gravely. Brigida married Matteo Zancari (1633), whom she and her sister Agata aided during his recovery from the 1630 plague. Four years later he died heirless while the couple was besieged in Tabiano Castle during a political upheaval. Thereafter Brigida fell gravely ill and vowed to devote her life to God should she recover. She fulfilled her obligation first by aiding the Franciscans of Salsomaggiore and the Jesuits of Piacenza, then by taking charge of Saint Ursula's House in Piacenza, which had been founded by Margherita de'Medici Farnese. On 17 February 1649, the women who assisted her formed the Ursuline Sisters of Mary Immaculate. Brigida cared for the poor and educated children despite continued ill health. On 18 December 1997, a miracle through the intercession of Brigida di Gesù was approved.

Before the Angelus following Mother Brigida's beatification, Pope John Paul II said: "In the Immaculate Mother of God Brigida Morello found inspiration and support for her work of Christian formation and the advancement of women, of evangelization and the quest for the unity of the Church."

Feast: 3 September.

Bibliography: *Acta Apostolicae Sedis,* no. 8 (1998): 399.

[K. RABENSTEIN]

MORENO Y DÍAZ, EZEQUIEL, ST.

Augustinian Recollect priest, missionary, bishop of Pasto (Colombia); b. 9 April 1848, Alfaro, Logroño, Spain; d. 19 August 1906, Monteagudo Monastery, Navarra, Spain; canonized in Santo Domingo, Dominican Republic, by John Paul II, 11 October 1992.

Ezequiel, the son of Felix Moreno and Josefa Díaz, joined the Augustinian Recollects at Monteagudo Monastery (21 September 1864) and pronounced his vows at Marcilla Monastery the following year. He was sent to the Philippine missions (1870), where he was ordained in Manila in 1871. After evangelizing the Philippines for fifteen years, he returned to Monteagudo to serve as prior and form future missionaries. In 1888, he travelled to Candelaria, Colombia to reorganize the Augustinian Recollects there. His success in reinvigorating the faithful of the region led to his appointment as the first vicar apostolic of Casanare, and in 1895 Moreno was consecrated bishop of Pasto in southern Colombia, where he actively defended the rights of the Church. After developing cancer, he returned to Spain in 1906 where he retired to Monteagudo Monastery to die.

Pope Paul VI beatified Bishop Moreno in Rome, 1 November 1975. Pope John Paul II cited the saint for his evangelical fervor, charity, and personal holiness. Patron of cancer victims.

Feast: 19 August.

Bibliography: *Epistolario del beato Ezequiel Moreno y otros agustinos recoletos con Miguel Antonio Caro y su familia,* ed. by C. VALDERRAMA ANDRADE (Bogotá 1983). E. AYAPE, *Semblanza de San Ezequiel Moreno* (Madrid 1994). E. L. A. ROMANILLOS, *Bishop Ezekiel Moreno: An Augustinian Recollect Saint among Filipinos* (Quezon City, Philippines 1993). C. VALDERRAMA ANDRADE, *Un capítulo de las relaciones entre el estado y la Iglesia en Colombia: Miguel Antonio Caro y Ezequiel Moreno* (Bogotá 1986). *Acta Apostolicae Sedis* (1976): 486–89; (1992): 1017. *L'Osservatore Romano,* Eng. ed. 45 (1975): 1–4.

[K. RABENSTEIN]

MOROSINI, PIERINA, BL.

A.k.a. Petrina, virgin martyr, lay woman; b. 7 January 1931, at Fiobbo di Albino (near Bergamo), Lombardy, Italy; d. there on 4 April 1957; beatified by John Paul II, 4 October 1987.

Pierina was the eldest child in a large, poor, farm family. After completing grammar school, she learned tailoring and quickly found work in a textile factory in Albino. Maria Goretti became a model for her life. Although Pierina's family obligations prevented her from becoming a missionary nun, she annually renewed her decision for celibacy as an oblation. Pierina sanctified her daily labors and participated in Catholic Action, evangelization, parish activities, and daily eucharist. She was attacked on her way home from work by a man who stoned her to death for refusing to comply with his wishes. She never regained consciousness and died two days later in hospital at the age of twenty-six. Her mortal remains rest in the place of her birth and death.

Feast: 6 April.

Bibliography: *Acta Apostolicae Sedis* (1987): 983. *L'Osservatore Romano,* Eng. ed. 40 (1987): 20. G. CARRARA, *La ragazza incredibile: Pierina Morosini nella sua epoca e nella sua valle* (Gorle, Italy 1989). F. ROSSI, *Pierina Morosini, Bienheureuse vierge et martyre* (Hauteville, Switz. 2000).

[K. RABENSTEIN]

MOSCATI, GIUSEPPE MARIO CAROLO ALPHONSE, ST.

Lay physician; b. 25 July 1880, Benevento, Italy; d. 12 April 1927, Naples, Italy; canonized by John Paul II, 25 October 1987.

Giuseppe Moscati, was seventh of the nine children of Francesco Moscati (d. 21 December 1897), a magistrate, and his wife Rosa (d. 25 November 1914). The family moved to Naples when his father was appointed (1884) president of the court. Following his graduation from secondary school with honors (1897), Giuseppe studied medicine at the University of Naples. He earned his degree with first-class honors (14 August 1903) by his thesis on hepatic urogenesis. At age twenty-three Giuseppe began his career at the Santa Maria del Populo Hospital for the Incurables in Naples. When Vesuvius erupted (April 1906), Moscati rushed to the hospital at Torre del Greco to help evacuate patients before the roof collapsed. Similarly, in 1911, he assisted in containing a cholera outbreak. That same year he finished his scientific preparation, passed the medical boards, was appointed to a university chair in biochemistry, and began lecturing on applied research and clinical research, as well as clinical medicine. He became known as one of the most outstanding researchers in his field.

In addition to his educational and scientific contributions, Giuseppe was a practicing physician and an administrator. In the course of time he was appointed director of military hospitals during World War I with the rank of major (1915), director of the Hospital for Incurables (16 July 1919), coadjutor ordinary, medical director of the United Hospitals, director of the department of tuberculosis, and associate of the Royal Academy of Surgery. Giuseppe Moscati is honored by the Church for the manner in which he practiced medicine. He required no payment from the poor, the homeless, religious, or priests, and, in fact, paid for their prescriptions himself. He used his time with patients to speak to them about the faith, often healing wounded souls as well as bodies. Moscati dedicated himself to the sacraments and prayer for his patients. He died peacefully of a stroke at age forty-seven. Three years later, his relics were translated to the church of Gesù Nuovo.

Moscati was declared venerable in 1973 and beatified by Paul VI in 1975. In canonizing Moscati, Pope John Paul II observed that "in his constant rapport with God, Moscati found the light to understand and diagnose illnesses and the warmth to be able to draw near to those who, in their suffering, looked for sincere participation on the part of the doctor assisting them. Patron of bachelors.

Feast: 16 November.

Bibliography: *Acta Apostolicae Sedis* (1976): 259–62. *Giuseppe Moscati nel ricordo dei suoi contemporanei* (Naples 1967). *L'Osservatore Romano,* Eng. Ed. 48 (1975): 5–7; 45 (1987): 10,12. A. MARRANZINI, *Giuseppe Moscati, modello del laico cristiano di oggi* (Rome: Ave 1989). F. D'ONOFRIO, *Joseph Moscati as Seen by a Medical Doctor* (Messina 1991). G. PAPÁSOGLI, *Giuseppe Moscati: vita di un medico santo* (2nd ed. Rome 1975). D. PARRELLA, *St. Joseph Moscati: the holy doctor of Naples* (Naples 1987). A. TRIPODORO, *Preghiere in onore di S. Giuseppe Moscati* (3rd ed., Naples 1994); *Giuseppe Moscati, il medico santo di Napoli* (2nd ed., Naples 1999).

[K. RABENSTEIN]

MOTRIL, MARTYRS OF, BB.

A.k.a. Vicente Soler and Companions, Augustinian Recollect Martyrs of Spain; d. 25-26 July and 15 August 1936, near Motril, Granada, Spain; beatified by John Paul II, 7 March 1999.

This group of seven Augustinian Recollects and a parish priest of Motril represent a small fraction of the 7,000 priests and religious killed for their faith during the

Spanish Civil War (1936–39). One week after the war began, revolutionaries attacked (25 July 1936) the Augustinian monastery, forced five priests out, and shot them in the street when they refused to renounce their faith. The next day two priests sought refuge in prayer in the Church of the Divine Shepherd next to the monastery. They were found and killed in the church courtyard. The final priest was captured later. All eight were decreed martyrs on 8 March 1997. In his beatification homily Pope John Paul II stressed that they "did not die for an ideology, but freely gave their life for Someone who had already died for them. They gave back to Christ the gift they had received from him." The blesseds include:

Diez, José Ricardo; Augustinian priest, d. 25 July 1936 in the streets of Motril.

Inchausti, Leon, Augustinian priest, d. 25 July 1936 in the streets of Motril.

Martin Sierra, Manuel, parish priest at the Church of the Divine Shepherd in Motril; d. 26 July 1936.

Moreno, Julian Benigno, Augustinian priest, d. 25 July 1936 in the streets of Motril.

Palacios, Deogracias, Augustinian priest, d. 25 July 1936 in the streets of Motril.

Pinilla, Vicente, Augustinian priest, d. 26 July 1936 with Father Manuel Martin in the church courtyard after praying in the parish church.

Rada, José, Augustinian priest, d. 25 July 1936 in the streets of Motril.

Soler, Vicente, Augustinian priest, b. 1867, Malon near Saragossa, Spain; d. 15 August 1936. He had been a missionary in the Philippines, provincial in Spain, and superior general of the order for seven months in 1926. He had been in the choir when five of his brothers were arrested and shot. He escaped but was caught and imprisoned on 29 July 1936. Throughout his incarceration he ministered to other prisoners and lead them in a Marian novena in the days before his death. He offered his life in exchange for that of a father of eight children, but the offer was declined. He was shot with sixteen others. One of the eighteen survived to relate the story of Vicente's martyrdom.

Bibliography: V. CÁRCEL ORTÍ, *Martires españoles del siglo XX* (Madrid 1995). W. H. CARROLL, *The Last Crusade* (Front Royal, Va. 1996). J. PÉREZ DE URBEL, *Catholic Martyrs of the Spanish Civil War,* tr. M. F. INGRAMS (Kansas City, Mo. 1993). *Acta Apostolicae Sedis* (1999): 310–12.

[K. RABENSTEIN]

MUTTATHUPANDATU, ALPHONSA, BL.

Baptized Anna and called Annakutty, also known as Sister Alphonsa of India, Alphonsa of the Immaculate Conception, Alphonsa of Bharananganam, mystic, virgin of the Syro-Malabar Poor Clares; b. 19 August 1910, Arpukara, India; d. 28 July 1946, Bharananganam, India; beatified at Kottayam, Archdiocese of Changanacherry, Kerala, India, by John Paul II, 8 February 1986, together with Blessed Kuriokose Chavara, the first Indians raised to the altars.

The fourth child of Joseph Muttahupadathu and his wife Mary, who died shortly after her birth; her family ensured Annakutty was well educated in preparation for a good marriage. Recognizing her vocation to religious life, Annakutty rejected her suitors and disfigured herself with fire so that she would be unmarriageable. Thereafter she was permitted to join the tertiary Clarist sisters in their convent at Bharananganam (Pentecost 1927). With the veil of the postulant she received the name Alphonsa of the Immaculate Conception (2 August 1928). She became a novice on 12 August 1935 and made final vows the following year. Throughout her life she endured repeated illness and physical pain, but received the consolation of mystical union. She possessed the gift of prophecy and experienced a vision of Saint Thérèse of Lisieux. Alphonsa's death after a prolonged illness went almost unnoticed. However, when miracles were granted to Alphonsa's beloved school children through her intercession, her tomb at Bharananganam became a pilgrimage site. The diocesan process for her beatification began, 2 December 1953, and a miracle wrought through Alphonsa's intercession was approved, 6 July 1985.

Feast: 8 February.

Bibliography: *Acta Apostolicae Sedis* (1986): 306. *L'Osservatore Romano,* Eng. ed. 7 (1986): 6–7.

[K. RABENSTEIN]

NASCIMBENI, GIUSEPPE, BL.

Priest, founder of the Little Sisters of the Holy Family (*Piccole Suore della Sacra Famiglia*); b. 22 March 1851, Torri del Benaco, Italy; d. 21 January 1922, Castelletto del Garda, northern Italy; beatified at Verona by John Paul II, 17 April 1988.

Giuseppe, the son of Antonio Nascimbeni and Amidaea Sartori, completed his seminary training at Verona, Venetia. Following his ordination in 1874, he taught and served as priest in the parish of San Pietro di Lavagno. On 2 November 1877, Nascimbeni was sent to the small village of Castelletto, where he remained the rest of his life as a teacher and associate, then as pastor. He was an exemplary parish priest, created protonotary apostolic by Pius X in 1911, who was active in advancing modernization in the area. He helped establish the local bank and post office, promoted the olive oil industry, urged the installation of modern utilities, and oversaw the construction of the parish church (1905–08), an oratory, a nursery school, an orphanage, and a nursing home. After trying and failing to persuade several congregations to send nuns to the area, on the advice of his bishop, Cardinal Bartolomeo Bacilieri, he founded (6 November 1892) the institute of Little Sisters of the Holy Family with four sisters, including Maria Mantovani. The congregation works in hundreds of institutes in Italy and abroad training girls, caring for the elderly, and teaching. Nascimbene, who cared for his flock spiritually and materially, died after a stroke (1916) and long illness. His mausoleum is in the chapel of the institute at Castelletto. Pope John Paul II praised Father Giuseppe as a pastor of consummate charity and virtue.

Feast: 20 January.

Bibliography: A. PRONZATO, *Il diritto di chiamarsi padre: profilo di mons. Giuseppe Nascimbeni, fondatore delle Piccole suore della Sacra Famiglia* (Turin 1980). *Acta Apostolicae Sedis* (1988): 586. *L'Osservatore Romano,* English edition, no. 15 (1988): 2, 5.

[K. RABENSTEIN]

NAVAL GIRBES, JOSEFA, BL.

Lay craftsperson, mystic, member of the Third Order Secular of Our Lady of Mount Carmel and St. Teresa of Jesus; b. 11 December 1820, Algemesi (near Valencia), Spain; d. 24 February 1893, Algemesi; beatified by John Paul II, 25 September 1988.

Following the death of her mother (1833), Josefa took over the running of her family's household. Five years later, she made a personal vow of perpetual chastity and became a Carmelite tertiary. To provide instruction for girls and young women, she started an embroidery workshop in her home (1850). While teaching them her art, she was able to evangelize her entourage. Josefa reinvigorated the spiritual life of those around her and actively encouraged vocations to religious life. In the course of her ministry to the terminally ill, Josefa display heroic courage during the cholera epidemic of 1885. She achieved mystical union with God at 55. Her mortal remains are enshrined in her parish church, Saint James in Algemesi.

In beatifying Josefa, Pope John Paul II noted her special characteristic as a member of the laity: Josefa's ''dis-

ciples filled the cloistered convents, [while she] remained as an unmarried woman in the world.''

Feast: 6 November (Carmelites).

Bibliography: *Acta Apostolicae Sedis* (1988): 1092.

[K. RABENSTEIN]

NENGAPETE, MARIE-CLÉMENTINE ANUARITE, BL.

Baptized Anuarite (Anawarite or Alphonsine), martyr of the Congregation of the Holy Family; b. 29 December 1939, Matali, Wamba, Belgian Congo, Africa; d. 1 December 1964, Isiro near Kisangani, Zaire; beatified at Kinshasa, Zaire (now the Democratic Republic of the Congo), by John Paul II, 15 August 1985.

Anuarte was baptized with her mother and sister. In 1954 at the age of fifteen, she entered the Congregation of the Holy Family at Bafwabaka and was professed (5 August 1959) as Sister Marie-Clémentine. Ten years later the Congo, which had gained its independence four years earlier, was in turmoil. General Olenga's rebels, who had assassinated Bishop Wittehois of Wamba (26 November 1964), arrived at the convent on 29 November 1964, to conduct the nuns and orphans to Isiro for safety. Soon after their arrival, Sisters Marie-Clémentine and Bokuma were separated from the rest for the pleasure of two colonels. When Mother Kasima protested, Colonel Yuma Deo threatened to kill all thirty-four women and children. Sister Marie-Clémentine offered herself as the victim, but refused the advances of Colonel Olombe. After being brutalized, she was shot in the chest but lingered in pain for another day. She was immediately revered as a virgin martyr.

Bibliography: *Acta Apostolicae Sedis* (1985): 923. *L'Osservatore Romano,* Eng. ed. 36 (1985): 7–8.

[K. RABENSTEIN]

NEURURER, OTTO, BL.

First priest martyred by the Nazis; b. 25 March 1882, Piller, Oberinntal, Austria; d. 30 May 1940 at Buchenwald concentration camp near Weimar; beatified by John Paul II in St. Peter's Basilica, 24 November 1996.

Otto, the youngest of twelve children of peasants, attended the Vincentian minor seminary and diocesan major seminary in Brixen (Bressanone), South Tyrol. He was ordained priest on 29 June 1907 by Archbishop Altenweisel. His first assignment was in Urdens (Zillertal), then he served in parishes in Fiß (Oberinntal), Kappl (Paznautal), and Innsbruck, among others. During Neururer's final assignment at SS. Peters and Paul in Götzens, the Nazis occupied Tyrol and subjected the Church to persecution. Neururer was arrested for interfering with a "German marriage" after he advised a girl against marrying a dissolute, divorced man who was a friend of the Tyrolean *Gauleiter,* the highest local Nazi official. He was tortured in Dachau concentration camp, then sent to Buchenwald, where he catechized other inmates, despite severe prohibition. A camp spy reported the priest's actions, and Neururer was hanged by his ankles. His cremated remains are enshrined under the altar of his parish church at Götzens.

In his beatification homily, Pope John Paul II praised Neururer for "defending the sanctity of Christian marriage in the most difficult and dangerous circumstances." He is the patron of preachers, marriage, and priestly service.

Feast: 30 May.

Bibliography: J. GELMI, *Kirchengeschichte Tirols* (Innsbruck-Wien-Bozen, 1986): 198, 257, 260. H. TSCHOL, *Pfarrer Neururer-Priester und Blutzeuge* (Innsbruck 1963); *Otto Neururer* (Innsbruck 1982). *L'Osservatore Romano,* English edition, no. 48 (1996): 1–3.

[K. RABENSTEIN]

Pope John Paul II celebrates Mass in St. Peter's Basilica on 24 November 1996, at a beatification ceremony in honor of Austrian priest, Otto Neururer, who died in a Nazi concentration camp. (AP/Wide World Photos. Photograph by Giulio Broglio.)

NICOLA DA GESTURI, BL.

Baptized Giovanni Angelo Salvatore, called "Giovanni Medda," Capuchin; b. 5 August 1882; Gesturi, Cagliari (archdiocese of Oristano, Sardegna), Italy; d. 8 June 1958, Cagliari; beatified by John Paul II, 3 October 1999.

Giovanni Medda, the sixth child of a poor family, felt called to religious life but lacked the means to pursue it. He was raised by his eldest sister following the death of his parents, Giovanni Messa Serra and Priama Cogoni Zedda. After completing his primary education he worked on the farm. With the help of his parish priest, he entered the Capuchin convent of San Antonio Gesturi as a tertiary oblate (1911) and took the habit and name Fra Nicola (30 October 1913). He pronounced his first vows the following year on 1 November and his solemn vows on 16 February 1919. During his first ten years of religious life, he served as cook in several Sardinian monasteries (Sassari, Oristano, and Sanluri). For the next thirty-four years (from 1924) Nicola was entrusted with collecting alms for the monastery in Cagliari and nearby Campidano. He developed an attitude of constant prayer, which animated all his actions. His spirituality and wisdom attracted others to him for counsel and comfort; however, he became most renowned as a miracle worker, especially for the sick. His body was buried in the cemetery of Bonaria. The ordinary process for his beatification was conducted from 1966 to 1971 and introduced in Rome in 1977. The declaration of Fra Nicola's heroic virtues came 18 years after his death (25 June 1996).

Pope John Paul II, at the beatification, said: "In a world satiated with words and poor in values, men and women like Blessed Nicola da Gesturi are needed, who will stress the urgency of recovering the capacity for silence and listening."

Feast: 8 June.

Bibliography: FILIPPO DA CAGLIARI, *Fra Nicola nel decennale della morte* (Sardinia 1968).

[K. RABENSTEIN]

NIEVES, ELÍAS DEL SOCORRO, BL.

Baptized Mateo Elías (Matthew Elijah), Augustinian martyr of Communist revolutionaries; b. 21 September 1882, on Isla San Pedro, Yuriria, Guanajuato, Mexico; d. 10 March 1928, near Cortazar, Mexico; beatified 12 October 1997 by Pope John Paul II.

Born into a modest peasant family and baptized with urgency because he was in danger of death, Nieves had an early, strong vocation to the priesthood. However, he contracted tuberculosis and was temporarily blind (age 12). He regained his sight, and he assumed the responsibilities as head of household upon his father's death. Nevertheless, he was admitted (1904) to the Augustinian college at Yuriria. When he professed his vows (1911), Mateo took the name Elías del Socorro (Elijah of Our Lady of Succor) in acknowledgment of the help he received overcoming his hardships. He was ordained in 1916.

Nieves served in various parishes within Guanajauto until he was assigned to the poor, isolated parish of La Cañada de Caracheo in 1921, where he helped to build the church—physically and spiritually. In disobedience to governmental orders (1926) forcing priests to abandon rural areas, Nieves courageously hid in a cave in the nearby hills of La Gavia in order to continue administering the sacraments to his parishioners under the cover of darkness.

After fourteen months of clandestine ministry, he was arrested together with two campesinos, José Dolores and José de Jesús Sierra. Although he was dressed in the rags of a peasant, the hem of his habit betrayed him. He was questioned, and since he immediately admitted being a priest, he was detained. A parishioner negotiated for the freedom of the laymen, but they refused to abandon their pastor. En route under guard to the provincial capital of Cortazar, the two companions were killed. At the next resting place, Nieves was taunted and then shot.

His body has been moved to the parish church at La Cañada de Caracheo. Beatified with Nieves was another Augustinian, Mother Maria Teresa Fasce, who documented Nieves's martyrdom for her convent.

In beatifying John Paul II declared that Nieves exercised his priestly ministry "with self-denial and a spirit of service, without letting himself be overcome by obstacles, sacrifices, or danger. . . . [He] did not want to abandon his faithful despite the risks he was taking. . . . He faced death with fortitude, blessing his executioners, and witnessing to his faith in Christ." He is a patron of Mexico.

Feast: 11 October.

Bibliography: *Acta Apostolicae Sedis,* no. 20 (1997): 999. *L'Osservatore Romano,* English edition, no. 42 (1997): 1, 2, 11, 12.

[K. RABENSTEIN]

NISCH, ULRIKA FRANZISKA, BL.

Baptized Francizka, a.k.a. Francizka of Hegne, virgin of the Sisters of Mercy of the Holy Cross of Ingenbo-hl (*Barmherzigen Schwestern vom Heiligen Kreuz*); b. 18 September 1882, Oberdorf-Mittelbiberarch (on the Ress River near Württemberg), Schwabia, Germany; d. 8 May 1913, Hegne near Rorschach am Bodensee; beatified by John Paul II, 1 November 1987.

Franziska was born into extreme poverty and neglected by her parents until she was seven. Her grandmother and aunt/godmother raised her until her parents took her home to assume the household duties. She became a farm servant at age twelve and in 1901 was sent to Rorschach, Switzerland, as a domestic servant. There she fell ill, was hospitalized, and was nursed by sisters of the Holy Cross of Ingenbohl, the Swiss congregation founded by Maria Theresia Scherer. Upon her recovery and despite having no dowry, she was accepted into the order at the German provincial house at Hegne (17 October 1904), where she was professed (24 April 1907). She served the order as cook at Bühl, then at Saint Vincent's in Baden-Baden, but later returned to Hegne. Sister Ulrike, known for her simplicity and joy, was gifted with profound mystical experiences, especially visions of the angels and saints, until 1912.

Following her death from tuberculosis at age thirty, her grave at Hegne became a pilgrimage site. Since 1991, her mortal remains have been housed in the convent church crypt at Hegne.

At her beatification, Pope John Paul II said that the hardships of her life "led Sister Ulrika to the purity of heart that could discover in little things the merciful hand of the heavenly Father. She accepted each instance of her life with childlike gratitude. . . . In her presence, people felt 'a heavenly atmosphere.'"

Feast: 8 May.

Bibliography: B. BAUR, *Kein Maß kennt die Liebe. Ulrika Nisch, Kreuzschwester von Hegne* (Constance 1963). W. BÜHLMANN, *Er hat auf meine Niedrigkeit geschaut: der Weg von Schwester Ulrika Nisch Kreuzschwester von Hegne, Mutterhaus Ingenbohl/Schweiz* (Beuron 1987). K. HEMMERLE, *Die leise Stimme: Ulrika Nisch ihr Weg und ihre Botschaft* (Freiburg 1987). G. MOSER, *Aus unserer Mitte: Rupert Mayer, Ulrika Nisch, Edith Stein* (Rottenburg, 1988). *Acta Apostolicae Sedis* (1987): 1117. *L'Osservatore Romano,* Eng. ed. 47 (1987): 7–8.

[K. RABENSTEIN]

NOWOGRÓDEK, MARTYRS OF, BB.

A.k.a. Sister Maria Stella Adela Mardosewicz and ten Companions, martyrs, members of the Congregation of the Holy Family of Nazareth; b. 14 December 1888, at Ciasnówka, Nieświesk, Poland; d. 1 August 1943, Nowogródek, eastern Poland (now Navahradak, Belarus); beatified in Rome by John Paul II, 5 March 2000.

In 1929, Bishop Zygmunt Łoziński invited the Sisters of the Holy Family of Nazareth to undertake the education of Nowogródek's children and care for the Church of the Transfiguration (Biała Fara). There they established (1931) a school. During the Russian occupation (1 September 1939 to 21 June 1941), the sisters were barred from their convent and school. When German forces ousted the Russians, the sisters again donned their habits and returned to their ruined Convent of Christ the King. On 18 July 1943, the Nazis arrested and sentenced 120 citizens to execution by firing squad. The sisters were dedicated to serving families and volunteered to exchange places with the fathers of children. The male hostages were released to their families, although some were interned later in German concentration camps. The second time they offered themselves in place of the only remaining priest in the region. On 31 July 1943 the Gestapo ordered Sister Stella and eleven of the twelve sisters (one was working in the hospital at the time of the arrest) to appear at the Gestapo headquarters. Without investigation, they were sentenced to death. The order was carried out the next day, when they were executed in the woods five kilometers from Nowogródek. Initially the martyrs were buried in a common grave. On 19 March 1945, Sister Maria Margaret Malgorzata, the only survivor of the community, oversaw the translation of their mortal remains to the Church of the Transfiguration.

Their process was officially opened in 1991. On 28 June 1999, in addition to the superior, S. Maria Stella, the following were declared martyrs. PAULINA BOROWIK (S. Maria Felicyta, b. 30 Aug. 1905 at Rudna, Lublin); JÓZEFA CHROBOT (S. Maria Kanuta, b. 22 May 1896 at Raczyn, Wielun); HELENA CIERPKA (S. Maria Gwidona, b. 11 Apr. 1900 at Granowiec, Odalanów); ELEANORA JÓŹWIK (S. Maria Daniela, b. 25 Jan. 1895, Poizdow, Poldlasie); ANNA KOKOŁOWICZ (Maria Rajmunda, b. 24 Aug. 1892, Barwasniszk, Vilnius); EUGENIA MACKIEWICZ (Maria Kanizja, b. 9 Sept. 1903, Suwałki); LEOKADIA MATUSZEWSKA (Maria Heliodora, b. 8 Feb. 1906, Stara Huta, Świecie); WERONIKA (VERONICA) NARMONTOWICZ (Maria Boromea, b. 18 Dec. 1916, Wiercieliszki, Grodno); JULIA RAPIEJ (Maria Sergia, b. 18 Aug. 1900. Rogoczyn, Augustów); and JADWIGA (HEDWIG) ŻAK (Maria Imelda, b. 29 Dec. 1892, Oświęcim).

At their beatification Pope John Paul II thanked the martyrs for their witness of love, their example of Christian heroism, and their trust in the power of the Holy Spirit: "You are the greatest inheritance of the Congregation of the Holy Family of Nazareth. You are the inheritance of the whole Church of Christ forever." They are patrons of Christian teaching.

Feast: 1 August.

Bibliography: A. ZIENKIEWICZ, *No Greater Love* (Pulaski, Wisc. 1968). *L'Osservatore Romano,* English edition, no. 10 (8 March 2000): 3, 9.

[K. RABENSTEIN]

ODDI, DIEGO, BL.

Baptized Giuseppe; Franciscan lay brother; b. 6 June 1839, Vallinfreda near Rome; d. 3 June 1919, Bellegra, Italy; beatified by John Paul II, 3 October 1999.

Born into a poor family, Giuseppe Oddi labored in the fields rather than attend school. At age twenty, he felt a mysterious spiritual calling and responded by praying each evening before the Blessed Sacrament. Shortly thereafter (1860) he made a pilgrimage to the Bellegra (Rome) hermitage of St. Francis of Assisi, where he was deeply impressed by the prayer life of the brothers. He returned in 1864 and was met by Mariano da Roccacasale (1778–1866; beatified with Oddi), who helped Oddi discern his vocation. Overcoming his parents' objections, Oddi entered the friary at Bellegra as a tertiary oblate (1871), but later professed solemn vows (1889). During his forty years as a brother, he begged alms throughout the Subiaco region. A miracle attributed to Brother Diego's intercession was approved 6 April 1998.

Pope John Paul II referred to Blessed Diego as a "real angel of peace and goodness toward all he met, especially because he knew how to identify with the needs of the poor and suffering" (beatification homily).

Feast: 6 June (Franciscans).

Bibliography: *Acta Apostolicae Sedis* 19 (1999): 965. *L'Osservatore Romano,* Eng. ed. 40 (1999): 1–3; 41 (1999): 2.

[K. RABENSTEIN]

ORIONE, LUIGI (LOUIS), BL.

Founder of the Congregation of the *Piccola Opera della Divina Providenza* (Little Work of Divine Providence); b. 23 June 1872, Pontecurone (Alessandria), Italy; d. 12 March 1940, San Remo (Imperia), Italy.

Orione joined the Franciscans at Voghera at an early age but left because of poor health. St. John Bosco accepted him into the Salesian Oratory in Turin (1886). In 1890 Orione entered the seminary in Tortona in his native diocese and began what was to be his main work in life by caring for poor boys. After ordination (13 April 1895) he opened a lodging house for needy seminarians. As the work expanded he accepted orphans and elderly and needy persons. His Little Work of Divine Providence, a network of laity and religious dedicated to charitable works and prayer, was modeled on the foundation of St. Giuseppe Cottolengo. To attain the goals of the Piccola Opera, Don Orione founded a number of religious congregations: the Sons of Divine Providence; the Little Missionary Sisters of Charity; the Hermits of Divine Providence; the Brothers of Divine Providence, who wear lay dress, but follow a common rule of life; and the blind Sacramentine Sisters, who dedicate themselves to prayer. By 2000 Orione's disciples in these related institutes had spread to 30 countries and were found on all five continents.

Worn out from his labors, he died. His remains repose in Tortona. The *Decretum super scripta* in his beatification cause was issued in 1956. Pope John Paul II declared Orione blessed on 26 October 1980, presenting him to the Church as a ''marvelous and genial expression of Christian charity . . . certainly one of the most eminent personalities of this century because of his Christian faith lived openly.'' The pope described him as ''having the character and heart of the Apostle Paul, tender and sensitive, indefatigable and courageous, tenacious, and dynamic.''

Feast: 12 March.

Bibliography: Works. 116 volumes of his writings, as well as voice recordings, are preserved in the Archives of the Piccola Opera della Divina Providenza in Rome. *A Priceless Treasure Don Orione. Letters & Writings,* 2 v. (London 1995). *Acta Apostolicae Sedis* 72 (1981): 477–480. *L'Osservatore Romano,* English edition, no. 44 (1980). G. BARRA,, *Don Orione* (Turin 1970). E. A. CUONO, *Don Orione* (Victoria, Argentina 1967). *Don Orione. L'apostolo tortonese a 100 anni dalla nascita* (Turin 1972). A. GEMMA,, *Don Orione: un cuore senza confini* (Gorle, Italy 1989); *I fioretti di Don Orione* (Rome 1994). A. GEMMA, ed., *La scelta dei poveri più poveri: scritti spirituali* (Rome 1979). *The Restless Apostle. From the Writings of Don Orione* (London 1981). D. A. HYDE,, *God's Bandit, The Story of Don Orione, ''Father of the Poor''* (Westminster, Md. 1957). G. PAPÀSOGLI, *Vita di don Orione,* fourth ed. (Turin 1994). G. PICCININI, *Luce dai colli* (Boston 1958).

[T. F. CASEY]

OSSÓ Y CERVELLÓ, ENRIQUE DE, ST.

Priest, founder of the Society of Saint Teresa of Jesus (*Compañia de Santa Teresa de Jesús*); b. 15 or 16 October 1840, Vinebre (village near Tarragona), Spain; d. 27 January 1896, Gilet near Valencia, Spain; beatified by John Paul II, 14 October 1979, and canonized by him, 16 June 1993, at Madrid, Spain.

The youngest of the three children of Jaime de Ossó and his wife Micaela Cervelló, Enrique was apprenticed at age twelve to his uncle, a Barcelona merchant, when he fell gravely ill and was sent home. Upon his recovery he was apprenticed with a businessman in Reus, Don Ortal, but Enrique left everything behind following his mother's death (15 September 1854). He began to study for the priesthood at Tortosa's seminary (1854–60), and then at Barcelona (1860–61, 1863–66), where he completed spiritual exercises for the subdiaconate (May 1866) under the direction of Saint Anthony Mary Claret. He was still a seminarian when he returned to the Tortosa seminary to teach in 1862. There he was ordained in 1867. In June 1870, Enrique made a pilgrimage to Rome in the company of two other later saints, Claret and Emmanuel Domingo y Sol. He began his catechetical work and offering popular missions in Tortosa in 1871, while continuing to teach mathematics in Tortosa's seminary until the bishop relieved him from his faculty duties.

Ossó y Cervelló founded several associations for lay people: the Association of the Immaculate Conception for farmers (1870); Association of the Daughters of Immaculate Mary and Saint Teresa of Jesus for youth (approved 1873); Brotherhood of Saint Joseph for men (1876); and Little Flock of the Child Jesus (*Rebañito del Niño Jesús,* 1876) for children. The inspiration for his greatest work came during his prayer in April 1876, and was realized several months later (23 June) when eight young women committed to help him found the Society of Saint Teresa of Jesus for Christian education. In 1878 the cornerstone was laid in Tortosa for the first house and the following year the eight founders pronounced their vows in the chapel of St. Paul in Tarragona (1 January 1879). The foundation quickly spread to Portugal and Latin America, and, in 1885, to Algeria, but was not without difficulties.

Ossó used modern methods to communicate the Gospel message. The weekly *El amigo del puebla* (*The People's Friend,* founded 1871), which responded to the prevailing anticlerical attitudes, was censured. In October 1872, he published the first edition of the monthly magazine *Santa Teresa de Jesús* as well as his first book, *Guía práctica del catequista* (*Practical Guide for Catechists*). In 1874, he produced the first edition of *El cuarto de hora de oración* (*Fifteen Minutes of Prayer*). He also published *Handbook of the Friends of Jesus, Treasure Chest for Children, Novena to Saint Joseph, The Spirit of Saint Teresa, A Tribute to Saint Francis de Sales, Novena to the Holy Spirit,* and *Novena to the Immaculate Conception,* as well as textbooks used by the sisters and many other publications.

On 2 January 1896, Enrique retired to the Franciscan convent of Santo Espiritu at Gilet, where he suffered a stroke and died. Initially he was buried in Gilet; in July

1908 his body was translated to the chapel of the Company of Saint Teresa in Tortosa, Spain. Ossó's cause for beatification was introduced in 1923, but suspended from 1927 until 1957, when it was reintroduced. He was declared venerable in 1976.

Feast: 27 January (Carmelites).

Bibliography: M. GONZÁLEZ MARTÍN, *The Power of the Priesthood: A Life of Father Henry de Ossó,* tr. by L. BONNECARRÈRE (Barcelona 1971). M. V. MOLINS, *Así era Enrique de Ossó: biografía del fundador de la Compañía de Santa Teresa* (Burgos 1993); *Henry de Osso, priest and teacher,* tr. O. DAIGLE, ed. J. ROXBOROUGH (Covington, La. 1993). *Acta Apostolicae Sedis* (1982): 673–76. *L'Osservatore Romano,* Eng. ed. 43 (1979): 13–14.

[K. RABENSTEIN]

OULTREMONT, EMILIE, BL.

In religion, Mother Mary of Jesus, a.k.a. Baroness Emilie Olympe Marie Antoinette van der Linden d'Hooghvorst, married woman, missionary, foundress of the Society of Mary Reparatrix; b. 11 Oct. 1818, at Wégimont, Liège, Belgium; d. 22 Feb. 1878, at Florence, Tuscany, Italy; beatified 12 Oct. 1997.

She was the daughter of Count d'Oultremont of Liège, who was later (1840) the Belgian minister to the Holy See. At age nineteen Emilie was married to Baron Victor van der Linden d'Hooghvorst and bore him four children before his early death ten years later (1847). Her family wanted her to remarry, but the baroness made a vow of chastity. Two of her daughters assisted her in the foundation of the Society of Mary Reparatrix. Under the spiritual direction of the Jesuits, particularly that of Paul Ginhac (1824–95), the society was canonically established in Strasbourg, Alsace-Lorraine, in 1857. The following year she took the name Mary of Jesus and made her first vows together with her daughters and eight other companions. The mission of the society is "to make known the tenderness of God's love for the world, to follow Jesus as Mary did, and to collaborate with Him in His mission of Redemption-Reparation." Her relics are enshrined in the Church of Santa Croce e San Bonaventura in Rome.

John Paul II underlined the centrality of the family when he beatified Emilie d'Hooghvorst: "She first fulfilled the mission of all Christian married couples: She made her home a 'sanctuary of family life.'" (*cf. Apostolicam actuositatem,* n. 11)

Feast: 11 October.

Bibliography: *Acta Apostolicae Sedis,* no. 20 (1997): 999. *L'Osservatore Romano,* English edition, no. 42 (1997): 1–2, 12. *Emilie d'Oultremont, Baroness d'Hooghvorst, Foundress of the Society of Mary Reparatrix and Her Two Daughters* (London 1932). *In the Silence of Mary: The Life of Mother Mary of Jesus* (London 1964). C. COUVREUR, *Témoignage pour tous les temps, vie, esprit, oeuvre d'Emilie d'Oultremont, fondatrice de la Société de Marie Réparatrice* (Toulouse 1967). V. DELAPORTE, *The Society of Marie Reparatrix* (Montreal 1919). P. SUAU, *The life of Mother Mary of Jesus, Emilia d'Oultremont, Baroness d'Hooghvorst* (London 1913).

[K. RABENSTEIN]

OZANAM, ANTOINE FRÉDÉRIC, BL.

Married layman, French historian and literary scholar, founder of the Society of St. Vincent de Paul; b. 23 April 1813, Milan, Italy; d. 8 September 1853, Marseilles, France; beatified by John Paul II, 22 August 1997, in Notre Dame Cathedral at Paris, France, during the World Youth Day celebrations.

A tradition of the Ozanam family traced its descent from a seventh-century Jew, Samuel Hosannam, converted by St. Desiderius of Cahors, whom he sheltered from persecution. Frédéric was brought up and educated in Lyons. In 1829 he underwent a "crisis of doubt," which he overcame with the assistance of his teacher, Abbé Noirot. This experience consolidated the intellectual basis of his faith and also imbued him with deep charity in controversy with unbelievers.

In 1831 he published his first work, a refutation of the socialist theories of the Saint-Simonians. In the same year he went to Paris to study law and made the acquaintance of the leaders of the Catholic revival—Chateaubriand, Montalembert, Lacordaire, Ampère, and others. He was concerned to refute the attacks on Catholicism that were widespread in the Sorbonne. It was in May 1833 that he and a few fellow students formed a "Conference of Charity" to undertake practical work among the poor. This is accepted as the foundation date of the Society of St. Vincent de Paul, although its formal title and rules were not adopted until 1835. Ozanam insisted that the Society should not restrict its charity to Catholics and that countries should assist each other; thus, the Paris Society aided Dublin during the Irish famine and Dublin reciprocated during the Revolution of 1848.

Ozanam completed his first degree in law in 1834, and was called to the bar in Lyons. However, his true bent was for literature and history. He returned to Paris, where he took his first degree in literature in 1835, his doctorate in law in 1836, and his doctorate in literature in 1839. During this period he was active in the Society of St. Vincent de Paul, the Society for the Propagation of the Faith, Catholic journalism, and many Catholic causes. He was instrumental in bringing about the first of Lacordaire's famous series of Lenten sermons in Notre Dame.

Three hundred cardinals and bishops from all parts of the world attended the beatification ceremony at Notre Dame, Paris, for Frederic Ozanam. (© Youth Day Pool/Liaison Agency.)

Ozanam became the first to hold a chair as professor of commercial law at Lyons in 1839, but returned to Paris the following year to teach foreign literature at the Sorbonne. He was elected professor in 1844. His studies of Dante, beginning with his doctoral thesis, revolutionized critical work on the poet. Although Ozanam is a neglected figure in nineteenth-century historiography, his research in the development of Christian Latin, literature, and art showed an acquaintance with the original texts and contemporary critical research in the major European languages which was remarkable in the French scholarship of his day.

Ozanam advocated that Catholics should play their part in the evolution of the democratic state and unsuccessfully stood for election to the National Assembly in 1848. He denounced economic liberalism and any form of socialism. Lecture 24 in his course of commercial law is a brilliant exposition of Catholic social doctrine, fore-shadowing *Rerum novarum* and antedating the *Communist Manifesto* in its attention to the social question. Ozanam's personal visitations to the poor and his reports of the St. Vincent de Paul Society antedated even Villermé's pioneer social investigation published in 1840.

Ozanam may justly be regarded as an exemplar of the lay apostolate in family, social, and intellectual life. His marriage (23 June 1841) to Amelie Soulacroix produced one daughter, Marie (b. 1845). Without neglecting family duties he worked for social justice. At his request, Ozanam was buried in the church crypt of Saint-Joseph-des-Carmes at the Catholic Institute of Paris, among the students to whom he gave the best of himself. His cause for beatification, introduced in 1925, was followed by the declaration of his heroic virtues (6 July 1993) and the approval of a miracle attributed to his intercession (25 June 1996).

Pope John Paul II reflected on this servant of God as "an apostle of that charity which is respectful of the human person, and a clear-sighted analyst of social problems."

Feast: 8 September.

Bibliography: Works by Frédéric Ozanam: *Oeuvres complètes,* 11 v. (Paris 1859–65). *Dante et la philosophie catholique au 13e siècle* (Paris 1839); *Études germaniques,* 2 v. (Paris 1847–49); *Les poètes franciscains en Italie au 13e siècle* (Paris 1852). *Lettres de Frédéric Ozanam. édition critique,* 5 v., ed. D. OZANAM (Paris 1961–97). Literature about Frédéric Ozanam: C. A. OZANAM, *Vie de Frédéric Ozanam* (Paris 1879). T. E. AUGE, *Frederic Ozanam and His World* (Milwaukee, Wisc. 1966). L. BAUNARD, *Ozanam d'après sa correspondance* (Paris 1912), a standard work published by the Catholic Truth Society of Ireland as *Ozanam in his Correspondence.* B. CATTANÉO, *Frédéric Ozanam le bienheureux* (Paris 1997). V. CONZEMIUS, *Frédéric Ozanam* (Freiburg, Switz. 1985). G. FORSANS, *Frédéric Ozanam 1813–53. Un précurseur de notre temps dans la fidélité à l'évangile* (Chambray-les-Tours 1991). I. GOBRY, *Frédéric Ozanam ou la foi opérante* (Paris 1983). G. GOYAU, *Frédéric Ozanam* (Paris 1925); et al., *Ozanam: Livre du centenaire,* rev. ed. (Paris 1931). H. GUILLEMIN, *La bataille de Dieu* (Geneva 1944). H. L. HUGHES, *Frederick Ozanam* (London 1933). F. MÉJECAZE, *Fr. Ozanam et l'église catholique* (Paris 1932). J.-A. LAMARCHE, *Frédéric Ozanam: fondateur de la Société Saint-Vincent-de-Paul* (Montréal 1997). K. O'MEARA, *Frederic Ozanam, Professor at the Sorbonne; His Life and Works* (Edinburgh 1876). E. RENNER, *The Historical Thought of Frédéric Ozanam* (Washington 1960). M. DES RIVIÈRES, *Ozanam. Un savant chez les pauvres* (Montréal 1984). A. P. SCHIMBERG, *The Great Friend: Frederick Ozanam* (Milwaukee, Wisc. 1946). M. VINCENT, *Ozanam. Une jeunesse romantique* (Paris 1994).

[T. MACMILLAN]

PADRE PIO (FRANCESCO FORGIONE), BL.

Capuchin-Franciscan priest, stigmatic; b. Pietrelcina, Italy, 25 May 1887; d. San Giovanni Rotondo, Italy, 23 September 1968. Beatified 2 May 1999 by Pope John Paul II.

From early childhood he exhibited a spiritual sensitivity bordering on mysticism. Later, he confided to his spiritual director that at the age of five he thought of consecrating himself to God forever, a desire that he felt materialized when he entered the Capuchin-Franciscan Order. In his formative years as a Capuchin physical ill-health and encounters with the devil plagued the quiet, gentle, and reserved friar.

After his ordination to the priesthood in 1910, his life was relatively uneventful, except for a brief stint—six weeks—in the medical corps of the Italian Army during World War I. He received a medical discharge after mistakenly being considered a deserter.

In 1918, he was officially assigned to the friary at San Giovanni Rotondo and in September of that year he

This photograph taken in 1964 shows Padre Pio as he celebrates a mass in the town of San Giovanni Rotondo. (© AFP/CORBIS)

was first gifted with the visible phenomenon of the stigmata. When the Vatican and the Capuchin Order intervened to ascertain the facts concerning the stigmata, Padre Pio had to face suspicion, embarrassment, and disciplinary action in addition to his crosses of ill-health and demonic affliction. Considerable controversy arose among doctors and the clergy over the natural and supernatural aspects of his stigmata. The Vatican began its investigation by forbidding Padre Pio to say Mass publicly. This action by the Holy See combined with rumors that Padre Pio would be transferred from San Giovanni Rotondo stirred violent riots by the townspeople resulting in fourteen deaths and eighty injuries. As a result, in 1920 Church authorities imposed restrictions that were to last thirteen years on his public activities. Through it all Padre Pio remained obedient and compliant. Finally in 1933, Pius XI lifted the ban telling the friar's archbishop: "I have not been badly disposed toward Padre Pio, but I have been badly informed about Padre Pio."

For 50 years Padre Pio never left San Giovanni Rotondo; yet his influence was felt everywhere as the world flocked to him for spiritual favors. Aside from saying Mass, preaching, hearing confessions, and being a victim of Christ's suffering, he did nothing extraordinary except for the creation of one mighty monument: Padre Pio's hospital, *Casa Sollievo della Sofferenza* which was the result of his zeal and inspiration. After his death in 1968, the impact of his life, sanctity, and spirituality remained a powerful influence on the faithful and on the Church.

On the occasion of the centenary of Padre Pio's birth, Pope John Paul II visited the tomb of the Capuchin stigmatic in 1987 and paid him this tribute: ". . . as a religious he generously lived out the ideal of the Capuchin friars, just as he lived out the ideal of the priest. . . . Were not the altar and the confessional the two poles of his life? This priestly witness contains a message as valid as it is timely."

Feast: 25 May.

Bibliography: C. RUFFIN, *Padre Pio: The True Story* (Huntington, Ind. 1982). J. A. SCHUG, *Padre Pio* (Huntington, Ind. 1976). D. GAUDIOSE, *Prophet of the People* (New York 1973). G. PAGNOSSIN, *Il Calvario di Padre Pio*, 2 v. (Padova 1978). PADRE PIO DA PIETRELCINA, *Epistolario-Corrispondeza con le Figlie Spirituali (1915–1922)* (San Giovanni Rotondo 1977); *Epistolario-Corrispondenza con i Direttori Spirituali (1910–1922)* (San Giovanni Rotondo 1971). G. FESTA, *Misteri di Scienza e Luci di Fede, le Stigmate Padre Pio da Pietrelcina* (Roma 1938).

[S. F. MIKLAS]

PALAU Y QUER, FRANCISCO, BL.

A.k.a. Francis of Jesus Mary Joseph; Discalced Carmelite (OCD); mystic priest, thaumaturge; founder of the Theresian Missionary Carmelite Sisters and the Missionary Carmelite Sisters; b. 29 December 1811, Aytona, Lérida (Lleida) Province of Catalonia, Spain; d. 20 March 1872, at Tarragona; beatified by John Paul II on 24 April 1988, Rome.

Born into a poor but devout family, Francis Palau entered the seminary at Lérida in 1828. After studying philosophy and completing one year of theology, he joined the Discalced Carmelites (OCD) (1832). He made his religious profession on 14 November 1833 and was ordained a priest on 2 April 1836.

Upheaval in Spain at the time caused him to live outside the cloister in France from 1840 to 1851. Upon returning to Spain, he preached and gave missions in the Balearic Islands and in Barcelona, where he founded his "School of Virtue," a model for catechetical instruction. The school was suppressed upon the accusation that it was being used to foment labor strikes, and Francis was forced into exile 1854-1860 on the small barren island of Vedrá off the coast of Ibiza.

When Francis was allowed to return to the mainland following the intervention of Queen Isabella II, he organized small communities of women (1860–61) in the Balearic Islands that later became the Theresian Missionary Carmelite Sisters and the Missionary Carmelite Sisters. He also founded the now-defunct Brothers of Charity. Fr. Palau traveled to Rome to present his concerns to the pope (1866) and to serve as consultor to the bishops gathered for Vatican Council I (1870). He died peacefully at age 60.

Feast Day: 7 November (Carmelites).

Bibliography: *L'Osservatore Romano,* English edition, no. 16 (1988). GREGORIO DE JESÚS CRUCIFICADO, *Braza entre cenizas: Biografía del R. P. Francisco Palau y Quer* (Bilbao, Spain 1956).

[K. RABENSTEIN]

PALMENTIERI, LUDOVICO DA CASORIA, BL.

Baptized Arcángelo; Franciscan priest; founder of the Brothers of Charity (Grey Franciscan Friars of Charity or *Frati Bigi*) and Sisters of St. Elizabeth (*Suore Bigie*); b. 11 March 1814, Casoria (near Naples), Campania, Italy; d. 30 March 1885, Pausilippo near Naples, Italy; beatified by John Paul II, 18 April 1993.

Arcángelo was a cabinetmaker in his youth. Attracted by the Franciscans at the nearby friary in Naples, Arcángelo entered the order at Avellino (17 June 1832) and took the name Ludovico (Louis). Shortly after the completion of the year's novitiate, he was appointed to study and teach philosophy, chemistry, and mathematics in San Pietro Convent, Naples. His affinity for science led him later to found a meteorological observatory, an Academy of Religion and Science, and five magazines. Other literary accomplishments included an Italian translation of the works of Saint Bonaventure and a pocket edition of the Bible.

Following the advice of his superiors, he instituted a branch of the Third Order at San Pietro from which he formed (1859) a religious institute, commonly known as the *Frati Bigi* because of their grayish-colored habits. In 1862, Ludovico instituted a congregation of religious women, known as the *Suore Bigie*, whom he placed under the protection of Saint Elizabeth of Hungary. These congregations made his many charitable works possible.

Ludovico was ordained to the priesthood on 4 June 1837. In 1847, during a mystical experience in prayer, he discerned a vocation to serve the poor actively. He opened a pharmacy in the friary and, later, infirmaries for the elderly and sick friars of the province. Additionally, he founded care centers for children; institutes for the blind, and deaf and dumb; hospices for travellers; agricultural colonies; and savings and loan societies for the poor. About 1852, he opened the first of two schools for the children of emancipated African slaves with the intention that they would return home to evangelize Africa. He later entrusted the continuance of this work to Anna Maria Fiorelli Lapini and her Stigmatine Sisters.

Ten years before his death he was attacked with a serious and painful illness, from which he never completely recovered. He died in the Marine Hospital he had established for elderly sailors. The numerous charitable institutions in Naples, Rome, Assisi, and Florence that owe their origin to Ludovico of Casoria, as well as his fame for sanctity even during his lifetime, account for the veneration in which he was held by all classes. His mortal remains were entrusted to his spiritual daughters, the *Suore Bigie*, in 1887. The cause for Ludovico's beatification was introduced in Rome in 1907, and he was declared venerable, 13 February 1964.

Pope John Paul II said that Ludovico "assumed an active responsibility for the gravest forms of poverty and intervened with Christian compassion" (beatification homily).

Feast: 30 March.

Bibliography: *Epistolario*, ed. G. D'ANDREA (Naples 1989). A. CAPECELATRO, *La vita del p. Lodovico da Casoria* (Naples 1887).

[K. RABENSTEIN]

PAMPLONA, DIONISIO AND COMPANIONS, BB.

Martyrs; Religious of the Order of Poor Clerics Regular of the Mother of God of the Pious Schools (Piarists); beatified 1 October 1995 by Pope John Paul II.

Born 11 October 1868 in Calamocha, Teruel, Spain, Pamplona made his solemn profession in 1889 and was ordained a priest in 1893. He taught in several Piarist schools in Spain and then Argentina. In 1934 he was appointed rector of the novitiate house in Peralta de la Sal, Huesca, Spain, where he also served as pastor of the church there. He was devoted to the rule and allowed the love of God to animate all he did. The religious persecution marking the Spanish civil war intensified in 1936. On 23 July 1936 the Revolutionary Committee placed the Piarist community under house arrest in a secluded home away from the church and school. The next day at dawn, Pamplona left the house unnoticed by the guards and returned to the church to celebrate Mass. As he was locking the church to leave, armed men seized him and later took him to the prison in Monzón. On 25 June around 11

o'clock in the evening, the soldiers removed Pamplona with several other prisoners, led them to the main square, and lined them up for execution. Pamplona was singled out and violently shot to death. Other members of the Piarist community martyred during the Civil War were beatified with Pamplona.

Manuel Segura López, b. 22 January 1881, Almonacid de la Sierra; d. 28 July 1936; ordained in 1907, Segura was the novice master in Peralta

David Carlos Marañón, b. 29 December 1907, in Asartam; d. 28 July 1936; professed as a lay brother in 1932 and made solemn profession in 1935. David was the cook and gardener for the community. He refused an offer of freedom and was shot along with Segura.

Faustino Oteiza Segura, b. 14 February 1890, in Ayegui; d. 9 August 1936; professed in 1907 and ordained in 1913; Faustino went to Peralta where he taught in the elementary school and later was novice master. He witnessed and chronicled the martyrdom of Dionisio, Manuel, and Brother David in a letter to the provincial written on 1 August 1936. He lived piously in the prison house until his execution.

Florentín Felipe Naya, b. 10 October 1856 in Alquézar; d. 9 August 1936. Felipe lived under house arrest with his confreres. Partially blind and in ill health in his advanced age, he devoted himself to constant prayer. Four kilometers from Peralta, on a hill about ten meters from the side of the road, he and Faustino were gunned down.

Enrique Canadell Quintana, b. 29 June 1890 ; d. in the night 17–18 August 1936. Enrique (Henry) Canadell Quintana was a Piarist from the community of Our Lady of Barcelona. At the start of the Revolution, he fled to his sister's house in Olat. There he spent his days reading and praying. On the night of 17 August some soldiers arrived, arrested him, and took him away in a car. During the journey, the soldiers cruelly beat him with their rifle butts. About ten kilometers down the road, they stopped the car, ordered him out, and shot him.

Matias Cardona Meseguer, b. 23 December 1902, in Vallibona; d. 20 August 1936. Matias had just been ordained on 11 April 1936. A member of the San Anton community in Barcelona, he went to his home town of Vallibona at the beginning of the persecution of religious. On 17 August he left his sister's house where he was staying to seek asylum at his uncle's farm in the mountains. He was arrested shortly thereafter by soldiers sent by the Revolution Committee. He turned himself in, and they imprisoned him. In the early morning of 20 August, soldiers took him from the prison in a truck along with a diocesan priest; the two were shot on the side of the road.

Francisco Carceller Galindo, b. 2 October 1901 in Forcall, Castile; d. 2 October 1936; Carceller was a priest assigned to the Collegium of Our Lady of Barcelona. In addition to his regular classes, he devoted himself to the religious formation of the older students who both loved and admired him. He fled to his parent home on 17 July 1936 for protection. On 29 July he was arrested and imprisoned at Castellon. In the middle of the night on 2 October, the soldiers removed from the prison thirty-five priests among whom was Canceller. They were lined up and executed by machine gun.

Ignacio Casanovas Perramón, b. 15 June 1893, Igualada; d. 16 September 1936. Ignacio taught at the Collegium of Our Lady of Barcelona from 1921 until his death. A good priest, he was also skilled in various kinds of woodworking. He went to his family home in July 1936 in Can Brunet where he stayed with his widowed mother. Soldiers arrested him on 16 September. They marched him out of town, ordered him to stop, and shot him while he prayed.

Carlo Navarro Miguel, 11 February 1911 in Torrente; d. 22 September 1936. Carlos was ordained to the priesthood in 1935 and served in Albacete. He sought refuge at his parent's home. On 12 September, soldiers seized him and imprisoned him. Early on 22 September he was shot along with two other priests of the town.

José Ferrer Esteve b. 17 February 1904, in Algemesí; d. 9 December 1936. The novice master in Albarracin for the province of Valencia, José was joyful, jovial man by nature, and his humor cheered his confreres daily. On 10 July he went to Algeneri to rest with his parents. He remained there until 9 December, when he was arrested. During the night he was taken to a roadside location and shot.

Juan Agramunt Riera, b. 13 February 1907 in Alzamora; d. 14 August 1936. Fr. Juan was assigned to the Castellon school four kilometers from his home in Almazora. He fled to his parents home at the end of July where he was arrested. The night of 13–14 August, he was taken to prison along with a diocesan priest. They were shot en route, six kilometers from Almazora at the intersection of two roads.

Alfredo Parte Saiz, b. 1 June 1899 in Cilleruelo de Bricia; d. 27 December 1936. Alfredo Parte was a priest from the Collegio Villacarriedo. In mid-August 1936, he fled to his uncle's home in Santander. On 15 November he was seized. He consoled his fellow prisoners and endured his suffering with patience. On 27 December he was shot.

At their beatification Pope John Paul II observed, ''They are not heroes of an inhuman war but teachers of youth who, as both religious and teachers, faced up to their tragic fate by authentic witness to the faith, giving by their martyrdom, the ultimate lesson of their life.''

Bibliography: ''Decreto Super Martyrio,'' *Acta Apostolicae Sedis* (1995): 651 656. *La Documentation Catholique* 2125 (5 November 1995): 924.

[LEONARD GENDERNALIK/EDITORS]

PAMPURI, RICCARDO, ST.

Baptized Erminio Filippo (Herman Philip), physician, lay brother of the Hospitallers of St. John of God; b. 2 August 1897, Trivolizi (near Pavia), Lombardy, Italy; d. 1 May 1930, Milan; canonized 1 November 1989 in Rome by John Paul II.

The second youngest of the eleven children of wine merchants Innocente Pampuri and Angela Campari, who died of tuberculosis when Erminio was three, Erminio was raised by his uncle Carlo Campari in Turin following his father's death (1907). There, Erminio became involved in Catholic Action. He studied medicine at the University of Pavia (1915–21) with an interruption for military service in the Italian Army Medical Corps (1917–18). In 1921, he joined his uncle Carlo's practice in Morimondo (Milan) as a general physician. He became an active member of the St. Vincent de Paul Society, joined the Third Order of Franciscans (1922), fostered the growth of a parish Catholic Action youth group, and organized spiritual exercises in preparation for the 1925 Jubilee. Under the spiritual direction of Fr. Riccardo Beretta, he entered the Hospitallers of St. John of God (22 June 1927). After receiving the habit and name Brother Richard (21 October 1927), he completed his novitiate and began his work as director of the dental clinic at St. Ursula's Hospital in Brescia (24 October 1928). He died at the age of thirty-three from bronchial pneumonia; his remains are venerated in a chapel dedicated to him in Trivolzio.

At Pampuri's beatification (process opened 1949), Pope John Paul II said: ''The short but intense life of Br. Richard is an incentive for all the People of God, but especially for the young, for doctors and for religious.''

Feast: 1 May.

Bibliography: *Acta Apostolicae Sedis* 74 (1982): 376–379. *L'Osservatore Romano,* English Edition, no. 41 (1981): 1, 12. L. CIONI, *Il santo semplice: vita di san Riccardo Pampuri* (Genoa 1996). N. MUTSCHLECHNER, *Ein Arzt wählt Gott—Der Heilige Frater Richard Pampuri aus dem Orden der Barmherzigen Brüder* (Munich 1991).

[K. RABENSTEIN]

PARADIS, MARIE-LÉONIE, BL.

Baptized Alodie Virginie, foundress of the Little Sisters of the Holy Family; b. 12 May 1840, at L'Acadie (Sainte Marguerite de Blairfindie, a suburb of Montréal), Québec, Canada; d. 3 May 1912, at Sherbrooke, Québec; beatified 11 September 1984.

She was the daughter of a miller, who sent her to a boarding school run by the Sisters of Notre Dame at Saint-Laurent. Paradis entered the religious life at age thirteen, taking vows in 1857 as a Holy Cross sister. She was sent to St. Vincent's Orphanage in New York City. For sometime she taught in various schools. In 1864, she was given charge of the domestic work in an Indiana household. Later she had the same responsibilities at St. Joseph's College, Memramcook, New Brunswick. Finding many young women eager to join her in this vocation, she formed a new community, Little Sisters of the Holy Family (1880), which received canonical approval in 1896 and papal approbation in 1905. The sisters work in the kitchens, laundries, and sacristies of colleges, seminaries, episcopal residences, and retirement homes for priests. They began with the household management of the apostolic delegations in Canada and Washington, D.C. In 1885, the novitiate was transferred to Sherbrooke, Québec, where the motherhouse was later established. Although Mother Marie-Léonie was frail and often ill, she continued her service until a few hours before her peaceful death.

At her beatification in Montréal, John Paul II declared that Marie-Léonie "never shied away from the various forms of manual labor which is the lot of so many people today and which held a special place in the Holy Family and in the life of Jesus of Nazareth himself."

Feast: 4 May (Canada).

Bibliography: *Acta Apostolicae Sedis* 78 (1986): 13–15. *L'Osservatore Romano,* English edition, no. 39 (1984): 9.

[K. RABENSTEIN]

PARAGUAY, JESUIT MARTYRS OF, SS.

Jesuit missionaries and martyrs; d. 15 and 17 November 1628, Rio Grande do Sul, Brazil; canonized at Asunción, Paraguay, by John Paul II, 16 May 1988.

Roch González de Santa Cruz, b. 1576 in Asunción, Paraguay; d. 17 November at Caaró he dedicated his life to the evangelization of the Indians. He was appointed priest of the cathedral and, in 1609, vicar-general of the diocese. On 9 May 1609, he entered the Society of Jesus.

In 1615 he began his missionary work by founding the *Reducción* of Itapúa and in subsequent years other such settlements. In 1620 he was appointed by his superiors to give religious instruction to the inhabitants of the area that is now the Brazilian state of Rio Grande do Sul. There he was martyred at the *Reducción* of Todos los Santos, the last one he founded. He had two companions in his martyrdom.

Alonso Rodríguez was born in Zamora, Spain, on 10 March 1598; d. 15 November at Caaró. He entered the Society of Jesus on 25 March 1614, and arrived in Buenos Aires on 15 February 1617. After completing his studies, he gave religious instruction to the Indians for four years.

Juan del Castillo died two days later (17 November), at Iyuí in the *Reducción* of La Asunción. He was born in Belmonte, Spain, 14 September 1596, and he entered the Society of Jesus on 22 March 1614. Assigned to Paraguay, he arrived in Buenos Aires with Rodríguez and worked among the Indians there for three years.

Their bodies were taken first to the *Reducción* of Candeleria and later transferred to that of the Immaculate Conception. These Jesuits became the first American martyrs to be beatified (28 January 1934 by Pius XI).

Pope John Paul II praised the Paraguayan martyrs because "neither the obstacles of the wilderness, the misunderstanding of people, nor the attacks of those who saw their evangelizing activity as a threat to personal interests could intimidate these champions of the faith" (canonization homily). The are patrons of native traditions.

Feast: 16 November.

Bibliography: L. G. JAEGER, *Os-bem aventurados Roque González, Alfonso Rodríguez e João del Castillo: Mártires do Caaró e Pirapó,* 2d ed. (Pôrto Alegre 1951). L. KOHLER, *Los tres héroes de Caaró y Pirapó* (Posadas, Argentina 1978). G. MÁRKUS, *The Radical Tradition: Revolutionary Saints in the Battle for Justice and Human Rights* (New York 1993): 143–50. C. J. MCNASPY, *Conquistador without Sword: The Life of Roque González* (Chicago 1984), tr. of *Roque González de Santacruz, un conquistador sin espada* (Asunción, Paraguay 1983). H. THURSTON, "The First Beatified Martyr of Spanish America," *Catholic Historical Review* 20 (1934–35): 371–83. J. N. TYLENDA, *Jesuit Saints & Martyrs* (Chicago 1998): 387–92. R. E. VELÁZQUEZ, *Roque González de Santa Cruz, colonia y reducciones en el Paraguay de 1600* (Asunción, Paraguay 1975).

[H. STORNI]

PELCZAR, JÓZEF SEBASTIAN, BL.

Bishop, founder of the Servants of the Most Sacred Heart of Jesus; b. 17 January 1842, Korczyna, Poland; d. 28 March 1924, Przemyśl, Poland; beatified at Rzeszów, Poland, by John Paul II, 2 June 1991.

Józef Pelczar founded the Servants of the Most Sacred Heart of Jesus (1894), which came to the United States in 1959. He was consecrated titular bishop of Meletopolis (20 February 1899) prior to assuming the see of Przemyśi, Poland (13 January 1901), which he guided through the horrors of World War I. He is remembered for his selfless heroism following the invasion of Russia (March 1915), as well as for opening medical centers to care for the wounded and victims of epidemics.

At his beatification, Pope John Paul II remembered Bishop Pelczar as "the man who did the will of the Father."

[K. RABENSTEIN]

PERBOYRE, JEAN-GABRIEL, ST.

Martyr, priest of the Congregation of the Mission of Saint Vincent de Paul; b. 6 January 1802, at Le Puech, Mongesty (diocese of Cahors), France; d. 11 September 1840, at Wuchangfu (near Hu-pei), China.

The eldest of eight children (five of whom became Vincentians) of the farmers, Pierre and Marie Rigal Perboyre, Jean-Gabriel attended minor seminary with his brother Louis at Montauban, founded by their uncle Jacques Perboyre, a Vincentian who had survived the French Revolution. In 1818 Jean-Gabriel became the first French Vincentian seminarian since the revolution. He studied theology in Paris, then accepted an appointment as professor at Montdidier College (1823), and was ordained in 1826. After working as a teacher, spiritual director, and in other capacities in various Vincentian seminaries and training centers in France, he went to east central China (1835) to replace his brother, Fr. Louis, who died en route. In the missions of Hunan and Hu-pei Provinces, he acquired a familiarity with the Chinese language and dedicated himself especially to instructing abandoned children. When persecution broke out, he was arrested (16 September 1839) at Cha-yuan-kou for entering China illegally to spread Christianity. Imprisoned at Wuchangfu, he was interrogated many times by mandarins and by the viceroy and tortured in a vain effort to make him reveal the hiding places of other priests. After eight months' imprisonment he was strangled to death Chinese-style (on a cross) on Ou-tch'ang (Red Mountain), and was buried in the nearby cemetery in Wuchangfu close to the remains of his confrere and fellow martyr, Bl. François Clet.

On 2 June 1996, Pope John Paul II canonized Perboyre, the first saint of China, declaring: "He ardently witnessed to Christ's love for the Chinese. . . . By daily imitation of his Lord, in humility and gentleness, he would be fully identified with him. . . . To the memory of Jean-Gabriel Perboyre, . . . we wish to add the memory of all those who down the centuries bore witness to the name of Jesus Christ in the land of China." Patron of the Vincentian missionaries.

Feast: 11 September (since 1969).

Bibliography: *Life of the Bl. Servant of God, the Heroic Martyr, John Gabriel Perboyre . . .* , tr. C. FEILDING (New Orleans 1894). *L'Osservatore Romano,* English edition, no. 23 (1996): 1–2, 5, 12. J.L. BAUDOT and L.CHAUSSIN, *Vies des saints . . . avec l'historique des fêtes,* 9: 252–255. A. CHATELET, *Jean Gabriel Perboyre, Martyr* (Paris 1943). L. CHIEROTTI, *Il beato Gian Gabriele Perboyre: Lo strangolarono ad una croce* (Genoa 1995). A. SYLVESTRE, *Jean-Gabriel Perboyre : prêtre de la mission, martyr en Chine* (Moissac 1994).

[J. KRAHL]

PÉREZ FLORIDO, PETRA DE SAN JOSÉ, BL.

Foundress of the Congregation of the Mothers of the Helpless and of St Joseph of the Mountain; b. 7 December 1845, Málaga, Costa del Sol, Spain; d. 16 August 1906, Barcelona, Spain; beatified by John Paul II, 16 October 1994.

From her youth Pérez desired the religious life. Full of compassion for the poor, she begged in the streets on their behalf despite her father's opposition. With the approbation of the bishop of Málaga, who also named the congregation, Petra and three companions formed (1880) the Mothers of the Helpless. Mother Petra labored (1895–1901) to build the royal sanctuary of Saint Joseph of the Mountain (Montaña Pelada), while guiding her growing religious communities.

Feast: 16 August.

Bibliography: F. DE LA HOZ, *Desde el valle a la montaña* (Seville 1961). MOTHERS OF THE HELPLESS, *Sobre la 'piedra'.* (Valencia 1972).

[K. RABENSTEIN]

PETER TO ROT, BL.

Martyr, married man, father, lay catechist; b. ca. 1912, at Rakunai, New Britain Island, northeast of Papua New Guinea; d. ca. 1945, at Vunaiara, Papua New Guinea; beatified at Port Moresby, Papua New Guinea, by John Paul II on 17 January 1995.

As the son of the local chieftain, Angelo To Puia and his wife Maria la Tumul, Peter was baptized by the Missionaries of the Sacred Heart when his father invited his people to become Catholics. During his 40 years as chieftain, Angelo promoted the faith but felt it was unwise for his son Peter—or any of the new Christians—to become priests or religious. He did allow Peter to study at Saint Paul's Mission School (1930–33) to become a catechist. After receiving his diploma, Peter taught effectively in Rakunai. He married (11 November 1936) another Catholic, Paula La Varpit, with whom he had three children (the last born shortly after Peter's death).

When the Japanese invaded (1942), the clergy and religious were imprisoned; however, Peter was allowed to continue his work. In the absence of priests, he led other laity in ministering to the extent permitted them: baptizing, witnessing marriages, visiting the sick with the presanctified Eucharist, conducting communion services, catechizing, and running charitable organizations. He even built a church from branches on the outskirts of the village to replace one destroyed by the Japanese. Peter protested against the 1945 Japanese prohibition against Christian religious instruction and worship, as well as the imposition of polygamy. For this he was arrested (1945) and beaten repeatedly during his two-month incarceration in a cave. Finally he was killed for refusing to espouse polygamy. A fellow prisoner, Arap To Binabak, testified to Peter's martyrdom.

During his address to the bishops of Papua New Guinea and the Solomon Islands during their *ad limina* visit (30 November 1998), Pope John Paul II pointed to Peter To Rot as an example that young people "have a role and responsibility in the Church's life" that must be encouraged.

Feast: 7 July.

Bibliography: *The Martyrs of Papua New Guinea: 333 Missionary Lives Lost during World War II*, ed. T. AERTS (Port Moresby 1994). *Acta Apostolicae Sedis* (1995): 166–68.

[K. RABENSTEIN]

PETRILLI, SAVINA, BL.

Foundress of the Sisters of the Poor of Saint Catherine of Siena; b. 29 August 1851, Siena, Italy; d. there 18 April 1923; beatified by John Paul II, 24 April 1988.

At the age of ten, Savina was introduced to and inspired by the life of Saint Catherine of Siena and the saint's eucharistic devotion. Her family, the parish Children of Mary Sodality, and her pastor all nourished her spirituality and encouraged her generosity toward the poor. During an audience with Pope Pius IX (1869), she was told to follow Saint Catherine. In 1873, she requested permission from the archbishop of Siena to found a religious order. He instructed her to draw up the Rule. With three friends Savina founded (1874) a small group to care for the poor, beginning in a small apartment with an abandoned baby. Mother Savina continued working with the Sisters of the Poor of Saint Catherine of Siena, approved by the Holy See in 1875, until her death from cancer. The order spread to India, Italy, the Philippines, and Latin America.

At her beatification, Pope John Paul II said that Mother Savina gathered "the most neglected brothers and sisters seeking along the ways of the world all those whom people despise, in order to lead every person to the joy of the banquet of the Kingdom."

Feast: 18 April.

Bibliography: *Acta Apostolicae Sedis* (1988): 583. *L'Osservatore Romano,* English edition, no. 16 (1988): 12.

[K. RABENSTEIN]

PIAMARTA, GIOVANNI BATTISTA, BL.

Diocesan priest, founder of the Congregation of the Holy Family of Nazareth and the Humble Servants of the Lord; b. 26 November 1841, Brescia, Italy; d. 25 April 1913, Remedello, Italy; beatified by John Paul II, 12 October 1997.

Born into a poor but pious family headed by a barber and a seamstress, Piamarta received his education in local schools until he entered the seminary in 1860. Following ordination (1865) his ministry, first in rural parishes (Carzago Riviera and Bedizzole) then in Brescia, focused on working class young people and their families. With Msgr. Petro Capretti he founded (1886) the *Istituto Artigianelli* to provide working class children with the moral foundation and professional skills needed in the newly industrialized society. He built housing and workshops for 100 boys whom he served as a father and spiritual director. With Fr. Bonsignori he established (1895) an agricultural research center on 140 hectares at Remedello to enhance the farming skills of peasants. Remedello gained an international reputation, and its structure was copied in many countries. In 1902, he founded the Congregation of the Holy Family of Nazareth to perpetuate his work. A women's community, the Humble Servants of the Lord, was established, with the help of his mother and Elisa Baldo Foresti, to strengthen rural and urban families in the region through education. Piamarta gave precedence to the material and spiritual needs of others, while finding his own consolation in prayer. He died peacefully surrounded by his brothers and Fr. Bonsignori.

During his beatification, Pope John Paul II pointed out that Piamarta brought "many boys and young men to meet the Lord's loving and demanding gaze. . . . [His] work has many facets and embraces many areas of social life: from the world of work to that of agriculture, from education to the publishing sector. . . . Assiduous and fervent prayer was the source of his tireless apostolic zeal and beneficial influence which he exercised on everyone he approached." He is a patron of families and workers.

Feast: 26 June.

Bibliography: *Acta Apostolicae Sedis,* no. 20 (1997): 999. *L'Osservatore Romano,* English edition, no. 42 (1997): 1–2. *Lettere di P. Giovanni Piamarta e dei suoi corrispondenti,* ed. by A. FAPPANI (Brescia 1994). *Giovanni Piamarta e il suo tempo: atti del colloquio di studio: Brescia, 12 settembre 1987* (Brescia 1987).

[K. RABENSTEIN]

PIDAL Y CHICO DE GUZMÁN, MARÍA MARAVILLAS DE JESÚS, BL.

Baptized María Christina Luisa Ildefonsa Patricia Josefa, also known as Mother Maravillas de Jesús, Discalced Carmelite; foundress of the Association of Saint Teresa; b. 4 November 1891, Madrid, Spain; d. 11 December 1974, in the Carmel of Aldehuela (Madrid); beatified by John Paul II, 10 May 1998.

María Pidal was born while her father, Luis Pidal y Mon, the marquis of Pidal, was the Spanish ambassador to the Holy See. Her mother, Cristina Chico de Guzmán, was also a devout Catholic. María did not enter religious life until she was nearly thirty. Drawn to the Carmelites after reading the works of John of the Cross and Teresa of Ávila, she entered (1920) and was professed (1921) at the Escorial Carmel, Madrid. In 1924, with three others, she founded the Carmel of Cerro de los Angeles at the geographical center of Spain, where she pronounced her solemn vows that same year. Because the carmel grew so quickly, other communities, including one in Kottayam (1933), India, evolved from it. During the Spanish Civil War (1936–39), the sisters lived in an apartment in Madrid and their number continued to grow. In September 1937, they opened a carmel in the Batuecas near Salamanca. Following the war, she restored Cerro de los Angeles and continued to found other carmels (Mancera de Abajo, Duruelo, Cabrera, Arenas de San Pedro, San Calixto, Aravaca, Talavera de la Reina, La Aldehuela and Montemar-Torremolinos) and restored that at El Escorial and Ávila. To bind these carmels together, Mother María obtained Vatican approval for the Association of Saint Teresa (1972). A miracle attributed to her intercession was approved 18 December 1997.

Pope John Paul II said María Maravillas de Jesús used her fame "to attract many souls to God. . . . She lived with heroic faith, formed in response to an austere vocation, by putting God at the center of her life."

Feast: 11 December (Carmelites).

Bibliography: *Si tu le laisses faire: mère Maravillas de Jésus, Carmélite Déchaussée* (Montsurs 1993), French tr. of *Si tú le dejas: vida de la Madre Maravillas de Jesus, Carmelita Descalza* (Madrid 1976). *Acta Apolstolicae Sedis,* no. 12 (1998): 599.

[K. RABENSTEIN]

PIETRANTONI, AGOSTINA LIVIA, ST.

Baptized Livia, nurse, a Sister of Charity of Saint Joan Antida Thouret (*Istituto delle Suore della Carità di Santa Giovanna Antida Thouret*); b. 27 March 1864 in Pozzaglia Sabina (between Rieti and Tivoli), Italy; d. 13 November 1894, Rome; canonized by John Paul II, 18 April 1999.

Livia, the second of the eleven children of farmers, received little formal education. Responding to a call, Livia entered the Sisters of Charity at Rome in 1886. Sister Agostina became a nurse in the pediatric ward at Holy Spirit Hospital near the Vatican, where she cared for the critically ill. Later she was transferred to the tuberculosis ward, where she contracted the deadly disease but was miraculously cured. Following a month of threatening notes, a former patient, Giuseppe Romanelli, stabbed Sister Agostina to death while attempting to rape her. As she died, she prayed for Romanelli's salvation and forgiveness. Agostina was beatified in 1972. The miracle required for her canonization was approved, 6 April 1998.

Pope John Paul II, during her canonization, said: "Sister Agostina understood that the love of Jesus requires generous service to one's brothers, in whose faces, especially that of the neediest, is reflected the face of Christ."

Bibliography: *Acta Apostolicae Sedis* 65 (1973): 229–235. *L'Osservatore Romano,* Eng. ed. 47 (1972): 1–2. A. PRONZATO, *Una certa suor Agostina. Suora della carità di S. Giovanna Antida Thouret* (Turin 1971).

[K. RABENSTEIN]

POLANCO FONTECHA, ANSELMO, BL.

Bishop of Teruel, Augustinian; martyr; b. 16 April 1881, Buenavista de Valdavia, Palencia, Spain; d. 7 February 1939, "Can Tretze" of Pont de Molins (near Gerona), Spain; beatified at Rome by John Paul II, 1 October 1995.

Born to modest farmers, Anselmo Polanco was professed as an Augustinian friar at Valladolid (1896), studied at Santa María of La Vid Monastery, and was ordained in 1904. He began his priestly career teaching theology in the seminary, then served as prior until he was sent to the Philippines as provincial councilor. He returned to Valladolid upon his election as provincial superior (1932) of the Philippines Province, which entailed sending missionaries to various parts of the world. In that position he travelled to China, Colombia, Peru, and the United States. Three years later he was named bishop of Teruel (Spain) and appointed apostolic administrator of Albarracín. Polanco remained in Teruel throughout the terrors of the Spanish civil war. In 1938, he was arrested and imprisoned by the Republican Army for refusing to remove his signature from a collective letter of the Spanish bishops denouncing the persecution of the Church. Shortly thereafter he was joined by his vicar general, Felipe Ripoll. After thirteen months incarceration the two were used as human shields as the soldiers disbanded at the end of the war. The bodies of both martyrs are enshrined in Bishop Polanco's cathedral.

During Bishop Polanco's beatification, Pope John Paul II observed: "As a presentiment, [Polanco] said on the day he took possession of his diocese: 'I have come to give my life for my flock.' This is why, together with Felipe Ripoll, he chose to stay at the side of his flock in the midst of danger and it was only by force that he was taken from them."

Feast: 7 February.

Bibliography: V. CÁRCEL ORTÍ, *Martires españoles del siglo XX* (Madrid 1995). J. PÉREZ DE URBEL, *Catholic Martyrs of the Spanish Civil War, 1936–1939*, tr. M. F. INGRAMS (Kansas City, Mo. 1993). *L'Osservatore Romano*, Eng. ed. 40 (1995): 1–3.

[K. RABENSTEIN]

POLAND, MARTYRS OF, BB.

Martyrs; d. 24 January 1874, Pratulin, Poland; beatified by John Paul II, 6 October 1996.

The background for the martyrdom was the the Union of Brest (1595–96) that marked the reunion of Polish Orthodox to the Church of Rome. It retained the Byzantine-Ukranian Rite, while permitting their priests to marry. When Poland fell under Russian domination, "Uniate" Catholics were systematically persecuted by the Tsarist regime. Bishops and priests who refused conversion to the Orthodox Church were deported to Siberia or detained in Siedlce or Biała Podlasie (now eastern Poland). By 1874, only the Byzantine Catholic Eparchy of Chelm remained.

When the Russian Kutanin, district prefect of Pratulin village, wanted to nominate an Orthodox priest to

A tapestry hanging in St. Peter's Basilica at the Vatican depicts Sister Agostina Livia Pietrantoni. (AP/Wide World Photos. Photograph by Massimo Sambucetti.)

replace the pastor of Pratulin, the parishioners objected. Kutanin brought Colonel Stein and his Cossack troops into the town to make the transfer by force. The unarmed parishioners surrounded the church to defend it and refused to disperse despite promises of favors and then threats. Thirteen Byzantine Catholics, led by Wincenty Lewoniuk, were martyred when the soldiers shot them to death for their fidelity to the Catholic Church, another 180 survived their wounds. The martyrs were buried without ceremony. The decree of martyrdom for the 13 killed was pronounced 25 June 1996. Those beatified were:

Andrzejuk, Jan (John), married, b. 1848, Derło; cantor in the church.

Bojko, Konstanty (Constantine), married, subsistence farmer, b. 25 September 1826, Derło.

Bojko, Łukasz (Luke), unmarried farmer from the village of Legi; b. 1852, Zaczopki. Łukasz, the son of Dymitra Bojko and Anastazji Wojda, spread the news of the arrival of the Cossacks to encourage others to defend the church in Pratulin and rang the church bells throughout the attack. He was shot in front of the church doors.

Franczuk, Ignacy (Ignatius), married layman, b. 1824, Derło (age 50). Ignacy, son of Daniel and Akacja Franczuk, had seven children by his wife Helena.

Hawryluk, Maksym (Maximilian), married farmer in Derło, b. 22 May 1840, Rolnik. Maksym and his wife Dominika had three children. He died at home of a wound in his stomach.

Hryciuk, Anicet, unmarried layman, b. 1855, Zaczopki. Anicet, the only son of Józef and Julianna Hryciuk, was shot in the head.

Łukaszuk, Konstanty (Constantine), married farmer, b. ca. 1829, ZaczopkI. Konstanty, husband of Irene and father of seven children, was pierced with a bayonet in the cemetery.

Karmasz, Daniel, married, layman; b. 1826, Odznaczał. He was the uneducated farmer from Legi who encouraged others to defend the church against the Cossacks and was shot holding the Cross in his hand.

Kiryluk, Filip (Philip), married farmer, b. 1830, Zaczopki. Shot.

Lewoniuk, Wincenty (Vincent), married layman; b. 1849, Krzyczewie. Vincent, husband of Marianna, was persecuted for supporting the Union of Brest. During the defense of Pratulin's church, he was shot to death.

Osypiuk, Bartołomiej (Bartholomew), married farmer; b. 1844, Bohukały. Son of Wasyla Osypiuk and Marty Kondraciuk; had two children of his own. He guarded the church, was wounded, and died at home praying for the pardon of his attackers.

Wasyluk, Onufry (Humphrey), married layman, village administrator; b. 1853, Zaczopki. Onufry's parents paid 800 rubles to the Russians to keep their son out of the army. He was shot in the head during the defense of the church.

Wawryszuk, Michał, layman, b. 1853, Derło. Michał had only recently been married in Olszyna before his martyrdom.

At their beatification Pope John Paul II declared: "The martyrs of Pratulin defended not only the parish church in front of which they were killed, but the Church that Christ entrusted to the Apostle Peter, the Church which they felt a part of, like living stones."

Feast: 24 January.

Bibliography: K. DEBSKI, *Bohaterstwo unitów podlaskich* Warsaw 1993). J. HAWRYLUK, *Z dziejów Cerkwi Prawoslawnej na Podlasiu w X-XVII wieku* (Bielsk Podlaski 1993). T. KRAWCZAK, *Zanim wróciła Polska* (Warsaw 1994). R. SOSZYNSKI, *400-lecie Unii Brzeskiej, 1596–1996* (Warsaw 1996). *Acta Apostolicae Sedis* (1996): 999.

[K. RABENSTEIN]

POLLO, SECONDO, BL.

Military chaplain, diocesan priest of Vercelli, martyr; b. 2 January 1908, Caresanablot (near Vercelli), Lombardy, Italy; d. 26 December 1941, on the plain of Dragali (near Montenegro), Yugoslavia; beatified by John Paul II, 23 May 1998 during a pastoral visit to northern Italy.

Secondo Pollo completed the minor seminary at Montecrivello, then studied philosophy and theology at the Pontifical Lombard Seminary in Rome. Following his ordination he taught at his alma mater in Montecrivello, while ministering in various parishes, including Cigliano, Borgo d'Ale, Saluggia, Livorno Ferraris, and others. He was particularly gifted as a catechist, preacher, and spiritual director. Later he taught philosophy and theology at the archdiocesan major seminary, served as chaplain of the Italian Youth of Catholic Action (September 1936), and ministered to prisoners. Pollo enjoyed parochial ministry and administered a parish in Larizzate (1940–41) until he was drafted as a military chaplain.

He was assigned to the Val Chisone battalion of the Alpine regiment, which was sent to Montenegro. He died on the battlefront between Italian and Yugoslav forces as he comforted a wounded soldier. The mortal remains of this priest, who was declared venerable 18 December 1997, were translated to Vercelli's cathedral in 1968.

During the beatification ceremony, Pope John Paul II explained that Fr. Pollo's holiness was rooted in "prayer and the most tender devotion to our heavenly Mother, Mary."

Bibliography: *L'Osservatore Romano,* English edition (26 May 1998): 2.

[K. RABENSTEIN]

PONTILLO, EGIDIO MARIA DI SAN GIUSEPPE, ST.

Baptized Francesco Antonio, a.k.a. Giles Mary of St. Joseph, Franciscan lay brother; b. 16 November 1729, near Taranto (Apulia), Italy; d. 7 February 1812, Naples; beatified by John Paul II at Rome, 2 June 1996.

He practiced his father's trade of rope making and supported the family with this skill after his father's death (1747). Before entering the Alcantarine Franciscans at Galatone, Lecce, Italy (1754) under the impetus of an extraordinary spiritual experience, he led a very devout life and participated zealously in the activities of the Sodality of Our Lady of the Rosary. From 1759 to 1812 Egidio lived at the friary of San Paolo a Chiara in Naples, where he labored as cook, porter, and alms gatherer (*quaestor*). His simplicity and serenity won him the affection of the Neapolitan sick and poor, among whom he propagated devotion to Mary and Joseph.

Pope John Paul II declared Egidio Maria was a "genuine spiritual son of St. Francis of Assisi, who obtained from the contemplation of Christ's mysteries the ardor of a charity without limits, inspiring his own spiritual charism with the humility of the Incarnation and the free gift of the Eucharist."

Feast: 7 February.

Bibliography: P. COCO, *Cenni della vita del beato Egidio Maria di S. Giuseppe, taumaturgo di Taranto* (Taranto 1931). M. A. HABIG, *The Franciscan Book of Saints* (Chicago 1959): 89–92. V. MUSARDO TALÒ, *S. Egidio Pontillo da Taranto: dalla marina tarantina a quella di Napoli* (Lecce, Italy 1996). *Acta ordinis minorum* (1888): 7:18–20.

[C. J. LYNCH]

POPPE, EDWARD JOHANNES MARIA, BL.

Diocesan priest of Ghent; b. 18 December 1890, Temse, East Flanders, Belgium; d. 10 June 1924 in Moerzeke, Belgium; beatified by John Paul II, 3 October 1999.

Edward Poppe, a baker's son, entered the diocesan seminary in May of 1909. His first assignment following ordination (1916) was the working-class Sainte Colette's parish in Ghent, where he exhibited a special love for children, the poor, and the dying. Poppe's concern regarding the secularization of society led him to emphasize catechesis and the formation of Eucharistic associations. He was appointed rector of a religious community in rural Moerzeke (1918) because of poor health. Although he was often too ill to get out of bed (1918–22), he used his time well for prayer, study, and writing about contemporary problems: ten short works, 284 articles, and thousands of letters. He adopted the "Little Way" of Saint Thérèse de Lisieux after a pilgrimage to her tomb in 1920 and began an intense campaign for re-evangelization centered around the Eucharist. Although he continued to concentrate on the religious instruction of young people, he also formed an association of priests, mobilized the laity, and invigorated social action in Flanders. He had a profound effect on a generation of Belgian priests when he was sent (October 1922) to Leopoldsburg as spiritual director to military chaplains. He died two years later at age thirty-four. On 3 July 1998, a miracle attributed to Poppe's intercession was approved.

At his beatification Pope John Paul II pointed to Poppe as one who "consecrated his life to Christ in the priestly ministry. . .nourished by intimate contact with the Divine Master."

Bibliography: O. G. JACOBS, *Edward J. M. Poppe*, 5th ed. (Averbode 1965). M. LEKEUX, *La dure montée* (Bruges 1964). F. VAN DE VELDE, *De wereld van Edward Poppe* (Antwerpen 1983); *Edward Poppe en de Vlaamse beweging* (Veurne 1994). *Acta Apostolicae Sedis*, no. 19 (1999): 965.

[K. RABENSTEIN]

POUSSEPIN, MARIE, BL.

Foundress of Dominican Sisters of the Presentation; b. 14 October 1653 near Chartres in the village of Dourdan, France; d. in Sainville, France, 24 January 1744.

Marie's well-to-do middle class parents, Claude and Julienne Fourrier, were hosiers and actively engaged in the local parish and in the Confraternity of Charity dedicated to works of mercy. When her mother died in 1675, Marie assumed responsibility for looking after her younger brother and rescued the family business from bankruptcy by expanding into the manufacture of woolen stockings and introducing the latest advances in looms. She also revolutionized the work place by abolishing the customary apprenticeship fee. In addition Marie was generous to the young employees, rewarding them with bonuses and offering them opportunities for advancement.

Sometime after 1690 she joined the Third Order of St. Dominic, and in 1696 she moved to Sainville where she gathered a community of women to serve in the local parish, educating girls and ministering to the sick poor of the area. Marie placed her sisters under the protection of Mary in the mystery of her Presentation in the Temple. They took simple vows, living according to the rule of the Third Order of St. Dominic, and they dedicated themselves to apostolic work at a time when most women religious lived a cloistered life. When Marie died at the age of ninety, the community had established twenty houses in northern France. Her tombstone bears the simple inscription: "She saw what was good in the eyes of God and accomplished it."

Pope John Paul II beatified her 24 November 1994, calling her a "social apostle of charity." He held her up as "one of our sisters in humanity . . . capable of understanding family problems and also showing where to seek their solution: in the love which spring from the heart of Christ, King of the universe."

Feast: 14 October (the anniversary of her baptism).

Bibliography: BERNARD PRÉTESEILLE, *Marie Poussepin*, translated from the French by MADELEINE CLEMENCE VAILLOT (Private printing). *L'Osservatore Romano*, English edition (23 November 1994).

[M. W. LAPOINTE]

POVEDA CASTROVERDE, PEDRO, BL.

Priest, martyr, scholar, founder of the Teresian Institute, Carmelite tertiary; b. 3 December 1874, Linares, Spain; d. 28 July 1936, Madrid, Spain; beatified 10 October 1993 by John Paul II.

Although Pedro desired to become a priest, his family experienced financial difficulties, and he lacked the means to continue his studies at the diocesan seminary at Jaen. Fortunately he was offered a scholarship by the bishop of Guadix to attend his seminary in southern Spain. Following his ordination in 1897, Father Poveda taught in that seminary. In 1900, he earned his licentiate in theology at Seville, then worked in Guadix and Madrid. In 1906, he was appointed canon of the Basilica of Covadonga in Asturias. He returned to his first seminary at Jaen to again teach theology.

Throughout his adult life, Poveda's primary apostolate was education. He built an elementary school and started workshops for the cave-dwellers of Guadix. In 1911, he founded Saint Teresa of Avila Academy as a residence for students, which became the basis for the Teresian Institute, an organization that was dedicated to the formation of teachers. It received diocesan and civil approval in Jaen and then Vatican approbation in 1924. Additionally, Poveda initiated pedagogical centers, opened the first university residence for women in Madrid (1914), and served as the spiritual director of Los Operarios Catechetical Center. He also continued to take an active role in teacher formation. He published articles and pamphlets and founded several periodicals to advance pedagogy in Spain.

After moving back to Madrid (1921), Poveda was appointed chaplain to the Royal Palace and sat on the Central Board Against Illiteracy. He continued to guide the growth of the Teresian Institute as it spread to Chile and Italy (1934), until he was killed at the beginning of the Spanish Civil War.

Pope John Paul II, upon beatifying Poveda, said "his apostolic desires focused on promoting the evangelizing presence of Christians in the world, mainly in the field of teaching and culture."

Feast: 28 July.

Bibliography: *La Radicalidad de una utopia: Pedro Poveda desde América* (Buenos Aires, Argentina 1993). P. ALASTRUÉ, *Inquietud y conquista* (Madrid 1976). D. GÓMEZ MOLLEDA, *La escuela, problema social: en el centenario de Poveda* (Madrid 1974); *Pedro Poveda et son temps* (Paris 1974); *Pedro Poveda, hombre interior* (Madrid 1971). D. MONDRONE, *Un prete scomodo*, 2d. ed. (Milan 1969). A. SERRANO DE HARO, *Una figura del pensamiento español: Don Pedro Poveda Castroverde* (Madrid 1974).

[K. RABENSTEIN]

PRAT Y PRAT, MERCEDES, BL.

Known in religion as María Mercedes; martyr of the Society of St. Teresa of Jesus; b. 6 March 1880, Barcelona, Spain; d. 24 July 1936, Barcelona; beatified by John Paul II, 29 April 1990.

Mercedes' Christian parents, Juan and Teresa, died while she was still a child. She combined her special talents as a painter, needleworker, and catechist to evangelize other girls. In 1904, she entered the novitiate of the Society of Saint Teresa of Jesus at Tortosa, where she pronounced her initial vows (1907) and served as a dedicated teacher. From 1920, she was assigned to the motherhouse at Barcelona, from which the community was forced to flee (19 July 1936) at the beginning of the Spanish Civil War. Stopped by militiamen, Mercedes was arrested on 23 July upon identifying herself as a religious and shot at dawn on 24 July on the road to Rabasada. Although mortally wounded she survived for some hours in extreme pain. Her cries attracted the attention of the passing militiamen, who shot her again.

At her beatification Pope John Paul II said: "Her great love for God and neighbor brought her to engage in the apostolic work of catechesis. . . . Her love for her neighbor showed itself above all in her act of pardoning those who shot her."

Feast: 24 July (Carmelites).

Bibliography: V. CÁRCEL ORTÍ, *Martires españoles del siglo XX* (Madrid 1995). J. PÉREZ DE URBEL, *Catholic Martyrs of the Spanish Civil War*, tr. M. F. INGRAMS (Kansas City, Mo. 1993). *Acta Apostolicae Sedis* (1990): 578.

[K. RABENSTEIN]

PRO JUÁREZ, MIGUEL AUGUSTIN, BL.

Mexican Jesuit martyr; b. Guadalupe, 13 Jan. 1891; d. Mexico City, 23 Nov. 1927. His parents were Miguel Pro and Josefa Juárez, a well-to-do, socially prominent couple. As a child, Pro was noted for his open and sympathetic nature and his firm piety. He entered the Jesuit novitiate in El Llano, Michoacán in 1911. He devoted himself fervently to the religious life, believing "that God wanted him among His saints." Because of the religious persecutions under President Carranza, he studied in Los Gatos, Calif., from 1914 to 1915. He was then sent to Spain, where he stayed until 1924 except for the years (1919–22) he taught in Granada, Nicaragua, a task that proved very difficult because of his ill health. In 1924 he went to Enghien, Belgium, for special studies in sociology and he was ordained there in 1925. He then became gravely ill. In 1926 he returned to Mexico City where public worship had ceased because of the persecutions of President Calles. Pro undertook so many religious duties that they would have exhausted even a well man. He was seized by the police on 13 November 1927 and executed with his brother Humberto ten days later amid much public uproar. Officially, he had been accused of plotting against General Obregón, but his innocence was clearly proved. Father Pro was beatified by Pope John Paul II on 25 September 1988.

Feast: 23 November.

Bibliography: A. DRAGON, *Vida intima del Padre Pro,* tr. R. MARTÍNEZ DEL CAMPO, 3d ed. (Mexico City 1961). R. MARTÍNEZ DEL CAMPO, *La prueba del Padre Pro y el proceso de su beatificación* (Mexico City 1952). F. ROYER, *Padre Pro* (New York 1954). J. CARDOSO, *Los mártires Mexicanos* (Mexico City 1953): 363–389. ANN BALL, *Blessed Miguel Pro: Twentieth-Century Mexican Martyr* (San Francisco 1996). JAVIER ESCALADA, *Miguel Agustine Pro: Alter Christus* (Mexico: Enciclopedia Guadalupana A.C., 1999). JOSEPH TYLENDA, *Jesuit Saints and Martyrs* (Chicago: Loyola University Press, 1984).

[R. RAMÍREZ TORRES]

PROTMANN, REGINA, BL.

Foundress of the Sisters of Saint Catherine (*Katharinenschwestern*); b. ca. 1552, Braunsberg, Warmia (Ermland; now Braniewo, Poland); d. there 18 January 1613; beatified in Warsaw, Poland, by John Paul II, 13 June 1999.

Regina, daughter of the merchants Peter Protmann and Regina Tingels, left her family in 1571 to serve God with two other young women, who were soon joined by others. They lived as Beguines in an inherited house and tended the sick daily in their homes. In 1583, Protmann wrote the group's ascetic rule and placed the fledgling congregation under the patronage of Saint Catherine of Alexandria. On 3 March 1583 their ministry received the approbation of Bishop Martin Kromer (ca. 1512–89) and spiritual direction from the Jesuits. Initially the Sisters of St. Catherine cared for plague victims in modern northeastern Poland. As they spread to Wormditt (1586), Heilsberg (ca. 1586), and Rössel (ca. 1593), their contemplative spirituality was combined with further active apostolates including instructing children and providing pastoral care to women. A new rule, written with the assistance of two Jesuits, was approved by the bishop and recognized by the papal nuncio (1602). Since that time the congregation has been closely associated with the Jesuits as acknowledged in the writings of Jesuit Superior General Claudius Acquaviva. The first *vita* (*Das Leben der gottseligen Jungfrau Regina Protmann,* 1623) of

Miguel Augustin Pro Juárez prepares for execution. (Catholic News Service.)

Mother Regina is presumed to have been written by her Jesuit spiritual director, Engelberg Keilert. Uncharacteristic for the period, Protmann had her spiritual daughters instructed in theology. By the time of her death, the order had 35 sisters in four convents. Regina Protmann was declared venerable, 17 December 1996, and a miracle attributed to her intercession approved, 6 April 1998.

According to Pope John Paul II, Regina Protmann "took an active part in the post-conciliar [Trent] reform of the Church, carrying out a humble work of mercy with great generosity" (beatification homily).

Feast: 18 January.

Bibliography: E. M. WERMTER, ed., *Quellen zur Geschichte der ersten Katharinenschwestern und ihrer Gründerin Regina Protmann* (Münster 1975). G. BELLGARDT, *Die Bedeutung der Kongregation der hl. Katharina für die Erziehung der Mädchen* (Berlin 1931). A. BOENIGK, *Regina Protmann und die Kongregation der Schwestern von der hl. Katharina* (Braunsberg 1933). J. GRUNENBERG, *Die Congregation der hl. Jungfrau und Märtyrin Katharina. Ihr Entstehen, ihr inneres Leben und Wirken, wie es durch den Wandel der Stifterin und durch die Satzungen der Ordenregel vorgezeichnet ist* (Braunsberg 1868; reprinted Berlin-Wilmersdorf 1961). M. TREU, *Die katholische Kirche ehrt eine Braunsberger Bürgertochter: Regina Protmann seliggesprochen* (Münster 1999).

[K. RABENSTEIN]

Upon completing her studies, she entered the same convent with their permission (1807). Renzi and her sisters were exclaustrated when the monasteries were suppressed by Napoleon before she could make her vows. From that time until 1824, Elisabetta engaged in charitable activities while living at home. Recognizing the need to provide youth with a Christian education in a society increasingly hostile to religion, she began teaching at a school for girls in Coriano near Rimini (April 1824). When Saint Maddalena Canossa declined to assume responsibility for the school and suggested that Elisabetta was the better candidate, Renzi gathered a group of women to undertake the task (1828). The association eventually became a religious congregation, approved by the Holy See, 10 December 1839, dedicated to education and care of the neglected in the villages of Romagna. Elisabetta, who was declared venerable in 1988, is buried in the chapel of the mother house at Coriano.

During the beatification ceremony for Mother Elisabetta, Pope John Paul II said that she perceived ''with prophetic insight, some of the most acute needs in the society of her day. . . . It was as if God himself had placed her close to the problems of the young girls of her land. Her rule of life was to abandon herself to God, so that he would decide the steps and times for the development of her work as he wished.''

Bibliography: *Acta Apostolicae Sedis* (1989) 764. *L'Osservatore Romano,* Eng. ed.. 10 July 1989: 4.

[K. RABENSTEIN]

REPETTO, MARIA, BL.

Sister of Our Lady of Refuge of Mount Calvary; b. 1 November 1807, Voltaggio, northern Italy; d. 5 January 1890, Genoa, Italy; beatified by John Paul II, 4 October 1981.

Maria, the eldest child of Giovanni Battista Repetto and his wife Teresa Gozzola, helped raise her siblings. Of the nine children, five girls became religious sisters and one boy, a priest. At age twenty-two Maria became a cloistered nun of Our Lady of Refuge in Genoa. There she served the community in various offices (infirmarian, laundress, laborer), but became known as a portress of unwearying charity and wisdom. She nursed the sick of Genoa through the cholera epidemics of 1835 and 1854. Revered for her holiness while she lived, her body was interred in the chapel of Our Lady of Refuge of Mount Calvary.

During Repetto's beatification, Pope John Paul II recalled her words: ''Jesus must be contemplated, loved, and served in the poor, at all moments of our life.'' Patroness of Genoa.

Feast: 5 January.

Bibliography: *Acta Apostolicae Sedis* (1982): 1100–03. *L'Osservatore Romano,* Eng. ed. 41 (1981): 1, 12.

[K. RABENSTEIN]

RICE, EDMUND IGNATIUS, BL.

Married educator, founder of the Irish Christian Brothers and the Presentation Brothers; b. 1 June 1762, near Callan (Westcourt), Co. Kilkenny, Ireland; d. 29 August 1844, at Mount Sion, Waterford; beatified 6 October 1996 by John Paul II.

The fourth of the seven sons of the wealthy farmer Robert Rice and his wife Margaret, Rice attended the Catholic school at Moat Lane, Callan, which despite the provision of the iniquitous penal laws, the authorities suffered to exist. After preparing at Kilkenny for a business career, he went to Waterford in 1778 to serve as apprentice to his uncle, Michael Rice, a successful export and import trader, and, after the latter's death, became sole proprietor. Edmund married in 1785, but his wife, Mary Elliot, died suddenly in 1789 during a hunting trip.

The death of his wife was a turning point in Rice's life. At first he thought of entering a contemplative order on the Continent or the nearby Cistercian monastery at Mellary, but his brother, an Augustinian who had but just returned from Rome, discountenanced the idea. Rice, thereupon, devoted himself to the extension of his business. Some years later, however, he again desired to become a religious, then decided that his vocation was among the oppressed, poverty-stricken, and uneducated Irish Catholics. He provided for his only daughter, and gave up his business career in order to dedicate himself to the service of God.

In 1796, he sought authorization from Pius VI to create a society to provide free education for poor boys. With papal encouragement and the permission of the bishop, Rice and three disciples opened a school in Waterford (1803). In 1809 they took vows and formed a religious society following the rule of the Presentation Sisters of Cork. This arrangement proved unsatisfactory, because each house was autonomous as to personnel and finances and subject directly to the local bishops. At the urging of Daniel Murray, then auxiliary bishop of Dublin, Rice successfully petitioned Pius VII to permit the adoption of the rule of the Christian Brothers, founded by St. John Baptist de La Salle. Rice made his religious profession once more, this time as Brother Ignatius (1821). He was then elected the first superior general of the Irish Christian Brothers.

As a citizen he was distinguished for his probity, charity, and piety; he was an active member of a society established in the city for the relief of the poor. He was known to be an intensely committed yet modest and spiritual man. Following his peaceful death, Rice was interred in the monastery cemetery (Mt. Sion) in Dublin and marked with a simple stone. Since then a chapel was erected on the site.

At Rice's beatification John Paul II called him ''an outstanding model of a true lay apostle and a deeply committed religious. The love which he first gave to his young wife and which, after her untimely death, he always showed for his daughter, blossomed into a host of spiritual and corporal works of mercy, as he helped the clergy of his parish meet the pressing needs of his fellow citizens oppressed by poverty and the weight of anti-Catholic legislation.''

Feast: 5 May.

Bibliography: *L'Osservatore Romano,* English edition, no. 27 (1996): 12–13. *A Time of Grace—School Memories: Edmund Rice and the Presentation Tradition of Education,* ed. by J. M. FEHENEY (Dublin 1996). A CHRISTIAN BROTHER, *Edmund Ignatius Rice and the Christian Brothers* (New York 1926). D. BURTON, *Edmund Rice, Merchant Adventurer* (London 1964). J. D. FITZPATRICK, *Edmund Rice* (Dublin 1945). D. KEOGH, *Edmund Rice* (Portland, Oregon 1996). D. RUSHE, *Edmund Rice: The Man and His Times* (Dublin 1981). P. R. WILSON, *Educating Street Kids: A Ministry to Young People in the Charism of Edmund Rice* (New York 1991).

[J. H. VAUGHAN]

RINALDI, FILIPPO, BL.

Salesian priest; b. 28 May 1856 at Lu near Monferrato, Piedmont, Italy; d. 5 December 1931, Turin, Italy; beatified by John Paul II, 29 April 1990.

The eighth of the nine children of the farmers Christoforo Rinaldi and Antonia Brezzi, Rinaldi attended the Salesian school at nearby Mirabello for a short time in 1866. Rinaldi became a priest because of the persistence of John Bosco, who recognized his vocation. Rinaldi began religious studies with the Salesians at Sampierdarena in spring 1877 and proved to be an outstanding student. From Sampierdarena he went to the novitiate at San Benigno Canavese (1879), where the novice master chose him as his assistant. Rinaldi pronounced his vows in 1880, then continued his studies of philosophy and theology, and was ordained priest in 1882. Immediately thereafter he was placed in charge of late vocations at Mathi (1883–88), then Turin.

Father Rinaldi was sent to Sarria, Spain (1889–92), to assist the rector. There he established schools and two new houses (Gerona and Santander), and attracted many vocations, including that of the future saint Joseph Calasanz. Thereafter he was provincial for Iberia (1892–1901), during which he set up sixteen houses in Spain and three in Portugal; founded *Lecturas Catolicas,* a weekly newspaper for youth, as well as a library for students; and fostered the expansion of the Daughters of Mary Help of Christians in Spain.

In 1901, Rinaldi returned to Turin when he was chosen prefect general, an office he held for twenty years under Rectors General Michael Rua and Paul Albera. He spurred the spiritual development and the commitment of Salesian cooperators by promoting congresses and organizing reunions of past pupils. Inspite of his other work Rinaldi was a popular confessor and spiritual director and taught regularly at the Foglizzo seminary.

On 24 May 1922, Father Rinaldi was elected the third successor of John Bosco. He directed the Salesians with perspicacity in answer to the appeal of Pope Pius XI, with special reference to the Asian and Eastern missions. He opened the Cardinal Cagliero Institute (1922 at Ivrea) to train new missionaries, and similar training centers at Penango (1925), Foglizzo (1926), Astudillo, Spain (1928), Shrigley, England (1929), and elsewhere, and fostered missionary vocations in various ways to staff the new missions in Porto Velho, Brazil (1926), Madras and Krishnagar, India (1928), Japan (1928), and Ratburi, Siam (Thailand, 1930). He also served as apostolic delegate to the Daughters of Mary Help of Christians and encouraged their expansion, as well as that of the Don Bosco Union among teachers. During his tenure as rector general, Don Bosco was beatified (2 June 1929). The order grew from 6,000 to 10,000 members during Rinaldi's tenure and added over 250 new houses. This dynamic leader of the Salesians died at age seventy-five. His cause for beatification was initiated in 1947.

In beatifying him Pope John Paul II declared: ''Don Rinaldi was an especially tireless promoter of the great Salesian family in its various groups and worked to help it develop increasingly into a worthwhile, organized, and adaptable force for Christian education of youth and of the popular classes.''

Feast: 5 December (Salesians).

Bibliography: Works: *Quaderno Carpanera,* verbali redatti da Luigina Carpanera, Documenti e testi V, Istituto Secolare Volontarie di Don Bosco (Rome 1980); *Don Rinaldi ci parla ancora* (Palermo 1984). Literature: *Lo spirito di Don Bosco nel cuore del beato Don Rinaldi,* ed. S. MAGGIO, (Turin 1990). R. ALBERDI, *Don Filippo Rinaldi en Barcelona-Sarriá (1889–92)* (Barcelona 1990). A. L'ARCO, *Il Beato Filippo Rinaldi* (Castellammare di Stabia, Italy 1990). J. M. BESLAY, *Le Pere Rinaldi* (Lyons 1950). T. BOSCO, *Profili di santità* (Turin 1977); *Die Güte Don Boscos in Person,* tr. R. DAFELMAIR (Vienna 1990). L. CÀSTANO, *Don Rinaldi. Vivente immagine di Don Bosco* (Turin 1980); *Beato Don Filippo Rinaldi* (Turin 1990). E. CERIA, *Vita del Servo di Dio Sac. Filippo*

Rinaldi terzo successore di San Giovanni Bosco (Turin 1951). M. COLLINO, *Il beato Filippo Rinaldi e l'Istituto delle Figlie di Maria Ausiliatrice* (Rome 1990). E. DAL COVOLO, *Il beato don Filippo Rinaldi, maestro di profondità interiore, testimone di vita* (Rovigo 1990). L. DALCERRI, *Un maestro di vita interiore* (Rome 1990). A. FANTOZZI, *Un uomo di fede Don Filippo Rinaldi* (Rome 1990). P. M. RINALDI, *Sospinto dall'amore* (Turin 1979, 1990); *By Love Compelled: The Life of Blessed Philip R., Third Successor of St. John Bosco* (New Rochelle, N.Y. 1992); *Droga milosci* (Krakow 1992). P. SCHINETTI, *La spiritualità di Don Filippo Rinaldi e la Volontaria di Don Bosco oggi* (Rome 1986). *Acta Apostolicae Sedis* (1990): 578.

[K. RABENSTEIN]

RIPOLL MORATA, FELIPE, BL.

Priest, martyr of the Spanish civil war; b. 14 September 1878, Teruel, Spain; d. 7 February 1939, "Can Tretze" of Pont de Molins (near Gerona), Spain; beatified at Rome by John Paul II, 1 October 1995.

Felipe, son of a poor family, was educated and ordained a priest for the diocese of his birth. He then served consecutively as professor, spiritual director, and rector of the seminary. Upon the elevation of Anselmo POLANCO to bishop of Teruel (1935), Father Ripoll was appointed his vicar general. The following year the Spanish Church experienced its most severe persecution. Undaunted, the bishop of Teruel and Father Ripoll remained with their flock. In 1938 Bishop Polanco was arrested for refusing to withdraw his name from a document signed by his brother Spanish bishops, which condemned the persecution of the Church by the Republican Army. Father Ripoll joined him in jail for thirteen months, until the Republican forces were in retreat. The two were taken as hostages and shot in a gorge near Gerona. Fr. Ripoll's body rests in the cathedral of Teruel together with those of his bishop.

Speaking of both Fr. Ripoll and Bishop Polanco, Pope John Paul II said: "Before the alternative of abandoning the requirements of the faith, or of dying for it, strengthened by God's grace, put their own destiny in his hands. The martyrs did not defend themselves, not because they thought little of life, but out of their total love of Jesus Christ" (beatification homily).

Feast: 7 February.

Bibliography: V. CÁRCEL ORTÍ, *Martires españoles del siglo XX* (Madrid 1995). J. PÉREZ DE URBEL, *Catholic Martyrs of the Spanish Civil War, 1936–1939*, tr. M. F. INGRAMS (Kansas City, Mo. 1993). *L'Osservatore Romano,* Eng. ed. 40 (1995): 1–3.

[K. RABENSTEIN]

RIVIER, MARIE-ANNE, BL.

Also known as Marinette, foundress of the Sisters of the Presentation of Mary; b. 19 December 1768, Montpezat-sous-Bauzon, France; d. 3 February 1838, Bourg-Saint-Andéol, Diocese of Viviers, France; beatified by John Paul II, 23 May 1982.

Marie-Anne Rivier, who had been crippled by a fall as a toddler, was miraculously healed through the faith of her mother and the intercession of the Blessed Virgin Mary (1774). By age eighteen, Rivier had opened a parish school, tended abandoned children, and engaged in evangelization. After the outbreak of the French Revolution, Rivier organized secret assemblies on Sundays. On 21 November 1796, the feast of the Presentation of Mary in the Temple, when the French Revolution was dissolving existing congregations, Rivier and four companions founded a community in the small village of Thueyts, Ardèche, France. With the assistance of Father Pontannier, they consecrated themselves to God and to the education of youth. Neither the Reign of Terror nor the absence of human assistance prevented them from spreading and expanding their apostolate to include adult education and, in 1814, orphanages. The motherhouse was established at Bourg-Saint-Andéol (1819). At the death of Marie-Anne Rivier, who was known for her faith, expansive joy, and courage, the congregation had 141 houses. The sisters arrived in Canada, 18 October 1853, at the invitation of the first bishop of St. Hyacinthe, Jean-Charles Prince, and began their first mission in the United States at Glens Falls, New York, in 1873.

At Rivier's beatification Pope John Paul II pointed to the many difficulties she suffered, noting: "But her life demonstrates well the power of faith in a simple, upright soul, which surrenders itself entirely to the grace of its baptism."

Bibliography: A.-C. PELLESCHI, *Une parole de feu* (Paris 1983). T. REY-MERMET, *In the Strength of Her Vision*, tr. G. DANSEREAU (Manchester, N.H. 1978). A. RICHOMME, *Marie Rivier* (Paris 1967). *Acta Apostolicae Sedis* 78 (1986): 707–710. *L'Osservatore Romano,* English edition, no. 24 (1982): 6–7.

[K. RABENSTEIN]

ROCCACASALE MARIANO DA, BL.

Baptized Domenico, Franciscan lay brother; b. 14 January 1778, Roccacasale (Aquila), Abruzzi, Italy; d. 31 May (Feast of Corpus Christi) 1866, Bellegra, Italy; beatified by John Paul II, 3 October 1999.

Mariano's life was characterized by simplicity and poverty. He was one of six children of Gabriel de Nicolantonio and Santa de Arcángelo. In tending the family flocks in the Morrone mountains as a young boy, he grew to love silence and reflection. He entered Saint Nicholas Friary at Arischia, Abruzzi, took the name Mariano (2 September 1802) and pronounced his solemn vows the following year. For twelve years he engaged in prayer and work, as a carpenter, gardener, cook, and porter, at Arischia. In 1814, Mariano asked and received permission to transfer to the more austere Saint Francis Friary at Bellegra, where he served as porter for forty years, welcoming pilgrims, other travelers, and the poor. Among those he greeted and inspired was Diego ODDI, who later became a Franciscan in the same friary. A miracle attributed to Blessed Mariano's intercession was approved by the pope, 6 April 1998, opening the way for his beatification.

Pope John Paul II, speaking about Blessed Mariano, declared: "His poor and humble life were constantly directed to his neighbor in the desire to hear and share the sufferings of each individual in order to present them later to the Lord during the long hours he spent in Eucharistic adoration. Blessed Mariano brought peace, which is God's gift, wherever he went" (beatification homily).

Feast: 30 May (Franciscans).

Bibliography: *Acta Apostolicae Sedis* 19 (1999): 965. *L'Osservatore Romano,* Eng. ed. 40 (1999): 1–3; 41 (1999): 2.

[K. RABENSTEIN]

ROCHEFORT SHIPS, MARTYRS OF, BB.

A.k.a. Martyrs of La Rochelle, 64 Priest Martyrs of the French Revolution; d. 1794; beatified by John Paul II, 1 October 1995.

In 1790, the authorities of the French Revolution passed legislation requiring all priests to swear to the Civil Constitution of the Clergy, which was intended to separate the Church of France from Rome. The following year the state considered as suspect those who would not take the oath, and began deporting them to French Guyana, South America (1792). A total of 827 priests and religious, who considered taking the oath an act of apostasy, were imprisoned to await deportation on hulk ships in the harbor of Rochefort (La Rochelle), particularly the *Deux-Associés* and the *Washington*. Departure was delayed by the British blockade of the French coast. Meanwhile conditions worsened aboard the hulks, which were previously used for storage or to house slaves, as more detainees were added. In addition to the physical hardships of hunger, thirst, and lack of sanitation was added the confiscation of all religious goods from the priests. The majority of the prisoners (542) died in captivity from maltreatment between 11 April 1794 and 7 February 1795, and were buried in the sand of Île d'Aix (226) or the Île Madame (254). The survivors testified to the heroism of some of their fellows, including these beatified as martyrs for whom there was sufficient testimony as to their manner of death.

During the beatification homily for these martyrs of the Rochefort Prison Ships, Pope John Paul II said: "They also experienced a long calvary for remaining faithful. . . . If they are dead, it is because they did all they could to affirm their close communion with Pope Pius VI. In deep moral solitude, they endeavored to maintain a spirit of prayer. 'Being in torment' (Lk 16:23) of hunger and thirst, they had not a word of hatred for their torturers. They gradually let themselves be identified with the sacrifice of Christ, which they celebrated by virtue of their ordination."

Feast: 18 August.

Adam, Louis-Armand-Joseph, OFMConv., Franciscan priest of Rouen; b. 19 December 1741; d. 13 July 1794.

Ancel, Charles-Antoine-Nicolas, C.J.M., priest; b. 11 October 1763; d. 29 July 1794.

Auriel, Antoine, pastor of Calviat, Diocese of Cahors; b. 19 April 1764; d. 16 June 1794.

Bannassat, Antoine, parish priest in Saint-Fiel, Diocese of Limoges; b. 20 May 1729; d. 18 July 1794.

Beguignot, Claude, O. Cart., Carthusian priest; b. 19 September 1736; d. 16 July 1794.

Bourdon, Jean, OFMCap, Capuchin priest; b. 3 April 1747; d. 23 August 1794.

Brigéat de Lambert, Scipion-Jérôme, deacon of the cathedral of Avranches (joined in 1854 to the Diocese of Coutances); b. 9 June 1733; d. 9 September 1794.

Brulard, Michel-Louis, O.C.D., Discalced Carmelite priest; b. 11 June 1758; d. 25 July 1794.

Brunel, Gervaise-Protase, OCist, Cistercian priest and prior of the monastery at Mortagne; b. 18 June 1744; d. 20 August 1794.

Charles, Paul-Jean, OCist, Cistercian priest, abbot of Sept-Fons Monastery, Diocese of Moulins; b. 29 December 1750; d. 25 August 1794.

Collas du Bignon, Charles-René, P.S.S., Sulpician priest, superior of the seminary in Bourges; b. 25 August 1743; d. 3 June 1794.

Conte, Noël-Hilaires le, priest from the cathedral of Bourges; b. 3 October 1765; d. 17 August 1794.

The storming of the Bastille during the French Revolution. (Hulton Getty/Archive Photos. Reproduced by Permission.)

Cordier, Jean-Nicolas, SJ, Jesuit priest; professor of theology; b. 3 December 1710, near Souilly, Lorraine, France; d. 30 September 1794, Île Madame, La Rochelle, France (age 83). Cordier joined the Jesuits at Nancy (1728), studied at the University of Pont-à-Mousson, where he received a doctorate in philosophy. He was a professor of theology at Dijon, Auxerre, Autun, Strasbourg, and Pont-à-Mousson. Later he was prefect of studies at Rheims (1757–61) and superior of the Saint-Mihiel community at Verdun (from 1761-62). Following the suppression of the Society until the suppression of all religious orders (1790), he acted as chaplain to a convent in Saint-Mihiel. The aged priest retired to Verdun, where he was arrested (28 October 1793). After a six-month imprisonment at Bar, he was taken to the *Washington* for deportation. He was the first of the prisoners to die on the Île Madame, which was used as a hospital.

Feast: 19 January.

Desgardin, Augustine-Joseph, OCist, Cistercian lay brother in Sept-Fons Monastery, Diocese of Moulins; b. 21 December 1750; d. 9 July 1794.

Dumonet, Claude, priest, Diocese of Autun; b. 1 February 1747; d. 13 September 1794.

Dumontet de Cardaillac, Florent, vicar general of the Diocese of Castres (joined in 1922 to the Diocese of Albi); b. 8 February 1749; d. 9. September 1794.

Dupas, Jacques-Morellus, priest, Diocese of Poitiers; b. 10 November 1754; d. 21 June 1794.

Duverneuil, Jean-Baptiste, O.C.D., Discalced Carmelite priest; b. 1737; d. 1 July 1794.

Faverge, Pierre-Sulpice-Christophe, F.S.C., in religion Brother Roger, Lasallian lay brother; b. 25 July 1745, Orléans, France; entered novitiate 1767; d. 12 September 1794.

François François, OFMCap, Capuchin priest; b. 17 January 1749; d. 10 August 1794.

Gabilhaud, Pierre, parish priest in Saint-Christophe, Diocese of Limoges; b. 26 July 1747; d. 13 August 1794.

Gagnot, Jacques, O.C.D., Discalced Carmelite priest; b. 9 February 1753; d. 10 September 1794.

Guillaume, Jean-Baptiste, F.S.C., in religion Brother Uldaric, Lasallian lay brother; b. 1 February 1755, Fraisans, France; entered novitiate 16 October 1785; d. 27 August 1794.

Hanus, Charles-Arnaud, deacon and canon of Ligny cathedral; Diocese of Verdun; b. 19 October 1723; d. 28 August 1794.

Hunot, François, canon of Brienon, Archdiocese of Sens; b. 12 February 1753; d. 8 October 1794.

Hunot, Jean, canon and parish priest of Brienon, Archdiocese of Sens; b. 21 September 1742; d. 9 October 1794.

Hunot, Sebastian-Loup, canon of Brienon, Archdiocese of Sens; b. 7 August 1745; d. 17 November 1794. Brother of Bl. Jean Hunot.

Huppy, Louis Wulphy, from the Diocese of Limoges; b. 1 April 1767; d. 29 August 1794.

Imbert, Joseph, SJ, Jesuit priest, apostolic vicar for the Diocese of Moulins; b. ca. 1720; Marseille, France; d. 9 June 1794 on the *Deux-Associés*. Imbert entered the Jesuits at Avignon (1748), took his first vows (1750), and was ordained (1754). Thereafter he was a teacher at Châlons-sur-Saône, Besançon, and Grenoble until the Society of Jesus was suppressed (1762). He then placed himself under the authority of the bishop of Moulins and accepted parochial responsibilities. Instead of fleeing the country during the persecution, he continued to minister covertly until his bishop was expelled and Imbert appointed apostolic vicar for the diocese. He was arrested (1793) and imprisoned locally until his deportation in early 1794 with twenty-four diocesan priests. During their several-month journey to Rochefort, Father Imbert wrote *The Priests' Marseillaise,* uplifting words to the Revolutionaries tune.

Feast: 19 January (Jesuits).

Jarrige, Barthélémy, from the Diocese of Limoges; b. 18 March 1753; d. 13 July 1794.

Jarrige, Jean-François, canon of Saint-Yrieix, Diocese of Limoges; b. 11 January 1752; d. 31 July 1794.

Jarrige, Pierre, canon of Saint-Yrieix, Diocese of Limoges; b. 19 April 1737; d. 10 August 1794.

Jean-Baptiste de Bruxelles, canon of Saint Leonard and pastor of St. Stefan's, Diocese of Limoges; b. 12 September 1734; d. 18 July 1794.

Jouffret de Bonnefont, Claude-Joseph, parish priest in Saint-Sulpice; b. 23 December 1752; d. 10 August 1794.

Juge de Saint-Martin, Jean-Joseph, canon of the cathedral of Limoges; b. 14 June 1739; d. 9 July 1794.

Labiche de Reignefort, Marcel-Gaucher, priest of the *Societas Missionarium Lemovicensium.*; b. 3 November 1751; d. 26 July 1794.

Laborier du Vivier, Jean-Baptiste, deacon and cathedral canon of Mâcon (joined in 1853 to the Diocese of Autun); b. 19 September 1734; d. 26 or 27 September 1794.

Labrouche de Laborderie, Pierre-Yrieix, canon of Auvergne, Diocese of Limoges; b. 24 May 1756; d. 1 July 1794.

Laplace, Claude, parish priest in Saint-Bonnet, Diocese of Moulins; b. 15 November 1725; d. 14 September 1794.

Lebrun, Louis-François, O.S.B., priest of the French Benedictine Congregation of Saint-Maurus (*Mauristene*); b. 9 April 1744; d. 20 August 1794.

Legroing de la Romagère, Pierre-Joseph, priest of the *Societas Navarrae* and vicar general of the Diocese of Bourges; b. 28 June 1752; d. 26 July 1794.

Leymarie de Laroche, Élie, prior of Saint-Jean, Diocese of Verdun; b. 8 January 1758; d. 22 August 1794.

Loir, Jean-Baptiste Jacques Louis Xavier, OFMCap, Capuchin priest; b. 13 March 1720; d. 19 May 1794.

Lombardie, Jacques, parish priest in St. Hilarius, Diocese of Limoges; b. 1 December 1737; d. 22 July 1794.

Marchand, Michel-Bernard, pastor of Vaurouy, Archdiocese of Rouen; b. 28 September 1749; d. 15 July 1794.

Marchandon, André-Joseph, parish priest in Marsac, Diocese of Limoges; b. 21 August 1745; d. 22 September 1794.

Mascloux, Claude-Barnabé de Laurent de, canon in Dorat, Diocese of Limoges; b. 11 June 1735; d. 7 September 1794.

Mayaudon, François, vicar general in the Diocese of Soissons; b. 4 May 1739; d. 11 September 1794.

Menestrel, Jean-Baptiste, canon of Remiremont, Diocese of Saint-Dié; b. 9 December 1748; d. 16 August 1794.

Mopinot, Jean, FSC, in religion Brother Léon, Lasallian lay brother; b. 12 September 1724, Rheims, France; entered novitiate 14 January 1744; d. 21 May 1794.

Noël, Pierre-Michel, associate pastor of Pavilly, Archdiocese of Rouen; b. 23 February 1754; d. 9 August 1794.

d'Oudinot de la Boissière, François, canon of Saint-Germain in Masseré, Diocese of Limoges; b. 3 September 1746; d. 7 September 1794.

Papon, Philippe, priest of Coutigny, Diocese of Moulins; b. 5 October 1744; d. 17 June 1794.

Pergaud, Gabriel, OSA, Augustinian priest; b. 29 October 1752, Saint-Priest-la- Plaine (Creuse), France; d. 21 July 1794.

Petiniaud de Jourgnac, Raymond, vicar general of the archdeacons of the Diocese of Limoges; b. 3 January 1747; d. 26 June 1794.

Rehm, Jean-Georges, OP, Dominican priest; b. 21 April 1752; d. 27 August 1794.

René, Georges Edme, canon of Vézelay, Archdiocese of Sens; b. 16 November 1748; d. 1 October 1794.

Retouret, Jacques, OCarm, Carmelite priest; b. 15 September 1746, Limoges, France; d. 26 August 1794, Île Madame, La Rochelle, France (age 47). Renowned as a preacher.

Richard, Claude, OSB, priest; b. 19 May 1741; d. 9 August 1794.

Savouret, Nicolas, OFMConv., Franciscan priest and spiritual director for the Poor Clares of Moulins; b. 27 February 1733; d. 14 July 1794.

Souzy, Jean-Baptiste, priest of the Diocese of La Rochelle; b. 19 November 1734, La Rochelle, France; d. 27 August 1794. He was named vicar general of the deported. He died after ten months of abuse and was buried on Madame Island.

Tabouillot, Nicolas, parish priest of Méligny-le-Grand, Diocese of Verdun; b. 16 February 1745; d. 23 February 1795.

Tiersot, Lazare, OCist, Cistercian priest; b. 29 March 1739; d. 10 August 1794.

Vernoy de Montjournal, Jean-Baptiste Ignace Pierre, canon of Notre-Dame in Moulins; b. 17 November 1736; d. 1 June 1794.

Bibliography: J. N. TYLENDA, *Jesuit Saints & Martyrs,* 2d ed. (Chicago 1998): 165–167. *Acta Apostolicae Sedis* (1995): 923–926. *L'Osservatore Romano,* no. 40 (1995): 3–5; Documentation Catholique 19 (1995): 923–26.

[K. RABENSTEIN]

ROJAS, SIMON DE, ST.

Trinitarian priest, founder of the Congregation of the Servants of the Most Sweet Name of Mary (a secular institute); b. 20 October 1552, Valladolid, Spain; d. 28 September 1624, Madrid, Spain; canonized by John Paul II, 3 July 1988.

The third of the four children of the noble Gregorio Ruiz de Navamanuel and Costanza de Rojas, Simon joined the Trinitarians at age twelve. He made his profession in Valladolid (1572) and was ordained priest upon completing his studies at Salamanca (1577). Thereafter he served the order in many capacities, including superior of the order; he became a famous preacher of missions; and, later in life, was appointed chaplain to the Spanish court of Philip III and tutor to the future King Philip IV (reigned 1621–65). He was offered, and declined, two bishoprics. His intense Marian devotion caused him to advocate for the liturgical inclusion of the feast of the Holy Name of Mary, promote the total consecration to the Blessed Mother throughout Germany and Spain, and found the Servants of the Most Sweet Name of Mary for the relief of the poor. When the priest affectionately known as ''Padre Ave Maria'' (''Father Hail Mary'') died, he was given royal honors. Although Simon was beatified in 1766, political turmoil delayed its furtherance until the twentieth century.

In canonizing Saint Simon, Pope John Paul II stated that he ''gave full meaning to his life as a Christian and a priest, in his contemplation of the mystery of the God of Love. Faithful to the redeeming and merciful charism of his Order . . . the poor saw in him their guardian, champion, and father.''

Feast: 28 September.

Bibliography: *Acta Apostolicae Sedis* (1988): 847.

[K. RABENSTEIN]

ROLAND, NICOLAS, BL.

Priest, founder of the Sisters of the Child Jesus (Holy Child) (*Soeurs du Saint-Enfant Jésus de Reims*); b. 8 December 1642, Rheims, France; d. there 26 or 27 April 1678; beatified at Rome by Pope John Paul II, 16 October 1994.

Roland was educated by the Jesuits in Rheims. When he discerned his priestly vocation, he went to Paris (1861) to study philosophy and theology. Upon returning to Rheims (1665), he was provided with a rich cathedral canonry. Roland was probably ordained in 1667 or 1668; the records were lost or destroyed during the French Revolution. Following his ordination, he went to Saint-Amand's in Rouen, where he lived in complete poverty.

Here Roland's life entwined with that of Nicolas BARRÉ, who had established the Sisters of Providence in Rouen for the education of poor girls. When Roland returned to Rheims, he was entrusted with a poorly maintained orphanage, which he transformed into a school. In 1670, Roland convinced Barré to send two women from Rouen, who were trained in his methods and acquainted with community life, to establish a similar foundation at Rheims. This became the Congregation of the Child Jesus, which provides girls with free education designed to instill Christian values in both the children and their parents. The incipient congregation attracted criticism for teaching Christian doctrine, usually reserved to the ordained; however, Roland so convinced Archbishop Maurice Le Tellier of the efficacy of the approach that schools were opened throughout Rheims. Roland also served as spiritual director to and encouraged the vocation of Jean Baptiste de la Salle.

Roland died from a fever contracted while ministering to victims of an epidemic. Before his death, he charged de la Salle with executing his last will and testament: to seek approbation for the Sisters of the Child Jesus (given 9 May 1678) and ensure the growth of the congregation. The sisters took their first vows in 1684.

At his beatification, Pope John Paul II said of Father Roland: "During his short but spiritually intense life, . . . he shared [Christ's] love for those he guided to the priesthood." He also noted Father Roland's motto: "Orphans represent us to Jesus Christ in his childhood."

Feast: 27 April (LaSallian Brothers).

Bibliography: L. AROZ, *Nicolas Roland, John Baptist de la Salle and Sisters of the Child Jesus of Reims* (Rheims 1972); *The Succession of Nicolas Roland, Canon Théologal of the Notre Dame Church of Reims* (Rheims 1995). É. RIDEAU, *Nicolas Roland, 1642–1678: hier et aujourd'hui* (Paris 1976).

[K. RABENSTEIN]

ROSAL VÁSQUEZ, MARÍA VICENTE, BL.

Baptized Vicenta, known in religion as María Encarnación del Corazón Jesús (Mary of the Incarnation of the Heart of Jesus), reformer of the Institute of Bethlehemite Sisters; first Guatemalan beata; b. 26 October 1820, Quetzaltenango, Guatemala; d. 24 August 1886, near Tulcán, Ecuador; beatified by John Paul II on 4 May 1997.

Vicenta recognized her religious vocation at age fifteen, as she reflected on the mystery of the Incarnation. On 1 January 1837, she entered the Bethlehemites, founded by Pedro de San José Betancur (1670). Distressed by the laxity of the Beatario de Belem—which drifted from its original charism—Vicenta (now Sister María Encarnación), migrated to the convent of the Catalinas. Finding that convent also unsatisfactory she returned to Belem resolved to reform it. She had her opportunity when she was elected prioress in 1855. She

revised the constitutions; the older sisters, however, refused to accept them. After her continued attempts at disciplinary reform were resisted, she founded a new *beatario* in Quetzaltenango (1861). Her devotion to the Sacred Heart led to the tradition within the order of dedicating the twenty-fifth of each month to prayers of reparation. The Bethlehemites are now active in Africa, Costa Rica, Ecuador, El Salvador, Guatemala, India, Italy, Nicaragua, Panama, Spain, the United States, and Venezuela.

While endeavoring to reform her congregation, Mother María Encarnación founded two schools in Quetzaltenango (1855). When Justo Rufino Barrios expelled various religious orders from the country (1873–85), she continued her work of reformation of the order and evangelization abroad. Arriving in Costa Rica in 1877, María Encarnación established the first women's college in Cartago, about fourteen miles from San José. She was a refuge again in 1884, when the Costa Rican government unleashed a persecution against religious groups, but returned to found an orphanage in San José (1886). She continued to Pasto, Colombia, to start a home for abandoned children. Untiring in her travels, she established the Bethlehemites in Tulcán and Otavalo, Ecuador.

On a trip from Tulcán to Otavalo, Mother María Encarnación fell from her horse and died. Her incorrupt body was translated to Pasto, where it is enshrined. After her cause for beatification was introduced, 23 April 1976, María Encarnación was declared venerable, 6 April 1995. On 17 December 1996, the decree was signed approving a miracle attributed to her intercession.

Speaking in Spanish at Mother Rosal's beatification, Pope John Paul II said: "After learning love, humility, poverty, generous surrender, and austerity in the school of the Incarnation, [María Encarnación] lived a splendid synthesis of contemplation and action."

Feast: 18 April.

[K. RABENSTEIN]

ROSAZ, EDOARDO GIUSEPPE, BL.

Bishop, secular Franciscan, founder of the Secular Franciscan Missionary Sisters of Susa; b. 15 February 1830, Susa (near Turin), Piedmont, Italy; d. there 3 May 1903; beatified in Susa by John Paul II, 14 July 1991.

Edoardo's parents were hard-working, devout refugees of the French Revolution. Because of his frailty, Edoardo was tutored at home until he was ten. He then attended the Gianotti di Saluzzo school in Turin from 1840 to 1845, until his family returned to Susa following the deaths of his father and brother. Edoardo entered the diocesan seminary in 1847, joined the Third Order of Saint Francis in 1853, and was ordained 10 June 1854. Thereafter, he dedicated himself to preaching, catechesis, social work, the ministry of reconciliation, and the spiritual direction of the Saint Joseph Sisters. His pastoral enthusiasm, which he shared with his friend John Bosco, led to Rosaz's appointment as director of Susa's seminary in 1874. Three years later (26 December 1877) he was consecrated as bishop of Susa, a position he held until his death. Immediately upon assuming the cathedra Bishop Rosaz began to renew the spirituality of the diocese, institute charitable programs, and establish educational institutions for the young. He founded the Secular Franciscan Missionary Sisters of Susa to assist with these ministries. In addition to his works, Bishop Rosaz is remembered for his pastoral zeal, dedication to the good of his clergy, his self-mortifications, and love of the poor.

Pope John Paul II recalled that Rosaz "responded to the hopes of his brothers, especially the poor, with the love of Christ's heart, without rhetoric, in a concrete way, paying personally. In order to follow the Lord, he made himself a pilgrim, a beggar, with the humility of a priest and bishop who is joyful and confident in divine providence" (beatification homily).

Feast: 3 May (Franciscans).

Bibliography: *Acta Apostolicae Sedis* (1991), 814.

[K. RABENSTEIN]

ROSCELLI, AGOSTINO, BL.

Founder of the Institute of Sisters of the Immaculata; b. 27 July 1818, Bargone di Casarza, Liguria, Italy; d. 7 May 1902, Genoa, Italy.

Agostino's family was poor, but the deep faith and peace that filled his home produced an introspective, contemplative soul open to the workings of God. He first felt called to the priesthood during a parish mission in 1835, but poverty made schooling difficult. With financial assistance, prayer, and hard work, he completed his seminary studies in Genoa and was ordained to the priesthood in 1846. He began his parish work at St. Martin d'Albaro, then in 1854 he was assigned to the Church of Consolation. In addition to spending countless hours hearing confessions and providing spiritual counsel, Roscelli established residential centers to provide moral and educational support for young women. In 1876, he founded the Institute of Sisters of the Immaculata to care for women at risk because of their poor circumstances. Beginning in 1874, he served 22 years as chaplain to the provincial orphanage, in addition to working with prisoners, especially those condemned to death.

Throughout his life Roscelli's contemplative spirit and mystical experiences spurred him to action for love of God. At the time of his beatification, 7 May 1995, Pope John Paul II said his "apostolic activity was truly fruitful because it flowed from a genuine mystical and contemplative life." The pope cited Roscelli as a special model for pastors on the World Day of Prayer for Vocations.

Bibliography: *Acta Apostolicae Sedis* (1995): 564. *L'Osservatore Romano,* English edition, no. 19 (1995).

[K. RABENSTEIN]

ROUSSEAU, SCUBILION, BL.

Baptized Jean-Bernard, catechist to slaves, Lasallian brother; b. 21 March 1797, Anny-Côte, Burgundy, France; d. 13 April 1867, Sainte-Marie, Isle de Réunion in the Indian Ocean; beatified on Réunion by John Paul II, 2 May 1989.

Eldest of the four children of Bernard Rousseau, a stone cutter, and his wife Reine Pelletier, Jean-Bernard was born during the height of the French Revolution. He received his early education from his parents, his pastor, Father Petitier, and later a tutor. When the parish school reopened (1819) following the revolution, Jean-Bernard began teaching. His success in the field, combined with his sense of religious vocation, led him to the Brothers of the Christian Schools, who had just opened a school nearby. He entered their novitiate at Paris in 1822, where he became Brother Scubilion. After teaching (1823–33) at Alençon, Poitiers, and Chinon, he was assigned (1833) with two other brothers to Bourbon (now Réunion). Here he initiated evening classes to teach slaves Christian doctrine and morality in preparation for receiving the sacraments. Following their emancipation (1848), he helped them to adapt to new freedom and responsibilities. Brother Scubilion cared for the marginalized until his death thirty-four years after his arrival on the island. A constant stream of pilgrims visits his tomb on the island, where he was immediately venerated.

When Pope John Paul II beatified this "slave to the slaves," he said Brother Scubilion "shone with a power of love that revealed the God of Love. . . . by his example and in particular by his catechesis among the slaves."

Feast: 27 September (Lasallian Brothers); 20 December (La Réunion, national holiday commemorating the abolition of slavery).

Bibliography: FRÈRE CONCORDE MARIE, *Le frère Scubilion* (St. Denis 1975). A. FERMET, *Jean-Bernard Rousseau, frère Scubilion* (Paris 1985). L. SALM, *Brother Scubilion Rousseau, FSC: Apostle of Freedom and Reconciliation* (Romeoville, Ill. 1986).

[K. RABENSTEIN]

RUBATTO, MARIA FRANCESCA, BL.

Baptized Ana Maria, a.k.a. Sister Mary Frances of Jesus; missionary of the Institute of Capuchin Sisters of Loano (of Mother Rubatto); b. 14 February 1844, Carmagnola, Italy; d. 6 August 1904, Montevideo, Uruguay; beatified by John Paul II, 10 October 1993.

After losing both her father (d. 1848) and mother (d. 1863) before she was twenty, Ana Maria Rubatto moved to Turin. Although she had little formal education, she was intellectually gifted. In the Piedmontese capital, she befriended noblewoman Marianna Scoffone, who soon became her patroness. Scoffone provided Ana Maria the time and means to teach children's catechism in several parishes, visit the sick in Cottolengo Hospital, and tend to the needs of the suffering.

Following Scoffone's death in 1882, Ana Maria discerned her true vocation. An act of charity for an injured worker brought Ana Maria to the attention of a newly forming community of women in Loano, Liguria. They recognized her as the leader for whom they were praying. She joined the sisters in Loano, Liguria, in 1885, took the name Maria Francesca of Jesus, and, under the obedience to Bishop Filippo Allegro, became their superior. The congregation quickly expanded to Genoa (1888) and San Remo (1888), Italy, and Montevideo, Uruguay (1892). They also established missions in Argentina and deep within the Brazilian rainforest. Mother Rubatto crossed the Atlantic seven times in order to be with her daughters on both sides of the ocean, opening eighteen houses in twenty years. She remained in America most of the last eight of her thirty-nine years. Mother Rubatto, known for her concrete love of the poor, was buried in Montevideo.

During Mother Rubatto's beatification, Pope John Paul II hailed her for ''having made her life a continual service to the lowliest, testifying to God's special love for children and the humble.''

Feast: 6 August.

[K. RABENSTEIN]

RUBIO Y PERALTA, JOSÉ MARÍA, BL.

Jesuit priest; b. 22 July 1864, Dalías, Almeria, Andalusia, southern Spain; d. 2 May 1929, Aranjuez, Spain; beatified in Rome, Italy, 6 October 1985 by John Paul II.

José María, the eldest of twelve children of farmers, began his studies for the priesthood in the minor seminary of Almería in 1876. He transferred to the seminary at Granada (1879), completed his training in Madrid, and

was ordained in 1887. Before teaching Latin, pastoral theology, and philosophy in the Madrid seminary for four years, he served as assistant pastor in Chinchón (1887–89) and pastor at Estremera (1889). In 1893, he became chaplain to Cistercian nuns in Madrid. On 11 October 1906, Fr. Rubio fulfilled a long held desire to become a Jesuit by entering the novitiate in Granada. Two years later he pronounced his vows and after a short time in Seville, returned to Madrid (1911), where he carried out his priestly ministry with distinction. Fr. Rubio was known for his exceptional ability as a spiritual director, as a preacher—especially on the Blessed Sacrament and the Sacred Heart of Jesus—and, late in his life, as a miracle worker. He organized a group of over 6,000 women, called the Marys of the Tabernacles, who provided and cared for altarware, linens, and vestments, and lived ascetic lives. As part of his apostolate of charity, he directed the Honor Guard of the Sacred Heart of Jesus. Its 5,000 members, like their chaplain, were devoted to corporal and spiritual works of mercy. Following his death from a heart attack while visiting the novitiate at Aranjuez, he was buried in its cemetery. In 1953, his remains were transferred to the Jesuit residence on the Calle Maldonado, Madrid.

Feast: 4 May (Jesuits).

Bibliography: P. M. LAMET, *De Madrid al cielo* (Santander, Spain 1985). J. A. DE SOBRINO, *Tres que dijeron 'si'* (Madrid 1985). J. N. TYLENDA, *Jesuit Saints & Martyrs* (Chicago 1998): 123–5. *Acta Apostolicae Sedis* 78 (1986): 971–974. *L'Osservatore Romano*, English edition, no. 42 (1985): 6–7.

[K. RABENSTEIN]

RUIZ DE LOS PAÑOS Y ANGEL, PEDRO, AND EIGHT COMPANIONS, BB.

Martyrs, Diocesan Labor Priests; Ruiz de los Paños b. 18 September 1881 at Mora, Toledo, Spain; d. 23 July 1936 at Toledo, Spain; beatified in Rome by John Paul II, 1 October 1995.

Pedro Ruiz de los Paños entered the seminary in Toledo at an early age. In 1904 he joined the Diocesan Laborer Priests, a union of priests founded in 1883 by Blessed Manuel Domingo y Sol, mostly dedicated to the formation of future priests. That same year he was sent to the Seminary of Málaga as dean of students. On 9 April 1905 he was ordained to the priesthood, and from 1905 to 1927 he served as dean of students in the seminaries of Málaga, Badajoz, and Seville. He published a number of books dealing with seminary education (including *El libro del seminarista*, *El estado sacerdotal*, and *La bon-*

dad educadora). In 1927 he was appointed rector of the Pontifical Spanish College in Rome, where he served until 1933. On 31 July 1933 he was chosen as the fourth general director of the Diocesan Laborer Priests. He continued his work in the National Secretariat of Seminaries, published the journal *Vocaciones,* and authored *Idea de la Hermandad de Sacerdotes Operarios Diocesanos.* On 16 July 1936 he went to Toledo to found a community of sisters (Discípulas de Jesús) to vocational ministry. However, two days later the Spanish Civil War began and on the morning of 23 July, he was arrested along with two other priests, and hours later they were killed on the streets of Toledo.

Eight other Diocesan Laborer priests were also killed during the Spanish Civil War. José Sala Picó (b. 24 June 1889 at Pons, Lleida) was the rector of the Minor Seminary in Toledo when he was killed with Pedro Ruiz de los Paños. Guillermo Plaza Hernández (b. 25 June 1908 at Yuncos, Toledo) was killed on 10 August 1936 at Argés, Toledo. Recaredo Centelles Abad (b. 23 May 1904 at Vall d'Uxo, Castellón) died in October 1936 after the militia men shot him twice. Martín Martinez Pascual (b. 11 November 1910 at Valdealgorfa, Teruel) had only been a priest for fourteen months when was martyred in his hometown on 18 August 1936. Antonio Perulles Estivill (b. 5 May 1992 at Cornudella, Tarragona) served in different seminaries in Spain before being killed on 12 August 1936 in Marsá. José Pascual Carda Saporta (b. 29 October 1893 at Villareal, Castellón) dedicated his life to the formation of priests in Spain and Mexico; he was killed in Villareal on 4 September 1936; Isidoro Bover Oliver (b. 2 May 1890 at Vinaros, Castellón) worked in Tortosa as the editor of *El Correo Josefino,* a magazine for seminaries, when he was killed on 2 October 1936. José Maria Peris Polo, also a musical composer (b. 1 November 1889 at Cinctorres, Castellón) died on 15 August 1936 in Alzamora, Castellón.

The process of beatification began in 1958 in two different places: Toledo and Tortosa. In 1988 they were united in a single process. At their beatification, Pope John Paul II remembered the urgency of vocational ministry and in a later audience he said: "They worked efficiently to promote and prepare priestly vocations. As exemplary educators, they did not spare any effort to prepare seminarians, guiding them personally and paying special attention to their families."

Feast: 23 July.

Bibliography: JUAN DE ANDRÉS, *Testigos de su sacerdocio* (Madrid: Atenas, 1990).

[RUTILIO J. DEL RIEGO]

SAGHEDDU, MARIA GABRIELLA, BL.

Also called Maria Gabriella of Unity; Trappistine nun; b. 17 March 1914, Dorgali, Sardinia, Italy; d. 23 April 1939, in Grottaferrata, Frascati; beatified by John Paul II on 25 June 1983.

After the death of her sister, Maria Gabriella became a young woman of prayer and charity, enrolling in Catholic Action, teaching catechism, and tending the aged. At twenty-one, she entered the monastery of Grottaferrata, then headed by Mother Pia Gullini. After her profession (1937) her life was marked by gratitude for her calling to religious life and a desire to submit completely to God's will. When the community was asked to pray for Christian unity, Maria Gabriella immediately undertook the task and offered her life as an oblation. After three and one-half years of religious life, she died after contracting tuberculosis. Her body rests in the monastery chapel of Vitorchiano (Viterbo), to which the community of Grottaferrata was transferred. The beatification of Sister Maria Gabriella ended the Week of Prayers for Christian unity (1983) and was attended by representatives of the Anglican, Lutheran, and Orthodox churches.

Pope John Paul II later wrote that he set her before the faithful because "she devoted her life to meditation and prayer centered on Chapter 17 of St. John's Gospel and offered her life for Christian unity. This is truly the cornerstone of all prayer: the total and unconditional offering of one's life to the Father, through the Son, in the Holy Spirit. The example of Sister Maria Gabriella is instructive; it helps us to understand that there are no special times, situations or places of prayer for unity. Christ's prayer to the Father is offered as a model for everyone, always and everywhere." (*Ut unum sint,* no. 27).

Feast: 22 April.

Bibliography: *L'Osservatore Romano,* Eng. ed. 5 (1983): 5–6. P. CUSACK, *Blessed Gabriella of Unity: A Patron for the Ecumenical Movement* (Portland, Oregon 1995). M. DRISCOLL, *A Silent Herald of Unity* (Kalamazoo, Mich. 1990). P. B. QUATTROCCHI, *A Life for Unity: Sr. Maria Gabriella,* tr. M. JEREMIAH (Brooklyn, NY 1990).

[K. RABENSTEIN]

SALA, MARIA ANNA, BL.

Religious of the Congregation of St. Marcellina; b. 21 April 1829, Brivio, Italy; d. 24 November 1891, Milan, Lombardy, Italy; beatified by John Paul II, 26 October 1980.

Maria Anna's parents, Giovanni and Giovannina Sala, sent her to school with Marcelline Sisters at Vimercate. However, she returned home to assist her ailing mother. At age twenty-one, circumstances enabled Sala to join the Marcellines, who staff hospitals, conduct social work, and engage in missionary activities. Following her novitiate and profession in 1852, she dedicated her life to teaching at Cernusco, Chambéry, Genoa, and Milan. Diagnosed with malignant throat cancer in 1883, Sister Maria Anna continued forming young girls into women of character, commitment, and obedience until died.

Pope John Paul II praised Sala for silent suffering in union with that of Christ.

Feast: 24 November.

Bibliography: M. FERRAGATTA, *Visse per le anime, vita della serva di Dio suor Maria Anna Sala* (Milan 1963). *Acta Apostolicae Sedis* 73 (1981): 532–534. *L'Osservatore Romano,* English edition, no. 44 (1980): 10–11.

[K. RABENSTEIN]

SALAWA, ANIELA (ANGELA), BL.

Domestic servant, Franciscan tertiary; b. 9 September 1881, Siepraw (near Krakow), Poland; d. 12 March 1922, Krakow, Poland; beatified by John Paul II, 13 August 1991, in the Market Square at Krakow.

Raised in a family of modest means, Aniela Salawa entered domestic service in Krakow at age sixteen (1897). Following the death of her sister Teresa (1899), Aniela was moved to dedicate her life to God. Thereafter she exercised an active apostolate among other servants in the city and fed her spiritual life through prayer, while never neglecting her duty to her employers. She joined the Third Order of Saint Francis in 1912, following the deaths of her mother and her mistress in 1911. During World War I, Aniela comforted wounded soldiers in Krakow's hospitals during her free time. After falling seriously ill in 1917, Aniela was forced into retirement. In the five years before her death at age forty, she offered her continual pain to God in expiation of sins and for the conversion of sinners.

Pope John Paul II said Blessed Aniela "showed an extraordinary responsiveness to the action of the Holy Spirit" (beatification homily).

Feast: 12 March.

Bibliography: I. BORKIEWICZ, *Aniela Salawa: opowiadania o zyciu* (Warsaw 1987). J. STABINSKA, *Charyzmat sluzby: zycie Anieli Salawy* (Warsaw 1988); *Z nadmiaru milosci: zycie wewnetrzne Anieli Salawy* (Warsaw 1987). A. WOJTCZAK, *Aniela Salawa* (Warsaw 1983).

[K. RABENSTEIN]

SALLÉS Y BARANGUERAS, MARÍA DEL CARMEN, BL.

Baptized Carmen Francisca Rosa, known in religion as Mary of Mount Carmel, foundress of the Conceptionist Missionary Teaching Sisters (*Concepcionistas Misioneras de la Enseñanza*); b. 9 April 1848, Vich near Barcelona, Catalonia, Spain; d. 25 July 1911, Madrid, Spain; beatified by John Paul II, 15 March 1998.

Daughter of José Sallés and Francisca Rosa Barangueras, Carmen studied pedagogy at *La Enseñanaza* school run by the Company of Mary, and began teaching young woman following her graduation. Combining the Dominican ideals of contemplation and action, she founded the Missionary Teaching Sisters of the Immaculate Conception (1892) to witness to the Blessed Mother in the secular world and form young Christians. Before her death, the congregation operated thirteen schools, including one in Brazil (opened in 1911). The Conceptionist Missionaries have since expanded to twelve countries. María del Carmen was declared venerable 17 December 1996, and a miracle attributed to her intercession was approved on 18 December 1997.

At her beatification, Pope John Paul II remarked that her "Christocentric and Marian spirituality was nourished by solid and sensible piety."

Bibliography: *Acta Apostolicae Sedis* 8 (1998): 399.

[K. RABENSTEIN]

SALVI, LORENZO MARIA, BL.

Known in religion as Lorenzo Maria of Saint Francis Xavier, Passionist priest; b. 30 October 1782, Rome, Italy; d. 12 June 1856, Capranica (near Viterbo), Italy; beatified by John Paul II, 1 October 1989.

The son of Antonio Salvi, steward to the counts of Carpegna, and Marianna Biondi, Lorenzo was raised in the faith. Salvi studied at the Jesuit Pontifical Gregorian University. After professing his vows as a Passionist (1802) and being ordained (1805), he participated in the governance of communities and the province. Salvi was a popular preacher and spiritual advisor and promoted devotion to the Infant Jesus by word and example. Dominic Barbieri, who had lived with Salvi, sought the superior general's permission to send Salvi to England because of the strength of his preaching and his leadership ability within the Passionist community. Permission was denied. Following his death Salvi was enshrined at Sant'Angelo di Vetralla.

Pope John Paul II declared Salvi "a man of God, not only in intense prayer, but also in untiring dedication to the priestly ministry" (beatification homily).

Feast: 12 June.

Bibliography: A. LIPPI, *Il beato Lorenzo Salvi: apostolo di Gesù bambino,* 2d ed., (Torino 1989). *Acta Apostolicae Sedis* (1989): 1030.

[K. RABENSTEIN]

SAN VITORES, DIEGO LUIS DE, BL.

Jesuit missionary priest, martyr; b. 12 November 1627, Burgos, Spain; d. 2 April 1672, at Tomhon Beach, Agana, Guam; beatified by John Paul II, 6 October 1985.

Born into the Spanish nobility, Diego attended the Imperial College, Madrid, and was raised in the royal court. From age eleven, Diego wanted to join the Society of Jesus and become a missionary despite his parents' hope that he would aspire to a political career. He entered the novitiate of the Jesuits at Villarejo de Fuentes in 1640, completed his studies at Huete and Alcalá de Henares, and was ordained in 1651. Thereafter he taught at Oropesa, Madrid, and Alcalá de Henares (1655), where he also undertook a ministry to the sick and gave parish missions. Given permission to go to the Philippines, Diego sailed via Mexico, where he landed at Veracruz (28 July 1660). Unable to secure passage to the Orient, he conducted missions and evangelized in the streets of Mexico City. After finally reaching Manila (10 July 1662), he studied Tagalog while serving as university dean and master of novices. In his spare time he engaged in missionary work in the interior of Luzon and on Mindoro Island.

With the permission of King Philip IV of Spain (reigned 1621–65), Diego sailed back to Mexico City to obtained permission and funds for a mission to the Ladrones Islands, renamed in 1668 to Marianas Islands in honor of the regent Mariana of Asturia. The missionaries left Acapulco, Mexico, on 23 March 1668, and arrived at the archipelago on 15 June 1668. The missionaries learned and adopted local customs, and converted some 50,000 people on Saipan, Tinian, and Guam, including High Chief Quipuha (Kepuha), whose clan provided the land for the basilica built in 1669. Diego also compiled a grammar and vocabulary of the *lingua Mariana,* opened two seminaries, and erected eight churches before the mission was beset with problems.

Prompted by false rumors spread about Christianity, some of the new converts abandoned the faith and others became hostile. These heightened suspicions and societal changes led to the martrydom of Diego and his catechist Pedro Calungsod. Influenced by this hostile climate, Chief Matapang did not consent to the baptism of his infant daughter—requested by his wife who did not other-

wise need his permission—and became irate at Diego and Calungsod. With his companion, Hirao, Matapang brutally attacked the priest and the catechist and threw them into the ocean tied to rocks. A memorial now stands on the site of their martyrdom.

Feast: 6 October (Jesuits).

Bibliography: *L'Osservatore Romano,* Eng. ed. 42 (1985): 6–7. *Father San Vitores, His Life, Times, and Martyrdom,* ed. E. G. JOHNSTON (Agana, Guam 1979). F. GARCÍA, *Sanvitores in the Marianas,* tr. F. PLAZA (Mangilao, Guam 1980). A. DEL LEDESMA, *Mission in the Marianas: An Account of Father Diego Luis de Sanvítores and His Companions, 1669–1670,* tr. WARD BARRETT of *Noticia de los progressos de nuestra Santa Fe, en las Islas Marianas . . . desde 15 de mayo de 1669* (Minneapolis 1975). P. MURILLO VELARDE, *The ''Reducción'' of the Islands of the Ladrones, the Discovery of the Islands of the Palaos, and Other Happenings,* tr. F. E. PLAZA (Mangilao, Guam 1987). F. PLAZA, *Sanvitores, bibliografía de las materias existentes en el Micronesian Area Research Center* (Agana, Guam 1975). A. RISCO, *The Apostle of the Marianas: The Life, Labors, and Martyrdom of Ven. Diego Luis de San Vitores,* tr. J. M. H. LEDESMA, ed. O. L. CALVO (Agana, Guam 1970). J. A. DE SOBRINO, *Tres que dijeron 'si'* (Madrid 1985). J. N. TYLENDA, *Jesuit Saints & Martyrs* (Chicago 1998): 337–339.

[K. RABENSTEIN]

SANCHO DE GUERRA, MARÍA JOSEFA DEL CORAZÓN DE JESÚS, BL.

Professed religious, co-foundress of the Servants of Jesus of Charity; b. 7 September 1842, Vitoria, Spain; d. 20 March 1912, Bilbao, Spain; beatified by John Paul II, 27 September 1992.

María's poor, pious family provided her a Christian education and contributed to the recognition of her religious vocation. She entered the Servants of Mary in 1864 and worked in the poorest districts of Madrid. In 1865 she helped plague victims without consideration for her own health and safety. She left the congregation with two other sisters to found (25 July 1871) in Bilbao, Spain, a new congregation—the Servants of Jesus of Charity—to serve the indigent and sick in hospitals, clinics, sanitariums, retirement homes, and daycare centers. At the time of her death the congregation had expanded to forty-one houses in Spain and one in Chile. Pope John Paul II declared Mother María Josefa venerable in 1989.

At her beatification he said: ''She founded the Servants of Jesus of Charity, entrusting to them the mission of finding the face of Christ in so many brothers and sisters, alone and sick, and soothing them with the oil of fraternal love.'' A second miracle attributed to her intercession was approved 28 June 1999, and her canonization was scheduled for 1 October 2000.

Feast: 18 May.

Bibliography: P. BILBAO ARÍSTEGUI, *La Beata María Josefa Sancho de Guerra: una vida al servicio de los enfermos* (Vitoria, Spain 1992). *Acta Apostolicae Sedis* (1992): 919.

[K. RABENSTEIN]

SANTAMARIA, GRIMOALDO OF THE PURIFICATION, BL.

Baptized Ferdinando, Passionist seminarian; b. 4 May 1883, Pontecorvo, Frosinone, Italy; d. 18 November 1902, Santa Maria di Corniano Abbey near Cecceano, Frosinone, Italy; beatified in Rome by John Paul II, 29 January 1995.

Ferdinando, the eldest of five, demonstrated his attraction to spiritual matters from an early age. At eight, he was serving regularly at Mass; the following year he joined in the religious exercises of the Congregation of the Immaculata; and, at twelve, he was catechizing his peers. He joined the Passionists at Pugliano, 5 March 1899, after attending retreats directed by the fathers. In 1900, he was professed with the name Grimoaldo, patron of his hometown, and began his seminary studies at Santa Maria di Corniano near Cecceano. The youth, known for his joy, died of acute meningitis before ordination. On 2 July 1994, a miracle attributed to Grimoaldo's intercession was approved, leading the way to his beatification.

During the ceremony, Pope John Paul II summarized Grimoaldo's spirituality as inspired by a few basic ideas: ''to give God priority, to show Jesus Crucified constant gratitude by concrete works of penance and humility; to persevere in goodness even at the cost of great sacrifice; to live with austerity and be content at all times: to be always available to others.''

Feast: 18 November.

Bibliography: PASSIONIST MISSIONARIES, *Curved Bridge to Calvary* (Union City, N.J. 1996). *Acta Apostolicae Sedis,* no. 5 (1995): 249. *L'Osservatore Romano,* English edition, no. 6 (1995): 3.

[K. RABENSTEIN]

SARKANDER, JOHN, ST.

Martyr of the seal of confession; b. Skoczów (Skotschau), Austrian Silesia, 20 December 1576; d. Olomouc (Olmütz), Moravia, 17 March 1620.

He attended Jesuit schools at Olmütz and Prague, where he completed his course of philosophy (1603). In 1606 he interrupted his course in theology to marry Anna Platska, a Lutheran, but his wife's death the following year strengthened his resolve to become a priest. Following his ordination (1609) he undertook pastoral ministry in the diocese of Olmütz.

After Baron Ladislaus Lobkovič (Lobkowitz) bought the estates of Holešov (Holleschau), Moravia, previously in the control of the Bohemian Brethren, he returned the church to the Catholics. Cardinal Franz von Dietrichstein appointed Sarkander pastor in 1616. Lobkovič also established a Jesuit College, formerly occupied by the Bohemian Brethren. The many converts made by Sarkander and the Jesuits increased the rivalry between the Baron and his anti-Catholic neighbors, especially Bitovsky of Bystrzyca (Bystritz). At the beginning of the Thirty Years' War (1618–1648) the Protestants seized power in Moravia. Sarkander made a pilgrimage to the Polish shrine of Our Lady of Częstochowa and remained in Cracow for some months before returning to his parish. In 1620 Sigismund III, King of Poland, sent Cossacks into Moravia to support Emperor Ferdinand II in his struggle with the Protestant Estates. They pillaged Protestant lands but spared Holešov when they met Sarkander carrying the Blessed Sacrament. Bitovsky accused him of conspiracy with the Poles, and imprisoned him while awaiting questioning. At his trial Sarkander denied any treasonable acts and defied his judges, who, in an attempt to implicate Lobkovič, demanded that he reveal confessional secrets. Sarkander was tortured for several days and a month later he died in prison. Sarkander was venerated as a martyr immediately afterward. The Silesian bishops opened his case for sainthood under Benedict XIV, and Pius IX beatified him on 6 May 1860. Sarkander's relics are in an altar dedicated to his name in the cathedral of Olmomouc. He is the patron of Moravia and Silesia.

On May 21, 1995, during his sixty-fourth international pastoral visit, John Paul II canonized at Olomouc's airport Zdislava Berka and Jan Sarkander, drawing sharp criticism from Czech and Slovakian Protestants. During the homily he said: ''Perhaps today more than ever . . . we are able to grasp the mysterious message of Jan Sarkander for the Church in Europe and the world. His canonization first of all gives honor to all those in this century, not only in Moravia and Bohemia but throughout Eastern Europe, who preferred the loss of property, marginalization and death, rather than submit to oppression and violence.''

Feast: 17 March.

Bibliography: BIRKOWSKY, *Positio super martyrio. . . .* (Rome 1825). F. LIVERANI, *Della vita e della passione del ven. servo di Dio, Giovanni Sarcander* (Rome 1855). F. SEIBT, ''Sarkander, Johannes,'' *Lexikon für Theologie und Kirche,* 2d. ed. 9: 330. C. TESTORE, ''Sarcander, Giovanni,'' *Enciclopedia cattolica,* 10: 1926–27.

[F. J. LADOWICZ]

SARNELLI, GENNARO MARIA, BL.

Januarius; lawyer, ascetical writer, Redemptorist priest; b. 12 September 1702, Naples, Italy; d. there, 30 June 1744; beatified 12 May 1996.

The fourth son of Baron Angelo Sarnelli of Ciorani, Gennaro was inspired at age 14 by the beatification of John Francis Regis to become a Jesuit himself. His father persuaded him instead to study canon and civil law, in which he earned a doctorate (1722). He succeeded admirably in the legal profession, while daily Mass, visits to the Blessed Sacrament, and attendance on the sick in the hospital of incurables filled his free time. He abandoned the bar at age 26, entered the seminary in 1728, and was assigned to catechize children at St. Anne di Palazzo parish. In 1730 he entered the novitiate in the Congregation of the Apostolic Missions, a society of secular missionary preachers. Throughout his seminary training he continued his catechetical work with children, visited the elderly in the Hospice of San Gennaro, and ministered to sick sailors. During this period he and Alphonsus Ligouri became friends and together organized the Evening Chapels (*cappelle serotine*), an association of workers and artisans formed for the purpose of mutual assistance, religious instruction, and works of apostolic zeal.

After his ordination in 1732, he served as director of religious education at a poor parish in the Spanish quarter of Naples, where he found employment for poor women to keep them out of prostitution. The year after Alphonsus's founding of the Congregation of the Most Holy Redeemer (9 Nov. 1732), Sarnelli defended his friend against unjust criticism and in June of that year joined him in Salerno. They gave missions together along the coast of Amalfi until Sarnelli's health failed. In April 1736, he officially entered the Redemptorists in Naples. Once his health improved he began a successful written crusade in defense of young girls in danger, again undertook missions, and promoted meditation in common among the laity until his precarious health forced him into retirement in April 1744.

Sarnelli composed 30 major works on various legal, pedagogical, and theological topics, including *Il Mondo santificato*, 2 v. (Naples 1738); *Il Mondo riformato* (Naples 1739); *Le glorie e grandezze della divina Madre* (Naples 1739); *Il Cristiano santificato* (Naples 1739); *L'Anima illuminata*, 3 v. (Naples 1740); *L'Anima desolata* (Naples 1740); *Discrezione degli spiriti* (Naples 1741); *L'Ecclesiastico santificato* (Naples 1741). In his spiritual works he insists that meditation is essential for perseverance and within reach of all Christians. His writings in this area occasioned Benedict XIV's granting an indulgence for meditation (16 Dec. 1746).

Sarnelli died at age 42 in the presence of his friend St. Alphonsus Ligouri, who reported that Sarnelli's body exuded the odor of sanctity that "remained in the room long after his interment." An urn containing his relics can be found in the Redemptorist church at Ciorani, S. Antonio a Tarsia.

At Sarnelli's beatification, Pope John Paul II said: "The new blessed never neglected to seek fresh forms of evangelization to respond to new challenges. . . . An example of an apostle who was open to accepting every useful innovation for a more penetrating proclamation of the eternal message of salvation."

Feast: 30 June (Redemptorists).

Bibliography: *Riproduzione di tutte le opere*, 14 v. (Naples 1848–55). A. M. DE' LIGUORI, *Compendio della vita del servo di Dio G. M. S.* (Naples 1752). *Neapolit. beatificationis et canonizationis p. J. M. S. positio* (Rome 1889). *Acta Apostolicae Sedis*, no.12 (1996): 551–53. *L'Osservatore Romano*, English edition, no. 11 (1996): 1–2. R. GIOVINE, *Vita del gran servo di Dio p. G. M. S.* (Naples 1858). F. DUMORTIER, *Le vénérable serviteur de Dieu, le p. J. M. S.* (Paris 1886). M. DE MEULEMEESTER, *Bibliographie générale des écrivains rédemptoristes*, v. 2 (Löwen 1935), 373–377; v. 3 (Löwen 1939), 379. G. SPARANO, *Memorie istoriche per illustrare . . . gli atti della Congregazione delle Apostoliche Missioni* (Naples 1768), 2:345ff. H. F.G. SWANSTON, *Saint Alphonsus and His Brothers: A Study of the Lives and Works of Seven Redemptorists* (Liguori, Missouri 2000).

[K. RABENSTEIN]

SATELLICO, ELISABETTA MARIA, BL.

Known in religion as Maria Crucifixa (Mary Crucified), Poor Clare abbess; b. 31 December 1706, Venice, Italy; d. 8 November 1745, at Ostra Vetere, Italy; beatified at Rome by John Paul II, 10 October 1993.

Elisabetta and her parents, Piero Satellico and Lucia Mander, lived with her maternal uncle, a priest who early encouraged her gifts for music and prayer. She studied under the Poor Clares at Ostra Vetere, where she sang and played the organ. In 1726, she received the religious habit there and took the name Maria Crucifixa. She undertook penances in order to become more like Jesus Crucified. She was elected abbess and employed her mystical gifts for the benefit of the community. Upon her death at age thirty-nine, she was buried in Santa Lucia, Ostra Vetere. The cause for her canonization was opened shortly after her death.

Pope John Paul II said that Mother Maria Crucifixa configured her life "to him who for love of humanity let himself be nailed to the Cross."

Feast: 8 November (Franciscans).

Bibliography: G. B. SCARAMELLI, *Vita di Suor Maria Crocifissa Satellico monaca Francescana nel monastero di Monte*

Nuovo, 5th ed. (Rome 1819). This work was originally published in Venice in 1750.

[K. RABENSTEIN]

SCALABRINI, GIOVANNI BATTISTA (JOHN THE BAPTIST), BL.

Bishop of Piacenza, "father of migrants," founder of the Congregation of the Missionaries of Saint Charles (Scalabrinians) and the Missionary Sisters of St. Charles Borromeo; b. 8 July 1839, at Fino Mornasco (near Como), northern Italy; d. 1 June 1905, at Piacenza, Italy.

On the Feast of the Dedication of St. John Lateran (9 November) 1997, the pope's cathedral church, John Paul II beatified Scalabrini and recalled his repeated saying: "Would that I could sanctify myself and all the souls entrusted to me!" The Holy Father continued: "Out of his love for the poor, particularly for emigrants, he became apostle of his many compatriots compelled to leave their country, often under difficult conditions and in concrete danger of losing their faith: for them he was a father and sure guide."

He was the third of the eight sons of Luigi Scalabrini, a wine merchant, and his wife Colomba Trombetta, a religious couple of modest means. After ordination (30 May 1863) he was a professor of History and Greek at St. Abundius Seminary in Como (where he had studied), and then rector (1867–70). As pastor of one of the largest parishes in Como (San Bartolomeo) he was distinguished for his solicitude for the working class as well as for his forward thinking on political, social, and economic matters. His published conferences on Vatican Council I brought him to the attention of Pius IX, who named him bishop of Piacenza (1875). As bishop he distinguished himself by frequent visitations of all 365 parishes and diocesan synods. In his eagerness to reorganize catechetical teaching throughout Italy, he instituted the first National Catechetical Congress at Piacenza. Pius IX referred to him as the "Apostle of the Catechism."

Unlike many churchmen, he was open-minded on the "Roman Question," which dominated the relations between church and state in Italy in the last part of the nineteenth and early twentieth century. It asked: should the lands of central Italy remain under the political control of the Church as they had since the Middle Ages, or should they become part of a united Italy? At Leo XIII's request he outlined possible approaches and solutions to the Roman Question in a memorandum which labeled as ruinous the policy of urging Catholics to refrain from participating in secular politics in protest against the Italian government's confiscation of the papal states.

To assist the huge number of Italians emigrating to various parts of the world, he founded the Scalabrinians (28 Nov. 1887) with Fr. Joseph and Mother Assunta Marchetti, and promoted the work of the congregation by journeying in 1901 and 1904 to North and South America. With the same aim, he convinced St. Frances Xavier Cabrini to travel to America (1889), founded (25 Oct. 1895) the Missionary Sisters of St. Charles Borromeo, and co-founded the Missionary Zelatrices of the Sacred Heart. To provide material and social aid to emigrants he established (1889) the lay Society of St. Raphael. Among his other charitable activities, he founded an institute to help mutual aid societies, rural banks, cooperatives and women who were hearing and speech impaired.

He encouraged frequent Communion and Perpetual Adoration. He also had a deep devotion to the Blessed Mother that he expressed in homilies and Marian pilgrimages. His heroic charity was demonstrated during a cholera epidemic and the fact that he sold everything he had, including his horse and pectoral cross to care for the poor. He died on the Solemnity of the Ascension saying: "Lord, I am ready. Let us go." His mortal remains are venerated in the cathedral of Piacenza. Scalabrini's cause for beatification was introduced by Bishop Menzani at Piacenza in June 1936. On 16 March 1987, Pope John Paul II promulgated a decree recognizing him as venerable, the first step to sainthood. The miracle required for his beatification was approved 7 July 1997.

John Paul II praised Scalabrini: "Deeply in love with God and extraordinarily devoted to the Eucharist, he knew how to translate the contemplation of God and his mystery into intense apostolic and missionary activity."

Feast: 1 June.

Bibliography: Sources for the study of Blessed John Baptist Scalabrini: *For the Love of Immigrants: Migration Writings and Letters of Bishop John Baptist Scalabrini,* ed. by S. M. TOMASI (New York 1999). *La Societá italiana di fronte alle prime migrazioni di massa* (New York 1975). Records of the Congregation of the Missionaries of St. Charles (Scalabrians), v. 8 of *A Guide to the Archives,* ed. N. FALCO (New York 1988). Literature about Blessed John Baptist Scalabrini: *L'Osservatore Romano,* English edition, no. 46 (1997): 1–3. M. CALIARO and M. FRANCESCONI, *John Baptist Scalabrini, Apostle to Emigrants,* tr. A. I. ZIZZAMIA (New York 1977). I. FELICI, *Father to the Immigrants, the Servant of God,* tr. C. DELLA CHIESO (New York 1955). M. FRANCESCONI, *Giovanni Battista Scalabrini, vescovo di Piacenza e degli emigrati* (Rome 1985); *Giovanni Battista Scalabrini. Spiritualità d'incarnazione* (Rome 1989). F. GREGORI, *La vita e l'opera di un grande vescovo, Giovanni Battista Scalabrini* (Turin 1934). G. LANDI, *Un vescovo e la legge sull'emigrazione* (Milan 1986). T. DE ROSA, *Bishop John Baptist Scalabrini, Father to the Migrants* (Darien, Conn. 1987). G. SARAGGI, *Giovanni Battista Scalabrini. Vescovo insigne e padre degli emigrati* (Cinisello Balsamo 1986). L. M. SIGNOR, *John Baptist Scalabrini and Italian Migration: A Socio-Pastoral Project* (New York 1994).

[L. SABATINI]

SCHÄFFER, ANNA, BL.

Lay mystic; Franciscan tertiary; b. 18 February 1882, Mindelstetten (between Regensburg and Ingolstadt), Bavaria, Germany; d. there on 5 October 1925; beatified by John Paul II, 7 March 1999.

Anna Schäffer was one of many children of a carpenter. Offering her life to God for the welfare of others, she began working in Regensburg to help support her family, although she had hoped to become a missionary sister. Following the death of her father (1896), she worked in Landshut, then in the laundry at Stammham, where on 4 February 1901 an industrial accident left nineteen-year-old Anna immersed in a tub of boiling bleach. After a year in the hospital, she was discharged (May 1902) because the specialists were unable to heal her wounds. She was virtually bedridden for the next 25 years. With disability came poverty. In time her anger turned to understanding that her suffering could be united with that of the Crucified Christ and offered as a sacrifice for others. Her confessor, Father Karl Rieger, said that he never heard Anna Schäffer complain during the twenty-five years he brought Communion to her daily. From spring 1910 she had many mystical experiences. She related that God gave her three keys with which she opened heaven's gates: her suffering, her sewing needle, and a pen. In her beautiful embroidery for churches, Anna would illustrate the Sacred Heart with the flames bent inward like a head of wheat. She used this symbol often on the letters she wrote to those seeking her prayers or counsel in Austria, Switzerland, and America. Anna suffered greatly in her last days. Soon after her death, her tomb in the churchyard at Mindelstetten became a popular pilgrimage destination. After her relics were identified and transferred into the church (26 July 1972), the diocesan process for her beatification was opened (1973). She was declared venerable in 1995.

Pope John Paul II noted during Anna's beatification that "between atrocious pains she became aware of the responsibility every Christian has for the salvation of his neighbor. . . . Her bedside became the cradle of a wide apostolate through correspondence."

Feast: 5 October.

Bibliography: *Acta Apostolicae Sedis* (1999): 310–12. *L'Osservatore Romano,* no. 10 (1999): 1–2. *L'Osservatore Romano,* English edition, no. 29 (1995): 5.

[K. RABENSTEIN]

SCHERER, MARIA THERESIA, BL.

Baptized Anna Maria Katharina, co-foundress of the Sisters of Mercy of the Holy Cross; b. 31 October 1825, Meggen (near Lucerne), Switzerland; d. 16 June 1888, Ingenbohl, Switzerland; beatified 29 October 1995.

Maria Theresia Scherer was seven years old when her father died, and she was placed in the care of two uncles, who provided her with a Christian education. A conscientious child, she began working in hospitals at age sixteen. Following a pilgrimage to Einsiedeln, she recognized her vocation and joined the Teaching Sisters of the Holy Cross, or Menzingen Sisters, an order founded in 1844 by Theodosius Florentini (1808–65). After teaching in three different parochial schools, and in an industrial school, she became superior of the congregation's first hospital (1852). Out of this institute developed the Sisters of Mercy of the Holy Cross, or Ingenbohl Sisters, founded in 1856 by Florentini to care for the poor, aged, and sick in their homes or in hospitals, and to train children mentally or physically handicapped. Maria Theresia, generally considered as cofoundress, was one of the first members. As the first superior general (1857–88), she was noted for her energy, sacrifice of self, and ability as organizer and administrator. Despite many material difficulties, she established and directed houses in her native land, in Germanic and Austrian-Hungarian territories, and in Rome. Throughout the growth of the Ingenbohl Sisters she retained her motto: "No work of Christian love of neighbor may be considered beyond the scope of this institute." At the time of her death (1888) following a prolonged, painful illness, her order had become one of the largest religious congregations.

In his homily at the beatification Pope John Paul II spoke of Scherer: "Through her life and work she reminds us of the essential place of the mystery of the Cross, . . . [that] raises the whole universe to Christ. . . . After becoming aware of the sufferings and lot of the sick, she resolved to dedicate her life to the Lord as a religious . . . so that she was eventually known as the 'mother of the poor.' She agreed to forsake her educational work, which gave her so much joy, in order to obey the will of God."

Feast: 16 June.

Bibliography: V. GADIENT, *Die Dienerin Gottes, Mutter M. Theresia Scherer* (Basel 1954). W. HEIM, *Briefe zum Himmel. Die Grabbriefe an Mutter M. Theresia Scherer in Ingenbohl* (Basel 1961). E. MARTIRE, *Madre M. Teresa Scherer* (Rome 1947). C. RUTISHAUSER, *Mutter Maria Theresia Scherer: Leben und Werk* (Ingenbohl, Switz. 1959), Fr. tr. R. M. MERMOD (Paris 1964). M. G. SECCHI, *Suor Maria Teresa Scherer e i suoi tempi* (Milan 1959).

[A. KUNZ]

SCHININA, MARIA OF THE SACRED HEART, BL.

Cofoundress of the Sisters of the Sacred Heart of Jesus; b. 10 April 1844, Ragusa, Sicily, Italy; d. there 11 June 1910; beatified by John Paul II, 4 November 1990.

Born into the nobility of Sicily, Maria received a good education and Christian upbringing from her parents. In 1860, Maria shocked her peers by recruiting several companions to work with her to relieve the suffering of prisoners of war and the peasantry tormented by the *Risorgimento*. With the approval of the bishop of Syracuse, Maria and five companions formed (1885) the Sisters of the Sacred Heart of Jesus to serve a variety of apostolates among orphaned girls, the elderly, the infirm, and prisoners. She also aided other religious institutes, such as the Ladies of Charity and the Carmelites, by providing a home when they were forced from their convents due to political unrest, financed seminaries, and sponsored educational programs. All in need received help from the Sacred Heart sisters.

According to the Pope John Paul II, Maria of the Sacred Heart responded to God's love by emphasizing "contemplation, adoration, and reparation" (beatification homily).

Bibliography: *Acta Apostolicae Sedis* (1990): 1091.

[K. RABENSTEIN]

SCHUSTER, ALFREDO ILDEFONSO, BL.

Cardinal archbishop of Milan, Cassinese Benedictine, liturgist; b. 18 Jan. 1880, Rome, Italy; d. 30 August 1954, at Venegono Seminary near Milan, Italy.

Although his father Johannes (d. 1888), a tailor in Rome, was born in Bavaria, and his pious mother Anna Maria (Tutzer) came from Bolzano in the Austrian South Tyrol, Alfredo Ludovico Schuster grew up a thorough Roman. He was accepted as a Benedictine monk by the Roman Abbey of St. Paul-outside-the-Walls (1891; age 11) and given the name Ildefonso; he made his monastic profession on 13 November 1899. After priestly studies at Sant'Anselmo, Rome, he was ordained on 19 March 1904. He then developed into a model religious, thanks in large measure to the counsel of his saintly confrère (Bl.) Placido Riccardi, O.S.B. Schuster served his abbey as master of novices (1904–16) and as prior (1916–18). From 1914 to 1929 he was procurator-general of the Benedictine Cassinese Congregation. On April 6, 1918, he was elected abbot-ordinary of the abbey *nullius* of St. Paul-outside-the-Walls.

Ildefhonso Alfredo Cardinal Schuster shown as he presided at the starting of building of the Church of Santa Rita in Milan, Italy. (© Bettmann/CORBIS)

Recognizing his talents, the popes gave him various assignments, including consultorships on the Congregation of Rites (Liturgy, Causes of Saints) and the Congregation for the Oriental Church. Additionally, he was censor of the Academy of Sacred Liturgy, president of the Commission for Sacred Art and Apostolic Visitator for Italian seminaries. Pius XI named him archbishop of Milan on 26 June 1929, created him cardinal priest of SS. Silvestro e Martino ai Monti on 15 July 1929, and personally consecrated him on 21 July 1929. The frail ascetic, with a spirit worthy of a successor of St. Charles Borromeo and St. Ambrose, embarked upon a tireless episcopal career notable for both its liturgical emphasis and its contemporary pastoral awareness. He emphasized catechetics and promoted the role of the laity in parishes and in Catholic Action. During the German military occupation of Lombardy (1943–45), the cardinal gave his flock strong and provident guidance, and the advice to surrender that he gave to the German commandant in 1945 had a decisive influence.

From 1938 on Schuster had stood firm against the racist views and other "Germanizations" of Italian Fascism. Prior to that, however, he had shown public benevolence toward the Fascist regime, to the particular chagrin of many Catholics in other lands. Whether rightly or wrongly—and he was content to let history judge—he had chosen this course for pastoral, not political, reasons. He also interpreted strictly the pledge of loyalty that he, before his consecration, had made to the king, pursuant to art. 20 of the Lateran Concordat of 1929. He was the first Italian prelate to be affected by that rule. Had he not maintained his punctilious personal concern for Mussolini, he might never have had that last interview of 25 April 1945, at which he urged the dictator to make peace with God and man. Unfortunately, Mussolini spurned the admonition, to his own quick disaster.

Although his spirituality is best characterized by his intense prayer life; his opposition to racism was simply a manifestation of his egalitarian spirit: He believed that the goal of all Christians is holiness. He worked toward this ideal by seeking justice during and after World War II and founding the Institute of Ambrosian Chant and Sacred Music to inspire the faithful through beautiful liturgy. Schuster also won great esteem as a liturgical and monastic historian. During his lifetime he wrote many scholarly articles and several books. Among the books were *Storia di San Benedetto e dei suoi tempi* (Viboldone 1943), which was translated into English as *St. Benedict and His Times* (St. Louis 1951), and the classic *Liber Sacramentorum* (9 v. Turin 1919–29). The latter, a most influential work, has been translated into several languages [Eng. ed., *The Sacramentary: Historical and Liturgical Notes on the Roman Missal* (5 v. New York 1925–31)].

Having tended his flock through nine turbulent postwar years, Schuster died in 1954 with a reputation for high sanctity. He was entombed in the metropolitan cathedral of Milan. The diocesan process for his canonization was initiated in 1957 by his successor, Giovanni Battista Montini, who became Pope Paul VI. A miracle attributed to his intercession was approved on 11 July 1995.

During Schuster's beatification on 12 May 1996, Pope John Paul II observed: "Schuster's pastoral ministry was motivated by the spirit of prayer and contemplation proper to the Benedictine tradition. His monastic spirituality, nourished by daily meditation on Sacred Scripture, thus expanded into active collaboration with the Holy See and into his generous service to the Ambrosian community, edified and consoled by him until the very end by the regular, devoted celebration of the sacred mysteries and by the example of a clear and consistent life" (Ambrosian Missal, Preface of the Memorial).

Feast: 30 August.

See Also: LATERAN PACTS

Bibliography: *L'Osservatore Romano,* English edition. no. 29 (1995): 5. *L'epistolario card. Schuster-don Calabria,* ed A. MAJO and L. PIOVAN (Milan 1989). *Scritti del Cardinale A. Ildefonso Schuster,* ed. G. OGGIONI (Varese 1959); *Gli ultimi tempi di un regime,* 2d ed. (Milan 1946). *Ildefonso Schuster: Cenni biografici* (Viboldone 1958). G. BASADONNA, *Cardinal Schuster. Un monaco vescovo nella dinamica Milano* (Milan 1996). D. A. BINCHY, *Church and State in Fascist Italy* (New York 1941). A. M. BOZZONE, "Schuster, A.I.," in Mercati-Pelzer, eds., *Dizionario ecclesiastico,* 3:756. E. CAVATERRA, *Salvate Milano! La mediazione del cardinale Schuster nel 1945* (Milan 1995). G. JUDICA CORDIGLIA, *Il mio Cardinale* (Milan 1955); *Così sorrideva il Cardinale Schuster* (Milan 1957). A. M. FORTUNA, *Incontro all'Archivescovado* (Florence 1971). A. MAJO, *Gli anni difficili dell'episcopato del card. A. I. Schuster* (Milan 1978); *Schuster: una vita per Milano* (Milan 1994); with G. RUMI, *Il cardinal Schuster e il suo tempo* (Milan 1979).

[R. F. MC NAMARA]

SCHWARTZ, ANTON MARIA, BL.

Piarist priest, founder of the Catholic Association of Apprentices *Katholischer Lehringsverein* and the Congregation of Christian Workers of St. Joseph Calasanz (*Kalasantiners*), apostle to working men; b. 28 February 1852, Baden (near Vienna), Austria; d. 15 September 1929, Vienna; beatified in Vienna's Heldenplatz by John Paul II, 21 June 1998.

The ministry of Anton Schwartz was shaped by his early life growing up in a large, working-class family. He was the fourth of thirteen children of a theater musician. While attending secondary school in Vienna, Anton sang at the Heiligenkreuz. He joined the Piarists at Krems (1869), but left when the prevailing *Kulturkampf* threatened the suppression of religious orders. After completing his studies in philosophy and theology at the diocesan seminary in Vienna, he was ordained (1875). His first assignment was as chaplain in Marchegg (1875–79); he was then appointed chaplain at the Daughters of Charity hospital at Vienna-Sechshaus, where he witnessed the suffering of young workers. In 1882, Schwartz became the "apostle of social justice" for working men decades before Pope Leo XIII issued the encyclical *Rerum Novarum*. Recognizing that no organization within the Church focused on the problems experienced by apprentices and young workers, Schwartz established an association in Vienna to educate them and advocate for their rights. Thereafter, he founded the Kalasantiners (24 November 1889) with four confreres to serve working-class men just days after the consecration of the first church built by Schwartz for workers (17 November 1889). The order of priests and brothers follows a modified Piarist Rule. They teach religion and practical skills, operate oratories, offer social services for workers, and diffuse literature, including Father Schwartz's prayer book for workers, biographies, and the monthly *Saint Calasanctius-Blätter* (since 1888). The order's constitutions were approved by the Vatican in 1939. Schwartz fought against exploitation by appealing to Christian ethics, advocated for compensation for overtime and free time on Sundays for worship, and defended the right to organize. In 1908, he withdrew from all public controversy, but continued his quiet assistance.

Anton Maria Schwartz was declared venerable by John Paul II (6 April 1995), who noted during the beatification ceremony that Schwartz was "sensitive to the needs of apprentices and workers, who frequently lacked support and guidance."

Bibliography: J. BRUCKNER, *Der Wiener Arbeiterapostel P. A. M. S.* (Vienna 1934). A. INNERKOFLER, *Anton Maria Schwartz* (Vienna 1931). F. ZIMMERMANN, *Die ersten 25 Jahre der Calasantiner-Congregation* (Vienna 1914). *Acta Apostolicae Sedis* (1998): 690.

[K. RABENSTEIN]

SCROSOPPI, LUIGI, BL.

A.k.a. Luigi of Udine, Oratorian priest, founder of the Sisters of Divine Providence (*Suore della Provvidenza*); b. 4 August 1804, Udine, Italy; d. there 3 April 1884; beatified by John Paul II, 4 October 1981.

Following Luigi's ordination in 1827, he immediately began an apostolate to tend the poor and abandoned by establishing the *Casa delle Derelitte*. Additionally, he founded the *Casa Provedimento* for the formation of young women and the *Opere* for deaf-mute girls. He formed the women who assisted him in his charitable work into the Sisters of Divine Providence, and placed them under the patronage of Saint Cajetan. The sisters continue to educate young girls in Argentina (since 1929), Bolivia (1980), Brazil (1927), India (1977), Italy (1837), Ivory Coast (1973), Romania (1992), Togo (1985), Uruguay (1929). Scrosoppi, known for his exceptional charity and prayer life, gave his family fortune to the poor and joined the Oratorians before he died at the venerable age of eighty. A second miracle attributed to his intercession was approved 1 July 2000, opening the way for his canonization.

Feast: 5 October.

Bibliography: *Acta Apostolicae Sedis* (1982): 534–37. *L'Osservatore Romano*, Eng. ed. 41 (1981): 1,12. G. BIASUTTI, *Tutto di Gesù!* (Udine, Italy 1968).

[K. RABENSTEIN]

SEELOS, FRANCIS XAVIER, BL.

Redemptorist missionary priest; b. 11 January 1819, Füssen, Bavaria, Germany; d. 4 October 1867, New Orleans, Louisiana, U.S.A.; beatified by John Paul II, 9 April 2000, St. Peter's Square, Rome.

The sixth of the twelve children of Mang Seelos, weaver and parish sacristan, and his wife Frances Schwarzenbach, Seelos spent six years at St. Stephen's Gymnasium, Augsburg, and three more at the University of Munich, Germany. He immigrated to America to join the Redemptorists in April 1843. He was professed 10 May 1844, ordained 22 December 1844, and he served at St. James, in Baltimore, Md., until August 1845. He was transferred then to St. Philomena's, in Pittsburgh, Pa., where he shared the rectory with St. John Neumann, his spiritual director, whom he succeeded as pastor (1851). During nine years there, as subject, master of novices, and rector, he won the highest praise from people, priests, and bishop. After three years as rector of St. Alphonsus, Baltimore, he became prefect of students and rector of the Redemptorist seminary at Cumberland, Md. (1857). When Bp. Michael O'Connor of Pittsburgh sought to have him named as his successor (1860), Seelos himself wrote to Pius IX to discourage the appointment. In 1862 the Civil War forced the seminary to move to Annapolis, Md., where Seelos cared for military and civilian victims of the conflict. From 1863 to 1865 he was superior of the Redemptorist missionary band, laboring with them from New England to Illinois. In September 1866, after nine months as an assistant at Old St. Mary's in Detroit, Mich., he went to New Orleans, where he died a year later of yellow fever contracted while making sick calls. He was enshrined in the sanctuary of St. Mary's Assumption, New Orleans, next to Brother Wenceslaus Neumann, St. John Neumann's brother.

At the beatification, Pope John Paul II declared that Seelos "sustained by God's grace and an intense life of prayer, . . . committed himself generously and joyfully to the missionary apostolate among immigrant communities in the United States. . . . Today [he] invites the members of the Church to deepen their union with Christ in the Sacraments of Penance and the Eucharist."

Feast: 5 October (Redemptorists).

Bibliography: B. BECK, *Goldenes Jubiläum des Wirkens der Redemptoristenväter an der St. Philomena Kirche in Pittsburg und Umgegend* (Ilchester, Md. 1889): 158–159, 192–211. M. J. CURLEY, *Cheerful Ascetic: The Life of Francis Xavier Seelos, C.SS.R* (New Orleans 1969); "The Nomination of Francis X. Seelos for the See of Pittsburgh," *Spicilegium Historicum Congregationis SSmi Redemptoris* 11 (1963): 166–181. W. GRANGELL, *Seelos and Sanctity. The 12 Monthly Virtues* (New Orleans 1968–69). C. W. HOEGERL & A. VON STAMWITZ, *A Life of Blessed Francis Xavier Seelos, Redemptorist* (Liguori, Mo 2000). J. SCHLEINKOFER, *Leben des ehrw. Dieners Gottes P. Franz Seelos aus der Congregation des allerheiligsten Erlösers* (Innsbruck 1901). A. VON STAMWITZ & C. W. HOEGERL, *Blessed Francis Xavier Seelos, Redemptorist* (Liguori,

Junípero Serra. (Library of Congress.)

Mo. 2000). P. ZIMMER, *Leben und Wirken des Hochwürdigen P. Franz Xaver Seelos* (New York 1887).

[M. J. CURLEY/EDS.]

SERRA, JUNÍPERO, BL.

Founder of Franciscan missions of California; b. Petra de Mallorca, Spain, 24 November 1713; d. Carmel, Calif., 28 August 1784; beatified 25 September 1988 by Pope John Paul II. His parents, Antonio Nadal and Margarita Rosa (Ferrer) Serra, were farmers. José Miguel, as he was baptized, joined the Franciscan Order in Palma de Mallorca, 14 September 1730, taking the name Junípero. Even before his ordination (1738), he was assigned to teach philosophy in his province. Later he received his doctorate in theology from Lullian University, Palma, and in 1743 was appointed to the Duns Scotus chair of philosophy there. In 1749 he sailed for Mexico to enter the Apostolic College of San Fernando, Mexico City. En route he preached his first American mission at San Juan, Puerto Rico. From 1750 to 1758, he worked successfully in the missions of the Sierra Gorda, built the central mission of Santiago de Jalpan, supervised the mission district for three years as president, and learned the Otomí language. In 1752 he was appointed commissary of the Holy

Office of the Inquisition. After returning to Mexico City in 1758, Serra was employed for the next nine years in administrative offices at the Apostolic College and as a missionary in the dioceses of Mexico, Puebla, Oaxaca, Valladolid, and Guadalajara.

In 1767, when the Spanish government exiled the Jesuits, Serra was designated *presidente* (administrator) of the Baja California missions, with headquarters at Loreto. When the conquest of Alta California was undertaken by Spain in 1769, Serra accompanied the military expedition under Don Gaspas de Portolá to San Diego where he founded his first mission in the territory on 16 July. In June 1770 he established his permanent headquarters at San Carlos Mission at Monterey-Carmel. Under his administration nine missions were founded in Alta California where Junípero served as *presidente* until his death. These missions were San Diego, San Carlos Borromeo (1770), San Antonio (1771), San Gabriel (1771), San Luis Obispo (1772), San Francisco (1776), San Juan Capistrano (1776), Santa Clara (1777), and San Buenaventura (1782).

In his California foundations, Serra insisted on the full activation of the Spanish mission system, which had been in use for several centuries. Frequent conflicts with the military and civil authorities over their treatment of Indians prompted him, in 1773, to present a *Representación* of thirty-two points for the better conduct of mission affairs to Viceroy Bucareli in Mexico City. Serra visited all the missions a number of times, administering the sacrament of confirmation after 1778. Contrary to legend, he did not travel exclusively by foot. Though he walked thousands of miles during his misson career, he did at times travel by packet boat, carriage, or mule, at times accompanied by a military guard or an Indian page.

The writings of Serra, confined almost exclusively to mission affairs, varied from factual reports to commentary that afford insight into his character. Though fundamentally robust, he suffered from an ulcerated leg and foot during his years in Mexico and California. His apostolate was characterized by a devotion to the Indians that resulted in over 6,000 baptisms and 5,000 confirmations, and in a marked improvement in their standards of living. Under his administration, agriculture and domestic animals, as well as European trades, were introduced to the indigenous peoples of California.

After his death, Junípero Serra was buried with military and naval honors in the sanctuary of San Carlos Mission, Carmel; his remains were identified in 1943. Since the middle of the 19th century, the literature on Serra has reached great proportions in both Europe and America. Many monuments and memorials have been erected in his honor. The most significant distinction came in 1931 when his statue was placed in the Statuary Hall in the Capitol at Washington, D.C. His cause was opened in 1934 at the request of the bishop of Monterey-Fresno and of the Franciscan provincial of the Province of St. Barbara.

Feast: 1 July.

Bibliography: Z. ENGELHARDT, *The Missions and Missionaries of California*, 4 v. (San Francisco 1908–15). F. PALÓU, *Life of Fray Junipero Serra*, tr. and annotated M. J. GEIGER (Washington 1953). M. J. GEIGER and F. WEBER, *The Life and Times of Fray Junipero Serra*, rev. ed. (Los Osos, Calif. 1989). M.N.L. COUVE DE MURVILLE, *The Man Who Founded California: The life of blessed Junipero Serra* (San Francisco 2000). *Escritos de Fray Junípero Serra*, ed. P. SALUSTIANO VICEDO (Mallorca 1984). M. HABIG, *Junípero Serra* (Chicago, Ill.1987) E. LOARCA CASTILLO, *Fray Junípero Serra y sus misiones barrocas del siglo XVIII: Sierra Gorda de Querétaro* (Mexico 1983).

[M. GEIGER/T. RUSCIN/F. WEBER]

SIEDLISKA, FRANCISZKA, BL.

In religion, Mary of Jesus the Good Shepherd; foundress of the Sisters of the Holy Family of Nazareth (Congregatio Sororum Sacrae Familiae de Nazareth [CSFN]); b. 12 November 1842, Roszkowa Wola, Poland; d. 21 November 1902, Rome; beatified by Pope John Paul II, 23 April 1989.

Frances Siedliska was born into a noble family; yet as a child she was gifted with a deep spiritual sensitivity that grew into an intense longing for God. She realized her call to religious life at age twelve, but her father was deeply disappointed by her rejection of the family's wealth and social status. She struggled courageously with his disapproval and her own poor health before finally fulfilling her vocation to become a nun at age thirty in 1872.

Siedliska's first spiritual advisor, Leander Lendzian, OFMCap, recognized the uniqueness of her vision and discerned that she was called to establish a new religious community. In 1875 she founded the Sisters of the Holy Family of Nazareth in Rome. She discovered within the Holy Family the perfect model for loving surrender to God. Committed to extending the reign of God's love on earth through ministry to families, she and her sisters established twenty-nine foundations across Europe and the United States before her death in 1902.

After authenticating a miracle attributed to her intercession, Pope John Paul II beatified Frances Siedliska in 1989, upholding Blessed Mary of Jesus the Good Shepherd as one who had consecrated her life to emulating the love of Jesus, Mary, and Joseph.

Feast: 21 November.

Bibliography: F. SIEDLISKA, *Autobiography* (preface by M. T. JASIONOWICZ, trans. M. P. KRASOWSKI) (Pittsburgh 1997). K. BURTON, *Where There is Love: The Life of Mother Mary Frances Siedliska of Jesus the Good Shepherd* (New York 1951). M. MICHAEL GECEWICZ, *Love Finds a Way: The Life of Mother Mary of Jesus the Good Shepherd,* illustrated by M. RITA KOBIEROWSKA (Philadelphia 1986). M. DECHANTAL, *Out of Nazareth: A Centenary of the Sisters of the Holy Family of Nazareth in Service of the Church,* foreword by JOHN CARDINAL KROL (New York 1974). A. RICCIARDI, *His Will Alone: The Life of Mother Mary of Jesus the Good Shepherd,* trans. R. N. BARWIG (Oshkosh, Wisc. 1970). M. I. STRZALKOWSKA, *Blessed Mary of Jesus the Good Shepherd Frances Siedliska,* trans. M. J. BASIEWICZ, M. R. BRADLEY et al. (Rome 1989). M. I. STRZALKOWSKA, *For Me to Live is Christ,* trans. M. P. KRASOWSKI, illustrated by G. DE SILVA (Pittsburgh 1995).

[LISA V. MIKOLAJEK]

SILVESTRELLI, BERNARD MARIA OF JESUS, BL.

Baptized Cesare, Passionist priest; b. 7 November 1831, Rome, Italy; d. there 9 December 1911, in Morricone Monastery; beatified by John Paul II, 16 October 1988.

Cesare was born into Roman nobility, the third of the seven children of Gian Tommasso and Teresa Silvestrelli. Cesare attended Jesuit schools, including the Collegio Romano. Although he entered the Passionist novitiate on Monte Argentaro (1854), he was forced to leave because of ill health. He continued his studies and was ordained a secular priest (1855). Four months later he asked and was given permission to re-enter the Passionists at Morrovalle, where he was given the name Bernard Maria of Jesus (28 April 1857) and studied with St. Gabriel Possenti.

Following the completion of his studies, Father Bernard Maria served the Passionists in various capacities: novice master (1865–69) and rector of the new Scala Santa (''Holy Stairs'') monastery next to the Lateran (1869–75); provincial consultator (1875–76); and viceprovincial (1876–78). Silvestrelli was elected and reelected superior general (1878–84, 1884–89, 1893–99, 1899–1905, 1905–07) and instituted a number of reforms within the order. To maintain the order's ideals, he published the *vitae* of the companions of St. Paul of the Cross. Additionally, he established preparatory schools to form future candidates for the novitiate. As superior general, he expanded the congregation into Spain, Mexico, and Latin America, established a novitiate in Bulgaria, and founded the international house of studies at Saints John and Paul in Rome. Silvestrelli visited all the Passionist provinces, including those in northern Europe, Spain, and, in 1896, the United States to better understand the difficulties pursuant to Passionist life in these localities. He was a man known for his prudence, gentleness, and charity.

During the beatification ceremony, Pope John Paul II praised Silvestrelli for remaining "steadfast in the profession of faith with exemplary strength and generosity."

Feast: 9 December (Passionists).

Bibliography: F. GIORGINI, *Bernardo Maria Silvestrelli Passionista* (Rome 1988); English tr. P. ROGERS (Rome 1990). F. G. ZICCHETTI, *Padre Bernardo M. Silvestrelli Passionista* (Recanati 1988).

[K. RABENSTEIN]

SIMON DE LONGPRÉ, MARIE CATHERINE OF ST. AUGUSTINE, BL.

Baptized Catherine, virgin of the Hospitallers of Mercy of St. Augustine; b. 13 May 1632, Saint-Sauveur le Vicomte, France; d. 8 May 1668, Québec, Canada; beatified at Rome by John Paul II, 23 April 1989.

Catherine's vocation was awakened by her grandparents, who lovingly tended the sick and poor in their own home. She joined a new order of Augustinian hospitaller sisters and received the habit, 24 October 1646, the same day her biological sister pronounced her vows. Marie Catherine made her own vows on 4 May 1648. The two sisters were among the first to respond to the call for women religious to minister in New France (now Canada). Marie Catherine set sail the day before her sixteenth birthday. Despite the hardships of colonial life, the young sister remained cheerful as she cooked for and tended the sick, sharing with them her medical knowledge and spiritual wisdom. Before her death at thirty-six, she was novice mistress for her community (1665–68).

Pope John Paul II praised Sister Marie Catherine's ability to be "ceaselessly present to God" and her generosity "in fulfilling her important responsibilities" (beatification homily).

Feast: 8 May (Canada).

Bibliography: G. BOUCHER, *Dieu et Satan dans la vie de Catherine de Saint-Augustin, 1632-1668* (Tournai 1979). A. MERLAUD, *L'épopée fantastique d'une jeune Normande: Catherine de Longpré* (Paris 1981).

[K. RABENSTEIN]

SISTERS OF CHRISTIAN DOCTRINE, MARTYRS OF, BB.

Angeles Lloret Martí and companions; religious of the Institute of Sisters of Christian Doctrine; d. Paterna, Valencia, Spain, September–November 1936; beatified 1 October 1995 by Pope John Paul II.

The third decade of the twentieth century in Spain was characterized by a social and political turmoil and antagonism toward the Catholic Church. The Sisters of the Institute of Christian Doctrine, founded by Mother Micaela Grau in 1880, devoted themselves to teaching catechism even in the midst of the difficult political climate. Dedicated to evangelization, the sisters followed the poor Christ by living in poverty and working arduously hard to alleviate the anguish of the poor.

While some of the sisters had been able to take refuge with their relatives, others who had no families, the elderly sisters, and their caretakers remained in the Mother House. The sisters who remained kept correspondence with the dispersed sisters during years 1931 to 1936, which intensified in the latter months. These letters witness that they were conscious of the events happening and the imminent danger. They kept faith and mutually encouraged one another. On 19 July 1936 they were forced to abandon the Mother House in Valencia. They remained a community led by Mother Angeles de San José and supported one another. Mother Amparo Rosat and Sister María del Calvario were executed on 26 September 1936, having been incarcerated at Carlet. During the month preceding their death, the sisters continued to trust in God and do works of charity, even knitting jerseys for their captors. On 20 November 1936 a bus came to collect the sisters, ultimately taking them to their death. They are:

Angeles (Francisca D.H. Lloret Martí), superior general; b. Villajoyosa, Alicante, 16 January 1875.

María del Safragio (Antonia María del Sufragio Orts Baldó); b. Altea, Alicante, 9 February 1888; vicar general and novice mistress.

María de Montserrat (María Dolores Llimona Planas), b. Molins de Rey, Barcelona, 2 November 1860; superior general from 1892 to 1931; advisor general in 1936.

María Teresa de San José (Ascensión Duart y Roig); b. Benifayó, Valencia, 20 May 1876; novice mistress and local superior of the Generalate when the revolution broke out.

Isabel (Isabel Ferrer Sabriá); b. Vilanova y la Geltrú, Barcelona, 15 Nov. 1852. Inspired by the ideals of the foundress Mother Micaela, she collaborated in the foundation of the Institute.

Amparo (Teresa Rosat Balasch); b. Mislata, Valencia, 15 Oct. 1873. Superior of the Colegio de Carlet, Valencia; martyred with María del Calvario on 26 September in the station at Llosa de Ranes, Valencia.

María de la Asunción (Josefa Mangoché Homs).; b. Ulldecona, Tarragona, 12 July 1859.

María Concepción (Emilia Martí Lacal); b. Carlet, Valencia, 9 Nov. 1861.

María Gracia (Paula de San Antonio); b. Valencia, 1 June1869.

Corazón de Jesús (María Purificación Gómez Vives); b. Valencia, 6 Feb.1881.

María del Socorro (Teresa Jiménez Baldoví); b. San Martín de Provençal, Barcelona, 13 March 1885.

María Dolores (Gertrudis Suris Brusola.); b. Barcelona, 17 January 1899.

Ignacia del Santísimo Sacramento (Josefa Pascual Pallardó); b. Valencia, 1862.

María del Calvario (Josefa Romero Clariana); b. Carlet, Valencia, 11 April 1871.

María del Rosario (Catalina Calpe Ibáñez); b. Sueca, Valencia, 25 Nov. 1855.

María de la Paz (María Isabel López García); b. Turía, Valencia, 12 August 1885.

Marcela de Santo Tomás (Aurea Navarro); b. Provincia de Albacete; a novice.

[AMPARO ROS]

SLOMŠEK, ANTON MARTIN, BL.

Slovenian archbishop, educator, writer, poet; b. 26 Nov. 1800, Slom, Ponikva, Lower Styria, Slovenia; d. 24 Sept. 1862, Maribor, Slovenia.

Born into a prosperous peasant family and received his secondary education in Celje (Zilli in Old Austria, now Slovenia), Ljubljana, and Senj, Slomšek finished his theological studies in the Carinthian capital of Klagenfurt and was ordained (1824). He ministered in two Slovene parishes in Styria and was appointed (1829) spiritual director at the theological seminary in Klagenfurt, where he also taught the Slovene language. In 1846, he became archbishop of the Lavant Valley (Carinthia), but in 1859 was transferred to Maribor (or Marburg, as the Austrian Germans called it) in the Slovene part of Styria. Slomšek was devoted to raising the cultural and moral level of the Slovene population. Schools were in a precarious state because of the Austrian suppression of the national language and the introduction of foreign teachers. Slovenian literature was forbidden out of fear of Panslavism. Following the adoption of the Constitution of 1848, granting national rights, he helped to found many schools, in which he also taught. His most important work, however, was the founding (1851-52) of the St. Hermagoras Society (*Druzba svetega Mohorja*), whose aim was to distribute inexpensive and good books among the people.

Working as a Christian moralist and educational author, he published in 1834 *Keršansko devištvo* (*Christian*

Charity). In the same lucid Slovene prose (the best of the period) was the educational narrative *Blaže in Nežica v nedeljski šoli* (1842, *Little Blase and Agnes in the Sunday School*), as well as essays and other books on a great variety of subjects. In 1846, he began the educational weekly *Drobtinice* (*Crumbs*), designed to serve village priests and teachers. In 1849, his collection of sermons, *Apostolska Hrana* (*Apostolic Food*), appeared. Slomšek was also, although less prominently, a poet. As a young priest of 26 he translated Schiller's *Das Lied von der Glocke*, and in 1833 was responsible for a collection of Slovene folk songs sung in Carinthia and Styria. His own poems are didactic, serene, and close to the style and rhythm of folk song. Although Slomšek was a zealous nationalist, his humility, childlike simplicity, and kindness won the admiration of foreigners.

Pope John Paul II beatified Slomšek on 19 September 1999, at Maribor, Slovenia. The pope praised Slomšek, the first Slovenian to be beatified, for his work of evangelization and his ecumenical efforts.

Feast: 24 September.

Bibliography: A. SLOMŠEK, *Zbrani spisi*, 5 v. (Celje 1876–90), collected works; *Izbrani spisi za mladino* (Celje 1924), selected works for youth. J. AMBROZIC, *Pastorale familiare di Mons. Anton Martin Slomsek* (Rome 1981). V. HABJAN, *Anton Martin Slomsek* (Ljubljana 1992). S. JANEZIC, *Slomsek in nas cas* (Maribor 1992). M. KLUN, *Fürstbischof Anton Martin Slomsek in Kärnten* (Klagenfurt 1969). F. KOSAR, *Anton M. Slomšek, Fürstbischof von Lavant* (Marburg 1863). F. KOVACIC, *Sluzabnik bozji A. M. Slomšek*, 2 v. (Celje 1934–35). D. MEDVED, *Knezoškof Lavantinski A. M. Slomšek* (Cakovec 1900). J. POGACNIK, *Kulturni pomen Slomskovega dela* (Maribor 1991). B. ZAVRNIK, *Anton Martin Slomsek* (Ljubljani 1990).

[J. LAVRIN/K. RABENSTEIN]

SMALDONE, FILIPPO MARIANO, BL.

Priest, cofounder of the Congregation of the Salesian Sisters of the Sacred Hearts (*Congregazione delle Suore Salesiane dei Sacri Cuori*); b. 27 July 1848, Naples, Sicily, Italy; d. 4 June 1923, Lecce, Apulia, Italy; beatified by John Paul II, 16 August 1996.

The eldest of the seven children of Antonio Smaldone and Maria Concetta de Luca, Filippo had decided by age 12 to become a priest, despite the persecution the Church was experiencing. He entered the minor seminary in Rossano Calabria (1862). His specific apostolate was determined while he was still a student following an encounter with the mother of a deaf-mute child in Saint Catherine's Church in Naples. From that time he evangelized and taught deaf-mutes. Overcoming some difficulties that required his transfer to the archdiocese of

Naples, Smaldone was ordained in 1871. While ministering to plague victims, Smaldone contracted the disease but was miraculously healed through the intercession of Our Lady of Pompeii. Frustrated by his inability to help deaf-mutes sufficiently, Smaldone considered undertaking a foreign mission; however, his spiritual director convinced him to recommit himself to his apostolate in Naples. On 25 March 1885, Smaldone cofounded an institute in Lecce with Father Lorenzo Apicella and some specially trained Grey Sisters, who became Salesian Sisters of the Sacred Heart dedicated to the education of deaf-mutes. Other institutes followed for deaf-mutes in Bari (1897) and throughout Italy, as well as centers for the blind, abandoned, and orphaned. Smaldone's love for the Blessed Sacrament was demonstrated by his founding the Eucharistic League of Priest Adorers and Women Adorers. In addition to his charitable activities and spiritual direction of many priests, seminarians, and religious communities, Smaldone served as superior for the Congregation of the Missionaries of Saint Francis de Sales and canon of the Lecce cathedral. He died at age 75 of cardiac complications from diabetes, and was declared venerable 11 July 1995.

Pope John Paul II remarked at his beatification that Smaldone's "intense, unwavering priestly spirituality, nourished by prayer, meditation, and even bodily penance, spurred him to provide a social service open to those advanced insights which true pastoral charity can inspire."

Feast: 4 June.

Bibliography: *Acta Apostolicae Sedis* (1996): 551–53. *L'Osservatore Romano,* no. 20 (1996): 1; 21 (1996): 4–5. *L'Osservatore Romano,* English edition, no. 29 (1995): 5.

[K. RABENSTEIN]

SOLMINIHAC, ALAIN DE, BL.

Reforming bishop of Cahors, France, canon regular of St. Augustine; b. 25 November 1593, Belet (near Périgueux) France; d. 31 December 1659, Mercuès (near Cahors), Quercy, France; beatified by John Paul II in Rome, 4 October 1981.

Named abbot of Chancelade (a foundation of Canons Regular of St. Augustine near Périgueux) in 1614, Alain gradually corrected the physical and spiritual deterioration of his monastery. He was consecrated bishop of Cahors on 27 September 1637, and worked vigorously and successfully for the reform of this huge but spiritually impoverished diocese. He was strongly pro-papal in the Gallican conflicts and actively anti-Jansenist. He was regarded as a saint by Vincent de Paul and others.

The cause of his beatification was introduced in 1783. Pope John Paul II, during the beatification ceremo-

ny, praised Solminihac for his "courage to evangelize the modern world fearlessly."

Feast: 3 January.

Bibliography: *Acta Apostolicae Sedis* 74 (1982): 261–63. *L'Osservatore Romano,* English edition, no. 41 (1981): 1,12. L. CHASTENET, *La Vie de Monseigneur Alain de Solminihac Eveque Baron, et Comte de Caors, et Abbé régulier de Chancellade* (Cahors 1663). C. DUMOULIN, *Au service de Dieu et de sa gloire* (Paris 1981). E. SOL, *Un prélat ultramontain du XVIIe siècle, Alain de Solminihac et le Saint-Siège* (Aurillac, France 1927); *Alain de Solminihac . . . : Lettres et documents* (Cahors 1928); *L'Église de Cahors à l'époque moderne* (Paris 1947).

[M. A. ROCHE]

SPINELLI, FRANCESCO, BL.

Priest, founder of the Sisters of Perpetual Adoration of the Blessed Sacrament; b. 14 April 1853, Milan, Italy; d. 6 February 1913, Rivolta d'Adda (near Cremona), Italy; beatified at Caravaggio, Italy, by John Paul II, 21 June 1992.

While he was still very young, Francesco's family moved from Milan, where he was baptized (15 April 1853), to Cremona. The family spent summers at Vergo (near Bergamo), where Francesco was cured of a severe spinal problem in 1871. His priestly vocation was fostered by the charity and devotion of his mother, his uncle, Peter Cagliaroli, and a friend, Luigi Palazzolo. Soon after his ordination (14 August 1875) at Bergamo, Spinelli made a pilgrimage to Rome, where he was inspired to create an order of nuns dedicated to prayer before the Blessed Sacrament for atonement and reconciliation. Upon returning to Bergamo, he met Gertrude Caterina Comensoli, who was pursuing the same calling. With Comensoli he founded the Sacramentine Sisters (1882). When the new congregation met with financial difficulties, the bishop of Bergamo severed Spinelli's connection with the sisters in the diocese. Spinelli was welcomed by Bishop Geremia Bonomelli of Cremona. At Rivolta d'Adda Spinelli founded (1889) the Sisters of Perpetual Adoration of the Blessed Sacrament, which is independent of the Sacramentine Sisters but uses the same Rule. Personally Spinelli was compelled by his love of the Eucharist to meet the needs of the suffering and marginalized, even while he himself was sick or troubled.

Spinelli's process for beatification, opened 25 January 1952, concluded with his beatification by Pope John Paul II, who offered Spinelli "as a model of an authentic apostle especially to you the priests whom Providence calls to be stewards of the mysteries of salvation."

Bibliography: P. G. BORGONOVO, *Il prête Francisco Spinelli,* (Milan 1939). E. LINGIARDI, "A quarant'anni dalla santa morte. Il venerabile. Francesco Spinelli verso la gloria degli altari,'' *La vita cattolica* (Cremona, 5 February 1955): 4. *Acta Apostolicae Sedis* (1952): 638–40; (1992): 764.

[K. RABENSTEIN]

SPÍNOLA Y MAESTRE, MARCELO, BL.

A.k.a. Marcello of Seville, cardinal archbishop, founder of the Conceptionist Handmaids of the Divine Heart; b. 14 January 1835, Isla de Spinola, San Fernando (near Cádiz), Spain; d. 19 January 1906, Seville; beatified by John Paul II, 29 March 1987.

Marcelo, the son of the Marquis Juan de Spinola and his wife Antonia Maestre, was a lawyer prior to his ordination as a diocesan priest (21 March 1864). On 21 March 1871, he was appointed parish priest of San Lorenzo in Seville, where he engaged in pastoral work and instituted programs for the sick and abandoned until Cardinal Archbishop de la Lastra y Cuesta named him cathedral canon (1879). Upon his consecration as auxiliary bishop of Seville (1881), he adopted the motto: ''Either sanctity or death.'' Three years later (1884) he was named bishop of Caria in Cáceres, then transferred to the see of Málaga (1886) until his appointment as archbishop of Seville (1896). As archbishop, Spínola concerned himself especially with educational reforms. To further this goal, he founded the Handmaids of the Divine Heart for the education of girls, an order that combines the active and contemplative life. This bishop, known for his devotion to duty, defense of the interests of the Church, and his concern for the poor, was named cardinal in 1905, but died before receiving the red hat.

Bibliography: J. M. JAVIERRE, *El arzobispo mendigo: biografía de Marcelo Spínola* (Madrid 1974); *Don Marcelo de Sevilla* (Barcelona 1963). *Acta Apostolicae Sedis* (1987): 598. *L'Osservatore Romano,* Eng. ed. 14 (1987): 1–2.

[K. RABENSTEIN]

STANGASSINGER, KASPAR, BL.

Also Gaspar, Caspar; Redemptorist priest, teacher; b. 12 January 1871, Unterkälberstein (near Berchtesgaden), Bavaria, Germany; d. 26 September 1899, Gars am Inn, Upper Bavaria; beatified 24 April 1988.

He was the second of 16 children of a farmer who owned a stone quarry and participated in local politics. At school in Freising he encountered difficulties in his studies, but his vocation to the priesthood remained strong. During summer vacations he organized friends for group religious activities: Mass, pilgrimages, and common prayer. He began his theological studies in the diocesan seminary at Freising, but he transferred to the Redemptorist seminary at Gars because of his desire to become a missionary. He was ordained in Regensburg (Germany) on 16 June 1895. Although he preferred missionary work, out of obedience he dedicated himself wholeheartedly to his assignment as vice-director of the minor seminary of Dürrnburg (near Hallein), where he taught and provided spiritual direction to his students. On weekends, he served nearby parishes, preparing his homilies in front of the Blessed Sacrament and often preaching on the consolation available in the Eucharist. In 1899 (age 28), he was appointed director of the order's new seminary in Gars. Shortly after the opening of the school year, he died of peritonitis. When his cause for canonization was opened in 1935, his body was translated into the side chapel of the church of Gars.

During the beatification Mass on 24 April 1988, Pope John Paul II described Stangassinger: ''Shaped by the deep religious spirit of his family and called very early to the priesthood, his life was wholly centered on God. . . . He did not seek the extraordinary, but wanted 'to do what the day demanded.'''

Feast: 26 September (Redemptorists).

Bibliography: *Der selige Kaspar Stanggassinger (1871–1899) in Selbstzeugnissen9) in Selbstzeugnissen und im Urteil seiner Zeitgenossen,* ed. O. WEISS (Rome 1995). *L'Osservatore Romano,* English edition, no. 16 (1988): 12. *Positio super causae introductione* (Rome 1959). *Positio super virtutibus* (Rome 1978). A. CUMMINGS, *A Shining Light. The Story of Fr. Kaspar Stanggassinger* (Dublin 1963). O. GAMBI, *Vida do Padre Gaspar Stanggassinger* (Aparecida 1991). J. HEINZMANN, *Suchen was droben ist* (Freiburg, Switzerland 1988). H. PFEILSTETTER, *Pater Kaspar Stanggassinger. Annäherungen* (Gars 1988). M. STÖBENER, *Du forderst mich heraus. Eine briefliche Begegnung mit Kaspar Stanggassinger* (Munich 1988). F. TATARELLI, *Un canto sulle Alpi: vita del servo di Dio P. Gaspare Stanggassinger, Redentorista* (Rome 1963). F. WETTER, *Leben und Wirken eines Seligen. Hirtenbrief zur Fastenzeit 1988* (Munich 1988).

[K. RABENSTEIN]

STEIN, EDITH (SAINT TERESA BENEDICTA OF THE CROSS), ST.

Martyr; Carmelite nun; philosopher and pedagogue; b. Wrocław (Breslau in Prussian Silesia), Poland, 12 October 1891; d. Birkenau section of Auschwitz death camp, 9 August 1942. Born of devout Jewish parents, Edith gave up her faith as a teenager and became interested in philosophy after dissatisfaction with her studies in psychology. She read the important philosophical treatise *Logical Investigations of Edmund Husserl,* the founder of

Edith Stein (Sister Teresa Benedicta of the Cross) wearing the habit of a Carmelite nun. (UPI/Corbis-Bettmann. Reproduced by permission.)

phenomenology, and went to Göttingen University to study with him. There, contacts with Husserl's former pupil Max Scheler began her acquaintance with Catholicism. After several years of searching, she asked to enter the Church upon reading the autobiography of St. Teresa of Avila, and was baptized 1 January 1922. She accepted a teaching post at a girls' school run by Dominican teaching sisters in the cathedral city of Speyer. Along with her teaching duties, she acquainted herself with Catholic philosophy and translated the treatise *On Truth* by St. Thomas Aquinas.

Stein traveled to several German-speaking countries to address Catholic audiences, especially on women's and educational topics. Her growing reputation led her to leave the school at Speyer to teach at a more specialized institution of higher learning. In 1932 she became a lecturer at the German Institute for Scientific Pedagogy in Munster, but in the next calendar year she had to leave this post because of anti-Semitic legislation introduced by the Nazi Party. Convincing her spiritual director the time had come, she now acted on a long-cherished wish and entered the Carmel of Cologne, taking the name of Sister Teresa Benedicta of the Cross. After her initial training at Cologne her monastic superiors invited her to

resume writing. She transformed an earlier philosophical essay, developed in an unsuccessful effort to obtain a university position a few years previously, into her major opus *Finite and Eternal Being,* in which she attempted to synthesize the philosophy of St. Thomas with modern thought, especially with phenomenology. From her monastery she remained a faithful correspondent with former colleagues, among them the Polish phenomenologist Roman Ingarden.

Soon after the Nazi persecution of the Jews turned violent in the nationwide Kristallnacht pogrom of 9–10 November 1938, she left Germany for exile in the Dutch Carmel of Echt on the last day of the year. Here she wrote another important work, *The Science of the Cross,* a presentation of the life and teaching of St. John of the Cross. This contained several sections that incorporate the phenomenological method. Nazi Germany invaded the Netherlands in 1940 and both Sr. Teresa Benedicta and her sister Rosa Stein, now living at the Echt Carmel as a lay assistant, had to comply with anti-Semitic regulations. SS agents arrested them both on a day she was putting the finishing touches on her *John of the Cross* manuscript (which was published posthumously). That round-up on Sunday, 2 August 1942, led to deportation of several hundred priests and religious and Catholic laity of Jewish origin as a reprisal for an outspoken pastoral letter written by Dutch bishops condemning the anti-Semitic measures of the German occupation forces. One week later they arrived at the Auschwitz concentration camp, where she and her sister died in the gas chamber.

Official introduction of her cause for canonization took place in 1962, leading to her beatification at Cologne by Pope John Paul II on 1 May 1987. He canonized her at St. Peter's Basilica in the Vatican on 11 October 1998. In the same week he recommended reading her works in his encyclical *Fides et Ratio.* The following year the pope declared her copatroness of Europe, the only twentieth-century saint to be so honored.

Bibliography: Works by Edith Stein: *Life in a Jewish Family* (Washington, 1986); *Essays on Woman,* rev. ed. (Washington 1997); *On the Problem of Empathy, 2d. ed.* (Washington, 1989); *The Hidden Life* (Washington 1992): 5. *Self-Portrait in Letters, 1916–1942* (Washington 1993); *Knowledge and Faith* (Washington 2000); *Edith Stein: Selected Writings,* tr. S. BATZDORFF (Springfield, Ill. 1990); *Edith Stein: Day Book,* tr. S. BATZDORFF (Springfield, Ill. 1994); *The Science of the Cross,* tr. H. GRAEF (Chicago 1960). Works about Edith Stein: S. BATZDORFF, *Aunt Edith: The Jewish Heritage of a Catholic Saint* (Springfield, Ill. 1998). *Never Forget: Christian and Jewish Perspectives on Edith Stein,* tr. S. BATZDORFF (Washington, 1998). C. BASEHEART, *Person in the World: Introduction to the Philosophy of Edith Stein* (Dordrecht 1997). *Holiness Befits Your House,* ed. J. SULLIVAN (Washington 2000).

[JOHN SULLIVAN]

The phrase on the main gateway to the Auschwitz concentration camp, where Edith Stein and her sister perished, translates as "Work Will Make You Free." (© Grzegorz Galazka/CORBIS.)

STENSEN, NIELS, BL.

(Nikolaus Steensen, Steno, Stens, or Stenonis), pioneer in the field of anatomy, founder of scientific paleontology, geology, and crystallography, bishop; b. 11 January 1638, Copenhagen, Denmark; d. 5 December 1686, Schwerin, Germany.

His parents were Lutheran; his father, a goldsmith, was the descendent of a long line of Lutheran pastors in Scania. At an early age Niels showed a strong interest in mathematics and science, and he began to study medicine in 1656 at the University of Copenhagen. His first discovery (1660) in Amsterdam was the excretory duct of the parotid gland (Steno's duct); it was followed by many more discoveries after he moved to Leiden (27 July 1660). These are described in the *Observationes anatomicae* (Leiden 1662) and *Observationum anatomicarum specimen* (Copenhagen 1664).

After the University of Copenhagen passed him over, the University in Leyden granted him the degree of doctor of medicine *in absentia* in 1664. In Paris (1665), in the house of M. Thévenot, he delivered his *Discours sur l'anatomie du cerveau* (Paris 1669) to the forerunners of the Académie des Sciences. There he gained a reputation as an embryologist and brain anatomist. The following year he was well received at the court of the Medici, and among the members of the Accademia del Cimento, which had been founded in the spirit of Galileo; he resumed anatomical research at the Ospidale de S. Maria Nuova in Florence. By sectioning the head of a large shark and by stating the organic origin of the *glossopetrae* (fossilized shark teeth) he was led to basic discoveries in the fields of paleontology and geology. These discoveries he published succinctly and hurriedly in the *Elementorum myologiae specimen seu musculi descriptio geometrica* (Florence 1667) and *Prodromus de solido intra solidum naturaliter contento* (Florence 1669).

While residing in the Netherlands he had begun to question Lutheran doctrines. A Corpus Christi procession in Livorno, Italy deeply impressed him and he decided to become a Catholic; and on 7 November 1667 he entered the Church. Shortly after, he received a letter from the crown of Denmark calling him home and offering him a high annual salary. But it was too late; he did not feel that he could return to Denmark as a Catholic.

After a journey covering half of Europe in 1669 and 1670, he returned to Italy for a time, then served as royal anatomist in Copenhagen from 1672 to 1674. Discerning a call to the priesthood, he went back to Italy and was ordained in Florence before Easter 1675. He was appointed tutor of the crown prince of Florence, but upon request of Duke Johann Friedrich of Hanover, Innocent XI made him vicar apostolic for the Nordic Missions on 21 August 1677, and he was consecrated bishop of Titiopolis on 19 September. His territory extended to the north of Norway, but it contained very few Catholics. In his dealings with Protestants in Hanover he showed both determination and mildness (e.g., his discussions with G. W. Leibniz).

After Johann Friedrich's death, Prince-Bishop Ferdinand von Fürstenberg of Paderborn requested Stensen as auxiliary bishop of Münster (appointed 7 October 1680). With great zeal he continued the work of reform begun by C. B. von Galen. His vibrant preaching led many back to Catholicism. In his *Parochorum hoc age* (Florence 1684) he exhorted both clergy and laity to follow the example of the early Church. In 1683 he left Münster in protest against a simoniacal election. After 2 years of strenuous activity in Hamburg, he spent the last year of his life as a missionary in Schwerin.

Stensen ranks with the most eminent scientists. Among other things, he discovered many glands and glandular ducts in the eye, mouth, nose, skin, chest, and the mucous canal system of fish. He described the structure in general and in particular muscles such as those of the tongue and esophagus. He pioneered in declaring the heart to be a muscle and in stating the function of the uterus and ovaries, and in new methods of research on the brain. His chief contributions were his scientific explanations of fossils, geological stratification, the development of mountains, the difference between organic and inorganic growth, and the law of the constancy of crystalline angles.

Stensen became a model for all times through his desire for certitude, combining, happily, the most exacting inductive method with ingenious deductive conclusions. Though enthusiastic about mechanical and mathematical methods, he contradicted Descartes from the biological point of view, and referred Spinoza, the friend of his youth, to the *philosophia perennis* in his *Epistola ad novae philosophiae reformatorem de vera philosophia.* His coat of arms reflect his ideals (a heart crowned with a cross), and his most quoted saying is: "Pulchra quae videntur, pulchriora quae sciuntur, longe pulcherrima quae ignorantur" ("Beautiful are the things that are seen; more beautiful are the things that are known; and most beautiful of all are the things that are not known").

As priest and bishop, Stensen was a reformer. He became most influential through his own personal striving for sanctification in poverty, strict asceticism, and a deep union with God. Of his 16 theological works the more interesting are his *Epistola de propria conversione* (Florence 1677) and *Defensio et plenior elucidatio epistolae de propria conversione* (Hanover 1680).

His 9 years of difficult labor in northern Germany eroded his health. When he died at age 48, he was venerated as a saint in the diocese of Hildesheim. After his death, Cosimo III had his remains transferred to the crypt of St. Lorenzo in Florence, from where they were solemnly removed to a chapel in the transept of this basilica in 1953. His canonization process was begun in Osnabrück in 1938. Pope John Paul II beatified him 23 October 1988.

During his beatification ceremony, Pope John Paul II proclaimed: "Blessed son of the Danish land! You enliven the choir of those great people who have preceded you on the way to holiness. With them you cry: 'He who is mighty has done great things for me.' This cry of yours is heard in heaven and on earth. May it be received in the hearts of your brothers and sisters today and cause in them an abundant harvest of good, in faith, charity, and communion."

Feast: 5 December.

Bibliography: Works: *Opera philosophica,* ed. V. MAAR, 2 v. (Copenhagen 1910); *Opera theologica,* ed. K. LARSEN and G. SCHERZ, 2v. 2d ed. (Copenhagen 1944–47); *Epistolae,* ed. G. SCHERZ, 2 v. (Copenhagen 1952); *The Prodromus,* tr. and ed. J. W. WINTER (New York 1916); *The Earliest Geological Treatise,* tr. C. CARCHARIAE, ed. A. GARBOE (New York 1958); *Chaos-manuscript, Copenhagen, 1659,* ed. A. ZIGGELAAR (Copenhagen 1997). Studies about Stensen: R. ANGELI, *Niels Stensen anatomico, fondatore della geologia, servo di Dio* (Florence 1968). M. BIERBAUM, *Niels Stensen: Anatom, Geologe u. Bischof,* 2d ed. (Münster 1979). R. CIONI, *Niels Stensen: Scientist-Bishop,* tr. G. M. CAMERA (New York 1962). A. GARBOE, *Nicolaus Steno and Erasmus Bartholinus* (Copenhagen 1954). U. HEIDA, *Niels Stensen und seine Fachkollegenin* (Berlin 1986). A. D. JÖRGENSEN, *Niels Stensen,* ed. G. SCHERZ, 2d ed. (Copenhagen 1958). V. MAAR, *To uudgivne Arbejder af Nicolaus Steno fra Biblioteca Laurentiana* (Copenhagen 1910). J. METZLER, *Die Apostolischen Vikariate des Nordens* (Paderborn 1919). H. MOE, *Nicolaus Steno: An Illustrated Biography,* tr. D. STONER (Copenhagen 1994). E. K. PÅLSSON, *Niels Stensen, scientist and saint,* tr. M. N. L. COUVE DE MURVILLE (Dublin 1988). W. PLENKERS, *Der Däne Niels Stensen* (Freiburg 1884). K. J. PLOVGAARD, *Niels Stensen: Anatom, Geologog Biskop* (Copenhagen 1953). N. QUATTRIN, *Nicola Stenone scienziato e santo (1638–1686)* (Vicenza 1987). S. DE ROSA, *Niccolò Stenone a Volterra, 1668,* tr. G. LAZZERI (Florence 1996). G. SCHERZ, *Dansk biografisk leksikon,* ed. C. F. BRICKA et al., v.22 (Copenhagen 1942); *Vom Wege Niels Stensens* (Copenhagen 1956); *N. Steno and His Indice* (Copenhagen 1958), with biography and essays on his scientific work; *Niels Stensen* (Würzburg 1962); *Pionier der Wissenschaft* (Copenhagen 1963), list of sources; *Niels Stensen: Forscher und Denker im Barock* (Stuttgart 1964). *Niels Steensen: The Goldsmith's Son from Copenhagen . . . ,* tr. R. SPINK (Copenhagen 1988).

[G. SCHERZ]

STEPINAC, ALOJZIJE VIKTOR, BL.

Cardinal, archbishop of Zagreb, martyr; b. 8 May 1898, at Brezaric (near Krašić), Croatia; d. 10 February 1960, in Krašić; beatified 3 October 1998.

Stepinac was the eighth of twelve children of wealthy peasants Barbara Penic and Josip Stepinac. Upon graduation from the Gymnasium in Zagreb (1916), he was drafted into the Austrian army. As second lieutenant he fought on the Italian front (1917–18). Taken prisoner by the Italians (September 1918), he joined the South Slav volunteers to fight against the Hapsburg rulers. Returning to Croatia (1919), by then a part of Yugoslavia, he studied agriculture in Zagreb. In 1924 he enrolled in the German College, Rome, and attended classes at the Gregorian University. In 1930, he obtained doctorates in philosophy and theology and was ordained a priest in Rome (26 October).

After returning to Zagreb in 1931 he was assigned to the chancery office, from which he administered several parishes and initiated the establishment of Caritas in the archdiocese. He became coadjutor of Zagreb in 1934 (the youngest bishop in the world at the time), and archbishop in 1937. As archbishop he promoted Catholic charities and Catholic Action, defended the Church's rights, and denounced Communism and National Socialism. On 31 December 1938, he founded the Relief Action for Refugee Jews under his protection. In April 1941 he welcomed the Croatian State, but continuously opposed the regime of Ante Pavelić, especially for its forced conversions and racial persecution. Thousands of persecuted Jews, Slovenes, and Serbs received his help. After the government was taken over by the Communist party in 1945, Stepinac and his fellow bishops refused to accede to the new regime's desire for a "national Catholic Church," independent of Rome, and spoke out against the persecution of the Church by the communists. He was arrested for denouncing the execution of priests by militant communists and later released. Josip Tito's government arrested him again in 1946 and tried him on trumped-up charges of collaborating with the Germans, Italians, and the fascist Ustasha regime,. He was sentenced to 16 years' imprisonment. For five years he was kept in Lepoglava prison; in 1951 Tito released him on house arrest in Krašić because of his health. Systematically harassed and urged by Tito to leave the country, Stepinac remained with his flock. When he was made cardinal by Pope Pius XII in 1953, he declined to go to Rome to receive the cardinal's hat, fearing that he would not be allowed back into Yugoslavia. He did not attend the conclave after Pius XII's death, for the same reason. During these years of internment and isolation he continued his practice of exercising his ministry in part through extensive letter-writing (more than 5000 letters in all).

Alojzije Viktor Stepinac (left) is accompanied by a soldier. (Catholic News Service.)

Stepinac's faith was nurtured by daily meditation on the whole Rosary and Holy Scripture—practices he recommended to the faithful. His spirituality is marked by gratitude for God's gifts, a desire to compensate for the sins of blasphemy and abortion, zeal for the Eucharist, and filial devotion to the Blessed Mother. He predicted that "Russia will be converted, and the statue of the Mother of God will be put in the Kremlin."

He died in 1960 of a rare blood disease (*polycythemia rubra vera*) from which he suffered acutely since 1953. He was buried behind the main altar in the cathedral in Zagreb.

Stepinac was beatified by John Paul II when the pope visited the Marian shrine of Marija Bistrica, near Zagreb, in 1998. During the general audience at the Vatican the following week (7 October), the Holy Father said that Stepinac "synthesized the tragedy that has scourged Europe in the course of this century, marred by the great evils of Fascism, Nazism and Communism . . . [and] the full splendor of the Catholic response: faith in God, respect for man, love and forgiveness for all, unity of the Church guided by Peter's successor. In his beatification we acknowledge the victory of the Gospel of Christ over totalitarian ideologies, the victory of God's rights and of conscience over violence and oppression, the victory of forgiveness and reconciliation over hatred and vengeance.''

Bibliography: *Alojzije Kardinal Stepinac, Nadbiskup Zagrebacki,* documentation for canonization (Zagreb 1996). S. ALEXANDER, *The Triple Myth* (New York 1987). D. BATON, *Mladi Stepinac. Pisma zarucnici* (Rome 1975). E. BAUER, *Aloisius Kardinal Stepinac* (Recklinghausen 1979). T. DRAGOUN, *Le Dossier du Cardinal Stepinac* (Paris 1958). F. ETEROVIC, *Aloysius Cardinal Stepinac: A Spiritual Leader* (Chicago 1970). N. ISTRANIN, *Stepinac-un innocenta condemnatio* (Vicenza 1982). A. H. O'BRIEN, *Archbishop Stepinac: The Man and His Case* (Westminster, Md. 1947). R. PATTEE, *The Case of Cardinal Aloysius Stepinac* (Milwaukee 1953). E. PEZET, *Stepinac-Tito* (Paris 1959). M. PIOVANELLI, *Un vincitore all'Est,* 2d ed. (Milan 1962). I. PRCALA and S. SKRTIC, *The Man of God and His People* (Cleveland 1961). M. RAYMOND, *The Man for this Moment: The Life and Death of Aloysius Cardinal Stepinac* (New York 1971).

[G. J. PRPIC/K. RABENSTEIN]

STOLLENWERK, HELENA, BL.

In religion, Maria and later as Adoration Sr. Maria Virgo, co-foundress of the Congregation of Missionary Sisters, Servants of the Holy Spirit (SSpS); b. 28 November 1852, in Rollesbroich (northern Eifel Region), Germany; d. 3 February 1900, at Steyl, the Netherlands; beatified 7 May 1995 by John Paul II.

Raised in a religious farm family headed by Johann Peter Stollenwerk and his third wife, Anna Maria Bongard, Helena had early aspirations to evangelization. In the autumn of 1881, she wrote to Bl. Arnold Janssen, founder of the Divine Word Missionaries, to help her realize her own dream of taking the Good News to China. He promised her nothing but accepted her as a kitchen maid in the Divine Word Seminary he had founded at Steyl. From 1882–89, she served in the kitchen with three other women who shared her missionary vocation.

With Helena Stollenwerk and Hendrina Stenmanns, Janssen founded the Congregation of Missionary Sisters, Servants of the Holy Spirit on 8 December 1889, in response to a call from Argentina for sisters. Stollenwerk became its first superior general when she received the religious habit and the name Sr. Maria in 1892. She professed her vows on 12 March 1894. As superior she remained in Steyl while the first sisters went to Argentina in 1895. In 1896, Janssen founded the cloistered Holy Spirit Adoration Sisters with a small group of Missionary Sisters. Stollenwerk expressed a desire to join the new branch immediately, but it was not until two years later he asked her to make the transfer and begin a second novitiate with the name Sr. Maria Virgo. Although she had hesitated between her missionary vision and a desire for a more contemplative life, her humility and obedience are demonstrated by her uncomplainingly relinquishing her position as superior and her desire to become a missionary.

Her motto indicates the depth of her spirituality: ''To God the honor, to my neighbor the benefit, and to myself the burden.'' At the time of her transfer to the Adoration Sisters she encouraged the sisters in Argentina: ''If you find things difficult at any time in the future, be comforted by the thought that, like Moses in the Old Testament, there is a Sister before the tabernacle raising her heart and hands to Heaven for you.''

Stollenwerk professed as a Holy Spirit Adoration Sister three days before she died.

Throughout his pontificate John Paul II has stressed the need to build a ''culture of life.'' In beatifying Mother Stollenwerk on 7 May 1995, he observed that she was ''particularly affected by the loss of those children who were deprived of the right to life.'' He also spoke of her as ''a great feminine personality and missionary pioneer.''

Bibliography: *Acta Apostolicae Sedis* (1995): 564. *L'Osservatore Romano,* English edition, no. 19 (1995): 2, 4. A. GRÜN, *Treue auf dem Weg. Der Weg der Helena Stollenwerk* (Münsterschwarzach 1995); *Faithful to the Spirit,* Eng. tr. P. G. LAFORGE (Techny, Ill. 1997). F. C. REHBEIN, *Helena Stollenwerk, A Charism Nurtured: Mission and Surrender* (Rome 1995). O. STEGMAIER, *M. Maria Stollenwerk: Aufzeichnungen* (Rome 1987); *M. Maria Stollenwerk: Berufsgeschichte* (Rome 1987), Eng. tr. *Mother Maria's Vocation* (Rome 1990); *M. Helena Stollenwerk Reifung und Sendung der Mitgründerin der Steyler Missionsschwestern im Licht ihres Christusbildes* (Augsburg 1994), *Brought Forth into Freedom,* Eng. tr. LJ. MULBERGE (Rome 1995).

[K. RABENSTEIN]

TADINI, ARCANGELO, BL.

Diocesan priest, founder of the Workers of the Holy House of Nazareth; b. 12 October 1846, Verolanuova near Brescia, Lombardy, Italy; d. 20 May 1912, Botticino Sera, Brescia; beatified by John Paul II, 3 October 1999.

The youngest in a noble family headed by Pietro Tadini, a widower with seven children by his first wife, and his second wife, Antonia Gadola, who bore four children. Arcangelo's father, the communal secretary and a patriot during the struggle for Italian independence, died in 1860. A sickly child, Arcangelo studied in the local schools until he entered secondary school at Lovere. He began his seminary studies in Brescia at age eighteen (1864). An accident during these years left him with a limp. He was ordained in 1870, and following recuperation from illness, he served as a parish priest and elementary school teacher in the mountain village of Lodrino in

Voltrompia (1871–73), Santa Maria della Noce near Brescia (1873–85), and for a brief time at S. Nazzaro in Brescia. In 1885, he was transferred to Botticino Sera, where he ministered for the rest of his life (1887–1912). There he proved himself a zealous pastor, who preached with a warmth and conviction that energized his parish to come alive with many activities, including a choir, catechetical classes for all ages, and various confraternities.

Tadini gave flesh to the teachings of *Rerum novarum* (Leo XIII, 1891) by promoting the sanctification of daily work. He established an agricultural cooperative (1893), built a textile mill with his own inheritance to provide work for the unemployed (1894), and acquired the adjacent villa to house the female workers. To ensure the continuance of his work, Father Tadini founded the *Suore Operaie della Santa Casa di Nazareth* in 1900. The sisters worked alongside those they sought to evangelize by their example. The order operates in Italy, England, Switzerland, Africa, and Latin America.

Tadini, the ''Apostle of the Working World,'' was buried in the cemetery of Botticino Sera. His cause for canonization was opened 13 January 1963.

At Tadini's beatification, Pope John Paul II praised him: ''In the school of the Eucharist he learned to break the bread of God's Word, to practice charity, and to respond with pastoral resourcefulness to the social and religious challenges that marked the end of the last century. . . . The needs arising then in the working world spurred his pastor's heart to search for new ways to proclaim and bear witness to the Gospel.''

Feast: 21 May.

Bibliography: DON LUIGI FOSSATI, *Arcangelo Tadini e la sua opera sociale* (Brescia 1977). MOLINARI FRANCO and A COMUZZI, *Il prete sociale e le Operaie di Dio,* (Brescia 1990). *L'Osservatore Romano,* daily edition (in Italian) (6 October 1999): 2.

[K. RABENSTEIN]

TANSI IWENE, CYPRIAN MICHAEL, BL.

Baptized Michael, Trappist priest; b. September 1903 at Igboezunu near Aguleri, southwestern Nigeria; d. 20 January 1964, Leicester, England; beatified at Onitsha, Nigeria, by John Paul II, 22 March 1998.

Named Iwene (''sorrow will not kill you'') by his parents, Tabansi (d. 1904) and Ejikwevi (d. 1922). After his father's death, Iwene was raised by relatives who sent him (1909) to Saint Joseph's school, where he was baptized Michael in 1912. Although an accident left him blind in his left eye, he completed school in 1919, began teaching at his alma mater (1919–22), and then at Holy Trinity Primary School in Onitsa (1922–24), and was appointed headmaster at Saint Joseph's in 1924. Michael entered the new seminary at Igbariam in 1925 and was ordained priest (19 December 1937) in Onitsha's cathedral, the second native priest of the diocese. During his years of active ministry he served in the parishes of Nnewi, Dunukofia (1939–45), Akpu (1945–49), and his hometown of Aguleri (1949–40). He catechized and baptized the future Cardinal Francis Arinze, who attended Tansi's funeral and concelebrated his beatification Mass.

Following a pilgrimage to Rome, Tansi joined (1950) the Trappistsas—an oblate at Mount Saint Bernard, Leicestershire, England—and took the name Cyprian. Administrative problems delayed his entry into the novitiate until 8 December 1953. He made his solemn profession 8 December 1956. In the silence of the monastery, Father Cyprian wrote voraciously. As he gained a reputation for holiness, many came to the monastery to seek his prayers on their behalf. In 1963 his abbot announced that he had been appointed novice master for a monastery opening in Cameroon, but Father Cyprian died before he could undertake the assignment.

Tansi was initially buried in Leicestershire, but in 1988 his remains were exhumed and interred in the priests' cemetery near Onitsha's cathedral in Nigeria. Following his beatification they were translated to the parish church at Aguleri. The archdiocesan process for Tansi's beatification began July 1981; the decree of his heroic virtues promulgated in 1995; and a miracle approved on 25 June 1996.

In war-torn Africa Pope John Paul II pointed to Cyprian Tansi during his beatification as a man of reconciliation, then added: ''Everyone who met [Father Tansi] was touched by his personal goodness. He was a man of the people: he always put others before himself, and was especially attentive to the pastoral needs of families.''

Bibliography: A. E. ISICHEI, *Entirely for God: The Life of Michael Iwene Tansi* (London and Kalamazoo, Mich. 1980; Ibadan, Nigeria 1981). V. O. C. UMEGAKWE, *Fr. Tansi Solidarity Prayer Movement* (Onitsha, Nigeria 1989).

[K. RABENSTEIN]

TEKAKWITHA, KATERI, BL.

First North American Indian to be declared blessed; b. ca. 1656, Ossernenon (Auriesville), N.Y.; d. 17 April 1680, Caughnawaga, Canada; beatified in Rome by Pope John Paul II, 22 June 1980.

Kateri's mother was a Christian Algonquin, who was raised among the French at Three Rivers, taken captive

Kateri Tekakwitha. (Catholic News Service.)

by the Iroquois, and made the wife of a pagan chief of the Mohawk tribe. Of this marriage two children were born, Tekakwitha and her younger brother. At four years of age the girl was taken into the home of an uncle after she had lost her father, mother, and brother in a smallpox epidemic. The disease left her disfigured and with impaired eyesight. In 1667 she had her first meeting with Christian missionaries, three of whom were given temporary lodging by her uncle. Although the girl was very favorably impressed by these Jesuit missionaries, shyness and fear of her uncle probably kept her from seeking instruction. In 1675, however, she met Rev. Jacques de Lamberville, who instructed her in the Christian faith and baptized her on Easter, 5 April 1676, giving her the name of Kateri, or Katharine.

Katharine's conversion and her exemplary life stirred up so much opposition that the priest advised her to flee to the Christian Indian village on the St. Lawrence River, where she would be able to grow in virtue without external hindrance. After a trek of nearly 200 miles she arrived at Sault St. Louis, near Montreal, in October 1677; she received her first Holy Communion there on Christmas Day. For the next three years, under the direction of Rev. Pierre Cholonec, and with the encouragement of an older Iroquois woman, Anastasia Tegonhatsihongo, she led a life of great austerity and charity. On 25 March 1679, Katharine gave herself completely to Christ by a private vow of chastity—a most exceptional act for an Indian woman, whose maintenance depended upon getting a husband. Her death at the age of 24 served as an inspiration to the Indian community and was followed by an extraordinary outburst of religious fervor among them. The three missionaries who knew her best, Jacques de Lamberville, Claude Chauchetière, and Pierre Cholonec, left a collection of biographical data, written during the thirty-five years following her death. This together with other sources provided the documentation for her cause of beatification, which was introduced in Rome on 11 July 1932. The Tekakwitha League, located at Auriesville, publishes a quarterly and directs other activities to disseminate knowledge of her.

During the beatification ceremony, John Paul II praised Kateri as "the Iroquois maiden, who in seventeenth-century North America was the first to renew the marvels of the sanctity of SS. Scholastica, Gertrude, Catherine of Siena, Angela Merici and Rose of Lima. She preceded along the path of Love, her great spiritual sister, Thérèse of the Child Jesus." Her tomb at Caughnawaga is a pilgrimage site. Patron of Native Americans, ecology, and the environment.

Feast: 17 April (Canada); 14 July (U.S.A.)

Bibliography: *Katharine Tekakwitha, the Lily of the Mohawks: The Positio of the S. Congregation of Rites on the Introduction of the Cause for Beatification* . . . (New York 1940). *Jesuit Relations and Allied Documents,* ed. R. G. THWAITES, 73 v. (Cleveland 1896–1901; New York 1959–). *Acta Apostolicae Sedis,* no. 73 (1981): 235–258. *L'Osservatore Romano,* English edition, no. 26 (1980): 10–11. M. C. BUEHRLE, *Kateri of the Mohawks* (Milwaukee 1954). M. R. and M. BUNSON, *Kateri Tekakwitha* (Huntington, Ind. 1993). É. LECOMPTE, *Glory of the Mohawks,* tr. F. RALSTON WERUM (Milwaukee 1944).

[J. D. L. LEONARD]

THAILAND, MARTYRS OF, BB.

A.k.a. Philip Siphong and Six Companions; d. December 1940 at Ban Songkhon on the banks of the Mekong River about 400 miles from Bangkok; beatified at Rome by John Paul II, 22 October 1989.

A small village of rice farmers about fifteen miles upstream from Mukdahan on the Mekong River was the home the first Thais to become Catholics. They were caught up in a persecution of Christians, particularly Catholics, that resulted in foreign missionaries being expelled from the country and religious pluralism actively suppressed by police who went from door to door. Two religious sisters and five catechists (one man and four women) were killed nearby for refusing to renounce their

faith. Today a new church, displaying the glass-topped caskets of the martyrs, and a memorial site serve the 2,000 Catholics of the parish and a steady stream of pilgrims. The martyrs include:

Agatha Phutta, wife and mother; b. 1881; d. 26 December 1940. She served the missionaries as cook prior to their banishment.

Agnes Phila, religious of the Servants of the Cross; b. 1909, Bangkok; d. 26 December 1940. Sister Agnes, a teacher, was appointed superior of the Songkhon Catholic school in 1932. She encouraged the other women to remain steadfast and wrote a defense of the faith before her execution.

Cecilia Butsi, catechist; b. 1924; d. 26 December 1940. She was martyred for publicly defending the faith in defiance of the police.

Lucy Khambang, religious of the Servants of the Cross; b. 1917, Viengkuk, Thailand; d. 26 December 1940. She entered the congregation in 1931 and was sent to Songkhon in 1917.

Mary Phon, mission helper, catechist; b. 1926; d. 26 December 1940 in the Songkhon cemetery.

Philip Siphong Onphitak, lay catechist, known as "the man of oak;" b. 30 September 1907, Nonseng, Thailand; d. 16 December 1940, shot in the woods near the village (age 33). Blessed Philip and his wife Maria Thong had five children. While the priests were banished, he led the community, taught in the school, and served as the catechist. Despite the known danger of his actions, he followed behind the police to encourage the threatened faithful.

Viviane (Bibiana) Khampai, catechist; b. 1925; d. 26 December 1940 in Songkhon cemetery.

Feast: 16 December.

Bibliography: *Acta Apostolicae Sedis* (1989): 1079.

[K. RABENSTEIN]

THÉVENET, CLAUDINE, ST.

Known in religion as Marie Saint-Ignace, foundress of the Congregation of the Religious of Jesus and Mary; b. 30 March 1774, Lyons, France; d. there 3 February 1837; both beatified (4 October 1981) and canonized (21 March 1993) by John Paul II.

Claudine's life, spent entirely in Lyons, was shaped by the French Revolution. From the age of nine until the outbreak of unrest, Claudine was entrusted to the Bene-dictines at Saint-Pierre Abbey for her education. Lyons was overrun by revolutionary troops 29 May 1793, leaving misery in its wake. Claudine witnessed her brothers—Louis-Antoine (age 20) and François-Marie (age 18)—executed while pardoning their executioner, and begging her to do the same (January 1794). Wishing to alleviate some of the distress around her, Claudine became involved in acts of charity. In 1815, a young priest, Father Coindre, brought her two orphans he had found in the cold, whom she placed in the care of Marie Chirat. In the next several days, the Providence of the Sacred Heart was founded when five more children were taken into Chirat's home. On 31 July 1816, the small community became the Association of the Sacred Heart of Jesus and Thévenet was elected president. Two years later the sisters became the Religious of Jesus and Mary, a second Providence was opened, and Claudine left her mother's home (5 October 1818) to become Sister Marie Saint-Ignace. The "Providences" were homes designed to provide education for young women, where they were taught household management, and to undertake the smallest chore with great care and love. As the congregation expanded, it established boarding schools, academies, and residences for poor girls and women involved in the literary profession.

Pope John Paul II explained during Thévenet's beatification that she was "moved to compassion by the misery left by the revolutionary upheaval. She wished to become a messenger of God's mercy and forgiveness in a society torn by hatred and to give her life to educate the young."

Feast: 3 February.

Bibliography: G. PAPÁSOGLI, *Una vita, una missione. Claudine Thévenet* (Vatican City n.d.). *Acta Apostolicae Sedis* (1981) 952; (1993) 404–06. *L'Osservatore Romano*, Eng. ed. 41 (1981): 1, 12.

[K. RABENSTEIN]

TLAXCALA, MARTYRS OF, BB.

A.k.a. Blessed Cristobal (Christopher), Antonio (Anthony), and Juan (John), protomartyrs of the New World; d. ca. 1527–29 in Tlaxcala (now the Archdiocese of Puebla), Mexico; beatified 6 May 1990, by John Paul II in the basilica of Our Lady of Guadalupe, Mexico City.

Tlaxcala, which is about sixty-five miles from Mexico City and twenty miles from Puebla, was the fifth diocese established in New Spain, the second in Mexico. The Franciscans evangelized the warrior Tlaxcalans, who were the first to enter a treaty with Hernán Cortés and assist the Spanish *conquistadores*. Although Cortés stood as godfather for four of the leading men of Tlaxcala in 1520, Christianity was not readily accepted by all. The three youths Cristobal, Antonio, and Juan were the first to die in America *in odium fidei.*

Cristobal (b. ca. 1514, Atlihuetzia near Tlaxcala; d. 1527) was the principal heir of Acxotécatl, a high-ranking nobleman. Following his baptism, Cristobalito served the Franciscans catechists as interpreter and repeatedly harassed his father to convert. His father reacted by beating his son and burning him over a fire. Cristobal died of his injuries the following morning.

Antonio (b. ca. 1516, Tizatlán; d. 1529, Cuauhtin-chán), another Tlaxcalan noble and interpreter for the Franciscans, was the grandson of Xicohténcati and heir to his title and estates. He was clubbed to death for destroying idols in the town of Tepeaca.

Juan (b. ca. 1516, Tizatlán; d. 1529, Cuauhtinchán) was servant to Antonio and died with his master.

In his beatification homily, Pope John Paul II said these martyrs were drawn at a tender age "to the words and witness of the missionaries and they became helpers, as catechists for other indigenous people. They are sublime and instructive examples of how evangelization is a task of all God's People, excluding no one, not even children."

Feast: 23 September.

Bibliography: Congregatio pro Causis Sanctorum, *Cristobalito, Antonio y Juan: niños mártires de Tlaxcala* (Mexico City 1990). G. DE MENDIETA, *Historia eclesiástica indiana,* ed. J. GARCÍA ICAZBALCETA (Mexico City 1980). T. DE BENAVENTE MOTOLINIA *Historia de los indios de la Nueva España,* ed. E. O'GORMAN (Mexico City 1979), 176–81. *L'Osservatore Romano,* English edition (14 May 1990): 5–6.

[K. RABENSTEIN]

TOMASI, GIUSEPPE MARIA CAROL, ST.

Cardinal, liturgical scholar, priest of the Clerks Regular of the Theatine; b. 12 September 1649, Alicata, Sicily, Italy; d. 1 January 1713, Rome; canonized by John Paul II, 12 October 1986.

Eldest son of the duke of Palermo; four of his sisters including Ven. Maria Crucifixa (1645–99), became Benedictines. Rather than attaching himself to the Spanish Court as his father desired, he renounced his inheritance, joined the Theatines in Palermo in 1665 and was ordained in 1673.

Delicate health prevented his engaging in the sacred ministry, so he dedicated himself to study at Messina,

Ferrara, and Rome. He was fluent in the classical as well as many Oriental languages. Energetic in research, he drew from the Vallicellian and Vatican Libraries' treasures of unedited works, among them: *Codices Sacramentorum nongentis annis antiquiores* (Rome 1680), containing the Sacramentarium Gelasianum (7th c.), Missale Gothicum, Missale Francorum, Gallicanum Vetus; *Psalterium* (Rome 1683), a comparison of the Gallican and Roman psalters; *Responsalia et Antiphonaria Romanae Ecclesiae* (Rome 1686), manuscripts of the 9th to 12th centuries; *Sacrorum Bibliorum tituli* (Rome 1688); and *Antiqui libri Missarum Romanae Ecclesiae* (Rome 1691), containing the Antiphonary and Lectionary of St. Gregory; *Officium Domicinae Passionis* (Rome 1695), used by Greeks on Good Friday and translated into Latin; *Speculum* (Rome 1679); *Exercitium Fidei, Spei et Caritatis* (Rome 1683); *Breviarium Psalterii* (Rome, 1683); *Vera Norma di Glorificar Dio* (Rome, 1687); *Fermentum* (Rome, 1688); *Psalterium cum canticis* (Rome, 1697); *Indiculus Institutionum Theologicarum Veterurn Patrum* (3 vols., Rome, 1709, 1710; 1712), an exposition of theological theory and practice, derived from original patristic sources. Tomasi di Lampedusa's profound erudition and critical power are apparent in the introductions and the dissertations he wrote for his editions of manuscripts. His scholarship would lay the groundwork for the science of liturgical studies that enabled the revision of the missal and breviary following Vatican II.

Tomasi was a consultor on many of the Roman Congregations, and on 19 May 1712, was created a cardinal by Clement XI, his friend whom he had encouraged to accept the Chair of Peter. Beyond his erudition and nobility, Tomasi was a humble man of great charity toward the poor. Many of his works were published under the pseudonym *Carus.* He introduced Gregorian chant and taught in his titular church, S. Martino ai Monti, Rome. He fell ill on Christmas Eve 1712. Upon his death one week later, he was buried in his titular church. He was beatified by Pius VII, 5 June 1803.

Pope John Paul II commented that his canonization was timely because of Tomasi's "importance in the field of liturgical worship, which he greatly promoted in his life and with his learned writings. . . . The saint whom we proclaim today helps us to understand and bring about this renewal [Second Vatican Council] in its proper sense." Patron of liturgy and liturgists.

Feast: 3 January.

Bibliography: F. ANDREU, *EncCatt* 12:236–38. P. A. RULLÁN, *Ephemerdies Liturgicae* 72 (1958) 181–98. I. SCICOLONE, *Il cardinale Giuseppe Tomasi di Lampedusa e gli inizi della scienza liturgica* (Rome 1981). *L'Osservatore Romano,* Eng. ed. 42 (1986) 8–9.

[A. BUGNINI/EDS.]

TOMMASO DA CORI, ST.

Baptized Francesco Antonio Placidi, Franciscan priest; b. 4 June 1655, Cori, Latina, Italy; d. 11 January 1729, Civitella (today Bellegra), Italy; canonized by John Paul II, 21 November 1999.

After the death of his parents when he was fourteen, Tommaso cared for his sisters and his flock of sheep in the Roman Compagna, while holding silently in his heart a desire to live totally for God through the Franciscan life. Once his sisters were married, he entered the Observant Franciscan novitiate in Holy Trinity Friary at Orvieto (1677), completed his theological studies, and was ordained priest (1683). He spent most of his life (1684–1729) in the friary of Civitella (today Bellegra) hidden among the mountains around Subiaco. Immediately after his ordination he was assistant novice master at Orvieto, and for a six-year period he was guardian at Palombara. He established hermitages at Civitella and Palombara. These were individual communities in which the Rule was observed strictly and austerely. He was renowned as a preacher, confessor, and miracle-worker throughout the Subiaco region. His entire life centered around the Eucharist. Although Tommaso was beatified in 1785, the decree for his canonization was not issued until 2 July 1999.

During the canonization ceremony, Pope John Paul II said that Bl. Tommaso "knew how to lead the brothers entrusted to his care toward the pastures of faith, ever inspired by the Franciscan ideal."

Feast: 19 January.

Bibliography: *Lettere inedite del B. Tommaso da Cori dei frati minori*, prepared by U. V. BUTTARELLI (Assisi 1993). Vatican Information Service (2 July 1999). *L'Osservatore Romano*, English edition, no. 47 (24 November 1999): 2.

[K. RABENSTEIN]

TORNAY, MAURICE, BL.

Religious priest, martyr; b. 31 August 1910, La Rosière, near Orsières, Valais Canton, Switzerland; d. 11 August 1949, To Thong, Tibet; beatified at Rome by John Paul II, 16 May 1993.

After completing school at St. Maurice Abbey, Maurice Tornay entered the novitiate of the Canons Regular of Great St. Bernard (Congregatio Ss. Nicolai et Bernardi Monti Iovis) (1931), made his solemn profession (1935), then volunteered for the Chinese missions (1936). He completed his theological studies while learning the local dialects at Weixi, Yunnan, China. Following his ordination at Hanoi (1938), he was given charge of the students at the minor seminary at Houa-Lo-Pa, China. In 1945, Tornay was assigned to Yerkalo, the only parish in the autonomous Himalayan theocratic kingdom of Tibet. Here, he met with opposition from Buddhist monks, who forced him to abandon his parish. Undaunted, Tornay maintained contact with his persecuted parishioners from a hiding place in Pamé. Finally, he decided to seek an edict of toleration from the Dalai Lama in order to protect the Christians. He was murdered (with his servant) by armed men—agents of the Lamistic monks—who had offered to escort him to Lhasa.

During the beatification homily, Pope John Paul II remembered Tornay as a man "who wanted to teach children and lead them to holiness."

Feast: 11 August.

Bibliography: R. LOUP, *Martyr au Thibet: Maurice Tornay, chanoine régulier du Grand-St-Bernard* (Fribourg 1950); *Martyr in Tibet: The Heroic Life and Death of Father Maurice Tornay, St. Bernard Missionary to Tibet,* tr. C. DAVENPORT (New York 1956). C. MARQUIS-OGGIER and P. DARBELLAY, *Maurice Tornay: Ein Schweizer Märtyrer im Tibet,* 2d ed. (Martigny 1999).

[K. RABENSTEIN]

TORRES MORALES, GENOVEVA, BL.

Religious, foundress of the Sisters of the Sacred Heart of Jesus and the Holy Angels (Angelicas); b. 3 January 1870, Almenara, Castile, Spain; d. 5 January 1956, Saragossa, Spain; beatified in Rome by John Paul II, 29 January 1995.

Young Genoveva endured many tragedies during her lifetime: by the time she was eight, four of her siblings and both her parents had died, and her left leg was amputated to the thigh in 1883. Spiritual reading and prayer strengthened her fortitude. Because of her disability, she was barred from joining the Carmelites of Charity, in whose Mercy Home she had lived from 1885 to 1894. Canon Barbarrós encouraged Genoveva and the two women with whom she lived to form a religious community to assist needy women. Thus, Genoveva founded the Angelicas in Valencia (1911). Despite the numerous obstacles of a new enterprise, the community soon spread to other parts of Spain: Barcelona, Bilbao, Madrid, Pamplona, Santander, and Saragossa. Several years before Mother Genoveva's death, the institute of the Angelicas received papal approval (1953).

When Pope John Paul II beatified Mother Genoveva, he stated that her love of the Sacred Heart "led her to devote her life to caring for retired women, to remedy the loneliness and deprivation in which many of them lived, looking after them materially and spiritually in a true home."

Bibliography: *Escritos personales de la Rdma. Madre Genoveva Torres Morales* ed. B. LLORCA (Barcelona 1973). B. LLORCA, *Angel de la soledad: la madre Genoveva Torres Morales fundadora de las Hermanas del Sagrado Corazón de Jesús y de los Santos Angeles* (Zaragoza 1970). M. A. MARRODÁN, *Loores a la madre Genoveva* (Tarragona 1996).

[K. RABENSTEIN]

TOVINI, GIUSEPPE ANTONIO, BL.

Married lawyer, journalist, politician, lay Franciscan tertiary; b. 14 March 1841, Cividate Camuno (near Brescia), Italy; d. 16 January 1897, Brescia; beatified there by John Paul II, 20 September 1998.

Giuseppe, the eldest of the seven children of Mosè Tovini and Rosa Malaguzzi, attended schools at Breno and Lovere (1852–58). His priest-uncle, Giambattista Malaguzzi, obtained a scholarship for him at a school in Verona, and then at the diocesan seminary. Following the death of his father (June 1859), Giuseppe enrolled in the law faculty at the University of Padua (1860–64). He continued his legal studies at the University of Pavia (1864–65) while working as an assistant director and teacher in a secondary school. Returning to Brescia in 1867, he worked in the law firm of Giordano Corbolani, whose daughter Emilia he married in January 1875. They had ten children, one of whom became a Jesuit and two who because religious sisters.

As mayor of Cividate (1871–74) he initiated several important public works, including the Bank of Vallecamonica (Breno) and a railroad connection to Brescia. From 1877, Giuseppe was especially involved in the Catholic Movement of Brescia. He collaborated in the creation of a Catholic daily paper, *Il Cittadino di Brescia*, where he later became manager. The paper's editor was Giorgio Montini, father of future Pope Paul VI. As president of the diocesan committee of *Opera dei Congressi*, a program designed to counter repression of the Church and anticlerical sentiment, he travelled throughout the region forming parochial committees. He later had regional (Lombardy) and national leadership roles in the organization. Beginning in 1879, he encouraged Catholic involvement in Brescian politics, invoking the ire of the liberal intelligentsia. He was elected provincial councilman for the district of Pisogne (1879) and city councilman in Brescia (1882). It was from these political positions that he able to defended the weak and poor peolple of his district.

In 1881, Tovini became a member of the Third Order of Saint Francis, which he found a providential way of living and serving in the world—living a life of voluntary poverty. Tovini became prior of the congregation in 1884, a post he held until his death. Of seemingly bound-less energy and wanting to imbue every aspect of labor and industry with Catholic values, Tovini organized local and national Catholic congresses, founded charitable institutions, initiated the *Banco Ambrosiano* (1896), *Banco S. Paulo* (Brescia, 1888), and an agricultural union. In 1881 he disseminated constitutions for the establishment of societies of Catholic workers, small farm loan banks, and mutual aid societies.

Tovini's other important contributions were in the educational arena. He defended religious education in the schools and advocated free education in order to form youth to fulfill their civic and social responsibilities. For this purpose he founded (1882) a kindergarten (*l'Asilo San Giuseppe*), an association of fathers of families, the *Società Cesare Arici*, and an academy (*l'Istituto venerabile Alessandro Luzzago*); invited the Canossian Sisters to open a girls school in Cividate Camuno (1894); and promoted and raised funds for the establishment of the Saint Antony of Padua University (1884), Artigianelli Institute (1891), and an international Catholic university in Rome (1891). He collaborated in the formation of the *Unione Leone XIII*, which was the foundation of the Federation of Italian Catholic Students (FUCI). Tovini used the media to spread Catholic faith by establishing pedagogical and religious periodicals, such as *Fede e Scuola* (from 1891), *Scuola Italiana Moderna* (from 1893), and *La Voce del Popolo* (from 1893).

Tovini, who had suffered from poor health throughout his life, died at age fifty-six. His mortal remains were solemnly translated to the church of San Luca at Brescia, 10 September 1922. He was declared venerable 6 April 1995. Pope John Paul II beatified Tovini at the end of the centenary celebration of the birth of Pope Paul VI, who spoke often of Tovini.

John Paul II stressed that Tovini "encouraged Catholics to affirm the values of the Gospel in society by creating schools and social works, cultural circles, operating committees, and singular economic initiatives. . . . He is resplendent for his strong personality, his profound lay and family spirituality, and for his generous efforts to improve society."

Feast: 16 January (Franciscans).

Bibliography: *Acta Apostolicae Sedis* 20 (1998): 956–958. *L'Osservatore Romano,* Eng. ed. 28 (1998): 1–2.

[K. RABENSTEIN]

TRICHET, MARIE-LOUISE OF JESUS, BL.

Baptized Louise Trichet; co-foundress of the Daughters of Wisdom (*La Sagesse*); b. 7 May 1684 at Poitiers,

France; d. 28 April 1759 at Saint Laurent sur Sèvre, Vendée, France.

She was the fourth of eight children of devout, bourgeois parents, who ensured that she was baptized on the day of her birth. Her family life and the Christian education that she received endowed her with virtue and an awareness of the needs of others. At age 17, the beautiful young woman met the already-esteemed Louis de Montfort in the hospital of Poitiers and spontaneously offered her services, confiding to him her desire for religious life. Two years later she responded to his invitation to commit herself totally to working with the sick. Although her mother opposed her decision to follow "this mad priest," she accepted the grey religious habit and the name Sister Marie-Louise of Jesus on 2 February 1703 and began her humble duty as a nurse.

Together with de Montfort, she founded the Daughters of Wisdom, the mainspring of whose spirituality was to be Jesus, the "Eternal and Incarnate Wisdom." After de Montfort's departure, she worked alone until she met Catherine Brunet in 1714. The following year the two women, who had now been joined by two others, established the order's first community at La Rochelle (Charente), where they continued to help the children of the poor, the neglected sick (both in hospitals and homes), and others in need. The order continued to grow, and by the end of the twentieth century the Daughters of Wisdom had more than 2,361 members on 5 continents.

Sister Marie-Louise of Jesus is buried next to the relics of St. Louis de Montfort in the parish church of Saint-Laurent, in Saint Laurent sur Sèvre, where both were venerated by Pope John Paul II during a visit 19 September 1996.

When the pope beatified her on 16 May 1993, he stated: "Marie-Louise of Jesus let herself be seized by Christ; she passionately sought the interior union of human wisdom with the Eternal Wisdom. The natural outcome of this bond of deep intimacy was an activity passionately devoted to the poorest of her contemporaries."

Feast: 7 May.

Bibliography: B. PAPASOGLI, *Wisdom of the Heart: The Story of Marie Louis Trichet* (Bay Shore, N.Y. 1993). M. T. PIERCE, *Marie Louise of Jesus: De Montfort's Spiritual Daughter* (Dublin 1963).

[K. RABENSTEIN]

TROIANI, CATERINA, BL.

Baptized Costanza (Constance), known in religion as Mary Catherine of Saint Rose of Viterbo, Poor Clare, foundress of the Institute of Franciscan Missionary Sisters of the Immaculate Heart of Mary; b. 19 January 1813, at Giuliano (near Rome), Italy; d. 6 May 1887, at Cairo, Egypt; beatified by John Paul II, 14 April 1985.

Upon the death of her mother (1819), Costanza was entrusted to the Poor Clares at the convent in Ferentino near Frosinone, Campania, Italy. In the course of her decade living with the sisters, she came to love the Rule. At age 16, she became a novice and made her profession the following year. She and five other sisters responded to the call of Bishop Guasco, apostolic vicar of Egypt, for missionaries. Upon arriving in Cairo (14 September 1859), the sisters established an elementary school that was open to all children. Troiani earned the affectionate title "mother of the poor" for her many acts of charity and her collaboration in the movement to emancipate slaves. In 1868, she founded the Sisters of the Immaculate Heart. Her poor house established in the Clot-Bey district became her headquarters; however, the generalate was later transferred to Rome and the sisters continue Troiani's work in Brazil, China, Egypt, France, Ghana, Iraq, Israel, Italy, Jordan, Lebanon, Malta, Morocco, Palestine, Syria, the United States, and West Africa. In 1967, her relics were translated from Cairo to the congregation's generalate in Rome.

In beatifying Maria Caterina Troiani, Pope John Paul II praised her courage in using the faith to bridge cultural differences for the benefit of the young and needy.

Bibliography: *Acta Apostolicae Sedis* (1986): 913–16. *L'Osservatore Romano,* English edition, no. 19 (1985): 6–8.

[K. RABENSTEIN]

TRUSZKOWSKA, ANGELA MARIA, BL.

Baptized Sophia (Zofia) Camille; foundress of the Felician Sisters; b. 16 May 1825, Kalisz, Poland; d. 10 October 1899, Krakow, Poland; beatified by John Paul II, 18 April 1993.

Joseph Truszkowski, a judge, and his wife Josephine had the means to educate their frail daughter Sophia at home. She enrolled in Madame Guerin's academy when her family moved to Warsaw (1837), but tuberculosis forced her to continue her studies in her father's extensive library after she recovered in a Swiss sanitarium. She considered joining the Visitation Nuns, but she remained at home to assist her ailing father.

Sophia came to understand her vocation was serving the poor, not cloistered contemplation, during a trip to Cologne, Germany (1848). At first she answered the call as a member of the Society of Saint Vincent de Paul. Later she became a lay Franciscan and took the name Angela. At age 29, she sought out and helped street children and the aged homeless in the Warsaw slums. Soon she and her cousin Clothilde were caring for six children in two attic rooms with the financial help of her father.

On 21 November 1855, Sophia and Clothilde made private vows before the icon of Our Lady of Częstochowa. They attracted other volunteers to form a congregation in 1857, which responds to the needs of the Church in social service or catechetical centers. Mother Angela's name is inexorably linked with that of Blessed Honorat Kozminski (1829–1916), who was appointed spiritual director for the new order. The congregation received its name—the Sisters of Saint Felix of Cantalice—because the sisters took their young charges to pray at the shrine of the patron of children. After three successive terms as superior general of the Felician sisters, Mother Angela (age 44) stepped aside because of her increasing deafness. She served another 30 years as a simple sister, but did continue to guide the order and inspire new ministries, including their mission to the United States (1874). Towards the end of her life, Sister Angela suffered from deafness and cancer; the latter eventually claimed her life. Her remains were enshrined in the motherhouse chapel on Smolensk Street, Krakow.

In his homily at Bl. Angela's beatification, Pope John Paul II, who had opened her cause as Cardinal Karol Wojtyła of Krakow, noted that ''Christ formed her spirit through great suffering, which she accepted with faith and truly heroic submission to his will: in seclusion and solitude, through a long, painful disease, and in the dark night of the soul.''

Feast: 10 October.

Bibliography: F. A. CEGIELKA, *The Pierced Heart* (Milwaukee 1955). M. WINOWSKA, *Go, Repair My House*, tr. C. QUINTAL (Lodi, N.J. 1976). M. B. DMOWSKA, *Matka Maria Angela Truszkowska: Założycielka Zgromadzenia Sióstr Felicjanek* (Buffalo 1949). M. J. ZIOLKOWSKI, *The Felician Sisters of Livonia, Michigan: First Province in America* (Detroit, Mich. 1984).

[K. RABENSTEIN]

TSCHIDERER ZU GLEIFHEIM, JOHANN NEOPMUK, BL.

A.k.a. John von (zu) Gleifheim or Giovanni Nepomuceno Tschiderer, bishop of Trent (Italy); b. 15 April 1777, Bolzano, South Tyrol, Italy; d. 3 December 1860, Trent, Italy; beatified 30 April 1995 by Pope John Paul II during a pastoral visit to Trent.

Tschiderer's family emigrated from the Grisons to the Tyrol in 1529 and was given a patent of nobility in 1620. He completed his secondary education under the Franciscans (1792), and then he rejoined his parents, Josef Joachim and Caterina de Giovanelli. They had moved to Innsbruck, Austria, where he studied philosophy and theology. On 27 July 1800 he was ordained priest by Emmanuel Count von Thun, bishop of Trent. After spending two years ministering in mountain parishes, he went for further training to Rome, where he was appointed Apostolic notary.

Upon his return north he took up pastoral work again in the German part of the Diocese of Trent, and from 1807 was professor of moral and pastoral theology at the seminary at Trent. In 1810 he was appointed pastor at Sarnthal (Sarentino) and in 1819 at Meran (Merano), where he was also school inspector. Wherever he went he gained a lasting reputation for zeal and charity. In 1827 he was appointed as a canon of the Cathedral of St. Vigilius, Trent, and pro-vicar of the diocese. On 20 May 1832, he was consecrated bishop of Heliopolis and auxiliary bishop of Bressanone and took up residence at Feldkirch. Two years later Emperor Francis I nominated him prince-bishop of Trent to replace Francis Xavier Luschin, who had been transferred to Lemberg (now Lviv, Ukraine) and named him as successor. From May 1835 until his death, Tschiderer governed his diocese with the same apostolic zeal and charity he had demonstrated in earlier endeavors. He devoted a considerable part of his revenues and personal wealth for the building or restoration of more than 60 churches, and the purchasing of good books for parish rectories. He provided for the continuous formation of priests, Christian education for youth, and the generous care of the poor and sick. He used the third centenary of the opening of the Council of Trent (1545–63) to promote a religious revival through popular missions and other pastoral activities. He intervened promptly and decisively to prevent the 20 March 1848 uprising from becoming a blood-bath; when his petition to the Austrians for clemency for 21 young members of the Franco-Italian forces was refused, he saw to their preparation for execution and Christian burial.

He lived in deep communion with God through long periods of prayer, the celebration of Mass, and meditation on Scripture, Magisterial teachings, and the Rosary. During his 25-year episcopacy he was distinguished for the exercise of virtue and charity, and for intense zeal in the fulfillment of the duties of his episcopal office. He was exceedingly simple and abstinent in his personal habits. His charity to the poor and sick was carried so far that he was often left without a penny, because he had given away everything he had. Twice (1836 and 1855) cholera raged in his diocese and on these occasions he set a shining example of Christian courage before his clergy.

He left his property to the institution for the deaf and dumb at Trent and to the seminary that he had founded, which was named after him the Joanneum. Directly after his death he was honored, and the process for his beatification was initiated by his successor Benedict Riccabona in 1873. His body now lies in the north transept of Trent's cathedral.

The Holy Father praised von Tschiderer as "a man who transcended borders. . . . [He] was able to bridge the gap between various social classes, different languages and diverse mentalities, and bring them together. The new blessed indeed worked in the heart of Europe and was able to preserve these identities in the shining example of his person, while promoting a sense of community."

Feast: 4 December.

Bibliography: *Acta Apostolicae Sedis,* 61 (1969): 121–125. *Mitteilungen über das Leben des. . .J. N. Tschiderer* (Bolzano 1876). *L'Osservatore Romano,* English edition, nos. 18 and 19 (1995). M. A. BUOL and V. BERENBERG, *Johann Nepomuk von Tschiderer und seine Zeit* (1934). A. COSTA, *I Vescovi di Trento* (1977): 238–248. A. TAIT, *Vita del Venerabile Servo di Dio Giovanni Nepomuceno di Tschiderer, Principe vescovo di Trento,* 2 v. (Venice 1904).

[K. RABENSTEIN]

TURÓN, MARTYRS OF, SS.

A.k.a. Martyrs of the Asturias, Martyrs of the LaSallian Christian Brothers, Cirilo Bertrán and Companions; d. 9 October 1934, Turón, Asturias, northern Spain; both beatified (29 April 1990) and canonized (21 November 1999) by John Paul II. They are the first saints of the Spanish Civil War.

Most of the 6,832 modern Spanish martyrdoms occurred during the persecutions of the Civil War itself (18 July 1936 to 1 April 1939). In 1931 a mild revolution overthrew Alfonso XIII, the last Bourbon, and instituted a republic. To combat the entrenched power of the Church, anticlerical legislation was enacted, generally removing education from the hands of the religious or forbidding religious education. The government tried to placate the peasantry through land reform, but not vigorously enough to satisfy the extremists. Dissatisfaction led to strikes and uprisings, especially in the mining areas of the Asturias, where the nine Martyrs of Turón died about two years before the July 1936 insurrection. During the fourteen bloody days of this first test of the revolution, ten diocesan priests, thirteen religious, and six seminarians were killed, including the Martyrs of Turón. They were caught in this political upheaval that was then fomenting in Spain.

Eight of the Martyrs of Turón were followers of Saint John-Baptiste de la Salle. They ran the LaSallian Christian School of Our Lady of Covadonga College in Turón for the sons of local miners. The last was a Passionist priest. After withstanding a victorious attack with heavy artillery on the forces of the Second Republic, revolutionary authorities broke into the house of the brothers on the pretext that arms had been hidden there (5 October 1934). The nine were arrested and held in the "People's House" over the weekend without a trial. The Revolutionary Committee decided that they must die because of their influence over the children of the region. A witness at their sentencing reported that the martyrs heard their fate calmly. On the evening of 9 October, they walked to the local cemetery under guard while softly praying. There they were executed by firing squad. The cause of Jaime Hilario Barbal Cosan was attached to that of the Martyrs of the Asturias, but it is dealt with separately in this volume because he was not martyred with this group.

The bodies of the LaSallian martyrs were buried in the cemetery of Bujedo near Burgos (26 February 1935), but that of Father Inocencio de la Immaculada, buried in the cemetery of Mieres, was destroyed in the bombings of 1936. Their cause for beatification began in the Diocese of Oviedo (9 October 1944 to 22 June 1945), and the decree of martyrdom was issued in Rome, 16 May 1989. At their beatification, Pope John Paul stated: "The Passionist priest met occasionally with the de la Salle Brothers. In that way God in his inscrutable providence wished to unite in martyrdom members of two congregations who worked in solidarity for the Church's one mission." The martyrs are:

Augusto Andrés, in the world Román Martín Fernández, LaSallian brother; b. 6 May 1910, Santander, Spain. An expressive child, Román joined the LaSallians after recovery from a grave illness (8 August 1922) and entered the novitiate (3 February 1926). After completing his formation (1929), he taught at Valladolid (1929–32), then completed his obligatory military service (1932–33) at Palencia. Brother Augusto was sent to Turón in 1933 when the school at Valladolid, to which he had returned following his military service, was closed by rebels.

Aniceto Adolfo, in the world Manuel Seco Gutiérrez, LaSallian brother, b. 4 October 1912, Celada Marlantes (on the border between Cantabria and Castilla), Spain. The son of Pio Seco, Anceito is the youngest of the martyrs. He followed his eldest brother Maximino into the LaSallians at Bujedo, and he himself was followed by his younger brother Florencio. Manuel joined the house of studies (6 September 1926), then entered the novitiate (1928), and received the habit together with the name Aniceto Adolfo (February 1929). He became known for his mercy and diligence. After finishing his studies at Bujedo, Aniceto Adolfo taught young children in Valladolid (August 1932–October 1933). He arrived in the mining town of Asturias to begin his new assignment in October 1933.

Benito de Jesús, in the world Héctor Valdivieso Sáez, LaSallian brother, first native Argentinian to be canonized; b. 31 October 1910, Buenos Aires, Argentina. His parents, Benigno Valdivielso y Aurora Sáez, came from La Bureba near Burgos, Spain. When life in Argentina proved unsatisfactory, they returned to Briviesca, Spain, where Héctor was raised. Héctor attended the city school, then the school of the Daughters of Charity, until he discovered and entered the LaSallian school at Bujedo (August 1923). Because of his brilliance as a student, he was sent to the international house of studies at Lembecq-les-Hall, Belgium, with three companions. He returned to Bujedo to begin his novitiate (26 October 1926). He began teaching at Astorga (24 August 1929), where he won acclaim from parents and students for his teaching methods. There he began to write as a means of propagating the faith, *La luz de Astorga* (*The Light of Astorga*). He also wrote beautifully about martyrdom in letters to his father, who had suffered in the recent persecutions in Mexico. He was sent to Turón in the summer of 1933.

Benjamín Julián, in the world Vicente Alonso Andrés, LaSallian brother; b. 27 October 1908, Jaramillo de la Fuente near Burgos, Spain. Vicente's parents, Lesmes and Tomasina, were simple farmers who encouraged his vocation, evoked by a LaSallian brother who visited his school in 1919 to invite the students to become Christian educators. He was received at Bujedo (7 October 1920) at a much younger age (age 11) than usual because of his enthusiasm. He found his studies difficult because of his lack of preparation, but he persisted and entered the novitiate 2 February 1924. He proved to be a masterful educator whose joy engaged his students in his first assignment at Santiago de Compostela (summer 1927). He was sent to Turón in the summer of 1933.

Cirilo Bertrán, in the world José Sanz Tejedor, LaSallian Christian brother; b. at Lerma near Burgos, Spain, March 20, 1888. Born of humble workers, José joined the order at Bujedo (12 July 1905) and entered the novitiate (4 March 1907). As Brother Cirilo Bertrán, he taught in Duesto near Bilbao (1909–10), the orphanage of the Sacred Heart of Jesus in Madrid (1910–11), Puente de Vallecas in Madrid (March-June 1911), Santa Susana in Madrid (June 1911–12), and many other places before making his final vows (1916). He served as director in Santander (1918, 1925), Riotuerto near La Cavada (1919, 1924), Valladolid (1930), and other places for thirteen years. In 1933, he began his assignment as director in Turón with a thirty-day retreat. He defied the government by continuing religious instruction and urging attendance at Mass.

Inocencio de la Immaculada, in the world Manuel Canoure Arnau, Passionist priest; b. 10 March 1887, Santa Cecilia y San Acisclo del Valle de Oro (between Ferreira and Foz near Lugo), Galicia, Spain. After joining the Passionists (1902), he made his novitiate at Peñafiel, Valladolid, then Deusto in Vizcaya. Upon professing his first vows (26 July 1905), Manuel became Inocencio de la Immaculada. He was ordained to the priesthood in 1913. In additional to his sacradotal duties, Innocencio taught philosophy, literature, and theology at various houses: Daimiel (Ciudad Real), Corella (Navarra), Peñaranda de Duero (Burgos), and three times at Mieres (Asturias), the last time in September 1934.

Julián Alfredo, in the world Vilfrido Fernández Zapico, LaSallian brother; b. 24 December 1902, Cifuentes de Rueda on the Esla River near León. Born into a humble, pious family, Vilfrido's uncle, a priest, convinced him to join the Capuchins at León. He was about to begin his novitiate at the Capuchin house at Bilbao when he had to return home because of illness. After a second attempt and a second illness, he decided to enter the LaSallian novitiate at Bujedo, 4 February 1926. Upon completing his studies, he began his first teaching assignment (24 August 1929) and was renowned for his joy in teaching children. He professed his perpetual vows during the summer of 1932. The following September (1933) he was assigned to Turón.

Marciano José, in the world Filomeno López y López, LaSallian brother; b. 15 November 1900, El Pedregal near Molina de Aragón, Guadalajara, Spain. Filomeno's parents were farmers, but his uncle was Brother Gumersindo, infirmarian at Bujedo, who inspired the young man's vocation. Filomeno did well in his studies at Bujedo, but had to return home due to a serious ear infection that left him functionally deaf. Although he was unable to engage in teaching with this disability, he wanted to serve the brothers in other ways. He retuned to Bujedo, entered the novitiate (20 September 1916) and made his first vows (3 April 1918). He served as gardener and housekeeper in Bujedo, and sacristan in the Premonstratensian church nearby. Thereafter he was sent as cook at Terán in Santander (28 May 1928), then to Caborana (Asturias), Valladolid, Colunga (Asturias), Gallarta (Biscay), and Mieres (Asturias). Before he was sent to Turón (April 1934) to replace a brother who was afraid to stay because of the mounting tension, he wrote to his relatives that martyrdom was likely in the current situation—and he was willing to die. He could have saved himself simply by stating he was a cook and not revealing that he was also a brother religious.

Victoriano Pío, in the world Claudio Bernabé Cano, LaSallian brother, b. 7 July 1905, San Millan de Lara near Burgos, Spain. His parents were farmers. He began his studies at Bujedo (26 August 1918) and continued into the novitiate (30 August 1921). Brother Victoriano passed nearly ten years (1925–34) at the school in Palencia, where he used his musical talents to teach others, formed a choir, and used music to motivate slow learners. He arrived in Turón about a month before his martyrdom to replace another frightened brother.

Feast: 9 October.

Bibliography: V. CÁRCEL ORTÍ, *Martires españoles del siglo XX* (Madrid 1995) J. PÉREZ DE URBEL, *Catholic martyrs of the Spanish Civil War*, tr. M. F. INGRAMS (Kansas City, Mo. 1993). L. SALM, *The martyrs of Turón and Tarragona: the De La Salle Brothers in Spain* (Romeoville, Ill. 1990).

[K. RABENSTEIN]

VANNINI, GIUSEPPINA, BL.

Josephine; baptized Giuditta Adelaides (Judith Adelaide); foundress of the Daughters of Saint Camillus; b. 7 July 1859, Rome, Italy; d. there 23 February 1911; beatified 16 October 1994, by John Paul II

Orphaned at age seven, Giuseppina was educated at the Torlonia orphanage at St. Onofrio until 1883. She joined the Daughters of Charity of St. Vincent de Paul (3 March 1883), but after four years she was compelled to leave, mainly because of ill health. In 1891, she met Fr. Luigi Tezza, a Camillian priest, and at his suggestion she founded a congregation (2 February 1892). It followed the rule of St. Camillus de Lellis and aimed, like the Camillians, to care for the sick in hospitals, clinics, and rest homes. Giuseppina took her vows privately (1895), since her application for official ecclesiastical approval was at first rejected. Papal approval of the congregation came in 1909. She died peacefully and was interred in Rome, but later translated to Grottaferrata.

At her beatification during the ninth general assembly of the Synod of Bishops dealing with the consecrated life, Pope John Paul II declared: "To belong totally to God, who is loved and honored in the needy, was her constant concern. . . . She invites all who are called to the consecrated life to respond generously, as she does all who fulfill their vocation in family life: God has a plan of holiness for everyone."

Feast: 16 October.

Bibliography: B. BRAZZAROLA, *Madre G. Vannini* (Rome 1956). G. SANDIGLIANO, *Madre G. Vannini* (Casale Monferrato 1925).

[F. G. SOTTOCORNOLA/EDS.]

VAZ, JOSEPH, BL.

Priest of the Oratory of St. Philip Neri, apostle of Ceylon (Sri Lanka); b. 21 April 1651, Benaulim, Province of Salcette, Goa, India; d. 16 January 1711, Kandy, Sri Lanka; beatified by John Paul II, 21 January 1995, Colomba, Sri Lanka.

Vaz, ordained in 1676, labored incessantly in his native Goa, though he desired to go to Ceylon, where the Dutch denied religious freedom to Catholics. In 1681, he undertook a difficult missionary assignment in Kanara. He returned to Goa in 1685 convinced that the task in Ceylon could best be accomplished by a religious society. Toward that end Vaz associated himself with a group of priests that under his leadership formed an Oratory of St. Philip Neri. In the spring of 1686, accompanied by a lay brother, Vaz arrived in Ceylon. Because of the persecution, he disguised himself as a beggar. Though hunted as a criminal and forced to endure many hardships, he ministered to souls there. Eventually he won the confidence of the king of Kandy through the working of a miracle, and religious liberty was restored. In 1697, fellow Oratorians joined him. Under his supervision the territory was geographically divided, each Oratorian being responsible for an assigned area. Through his efforts more than 70,000 openly professed the faith in Ceylon. Because of his success ecclesiastical authorities wanted to heap honors upon him, but he managed to resist. By the time he died, he was revered for holiness. He was buried in the church he built in Kandy, which has since been destroyed and the relics lost. A shrine in his honor was inaugurated in Mangalore 6 February 2000. Vaz's cause for beatification was opened in Ceylon in 1737; the necessary miracle attributed to his intercession was approved 6 July 1993.

Pope John Paul II praised Vaz, Sri Lanka's first blessed, who "answering the call of the Holy Spirit, left his homeland for a country where the Church had no priests for more than three decades. He came in absolute poverty and lived like a beggar, guided by a burning desire to lead people to Christ." He is the patron of Goa, India.

Feast: 16 January.

Bibliography: P. COURTENAY, *History of Ceylon,* tr. M. G. FRANCIS, abridged translation (New Delhi 1999). C. GASBARRI, *A Saint for the New India* (Allahabad 1961). S. G. PERERA, *Life of the Venerable Father Joseph Vaz* (Galle, Ceylon 1953); *The Oratorian Mission in Ceylon* (Colombo, Ceylon 1936). W. L. A. DON PETER, *Star in the East* (Colombo, Sri Lanka 1995). G. SCHURHAMMER, *Lexikon für Theologie und Kirche*, first edition, 10;511.

[J. WAHL/EDS.]

VENDRAMINI, ELISABETTA, BL.

Foundress of the Franciscan Tertiary Sisters of Saint Elizabeth of Hungary; b. 9 April 1790, Bassano del Grappa (near Treviso), Italy; d. 2 April 1860, Padua; beatified in Rome by Pope John Paul II, 4 November 1990.

Elisabetta was educated in an Augustinian convent, where she was imbued with an intense spirituality. In 1917, Elisabetta broke off her six-year engagement on the evening before her wedding because she felt a strong, clear calling to dedicate herself to the poor. She cared for children in her hometown, then joined the staff of the Capuchin orphanage (1820). In 1821 she assumed the habit of the Third Order of St Francis. After moving to Padua (1827), she again worked with children and opened a tuition-free school at Padua with two friends (1829). She then founded the Sisters of St. Elizabeth, a religious institute to care for orphans, elderly women, and the sick (1830). The congregation's constitution, using the rule of the Third Order Regular of St. Francis, was completed 4 October 1830, and the first sisters were professed the following year. Elisabetta served as superior for more than three decades before her death.

Speaking of Blessed Elisabetta at her beatification, Pope John Paul II explained that she "teaches us that wherever faith is strong and sure, our charitable outreach to our neighbor will be more daring. Wherever our sense of Christ is more acute, our sense of the needs of our brothers and sisters will be more correct and on target."

Feast: 2 April (Franciscans).

Bibliography: *Madre Elisabetta Vendramini e la sua opera nella documentazione del tempo* (Padua 1972). *L'Osservatore Romano,* English edition, no. 6 (1990):1.

[K. RABENSTEIN]

VENEGAS DE LA TORRE, MARÍA DE JESÚS SACRAMENTADO, ST.

Baptized María Natividad; virgin, nurse, foundress of the Congregation of Daughters of the Sacred Heart of Jesus; b. 8 September 1868, La Tapona near Zapotlanejo, Jalisco, Mexico; d. 30 July 1959, Guadalajara; canonized 21 May 2000 at Rome by John Paul II.

When María was nineteen years old, her parents, both practicing Catholics, died and she was placed in the care of her paternal aunt and uncle. She had devotion for the Blessed Sacrament and participated in parish life. Two years later she joined the flourishing Association of the Children of Mary (8 December 1889) in her hometown. Following spiritual exercises in November 1905,

she decided to enter the Daughters of the Sacred Heart of Jesus, a pious union originally founded by Guadalupe Villaseñor de Perez Veria to care for patients in Guadalajara's Sacred Heart Hospital, which had recently been founded by the future bishop Atenógenes Silva y Alvarez Tostado (2 February 1886). Sister María lived in the hospital from 5 December 1905 until her death at age ninety-one. Her simplicity, tender love, and obedience to her superiors attracted others to her. In 1912, she was elected vicaress and maintained that position until 25 January 1921, when she was elected superior general. Because Mother María wrote the constitutions that gained canonical approval (1930) for the congregation, she is regarded as its foundress. Her cause for canonization was opened in 1978.

When John Paul II declared Venegas the first female saint of Mexico, he said: "Most faithful in observing the constitutions, most respectful toward bishops and priests and solicitous of seminarians, Saint María of Jesus of the Blessed Sacrament is an eloquent testimony of absolute consecration to the service of God and suffering humanity."

Feast: 30 July.

[K. RABENSTEIN]

VERSIGLIA, LUIGI, BL.

A.k.a. Aloysius of John Bosco, missionary bishop, Salesian protomartyr; b. 5 June 1873, Oliva Gessi (near Pavia), Italy; d. 25 February 1930, Lin-Chow Tsieu, southern China; beatified in Rome with Callisto Caravario by John Paul II, 15 May 1983.

Luigi studied at the oratory of St. John Bosco in Valdocco (1885–89), before joining the Salesians at age sixteen. He earned a doctorate in philosophy from the Gregorian University (1893), received presbyteral ordination in 1895 (with a dispensation because he was only twenty-two), then served as the rector and the demanding, but idolized, novice master at the Genzano, Rome (1896 to 1905). On 7 January 1906, he arrived in Macao as head of the first Salesian mission to the Far East. In the Portuguese colony he founded an orphanage, which later became the Salesian motherhouse in the Orient. After his consecration (9 January 1921) in Canton cathedral as vicar apostolic, he took up his work in Shiu Chow. All his many skills were engaged to found schools, a seminary, two leper colonies, and medical facilities; he served as printer, catechist, sacristan, gardener, builder, painter, and barber, in addition to his priestly duties. The turmoil following the 1902 overthrow of the last emperor permitted armed bands and pirates to roam the countryside. In 1930, the river boat on which Bishop Versiglia, Fr. Caravario, and four young teachers traveled to the Lin-Chow mission was ambushed. The bishop successfully intervened to save the female teachers. He pleaded for Caravario's life to be spared, but both bishop and priest were shot to death. Versiglia's body was enshrined at the cathedral of Lin Kong-How, which was vandalized by the Red Guards during the Cultural Revolution.

John Paul II declared in his homily during their beatification that the blood of Versiglia and Caravario "is at the foundation of the Chinese Church, as the blood of Peter is at the foundation of the Church of Rome."

Feast: 13 November (Salesians).

Bibliography: *Acta Apostolicae Sedis* 78 (1986): 137–39. *L'Osservatore Romano,* English edition, no. 21 (1983): 1. G. BOSIO, *Monsignor Versiglia e Don Caravario* (Turin 1935); *Martiri in China* (Turin 1977). B. LARENO, *Assassinio di Mons. Luigi Versiglia e di Don Callisto Caravario* (Hong Kong 1933). T. LEWICKI, *"Ten kielich mam wypelniać krwią": opowiesc o pierwszych meczennikach salezjanskich* (Warsaw 1985). A. J. ORTAS, "Protomartiri Salesiani in missione" in *Martirio e spiritualità apostolica* 12 (1983): 17–65. M. RASSIGA, *Blood on the River Bank,* tr. J. CARPELLA (Hong Kong 1980).

[K. RABENSTEIN]

Joseph de Veuster. (The Library of Congress.)

VEUSTER, JOSEPH DE (FR. DAMIEN), BL.

In religious life, Damien; Picpus (SS.CC.) priest, missionary to lepers; b. 3 January 1840, Tremeloo, Belgium; d. 15 April 1889, Molokai, Hawaii, USA.

Joseph, one of many children of prosperous peasants, was sent to college at Braine-le-Comte, to prepare for a commercial career, but he decided to follow his eldest brother, Auguste (later Fr. Pamphile), into the Congregation of the Sacred Hearts of Jesus and Mary (Picpus Fathers) at Louvain. He was professed on 7 October 1860, taking the name Damien. When Fr. Pamphile was unable to sail for the missions, Damien received permission to go in his place. He arrived in Honolulu, Hawaii, in 19 March 1864, and was ordained 21 May in Our Lady of Peace Cathedral.

Damien served for 8 years as a missionary on the island of Hawaii at Puna and Kohala. In 1873, when the vicar apostolic, Louis Maigret, decided to supply a priest for Kalaupapa, the Molokai leper settlement, Damien volunteered. On 10 May 1873, he went to Molokai and was subsequently given permission to remain there permanently. The colony's 800 lepers had only the clothing and food rations supplied by the government. Officially, Damien was the pastor of the Catholics in the colony, but actually he served as the lepers' physician, counselor, teacher, house-builder, sheriff, maker of musical instruments, gravedigger, and undertaker in order to transform their prison into a home. For 10 of his 16 years with the lepers, he was without the companionship of other priests. He founded two orphanages at the leprosarium, and effectively fought the immorality, drunkenness, and lawlessness that he found among the adult lepers when he came. Most importantly he instilled in his flock a sense of their human dignity; he taught them to live rather than simply await death.

By 1884, when he had contracted leprosy (Hansen's disease), he wrote that he would not wish to he cured if the price of his cure involved leaving the island and giving up his work. He continued that work untiringly until the month before his death. He was buried next to the Church he built, St. Philomena. In 1936 his relics were translated to Louvain, Belgium, where they were placed in a crypt of his congregation's church.

John Paul II beatified Fr. Damien on the Sacred Heart Basilica esplanade in the Koekelberg neighborhood of Brussels, Belgium, Pentecost Sunday, 4 June 1995. After the beatification ceremony, Fr. Damien's right hand was returned to the Hawaiian people, who placed it in his original grave at Kalaupapa, Molokai. In

1965, his sacrifices were honored with the placement of a bronze statue of Damien in Statuary Hall in the U.S. Capitol to represent Hawaii. Less than two months after his death, a "leprosy fund" was established in London, the first such organized effort devoted to helping the victims of this disease.

Before and after his death, derogatory rumors circulated regarding Damien's morals, primarily because some held the mistaken notion that Hansen's disease was sexually transmitted. He was completely exonerated by a thorough investigation made shortly after he died. During his last years he also suffered from the misunderstanding of his superior and some fellow priests because of his fund raising efforts and invitation to a secular priest to join him. One attack upon Damien's reputation by a Protestant clergyman was answered by R. L. Stevenson in his *Open Letter to Dr. Hyde* (Boston 1900). He is the patron of lepers and those with incurable diseases, particularly AIDS.

Feast: 15 April.

Bibliography: *Acta Apostolicae Sedis* (1995): 633–644. Archives, Hawaii Catholic Mission. P. BRADLEY, *Father Damien, SS.CC., Missionary* (Rome 1990). E. BRION, *Comme un arbre au bord des eaux. Le Pére Damien, apôtre des lépreux* (Paris 1994); *Un étrange bonheur. Lettres du Père Damien lépreux* (Paris 1988). M. R. BUNSON, *Father Damien: The Man and His Era* (Huntington, Ind. 1989). G. DAWS, *Holy Man. Father Damien of Molokai* (Honolulu 1984). H. EYNIKEL, *Het zieke paradijs. De biografie van Damiaan,* 2d. ed. (Antwerp 1994). V. JOURDAN, *The Heart of Father Damien* tr. F. LARKIN and C. DAVENPORT, rev. ed. (New York 1960). *L'Osservatore Romano,* English edition, no. 23 (1995). L. DE REYES, *Damien De Veuster SSCC, un homme aux relations théologales* (Montréal 1989). D. THOMAS, *Crusaders for God* (New York 1952), 22–50. R. YZENDOORN, *History of the Catholic Mission in the Hawaiian Islands* (Honolulu 1927). J. FARROW, *Damien the Leper* (New York 1937).

[R. E. CARSON]

VICUÑA, LAURA, BL.

Virgin, martyr; b. 5 April 1891, Santiago, Chile; d. 22 January 1904, Junín de los Andes, Argentina; beatified at Turin, Italy, by Pope John Paul II, 3 September 1988.

Following the death in 1895 of her soldier father, José Domingo Vicuña, Laura's mother Mercedes Piño moved the family to Junín de los Andes, Neuquén, Patagonia. Because of the family's poverty and her inability to find work, Mercedes became the mistress of a local *hacendero*, Manuel Mora. In Junín Laura and her younger sister Julia Amanda were accepted into the new school run by the Daughters of Mary Help of Christians (1900). Laura came to understand that her mother's illicit union

endangered her soul. Laura pledged her life for her mother's conversion before her confessor. Laura fell ill during the winter of 1903 and died at age thirteen from internal injuries inflicted by Manuel Mora during a final confrontation. After Laura admitted on her deathbed the promise she had made to God—her life for Mercedes' salvation—her mother left Mora and returned to the Church. Vicuña's body rests in the María Auxiliadora Chapel.

Pope John Paul II called her the "Eucharistic flower of Junín de los Andes, whose life was a poem of purity, sacrifice, and filial love" (beatification homily). Patron of Argentina.

Feast: 22 January (Salesians).

Bibliography: A. AUFFRAY and A. SWIDA, *Pszeniczne klosy: opowiesc o niezwyklym zyciu trojga wychowanków salezjánskich,* 2nd ed. (Łodz 1982). J. M. BLANCO, *Laura, la flor del paraíso* (San José Costa Rica 1942).

[K. RABENSTEIN]

VIETNAM, MARTYRS OF, SS.

A.k.a. Andrew Dung-Lac An Tran and 116 Companions, martyrs of Tonkin; martyrs of Indo-China; d. 18th-19th centuries. Canonized 19 June 1988 by Pope John Paul II.

For centuries, Indochina was divided into five regions: Tonkin (Bắc Việt, north Vietnam), Annam (Trung Việt, central Vietnam), Cochin-China (Nam Việt, south Vietnam), Laos, and Cambodia. Not long after the Portuguese arrived in Indochina, Christianity was introduced in 1533 by Inigo (Ignatius), who was apparently a European religious on his way to China. Inigo remained in the region for two years. Other missionaries labored intermittently in this little-frequented region for several decades. The Jesuits opened the first stable mission in 1615 at Đà Nẵng (Trung Việt) with the arrival of the Neopolitan Francesco Buzomi and Portuguese Diego Carvalho. They ministered to Japanese converts who had been driven from Japan by persecution. Alexander de Rhodes, SJ (1591–1660), the "apostle of Vietnam," arrived in 1624, and in 1627 went to Hanoi, capital of Tonkin. His success was extraordinary. The first year he baptized several thousand, including the king's sister. In 1630, he was expelled and the first Christian (unnamed) was beheaded for the faith. Rhodes returned to Vietnam in 1639, reporting that there were now 100,000 Vietnamese Catholics. In 1645, he was banished again, returned to France, and founded the Paris Seminary for Foreign Missions. The influx of new missionaries from the Society for Foreign Missions led to a period of swift growth; in 1658, there were 300,000 Catholics in Tonkin alone. The first seminary opened in 1666, and the first two native priests were ordained in 1668. A native religious congregation of women, the Lovers of the Cross *(Amantes de la Croix, Dòng Mến Thánh Giá)*, began in 1670.

Sporadic persecutions occurred up to 1698, when the first severe one erupted. Others followed (notably 1712, 1723, and 1750) during which at least 100,000 Christians, including the first of the canonized (Gil and Lenziniana, 1745), were martyred. A temporary peace took effect when the vicar apostolic arranged a treaty (1787) between France and a pretender to the Vietnamese throne, Nguyện-Ánh, who was given French military aid to become Emperor Gia- Long (1806). His successors, Minh Mạng and Tự-Đức, increased the ferocity of the persecutions. Minh banished all foreign missionaries and required Vietnamese Christians to apostatize by trampling a crucifix underfoot. After abating for a time, in 1847, suppression of Christianity was renewed when the emperor suspected foreign missionaries and Vietnamese Christians of aiding in the rebellion of one of his sons. Christians were marked on their faces with the words *tả đạ* ("false religion"); husbands were separated from their wives, and children from their parents. During the 19th century, between 100,000 and 300,000 Christians suffered for their faith, including most of those canonized. Catholic resistance, shown notably in hiding priests, was heroic. In the five years between 1857 and 1862, it is estimated that more than 5,000 faithful were martyred in addition to 215 native priests and nuns, and about 40,000 Catholics were dispossessed and exiled from their home regions. In 1917 no less than 2,078 causes from this last group were introduced; 25 of these were beatified in 1951.

Although the records of most who suffered have been destroyed, a total of 117, including 96 Vietnamese, 11 Spanish Dominicans, and 10 French members of the Paris Society for Foreign Missions *(Missions Étrangères de Paris)* (MEP) were canonized. Among them were 8 bishops, 50 priests (15 Dominicans, 8 members of the Paris Foreign Mission Society, 27 seculars), 1 seminarian, and 58 lay people (9 Dominican tertiaries and 17 catechists). The names of this representative sample of 117 martyrs follows. These martyrs were beatified on four separate occasions: 64 in 1900 by Pope Leo XIII; 8 in 1906 by Pope Pius X (all Dominicans); 20 in 1909 also by Pius X; and 25 in 1951 by Pope Pius XII. The corporate feast of the saints is 24 November. A personal feast day is shown only when it is not the *dies natalis*. This date is given to aid further research in older documents.

Almato, Pedro (Phêrô Almato Bính), Dominican priest; b. 1830 at Sassera (Vich), Spain; d. 1 November 1861, at Hải Dương, Tonkin. He was first sent to the Phil-

A martyrs' cemetery in Vietnam. (© Tim Page/CORBIS.)

ippines upon his profession as a Dominican. Thereafter he was sent to Ximabara under Jerome Hermosilla, with whom he was beheaded. Beatified 1906.

Berrio-Ochoa, Valentín (Valentine Berriochoa, Valentinố Berrio-Ochoa Vinh), Dominican bishop of Central Tonkin; b. 1827 at Ellorio (Vitoria), Spain; d. 1 November 1861 at Hải Dương, Tonkin. Following his profession in the Order of Preachers, he was sent to the Philippines, where he was known as an especially devout member of the order. In 1858, he was consecrated titular bishop of Tonkin and appointed vicar apostolic. Upon his arrival in Vietnam, he faced persecution by the government and worked in extremely difficult conditions. Like his Master, the bishop was betrayed by one of his own who had apostatized. In 1861, he was arrested, degraded, imprisoned, tortured, and beheaded with Bishop Hermosilla and Fr. Almato. For a time Valentine's cause was separated from the group because his intercession was credited with several miracles. Beatified 1906.

Bonnard, Jean-Louis (John Louis Bonnard Hương), priest; b. 1824 at Saint-Christo-em-Jarez, France; d. 1 May 1852 Nam Định, Tonkin. He was a attached to the MEP during his work in Annam. While awaiting execution, he wrote a letter of farewell to his family. He was beheaded at the age of 28. Beatified 1900.

Buong Viet Tong, Paul (Paul Doi Buong, Paul Tong Viet Buong, Phaolô Tổng Việt Bường), soldier; b. in Phủ Cam, Huế (Trung Việt); d. 23 October 1833, in Thủ Đức (Nam Việt) He was the captain of the Emperor Minh Mạng's bodyguard. As a Christian he became attached to the MEP. He was arrested in 1832, degraded, and suffered for months before he was beheaded. Beatified 1900. Feast: 22 October.

Cam, Dominic (Đaminh Cẩm), priest, Dominican tertiary; b. at Cẩm Chương, Bắc Ninh, Tonkin; d. 3 March 1859, at Hưng Yên, Tonkin. Beatified 1951.

Can Nguyen, Francisco Javier (Francis Xavier Can, Phanxicô Xaviê Cẩn), lay catechist; b. 1803 at Sơn Miêng, Hà Đông, West Tonkin; d. 20 November 1837, at Ô Cầu Giấy, Tonkin. He was a catechist for the fathers of the MEP. Strangled in prison. Beatified 1900.

Canh Luong Hoang, José (Joseph Canh, Giuse Hoàng Lương Cảnh), physician, Dominican Tertiary; b. ca. 1763-1765 at Làng Văn, Bắc Giang, Tonkin; d. 5 September 1838, at Bắc Ninh, Tonkin. Beheaded. Beatified 1900.

Castaneda, Jacinto (Jacinto Castaneda Gia), Dominican priest; b. 1743 at Jávita (Valencia), Spain; d. 7 November 1773 at Đồng Mỏ, Tonkin. After his profession as a Dominican, he was sent to the Philippines. An extant account tells of the difficulties of their sailing across the Atlantic, their march across Mexico, and a difficult final voyage across the Pacific. When they finally arrived, Manila was in the hands of the English. After months of searching for his Dominican brothers, he located the community and was ordained. Thereafter he travelled by ship another 66 days to China, from where he was deported to Tonkin. His ministry lasted for only a very short time before he was arrested and imprisoned for three years. He was beheaded with Vincent Liem. Beatified 1906.

Chieu van Do, Francisco (Francis Chieu, Francis Do van Chieu, Phanxicô Đỗ Văn Chiểu), Dominican tertiary, lay catechist; b. ca. 1796-97 at Trung Lễ, Liên Thủy, Nam Định, Tonkin; d. 12 June 1838 at Nam Định. Francis aided the Dominican priests in their Vietnamese mission. He was captured in the village of Kiên-Lao with Bishop Domingo Henares, whom he was serving as catechist, and beheaded with him. His remains were also retrieved by Christians seeking their preservation. Beatified 1900. Feast: 25 June.

Con, John Baptist (Gioan Baotixita Cồn), married man, lay catechist; b. 1805 at Kẻ Bàng, Nam Định (near Hanoi, Tonkin); d. 8 November 1840, at Bảy Mẫu, Tonkin. Beheaded. Beatified 1900. Feast: 7 November.

Cornay, Jean-Charles (John Cornay, John Corny, Jean-Charles Cornay Tân), priest; b. 1809 at Loudun (Poitiers), France; d. 20 September 1837, at Sơn Tây (West Tonkin). Cornay worked in Annam as a member of the MEP. He was arrested at Bản-no, Tonkin. He had been framed by the wife of a brigand chief, who had planted weapons in a plot of land that he cultivated. Thereafter Cornay was kept in a cage for three months and taken out only to be bound and brutally beaten. He was compelled to use his fine voice to sing to his captors. Beatified 1900. Feast: 8 February.

Cuénot, Étienne-Théodore (Stephen Cuénot, Étienne-Théodore Cuénot Thể), bishop, vicar apostolic; b. 1802 at Beaulieu, Besançon, France; d. 14 November 1861, at Bình Định, Cochin-China. He was ordained, became a member of the MEP, and was sent to Annam. In 1833, he was appointed vicar apostolic of East Cochin-China and consecrated bishop in Singapore. He labored in the missions, establishing three vicarates during his 25-year episcopate. When the persecutions heightened he was safely hidden until he had to emerge for water at which time he was arrested. He died of dysentery just before the edict for his execution arrived. Beatified 1909. Feast: 8 February.

Dac Nguyen, Matthew (Matthew Nguyen van Phuong, Matthew Phung, Matthêô Nguyễn Văn Đắc (Phủng), lay catechist; b. ca. 1801 at Kẻ Lai (Ke-lay), Quảng Bình (Trung Việt); d. 26 May 1861, near Đồng-Hới (Trung Việt). Like Andrew Dung Lac, he used an alias. Beheaded. Beatified 1909.

Da, Peter (Peter Da, Phêrô Đa), lay catechist; b. at Ngọc Cục, Nam Định, Tonkin; d. 17 June 1862, in Định. He was burnt alive in a bamboo hut with two Catholic fishermen. Beatified 1951.

Dat Dinh, Domingo Nicolás (Dominic Nicholas Dat, Đaminh Đinh Đạt), soldier; b. 1803 in Phú Nhai, Nam Định, Tonkin; d. 18 July1838, in Nam Định. When it was discovered that Dominic was a convert to Christianity, he was arrested, and stripped of his military position for embracing the faith. He may have been a Dominican tertiary. Strangled. Beatified 1900.

Dat, Juan (John Dat, Gioan Đạt), priest; b. ca. 1764 in Đồng Chuối, Thanh Hóa (Trung Việt); d. 28 October 1798, in West Tonkin. Đạt, described as a man of great serenity, was ordained to the priesthood in 1798. Following his arrest as an outlawed priest, he was held in captivity for 3 months, then beheaded. He and Manuel Trieu were the first Vietnamese diocesan priests for whose martyrdom a written account has been preserved. Beatified 1900.

De Van Nguyen, Tomás (Thomas De, Tôma Nguyễn Văn Đệ), tailor, Dominican tertiary; b. 1810, in Bồ Trang, Nam Định, Tonkin; d. 19 December 1839, in Cổ Mê, Tonkin. He was strangled with four others for giving shelter to the missionaries. Beatified 1900.

Delgado y Cebrian, Ignacio (Ignatius Delgado, Clemente Ignatius Delgado, Clementé Ignaxiô Delgado Hy); Dominican bishop of East Tonkin; b. ca. 1761 at Villa Felice, Spain; d. 21 July 1838, at Nam Định, Tonkin. Most of the information on Delgado derives from the decree of condemnation. After professing himself as a Dominican, he was sent to the Tonkinese mission, where he labored for nearly 50 years and was appointed vicar apostolic of East Tonkin. He had been hidden in the village of Kien-Lao until he was betrayed through the artful questioning of a young boy. The bishop was locked in a cage. When questioned he answered truthfully about himself but would reveal nothing about other Christians. For this the 76-year-old bishop died of dysentery and hunger in a cage exposed to the summer sun. After his death soldiers cut off his head and tossed his remains into the river, where they were recovered by fishermen and honorably buried by Jerome Hermosilla. Beatified 1900. Feast: 11 July.

Diaz Sanjurjo, José (Joseph Diaz, Giuse Maria Diaz Sanjuro An), Dominican bishop, vicar apostolic; b. 1818 at Santa Eulalia de Suegos, Lugo, Spain; d. 20 July 1857 in Nam Định, Tonkin. His parents had determined that he would have a successful career using his literary skills. He secretly entered the Dominicans at Ocada, Spain. There he was trained for the missions. He made his vows at Cadiz prior to undertaking the 120-day voyage to Manila, where he was assigned teaching duties at the University of Santo Tomás. After six months, he entered Tonkin with Melchoir Garcia-Sampedro under the cover of night disguised in native dress. Shortly thereafter, Diaz was appointed vicar apostolic of Central Tonkin with Garcia as his coadjutor. Although the Christian community tried to hide them as the persecution intensified, Sanjuro was arrested in a surprise raid and imprisoned for two months during which he demonstrated his forgiveness of his betrayer. He was beheaded and his body thrown into the sea. Beatified 1951.

Dich Nguyen, Anthony (Anthony Nguyen Dich, Antôn Nguyễn Đích), farmer; b. in Chi Long, Nam Định, Tonkin; d. 12 August 1838, Bảy Mẫu, Tonkin. Anthony used his wealth from agriculture generously to assist the work of the MEP. He was arrested for sheltering priests, including James Nam, who were fleeing government persecution. Beheaded. Beatified 1900.

Diem The Nguyen, Vincent (Vinh Sơn Nguyễn Thế Điểm), priest; b. 1761 at An Đô, Quảng Trị (Trung Việt); d. 24 November 1838, at Đồng Hới (Trung Việt). Beheaded. Beatified 1900.

Du Viet Dinh, Tomás (Thomas Du, Tôma Đinh Viết Dụ), priest, Dominican tertiary; b. 1774 at Nam Định, Tonkin; d. 26 November 1839, at Bảy Mẫu, Tonkin. After his ordination Thomas worked in the Province of Nam Định. He underwent horrible tortures before he was beheaded. Beatified 1900. Feast: 31 May.

Due Van Vo, Bernardo (Bernard Vo van Due, Bênađô Vo Văn Duệ), priest; b. 1755 at Quần Anh, Nam Định, Tonkin; d. 26 November 1838, at Ba Tóa, Tonkin.

Bernard converted to the faith, studied in the seminary, and was ordained. After laboring for many years in the mission, Bernard retired. He was living quietly until he felt called to offer himself to the soldiers as a Christian priest. Beheaded at age 83. Beatified 1900. Feast: 1 August.

Dumoulin-Borie, Pierre (Peter Dumoulin, Phêrô Dumoulin-Borie Cao), missionary priest of the MEP; b. 1808 at Cors (diocese of Tulle), France; d. 24 November 1838, at Đồng Hới (Trung Việt). Peter studied for the priesthood in Paris, was ordained in 1832, and sent to Tonkin. He was arrested in 1836. While in prison he was appointed vicar apostolic and titular bishop of Western Tonkin, but was never consecrated. Beatified 1900.

Dung Lac An Tran, Andrew (Anrê Trần An Dũng (Lạc), priest; b. ca. 1795 in Bắc Ninh, Tonkin; d. 21 December 1839, Cầu Giấy, Tonkin. When Dung An Tran was 12, his family moved to Hanoi to find work. His non-Christian parents allowed their son to receive instruction from a lay catechist so that he might benefit from the education generally denied the poor. He was baptized Andrew at Vĩnh-Tri. He studied Chinese and Latin, served as a catechist for ten years, and then was ordained to the priesthood in 1823. He was a tireless preacher both by word and example in several parishes until his arrest in 1835 as a Christian. His parishioners gathered the money needed to purchase his release. Thereafter, he changed his name from Dũng to Lạc in order to disguise his identity and went to another area to continue his ministry. On 10 November 1839, he was again arrested with another Vietnamese priest, Peter Thi. Both were freed once ransom was paid on their behalf, but they were soon arrested again and taken to Hanoi, where priests of the MEP were singled out for especially harsh punishment. Beheaded. Beatified 1900. Feast formerly on 26 December.

Dung Van Dinh, Peter (Phêrô Dũng), lay catechist; b. in Đồng Hào, Thái Bình, Tonkin; d. 6 June 1862, in Nam Định, Tonkin. Beatified 1951.

Duong, Paul (Paul Dong, Phalô Vũ Văn Dủong), layman; b. 1792 at Vực Đường, Hưng Yên, Tonkin; d. 3 June 1862, in Nam Định, Tonkin. Beatified 1951.

Duong Van Truong, Peter (Peter Truong Dang Duong, Phêrô Trưởng Văn Đuong), lay catechist; b. 1808 at Kẻ Sở, Hà Nam, Tonkin; d. 18 December 1838, at Sơn Tây (West Tonkin). He was strangled together with another catechist, Peter Truật. Beatified 1900.

Duong, Vincent (Vinh-sơn Dương), layman; b. in Doãn Trung, Thái Bình, Tonkin; d. 6 June 1862, at Nam Định, Tonkin. Beatified 1951.

Fernández, José (Joseph Fernández, Giuse Fernández Hiển), Dominican priest; b. 1775 at Ventosa de la

Cueva, Spain; d. 24 July 1838 in Nam Định, Tonkin. After his profession as a Dominican friar, he studied in the seminary expressly to serve in the Vietnamese mission. In 1805, he was sent to Tonkin, where he was ordained. He was appointed provincial vicar there and arrested shortly thereafter. Beheaded. Beatified 1900. Feast: 11 July.

Gagelin, François (Francis Isidore Gagelin, Francois-Isidore Gagelin Kinh), priest; b. 1799 at Montperreux (Besançon), France; d. 17 October 1833 in Bãi Dâu (Bồng Sổn). Belonged to the MEP. Sent to Cochin-China in 1822 (age 23), where he was ordained to the priesthood upon his arrival. He worked zealously until the outbreak of persecution, when he gave himself up to the mandarin of Bồng Sổn and was strangled. Beatified 1900.

Gam Van Le, Matthew (Matthew Le van Gam, Matthêô Lê Văn Gẫm), merchant; b. ca. 1812 in Gò Công, Biên Hòa, Cochin-China; d. 11 May 1847, in Chợ Đũi. As a dedicated member of the MEP, he carried the missionaries in his fishing boat from Singapore to Annam. He was captured in this illegal act in 1846, imprisoned, tortured, and beheaded. Beatified 1900. Feast: 26 May.

Garcia Sampedro, Melchoir (Melchior Garcia-Sampedro Xuyên), Dominican, vicar apostolic; b. 1821 at Cortes, Asturias, Spain; d. 28 July 1858, in Nam Định. Melchoir was born into a poor family that was unable to provide him with an education. He earned his way through school by teaching grammar to younger students. He opted to become a Dominican (1845) and was prepared for the missions at the novitiate at Ocada. He went to the Philippines, and then to Tonkin in an arduous journey (with José Diaz Sanjurjo). Shortly after their arrival Garcia was named coadjutor to Diaz, the vicar apostolic. While Garcia wanted to proclaim publically that he was a priest, the local Christian community convinced him that his presence with them was needed, and they kept him in hiding. Eventually Garcia was found, arrested, and put in a cage with two native brothers. He was hacked to death, the brothers beheaded, and their remains were thrown into a ditch. Some of their relics were recovered. Beatified 1951.

Gil de Federich, Francisco (Francis Gil, Phanxicô Gil de Fedrich Tế), Dominican priest; b. 1702 in Tortosa, Cataluda, Spain; d. 22 January 1745 at Thăng Long, Tonkin. Francis was educated in Barcelona and became a Dominican there before being sent to the Philippines. In 1732, he continued on to Tonkin, where he was arrested in 1742. During his confinement Gil directed a fruitful apostolate, then he was beheaded. He is the earliest martyr of whom there is substantial documentation. Beatified 1906. Feast: 29 January.

Hanh Van Nguyen, Domingo (Dominic Du, Dominic Nguyen van Hanh, Đaminh Nguyễn Văn Hạnh),

Hạnh is his alias; his real name is Domingo Dụ, Dominican priest; b. 1772 in Năng A, Nghệ An (Trung Việt); d. 1 August 1838, in Ba Tóa, Tonkin. He ministered as a priest to persecuted Christians for decades before his arrest and execution as a Christian at age 67. Beatified 1900.

Hanh, Paul (Phaolô Hạnh), layman; b. 1826 in Chợ Quán, Gia Định, Cochin-China; d. 28 May 1859 near Saigon (Ho-Chi-Minh City). He abandoned formal practice of his faith to join a band of outlaws, although he secretly assisted the Christian community. When he was arrested for his crimes, he professed his faith and, after torture, was beheaded. Beatified 1909.

Henares, Domingo (Dominic Henarez, Đaminh Henares Minh); Dominican auxiliary bishop; b. 1765 in Baena, Cordova, Spain; d. 25 June 1838, in Nam Định, Tonkin. He was appointed bishop-coadjutor (1803) to Ignatius Delgado, vicar apostolic of Tonkin. After working for about 50 years in Vietnam, Bishop Henares hid himself in the village of Kiên-Lao with his bishop during a renewed outbreak of persecution. He managed to escape immediate arrest by hiding himself in a fishing boat. The boatman betrayed him, and a detachment of 500 soldiers was sent to arrest Henares and his catechist Francis Chiểu. They were kept separate from Delgado and beheaded two weeks after their bishop's death. His body was recovered and buried by Hermosilla. Beatified 1900.

Hermosilla, Jeronimo (Jerome Hermosilla, Jêrônimô Hermosilla Liêm), Dominican bishop East Tonkin; b. 1880 at Santo Domingo de la Calzada, Old Castile, Spain; d. 1 November 1861, Nam Định, Tonkin. After his profession as a Dominican, he was sent to Manila, where he was ordained. In 1828, he was appointed to the mission at East Tonkin. In April 1841, he succeeded Ignatius Delgado as vicar apostolic and consecrated bishop, which marked him for persecution. Nevertheless, he was able to serve his flock for 20 years. As his first episcopal task, he gathered the relics of his two predecessors and recorded the eyewitness accounts of their martyrdoms. After many trials and the loss of some of his finest supporters, Hermosilla was betrayed by an apostate. He and Berrio-Ochoa had been hidden aboard a ship that would take them to a group of Christians. They were captured, humiliated, and finally beheaded. Their bodies were guarded for several days to prevent Christians from rescuing the relics. Beatified 1906.

Hien Quang Do, José (Joseph Hien, Joseph Yen, Giuse Đỗ Quang Hiển), Dominican priest; b. 1775 in Đồng Chuổi, Ninh Bình, Tonkin; d. 9 May 1840, at Nam Định, Tonkin. Beheaded. Beatified 1900. Feast: 27 June.

Hieu Van Nguyen, Peter (Peter Nguyen van Hieu, Phêrô Nguyễn Văn Hiếu, lay catechist; b. 1783 in Đông

Chuối, Ninh Bình, Tonkin; d. there on 28 April 1840. His attachment to the MEP led to his beheading during the persecution of Minh Mạng. Beatified 1900.

Hoa Dac Phan, Simon (Simon Phan Dac Hoa, Simon Phan Dac Thu, Simon Phan Đắc Hòa), lay physician; b. 1778 in Mai Vĩnh, Thừa Thiên (Trung Việt); d. 12 December 1840, in An Hòa (Trung Việt). In addition to serving his community as a doctor, Simon was mayor of his native village. A married man with 12 children, he also assisted the evangelization efforts of the MEP. He persisted in coming to the aid of the persecuted clergy, which led to his arrest, torture, and execution. Beatified 1909.

Hoan trinh Doan, John (John Doan trinh Hoan, Gioan Đoàn Trinh Hoan), priest; b. ca. 1790 at Kim-Long, Thừa Thiên (Trung Việt); d. 26 May 1861 near Đồng Hới (Trung Việt). He received his education from the missionaries ministering in his land, continued his education through the seminary, and was ordained. Beheaded under King Tự-Đức. Beatified 1909.

Huong Van Nguyen, Lawrence (Lorenzo Huong, Laurensô Nguyễn Văn Hưởng), priest; b. ca. 1802 in Kẻ Sài, Hà Nội, Tonkin; d. 13 February 1855 or 1856, near Ninh-Bình, West Tonkin. Beatified 1909. Feast: 27 April.

Huy Viet Phan, Agustin (Augustine Phan Viet Huy, Augustinô Phan Viết Huy), soldier; b. 1795 in Hạ Linh, Nam Định, Tonkin; d. 12 June 1838, Thừa Thiên (Trung Việt). Beatified 1900. Feast:13 June.

Huyen, Dominic (Đaminh Huyện), layman; b. 1817 in Đông Thành, Thái Bình, Tonkin; d. 5 June 1862, in Nam Định, Tonkin. Beatified 1951.

Hy-Dinh-Ho, Michael (Michael Ho dinh Hy, Micae Hồ Định Hy), mandarin (high government official); b. ca. 1808 at Như Lâm; d. 22 May 1857 at An-Hòa near Huế (Trung Việt). Michael was born into a noble, Christian family. He became a great mandarin and superintendent of the royal silk mills. For a long time he did not practice his faith, but eventually he became a leader and protector of his fellow Christians. Beheaded. Beatified 1909.

Jaccard, François (Francis Jaccard, Phanxicô Jaccard Phan), priest; b. 1799 at Onnion, Annecy, Savoy, France; d. 21 September 1838, at Nhan Biểu (Trung Việt). He entered the seminary for MEP in Paris, was ordained, and was sent to Cochin-China in 1826. Strangled. Beatified 1900.

Kham Viet Pham, Dominic (Dominic An-Kham, Đaminh Phạm Viết Khảm), judge, Dominican tertiary; b. 1799 at Quần Cống, Nam Định ; d. 13 January 1859 in Nam Định, Tonkin. He was a wealthy, respected member of the community, as well as the prior of the Dominican

Confraternity. He died with his son and several other wealthy members of the confraternity who were protecting missionaries. Beatified 1951.

Khang Duy Nguyen, José (Joseph Klang, Giuse Nguyen Duy Khang), servant, Dominican tertiary; b. 1832 at Trà Vi, Nam Định, Tonkin; d. December 6, 1861, at Hải Dương, Tonkin. Joseph was Bishop Hermosilla's servant. While trying to rescue his master from prison, he was caught, punished, futher tortured, and finally beheaded. Beatified 1906.

Khanh, Peter (Phêrô Khanh), priest; b. 1780 at Hòa Duệ, Nghệ An (Trung Việt); d. 12 July 1842, Hà Tĩnh (Trung Việt). Beheaded. Beatified 1909.

Khoa, Pedro (Peter Khoa, Phêrô Võ Đăng Khoa), priest; b. 1790, in Thuận Nghĩa, Nghệ An (Trung Việt); d. 24 November 1838 at Đồng-Hới. Strangled. Beatified 1900.

Khoan Khan Pham, Paul (Phaolô Phạm Khắc Khoan), priest; b. 1771 in Duyên Mậu, Ninh Bình, Tonkin; d. there, 28 April 1840. Paul studied with the MEP, was ordained, and labored with the missionaries for 40 years. He was imprisoned and tortured for two years prior to his decapitation. Beatified 1900. Feast: 28 April.

Khuong, Thomas (Thomas Huong, Tôma Khuông), priest, Dominican tertiary; b. 1789 at Nam Hào, Hưng Yên, Tonkin; d. there January 30, 1860. Son of a mandarin, he suffered great tortures before his death. Beatified 1951.

Phung van Le, Emmanuel (Manuel Phung, Emmanuel Lê Văn Phụng), mandarin, catechist; b. 1796 at Đầu-Nước, Cù Lao Giêng (Nam Việt); d. 31 July 1859, near Châu Đốc (Nam Việt). Emmanuel was the father of a family. Garrotted. Beatified 1909.

Lenziniana, Mateo Alonzo (Matthew Leziniana, Matthew Liciniana, Matthêô Alonzo-Leciniana Đậu), Dominican priest; b. 1702 at Navas del Rey (Valladolid), Spain; d. 22 January 1745, at Thăng Long, Tonkin. Matthew was sent to Philippines after his ordination, then to Tonkin. There he ministered furtively to the Christian community while dodging the authorities for 13 years. He was beheaded with Francisco Gil and is one of the earliest of the canonized martyrs of Vietnam. Beatified 1906.

Liem de la Paz, Vicente (Vincent Liem da Pace, Vinh-sơn Lê Quang Liêm), Dominican priest; b. 1732 in Trà Lũ, Nam Định, Tonkin; d. 7 November 1773, in Đồng Mo, Tonkin. Vincent was born into the nobility of Tonkin. He labored as a priest for 14 years with Dominican Bishop Hyacinth Casteñeda prior to his arrest and execution by decapitation. Liêm is the first Indo-Chinese Dominican known to be martyred for the faith. Beatified 1906. Feast: 7 November.

Loan Ba Vu, Luke (Luca Vū Bá Loan), priest; b. 1756 in Trại Bút, Phú Đa, Tonkin; d. 5 June 1840, at Ô Cầu Giấy, Tonkin. Luke was raised in a Christian family. He ministered for decades to a people who revered him; beheaded for his priesthood. Beatified 1900. Feast: 4 June.

Loc Van Le, Paul (Paul Lok, Paul Le van Loc, Phaolô Lē Văn Lộc), priest; b. ca. 1830 at An Nhồn, Gia Định; d. 13 February 1859 at Gia Định (Saigon or Ho-Chi-Minh City). He served in the army prior to entering the seminary; beheaded shortly after his ordination to the priesthood. Beatified 1909.

Luu van Nguyen, Joseph (Joseph Nguyen van Luu, Giuse Nguyễn Văn Lụu), lay catechist; b. ca. 1790 at Cái-Nhum (Nam Việt); d. 2 May 1854 or 1855, at Vĩnh-long (Nam Việt). He died in prison from torture and abuse. Beatified 1909.

Luu, Peter (Phêrô Nguyễn Văn Lụu), priest; b. 1812 at Gò Vấp, Gia Định (Nam Việt); d. 7 April 1861, at Mỹ Tho (Nam Việt). Beatified 1909.

Mao Trong Ha, Dominic (Đaminh Maọ), layman; b. 1818 in Ngọc Cục, Nam Định, Tonkin; d. 16 June 1862, in Làng Cốc, Tonkin. Beatified 1951.

Marchand, Joseph (Giuse Marchand Du), priest; b. 1803 at Passavant, Besançon, France; d. 30 November 1835, in Thọ Đức near Saigon (Ho-Chi-Minh City). Joseph completed his theological studies at the seminary of MEP, was ordained, and sent to Annam (Vietnam). He was arrested at Saigon. Beatified 1900.

Mau, Dominic (Dominic Mau, Đaminh Mẫu), Dominican priest; b. 1808 in Phú Nhai, Nam Định, Tonkin; d. 5 November 1858, in Hưng Yên, Tonkin. He died after a long torture. Beatified 1951.

Mau, Francisco Javier (Francis Xavier) (Phanxicô Xaviê Hà Trọng Mậu), Dominican tertiary, catechist; b. 1790, in Kẻ Điểu, Thái Bình, Tonkin; d. 19 December 1839, in Cổ Mê, Tonkin. He was strangled with four companions, including Stephen Vinh and Dominic Uy. Beatified 1900.

Minh Van Phan, Philip (Philip Phan van Minh, Philiphê Phan Văn Minh), priest; b. 1815 in Cái Mỏn, Vĩnh Long (Caimon); d. 3 July 1853, at Định Khao. Philip joined the MEP and was ordained a priest for East Cochin-China. Beheaded. Beatified 1900.

Moi Van Nguyen, Agustín (Augustine Moi, Augustinô Nguyễn Văn Mới), day-laborer, Dominican tertiary; b. 1806 at Phù Trang, Nam Định, Tonkin; d.19 December 1839, in Cổ Mê, Tonkin. Agustín was known for his piety and charity, though a poor man himself. Strangled. Beatified 1900. Feast: 18 December.

My Huy Nguyen, Michael (Michael Mi, Michael Nguyen Huy My, Micae Nguyễn Huy Mỹ), married farmer; b. 1804 in Kẻ Vĩnh, Hà Nội, Tonkin; d. 12 August 1838, in Bảy Mẫu, Tonkin. Michael had been mayor of Vĩnh-Tri, where several of the saints were arrested. He served the Church faithfully, but gave special assistance to Anthony Đích, his son-in-law, to protect the missionaries during the persecution. When Đích tried to hide Fr. James Nam in 1838, they were all arrested and beheaded. Beatified 1900.

My Van Nguyen, Paul (Paul Mi, Phaolô Nguyễn Văn Mỹ), layman; b. 1798 at Kẻ Non, Hà Nam, Tonkin; d. 18 December 1838, at Sồn Tây. He was attached to the MEP. Strangled. Beatified 1900.

Nam, James (Jacob Nam, James Mai Nami, Giacôbê Đỗ Mai Năm), priest; b. 1781 in Đồng Biên, Thanh Hóa (Trung Việt); d. 12 August 1838, in Bảy Mẫu, Tonkin. James, a priest attached to the MEP, found refuge from persecution for a long period in the home of Anthony Đích. He was discovered and both were arrested together with Anthony's father-in-law, Michael Mỹ. Beheaded. Beatified 1900.

Néron, Pierre-François (Peter Francis Néron, Phêró Phanxicô Néron Bắc), priest; b. 1818 at Bornay, Saint-Claude (Jura), France; d. 3 November 1860, in Sồn Tây (West Tonkin). He entered the MEP in 1846, was ordained two years later (1848), and sent to Hong Kong. He labored in West Tonkin as director of the central seminary until his arrest and decapitation. Beatified 1909.

Ngan Nguyen, Paul (Phaolô Nguyễn Ngân), priest; b. 1771 in Kẻ Biên, Thanh Hóa (Trung Việt); d. 8 November 1840, in Bảy Mã, Nam Định, Tonkin. Beatified 1900.

Nghi, Josá (Joseph Nien Kim, Giuse Nguyễn Đình Nghi), priest; b. 1771 in Kẻ Vễ, Hà Nội, Tonkin; d. 8 November 1840 in Bảy Mẫu, Tonkin. He was beheaded because he was a member of the MEP. Beatified 1900.

Ngon, Lorenzo (Lawrence Ngon, Laurensô Ngôn), layman; b. at Lục Thủy, Nam Định; d. 22 May 1862, in Nam Định. Beatified 1951.

Nguyen, Domingo (Dominic Nguyen, Đaminh Nguyện), layman; b. 1802 in Ngọc Cục, Nam Định, Tonkin; d. 16 June 1862, in Làng Cốc, Tonkin. Beatified 1951.

Nhi, Domingo (Dominic Nhi, Đaminh Nhi), layman; b. at Ngọc Cục, Nam Định, Tonkin; d. 16 June 1861, in Làng Cốc, Tonkin. Beatified 1951.

Ninh, Dominic (Đaminh Ninh), layman; b. 1835 in Trung Linh, Nam Định, Tonkin; d. 2 June 1862, at An Triêm. Beatified 1951.

Quy Cong Doan, Pedro (Peter Qui, Phêrô Đoàn Công Quý), priest; b. 1826 in Búng, Gia Định (Nam Việt); d. 31 July 1859, in Châu Đốc (Nam Việt). Beheaded. Beatified 1909.

Quynh, Antonio (Anthony Quynh-Nam, Anthony Nguyen Huu Nam, Antôn Nguyện Hữ Quỳnh), physician, lay catechist; b. 1768 in Mỹ Hưởng, Quảng Bình (Trung Việt); d. 10 July 1840, Đồng Hới (Trung Việt). He was arrested in 1838 because of his attachment to the MEP. During his two-year imprisonment he tended the inmates and endured tortures. Strangled. Beatified 1900. Feast: 24 November.

Schoeffler, Agustin (Augustine Schoeffler Đông), priest, Dominican tertiary; b. 1822 at Mittelbronn (Nancy) Lorraine, France; d. 1 May 1851 in Sởn Tây (West Tonkin). Augustine joined the MEP and was sent to Vietnam in 1848. He labored in the missions for only a short time before his arrest and beheading. Beatified 1900.

Ta, José (Joseph Cai Ta, Cai Tả, Giuse Phạm Trọng Tả), soldier; b. 1800 at Quần Cống, Nam Định, Tonkin; d. 13 January 1859, in Nam Định. Tortured to death. Beatified 1951.

Thanh Van Dinh, Juan-Baptist (John Baptist Thanh, Gioan B. Đinh Văn Thành), lay catechist; b. 1796 in Nộn Khê, Ninh Bình, Tonkin; d. 28 April 1840, Ninh Bình. He was beheaded with Peter Hieu and Paul Khoan because of his attachment to the MEP. Beatified 1900.

Thanh Thi Le, Inés (Agnes De, Inê Lê Thị Thành Bà Đe]), married woman; b. 1781 at Bái-Đến, West Tonkin; d. 12 July 1841, at Nam Định. She was born into a Christian family and was the mother of six. She was caught carrying letters from the Christians in prison and arrested. Died in prison. Beatified 1909. Feast: 18 February.

Thé, Nicolás (Nicholas Duc Bui, Nicholas Bui Buc The, Nicôla Bùi Đức Thế), soldier, b. 1792 in Kiên Trung, Nam Định, Tonkin; d. 12 June 1838, at Thừa Thiên (Trung Việt). Beatified 1900. Feast: 13 June.

Thi Dang Le, José (Giuse Lê Đăng Thi), soldier; b. 1825 at Kẻ Văn, Quảng Trị (Trung Việt); d. 25 October 1860 at An-Hòa (Trung Việt). A captain in the army of King Tự-Đức. Once it was discovered that he was a Christian and he refused to deny his faith, he was garrotted. Beatified 1909. Feast: 24 October.

Thi van Truong, Pedro (Peter Pham Thi, Phêrô Trưởng Văn Thi), priest; b. 1763 at Kẻ Sở, Hà Nội, Tonkin; d. 21 December 1839, at Ô Cầu Giấy, Tonkin. Beheaded. Beatified 1900. Feast: 20 December.

Thien van Tran, Tomás (Thomas Tran Dien, Thomas Tran van Thien, Tôma Trẳn Văn Thiện), seminarian, lay catechist; b. 1820 at Trung Quán, Quảng Bình (Trung Việt); d. 21 September 1838, in Nhan Biểu (Trung Việt). He was studying with MEP, preparing for ordination at the time of his arrest. After being scourged, he was strangled at the age of 18. Beatified 1900. Feast: 21 September.

Thin Trong Pham, Luca (Lucius Cai Thin, Luca Phạm Trọng Thìn), layman; b. 1819 in Quần Cống, Nam Định ; d. 13 January 1862, in Nam Định. Beatified 1951.

Thinh, Martin (Matthew Ta Duc Thinh, Martin Thinh, Martinô Tâ Đức Thịnh), priest; b. 1760 in Kẻ Sặt, Hà Nội, Tonkin; d. 8 November 1840, in Bảy Mẫu, Tonkin. Martin, a member of the MEP, labored for decades as a priest to his own people. Beheaded with Martin Tho. Beatified 1900.

Tho, Martin (Martinô Tho), tax collector; b. 1787 at Kẻ Bèng, Nam Định, Tonkin; d. 8 November 1840, in Bay Mẫu, Tonkin. Martin, the head of his parish council, was martyred with Martin Thinh, an 80-year-old native priest, and Joseph Nghi. Beatified 1900.

Thong Kim Nguyen, Andrew (Andrew Thong Kim Nguyen, Anrê Nguyễn Kim Thông (Năm Thuông), politician, lay catechist; b. ca. 1790 in Gò Thị, Bình Định (Trung Việt); d. 15 July 1855, in Mỹ Tho (Miễn Tây Nam Việt). Andrew, the chief of his village, was exiled at the beginning of the persecution because of his devotion to the Catholic faith. He died from exhaustion and dehydration en route to exile at Mỹ-Tho. Beatified 1909. Feast: 18 February

Thuan, Peter (Phêrô Thuấn), fisherman; b. at Dông Phú, Thái Bình, Tonkin; d. 6 June 1862, in Nam Định, Tonkin. Burnt alive with Peter Đa. Beatified 1951.

Tinh Bao Le, Paul (Paul Le Bao Tinh, Phaolô Lê Bảo Tịnh), priest; b. 1793 at Trinh-Ha, Tonkin; d. 6 April 1857 at Sởn Tây (West Tonkin). He wrote a letter to the seminary of Kẻ Vĩnh in 1843 detailing the sufferings of Christian prisoners. Beheaded. Beatified 1909. Feast: 6 April.

Toai, Domingo (Dominic Toai, Đaminh Toái), fisherman; b. 1811 in Đông Thành, Thái Bình, Tonkin; d. 5 June 1862, in Nam Định, Tonkin. Burnt alive with Peter Da and Peter Thuan. Beatified 1951.

Toan, Tomás (Thomas Toan, Tôma Toán), Dominican tertiary, lay catechist; b. 1767 in Cẩn Phan, Nam Định, Tonkin; d. 27 June 1840, in Nam Định. Although he was teaching the faith to others, Thomas's faith waivered. After showing signs of apostatizing, he repented. In consequence, he was tortured and starved to death. Beatified 1900.

Trach, Domingo (Dominic Doai, Đaminh Trạch [Đoài]), priest, Dominican tertiary; b. 1792 in Ngoâi Bôi,

Nam Định, Tonkin; d. 18 September 1840, at Bảy Mẫu, Tonkin. Dominic, a native Dominican priest, had labored to evangelize his own land until his arrest. The following year Dominic was given the choice to renounce the faith and go free or suffer death. He confessed and encouraged his friends before his own beheading. Beatified 1900.

Trieu van Nguyen, Manuel (Emmanuel Nguyen van-Trieu, Emmanuel Nguyễn Văn Triệu), priest; b. ca. 1756 in Saigon (Ho-Chi-Minh City), Phú Xuân, Huế; d. 17 September 1798, in Bã Dầu (Bồng Sơn). Emmanuel, who had been born into a Christian family, joined the army. Later he was ordained to the priesthood at Pong-King and worked with his brother priests in the Paris Foreign Mission Society. He was arrested while visiting his mother and beheaded, becoming one of the first Vietnamese diocesan priests to die for the faith. Beatified 1900.

Trong Van Tran, Andrew (Andrew Tran van Trong, Anrê Trần Văn Trôg), soldier; b. 1817 in Kim Long, Huế (Trung Việt); d. 28 November 1835 at An Hòa, Huế. Trong was a young native soldier or silk-weaver to the king of Annam and attached to the MEP. When this affiliation was discovered by the authorities in 1834, he was arrested, stripped of his military rank, and imprisoned. Beatified 1900. Feast: 18 November.

Truat Van Vu, Peter (Peter Truat, Phêrô Vũ Văn Truật), lay catechist; b. 1816 in Kẻ Thiếc, Hà Nam, Tonkin; d. 18 December 1838, in Sỏn Tây (West Tonkin). Beatified 1900.

Trung Van Tran, Francisco (Francis Tran van Trung, Phanxicô Trần Văn Trung), soldier; b. 1825 in Phan-Xả; d. 2 May 1858, at An-Hòa (Trung Việt). Francis was a corporal in the army, who converted to Christianity. Beheaded. Beatified 1909. Feast: 6 October.

Tu Khac Nguyen, Pedro (Peter Tu, Phêrô Nguyễn Khắc Tụ), lay catechist; b. 1811 in Ninh Bình, Tonkin; d. 10 July 1840, in Đồng Hới (Trung Việt). Beheaded. Beatified 1900.

Tu Van Nguyen, Peter (Phêrô Nguyễn Văn Tự), Dominican priest; b. 1796 in Ninh Cường, Nam Định, Tonkin; d. 5 September 1838, in Bắc Ninh, Tonkin. Beatified 1900.

Tuan van Tran, Joseph (Giuse Tuân), Dominican priest; b. 1821 in Trần Xà, Hưng Yên, Tonkin; d. there 30 April 1861, after a long torture. Beatified 1951.

Tuan, Joseph (Giuse Tuẩn) (2nd of the name), layman; b. 1825 in Nam Điền, Nam Định; d. 7 January 1862, in Nam Định. Beatified 1951.

Tuan Ba Nguyen, Pedro (Peter Tu, Phêrô Nguyễn Bá Tuẩn), priest; b. 1766 in Ngọc Đồng, Hưng Yên, Tonkin; d. 15 July 1838, at Ninh Tai, Nam Định. Beatified 1900.

Tuc, Joseph (Giuse Túc), layman; b. 1852 in Hoàng Xá, Bắc Ninh, Tonkin; d. there on 1 June 1862. A child of 9 who was martyred for the faith. Beatified 1951.

Tuoc, Domingo (Dominic Tuoc, Đaminh Tước), priest; Dominican tertiary, b. 1775 in Trung Lao, Nam Định, Tonkin; d. 2 April 1839, in Nam Định. Died from wounds in prison. Beatified 1900.

Tuong, Andrew (Andrew Thuong, Anrê Tưởng), lay catechist; b. 1812 in Ngôc Cúc, Nam Định, Tonkin; d. 16 June 1862, in Làng Cốc, Tonkin. Beatified 1951.

Tuong, Vincent (Vincent Truong, Vinh-Sơn Tưởng), judge, layman; b. 1814 in Ngôc Cưc, Định, Tonkin; d. 16 June 1862, in Làng Cốc, Tonkin. Beatified 1951.

Tuy Le, Pedro (Peter Tu, Peter Le Tuy, Phêrô Lê Tùy), priest; b. 1773 in Bằng Sở, Hà Đông (West Tonkin); d. 11 October 1833, in Quan Ban. Arrested after many years of ministry and beheaded. Beatified 1900.

Uy Van Bui, Domingo (Dominic Uy, Đaminh Búi Văn Úy), Dominican tertiary, lay catechist; b. 1813 in Tiên Mon, Thái Bình, Tonkin; d. 19 December 1839, Cổ Mê, Tonkin. He was seized as a Christian with Thomas Đệ and strangled for refusing to abjure the faith. Beatified 1900.

Uyen Dinh Nguyen, José (Joseph Nguyen Dinh Uyen, Joseph Peter Uyen, Joseph Yuen, Joseph Uen, Giuse Nguyễn Đính Uyển), Dominican tertiary, lay catechist; b. ca. 1775 in Ninh Cưởng, Nam Định, Tonkin; d. 4 July 1838 in Hưng Yên, Tonkin. After a year's tortuous imprisonment, he was strangled in his cell. Beatified 1900. Feast: 3 July.

Van Van Doan, Peter (Peter Doan van Van, Phêrô Đoàn Văn Vân), lay catechist; b. ca. 1780 in Kẻ Bói, Hà Nam, Tonkin; d. 25 May 1857, at Sỏn Tây, West Tonkin. Beheaded. Beatified 1909.

Vénard, Jean-Théophane (Théophane Vénard, Giuse Theophanô Vénard Ven), priest; b. 21 November 1829 in St.-Loup-sur-Thouet (Deux-Sèvres), Poitiers, France; d. 2 February 1861, in Ô Cầu Giấ, Tonkin. This son of the village schoolmaster studied at the College of Douela-Fontaine, and at the seminaries at Montmorillon and Poitiers, where he was ordained subdeacon (1850). He transferred to the MEP (1851), was ordained priest on 5 June 1852, and departed for Hong Kong on 19 September. After fifteen months studying Vietnamese at Hong Kong he arrived (1854) secretly at his mission in West Tonkin, where the Christians had recently been tried by a series of persecutions under Minh Mạng. In 1856, he was expelled from Nam Định and went to Hanoi. Shortly after Vénard's arrival a new royal edict was issued against Christians; bishops and priests were obliged to seek refuge in caves, dense woods, the hulls of sampans, and elsewhere. Vénard, whose constitution had always been delicate, suffered almost constantly, but continued to exercise his ministry at night, and, more boldly, in broad day because he was greatly impressed by the courage of the Vietnamese Catholics who had been suffering since 1848. On 30 November 1860, he was betrayed by a Christian and captured at Kim Bàng. Tried before a mandarin, he refused to apostatize and was sentenced to be beheaded. While chained in a tiny bamboo cage, he wrote to his family beautiful and consoling letters.

Viên Đinh Dang, Joseph (Joseph Dang Dinh Vien, Joseph Nien, Giuse Đặng Đình Viên), Dominican tertiary, lay catechist; b. ca. 1786 in Tiên Chu, Hưng Yên, Tonkin; d. 21 August 1838, in Bảy Mẫu, Tonkin. Beatified 1900.

Vinh, Esteban (Stephen Vinh, Stephanô Nguyễn Văn Vinh), lay catechist, Dominican tertiary; b. 1814 in Phú Trang, Nam Định, Tonkin; d. 19 December 1839, at Cổ Mễ, Tonkin. Devout peasant; strangled with 4 companions, including Thomas Đệ. Beatified 1900.

Xuyen Van Nguyen, Domingo (Dominic Doan, Dominic Xuyen, Đaminh Nguyễn Văn Xuyên), Dominican priest; b. ca. 1787 in Hưng Lập, Nam Định, Tonkin; d. 26 November 1839, in Bảy Mẫu, Tonkin. Beheaded with Thomas Dụ. Beatified 1900. Feast: 26 October.

Yen Do, Vicente (Vincent Do Yen, Vinh Sơn Đỗ Yến), Dominican priest; b. ca. 1764 in Trà Lũ, Nam Định, Tonkin; d. 30 June 1838, in Hải Dương, Tonkin. After becoming a Dominican in 1808, he labored in the mission field until his martyrdom. From the publication of the edict of persecution in 1832, he lived six years in hiding and continued to minister secretly. He was finally betrayed and beheaded. Beatified 1900.

On 19 June 1988, some 8,000 exiled Vietnamese Catholics participated in the canonization ceremony in Rome. They heard Pope John Paul II announce: "The Vietnamese Church, with its martyrs and its witness, has been able to proclaim its desire and resolve not to reject the cultural traditions and the legal institutions of the country; rather, it has declared and demonstrated that it wants to incarnate them in itself, in order to contribute faithfully to the true building up of the country."

Bibliography: B. BLOOMFIELD, *Martyrs of Vietnam* (London 1995). M. J. DORCY, *Saint Dominic's Family* (Dubuque, Iowa, 1963) 498ff. V. GOMEZ, *Pedro Almato y Ribera, OP, Martir del Vietnam: Letters to Family and Friends* (Valencia 1987). *Kỷ Yếu Phong Thánh Tử Đạo Việt Nam* (Canonization of The Vietnamese Martyrs), prepared by the Canonization Committee (Vatican City 1989). MISSION ÉTRANGÈRES DE PARIS, *Le Clergé Annamite et ses Prêtres Martyrs* (Paris 1925). NGUYỄN BÁ TÒNG, *Les Martyrs de l'Annam*, (Hanoi 1937). TRẦN VĂN TRIẾT, *Histoire des Persecutions au Vietnam*, (Paris 1955). VINCENT TRẦN NGỌC THỤ, *Giáo Hội Việt Nam: Tập 1: Vụ Án Phong Thánh* (Vietnamese Church, Vol 1: Canonization Proceeding) (Vietnam 1987). TRỊNH VIỆT YÊN, *Máu Tử Đạo Trên Đất Việt Nam* (Blood of the Martyrs in the Land of Vietnam) (National Canonization Committee, U.S.A., 1987). *Witnesses of the Faith in the Orient* (Hong Kong 1989).

[THU BUI/K. RABENSTEIN]

VILAR DAVID, VICENTE, BL.

Martyr; married lay man; industrial engineer; b. 28 June 1889, Manises, Valencia, Spain; d. there on 14 February 1937; beatified by John Paul II, 1 October 1995.

Vicente, husband of Isabel Rodes Reig (d. 1993), was the youngest of eight children of a family that owned a ceramics factory. He received his initial education from the Piarists, then studied industrial engineering in Valencia. While working in his family's business, Vicente undertook charitable work among the poor, involved himself in parish activities and enacted some of the Church's social teaching during his tenure in several municipal positions. Beginning in 1931, he openly and courageously offered refuge to persecuted religious during the surge of anti-ecclesial sentiment and refused to moderate his own religious practices. He was killed "*in odium fidei*"; shot in the street a few yards from his home.

In beatifying Vicente, Pope John Paul II pointed to the new blessed's example, saying, "The activities of lay people are ways that lead to holiness if they are lived with sincerity and evangelical commitment."

Bibliography: V. CÁRCEL ORTÍ, *Martires españoles del siglo XX* (Madrid 1995). J. PÉREZ DE URBEL, *Catholic martyrs of the Spanish Civil War, 1936-1939*, tr. M. F. INGRAMS (Kansas City, Mo. 1993). *Acta Apostolicae Sedis* 19 (1995): 923–26. *L'Osservatore Romano*, English edition, no. 40 (1995): 1–3.

[K. RABENSTEIN]

VISINTAINER, AMABILE LUCIA, BL.

Known in religion as Mother Paolina of the Agonizing Heart of Jesus; foundress of the Daughters of the Immaculate Conception (*Irmazinhas da Imaculada Conceiçao*); b. 16 December 1865, Vigolo Vattaro, Trentino, Italy (then Austria); d. 9 July 1942, at Sao Paolo, Brazil; beatified by John Paul II, 18 October 1991, at Florianópolis, Sao Paulo, Brazil.

For two years before emigrating to Brazil with her family (1875), Amabile, the daughter of Antonio Napoleone Visintainer and Anna Pianezzei, worked in the local silk mill. With other immigrants they established the village of Vigolo (now part of Nova Trento, sixty miles from Florianópolis) in Santa Catarina Province. Upon her mother's death in 1886, Amabile assumed household responsibilities and cared for her twelve siblings. When her father remarried, Amabile was free to respond to her recurring dream of religious life. Together with Virginia Nicolodi and Teresa Maoli, Amabile pronounced religious vows 7 December 1895 before Bishop José de Camargo Barros of Curitaiba and assumed the name Paolina. The bishop approved the religious order that began in 1890 with Amabile and Virginia nursing a woman with cancer in an abandoned shack. The Sisters of the Immaculate Conception soon spread to nearby towns and to Sao Paolo, where they directed hospitals and asylums and assisted the recently emancipated slaves. In 1909, after difficult internal conflicts in the order, Mother Paolina accepted her removal from the office of mother general ''ad vitam'' by the archbishop, Duarte Leopoldo da Silva. For the next ten years she humbly served her sisters at Santa Casa de Bragança Paulista and remained assiduous in prayer. Although she never reclaimed her office as superior, Mother Paolina's reputation was rehabilitated, and she was venerated during her lifetime as the congregation's founder. Beginning in 1938, she suffered complications from illness and cancer that lead to her death.

During the ceremony of the first Brazilian citizen to be beatified, Pope John Paul II said: ''She was able to convert all her words and actions into a continual act of praise to God. . . . This being-for-others is the background for her whole life.''

Feast: 9 July (Bolzano).

Bibliography: F. A. FARACE, *Love's Harvest: The Life of Blessed Pauline*, ed. J. KINDEL and B. LEWIS (Milford, Ohio 1994). *L'Osservatore Romano*, English edition, no. 19 (1995): 6.

[K. RABENSTEIN]

VISITATION SISTERS, MARTYRS OF, BB.

Maria Gabriela de Hinojosa Naveros, and six other members of the Order of the Visitation of Holy Mary; b. 24 July 1872, in Alhama, Granada, Spain; d. 18 November 1936. Five of her sister companions died with her: Josefa Maria Barrera Izaguirre, b. 23 May 1881 in El Ferrol, La Coruna; Teresa Maria Cavestany y Anduaga, b. 30 July 1888 in Puerto Real, Cadiz; Maria Angela Olaizola Garagarza, b. 12 November 1893 in Azpeitia, Guipuzcoa; Maria Engracia Lecuona Aramburu, b. 2 July 1897 in Oyarzun, Guipuzcoa; and Maria Ines Zudaire Galdeano, b. 28 January 1900 in Echavarri, Navarra.

Maria Cecilia Cendoya Araquistain, b. 10 January 1910 in Azpeita, Guipuzcoa escaped execution with the rest and was martyred five days later, 23 November 1936. Beatified 10 May 1998 by John Paul II.

All of the nuns had been brought up in deeply Christian families, but they represented varying social and economic backgrounds. They were bonded in their vocation to the Order of the Visitation, in their communal and contemplative prayer, and in the value they placed on life lived in community, where they performed the ordinary tasks of daily life with great love and fidelity.

The religious persecution marking the Spanish civil war intensified during the first months of 1936, and convents and churches were looted and burned. The Sisters of the Visitation realized that it was too dangerous for their community—numbering more than 80 sisters—to stay in Madrid and decided to move to Oronoz, a small town in Navarra. However, they felt called to maintain a presence in the capital, where the monastery church was one of the few still open for worship; thus seven nuns were asked to remain. Before leaving, the superior of the community rented a basement apartment nearby to serve as a shelter if the sisters who were to stay ever needed a place of refuge. S. Maria Gabriela de Hinojosa was given charge of the group.

The sisters were able to continue in the monastery for only one month. On 13 July 1936 they moved to the apartment, but spent their days in the monastery—ringing the bells, trying to give the impression that it was lived in. The situation deteriorated, however, and by the end of July it was impossible for the sisters to leave the apartment. Occasionally a priest slipped in and celebrated Mass, and the extern sisters attempted to do errands, but it was dangerous: S. Maria Angela was arrested, booked, and warned. The sisters could be seen from the street as they moved about, and friends warned them to apply to foreign consulates for refuge. The Visitandines were convinced that the neighbors who had seen them in the interior courtyard respected them and would keep their secret. They refused to consider separating. However, they were reported and both they and those who had helped them were denounced.

On 14 August the apartment was searched and soldiers carried off their belongings. After this, the community became entirely dependent on others for provisions. The house was searched again; S. Teresa Maria Cavestany was taken captive and S. Josefa Maria Barrera, who had previously declared herself fearful now bravely offered to accompany her. The police detained both nuns for twenty-four hours.

The militia searched the apartment yet again on 17 November, remarking as they left that they would return the following day. S. Maria Gabriela called the sisters together and offered them a chance to seek refuge in foreign consulates, but they refused. They spent that night in prayer, preparing themselves for death. On the evening of 18 November, a patrol of the Iberian Anarchist Federation broke into the apartment. They ordered the sisters out. A mob gathered in the street, demanding that they be shot immediately. Each had made the sign of the cross as she entered a waiting van—an act of defiance in the eyes of the government. They were driven to a vacant lot on Lopez de Hoyos Street in Madrid. As the nuns emerged two by two, clasping hands to support one another, a barrage of gunfire shattered their bodies.

S. Maria Cecilia, 26 years old, felt S. Maria Gabriela fall next to her and dropped her hand. She took off running, fleeing instinctively. A short time later she surrendered herself to the militiamen, declaring that she too was a nun and wanted to die as her sisters had. She was held in a crowded cell for five days before being shot against the wall of the cemetery in Vallecas in the outskirts of Madrid. S. Maria Cecilia's cross, worn over her heart as a sign of her religious profession, was retrieved, pierced by a bullet. Because of S. Maria Cecilia's incarceration, the story of the sisters' martyrdom became public. Prisoners held in the same cell with her later shared her story with others.

Speaking of the Visitation Martyrs at their beatification, Pope John Paul II emphasized their fidelity to their own charism of gentleness and nonviolence. "I beg God that the marvelous example of these women who shed their blood for Christ, pardoning from their hearts their executioners . . . may succeed in softening the hearts of those who today use terror and violence to impose their will upon others."

Feast: 18 November.

Bibliography: JOHN PAUL II, "Allocution" (Remarks at the End of the Mass and Rite of Beatification of Visitation Martyrs and Others) 10 May 1998.

[MADA-ANNE GELL]

WIAUX, MUTIEN-MARIE, ST.

Baptized Louis Joseph Wiaux; religious of the Institute of the Brothers of the Christian Schools; b. 20 March 1841, Mellet (near Gosselies) Belgium; d. 29 January 1917, Malonne, Belgium; canonized in Rome by John Paul II, 10 December 1989.

Louis was the third of the six children of a blacksmith and his wife, who ran a small café in their home. After attending the village school, he unsuccessfully undertook an apprenticeship in his father's forge. On 1 July 1865 he joined the Brothers of the Christian Schools, who had just arrived in the area. Following his novitiate at Namur, he made his profession, took the name Mutien-Marie, and taught for three years (1856–58) in parish schools at Chimay and Brussels. For the next fifty-eight years he taught art and music at St. Bertuin's at Malonne, and served as parish catechist during his free time. Soon after the death of the man called by his students "the brother who is always praying," miracles were attributed to his intercession. His tomb, moved into St. Bertuin's in Malonne, draws many pilgrims. In 1923, Bishop Heylen of Namur opened his cause, and he was beatified in 1977 by Paul VI.

Mutien-Marie was not canonized for great works but for his transformation of the routine into moments of devotion. Pope John Paul II said during the canonization Mass that Br. Mutien-Marie shows "the true fruitfulness of a life that is humbly offered."

Feast: 30 January (De la Salle Brothers).

Bibliography: *L'Osservatore Romano,* English edition, no. 45 (1977): 8–9. L. SALM, *Brother Mutien-Marie Wiaux, FSC: Sanctity in Simplicity* (Romeoville, Ill. 1989).

[K. RABENSTEIN]

YBARRA DE VILLALONGA, RAFAELA, BL.

Widow, mother, foundress of the Institute of Holy Guardian Angels; b. 16 January 1843, Bilbao, Spain; d. there 23 February 1900; beatified by John Paul II, 30 September 1984.

Born into a noble, pious family, Rafaela married while still young. With the approval of her husband, she pronounced vows of poverty, chastity, and obedience (1890). In order to assist abandoned girls, she founded the Holy Guardian Angels (8 December 1894) with three other women. Although her duties as the mother of seven children prevented her from living in community, Rafaela directed the formation of the first nuns, organized the community, built its first residential school in Bilbao at her own expense (1899), and wrote its first Rule. The institute provides moral and economic support for disadvantaged youth, especially young women, through schools and residences. Rafaela, known for her social conscience and activity, died at age fifty-seven following a serious illness.

Pope John Paul II said at Rafaela's beatification: "Her unconditional dedication to God and others in the different circumstances of her life is admirable. . . . From the Cross and prayer she was able to draw strength to offer herself on the altars of Christian love."

Feast: 8 March.

Bibliography: J. E. SCHENK, *Rafaela Ybarra* (Valencia, Spain 1984). *Acta Apostolicae Sedis* (1984): 1104. *L'Osservatore Romano,* English edition, no. 44 (1984): 6–7.

[K. RABENSTEIN]

YERMO Y PARRES, JOSÉ MARÍA DE, ST.

Founder of the Christian Mercy Program and the Congregation of the Servants of the Sacred Heart of Jesus and the Poor (*Congregación de las Servidoras del Sagrado Corazón*); b. 10 November 1851, Hacienda de Jalmolonga, Malinalco, Mexico; d. 20 September 1904, Puebla de los Angeles, Mexico; both beatified (6 May 1990, Basilica of Nuestra Señora de Guadalupe, Mexico City) and canonized (21 May 2000, Jubilee of Mexico, Rome) by John Paul II.

José María was the only child of a lawyer, Manuel de Yermo y Soviñas, and his wife María Josefa Parres, who died 50 days after his birth. Under careful religious training by his father and his paternal aunt, José María soon discovered his vocation. He received his academic education from tutors, then by members of the Congregation of the Mission (Vincentians) (1861–67). Emperor Maximilian gave him a medal for his academic excellence. At age 16 he left home to join the Vincentians in Mexico City. In 1873, he founded a youth group called the "Angel of Purity." José María was sent to Paris for his theological studies. After his return to Mexico and a vocational crisis, he left the Vincentians to study in the diocesan seminary of León, Guerrero, and was ordained (24 August 1879).

Early in his career José María was known for his eloquence, promotion of catechesis for children, and care in fulfilling diocesan duties as secretary of the diocesan seminary, master of ceremonies, choir chaplain, and prosecretary to the bishop. When his health began to fail him in 1885, the new bishop assigned Father José María to the outlying churches of El Calvario (Calvary) and El Santo Niño (Holy Child). The young priest wanted to resign upon being confronted with the misery of poverty, but accepted his assignment as God's will. On 13 December 1885, he founded the Asilo del Sagrado Corazón (Sacred Heart Shelter) at the hilltop near Calvary Church with the help of four women and a doctor. These women became the nucleus of the Servants of the Sacred Heart of Jesus and the Poor as they began their novitiate (19 June 1888). The following year the congregation was transferred to Puebla de los Angeles, where it grew rapidly and spread throughout Mexico. Despite many tribulations during the rest of his short life, José María founded schools, hospitals, and homes for the elderly, orphans, and repentant women. His Christian Mercy program at Puebla freed women from lives of prostitution. On 20 September 1904 he established the mission among the indigenous Tarahumaras of northern Mexico.

The saint left behind many writings, not all of which have been published, despite his having obtained printing equipment from Italy and France. He edited the first magazine for the formation of Mexican clergy (*El reproductor eleciástico*).

Father José María, known for his personal asceticism, obedience, and love of the poor, died at age 52. His mortal remains lie beneath the main altar of the congregation's convent chapel in Puebla.

At his canonization Pope John Paul II said that Father Yermo distinguished himself "by an essentially prayerful and contemplative attitude. In the Heart of Christ he found guidance for his spirituality and, in reflecting on his infinite love for men, he desired to imitate him by making charity the rule of his life."

Bibliography: *Acta Apostolicae Sedis* (1990): 588–90.

[K. RABENSTEIN]

YOUVILLE, MARIE MARGUERITE D', ST.

Foundress; first native Canadian saint; b. Varennes, Canada, 15 October 1701; d. Montreal, Canada, 23 December 1771. Marguerite was the eldest of six children born to Christophe Dufrost de Lajemmerais and Marie-Renée Gaultier. Her father died when she was seven years old leaving this family of six in great poverty. Through the influence of her great grandfather, Pierre Boucher, she was enabled to study for two years at the Ursulines in Quebec. Upon her return home, she became an invaluable support to her mother and undertook the education of her brothers and sisters.

Marguerite married François d'Youville in 1722, and the young couple made their home with his mother who made life miserable for her daughter-in-law. Marguerite soon came to realize that her husband had no interest in making a home life. His frequent absences and illegal trading with the natives caused her great suffering and brought him infamy. She was pregnant with their sixth child when François became seriously ill. She faithfully cared for him until his death in 1730. By the age of twenty-nine, she had experienced desperate poverty and suffered the loss of her father and husband. Four of her six children had died in infancy. In all these sufferings,

Marguerite grew in her belief of God's presence in her life and God's love for every human person. She, in turn, wanted to make known God's compassion to all, undertaking many charitable works with complete trust in God.

Marguerite provided for the education of her two sons, who later became priests. As a Lady of Charity in her parish, Madame d'Youville helped the sick, buried the bodies of hanged criminals, and welcomed a blind woman into her home. Marguerite was soon joined by three young women who shared her love and concern for the poor. On 31 December 1737, they consecrated themselves to God and promised to serve God in the person of the poor. Marguerite, without realizing it, had founded a group that would become the Sisters of Charity of Montreal, "Grey Nuns."

D'Youville always fought for the rights of the poor and broke with the social conventions of her day, making her the object of ridicule and taunts by her own relatives. Her small society was publicly refused Holy Communion, stoned, and insulted. When fire destroyed their home, they pledged on 2 February 1745 to put everything in common in order to help a greater number of persons in need. In 1747, this "mother of the poor" as she was called, was asked to become director of the Charon Brothers Hospital in Montreal, which was falling into ruin. She and her sisters rebuilt the hospital and cared for those in most desperate human misery. With the help of lay collaborators, Marguerite laid the foundation for service to the poor of a thousand faces.

In 1765 a fire destroyed the hospital, but Marguerite's faith and courage remained firm. She asked her sisters and the poor who lived at the hospital to recognize the hand of God in the disaster and to offer praise. At the age of sixty-four, she undertook the reconstruction of this shelter for those in need. Totally exhausted, she died six years later. She was declared venerable in 1890, beatified on 3 May 1959 by Pope John XXIII, who called her "Mother of Universal Charity."

Marguerite d'Youville was canonized by John Paul II on 9 December 1990. He extolled Marguerite's fortitude: "More than once the work which Marguerite undertook was hindered by nature or people. In order to work to bring that new world of justice and love closer, she had to fight some hard and difficult battles."

Feast 16 October (Canada).

Bibliography: Archives, Grey Nuns of Montreal. A. FERLAND-ANGERS, *Mère d'Youville* (Montréal 1945), approved Fr. biog. for beatification. M. P. FITTS, *Hands to the Needy; Blessed Marguerite d'Youville, Apostle to the Poor* (Garden City, N.Y. 1971), approved Eng. biog. for beatification. B. JETTÉ, *Vie de la vénérable mère d'Youville, fondatrice des Soeurs de la charité de Montréal, suivie d'un historique de son institut* (Montréal 1900). A. FAUTEUX, *Love Spans the Centuries*, 4 vols. (Montreal, 1987). E. MITCHELL, *Marguerite d'Youville, Foundress of the Grey Nuns*, tr. H. NANTAIS (Montreal 1965); *Le vrai visage de Marguerite d'Youville* (Montréal 1973); *The Spiritual Portrait of Saint Marguerite d'Youville* (Montreal 1993).

[SUZANNE FORGET]

ZDISLAVA OF LEMBERK, ST.

Married member of the Dominican lay tertiary; b. ca. 1220, Krizanov, Moravia (now Letomerice, Bohemia, Czech Republic); d. 1 January 1252, Jablonné v Podjestìdí, Bohemia; canonized by John Paul II at Olomouc, Czech Republic, 21 May 1995, during his second pastoral visit.

Zdislava, daughter of Privislav, was born into the Czech aristocracy. Her mother Sibila was a lady-in-waiting to Queen Cunegunda of Hohenstaufen. About 1236, Zdislava married Count Havel of Lemberk (d. 1253), a soldier in command of the frontier fortress at Gabel (Jablonné v Podjestìdí), to whom she bore four children (Havel, Margarita, Jaroslav, and Zadislav). Through the preaching of St. Hyacinth and Bl. Ceslaus of Silesia, Zdislava became the first Slavic Dominican tertiary. She encouraged her husband to build a hostel for homeless pilgrims, visited and interceded for prisoners, cared for the poor, taught the faith to her servants' children, and built a church and priories at Turnov and Jablonné. Not content with merely funding charitable works, she personally bathed the sick and carried some of the materials for the church. During the Mongol invasions she eased the distress of the suffering who sought refuge with her. According to her fourteenth-century chronicler Dalimil, Zdislava raised five dead men to life, healed many through her touch, and was gifted with visions and ecstasies. Her body is venerated in the church she had built, now called SS. Lawrence and Zdislava at Jablonné v Podjestìdí.

Following Zdislava's canonization, Pope John Paul II called her a heroine of charity and the family, who "imitated Mary's tenderness and concern for neighbor, especially the poor and sick." She is the patroness of the sick and poor of Bohemia, and of families in Bohemia and Moravia.

Feast: 4 January (Dominicans); 30 May (Czech Republic).

Bibliography: M. J. DORCY, *Saint Dominic's Family* (Dubuque, Iowa 1964), 47–48. T. EDEL, *Príbeh ztraceného klóstera blahoslavené Zdislavy* (Prague 1993). J. SALLMANN, *Festschrift zum 200 jährigen Jubiläum der Dekanalkirche zum Hl. Laurentius in Deutsch Gabel* (Gabel 1929). *L'Osservatore Romano*, English edition, no. 21 (1995): 1–2, 12; no. 23 (1995): 9.

[K. RABENSTEIN]

Patron Saints

The custom of designating patron saints arose from the practice of building churches over the tombs of martyrs. Constantine was responsible for the great Roman basilicas of St. Peter and St. Paul-Outside-the-Walls. Similarly the basilicas of St. Lawrence in Agro Verano, St. Sebastian, St. Agnes on the Via Nomentana, among others, were built on sites where their bodies were buried. The saints came to be regarded as the special advocates and intercessors for the churches and the people who assembled in them. Dedication of churches to saints and angels followed. The reference to the seven angels of the seven churches in the Book of Revelation (1:20 ff) may have provided a precedent for the practice of churches seeking the patronage of angels. A church in Ravenna was dedicated to St. Michael the archangel as early as 545.

Over time the choice of a particular patron has depended upon many factors. In summary, patrons have been chosen for one or more of the following reasons: (1) A church or chapel is the burial place of a martyr or confessor; (2) a church or chapel is the repository of an important relic of the saint; (3) saints who were the first to bring the Gospel message to a region or a people as, for example, St. Patrick in Ireland, St. Ansgar in Scandinavia; (4) the cult of a saint fostered by national pride and tradition; (5) the popularity of a saint at a given time, e.g. St. Thérèse of Lisieux in the twentieth century; (6) the personal devotion and priorities of a pastor or important benefactor; (7) the identification of a saint with a particular situation or condition in his lifetime or heritage.

The 1917 Code of Canon Law spoke of *titles,* that is, the permanent names assigned to churches to distinguish one from another. If the title was the name of a saint, the person was called a *patron,* an advocate (CIC c. 1168), and the titular feast was to be celebrated annually in the church. Blessed were able to be named patrons only with permission of the Holy See, generally granted to places and groups associated with the individual. The 1983 code is silent on the matter of titular patrons.

Patrons found their greatest popularity in the high Middle Ages. Towns were named after saints and nearly every institution and circumstance of life had its heavenly protector. The choice of heavenly patrons by guilds of artisans and craftsmen was dictated by some attribute or legend associated with the name of saint that linked their members to him or her. St. Vitus who was said to have been martyred in a caldron appealed to kettle-makers. Archers venerated St. Sebastian. Wagon-makers chose St. Catherine of Alexandria because a wheel was the means of her martyrdom. Tailors sought the patronage of St. Martin of Tours because he was said to have cut his mantle in half, giving one part to a beggar who turned out to be Christ. The intercession of other saints was implored for particular illnesses because they themselves had suffered from a particular malady or they ministered to those who had.

The practice of giving a child a Christian name at baptism is of medieval origin. As late as the ninth century, children in Germany were customarily given old Teutonic names, but gradually the sentiments of the people led to the custom of conferring the name of saints at baptism. The name of John the Baptist was very widely invoked in the eleventh century, then the names of the apostles, and eventually the names were taken from litanies of the saints and the liturgical calendar. The importance given in medieval times to patron saints is reflected in a decree of the Council of Benevento (1374) that forbade the practice of repeating the baptismal rite in a case where a name had been omitted in the original administration. The Catechism of the Council of Trent strongly urged that the name given at baptism be from the catalogue of saints. The saint after whom one is named is held up as a model for imitation as well as being one's guardian and advocate (II, s.v., Baptism, n. 76). The 1917 Code of Canon Law encouraged parents to choose a saint's name and, if they refused, the pastor was to enter both the given name and the name of a saint in the in the baptismal register (c. 761). The 1983 Code states that "parents, sponsors, and the pastor are to see that a name is not given which is foreign to Christian sentiment" (CIC c. 855).

The patron serves as a model of holiness and charity for the neophyte. The *Catechism of the Catholic Church,* explains at baptism that people are sanctified by the Lord's name, and Christians receive their name in the Church. "This can be the name of a saint, that is, of a disciple who has lived a life of exemplary fidelity to the Lord. The patron saint provides a model of charity; we are assured of his intercession" (no. 2156).

Dates in parentheses represent the date that an individual was declared to be patron; most patronages have developed in a less formal manner.

Patrons

Academics: Thomas Aquinas
Actors: Genesius
Adopted children: Clotilde, Thomas More
Advertisers: Bernardine of Siena (20 May 1960)
Alpinists: Bernard of Montjoux (or Menthon) (20 August 1923)
Altar servers: John Berchmans
Anesthetists: René Goupil
Animals: Francis of Assisi
Archaeologists: Damasus
Archers: Sebastian
Architects: Thomas Apostle
Art: Catherine de Virgi of Bologna
Artists: Luke, Catherine of Bologna, Bl. Fra Angelico (21 February 1984)
Astronomers: Dominic
Athletes: Sebastian
Authors/Writers: Francis de Sales (26 April 1923), Lucy
Aviators: Our Lady of Loreto (1920), Joseph of Cupertino

Bakers: Elizabeth of Hungary, Nicholas
Bankers: Matthew, Bl. Joseph Tardini
Barbers: Cosmas and Damian, Louis
Basket-makers: Anthony, Abbot
Bees: Ambrose
Beggars: Martin of Tours
Blacksmiths: Dunstan
Blood banks: Januarius
Bookbinders: Peter Celestine
Bookkeepers: Matthew
Booksellers: John of God
Boy Scouts: George
Brewers: Luke, Nicholas of Myra
Bricklayers: Stephen
Brides: Nicholas of Myra
Bridges: John Nepomucene, Bénézet
Broadcasters: Gabriel
Builders: Vincent Ferrer
Butlers: Adelelm

Cabdrivers: Fiacre of Breuil
Canonists: Raymond of Peñafort
Carpenters: Joseph
Catechists: Angela Merici, Charles Borromeo, Peter Canisius, Robert Bellarmine
Catechumens: Ambrose of Milan, Augustine of Hippo

Catholic Action: Francis of Assisi (1916)
Catholic Press: Francis de Sales
Charitable societies: Vincent de Paul (12 May 1885)
Chastity: Thomas Aquinas
Chefs (Italian): Francis Caracciolo (1996)
Chefs (Pastry): Honoratus: Felicity, Raymond Nonnatus, Gerard Majella, Margaret of Antioch, Bl. Marie d'Oignies
Children: Nicholas of Myra
Choirboys: Dominic Savio (8 June 1956)
Church Universal: Joseph (8 December 1870)
Civil Disorder/Riots: Andrew Corsini
Circus people: Julian the Hospitaller
Colleges and Universities: Thomas Aquinas, Bl. Contardo Ferrini
Comedians: Vitus
Communications personnel: Gabriel
Computer Users: Isidore of Seville
Confessors: Alphonsus Liguori (26 April 1950)
Converts: Justin, Elizabeth Seton
Cooks: Martha
Coppersmiths: Maurus

Dairy workers: Brigid of Ireland
Dancers: Vitus
Dentists: Apollonia
Desperate situations: Gregory Thaumaturgist, Jude Thaddeus, Rita of Cascia
Difficulties: Eustace
Divorce: Helena
Dyers: Maurice, Lydia

Ecologists, Environmentalists: Francis of Assisi (29 November 1979)
Ecumenists: Cyril and Methodius, Bl. Elizabeth Hesselblad, Bl. María Gabriella Sagheddu
Editors: John Bosco
Educators, Catholic: Bl. Karolina Gerhardinger
Emigrants: Frances Xavier Cabrini (8 September 1950)
Engineers: Ferdinand Ill
Epilepsy: Vitus, Willibrord
Epidemics and Pestilence: Christopher and Giles
Eucharistic Devotion: Pierre Julien Eymard, Paschal Baylon (28 November 1897)
Expectant mothers: Raymond Nonnatus, Gerard Majella

Falsely accused: Raymond Nonnatus
Families: Bl. Gianna Beretta Molla, Bl. Giuseppina Bonino, Bl. Giovanni Piamarta
Farmers: George, Isidore
Fathers: Joseph (1899)
Firemen: Florian
Fire prevention: Catherine of Siena
First communicants: Tarcisius
Fishermen: Andrew
Flight Attendants: Bona of Pisa (2 March 1962)
Florists: Thérèse of Lisieux
Forest workers: John Gualbert
Foundlings: Holy Innocents
Friendship: John the Divine, Aelred of Rievaulx
Funeral directors: Joseph of Arimathea, Dismas

Gardeners: Adelard, Tryphon, Fiacre, Phocas
Glassworkers: Luke
Goldsmiths: Dunstan, Anastasius
Gravediggers: Anthony, Abbot
Gypsies: Bl. Zeferino Jimenez

Hairdressers: Martin de Porres
Hagiographers: Athanasius, Gregory the Great
Homeless: Margaret of Cortona, Benedict Joseph Labré
Home Missions: Katharine Drexel
Horses: Giles
Housekeepers: Zita
Hospital administrators: Basil the Great, Frances X Cabrini
Hospitals: Camillus de Lellis and John of God (22 June 1886)
Hospitality/Lodgings: Gertrude of Nivelles, Julian the Hospitaller
Hunters: Hubert, Eustachius

Infantrymen: Maurice
Innkeepers: Amand, Julian the Hospitaller

Janitors: Theobald
Jewelers: Eligius, Dunstan
Journalists: Francis de Sales (26 April 1923), Bl. Titus Brandsma
Jurists: John Capistrano

Laborers: Isidore, James, John Bosco
Lawyers: Ivo (Yves Helory), Genesius, Thomas More
Librarians: Jerome
Lighthouse Keepers: Venerius of Milan (10 March 1961)
Linguists: Gottschalk
Locksmiths: Dunstan
Lost Articles: Anthony of Padua, Arnulf of Metz, Daniel of Padua
Lovers: Raphael, Valentine

Maids: Zita
Mariners: Michael, Nicholas of Tolentino
Marriage: John Francis Regis, Bl. Otto Neururer, Ursla of Cologne, Bl. Benedetta Frassinello, Bl. Elizabeth Canori Mora, Bl. Giuseppe Tovini
Married Couples: Joachim and Anne, Bl. Luchesius and Buona of Poggibonsi
Merchants: Francis of Assisi, Nicholas of Myra
Messengers: Gabriel
Metal workers: Eligius of Noyon
Military chaplains: John Capistrano (10 February 1984)
Millers: Arnulph, Victor
Missionaries: Francis Xavier (25 March 1904), Thérèse of Lisieux (14 December 1927), Peter Claver (1896, Leo XIII), Benedict the Moor
Missions, parish: Leonard of Port Maurice (17 March 1923)
Mothers: Monica
Motorists: Frances of Rome
Music: Arnulf of Metz, Cecilia of Rome, Dunstan of Canterbury, Philip Neri
Musicians: Gregory the Great, Cecilia, Dunstan
Mystics: John of the Cross, Teresa of Avila, Bl. Rafqa

Native Americans: Bl. Kateri Tekawitha
Notaries: Luke, Mark
Nurses and Nursing: Agatha, Catherine of Siena, Elizabeth of Hungary, John of God (1930, Pius XI), Camillus de Lellis, Raphael

Orators: John Chrysostom (8 July 1908)
Organ builders: Cecilia
Orphans, Abandoned Children: Jerome Emiliani (1928), Bl. Daniel Brottier

Painters: Bl. Fra Angelico
Parenthood: Adelaide of Burgundy, Rita of Cascia

Pharmacists: Cosmas and Damian, Gemma Galgani
Philosophers: Justin, Edith Stein
Physicians: Pantaleon, Cosmas and Damian
Pilgrims: James the Greater
Poets: Brigid of Ireland, John of the Cross
Poor: Lawrence, Anthony of Padua, Bl. Giacomo Cusmano, Bl. Maria Bernardina Jablonska
Poor souls: Nicholas of Tolentino
Possessed: Bruno, Denis
Postal employees: Gabriel
Priests: Jean-Baptiste Vianney (23 April 1929)
Printers: John of God
Prisoners: Dismas, Joseph Cafasso
Public relations: Bernardine of Siena (20 May 1960)
Publishers: Bl. Timothy Giaccardo, Bl. Joseph Tardini

Race relations: Martin de Porres
Radiologists: Michael (15 January 1941)
Refugees: Bl. Angela Truszkowska, Bl. Kateri Tekakwitha
Retreats: Ignatius Loyola (25 July 1922)

Sailors: Cuthbert, Brendan, Eulalia, Christopher, Peter González, Erasmus, Nicholas
Scholars: Bede the Venerable
Schools, Catholic: Thomas Aquinas (4 August 1880), Joseph Calasanz (13 August 1948)
Scientists: Albert the Great (13 August 1948), Bl. Niels Stensen
Sculptors: Four Crowned Martyrs
Seamen: Francis of Paola
Searchers of lost articles: Anthony of Padua
Secretaries: Genesius
Secular Franciscans: Louis of France, Elizabeth of Hungary
Seminarians: Charles Borromeo
Senior Citizens: Polycarp, Marie Poussepin
Shepherds: Drogo
Shoemakers: Crispin and Crispinian
Sick: John of God and Camillus de Lellis (22 June 1886)
Silversmiths: Andronicus
Single mothers: Margaret of Cortona
Skaters: Lydwina
Skiers: Bernard of Montjoux (or Menthon)
Social workers: Louise de Marillac (12 February 1960), John Francis Regis
Soldiers: Hadrian, George, Ignatius, Sebastian, Martin of Tours, Joan of Arc
Spelunkers: Benedict
Stenographers: Genesius, Cassian
Stonecutters: Clement
Stonemasons: Stephen
Students: Thomas Aquinas
Surgeons: Cosmas and Damian, Luke
Swordsmiths: Maurice

Tax collectors: Matthew
Teachers: John Baptist de la Salle (15 May 1950)
Telecommunications workers: Gabriel (12 January 1951)
Television: Clare of Assisi (14 February 1958)
Thieves, Repenant: Dismas
Theologians: Augustine, Alphonsus Liguori, Thomas Aquinas
Tour Guides: Bona of Pisa
Toymakers: Claude
Translators: Jerome
Travelers: Nicholas of Myra, Christopher, Raphael, Julian the Hospitaller

Contributors

ABOU MOUSSA, RICHARD, M.B.A., Maronite Archdiocese of Antelias, Lebanon. **Article:** Rafqa de Himlaya, Bl.

ABRUZESSE, MSGR. JOHN, *Minutante*, Special Council for Europe, General Secretariat of the Synod of Bishops, Vatican City. **Articles:** Synod of Bishops; Synod of Bishops, Special Assembly for America.

*AHERN, BARNABAS, C.P., Consultor, Congregation for the Doctrine of the Faith. **Article:** International Theological Commission.

ALVARÉ, HELEN M., Esq., Professor of Law, Columbia School of Law, The Catholic University of America, Washington, D.C.; former Director of Planning and Information for the National Conference of Catholic Bishops' Secretariat for Pro-Life Activities, Washington, D.C. **Article:** From Rome to Cairo and Beijing: John Paul II on Family and Human Rights.

*ANDERSON, CARL A., Dean, John Paul II Institute for Studies on Marriage and Family, Washington, D.C. **Article:** John Paul II Institute on Marriage and Family.

AUMANN, JORDAN, O.P., S.T.D., Ph.L., Professor Emeritus, University of St. Thomas, Rome; Director (ret.), Institute of Spiritual Theology, River Forest, Illinois. **Article:** Amantissima providentia.

BARBIERI, WILLIAM A., Ph.D., Assistant Professor of Religion and Religious Education, The Catholic University of America, Washington, D.C. **Article:** Sollicitudo rei socialis.

BAUM, GREGORY G., D.Th., Professor Emeritus, Faculty of Religious Studies, McGill University, Montreal, Canada. **Article:** John Paul II's Economic Teaching: A Call for Spiritual, Moral, and Structural Conversion.

BEGGIANI, CHORBISHOP SEELY, S.T.D., Rector, Our Lady of Lebanon Maronite Seminary, Washington, D.C. **Articles:** Esperance Nouvelle pour le Liban, Une; Synod of Bishops, Special Assembly for Lebanon.

BORELLI, JOHN, Ph.D., Associate Director, Secretariat for Ecumenical and Interreligious Affairs, National Conference of Catholic Bishops, Washington, D.C. **Article:** John Paul II and Interreligious Dialogue.

BRANDL, GARY, General Manager, New City Press, Hyde Park, New York. **Articles:** Focolare Movement; Lubich, Chiara.

*BROCKMAN, JAMES R., S.J., M.A., Ph.L., S.T.B., St. Ignatius Parish, Chicago, Illinois. **Article:** Romero, Oscar A.

BROWN, LEN, C.M.F., Provincial Superior, Claretian Missionaries, Oak Park, Illinois. **Article:** Barbastro, Martyrs of, Bl.

*BROWN, RAPHEAL, Senior Reference Librarian, Library of Congress, Washington, D.C. **Article:** Assisi.

BROWNE, MAURA, S.N.D., M.A., J.D., Justice and Peace Coordinator, Sisters of Notre Dame de Namur International Communications Office. **Article:** Ecclesia in Africa.

BSTEH, PETRUS, Director, Kontaktstelle für Weltreligionen, Vienna, Austria. **Article:** König, Franz Borgia.

BUGARIN, G. MICHAEL, Director, Pope John Paul II Cultural Center, Washington, D.C. **Articles:** Pope John Paul II Cultural Center; Maida, Adam Joseph.

BUI, THU, Ph.D. Vienna, Virgina. **Article:** Vietnam, Martyrs of, SS.

*BULL, GEORGE ANTHONY, M.A., OBE, FRSL, Director, Anglo-Japanese Economic Institute; editor, Internation Minds, London, England. **Article:** Sistine Chapel, Restoration of.

*BURKHARD, JOHN J., O.F.M.Conv., S.T.L., Ph.D., Assistant Professor of Systematic Theology, Washington Theological Union, Silver Spring, Maryland. **Article:** Synod of Bishops, Eighth General Assembly, 1990.

BURTON, MSGR. RICHARD, M.A., Pastor, St. Anthony's Church, Washington, D.C. **Article:** Baum, William Wakefield.

BUTLER, SARA, M.S.B.T., S.T.L., Ph.D., Associate Professor of Systematic Theology, Mundelein Seminary, University of St. Mary of the Lake, Mundelein, Illinois. **Article:** Ordinatio sacerdotalis.

CALDECOTT, STRATFORD, Director, Centre for Faith & Culture, Plater College, Oxford, United Kingdom. **Articles:** Centesimus annus; Common Good and Catholic Social Teaching, The.

CAMELI, LOUIS J., Director of Ongoing Formation of Priests, Archdiocese of Chicago, Chicago, Illinois. **Article:** George, Francis E.

CARRIER, HERVÉ, S.J., S.T.L. Professor Emeritus of Sociology of Religion and Culture, Gregorian University, Rome. **Articles:** Dezza, Paolo; New Evangelization.

CARSON, THOMAS. **Article:** Szoka, Edmund C.

CESSARIO, ROMANUS, O.P., S.T.D., Professor of Theology, St. John's Seminary, Brighton, Massachusetts. **Article:** Schönborn, Christoph.

*CHANTRAINE, GEORGES, S.J., Professor of Church History and Dogmatic Theology, Faculté SJ de Théologie, Belgium. **Articles:** Balthasar, Hans Urs von; Lubac, Henri de.

CLARK, DOUGLAS K., S.T.L., Editor, *The Southern Cross*, Savannah, Georgia. **Articles:** Evangelium vitae; Law, Bernard F.; Pastores dabo vobis.

CLOONEY, DAVID, Rector, St. Josaphat Ukrainian Catholic Seminary, Washington, D.C. **Articles:** Union of Brest; Slavorum apostoli.

COLERIDGE, MSGR. MARK, S.S.D., Official of the First Section (General Affairs), Secretariat of State, Vatican City. **Articles:** Cassidy, Edward Idris; Clancy, Edward Bede; Domus Sanctae Marthae.

COLLINGE, WILLIAM J., Ph.D., Father James M. Forker Professorship in Catholic Social Teaching, Theology and Philosophy, Mount Saint Mary's College, Emmitsburg, Maryland. **Article:** Fides et ratio.

COYNE, GEORGE V., S.J., Ph.L, S.T.L., Ph.D., Director of the Vatican Observatory (Specola Vaticana). **Article:** The Church in Dialogue with Science: The Wojtyła Years.

CUNNINGHAM, LAWRENCE S., Ph.D., Professor of Theology, Department of Theology, University of Notre Dame, Notre Dame, Indiana. **Article:** Universal Call to Holiness: Martyrs of Charity and Witnesses to Truth.

CURRAN, CHARLES E., S.T.D., Scurlock Professor of Human Values, Perkins School of Theology, Southern Methodist University, Dallas, Texas. **Article:** McCormick, Richard A.

DEMPSEY, MSGR. ROBERT J., Editor, *L'Osservatore Romano*, English edition, Vatican City. **Article:** Marcinkus, Paul Casimir.

*DE WALD, ERNEST THEODORE, Ph.D., L.H.D., Professor Emeritus, Department of Art and Archaeology, and Director Emeritus, Art Museum, Princeton University, Princeton, New Jersey. **Article:** Assisi.

DIAS, MARIO SATURNINO, S.T.L., Ph.D., Executive Secretary, Office of Evangelization, Federation of Asian Bishops' Conferences, New Delhi, India. **Article:** Ecclesia in Asia.

DICK, JOHN A., Ph.D., S.T.D., Coordinator of International Research and Programming, European Centre for Ethics, Catholic University of Leuven, Belgium. **Articles:** Cologne Declaration; Daneels, Godfried; Hamer, Jean Jérome; Schotte, Jan Pieter.

DINGES, WILLIAM D., Ph.D., Associate Professor of Religion and Religious Education, The Catholic University of America, Washington, D.C. **Articles:** Catholic Traditionalism; Lefebvre, Marcel; New Age Movement; New Religious Movements.

DINOIA, J. A., O.P., Ph.D., Executive Director, Secretariat for Doctrine and Pastoral Practices, National Conference of Catholic Bishops, Washington, D.C. **Article:** Neocatechumenal Way.

DOLAN, MSGR. TIMOTHY M., Ph.D., Rector, Pontifical North American College, Rome. **Article:** Laghi, Pio.

DOOLEY, CATHERINE A., O.P., Associate Professor of Religion and Religious Education, The Catholic University of America, Washington, D.C. **Article:** Lectionary for Masses with Children.

DRUMM, JOACHIM, Ordinariatsrat, Diocese of Rottenburg-Stuttgart, Germany. **Article:** Kasper, Walter.

DULLES, AVERY, S.J., S.T.D., McGinley Chair in Religion and Society, Fordham University, Bronx, New York. **Article:** Lima Text.

EADS, JOAN, Zone Coordinator, L'Arche U.S.A. **Article:** L'Arche International.

ELDAROV, GIORGIO, O.F.M.Conv., S.T.D., S.E.O.D., Director of AGABAR (*Archivio cattolico bulgaro di Roma*), Professor Emeritus of Ecclesiology, Seraphicum, Rome. **Articles:** Bossilkov, Vincent Eugene, Bl.; Casaroli, Agostino; Slipyj, Josyf.

ESPELAGE, ARTHUR, O.F.M., J.C.D., Executive Coordinator, Canon Law Society of America, Washington, D.C. **Articles:** Apostolos suos; Camerlengo; Episcopal Conferences; Sacrae disciplinae leges; Sacri canones.

FISHER, EUGENE J., Ph.D., Associate Director, Secretariat for Ecumenical and Interreligious Affairs, National Conference of Catholic Bishops, Washington, D.C. **Article:** A Pilgrimage of Reconciliation: From Wadowice to the Wailing Wall.

FORD, JOHN T., S.T.L., S.T.D., Professor of Systematic Theology, The Catholic University of America, Washington, D.C. **Article:** Dulles, Avery.

FORD, MICHAEL, B.A., Reglious Affairs Journalist, BBC, England. **Article:** Nouwen, Henri.

FORGET, SUZANNE, S.G.M., Sisters of Charity of Montreal, "Grey Nuns," St. Joseph Province, Provincial Administration, Lexington, Massachusetts. **Article:** Youville, Marguerite d', St.

FRAZE, BARB, International Editor, Catholic News Service, Washington, D.C. **Article:** The Papacy:1995–2000.

*FREEMAN, LAURENCE, O.S.B., M.A. (oxon.), Monastery of Christ the King, London; Director, World Community for Christian Meditation. **Article:** Griffiths, Bede.

*GALLAGHER, MICHAEL PAUL, S.J., M. Litt., Ph.D., Former Lecturer in Literature, University College, Dublin, Ireland; staff member, Pontifical Council for Culture. **Article:** Pontifical Council for Culture.

*GARCIA, JAVIER, L.C., Prefect, Center of Higher Studies of Legionaries of Christ, Rome. **Article:** Legionaries of Christ.

GELL, MADA-ANNE, V.H.M., Department of Religion, Georgetown Visitation Preparatory School, Washington, D.C. **Article:** Visitation Order, Martyrs of the, BB.

GENDERNALIK, LEONARD, Sch.P, Provincial Office, Piarist Fathers, USA Province, Washington, D.C. **Article:** Pamplona, Dionysio and XIII companions.

GIBSON, DAVID E., Catholic News Service, Washington, D.C. **Articles:** Challenge of Peace; Christifideles laici; Familiaris consortio.

GODFREY, KEVIN, O.F.M.Conv., Ph.D., Assistant Professor of Philosophy and Theology, Alvernia College, Reading, Pennsylvania. **Articles:** Reconciliatio et paenitentia; Salvifici doloris.

GROS, JEFFREY, F.S.C., Ph.D., Associate Director, Secretariat for Ecumenical and Interreligious Affairs, National Conference of Catholic Bishops, Washington, D.C. **Articles:** Ecumenical Formation of Pastoral Workers; Ut unum sint.

HAYES, PATRICK, M.A., Editorial Assistant, *The Living Light*, Washington, D.C. **Articles:** Mello, Anthony de; Pontifical Academies; Pontifical Councils.

HAYES, ZACHARY, O.F.M., Dr. Theol., Litt. D., Professor of Doctrinal Theology, Catholic Theological Union, Chicago, Illinois. **Article:** Ratzinger, Joseph.

*HENNELLY, ALFRED T., S.J., Ph.D., Professor of Theology, Fordham University, Bronx, New York. **Article:** Santo Domingo (1992).

*HERBST, CLARENCE ANTHONY, S.J., S.T.L., Ph.D., Professor of History, Sogang Jesuit College, Seoul, Korea. **Article:** Korea, Martyrs of, SS.

HIGGINS, MICHAEL, Ph.D., Professor of English and Religious Studies, St. Jerome's University, Waterloo, Ontario, Canada. **Articles:** Carter, Gerald Emmett; Gagnon, Edouard, P.S.S.; Vachon, Louis-Albert.

HITTINGER, F. RUSSELL, Ph.D., Warren Professor of Catholic Studies and Research Professor of Law, University of Tulsa, Tulsa, Oklahoma. **Article:** Solidarity.

HOAGLAND, VICTOR, C.P., St. Michael Residence, Union City, New Jersey. **Article:** Daimiel, Martyrs of.

*HOGAN, JOHN P., Ph.D., Associate Director of the Peace Corps, former Director of Catholic Relief Services in Haiti. **Article:** Puebla.

*HOLLAND, SHARON L., I.H.M., J.C.D., Office head, Congregation for Institutes of Consecrated Life and Societies of Apostolic Life; Professor of Canon Law, Regina Mundi Institute, Rome, Italy. **Article:** Synod of Bishops, Ninth General Assembly, 1994.

*HOTCHKIN, JOHN F., S.T.D., Executive Director, Secretariat for Ecumenical and Interreligious Affairs, National Conference of Catholic Bishops, Washington, D.C. **Article:** Ecumenical Directory.

*HUG, JAMES E., S.J., Ph.D., Director of Research, Center of Concern, Washington, D.C. **Article:** Economic Justice for All.

HUYSMANS, RUDD, Professor, Faculty of Canon Law, Catholic University of Louvain, Belgium. **Article:** Synod of Bishops, Particular Assembly for Holland.

*IWELE, GODÉ, O.M.I., S.T.L., D.E.S., African Institute of Mission Studies, Kinshasha, Zaire. **Article:** Synod of Bishops, Special Assembly for Africa.

JELLY, FREDERICK M., O.P., S.T.D., S.T.Lr., S.T.M., Professor of Systematic Theology, Mount St. Mary's Seminary, Emmitsburg, Maryland. **Articles:** Redemptoris custos; Redemptoris mater.

*JOHNSTONE, BRIAN V., C.Ss.R., S.T.D., Professor of Moral Theology, Accademia Alphonsiana, Rome. **Article:** Häring, Bernard.

*KAUFFMAN, CHRISTOPHER J., Ph.D., Catholic Daughters of the Americas Professor of American Church History, The Catholic University of America, Washington, D.C. **Article:** Keeler, William Henry.

KELLY, MOST REVEREND THOMAS C., O.P., D.D., J.C.D., Archbishop of Louisville, Kentucky. **Article:** Ad limina visit.

*KERR, FERGUS, O.P., S.T.M., Prior of Blackfriars, Edinburgh, Scotland. **Articles:** Chenu, Marie-Dominique; Schillebeeckx, Edward.

KIRBY, MARC-DANIEL, O.Cist., M.A., S.T.L., Instructor in Liturgy, Holy Apostles Seminary, Cromwell, Connecticut. **Article:** Orientale lumen.

KIRK, PAMELA, Dr.Theol., Associate Professor of Theology, St. John's University, Jamaica, New York. **Article:** Mulieris dignitatem.

KOMONCHAK, JOSEPH A., S.T.L., Ph.D., Professor of Religion and Religious Education, The Catholic University of America, Washington, D.C. **Articles:** Congar, Yves Marie-Joseph; Ex corde Ecclesiae; Synod of Bishops, Second Extraordinary Assembly, 1985.

KONSTANT, RIGHT REVEREND DAVID EVERY, Bishop of Leeds, Great Britain. **Article:** Hume, George Basil.

*KRESS, ROBERT, Ph.D., S.T.L., Professor, Department of Philosophy and Religion, University of Evansville, Evansville, Indiana. **Article:** Communio.

KROEGER, JAMES H., M.M., Ph.D., Professor of Systematic Theology, Missiology, and Islamics, Loyola School of Theology, Manila, Philippines. **Articles:** Redemptoris missio; Synod of Bishops, Special Assembly for Asia.

KUTYS, DANIEL, M. Div., Executive Director, Office for the Catechism, National Conference of Catholic Bishops, Washington, D.C. **Articles:** Catechism of the Catholic Church; Fidei depositum.

*LAGHI, MOST REVEREND PIO, S.T.D., J.C.D., Apostolic Pro-Nuncio to the United States of America, Washington, D.C. **Article:** Lateran Pacts 1985.

*LAMBRECHT, JAN, S.J., Professor Emeritus, Katholieke Universiteit Leuven; Member, Pontifical Biblical Commission. **Article:** Pontifical Biblical Commission.

LANAVE, GREGORY F., M.A., Assistant Editor, *New Catholic Encyclopedia*; Managing Editor, *The Thomist*, Washington, D.C. **Article:** Veritatis splendor.

LAPOINTE, MARIE WILLIAM, O.P., Provincial Council of the Dominican Sisters of the Presentation in the U.S.; Administrator, Rosary House of Studies, Washington, D.C. **Article:** Poussepin, Marie, Bl.

LASZOK, ANN, O.S.B.M., M.A., Coordinator of the Pastoral Ministry Office, Ukrainian Catholic Diocese of St. Josaphat in Parma, Pittsburgh, Pennsylvania. **Article:** Lubachivsky, Myroslav Ivan.

*LAWRENCE, FREDERICK G., D.Th., Associate Professor of Theology, Boston College, Chestnut Hill, Massachusetts. **Article:** Lonergan, Bernard.

*LEBEAU, PAUL, S.J., President, Institut d'Etudes Théologiques, Brussels. **Article:** Suenens, Leo Jozef.

*LEFLON, RIGHT REVEREND JEAN ADOLPHE MARIE, Professor Emeritus, Institut Catholique, Paris. **Article:** Mazenode, Charles Joseph Eugène de.

LETSON, DOUGLAS, Ph.D., Professor of English, St. Jerome's University, Waterloo, Ontario, Canada. **Articles:** Ambrozic, Aloysius; Gregoire, Paul; Turcotte, Jean-Claude.

LINGLEY, ANNE, Editorial Director, *Living City Magazine*, Hyde Park, New York. **Articles:** Focolare Movement; Lubich, Chiara.

MACGREGOR, MORRIS J., M.A., Historian (ret.), Joint Chiefs of Staff, Department of the Army, Washington, D.C. **Article:** Hickey, James Aloysius.

*MACNAMARA, ROBERT FRANCIS, A.M., S.T.L., Professor of Church History, Lecturer in History of Christian Art, and Instructor in Italian, St. Bernard's Seminary, Rochester, New York. **Article:** Schuster, Ildephonse Alfredo, Bl.

MADDEN, MARY RODGER, S.P., M.A., Pilgrimage Coordinator, Sisters of Providence, Saint Mary-of-the-Woods, Indiana. **Articles:** Bradley, Ritamary; Guerin, Théodore-Anne-Thérèse, Bl.

*MALANOWSKI, GREGORY, O.F.M.Conv., S.T.D., Assistant Professor of Theology, The Catholic University of America, Washington, D.C. **Article:** Communio.

MARQUES, LUIZ CARLOS, C.Ss.R., Ph.D., São Paolo, Brazil. **Article:** Camara, Helder.

MARTHALER, BERARD L., O.F.M.Conv., S.T.D., Ph.D., Executive Editor, *New Catholic Encyclopedia*, Professor Emeritus of Religion and Religious Education, The Catholic University of America, Washington, D.C. **Articles:** Missionaries of Charity; Mother Teresa of Calcutta; Synod of Bishops, Seventh General Assembly, 1987; Tertio millennio adveniente; World Youth Day.

MATEO, R. P., Sch.P., Piarist Fathers, Rome. **Article:** Casani, Pietro, Bl.

*MAY, WILLIAM E., Ph.D., Michael J. McGivney Professor of Moral Theology, Pope John Paul II Institute for Studies on Marriage and Family, Washington, D.C. **Article:** International Theological Commission.

MCCARRON, RICHARD E., Ph.D., Assistant Professor of Liturgy, Catholic Theological Union, Chicago, Illinois. **Article:** Inculturation, Liturgical.

MCCURRY, JAMES, O.F.M.Conv., M.A., National Director of the Militia of Mary Immaculate, Granby, Massachusetts. **Articles:** Częstochowa; Kolbe, Maximilian, St.

MCDERMOTT, JOHN, S.J., Ph.D., Laghi Chair Research Professor, Pontifical College Josephinum, Columbus, Ohio. **Article:** Incarnationis mysterium.

MCDERMOTT, ROSE, S.S.J., J.C.D., The Catholic University of America, Washington, D.C. **Articles:** Redemptionus donum; Vita consecrata.

*MCMANUS, MSGR. FREDERICK R., J.C.D., LL.D., Professor Emeritus and Professorial Lecturer in Canon Law, The Catholic University of America, Washington, D.C. **Articles:** Profession of Faith & Oath of Fidelity; Sapientia Christiana.

MCMANUS, THOMAS J., S.T.L., Adjunct Professor, Saint Charles Borromeo Seminary, Overbrook, Pennsylvania. **Article:** Krol, John Joseph.

MCNALLY, MICHAEL J., Saint Charles Borromeo Seminary, Overbrook, Pennsylvania. **Article:** Bevilacqua, Anthony Joseph.

MCPARTLAN, PAUL, S.T.L., D.Phil., Lecturer in Systematic Theology, Heythrop College, University of London. **Article:** The Legacy of Vatican II in the Pontificate of John Paul II.

MEEKING, MOST REVEREND BASIL, S.T.D., Bishop Emeritus of Christchurch, New Zealand. **Article:** Willebrands, Johannes Gerardus Maria.

MESKO, LOUIS, Sch.P., Piarist Fathers, Rome. **Article:** Casani, Pietro, Bl.

MESSBARGER, PAUL R., Ph.D., Professor Emeritus of English Literature, Loyola University of Chicago, Chicago, Illinois. **Article:** West, Morris.

MIKOLAJEK, LISA V., Communications Specialist, Sisters of the Holy Family of Nazareth, St. Joseph Province, Pittsburgh, Pennsylvania. **Article:** Siedliska, Maria of Jesus, Bl.

MILLER, R. BRUCE, M.S.L.S., Head, Theology/Philosophy, Canon Law Libraries, The Catholic University of America, Washington, D.C. **Articles:** Annuario Pontificio; Euntes in Mundum.

MINNIHAN, PAUL D., S.T.L., Oakland, California. **Article:** Ecclesia in America.

MIRANDA, SALVADOR, M.A., M.S., Assistant Director for Collection Management, Florida International University Library, Miami, Florida. **Articles:** *Contributing editor for cardinals.*

MISCAMBLE, WILSON D., C.S.C., Associate Professor, Department of History, University of Notre Dame, Notre Dame, Indiana. **Article:** Hesburgh, Theodore Martin.

MOLONEY, FRANCIS J., S.D.B., D.Phil., Professor of New Testament, The Catholic University of America, Washington, D.C. **Article:** International Theological Commis-sion.

MORRISEY, FRANCIS G., O.M.I., S.T.L., Ph.D., J.C.D., Professor of Canon Law, St. Paul University, Ottawa. **Articles:** Canon Law, 1983 Code; Introduction to Magisterial Documents.

*O'BRIEN, THOMAS C., S.T.D., International Commission on English in the Liturgy; Executive Editor, *New Catholic Encyclopedia*, Vol. 17, The Catholic University of America, Washington, D.C. **Articles:** John Paul I, Pope; Tridentine Mass.

*O'CONNELL, TIMOTHY E., S.T.L., Ph.D., Professor of Pastoral Studies, Loyola University, Chicago, Illinois. **Article:** Fuchs, Josef.

O'DONNELL, GABRIEL B., O.P., S.T.D., Postulator of the Cause of Father Michael J. McGivney. **Article:** Divinus perfectionis magister.

*O'DONOGHUE, PATRICK, M.M., Ph.D., Editor, *Japan Mission Journal*, Tokyo, Japan. **Article:** Endo, Shusaku.

*O'DONOVAN, LEO J., S.J., S.T.L., Th.D., Professor, Weston School of Theology, Cambridge, Massachusetts. **Article:** Rahner, Karl.

*O'KEEFE, VINCENT T., S.J., S.T.D., Assistant General of the Society of Jesus, 1965–1982, New York, New York. **Article:** Arrupe, Pedro.

*PARACHINI, PATRICIA A., S.N.J.M., D.Min., Coordinator, Spiritual Development, Paulist Seminary, Washington, D.C. **Article:** Durocher, Rose Marie.

PARRON MARIA, JOAQUIM, C.Ss.R., M.Ed., M.Th., Lecturer, Universidade Paranaense, Umuarama, Brazil. **Article:** Boff, Leonardo.

*PASKA, MSGR. WALTER, St. Michael's Ukrainian Catholic Church, Cherry Hill, New Jersey. **Article:** Oriental Code of Canon Law, Revision of.

PELLITERO IGLESIAS, RAMIRO, D.Th., Professor of Pastoral Theology, University of Navarre, Pamplona, Spain. **Article:** Opus Dei.

PELZEL, MORRIS, Ph.D., Associate Professor of Systematic Theology, Saint Meinrad School of Theology, Saint Meinrad, Indiana. **Articles:** Dives in misericordia; Dominum et vivificantem; Redemptoris hominis.

*PETER, CARL J., Ph.D., S.T.D., Professor of Theology, The Catholic University of America, Washington, D.C. **Article:** Synod of Bishops, Sixth General Assembly, 1983.

*PFNAUSCH, EDWARD G., J.C.D., Executive Coordinator of the Canon Law Society of America, Washington, D.C. **Article:** Directory for Ministry and Life of Priests (1994).

PHAN, PETER C., S.T.D., Ph.D., D.D., Warren-Blanding Professor of Religion and Culture, School of Religious Studies, The Catholic University of America, Washington, D.C. **Article:** God in the World: A Trinitarian Triptych.

*POLLARD, JOHN E., S.T.L., Representative for Catechesis and Leadership Development, Department of Education, United States Catholic Conference, Washington, D.C. **Articles:** Catechism of the Catholic Church; International Council for Catechesis (COINCAT).

*PRITCHARD, WILLIAM, Foreign Editor, Catholic News Service, Washington, D.C. **Article:** The Papacy: 1988–1994.

PURCELL, MICHAEL, Ph.B., Ph.L., Ph.D., Lecturer in Systematic Theology, University of Edinburgh, Scotland. **Articles:** Gray, Gordon Joseph; Winning, Thomas Joseph.

QUINN, KEVIN P., S.J., J.D., S.T.L., Ph.D., Associate Professor of Law, Georgetown University Law Center, Washington, D.C. **Article:** Drinan, Robert Frederick.

RABENSTEIN, KATHERINE I., Washington, D.C. **Articles:** Contributing editor for saints and beati.

RADANO, JOHN A., S.T.B., M.A., Ph.D., Head of the Western Section, Pontifical Council for Promoting Christian Unity, Vatican City. **Article:** Ut Unum Sint: John Paul II's Ecumenical Commitment.

RADZILOWSKI, PAUL, Ph.D., Assistant Professor of History, Saint Mary's College, Orchard Lake, Michigan. **Articles:** Dziwisz, Stanisław; Glemp, Jozef; Lublin, Catholic University of; Macharski, Franciszek; Rubin,

Władisław; Sapieha, Adam Stefan; Tischner, Jozef.

*RAMÍREZ TORRES, RAFAEL, S.J., Ph.D., Professor of Oratory and Greek, Director, Curso de Cultura Helena, Instituto de Literatura, Puente Grande, Jal, Mexico. **Article:** Pro, Miguel Agustin, Bl.

RAPADAS, DON ZANDRO G., Office of Communications, Archdiocese of Manila, Philippines. **Article:** Sin, Jaime L.

*REGAN, JANE E., Ph.D., School of Theology, St. John's University, Collegeville, Minnesota. **Article:** Catechesi tradendae.

RIEGO, RUTILIO J. DEL, Diocesan Laborer Priests House of Studies, Washington, D.C. **Article:** Ruiz de los Paños, Pedro, and Companions.

RINERE, ELISSA, C.P., J.C.D., Associate Professor of Canon Law, The Catholic University of America, Washington, D.C. **Articles:** Ad tuendam fidem; Pastor bonus.

ROS LLOPIS, AMPARO, H.D.C., Superior General, Hermanas de la Doctrina Cristiana, Mislata, Valencia, Spain. **Article:** Sisters of Christian Doctrine, Martyrs of, BB.

RUBIO, JOSE ANTONIO, Director of Ecumenical and Interreligious Affairs, Diocese of San Jose, Santa Clara, California. **Article:** Juan Diego.

RUSCIN, TERRY, Researcher and Author, San Diego, California. **Article:** Serra, Junípero, Bl.

SAMMUT, PIUS EDWIN, O.C.D., Former Provincial of the Discalced Carmelites in Malta. **Article:** Arguello, Kiko.

SCHINDLER, DAVID L., Ph.D., Editor, Communio (North American edition); Gagnon Professor of Fundamental Theology, John Paul II Institute for Studies on Marriage and Family, Washington, D.C. **Article:** Communio: International Catholic Review.

SCHIPPE, CULLEN, Publisher, Glencoe/ Benziger, Woodland Hills, California. **Article:** Mahony, Roger M.

SCHMITZ, KENNETH L., Ph.D., Professor Emeritus of Philosophy and Fellow of Trinity College, University of Toronto, Toronto, Ontario, Canada. **Article:** The Personalist Philosophy of Karol Wojtyła.

SCHRECK, CHRISTOPHER J., Ph.D., S.T.D., Professor of New Testament, Saint Charles Borromeo Seminary, Overbrook, Pennsylvania. **Article:** Scriptuarum thesaurus.

*SELLING, JOSEPH A., S.T.D., Professor of Moral Theology, Katholieke Universiteit Leuven, Belgium. **Article:** Synod of Bishops, Fifth General Assembly, 1980.

SHELLEY, MSGR. THOMAS J., Ph.D., Church of St. Thomas More, New York, New York. **Article:** O'Connor, John Joseph.

*SHORTER, AYLWARD, M. Afr., Ph.D., President, Missionary Institute London. **Article:** Inculturation, Theology of.

SPALDING, THOMAS W., C.F.X., Ph.D., Professor Emeritus of History, Spalding University, Louisville, Kentucky. **Article:** Stafford, James Francis.

*STASIEWSKI, BERNHARD CLEMENS, Dr. Phil., Dr. Theol., Professor of Modern and Contemporary Church History and Church History of Eastern Europe, University of Bonn, Germany; Head Institut für ostdeutsche Kirchen-und Kulturgeschichte. **Article:** Poland, History of (to 1965).

SULLIVAN, JOHN, O.C.D., S.T.D. Publisher, Institute of Carmelite Studies, Washington, D.C. **Article:** Stein, Edith.

*SURLIS, PAUL, S.T.D., Associate Professor, Moral Theology and Social Ethics, St. John's University, New York. **Article:** Option for the Poor.

TABORSKI, BOLESŁAW, M.A., Poet, Writer, Theater Critic. **Article:** Karol Wojtyła: Poet, Playwright, Philosopher, and Patriot.

*TETREAU, RICHARD D., Ph.D., Director of Library, St. Peter's College, Jersey City, New Jersey. **Article:** Focolare Movement.

THAVIS, JOHN M., Rome Bureau Chief, Catholic News Service, Rome. **Article:** Navarro-Valls, Joaquin.

TREANOR, NOËL, S.T.L., Secretary General, Commission des épiscopats de la Communauté Européene. **Article:** Synod of Bishops, Second Special Assembly for Europe.

WALL, A. E. P., Former Editor and President of the *Chicago Catholic*. **Article:** Bernardin, Joseph Louis.

WEBER, MSGR. FRANCIS J., Archivist, Archdiocese of Los Angeles. **Article:** Serra, Junípero, Bl.

WEIGEL, GEORGE, Senior Fellow, Ethics and Public Policy Center, Washington, D.C. **Article:** The Church, the Collapse of Communism, and the Challenge of New Democracies.

WHALEN, MICHAEL D., C.M., S.T.D., Assistant Professor of Theology, St. John's University, Jamaica, New York Article: Dies Domini.

WILLIAMS, BRUCE, O.P., S.T.D., Professor of Moral Theology, Pontifical University of St. Thomas Aquinas, Rome. **Article:** Homosexuals, Pastoral Care of.

*WILLIAMS, GEORGE H., Hollis Professor of Divinity Emeritus, Harvard University. **Article:** The Papacy: 1978–1988.

WILLIAMS, HIS EMINENCE THOMAS STAFFORD, D.D., Archbishop of Wellington, New Zealand. **Article:** Synod of Bishops, Special Assembly for Oceania.

WUERL, MOST REVEREND DONALD W., S.T.D., D.D., Bishop of Pittsburgh, Pennsylvania. **Article:** Synod of Bishops, Fourth General Assembly, 1977.

ZIELINSKI, REV. ZYGMUNT, Katholic University of Lublin, Poland **Article:** Poland, History of (from 1965).

ZUKOWSKI, ANGELA ANN, M.H.S.H., M.A., D.Min., Associate Professor, Department of Religious Studies, University of Dayton, Dayton, Ohio. **Article:** Eternal Word Television Network (EWTN).

Subject Index

Article titles are indicated by all capital letters; page references for the main article for each are given in boldface type. Page references in italic type indicate illustrations.

A

A Graça Libertadora no Mundo (Boff), 261

Abadesa de las Huelgas, La (Escrivá de Balaguer), 489

Abdullah II (King of Jordan), *83*

Aborigine people, 175

Abortion, 133, 138, 141, 168
    Drinan on, 292
    Evangelium vitae on, 55, 207
    McCormick on, 355
    O'Connor on, 369
    post-Communist Poland, 12
    world conferences, 57, 58-59, 60

Absolution, 155

Abuna Paulos (Ethiopian Orthodox Patriarch), 77

Academic Pastoral Care (*Duszpasterstwo Akademickie*), 7

Acta Apostolicae Sedis, 22, 178, 182

Acting Person, The (Wojtyła), 30, 41, 42, 63

Acton, Charles, 322

Acts of the Apostles, 164, 283

Actus humanus, 30-31

Ad gentes, 231, 283, 317, 320

AD LIMINA VISITS, 221, **247-248**

AD TUENDAM FIDEM (motu proprio, John Paul II), **182-183**

Adalbert of Prague, St., 140, 374

Adam, Louis-Armand-Joseph, Bl., 583

Adame Rosales, Román, St., 549

Adams, John, Bl., 477

Adradas Gonzalo, Juan Jesús, Bl., 509

Adult Catechesis in the Christian Community, 321

Aeterni patris (encyclical, Leo XIII), 212

Africa
    beatifications and canonizations, 113, 438, 464, 558, 611
    cardinals, 251-252, 303-304
    Ecclesia in Africa, 58, 168, 197-198
    John Paul II pilgrimages, 87, 125-126, 127, 130-131, 135, 136, 137
    martyrs, 438
    missionaries, 198, 431-432, 464
    Synod of Bishops Special Assembly, 58, 138, 165-168, *166*, 197-198, 315

African Americans, *193*, 318 319, 470-471

Agape, 40

Agça, Mehemet Ali, 127

Aggiornamento. See Vatican Council II

AGNES OF BOHEMIA, ST., **430**

AGOSTINI, ZEFERINO, BL., **431**

Agramunt Riera, Juan, Bl., 568

Aguilar Alemán, Rodrigo, St., 549

Ahern, Barnabas, 322

AIDS, 312

Alacoque, Margaret Mary, St., 132

Alberione, James, 501

ALBERT, FEDERICO, BL., **431**

Albertine Brothers and Sisters, 25, 460

Alcalde, Juan Alcalde, Bl., 509

Alcalde Negredo, Pedro María, Bl., 509

Alexander I (Czar of Russia), 378

Alexander II (Czar of Russia), 378

Alexander III (Czar of Russia), 379

Alexander III, Pope, 242, 267-268

Alexander VII, Pope, 377

Alexei II (Patriarch), 12, 140

Alfonsin, Raul, 132

Alfrink, Bernard (card.), 406

Algabid, M. Hamid, 85

Alguire, Frances, 74

ALLAMANO, GIUSEPPE, BL., **431-432**

Almato, Pedro, St., 625

ALMERÍA, MARTYRS OF, BB., **432**

Alvarado Cardozo, Laura Elena, Bl., **433**

Alvarez Mendoza, Julio, St., 547

AMANTISSIMA PROVIDENTIA (apostolic letter, John Paul II), **183-184**

Ambassador, The (West), 422-423

AMBROZIC, ALOYSIUS M. (card.), 141, **248-250**, *249*

Americanization. *See* Inculturation

Amoris officio (letter, Paul VI), 392

Amorós Hernández, José María, Bl., 442

Ancel, Charles-Antoine-Nicolas, Bl., 583

Anchieta, José (Joseph) de, Bl., *433*, **433-434**

ANDREW THE CATECHIST, BL., **434-435**

Andropov, Yuri, 11

Andrzejuk, Jan, Bl., 573

Angelica, Mother, 298

Angelico, Fra (Guido da Fiesole), 493-494

Anglican-Catholic International Commission (ARCIC), 76, 128

Anglican-Catholic relations
    Anglican-Catholic International Commission, 76
    Anglo-Welsh martyrs, 112, 476-477
    Hume, 314
    shared Christian heritage, 73
    women's ordination, 75, 131, 136, 138, 140, 314
    See also Ecumenism

Aniceto Adolfo, St., 619-620

Anima desolata, L' (Sarnelli), 594

Anima illuminata, L' (Sarnelli), 594

Animism, 131

ANNUARIO PONTIFICIO, **250**, 321

Annunciation, 18, *227*

Anthropocentrism, 33, 35-36, 39

Anthropology, 35-36, 41

B

Copernicanism, 102-103

Corazón de Jesús, Bl., 603

Corbon, Jean, 187, 322

Corby, Ralph, Bl., 511

Cordeiro, Joseph (card.), 155, 160

Cordes, Paul Josef (bp.), 359

Cordier, Jean-Nicholas, Bl., 584

Co-responsibility in the Church (Suenens), 417

Corinthians, Epistles to the, 67, 283, 312

CORMIER, HYACINTHE-MARIE, BL., **465-466**

Cornay, Jean-Charles, St., 626

Cornelius, John, Bl., 511

Corpus canonum ecclesiarum orientalium, 164

Corpus Mysticum (Lubac), 347, 400

Correa Magallanes, Mateo, St., 548

Corrective Vision: Explorations in Moral Theology (McCormick), 355

Correia, Simao, Bl., 451

Corres Díaz de Cerio, Braulio María, Bl., 507

Cortés, Hernán, 613-614

Cortesi, Filippo, 380

Cosmology, 102

Cottier, Georges, 322

Council of European Bishops' Conferences (CCEE), 177

Counter Reformation, Poland, 376-377

Craft of Theology, The (Dulles), 294

Craxi, Bettino, 336

CRISPIN OF VITERBO, ST., **466**

Cristero Movement, 545-550

Cristianism, socialismo, capitalismo (Camara), 264

Cristiano santificato, Il (Sarnelli), 594

Cristobal, Bl., 614

Critical Calling, The: Moral Dilemmas Since Vatican II (McCormick), 355

Croatia, 537, 609-610. *See also* Yugoslavia

Crossing the Threshold of Hope (John Paul II), 84, 89, 138

Crow, Alexander, Bl., 479

Crowe, Frederick E., 343

Crucifixion, 35, 40, 42, 234-235, *234*

Crusades, 66

Cruz, Oscar (abp.), 171

Cruz Alvarado, Atilano, St., 546

Cry of the Oppressed: The History and Hope of the Human Rights Revolution (Drinan), 292

Cuartero Gascón, Jose Maria, Bl., 467

Cuartero Gascón, Tomas, Bl., 467

Cuarto de hora de oración, El (Ossó y Cervello), 562

Cuba, 141, *187*, 275, 337, 358-359

Cubells Minguell, Protasio, Bl., 508

Cuénot, Étienne-Théodore, St., 626

Cuesta Redondo, Justiniano, Bl., 467

Cults. *See* New religious movements

Culture, 299-300, 319-320, 390-391. *See also* Inculturation

"Culture of death", 111, 132, 138, 192, 207

Cum iuris canonici (motu proprio, Benedict XV), 393

Cuomo, Mario, 369

Curia, 68, 134, 182, 220-221, 391. *See also specific congregations*

Curran, Charles, 123, 334, 355

CUSMANO, GIACOMO, BL., **466-467**

Cyprian, 282

Cyril, St., 73, 206-207, 237-238, *237*

Czartoryski, August, 380

Czechoslovakia, 10, 13, 154-155, 274, 275, 329-330, 419

beatifications and canonizations, 430, 526-527, 637

See also Eastern Catholic Churches; Eastern Europe

Czesław, 374

CZĘSTOCHOWA, **287-289**, *288*

D

Da, Peter, St., 626

Dac Nguyen, St., 626

Dalai Lama, 84, *243*

Dalbor, Edmund (abp.), 380

Dalle api alle rose (Fasce), 491

Dalmau Rosich, Antonio María, Bl., 441

Daly, Leo A., 324

DAMIEL, MARTYRS OF, BB., **467**

DANNEELS, GODFRIED (card.), 146, 148, *289*, **289**

Darlap, Adolf, 397, 398

Darmaatmadja, Julius (card.), 171

Darowska, Marcelina, 380

DAROWSKA, MARCELINA KOTOWICZ, BL., **467-468**

Dat, Juan, St., 626

Daughters of Charity of Canossa, 456

Daughters of Divine Zeal, 494

Daughters of Jesus, 462

Daughters of Mary, 553

Daughters of Mary Immaculate, 431

Daughters of St. Anne, 499

Daughters of St. Camillus, 621

Daughters of St. Joseph, 539

Daughters of St. Paul, 501

Daughters of the Holy Cross of Liège, 504

Daughters of the Immaculate Conception, 634

Daughters of the Sacred Heart of Jesus, 468-469

Daughters of Wisdom, 617

Daveluy, Antoine, St., 524

David, David Oghlou, 436

David, Toros Oghlou, 436

David (Wojtyła), 23

Davies, Norman, 8

Davies, William, Bl., 479

Day of Pardon (2000), 66, 70, 79

De anima (Duns Scotus), 472

De Castro Mayer, Antonio (bp.), 340

De constitutione Christi ontologica et psychologica supplementum (Lonergan), 342

De Deo trino (Lonergan), 342

De fide catholica, 373

De gentes, 86-87

De la Salle, John, St., 443

De lege (Cicero), 266

DE MELLO, ANTHONY, **290**

De Pauw, Gommar, 278

De potestate papae et imperatoris respectu infidelium (Paul Vladimiri), 375

De praedicamentis (Duns Scotus), 472

De sacerdotali ordinatione viris tantum reservanda (apostolic letter, John Paul II), 138

De salute animarum (bull, Pius VII), 379

De Servorum Dei beatificatione et Beatorum canonizatione (Benedict XIV), 429

De Van Nguyen, Tomás, St., 626

De Verbo incarnato (Lonergan), 342

Death, 17, 38

Death penalty, 141, 187, 207

Dechant, Ann, 156

Dechant, Virgil, 156

Declaration on Religious Freedom. *See Dignitatis humanae*

Declaration on the Relation of the Church to Non-Christian Religions. *See Nostra aetate*

Decree on Ecumenism. *See Unitatis redintegratio*

Decree on the Pastoral Office of Bishops in the Church. *See Christus Dominus*

Deep River (Endo), 295

ECCLESIA IN ASIA (apostolic exhortation, John Paul II), 88, 113, 173, **200-201**

Ecclesiae sanctae (motu proprio, Paul VI), 185, 295

Ecclesiam Suam (encyclical, Paul VI), 81, 82-83

Ecclesiastico santificato, L' (Sarnelli), 594

Ecclésiologie du haut moyen-age, L' (Congar), 287

Ecclesiology, 320. *See also* Communion

Echarri Vique, Juan, Bl., 441

Eck, John, 376

Ecole de Fourvière, 346

École de The'ologie, Une: Le Saulchoir (Chenu), 279

Ecology. *See* Environmental issues

Economic inequality, 36, 39, 51, 139, 277

ECONOMIC JUSTICE FOR ALL (National Conference of Catholic Bishops), **201-203**, 371

Economics. *See* Capitalism; Economic inequality; Social/economic thought

Ecuador, 130, 492, 552. *See also* Latin America

Ecumenical Commemoration of Witnesses to the Faith in the Twentieth Century, 80

ECUMENICAL DIMENSION IN THE FORMATION OF PASTORAL WORKERS, THE (Pontifical Council for Promoting Christian Unity), 204

ECUMENICAL DIRECTORY, **203-204**, 243

Ecumenical formation. *See Ecumenical Dimension in the Formation of Pastoral Workers, The*

Ecumenism, 71-80, 83, 139

  beatifications and canonizations and, 73, 112

  Christology disputes, 77-78

  communion, 283-284

  conciliar anniversary message (1981), 127

  Congar, 286

  Danneels, 289

  dialogue, 75-76

  Ecumenical Directory, 203-204, 243

  Focolare Movement, 301

  Hume, 314

  indulgences, 213-214

  John Paul II personal contacts, 74-75

  John Paul II pilgrimages, 69, 126-128, 129, 130

  Joint Declaration on the Doctrine of Justification, 78, 213, 276

  Jubilee, 79-80

  papal primacy, 68-69, 75, 78-79, 129, 138

  personalism and, 32

  Pontifical Council for Promoting Christian Unity, 76, 203, 213, 392

  Redemptor hominis, 73, 229

  shared Christian heritage, 71, 73-74

  Synod of Bishops for Europe, 177

  Vatican Council II, 69-70, 76, 77, 126, 203, 241, 283-284

  Willebrands, 131, 423-424

  women's ordination, 75, 131, 136, 138, 140, 314

  See also Anglican-Catholic relations; Interreligious dialogue; Orthodox-Catholic relations; *Ut unum sint*

Ecumenism and Charismatic Renewal (Suenens), 417

Editora Vozes, 261

Edmund, Bl., 480

Education, 56, 330-331

  Catholic universities, 136-137, 208-209, 235-236, 308-309, 349

  See also Catechetics; Religious education

Église de Saint-Augustin à l'époque moderne, L' (Congar), 287

Egozcuezábal Aldaz, Juan Bautista, Bl., 508

Egregiae virtutis, 237

Egypt, 142

El Salvador, 401-402. *See also* Latin America

ELIZABETH OF THE TRINITY, BL., **474-476**

Eminence (West), 422

Encounters with Silence (Rahner), 397

ENDO, SHUSAKU, **294-295**, *296*

ENGLAND, SCOTLAND, AND WALES, MARTYRS OF, BB., 112, **476-488**

Environmental issues, 36, 48

Ephesians, Epistle to the, 56, 218

Ephesus, Council of, 78, 230

EPISCOPAL CONFERENCES, 184-185, **295-297**. *See also* Synod of Bishops

Epistola de propria conversione (Stensen), 608

Eremo delle Carceri (Assisi, It.), 255

Errington, George, Bl., 480

Eschatology, 40

ESCRIVÁ DE BALAGUER Y ALBÁS, JOSEMARIA, BL., 372, **488-489**, *489*

ESPÉRANCE NOUVELLE POUR LE LIBAN, UNE (apostolic exhortation, John Paul II), **205-206**

Esqueda Ramírez, Pedro, St., 549

Estalayo García, Jose, Bl., 467

Estepa, José (bp.), 187

ETCHEGARAY, ROGER (card.), 155, *297*, **297-298**

ETERNAL WORD TELEVISION NETWORK (EWTN), **298**

Ethical Reflections on the Economic Crisis (Canadian bishops), 45-46

Ethiopia, 74, 77. *See also* Africa

Eucharist

  catechetics, 150

  communion, 284

  divorce and, 210

  inculturation, 318

  Lima text, 215, 216

  Vatican Council II on, 69

  in Wojtyła's poetry, 16

Eucharistic Congress (Philadelphia, 1976), 8, 122

Eugene III, Pope, 267

Eugene IV, Pope, 268

EUNTES IN MUNDUM UNIVERSUM (apostolic letter, John Paul II), 135, **206-207**

Europe

  episcopal conferences, 295

  European Union, 57, 58, 176-177, 192

  patrons/patronesses of, 73, 74, 112, 177, 184, 207, 237-238, 506

  Synod of Bishops Special Assembly (1999), 141, 144, 176-178

European Union (EU), 57, 58, 176-177, 192

EUSE HOYOS, MARIANO DE JESÚS, BL., **489-490**

Euthanasia, 55, 132, 133, 138, 207-208, 355

Evaluation of the Possibility of Constructing a Christian Ethics on the Basis of the System of Max Scheler (Wojtyła), 121-122

Evangelii nuntiandi (apostolic exhortation, Paul VI), 158, 186, 300, 390, 395

  Redemptoris missio and, 87, 231, 232

EVANGELIUM VITAE (encyclical, John Paul II), 31, 55, 111, 138, 187, **207-208**, 415

Evangelization, 137, 231-232

  Africa, 198, 431-432, 464

  Asia, 200-201

  catechetics and, 149

F

G

H

Karekin I of Etchmiadzin (Armenian Patriarch-Catholicos), 74, 78, 141

Karl Barth (Hamer), 307

Karlic, Estanislao Esteban (bp.), 187

KARLOWSKA, MARIA, BL., **518**

Karmasz, Daniel, Bl., 574

Karnkowski, Stanisław (abp.), 377

Karol Wojtyła negli scritti, 123

Karotemprel, Sebastian, 322

Karska, Jozefa, 380

KASPER, WALTER (bp.), 322, **327**

KASSAB, NIMATULLAH AL-HARDINI YOUSEF, BL., **519**

Katolicky katechismus (Tomášek), 419

KAZIMIERCZYK, STANISLAW YOUSEF, BL., **519**

Kearney, John, Bl., 511

KEELER, WILLIAM HENRY (card.), 138-139, 162, **327-328**, *328*

Keilert, Engelberg, 577

KEK (Conference of European Churches), 177

Kelly, Francis, 321

KERN, JAKOB FRANZ, BL., **519-520**

Kern, Walter, 397

Keršansko devištvo (Slomšek), 603

Kham Viet Pham, Dominic, St., 629

Khambang, Lucy, Bl., 613

Khang Duy Nguyen, José, St., 629

Khanh, Peter, St., 629

Khoa, Pedro, St., 629

Khoan Khan Pham, Paul, St., 629

Khuong, Thomas, St., 629

KIK (*Klub Inteligencji Katolickiej*), 7-8, 9

Kim, Agatha A-gi, St., 523

Kim, Agnes Hyo-ju, St., 523

Kim, Andrew Te-gon, St., 522-523

Kim, Anna Chang-gum, St., 524

Kim, Anthony Song-u, St., 524

Kim, Barbara, St., 524

Kim, Columba Hyo-im, St., 524

Kim, Ignatius Che-jun, St., 524

Kim, Julietta, St., 525

Kim, Lucy, St. (I), 525

Kim, Lucy, St. (II), 525

Kim, Magdalena Ob-i, St., 525

Kim, Martha Song-im, St., 525

Kim, Rosa, St., 526

Kim, Teresa Im-i, St., 526

Kim, Teresa, St., 526

KINGA, ST., 375, **520**

Kiryluk, Filip, Bl., 574

KITBAMRUNG, NICHOLAS BUNKERD, BL., **520-521**

Kloppenburg, Bonaventura, 322

Klub Inteligencji Katolickiej (KIK) (Club of the Catholic Intelligentsia), 7-8, 9

Kluger, Jerzy, 89-90

Knight, William, Bl., 482-483

Knox, John (card.), 153

Ko, Barbara Sun-i, St., 524

Kocisko, Stephen (abp.), 149, 152, 154, 160

Kokołowicz, Anna, Bl., 561

Kolakowski, Leszek, 8

KOLBE, MAXIMILIAN, ST., 111-112, 115, 381, **521**

Kołłątej, Hugo, 377

KOLPING, ADOLF, BL., **521-522**

Kolvenbach, Peter-Hans, 254

Konarski, Stanisław, 377

KÖNIG, FRANZ (card.), 274, **328-329**, *329*

Konstant, David, 187

Kopp, Georg (card.), 379

Korea, 129

MARTYRS OF, SS., 113, **552-557**

KOREC, JÁN CHRYZOSTOM (card.), **329-330**

Kosciol, Lewica, Dialog (Michnik), 8

KOŠICE, MARTYRS OF, SS., **526-527**

KOSTISTK, GEREMIA OF VALACHIA, BL., **527-528**

Kotlarczyk, Mieczysław, 22-23, 119, 121

KOWALSKA, FAUSTINA, ST., **528-529**, *529*

KOZAL, MICHAŁ, BL., 381, **529**

KÓZIMÍNSKI, HONORAT, BL., **529-530**

KOZKA, KAROLINA, BL., **529**

KPN (Confederation of Independent Poland), 384

Krąpiec, Mieczysław, 349

Krasiński, Adam Stanisław (bp.), 377, 378

Krause, Christian (bp.), 74

Križín, Marek, St., 527

KROL, JOHN JOSEPH (card.), 146, **330-331**, *331*

Kromer, Martin, 377

Krzaklewski, Marian, 387

Krzycki, Andrzej (bp.), 376

Kuncevyč, Josephat, St., 376

Küng, Hans, 123, 280

KUNG, PIN-MEI IGNATIUS (card.), *332*, **332-333**

Kwasniewski, Aleksander, 386-387

Kwon, Agatha Chin-i, St., *523*

Kwon, Peter Tug-in, St., 526

L

Labiche de Reignefort, Marcel-Gaucher, Bl., 585

Labor movement, 47-48, 214

O'Connor, 369

Solidarity, 8-9, 44-46, 48, 50, 124

LABOREM EXERCENS (encyclical, John Paul II), 9, 44-46, 47, 50, 127, **214**

family, 53, 55

personalism, 32

solidarity, 414

Tischner and, 418

Labre Mañoso González, Benito José, Bl., 507

Labrouche de Laborderie, Pierre-Yrieix, Bl., 585

Laetamur magnopere (apostolic letter, John Paul II), 187

LAGHI, PIO (card.), 161, *333*, **333-334**

Lais, Giuseppe, 101

Laity, 134, 156-159

Christifideles laici, 55, 136, 179, **190-191**

Pontifical Council for the Laity, 391-392

Lambert, Matthew, Bl., 511

Lambeth Conference (1989), 75

Lambton, Joseph, Bl., 483

LAMENT, BOLESLAWA MARIA, BL., **530**

Lampley, William, Bl., 483

Lanfranco, Giovanni, *244*

Langevin, Gilles, 322

Laos, 154

Laplace, Claude, Bl., 585

Lara Puente, Salvador, St., 549

Largo Redondo, Pedro, Bl., 467

Lasheras Aizcorbe, Rufino, Bl., 508

Łaski, Jan (abp.), 376

Last Judgment (Michelangelo), 409-410, *410*

Last Retreat on the Praise of Glory (Elizabeth of the Trinity), 475

Last Supper, 36

LATERAN PACTS (1985), 129, 275, **334-337**

Latin America

Ecclesia in America, 111, 141, 171, 198-200

family policies, 55

John Paul II pilgrimages, 124, 126, 128, 130, 131-132, 132, 135, 137

liberation theology, 46, 110, 124, 129-130, 261, 360, 370, 395